Third Edition

THE AMERICAN POLITICAL SYSTEM

2018 Election Update

Ken Kollman
University of Michigan

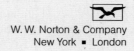
W. W. Norton & Company
New York ■ London

W. W. Norton & Company has been independent since its founding in 1923, when William Warder Norton and Mary D. Herter Norton first published lectures delivered at the People's Institute, the adult education division of New York City's Cooper Union. The firm soon expanded its program beyond the Institute, publishing books by celebrated academics from America and abroad. By midcentury, the two major pillars of Norton's publishing program—trade books and college texts—were firmly established. In the 1950s, the Norton family transferred control of the company to its employees, and today—with a staff of four hundred and a comparable number of trade, college, and professional titles published each year—W. W. Norton & Company stands as the largest and oldest publishing house owned wholly by its employees.

Editor: Peter Lesser
Assistant Editor: Anna Olcott
Managing Editor, College: Marian Johnson
Project Editor: Laura Dragonette
Manuscript Editors: Christianne Thillen
  and Gwen Burda
Managing Editor, College Digital Media:
  Kim Yi
Media Project Editor: Marcus van Harpen
Media Editor: Spencer Richardson-Jones
Associate Media Editor: Michael Jaoui
Media Editorial Assistant: Tricia Vuong

Marketing Manager, Political Science:
  Erin Brown
Production Manager: Elizabeth Marotta
Design Director: Lissi Sigillo
Photo Editor: Agnieszka Czapski
Photo Researcher: Julie Tesser
Director of College Permissions: Megan
Jackson Schindel
Permissions Assistant: Patricia Wong
Composition: Westchester Publishing Services
Manufacturing: TC-Transcontinental Printing

Permission to use copyrighted material is included in the Credits section of this book.

Library of Congress Cataloging-in-Publication Data

Names: Kollman, Ken, 1966- author.
Title: The American political system. Election update / Ken Kollman,
  University of Michigan.
Description: Third Edition. | New York: W. W. Norton & Company, Inc., [2019] |
  Includes bibliographical references and index.
Identifiers: LCCN 2018057915 | **ISBN 9780393675283** (paperback)
Subjects: LCSH: United States—Politics and government—Textbooks.
Classification: LCC JK276 .K66 2019 | DDC 320.473—dc23 LC record
  available at https://lccn.loc.gov/2018057915

W. W. Norton & Company, Inc., 500 Fifth Avenue, New York, NY 10110

wwnorton.com

W. W. Norton & Company Ltd., 15 Carlisle Street, London W1D 3BS

1 2 3 4 5 6 7 8 9 0

This book is dedicated to my many wonderful colleagues and students at the University of Michigan.

CONTENTS

Preface   xix

CHAPTER 1 Introduction 3

What can the tools of political science tell us that
we don't already know?

- **Understanding American Politics**   5
  Institutions   6

- **Collective Dilemmas and the Need for Government**   9

- **Types of Collective Dilemmas**   12
  Collective Action Problems   12
  Prisoner's Dilemma Situations   13
  Coordination Problems   16
  Comparing Collective Action Problems and Coordination Problems:
    Example from Voting   18
  Unstable Coalitions   19

- **Principal-Agent Problems**   21

- **Designing Institutions**   23

- **In Comparison: Types of Government Institutions**   25

- **Analyzing Politics and Government Using the
  Tools of Political Science**   29

Further Reading   30
Key Terms   31

CHAPTER 2 The Constitution 33

How does the Constitution strike a balance between
preserving order and protecting liberty?

- **What Do Constitutions Accomplish?**   35

- **Origins of the American Political System**   36
  The Revolution   37

The Declaration of Independence   39
The Colonial and State Constitutions   40
The Articles of Confederation   40
The Constitutional Debates   41
Difficult Compromises   44

■ **Institutional Features of the Constitution**   46
A President as Executive   47
A Bicameral Legislature   47
An Independent Judiciary   48
Separation of Powers   49
Checks and Balances   49
Federalism with National Authority over the States   50
Reserved Powers for the States   51
Amending the Constitution   51

■ **The Ratification Debate**   52
Federalists versus Antifederalists   52
The Bill of Rights   54

■ **In Comparison: National Constitutions**   56

■ **Constitutional Evolution**   57
Relative Powers of the Branches of Government   57
INTERESTS, INSTITUTIONS, AND OUTCOMES The Constitution and
    Religion in Politics   58
National Power versus States' Rights   61
Direct Election of the President and Senators   62
Rights and Liberties   62

■ **Consequences of the Constitution**   63
DATA EXPLORATION The Costs and Benefits of a Longer Constitution   65

Further Reading   69
Key Terms   69

CHAPTER 3 Federalism **71**
Why have the states and the American people allowed the federal
government to become more and more powerful?

■ **Federation and Confederation**   73
Federalism as a Response to Collective Dilemmas   75

■ **The Dynamics of American Federalism**   76

■ **The Courts and the Constitution**   78

■ **Toward a Stronger National Government**   82
Progressive Era, 1896–1913   82
New Deal Era, 1933–52   82
Great Society Era, 1964–77   83
Recent Trends   84

■ **Federal Financing**   85

■ **Federalism and Race**   88

   DATA EXPLORATION Where Does Federal Money Go, and Why?   89

■ **State Governments**   90

   The Institutions of State Government   91

   State Power   92

■ **Local Governments**   93

   INTERESTS, INSTITUTIONS, AND OUTCOMES Federal and State
     Conflicts over Marijuana   94

   Special Districts   96

■ **In Comparison: American Federalism**   97

■ **Evaluating American Federalism**   99

   Avoiding Tyranny   99

   Preserving Diversity   100

   Fostering Competition   101

   Promoting Unity and Experimentation   102

   Negative Consequences of Federalism   103

   Federalism as a Difficult but Important Balance   104

Further Reading   104

Key Terms   105

CHAPTER 4 Civil Rights and Liberties 107

  What rights and freedoms
  do Americans have?

■ **Defining Civil Rights and Liberties**   109

■ **The Origins of Rights and Liberties**   110

■ **The Special Role of the Courts**   113

■ **Race, Ethnicity, and Nationality**   117

   Slavery and African Americans   118

   The Treatment of Immigrants   119

   Other Failures   120

■ **Popular Demands for More Rights**   122

   The Civil Rights Movement   122

   Other Movements   124

■ **Incorporating the Bill of Rights into the Fourteenth Amendment**   126

■ **Government Responses to Discrimination**   128

   Affirmative Action   131

   Abortion Rights   132

   INTERESTS, INSTITUTIONS, AND OUTCOMES Access to What Others Have:
     Rights of the Disabled   134

   Rights Related to Sexual Identity   136

■ **In Comparison: Rights and Liberties around the World**   138

DATA EXPLORATION Civil Liberties and National Security: A Trade-Off   141

■ **Why Protect Rights and Liberties?**   142

Further Reading   145
Key Terms   145

CHAPTER 5 Congress **147**

How do legislators rise above self-interest and the narrow
interests of their districts to pass important legislation?

■ **Congress and the Constitution**   149
Bicameralism   150
Making Law   150

■ **Congressional Elections**   151
Causes of Individualism in Congress   152
Representing the District or State   159

■ **Internal Institutions of Congress**   165
An Increasingly Institutionalized Congress   166
Party Leaders   168
Committees   170
Other Internal Features   173

■ **The Process of Lawmaking**   176
Proposals   176
Referrals   176
Committee Action   178
Moving Bills to the Floor   178
Senate Distinctiveness   180
INTERESTS, INSTITUTIONS, AND OUTCOMES A Sit-In for Gun Control   182
Floor Action   184
Conference Committees   184
Presidential Signature   185

■ **Making Law in a System of Separation of Powers**   185

■ **In Comparison: Legislative Institutions**   186
DATA EXPLORATION Does Gerrymandering Matter?   187

■ **Analyzing Collective Dilemmas in Congress**   188
Three Models for Analyzing Congress   190

Further Reading   196
Key Terms   197

CHAPTER 6 The Presidency **199**

How and why has presidential
power grown?

■ **Sources of Presidential Power**   201
Constitutional Bases of Presidential Power   201
Solving Collective Dilemmas and Principal-Agent Problems
  since the Founding   205

■ **Shaping the Modern Presidency** 207

Nineteenth-Century Changes 207

Through the Twentieth Century and into the Twenty-First 210

■ **Enhancing Presidential Power through Military and Economic Means** 214

■ **Today's Powerful Presidency** 218

The Veto 220

Executive Orders, Executive Agreements, and Signing Statements 222

Appointments 224

INTERESTS, INSTITUTIONS, AND OUTCOMES Abortion Funding and the Use of Executive Orders 226

Solving Collective Dilemmas with Administrative and Financial Resources 228

■ **In Comparison: Executive Forms** 232

DATA EXPLORATION The Politics of Executive Orders 235

■ **Checks on Presidential Power** 236

Investigations and Impeachment 237

Electoral Pressures 239

Institutionalizing Presidential Power to Solve Collective Dilemmas 240

Further Reading 240

Key Terms 241

CHAPTER 7 The Bureaucracy 243

Who controls the bureaucracy?
And does it work?

■ **What Is the Federal Bureaucracy?** 245

■ **Why Do We Need a Federal Bureaucracy?** 248

Solvers of Collective Dilemmas 248

■ **Principals and Agents in the Executive Bureaucracy** 251

The Motivations of Bureaucrats 251

Bureaucracy's Principal-Agent Problems 252

Bureaucrats as Policy Makers 256

■ **How Has the Bureaucracy Changed?** 258

The Early Years 258

Growth in Size 259

The Spoils System 261

Civil Service Reform 262

Modern Reforms of the Bureaucracy 264

Privatization and Marketization 267

■ **Shaping and Influencing the Bureaucracy** 269

Appointments 269

Budgeting 270

Oversight 271

INTERESTS, INSTITUTIONS, AND OUTCOMES Bureaucratic Budget Battles 272

The Courts' Influence 274
Interest Groups 275

■ **In Comparison: Bureaucratic Traditions** 276
DATA EXPLORATION Do Bureaucrats Behave Differently than Elected Officials? 277

■ **Two Views of Bureaucracy** 278
The Progressive Vision of a Fair, Competent, and Impartial Bureaucracy 279
The Democratic Vision of a Bureaucracy Responsive to the Wishes of Politicians Elected by the People 280

Further Reading 282
Key Terms 283

CHAPTER 8 The Judiciary 285

Are the courts above politics?

■ **Courts and Collective Dilemmas** 287
Prisoner's Dilemmas 287
Coordination Problems 287
Independence and Legitimacy 288

■ **Constitutional Basis** 289

■ **Establishing Judicial Power** 290
Judicial Review 290
Supremacy of Federal Courts and Federal Law 293
The Court of Last Resort 294

■ **Organization of the American Judiciary** 297
Types of Cases 297
Standing and Class Actions 297
Federal Courts 298
State Courts and the Electoral Connection 299
Jurisdiction at the Federal and State Levels 301
Common Law and Legal Precedent 302

■ **Path of a Supreme Court Case** 303
Choosing Cases 304
Legal Briefs 305
Oral Arguments 306
The Conference 307
Opinion Writing 309

■ **In Comparison: The Judiciary** 311
Selecting Judges 311
Judicial Review 312

■ **How Political Are the Courts?** 313
Minority Rights versus Majority Rule 313
Analyzing Judicial Behavior 314
DATA EXPLORATION Ideology on the Supreme Court 315

Public Opinion, Congress, and the Federal Courts 317
The Politics of Judicial Appointments 318
INTERESTS, INSTITUTIONS, AND OUTCOMES The Politics and
    Strategies of Judicial Confirmations 322
Further Reading 324
Key Terms 325

CHAPTER 9 Public Opinion 327

What is the link between public opinion
and politicians' behavior?

■ **Public Opinion in a Democratic System** 329

■ **What Is Public Opinion?** 330
The Challenge of Having Many Principals 331

■ **Measuring Public Opinion** 333
Early Attempts at Measurement 334
Random Sampling 335
Possible Biases 336
Alternative Methods to Surveys 340

■ **Where Do Political Attitudes Come From?** 341
Socialization 341
INTERESTS, INSTITUTIONS, AND OUTCOMES Meta-Analysis:
    A Response to the Cell Phone Era 342
Interests and Rationality 345
Group Attachments 347
Emotions 348
Influence of Elites 348

■ **Predispositions** 350
Ideology 351
Party Identification 353
Other Predispositions 354

■ **Opinions on Policies and Politicians** 355
Policy Opinions 355
Evaluations of Politicians and Government Institutions 357

■ **Apathy and Lack of Knowledge** 358
Rational Ignorance? 360
Apathy and Non-Attitudes 361

■ **In Comparison: Public Opinion** 362

■ **Public Opinion and Policy Making** 364
DATA EXPLORATION Income, Policy Preferences, and Outcomes:
    Do the Rich Win? 365
Does Government Policy Follow Public Opinion or Vice Versa? 366

Further Reading 370
Key Terms 371

CHAPTER 10 Political Participation............373

Why do groups with the greatest interest in changing the status quo have relatively low turnout rates?

■ **Participation and Democratic Politics** 375
Conventional and Unconventional Participation 376

■ **Collective Dilemmas in Participation** 377

■ **Tallying the Costs and Benefits of Participating** 380
Registering to Vote 381
Gathering Information 382
Voting 383
Participation beyond Voting 385
INTERESTS, INSTITUTIONS, AND OUTCOMES Voter Turnout 386

■ **The Struggles for Voting Rights** 389
Restricting the Right to Vote 389
Challenges to Reforms Intended to Increase Turnout 391
Removing Barriers to Voting 392
Group Struggles 393

■ **Patterns of Participation in the United States** 395
Trends in Voter Turnout 395
The Demographics of Participation 397

■ **In Comparison: Political Participation** 401
DATA EXPLORATION Does the Cost of Voting Affect Turnout? 405

■ **The Crucial Role of Institutions and Mobilization** 406

Further Reading 409
Key Terms 409

CHAPTER 11 Interest Groups and Social Movements............411

How can well-organized, narrow interests influence government in ways that go against the preferences of a majority of Americans?

■ **What Are Interest Groups, and What Do They Do?** 413
Inside and Outside Lobbying 417
Campaign Financing 419
INTERESTS, INSTITUTIONS, AND OUTCOMES The Costs, Benefits, and Politics of Tax-Exempt Status 420

■ **Collective Dilemmas and Interest Group Politics** 424
Collective Action Problems 424
Overcoming Collective Action Problems 425
Coordination Problems 427

■ **Determining Interest Group Influence** 428

■ **Social Movements** 432
Deeper Analysis of Social Movements 437

- **In Comparison: Group Politics** 440
    - DATA EXPLORATION What Does Lobbying Look Like Up Close? 441
- **Organized Forms of Public Pressure** 442

Further Reading 444
Key Terms 445

CHAPTER 12 Political Parties 447

Why are political parties and partisanship so widely criticized,
but also so indispensable in a democratic system?

- **What Are Parties?** 449
    - Parties in Government 450
    - Parties as Organizations 456
    - Parties in the Electorate 461
- **The History of the American Party System** 464
    - The First Party System 464
    - The Second Party System 465
    - The Third Party System 466
    - The Fourth Party System 467
    - The Fifth Party System 469
    - The Sixth Party System 470
    - Understanding Transitions to New Party Systems 474
- **Why Two Parties?** 477
    - The Electoral System 478
    - National–State Political Relations 479
    - INTERESTS, INSTITUTIONS, AND OUTCOMES Sore-Loser Laws:
      Anti-Democratic, Smart Tactics, or Both? 480
    - Major-Party Actions 482
- **In Comparison: Parties** 482
    - Two Parties versus More Parties 482
    - Party Discipline 483
    - DATA EXPLORATION Do the Rich (Candidates) Get Richer?
      Fund-Raising and Political Parties 485
- **Key Intermediate Institutions of Democracy** 486

Further Reading 487
Key Terms 489

CHAPTER 13 Elections and Campaigns 491

Do campaigns matter in national elections,
and if so, how?

- **What Do Elections Accomplish?** 493
    - Determining Policy Direction and Ideology 493
    - Choosing Competent, Non-Corrupt Leaders 497
- **American Electoral Institutions** 500
    - State-Level Election Laws 501

Plurality Rule   504
Election Ballots   505
Direct Democracy   505

■ **American Electoral Campaigns**   507
Getting on the Ballot   507
Raising Campaign Money   510
Campaign Rhetoric and Prisoner's Dilemmas   515
INTERESTS, INSTITUTIONS, AND OUTCOMES Caucuses and Primaries:
    Who Goes First?   516
Campaigning with Modern Technologies   518
Voter Decision Making   522

■ **In Comparison: Elections**   525
Different Formal Electoral Institutions   525
Party-Centered, Ideological Elections   526
DATA EXPLORATION Which Candidates "Go Negative"? And When?   527
Limited Campaigning   528
Public Financing of Campaigns   528

■ **Is There a Need for Reform?**   529

Further Reading   531
Key Terms   533

CHAPTER 14 Mass Media and the Press. **535**
    Is media bias a problem in
    American politics?

■ **Mass Media and the Press in a Democracy**   537
Providing Essential Information   538
Evaluating and Interpreting   538
Helping Solve Collective Dilemmas   539
INTERESTS, INSTITUTIONS, AND OUTCOMES Verifying Political
    Statements   540

■ **Trends in Media and the Press**   542
The Eighteenth and Nineteenth Centuries   543
Network Television Comes to Predominate   544
Rise of New Media   545

■ **Mass Media Companies and the Profit Motive**   549

■ **Government Regulation**   551

■ **In Comparison: Mass Media**   554

■ **Are the American Press and Mass Media Biased?**   556
Discerning Bias   556
Ideological versus Other Kinds of Bias   558
How Can Bias Occur?   560

■ **Media Effects**   561
Who Chooses Which Media Content and Why?   561

What Is the Effect of Specific Media Content?   563

DATA EXPLORATION Do Fact-Checking Organizations Change
   Candidate Behavior?   565

Politicians and the Government as Sources   566

■ **The Media as Principals and Agents**   567

The Press and Mass Media as Principals   568

The Press and Mass Media as Agents   569

Further Reading   570

Key Terms   571

CHAPTER 15 Economic Policy **573**

What can governments do about the economy?
Why do they sometimes favor one approach over another?

■ **Government and the Economy: Ideas and Historical Trends**   575

Prominent Economic Philosophies   575

Economic Policy in the Early United States   578

A Growing Role for Government   580

■ **Benefits and Costs**   583

Types of Public Goods   583

Externalities   585

■ **Purposes of Economic Policies**   585

Distributing Benefits   586

Redistributing Benefits   586

Stabilizing the Economy   587

Regulating Commerce   590

Promoting Economic Growth   592

■ **Types of Policies**   593

Monetary Policies   593

Fiscal Policies   597

INTERESTS, INSTITUTIONS, AND OUTCOMES Independence and
   Accountability at the Federal Reserve   598

Trade Policies   605

■ **In Comparison: Economic Policy**   608

■ **The Politics of Economic Policy Making**   610

DATA EXPLORATION Income Inequality and Politics   611

Further Reading   613

Key Terms   615

CHAPTER 16 Social Policy **617**

Why are social policies
so controversial?

■ **What Are Social Policies?**   619

■ **Historical Perspective**   621

Social Policies at the State and Local Levels   621

The Growing Role of the National Government   623

■ **Major Areas of Social Policy**   626
Basic Provisions for the Poor   626
Social Insurance   628
Education   630
Health Care   631
INTERESTS, INSTITUTIONS, AND OUTCOMES Inequality in
  Public Education: Roots and Reforms   634
Housing   636
Crime Prevention   639

■ **Political Ideologies and Social Policies**   642

■ **In Comparison: Social Policy**   645
DATA EXPLORATION Who Deserves Social Services?   649

■ **Interest Groups, Parties, and Social Policy Making**   650
Collective Dilemmas among Sectors of Society   650
The Major Parties and Social Policies   651

■ **Explaining Political Outcomes**   652

Further Reading   654
Key Terms   655

CHAPTER 17 Foreign Policy **657**

What tools does the United States have to craft
foreign policy? When and why does it use them?

■ **Collective Dilemmas and Foreign Policy**   659
Domestic Dilemmas   659
International Dilemmas   660

■ **Theories and Strategies of Foreign Policy**   661
Realism   662
Idealism   662
Internationalism versus Isolationism   662
Unilateralism versus Multilateralism   663
The Democratic Peace as a Motivation   664
Contemporary Political Science Approaches   665

■ **Historical Perspective**   666

■ **Tools of Foreign Policy**   670
Basic Tools   670
Crisis Tools   677

■ **Making Foreign Policy**   682
Elected Leaders   682
Bureaucracies   683
DATA EXPLORATION Who (Do the American People Think) Makes
  Foreign Policy?   685
INTERESTS, INSTITUTIONS, AND OUTCOMES The Politics of
  Military Base Closings   686

Domestic Political Pressures   689

■ **Foreign Policy Doctrines**   691

■ **Domestic and International Constraints on Foreign Policy**   692

Further Reading   694
Key Terms   695

Appendix   A-1

The Declaration of Independence   A-1
The Articles of Confederation   A-5
The Constitution of the United States of America   A-12
Amendments to the Constitution   A-24
The Federalist Papers   A-34

Glossary   G-1
Credits   C-1
Index   I-1

PREFACE

D onald Trump's presidency has ushered in a new era in American politics. Many students were heavily invested emotionally and intellectually in the 2016 and 2018 elections, and there is and will continue to be a wide range of reactions to the Trump presidency.

A common impression used to be that students entering colleges and universities today did not care about politics and were uninformed. In fact, for many students the 2016 and 2018 elections mean a new sense of urgency to become informed and active. Even before they arrive at college, students are awash in details about politics, public opinion, and international events. They regularly encounter information or opinions about the political world, whether online; through traditional media, personal conversations, and public speeches; or within their clubs and other associations. And in recent years, they have witnessed repeated attacks on the quality of information they were getting from media sources. What are they to believe? The information from the typical media sources? Or those attacking the credibility of those typical sources?

Students thus face a confusing information environment about politics. Consider the conflicting—and often negative and misleading—messages about the American political system that are broadcast widely and likely to reach the typical student in the United States. Even giving brief attention to the news or other political programming might lead a person to believe some subset of the following: Politicians are venal and corrupt. Lobbyists are venal and corrupt. Congress cannot get anything done. The government meddles too much in the economy and/or in people's lives. The federal government cannot close a military base, reform a bureaucracy, or coordinate relief efforts effectively. The government does not promote jobs effectively enough. No politician wanting to keep his or her job would ever want to raise taxes. Americans' taxes are outrageously high. The Social Security program is going broke. The government spends too much beyond its budget. Political parties get in the way of effective compromise. The Supreme Court is out of touch with public opinion. Interest groups essentially bribe politicians.

Students may try to make sense of the American political system, but understanding can be elusive. The challenge of getting an accurate, coherent picture of American politics is exacerbated by the enormity of the American political system. The bombardment of information about a broad range of topics across different institutions and levels of government may give the impression of incoherence or disorder. The political system can look chaotic, random, and complex, making useful understanding nearly impossible.

Students entering introductory courses often lack a coherent intellectual framework and a set of logical concepts for making sense of political information. I wrote this book to provide such a framework, and this third edition sharpens the original framework even more. My goal is to deliver a clear introduction to the core facts about American government and an intellectual toolkit to navigate the extraordinarily complex political system in the United States. I want my students to be able to take that toolkit with them after the course, and I hope readers of this book will too. The tools in this book can help students understand the political issues and information they encounter throughout their lives—in the news as well as in their own experiences.

Analytical Tools for Understanding American Politics

This textbook conveys the core theoretical insights and analytical tools from modern political science and applies them to the American political system. Political science is a diverse discipline, so this textbook focuses on three core insights:

1. People face recurrent collective dilemmas and principal-agent problems.

2. Political institutions, including those in the United States, are intended to solve collective dilemmas and principal-agent problems.

3. The specific details of those institutions affect how costs and benefits are allocated in society. In other words, institutional details matter for who gets what in society.

After learning about this core and studying various kinds of collective dilemmas and principal-agent problems, students can make better sense of the major topics in American politics. For example, as they learn about Congress in Chapter 5, they can consider the institutional features of Congress—including the use of primary elections and legislative action such as agenda control by the Rules Committee in the House—with a keen eye toward how those features are intended to (but do not always) successfully solve social dilemmas. Students learn the consequences of having specific institutions in place in Congress, such as which states will benefit when the filibuster is used on spending bills. They can make sense of why members of Congress are typically reelected even when a large majority of Americans are unhappy with Congress as a whole. Or how internal congressional politics affects bargaining between the two chambers and between Congress and the president. In every chapter, the analytical tools from Chapter 1 are used to provide insight into the topic at hand.

A Problem-Oriented Approach

Each chapter starts with a puzzle, illustrated through a story about American politics, then uses the concepts and information in the chapter to help "solve" it. Chapter 1, for example, uses the story of the ongoing budget battles between Democratic and Republican party leaders, and asks how the two parties can consistently fail to solve long-term problems. Most Americans complain simultaneously about high deficits, their tax burdens, and not enough government spending on programs like education and infrastructure. At first the situation does not appear to make sense. If deficits are caused by the government spending more than it collects in taxes, then increased spending and lower taxes will increase the deficit. So it seems illogical that majorities support both maintaining current levels of spending and retaining existing tax rates, instead of raising more revenue from taxes. Only by further exploring the issue using concepts such as free riding, public goods, and collective dilemmas does the budget conflict (and the public's reaction) begin to make sense.

These types of puzzles motivate not only what follows in the chapters but also the priorities of political science researchers. The book reflects some of the best contemporary scholarship with rich citations, reference lists, and carefully annotated sources for the charts and tables. Students will find the information accessible, accurate, and clearly specified.

Insights through Comparison

To gain insights into how specific institutional details matter, each chapter includes an "In Comparison" section that describes features of the American system as they compare to those in other countries. Students will read about research findings on the consequences of having different institutions and social circumstances in other countries. For example, a section in Chapter 4 explores how France and the United States differ over the interpretation of the separation of church and state. A section in Chapter 13 looks at the differences between simple plurality and proportional electoral systems, and the research connecting those institutional details to certain political and policy outcomes. Sections in other chapters provide data and analysis comparing the United States to other countries on political participation, party systems, public opinion, and constitutional design. While instructors often do not have time to cover comparative material, the comparisons made in this textbook will help students understand the American system better by highlighting the impact of certain kinds of institutions.

Pedagogical Features

This textbook uses innovative pedagogy to help students grasp important concepts and master basic factual material. In each chapter, the following features reinforce the information in the chapter text.

NEW Data Exploration features in every chapter analyze a key piece of contemporary data that connects to the chapter's big ideas and help to answer the chapter puzzle. Here are some examples:

- How does public opinion about civil liberties and privacy change in reaction to domestic terrorist attacks? (Chapter 4: Civil Rights and Liberties)

- Do Republican presidents delegate authority to different agencies than Democratic presidents? (Chapter 6: The Presidency)

- Does the government listen more to wealthy people than to middle-class and poor people? (Chapter 9: Public Opinion)

Expanded and reconceived Interests, Institutions, and Outcomes features in every chapter provide students with real-world examples of how institutions work on collective dilemmas to foster specific outcomes. These can serve as models for students' own analysis or as prompts for classroom discussion. Here are some examples:

- How do state and federal policy around marijuana use differ? (Chapter 3: Federalism)

- Why does the budget of the Defense Department contain some strange expenditures, such as research on beef jerky? (Chapter 7: The Bureaucracy)

- Why should Iowa and New Hampshire have the early presidential election caucuses and primaries? (Chapter 13: Elections and Campaigns)

Know the Facts boxes give the nuts and bolts of American government without cluttering the text with excessive details on features that are relatively straightforward. Using clear tables and outlines, these boxes cover basic factual information that every student taking an American government course should know.

Historical Path boxes highlight important events in history that students should be familiar with, helping them to put these events in historical context and see long-term trends.

A rich art program includes tables and figures that are an integral part of each chapter, carefully chosen photos that illustrate key points, and marginal definitions of key terms.

New in the Third Edition

In preparing this third edition (election update), I was attentive to the feedback I received from professors who have used the textbook in their courses and from students in my own course. The new Data Exploration sections respond to a concern among faculty that students are reluctant to read or study charts and tables of data. The sections are straightforward in their exposition, but they also challenge students to make sense of data presentations. Likewise, as discussed earlier, the Interests, Institutions, and Outcomes feature offers additional material for students to consider in applying core concepts from the book, while new opening stories and contemporary examples keep the text fresh and compelling. As an example, Chapter 3 (Federalism) opens with a story about states' attempts (as in Arizona) to adopt immigration laws that may be at odds with federal policy. It poses the puzzle of why, in general, centralization has prevailed in conflicts between the national government and the states.

All chapters have new citations with contemporary scholarship, refreshed "Further Reading" lists, and updated data for charts and tables whenever possible. Finally, professors and students asked for more examples of contemporary real-world events that illustrate the concepts in the book. The Interests, Institutions, and Outcomes feature and the puzzle examples based on real-world events provide plenty of material for lectures, discussions, test questions, and topics for papers.

Support Materials for Students and Instructors

This textbook is accompanied by an extensive set of resources developed specifically for instructors and students to use with *The American Political System.*

Coursepacks Available at no cost to professors or students, Norton coursepacks for online or hybrid courses are available in a variety of formats, including Canvas, Desire2Learn, Moodle, and all versions of Blackboard. Content includes review material, chapter quizzes, Data Exploration exercises, and video exercises.

Instructor's Resource Disc

- *PowerPoints:* Written by Kimberly Rice (Western Illinois University), these PowerPoint slides feature concise text slides, helpful notes and suggestions for instructors, all the figures and photos from the text, and researcher videos.

- *Researcher Videos:* Prominent political scientists talk about key concepts in the text.
- *Art Files:* All figures, tables, and photos are available in JPEG and PowerPoint formats.

Instructor's Manual Written by Donald Gooch (Stephen F. Austin State University), the Instructor's Manual includes chapter outlines, lecture ideas, teaching suggestions, in-class activities based on the researcher videos and suggested web activities, supplementary readings, and in-class and home-work assignments.

Test Bank Written by Elizabeth Coggins (Colorado College), the Test Bank includes multiple-choice, true/false, and essay questions for every chapter, all labeled for question type, difficulty, and concept. Available in the following formats: PDF, RTF, LMSes like BlackBoard, Canvas, and Moodle, as well as ExamView Assessment Suite.

Ebook An affordable and convenient alternative, Norton ebooks retain the content and design of the print book and allow students to highlight and take notes with ease, print chapters as needed, and search the text for references. Norton ebooks are available online and as downloadable PDFs.

Acknowledgments

I am grateful for the comments, suggestions, and constructive criticisms provided by the following reviewers at various stages of this book's development:

Scott Adler, *University of Colorado Boulder*

Scott Ainsworth, *University of Georgia*

John Anderson, *University of Nebraska at Kearney*

Tama Andrews, *University of New Hampshire*

John Aughenbaugh, *Virginia Commonwealth University*

Julia Azari, *Marquette University*

Paul Bellinger, *Stephen F. Austin State University*

Michael Berkman, *Pennsylvania State University*

Robert Boatright, *Clark University*

Frederick Boehmke, *University of Iowa*

Walt Borges, *University of North Texas at Dallas*

Michael Brown, *Emerson College*

Brian Brox, *Tulane University*

Justin Buchler, *Case Western Reserve University*

Graham Bullock, *Davidson College*

Peter Burns, *Loyola University New Orleans*

Michael Burton, *Ohio University*

Jamie Carson, *University of Georgia*

Dan Cassino, *Fairleigh Dickinson University*

Matt Childers, *University of North Florida*

Suzanne Chod, *North Central College*

Jeffrey Christiansen, *Seminole State College*

Ann Cohen, *CUNY Hunter College*

Martin Cohen, *James Madison University*

M. Jeffrey Colbert, *University of North Carolina at Greensboro*

Paul Collins, *University of North Texas*

Michael Crespin, *University of Texas at Dallas*

Sharon Deubreau, *Rhodes State College*

Casey Dominguez, *University of San Diego*

Jamie Druckman, *Northwestern University*

David Dulio, *Oakland University*

Ralph Durham, *Kennesaw State University*

Justin Dyer, *University of Missouri*

Chris Ellis, *Bucknell University*

Matthew Eshbaugh-Soha, *University of North Texas*

William Ewell, *Stonehill College*

Emily Farris, *Texas Christian University*

Kathleen Ferraiolo, *James Madison University*

Femi Ferreira, *Hutchinson Community College*

Brian L. Fife, *Indiana University–Purdue University Fort Wayne*

Gina Flakes, *University of Kentucky and Eastern Kentucky University*

John Franklin, *Graceland University*

Rodd Freitag, *University of Wisconsin–Eau Claire*

Brad Gomez, *Florida State University*

Donald M. Gooch, *Stephen F. Austin State University*

Craig Goodman, *University of Houston–Victoria*

Andrew Green, *Central College*

Thad Hall, *University of Utah*

Edward Hasecke, *Wittenberg University*

Danny Hayes, *George Washington University*

Diane Heith, *St. John's University*

Roberta Herzberg, *Utah State University*

Matthew P. Hitt, *Louisiana State University*

James Hurtgen, *SUNY Fredonia*

Jessica Ice, *West Virginia University*

Dorothy James, *Connecticut College*

Marc James, *Brock University*

Richard Jankowski, *SUNY Fredonia*

Timothy Johnson, *University of Minnesota*

David Jones, *James Madison University*

Michael Julius, *Coastal Carolina University*

Kristin Kanthak, *University of Pittsburgh*

Josh Kaplan, *University of Notre Dame*

William E. Kelly, *Auburn University*

David Konisky, *Georgetown University*

Chris Koski, *Reed College*

Douglas W. Kuberski, *Florida State College at Jacksonville*

Chris Kypriotis, *Ohio State University*

Christopher Lawrence, *Texas A&M International University*

Beth Leech, *Rutgers University*

Jan Leighley, *University of Arizona*

Renan Levine, *University of Toronto, Scarborough*

Christine Lipsmeyer, *Texas A&M University*

Daniel Lipson, *SUNY New Paltz*

James Lutz, *Indiana University–Purdue University Fort Wayne*

Jason MacDonald, *West Virginia University*

Ellie Malone, *United States Naval Academy*

Tom Martin, *Eastern Kentucky University*

Andrea Mayer, *Georgetown University*

Corrine McConnaughy, *The Ohio State University*

Ian McDonald, *Duke University*

Amy McKay, *Georgia State University*

Seth C. McKee, *Texas Tech University*

Will Miller, *Southeast Missouri State University*

William Mishler, *University of Arizona*

Jamie Monogan, *University of Georgia*

Joanna Mosser, *Drake University*

Ken Mulligan, *Southern Illinois University*

Michael Nelson, *Rhodes College*

James Newman, *Idaho State University*

Hans Noel, *Georgetown University*

Timothy Nokken, *Texas Tech University*

Paul Nolette, *Marquette University*

Catherine Paden, *Simmons College*

Evan Parker-Stephen, *Texas A&M University*

Justin Phillips, *Columbia University*

Jeremy Pope, *Brigham Young University*

Michael Reinhard, *Millsaps College*

Kimberly Rice, *Western Illinois University*

Jesse Richman, *Old Dominion University*

Travis Ridout, *Washington State University*

Jason Roberts, *The University of North Carolina at Chapel Hill*

Robert Robinson, *The University of Alabama at Birmingham*

Mark Rom, *Georgetown University*

Beth Rosenson, *University of Florida*

Robert Sahr, *Oregon State University*

Debra Salazar, *Western Washington University*

Pamela Schaal, *Ball State University*

Scot Schraufnagel, *Northern Illinois University*

Amy Semet, *Dartmouth College*

Jungkun Seo, *University of North Carolina Wilmington*

Emily Shaw, *Thomas College*

James Sheffield, *The University of Oklahoma*

Valeria Sinclair-Chapman, *Purdue University*

Fred Slocum, *Minnesota State University*

Keith Smith, *University of the Pacific*

Stephen Swindle, *Lee University*

Barry Tadlock, *Ohio University*

Terri Towner, *Oakland University*

Sarah Treul, *University of North Carolina at Chapel Hill*

Jessica Trounstine, *University of California, Merced*

Joseph Ura, *Texas A&M University*

Abby Van Horn, *North Central College*

Renee Van Vechten, *University of Redlands*

Justin Vaughn, *Boise State University*

Greg Vonnahme, *University of Missouri–Kansas City*

Charles Walcott, *Virginia Tech*

Timothy Werner, *University of Texas at Austin*

Kenneth C. Williams, *Michigan State University*

Stephen Wirls, *Rhodes College*

Patrick Wohlfarth, *University of Maryland, College Park*

Frederick Wood, *Coastal Carolina University*

Gina Woodall, *Arizona State University*

Thanks are also due to the following people for helping to put the first edition of the book together: Daniel Magleby, Sang-Jung Han, David Cottrell, Molly Reynolds, Semra Koknar, Sarah Neuman, Michael Robbins, Phil Clark, Nick Marcus, Hannah Bozian, Sarah Danserau, Josh Deyoung, Emma Rew, Peter Gutsche, Zachary Goldsmith, Charles Doriean, Jennifer Miller-Gonzales, Paul Poast, and Tim Ryan. Paul Gargaro was especially helpful in the initial drafting of chapters. The second edition was put together with the help of David Cottrell, Phil Schermer, Richard Anderson, and Erica Mirabitur.

In creating this third edition, I received substantial assistance from Erica Mirabitur, who deserves credit for finding much of the information for the new Data Exploration sections and any new Interests, Institutions, and Outcomes boxes, as well as my deep thanks for her professionalism and collegiality. As she launches her own career in research, I commend her and express my admiration for her talent and doggedness. The team at Norton—including project editor Laura Dragonette and production manager Elizabeth Marotta—did a superb job keeping track of the myriad details throughout the development and production process and ensuring the high quality of the printed book. Thanks to Steve Dunn for supporting the original idea, to Roby Harrington for key moments of inspiration during lively conversations, and to Ann Shin, a talented, demanding editor who confidently guided me to the end of a long process for the first edition. With the second edition, Ann began the process as editor, and then handed things over to Pete Lesser, who has been a terrific creative partner. Pete has been an excellent editor of this third edition, pushing me when necessary to improve the text and the features. Samantha Held also deserves my gratitude for handling the details of this third edition and doing wonderful work in editing and putting the final product together. This election update was helped along tremendously by Max Housner's hard work, and by the able assistance of Anna Olcott.

Ken Kollman

Third Edition

THE AMERICAN POLITICAL SYSTEM

2018 Election Update

Republican businessman Donald Trump won the 2016 presidential election after vowing to "make America great again." A large part of this promise centered around improving the economy. Although Trump won the presidency and Republicans maintained control of both houses of Congress for two years, economics and taxes remained highly contentious. How can the tools of political science help us explain the deep divisions and obstacles we see in American political life?

Introduction

What can the tools of political science tell us that we don't already know?

After a bitter, divisive election campaign, Republican Donald Trump won the election to the presidency of the United States and upended the American political system. His victory was a dramatic surprise that caught many people off guard, including election analysts, pollsters, politicians in Washington, D.C., and the state capitals around the country.

After the shock of Trump's win wore off, focus turned quickly to what his presidency would look like, especially in light of the deep political divide in the country, and the Democrats poised to contest the 2018 elections with momentum. During his campaign, Trump promised to change many things if elected. Among his promises were to lower taxes, improve the country's infrastructure, bolster the military and veterans' benefits, and rebuild the economy in financially depressed areas. Trump was not specific on how he planned to do all this at the same time and was only able to pass one major piece of legislation in spite of having Republican control of Congress for the first two years.

Budgeting has been a source of deep conflict within the government. For more than a decade before 2016, the U.S. government experienced one budgetary crisis after another. Every time a major decision loomed over the government's budget and borrowing capacity (its debt ceiling, as it is known), deadlines were set, grandstanding among political adversaries ensued, pundits threatened economic doom, and intense negotiations among politicians lasted into the early morning hours. Government officials used stark words and phrases to describe the consequences of the government's actions, or inactions, in dealing with the basic disagreements between the two major political parties over the budget. For example, they claimed that if leaders of the two political parties did not come to an agreement over taxes and spending, the government might fall off a "fiscal cliff," funding for many government programs would be subject to "sequestration" (mandatory budget cuts), or the government might default on its debt obligations.

OUTLINE

- Understanding American Politics

- Collective Dilemmas and the Need for Government

- Types of Collective Dilemmas

- Principal-Agent Problems

- Designing Institutions

- In Comparison: Types of Government Institutions

- Analyzing Politics and Government Using the Tools of Political Science

Disagreements between Republicans and Democrats over budgets are not petty or trivial but reflect fundamental differences in policy goals and society outcomes. Leaders of both parties recognize that large deficit spending cannot continue indefinitely. In general, Democrats seek targeted increases in government spending and increased taxes on the wealthy, while Republicans seek deep cuts to government spending and no tax increases on anyone. Compromises are hard fought, and when they come, they follow bitter negotiations. All this leads to a general feeling that nobody wins. Many economic problems get put off until later, and the essential decisions over how to ensure sustainable government budgets are postponed.

A key component of budget planning is tax policy and, in general, Americans do not like to pay taxes. It has never been popular for politicians of either major party to call for an increase in taxes. At the same time, however, Americans ask a lot of their government. They want it to educate children, preserve public order, provide health care for the elderly and the poor, regulate products and services, build roads and bridges, and provide student loans for college; and also fight terrorism and protect the country and its interests abroad. Moreover, most Americans prefer that it operate on a balanced budget, spending no more than it collects in taxes and other revenue.

The expectations Americans have for their government often seem incompatible with their dislike of taxes. Politicians commonly complain that the American people want the government to do more than what they are willing to pay. This conflict, coupled with partisan rancor over the proper long-term solution, often leads to stalemates and inaction on many issues, including the budget. Many Americans wonder why politicians cannot just come to an agreement on a long-term solution. But the reasons are not mysterious, given how social scientists think about political systems and institutions.

The Trump administration began with a "unified" government, meaning that Republicans controlled both houses of Congress and the presidency. Presumably, that would give him a good chance of passing a budget that reflects his preferences and policy goals. However, deep conflicts among the Republicans derailed much of his economic agenda. Then, the 2018 elections brought Democrats to majority power in the House. People wondered whether the Democrats would try to work with Trump and Senate Republicans or attempt to stonewall any new economic policies.

When it comes to critical issues like how to raise and spend the federal government's money, conflicts are inevitable, even within the same political party. In this chapter, and throughout this book, we will ask—and answer—the question: How can basic concepts in political science help us understand the complexities and apparent contradictions of the American political system? The tools presented here will help you understand the processes and outcomes we see in American political life.

Understanding American Politics

Politics refers to the process of making collective decisions, usually by governments, to allocate public resources and to create and enforce rules for the operation of society. A **political system** is the way a society organizes and manages its politics across various levels of public authority. This book will deepen your understanding of the American political system.

The political scientist Harold Lasswell once offered an alternative definition of politics as the struggle over "who gets what, when, [and] how."[1] Lasswell's curt definition highlights the fact that people have **preferences** over things that government can potentially provide, and they take actions to satisfy those preferences. Generally speaking, people prefer more benefits and fewer costs, and they understand that they live in a society with others who

politics The process of making collective decisions, usually by governments, to allocate public resources and create and enforce rules for the operation of society.

political system The way a society organizes and manages its politics across various levels of public authority.

preferences The outcomes or experiences people want or believe they need.

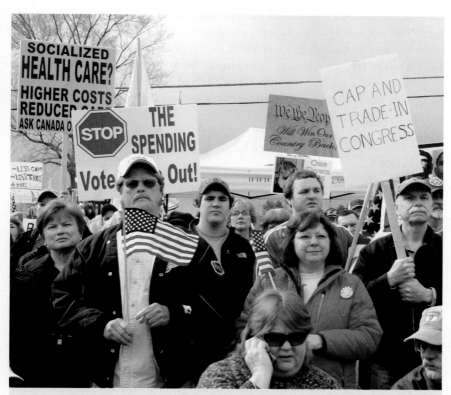

Conflicts over the nation's debt limit, taxes, and spending priorities seem to exemplify chaos and contradictions in American politics. However, when we look deeper, we begin to see the often predictable ways that American political institutions shape debates about current events and the policy outcomes that ensue.

[1] Harold D. Lasswell, *Politics: Who Gets What, When, How* (New York: Whittlesey House/McGraw-Hill, 1936).

have their own, sometimes competing, preferences. For example, we want more money for our families and we wish to pay less in taxes, though we also understand that we need to pay some taxes in order for society to function. Peoples' preferences, including how strongly they prefer some things over others, shape their ideas about how society should be run and what actions governments should take. If I strongly prefer to pay less in taxes and am willing to live with fewer government services, then I will try to convince the government to cut taxes for people like me. Alternatively, if I strongly prefer more government services and am willing to pay more in taxes for those services, I will try to convince the government to bolster services for people like me.

Politics determines the distribution or redistribution of benefits and costs to satisfy those preferences, and therefore it often involves considerable conflict. It goes without saying that people often do not share the same preferences. One person's costs could be another person's benefits. Nor do people share the same ideas about how society should be run. The people who want more government services are in conflict with those who want lower taxes. It is rare to observe a governmental decision where everyone believes that the government has taken the correct action to satisfy his or her preferences. Much of the time in politics, some people win more benefits and some people pay more costs, and even if everyone wins some benefits, certain people win more than others.

Institutions

institutions Rules or sets of rules or practices that determine how people make collective decisions.

In light of people's conflicting preferences and disagreements, there must be means of making collective decisions. Those decisions happen because of the workings of institutions. In politics, **institutions** are the rules or sets of rules or practices that determine how people make collective decisions. Institutions include the rules and procedures for passing laws, interpreting laws, enforcing laws, counting votes and electing governments, and appointing government employees, among many other functions. The institutions of government vary across countries, states, and parts of the world, and they can change over time with important implications for societies. They determine who can legally do what, when, and how, and they affect how the political system distributes benefits and costs among people in society.[2]

The term *institution* may be confusing because it is abstract and can be used in multiple ways. It can refer to large parts of the government or to specific procedures or organizations. The three major branches of the U.S. government—the executive (the White House and the presidency), the legislative (Congress), and

---

[2] Kenneth A. Shepsle, *Analyzing Politics: Rationality, Behavior, and Institutions,* 2nd ed. (New York: Norton, 2010).

Political Institutions

Political institutions include

- **Branches of Government**
  Examples: Congress
  The president
  The federal courts

- **Organizations**
  Examples: The Internal Revenue Service
  The Rules Committee in the House of Representatives
  The electoral college
  Political parties
  Interest groups

- **Rules and Procedures**
  Examples: Simple plurality election rules
  Separation of powers
  Judicial review
  Campaign finance laws

the judicial (the Supreme Court)—are each important institutions in American politics, but formal institutions do not always refer to a branch of government or a particular level of government. The methods of electing people to offices, for example—the voting rules, including the electoral college—and the codified procedures adopted for bargaining between the branches of government are also key institutions of government.

Informal institutions, which are not codified in written form and are not required to exist according to the Constitution or the law, are also central. Examples include the major political parties; they are considered crucial to the functioning of Congress and of elections. Interest groups play a vital role in determining which policies get chosen. Media companies, the press, and other communication organizations inform citizens and expose government actions. Alongside the formal institutions of government, these political organizations outside of the legal framework of the government help make the political system operate.

One way to think of a political system is as a bundle of institutions, both formal and informal, within which many diverse people pursue the satisfaction of their preferences. The national government in the United States sits atop the American political system, but there is much more to a **federal system** like that of the United States. In federal systems, there are multiple levels

federal system A political system with multiple levels of government, in which each level has independent authority over some important policy areas.

An institution can be as big as an entire branch of government, such as Congress, or it can be as specific as a rule for making a particular decision, such as how the Speaker of the House of Representatives is chosen. In 2019, Nancy Pelosi (D-CA) was chosen as Speaker through codified rules for electing party leaders.

of government with independent authority over important areas of policy. Each resident of the country is also affected by the policies of the nearly 90,000 state and local governments. People's lives are changed daily by the regulations and budgets decided on by city, county, state, and regional governments, and by the day-to-day decisions of governors, mayors, council members, attorneys general, prosecutors, assessors, and comptrollers at lower levels of government.

We will see in this book that the specific nature of these political institutions matters. It is not enough to explain a political outcome by saying that it occurred because "people wanted it that way." *How* they make their collective decisions has consequences. Institutions of government profoundly shape political outcomes.

Consider the example of the electoral college, an institution that determines which person wins the presidency of the United States. Had the institution for choosing the president been different—in particular, if the presidency were decided purely by which candidate received the most votes—the election of 2016 would have put Hillary Clinton in the White House. Clinton won more popular votes than Donald Trump in 2016, but she lost the presidency because Trump received more votes in the electoral college. (We will discuss the electoral college in more detail in later chapters.)

In fact, the collection of procedures used to select the president of the United States—the voting rules used by the states, the rules governing the electoral college, the rules the two major parties use to choose their candidates, the tie-breaking rules, and the methods for settling the outcome when it is not determined simply—constitutes a bundle of institutions with major consequences for determining the winner of the ultimate prize in American politics.

As another example, the institutions described by the U.S. Constitution specify that two senators are to be elected from each state, regardless of population size. Thus, the politics of the Senate are constrained by institutional rules that have had the important effect of giving more representation to people from smaller, more rural states than to those from larger, more urban states. Wyoming, with approximately 580,000 residents, has the same number of senators representing its citizens as California, with approximately 40 million residents. Consequently, the Senate has traditionally been the unit of the U.S. government that is most prone to ensuring generous benefits for farmers. A central question that this book will help answer is how the institutions of the American political system lead to disparities in the apportionment of benefits and costs among people. These benefits and costs are not equitably distributed throughout the United States, and most scholars point to persistent biases in the system as the source of such disparities.

Without a framework for understanding the American political system, its complexity can seem overwhelming. To begin making sense of this system, let's look first at individual behavior and then institutional design and collective choices. We start by focusing on the "micro" level of politics—the social dilemmas arising among individuals and organizations that require some level of authority to solve.

Collective Dilemmas and the Need for Government

Suppose you live in a house with several other students and share a kitchen. The kitchen is always a mess—dirty dishes in the sink, food on the counters and floor, and garbage spilling out of the wastebasket. Moreover, the kitchen needs new equipment, particularly a new refrigerator that the landlord refuses to buy. You and your housemates all agree that you want a clean kitchen and a new refrigerator. Yet despite this understanding, the kitchen remains dirty and no one bothers to buy the refrigerator. Why won't anyone take care of these problems?

Imagine that you get mad enough to do something about the situation. You wake up one morning, clean the kitchen, and buy the refrigerator on your credit card. You ask your housemates to help pay for the refrigerator, but only some pay their share. You wish you had a way to enforce a rule that only those who paid for the refrigerator could use it. Furthermore, you wish there was a rule restricting kitchen use to those who will clean it. You cannot, however, enforce these rules, so all of your housemates enjoy the newly cleaned kitchen and the new refrigerator, regardless of their contributions.

Your frustration ultimately leads you to propose rules that determine who has to clean the kitchen and when, and who has to pay for the new equipment. Some housemates object, claiming that they don't mind a dirty kitchen and don't use the refrigerator very often. They propose to leave things as they are. Soon after, the kitchen becomes dirty, and when the need arises to replace a broken microwave oven, no one bothers to buy it. The problems begin to mount once again.[3]

collective dilemma A situation in which there is conflict between group goals and individual goals or self-interest.

Even if you haven't faced this precise situation, you have likely encountered something similar. A group is challenged by a **collective dilemma** when there is a conflict between group goals and individual goals or self-interest. Such dilemmas can be found everywhere.[4] Take, for example, the economist Thomas Schelling's story of the mattress in the middle of the road.[5] A traffic jam arises as cars slow to a crawl to bypass the mattress. One after another, each driver makes the decision to drive around the mattress and continue on his or her way, and the traffic jam persists. Had one driver taken the time to stop and move the mattress off the road, the traffic snarl would have been eliminated. But for each driver individually, it is easier and faster to simply drive around the mattress.

Maybe you know of a park with trash on the ground that no one will pick up. Or you may belong to an organization that has difficulty recruiting volunteers to work at events or to help pay for food or equipment. These are all situations in which a group of individuals would be better off if some action were taken to resolve the collective dilemma—clean the kitchen, buy the refrigerator, move the mattress, clean the park—yet group goals are often thwarted by individual self-interest. People may be incapable of solving their collective dilemmas without the presence of some authority, or they may lack a personal incentive to resolve the issue for the betterment of the group.

These stories help illustrate the need for government. Some people argue that government is unnecessary because members of society can self-govern by organizing activities that contribute to the common good. Most philosophers and political theorists, however, disagree. In the absence of government, they argue, chaos reigns. Many would concur with Thomas Hobbes, the

[3] For a general statement of one version of this problem, see Garrett Hardin, "The Tragedy of the Commons," *Science* 162 (December 1968): 1243–48.

[4] Russell Hardin, *Collective Action* (Baltimore: Johns Hopkins University Press, 1982).

[5] Thomas Schelling, *Micromotives and Macrobehavior* (New York: Norton, 2006).

seventeenth-century English philosopher, who claimed that without a sovereign, society would become a "war of all against all."[6] By sovereign, Hobbes meant a person, group, or government with a monopoly control of force over a well-defined territory. In other words, a sovereign is the final authority—the decision maker of last resort—that can enforce its decisions over others. Imagine a society lacking such authority. There would be no courts or governments to enforce contracts; theft would be rampant, with no threat of prosecution; victims would pursue their own justice, sinking society into a swirl of destruction and unhappiness. A sovereign, therefore, is necessary for an ordered, stable society. Government is not only necessary to solve the fundamental problem that Hobbes identified, it is also essential for solving many of the collective dilemmas that arise in everyday life, such as funding for park maintenance, police protection, education, national defense, and care for the poor. Without the coercive power of government, few services of collective benefit would be provided.

Today, most of us take the need for government for granted. It is true that many governments throughout history have been oppressive and have mistreated their people. All too many have started wars with other countries without justification. The *absence* of government, however, can be at least as bad, if not worse. The idea that societies fall apart without government does not merely spring from the fanciful imagination of philosophers. In recent decades, some societies have exemplified Hobbes's war. In Somalia in the 1990s, parts of the Congo in the 2000s, and recently in some parts of Afghanistan, Mali, and Yemen, the lack of sovereign governments led to long periods of competition among unchecked militias or roving bands of thugs led by warlords that terrorized people and destroyed cities and towns without regard for loss of life.

Contemporary debates over the appropriate size of government tend not to be about whether we need government at all, but rather about what part the government should play in people's economic, social, and personal lives. Such debates hinge on concerns about the amount of government involvement in resolving collective dilemmas, and whether people should be left alone to solve those dilemmas themselves. Toward one end of the spectrum, libertarians believe that governments should do only the bare minimum to address collective social concerns, such as building roads and bridges and maintaining a small standing army to defend the country. Toward the other end of the spectrum, socialists believe government should provide an extensive social safety net, including generous unemployment benefits; free health coverage, education, and child care; and heavily subsidized utilities, housing, and transportation.[7] Most of the debate within the United States occurs between these two ends of the spectrum; disagreements are matters of degree.

---

[6] Thomas Hobbes, *Leviathan* (1651; repr., New York: Oxford University Press, 2009).

[7] We will discuss these and other political philosophies in later chapters, especially Chapters 9 and 16.

Types of Collective Dilemmas

As we study the American government and political system, it will be useful to consider four types of collective dilemmas common in politics.

Collective Action Problems

In the housemates example, a clean kitchen is a collective good, or what economists call a public good. A **public good** refers to a benefit provided to a group of people that each member can enjoy without necessarily having to pay costs for it, and for which one person's enjoyment of it does not inhibit the enjoyment of it by others.[8] A classic example of a public good is clean air to breathe. Something like the bite of a hamburger or a sip of a soft drink is a **private good**, which refers to a product or benefit provided to you such that your consumption of it precludes others from consuming it.

The problem is that public goods can be hard to produce without some external enforcer (for example, government) requiring that people pay for them. People will be tempted to **free ride**, which means they will benefit from the public good while avoiding the costs of contributing to it. As with producing the clean kitchen that you and your housemates desire, the public good clashes with individual incentives.[9] A **collective action problem** is any situation in which people are individually better off when free riding and enjoying the public good that others produce without contributing toward the production of that public good.

Your free-riding housemates enjoyed the clean kitchen, and that made you angry because you paid the price and they did not. Likewise, governments produce public goods—such as parks, national defense, clean air and water, public beaches, traffic lights, and streetlights—that benefit anyone in the vicinity, even if he or she did not pay the taxes to produce those goods.

If there is effective enforcement, however, public goods can be produced with fair systems of payment or contribution by all those who enjoy them. Some kind of authority can be necessary even at the most basic level. Without some form of governance applied to you and your housemates, the kitchen will probably remain dirty. Without some kind of enforcement by the Internal Revenue Service, people would not pay enough taxes to support basic government services.

In later chapters, we will explore a variety of collective action problems that occur in all modern political systems, including the American system.

public good A benefit provided to a group of people such that each member can enjoy it without necessarily having to pay for it, and one person's enjoyment of it does not inhibit others from enjoying the benefit.

private good A product or benefit provided such that its enjoyment can be limited to specific people, and one individual's consumption of it precludes others from consuming it.

free riding Benefiting from a public good while avoiding the costs of contributing to it.

collective action problem A situation in which people would be better off if they all cooperated; however, any individual has an incentive not to cooperate as long as others are cooperating.

[8] Mancur Olson, *The Logic of Collective Action: Public Goods and the Theory of Groups* (Cambridge, MA: Harvard University Press, 1971).

[9] Many goods considered public are not pure, in the sense that they contain elements of a private good. For example, the new refrigerator can be subject to crowding: the availability of the refrigerator is a public good to you and your housemates, but each space on a shelf is more of a private good during the period you use it. Public parks are considered public goods, but at some point one person's enjoyment may impinge on another's enjoyment.

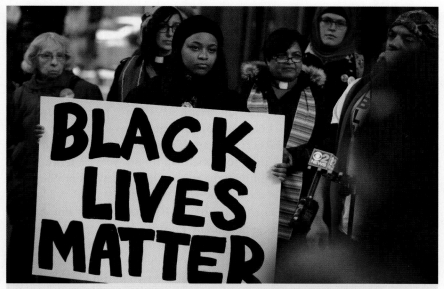

The #BlackLivesMatter movement represents a collective action problem. Those who actively protest absorb the costs of doing so while many others who do not nonetheless benefit from the attention the movement draws to race-driven police fatalities and police reform.

You will discover that collective action problems are endemic in politics. For example, protests by the #BlackLivesMatter movement require active participants who are willing to gather in big cities like Chicago, Milwaukee, St. Louis, and Dallas in response to the shooting deaths of black teenagers by police. Many of the participants in these protests are from other states. For instance, protesters in Ferguson, Missouri, arrived on busses with others united by the cause. Although the movement is for all black Americans and anyone who feels a need for police reforms around racial profiling, the protesters pay the costs of participating while having to share the benefits—increased attention to race-driven police fatalities—with those who choose not to participate.

All voluntary organizations, including movements like #BlackLivesMatter, face collective action problems daily as they seek contributors to their cause. If a voluntary organization cannot solve such problems, it will cease to exist. This is just one example of how collective action problems occur in politics; they also present challenges in other types of groups and other situations.

Prisoner's Dilemma Situations

A famous parable in modern social science tells the story of two criminal suspects caught after a burglary. The police separate the suspects (we will call them John and Frank) so that they cannot communicate with each other, and interrogate them individually to try to induce confessions. The police have enough evidence on each man that even if no confessions are forthcoming, they can get them sentenced to a year in prison. However, if either John or Frank provides more evidence against the other man, the police can get a harsher sentence for the one implicated (and get closer to solving the crime). In this context, each man is offered a stark choice: implicate your partner or stay silent. If John implicates Frank and Frank stays silent, John goes free and Frank gets six years in prison. Likewise, if Frank implicates John and John stays silent, Frank goes free and John gets six years. If they both implicate each other, then they each get three years in prison (less than the six-year sentence, to reward their individual cooperation with the police). If both stay silent, they each get one year. Figure 1.1 shows the four possible outcomes.

The situation is troubling for the prisoners. No matter what Frank does, John receives a lighter sentence—potentially no prison time at all—by implicating Frank. The same goes for Frank. Therefore, both prisoners, if they decide to serve their individual interests, implicate their partner. The expected outcome of this situation is the convergence of the two selfish strategies: each prisoner will implicate the other, and both will receive three years in prison. But note that the expected outcome is not the best outcome for the prisoners together. The **prisoner's dilemma** is that each of them would be better off if they cooperated and remained silent, but they cannot achieve the better collective outcome unless there is a way to enforce their cooperation.[10] Moreover, social scientists pay attention to **transaction costs**, which are the challenges people face when they try to exchange information or use other means to cooperate with each other. In the case of the prisoners, they cannot communicate at all, so no transactions can happen to achieve the better outcome.

Note the similarity between the prisoner's dilemma and the collective action problem. In both situations, what is good for the group is difficult to achieve because of individual temptations. In the prisoner's dilemma, the overriding individual temptation is to implicate your partner (to "defect"), but in the collective action problem, the temptation is to free ride off the members of your group who are contributing. Collective action problems, therefore, are multi-person versions of prisoner's dilemmas.

The prisoner's dilemma is also a generic version of situations that regularly occur in American politics. Two candidates campaigning for election to the same office, for example, would both benefit if neither spent much money on television advertising. It is quite possible that the election outcome would be the same if neither one advertised or if both advertised. Yet if one candidate advertises and the other does not, then the former is likely to win. Neither candidate can escape the trap of spending large amounts on television adver-

prisoner's dilemma An interaction between two strategic actors in which neither actor has an incentive to cooperate even though each of them would be better off if they both cooperated.

transaction costs The challenges people face when they try to exchange information or use other means to cooperate with each other.

[10] Robert Axelrod, *The Evolution of Cooperation* (New York: Basic Books, 1984).

The Prisoner's Dilemma: The Concept in Context

A classic collective action problem is the prisoner's dilemma. We use the figure here to illustrate the choices and outcomes for two hypothetical prisoners, John and Frank, and two candidates.

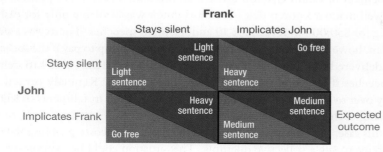

John gets the red jail sentence and Frank gets the blue for any of the four combinations of actions. No matter what action Frank takes, John is always better off implicating Frank. Likewise, no matter what action John takes, Frank is always better off implicating John. The expected outcome, therefore, is for both to implicate each other (bottom right). However, if they could cooperate with each other and stay silent, they both could have a better outcome (upper left). The dilemma is that their individual interests always tug them toward the worse (collective) outcome.

The logic is similar for two candidates locked in an electoral competition and deciding how to spend their campaign money. Each is better off running expensive TV advertisements against the opponent, no matter what the opponent does. But they both could be better off collectively if they save their campaign funds and run no TV ads. This scenario assumes that the outcome would be the same (toss-up election) if either the upper left or the lower right scenario occurs.

tising. The result is expensive advertising by both sides, often with little effect on the election outcome (see Figure 1.1).

An external authority or a neutral party, however, can enforce cooperation among people to overcome collective action obstacles. The political scientist Dennis Chong offers as an example the prisoner's dilemma that arose during the 1960 presidential campaign, when candidate John F. Kennedy sought the endorsement of Adam Clayton Powell, an influential New York politician.

Powell made it known that his endorsement was available only for cash—settling for $50,000 in return for 10 endorsement speeches. There was a small problem, however: Powell did not trust the Kennedy camp to pay if the speeches were delivered first, and the Kennedy camp did not trust Powell to deliver the speeches if he were paid in advance. The solution? Kennedy turned the money over to an intermediary, who would pay it out in installments of $5,000 following each endorsement speech.[11]

In this case, the intermediary reduced the transaction costs, enabling the two men to overcome a collective dilemma. This situation could be categorized as a repeated prisoner's dilemma, where each faced an individual temptation to "defect" from the agreement to cooperate. Yet even the intermediary could not ensure resolution of the problem's final stage. As Chong adds in an intriguing postscript, "What incentive did Kennedy have to make the final payment?"[12]

Governments play the role of external authorities in many related situations, including the enforcement of contracts among people or organizations. For example, the government helps labor unions and corporations in their negotiations over wages and working conditions by making sure that each side lives up to the agreements reached during labor talks.

Coordination Problems

People often fail to coordinate on a course of action even though they all wish they had. If you and a friend agree to meet downtown for lunch at noon but forget to specify the location (and at least one of you does not have a cell phone, so you cannot communicate), where would you meet? Perhaps you would go to the last place you had lunch together. Or maybe you would look for your friend at her favorite place. In the end, you are unlikely to find each other.

A **coordination problem** is any situation in which each individual in a group prefers to act in common with the others, but there are multiple possible common actions to take; and for a variety of reasons (usually incomplete information), the individuals might have difficulty coordinating on a single, cooperative action. People often face coordination problems either because

coordination problem A situation in which two or more people are all better off if they coordinate on a common course of action, but there is more than one possible course of action to take.

[11] Dennis Chong, *Collective Action and the Civil Rights Movement* (Chicago: University of Chicago Press, 1991), p. 38.

[12] Chong, *Collective Action and the Civil Rights Movement*, p. 38.

they cannot communicate or because there is a fundamental disagreement over the best action to take. Such situations differ from prisoner's dilemmas, where the expected outcome is for both prisoners to implicate the other. With the prisoner's dilemma, there is one expected outcome: the pair does not cooperate with each other. In coordination problems, each member of the group wants to coordinate on a single outcome with the others, even though more than one outcome is possible.

As mentioned, people are frequently conflicted about the desirability of a given behavior, making it hard to coordinate. For example, let's say your friend prefers to eat Chinese food and you prefer pizza. What is most important to each of you, however, is that you eat together rather than eating alone, even at your preferred restaurant. This reflects an important type of coordination problem in which members of a group have a strong desire to coordinate, but they disagree over the precise behavior on which to coordinate (Figure 1.2).

FIGURE 1.2

Coordination Problems: The Concept in Context

We often see coordination problems in everyday life. This figure illustrates the challenges of coordinating what kind of food to eat with friends. It helps to walk through all scenarios one by one. For any of the four outcomes you get the red "satisfaction level" and your friend gets the blue. You like pizza better than Chinese food but you want to eat with your friend. Your friend likes Chinese food better than pizza but wants to eat with you. Assume for the moment that the two of you cannot communicate, but must show up at one of the two restaurants. Where will you go? While any of the four outcomes are possible, the upper left and the lower right outcomes are better collectively than the other two outcomes. Now, assume that you can communicate. What will you say to make sure that both of you coordinate on going to the same restaurant? It will likely depend on the nature of your relationship with your friend, which is another way of saying that it will depend on the institutionalized patterns of behavior that you have with your friend. Do you always get your way? Does your friend? Where do you always go on this day of the week? Do you alternate who gets to choose the restaurant? These are examples of mechanisms used by friends to make decisions and, more generally, for groups of people to solve coordination problems.

A classic example from politics is when members of a political party in Congress want to coordinate their support and get behind one bill and pass it into law. Members of the same political party in Congress, even if they have a majority of votes, may disagree over which bill to support. The negative scenario for the party is a failure to coordinate, meaning they split their votes among rival bills, and undermine the passing of either bill because of internal party squabbling. Failure to coordinate on a common legislative strategy will enable the opposition party to exploit the divisions and keep both bills from passing. In the positive scenario, party members effectively unite behind a single bill and pass it with enough affirmative votes.

Because people are sometimes indifferent regarding how best to coordinate, many coordination hurdles are easily overcome. Most people simply want a decision to be made so that they can accurately anticipate how others will behave. In the early twentieth century, countries had to choose the side of the road on which cars would drive. Some countries, especially the former British colonies, chose the left side. This is a simple example of government establishing a rule to coordinate people's behavior for everyone's benefit. In terms of safety, it does not matter which side people drive on as long as there is a consistent rule that everyone follows. A more widespread example of coordination is the worldwide adoption of traffic signals, where red lights mean stop and green lights mean go. If governments did not make and enforce consistent rules to coordinate such behavior, the world's roadways would be far more dangerous places.

Comparing Collective Action Problems and Coordination Problems: Example from Voting

We see collective action and coordination problems all around us, and sometimes they encourage us to act alone or to stand with others—even when facing the same situation. Consider the case of voting for student government. Suppose two of your friends, Jane and Marie, both want to be elected to the same student council position, as does Tina—someone you and your friends do not know at all. First, you are faced with a collective action problem: Is it in your best interest to vote or not? Voting takes time, and unless the outcome of voting is an exact tie, your vote will not be decisive. So why not save time and let others vote—in other words, free ride? Second, if you do decide to vote, you and your friends face a coordination problem. Your friends may disagree over which of your friends to support—Jane or Marie. A failure to coordinate would lead you and your friends to split your votes between Jane and Marie, possibly enabling Tina—the rival candidate from a more united group of voters—to win the election. Alternatively, your friends effectively could unite behind a single candidate (either Jane *or* Marie) and defeat the rival contestant (Tina). Interestingly, while in the collective action problem, your incentives are to do the opposite of what the others do (you wanted to free ride while the others voted); in the coordination problem, your incentives are to do the same thing as your friends (vote for the same candidate).

Unstable Coalitions

Politics is about dividing and uniting people. Different interests divide members of society or groups within that society, resulting in disagreements over the best courses for implementing collective action. The ability to accomplish anything in politics, however, demands that people unite into effective coalitions. Unless you are an all-powerful dictator who can force people to bend to your will, a collective effort typically is required to take action for a common cause. The process of forming coalitions, therefore, is a fundamental feature of all politics.

Understanding how coalitions form is not as straightforward as it may sound, however, and collective dilemmas are prevalent. We have already learned about the need to overcome collective action problems by motivating people to contribute to a public good. Forming a coalition of any kind to create a public good requires solving the basic collective action problem. We also know that coordinating on a common strategy can be difficult.

Maintaining your coalition in the face of competition presents an additional dilemma, particularly when other coalition leaders make better offers to your coalition partners. To illustrate such instability in coalitions, we can embellish the housemates story. Suppose that there are nine of you in the house but only five parking spaces available, for which you must pay the landlord a flat fee. It is clear to everyone that unless you contribute financially to renting the parking spaces, no one can use them. Let's further suppose that the parking spaces altogether cost $500 to rent for a year. You and four others have formed a coalition, and each member of your group promises to contribute $100 toward the parking spaces. Note that you have formed a **minimum winning coalition**, or the smallest-sized coalition necessary to achieve your goal. In many situations, minimum winning coalitions are the most desirable, because larger membership tends to dilute the overall benefits of winning. In this case, for five people and five parking spaces, if you are in the winning coalition, you will always have a place to park your car. If there are any more people in the coalition, you may not have a space when you need it, because there will be more people than spaces.

Problems for your coalition quickly emerge. Just before you make your rent payment for the parking spaces, two of the excluded housemates, who want to park their cars, make the following offer to three members of your coalition: "If three of you pay only $90, we will pay $115 each." In effect, they

minimum winning coalition
The smallest-sized coalition necessary to achieve a goal.

unstable coalition An instance in which three or more people must make a collective choice from a set of alternatives, but any voting coalition in favor of an alternative can be divided by consideration of another alternative.

agenda setter An authority that controls what options are decided on by a group.

have formed a second coalition by "raiding" your coalition. Soon after, two more housemates raid this second coalition by each offering to pay $130—so the remaining three members will pay $80 apiece. This third coalition, however, is quickly destabilized when a couple of additional housemates make a better offer to some of its members.

The coalition raiding can continue indefinitely, and in fact, any coalition of five is susceptible to raiders with a better offer. As a result, no coalition will remain in place long enough to accomplish its goal. This collective dilemma is referred to as a problem of **unstable coalitions**. A coalition is unstable if the people in the coalition can be easily divided into two or more groupings by another proposal.

As with other kinds of collective dilemmas, unstable coalitions are a natural part of politics, yet they can be stabilized by external enforcers and by effective institutions. For example, an outside authority (perhaps the landlord) can set up an effective voting system (that is, an institutional solution) and grant one of you status as an **agenda setter** to control what options your group will vote on. Say, for example, that there will be a single, binding vote with a majority deciding the outcome. The agenda setter then uses his or her power to restrict to two the available options of paying for the parking spaces. This arrangement enables a decision to be made over payments, and the parking spaces can be allocated.

Agenda-setting power is essential to avoid coalition raiding, yet those who possess it can use it in a variety of ways. A manipulative agenda setter may rig the results so that he or she pays less for the parking spaces than everyone else while gaining equal access to them. A more beneficent agenda setter with enforcement powers will ensure that a fair scheme emerges, including one option where each of the nine housemates pays just $55.56 for the parking spaces and enjoys access to their use. This type of agenda-setting approach rejects the minimum winning coalition strategy, opting instead to create a consensus among all to enact a program with a unanimous coalition.

In politics, unstable coalitions potentially can occur in legislatures, agency boards, and elections; among groups of judges on the Supreme Court; and within political parties. In the U.S. Senate, for example, it is common for senators who want to defeat a bill to introduce a "killer" amendment, which reduces support for the bill enough to defeat it. The amendment splits apart the original coalition of senators in favor of the bill, and some senators now want to vote against the bill. Introducing killer amendments is a form of co-alition raiding by opponents. We usually do not witness coalitions being raided and constantly falling apart, however. This is largely because members of vulnerable coalitions anticipate the potential problems and minimize their occurrence by adopting voting rules and granting agenda-setting powers to make raiding difficult. The granting of agenda-setting powers and the estab-lishment of effective voting rules are examples of institutional features to resolve collective dilemmas—in this case, the problem of unstable coalitions.

Principal-Agent Problems

Another kind of situation that commonly arises in politics is called the **principal-agent problem**. It is sometimes referred to as a delegation prob-lem. It is not technically a collective dilemma, because it does not at its core involve a conflict between collective goals and individual incentives. Rather, it is a dilemma arising from a direct conflict between at least two individuals. Like the collective dilemmas discussed earlier, the principal-agent problem is found in various guises in politics and can require careful institutional design to solve.[13]

Principals are those who hire others (agents) to work for them. A classic principal-agent dilemma goes something like this: Suppose your car has a knocking sound that worries you. You hire a mechanic to fix whatever is causing the knocking. In this simple example, you are the principal and the mechanic is the agent. You have delegated the task of fixing your car to him. The me-chanic tells you that he has found the source of the sound and needs to replace

principal-agent problem (delegation problem) An instance in which one actor (a principal) contracts another actor (an agent) to act on the principal's behalf; but the actors may not share the same preferences, and the principal lacks the means to observe all of the agent's behavior.

---

[13] D. Roderick Kiewiet and Matthew McCubbins, *The Logic of Delegation: Congressional Parties and the Appropriations Process* (Chicago: University of Chicago Press, 1991).

several parts. He promises to order new, high-quality parts from the car's manufacturer. He goes ahead with the work. You get your car back and pay him for his services and for the parts. A happy ending would be that the knocking has gone away and your car is in fine shape.

However, you remain concerned, because you do not know anything about car engines. More troubling, perhaps, is that you did not watch everything the mechanic did to your car. For all you know, he tightened a few screws and did not put in any new parts (but charged you for some), or he put in used parts, or he did a sloppy job. Perhaps the car will be back in the repair shop within weeks.

This "problem" or "dilemma," as economists like to point out, is inherent in any relationship between a principal and an agent who does not have exactly the same interests as the principal. You as the principal have limited information about what the agent does in your interests. Without laws to protect you, you are at risk of being taken advantage of by an unscrupulous agent. For a variety of possible reasons, a principal in a contractual relationship may not be able to observe all of an agent's actions. This gives the agent some leeway. He or she could act in a manner that the principal would not want: the agent could shirk his or her responsibilities to the principal, or even steal from the principal. One solution would be to give the principal more information about the agent's actions, but this may be difficult to do. After all, you would need to learn a lot about auto repair to be able to determine what the mechanic was doing, even if you could watch him.

What does the principal-agent problem have to do with politics and government? Much of government involves the delegation of responsibility by principals to agents. Military leaders expect lower-level commanders to carry out overall strategies with tight precision. Judges expect their hired law clerks to conduct research and help write opinions consistent with the judges' overall philosophy. The president expects advisers to give advice diligently and with the interests of the president foremost in mind. Ideally for the principal, an agent is a substitute, acting as the principal would if the principal were in the situation the agent faces while bringing expertise and judgment to bear that the principal sometimes lacks.

A prominent example of a principal-agent problem in politics is the relationship between a bureaucratic agency and elected members of the government. Anyone working for the government who is not part of the ruling powers is called a **bureaucrat**. A **bureaucracy** is an agency or office devoted to carrying out tasks for the government in a manner consistent with the law. In any political system, even nondemocratic ones, bureaucracies can be considered the agents of the sovereign government, as when a king hires an army to fight his wars. In democracies, however, bureaucracies are supposed to carry out the work that elected representatives—the ones who make the rules—want them to do.

bureaucrat Any government employee who is not part of the ruling powers.

bureaucracy An agency or office devoted to carrying out tasks for the government in a manner consistent with the law.

In the United States, Congress and the president together pass legislation, and the jobs of the executive-branch bureaucracies are to execute, administer, and enforce the laws. The principal-agent problem looms, however. Executive-branch bureaucracies (the agents) may not always execute the laws in a manner that Congress or the president (the principals) wants. Leaders in government cannot observe all that the millions of employees of the executive-branch bureaucracies do. Like the auto mechanic in the preceding example, bureaucrats can shirk their duties, misrepresent their effort, and steal from taxpayers. (We will study these situations in Chapter 7.)

Economists, political scientists, and other social scientists consider ways of setting up institutions so that agents have incentives to do what principals want them to do. The principal-agent problems inherent in any political system require institutional solutions. So Congress requires bureaucratic agencies to adhere to strict rules for documenting administrative decisions. In the realm of auto mechanics, many states have laws requiring warrantees on repair work. Warrantees improve the situation because mechanics have an incentive to get the repair right the first time and avoid returns. Some states require that mechanics show the customer the parts being replaced. Of course, one way to hold an agent accountable is to pass along information about the agent to other potential principals. Agents' reputations depend on satisfied principals (or customers, in the case of the mechanic). Honest mechanics hope to get more business over time, because people talk among themselves or can blog about who does good work.

Designing Institutions

We have noted that governments are necessary to solve the most fundamental of all collective dilemmas—namely, the dangerous breakdown in social order. But governments are also necessary to solve many everyday dilemmas, including challenges that arise from prisoner's dilemmas, coordination and coalition problems, and principal-agent problems. Governments accomplish this by establishing rules for decision making or by creating institutions. In the abstract, institutions can be thought of as long-term solutions to the problem of keeping social order, as well as day-to-day solutions to routine collective dilemmas. Without effective institutions that survive over the long term, societies can become unstable and fall apart due to people's inabilities to self-organize on a daily basis. The dilemmas described earlier, if unsolved, can destroy a society.

It is not enough to know that institutions solve collective dilemmas and principal-agent problems, however. The *way* they solve these dilemmas matters in determining whose interests are served. In other words, different kinds of institutions will lead to different kinds of outcomes over the long run. Specific institutional designs affect the distribution of power, wealth, status, and other things people prefer and care about in politics.

There is a contrast, at least conceptually, between **public policies** and institutions. Public policies can distribute benefits and costs to people too. Policies are rules for day-to-day life, such as those that establish whether we can turn right on a red light when we are driving, how much we pay in sales tax for a new pair of shoes, or how much the government pays retirees in Social Security benefits. These are policies (which usually take the form of laws) that determine specific conduct in one part of our lives.

Institutions are broader, more stable rules that determine how policies or laws are made and enforced. They are the relatively fixed "rules of the game"— the fundamental rules that dictate how we govern and make future rules or decisions (including public policies). The Constitution, for example, describes in detail the basic institutions of American government, such as the methods for passing laws and electing representatives and presidents, the authority of the states vis-à-vis the national government, and the fundamental rights of citizens in relation to their government. In short, the Constitution lays out the long-term set of rules (institutions) for making the everyday rules (policies).

Institutions of government are designed purposefully by people who believe such institutions will help them achieve their policy goals.[14] When the leaders of small states argued in the Constitutional Convention of 1787 over the need for a Senate with two senators from each state, they understood that this institutional design would help protect them against policies and laws that would benefit large states at the expense of small states. The leaders of large states understood this, too, and insisted on an institutional design for the House of Representatives that offered them an advantage: representation by the states based on population. The resulting compromise—two legislative houses that are both necessary to approve legislation—was a deliberate attempt to create institutions of government that would allow small and large states to benefit from the union and would encourage all the states to approve the new Constitution. And historians would generally agree that the design of the Senate has ensured that smaller, more rural states have used their Senate delegations to their benefit. Because sparsely populated farm states have as many senators as highly populated urban states, the Senate historically has been more sensitive to the plight of farmers than have other parts of the national government, and it has tended to thwart changes in policy that threaten farmers' incomes, even when most of the population favored such changes.

Institutions can be designed or can evolve over time. They continue to shape outcomes long after those who originally designed the institutions have

public policies Programs and decisions by the government that are enforced by the rule of law.

[14] Daniel Diermeier and Keith Krehbiel, "Institutionalism as a Methodology," *Journal of Theoretical Politics* 15 (2003): 123–44.

departed the scene. Institutions have lasting effects on societies because they channel political, economic, and social behavior into patterns that can be enduring. As an example, after the national government began to spend a lot of money on space research in the 1950s, a set of interest groups, such as those representing scientists, universities, and research companies, formed to pressure the government to continue these spending policies. In this way, the institutions created to promote space research—new agencies like NASA—became self-reinforcing in that they spawned groups in society applying public pressure for robust budgets for more space research. More generally, the policies chosen as a result of an institutional design create interest groups that resist any institutional changes that would threaten the policies that benefit them. Social scientists often refer to this idea as **path dependence**. Path dependence in this context means that institutional decisions made early on deeply affect current and future policy decisions. The system begins down a "path." Past decisions about institutions leave legacies for the present that make it difficult to change direction, even if that change seems desirable in the present.

path dependence The notion that earlier events or decisions deeply affect current and future policy decisions or outcomes.

Consider our discussion of how representation in the Senate was designed and the consequences of this design: the decision in 1789 to grant each state in the new United States equal representation in the Senate has profoundly shaped the policies of the national government. As we will see in Chapter 5, the Senate provides opportunities, under its institutional rules, for a small minority of senators to halt legislation they do not like. So once policies are set that happen to favor rural areas, perhaps helped along because of the overrepresentation of smaller states, a few senators from those states can block later attempts to undo the policies. In this way, certain institutional design features—such as equal representation by state in the Senate and strong rights of a minority of senators to stop legislation action—not only can cause certain policies to occur but also can freeze those policies in place once they do occur.

In Comparison: Types of Government Institutions

Comparing the American political system with other political systems can help us to understand and evaluate it. We can learn about the consequences of having different institutional forms by examining what happens in other countries. Throughout this book, we will compare the United States to other countries.

The institutions of government shape the operation of the overall political system, and they differ across countries.[15] All governments, even nondemocratic ones, have some kind of basic institutional structure. A common feature

---

[15] Plato's *Republic* is an excellent place to begin a discussion of the various kinds of political systems.

authoritarianism A political system in which there is no expectation that the government represents the people, and the institutions of government do not give the people a direct voice in who will lead.

dictatorship An authoritarian political system in which sovereign power is vested in one individual.

monarchy A political system in which a ruler (usually a king or queen) is chosen by virtue of being the heir of the previous ruler.

oligarchy A political system in which power resides in a small segment of society.

one-party state A political system in which one party controls the government and actively seeks to prevent other parties from contesting for power.

democracy Rule by the people; in practice today, this means popular election of the government and basic protections of civil rights and liberties.

republic A political system in which public officials are chosen to represent the people in an assembly that makes important policy decisions.

of the various types of **authoritarianism** is the absence of any expectation that the government represents the people. Furthermore, the institutions of government do not give the people a direct voice in choosing their leaders. The institutions within these countries, however, can be different.

Some authoritarian countries are **dictatorships**, vesting sovereign power in one individual. The leader of North Korea, Kim Jong-un, has ruled uncontested as a dictator since he took over from his father in 2012. He has maintained final authority over the government and dealt harshly with his political opponents. In **monarchies**, such as in Saudi Arabia and Jordan, the king (or queen in some instances) rules on the most critical matters, and there is no competition for his (or her) position. Most authoritarian countries are **oligarchies**, meaning that the political power resides in a small segment of society. In the major Middle Eastern monarchies, a parliament that is partially elected and partially appointed shares power with the monarch, and the parliament makes many of the day-to-day policy decisions. Other nations are **one-party states**, another form of oligarchy. In China, for example, the Communist Party runs the government and represses any opposition. It is not subject to real competition in elections. The leader of the Chinese Communist Party conducts foreign policy, but shares with various party committees the responsibility for day-to-day governing.

In parts of the world accustomed to democratic government, people want governmental institutions not only to solve collective dilemmas—even the most totalitarian governments can do that—they also demand specific institutions based on democratic principles that will improve the welfare of everyone in society.

Democracy means rule by the people. Although there is disagreement over exactly what democracy means in practice, some consider it an ideal situation where everyone has an equal voice in all public decisions—a goal that has never been attained and perhaps never will be. There is widespread consensus that, at a minimum, democracy means that the people leading the government are chosen by popular election to rule for a specific period.

Nearly all governments in the world's democracies are also **republics**, meaning that public officials are chosen to represent the people in an assembly, which makes important policy decisions.[16] This is in contrast to direct democracies, in which citizens can vote directly on policy matters. No country operates purely by direct democracy, though some countries, such as Switzerland, and even

---

[16] This use of the word *republic* should not be confused with the distinction made between a republic and a constitutional monarchy. A republic, of which the United States, Germany, and France are examples, has no monarch, and the head of state is chosen by the people or by representatives of the people. A constitutional monarchy, such as in the United Kingdom or Belgium, formally has a king or queen as its head of state. In practice, there is little difference between these two forms of democratic governance because monarchs have long since become figureheads and do not retain governing power.

many of the states in the United States (such as California and Oregon), rely extensively on direct democracy to decide major policy issues.[17]

Today, most people—even those living under authoritarian rule—believe that democracy is a desirable form of government. This belief is based on the simple notion that when compared with other systems, democratic government tends to produce better standards of living and satisfies people's preferences more widely among the population.[18]

In democratic systems, large-scale conflicts among groups of people typically are settled peacefully through legislatures, courts, elections, and administrative agencies. Although peaceful conflict settlement can be reached even in the most authoritarian or dictatorial regimes, democratic regimes offer a better track record of preventing wars, human rights abuses, and oppression. They also tend to be less corrupt than authoritarian regimes.

What makes a country more or less democratic? In classifying political systems, international organizations use specific criteria. For example, Freedom House, a nonprofit organization that monitors the democratization of countries, relies on two general criteria:

- *Political rights*—the degree to which a country's political process allows for open and extensive participation of citizens, with free and fair elections.

- *Civil liberties*—the degree to which a country's people are free to express their views and organize into political parties and other groups, to run for office, to pressure the government, and to insist on the independence of the judiciary.

There is disagreement over how democratic the United States has been in the past, and even how democratic it is today. Some critics argue that the United States is less than a full democracy because, for example, it has mistreated—and continues to mistreat—specific groups of minorities, or because wealthy people have advantages in influencing electoral politics. We will discuss the first point in Chapter 4 and the second in Chapters 5, 11, and 16.

There is great variety in democratic institutions around the world. In fact, the institutional features of American government are quite rare. Figure 1.3 lists some basic elements of the American political system and shows that most other countries have different institutions. In later chapters, we will study and compare these institutions in more detail.

Although many other countries share one or several institutional features with the United States, none has the identical institutional structure. For example, the Canadian system is also federal and republican, but it is not presidential, nor does it have separation of powers. The American system is unusual

---

[17] Referendums are direct elections in which voters choose whether to support a law passed by a parliament or legislature. Initiatives are direct elections in which voters choose whether to support a law proposed by a group of fellow citizens.

[18] For evidence on the links between democracy and quality of life, go to www.freedomhouse.org.

FIGURE 1.3

Institutional Features of Select Democracies

	Federalism	Executive			Legislature		Party System		Legal System		
		Parliamentary	Premier-presidential	Presidential	Bicameral	Unicameral	Two-party	Multiparty	Civil Law	Hybrid	Common Law
Australia	X	X			X			X			X
Brazil	X			X	X			X	X		
Canada	X	X			X			X			X
France			X		X			X	X		
Germany	X	X			X			X	X		
India	X	X			X			X			X
Ireland			X		X			X			X
Italy		X			X			X	X		
Japan		X			X			X		X	
Mexico	X			X	X			X		X	
Poland			X		X			X	X		
South Korea				X		X		X		X	
Spain		X			X			X	X		
Sweden		X				X		X	X		
Turkey		X				X		X	X		
United Kingdom		X			X			X			X
United States	X			X	X		X				X

in its combination of federal and presidential structures, as well as in having only two major political parties.

Political scientists have demonstrated that institutional differences shape not only the nature of politics but also the kinds of policies adopted and the impact of those policies on people's lives. For example, political scientists draw on comparative data to argue that if the United States were to change its method of electing presidents and members of Congress to be more like the methods used in European countries, the country would have more than two major political parties. And systems with more than two major political parties tend to be characterized by more generous government spending on social programs.

Analyzing Politics and Government Using the Tools of Political Science

The concepts that we have covered in this chapter are those that political scientists use to analyze and understand politics and government. Let's now return to the opening story of the budget crises during previous administrations and the situation now under President Trump to see how these concepts help us make sense of the apparent puzzle in the story.

Two collective action problems lie at the heart of the story. The first is among the public, who in general do not like to pay taxes despite wanting the government to maintain programs and services at a high level. Each person would prefer that others pay for the government's programs, as long as the benefits of those programs and a stable economy are available to everyone. In fact, the national government often borrows money rather than raise taxes to pay for its new programs, thus leading to the large deficit. When the government borrows money to pay for services instead of taxing citizens, it is in effect asking future generations (who will have to pay back the loans) to bear the cost of current government programs. Thus, contemporary beneficiaries of the stimulus plan are free riding off their children! The more general point is that it is always tempting for taxpayers to support tax cuts *and* generous government programs on the assumption that citizens other than themselves will pay the bill.

The second collective action problem occurs among politicians. Suppose a politician prefers to balance the budget by cutting back a popular and expensive program like Medicare, as opposed to raising taxes or cutting other programs. Any politician who takes this stand and declares his or her support for reduced government services runs the risk of losing the next election. If a large group of politicians joined together to advocate for reductions in Medicare, then each politician in that group would be somewhat protected. But it is hard for any individual politician to overcome the temptation to go along with the crowd, because that is the easier course of action. From the perspective of those who do not favor continued funding at current levels, fear of the wrath of voters prevents them from publicly supporting deficit-reducing policies like cutting programs or raising taxes. We learned earlier that public goods are hard to produce because of collective action problems. In this case, the public good—such as a balanced budget—does not happen, because the individual costs of participating in the collective action are high enough that the joint effort to stop the growth of expensive government programs and services never gets off the ground.

We also know that institutions are designed or evolve in response to collective dilemmas and principal-agent problems. The main theme of this book is that the specific political institutions chosen to solve collective dilemmas and principal-agent problems have important consequences for society. Generally, conflicts over budgets indicate that political institutions designed to solve *some* problems cannot solve *all* problems, and so other collective dilemmas will arise. The budget deficit continues to be very large, and politicians continue their battle over which policies are necessary to balance the budget, such as cutting services and programs or raising taxes.

Many details about the institutions in the American political system help to explain the continued recurrence of budgetary battles, but we would be getting ahead of our story if we tried to incorporate them all here. We will study these institutions in later chapters, but first, we take a closer look at the challenges the Founders faced in designing the basic institutions of American government.

FURTHER READING

★ = Included in *Readings in American Politics*, 5th ed.

Acemoglu, Darren, and James Robinson, *Why Nations Fail: Origins of Power, Poverty and Prosperity* (New York: Crown Publishers, 2012). Nations will fail unless their political and economic institutions encourage the government to serve the needs of most people, as opposed to catering to a small number of elites.

Axelrod, Robert, *The Evolution of Cooperation* (New York: Basic Books, 1984). A close analysis of the prisoner's dilemma, especially situations where people have repeated interactions with one another; tit-for-tat strategies arise over time when people face each other repeatedly in prisoner's dilemma situations.

★ Hardin, Garrett, "The Tragedy of the Commons," *Science* 162 (December 1968): 1243–48. Applies the collective action problem to the study of common-pool situations.

Hirschman, Albert, *The Passions and the Interests: Political Arguments for Capitalism before Its Triumph* (Princeton, NJ: Princeton University Press, 1977). An intellectual history showing the relatively recent acceptance of the legitimacy of publicly striving to protect the individual's material interests.

★ Olson, Mancur, *The Logic of Collective Action: Public Goods and the Theory of Groups* (Cambridge, MA: Harvard University Press, 1971). A classic account defining the collective action problem and applying it to the study of political organizations.

Ostrom, Elinor, *Governing the Commons: The Evolution of Institutions for Collective Action* (New York: Cambridge University Press, 1990). Under certain conditions, communities are capable of self-regulation, allowing them to sustain long-term yields of a common resource and effectively overcoming the tragedy of the commons.

Shepsle, Kenneth A., and Mark S. Bonchek, *Analyzing Politics: Rationality, Behavior, and Institutions*, 2nd ed. (New York: Norton, 2010). A comprehensive treatment of models of politics using rational choice assumptions, written at a level appropriate for undergraduate students.

KEY TERMS

agenda setter (p. 20)

authoritarianism (p. 26)

bureaucracy (p. 22)

bureaucrat (p. 22)

collective action problem (p. 12)

collective dilemma (p. 10)

coordination problem (p. 16)

democracy (p. 26)

dictatorship (p. 26)

federal system (p. 7)

free riding (p. 12)

institutions (p. 6)

minimum winning coalition (p. 19)

monarchy (p. 26)

oligarchy (p. 26)

one-party state (p. 26)

path dependence (p. 25)

political system (p. 5)

politics (p. 5)

preferences (p. 5)

principal-agent problem (delegation problem) (p. 21)

prisoner's dilemma (p. 14)

private good (p. 12)

public good (p. 12)

public policies (p. 24)

republic (p. 26)

transaction costs (p. 14)

unstable coalition (p. 20)

Events like Shays's Rebellion, in which poor farmers took up arms against the government in 1786–87, pointed to the need for a strong national government. However, at the time of the Founding, many people were afraid of putting excessive power in the hands of the national government, and this debate over governmental power shaped the Constitution.

2

The Constitution

How does the Constitution strike a balance between preserving order and protecting liberty?

I n 1786, not long after the United States won independence from Britain, a group of several hundred debt-laden, cash-poor farmers in Massachusetts took up arms against their new government. They were led by Daniel Shays, a veteran of the Revolution, who faced the threat of debtor's prison when he returned home from the war. Shays's Rebellion pitted poor farmers like Shays—who had been hurt financially by an economic downturn after the war—against the Massachusetts state militia. The farmers resented the state government's enforcement of foreclosure rules and its alignment with Boston-area merchants. The rebels closed down courts across Massachusetts in an attempt to prevent debt collection. In 1787, Shays led a march to Springfield, Massachusetts, with the intention of seizing the federal arsenal there. Along the way, more farmers, including many war veterans and even some state militia members, joined the rebels, bringing their numbers to around 1,400. The rebellion was eventually crushed in Springfield by a privately funded government militia, but the armed resistance by civilians against state troops alarmed political leaders throughout the young country.

Shays's Rebellion severely tested the governmental institutions in place at the time, which had been established by the Articles of Confederation (ratified in 1781). As Shays's Rebellion and other events following independence showed, the Articles did not provide for effective security in the new country. The rebellion was emblematic of the many collective dilemmas facing the new country. Under the Articles, there was a *unicameral* (one-house) Congress with two to seven delegates from each state. But there was no executive branch to enforce the laws passed by Congress, to protect the states from internal or external threats, or to represent the country in foreign relations. And Congress could not raise revenue by passing direct taxes, customs, duties, or levies. Instead, it had to "requisition" the states for money and then wait for them to raise funds and forward those to the national government. Finally,

OUTLINE

- **What Do Constitutions Accomplish?**

- **Origins of the American Political System**

- **Institutional Features of the Constitution**

- **The Ratification Debate**

- **In Comparison: National Constitutions**

- **Constitutional Evolution**

- **Consequences of the Constitution**

the procedure for amending the Articles was too onerous, making it nearly impossible to address these shortcomings under the Articles.

When delegates from the various states gathered at the Constitutional Convention in Philadelphia in 1787 to improve the institutions of government, they quickly decided to write a new constitution. In summarizing the defects of the Articles, they had events like Shays's Rebellion in mind. They understood that they needed to strengthen the national government so that it could respond to crises like these, and to other collective dilemmas such as the state-by-state economic policies that, by operating distinct from and sometimes at odds with other states, were harming the country as a whole.

A major concern, resulting from the national government's lack of enforcement and direct taxing powers, was that financial free riding among the states was common. Here we see a clear example of a collective action problem as described in Chapter 1. All of the states would benefit from a stronger national government able to enforce order, but it was in each state's interest to let the other states pay for the military power necessary to keep order. As a result of the incentives to free ride, the national government failed to raise more than 20 percent of the funds owed to it by the states; and some states paid none of what they owed. Moreover, a series of ominous events, including Shays's Rebellion, quickly revealed the problems inherent in having a national government without an executive that could wield military powers.

At the same time, the Founders were acutely aware of Americans' fear of excessive governmental power. The Revolution that secured independence from Britain was justified as a fight against tyrannical power, and state leaders had agreed to the Articles of Confederation because they wanted a weak national government that would not interfere too much with the states or individual freedoms. Most citizens believed that the Revolution would lead to less-intrusive government and thus to more liberty than they experienced under British colonial rule.

The task for the Founders at the Constitutional Convention was to agree on a set of governmental institutions that were powerful enough to resolve collective dilemmas among the states in times of crisis, but not so powerful as to become dictatorial or dangerous to liberty. As we will learn in this chapter, the Founders held different views about how this balance should be struck. Some wanted much stronger national powers than were allowed under the Articles, but others preferred to keep national powers weak while perhaps strengthening the state governments. In the end, the former group (called Federalists) won out. Why did the Federalists triumph when there was so much distrust of government among the people? Did the Constitution, which created a set of relatively strong national institutions, strike an effective balance among the competing views of appropriate governmental authority?

What Do Constitutions Accomplish?

How successful was the Constitution in solving the early United States' collective dilemmas and principal–agent problems resulting from the Articles of Confederation? Before we consider that question, let's examine what role constitutions play in society in general.

In societies governed by the **rule of law**, legal codes are intended to be applied to everyone in an unbiased manner. Rule of law implies not only that legal principles guide the behavior of citizens but also that the government, and the officials in that government, are subject to the law and cannot make arbitrary decisions contrary to the law in their capacity as public authorities.

rule of law A system in which all people in a society, including governing officials, are subject to legal codes that are applied without bias by independent courts.

In authoritarian regimes or dictatorships, leaders are often not subject to the same rules that apply to all other citizens. The law in such systems can be what the leaders say it is at any time. A distinctive feature of democratic systems, by contrast, is governance by a body of laws that has been established by the people or their representatives.

Written constitutions form the basis of most societies governed by the rule of law. They establish the basic institutions of government and represent the country's legal core. Legal scholars worldwide share an understanding of a hierarchy of law, which sets constitutional law above statutory law. Statutory laws are those passed by legislatures or by administrative agencies empowered by legislatures. Constitutional law is seen as the collection of fundamental rules for making statutory laws and regulations.

In essence, constitutions specify the most basic institutional rules for making policies. For example, legislatures make statutory law, but constitutions determine who is eligible to be in the legislature, what authority the legislature has, and in many cases, what rules legislators must follow to make decisions. Although the officials elected to legislatures may disagree about what public policy should be, they should not routinely disagree about *who* can make the decisions and *how* those policy decisions should be made. A legitimate constitution reflects a shared understanding of who can wield public authority and what kinds of authority public officials should have.

A constitution is therefore a prerequisite for a society based on the rule of law. The U.S. Constitution is like a skeleton; it provides the fundamental shape and structure of the whole political system. The backbone of that skeleton is the set of institutions of government specifying who has ultimate legislative, executive, and judicial authority, and how those in authority are subject to the laws.

Recall from the last chapter that governments exist to solve the basic collective dilemmas of human societies. Without sovereign authorities running the government, society would descend into chaos and few or no public goods would be provided. In establishing the basic form of government, a constitution provides the means for solving troublesome collective dilemmas. Indeed, we could regard a constitution as a series of prescriptions for such problems.

Origins of the American Political System

Among the types of collective dilemmas we discussed in Chapter 1 were collective action problems and coordination problems. Let's now examine these dilemmas in the context of the 13 new states organized under the Articles of Confederation before the writing and ratification of the Constitution.

Under the Articles of Confederation, the national government could not compel the states to do much of anything. When these states faced a collective action problem, each had a strong incentive to free ride off the efforts of others. Many states failed to pay their share of the debt incurred during the Revolutionary War, even though all the states enjoyed the benefits of independence from Britain. Likewise, some states refused to participate in cooperative efforts intended to boost the national economy. When several New England states agreed to close their ports to British goods in order to protect their own industries, Connecticut took advantage of the situation by welcoming British goods and securing more favorable terms of trade from England than those extended to other states. Connecticut even imposed a tax on goods from Massachusetts after leaders from that state complained. Such collective action problems often descended into rounds of punishment, recrimination, and mistrust.

In the case of coordination problems, all states are worse off if the group fails to act in unison. The states may disagree on how precisely to coordinate, but they all have an incentive to pursue a common course of action. For example, under the Articles of Confederation, states had their own types of currency for buying and trading. This not only made it difficult for people from foreign countries to trade with or conduct business in the United States, it also led to rampant inflation because states had incentives to increase amounts of their own money to pay off debts. Most leaders recognized that if the colonies could agree to use one national currency, it would make trading and business investment more attractive to foreigners and also lead to unified policies on inflation.

The Constitutional Convention was called in 1787 largely because leaders in the Continental Congress and in the states acknowledged that the weakness of the national government under the Articles made it impossible to solve these types of collective dilemmas. Most believed that a stronger national government was necessary. Three of the ultimate features of the Constitution—the presidency, the specified national government powers, and an independent judiciary—were

Under the Articles of Confederation, states printed their own currency, such as North Carolina's four-dollar bill pictured here. This system led to a coordination problem that hindered foreign trade with the United States and caused massive inflation, a problem that leaders under the Articles of Confederation were unable to rectify.

specifically designed in response to previous failures to solve free riding and coordination problems. We will start our analysis earlier in history, however, with the Revolutionary era and the Declaration of Independence.

The Revolution

In the mid-eighteenth century, the American colonies were part of the British Empire. Tensions between the British government and the colonies escalated in the 1760s as the colonists grew increasingly weary of being exploited for the economic benefit of England. Many of them especially resented the repressive taxes and unfair trade rules imposed by London. They rebelled against the Crown by various means, including boycotts, riots, attacks on British troops, and formal declarations that the colonies had sole authority to tax themselves ("No taxation without representation"). The colonies ignored or flouted a series of measures by which the Crown demonstrated its authority. Radical groups of colonists, such as the Sons of Liberty in Boston, planned public events to highlight the abusive actions of the British government. In one such event, known as the Boston Tea Party, rebels raided British ships in Boston Harbor and dumped hundreds of chests of tea into the water to protest increasingly onerous taxes on tea from the East Indies.

In 1774, the Continental Congress, which represented the colonies in communications with the British government, repeatedly passed resolutions deploring the

By the 1760s, American colonists were increasingly resistant to the taxes and other rules imposed by the British government. Here, British troops arrive in Boston to enforce compliance in the colonies. Despite the resentment toward British rule, the states later adopted some of the institutions of colonial government in the U.S. Constitution.

actions of the Crown, asking for relief, and expressing continued loyalty. At the same time, it approved broad boycotts of British goods and indicated that the colonies were willing to risk war with Britain to be free of its tyrannical control. The British government responded to these provocations not through dialogue or by seeking compromises, but by sending troops to America and threatening to arrest the leaders of the rebellious colonies.

In the spring of 1775, under orders to arrest John Hancock and Samuel Adams—two Massachusetts leaders who had been urging the colonies to declare independence—700 British troops confronted 70 Massachusetts militiamen in Lexington, outside Boston. When the militia refused to disperse, the British redcoats fired, killing eight Americans. The British troops then advanced on nearby Concord and exchanged gunfire with another group of militiamen on a bridge over the Concord River. The British subsequently retreated, only to be attacked by more than 1,000 Americans. By the end of the battle, 73 British troops had been killed and 200 wounded. These opening battles of the war for American independence were humiliating setbacks for the British.

News of the battles spread rapidly on both sides of the Atlantic. The British and the Americans mobilized additional troops, and over the next year they fought to capture key cities and forts from each other. Neither army gained the upper hand, but the escalating war inflamed passions on both sides. Violence by the two armies became more wanton and brutal. In the spring of 1776, realizing that it had a real fight on its hands, the Crown sent tens of thousands of additional troops to put down the troublesome colonists. Throughout the year, thousands of British-paid Hessian mercenaries were dispatched to invade and occupy New York City. It was widely assumed that they would then proceed to conquer the capital city of Philadelphia.

As the colonies prepared for a new British onslaught, they formally announced their separation from Britain in July 1776. Implicitly, the Declaration of Independence was also a declaration of full-scale war against Britain. Discussion within the Continental Congress before the signing of the Declaration revealed a bitterly divided group of colonial leaders. There were moments when men charged others with treason and stormed out of the chamber. Those who remained and signed the document did so with considerable trepidation. Had the Revolution failed and the men been captured by the British, they would surely have been shot or hanged as traitors to the Crown. In fact, they wrote a secret agreement into the records of Congress: "To prevent traitors and spies from worming themselves amongst us, no person shall have a seat in Congress until he should have signed the Declaration."[1]

After the Declaration, the war raged for five more years along the Atlantic seaboard, at various locations in the interior of the continent, in the West Indies,

---

[1] Cornel A. Lengyel, *Four Days in July: The Story behind the Declaration of Independence* (Garden City, NY: Doubleday, 1958), p. 250.

and in what is now Canada. With considerable help from the French, who provided badly needed naval power, the Americans eventually were able to isolate British forces and destroy them or induce their surrender.

The Declaration of Independence

The Declaration of Independence and the U.S. Constitution are famous all over the world, not only for being the founding documents of the United States but also for their influence in promoting specific philosophies of government. Both have been widely imitated or referred to in other countries' founding documents. Because it determined the institutions of American government, the Constitution plays by far the more important role in our daily lives. However, the Declaration of Independence, credited to Thomas Jefferson and John Adams, among others, was written in bold, memorable prose. It has long been widely quoted in defense of revolution and in defiance of abusive authority. It was and continues to be enormously influential in proposing that by virtue of their natural rights, people ought to be self-governing and free from subjugation by foreign powers or tyrannical leaders.

The Declaration comprises three parts (see Appendix, page A-1). The first offers an argument for rebellion. The more learned members of the Founding generation, including Jefferson, were influenced by the English philosopher John Locke (1632–1704), who was well known for declaring that government was legitimate only if it was based on the consent of the governed. Locke wrote that government exists to protect people's natural rights, which include the right to life and the enjoyment of their property. He also was a proponent of "social contract theory," or the idea that by entering into a society ruled by a popularly elected government, people were obliged to obey the rules determined by the majority. For Locke, decision making by majority rule logically followed from the idea that all humans ought to be treated equally. A government formed by people consenting to being constrained could, in Locke's words, lead to "peace, safety, and public good." These ideas by Locke influenced Jefferson when he wrote the Declaration's famous opening paragraphs asserting that "all men are created equal"; that people have the right to "Life, Liberty and the pursuit of Happiness"; and that governments derive their "just powers from the consent of the governed."

The Declaration's second and lengthiest section provides political justification for rebellion. It calls King George III a tyrant and cites a litany of grievances against him. In the document's third part, the former colonies took the fateful step: "We, Therefore, the Representatives of the United States of America . . . solemnly publish and declare, That these United Colonies are, and of Right ought to be Free and Independent States; that they are Absolved from all Allegiance to the British Crown."

After considerable debate, the Continental Congress approved the Declaration by an affirmative vote by representatives from 12 of the 13 colonies on July 4, 1776. The New York delegation approved the document two weeks later, after receiving approval to do so from their state convention (as their legislature was called at the time).

The Colonial and State Constitutions

Each colony under the British Empire had a charter describing the powers and responsibilities of the different branches of government. These charters, and the institutional design they described, presaged later state constitutions and the U.S. Constitution. The North American origins of separation of powers, a single executive, and a two-chambered legislative branch lie in these colonial governments and charters. Then, after the Revolution, these colonial charters were amended or rewritten entirely so leaders of the new states could govern without imperial control from Britain. In fact, many delegates to the Constitutional Convention had written their own state constitutions. The writers of the U.S. Constitution drew much of their inspiration for institutional design from the state constitutions drafted following independence.

Between 1776 and 1784, after the Revolution and Declaration of Independence, many of the states ratified constitutions establishing forms of government that looked partly, if not entirely, like today's national government. The states typically had separation of powers between a single executive and a legislative assembly, as well as an independent judiciary. These similarities reflected a widespread appreciation for the ideas of the French philosopher Montesquieu (1689–1755) and of Locke, who believed that power should be fragmented and that to lodge power in one branch of government was to invite abuse of authority and even tyranny. Most states also had the equivalent of a bill of rights designed to protect freedom of speech, press, and religion, and to guarantee rights for criminal defendants. The description of basic rights and liberties protected under law given in the Virginia Declaration of Rights (1776), which was attached to the Virginia constitution, formed the basis for the first 10 amendments to the U.S. Constitution, known as the Bill of Rights.

Articles of Confederation
The constitution drafted by the Second Continental Congress in 1777 and ratified by the states in 1781. It set up a weak central government consisting of a congress with limited legislative power and virtually no authority over the execution of its laws.

The Articles of Confederation

As we saw at the start of this chapter, in their first attempt to create a national constitutional system the representatives from the states agreed on a set of institutions that largely failed to address their underlying collective dilemmas. The **Articles of Confederation**, ratified in 1781, created more of a cooperative framework among sovereign states than a sovereign national government with power to govern effectively (see Appendix, page A-1).

In principle, the Congress established by the Articles had meaningful powers, but in fact it had little means to enforce its laws. Under the Articles, the states agreed on actions that they should not take independently, such as conducting foreign policy or undertaking military operations. They also agreed on how states would respect one another's prerogatives, such as by returning fugitives or honoring each other's contracts. Each state had two to seven delegates but only one vote in the Congress under the Articles, and the voting rules were such that 9 of 13 state delegations were required to approve legislation.

As noted in the opening story of this chapter, in the absence of an executive with powers to enforce the rule of law, and without the power to raise revenue for common action, the Confederation under the Articles proved ineffective. Moreover, it lacked the means to correct its shortcomings. The requirement of unanimous consent for any amendments to the Articles meant that any single state could block institutional change. For example, 12 of the 13 states approved an amendment allowing for a levy on imported goods to raise funds for the common defense. Yet when Rhode Island failed to approve the measure, the Confederation was forced to continue to rely on the goodwill of the states to pay what they owed. Inevitably, states were free riders and collective action problems persisted.

Leaders in several states called for a convention to discuss problems among the states related to trade and finances. A first attempt to hold a convention in Annapolis in 1786 failed when only five state delegations showed up. That meeting, however, resulted in a statement calling for a true national convention. The Continental Congress approved the idea, and the meeting was set for May 1787. Eventually, 55 delegates from all the states except Rhode Island convened in Philadelphia, ostensibly to amend the Articles.

The Constitutional Debates

It quickly became clear at the 1787 Constitutional Convention that amending the Articles would not be sufficient to address the collective dilemmas that the states faced. A new constitution was in order. The document ultimately drafted in Philadelphia that summer was the product of intense negotiations among competing interests represented by the men who wrote and ratified it.

Despite the Constitutional Convention's secretive deliberations, we know a lot about what occurred there thanks to James Madison's detailed journal. His notes reveal major cleavages among both the states and their political leaders. These divisions related to three major issues: liberty versus strong government, large states versus small states, and slavery.

Liberty versus Strong National Government. One cleavage existed between those who wanted to preserve the philosophy of individual liberty that animated the Revolution and those who believed that a more vigorous national government was necessary. Individual liberty tended to mean weak government, primarily at the national level but also at the state levels. Several prominent men of the revolutionary generation—including John Hancock, the first signer of the Declaration, and Patrick Henry, a prominent Virginian who had led the fight against the Stamp Act in 1765—declined to attend the convention. They wished to preserve the "spirit of 1776," which reflected a government philosophy more consistent with the Articles—namely, that free and independent states should retain full sovereignty with no external constraints. To Henry and others like him, freedom from the dictates of an American national government was as important as freedom from British tyranny.

In contrast, a majority of Henry's fellow Virginians who attended the Philadelphia gathering proposed a plan for a set of institutions that would replace the Articles and create a stronger national government. The basic framework of the so-called **Virginia Plan** was eventually incorporated in the Constitution, although important and consequential changes were made to the plan throughout the convention. The plan called for legislative supremacy and an independent executive. The legislature would have two houses, whose representation would be accorded to the states in proportion either to their population or to their contributions to the national treasury. A lower house would be elected by the people, and an upper house would be nominated by the states and elected by the lower house. Finally, the original plan contained the provision that the national legislature could nullify state laws that contradicted the Constitution (Figure 2.1).

Large States versus Small States. The debate over the Virginia Plan exposed another cleavage, this time between large and small states. The plan did not sit well with those from smaller states who worried about a legislature that apportioned seats by population size. The New Jersey delegation proposed its own plan, an attempt to forge a coalition among the smaller states to defeat the Virginia Plan. The New Jersey Plan, which was debated for only one day but nevertheless played a crucial role in the outcome, was essentially a series of amendments to the Articles that provided for a single legislative house with equal representation among the states. There would be no separation of powers between the executive and the legislature under the **New Jersey Plan**, in the sense that the legislature would appoint a plural (multi-person) executive. The legislature would, however, have strong powers to regulate commerce and would retain supreme authority over the states on certain matters. Except for a few aspects, the New Jersey Plan was rejected. The large- and medium-sized states did not approve of equal representation as proposed under the New Jersey plan.

Slavery. A third cleavage divided northern and southern states over slavery. This issue was deeply intertwined with the question of representation. If representation in the legislature was to be based on population, as proposed by the Virginia Plan, how were slaves to be counted? Naturally, the southern states, with large slave populations, wished for the slaves to be counted fully for

Virginia Plan A plan proposed at the Constitutional Convention by Edmund Randolph of Virginia outlining a stronger national government with an independent executive and a bicameral legislature whose membership in both houses would be apportioned according to state population.

New Jersey Plan A plan proposed at the Constitutional Convention by William Paterson of New Jersey to amend, rather than replace, the standing Articles of Confederation. The plan called for a unicameral legislature with equal representation among the states, along with a plural (multi-person) executive appointed by the legislature.

FIGURE 2.1

The Virginia and New Jersey Plans and the Connecticut Compromise

Virginia Plan

Upper house	Lower house	Executive
• Members nominated by the state legislatures and elected by the lower house	• Members elected by the people	• Single, independent executive
• Number of representatives determined by state population (or quotas of contribution)	• Number of representatives determined by state population (or quotas of contribution)	• Appointed by the legislature

New Jersey Plan

Unicameral legislature	Executive
• Members appointed by the states	• Multi-person, independent executive
• One representative from each state	• Appointed by the legislature

Connecticut Compromise

Senate	House of Representatives	Executive
• Members appointed by state legislatures	• Members elected by the people	• Single, independent executive
• Equal number of senators (two representing each state)	• Number of representatives determined by state population; slaves are counted as three-fifths of a person	• Elected by the state legislatures through the electoral college

purposes of representation. However, as their northern colleagues pointed out, the same southern states wanted slaves to count for considerably less than full persons in determining the apportionment of taxes and duties owed by the states to the national government. This contradiction between the southern states' position on legislative representation and financial matters bedeviled the negotiations for some time, and it was exacerbated by the discomfort many representatives (mostly from the North) felt toward slavery, and especially toward the continuing slave trade. The pro-slavery delegations generally supported equal representation and voted that way in the convention.[2]

[2] Jeremy Pope and Shawn Trier, "Voting for a Founding," *Journal of Politics* 77 (April 2015): 519–34.

Difficult Compromises

Although these three cleavages—over the nature of federation, the representation of big and small states, and slavery—overlapped, the opposing groups were not always the same across all three issues. For instance, some delegates found themselves opposing their colleagues on the question of representation while agreeing with them on the question of slavery.

The nationalists—later known as Federalists for their support of a stronger federal (national) government—largely triumphed at the convention, though only after the idea that the national government could nullify state laws was dropped. As we saw earlier in this chapter, a series of events, including Shays's Rebellion and the states' failure to cooperate on important matters such as international trade, gave increasing momentum to the belief that a stronger national government could solve collective dilemmas. Nonetheless, the question of the national government's power would continue to be debated, as we will see later in this chapter.

The other two cleavages resulted in painful compromises. The Constitution would not have been approved by the convention or ratified by the states had the delegates stuck firmly to their positions on the issues of representation and slavery.

Connecticut Compromise
An agreement reached at the Constitutional Convention to establish a bicameral legislature with an upper house (the Senate) composed of equal representation from each state and a lower house (the House of Representatives) composed of representation from each state in proportion to its population.

The Connecticut Compromise. The issue of representation was the most difficult to resolve. Delegates remained deadlocked over it for several weeks. Finally, a committee composed of one delegate from each of the participating states hammered out the **Connecticut Compromise**. It was a compromise that incorporated one key element of the New Jersey Plan, equal representation of the states, into the Virginia Plan. The compromise determined that Congress would be composed of two houses: representation in the lower house would be apportioned by population, and the upper house would have equal representation across the states. The nationalists insisted that the lower house, elected by the people, would initiate all spending bills. The southern states insisted, for the purposes of representation in the lower house, that slaves would have to be counted in some fashion acceptable to them. Ultimately, on the question of slave representation, northern and southern delegates compromised on a formula such that five slaves were to be counted for representational purposes as three people. Only after the southern states accepted a northern counterproposal did they come to agreement. Northern delegates insisted that for them to go along with the so-called three-fifths compromise on lower house representation, in a similar way five slaves would count as three persons for the purposes of apportioning financial levies on the states. After all finally agreed on the compromises on these representational issues, which were immensely important to the design of the new government, the convention could move forward on other issues.

Compromising on Slavery. The issue of slavery came up several more times in the convention, and each time delegates recognized that the fate of the Constitution depended on compromise. Even delegates from the North, who generally favored abolishing the slave trade (or banning slavery altogether), understood that any move to change the status quo in the South would doom the entire constitutional enterprise. Neither delegates from the major slaveholding states nor southern state legislatures would have approved the Constitution without the inclusion of protections of the institution of slavery. And notably, all but one state (Pennsylvania) in the north still allowed for some form of slavery within their borders in 1787. A portion of the northern delegates who personally opposed slavery deeply regretted having to compromise on this particular issue but expected that the issue would eventually go away, either because slavery would become economically less feasible or because future generations would settle this delicate matter.

As a result of the southerners' intransigence, four articles in the Constitution were included that implicitly sanctioned slavery (although the word *slavery* does not appear in the document). The first was Article I, Section 2, which, as mentioned earlier, declared that for purposes of representation in the House and the electoral college, and for apportionment of direct taxes owed by the states, every five slaves were to be counted as three persons. (This was superseded by the Thirteenth and Fourteenth Amendments after the Civil War.) The second was Article I, Section 9, which stated that the importation of slaves could not be prohibited by Congress until after 1807, although Congress could approve a limited tax on the importation of slaves. (Congress did in fact ban the importation of slaves in 1808.) Third, Article V said that no constitutional amendment was allowed that would change Article I, Section 9, until after 1807. Finally, Article IV, Section 2, stated that fugitive slaves fleeing to another state were to be returned to their owners (superseded by the Thirteenth Amendment).

The Constitution was finally agreed to and signed by all but three of the delegates present in Philadelphia. Delegates gave speeches, some indicating that they were unhappy with specific aspects of the Constitution but felt it was important to approve the document as it stood. The last signer was Benjamin Franklin, old and frail, but still eloquent. He said to those present that, throughout the convention and its debates, he had been concerned that the divisions in the young country might doom it to failure. Now, he said, comparing the young country to the sun pouring into the chamber, he had "the happiness to know that it is a rising, and not a setting sun."

Though the delegates had worked out their differences—or at least agreed to a constitution despite them—big questions remained. Would this constitution provide an effective framework for governing the new nation? Would the new constitution solve the United States' collective dilemmas and principal-agent problems?

Institutional Features of the Constitution

The U.S. Constitution is the oldest written constitution among those in use by nation-states around the world. Having a written constitution was rare at the time it was crafted, and it was due largely to an American practice born out of the experience of the colonies and the states after the Revolution. Although the U.S. Constitution has served as a model for many other constitutions, the form of government it established also remains, on the whole, distinctively American. Upon its ratification in 1788, the Constitution provided the new country with the critical governance features it had lacked under the Articles of Confederation. These features helped to strengthen the national government by enabling it to overcome collective dilemmas among the states and the people. The Founders, however, deliberately designed a constitutional system with limited popular control because they feared that too much democracy would lead to poor government and mob rule. Only one unit of government, the House of Representatives, was directly elected; the Senate, the president, and federal court judges were appointed by officials chosen in some way by the people—the Senate by state governments, the president by the electoral college, and federal court judges by the president and the Senate.

The complete text of the Constitution is included in the Appendix. Here we consider its main institutional features.

A President as Executive

Various ideas were proposed at the Constitutional Convention regarding the executive branch. They ranged from a plural executive, consisting of three or more people, to a president who served for life. The delegates eventually settled on the idea of one person serving as president for a four-year term. The Articles of Confederation had made it difficult for the states to join together to quell rebellions and negotiate with foreign powers. With the new constitution, having one individual hold the executive powers was intended to bring decisiveness to the national government when the country faced collective dilemmas. Under the Constitution, the president has relatively broad powers to execute laws, protect the country against internal and external military threats, negotiate with foreign countries, and appoint officials to the executive branch.

The president is indirectly elected by state-level groups of electors, which together make up the **electoral college**. This method of presidential selection reflects the logic of the Connecticut Compromise over representation, whereby smaller states get substantial representation but not as much as larger states. Each state is granted the number of electors totaling the number of senators and members of the House of Representatives. Thus, the smallest states (like Wyoming today) are guaranteed at least three electors, while the larger states have more electors according to their relative size by population. (California today has the most electors: 55 in 2016.)

electoral college The electors appointed by each state to vote for the president.

A Bicameral Legislature

The delegates agreed on a Congress with two chambers or houses (we call this a **bicameral legislature**), both of which must approve legislation before it can become law. Because the House of Representatives is intended to represent the people, its members are directly elected by the voters. Representation in the House is in proportion to state population, and each representative serves a two-year term. The Senate is intended to represent the states. Each state has two senators, who originally were appointed by the state governments for six-year terms. Since 1913, after ratification of the Seventeenth Amendment to the Constitution, senators have been directly elected by the people in their respective states.

bicameral legislature A legislature consisting of two chambers or houses.

The Founders intended Congress to be the center of the national government, and they endowed it with the greatest number of **expressed powers** in the Constitution—more than those given to the executive or judicial branch. The general language of the so-called **elastic clause**, referring to the power to make "all laws necessary and proper," grants Congress wide authority to legislate to provide the means to carry out its enumerated powers.

expressed powers (enumerated powers) Those powers specifically described in the Constitution.

elastic clause (necessary and proper clause) The provision in Article I, Section 8, of the Constitution stating that Congress can make whatever laws are "necessary and proper" to provide the means to carry out its enumerated powers.

The constitution that was signed in Philadelphia in 1787 was the product of bargaining and compromise. Although delegates to the convention did not agree on all the institutional features of the new government, in the end, most felt that it was important to establish a more effective government than the one under the Articles of Confederation.

An Independent Judiciary

Judicial power for the entire country rests with the federal courts, headed by the Supreme Court, which has very broad jurisdiction, including all cases "arising under this Constitution." Congress, charged by the Founders to decide whether to establish "inferior" federal courts, early on set up a system of federal district and appeals courts. Courts that are independent of other branches of government and of the interests of their particular states or localities play a crucial role in maintaining social order and promoting the common good in modern societies. The courts settle disputes over the meaning and applicability of laws and contracts. Without neutral, unbiased courts, people, states, or organizations would regularly settle their conflicts by other means, including violence or intimidation.

Furthermore, a federal court can resolve disputes among states or among subunits of the national government. A strong Supreme Court was seen as necessary to settle conflicts among the states, as much as to resolve cases involving more general legal or constitutional issues. The states have maintained their own court systems to manage state-level matters, but cases involving conflicts among states, between citizens residing in different states, and between representatives of foreign countries and the United States are all the prerogative of the federal courts.

Soon after the Founding, the Supreme Court took the further step of declaring that it had the authority to determine the constitutionality of actions by any government within the United States. Although the Court's power to review the constitutionality of laws or acts of government was not mentioned in the Constitution, it was asserted by the Federalists and applied by the Supreme Court in the *Marbury v. Madison* decision of 1803, as we will see in Chapter 8.

Separation of Powers

The executive, legislative, and judicial functions are separated into three distinct branches of government in the United States. This is known as **separation of powers**. One way to think of separation of powers is to consider what it is not. Separation of powers does not have the various branches as part of a hierarchy with one branch above the others. No single branch can determine the people leading any other branch. Rather, the branches are coequal and have different functions to perform. When the Founders chose to devise a system using separation of powers, they were deliberately avoiding a model of government with a single sovereign, based on their experiences with the British government. For the Founders, dividing governmental authority was a bulwark against oppression.

separation of powers An arrangement in which specific governmental powers are divided among distinct branches of government; typically, this means having an executive who is chosen independently of the legislature, and thus executive power and legislative power are separated.

Checks and Balances

The concept of **checks and balances** (as distinct from the notion of separation of powers) refers to the ways in which the three branches of government share power (Figure 2.2). The Founders built various "checks" into the political system to help ensure that power would not be concentrated anywhere within the three branches. No one branch can conduct its core business without the approval or acquiescence of the others. While separation of powers divides the primary functions among multiple branches, checks and balances ensures that no one branch has total control over any function. For example, Congress primarily legislates, but the president (or the executive branch) has some legislative powers, including the power to veto legislation and to call Congress into special session in emergencies. The judicial branch runs the courts and interprets the law, but the president appoints judges to federal courts with Senate approval. Congress (or the legislative branch) can override the president's veto, impeach the president and federal judges, and set up new federal courts. It must also pass laws to raise funds for anything the other branches wish to do. The Senate must approve many executive-branch appointments, including federal judges, as well as all treaties. The Supreme Court, under

checks and balances An arrangement in which no one branch of government can conduct its core business without the approval, tacit or expressed, of the other branches.

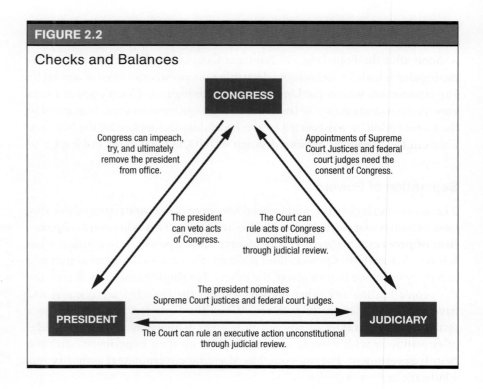

FIGURE 2.2

Checks and Balances

CONGRESS

Congress can impeach, try, and ultimately remove the president from office.

Appointments of Supreme Court Justices and federal court judges need the consent of Congress.

The president can veto acts of Congress.

The Court can rule acts of Congress unconstitutional through judicial review.

The president nominates Supreme Court justices and federal court judges.

The Court can rule an executive action unconstitutional through judicial review.

PRESIDENT

JUDICIARY

the doctrine of judicial review, can declare acts of Congress or the president unconstitutional. The chief justice on the Supreme Court presides over impeachment trials in Congress.

Federalism with National Authority over the States

There was never any doubt among the delegates to the Constitutional Convention that the states would retain considerable authority over their own affairs. The issue of the national government's authority, however, was highly controversial. Proponents of a stronger national government eventually held sway because they were able to convince enough leaders that a weak national government, such as existed under the Articles of Confederation, would lead to continued squabbling among the states, ineffective response to threats, and lack of coordination on appropriate policies. (These same arguments were used to support the creation of a single executive.)

By acknowledging the need for a central government to solve the collective action problem inherent in getting states to contribute to national defense, the delegates included in Article IV, Section 4, of the Constitution the declaration that the national government (rather than individual states through state militias) is responsible for protecting the states against invasion. Under Sections 2 and 3 of the same article, the national government has the power to approve the boundaries of new states coming into the union and to enforce the rule that states return fugitives to the state from which they fled. These important coordination and enforcement functions were designed to avoid disputes between the states and/or new territories that might lead to war. Article VI of the Constitution contains the most important such language, the **supremacy clause**, which states that the laws and treaties of the United States are supreme throughout the land, including superseding rulings by state courts. Moreover, all government officials in the states must swear allegiance to the Constitution. Finally, Article I, Section 10, lists a series of actions that states cannot take, such as making treaties with foreign nations, placing tariffs on foreign goods, and coining their own money. If taken by the states individually, such actions would harm the collective good of the entire group of states.

supremacy clause The section of Article VI of the Constitution stating that the Constitution and the subsequent laws of the United States are to be the "supreme law of the land," meaning that they supersede any state and local laws.

Reserved Powers for the States

Although the Constitution lists things that the states cannot do, it also protects them in critical ways from intrusion by the national government or by other states. States cannot be subdivided into other states. One state cannot have fewer senators than any other state unless that state approves. That is, according to Article V, the Constitution cannot be amended to allow for unequal representation in the Senate unless states receiving less representation approve. The states are guaranteed protection as republican forms of government. Most directly, as part of the Bill of Rights, the Tenth Amendment decrees that all powers not granted to the national government in the Constitution are reserved to the states (and therefore known as **reserved powers**). For a long time, this amendment was seen as having little meaning, especially in light of the previously mentioned elastic clause. In recent years, however, the Supreme Court has used the amendment to limit the power of the national government relative to the states on certain matters.

reserved powers Those powers not granted to the national government by the Constitution, and therefore reserved to the states.

Amending the Constitution

The delegates to the Constitutional Convention agreed on the need for a process to amend the Constitution. Unlike the Articles of Confederation, amendments did not need unanimous approval of the states. The delegates designed two methods for amendment. Under the first method, an amendment becomes law when two-thirds of both houses of Congress and three-quarters of the state legislatures approve it. Under the second method, two-thirds of the state legislatures can together call for a national convention to propose an amendment or a set of amendments, any of which must be approved by three-quarters of the state legislatures. Only the first method has been used in a successful amendment.

The very fabric of the country has been changed by constitutional amendment, including the Thirteenth, banning slavery (1865), the Fourteenth, which laid the basis for antidiscrimination laws (1868), and the Sixteenth, permitting a national income tax (1913). Amendments have greatly expanded the right to vote, declaring that racial minorities (1870), women (1920), people of Washington, D.C. (1961), and 18- to 20-year-olds (1971) can vote in all elections. In recent years, Congress has debated amendments banning the burning of the American flag, another one banning abortion, and yet another banning same-sex marriage. In 2018, there were dozens of proposed constitutional amendments by members of Congress to require a balanced budget for the federal government, but even with Republican control of Congress at the time, these did not get very far. Only 27 amendments, out of the thousands that have been proposed, have made it through the process. The first 10 (the Bill of Rights) were approved together in one process soon after the ratification of the Constitution, as we will see later in this chapter.

The Ratification Debate

According to Article VII, the Constitution required the approval of conventions in nine states for it to take effect. By implication, any state that withheld its approval would be excluded from the federation. Those who favored adopting the Constitution as written, with its stronger national institutions, became known as the **Federalists**; those opposed were called **Antifederalists**. In the seven states dominated by Federalists, the Constitution was ratified by the spring of 1788 with comfortable majorities, but there was serious opposition in all the other states. Three—Virginia, Massachusetts, and New York—had strong Antifederalists among their leadership. Rhode Island didn't even send delegates to the convention and remained opposed to the Constitution for several more years.

Federalists versus Antifederalists

The Antifederalist positions were published as letters in various periodicals and summarized in a pamphlet titled "Letters from the Federal Farmer to the Republican," written anonymously.[3] These letters complained that the new

Federalists Those who favored adopting the Constitution as written because they believed that a strong national government was needed to solve the collective dilemmas facing the states.

Antifederalists Those who opposed adopting the Constitution as written because they feared that it created an overly strong national government.

[3] Its full title was "Observations Leading to a Fair Examination of the System of Government Proposed by the Late Convention; and to Several Essential and Necessary Alterations in it. In a Number of Letters from the Federal Farmer to the Republican." Historians now know that the letters were written by Richard Henry Lee of Virginia.

constitution trampled on the sovereignty of the states, that the Constitutional Convention had gone far beyond its mandate to amend the Articles of Confederation, and that the people of the states could potentially be tyrannized by a new national government.

The Antifederalists adamantly opposed ratifying the new constitution because they felt it betrayed the principle of the Revolution—namely, that people should live in freedom apart from strong, vigorous government, such as the one they believed would be established by the Constitution. They were particularly opposed to the elastic clause and the supremacy clause (see the preceding text) because they believed that together, the clauses gave the national government such power that "there is no need of any intervention of the state governments . . . with this constitution . . . the government then, so far as extends, is a complete one, and not a confederation."[4] To the Antifederalists, federalism as described in the Constitution meant a return to what they despised about the British: remote government with overriding authority to tax without the approval of popularly elected local or state governments, a standing army ready to oppress the people, and one-size-fits-all policies that did not recognize the diversity of the various states spread across a huge land area.

In response, three proponents of the Constitution—James Madison, Alexander Hamilton, and John Jay—published (under a pseudonym) a series of articles in New York newspapers extolling the virtues of the proposed constitution. These articles, which eventually became known as the *Federalist Papers*, not only urged approval of the Constitution but also advanced a political philosophy that provided much of the intellectual basis for the American form of government. Among other themes raised in the *Federalist Papers*, a stronger national government was considered crucial to solving collective dilemmas facing the states and the people.

Several of the *Federalist Papers* have become classics in political theory across the world. The institutions of government, the Federalists argued, should be designed to constrain the behavior of ambitious people and lead to better collective outcomes. The writers believed that people, both leaders and those being led, were rational and would pursue their self-interest. If not constrained by legitimate sovereign governments, some individuals and groups ("factions") would dominate, oppress, or even tyrannize others. The same logic applied to relationships between the states, in that the states needed protection from each other and from outside threats. A stronger national government was essential to protect states from threatening foreign powers, to prevent war between the states, and to forestall damaging internal competition among the states for trade and commerce with other countries. Furthermore, a combination of federalism with separation of powers was desirable to ensure that power did not become

[4] Brutus, "*Antifederalist* No. 1," in *The Complete Anti-Federalist*, vol. II, ed. Herbert J. Storing (Chicago: University of Chicago Press, 1981), p. 365.

1775–81
Revolutionary War

1787 Constitutional
Convention

1791 Bill of Rights
ratified

1770 — 1780 — 1790 — 1800

1776 Declaration of
Independence

1781
Articles of Confederation

1788
Constitution ratified

lodged in one branch of the government, where it could be controlled by one faction of the society. Finally, the Federalists sought to dispel the fears of those opposed to a stronger national government by arguing that the Constitution reserved important powers for the states, and that citizens would retain their loyalties to the states and not transfer that loyalty to the national government.

Massachusetts and New Hampshire approved the Constitution in early summer, providing the two additional approvals required for ratification. June 21, 1788, the date of New Hampshire's ratification, marks the formal beginning of the new constitutional era. However, it was not until Virginia and New York, the two largest and most important states, ratified the Constitution later that summer that the Federalists knew they had won their struggle. A new Congress and the new president, George Washington, took office on April 30, 1789. Eventually, North Carolina (in November) and Rhode Island (in 1790) approved the Constitution and joined the rest of the states within the new system. The Historical Path box above shows the timeline of major developments in the Founding era.

The Bill of Rights

In the debates over ratification, the Antifederalists complained that the Constitution did not contain a list of individual rights to be protected against government intrusion. Many of the state constitutions contained such lists, particularly Virginia's. To address these concerns, supporters of the Constitution promised that a list of rights would be added as amendments soon after ratification. Consequently, the first 10 amendments were approved by Congress in September 1789 and ratified by three-quarters of the states in December 1791.[5]

Bill of Rights The first 10 amendments to the Constitution, which enumerate a set of liberties not to be violated by the government and a set of rights to be protected by the government.

These 10 amendments, known as the **Bill of Rights**, specify the limits of government action. Among the rights listed are freedom of speech, assembly,

[5] In fact, Congress approved 12 amendments in 1789, but only 10 were ratified by the states. One of the two remaining amendments, concerning congressional salaries, was finally ratified by the states in 1992 as the Twenty-seventh Amendment.

and religious practice; a criminal defendant's right to counsel; the right to bear arms; and the right to security against government intrusion on private property unless a warrant is granted by a court of law. The Bill of Rights is as fundamental to the American political system as the governmental institutions established by the original Constitution. Its protections have been central in determining how individuals and government relate to each other in American society, operating as a kind of buffer against government intrusion on individual liberty.

Figure 2.3 shows how the Constitution created a national government that was stronger than under the Articles of Confederation, but the Bill of Rights put limits on government power. As we will discuss in more detail in Chapter 4, controversies over whether the Bill of Rights applies to state as well as

FIGURE 2.3

The Strength of the National Government

The Founders attempted to establish a national government that was strong enough to hold the Union together, but not so strong as to infringe on state prerogatives and individual freedoms. The Articles of Confederation represented a step toward unity, but its provisions were not strong enough to solve the states' collective dilemmas. The Constitution created a stronger national government that could effectively hold the states together. The Bill of Rights then placed limits on the national government, reducing its powers toward the minimum strength needed to maintain unity.

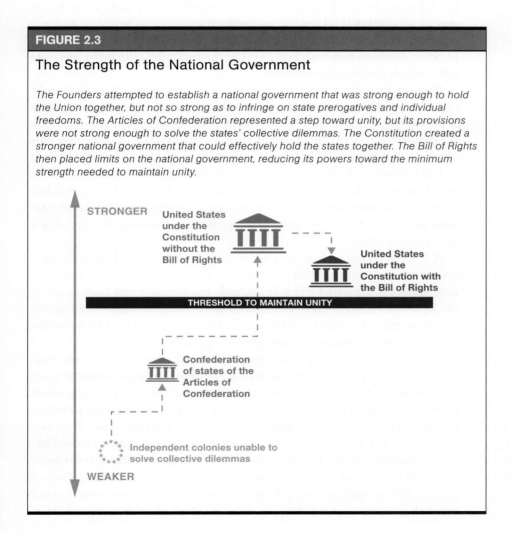

to national laws, and over the meaning of the particular rights listed, have occurred throughout American history. These controversies underlie many of the most important political struggles past and present over federalism, slavery, voting rights, taxation, discrimination, and abortion.

In Comparison: National Constitutions

Although our main focus is on the U.S. Constitution, it is useful to consider how it differs in structure and purpose from the constitutions of other countries. There is great diversity among the world's constitutions, mirroring the differences in the institutional structures of the countries discussed in Chapter 1. For instance, separation of powers contrasts with a parliamentary system (as in the UK), where the executive (typically the prime minister) is chosen by the parliament and remains in power at the parliament's discretion. In other words, in parliamentary systems, the parliament sits atop a hierarchy and can hire and fire the executive.

Thus, in practice, having a president elected independently of the legislature is the distinctive feature of a system based on separation of powers. The American-style system of separation of powers, whereby the legislature does not choose the executive but rather determines the laws that the executive must carry out, is increasingly common among new democracies around the world. In Latin America, Africa, and Asia, many countries have systems with elected presidents who hold considerable powers. Among older democracies, especially in Europe, parliamentary systems—in which the legislative and executive functions are fused together by virtue of the parliament choosing the executive— are more common.

A few countries, such as the United Kingdom, Israel, and New Zealand, do not have written constitutions. Instead, the "constitutional structure" of government is expressed either in multiple documents or by laws passed by the legislature that are given constitutional stature. In the United Kingdom, basic principles of conduct and laws born of traditional practices (the so-called common law) constitute the foundational legal structure.

Some countries have written constitutions that are essentially meaningless. For example, the North Korean constitution guarantees equal rights "irrespective of sex, race, occupation, length of residence, property status, education, party affiliation, political views or religion" and claims to protect freedom of speech, press, assembly demonstration, and association. However, these rights and protections exist only on paper. North Korea established a communist dictatorship following World War II and mandated that the country "shall conduct all activities under the leadership of the Workers' Party of Korea." The country has one of the world's most repressive governments, which regularly jails or executes dissidents and critics of the ruling regime. Iran's constitution guarantees equal rights for men and women and divides power equally among three branches of government. In fact, all power in Iran resides with the religious hierarchy, and men and women are treated very differently, both legally and in the broader society.

The U.S. Constitution, at approximately 4,600 words in its original form (approximately 8,000 words including the amendments), is reported to be the shortest among any of the world's nation-states. Unlike some constitutions, such as those of Brazil and Portugal, the U.S. document does not delve into detailed social and political goals. And unlike those of many other countries, the U.S. Constitution does not describe much in the way of citizens' duties. Rather, it focuses on the powers of government and the rights of individuals that are to be protected by the government and from the government. The U.S. Constitution is less specific about several important matters than those of other countries. For instance, it is vague on the powers of the Supreme Court relative to the other branches of government; as we have seen, it was only through later court decisions that the principle of judicial review—the power of the Supreme Court to declare acts of government at any level unconstitutional—was established. The U.S. Constitution is also relatively vague on the exact powers of the president to wage war. Although the document appears highly specific about Congress's powers, in practice the president's war powers relative to those of Congress go far beyond what the Constitution states.

Nevertheless, many other countries have adopted the basic elements of the U.S. Constitution. Following the American model, nearly all constitutions contain a preamble that sets forth guiding principles, a section that describes the institutions of government and how they are to function, and guidelines for amending the constitution.

Constitutional Evolution

The text of the Constitution should be understood as a starting point and not the entire story of constitutional government in the United States. Amendments, court decisions, and the practices of politicians have significantly shaped the constitutional structure of government as it applies to the political system today. Let's consider some of the major areas in which the Constitution, its meaning and its application, have evolved.

Relative Powers of the Branches of Government

Take, for instance, the military powers of the president. They have changed significantly from what the Founders delineated in the Constitution, mostly through the actions of presidents and decisions of Congress and the federal

The Collective Dilemma

The U.S. Constitution is often said to have created a political system with separation of church and state. Yet public religious expression is common, and religious symbolism pervades some government buildings and schools throughout the country. What leads to religious expression being tolerated and even promoted in American politics?

Interests

Compared to populations in most other industrialized countries, Americans are notably religious. According to national surveys, 80 to 90 percent of Americans say they believe in God. Further, the importance of religion in the United States is greater than in other industrialized nations. For example, 54 percent of Americans affirmed this importance, while only 24 percent did in Canada, 21 percent in Australia, and 21 percent in Germany.[a] Many Americans who are religious support candidates with similar views and who invoke God and religious beliefs in public life. A majority of Americans expect that viable presidential candidates be Christians who practice their faith. Alternatively, there are other Americans (even many who are religious) who oppose the promotion of religion in public life. They advocate a strict separation of church and state and want religion to be a private matter, and not promoted in any way by government.

Institutions

The words of the Constitution matter greatly, and this can be seen when we contrast the United States with France on religious liberties. In France, the words in its Declaration of the Rights of Man and of the Citizen guide French constitutional law: "No one shall be disquieted on account of his opinions, including his religious views, provided their manifestation does not disturb the public order established by law." By comparison, the relevant language of the First Amendment in the U.S. Constitution reads: "Congress shall make no law respecting an establishment of religion, or prohibiting the free exercise thereof." Unlike the French declaration, the American text makes no mention of public order. Instead, it precludes the law from interfering in the free exercise of religion. This language—"Congress shall make no law . . . prohibiting the free exercise thereof"—is referred to as the free exercise clause. It is interesting to note that both the United States and France are widely considered secular states in that there is not an established religion and both are neither against nor seeking to control religion.

Outcomes

Religious expression is common in American society, and religion is embedded in many of its institutions and laws. The free exercise clause encourages religious expression and gives it wide latitude in decision making. More than half of the major airports in the United States have places of worship; almost every state allows religious exemptions for vaccines; open religious expression, even by politicians, is tolerated and common; legislative sessions in Congress regularly feature prayers; "In God We Trust" is engraved and printed on U.S. currency; and a number of court cases hinge on religious freedom and its parameters. Consider, for instance, a 2004 court case in which an Oklahoma school suspended a sixth-grade student for wearing a hijab to school, citing that it violated the school dress code.[b] The U.S. Justice Department intervened and became a plaintiff in the case. The case was settled by a consent order, with a stipulation that the school district must allow the student to wear her hijab and must allow other students to deviate from the dress code on religious grounds.

By contrast, Eleanor Beardsley, Paris correspondent for NPR, describes what French secularism—*laïcité*—means in everyday life in France:

The Constitution and Religion in Politics

[Y]ou would never hear the president say, God bless France. You would never have a congressional prayer breakfast of lawmakers. People do not pray in public. It is not seen as an added value to talk about your relationship to God—never. That is your private, personal business, and in the public sphere, that is no one else's business.[c]

Further, for over 10 years, the French government has prohibited students in public schools from wearing conspicuous religious items, such as Muslim head scarves or larges crosses around their necks. In 2010, French law prohibited the covering of the face in public spaces, which include public transportation, restaurants, and movie theaters. It is important to note that this law does not exclusively target religion or mention Islam. Face covering for religious reasons is treated the same as wearing a mask: neither is tolerated. In 2016, some French cities banned the wearing of burkinis—full-covering swimsuits worn sometimes by Muslim women—on public beaches, based on the idea that they were religious expressions and meant to provoke non-Muslims.

The United States and France have thus responded differently to the challenges of the separation of church and state; the former has favored the coexistence of varied religious expression in the public sphere while the latter has favored the removal of all religious expression. Put another way, France has responded to the question of separation of church and state with "assertive secularism"; the United States, with "passive secularism."[d] Due to differences in the language enshrined in their constitutional law, a public-school student of the Islamic faith in the United States enjoys the constitutional guarantee to wear a religious head scarf to express her religious belief, whereas a similar student in France does not.

A woman sports a burkini while swimming in Marseille, France.

Think About It

Is American implementation of the separation of church and state appropriate given the language of the First Amendment? Is the French model better by keeping religious expression out of the public sphere?

a. George Gao, "How Do Americans Stand Out from the Rest of the World?" Pew Research Center, March 12, 2015, www.pewresearch.org/fact-tank/2015/03/12/how-do-americans-stand-out-from-the-rest-of-the-world (accessed 10/29/15).

b. U.S. Department of Justice, "Case Summaries: *Hearn & United States v. Muskogee Public School District*," October 14, 2015, www.justice.gov/crt/case-summaries#hearnok (accessed 10/25/15).

c. Audie Cornish, "French Law 'Laicite' Restricts Muslim Religious Expression," NPR, March 4, 2015, www.npr.org/2015/03/04/390757722/french-law-laicite-restricts-muslim-religious-expression (accessed 10/25/15).

d. Ahmet T. Kuru, "Ideologies, Institutions, and Laws: Religious Freedom in Secular States," in *Secular States and Religious Diversity*, ed. Bruce J. Berman, Rajeev Bhargava, and André Laliberté, (Vancouver, British Columbia: University of British Columbia Press, 2013), pp. 165–83.

courts. After much debate, the Founders decided to divide responsibilities on matters of war, foreign policy, and domestic peace between Congress and the president.

The Constitution states in Article I, Section 8, that Congress has the power to

- declare war;
- make rules concerning captures on land and water;
- call forth the militia to execute the laws of the union, suppress insurrections, and repel invasions;
- raise and support armies;
- provide and maintain a navy.

The president's powers, in contrast, are tersely summarized in the first clause of Article II, Section 2: "The President shall be Commander in Chief of the Army and Navy of the United States, and of the Militia of the several States, when called into the actual Service of the United States."

One might assume that the last phrase, "when called into the actual Service," in combination with the powers granted to the Congress, implies that, under the Constitution, Congress alone is empowered to call the military into service, while the president's duty is to determine *how* the military will carry out its task. The Constitution clearly states that Congress shall play the preeminent role in military decision making, while the president is in charge of implementing congressional decisions.

The Constitution's words, however, do not match up against the events that have taken place since its ratification. As a result of important court rulings and acts of Congress dating back to the 1790s, the president has had predominant authority and wide discretion over executing the law, and over foreign policy and defense matters. George Washington set the tone in 1794 by vigorously suppressing a rebellion against a tax on whiskey in rural Pennsylvania. Indeed, Washington deliberately set out to demonstrate that the national government, which had been exposed as weak at the time of Shays's Rebellion seven years earlier under the Articles of Confederation, had gained considerable strength under the new Constitution.

Recent presidents have exercised broad war powers. President George W. Bush ordered that American troops, in coalition with other countries, invade Iraq and topple Saddam Hussein's government in 2003 after receiving a vaguely worded congressional authorization to use force under certain conditions. President Barack Obama authorized the bombing of Libyan armed forces in 2011 to oust dictator Mu'ammar Qaddafi. President Obama claimed that he did not need congressional approval to do so. He ordered the bombing of Syrian rebels and positions of ISIS in various countries in the Middle East during his last two years in office, all with only vague approvals by Congress. Congress sometimes passes resolutions giving presidents wide latitude as international crises unfold; when that happens, these decisions are the presidents' to make without any legal controversy. While the decisions to use military force can be controversial, and opponents complain because they believe either the decision was wrong or presidential authority was overstepped, recent presidents have ordered troops into battle with little or no legal consequence.

This may all seem strange to those who look to the words of the Constitution for guidance on the conduct of foreign affairs and defense. Why is there such divergence between what the Constitution says and what presidents actually do? In fact, any constitutional text, regardless of what country it covers or when it was written, invariably contains passages that are ambiguous in their application to real situations, or that will become outdated by historical events. Military policy is not the only area where the operation of American political institutions has departed from the original text of the Constitution. In later chapters, we will discuss how historical events have changed the relative authority of different parts of the American political system as set forth in the Constitution. We must bear in mind, however, that it is not only the meaning of a given constitutional text that is subject to change over time, but the text itself.

National Power versus States' Rights

The Constitution itself contains a number of apparent contradictions. For instance, the elastic clause (Article I, Section 8) states that Congress has the power to make laws to carry out a wide range of powers listed in the Constitution, including those providing for "the common Defence and general Welfare of the United States." This could in principle mean that Congress can pass any law with the common good of the country as its goal, leaving little power to the states. The Tenth Amendment, however, appears to contradict this interpretation. It reserves all residual powers not mentioned in the Constitution to the states or to the people. Without the benefit of judicial interpretation over the years, such contradictions could be problematic in the elastic clause's application for governance. Only in later decisions did the courts rule on the kinds of national laws that are allowable under the standard of providing for the "general Welfare."

The courts have mainly focused on the **commerce clause** (Article I, Section 8) as a guide to what policy areas Congress is allowed to act on. Under this clause, the Constitution grants Congress the power to regulate commerce when it is conducted with foreign nations and when it involves more than one state. Court decisions in the twentieth century made it clear, however, that just about any commercial activity occurring in the United States constitutes interstate commerce and thus is fair game for regulation by the national government. Beginning in the 1930s, the courts gave all but complete discretion to the national government to regulate business and commercial activity, stretching

commerce clause An enumerated power listed in Article I, Section 8, of the Constitution that grants Congress the power to "regulate Commerce with foreign Nations, and among the several States, and with the Indian Tribes."

congressional authority far beyond what earlier Courts interpreted the original text of the commerce clause to imply. Recent Supreme Court decisions (on health care, for example), however, have opened up legal debate over further refinement of the application of the commerce clause. The Roberts Supreme Court has recently offered a somewhat different rendering of the commerce clause, a subject we return to in later chapters.

Direct Election of the President and Senators

The institutions described by the first version of the Constitution were designed to limit popular participation and shield policy makers from public pressure. Among the major branches of the national government, only the House of Representatives was directly elected. The president and senators were not elected directly by the people, but were appointed by the states through a group of electors or legislators. The president and senators were given longer terms in office to protect them from short-term changes in the popular will. Furthermore, the right to vote, known as suffrage, was controlled by the state governments that mostly restricted voting to property-owning white males. Overall, the original Constitution did not specify or encourage a highly democratic political system sensitive to public opinion.

Over the course of American history, however, constitutional amendments and court decisions provided for—and even encouraged—popular participation in government. This evolution not only enabled new groups in society to vote, such as former slaves, women, and 18- to 20-year-olds, it also empowered the national government to enforce this right. Since the early twentieth century, the Constitution also has been applied by the courts to protect vigorously the rights of people to organize, speak out, and protest against the government.

Rights and Liberties

The Bill of Rights clearly stated our rights of free speech, assembly, and the press. The application of those rights to specific circumstances, however, is not always so clear. Thus, as one Supreme Court decision states, freedom of speech does not permit someone to yell "Fire!" falsely in a crowded theater. The lines defining what is permissible and what is not continue to be drawn and redrawn by the courts and by constitutional amendments. The Nineteenth Amendment established women's right to vote. The requirements for how criminal defendants are to be treated—the quality of their jail cells, for example—have evolved as the federal courts have interpreted the meaning of the ban on "cruel and unusual punishment" in the Eighth Amendment, part of the Bill of Rights.

Other rights not specified in the text have been declared by courts to be implied by the Bill of Rights. For instance, the federal courts identified a "right to privacy," which has been used to protect people from certain kinds of warrantless searches by police and to strike down laws banning birth control, abortion, homosexual sex, and sodomy. Nowhere is the right to privacy mentioned in the Constitution. But, according to the Supreme Court in *Griswold v. Connecticut* (1965), marital privacy is a fundamental right that exists due to the Ninth Amendment ("certain rights shall not be construed to deny or disparage others retained by the people") and also "within the penumbra of the specific guarantees of the Bill of Rights."[6] In the *Griswold* case, the Court discovered meanings in the text to establish that the right to privacy exists, and then used the concept to strike down state laws banning contraception that had been in place for decades.

Under the original Constitution, senators were appointed by state legislatures. Since the passage of the Seventeenth Amendment in 1913, senators have been elected directly by the people. In 2018, Jacky Rosen (D) narrowly defeated incumbent Dean Heller (R) for a highly contested U.S. Senate seat in Nevada.

Later court rulings have used other reasoning based on constitutional text to support rights, such as the right to have access to abortion services and the right to engage in private homosexual behavior.

Despite the evolution of constitutional law, the original document and the constitutional framework it established in 1789 remain important today. The institutions set forth in the original Constitution remain the most critical factors in shaping the nature of conflict and cooperation within the American political system. The document was written by people who disagreed bitterly over the fundamental structure of government because they knew that structure would help determine who wins and who loses in American society as a result of government decisions. In short, the Founders understood the importance of institutional design for shaping the country's future.

Consequences of the Constitution

We began this chapter by puzzling over why the Federalists ended up winning most of the conflicts surrounding constitutional design at the Founding. After all, Americans at the time were, and to some extent still are, distrustful of stronger government. Yet the Federalists wanted a stronger national government than the one that existed under the Articles of Confederation. In light of what we

---

[6] From Justice Arthur Goldberg's concurring opinion in *Griswold v. Connecticut*, 381 U.S. 479 (1965).

have learned in this chapter, the answer to our puzzle comes down to this: the Federalists provided convincing arguments to enough groups in society that a government that was too weak would not work to solve collective dilemmas. Unsolved collective dilemmas, leading to events like Shays's Rebellion and to possible threats from foreign powers such as France and Britain, were considered worse than the potential threats from the stronger government put in place by the new Constitution.

Were the Federalists correct that the new Constitution would improve things dramatically for the new country? Most political scientists believe that governmental institutions, especially those established by constitutions, have real consequences. Certainly, the Founders believed this, as do the people who write or amend constitutions in other countries or in the United States. So what have been the consequences of the governmental institutions that were established by the original U.S. Constitution?

Answering this question is not as straightforward as it seems. First, we cannot simply rerun American history multiple times under different institutional conditions and see how it would play out in each scenario. How would American history have been different if the country had not had a strong president, but a weak figurehead appointed to a ceremonial position by Congress? We can never know the answer to such questions with certainty. Second, we cannot know for certain if outcomes were caused by the original aspects of the Constitution, by the Constitution as it was amended later, or by other factors in society. As previously discussed, the structure of the American political system only partly reflects the text of the original Constitution. Later developments, including court cases, constitutional amendments, legislation, and even the Civil War, have reshaped its meaning over time, leading to a constitutional system that is different today than the one the Founders intended.

Despite these obstacles to determining cause and effect, there are two promising approaches to understanding the consequences of governmental institutions. One is to compare what happens in other countries that have different constitutional or institutional frameworks. Another is to compare what happens over time as institutions change.

Extensive research has focused on the consequences of having specific institutional features in place. This research confirms that there is an overall benefit to having a democratic system, or what the Founders called a *republican system* (meaning that representatives of the people govern). Political scientists have learned, for example, that democratic institutions across the world tend to lead to better economic growth, improved health among citizens, a higher level of educational achievement, and lower incidences of infant mortality.[7]

---

[7] William R. Clark, Matt Golder, and Sona N. Golder, *Principles of Comparative Politics* (Washington, DC: CQ Press, 2009).

Two political scientists analyzed constitutions around the world, comparing their length by the number of words, and concluded that "longer constitutions ultimately generate more opportunities for corruption and exploitation."[a]

What about the state constitutions in the United States? We can compare the length of the constitutions across the 50 states. Figure A displays the number of words in each state's current constitution. All of them—especially the longer ones—contain more than just statements of a state's core principles. They also often include what amounts to legislation, sometimes around very specific issues like education, taxation, government spending, wages for public workers, pensions, abortion, and gun policy. Some states have long constitutions for a simple reason: they make it easier (less steps and hurdles) to add amendments. For instance, a constitution that can be changed with an act of the legislature alone is easier to amend than one that requires any amendment be approved by both the legislature and a referendum, which must be approved by a majority of voters in a popular election.

B. Average Length of State Constitutions by Number of Constitutions

53,749 words

29,979 words

States that Have Had One or Two Constitutions

States that Have Had More than Two Constitutions

Some states also have changed their constitutions a number of times, scrapping the old one and rewriting and approving a completely new one. Figure B shows the average number of words in state constitutions according to the number of constitutions the states have had over time.

A. Length of Selected State Constitutions as of January 2018

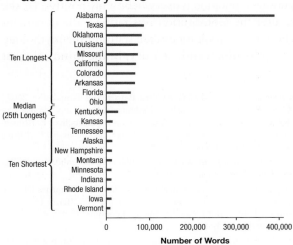

Think About It

What are some possible benefits to having a shorter or longer state constitution? What may happen in Alabama state politics that might not happen in Vermont? Why do you think "longer constitutions ultimately generate more opportunities for corruption and exploitation," as concluded by the political scientists mentioned above? The U.S. Constitution has less than 8,000 words, including amendments. Should it be longer?

Source: Council of State Governments, *Book of the States 2017*, http://knowledgecenter.csg.org/kc/category/content-type/bos-2017 (accessed 10/19/18).

a. George Tsebelis and Dominic J. Nardi, "A Long Constitution Is a (Positively) Bad Constitution: Evidence from OECD Countries," *British Journal of Political Science* 46, no. 2 (2016): 457–78.

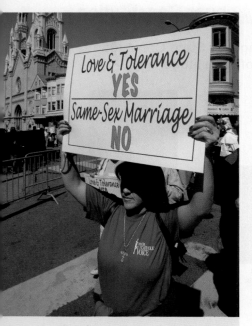

The Constitution and the Bill of Rights are very clear about some rights and liberties, but somewhat vague about others, leaving the door open to interpretation and debate. Opponents of same-sex marriage have tried to pass a constitutional amendment limiting marriage to one man and one woman in order to clarify the limits of gay rights.

In addition, researchers who have studied emerging democracies have demonstrated that those with presidential systems have different kinds of public policies in comparison with parliamentary democracies. More specifically, presidential systems, relative to parliamentary systems, have more incremental changes in governmental budgets and fall back into authoritarian rule more often.[8] Democracy is significantly less likely to be sustained under a presidential system than a parliamentary system[9] (Figure 2.4), and there are more instances of scrapping and replacing constitutions under presidential systems.[10]

There is compelling evidence that countries with longer constitutions, more words and sections, fare worse than countries with shorter ones. Countries with longer constitutions tend to have worse economic outcomes and more corruption.[11] The reason is not entirely agreed upon. Some scholars have argued that longer constitutions contain many specific rules and amendments that protect special economic interests at the expense of the broader public good.

Finally, there is widespread agreement among scholars that the rule of law, with independent courts and enforcement of individual rights and liberties such as those in the Bill of Rights, leads to better economic growth and to richer associational life in the country.[12] In other words, people living under the rule of law tend to be more active in local and national governance in their societies by belonging to civic organizations and participating in politics, in comparison with those in countries without such constitutional protections and judicial independence.

Taking a more historical approach, it is worth stating the obvious point that the U.S. Constitution's reputation is overwhelmingly positive. By the 1820s, three decades after the Constitution was ratified, the document itself and the men who wrote it took on exalted status in the mythology of the country. By the mid-nineteenth century, in the minds of most

[8] George Tsebelis, *Veto Players: How Political Institutions Work* (New York: Russell Sage Foundation, 2002); Matthew S. Shugart and John M. Carey, *Presidents and Assemblies: Constitutional Design and Electoral Dynamics* (Cambridge, UK: Cambridge University Press, 1992); Adam Przeworski, Michael E. Alvarez, José A. Cheibub, and Fernando Limongi, *Democracy and Development: Political Institutions and Well-Being in the World, 1950–1990* (New York: Cambridge University Press, 2000).

[9] Alfred Stepan and Cindy Skach, "Constitutional Frameworks and Democratic Consolidation: Parliamentarianism versus Presidentialism," *World Politics* 46, no. 1 (1993): 1–22.

[10] Bernd Hayo and Stefan Voigt, "Determinants of Constitutional Change: Why Do Countries Change Their Form of Government?" *Journal of Comparative Economics* 38 (2010): 283–305; Bernd Hayo and Stefan Voigt, "Endogenous Constitutions: Politics and Politicians Matter, Economic Outcomes Don't," *Journal of Economic Behavior & Organization* 88 (2013): 47–61.

[11] George Tsebelis and Dominic Nardi, "A Long Constitution Is a (Positively) Bad Constitution: Evidence from OECD Countries," *British Journal of Political Science* 46 (April 2016): 457–78.

[12] Douglass C. North, *Institutions, Institutional Change, and Economic Performance* (Cambridge, UK: Cambridge University Press, 1990); Robert D. Putnam, *Making Democracy Work: Civic Traditions in Modern Italy* (Princeton, NJ: Princeton University Press, 1993).

FIGURE 2.4

Parliamentary versus Presidential Systems

Presidential systems have a popularly elected executive who cannot be removed by the parliament for political reasons. Parliamentary systems have an executive who is chosen by the parliament. Semi-presidential systems have a popularly elected executive who can be removed by parliament for political reasons.

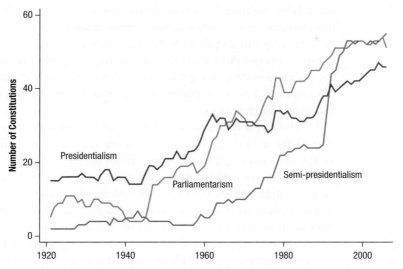

Source: José Antonio Cheibub, Zachary Elkins, and Tom Ginsburg, "Beyond Presidentialism and Parliamentarism," *British Journal of Political Science* 44, no. 3 (November 2013): 1–30.

Americans, the Constitution was fundamental to the thriving of the country.

Historians and political scientists in our own era credit the Constitution with establishing a stable political system that became more democratic over time, and that has enabled the country to grow in three important ways: geographically, by population, and by wealth. The Founders fully expected westward expansion of the country to take place and included provisions for expanding the size of Congress and the electoral college to keep up with the increasing number of states, making it relatively easy for new states to join the union. The Constitution, especially through the Bill of Rights, also paved the way for the nation to grow as wave after wave of immigrants swelled the population. Finally, economic historians widely agree that the constitutional basis for protection of private property, for enforcing contracts and bills of credit, and for ensuring that courts remained independent of political manipulation was instrumental in the unprecedented economic growth experienced by the United States throughout its history, especially in the nineteenth century.[13]

The institutions established by the Constitution have survived, even if not working exactly in the way the Founders intended. To answer one of the questions posed at the beginning of this chapter, the Constitution, by its flexibility, seems to have survived by virtue of striking a workable, amendable balance between strong government and liberty. Although it has changed in many ways, the Constitution—if measured objectively by its longevity and its role in fostering a strong, wealthy country—has been a rousing success. And with the important exceptions of the Civil War and the political system's long tolerance of racial and gender discrimination, the Constitution has been able to solve the most threatening collective dilemmas faced by the states.

Is this conclusion too rosy? The Constitution and the consequences that flow from it have their critics. Among the most notable are those, such as the historian Charles Beard, who believe that the Founders—who were almost entirely wealthy men with large landholdings or considerable capital—deliberately wrote a Constitution to protect the economic interests of people in their own class.[14] Other critics have complained that the American system of government, supported by the legal and political institutions established by the Constitution, has led to extreme inequality and racial subjugation.[15] These criticisms, especially of the Constitution's implicit sanctioning of slavery, undoubtedly have merit. The Constitution generally changes slowly. Even slower has been the appropriate application by courts and legislatures of constitutionally enshrined protections for individual rights and liberties, such as freedom of speech and the right to vote.

Other critics of the American constitutional system suggest that it creates partisan conflict that does not adequately represent public opinion, or that it encourages inefficient government that is better at doling out benefits to special interests than at formulating policies that promote the public good.[16] We will be in a better position to evaluate such criticisms after examining in later chapters the consequences of specific features of the American political system.

[13] North, *Institutions, Institutional Change, and Economic Performance.*

[14] Charles A. Beard, *An Economic Interpretation of the Constitution of the United States* (New York: Macmillan, 1913).

[15] Mary F. Berry, "Slavery, the Constitution, and the Founding Fathers: The African American Vision," in *African Americans and the Living Constitution*, ed. J. H. Franklin and G. R. McNeil (Washington, DC: Smithsonian Institution Press, 1995); Howard Zinn, *A People's History of the United States: 1492–Present* (repr., New York: Harper Perennial, 2005).

[16] Michael Bailey and Mark Carl Rom, "A Wider Race? Interstate Competition across Health and Welfare Programs," *Journal of Politics* 66, no. 2 (2004): 326–47. See also Barry Weingast, "The Economic Role of Political Institutions: Market-Preserving Federalism and Economic Development," *Journal of Law, Economics, and Organization* 11 (1995): 1–31.

FURTHER READING

★=Included in *Readings in American Politics*, 5th ed.

Anonymous, *Letters from the Federal Farmer*, No. 2, 1788. Critics of the Constitution (the Antifederalists) wrote under pseudonyms urging state legislatures not to approve the new Constitution.

Beard, Charles, *An Economic Interpretation of the Constitution* (New York: Macmillan, 1913). A classic account arguing that the Founders intentionally created a document that primarily led to preserving their own wealth and position.

★ Dahl, Robert, *How Democratic Is the Constitution?* 2nd ed. (New Haven, CT: Yale University Press, 2003). A critical look at the Constitution, arguing that the Senate and the judiciary are highly undemocratic features.

Hamilton, Alexander, James Madison, and John Jay, *The Federalist Papers*, No. 10 and No. 51, 1788. Letters written by Madison (under a pseudonym) describing the virtues of republican government. Other *Federalist Papers* were written by Alexander Hamilton and John Jay (also under pseudonyms).

Pope, Jeremy C., and Shawn Treier, "Voting for a Founding: Testing the Effect of Economic Interests at the Federal Convention of 1787," *The Journal of Politics* 77, no. 2 (April 2015): 519–34. After examining Charles Beard's thesis using new data on the personal attributes and the votes of each of the Founders at the Constitutional Convention, Pope and Treier find that voting based on economic interests among the Founders was uneven and depended on the specific issues at stake.

Rakove, Jack, *Original Meanings: Politics and Ideas in the Making of the Constitution* (New York: Alfred Knopf, 1996). A careful, detailed examination of the debates and intentions of the Founders.

Schwarzenbach, Sibyl A., and Patricia Smith, eds., *Women and the U.S. Constitution: History, Interpretation, and Practice* (New York: Columbia University Press, 2004).

KEY TERMS

Antifederalists (p. 52)

Articles of Confederation (p. 40)

bicameral legislature (p. 47)

Bill of Rights (p. 54)

checks and balances (p. 49)

commerce clause (p. 61)

Connecticut Compromise (p. 44)

elastic clause (necessary and proper clause) (p. 47)

electoral college (p. 47)

expressed powers (enumerated powers) (p. 47)

Federalists (p. 52)

New Jersey Plan (p. 42)

reserved powers (p. 51)

rule of law (p. 35)

separation of powers (p. 49)

supremacy clause (p. 51)

Virginia Plan (p. 42)

The views of many states and the federal government conflict on the issue of Syrian refugee resettlement. Governors of some states, such as Greg Abbott of Texas, took steps to ban the settlement of refugees in their states. Here, pro-refugee groups protest Abbott's decision outside the Texas State Capitol.

3

Federalism

 Why have the states and the American people allowed the federal government to become more and more powerful?

After a string of attacks claimed by the Islamic State of Iraq and the Levant (ISIL) killed and injured thousands of people in train stations, airports, and popular tourist destinations in Europe in 2015 and 2016, there was speculation that some of the individuals responsible entered the continent pretending to be Syrian refugees.

After the attacks in Paris, more than half of the governors in the United States announced bans on Syrian-refugee resettlement in their states.[1] For instance, in Georgia, Governor Nathan Deal ordered state agencies to halt any refugee-resettlement activity, which meant that Georgia's Division of Family and Children Services was prohibited from processing Syrian refugees' applications for benefits. In Indiana, then Governor Mike Pence's ban meant that state agencies would withhold funds to nonprofit organizations involved in Syrian-refugee resettlement. And, in Texas, Governor Greg Abbott ordered the Texas Health and Human Services Commission's Refugee Resettlement Program to halt any activity related to Syrian-refugee resettlement.[2]

Some states even brought lawsuits against the federal government. For example, Texas sought an injunction against the federal government for failing to consult with the state on matters of resettlement, arguing that according to the Refugee Act of 1980, the federal government "shall consult regularly with State and local governments and private nonprofit voluntary agencies concerning the sponsorship process and the intended distribution of refugees among the States and localities."[3] But the U.S. District Court for the Northern District of Texas rejected the injunction twice,

[1] Ashley Fantz and Ben Brumfield, "More than Half the Nation's Governors Say Syrian Refugees Not Welcome," CNN, November 16, 2015, www.cnn.com/2015/11/16/world/paris-attacks-syrian-refugees-backlash (accessed 11/17/15).

[2] Greg Abbott, Letter to Barack Obama, Governor of Texas Press Office, November 16, 2015, http://gov.texas.gov/files/press-office/SyrianRefugees_BarackObama11162015.pdf (accessed 3/30/16).

[3] 8 U.S.C. § 1522 (1980).

OUTLINE

- Federation and Confederation
- The Dynamics of American Federalism
- The Courts and the Constitution
- Toward a Stronger National Government
- Federal Financing
- Federalism and Race
- State Governments
- Local Governments
- In Comparison: American Federalism
- Evaluating American Federalism

stating that it "cannot interfere with the executive's discharge of its foreign affairs and national security duties based on a possibility of harm, but only on a proper showing of substantial threat of irreparable injury and a legal right to relief."

Then-governor Rick Scott of Florida, recognizing the power of the federal government, tried to halt Syrian-refugee resettlement through legislative means. In a letter to leaders in Congress, he urged congressional leaders to take legislative action, saying, "[i]t is our understanding that the state does not have the authority to prevent the federal government from funding the relocation of these Syrian refugees to Florida even without state support."[4]

Compared to these governors, President Barack Obama responded very differently to the Syrian refugee crisis. In a press conference he said, "Slamming the door in their faces would be a betrayal of our values."[5] Further, he promised that the United States would accept 10,000 Syrian refugees.[6] An open letter from the director of Office of Refugee Resettlement (ORR) said, "States that continue to use ORR funding must ensure that assistance and services are delivered without regard to race, religion, nationality, sex, or political opinion. States may not deny ORR-funded benefits and services to refugees based on a refugee's country of origin or religious affiliation."[7]

The conflicting statements around the Syrian refugee crisis articulate a central tension of the American federal system: states can enjoy certain benefits (federal funds, for example) but at a cost to their policy autonomy. Moreover, it is often unclear where state authority ends and federal authority begins.

The boundaries between state and federal authority have been contested throughout American history due, in part, to the Constitution's fundamental ambiguity about the nature of American federalism. Throughout the twentieth century, federalism questions were most often decided in favor of the national government. As a result, the national government has grown in power over time relative to the states. Perhaps surprisingly, this centralization of authority is largely the result of public pressure and even some state governments requesting and assenting to increased national power. In general, the representatives of the people in the states (in Congress) consent to national authority and keep it in place. Given the states' interest in protecting their own sovereignty and the people's traditional fears of excessive centralized power, why have they allowed the federal government to become more powerful in the last century?

---

[4] Rick Scott, Letter to Paul Ryan and Mitch McConnell, Office of the Governor of Florida, November 16, 2015, www.flgov.com/wp-content/uploads/2015/11/Letter-11.16.15.pdf (accessed 2/11/16).

[5] The White House, Office of the Press Secretary, "Press Conference by President Obama—Antalya, Turkey," November 16, 2015, www.whitehouse.gov/the-press-office/2015/11/16/press-conference-president-obama-antalya-turkey (accessed 2/6/16).

[6] Amy Pope, "How We're Welcoming Syrian Refugees While Ensuring Our Safety," The White House, November 17, 2015, www.whitehouse.gov/blog/2015/11/17/how-were-welcoming-syrian-refugees (accessed 3/8/16).

[7] Robert Carey, "Resettlement of Syrian Refugees," Office of Refugee Resettlement, November 25, 2015, http://judiciary.house.gov/_cache/files/ad1921a5-383c-4053-8599-8c752ec484ea/orr-syrian-resettlement-letter.pdf (accessed 3/8/16).

Federation and Confederation

Federalism can be defined as a political system that includes multiple levels of government where subunit governments exercise independent authority over important areas of policy and at least one level of subunit government has constitutionally protected status.[8] "Constitutionally protected status" means that subunit governments (such as states or provinces) coexist with the central government according to constitutional tradition and cannot be abolished unilaterally by the central government. In the United States, for example, the states have always been the constituent units of the federation, and Congress is explicitly forbidden under the Constitution from unilaterally changing an existing state's boundaries or altering its government so long as it is of a republican nature.[9]

Compared with a federation, a **confederation** is a weaker form of union. As commonly used, the term *confederation* implies that the subunit governments retain full sovereignty and that the national government cannot compel them to act. In practice, united action by a confederation requires voluntary compliance. In this situation, as when the American colonies operated under the Articles of Confederation (discussed in Chapter 2), subunit governments typically face serious collective action problems that inhibit them from achieving the common good. If confederation was as far as the states would allow the country to go down the path of centralization, the states could refuse to pay the costs of union—as many did under the Articles—or even leave the Union, as the 11 Confederate states did in 1860 and 1861.

After the Founding, the Civil War was the most important event in the development of the American political system. The war began after the southern states left and formed a new country called the Confederate States of America. In response, the U.S. government, composed of the remaining states and led by President Abraham Lincoln, mobilized an army and invaded the South to preserve the Union. Approximately 620,000 Americans died in the Civil War; 1 out of every 10 able-bodied men in the North and 1 out of 4 in the South were killed or injured. The Union army finally defeated the Confederate army in 1865, ending the war and southern secession.

The Civil War stemmed from a variety of deep splits between the states of the North and the South during the first 80 years of the nation's history, including slavery and economic policies. The two sides also interpreted the Constitution differently when it came to the relationship between the states and the federal government. In deciding to secede, the leaders of the Confederacy relied on a view of American federalism that held that the country was created

federalism A political system with multiple levels of government in which each level has independent authority over some important policy areas.

confederation A political system with multiple levels of government in which lower-level governments retain full sovereignty and cannot be compelled by the national government to act.

[8] See William H. Riker, *Federalism: Origin, Operation, Significance* (Boston: Little, Brown, 1964).

[9] In contrast, U.S. cities and counties do not have the same protected status that states have. They are "creatures" of the states, which means they can be set up, abolished, or amended in form by state law.

by agreement among sovereign states. They took the position that the United States are together *voluntarily* under one confederation and, as sovereign states, could leave the Union if they wished.[10] Unless the Constitution expressly forbade states from taking certain actions or adopting certain policies—such as making treaties with foreign countries—the national government, according to the Tenth Amendment, granted them full discretion. In the Confederate view, state sovereignty was the hallmark of the American federal republic.

Reflecting on what we learned in Chapter 2, we can see that this interpretation of the Constitution springs from a view resembling the Antifederalists' philosophy. The Confederation's subsequent defeat at the hands of the Union army could be seen as vindication of the Antifederalists' prediction that the Constitution would lead to the trampling of states' rights. While the Antifederalists after the Founding pushed the Bill of Rights, including the Tenth Amendment designed to protect the states from a vigorous national government, Confederation leaders could only conclude that the Tenth Amendment was not enough.

The Lincoln administration and most northern politicians, particularly members of Lincoln's Republican Party, promoted a different version of federalism and the Constitution. In their view, the Constitution meant the United States *is* a sovereign country, and the preamble declared that "the people" had created an indissoluble union. The national government had authority granted to it by the sovereign people of the United States as a whole. As such, the national government could make decisions and expect compliance even if a united South was opposed to those decisions. More important for Lincoln, secession was not only an illegal act, but it also broke the "sacred" bond created at the Founding. Lingering notions from the Antifederalists, in this view, were dangerous precisely because they could lead to disorder, including secession. The Civil War and its aftermath settled the issues of secession and slavery and emphatically shifted the country in a more federal direction.

Figure 3.1 illustrates the continuum in the centralization of political control from a loosely organized confederation to a highly centralized "unitary system" of government.[11] Moving toward the left along the continuum, the central government's power increases relative to that of the subunit governments. During the ratification debates between Federalists and Antifederalists following the Constitutional Convention, much of the discussion centered on where along this continuum the United States should stand. The issue continued to be debated up to and during the Civil War.

An example from another part of the world can help clarify the distinction between federation and confederation. Most scholars consider the European

[10] Geoffrey Ward, with Ken Burns and Ric Burns, *The Civil War: An Illustrated History* (New York: Alfred Knopf, 1996), p. 404.

[11] See Daniel Elazar, *American Federalism: A View from the States* (New York: Crowell & Company, 1966).

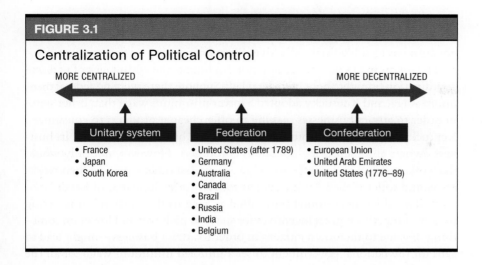

FIGURE 3.1

Centralization of Political Control

MORE CENTRALIZED ←——————————————————————→ MORE DECENTRALIZED

Unitary system	Federation	Confederation
• France	• United States (after 1789)	• European Union
• Japan	• Germany	• United Arab Emirates
• South Korea	• Australia	• United States (1776–89)
	• Canada	
	• Brazil	
	• Russia	
	• India	
	• Belgium	

Union (EU) to be a confederation. The member countries have agreed to join together to create a single economic market. To that end, they have developed a set of political institutions, such as a European parliament, an executive commission, and a court, to coordinate action and solve their collective dilemmas. The EU government in Brussels, however, cannot compel the member countries to act in the same way that the national governments of the world's federations can compel states and provinces. Brussels exacts fines from member countries when they do not comply with EU decisions, but there is no legal basis for the idea that the EU government in Brussels has authority over the territory of the countries in the European Union. If the member countries were to vest sovereign military authority in the Brussels government, then Europe would begin to look more like other federations around the world. Until then, however, compliance is essentially voluntary because punishments for noncompliance are financial (and typically moderate) and do not entail force. In 2016, the citizens of the United Kingdom voted to leave the EU effective in March 2019.

Federalism as a Response to Collective Dilemmas

The United States and the European Union provide stark examples of how centralization evolves when subunit governments cannot solve certain problems on their own. Central governments often gain power and become either confederated or federated when the subunits face collective dilemmas. The European Union originated in the 1950s as a confederation among six countries, largely in response to two devastating world wars resulting from conflict between Germany and France. The idea was that a political confederation, even a weak one, would prevent wars between member countries. Likewise, we saw in Chapter 2 how the creation of the American federation under the Constitution was largely a response to fears among the states that they could not protect themselves from foreign invasion or internal strife without a stronger national government to solve their collective dilemmas.

The following hypothetical situation highlights the advantages of national coordination brought about by federal law. Suppose there were no federal minimum wage, and Kentucky adopted a lower minimum wage than other states in order to attract businesses seeking to offer cheaper products to consumers. Kentucky might benefit from the influx of new businesses, as would its business owners and their price-conscious consumers. However, not only would the workers in Kentucky suffer from low wages, but other states and their workers would suffer if their businesses left for Kentucky in search of lower labor costs. This dilemma—sometimes called a "race to the bottom" in referring to how competition gives incentives for states to go lower and lower on something of value to their own citizens in order to attract business—might lead to calls for the national government to set a uniform minimum wage for all the states, eliminating the collective action problem by reducing the temptation to free ride off states with a higher minimum wage. In fact, the United States *does* have a national minimum wage. Congress first established it in 1938 to resolve the collective action problem among states and city governments. By passing a national law mandating a minimum wage enforceable everywhere, the national government uses its authority over the states to solve a problem that they cannot solve on their own.[12]

Most people would agree that the states often need coordination and enforcement to avoid the problem of free riding, but not always and not on every issue. When and on what issues should the national government make policies that apply to all the states? On what issues should the states be given the discretion to adopt their own policies? Most controversies over federalism stem from differences of opinion about these questions. It is fair to say that, although the balance of power between the states and the national government is constantly in flux, depending on the nature of the times and the issues that confront the nation, the historical trend has been toward greater centralization, shifting more power to the national level.

The Dynamics of American Federalism

dual federalism A political system in which each level of government—national and state—is sovereign in its own sphere of policy authority.

Some scholars have depicted the set of American governmental institutions as a system of **dual federalism**, whereby each level—national and state—is sovereign in its own sphere and operates largely independently of the other. This kind of federalism is often likened to a layer cake. Critics of this depic-

---

[12] The federal government's minimum wage is the *minimum* legal wage. However, states and localities can impose a *higher* minimum wage than the national standard, and many have in recent years.

tion describe the system instead as **cooperative federalism**, whereby both national and state governments are active in nearly all spheres, sharing powers and working together to solve problems. A marble cake is a more apt metaphor for this kind of federalism, because no matter how you slice it, both levels of government are present in every piece.

In fact, the American political system is a mixture of dual and cooperative federalism, although as the national government has grown stronger over time, the system has come to more closely resemble a marble cake. As Figure 3.2 shows, some policy areas are almost completely the prerogative of one or the other level of government. In many policy areas, however, the two levels cooperate or share resources. This is sometimes called **intergovernmentalism**. When both the states and the national government are active in a given area, the precise boundaries of their authority can be difficult to define, or subject to "back and forth" swings between national control and state control. One example is education policy. Congress has in the past mandated federal standards for states in designing and operating school systems. Schools are run by the states and by local school districts, but the federal government has used strong financial incentives (fines as punishments in some cases and grants as rewards in others) to induce the states to comply with federal standards. Because

cooperative federalism A political system in which both levels of government—national and state—are active in nearly all areas of policy and share sovereign authority.

intergovernmentalism A system in which multiple levels of government are active in a given policy area.

FIGURE 3.2

Responsibilities of National, State, and Local Governments

**Prerogatives of the
National Government**

**National
government only**

Examples:
- National defense
- Currency
- Tariffs and trade
- Negotiate treaties

**Shared
prerogatives**

Examples:
- Social welfare
- Tax collection
- Research and development
- Business regulation

**Mostly state
and local**

Examples:
- Traffic regulation
- K–12 education
- Zoning
- Marriage
- Insurance regulation

**Prerogatives of the
State and Local Governments**

the education of children has long been the prerogative of the states, the extension of federal power into the domain of education remains controversial, and subject to repeated changes between national and state assertions of authority. In the early 2000s, the national government established strong, uniform standards on all states in education through the No Child Left Behind Act (2001). By 2015, through a new law passed by Congress and signed by the president, No Child Left Behind was largely repealed and authority reverted to the states on many issues regarding educational standards.

The Courts and the Constitution

Throughout American history, the federal courts have helped determine the balance between the national government and the states. Decisions by the Supreme Court and other federal courts have played a large role in enabling the national government to increase its authority, while also maintaining state authority over certain policy areas. In other words, the courts have generally sought to maintain some balance between national power and state power, though it allowed the balance to tilt toward national power over the long run.[13]

The courts rely on the language of the Constitution for guidance, but as we have seen, there has always been ambiguity about how that language applies to actual practice. Recall our discussion of national power versus states' rights in Chapter 2. In various places, the Constitution specifically defines the limits of state and federal authority. For example:

- Article I, Section 10, clearly lists the things states cannot do, such as negotiate treaties with foreign countries or coin money.

- Article IV, Sections 2–4, declare that the national government has key responsibilities to protect the states, to approve state boundaries and new states joining the Union, and to enforce laws about fugitives crossing state boundaries.

- Article VI contains the "supremacy clause," which declares national law supreme over the entire nation (that is, if state law conflicts with federal law, federal law overrides it) and mandates that all public officials, including state officials, swear allegiance to the United States.

In the main, however, the Founders left it for later generations to decide what the national government and the states can do. For instance, the Constitution gives Congress broad powers to make all laws "necessary and proper for carrying into Execution the foregoing Powers" (Article I, Section 8,

---

[13] William Eskridge and John Ferejohn, "The Elastic Commerce Clause: A Political Theory of American Federalism," *Vanderbilt Law Review* 47 (1994): 1355.

Clause 18) and says that Congress has the power to "regulate Commerce . . . among the several States" (Article I, Section 8, Clause 3). These are referred to as the **elastic clause** and the **commerce clause**, respectively. People ever since have struggled to define the boundaries of authority prescribed by these words. Furthermore, the Tenth Amendment reserves to the states all powers not specified as the prerogative of the national government. But what powers are *not* the prerogative of the national government? The text of Article I, by itself, does not provide a conclusive answer.

The Antifederalists thought they had the answer, which was that the national government ought to have very limited powers. The Constitution as written, they argued, would lead to national government domination over the states and ultimately make the states powerless. In their writings, they focused on the elastic clause and the commerce clause, and indeed subsequent tensions over federalism have occurred largely because of interpretations of those parts of the Constitution. The elastic clause in particular, they feared, could open the door for the national government to make policies that override state law in virtually any domain. The Antifederalists may have predicted accurately the rising power of the national government as a whole, but they were most worried about Congress. They failed to anticipate the role of the courts not only in fostering national authority but also at times in maintaining some balance.

When there is disagreement over the limits of American federalism, the courts are often called in to adjudicate between states, or between states and the national government. In fact, legal wrangling over where sovereignty should lie is a constant feature of the American federal system. In perhaps the two most important Supreme Court cases concerning national government authority over the states, the majority opinions in *McCulloch v. Maryland* (1819) and *Gibbons v. Ogden* (1824) declared that the national government had wide latitude to regulate commercial activity, even within the states. In *Gibbons*, for instance, the Court took a particularly expansive view of the commerce clause. It decided that national power over interstate commerce includes commerce that occurs within state boundaries but involves enterprises from other states. In the increasingly nationalized economy of the 1820s, this ruling meant that virtually any commercial activity occurring anywhere in the country was subject to national regulation.

The courts have also helped the states preserve their autonomy in many areas. In the late nineteenth and early twentieth centuries, the Supreme Court limited the scope of national powers to regulate certain forms of commerce. Taking a narrow view of the commerce clause, the Court struck down efforts by the national government to regulate things like working hours and child labor, and to impose a national minimum wage. Only in the 1930s, at the height of the New Deal, did the Court begin to expand its reading of the commerce clause. In particular, new judicial theories led the Court increasingly to view "Commerce . . . among the several States" as incorporating nearly

elastic clause (necessary and proper clause) The provision in Article I, Section 8, of the Constitution stating that Congress can make whatever laws are "necessary and proper" to provide the means to carry out its enumerated powers.

commerce clause An enumerated power listed in Article I, Section 8, of the Constitution that grants Congress the power to "regulate Commerce with foreign Nations, and among the several States, and with the Indian Tribes."

any activity related to commerce, including employment and wages, the purchasing of products, and even racial exclusion. This was the legal opening the Roosevelt administration needed to assert substantial powers to regulate and stabilize the economy within and across the states with virtually no restrictions imposed by the Tenth Amendment. In recent decades, however, the Supreme Court has begun to return to a narrower interpretation of the commerce clause, a topic we expand on later.

Know the FACTS — Sources of National Government Power and State Power

CONSTITUTIONAL PROVISIONS The Constitution outlines national and state authority, leaving some areas ambiguous.

- **Centralization of power**

  - *The commerce clause*—Article I, Section 8, enumerates the responsibilities of Congress, giving Congress significant powers over the states.

  - *The elastic (necessary and proper) clause*— This clause, also found in Article I, Section 8, grants Congress the authority to do whatever is "necessary and proper" to execute its powers enumerated within the Constitution.

  - *Article I, Section 10*—This section of the Constitution lists numerous restrictions on the powers of the states.

  - *The supremacy clause*—Through this clause, the Constitution, subsequent federal law, and all U.S. treaties become the "supreme law of the land" to which all states are bound.

- **Decentralization of power**

  - *Article I, Section 9*—Much like Section 10 for the states, this section lists restrictions placed on federal power.

  - *The Bill of Rights*—The first 10 amendments to the Constitution place further limits on the actions of the federal government. The First Amendment begins with "Congress shall make no law . . ."

- *The Tenth Amendment*—The Tenth Amendment establishes what are referred to as the reserved powers. It says that "the powers not delegated to the United States by the Constitution, nor prohibited by it to the states, are reserved to the states respectively, or to the people."

MAJOR SUPREME COURT DECISIONS The text of the Constitution is not always clear in its meaning, and disputes over federalism are often settled in court.

- **Centralization of power**

  - *McCulloch v. Maryland* (1819)—The Court ruled that although this power is not expressed in the Constitution, Congress has the authority to establish a national bank according to the powers implied by the necessary and proper clause, giving the national government wide latitude.

  - *Gibbons v. Ogden* (1824)—The Court affirmed that Congress has the authority to regulate commerce as long as it involves more than one state.

- **Decentralization of power**

  - *United States v. Lopez* (1995)—The Court ruled that the Gun-Free School Zones Act passed by Congress in 1990 is unconstitutional because regulating firearms in public schools is not regulating interstate commerce. Thus the Court recognizes limitations on national government authority granted by the commerce clause.

To be sure, court decisions, and even changes to the Constitution, are often limited in their impact. In part, this is because courts generally lack the means to enforce their rulings and must rely instead on other branches of government. In many instances, the executive and legislative branches are responsible for enforcing court decisions. But which level of executive or legislative authority shoulders this responsibility: the local, state, or federal? Uncertainty and disagreement over such jurisdiction within the federal system can lead to dangerous confrontations. For example, in 1957 a Little Rock, Arkansas, school district failed to comply with federal court rulings mandating racial integration of its schools. The state of Arkansas likewise refused to enforce the federal law. President Dwight D. Eisenhower as a last resort sent federal troops to Little Rock to enforce the court order. The president's decision was controversial not only because it involved the issue of race relations in the South in the 1950s but also because it involved the federal government using force to bring a state into compliance on an issue usually reserved for the states—education. In a different realm of law, beginning in the mid-1960s, federal courts ruled on a number of cases concerning poor conditions in state prisons. To ensure compliance by the states, the courts set up a system whereby state officials who do not comply will face arrest on charges of contempt of court.

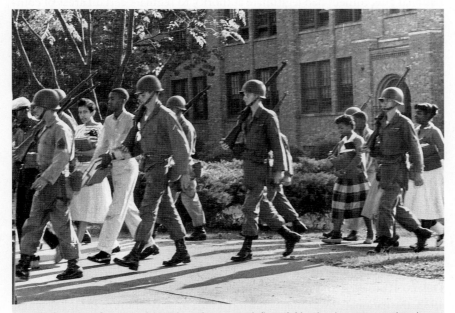

While Supreme Court decisions have been very influential in shaping state–national relations, they have often relied on the actions of the other branches of government to achieve their impact. Despite the Court's ruling in Brown v. Board of Education *that public schools were required to integrate, it took President Eisenhower's sending of federal troops into Little Rock, Arkansas, to escort black students into Little Rock Central High to ensure state compliance.*

Toward a Stronger National Government

Although the courts have at times interpreted the Constitution in favor of national power and at other times in favor of states' rights, the overall trend, in court decisions and in subsequent legislation and executive action, has been toward greater power for the national government. Since the Civil War, broad political movements in three distinct eras have shifted the balance toward the national government. Each of these movements culminated in sweeping legislative changes, and each were the product of public pressure in favor of national government action to solve problems that were seen as beyond the scope of the states either individually or collectively.

Progressive Era, 1896–1913

Around the turn of the twentieth century, the national government began to develop a substantial administrative capacity to regulate the newly industrialized, urbanized economy. Although some Supreme Court cases upheld states' rights, and thus slowed down the efforts of the national government, both major political parties and the public increasingly accepted the idea that the national government had legitimate authority to regulate certain areas of commerce: the safety of food, medicine, clothing, and household fabrics; the control or breakup of monopolies in oil, railroads, and utilities; and the management of mineral and wood extraction from federal lands. Although some national bureaus, such as the Interstate Commerce Commission (1877), were created earlier, it was not until the administration of President Theodore Roosevelt (1900–1908) that these units were given much real authority or substantial personnel to regulate interstate business activity. To cap off the so-called Progressive Era, the national government was granted authority by constitutional amendment to institute an income tax on individuals in 1913. This meant that for the first time, the national government could tax individuals directly—a power the states had always had.

New Deal Era, 1933–52

The New Deal Era saw the most far-reaching political and economic centralization in American history. Following the election of President Franklin Delano Roosevelt and overwhelming Democratic majorities in Congress in 1932, the national government embarked on a massive effort to bring the country out of the Great Depression and to prevent such shocks to the economic system in the future. It established bureaus to regulate the activities of banks, financial trading companies, public employees, airlines, railroads, unions, and utilities. It set up programs to promote the building of transportation, recreation, and utilities infrastructure nationwide. It also created a social security system that for the first time guaranteed a minimum level of income for retirees and the disabled. The national government grew to unprecedented size with the creation of numerous advisory agencies and oversight boards to help make informed decisions on macroeconomic and fiscal policies. By the end of the era, the federal budget was 14.5 times larger than it had been in 1932, and the number of federal employees (excluding military personnel) had increased more than threefold.

To understand the long-term trend in American federalism, it is vital for us to focus on the transition that occurred between 1900 and 1950. Most people saw their state governments as more important than the federal government. The states taxed them and provided most of the governmental services that affected their lives. By the late 1940s, however, the national government had become the more important level of government in citizens' lives. It taxed them directly, provided Social Security payments, regulated many household products, and was responsible for the overall health of the economy. The changes that took place in the early twentieth century gave the national government preeminent authority not only over the status of the Union itself, which had been settled by the Civil War, but also over the country's entire economic system.

FDR's New Deal programs greatly expanded the size of the national government in the 1930s and 1940s. In this 1938 cartoon, various new national programs were depicted as young children with the caption, "Ring a round a Roosevelt, pockets full of dough."

Great Society Era, 1964–77

Continuing the legacy of the New Deal, Presidents John F. Kennedy, Lyndon B. Johnson, and Richard M. Nixon—supported (or sometimes compelled) by Democratic majorities in Congress—sought to use the powers of the national government to correct various social problems such as poverty and inequality across groups in housing, education, and health care. Even more than during the New Deal, the national government of the Great Society Era worked directly with state and local governments to enact new programs. States and cities received large grants and loans from the national government to improve conditions in inner cities, build transportation infrastructure, enforce racial integration, and provide basic health care and education.

Moreover, the period was defined by another surge in the creation of federal bureaucracies, this time to enforce regulatory laws relating to the natural environment, worker safety, highway safety, health care, product safety, and access to education and housing. Finally, given the nature of the grants and loans to states and cities, and the complexity of problems that the national government sought to address, intergovernmental cooperation became vital for many areas of public policy. In the areas of law enforcement, medical care, education, transportation, energy, environmental protection, and land use, it became common

Note: This figure is a conceptual depiction of the increases in national government power corresponding to important historical eras. It is not intended to be a historical timeline.

in the United States for national, state, and local governments to work together, or at least coordinate their activities. The tendency toward this intergovernmentalism presents opportunities and challenges, which we discuss shortly.

Recent Trends

Since the 1990s, the development of American federalism has been characterized by two opposing trends. On the one hand, in the federal courts the balance between the national government and the states has tipped back toward the states. Between 1995 and 2015, the Supreme Court handed down decisions favoring state autonomy under federal laws regarding gun control, violence against women, rights of the disabled, medical marijuana, endangered species, and voting rights. In *United States v. Lopez* (1995), for example, the majority asserted states' rights against the national government by striking down a national law banning handguns near schools, deciding that the commerce clause did not justify congressional regulation of this issue area. In *National Federation of Independent Business v. Sebelius* (2012), the majority, while upholding President Obama's signature health care law on other grounds, also declared that the law violated the commerce clause because the Founders "gave the Congress power to *regulate* commerce, not *compel* it." A 2016 decision (*United States v. Texas*) invalidated an action by the Obama administration to postpone deportation of immigrants who are in the country unlawfully but are parents of citizens. The Supreme Court let stand a lower court ruling that, with this action, the federal government, and especially the presidency, had over-reached its constitutional authority and infringed on certain powers right-fully belonging to the states. Thus, in specific areas, the courts have reserved powers for the states, causing consternation among some national lawmakers who believe that the states cannot do it themselves and that the national gov-ernment's power is needed to solve specific social and economic problems.

On the other hand, enormous increases in federal spending resulting from the terrorist attacks on September 11, 2001, and the financial crisis in 2008 have made the states increasingly dependent on the national government for funding. Beginning in 2002, a series of homeland security policies by the na-tional government infused state budgets with money for policing, monitor-ing of potential criminal activity, and disaster-response preparedness. The money came with requirements for cooperation with other states and com-pliance with federal guidelines. Following the major economic downturn in 2008, the economic stimulus policies of the George W. Bush and Obama ad-ministrations again channeled huge amounts of federal money to the states, this time for education, research, small-business development, and incentives to hire new workers both in the private sector and in government.

Proponents of these policies argued that both of these situations called for strong responses at the national level, and by and large their arguments won the day. Public pressure to have the national government act came from those con-vinced that the states themselves would not be able to take strong enough ac-tion, because the states either would not be able to unite around coordinated policies or would not have the capacity to deal with problems at such a grand scale. Critics, such as those in the Tea Party movement beginning in 2009 and continuing through the 2012 and 2016 elections, harkened back to the symbols from the Founding and lamented the increasing power of the national govern-ment relative to the states. In their interpretation, the national government had far overreached its appropriate authority under the Constitution. Reflecting some of the contradictory trends about federalism in recent years, Donald Trump proposed and adopted some policies that would strengthen the national government and some that would give authority over spending to the states. Some also claimed that the large-scale national-level solutions were simply too expensive for taxpayers. Let's now examine the role of federal money in more detail.

Federal Financing

As part of the overall shift toward greater national power, the federal govern-ment since the 1950s has provided significant funding to states and cities for such things as highways and roads, education, research and development,

grants-in-aid Money that is distributed to lower-level governments with the purpose of funding special projects.

categorical grants Grants that narrowly define how the funds are to be spent. These grants normally come with conditions that need to be satisfied in order for the money to be used.

revenue sharing A principle whereby the national government and the lower-level governments cooperate in funding a project.

block grants Sums of money transferred to lower-level governments such that, as long as the general purpose of the grant is met, the lower-level governments are allowed considerable freedom in deciding how the money is spent.

environmental cleanup, urban renewal, and mass transportation. **Grants-in-aid** are given to state or local governments to fund special projects, such as school lunch programs or new transportation infrastructure. The national government often awards **categorical grants**, which specify exactly how the money is to be spent and attach many conditions. For example, a state can receive federal grant money for school lunches, but the national government attaches regulations on the kinds of food that must be served, the nutritional value, and the total number of calories per child. These grant programs frequently operate on a **revenue-sharing** principle, which means that the state or local government must partner with the national government to fund a project.

The national government gives **block grants** for more general purposes. With block grants, states or localities have considerable freedom to use the money as they see fit, as long as the purpose is in line with the broad goals set by the national government. Block grants were created in the 1970s in part because of complaints by the states that other kinds of federal grants had too many strings attached and led to excessive meddling by the national government in state affairs. In some circumstances, the national government provides loans to state or local governments on more favorable terms than are available on the private financial market, such as loans to rebuild after natural disasters.

Figure 3.3 shows the proportion of state revenues that came from national government grants (also called *transfers*) in 2014. Such grants represent a double-edged sword for state and local governments. Because the original legislation authorizing much of this funding—especially for block grants—was intended to give states and localities more autonomy relative to the national government, it was supported by state governments. However, the national government can always threaten to deny states money if the states do not comply with national standards. One classic example occurred in 1984–85 when President Ronald Reagan effectively mandated that states failing to comply with the national standard drinking age of 21 would not receive federal highway funds. South Dakota resisted and then appealed to the federal courts, claiming that the national government had overreached its powers. The courts sided with Reagan, but the Supreme Court recently clarified its position. In a 2012 decision on a major health care law, the Court said that the federal government can use money as a "mild encouragement" to the states but cannot use money as a "gun to the head." By this, the Court meant that financial penalties cannot be so severe that a state failing to comply with a federal requirement would need to eliminate core services due to budget losses.

Despite the Court's prohibition against onerous financial penalties on the states, the question arises: Are the states so dependent on the federal government in total that they have lost their freedom to act based on their own populations' preferences? Since the early 2000s, federal funding for homeland

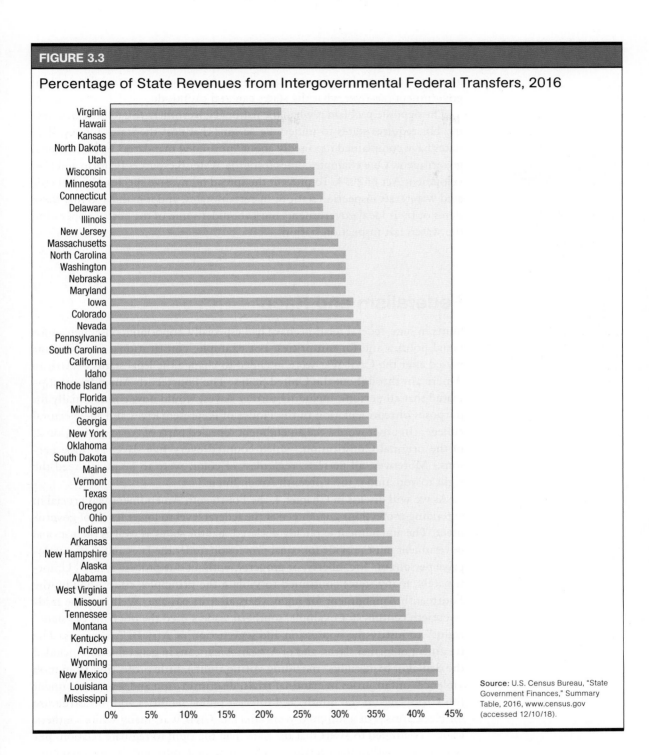

FIGURE 3.3

Percentage of State Revenues from Intergovernmental Federal Transfers, 2016

Source: U.S. Census Bureau, "State Government Finances," Summary Table, 2016, www.census.gov (accessed 12/10/18).

security and for stimulating the economy has come to make up a large portion of state budgets. The more states and localities start to depend on national grants to conduct their day-to-day operations, the more control the national government has over what the states can and cannot do.

The opposite problem is when the national government *fails* to provide funding but requires states to undertake actions that cost the states money. The states have complained repeatedly about "unfunded mandates" by the national government. One example comes from the Water Resources Reform and Development Act of 2014. To prevent the spread of invasive species, this bill created watercraft inspection stations in certain states, and it mandated that these states or their local governments must shoulder some of the costs of operating the watercraft inspection stations.

Federalism and Race

Shifts in state-federal relations have had especially important consequences for racial politics and for minorities. For example, constitutional amendments passed after the Civil War were intended to change the legal status of African Americans throughout the United States. The Fourteenth Amendment stipulated that all persons, including former slaves, would now count equally for purposes of representation in the House of Representatives and the electoral college. (In other words, the amendment repealed parts of Article I, Section 2, of the original Constitution, which counted every five slaves as three persons.) Moreover, all persons, regardless of color, were to be guaranteed the right to vote under the Fifteenth Amendment.

As we will discuss in Chapter 4, the Fourteenth Amendment was crucial in extending protections guaranteed at the federal level to lower levels of government. The amendment explicitly declared that the states as well as the national government must provide for equal protection under the laws and shall not deprive persons of "life, liberty, or property, without due process of law." Unfortunately, many states continued to violate the principles established by the Fourteenth Amendment for many years after its passage. Well into the mid-twentieth century, for example, southern leaders used the doctrine of "states' rights" to justify the oppression and segregation of African Americans. The treatment of former slaves, and of African Americans in general, often included the denial of basic rights (including voting rights), little protection from mob violence, unfair juries in criminal trials, discrimination and separation under Jim Crow laws in the South, and inferior public facilities and infrastructure for black areas. For a hundred years after the Civil War, many white southern leaders continued to assert that the states had the right to regulate relations between races within their territory. The Supreme Court and the national gov-

Where Does Federal Money Go, and Why?

The federal government has grown stronger relative to the states over the course of American history. One manifestation of this change has been the growing reliance of states and local communities on grants, loans, and contracts from the federal government. In 2015, for instance, over $600 billion in federal grant money was allocated across the country. What determines how much each state or locality receives? How much do political considerations, including election-related competition, determine federal grant allocations?

"Core" vs. "Swing" States, and Timing

Using data on federal grants to counties from 1984 to 2008, researchers sorted counties by whether they were in states with solid and consistent support for the president's party, and by whether they were in states that were highly competitive between the two major political parties in presidential elections. A "core state" was one where the president's party took 55 percent or more of the presidential vote in the past three election cycles. "Swing states," were those where the losing candidate in a presidential election won 45 percent or more over the past three election cycles. Figure A shows how much *additional* federal money a county received on average annually if it was in a core or swing state within those categories.

The political timing can also affect where federal money flows. Figure B shows where grants go in election and non-election years.

Think About It

Why do you think core states receive more federal grant money than swing states? Do you think it is fair that counties in swing states get more during election years?

A. Federal Grants to Counties in Core and Swing States* (in millions)

B. Federal Grants to Counties in Core and Swing States by Election Timing* (in millions)

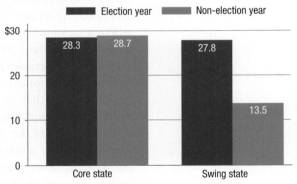

* Average additional grant amounts per year, 1984–2008, controlling for other factors.

Source: Douglas L. Kriner and Andrew Reeves, "Presidential Particularism and Divide-the-Dollar Politics," *American Political Science Review* 109, no. 1 (2015): 155–71.

ernment ultimately rejected that interpretation of the law in the latter part of the twentieth century because it led to systematic civil rights violations.

Starting in the 1940s, and especially in the 1960s, the national government began to use its power to enforce the ideals stated in the Fourteenth Amendment. Through additional constitutional amendments, enforcement of Supreme Court decisions, and civil rights legislation, authority tilted strongly in the direction of the national government on matters of race. By the 1970s, the national government had become the main protector of racial equality. In the wake of the 1965 Voting Rights Act, for example, the national government used the full power of the Justice Department to oversee elections in the southern states. In some cases, federal workers manned polls and counted ballots in southern counties.

The writers of the *Federalist Papers* argued that federalism had the advantage over other forms of government in that one level of government can check the abuses of another level. In theory, governments at any level can oppress or fail to protect the vulnerable. The national government has in its past been complicit or actively involved in the unjust killing and mistreatment of Native Americans, immigrants, slaves, and enemy combatants. But beginning in the mid-twentieth century, racial oppression and discrimination were undoubtedly lessened because of the national government's active role in upholding individual rights and liberties that were flouted by the states. This is an area where arguments in favor of states' rights in the past were made to protect those violating basic human rights.

On issues of crime control and policing, vigorous debates take place about whether the national government needs to do more to protect racial minorities who believe they are mistreated by local police forces. In Chicago, St. Louis, and Baltimore, local police departments have been accused of systematic racial profiling and the unnecessary use of force, wielded disproportionately against minority suspects. In heated debates over possible reforms of local political departments, the issue of national versus state and local authority is never far from the surface. As in many matters, localities often seek to preserve their autonomy in policing, while those populations with grievances against local police forces ask for national intervention.

In the next chapter, we will take a closer look at how federalism issues become intertwined with the politics of civil rights and liberties.

State Governments

The growth of the national government's power does not mean that the American states are powerless. As we have seen, the states retain important powers and have control over many aspects of the political system that touch the everyday lives of Americans. State government continues to flourish under American federalism, despite the increasing centralization since the Civil War. In fact, both federal and state governments in general play a larger role in people's lives today than they did in the late nineteenth century.

The Institutions of State Government

The institutions of state governments are very similar to those of the national government. All state governments have separation of powers, a directly elected governor as executive, a legislative branch with powers of the purse, and a judicial system headed by a state supreme court. Except for Nebraska, every state has two chambers in the legislature, typically a house and a senate. (Nebraska eliminated its senate in 1937 in a statewide referendum.)

Governors' powers vary from state to state, as do the structures of legislatures. For example, in states such as Texas and New Hampshire, the legislatures meet irregularly and members receive very low pay for what is often their second job. In other states such as New York, California, Illinois, and Michigan, legislators are well paid, have large staffs, and work full-time year-round.

By and large, state-level governance, like national governance, is accomplished by elected representatives in the executive and legislative branches. Unlike the national government, however, several states allow for direct democracy—citizens vote directly on laws, or vote to remove an elected official before completion of his or her term. Such action is often achieved through **ballot initiatives**, **referendums**, or **recall elections**. For instance, in 2018, the people in four states (Michigan, Missouri, North Dakota, and Utah) were asked to vote in ballot initiatives to decide whether marijuana should be legal for either recreational or medicinal purposes. In three of the four states (all except North Dakota), voters approved the initiatives. We will take a closer look at these forms of direct democracy in Chapter 13.

Governors and (in most states) other officers, such as state attorneys general and secretaries of state, are chosen in statewide elections. Representatives and senators are usually selected in a manner similar to U.S. House and Senate elections. For each chamber, the states are divided into electoral districts and one person is elected from each district.

Electoral politics in the states was changed drastically by the U.S. Supreme Court decisions in *Baker v. Carr* (1962) and *Wesberry v. Sanders* (1964). Together, these rulings mandated that all electoral districts of state and national legislatures (with the important exception of the U.S. Senate) must be equal in size by population within each state. When districts for state houses and senates were subsequently redrawn to reflect equality by population, cities immediately had a dramatic increase in representation in state legislatures. Before that change, many state legislatures were well known to be biased toward rural interests at the expense of urban interests.

ballot initiative An election in which citizens vote directly on a proposition raised by a group of fellow citizens.

referendum An election in which citizens vote directly on whether to overturn a bill or a constitutional amendment that has been passed by the legislature.

recall election An election during the term of an elected government official in which citizens vote directly on whether to remove the individual from office.

State Power

Over the past three decades, the states have begun to play a somewhat larger role in the American political system. This resurgence in state power stems from several sources. First, the Supreme Court in the 1990s handed down a series of decisions that narrowly interpreted federal powers, thereby granting states more discretion in complying with national law. Second, the national government in the mid-1990s shed some of its responsibility for social welfare programs, giving states considerably more freedom than before to adopt their own welfare standards (see Chapter 16). Third, the national government has become increasingly strained financially as a result of cuts in federal tax rates since the 1980s and international military interventions since the early 2000s. Except for the temporary economic stimulus funding enacted in 2009, Washington has cut back spending in many categories, including scientific and industrial research, roads and highways, job training, loans to students and businesses, and enforcement of antidiscrimination laws. In states where voters tend to favor such programs, the states have had to pick up where the federal government has left off. State budgets have generally grown since the 1980s (Figure 3.4).

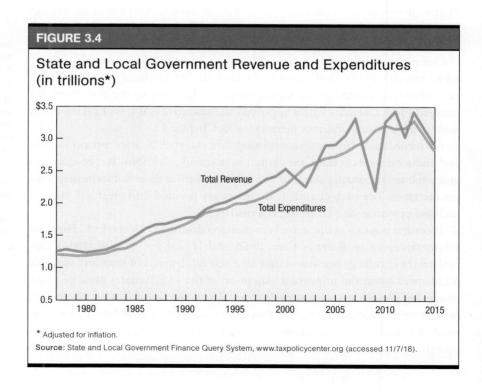

FIGURE 3.4

State and Local Government Revenue and Expenditures (in trillions*)

* Adjusted for inflation.

Source: State and Local Government Finance Query System, www.taxpolicycenter.org (accessed 11/7/18).

Local Governments

There are nearly 90,000 local governments in the United States. They include the most recognizable types: cities, towns, and counties. They also include school districts, regional councils, and special districts that deal with particular issues such as water, zoning and urban planning, transportation, business development, port and lake management, and utilities. The boundaries of special districts typically overlap or cut across multiple cities or counties, and they are often dedicated to coordinating the efforts of several local governments. There are even instances of cross-state regional governments, such as the Port Authority of New York and New Jersey, which operates within both states' territories and is governed by a 12-person board appointed by the governors of each state. In this case, the two states have agreed to grant the Port Authority considerable leeway in regulating transportation, water management, and commercial interactions within their territories, although with oversight by the individual state governments.

Although some leaders, managers, and representatives are appointed, nearly all local governments are led by elected officials. Thus, Americans vote to elect an enormous number of people to run local governments. Sometimes these elections are small in scope and occur throughout the year, with low voter turnout. Yet even when Americans go to the polls in November for national elections, their ballots are often long due to the large number of local races. They vote not only for mayors, council representatives, and state and county judges but also for coroners, sheriffs, drainage commissioners, zoning board members, and dogcatchers.

City governments can take on various forms. Many cities have a *mayoral* form with direct elections for a mayor and a city council; this is essentially a local version of separation of powers. For instance, the mayor appoints people to head administrative departments, but the council must approve those appointments. This form of city government is common among small cities with fewer than 10,000 people, and in large cities of more than 250,000. The most common form of government for cities, however, is *council-manager*. Under this setup, the city council is directly elected and then appoints a city manager to run the day-to-day operations of the city and to appoint heads of departments.

Scholarship on city politics has demonstrated that the type of governmental institutions in cities affects who is represented in city government, the quality of services delivered to residents, and overall success in attracting investment and jobs. For example, numerous studies have shown how at-large election rules—which require city council members to be elected by the city as a whole, rather than by district—lead to councils with fewer racial minorities and advocates for the poor than those relying on districted elections.[14] Also, different

---

[14] Bernard Grofman, Lisa Handley, and Richard Niemi, *Minority Representation and the Quest for Voting Equality* (New York: Cambridge University Press, 1992).

The Collective Dilemma

According to the Controlled Substance Act (1970), U.S. federal law prohibits the cultivation, sale, distribution, or possession of marijuana. Lawmakers at the time wished for uniform policies across the states on marijuana, and this law was one way to achieve that by coordinating and enforcing laws applicable to all states. Yet in recent years nearly half of the states have established policies that legalize medical marijuana. Moreover, between 2012 and 2015, Washington, Colorado, Oregon, and Alaska legalized recreational use of marijuana. How have these states been able to deviate from federal policy?

Interests

Leaders in the federal government have a strong interest in preserving public safety while appearing tough on crime. They also have an interest in preserving national power over the states. Yet they are not insulated from public opinion, which means they do not want to appear old-fashioned on policies that enjoy increasing popular support. In 2018, more Americans supported marijuana legalization than opposed it (62 percent compared to 34 percent).[a]

This popular support, which is higher in some states than others, pressures leaders in the states to support legalization. Supporters of legalized marijuana make several arguments: that marijuana is necessary to reduce pain and discomfort for certain diseases, that recreational use is no more harmful than alcohol or tobacco, and that the issue of marijuana legalization rightfully belongs under state jurisdiction, not federal. Many state leaders have decided to risk the consequences of not complying with national policy.

Institutions

Three institutional features of American federalism are especially relevant in this issue. First, the supremacy clause of Article VI of the Constitution and subsequent court decisions interpreting its application establish that the federal government's laws have ultimate authority over state laws. This clause gives the national government power to enforce national law prohibiting marijuana, even in states that have legalized it. In other words, the federal government could, if it chooses, enforce laws in all states against marijuana.

Second, direct democracy in the states allows citizens to pass laws through an initiative or referendum. In Colorado and Washington, the legalization of recreational marijuana was decided through voter initiatives. These public driven efforts cue officials at both the state and federal levels about their constituents' preferences. If federal officials believe the public would react negatively to attempts to assert federal power in this matter, they may decide to leave the states alone to implement their own policies.

Further, limited federal and state resources and the priorities of law enforcement redirect attention to other issues that often are more pressing. The U.S. Justice Department's agenda includes immigration, civil rights violations by police, and terrorism. States do not always have the resources to track drug trafficking and sales, especially for marijuana with its widespread use among so many people. The federal government in particular must decide the issues that merit federal resources and defer to the states on issues that are less immediately dangerous or significant.

Outcomes

The Obama administration assumed an ambiguous and sometimes conflicting posture on the issue of state-level marijuana legalization. This ambiguity and conflict can be observed in a document known as the Cole Memorandum II, named after the Deputy Attorney General who authored it.[b] The memorandum aptly illustrates the competing interests at play with sub-federal marijuana legalization in a federation that bans it.

Federal and State Conflicts over Marijuana

Cole Memorandum II (2013) states that the federal government has specific marijuana-related enforcement imperatives: the federal government is interested in, above all, marijuana-related enforcement to curtail marijuana possession by certain populations (minors, gangs, cartels), to prohibit marijuana harvesting on public or federal land, and to interfere when marijuana operations are used as a pretext for other drug operations.

In states that have legalized marijuana, the federal government expects that these states will "implement strong and effective regulatory and enforcement systems that will address the threat those state laws could pose to public safety, public health, and other law enforcement interests." The specifics of this expectation are unclear; what, in practice, constitutes these effective regulatory and enforcement systems?

The memorandum goes on to acknowledge that a rigorous federal enforcement calls for resources that the federal government is unable to supply, stating, "The Department is also committed to using its limited investigative and prosecutorial resources to address the most significant threats in the most effective, consistent, and rational way."

Finally, the memorandum affirms that federal purview of marijuana supersedes that of the states: "This memorandum does not alter in any way the [Justice] Department's authority to enforce federal law, including federal laws relating to marijuana, regardless of state law."

The memorandum makes clear that the U.S. Justice Department during the Obama administration would not interfere in places that have established a rational system to regulate and enforce marijuana-related conduct. This position strikes a balance between the federal government's conflicting interests to avoid unpopular law enforcement actions while also being seen as retaining its supremacy over the states and being strong on crime.

Perhaps the current ambiguous situation is untenable in the long run. People who use marijuana in many states are simultaneously breaking federal law *and* acting consistently with state law. They face risks of prosecution but do not know what to expect from law

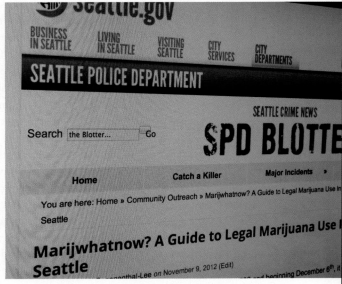

After Washington voters legalized recreational use of marijuana, the Seattle Police Department published guidelines for new enforcement rules.

enforcement at federal and state levels. Not only are states not complying with federal law, but overall coordination on marijuana policies is failing. The federal government has tried through its laws to coordinate a single, national policy; but with its unwillingness to enforce those laws, the coordinated outcome has unraveled and left a patchwork of policies that differ by state.

What Do You Think?

How do you think this situation will be resolved? Will the national ban on marijuana be preserved and the state laws negated? Or will the states be able to keep their laws making marijuana legal for recreational use?

a. Hannah Hartig and Abigail Geiger, "About Six-in-Ten Americans Support Marijuana Legalization," Pew Research Center, October 8, 2018, www.pew research.org/fact-tank/2018/10/08/americans-support-marijuana-legalization/ (accessed 11/7/18).

b. James M. Cole, "Guidance Regarding the Ogden Memo in Jurisdictions Seeking to Authorize Marijuana for Medical Use," U.S. Department of Justice, Office of the Deputy Attorney General, June 29, 2011, www.justice.gov/sites /default/files/oip/legacy/2014/07/23/dag-guidance-2011-for-medical -marijuana-use.pdf (accessed 11/2/15).

methods of budgeting have led to systematically different distributions of services among rich and poor neighborhoods.[15]

Regarding the powers of local government relative to the states, the prevailing legal theory, known as Dillon's Rule, holds that local governments are the "creatures" of the states, that states have sovereign authority to create, abolish, or amend local governments, and that all local matters must be approved by the states. If interpreted literally, this theory would mean that state governments have to deal constantly with minute decisions for every local government. In practice, it means that when there is a dispute over jurisdiction between states and local governments, the courts usually side with the states. When states set up a local government or a special district, for example, they authorize the new government to make decisions in accordance with state law. Nearly all states also have **home rule** as part of their constitutions or laws. Home rule gives a local government wide authority and even forbids states from interfering in local matters. In many states, for example, counties have home rule. Most of the nation's largest cities have home rule. States can revoke home rule either by legislation or by constitutional change, depending on the state. Also, states do sometimes infringe on cities' home rule, and courts have allowed that under certain circumstances.

home rule The constitutional or legal authority held by local governments that allows them to govern themselves with little or no interference from the state.

Special Districts

Growth in the number of special districts is one of the most striking recent developments in American local government (Figure 3.5). It signifies recognition by local politicians and public administrators that many problems—such as the management of transportation and waterways—call for solutions that cut across the boundaries of cities, towns, and counties. In fact, many of these special districts are created in response to collective dilemmas occurring among local governments. Problems such as polluted waterways or lakes, overcrowded airports, or terrible traffic require multiple governments to coordinate their efforts, or a central enforcer to make sure that local governments pay their fair share for the public good. Special districts can play the role of coordinators or enforcers.

There is also a downside to creating special districts. Some research has shown that a large portion of new governments in the United States created between the 1960s and the 1980s—especially school districts and special districts—occurred in response to demands by whites to separate themselves politically from cities with diverse populations that included many blacks and immigrants.[16] On the one hand, we can praise the flexibility of the American federal system in enabling groups of citizens and of local governments to craft

[15] Paul Peterson, *The Price of Federalism* (Washington, DC: Brookings Institution, 1995).

[16] Nancy Burns, *The Formation of American Local Governments: Private Values in Public Institutions* (New York: Oxford University Press, 1994).

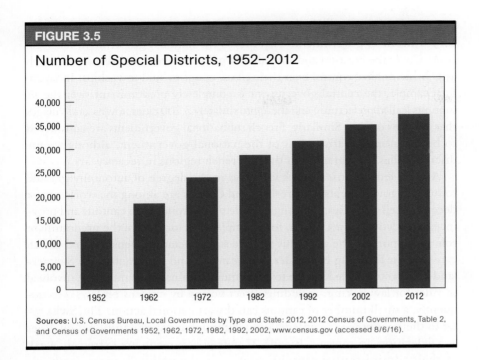

FIGURE 3.5

Number of Special Districts, 1952–2012

Sources: U.S. Census Bureau, Local Governments by Type and State: 2012, 2012 Census of Governments, Table 2, and Census of Governments 1952, 1962, 1972, 1982, 1992, 2002, www.census.gov (accessed 8/6/16).

new governmental institutions to deal with problems that span multiple jurisdictions. On the other hand, that same flexibility also allows groups that no longer want to be part of jurisdictions struggling to manage problems associated with poverty, immigration, and racial diversity to exit those jurisdictions and create a new space and a new government that faces fewer social problems.

In Comparison: American Federalism

Some countries have strong central governments while others are looser federations with relatively weak national governments. In studying American federalism, it is useful to consider how other political systems are structured and whether institutional structure makes a difference in policy outcomes. Countries or international organizations can be placed somewhere along the continuum illustrated in Figure 3.1. Those toward the right are more like the European Union (which is not a country, or what is referred to formally as a nation-state, but rather a collection of sovereign nation-states). Moving toward the left, countries range from federations like the United States and Canada to unitary countries such as Japan and France.

Countries divide authority among levels of government in different ways. Local governments everywhere exercise some degree of authority and responsibility for such functions as maintenance of local police, trash collection, and

unitary system A political system in which the national government holds ultimate authority over all areas of policy and over the actions of subunit governments.

street cleaning. But on the basis of our continuum, most countries have a **unitary system** of government. This means the national government has legal control over the creation and amendment of lower levels of government, much as U.S. states have control over their cities, counties, and townships. In Japan, for example, the central government is completely predominant over the 47 subunits (called prefectures) and the approximately 3,200 cities, towns, and villages that dot the country. Similarly, French subnational governments are considered to be the administrative arms of the national government, although some discretion has been granted to the 22 French regions in recent years.

Among federations, there is variation in the degree of autonomy granted to subunit governments. Switzerland and Canada are among the world's most decentralized countries, granting considerable autonomy to cantons and provinces, respectively. In Canada, for example, provinces have the predominant role in supporting the generous welfare state, including pensions and health care, and in licensing businesses. The cantons and half-cantons in Switzerland are granted wide latitude to implement national laws and to be involved in rules for lawmaking, including direct voting by citizens on laws. Consequently, a small number of cantons can thwart national action. The Swiss refer to their country as a confederation, although by our definition it qualifies as a federation. In contrast, Brazil's 27 state governments are extremely weak in their administrative capacity relative to the national government, although the political clout and electoral independence of Brazilian governors make them heavyweights in Brazilian politics. Most scholars consider the United States somewhere between these two extremes among federations because it has both a strong national government and important **reserved powers** for the states, which have substantial administrative capacity.

reserved powers Those powers not granted to the national government by the Constitution, and therefore reserved to the states.

Why have some countries set up federations instead of establishing a weaker form of union among sovereign states or provinces, as with the European Union? Alternatively, why have they not chosen a unified form of government in which the national government holds complete sovereign authority, as in Japan? It may seem at times as if the founders of countries had a lot of choice in the matter. But in the United States, for example, there was never any doubt at the Founding that the country would be federal (or, some thought, strongly confederal). The Founders debated how powerful the national government should be relative to the state governments, but they never considered setting up a unitary government.

To understand why one country is federal and another is unitary, it is most useful to consider the conditions at the time of their founding. (Recall our discussion of path dependence in Chapter 1.) For most federal countries, including the United States, their founding involved the uniting of disparate units under one central government for purposes of security or economic prosperity. The Canadian federation, for instance, was formed in 1867 to unite English and French Canada. It was simply assumed that the provinces would have considerable sovereign authority. The same goes for such countries as Belgium, Switzerland, and Germany. Following the breakup of the Soviet Union, the Russian federation was formed among existing subunits that chose, or were forced, to remain under Moscow's umbrella. Although these subunits have varying levels of autonomy, it has always been assumed that they would be separate parts of the federation with constitutionally protected status.

Does it make a difference if a country is federal or not? Scholars who have studied this question have generally agreed that federalism matters, but they come to mixed conclusions about whether it is good or bad. There is evidence that among low-income countries, federalism leads to more regime stability, including fewer coups and civil wars. But there is also evidence that federal countries have historically had higher rates of corruption and less-effective government in producing public goods.[17]

Evaluating American Federalism

The American federal system has been influential around the world and often serves as a model when constitutions are designed for new democracies. Scholars have argued that the American system has both advantages and disadvantages.

Avoiding Tyranny

One of the original justifications for the American system given by the writers of the *Federalist Papers* was that, just as with the separation of powers among the three branches of government (executive, legislative, and judicial), federalism fragments power and protects against tyranny. By dividing authority between the states and the national government, constitutional federalism has helped different levels of government check each other's power so that one level cannot dominate. The *Federalist Papers* claim repeatedly, in response to the Antifederalist fears of national government dominance, that the important powers reserved for the states check the power of the national government.

This observation brings us back to the puzzle set forth at the beginning of this chapter: If one advantage of federalism is that each level of government has the ability to check the other, why has the United States centralized authority and granted more power to the national government over time? And has the increase in national power protected citizens from bad government (as someone sympathetic to the Federalists might conclude) or made government worse and even more threatening (as an Antifederalist would have predicted)?

[17] For the relationship between regime stability and federalism, see Alicia Adsera and Carlos Boix, "Constitutions and Democratic Breakdowns," in *Controlling Governments*, ed. José M. Maravall and Ignacio S. Cuenca (New York: Cambridge University Press, 2008), pp. 247–301. For a summary of research linking federalism to corruption, see Daniel Treisman, *The Architecture of Government* (New York: Cambridge University Press, 2007), pp. 247–69.

As we have seen, the national government has become dominant in response to public pressure amid collective dilemmas among the states. During urgent crises, such as wars, depressions, and labor unrest, the states and the people in the states often come to recognize that collective dilemmas make it difficult to mobilize and coordinate effectively. When voters elect national leaders who propose *national* solutions to problems, they support authorizing the *national* government to lead the country out of trouble. In doing so, the national government amasses resources and capacity to carry out policies to deal with the crisis. And those resources and capacity often stay in place after the crisis passes.

Nevertheless, there have been institutional checks on national government powers. The Supreme Court, for example, has protected the states from national government encroachment on a variety of occasions. More generally, courts have been careful to define areas where, under the Constitution and existing national law, the states retain virtually complete sovereign authority. A federal court system independent of interference from the other branches of the national government is a critical institutional feature that preserves balance in the federal system.

Holding elections at multiple levels of government provides another important institutional check on the national government's power. Political scientists have long argued that federalism opens the door for voters to choose different types of politicians for different levels of government. For instance, a voter may prefer strong law-and-order politicians at the local level (let's say they are Republicans, for the sake of argument), but relatively liberal politicians who might restrict gun sales at the national level (Democrats, in this example). Thus, instead of pursuing one party's dominance at all levels of government, some voters may have different ideological preferences for different levels of government and can "split" their partisan loyalties accordingly. This idea indicates that federalism allows for a curious kind of partisan competition. Political scientists have found evidence that some voters intentionally split their votes between the parties in state and national elections so that no one party has complete control over all levels of government.[18]

Preserving Diversity

Federalism enables the citizens of a country to have it both ways: it preserves *diversity* across geographic areas while instilling *unity* to fight common enemies and solve collective problems. Furnishing states with powers preserved by constitutional mandate and court rulings allows people to live under different laws appropriate for their unique circumstances, requirements, or geographic location. For example, residents of Utah may prefer more restrictive

---

[18] Morris Fiorina, *Divided Government,* 2nd ed. (New York: Longman, 1995); Alberto Alesina and Howard Rosenthal, *Partisan Politics, Divided Government, and the Economy* (Cambridge, UK: Cambridge University Press, 1995).

laws regarding liquor, pornography, or drug treatment than residents of New York State. California residents may be more willing than Texans to pay higher gasoline prices to provide for tighter pollution regulations, while rules regulating farming may be different in Vermont than in Florida.

Yet this capacity for diverse policies across states or regions can be problematic. Some of these problems can be traced to what economists call *externalities*, which are the costs or benefits experienced by people who are not directly engaged in a specific activity (see Chapter 15).[19] Our earlier example of Kentucky potentially having a lower minimum wage than other states is an instance of externality: Kentucky's policies would indirectly affect the actions of businesses in other states. It might lead to a "race to the bottom," as discussed earlier. As another example, if a factory pollutes the water in Pennsylvania and the pollution floats down the Ohio River to parts of Ohio and Kentucky, then people in those two states would suffer negative externalities caused by the factories in Pennsylvania. Negative externalities in a federal system arise when states can take actions or conduct business irrespective of the consequences for other states. This is essentially a form of free riding in that all states might generally agree to keep the air and water clean, but one state might avoid paying the costs of regulation because the externalities fall elsewhere. Midwestern states, for example, may oppose onerous pollution control laws that deter business investment if most of the air pollution—from coal-burning power plants, for example—flows toward states to their east.

Fostering Competition

Economist Charles Tiebout argued that competition among states or localities for people and business leads to more efficient government and more generous public programs.[20] Because people and businesses can migrate to whatever town, city, or state they choose, those entities compete among each other to find the mixture of taxes and public policies that promotes the greatest efficiency. If taxes are too high relative to what residents receive from the government in services, then another city, town, or state will find a better set of policies to attract those people. In Tiebout's view, competition induces innovation in government and leads to better outcomes.

Some scholars, notably Paul Peterson, argue that competition among states or local areas for business investment creates a countervailing negative effect—

[19] Michael Bailey and Mark Carl Rom, "A Wider Race? Interstate Competition across Health and Welfare Programs," *Journal of Politics* 66, no. 2 (2004): 326–47. See also Barry Weingast, "The Economic Role of Political Institutions: Market-Preserving Federalism and Economic Development," *Journal of Law, Economics, and Organization* 11 (1995): 1–31.

[20] Charles M. Tiebout, "A Pure Theory of Local Expenditures," *Journal of Political Economy* 64, no. 5 (1956): 416–24. See also Craig Volden, "The Politics of Competitive Federalism: A Race to the Bottom in Welfare Benefits?" *American Journal of Political Science* 46, no. 2 (2002): 352–64; and Michael Bailey and Mark Carl Rom, "A Wider Race?" p. 326.

Today, disputes over federalism persist in several areas. For example, as of 2018, 33 states and the District of Columbia allow the use and sale of medical marijuana in defiance of federal drug laws, as shown in this Washington state dispensary.

namely, harm to the poor.[21] As in our Kentucky example, areas will compete actively with each other for business investment, not only by reducing the burden of regulations but also by lowering taxes on businesses and on wealthy people who run or own those businesses. Lower taxes on businesses and on wealthy people mean fewer funds to pay for social programs for the poor and for public goods, such as schools and parks, that benefit poor people who cannot afford to pay for them privately. In much the same way, migration of people and investment can also harm the poor. Cities or states with generous social programs for the poor (and higher taxes to pay for those programs) will lose wealthier residents and businesses to other cities or states with lower taxes and less generous programs, thus reducing the resources available for the poor in the former locales.

The Tiebout and Peterson theories are difficult to reconcile. Peterson argues that migration from the 1960s through the 1990s has overwhelmingly occurred among wealthier people leaving inner cities to live in suburbs, which have historically offered lower taxes and fewer social services. He notes that large urban areas with many poor residents have struggled to retain business investment as well as their upper-middle-class and wealthy inhabitants. Some economists in the Tiebout tradition argue that such migration is inevitable as people seek out better places to live, and that it forces urban areas to reform their governments. From either perspective, finding the right mixture of taxes and public policies to attract business investment and maintain generous social programs is very difficult for a city or state, and many cities have fared poorly as a result. Cities like Detroit, Gary (Indiana), and Newark (New Jersey) have suffered as people with higher incomes migrated to the suburbs, leaving behind large poor populations that have little means to pay for the services they need.

Promoting Unity and Experimentation

The national government promotes unity and helps to solve collective dilemmas in three ways.[22] First, it sets common national standards to avoid the prob-

---

[21] Peterson, *The Price of Federalism.*

[22] For a paper that addresses these issues in depth, see Rui J. De Figueiredo Jr. and Barry R. Weingast, "Self-Enforcing Federalism: Solving the Two Fundamental Dilemmas," *Journal of Law, Organizations, and Economics* 21 (2005): 103–35.

lem of negative externalities that result from differing state standards. Thus national pollution standards have become the norm, and states have the freedom to set even stricter standards.

Second, many national agencies cooperate with the states to coordinate activity for better effectiveness. The Department of Homeland Security attempts to coordinate the activities of state and local police forces to establish procedures for preventing and responding to terrorist attacks. Other national agencies that work closely with state agencies to coordinate efforts include the Department of Transportation, the Environmental Protection Agency, and the Department of Agriculture. These national-level agencies often work with parallel state-level agencies to design and implement policies passed by the national government.

The national government can also encourage states to try out new policies and report on the experiments for the benefit of all the states.[23] Former Supreme Court Justice Louis Brandeis wrote that one justification for maintaining strong states was that they can be "laboratories of democracy." For example, national welfare reform in the 1990s that gave greater authority to the states was modeled on initiatives in Michigan and Wisconsin that were deemed largely successful.[24]

Third, the national government can subsidize state efforts, and does so with regularity and purpose. It can also use that funding to give states incentives to go along with the rest of the country, as the Reagan administration did in establishing a national drinking age and as the Obama administration did with education standards. Although such federal funds have been unreliable in recent years—the huge boost provided by the stimulus package in 2009 soon dropped off—they are substantial even during economic downturns.

Negative Consequences of Federalism

Some have argued that a unified form of government would be better at managing the immense challenges of our time. We learned earlier about intergovernmentalism, when multiple levels of government need to cooperate with each other for a set of policies to be effective. However, history shows that in some instances intergovernmentalism failed spectacularly and tragically. In 2005, Hurricane Katrina hit the Gulf Coast and ravaged coastal areas of Mississippi and Louisiana, leading to mass flooding of New Orleans, killing 1800 people and driving tens of thousands of people from their homes. By most accounts, despite some successes, the responses of multiple levels of government after Katrina were slowed and less effective due to failures of coordination. The state governments, especially in Louisiana, felt hampered by federal

---

[23] Charles Shipan and Craig Volden, "Bottom-Up Federalism: The Diffusion of Antismoking Policies from U.S. Cities to States," *American Journal of Political Science* 50 (2006): 825–43.

[24] For an interesting and different approach to studying innovation, see Virginia Gray, "Innovation in the States: A Diffusion Study," *American Political Science Review* 67 (1973): 1174–85.

intrusions and lack of clear lines of authority, while the national government agencies complained of incompetence at state and local levels.

The governments' responses to Katrina are held today as symptoms of intergovernmental failure. It is difficult to know if a similar emergency requiring quick action on such a massive scale would be more successful due to lessons learned, or if the problem is more directly a consequence of federalism. Some critics of American federalism say that in matters like emergency responses to terrorism, natural disasters, and storms, there ought to be more direct hierarchy and less division of responsibilities.

Federalism as a Difficult but Important Balance

The federal aspects of the American political system contain tensions in design and implementation. The nation is comprised of states with considerable authority. Yet over time, the national government has grown in authority and power, often eclipsing the role of the states. The system honors diversity across geographic areas, but the states need, and their residents demand, a high degree of uniformity in coordination and enforcement by the national government to solve their collective dilemmas. In reality, the basic requirements and actions of the various states are not all that different. They tend to copy each other and to converge on similar policies.

The United States operates on the principle of two levels of sovereignty—the people of Iowa, for example, are sovereign over the territory of Iowa, and the people of the United States are sovereign over the entire country. Contrary to what the Founders envisioned, however, most Americans are not primarily loyal to their states; they relocate from state to state with regularity and, with few exceptions, patriotism among Americans is reserved more for the nation as a whole than for individual states. Studies show that more people pay attention to national politics than to their own state politics and recognize their national leaders more readily than their state leaders.[25]

All of these characteristics are consistent with the notion that the political system in the United States has tipped strongly in the national government's direction, but it has not tipped so far as to undo the fundamental federal design.

FURTHER READING

★ =Included in *Readings in American Politics*, 5th ed.

Arizona v. United States (2012). A Supreme Court decision that struck down aspects of an Arizona law that empowered local police to enforce immi-

---

[25] For a paper that addresses some of these issues, see Cindy D. Kam and Robert A. Mikos, "Do Citizens Care about Federalism? An Experimental Test," *Journal of Empirical Legal Studies* 4, no. 3 (2007): 589–624.

gration regulations, thus siding with national government authority over the states on matters of immigration.

Bednar, Jenna, *The Robust Federation: Principles of Design* (New York: Cambridge University Press, 2009). Details the tensions and dynamics of federalism.

Hamilton, Alexander, James Madison, and John Jay, *The Federalist Papers*, No. 39, 1788. Madison's classic account of the differences between American political institutions that reflect the will of the people and political institutions that represent the states.

★ Hammons, Christopher, "State Constitutions, Religious Protection, and Federalism," *University of St. Thomas Journal of Law and Public Policy* 7 (2013): 226–39. Hammons argues that the Founders of the U.S. Constitution likely considered religion to be mostly a state-level issue and thus favored keeping the national government out of regulation of religious institutions and practices.

Peterson, Paul, *The Price of Federalism* (Washington, DC: Brookings Institution, 1995). The argument that cities lose their taxpaying residents to suburbs and keep their poorer residents, thus reducing resources at the local level for services that benefit the poor.

★ Riker, William, *Federalism: Origin, Operation, Significance* (Boston: Little, Brown, 1964). A classic account of American federalism in comparative context, with special emphasis on civil rights.

Rodden, Jonathan, *Hamilton's Paradox: The Promise and Peril of Fiscal Federalism* (New York: Cambridge University Press, 2006). Describes the problems that arise when state governments take bad risks, knowing that the national government will bail them out if things go poorly.

KEY TERMS

ballot initiative (p. 91)

block grants (p. 86)

categorical grants (p. 86)

commerce clause (p. 79)

confederation (p. 73)

cooperative federalism (p. 77)

dual federalism (p. 76)

elastic clause (necessary and
    proper clause) (p. 79)

federalism (p. 73)

grants-in-aid (p. 86)

home rule (p. 96)

intergovernmentalism (p. 77)

recall election (p. 91)

referendum (p. 91)

reserved powers (p. 98)

revenue sharing (p. 86)

unitary system (p. 98)

Civil liberties, such as the right to bear arms, are protected from improper government interference. However, the meanings and boundaries of such rights are often unclear and in dispute. Moreover, when the rights and liberties of one group (for example, gun owners) threaten the rights and liberties of others (potential victims of gun violence), a question arises over what action the government should take.

4

Civil Rights and Liberties

 What rights and freedoms do Americans have?

In 1975, in response to rising rates of crime, the District of Columbia (Washington, D.C.) passed a law that severely limited the freedom of people to buy and own handguns. The stated objective was simple: to reduce the number of guns and thus reduce crimes involving guns.

To some, the new gun restrictions and others like them passed by other cities were justified because a major purpose of government is to protect the safety of its citizens. Citizens have an interest in security and order. But to others, the restrictions violated individual liberty, and some argued that gun restrictions do little to deter crime and may even permit more crime to occur. As a matter of constitutional interpretation, they argued, restricting the possession of handguns is a violation of the fundamental right to own a firearm, as enshrined in the U.S. Constitution. This right, they said, is protected by the Second Amendment of the Constitution, which says, "A well regulated Militia, being necessary to the security of a free State, the right of the people to keep and bear Arms, shall not be infringed."

The appropriate interpretation of this amendment, especially with regard to how much the government can restrict gun ownership, has been a subject of intense political and legal controversy. Political conflicts over these laws often pit hunters and sporting organizations, who oppose gun control, against police associations and big-city mayors, who favor more restrictions on gun ownership. There is always the question of what kinds of guns fall under the purview of the amendment. After all, it has never been controversial for the government to ban ownership of howitzers or machine guns, weapons that can kill indiscriminately and that require intensive training to use properly. But what about handguns or assault rifles?

D.C.'s law remained in effect for 33 years until Dick Heller, a local police officer who was denied a registration for his personal firearm, took his case against the law all the way to the Supreme Court. In 2008, the Court agreed to decide on the case

OUTLINE

- Defining Civil Rights and Liberties

- The Origins of Rights and Liberties

- The Special Role of the Courts

- Race, Ethnicity, and Nationality

- Popular Demands for More Rights

- Incorporating the Bill of Rights into the Fourteenth Amendment

- Government Responses to Discrimination

- In Comparison: Rights and Liberties around the World

- Why Protect Rights and Liberties?

to determine what exactly the Constitution's Second Amendment protects when it comes to possession of firearms. Does it protect an individual's right to keep and bear arms, or is it a protection that applies only in the context of those acting in common defense—as in a state militia? If it is an individual's right, does it protect all individuals—including felons and the mentally ill—or can governments limit who is allowed to own guns? Does the protection apply everywhere, such as in a school or in a government building? And what, exactly, constitutes a firearm? If possession of handguns is protected, what about possession of assault rifles?

Justice Antonin Scalia wrote the majority opinion and provided the Court's answers to these questions. With the support of four other judges, he wrote that the Washington, D.C., law violated the Second Amendment. The amendment guarantees individual rights to possess a firearm, even for purposes unconnected to a militia. However, this right, as is the case with all rights or liberties, has its limits. Although the right does protect the possession of firearms, it does not protect the ability of anyone anywhere to possess any type of firearm for whatever purpose. Rather, the Court determined that the right applies to gun possession only in the context of traditionally lawful purposes, such as self-defense in one's home. It determined that not all weapons were covered under the term *firearms*, but rather only those "in common use at the time." This ruling includes handguns, but it excludes machine guns. The Court determined that local governments prohibiting felons and the mentally ill from possessing firearms is constitutional, as is prohibiting the possession of concealed weapons in sensitive locations. In a later case, *McDonald v. Chicago* (2010), the Court held that its legal reasoning in the *Heller* decision applies to any jurisdiction in the United States, not just Washington, D.C., and federal property.

The coexistence of some legal restrictions on gun ownership and the Court's rulings limiting government regulation of guns is emblematic of the difficult balancing act that often occurs when rights and liberties conflict. The trade-offs among rights and goals can be stark. We can protect people's rights to own a gun; but a gun can be used to harm others, infringing on their right to security. The government is at once responsible for protecting an individual's life and property while also respecting his or her freedom to be armed. Thus, the principles of liberty and security can be viewed as in opposition. The Court was split 5–4 in the *Heller* decision, and the controversy continues in fierce public and legislative debate today. Some want to overturn *Heller* or change laws to work around it. And in spite of and in response to court decisions, powerful interest groups—such as the National Rifle Association (see Chapter 11) and the Brady Campaign to Prevent Gun Violence—put enormous pressure on Congress and state legislatures to influence gun control laws.

Ultimately, for controversies like these, the questions must be asked: Which principle should be upheld? How do we determine the proper balance between opposing rights and liberties? How have the courts and other branches of government resolved these controversies?

Defining Civil Rights and Liberties

To answer our chapter-opening questions, we need to learn how the boundaries on governmental behavior and on individuals' rights and liberties arose and continue to change within the United States. In Chapter 3, we focused on federalism, which has to do with the relationships among the states and between the states and the national government. Now we will build on that discussion to address the relationships between individuals and the government.

Typically in contemporary legal circles, **civil rights** are considered guarantees that individuals can engage in activities central to participation in society, such as the citizen's right to vote or petition the government, and that individuals are assured due process and equal protection under the law. Rights generally refer to protections that the government must actively provide. As an example, when people are charged with a crime, they have rights as criminal defendants to certain protections, like a court-appointed lawyer if necessary, that the government is obligated to make available. And the government is obligated to ensure equal rights for citizens qualified to vote to participate in popular elections.

Civil liberties are typically considered to be guaranteed freedoms from undue or unjust interference by government, such as interference with citizens' freedom of speech, right to bear arms, or freedom of religion. This category refers to protections from government, and thus legally requires the government to refrain from taking certain actions, such as censoring your artistic expression or your speech at a political rally.

Sometimes, the terms get used interchangeably, especially in older writings. In the Founding Era, "rights" included both categories; thus, the Bill of Rights included both rights and liberties. Even today, people refer to the right to bear arms or the right to free expression, even though in precise terms they are referring to liberties. For clarity and simplicity, in today's terminology, we can think of rights as requiring obligations by the government and liberties as establishing boundaries on the government. Consider, for instance, rights against gender discrimination and liberties surrounding reproduction. The government is obligated to protect the rights of women to be free from most forms of discrimination in the workplace and in education. At the same time, no level of government in the United States is allowed under current constitutional law to prevent women or men from using birth control or to prevent women from having a medically proscribed abortion during the first trimester of pregnancy.

These obligations and boundaries on behavior become vital pieces of the institutional framework in the American political system. They change over time. The laws and constitutional interpretations about rights and liberties change due to new legislation or to court decisions reinterpreting specific language in laws or in constitutional passages. Consider the *Heller* case, which

civil rights Rights that (1) enable individuals to engage in activities central to citizenship or legal immigrant status, such as voting or petitioning the government; (2) ensure all individuals receive due process and equal treatment under the law; or (3) guarantee freedom from discriminatory actions by others that seek to deny an individual's full status as an equal member of society.

civil liberties Freedoms protected from interference by the government, such as freedom of speech, the right to bear arms, and freedom of religion.

determined that state and city governments are able to regulate where hand-guns are allowed to be possessed (for example, not in schools) but not to ban all handgun ownership. The Court's decision clarified, in light of the Second Amendment, where the constitutional boundary exists for states and cities writing laws, and for lower-level courts in future legal cases.

Decisions by courts or other branches establishing these boundaries are often highly controversial and, as we have seen, involve difficult trade-offs. The set of civil rights and liberties to be protected is not always obvious. Moreover, the rights and liberties evolve in response to changing social conditions, values, and norms of behavior, as well as occasional emergencies and threats. In the context of voting rights, consider that at one time it was widely accepted that only men should be permitted to vote. In our own time, most people in nearly every country agree that men and women should have an equal right to vote in all public elections. The United States, through the Nineteenth Amendment, mandated in 1920 that women be allowed to vote. In Switzerland, however, women were not guaranteed the right to vote until 1971, and in Lichtenstein not until 1984. Rights and liberties vary across countries and over time, and these variations have consequences for the entire political system and for who can legally do what in society.

The Origins of Rights and Liberties

The values of equality and human dignity stand at the heart of the intellectual tradition that the Founders relied on when they debated and ultimately crafted the Declaration of Independence and the Constitution, especially in appending the Bill of Rights at the end of the Constitution. The Founders followed a long line of thinking from specific theologians and philosophers who since ancient times have written that all humans are born equal. These ideas have theological roots, and most of the Founders would have believed in a God-given "natural law" that exists independent of government. Because God created them thus or because of their inherent value as human beings (or both), all persons ought to be treated equally by governments. Similarly, values associated with the eighteenth-century Age of Enlightenment, and embodied in the principles expressed by leaders of the American and French Revolutions, placed special emphasis on limiting the powers of government—in particular, on protecting unpopular minorities from oppression by majorities or majority-elected governments.[1] Because of inherent human dignity and equality, people deserve protection from oppression. The Declaration of

[1] Many of these principles have their modern origins in the writings of John Locke, the English political philosopher. See John Locke, *Second Treatise on Government* (1690; repr., Indianapolis: Hackett, 1980), and *A Letter Concerning Toleration: Humbly Submitted* (1689; repr., Indianapolis: Hackett, 1983).

Independence, for example, states that "all men are created equal" and enjoy "certain unalienable rights" that no government should infringe on. Among these are the rights to "Life, Liberty, and the pursuit of Happiness." Similarly, the French revolutionaries' slogan of "Liberty, Equality, Fraternity" reflected an emphasis on individual rights and shared norms to protect them.[2]

Following the American Revolution, the Commonwealth (State) of Virginia paved an important path by including in its constitution a bill of rights, which is a detailed list of rights and liberties that the state government was obligated to protect. The Virginia Declaration of Rights in that constitution instantly became the reference for other state constitutions and served as the basis for the U.S. Bill of Rights. As discussed in Chapter 2, the U.S. Bill of Rights was ratified in 1791 as the first 10 amendments to the U.S. Constitution.

The rights and liberties specified in the U.S. **Bill of Rights** fall into several categories:

- Basic individual liberties, such as freedom to practice religion and the right to bear arms

- Rights and liberties having to do with the process of republican government, such as freedom of speech, assembly, and the press, and the right to petition the government

- Rights of criminal defendants, such as the right to a fair trial and to a trial by an impartial jury, and freedom from unreasonable search and seizure

- Liberties protecting citizens against excessive government force—for example, against seizure of property without just compensation, against soldiers occupying private property in times of peace, and against deprivation of "life, liberty, property, or without due process of law"[3]

Subsequent constitutional amendments either added to or clarified the rights and liberties enumerated in the Bill of Rights. Amendments ratified in the late nineteenth and twentieth centuries have been particularly important in making the American political system more democratic. Specifically, these amendments have

- abolished slavery (Thirteenth Amendment),

- expanded the right to vote to new groups (Fifteenth, Nineteenth, Twenty-fourth, and Twenty-sixth Amendments), and

- required the states to abide by the U.S. Bill of Rights and granted former slaves full rights of citizenship (Fourteenth Amendment).

Bill of Rights The first 10 amendments to the Constitution, which enumerate a set of liberties not to be violated by the government and a set of rights to be protected by the government.

[2] Max Ferrand, *The Framing of the Constitution of the United States* (1930; repr., Frederick, MD: Beard Books, 2000).

[3] The Tenth Amendment mostly concerns federalism, but its application has been important to the development of civil rights and liberties, as discussed later in this chapter.

In addition to expanding the right to vote and freeing the slaves, these amendments required all governments at any level to enforce the laws that applied to individuals and governments. The Fourteenth Amendment in particular advanced critical issues of federalism that not only gradually enhanced the role and stature of the national government but also resulted in a more humane and morally defensible government.

Beyond those rights and liberties directly mentioned in the Constitution, there are others that are set forth in statutory laws (for instance, laws passed by legislatures or other elected assemblies). Laws concerning civil rights and liberties have been passed by legislatures at the national and state levels, and by city and council governments. These laws can exist, according to the courts, as long as they do not violate the Constitution. For example, numerous laws at all levels of government in the United States ban discrimination in public places on the basis of race, ethnicity, religion, place of origin, gender, sexual orientation, political beliefs, or disability.

Other rights and liberties not explicitly mentioned in the Constitution have been "discovered" by courts in vague phrases in the Constitution or established by reference to tradition. For example, the Supreme Court declared in

Know the FACTS   Major Provisions of the Bill of Rights

The Bill of Rights is made up of the first 10 amendments to the Constitution and includes the following protections.

- **First Amendment:** protects the freedoms of religion, speech, press, assembly, and petition.

- **Second Amendment:** guarantees the states the right to establish a militia, and individuals the right to bear arms (own weapons).

- **Third Amendment:** ensures that citizens are not required to quarter troops in their home.

- **Fourth Amendment**: protects individuals from unreasonable search and seizure by government agents.

- **Fifth Amendment:** guarantees that an individual will not stand trial more than once for the same offense or have to testify against him- or herself. Also ensures that no individual is deprived of "life, liberty, or property" without a fair procedure or compensation.

- **Sixth Amendment:** guarantees criminal defendants the right to a speedy and public trial by an impartial jury.

- **Seventh Amendment:** provides the right to a trial by jury in civil cases.

- **Eighth Amendment:** protects the accused from excessive bail and cruel and unusual punishments.

- **Ninth Amendment:** guarantees rights not specifically enumerated in the Constitution or Bill of Rights.

- **Tenth Amendment:** reserves powers not specifically given to the national government for the states and the people.

Griswold v. Connecticut (1965) that the Constitution implies a right to privacy, making laws banning contraception unconstitutional. Also implied are the right to travel within the United States (if not fleeing justice) and the right to marry someone of the opposite sex as an individual chooses. (This has been expanded now to include the right to marry someone of the same sex.) The justification for treating these rights as constitutionally protected is a combination of constitutional interpretation, history, and tradition. For example, the courts have inferred that the right to marital privacy exists in the Ninth Amendment clause stating that other rights not mentioned in the Constitution are "retained by the people."

The Special Role of the Courts

The Founders understood well the dangers that a government elected by a majority might pose in oppressing minorities or in permitting mistreatment of minorities in society. Through civil rights and liberties protections, including the Bill of Rights, they attempted to design the American system to protect minorities, even from the government.[4] During debates over ratification of the Constitution, the minorities often mentioned by the Founders as needing protection were property owners whose rights to own and enjoy property were threatened by local and state governments' ability to impose onerous taxes or even redistribute property.

Not long after the Founding and the ratification of the Bill of Rights, however, another kind of threat to rights and liberties emerged. The presidential administration of John Adams blatantly violated the First Amendment by passing the Alien and Sedition Acts in 1798. The acts permitted the harassment and jailing of people critical of the administration and its policies. In the heat of political competition, the Adams administration forbade certain kinds of legitimate political assembly and speech guaranteed by the First Amendment.[5] Critics at the time claimed that the acts also violated the Tenth Amendment by giving the national government more power than the Constitution allowed. The acts became an embarrassment to Adams and did not ultimately result in large-scale oppression of dissent. The legislation expired in 1801, when Adams left the presidency.

Legislatures and executives, in trying to be responsive to majorities that elected them, can be tempted to violate basic freedoms of minorities. For that reason, the courts as unelected bodies interpreting the law are often considered the protectors of individuals against the government and against other

[4] Robert Dahl, *How Democratic Is the American Constitution?* (New Haven, CT: Yale University Press, 2001).
[5] Leonard Levy, *Freedom of Speech and Press in Early American History: Legacy of Suppression* (New York: Harper & Row, 1963).

individuals. Not only do courts act as independent enforcers of behavior by both individuals and governments, they also play a crucial role in defining the obligations and boundaries of behavior.[6] Governments sometimes violate their own rules or try to change them. The courts can overturn rule violations or decide whether a rule change is constitutional. As the final arbiters of what the law means, including the legal protections or rights and liberties enshrined in the Bill of Rights and other parts of the Constitution, the federal courts have often drawn the lines between acceptable and unacceptable laws or government actions.

As an example, the Supreme Court in *United States v. Jones* (2012) ruled that attaching a global positioning system (GPS) device to the car of someone being investigated for crimes (without the person's knowledge) constituted "search" under the Fourth Amendment. That amendment bars search and seizure by the government without probable cause (and usually a warrant). The question for the Court was, given new technologies enabling law enforcement to track movements using GPS devices, whether installing these devices was legally considered to be searching for evidence and thus subject to the restrictions mandated by the Fourth Amendment. The Court ruled that GPS devices do indeed fall into that category.[7] Through hundreds of such cases, the Supreme Court has played a key role in defining the institutional boundaries on individual and governmental conduct, having to make new rulings in response to changes in technologies and in the nature of people's behavior.

Other examples are in the areas of freedom of speech and freedom of association. As the example of the Alien and Sedition Acts shows, the government can be tempted to suppress the critical speech of an unpopular minority group. Governments especially come under pressure to crack down on dissent in times of crisis such as wars, after terrorist attacks, or amid fear of sabotage. During the so-called McCarthy era in the late 1940s and early 1950s, numerous members of Congress, led by Senator Joseph McCarthy of Wisconsin, falsely accused hundreds of people in the U.S. State Department and other federal agencies of conspiring against the United States. Many of those accused of belonging to the Communist Party lost their jobs or experienced other forms of harassment. In addition, the government banned more than 30,000 books from library shelves and pressured newspapers and magazines not to publish the writings of accused communists. The government later rescinded all its censorship provisions, and in 1954 the Senate put an end to the "witch hunts" by officially censuring McCarthy.

The McCarthy era treatment of suspected communists is now widely considered to be unjust, but at the time there was widespread fear of communist

---

[6] Howard Gillman and Cornell Clayton, *The Supreme Court in American Politics: New Institutionalist Interpretations* (Lawrence: University Press of Kansas, 1999).

[7] *United States v. Jones*, 132 S. Ct. 945 (2012).

Evolving technology and social norms have required the courts to continually revisit certain civil rights and liberties issues in new contexts. In 2012, the Supreme Court decided that police affixing GPS devices to the cars of unwitting investigation subjects violated the Fourth Amendment.

infiltration of the U.S. government. In some circumstances, it can be difficult to find the right balance between maintaining order and security while preserving rights and liberties, and there can be legitimate disagreements over appropriate government action. Groups can move beyond engaging in legitimate criticism to spreading damaging rumors or, more seriously, advocating violence or other illegitimate means of bringing down the government. Such actions risk provoking the government into cracking down on dissent. In the 1960s, for example, some fringe anti–Vietnam War groups that advocated violence against government institutions elicited fierce reprisals from the police and other government agencies. A few groups actually bombed government offices, and the reaction of some law enforcement agencies was to spy on and infiltrate many groups that were critical of the government's policies, even if most of them did not advocate violence. Elected officials disagreed, and historians still disagree, over whether this was legitimate law enforcement or a violation of civil rights and liberties.

Although popularly elected branches of government can pass laws proposing specific means of restricting actions in order to maintain security or to respond to majority sentiment, it is often left to the courts to decide whether the rules passed by governments are constitutional. In the area of freedom of speech, because of Supreme Court decisions beginning in the early twentieth

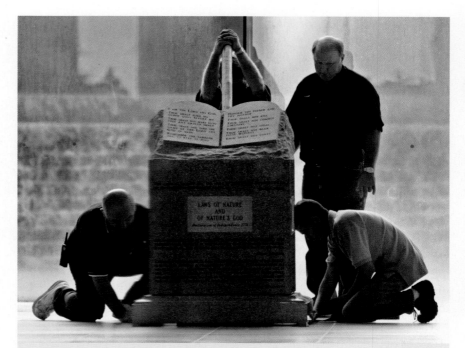

The First Amendment protects religious freedom partly by prohibiting the establishment of an official state religion. The courts have interpreted this to mean that religious displays in government offices—such as this monument of the Ten Commandments in an Alabama courthouse—are unconstitutional, even if a majority of people like them.

century, generally people today are free to express their opinions with few legal limitations. Exceptions defined by the courts include pronouncements advocating the overthrow of the government or the killing of people in positions of public authority, or speeches designed to incite immediate violence or panic. For its part, because of court decisions interpreting the Constitution, the government is not allowed to engage in most forms of censorship, even of very unpopular opinions.

The courts can play this role because of the establishment of an independent judiciary, a key institutional hallmark of most modern democracies. (We discuss this in more detail in Chapter 8.) Because courts make decisions but cannot enforce the law themselves, they must rely on the branches of government that control the military and the police—usually the executive branch. So even when ruling against the majority-elected government, the courts still have to count on parts of that government to enforce the decision. Therefore, the courts must have enough legitimacy in society to ensure that their decisions are ultimately enforced by the executive branch or by the states. This legitimacy has long been in place in the United States, where even the most unpopular court decisions eventually have been enforced.

As an example, opinion polls indicate that a clear majority of Americans support allowing religious prayer in public schools and the display of the biblical Ten Commandments on public buildings (see Chapter 9). If it were up to the elected branches of the national government—the Congress and some recent presidents—or to individual school districts, prayer in public schools would most likely be allowed, and courts would be free to display the Ten Commandments on their buildings and in their courtrooms. However, following two cases—*Engel v. Vitale* (1962) and *Abington School District v. Schempp* (1963)—the Supreme Court has maintained that school-sponsored prayer violates First Amendment prohibitions against the establishment of an official state religion.[8] The First Amendment includes the restriction that "Congress shall make no law respecting an establishment of religion, or prohibiting the free exercise thereof." In two cases decided in 2005, the Court ruled that unless the display of the Ten Commandments was clearly part of a secular exhibit of lawmaking throughout human history, such displays on publicly funded buildings violated the "Establishment Clause" of the First Amendment (that is, banning active government establishing religion).[9] Despite the unpopularity of the Court's rulings, state and local governments have taken down such displays. Likewise, most school districts throughout the country comply with the Court's mandate to keep organized prayer out of public school activities, even though many districts would receive overwhelming public support for allowing prayer in the schools. This compliance is an indication of the courts' legitimacy in the United States.

Race, Ethnicity, and Nationality

On issues of race, ethnicity, and nationality, American history has been fraught with deep controversy and conflict over rights and liberties. There is widespread agreement that American political institutions clearly failed to protect basic rights and liberties of minorities in the past, and controversies over the need for additional protections continue.

Courts, for instance, are not perfect arbiters, and they can make decisions that later generations consider morally wrong. In one of the most notorious Supreme Court decisions, the majority opinion in the *Dred Scott* case in 1857, written by Chief Justice Roger Taney, stated that the Founders did not consider African Americans to be part of the "people of the United States." Thus, blacks did not possess the rights and privileges granted to the people under the Constitution. By providing legal justification for the continued oppression of

---

[8] *Engel v. Vitale*, 370 U.S. 421 (1962); *Abington School District v. Schempp*, 374 U.S. 203 (1963).

[9] *Van Orden v. Perry*, 545 U.S. 677 (2005); *McCreary County v. ACLU of Kentucky*, 545 U.S. 844 (2005).

blacks, the Court's decision went against the norms of human rights and liberties that were generally promoted during the Founding era. *Dred Scott* was soon overturned by the Fourteenth Amendment in 1868, but the civil rights of African Americans were not well protected in practice for another 100 years.

Like the courts, American legislatures and executives have also grossly violated the principles enshrined in the Bill of Rights and failed at various times to protect the basic civil rights and liberties of certain groups in society. We have already considered the Alien and Sedition Acts that Congress passed in 1798 and the actions of the government during the McCarthy era. Even worse have been legally sanctioned systemic patterns of oppression and discrimination based on race, ethnicity, or national origin. With widespread public support among citizens, the U.S. government in the nineteenth century forcibly relocated or killed a substantial portion of the Native American population in order to settle the continent for white Americans. Two other shameful episodes have concerned slavery and its aftermath, and the treatment of immigrants.

Slavery and African Americans

The existence of slavery and the continuing discrimination against black people following the Civil War represent terrible breaches of the principles expressed in the Founding documents. In the eyes of many who participated in the debates over the drafting and ratification of the Constitution and the new institutions of American government, slavery, the slave trade, and the mistreatment of former slaves were fundamentally at odds with the ideals of the American Revolution and the new United States.[10] How could the institution of slavery be allowed to exist, they argued, in a land governed by a Constitution that was based on the revolutionary idea that all men are created equal? Proposals were made at the Constitutional Convention to outlaw slavery throughout the country, but in the end the issue was left to the states to resolve, ensuring the continuance of slavery for the next several decades.[11] Although owning or trading slaves was gradually outlawed in the northern states between 1790 and 1804, it remained a basic feature of southern society and the region's economy for another half-century and more.

By the start of the Civil War, slaves accounted for one-third of the total southern population. Among white leaders in the South, there were deep fears of slave uprisings and of the revenge that slaves would exact if they were freed en masse. Even after slavery was formally abolished throughout the United States in 1865, most black Americans were still denied their basic rights in many parts of the country. Segregated into areas with poor infrastructures and inadequate

[10] James D. Anderson, "Race-Conscious Educational Policies versus a 'Color-Blind Constitution': A Historical Perspective," *Educational Researcher* 36, no. 5 (2007): 249–57.

[11] David Waldstreicher, *Slavery's Constitution: From Revolution to Ratification* (New York: Hill & Wang, 2009).

public institutions, blacks were discriminated against in schools, in the workplace, and in hospitals, stores, government offices, restaurants, and courts of law.

It was common for former slaves to continue working as poorly paid servants on farms in the South, often living in hovels and shacks with little access to education and basic services. Many southern states enacted **Jim Crow laws** that codified the second-class citizenship of blacks. Blacks living in the North and in cities also suffered relative to other racial groups. Ever since the Civil War and the emancipation of slaves, American blacks have consistently experienced higher levels of unemployment; been poorer, less educated, and more disease prone; been subject to greater rates of discrimination in education, housing, and employment; and been incarcerated and subject to police brutality at higher rates than any other major racial group in the United States, particularly whites.

Black-white racial cleavages in American society remain the nation's most enduring and troublesome divide. Slavery, the discriminatory post–Civil War social and economic system, and long-standing prejudice have scarred the African American population.[12] The legacy of slavery represents a massive systemic failure of the country's political institutions and is the worst stain on its reputation for democratic governance.

> **Jim Crow laws** Laws passed after the Civil War to establish a system of segregation of public facilities and private establishments that made African Americans second-class citizens.

The Treatment of Immigrants

The treatment of immigrants, and their experiences of discrimination throughout the nineteenth and early twentieth centuries, similarly defies justification in light of constitutional principles. Since the sixteenth century, the American nation has been built on successive waves of immigration. Immigration peaks occurred in the 1840s when 1.7 million newcomers arrived, amounting to more than 6 percent of the total population. (In 1850, the nation's total population was just 27 million.) In sheer number of immigrants, the flow peaked between 1900 and 1910, when nearly 9 million arrived—approximately 10 percent of the total population—and again in the decade of the 1990s, when a similar number arrived (though about 4 percent of the total population).

Racial, ethnic, or religious discrimination against immigrants was common in each of these eras. Established residents—most of them English or Scottish in origin—justified their hostility by claiming that the immigrants were of inferior genetic stock and had strange religions, languages, accents, and dress. It did not help that most immigrants until the mid-twentieth century arrived poor. Residents resented competing with the new immigrants for jobs.

Irish immigrants endured some of the harshest discrimination. It was common in the 1850s for businesses in Boston and New York to post help-wanted

---

[12] Michael Klarman, *From Jim Crow to Civil Rights: The Supreme Court and the Struggle for Racial Equality* (New York: Oxford University Press, 2004).

signs that read, "Irish need not apply." The Chinese who came to work on the railroads in the West in the nineteenth century also suffered terrible exploitation, mistreatment, and denial of citizenship for years after their arrival. Italians and Greeks who arrived in the early twentieth century were often denied access to jobs and housing close to that of the better-established ethnic groups. Mexican Americans who arrived in the twentieth century to fill low-wage jobs in the South and Southwest often found living and employment conditions difficult at best. In the wake of the September 11, 2001, terrorist attacks, many Arab immigrants reported intimidation by immigration officials, employers, and law enforcement agents and were deported for such minor infractions as making typos on their immigration forms.

In a blatant act of state-sponsored discrimination during World War II, the U.S. government, responding to fears that Japanese Americans would sabotage the American war effort, set up prisonlike internment camps to isolate them from society. Over the course of the war, more than 120,000 Japanese Americans—a large majority of whom were American citizens—were confined to 10 relocation camps in the western United States. In 1944, the Supreme Court upheld the government's internment policy in its controversial decision in *Korematsu v. United States*. The Court majority held that during wartime the needs of national security trumped the individual rights of Japanese Americans and Japanese immigrants.

Hispanics now represent the largest nonwhite demographic group in the United States, comprising approximately 17 percent of the total population. Although the vast majority of Hispanics are in the United States legally, and many are American citizens, the large number of illegal Hispanic immigrants in recent years has sparked a backlash from citizens demanding that the government crack down on illegal immigration.

Historically, most immigrants have not had citizen status when they arrived in the United States and therefore were not entitled to all the civil rights and liberties protections afforded by the American legal system. However, a series of Supreme Court decisions has established that all immigrants are entitled to certain protections, including the right to life, the pursuit of material gain, and a basic education.[13]

Other Failures

There have been many other controversies over rights and liberties in American history besides those based on race or ethnicity. For instance, states and localities have denied voting rights to various other groups. Not only African Americans but also vagrants, Catholics, Mormons, women, Native Ameri-

[13] For example, the Supreme Court's decision in *Plyler v. Doe* (1982) affirmed that the children of illegal immigrants had a constitutional right to primary education.

cans, paupers, and illiterates were systematically denied the right to vote by some or all states at various stages in the nation's history. These rights were recovered or won through mass political action and sometimes turbulent struggle, as we will see below and in Chapter 10.

Various governments within the United States have also made repeated attempts—some successful—to harass political opponents or those deemed (but not proven) to be dangerous, to grant police broad powers to investigate legitimate democratic activities, or to suppress freedom of the press.

In the 1970s, for example, the U.S. Justice Department tried unsuccessfully to prevent the *New York Times* and *Washington Post* from publishing the documents known as the *Pentagon Papers*, which cast the government's conduct of the Vietnam War in an unfavorable light. In another example, from the 1950s into the 1970s, the Federal Bureau of Investigation (FBI), led by J. Edgar Hoover, adopted McCarthyesque tactics in investigating and harassing hundreds of people whose activities were deemed to threaten public order, including Martin Luther King Jr. and Albert Einstein. More recently, Congress responded to heightened fears of terrorism in the post–9/11 era by passing the controversial USA PATRIOT Act, some provisions of which have been ruled unconstitutional by the courts.

These examples highlight first, that democratic government is not a guarantee of protection from unjust government, and second, that the obligations and boundaries placed on individual and government conduct are fluid in nature. The legal obligations and boundaries have important effects on American politics, but they can and do change over time in response to historical circumstances. In this respect, they resemble other aspects of government that have changed through the years, such as federalism (that is, the relationship between the states and the national government).

Egregious violations of the Bill of Rights, such as the Alien and Sedition Acts of 1798 or the internments of Japanese Americans in World War II, seem embarrassing and even absurd today. Such actions highlight the need for perspective and wariness when political leaders consider restrictions of basic rights and liberties, even in the face of such real threats as terrorism. Although few people deny in principle that rights and liberties ought to be protected vigorously, the obligations and boundaries in any era are hotly contested. What seems obvious to us today—for instance, the right of women to vote—was very controversial as late as the 1910s, and it required many decades of concerted political action to win that right (see Chapter 10).

Often, competing rights have to be traded off against each other, and there can be deep tensions between broader societal benefits and individual rights and liberties. Where should the boundaries be set when the government through its elected representatives wants to restrict some people's freedom of action so that others are satisfied? How active can the government be in trying to achieve equality, even when it infringes on others? Do individuals have a right to say offensive things, even if it makes others uncomfortable or threatened? Under what circumstances, if any, can the government restrict what you read on the Internet, the guns you own, the medicines or drugs you take, the fireworks you set off, the vehicles you drive, the clothes you wear or do not wear, or the locations of your political rallies?

Three areas that continue to be particularly controversial—affirmative action, abortion, and rights of sexual minorities—will be discussed later in this chapter.

Popular Demands for More Rights

Democratic political systems permit legitimate expressions of dissent, and institutions of government can change the meanings and address the violations of rights and liberties. In other words, the political system can adapt and move the obligations and boundaries when called for. However, expanded rights and better-protected liberties have rarely been won by oppressed groups without a long struggle and major political action leading to changes in laws.

The Civil Rights Movement

civil rights movement A social movement of the 1950s and 1960s focused primarily on the situation of African Americans, but also promoting the goals that all people be treated as equals under the law and that discrimination based on race, religion, ethnicity, gender, and place of origin be eliminated.

The **civil rights movement** in the 1950s and 1960s focused on the rights of African Americans, but it also promoted broader goals, such as the principle that all people should be treated as equals under the law; that discrimination based on race, religion, ethnicity, gender, and place of origin should be eliminated; and that more generous programs should be created to help oppressed minorities and the impoverished. The results of the civil rights movement go well beyond the winning of basic civil and political rights for African Americans. The movement continues to serve as a model for efforts to expand access by minority groups to the American and other political systems and the economic rewards these societies offer. Other groups have applied the tactics used by civil rights leaders to force changes in government policy, establish new institutions, and open representational assemblies and voting booths to communities that formerly were disenfranchised.

The civil rights movement presented the case to the American people and political leaders that the national government had the obligation and the authority to protect the basic civil and political rights of citizens, even overriding state and local laws. Rather than support governmental institutions that perpetuated racial discrimination by deferring to state or local authority, civil rights leaders called for stronger federal institutions that would prevent unequal treatment and living conditions for blacks. The leaders' argument was based on the ideal of equal rights for all.

Activists in the civil rights movement of the 1950s and 1960s, like Martin Luther King Jr., argued that the national government has an obligation to protect the constitutional rights of all Americans, including African Americans and other minorities.

Southern political leaders in the first half of the twentieth century used the federated nature of the American system of government to perpetuate practices of racial discrimination and oppression that contradicted the basic ideals of the American Revolution and the Constitution. Many leaders justified the government's failure to take action against the mistreatment of African Americans by claiming that the authority to regulate race relations rested with the states. They maintained that the national government had no business stepping in to protect voting rights, the right of children to decent education, and the right to equal treatment before the law.

Opposition to this viewpoint gathered momentum in the 1950s, led by figures such as Martin Luther King Jr., who advocated nonviolent protest as a means to draw attention to the civil rights cause. Through boycotts, marches, and sit-ins, members of the movement pressured government to change the laws and practices of the United States, especially in the Deep South. They worked to eliminate racial segregation while protecting the basic civil and political rights of blacks and other minorities and improving their economic condition.[14]

The movement sparked a violent reaction from white supremacists, states' rights advocates, and others. Medgar Evers, a prominent civil rights leader from Mississippi, was killed in front of his house in 1963. In Birmingham, Alabama, that summer, police were televised beating, kicking, and unleashing attack dogs against peaceful civil rights advocates. Not long after, four young black girls died in the bombing of a Birmingham Baptist church.

Yet despite this brutal opposition, the movement largely achieved its legal goals. It set in motion a series of monumental changes in the American political system, including landmark legislation in civil rights and voting rights that left deep imprints on race relations throughout the United States. As a result of the movement, the U.S. Justice Department played a major role over the next three decades in enforcing voting rights for racial minorities; equal access to housing, education, and public benefits for all; and even affirmative action in university admissions and government contracts. (We will learn more about affirmative action later in this chapter.) By the late 1970s, significant progress had been made in the eradication of discriminatory laws and in the enforcement of regulations banning discrimination in many aspects of political, economic, and social life.

The civil rights movement highlights the importance of popular movements in pressing for political institutions to change and reset the boundaries of government action in support of civil rights. Early institutions of American government, although created out of the principles enshrined in the Constitution, failed to protect certain vulnerable minorities and to promote the common good that can be enjoyed by all persons. In other words, these initial institutions failed to safeguard minorities from the "tyranny of the majority," a mission outlined by the Founders.

Although contemporary civil rights leaders acknowledge the progress that has been made on the legal and regulatory front, many remain disappointed by the limited progress made in advancing racial equality in education and the workplace. Such gaps are still among the most troubling and urgent problems in American society.

Other Movements

As we will see in Chapter 11, along with the civil rights movement other social movements have successfully expanded the civil and political rights of groups experiencing discrimination. Prominent examples include the efforts of women

---

[14] David J. Garrow, *Bearing the Cross: Martin Luther King, Jr., and the Southern Christian Leadership Conference* (New York: William Morrow, 1986).

and of 18- to 20-year-olds to win the right to vote. Both initiatives culminated in constitutional amendments expanding the franchise. For women, the movement to win voting rights started in the mid-nineteenth century and only came to fruition in 1920. Women's rights activists in the mid-twentieth century sought another constitutional amendment banning all discrimination based on sex. The Equal Rights Amendment was passed by Congress in 1972 and submitted to the states for approval, but it narrowly failed a decade later after falling two states short of the 37 required for ratification.[15]

The national government often needs prodding to improve the lot of minorities who have experienced discrimination. Groups throughout American history, especially since the 1960s, have sought laws to prohibit discrimination, promote respect from the rest of the population, and provide for the concrete, economic rewards that

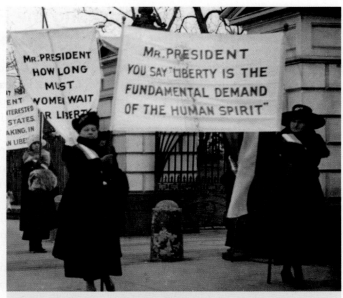

Women also faced a long struggle to achieve equal rights and liberties in the United States. In the late nineteenth and early twentieth centuries, the movement for women's political rights intensified and resulted in passage of the Nineteenth Amendment in 1920, which guaranteed women the right to vote.

flow from being part of the mainstream of American society. Only after public protests in the 1960s, for instance, did the federal government respond to repeated demands by Native Americans for more rights. In recent years, gays and lesbians have organized to pressure governments within the United States to extend to them basic civil rights protections and privileges, such as the rights to adopt children, marry, and serve as openly gay in the military. Christian conservatives have pressured governments to allow for more freedom of religious expression in public schools, and groups representing the disabled were successful in getting the national government to pass laws requiring easy access to all public buildings.

Equal treatment, however, is in the eye of the beholder, and the line between it and special treatment is fiercely debated. As we will discuss later when we examine the controversies over affirmative action, abortion, and gay rights, the boundaries for how far government can or should go to ensure equal rights end up being settled by political struggles waged in legislatures, elections, and courts.

---

[15] Judith Baer and Leslie Goldstein, *The Constitutional and Legal Rights of Women: Cases in Law and Social Change* (Los Angeles: Roxbury, 2006).

Incorporating the Bill of Rights into the Fourteenth Amendment

In Chapters 2 and 3, we learned that the Constitution is ambiguous on certain key points and that the American constitutional system continues to evolve. Particular historical circumstances are important in determining how constitutional institutions or ideals are applied in practice. The gun control issue shows that the Supreme Court must decide among various possible interpretations of the Second Amendment's protection of the right to "keep and bear arms," including the allowable policies of local governments. This is one example of how the Court rules on major issues of federalism as they relate to civil rights and liberties.

Before the Civil War, the Bill of Rights applied only to national laws and actions by the national government, not to the actions of state or local governments. The Supreme Court affirmed this view in *Barron v. Baltimore* (1833) when Chief Justice John Marshall, writing for the majority, ruled that a Maryland man would have been entitled to government compensation under the Fifth Amendment if the national government had ruined his property. Instead, because Maryland did not have a similar guarantee in its constitution, and because the harm to his property occurred as a result of actions by the city of Baltimore (a "creature" of the state of Maryland), the man was not legally protected under the Fifth Amendment.

The Fourteenth Amendment, ratified in 1868, began a process that dramatically changed the nature of civil rights and liberties in the United States. The key passage in the amendment declares, "No State shall make or enforce any law which shall abridge the privileges or immunities of citizens of the United States; nor shall any State deprive any person of life, liberty, or property, without **due process** of law; nor deny to any person within its jurisdiction the **equal protection** of the laws."

due process The right to legal protections against arbitrary deprivation of life, liberty, or property.

equal protection The principle that laws passed and enforced by the states must apply fairly to all individuals.

The language would seem to be clear in stating that the Bill of Rights, which summarizes all the "privileges and immunities of citizens," should apply to the states. The Supreme Court, however, was slow to embrace this idea, with unfortunate consequences. In the famous *Slaughter-House Cases* (1873), the Court ruled that the Fourteenth Amendment applied only to discrimination against African Americans, thus severely limiting its reach.[16] Furthermore, the Court decided soon thereafter that the language about equal protection applied only to laws and not to private conduct, even in the case of African Americans. It reasoned in both cases that the authors of the Fourteenth Amendment could not possibly have meant it to apply to the entire Bill of Rights. This legal understanding held sway for more than 60 years and opened the way for states, mostly in the South, to permit blatant discrimina-

[16] *Slaughter-House Cases*, 83 U.S. 36 (1873).

Freedom/Right	Amendment	Case	Year
Of speech and press	First	Gitlow v. New York	1925
To have attorney in capital cases	Sixth	Powell v. Alabama	1932
To exercise any religion	First	Hamilton v. Regents of the University of California	1934
Of assembly and petition	First	DeJonge v. Oregon	1937
From establishment of religion	First	Everson v. Board of Education	1947
To have a public trial	Sixth	In re Oliver	1948
From unreasonable searches and seizures	Fourth	Mapp v. Ohio	1961
From cruel and unusual punishments	Eighth	Robinson v. California	1962
To have attorney for felony cases	Sixth	Gideon v. Wainwright	1963
From self-incrimination	Fifth	Malloy v. Hogan	1964
To confront witnesses	Sixth	Pointer v. Texas	1965
To have an impartial jury trial	Sixth	Parker v. Gladden	1966
To have a speedy trial	Sixth	Klopfer v. North Carolina	1967
To compel witnesses to testify	Sixth	Washington v. Texas	1967
To trial by jury	Sixth	Duncan v. Louisiana	1968
From double jeopardy	Fifth	Benton v. Maryland	1969
To have attorney for charges that could result in jail time	Sixth	Argersinger v. Hamlin	1972
To bear arms	Second	McDonald v. Chicago	2010

tion of African Americans under Jim Crow laws. Those laws established a system of segregation of public facilities and private establishments that made African Americans second-class citizens. Other laws and practices in the rest of the country were patently discriminatory toward immigrants and other racial and ethnic minorities. The Supreme Court's initial refusal to apply the Fourteenth Amendment to the states set back progress on civil rights for many decades.

Nevertheless, court rulings and congressional legislation in the century following the ratification of the Fourteenth Amendment gradually **incorporated** into the amendment many of the protections for rights and liberties established by the Bill of Rights, so that they applied to state and local governments as well as to the national government. By the 1970s, the amendment had incorporated nearly all of the Bill of Rights, including freedom of speech and assembly, and the rights to counsel, privacy, and just compensation for

incorporation The process by which rights and liberties established by the Bill of Rights are applied to state and local governments through the Fourteenth Amendment.

forfeiture of property. It incorporated rights against warrantless searches, double jeopardy (being tried twice for the same offense), self-incrimination, the admission of illegal evidence, and forced confessions in criminal cases. In our own era, the Fourteenth Amendment's due process and equal protection clauses essentially apply to the entire Bill of Rights.[17]

This evolution in legal doctrine affected the progress of civil rights and liberties in the United States. It also altered the nature of American federalism. The incorporation of most of the Bill of Rights has been important in tipping the balance of authority in the United States away from the states and toward the national government. The national government has the authority through the Court to enforce the Bill of Rights in the states as well as the obligation to protect civil rights actively through legislation and administrative procedures.

Government Responses to Discrimination

American governmental institutions are both *restrained* from interfering in certain individual activities, such as practicing a religion or expressing dissent over government policies, and *empowered* or *obligated* to protect individuals when they exercise their rights as citizens or residents of the country. Since the mid-twentieth century, the emphasis has been on the latter role. Governmental institutions have stepped in to protect people in certain groups (especially racial, ethnic, or religious minorities; women; and the disabled) from discrimination. And in many cases, legislation and court decisions have required some governments in the United States to provide expensive and vital services to criminal defendants, minority schoolchildren, illegal immigrants, and prisoners. Indeed, in the area of civil rights, especially in relation to the equal protection and due process clauses of the Fourteenth Amendment, governments in the United States have become notably active in trying to limit discrimination and support vulnerable people.

New laws beginning in the mid-twentieth century were crucial. Of foundational importance was passage of the Civil Rights Act of 1964, a sweeping law that banned most forms of discrimination on the basis of race, color, national origin, or religion and required the government to be active in guaranteeing equal treatment of people traditionally discriminated against in employment, housing, educational admissions, and public funding. Passing the law took several years and started before President John Kennedy was assassinated in 1963. The law was passed by Congress after Kennedy's assas-

---

[17] Sue Davis and J. W. Peltason, *Corwin and Peltason's Understanding the Constitution* (Belmont, CA: Wadsworth, 2007). There are some exceptions: the Fifth Amendment right to indictment by a grand jury and the Eighth Amendment right against excessive bail have not yet been incorporated.

sination, following intense public pressure brought by the civil rights movement and by the culmination of changes in public opinion overall toward tolerance of and sympathy for oppressed minorities. Martin Luther King Jr., in late 1963, gave his famous "I Have a Dream" speech urging passage. It took sustained effort by proponents of the law in the government, including President Lyndon Johnson, to overcome opposition among southern senators.

The 1964 act formed the basis upon which many other national and state-level laws have been passed since banning discrimination and requiring government redress of past discrimination. The law in 1964 included some bans on discrimination based on gender, but it applied those bans only to public institutions or those supported by public funds or engaging in interstate commerce. Since then, however, many other protections for women and other groups, including the disabled, Native Americans, veterans, and homosexuals, have been included in certain states and localities. Moreover, the government has moved beyond protection to actively promoting minority well-being through affirmative action (discussed later in this chapter).

New laws have reshaped the landscape of civil rights and liberties, and so have court decisions. The Supreme Court, in wrestling with how to interpret the Constitution and the new laws about discrimination, has applied the equal protection and due process clauses of the Fourteenth Amendment by devising a three-tiered classification scheme to evaluate whether a state law or state government action violates someone's constitutional rights. If confronted with a case involving a potential violation of the equal protection clause, all courts in the nation must use this three-tiered scheme as guidance.

To understand the Court's scheme for making decisions, we first need to acknowledge that laws about civil rights do not prohibit *all* discrimination. In fact, many laws allow for, and certain situations require, discrimination. Only Native Americans can receive benefits accorded specifically to members of recognized Indian tribes. Insurance companies can discriminate by charging men higher auto insurance rates than women, and hairstylists can legally charge higher rates for women than for men. Movie studios are allowed to search for actors of particular races for parts in movies. Colleges and universities are allowed to employ a form of sex discrimination by admitting an incoming freshman class divided more or less equally between male and female students.

Nevertheless, the Supreme Court has declared that if a state law or state government action allows for discrimination (or results in discrimination) based on what are called "suspect" classifications such as race, ethnicity, religion, creed, or national origin, or involves a fundamental right, it is subject to **strict scrutiny**. If the Court uses this standard, it means that the law is presumed to be unconstitutional unless the government can convince the Court that it advances a "compelling state interest" and that the means used to achieve the

strict scrutiny The highest-level standard used by the Supreme Court to determine whether a law is compatible with the Constitution. A law subject to this standard is considered unconstitutional unless it advances a "compelling state interest" and represents the least intrusive means.

state's ends are the least intrusive on the fundamental right. This strict scrutiny standard is the highest of the three tiers. Laws allowing for or resulting in discrimination rarely pass this constitutional standard; in other words, most such laws or government actions are struck down by the Court.

When state laws or government actions discriminate (or result in discrimination) based on what are called "disfavored" criteria—usually economic in nature, such as income levels—then the Court uses the **rational basis test**, which presumes the law is constitutional as long as there is a reasonable link between the means and the goals of the law or action. Most laws or actions pass this hurdle, the lowest of the Court's prescribed tests.

Since the 1970s, the Supreme Court has also used an **intermediate scrutiny** standard in cases of discrimination that are not suspect but are nevertheless disfavored. If a law serves "an important government objective" and "is substantially related to the achievement" of the objective, then the law can stand. Otherwise, it is unconstitutional. Since the 1980s, for example, the Court has tended to use this intermediate standard for laws that allow for (or result in) discrimination based on sex. This means that the Court has yet to make sex difference a suspect classification that deserves strict scrutiny, but examines such laws more closely than those involving discrimination based on economic differences, for which it uses the rational basis test.

To summarize, the U.S. legal code has made it virtually impossible for state or local governments to tolerate or promote discrimination based on certain characteristics such as race or religion; the exceptions include certain kinds of affirmative action (discussed in the next section). But interpretations of the legal code have made it easy to discriminate based on economic criteria, and moderately easy to discriminate in categories such as sex. This three-tiered scheme has been criticized for being arbitrary and giving the Court too much leeway in defining which discriminatory categories fit into each tier. Critics, however, often miss the point that the obligations and boundaries drawn in the areas of civil rights and liberties, while meaningful and consequential, are continually being redrawn in response to particular historical circumstances and political trends.

When the Court declares that past discrimination or injustice has harmed a particular group in society, it often mandates that governments either change the laws to make discrimination illegal or provide remedies for that group. For example, when the Supreme Court decided in *Estelle v. Gamble* (1976) that the Eighth Amendment's prohibition against "cruel and unusual punishments" was violated when states packed prisoners into jail cells and denied them adequate food and sanitary conditions,[18] some lower federal courts subsequently forced states to submit plans for improving prison conditions so that the courts could decide whether the plans met constitutional standards. Start-

[18] *Estelle v. Gamble*, 429 U.S. 97 (1976).

rational basis test The lowest-level standard used by the Supreme Court to determine whether a law is compatible with the Constitution. A law subject to this standard is assumed to be constitutional as long as its goals are clearly linked to its means.

intermediate scrutiny An intermediate standard used by the Supreme Court to determine whether a law is compatible with the Constitution. A law subject to this standard is considered constitutional if it advances "an important government objective" and is "substantially related" to the objective.

ing in the 1970s, when local districts were seen to be operating highly segregated schools, contrary to the *Brown v. Board of Education* (1954) decision and subsequent rulings that racial segregation in schools violated the equal protection clause, the federal courts required the districts to bus students to various locations to ensure a more integrated and racially diverse student body among the schools.[19] The controversy over busing was particularly bitter, given that the government's attempts to force school districts to comply with court decisions mandating desegregation meant that children were often sent to schools far outside their neighborhoods and apart from their friends or siblings.

The trade-offs that governments have to make in pursuit of civil rights and liberties make many issues in this area controversial. Now let's take a closer look at three issues in which the proper degree of government activism or restraint is often debated.

Affirmative Action

Among the most controversial issues in the area of civil rights and liberties is **affirmative action**, defined in the American context as the effort to redress previous discrimination against women and minorities through active measures to promote their employment and educational opportunities. Many U.S. colleges and universities, for instance, have programs designed to bolster the admission of students from certain racial or ethnic groups, including African Americans, Latinos, and Native Americans. Departments in certain disciplines, especially in the sciences, actively try to attract women to undergraduate and graduate programs. Government agencies at the federal and state levels typically request bids from companies owned by women or racial minorities and give those bids special consideration when awarding contracts. Fire departments and police forces are required by local and federal laws to take steps to hire women and minorities and to maintain a certain proportion of such people in their ranks even when they have to lay off workers.

The rationale for affirmative action is that certain groups in society, having faced previous discrimination, are disadvantaged in employment and education and need active government intervention to promote equal opportunities. Merely allowing social processes, such as admissions to colleges or the awarding of government contracts, to operate normally perpetuates inequalities and the discrimination that underlies them.[20] Yet affirmative action, it has been argued, creates one form of discrimination in the interest of redressing another. Critics charge that when a college devotes special efforts to

affirmative action Efforts to redress previous discrimination against women and minorities through active measures to promote their employment and educational opportunities.

[19] *Brown v. Board of Education of Topeka*, 347 U.S. 483 (1954).
[20] W. Avon Drake and Robert Holsworth, *Affirmative Action and the Stalled Quest for Black Progress* (Urbana: University of Illinois Press, 1996).

recruit African American or Hispanic students, it can have the effect of discriminating against whites because of their race. Much of the criticism of affirmative action comes from people who claim that the government should not be using race, sex, or ethnic heritage to make decisions about access to education, government contracts, or jobs. They argue that even if the goal of equal opportunity is worthwhile, open preference for people based on race, sex, or ethnicity detracts from other goals, such as promotion of a society in which merit is the only criterion for educational or professional success.

Courts and other branches of government at all levels in the American political system have wrestled with the challenges raised by affirmative action. Can organizations set quotas for racial minorities or women? Should affirmative action for a particular group go on indefinitely, or should it end after a set period? These are only two of the many thorny questions that confront lawmakers and judges. The Supreme Court has issued a number of rulings on affirmative action that have attempted to define the boundaries of acceptable promotion of group attainment. In its *Regents of the University of California v. Bakke* decision (1978), the Court permitted affirmative action in university admissions as long as race or sex was only one consideration among others.[21] Quotas, however, were declared unconstitutional. In its several *Bollinger* cases (2003) and *Fisher* cases (2013 and 2016), the Court drew the line between university admissions policies that gave extra points to people if they were a racial minority (not allowed)[22] and policies that, consistent with *Bakke*, treated race as one of several factors considered in deciding on admission (allowed).[23]

Abortion Rights

The politics surrounding abortion rights have been among the most divisive of all issues in the American political system since the 1970s. At its core, the controversy over abortion entails differing understandings of whose rights and liberties deserve protection from government or by government.

Abortion, or the deliberate termination of a pregnancy, was only in recent history permitted under the law. Some states in the 1960s began allowing abortion. In 1973, with the decision *Roe v. Wade*, the Supreme Court mandated that no governments in the United States could restrict women from having abortions within the first trimester of their pregnancy.[24] This "right to choose" abortion was established as a matter of constitutional law under the interpre-

---

[21] *Regents of the University of California v. Bakke*, 438 U.S. 265 (1978).

[22] *Gratz v. Bollinger*, 539 U.S. 244 (2003).

[23] *Grutter v. Bollinger*, 539 U.S. 306 (2003). See also *Fisher v. University of Texas*, 570 U.S. 345 (2013), and *Fisher v. University of Texas*, 579 U.S. ___ (2016).

[24] *Roe v. Wade*, 410 U.S. 113 (1973).

tation of several amendments implying, in the Court's view, a right to privacy (discussed in Chapter 2).

For those opposed to abortion rights, attention on women's rights to choose abortion is misplaced, and instead focuses on the idea that unborn fetuses need protection by government. Many (though certainly not all) opponents are motivated by religious convictions that the life of a person deserving of protection begins at the moment of conception, and that allowing abortion amounts to the killing of a human being. To them, unborn fetuses should be included when the Constitution says governments should protect "life, liberty, and the pursuit of happiness." The Supreme Court in *Roe* rejected the idea that fetuses are included in this constitutional language. Those supporting abortion rights instead focus attention on the rights of women to control their reproduction, and that intrusion into women's freedom to choose abortion amounts to governmental invasion of privacy. For the majority in *Roe*, they mostly justified their decision by saying that women have a right to private decisions over their reproduction in consultation with their physicians.

Political battles over abortion continue. The controversy has been front and center in presidential politics, in the differences between the two major political parties, and in Supreme Court nominations. In general, Republicans have defined themselves as *pro-life*, meaning that they oppose abortion rights or at least support more restrictions on abortion. Democrats have mostly defined themselves as *pro-choice*, meaning that they support the legal reasoning in *Roe* and work to protect women's reproductive rights as defined by that decision. Supreme Court justices are known to have legal positions either for or against the legal reasoning in *Roe*, and recent Court cases on abortion rights have been very close (typically 5–4 or 6–3). Meanwhile, at the state and local levels, policies are passed to restrict access to abortion—and sometimes they are struck down by the federal courts, and sometimes they are allowed to stand. The U.S. Supreme Court recently struck down a Texas law, which the majority of the Court believed put undue burdens on facilities providing abortions, claiming that the intention of the law was to limit women's constitutional right to abortion.

Should government protect the right of women to terminate their pregnancies toward the beginning of term? Or should government protect unborn fetuses from being aborted? These are deep questions that people view passionately. For our purposes we can ask, Why did the Court choose the boundary between the first and second trimester as the point when governments could and could not regulate abortion access? The majority in the *Roe* decision reasoned that as a pregnancy progresses, the state has increasing room to regulate abortion, and the rights of the mother to privacy in determining her reproduction decrease relative to the right of states to protect the life of the fetus. Defining the line as between the first and second trimester was the Court's attempt, in effect, to balance the rights of the woman and the rights

The Collective Dilemma

It would seem unobjectionable to create buildings and provide services that accommodate people with disabilities. If workplaces did not have ramps and elevators to accommodate people with wheelchairs, many disabled people would not be able to work, even if they were qualified. If schools did not provide textbooks in Braille or texts of audio recordings, blind and deaf students would not be able to learn. Yet, as of the late 1980s, there was no recourse for the disabled to sue a person or an institution when faced with blatant discrimination.

As admirable as it is to provide access to people with disabilities, however, offering access to anything for anyone with any disability is, according to some, unreasonably expensive. And making such changes takes money away from serving the vast majority of people without disabilities.

Interests

People with disabilities want access to what others experience and enjoy. They want to travel, attend baseball games, and enjoy parks, movies, and the latest technology. Interest groups that lobby on behalf of people with disabilities have long pressured the government to have strict laws requiring businesses and all public institutions to change their facilities and programs to allow people with disabilities full access. Meanwhile, people who own businesses and run facilities that admit the public and numerous employees have interest in keeping costs down. They may claim that they can make reasonable accommodations but cannot afford expensive changes for a few people with disabilities.

One example that exposes these different interests is in the area of university study abroad programs. Many students attending American universities study in a foreign country for a semester or a summer term; Italy, France, and the United Kingdom are popular destinations, but there are programs all over the world. Yet, in these foreign locations, it is often the case that accommodations are in older buildings without ac-

cessibility for people in wheelchairs or other help aids, or in locations that do not require accessibility by law. American universities can try to accommodate students with disabilities for programs in, say, Rome or Paris, but in doing so it may make the program cost prohibitive for students and risk shutting down the programs entirely.

Institutions

The Fifth and Fourteenth Amendments to the U.S. Constitution mandate the protection of liberties and equal protection of the laws. These two amendments provide a legal framework from which Congress can act to protect the liberties of people with disabilities. Also, since the 1960s, Congress has tried to "fill in" the details on how government ought to protect liberties and determine equal protection of the laws. Instead of waiting for courts to settle disputes over discrimination, Congress passed legislation that required governments and all public institutions to avoid unjust discrimination and also bring about changes leading to equal treatment. Finally, the supremacy clause of the Constitution allowed the federal government to pass laws mandating all jurisdictions in the country be responsible for implementing changes in favor of the rights of the disabled.

Outcomes

Congress passed the Americans with Disabilities Act (ADA) in 1990 and subsequently amended and updated

Access to What Others Have: Rights of the Disabled

the act in 2008. This landmark law banned discrimination of people with disabilities in many circumstances, such as employment, schools, and public spaces, and required that most entities in society make reasonable accommodations for people with disabilities. Among the many sections of the law are descriptions of who and what places in society are exempt from the requirements, what aspects of technology have to conform, and what bodily functions count as major life activities that people are entitled to enjoy, even if it is costly for society to ensure that they can. The law has been criticized as burdening businesses and public institutions with enormous costs; still, the law and the regulations by agencies to implement the law are highly detailed as they try to strike a balance between the overall costs of complying with the law and ensuring equal access to those with disabilities.

A key word in the law is "reasonable." Businesses, educational institutions, public buildings, and government agencies must make reasonable accommodations for people with disabilities. In court decisions, if providing such accommodations means raising costs so high that it would lead to a business or a program shutting down, then that is not considered reasonable. So, in the case of university study abroad programs, to defend itself against a lawsuit on behalf of disabled students requiring that universities make programs accessible, a university would have to show that making such accommodations would entail costs that make its program financially untenable. Many universities, in fact, have study abroad programs that

Should universities have study abroad programs that are all accessible to this student?

are accessible, though it is typical for them to have some programs that are not due to the nature of the buildings housing or educating students in foreign countries.

Think About It

How far should society go to accommodate people with disabilities? What requirements should government set for society? Does American society, following passage of the ADA in 1990, strike the right balance?

of the state to protect the fetus if that is what state governments through their democratic processes decide to do. The line was set to establish a boundary at the moment when a fetus could be, given medical technology available at the time, viable outside of the womb. The author of the *Roe* decision, Justice Harry Blackmun, stated that "the end of the first trimester . . . is arbitrary . . . but perhaps any other selection point . . . is equally arbitrary."[25]

Rights Related to Sexual Identity

The treatment of gays, lesbians, and transgender people is an increasingly important area of civil rights. Until a few decades ago, homosexuality and transgender behavior were taboo topics, little discussed in public. Very few people were openly gay. People known to be gay often faced discrimination. Transgender individuals stayed hidden from public in most cases. Violence against gays, lesbians, and transgender people was not only widespread, but local governments in some places often looked the other way. Discrimination continues in many situations, but homosexuality and alternative sexual identities are now widely discussed. According to recent studies, for instance, millions of Americans acknowledge being gay and have stable homosexual relationships. Compared with past decades, homosexuality in many parts of American society is out in the open and accepted.

Nevertheless, there is still widespread hostility toward homosexuality and homosexuals, and toward transgender people, especially outside of the largest cities and in more traditional communities. Even the many Americans who claim to be sympathetic to the rights of sexual minorities to be free of discrimination often feel discomfort arising from religious or traditional beliefs about sexual practices, the importance of the traditional family, and child-rearing.

The sexuality rights movement (which we will discuss further in Chapter 11) has pushed for a variety of policy changes. A major effort has been made to add bias against homosexuals and transgender individuals to the list of discriminatory practices in housing, school admissions, and employment proscribed by national and state laws. Many cities and some states have outlawed discrimination based on sexual orientation (as well as race, ethnicity, sex, or religious belief), and the sexuality rights movement seeks to expand the reach of such laws.

One change was, and in some places remains, particularly controversial: expanding the legal definition of marriage to include same-sex unions. Marriage confers on a couple substantial legal and financial benefits, including the right of inheritance and the right to pass on Social Security benefits if one member of the couple dies. As important as the financial stakes for gay rights groups is the basic recognition of equality before the law. The movement for same-sex marriage has experienced growing success. The national govern-

[25] Bob Woodward, "The Abortion Papers," *Washington Post*, January 22, 1989.

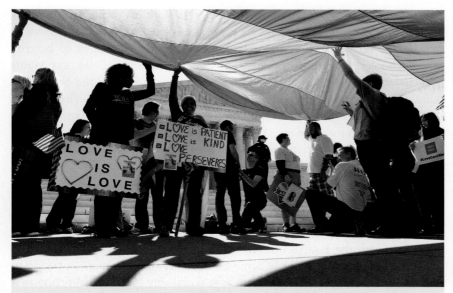

Outside the Supreme Court demonstrators try to influence the Court and public opinion on the issue of gay marriage. Throughout the early 2010s, gay marriage was a controversial issue, pitting those seeking equality for gay couples against those seeking to preserve traditional definitions of marriage in the law.

ment passed the Defense of Marriage Act (DOMA) in 1996, which defined marriage as between a man and a woman. A move that represented a major boost for gay rights activists was when President Barack Obama expressed his support for allowing same-sex marriage during the 2012 presidential election campaign. The Supreme Court in 2013 struck down the core of DOMA, which denied federal benefits to gay married couples even when legally married in their home states. The Court stated that DOMA violated the liberty protections of the Fifth Amendment. Then, in 2015, the Court in *Obergefell vs. Hodges* ruled that denying same-sex couples the right to marriage violated the Fourteenth Amendment guaranteeing equal protection and due process of the laws. This decision was a watershed, mandating that same-sex marriage was to be legal anywhere in the United States. Local and state governments have to offer marriage licenses to same-sex couples in the same manner in which they offer them to heterosexual couples.

For some people, same-sex marriage still presents a difficult trade-off between their freedom to practice their religion and the freedom of homosexuals to enjoy the benefits of marriage. A large proportion of Americans belong to religious faiths that consider homosexual practices to be morally wrong. Both in doctrine and among church leaders, several major religions oppose same-sex marriage. If a religious person agrees with his or her religious authorities on the issue, and same-sex marriage is legal, should that person be required to recognize homosexual couples as legally equivalent to heterosexual couples? For those opposed to same-sex marriage, the gay rights movement may pit religious freedom against equal rights to the benefits of marriage. Kim Davis, a county clerk in Rowan County, Kentucky, refused in 2015 after the Supreme Court ruling to issue any marriage licenses because doing so for same sex couples, she said, violated her right to practice her religion. She was briefly jailed for refusal to act in accordance with her duties and then was released when she agreed to resign her post. For some opposed to same-sex marriage, Davis was considered a hero who stood up for her religious freedom. To others, she stood in favor of unjust discrimination.

The challenge of trading off the rights of different people is apparent in all three of these policy areas. In trying to redress past discrimination, is it acceptable, given the Fourteenth Amendment, to tilt competition for admission or employment in favor of some groups over other groups? In trying to protect women's reproductive rights, is it acceptable to permit abortion that kills a fetus? In trying to allow for equal access to the benefits of marriage, is it acceptable, given the First Amendment, to force members of religious groups to recognize gay marriage contrary to their doctrines or the advice of their religious authorities?

In Comparison: Rights and Liberties around the World

Other countries face similarly controversial issues, and often the same issues. Comparison helps to put the American experience in context and enables us to consider more systematically the consequences of specific American interpretations of rights and liberties.

Compared with the rest of the world, people living in the United States today are remarkably free to speak, practice religion, publish, or assemble. In terms of liberty from government interference, the American political system places fewer restrictions on its citizens than the systems in most other democratic countries. Of course, civil rights and liberties are not absolute, and all countries place boundaries somewhere. Note the line drawn by the Supreme Court on owning guns. Other countries draw slightly different boundaries across a variety of issues that are typically tighter than in the United States. For instance, all advanced industrial democracies have tighter restrictions on individual gun ownership rights than the United States.

Germany, France, and Canada, for example, prohibit any speech that incites hatred, especially hatred based on ethnicity or religion. In Germany and

France, it is illegal to deny that the Holocaust (the Nazi genocide of Jews in World War II) occurred; and in both countries, items with the Nazi swastika cannot be sold or displayed in public. In 2005, the United Kingdom passed a law banning speech inciting religious hatred in response to bombings in London by Islamic extremists. The United States, on the other hand, permits such expressions in most situations; you are permitted to burn crosses (a long-standing practice of racist groups including the Ku Klux Klan) as long as you are not directly intimidating someone but are instead making a political statement.

The United States has relatively tolerant laws regarding assembly and the press, including organizing and publishing by groups that may advocate radical mass action or violence, such as communists, Nazis, and the Ku Klux Klan. More generally, the United States has liberal laws regarding pornography and strictures against "prior restraint" (government prohibition of speech in advance of publication). As for libel, nearly every other country has laws that make it easier for people to sue journalists or the press successfully for spreading false information about them. In the United States, the hurdle for winning a libel lawsuit is relatively high; plaintiffs must demonstrate that the defendant not only published false information, but knowingly published it with the intention of harming the plaintiff. This standard is almost never met, and libel lawsuits in the United States rarely succeed. Many other countries require plaintiffs to meet a lower standard in libel suits. For instance, the defendant may have to show that the accusation made in print is true, placing the onus on the journalist or author. Such standards give the U.S. press far more freedom than those in other countries to publish criticism of public figures.

The United States is not as distinctively vigorous in the protection of civil rights, although the nation has earned its place as a leader in some respects. Through the early twentieth century, the United States was historically at the forefront on the issue of voting rights. It extended the voting franchise earlier to major groups of people (non-property holders, religious minorities, women) than any other major country except Great Britain. Of course, from the late nineteenth century until well into the 1960s, the United States also allowed states and localities to inhibit voting by many of their citizens, especially African Americans and other racial minorities. The United States also grants criminal defendants more rights than do most other countries. Many countries, such as Germany, do not have jury trials. In Europe, criminal defendants commonly do not have the right to refuse self-incrimination, and prosecutors in many countries, unlike their American counterparts, may introduce evidence at trial that has been gathered illegally.

In contrast to legal traditions in such countries as Norway, Denmark, India, Brazil, and Canada, the U.S. courts have specifically declared that so-called social rights—such as the right to shelter, food, education, or health care—are not fundamental and do not have the same status as those rights mentioned in the Bill of Rights or declared in later court decisions. Of course, American governments at any level may legally provide these social benefits, but they are not mandated to do so. In the late twentieth century, however, the Supreme Court placed education in a somewhat intermediate category by implying in several rulings that, under equal protection clauses, the right to a minimal education enabling someone to read and write might approach the status of a fundamental right in the contemporary United States.

Why do such differences exist across countries? Why is the United States comparatively vigorous in protecting liberties and more typical with regard to rights? The latter question is not easy to answer. In such areas as freedom of speech, religion, and the press, the differences among countries may well exist because the United States is one of the few nations (even among democracies) that does not have a state-sponsored religion or a monarchy. Countries with state-sponsored religions and/or monarchies are more likely than nations that do not have such institutions to place greater restrictions on at least some of these civil liberties. Moreover, countries whose constitutions were designed after their loss in a war—Germany and Japan, for instance—are likely to place more restrictions on allowable political speech or publications.

France may be the largest nation that closely resembles the United States in both its history and its approach to civil rights and liberties. It has no state religion or monarchy and was founded by a revolution based on Enlightenment principles. France, like the United States, has a relatively liberal record on civil rights and liberties. There is, however, an important distinction between the French and American approaches to religious freedom. In the United States, the government may not support any particular religion, yet it vigorously protects people's rights to be religious and to express religious points of view. In France, the government also may not support any particular religion, and it protects the rights of people to be religious. Both societies have a constitutional tradition of maintaining separation of church and state. However, in state-supported public buildings in France, such as schools or courts, people may not express their religious views openly because these places are considered secular. Thus, bitter controversy has arisen in recent years when France banned Muslim girls from wearing head scarves and Christian students from wearing large crosses in public schools. There are further efforts to ban all Muslim women from wearing certain head coverings in public, including certain swimsuits ("Burkinis") on some beaches. According to French law, secular society is to be protected from religious zealotry. Under American law, government can neither promote nor inhibit religion. These are two fundamentally different ways to conceive of and apply meaning to "separation of church and state" and freedom of religion (see the Institutions, Interests, and Outcomes box in Chapter 2).

Policy makers in a democracy face a trade-off in adopting policies to enhance security versus protecting civil liberties. They can conduct surveillance of people they think might be a danger to the public, but in doing so possibly infringe on civil liberties. Or they can treat civil liberties as sacrosanct, which may leave the country vulnerable to terrorist attacks. How do Americans view the trade-off? Have their opinions changed over time?

Using data from Pew Research Center, the figure below tracks public opinion on this trade-off, and how the public balances security and liberties.[a]

Public Opinion on Civil Liberties and National Security, 2004–16

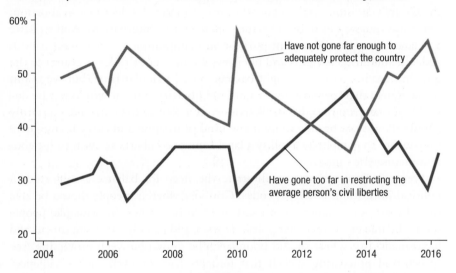

Source: Pew Research Center, "Public Uncertain, Divided over America's Place in the World," May 5, 2016, www.people-press.org/files/2016/05/05-05-2016-Foreign-policy-APW-release.pdf (accessed 7/11/16).

Think About It

As you can see, the trends move up and down over time.[b] What might explain these changes in opinion? Do Americans generally side with security over civil liberties, or vice versa? What events can change public opinion on this trade-off?

a. Pew Research Center, "Public Uncertain, Divided over America's Place in the World," May 5, 2016, www.people-press.org/files/2016/05/05-05-2016-Foreign-policy-APW-release.pdf (accessed 7/11/16).

b. Darren W. Davis and Brian D. Silver, "Civil Liberties vs. Security: Public Opinion in the Context of the Terrorist Attacks on America," *American Journal of Political Science* 48, no. 1 (2004): 28–46. Blake E. Garcia and Nehemia Geva, "Security versus Liberty in the Context of Counterterrorism: An Experimental Approach," *Terrorism and Political Violence* 28, no. 1 (2016): 30–48. Darren W. Davis, *Negative Liberty: Public Opinion and the Terrorist Attacks on America* (New York: Russell Sage Foundation, 2007).

Why Protect Rights and Liberties?

 Situations constantly arise that pit people's competing civil rights or liberties against each other. It may seem at times as if the Supreme Court splits hairs with its rulings. In the gun control cases discussed at the beginning of this chapter, for example, the Court drew a boundary between governmental laws that violated the Constitution and those that did not. Court decisions on difficult cases often expose trade-offs inherent in a democratic society's values. The Court defined the group needing protection to be gun owners, the people wanting to use firearms to protect themselves—not the people who might be harmed, even inadvertently, by gun violence.

This is the key to answering our questions at the beginning of the chapter: the Court's decision might seem arbitrary, as in the *Roe* decision on abortion, but it was one way to strike a balance between two alternatives. And striking a balance serves an important purpose in maintaining a society that is both ordered and protects rights and liberties. We may not think the courts or the government has struck the right balance on a particular issue, but we ought to recognize that for most civil rights and liberties issues it would not be desirable if one group's rights or liberties were taken to the extreme. Certainly people should not be able to own any kind of weapon and carry it anywhere they want. To paraphrase a folksy adage, someone's liberty to swing a fist ends at someone else's nose.

Free speech situations can illustrate the need for balance as reflected in political institutions and legal codes. Consider whether people should be able to call each other names, even racist or offensive names. In principle, people should be free to express their political views, and equally free from threats and harassment. But where should boundaries be drawn between protecting free speech and preventing speech that foments hate or even incites violence? Shouldn't people be free from hate speech? Should people be allowed to publicize and even broadcast racist messages? Should the government restrict speech by groups preaching hate? The federal courts have balanced the competing interests by saying (over many cases) that governments in the United States can restrict speech that is directly intimidating, but in almost all situations they cannot restrict political speech—for example, by candidates during a campaign—even if that speech is offensive. Moreover, constitutional protections of speech depend on whether the target of critical speech is someone well known to the public, and whether the speech occurs in a situation that could become disorderly or violent. In drawing legal boundaries on behavior and taking contexts into account, courts and governments are institutionalizing expectations among people over what is permitted for the intended purpose of ensuring order and freedom together. Not one without the other, but both.

Consider that we can divide justifications for protecting civil rights and liberties into two categories: those based on moral claims of inherent human dignity, and those based on "utilitarian" claims. Utilitarianism is a general philosophy that promotes social institutions in order to create the most good for the greatest number of people. The Founders were motivated by both justifications; let's discuss them in more detail.

The traditional moral justification for protecting civil rights and liberties as stated in the Declaration of Independence, and in the writings of philosophers such as John Stuart Mill or Isaiah Berlin, is that people possess certain rights simply by virtue of being human. Those rights could come from religious sources (as claimed in the writings of Saint Thomas Aquinas, for instance) or from a sense of shared values or experience as human beings (as claimed in the writings of Isaiah Berlin[26]). Many of us experience a sense of shame or anger at the way groups in American society have been treated in the past. Such responses undoubtedly come from a notion that discrimination, oppression, torture, or unjust bondage is morally wrong. We are offended by stories of slavery, of the Japanese American internments, and of failings by various American governments to protect people's voting rights regardless of their race, ethnicity, sex, or religion. It is hard to explain why we feel offended without some reference to an ethical system that is shared by a vast majority of people not only in the United States but also around the world. Simply put, most of us believe in the basic morality of a political system where the government is obligated to protect fundamental liberties and equal treatment of persons under the law.

Beyond the general moral claims of basic rights and liberties as fundamental to human dignity, there exist utilitarian justifications for the protection of liberties—specifically for freedom of speech, travel, assembly, and the press. These justifications share the idea that the entire society benefits from allowing many voices to be heard and from giving people the freedom to be creative. To stifle these freedoms is to stifle innovation, creativity, and the ability to learn from others.

On the political and social side, a system of government characterized by vigorous protection of civil rights and, especially, civil liberties fosters discussion, debate, deliberation, and competition among ideas. Thus, closed societies—those with few protections for rights and liberties—tend to stifle innovation, have little creativity and entrepreneurship, and, not incidentally, have low economic growth rates and fewer healthy and wealthy people. On the economic side, the arguments are similar. The freedoms to assemble, speak, and travel are related to the freedom to create new products and make associations with business partners, which spurs economic growth. Such freedoms, especially from government intrusion, regulation, and monopoly on investment, allow for creativity and entrepreneurship.

The utilitarian justification for protecting civil rights and liberties would not only say that the institutional boundaries on individual and governmen-

[26] Isaiah Berlin, *Liberty* (New York: Oxford University Press, 2002).

tal behavior that evolved in the United States have been successful in creating a dynamic, wealthy, and free society. It would also say that the boundaries were deliberately designed to achieve these goals. Far from enforcing freedoms to tolerate dissent merely because it is morally the right thing to do, dissent is tolerated because it is the smart thing to do.

It might be said that there is a downside, especially with regard to economic inequalities, to allowing too much freedom. Some might argue that allowing more economic freedom creates inequalities and allows people with the most resources to have the loudest voices and the most influence in a democracy. Instead of allowing for the orderly operation of a society, extreme versions of freedom of speech can stack the deck against real dissent. This topic arises again in Chapters 11 and 13 in our discussions of campaign finance.

Finally, consider the political interests that pursue changes in civil rights and liberties. Many expansions of civil liberties and rights, especially voting rights, have occurred because of opportunistic behavior by groups of politicians, and specifically by political parties seeking to expand their electoral support. In the early to mid-1800s, for example, both major parties—the Democrats and the Whigs—sought the support of immigrant groups, often by promising or providing them with an expansion of the franchise. Moreover, Democrats reasoned in the 1960s and 1970s that promoting voting rights for African Americans in the South would bring more Democratic voters to the polls in those regions. Undoubtedly, part of President Lyndon Johnson's motivation in seeking to expand the franchise to 18- to 20-year-olds in the late 1960s was to improve Democratic vote totals nationwide.

That rights frequently are expanded as a consequence of politicians seeking to achieve their goals does not necessarily mean that the expansion was wrong or led to bad consequences. This observation helps us understand that the institutions of government are typically designed intentionally and are not neutral regarding boundaries on individual and government behavior.

To return to our questions from the opening of the chapter, there is no definitive answer to the question of where the lines should be drawn in civil rights and liberties issues. The obligations of and boundaries on governmental behavior shift in response to changing values in society and among governmental leaders. But defining obligations and boundaries is often important, if not critical, for society to maintain a balance among competing rights and liberties. The obligations and boundaries have consequences for how people live day-to-day and make up vital institutional pieces of the American political system.

FURTHER READING

★=Included in *Readings in American Politics*, 5th ed.

★ *Brown v. Board of Education* (1954). The ruling that nullified the logic of *Plessy v. Ferguson* (1896) and declared "separate but equal" educational institutions for different races unconstitutional.

Katznelson, Ira, *When Affirmative Action Was White* (New York: Norton, 2005). A revealing examination of how federal social policies from the 1930s to the 1960s discriminated against African Americans.

King, Martin Luther, Jr., "I Have a Dream" Speech on the Mall, Washington, D.C., August 28, 1963. King's electrifying speech laying bare the inequalities in American society that were contrary to common sense and common values.

Obergefell v. Hodges (2015). The ruling that legalized same-sex marriage in all 50 states.

Plessy v. Ferguson (1896). The ruling that declared it constitutional for states to have "separate but equal" facilities for different races; overturned by *Brown v. Board of Education* (1954).

Roe v. Wade (1973). The ruling that established that women have a right to an abortion during the first trimester of their pregnancy.

Rosenberg, Gerald, *The Hollow Hope: Can Courts Bring about Social Change?* (Chicago: University of Chicago Press, 1991). A controversial book that questions the view that the federal courts led the way on civil and political rights, instead arguing that the courts lagged behind the elected branches in improving matters for minorities.

★ Tesler, Michael, *Post-Racial or Most-Racial: Race and Politics in the Obama Era* (Chicago: University of Chicago Press, 2016). Tesler's analysis shows that a substantial portion of the political polarization of American society stems from differences based on race and that this polarization has only increased since Obama's presidency.

KEY TERMS

affirmative action (p. 131)

Bill of Rights (p. 111)

civil liberties (p. 109)

civil rights (p. 109)

civil rights movement (p. 122)

due process (p. 126)

equal protection (p. 126)

incorporation (p. 127)

intermediate scrutiny (p. 130)

Jim Crow laws (p. 119)

rational basis test (p. 130)

strict scrutiny (p. 129)

Legislation filled with special "pork barrel" programs is frequently criticized by citizens and politicians. However, these bills are often hard for members of Congress to vote against because they usually want to "bring home the bacon" to their constituents. Here, Senator Jeff Flake (R-AZ) takes a selfie with Faye, a pot-bellied pig, after an event held by Citizens Against Government Waste, a nonprofit organization that works to reduce pork-barrel spending.

5

Congress

 How do legislators rise above self-interest and the narrow interests of their districts to pass important legislation?

Regardless of their party or ideology, legislators find some bills in Congress tough to vote against. Take, for example, the Continuing Resolution (CR) passed by both chambers in late 2016 to continue to spend money and avert a government shutdown. The spending bill provided $1.1 billion in funding for Zika research, as well as funds for flood relief in Louisiana and for improvements to the water supply in Flint, Michigan. It also approved full funding for a year for veterans and military contruction. While not all members of Congress were happy, the bill passed both chambers of Congress in September with strong bipartisan support. Some members voted against because it did not fund enough of what they wanted. For example, the two Democratic senators from Michigan, neither of whom were up for reelection that year, voted against the bill because in their view it did not provide enough funding for Flint; they had insisted on much more money for Flint than what was in the final bill.

Few doubted that some kind of bill maintaining the government spending would pass before the 2016 elections. And, as is often the case with such legislation, representatives and senators made sure that the bill contained what they wanted, some pork-barrel projects. (The term *pork barrel* refers to government spending that benefits a narrow constituency in return for electoral or some other kind of political support.) The portions on military construction, for example, averted what would have been a halt to popular military construction projects in many congressional districts.

Taken individually, each of these special-funding military construction projects may have merit. It is also difficult to argue against funding for the Zika virus research and the relief for the Gulf Coast flood victims. Funding for such critical needs is politically difficult to oppose. Indeed, not many members of Congress who are up for reelection would want to go on record for voting against support for veterans or for military construction in their states. But when the other spending items are lumped

OUTLINE

- Congress and the Constitution

- Congressional Elections

- Internal Institutions of Congress

- The Process of Lawmaking

- Making Law in a System of Separation of Powers

- In Comparison: Legislative Institutions

- Analyzing Collective Dilemmas in Congress

together with such funding, it raises the question of whether the legislation had more to do with pork-barrel projects than with critical needs.

Bills like this may inspire cynicism regarding the motivations and behavior of federal lawmakers. Opinion polls show that the public has little confidence in the institution of Congress. In fact, Americans' trust in the legislative branch of government has long been declining. More than a century ago, Mark Twain captured the view of many people when he wrote, "It could probably be shown by facts and figures that there is no distinctly American criminal class except Congress." Media coverage of Congress is often critical, and headline-grabbing scandals have beset the institution throughout its history. Leaders of every major political party have been found guilty of well-publicized misdeeds, ranging from influence peddling and bribery to sexual impropriety and extortion.

When political scientists question legislators' commitment to broad national goals, their doubts are not necessarily rooted in a belief that members of Congress are more prone to criminal activity than other professionals. Rather, they believe that congressional lawmakers place the interests of their districts and their own prospects for winning reelection ahead of the welfare of the country as a whole. It is widely assumed that members of Congress expend most of their energy on massive public relations efforts aimed at their constituents, rather than on making laws that benefit the entire nation.[1] If given the choice between delivering targeted benefits to people in their district or working with their colleagues to craft careful, meaningful legislation, members of Congress will choose the former. The political payoffs are simply much higher for helping constituents with specific requests than contributing to broad national policy outcomes. As one representative stated, "Before you save the world, you have to save your seat."[2]

This is one version of what we will describe later as the distributional model of congressional politics, and it has more than a kernel of truth to it. Instead of producing the best, most efficient public goods, members spend time cooperating with each other to produce pork for their districts and to ensure reelection.

Yet, if this model is accurate, and members of Congress focus mostly on the needs of their own districts above broader goals, how are they ever able to pass meaningful legislation? How do historic laws get passed, such as the legislation establishing the New Deal, the Civil Rights Act of 1964, and the Voting Rights Act of 1965; or various stimulus bills, health care and financial reforms, and the major budget agreement that Congress passed giving guidance on funding decisions through 2017? What explains the occasions when the members rise above their individual self-interest or the interests of their district to create meaningful, lasting legislative accomplishments?

[1] David R. Mayhew, *Congress: The Electoral Connection*, 2nd ed. (New Haven, CT: Yale University Press, 2004).

[2] Representative George Miller, quoted in Leroy N. Rieselbach, *Congressional Politics: The Evolving Legislative System*, 2nd ed. (Boulder, CO: Westview, 1995), p. 39.

Congress and the Constitution

The Founders intended Congress to be the most powerful branch of the national government. The Constitution describes dozens of specific congressional responsibilities and powers, and it also gives Congress broad authority as the primary lawmaking body in the national government. Specific congressional powers outlined by the Founders and listed in Article 1, Section 8, include the authority to tax, borrow and coin money, operate a postal service, promote science and the arts, declare war, raise and support armies and a navy, suppress insurrections, and build a capital city.

Broad responsibility, however, is found in the concluding clause of Article I, Section 8, which states that Congress has the power to "make all Laws which shall be necessary and proper for carrying into Execution the foregoing Powers, and all other Powers vested by this Constitution in the Government of the United States, or in any Department or Officer thereof." This elastic clause (also called the necessary and proper clause) grants Congress virtually blanket authority to make laws in the national interest, as long as those laws do not violate other precepts of the Constitution. No phrase in the Constitution gives any other branch such substantial powers.[3]

From the *Federalist Papers*, we know that leading constitutional advocates James Madison, Alexander Hamilton, and John Jay believed not only that Congress would play a preeminent role in a strong national government but also that a strong legislative branch was essential to proper functioning of the new government and protection of the population from injustice. Using the *Federalist Papers* to argue against skeptics who feared that under the new Constitution the presidency would be too powerful, or that the states would lose their identities, Madison, Hamilton, and Jay repeatedly claimed that strong congressional authority was vital to a functioning federal republic under a system of separation of powers that prevented the rise of a tyrannical president.

Yet, as with all the branches of the government, limits were placed on the power of Congress, and thus on any laws passed by the national government. Specifically, the Constitution forbids Congress from taxing goods that flow from one state to another, or from placing taxes or tariffs on goods exported from any state. Furthermore, Congress cannot pass laws that declare a person or group guilty of crimes without trial (called bills of attainder), and it cannot pass laws that make illegal any action that was committed before the law was passed (called ex post facto laws).

---

[3] The "Take Care" clause for the president (discussed in Chapter 6) is similarly broad and under a reasonable interpretation gives the president substantial discretionary power. But given that we know the Founders generally preferred Congress to be the primary locus of power in the national government, and given how federal courts have interpreted the Constitution, the elastic clause has had the biggest effect on national power relative to the states and on the relative powers of branches within the national government.

Bicameralism

The Constitution specifies that Congress will consist of two legislative chambers, the House of Representatives and the Senate. The **bicameral legislature** reflects the dual character of the American republic, blending popular government with federalism.[4] Congress not only makes the laws, it also plays the critical role of representing the people and the states in the national government.

In *Federalist 39*, for example, Madison compares the House to the Senate. Because the House was intended to represent the people, states are apportioned seats in the House according to the size of their population. Furthermore, members of the House have two-year terms of office, and all members can stand for reelection every two years to ensure that they remain responsive to the people. If their behavior diverges significantly from the wishes of their constituents, voters have frequent opportunities to replace them. For the House, the principals (voters) hold the agents (representatives) on a tight leash.

The Senate, in contrast, was designed to represent the states. Each state has two senators, regardless of size. Senators serve six-year terms and were originally appointed by the state governments. (Senators began to be elected directly by the people in the early twentieth century, as we will see later.) Although each Senate seat is up for renewal after six years, in any given even-numbered year, only one-third of the members' terms expire. Thus, in 2016, 34 senators faced reelection; in 2018, a different set of 33 senators faced reelection; and in 2020, the final set of 33 senators faces reelection. This design—longer terms in office and rotation of term-expiration dates—reflects the Founders' intention to make the Senate the more deliberative chamber, acting to maintain continuity in government in the face of popular whims and shifts in public opinion. For the Senate today, the principals (voters) hold the agents (senators) on a looser leash than is the case for the House.

Making Law

Congress, by constitutional mandate, bears ultimate responsibility for lawmaking. Both chambers of Congress must approve a piece of legislation, which can then be signed by the president to become law. Although the Constitution does not specify how a chamber approves the initial passage of bills, tradition and practice dictate that at least a majority in each chamber must be in favor of a bill before it can become law.[5] After both chambers approve a bill, the president can choose to sign it into law, ignore it (whereupon it becomes law after ten days if Congress is in session), or veto it. The Constitution specifies

[4] George Tsebelis and Jeannette Money, *Bicameralism* (New York: Cambridge University Press, 1997).

[5] The chambers can impose other rules for debate that make passage of a bill in practice require more than a majority. The Senate's cloture rule, for instance, requires three-fifths of the members' support for a bill to be introduced on the floor for debate. We will discuss this subject later in the chapter.

that Congress can "override," or overturn, a presidential veto by a vote of two-thirds of the members in each chamber. (We will look at the lawmaking process more closely later in this chapter.)

The Constitution also specifies voting rules for approval of treaties, which require the votes of two-thirds of the Senate. The House must be the formal originator of all taxing and spending decisions for the American national government.

Constitutional prerogatives aside, in some areas, especially foreign policy and war making, the president's power has eclipsed congressional authority. Over time, the presidency has become the locus of many legislative initiatives, federal budget planning, and foreign policy decision making. Madison, Hamilton, and Jay, therefore, were mistaken about what the relative powers of the Congress and the president would be. In particular, they failed to foresee how those powers would evolve over the course of the twentieth century. We will take a closer look at the expansion of presidential power in Chapter 6.

Congressional responsibilities as outlined in the Constitution and the growing role of the national government (see Chapter 3) mean that much of national politics swirls around Congress. As the formal originator of all taxing and spending decisions for the American national government, and as the locus of debate over business regulation, foreign and domestic aid, public works, approval for executive appointments and treaties, and the general direction of government, Congress is subject to intense media scrutiny. It attracts more lobbyists than any other national legislative body in the world. Congress also draws the attention—either ire or appreciation—of the voters who elect its members. We turn now to the choosing of members of Congress.

Congressional Elections

According to the Constitution, the states are responsible for deciding how to choose their congressional representation. These methods must comply with constitutional tenets, such as the requirement that representatives must be at least 25 years old and senators at least 30.

Distinctive features of congressional elections have emerged over time as a result of laws passed by Congress and of traditions dating back to the eighteenth century. In the following sections, we will see how plurality elections, primaries, and redistricting every 10 years encourages individualism in Congress. Individualism in this context means that members of Congress largely see their own political fortunes as tied primarily to their own behavior and to managing their reputations with their constituents. Voters consider their representation in Congress to be tied to individual legislators. Voters expect their representatives to belong to political parties or ideological groupings and to serve the specific needs of their local area. We will learn how institutional features and demographic trends have led to high incumbency reelection rates as well as to increasing minority representation in Congress.

The features of congressional elections have exacerbated the collective dilemmas that members face once they are inside their respective chambers. As we will see, the specific electoral *institutions* encourage candidates and members of Congress seeking reelection to maintain personal reputations among voters. In most other democracies, candidates for national legislatures are more closely linked to the reputations of their political parties. There is more individualism among members of the U.S. Congress than there is among legislators in most other democracies, and this individualism increased during the twentieth century.

Causes of Individualism in Congress

Several causes of individualism in Congress are institutional. The nature of electoral districts is one factor that leads to individualism, and other electoral rules also create incentives for legislators to make strong personal connections to voters in their districts.

Single-Member Districts and Plurality Rule. Drawing on the example set by the British House of Commons, nearly all states have elected their representatives for the House and Senate using **single-member districts** and **plurality rule**, sometimes known as "first past the post." In single-member districts, each electoral district or state chooses one representative. The plurality method of voting means that whoever receives the most votes wins. Note that this is not the same as a majority-rule voting method. Under majority rule, if no candidate receives at least 50 percent of the total vote, then there is a runoff between the top two vote-getters. Under plurality rule, there is no need for a runoff election.

Strictly speaking, under the current system, senators are elected in double-member districts (states have two senators), but each senatorial election occurs as a contest for one seat only, based on plurality voting rules. These elections are also first past the post. Until the early twentieth century, senators were not elected by popular vote; they were appointed by their state governments. This process was revised in 1913 by the Seventeenth Amendment, which provided for direct election of senators.

For Americans, the single-member simple plurality system is so familiar that it may be surprising to learn that few other countries use it. France, for example, requires that candidates win an outright majority of the votes in a district, which means that runoff elections between the top two vote-getters are held if neither candidate wins a majority. Many other countries elect multiple candidates from a district, use a form of **proportional representation**, or do

single-member district An electoral district in which a single person is elected to a given office.

plurality rule A method for determining an election's winner in which the candidate who receives the most votes wins.

proportional representation A method for allocating seats in a legislature in which the number of seats a party receives in a district or nationwide is proportional to the votes it receives in the elections.

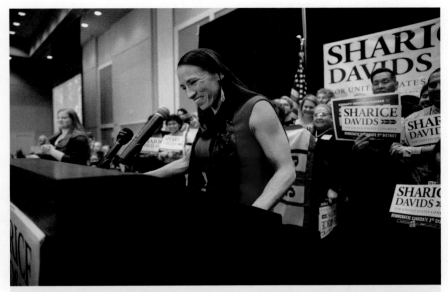

In the 2018 midterm elections, a record number of women ran for and won seats in Congress. Among those women is Sharice Davids, who represents Kansas's 3rd District and is one of the first Native American women to serve in Congress.

both. Under proportional representation systems, the number of seats a party receives in a district or nationwide is proportional to the votes it receives in the elections. For instance, if a party receives 30 percent of the vote under proportional representation, it can expect to hold about 30 percent of the legislative seats. Under single-member simple plurality systems, the winning candidate receives 100 percent representation of that district (its one and only seat) simply by getting more votes than any other candidate.

Historically, in a few cases states have elected representatives using methods other than plurality rule, and some states have recently switched to a system not unlike the French one, which requires a runoff election if no one wins a majority. Nevertheless, pervasive use of the plurality rule and single-member districts has strongly influenced the nature of the U.S. Congress, especially in combination with other features such as primary elections and redistricting.

Primary Elections. For both chambers, being chosen to run for Congress once depended on establishing a record of loyalty to state-level political parties. Party leaders in the states controlled which candidates got on the ballot and who was nominated to serve in the Senate. Beginning in the first half of the twentieth century, however, states began using the primary election process to select which congressional candidates would appear on ballots. Primary elections allow voters to choose who will appear under the party label on general election ballots. These primary elections are akin to the semifinals of a sports tournament because competition takes place *within* the parties (as in a sports conference), whereas the finals are the general election *between* the candidates of the parties (as when naming an overall champion). As long as someone wins a primary election, he or she can run for Congress under that party label without having to please the party leadership.

One consequence of single-member simple plurality election rules in combination with primary elections is that representatives and senators work extremely hard to cultivate reputations as individualistic politicians who are not completely beholden to their political parties. Candidates for Congress in the United States can focus mostly on satisfying voters in their own constituencies, whereas in most other countries politicians are much more loyal to their parties because they depend on party leadership for their job security.

Drawing District Boundaries. Congressional district boundaries determine the actual constituencies for representatives to the House. American states are allocated seats in the House according to population, but no state can have fewer than one representative. For example, with a half-million people, Wyoming has one representative for the entire state. Six other states also have a single representative in the House—Alaska, Delaware, Montana, North Dakota, South Dakota, and Vermont. Voters in the remaining 43 states are divided into districts.

House districts, according to Article I, Section 2, of the Constitution, cannot have fewer than 30,000 people. This number was stipulated at the time to ensure that state governments would not create tiny districts easily controlled by a given political faction or interest groups, something that was a problem in the British system. The British House of Commons for a long time contained representatives from so-called rotten boroughs, which were tiny electoral districts dominated by one person who could bribe the small number of voters to win reelection. The Founders used the 30,000-person minimum to avoid the American equivalent of rotten boroughs and also to set the size of the House at a bit more than twice the size of the Senate at the time (64 members in the House as compared to 26 members in the Senate). As the country grew in population, Congress occasionally increased the size of the House, until it was decided to cap the number permanently. The total number of representatives was set at 435 in 1911; the main argument for fixing the number then was that a legislature approaching 500 members in size would be unworkable.

The number of representatives allocated to each state and the boundaries of congressional districts are reset every 10 years, after the national census is taken. A state can gain or lose seats if its population grows or shrinks relative to other states. If a state gains or loses seats, it must redraw its district bound-

FIGURE 5.1A

Partisan Redistricting

Imagine a rectangular state with nine voters and three House seats. If the district lines are drawn one way, there is a mix of Republicans and Democrats in each district. In this scenario, Republicans have a majority in each district and will likely win all three seats.

However, district boundaries could also be drawn to give Democrats a majority in at least one district. In this second scenario, Democrats would be expected to win one of the three seats.

aries. Because of population shifts within the states, most states redraw their district boundaries every decade regardless of whether they have gained or lost seats.

For much of American history, states could draw their boundaries as they wished. This meant that districts were of varying population size even within states, and that it was possible (and common) for rural districts with few residents to have representation equal to the more populous urban districts. In the 1960s, however, the national government, through legislation (discussed later in this chapter) and through Supreme Court rulings, began to place restrictions on the states. The Court's rulings in *Baker v. Carr* (1962) and *Wesberry v. Sanders* (1964) paved the way for a major change in congressional districts. The Court concluded in those two cases that all House districts and all state house and senate districts in a given state must be of approximately equal population size. The *Baker* and *Wesberry* rulings not only mandated a dramatic change in districts all over the country, they also strengthened congressional representation of heavily populated cities. Following the ruling, large cities were divided into multiple congressional districts, each with one representative in the House.

Determining congressional district boundaries is fraught with politics, because districts can be drawn in ways that give one political party or population group more representation or power (Figure 5.1A).[6] For many states, the political party in control of the state government appoints a commission to redraw the boundaries. These commissions tend to draw the boundaries to the advantage of the political party that appointed them. In states with divided government—one party controls the governorship while another party controls the state legislature—the makeup of the commission typically reflects

[6] David Butler and Bruce Cain, *Congressional Redistricting: Comparative and Theoretical Perspectives* (New York: Macmillan, 1992).

FIGURE 5.1B

Racial Gerrymandering

Redistricting has been used in efforts to manipulate the voting power and representation of minorities. In a hypothetical state with six white voters and three black voters, lines could be drawn such that black voters do not constitute a majority in any district.

Or, boundaries could be drawn to create at least one "minority-majority" district, where members of the minority group constitute a majority of voters. Although this configuration may result in a black candidate being elected from the minority-majority district, some scholars have questioned whether this approach ultimately improves the overall representation of minorities in legislatures.

the proportion of each party's representation in government. Some states try to divorce the process from partisan politics by appointing a bipartisan commission to decide on district boundaries.

To see how politics can easily intrude into the drawing of district boundaries, consider the simplified example in Figure 5.1B. In this case, drawing boundaries one way results in a situation where African Americans do not have a majority in any district, while drawing boundaries another way ensures that there is a majority of African Americans in one district. If we assume, for the sake of argument, that blacks are more likely than whites to support an African American candidate, then the latter set of boundaries will virtually ensure that at least one African American is elected.

gerrymandering Drawing strangely shaped district boundaries to gain political advantage.

The process of drawing strangely shaped district boundaries to gain political advantage is known as **gerrymandering**. The term is derived from a district drawn for the 1812 election in Massachusetts to ensure the election of Governor Elbridge Gerry's allies, known as the Jeffersonians. The district looked like a salamander, or so Gerry's opponents thought. They accused the Jeffersonians of drawing not a salamander, but a "Gerrymander." One district in Texas in the 1990s was accused of looking like "four spiders having an orgy"[7] (Figure 5.2).

The Supreme Court has generally allowed gerrymandering by state governments, but only within limits. Congressional districts must be contiguous, or "all of one piece" geographically. Although the Supreme Court still allows state governments to draw districts to give a particular political party an advantage in elections, districts cannot be drawn by any state in ways that systematically disadvantage population groups that historically have been discriminated against in elections. The Court, for example, carefully examines districts drawn in southern states because of the region's long history of discrimination against

[7] Sam Roberts, "Will District Mappers Ever Draw the Line?" *New York Times*, March 23, 1992.

FIGURE 5.2

Texas Congressional District 18, 1992

In most states, the state legislature approves boundaries of electoral districts for the U.S. House and other offices. However, districts that fail to meet the guidelines established by the Constitution and subsequent Supreme Court decisions may be found unconstitutional. This strangely shaped Houston-area district was designed by the state legislature to give African Americans a majority in the district, but the Supreme Court found it went too far, making race the predominant factor.

African Americans. In fact, the Court has permitted states to draw districts for the express purpose of enhancing minority group representation. It has struck down redistricting efforts that led to reductions in the number of black representatives and other minority representatives to state legislatures or the U.S. Congress, and it has allowed redistricting that has deliberately led to increases in the number of black or Latino representatives. In 2015, for instance, the Court struck down an Alabama redistricting plan because the judges determined that it had been motivated by a desire to limit minority representation, as opposed to enhance it.

Certain U.S. counties and states with histories of discrimination in elections against minorities for many years had their districting plans subject to automatic review by the federal government due to the 1965 Voting Rights Act. A key Supreme Court ruling in 2013 (*Shelby County v. Holder*) invalidated the automatic process by which those areas had to have their districting plans reviewed. The ruling indicated that the original section of the Voting Rights Act (Section 5) was no longer based on current data about the demographics of those states and countries, and that Congress would have to write a new law reflecting contemporary information. As of early 2019, Congress had not passed such a law updating Section 5 of the Voting Rights Act.

As for individualism in Congress, districting for House seats can certainly intensify the need for members of Congress to make personal connections to voters. Redistricting after a census can sometimes make an incumbent safer in his or her seat by drawing the lines so that voters of the other party are now in another district. Conversely, redistricting can make the incumbent's district more competitive and thus hurt reelection efforts. Not surprisingly, the redistricting process is closely watched by members of Congress, who often feel that state-level politics determines their reelection fate. The best way for incumbents to protect themselves against the vagaries of redistricting is to make sure that constituents appreciate the members' work on their behalf regardless of party affiliation.

Other Electoral Factors. The individualism of American congressional candidates and members of Congress has increased over time, not only because of institutional changes such as the rise of primary elections for ballot access but also because of methods of campaigning and the kinds of policies the national government adopts. Since the latter half of the twentieth century, candidates have increasingly used television advertising to gain personal name recognition. Television advertising takes a lot of money, and to earn a seat in Congress candidates need to raise money from individual donors, interest groups, corporations, and political party fund-raising organizations so that they can hire a campaign staff and advertise their candidacy. Congressional candidates have to raise their own money for campaigns, and critics of Congress focus on the potential benefits that Congress can bestow on specific industries or companies that donate money to campaigns. Critics argue that members of Congress rely on wealthy donors to win and retain their seats, and therefore the legislation they pass mostly benefits contributors to campaigns. (We will discuss the ideas of these critics in more detail at the end of this chapter.)

The growth of the national government's power has also contributed to making elections more candidate centered. In the nineteenth century, when the federal government played a smaller role in the economic life of the country than it does now, state-level parties dominated congressional elections. In the early twentieth century, about the same time as the switch toward primary elections, the federal government began to enact legislation affecting the economic well-being of every congressional district in the country. The increase in national government power and wealth relative to the states meant that members of Congress could plausibly take credit as individual politicians for protecting their districts from such potentially harmful legislation such as new taxes or regulations. They could also claim credit for bringing home as many government benefits as possible, such as research grants or public works projects.

Recall our brief discussion of the distributional model of Congress (discussed in more detail later). Those who favor this model find the most convincing evidence to be from the era post-1930s.

The individualism in Congress is real and consequential, and as we will discuss shortly, it makes solving collective dilemmas inside the chambers a daunting task. But this individualism should not be overstated. Members of Congress do cooperate and do feel constrained by collective goals.[8] In fact, legislators work closely with their fellow party members, as we will see later and again in Chapter 12. Nevertheless, Congress needs effective institutions inside its chambers to do anything collectively.

Representing the District or State

Those who sit in Congress win their seats because they are good at determining what their constituents want from government. If they are effective enough as representatives, they will be reelected as a matter of course. As a rule, conservative representatives come from relatively conservative districts, and liberal representatives from relatively liberal districts. If representatives or senators are consistently out of step with their constituents, they will likely lose their jobs.

As noted earlier, a representative or senator is essentially an agent of the voters (the principals). What kinds of agents should members of Congress be for their principals? The principal-agent problem is a modern conceptualization, but political philosophers have long sought to answer the question of how best to represent constituents in a representative democracy. Edmund Burke, a nineteenth-century British member of Parliament and prominent theorist of government, proposed that representatives of a constituency sometimes act like trustees and at other times like delegates. **Trustees** make decisions within the legislature—voting, crafting bills, adding amendments—using their own judgments about what is best for their constituents. **Delegates** listen carefully to what their constituents want and make decisions based on feedback. We can think of trustees as being agents with more discretion to make their own decisions in comparison to delegates, who need to obey principals closely.

When asked in surveys, members of Congress claim that they try to balance these competing visions of representation.[9] The trustee-delegate trade-off is conspicuous when members publicly take policy positions in a manner inconsistent with what most of their constituents want. Four incumbent members of the House lost their seats in primary elections in 2018, presumably because they were not in sync with their own party voters. For example, Joseph Crowley, a Democrat of New York, lost his seat to a democratic socialist,

trustees Representatives who make decisions using their own judgments about what is best for their constituents.

delegates Representatives who listen carefully to what their constituents want and make decisions based on feedback from constituents.

[8] Nelson Polsby, *How Congress Evolves* (New York: Oxford University Press, 2004).

[9] John Kingdon, *Congressmen's Voting Decisions* (New York: Harper and Row, 1981); Richard Fenno, *Home Style: House Members and Their Districts* (Boston: Little, Brown, 1978).

Alexandria Ocasio-Cortez, because voters believed he did not adequately represent his left-leaning district.

The use of primary elections, however, means that the principals (voters) in the local election within a candidate's state or district may not exactly match the principals (voters) in the general state or national election. Indeed, primary election voters tend to be more intensely partisan than general election voters, and it can be hazardous for a candidate to vote in a manner inconsistent with what his or her party's primary voters want, even if doing so makes it harder to appeal to the broader electorate for the general election campaign. For example, Senator Richard Lugar (R-IN) voted in favor of President Obama's stimulus policies in 2009 and 2010, publicly announced his support for the practice of earmarking (inserting pork into a bill), and came out in favor of an immigration plan that many in his party felt offered amnesty to illegal immigrants. Lugar was well aware that many people who voted for him, especially Republican primary voters in his state, would be upset with him; nonetheless, he chose to act as a trustee and use his own judgment about what he thought was best for the country. Indiana has a strongly conservative state-level Republican Party, and in March 2012 Republican voters in Indiana ousted Lugar in the primary election in favor of a more conservative candidate, Richard Mourdock. Mourdock subsequently lost in the general election to the Democratic candidate, Joe Donnelly, in part because of comments Mourdock made about abortion that made him seem too extreme to many voters.

Constituency Service. An important part of the job of members of Congress is to help constituents in their interactions with the federal government. As an example, if a business owner believes that his or her company has been treated unfairly by the tax authorities or by another federal agency, it is common for that person to ask the congressional representative or senator to help clear things up, perhaps write a letter to the appropriate people in the agency or make a phone call on behalf of the business owner. Or if someone has been waiting too long to get a passport for foreign travel, a phone call from a senator's office to the Department of State (which issues passports) can speed things along. Complaints from ordinary people about the federal bureaucracy are plentiful; but when a federal agency receives a communication from a member of Congress, especially from a member of Congress on the relevant congressional committee with jurisdiction over that agency, people in that agency will pay more attention. Members of Congress of course wish to avoid being known as uncaring or unhelpful. Thus they devote staff time to what is called **constituency service**, the direct help of specific constituents with governmental matters.

If done effectively, constituency service can build tremendous goodwill among constituents. Developing a reputation for being a helpful, concerned representative or senator, especially among constituents who might be influential with other constituents (such as business owners or union leaders) or who

constituency service A legislator directly helping a constituent in dealing with government bureaucracy.

might make generous campaign donations, can bolster reelection chances considerably. Along with delivering pork to the local area or state, constituency service forms part of the individual reputations of members of Congress. However, if a member's staff devotes many hours to constituency service, and the member likewise devotes time in making phone calls or writing letters to federal agencies, less time is available to engage in collective activities such as working on legislation with broad benefits for the country or for the home state, or working with partisan allies inside Congress to pull the party together to pass or block legislation. In other words, constituency service provides individual benefits to constituents and to members of Congress, and helps with individual reputations, yet often competes with the pursuit of collective goals.

As the role of the federal government in people's lives has grown since the early twentieth century, members of Congress have had many more opportunities to come to the rescue of constituents vis-à-vis the federal government. This is one of the reasons that incumbent members of Congress have advantages over their challengers at election time.

The Incumbency Advantage. Members of Congress, especially in the House, are reelected in very high numbers. This **incumbency advantage** is indicated by Figure 5.3, which shows the proportions of incumbent House and Senate candidates that win reelection. In a typical election, it is extremely rare to defeat a sitting House member, and it is only somewhat more common to unseat a senator. The elections immediately following a census reapportionment, such as in 2012, produce more incumbent losses simply because redistricting often leads to situations where incumbents are running against incumbents, either in the primary or general election. Thus, because Ohio lost two House seats after the 2010 census, Democrats Dennis Kucinich and Marcy Kaptur were forced to run against each other in the 2012 Democratic primary. Kaptur won the primary and then went on to win the general election. Kucinich, after the redrawing of his Cleveland-area district led to his defeat, said that he briefly considered moving to Washington state and running in the district that Washington gained through reapportionment.

This measure of the incumbency advantage shown in Figure 5.3 probably overstates, though, the extent to which incumbent legislators are protected from electoral pressures. When considering whether to run for reelection, members consider their probability of winning. A political campaign is a grueling process, and few would willingly subject themselves to a campaign if they were certain they would ultimately lose. Therefore, counting only incumbents who decide to run removes from the sample several members who likely would have lost had they decided to run. Despite this, the overall levels of incumbent reelection are remarkably high and have been trending upward.

Political scientists have proposed various theories to account for this upward trend. First, state parties have had growing success, through enhanced

incumbency advantage
The advantage current officeholders have in an election, in particular as it relates to the high rates at which congressional legislators win reelection.

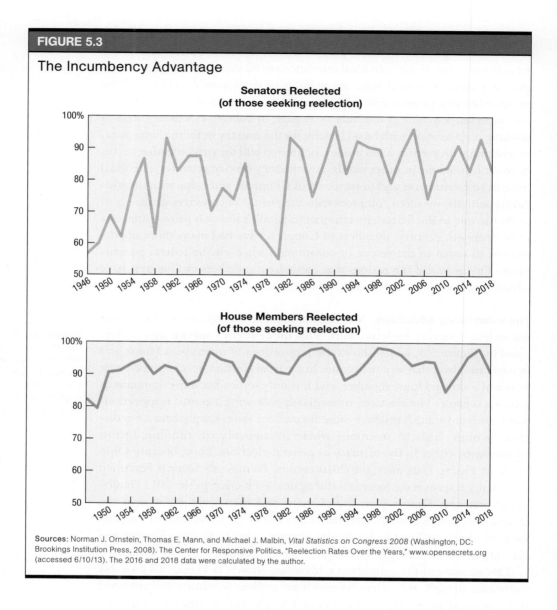

FIGURE 5.3

The Incumbency Advantage

Senators Reelected
(of those seeking reelection)

House Members Reelected
(of those seeking reelection)

Sources: Norman J. Ornstein, Thomas E. Mann, and Michael J. Malbin, *Vital Statistics on Congress 2008* (Washington, DC: Brookings Institution Press, 2008). The Center for Responsive Politics, "Reelection Rates Over the Years," www.opensecrets.org (accessed 6/10/13). The 2016 and 2018 data were calculated by the author.

computing technology, in gerrymandering districts to ensure their incumbents' reelection. Second, congressional members have demonstrated increasing skill, aided by the growth and sophistication of their staffs, in delivering pork and constituency service. This has been especially true in the decades since the 1960s, when the size of congressional staff doubled in the House and increased fourfold in the Senate. Third, members of Congress have had increasing opportunities since the 1950s to flood constituents with inexpensive or free television appearances to enhance name recognition. Throughout a session of Congress, members can grant interviews and hold press conferences to earn local television or newspaper coverage and ensure that constituents regularly hear or read their names. Such opportunities are generally unavailable to challengers, who must typically pay for advertising to gain name recognition among constituents.

Fourth, campaign finance laws have enabled incumbents to amass huge amounts of money ("war chests") and ward off potential challengers. The laws permit candidates to roll over money not spent in one election for use in the next election and also to raise money continuously during the congressional session. The fund-raising needs for challengers just to compete with well-funded incumbents can be discouraging. Fifth and finally, the national political parties have improved their organizations to target campaign money to incumbents in danger of defeat. Beginning in the 1980s, the national parties have themselves amassed large campaign war chests that they devote to protecting incumbents from their ranks.

Most political scientists argue that all of these factors—gerrymandering, pork and constituency service, television access, campaign finance, and national party efforts—contribute to the huge incumbency advantage, especially in the House. Yet scholars continue to debate which factor is the most important. Many critics of Congress see the incumbency advantage—especially as it is fueled by readily available campaign funding from wealthy segments of society—as evidence of a bias in American government toward entrenched, moneyed interests. Members of Congress and other defenders of the institution argue that the incumbency advantage is so strong because members are good at discerning and acting on constituents' preferences. Besides, the counterargument goes, the money members of Congress receive for reelection comes from people and organizations on all sides of controversial policy issues.

Minority Representation. Although incumbents win at high rates, changes since the mid-twentieth century have also increased the rates of election of minorities and women, as evidenced by the surge in women and minorities elected in 2018. An increase in minority voting followed the Voting Rights Act of 1965 and the heightened federal court scrutiny of congressional redistricting. Some scholars have speculated that the increased representation of minorities stems from efforts by state Republican parties to concentrate minority voters (who tend to vote Democratic) into a few predominantly urban districts. This strategy allegedly grants voters in those districts the minority representatives they seek, while enabling the Republicans to remain dominant in the state's other districts. This claim, however, remains controversial.[10]

---

[10] Carol Swain, *Black Faces, Black Interests* (Cambridge, MA: Harvard University Press, 1993); David Lublin, *The Paradox of Representation: Racial Gerrymandering and Minority Interests in Congress* (Princeton, NJ: Princeton University Press, 1997); David Epstein and Sharyn O'Halloran, "Measuring the Electoral and Policy Impact of Majority-Minority Voting Districts," *American Journal of Political Science* 42 (1999): 367–95.

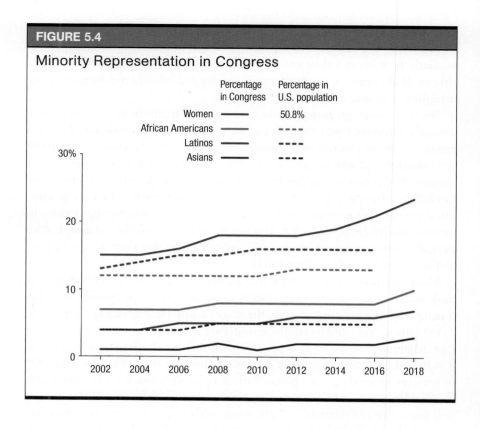

FIGURE 5.4

Minority Representation in Congress

	Percentage in Congress	Percentage in U.S. population
Women	——	50.8%
African Americans	——	- - - -
Latinos	——	- - - -
Asians	——	- - - -

Scholars do not dispute that the increase in minority representation has had notable consequences both for Congress and for American politics in general. The Congressional Black Caucus (discussed later in this chapter) has become an important organization on Capitol Hill, especially within the Democratic Party. The voting behavior of minority and women members of Congress has differed on a range of policy issues from that of their white male counterparts.[11] And the first female Speaker of the House, Nancy Pelosi, rose to that position in 2007 after the Democrats gained majority status in the 2006 election, and again in 2019.

The demographics of Congress today reflect decades of change in electoral institutions and in the U.S. population. In the 1950s, Congress was almost entirely white male. Today, as shown in Figure 5.4, noticeable proportions of the chambers are made up of minority groups traditionally facing discrimination, and of women. Congress does not mirror the general population in demographic

---

[11] Katrina L. Gamble, "Black Political Representation," *Legislative Studies Quarterly* 32, no. 3 (2007): 421–47; Michele L. Swers, "Are Women More Likely to Vote for Women's Issue Bills than Their Male Colleagues?" *Legislative Studies Quarterly* 23, no. 3 (1998): 435–48.

makeup, but it is much closer than it was half a century ago. Recent research suggests that women in Congress have been quite effective in achieving their policy goals and also critical to the success of bipartisan legislation.[12] This is increasingly relevant, as by 2019, 24 percent of members of Congress were women, its highest total ever.

The trend toward more women and minorities in Congress results from many factors. Some factors can be found in society as a whole; they include changing roles of women in society and more tolerance toward minorities in the general population. Other factors are related directly to electoral politics, such as mobilization and activism by minorities and women's rights groups, and outreach by the political parties toward new groups in order to win elections. Finally, institutional factors have mattered, such as federal and state enforcement of antidiscrimination laws in elections and voting rights, and revision of House of Representative election district boundaries.

Internal Institutions of Congress

As we have seen, several features of congressional elections have tended to promote highly individualistic behavior by members, at least in comparison to legislative behavior in most other democracies. The free-riding problem among members, for example, presents one kind of collective dilemma. When a party's leaders and most of its members in Congress agree on the need to raise taxes, to raise the pay of federal employees, or to cut spending on popular programs, it is tempting for individual members to free ride and let others in their party pay the political costs of casting the difficult votes. In other words, members have a strong incentive to do the most popular thing in the eyes of their constituents, rather than to support legislation that is seen within the party as best for the country as a whole.

The problem of unstable coalitions represents another kind of collective dilemma. Recall from Chapter 1 the problem in voting situations where any coalition can be "raided" by an alternative proposal. This problem always lurks in legislative bodies. Even if a coalition of people agrees to vote in favor of a bill, if opponents are able to propose any alternative bill they wish, it is possible that some supporters of the original bill will vote for the alternative and thus defect from their previous agreement.

The possibility of unstable coalitions highlights the importance of agenda control: who controls the agenda often determines which group wins its favored policies. If a group controls the agenda and wants the status quo to prevail, that group can prevent any vote on alternative policies. Or, if a group wants a

[12] Craig Volden, Alan Wiseman, and Dana Wittmer, "When Are Women More Effective Lawmakers than Men?" *American Journal of Political Science* 57 (April 2013): 326–41.

specific change to the status quo, it can control the alternatives being voted on to get its preferred policy outcome. A group needs to control not only what alternatives are proposed but also the order of the votes. The key insight is in the importance of maintaining agenda control and not giving it up. If the floor is open for anyone to propose any alternative and no one controls the agenda, cycling between different alternatives can continue indefinitely.[13]

The institutions and procedures of Congress are designed to grant agenda control to a small subset of people who carefully manage the flow of legislation. These institutions help overcome free-riding problems, and they also help prevent potential coalition raiding in legislation. As we will see, the institutions inside Congress solve many kinds of collective dilemmas and principal-agent problems. Before examining these institutions in detail, let's gain some historical perspective.

An Increasingly Institutionalized Congress

The Constitution says virtually nothing about how Congress should conduct its internal business apart from specifying a few voting rules, such as the two-thirds requirement to overcome vetoes or pass treaties. The first meeting of Congress in 1789 in New York City included 65 members in the House and 26 members in the Senate. It was composed of leading politicians of the day, including many of the Founders. To conduct business, members initially met as a full body rather than breaking into smaller committees. The House, however, quickly established its first committee, Ways and Means, and went on to develop several others. Only 144 bills were proposed in the first Congress (as compared with thousands today), though they involved such weighty matters as the future location of the nation's capital, Revolutionary War debt, foreign relations, domestic relations with Native Americans, national expansion, and postal services.

Congress changed over time in ways that mirrored the nation's development. Congress grew larger as new states were added. As discussed, House membership reached its peak and was capped in 1911 at 435 voting members. There are now 100 Senators, two from each of the 50 states. As the national government's responsibilities expanded in relation to those of the states, so too did the prestige of congressional membership versus membership in state legislatures. It was common in the early nineteenth century for state-level politicians to spend short spells in Congress and then return to the state level

---

[13] There are real examples of cycles occurring in Congress. See William Riker, "The Paradox of Voting and Congressional Rules for Voting on Amendments," *American Political Science Review* 52 (1958): 349–66; or John Blydenburgh, "The Closed Rule and the Paradox of Voting," *Journal of Politics* 33 (1971): 57–71.

where they could exert real influence. Between the mid-nineteenth century and the 1960s, however, the average tenure for a member of the House increased from two to five terms.

Furthermore, as the country became an industrial and military power, and as the national government took on greater responsibilities, Congress developed an increasingly elaborate committee system to deal with the volume and complexity of legislation. Its operations became more organized and rule based. Political scientists have summarized this process by saying that Congress became increasingly *institutionalized* over time.[14] The Congress we know today would not be recognizable to the Founders. Although the atmosphere on the floor of the House and Senate on the whole might seem dignified and relatively quiet, behind the scenes Congress is a very busy place. Hallways, members' offices, and committee meetings swarm with politicians, lobbyists, reporters, foreign dignitaries, experts, and citizens. Yet through remarkably efficient organization Congress manages, in an average year, to deal with approximately 9,000 proposed bills and pass 400 to 500 into law (though fewer bills have been passed in recent years). Its professional, well-paid legislators are assisted by some 11,000 staff members and a large number of congressional bureaus that conduct research and provide other services. Roughly 250 committees and subcommittees work in both chambers. More than 10,000 officially registered lobbyists try to influence congressional policy making.

The internal operations of Congress are highly bureaucratic and follow codified rules. Recall our definition of a political institution from Chapter 1: a rule or set of rules or practices that determines how people make collective decisions. Congress, especially the House, is considered to be highly institutionalized today because it has elaborate, codified rules of conduct.

These codes for behavior are expressed both in the internal rules of the two chambers, which are voted on by all the members, and in rules established by the political parties. Two institutional aspects of internal congressional politics are paramount: party leadership and committees. Party leaders, especially those from the majority, are like orchestra conductors: they make sure that things run smoothly, and they allocate resources and time to different members of the legislature. The committees function more like specific sections of the orchestra by doing their part to contribute to the overall performance. The party leaders orchestrate while the committees specialize. Their combined efforts provide the final product.

---

[14] Nelson W. Polsby, "The Institutionalization of the U.S. House of Representatives," *American Political Science Review* 62, no. 1 (1968): 144–68.

Party Leaders

The majority and minority parties in Congress each elect their leaders in the House and Senate. Leaders are elected at their party's caucus (meetings of all the party members within each chamber), which typically occurs at the beginning of each two-year congressional session. By orchestrating the conduct of members, party leaders can be seen as repeatedly solving coordination problems. They do this partly by trying to enforce **party discipline**—pressuring party members to vote on bills that have the support of the party leadership—on important votes, but they also help organize congressional business in other ways. If different committees or factions in Congress fail to coordinate, then nothing can get done and all members of the parties will be worse off. The party leaders make their members better off by getting them to coordinate on common action.[15]

House members vote to choose the **Speaker of the House**, the most important legislator in that chamber and in the country. The Speaker's position is considered so central to American politics that by law, he or she is second in line behind the vice president in the presidential succession. Should the president and vice president both die or otherwise become unable to serve out the term, the Speaker automatically becomes president. In fact, the Speaker of the House and his or her counterpart in the Senate, the Senate majority leader, often meet together and with the president on weighty matters of state.

In the 1890s, Congress began to follow rules adopted by then Speaker of the House Thomas Reed, perhaps the most feared and powerful person ever to hold that post. Congress was deadlocked on tariff policy because coalitions continually unraveled due to free riding and coalition raiding. The minority party used tactics repeatedly to derail legislation favored by the majority. By controlling the agenda more effectively in the House, Reed achieved his goal of raising tariffs. This is a classic example of how institutional changes within the House can bring about policy consequences that have important effects on the economy. **Reed's Rules**, which are still in place, specify procedural guidelines for how the majority party leadership should determine who sits on which committees, how the order of business should be decided, and how the majority party should limit the powers of the minority party. Congress today largely operates under the broad guidelines of these rules.

Below the House Speaker in the majority party are the **majority leader** and **whip**, who help the Speaker organize the chamber for business, raise money for elections, and encourage party members to vote for party-sponsored bills. The minority party also elects its leaders, the minority leader and the minority

party discipline Pressure on party members to vote on bills that have the support of the party leadership.

Speaker of the House The constitutionally designated leader of the House of Representatives. In the modern House, he or she is always the leader of the majority party.

Reed's Rules Procedural guidelines used by the majority party leadership for determining who sits on which committees, how the order of business should be decided, and how the majority party should limit the powers of the minority party.

majority leader The head of the party holding a majority of seats and, in the Senate, the leader of the Senate. In the House, the majority leader is second to the Speaker of the House.

whip A member of the House or Senate who is elected by his or her party to help party leaders coordinate party members' actions, including enforcing party discipline.

[15] Gary Cox and Mathew McCubbins, *Legislative Leviathan*, 2nd ed. (New York: Cambridge University Press, 2007).

HISTORICAL PATH Major Developments in Congress

1806 The Senate agrees to a rule that limits the use of calling the previous question, a dilatory tactic commonly used to thwart legislative action.

1850 The Missouri Compromise unravels, throwing off the balance of power in the Senate and setting the stage for the Civil War.

1917 The Senate agrees to a cloture rule, which ends debate if 2/3 of the senators agree to proceed to a vote.

1913 The Seventeenth Amendment provides for the direct election of senators.

2013 The Senate cloture rule is changed so that only 51 votes are needed to invoke cloture on executive and judicial appointments (except appointments to the Supreme Court).

1947 The number of standing committees in the House is reduced from 48 to 19.

1974 The number of votes required to end debate is reduced from 2/3 to 3/5 of the Senate.

1800　　　　　　　　　　**1900**　　　　　　　　　　**2000**

1789 The First Congress meets in New York City.

1820 The Missouri Compromise ensures that pro-slavery and antislavery forces will be numerically balanced in the Senate.

1890 Reed's Rules take effect, dramatically increasing the majority party's power and that of the Speaker of the House.

1911 A revolt against Speaker Cannon installs seniority system for determining chairmanship of House committees.

1911 The size of the House is capped at 435.

1947 The number of standing committees in the Senate is reduced from 33 to 15.

1995 Speaker Newt Gingrich introduces term limits for committee chairs, and partially abandons the seniority system for choosing them.

whip. (The term *whip* is derived from the British word for the person who keeps the dogs in line during foxhunts.)

In the Senate, the majority party chooses the Senate majority leader and also a party whip, while the minority party elects the minority leader and minority whip. Additional leadership posts include the chairs of the four party caucuses (one for each party in each chamber) and the four fund-raising committees (again, one for each party in each chamber). Together with the top leaders, these legislators gather often to plan legislative and electoral strategy. The majority party leaders determine the content and order of business. For example, they choose which proposed bills will be considered and when, and which bills will be ignored. Both the majority and the minority leaders appoint committee members and select who will be allowed to speak from the floor and in what order.

Although it is hard to deny that party leaders are extremely important, their power is limited by the persistent individualism of their members. As a result, political parties in Congress are relatively weak in contrast to their parliamentary counterparts in other countries. This means there is less party unity in voting. It is not uncommon in Congress for as many as 20 percent of a party's members to vote against their party's stated position and the majority of their colleagues. As discussed earlier (and in the following pages), this type of voting defection is rare in other countries because party leaders effectively choose who can serve in parliament by controlling who gets on the ballot at election time.

Coordination among party leadership is an important institutional element that shapes legislative behavior and outcomes and helps solve inherent collective dilemmas in Congress. Pictured here are the Republican House leadership. House Minority Leader Kevin McCarthy (R-CA), standing in front, is joined by: Conference Chair Liz Cheney (R-WY, left), Minority Whip Steve Scalise (R-LA, second from right), among other members of the leadership.

Committees

While the leadership orchestrates business, much of the detailed legislative work in Congress occurs in committees. Committees have jurisdictions, which means they have discretion over certain policy areas. For instance, foreign aid bills are sent to the Senate Foreign Relations Committee in that chamber, and most likely to the Appropriations Committee in the House. Farm–related bills go to the agriculture committees, and those for science funding are sent either to the Science Committee in the House or to the Commerce, Science, and Transportation Committee in the Senate.

Types of Committees. There are several types of congressional committees. The most well known are the **standing committees**, which remain in existence permanently unless they are formally abolished. Among these are the important House Ways and Means Committee and Senate Finance Committee, which deal with taxes and spending. Committees with more specialized jurisdictions, such as agriculture, science, veterans' affairs, small business, or

standing committee A group of legislators given permanent jurisdiction over a particular issue area or type of policy.

foreign relations, tend to attract members whose constituents care deeply about or are directly affected by policy in these areas. Agriculture committees, therefore, are primarily composed of members who represent states with large farming sectors while committees that deal with federal government operations are heavily populated by legislators from Maryland, Virginia, and West Virginia, which are home to most of the federal government's offices.[16]

Special (or select) committees are formed for a specific purpose and in principle are dissolved after accomplishing their tasks. An example is the Joint Select Committee on Deficit Reduction (or its nickname, the Supercommittee), which was created in 2011 to avoid partisan gridlock on budget matters that could have led to the United States defaulting on its loans. The Supercommittee was also an example of a joint committee. **Joint committees** include members from both the House and the Senate—there is a Joint Committee on Taxation, for instance. In recent years, the House and Senate Select Intelligence Committees have acted in tandem, submitting joint reports and regularly meeting together. In practice, many select committees end up being as permanent as standing committees. Three Senate select committees—on Indian affairs, intelligence, and aging—have existed for decades.

Conference committees consist of members of both chambers and are sometimes formed when each chamber passes a different version of the same bill. These committees, which are formed specific to a given bill and at the point in the process when the two chambers agree that reconciliation of the two bills is necessary, play a crucial role in congressional lawmaking. Most bills that pass do not require the formation and use of a conference committee, and often the two chambers work out their differences without conference committees. But conference committees become necessary for many important and controversial bills. Their job is to craft a compromise bill that both chambers will eventually approve.

The House Rules Committee, the traditional vehicle used by the majority party leadership to control House business, deserves special note. It determines which bills get considered for votes, under which amendment rules, and in which order. (We will discuss this committee in more detail later.) In general, since the late nineteenth century, the Rules Committee has been dominated by majority party members with close ties to the party leadership and has served as a means for the leadership to stop and start legislative action. The Rules Committee can prevent a bill from being voted on by the chamber. By tradition, the majority party holds 9 of the 13 seats on the Rules Committee, and the Speaker tightly controls which majority party members sit on the committee.

special (or select) committee A committee appointed to consider a special issue or serve a special function that disbands once it has completed its duties.

joint committee A committee made up of members of both the House and Senate.

conference committee A meeting of legislators from the House and Senate to reconcile two bills passed on the same topic.

---

[16] The boundaries among committees' responsibilities shift over time. Frequently, committees jockey for control of a particular type of policy. The Speaker of the House or the Senate majority leader arbitrates disagreements in the respective chambers. Control over the outcome of these disagreements is one of the sources of a chamber leader's power. See David C. King, *Turf Wars: How Congressional Committees Claim Jurisdiction* (Chicago: University of Chicago Press, 1997).

Committee Membership. Each committee has a chair who oversees its work. Chairs of the major committees are powerful people in the American political system. In many instances, they can by themselves determine the fate of legislation. They can defeat a bill by slowing it down in the committee, ignoring it, or encouraging colleagues to amend it to death by watering it down until it no longer accomplishes its original purpose. Chairs can also insert items into bills with dramatic consequences. In one instance of major historical importance, Howard Smith of Virginia, chair of the House Rules Committee in the early 1960s, single-handedly inserted into the bill that eventually became the Civil Rights Act of 1964 a provision that gender was to be a protected category similar to race. This meant that people could be sued for discriminating against people because of their sex. He made the provision a requirement of his support for the bill. Many historians believe that Smith, who generally opposed new federal civil rights laws for blacks, actually made the addition to kill the bill. He mistakenly thought that his colleagues would reject the new provision and thus the bill.

Furthermore, most standing committees have subcommittees to address specific topics. Composed of members of the full committee, subcommittees can be quite important, and subcommittee chairs wield considerable power over legislation in their jurisdiction.

Determining committee assignments is a highly political process. As previously noted, members on all committees are assigned by their party leaders, and majority party members hold most of the seats on each committee.

Consequences of the Committee System. The committee system is well suited to accomplishing two somewhat contradictory goals: creating better public policy and assisting members in their reelection efforts. First, the committee system provides expertise to improve lawmaking and is the key, distinctive institutional feature of Congress. Crafting effective public policy that will make constituents content and want to reelect incumbents is difficult. The average member of Congress may not know much about agricultural price supports, or the finer points of nuclear power, or defense strategy in the Middle East. But by creating a committee system and enabling members to specialize, both the entire legislative body and the entire country benefit.

Second, the committee system is well suited to members' individualism. The system fragments political power and redirects the limelight, enabling members to play a role in crafting legislation and earn credit from constituents. Each member, through his or her role on key committees of concern to constituents, can credibly claim to be powerful and important. Furthermore, committees give special opportunities to their members to insert into legislation language granting government projects specifically to one district or state.[17]

[17] Kenneth A. Shepsle, *The Giant Jigsaw Puzzle: Democratic Committee Assignments in the Modern House* (Chicago: University of Chicago Press, 1978).

The internal makeup of the U.S. Congress varies from that of parliaments in other countries mostly because of the power of its committees. Congressional committees act as gatekeepers for nearly all legislation proposed for the national government. Although there are committees in most nations' parliaments, they play a less important role. This is because drafting, amending, and debating legislation usually occur in the cabinet of the head of government before the legislation is sent to the parliament for approval. The main personnel in the executive departments and the leaders of the government, therefore, have already vetted legislation introduced to the parliaments. Bills are presented to the parliament as faits accomplis, to be voted "up" or "down" (almost always up) with little need for committee work. Political party leaders in other countries are far and away the most powerful actors in the legislature, serving as arbiters of which legislative members may speak, propose amendments to legislation, or run for reelection. In short, the existence of powerful committees is a feature that makes the U.S. Congress less hierarchical than its foreign counterparts. Table 5.1 shows the major committees in Congress, plus a few smaller ones.

The role of committees in allowing members to examine specialized information in specific policy areas is central to the expertise model of Congress. Here, Loretta Lynch, Attorney General under President Obama, testifies in the Senate on a plan to expand background checks on firearms purchases.

Other Internal Features

Besides parties and committees, other elements make up the institutional machinery inside Congress. Nonparty caucuses, congressional staffers, and bureaus that carry out research services and other activities play important roles.

Caucuses. In addition to the party caucuses in each chamber (made up of the members of that party), nonparty **caucuses** represent a third way for members to group themselves and conduct business. Unlike committees, caucuses are not given formal legislative power, nor do they command much in the way of resources or disciplinary mechanisms to hold their members in line. Rather, they are a means by which groups of members can push agendas that are not pursued within the parties or the committees. Several important caucuses align by racial identity, such as the Congressional Black Caucus, or by ideology, such as the conservative House Freedom Caucus.[18]

caucus In a legislature, a group of legislators that unites to promote an agenda not pursued within the parties or the legislative committees.

Staff. Congressional staff play a large role in Congress. Hired by representatives and senators who have many competing demands on their time, staffers are indispensable. They operate members' offices; communicate with constituents,

[18] The term *caucus* can be confusing. A party caucus is a meeting of party members. Nonparty caucuses are groups of legislators who pursue common policy goals that are more specific than the broad ideological goals pursued by parties.

TABLE 5.1

Selected Congressional Committees, 2018

Committee	Description	Number of Members
House Committee on Financial Services	Addresses issues pertaining to the economy, banking system, housing, insurance, and securities and exchanges	60
House Committee on Appropriations	Appropriates all funds that the U.S. Treasury will spend	51
House Committee on Ways and Means	Serves as the chief tax-writing committee in the House	40
House Committee on Homeland Security	Crafts legislations and holds hearings for matters of domestic security	30
House Committee on Rules	Determines the rules under which the House will receive a piece of legislation	13
Senate Committee on Finance	Responsible for tax policy and health care policy	27
Senate Committee on Armed Forces	Responsible for the common defense and all branches of the U.S. military	27
Senate Committee on Banking, House, and Urban Affairs	Charged with the policy areas that include banking, insurance, financial markets, mass transit, housing, and urban development	25
Senate Committee on the Judiciary	Considers presidential nominations for federal judgeships, and oversees the Department of Justice	21
Senate Committee on Foreign Relations	Considers all diplomatic presidential nominations; also responsible for treaties and legislation related to foreign relations	21
Senate Committee on Indian Affairs	Oversees issues pertaining to American Indian education, health care, economic development, land management, and claims against the United States	15
Senate Commission on Security and Cooperation in Europe	Monitors and aims to advance European security	9

the press, and other staffers on the members' behalf; organize the members' schedules; and even advise members and help them write legislation. Senior staffers, who make a career of working on Capitol Hill, tend to work directly for a committee and can be very influential in shaping how the committee operates and makes decisions. Staff sizes have grown substantially since the 1950s, although that growth has recently tailed off. Currently over 12,000 staffers are working for members of Congress.

Separate from staff who work directly on legislative business, members of Congress also hire staff to manage their reelection campaigns. Funding and staffing for legislative work and for campaign work must be kept separate by law, but the growth in numbers of both kinds of staff help explain the sub-

The Congressional Hispanic Caucus focuses on issues that affect minority groups, especially the Hispanic community. Here, Rep. Nydia Velázquez (D-NY) and other members of the Caucus hold a news conference to speak about the recovery effort in Puerto Rico after Hurricane Maria devastated the area in 2017.

stantial incumbency advantage. The legislative staff can help work on pork-barrel aspects of legislation and constituency service, while campaign staff can help with the direct work of running the reelection campaign, such as raising money and appealing to constituents for their vote.

Research Services. Congress has created its own internal bureaucracy to help its members conduct research and carry out other duties. These congressional bureaus have become increasingly important as counterweights to the bureaus that formally reside in the executive branch. The congressional bureaus, such as the Congressional Budget Office (CBO), were created because members of Congress—especially in the wake of the Nixon administration's Watergate scandal in the 1970s—had become suspicious of the data presented by executive branch agencies. The CBO, for example, was established as a balance to the executive Office of Management and Budget (OMB), which was regarded as too closely tied to the president's own political goals. The Congressional Research Service provides reports on policy topics upon request for members of Congress. One example of such reports is an analysis that shows how well Veterans Administration hospitals are meeting the needs of soldiers returning from war who have experienced trauma leading to mental illness. This report is designed to help the House and Senate Veterans Affairs Committees write legislation to improve matters in these hospitals.

The Process of Lawmaking

We have learned about the incentives that motivate members of Congress and the institutions inside of Congress. Let's now turn to the process of lawmaking. In this section, we will see how the institutions inside of Congress work to assist members in overcoming their collective dilemmas and principal-agent problems to pass legislation.

Proposals

Passing a law in Congress begins with at least one member of either the House or the Senate submitting a bill to his or her respective chamber. Only legislators themselves can formally submit a bill; no one else, not even the president, can do so. Some bills are proposed that everyone knows were written by the Office of the President, executive branch agencies, or interest groups, but they must always be submitted by surrogates in Congress. Bills can have multiple sponsors. Sponsoring a popular bill can earn kudos from constituents, and sometimes there are dozens and even hundreds of sponsors of a bill.

The volume of proposed bills is huge—around 9,000 per year in recent sessions. Once submitted in either the House or Senate, bills are given a number in each chamber and assigned to a committee and then usually to a subcommittee. With 9,000 bills per year proposed, party leaders have to solve a massive coordination problem. The only way to focus members' attention and effort is to ignore most of the proposed bills so that members of their party can coordinate action on a select few. Otherwise, members will divide their efforts among too many bills competing for attention. Given the work needed to pass legislation, this approach would risk none of the bills being passed. In fact, thousands of bills are proposed every year by members who know they will not be acted on. But the members have their own reasons for submitting bills, typically to brag to specific constituents that they did so.

Referrals

The nonpartisan parliamentarian routinely doles out the proposed bills, where a bill's topic usually determines which committee receives it. But for important or controversial bills, the Speaker of the House and Senate majority party leaders can strategically use the process of committee referral. For instance, if the Speaker does not like a bill about agricultural trade and has a choice between sending it to the Agriculture Committee or the International Relations Committee, he or she can send it to the one where it is more likely to

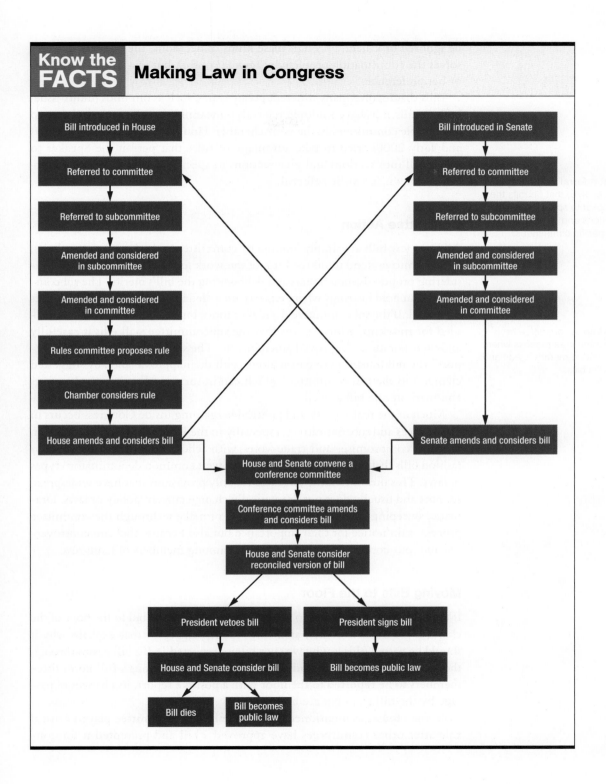

Know the FACTS: Making Law in Congress

Bill introduced in House
↓
Referred to committee
↓
Referred to subcommittee
↓
Amended and considered in subcommittee
↓
Amended and considered in committee
↓
Rules committee proposes rule
↓
Chamber considers rule
↓
House amends and considers bill

Bill introduced in Senate
↓
Referred to committee
↓
Referred to subcommittee
↓
Amended and considered in subcommittee
↓
Amended and considered in committee
↓
Senate amends and considers bill

House and Senate convene a conference committee
↓
Conference committee amends and considers bill
↓
House and Senate consider reconciled version of bill

President vetoes bill
↓
House and Senate consider bill
↓
Bill dies / **Bill becomes public law**

President signs bill
↓
Bill becomes public law

be ignored or killed. Through these kinds of decisions, the Speaker in effect solves the coordination problem by agenda control, but in a way that suits his or her preferences.

Bills that involve many different policy issues, such as omnibus (multi-issue) budget bills, can have multiple referrals—meaning that the same bill can go to multiple committees in the same chamber. House Republicans in the 1990s and early 2000s tried to take advantage of rules that permit the Speaker to split a bill into sections and give sections to specific committees. This strategy is known as a **split referral**.

split referral A rule (in place since 1975) that permits the Speaker to split a bill into sections and give sections to specific committees.

Committee Action

All but a few bills are simply ignored by committee and subcommittee chairs. Subcommittees tend to do the bulk of the work for bills taken seriously, considering proposed amendments and deliberating the bill's merits. The subcommittee can hold hearings where experts are called in to testify about the merits of the bill. If the subcommittee decides to move forward, then the bill is scheduled for **markup**, which means that the subcommittee will edit it carefully and incorporate any approved amendments. The subcommittee can then "report" the bill (meaning to pass it along with their approval and any suggested changes) to the full committee, which can in turn conduct its own hearings and mark up the bill as well.

markup A committee or subcommittee process where committee members edit and amend bills.

Much of the real activity and political bargaining inside Congress occurs in committees and subcommittees, especially in the House. Members must often bargain, compromise, and trade votes with fellow committee members to fashion bills that seem, in the end, to be "lowest common denominator" types of laws. This means that the bill includes only provisions that have widespread support and usually does not dramatically change current policy or laws. Dramatic, sweeping changes that become law, or make it through the committee process, gain notice for their importance but also because they are controversial and spur conflict among lobbyists and among members of Congress.

Moving Bills to the Floor

If the full committee wishes to move forward, it sends the bill to the floor of the chamber for a possible vote, along with a written report that explains why it should be passed (this is why we say a bill is "reported"). If a bill passes through the subcommittee process and gathers the support of enough full committee members to be reported to the floor with a positive report, its chances of passage by the full chamber are high.

In the House, as mentioned earlier, the Rules Committee plays a critical role after other committees have approved a bill and presented it for consideration by the entire chamber floor. The Rules Committee formally decides the bills to be considered for votes on the floor, what rules will be applied—such as the types of amendments that are permitted as the proposed legislation comes out of committee markup—and how much time will be allotted for debate. Through this committee, House party leaders have greater authority than their Senate counterparts over what happens on the floor of the chamber. Scholars argue that having something like a Rules Committee is vital to the proper functioning of a large chamber like the House. Without an agenda setter, the House would be far more vulnerable to the problems of unstable coalitions and other collective dilemmas, such as a lack of coordination among different committees working on the same bill.

The House Rules Committee's options for amendments allowable on the floor, for example, include

- **Open rule**, which means any amendment can be proposed.
- **Closed rule**, which means no amendments can be proposed.
- **Restricted (or modified) rule**, which specifies that only certain kinds of amendments are allowed. This typically is a "germaneness rule," which means that only amendments pertaining to the original purpose of the bill can be proposed.

open rule A provision that allows any amendment to be proposed once a bill comes to the chamber floor.

closed rule A provision that allows no amendments to be proposed once a bill comes to the chamber floor.

restricted (or modified) rule A provision that allows only certain kinds of amendments to be proposed once a bill comes to the chamber floor, typically only amendments that pertain to the original purpose of the bill.

Majority party leadership in the House, through the Rules Committee, can choose an amendment rule to thwart its opponents on a bill. Those opponents could be within the majority party or among the minority party members. Let's consider several scenarios.

First, assuming the leadership likes a bill and wants to see it passed in something similar to its present form, it may worry about the bill being amended to death on the floor and having its main effects gutted. In this case, the Rules Committee would adopt either a closed or a restricted rule. Second, assuming the leadership does not like a bill in its present form but wants to pass something along the same lines, then it would adopt a restricted or open rule and let allies on the floor offer amendments to change the bill accordingly. Third, assuming the leadership does not like a bill and wants to see it killed but feels public pressure to allow a floor vote, it may permit the bill to go to the floor under an open rule and let an unrestricted amendment process gut and perhaps even kill the bill.

Scholars in favor of the view that political parties are central to the working of the Congress (the *partisan* model of Congress discussed in the last section of this chapter) often use the centrality of the Rules Committee in the legislative process as evidence to support their claims. Majority party leadership can use the committee's powers over debate and amendment to get what it wants. The Rules Committee can itself kill a bill, even if that bill has been reported out of another committee.[19]

The Senate's process of moving a bill from committee to the floor is different from that of the House and gives less control to the majority party in that chamber. The Senate has a long tradition of giving more power to individual senators, even those from the minority party, to raise objections, propose amendments, and even halt legislation. Thus the Senate has a reputation for being the slower, more cautious chamber, where more potential roadblocks are put up by senators objecting to a bill.

There is no rules committee in the Senate, and in theory there are no limits on debate or on amendments from the floor. In the House, most of the real action is in the committees, whereas in the Senate, it is at least as common for real action to occur on the floor of the chamber as in committees. Less work happens in committees in the Senate than in the House due to the long-standing tradition of debate and amendment of bills on the Senate floor. Why should a committee bother to devote a lot of time to markups if their work will be undone on the floor? Let's look closer at these aspects, and others, of the Senate.

Senate Distinctiveness

Individual senators even have certain powers to halt the progress of a bill they do not like. In allowing "nongermane amendments" in the Senate, individual senators retain a great deal of power because they can add amendments that determine the fate of a given bill, even if those amendments have nothing to do with the purpose of the legislation. Or they can **filibuster**, which means that once recognized to speak on the floor, a senator can prevent any other action from happening on the bill. The filibustering senator can "hold" the floor in hopes that the bill's proponents will get tired or frustrated and drop the proposed legislation. The current record is held by the late Strom Thurmond of South Carolina, who spoke for more than 24 hours straight to prevent his colleagues from voting on a civil rights bill in 1957. In 2016, a group of Democratic senators, led by Connecticut senator Chris Murphy, held the floor for 15 hours. They took turns to speak and refused to let any other business be conducted in the Senate until the chamber agreed to vote on gun control legislation. Although this filibuster did not lead to any significant gun control legislation (the Republican-led House and Senate did not pass any

filibuster Instances in which senators, once recognized to speak on the floor, talk for an extended period ("hold the floor") in an attempt to block the rest of the Senate from voting on a bill.

[19] In rare instances, a majority of the House has used a *discharge petition* to force a regular standing committee or the Rules Committee to report out a bill that would otherwise die in committee. When that happens, members can petition to require a floor debate or a floor vote. If the petition gets a majority of votes, then the Speaker must comply. In a famous example, the Bipartisan Campaign Finance Act (known as the McCain-Feingold Act, after its authors) was discharged several times over a four-year period, forcing debate and votes on the floor against the wishes of party leaders, including the Speaker. The bill eventually passed in 2002. The discharge petition is rare enough that we can still ascribe very strong agenda-setting powers to the Rules Committee.

bills on the topic 2016–18), it did ignite support from many Americans in favor of gun control.

Senate rules currently include allowing a filibuster to occur simply by invoking it for a specific bill without requiring someone to actually speak on the floor. This rule allows Senate business to continue on other bills while a given bill is being filibustered. Fellow senators can stop a filibuster by voting to invoke **cloture**, which is a rule to limit debate on a bill to a specific number of hours. For many years it took two-thirds of the Senate to invoke cloture, but that was changed in 1975. It now takes 60 votes to approve cloture. In practice, this rule means that (with rare exceptions) any bill that is not supported by at least 60 senators will not be approved and will therefore not become law. In 2013 the Democratic majority in the Senate changed the cloture rules so that only 51 votes would be required to invoke cloture when confirming judicial and executive branch appointees (with the exception of Supreme Court justice nominees).

Senate procedures tend to keep legislation flowing despite the powers of senators to stymie legislation. Although unlimited debate and open amendment rules are in theory the way of the Senate, in practice the Senate uses **unanimous consent agreements** for relatively uncontroversial bills. These agreements describe rules for a given bill regarding debate and amendments on the floor. They are unanimous in that all senators must agree to them, and any senator can object and halt progress on a bill. Like the House Rules Committee, these agreements are an institutional means by which Senate members in the chamber can restrain individual action and solve collective dilemmas. In the absence of a unanimous consent agreement, for instance, the Senate could keep voting repeatedly for newly amended bills, producing voting cycles, because each senator could in theory keep proposing new amendments under the open rules.

Moreover, to a greater degree than members of the House, senators have developed norms for cooperation and for collegiality in their everyday interactions with each other. Most of the time senators, even from the opposing party, do not object to rules of debate and voting on the floor proposed by the majority party leadership. They typically give their approval to a unanimous consent agreement by not objecting, unless they feel very strongly about the bill. In other words, the norm among senators is not to abuse their individual prerogatives on issues that are not all that important to them. These norms are one way that senators can overcome the various collective dilemmas arising from their temptations to halt any collective actions that they do not like.

There is some evidence in recent decades, as the major political parties in Congress have polarized ideologically, that the norms just described have frayed somewhat. The use of holds, filibusters, and arcane parliamentary maneuvers to achieve legislative goals has increased, according to scholars. We will discuss these trends in more detail shortly.

cloture A rule that limits the debate on a bill to a specific number of hours. Senate rules require 60 senators to support such a motion to end the debate (including filibusters) and proceed to a vote.

unanimous consent agreement Rules under which the Senate debates, offers amendments, and votes on a given bill. All members of the chamber must agree to them, so any senator can object and halt progress on a bill.

The Collective Dilemma

O
n June 22, 2016, Democrats staged a sit-in on the House floor to demand that the House vote on an amendment that would ban anyone on the government's no-fly list from purchasing a gun. The idea was colloquially referred to as "no fly, no buy." In response, Speaker of the House, Republican Paul Ryan, called for a recess. Accordingly, the video cameras that film the House in session stopped rolling to avoid giving publicity to the sit-in. One of the participating representatives, however, began streaming the protest on a cell phone, allowing outside observers to witness what would become a 26-hour sit-in. Filming on the House floor using personal electronic devices is in violation of the rules. Yet, the Democrats endorsed this as a way to publicize the event and remained unapologetic for doing so. House Minority Leader Nancy Pelosi called the sit-in a "discussion heard around the world."[a] She and her colleagues scoffed at the possibility of a punitive response from House Republicans.[b] How do these tactics fit in with procedural rules? Why do legislators resort to these unconventional tactics from time to time?

Interests

The Democratic sit-in was an expression of their frustration over alleged Republican inaction after frequent gun violence in the United States. The sit-in took place in a time of nationwide despair after an Orlando, Florida, shooting that killed 49 people at a nightclub. The Democrats felt they had the public on their side. Indeed, as a poll taken in June 2016 found, more than 80 percent of the public supported this measure.[c] By engaging in the sit-in, House Democrats communicated that they were in line with the public and that they were willing to risk censure or some form of punishment from the majority Republicans.

Republicans, meanwhile, faced a dilemma. Almost to a person, Republicans in Congress opposed additional gun control measures. On the one hand, they wanted to avoid a vote on this gun control legislation because doing so would force them to oppose a popular proposal in a highly public fashion. As political scientist Gary W. Cox writes, "The majority party does not frequently ask its members to cast public votes, or to take public actions, that directly conflict with their constituents' interests (thereby worsening their prospects for reelection)."[d] On the other hand, voting on the legislation would have prevented the sit-in from happening, thereby denying Democrats the opportunity to create a highly publicized demonstration.

Institutions

The issues around the Democratic sit-in and the Republicans' response focus on the majority and minority party powers in Congress. The minority party can try to "amend, debate, or obstruct the majority's agenda,"[e] but they are mostly helpless in setting the agenda and can only try to embarrass the majority, while the majority party controls the agenda and tries to help its members. The majority party has enough votes to pass legislation, but sometimes public pressure forces its members to avoid tough votes. The Rules Committee, dominated by the majority party, determines which bills are put on the floor for a vote. The Republicans in this case were not only able to avoid voting on the measure but also to recess the chamber.

A Sit-In for Gun Control

Furthermore, the sit-in sheds light on the role of amendments as a possible tool to affect policy change and the further limits of the minority party. Amendments often serve as means to insert text into an unrelated bill to push party goals, and the "no fly, no buy" amendment would have been inserted into a large piece of legislation intended to combat the Zika virus. In this incident the institutions were strained, and some would say that they temporarily failed, as House Democrats opted to commit civil disobedience by refusing to comply with the normal rules. News coverage of this sit-in likened it to the Civil Rights era.[f]

House Democrats, led by John Lewis (D-GA, left), staged a sit-in to try to force a vote on gun control legislation. They were ultimately unsuccessful, but the event gained significant media attention.

Outcomes

Despite the Democratic sit-in, nothing was done on gun control in 2016 in Congress. During the 2016 elections, the Democrats criticized the Republicans for their intransigence on gun control, but the Republicans held firm. We can see from the sit-in that not only does the content of the legislation cause contention in Congress but so do the rules and procedures that determine what is taken up for a vote.

a. David M. Herszenhorn and Emmarie Huetteman, "House Democrats' Gun-Control Sit-In Turns into Chaotic Showdown with Republicans," *New York Times,* June 22, 2016, www.nytimes.com/2016/06/23/us/politics/house -democrats-stage-sit-in-to-push-for-action-on-gun-control.html?_r=0 (accessed 8/23/16).

b. Scott Wong and Mike Lillis, "Pelosi Scoffs as GOP Eyes Punishment for Gun Sit-In: 'Make my Day'," *The Hill,* July 7, 2016, http://thehill.com/homenews /house/286859-pelosi-scoffs-as-gop-eyes-punishment-for-gun-sit-in-make -my-day (accessed 8/23/16).

c. Quinnipiac University Polling Institute, Quinnipiac University Poll, June 2016. Produced by Quinnipiac University Polling Institute. Distributed by Cornell University, Ithaca, NY. Roper Center for Public Opinion Research, iPOLL.

d. Gary W. Cox, "Agenda Setting in the U.S. House: A Majority-Party Monopoly?" *Legislative Studies Quarterly* 26, no. 2 (2001): 204.

e. Sarah A. Binder, "The Partisan Basis of Procedural Choice: Allocating Parliamentary Rights in the House, 1789–1990," *American Political Science Review* 90, no. 1 (1996): 8–20.

f. See, for example, David Smith and Sabrina Siddiqui, "House Democrats End Gun Control Sit-In after 26 Hours," *Guardian,* June 23, 2016, www .theguardian.com/us-news/2016/jun/23/house-democrats-gun-control-sit-in -civil-disobedience (accessed 8/28/16).

Think About It

At what point do the rules encumber legislators from representing the interests of those who elected them? Do you think the rules serve to prevent theatrics or to prevent routine gridlock? How much influence should the minority party have on the House agenda?

Floor Action

Floor debate can be a dramatic event in either chamber, and some of the most memorable moments in congressional history have occurred when members gave rousing speeches about historic pieces of legislation. Particularly eloquent members, such as Senator Henry Clay of Kentucky in the nineteenth century, could compel their colleagues to compromise over deeply divisive issues like slavery and tariffs by the sheer force of their rhetoric. But often floor debates are dull, especially in the House, as members take turns to enhance their reputations back home in front of the television cameras. Members sometimes hold the floor when the chamber is virtually empty—when everyone else is either in committee meetings or otherwise engaged—and talk to a camera so that constituents back home can catch a glimpse of their legislator in action.

After all the debating and amending ends, the leadership schedules a vote, which on important pieces of legislation occurs by roll call. With a roll-call vote, each member's name is called and he or she responds "yea," "nay," or "abstain." ("Abstain" usually indicates that the member doesn't want to take a position on an issue for political reasons.) The roll call is taken electronically in the House and verbally in the Senate. These final roll-call votes are reported publicly and are important in building a member's reputation with constituents and interest groups. Many interest groups tally the roll-call votes on key bills and use them to craft members' "scores" to determine which members are friends and foes of the group.

Conference Committees

Although both chambers start the entire process with the same text for a bill, the bills that emerge from each chamber may be significantly different from the original bill and from each other. Often the two chambers work it out through informal negotiations or by one chamber just adopting the other chamber's version of the bill. Or sometimes it is clear that one chamber will not compromise, and the bill may just die. But at other times, the bill goes to a formal negotiating process in a House–Senate conference committee to be "reconciled"—that is, for the differences to be ironed out. If the conference committee cannot reconcile the two versions of the bill into one common bill, then the proposed legislation dies. The death of legislation after going to a conference committee is uncommon, because both chambers have devoted so much energy to the bill already and have built considerable steam behind its passage. More typically, the conference committee agrees on a single text, perhaps after much compromise and haggling among committee members. Very few bills are defeated at this point, because conference committee members tend to be careful to approve compromises that their own chamber will support. However it happens, through a conference committee or through less formal bargaining processes, the identical bill passed by both chambers is called the enrolled bill. The enrolled bill must be voted on by both chambers.

Presidential Signature

At this point, the bill's long journey is almost over. It now goes to the president's desk, whereupon the president has several options. He or she can sign the bill and it becomes law. The president can veto the bill and send it back to Congress, where it can still become law if two-thirds of the members of both chambers override the veto. If the president does not sign the bill within 10 days, it automatically becomes law if Congress is still in session. If Congress adjourns before the 10 days have passed, and the president has not signed the bill, the bill is effectively vetoed in what is called a **pocket veto**. Since the outgoing Congress has no opportunity to override a pocket veto, the legislation must wait until the next session, when the new Congress can pass a similar bill and force the president to make an explicit choice between signing and vetoing it. Congress in recent decades has become more careful in the timing of legislation, paying attention to the 10-day deadline before adjournment. Thus, the use of the pocket veto has become rare.

pocket veto A veto that occurs automatically if a president does not sign a bill for 10 days after passage in Congress and Congress has adjourned during that 10-day period.

Making Law in a System of Separation of Powers

In considering how Congress makes law, it is important to note that Congress does not act independently of the other two branches. Its actions do not have much meaning or effect without them. In fact, the executive branch also has legislative powers. The president can determine the fate of a law by either signing it or vetoing it (a veto can be overturned by Congress, but it is difficult to do). Furthermore, Congress has no capacity to carry out its laws. The executive branch, through executive agencies under the direction of the president, enforces, executes, and promulgates policies described in the laws passed by Congress.[20] As for the judiciary, Congress has no authorized powers or capacity to adjudicate disputes that arise over interpretations of laws or in enforcement of laws. Rather, it must rely on the courts that make up the judicial branch to perform this critical task. (A noteworthy exception is a presidential

[20] D. Roderick Kiewiet and Mathew D. McCubbins, *The Logic of Delegation: Congressional Parties and the Appropriations Process* (Chicago: University of Chicago Press, 1991); David Epstein and Sharyn O'Halloran, *Delegating Powers: A Transaction Cost Politics Approach to Policy Making under Separate Powers* (New York: Cambridge University Press, 1999).

impeachment trial, which occurs in the Senate and is presided over by the chief justice of the Supreme Court.)

The most contentious and consequential interactions among branches in the national government occur between Congress and the president. The separation of powers often requires that Congress repeatedly bargain with the president over policies. The two branches represent different constituencies and see their roles in the American political system as distinct. We will discuss interbranch politics in greater detail in Chapter 6.

In Comparison: Legislative Institutions

At various points in this chapter, we have highlighted differences between the U.S. Congress and other legislatures around the world. We have discussed why members of Congress see their career success as being closely linked to their individual reputations as good agents for the voters in their constituencies. In most other democracies, legislators succeed or fail based on how loyal they are to party leaders. Furthermore, inside Congress much of the action in crafting policy occurs in committees. The details of legislating happen in negotiations among committee leaders, party leaders, and sometimes people in the White House, including the president. In most other democracies, legislation is crafted by the executive and then simply voted on by the parliament.

Compare, for instance, how the French legislature works. French lawmakers get elected to the lower house, the National Assembly, mostly by virtue of working as loyal party members and being nominated by local party committees to run for office in a given district. France has single-member districts but uses a majority runoff system. Party leaders can prevent a legislator from running in a district if that legislator is disloyal to the party. Little of what occurs inside the French parliament resembles the operations of the American Congress. The National Assembly receives proposals for legislation from the French prime minister and the executive cabinet (the heads of the various national bureaucratic ministries). Prime ministers in countries like France are chosen from among parliamentary members by the parliament itself, so the prime minister's government has the support of a majority in the parliament. The Assembly, after receiving the proposed legislation, has a short time to offer suggested revisions and comment on the draft. Assembly members, in public sessions, question members of the prime minister's cabinet about policy matters, but these sessions are largely for show. Then the Assembly votes on the proposed legislation and nearly always approves it. Unlike in the United States, where the work of legislating happens inside the congressional chambers, in France the work of legislating happens inside the prime minister's

Gerrymandering allows party leaders or state government officials to draw district boundaries for political advantage. As we saw in Figure 5.2, sometimes extreme gerrymanders lead to districts that better resemble animals than they do natural geographic areas. But what real effect does gerrymandering have? Consider the figure below, which shows data from political scientist Nicholas Goedert.[a]

As you explore these data, consider the following:

1. The figure shows the relationship between Democratic national vote share (*x*-axis) with Democratic congressional seat share (*y*-axis) from 1972 to 2014. A dot on the 45-degree line would indicate a year when Democrats were awarded a seat share in the House of Representatives perfectly proportional to their vote share.
2. During the 1970s, Democrats controlled redistricting in the South and in some other parts of the country. In years after 1996, Republicans had more control over state redistricting.

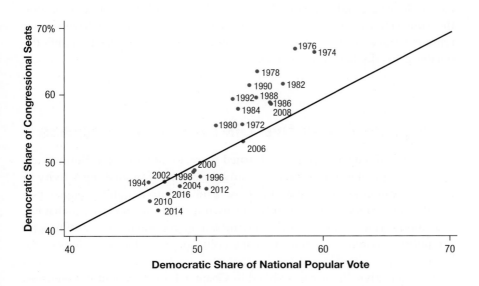

Votes to Seats: Democratic Performance in Congressional Elections, 1972–2016

Think About It

In what years did Democrats win proportionately more seats than their vote? When did they win fewer? Do the data here support the claim that gerrymandering provides parties with political advantage? Why or why not?

a. Nicholas Goedert, "Gerrymandering or Geography? How Democrats Won the Popular Vote but Lost the Congress in 2012," *Research and Politics* 1, no. 1 (2014): 1–8. Nicholas Goedert, "The Case of the Disappearing Bias: A 2014 Update to 'Gerrymandering or Geography' Debate," *Research and Politics* 2, no. 4 (2015): 1–6. Replication data available at https://dataverse.harvard.edu (accessed 5/19/16).

government. The legislature more or less rubber-stamps what the executive officers propose.

The French system is similar to that of most other democracies. Even in countries with a president and a system of separation of powers, such as Brazil or Argentina, parliaments rarely have the kinds of active legislation-writing duties that fall upon the U.S. Congress.

It is also worth noting how state legislatures compare to Congress. The states have intentionally modeled their state-level legislatures on the national Congress. With the sole exception of Nebraska, all states have bicameral legislatures.[21] The lawmaking procedures, the organization of chambers, and the electoral rules used to elect state representatives and senators are all similar to those in the U.S. Congress. There is one important exception to these similarities. In the U.S. Senate, as mandated by the Constitution, each state has two senators, regardless of population size. As we discussed earlier in this chapter, with the *Baker* and *Wesberry* rulings, the Supreme Court declared that the principle of *one person, one vote* must apply to state legislative houses and the U.S. House (but not to the U.S. Senate). This means that state senates have to be organized so that each electoral district within the state is roughly the same size by population. So, state houses and state senates have similar representational schemes (and therefore similar political pressures), though the senates generally have fewer members.

Analyzing Collective Dilemmas in Congress

In reading this chapter, you have learned more about Congress. But how do we make sense of it? Congress is not only the center of lawmaking activity in the American political system, it has also evolved into a highly complex political system in its own right. It has its own institutions, norms of behavior, and cultural practices. It is worth studying as a microcosm of the entire American political system and, indeed, of any political system based on democratic principles.

The collective dilemmas outlined in Chapter 1 are prevalent in Congress. Members of Congress face recurring collective action problems. They have incentives to free ride off the efforts of their colleagues—for example, by taking credit for producing public goods while spending most of their time working on bills that benefit their district, even though these bills may not be good for their party or for the country as a whole. Members of Congress also face coordination problems. To accomplish anything, they must find ways to coor-

---

[21] Nebraska has only one chamber, as a result of a 1937 ballot initiative that abolished the state senate. This initiative succeeded when enough voters became convinced that it would save taxpayers' money.

dinate their behavior. Coordination can include voting for one another's **pork-barrel** bills, but it can also include coordinating efforts on a compromise bill that no one is perfectly happy with. Moreover, members face the possibility of coalition raiding. If there were no one to control the agenda and prevent repeated introductions of competing bills, then coalition raiding could continue indefinitely as members presented alternative versions of bills in an effort to attract support for their favored version.

Consider the collective action problem highlighted in our opening story: How can we get members of Congress to work for the common good of the country as opposed to that of their own district or state? As a group, members want to pass broad legislation and earn a collective reputation as an efficient body. As members of a political party, they want their party to have a good reputation among voters. As individual representatives, however, they engage in activities to sustain their political popularity by delivering pork to their constituents and supporters.[22] Pork-barrel projects and constituency service can undercut their collective goals. The collective action problems spring from this disconnect between individual and group interests: Each legislator would prefer that his or her colleagues do the hard and sometimes unpopular work of crafting legislation for the good of the entire country. At the same time, each legislator is tempted to free ride off the efforts of the group and bring home as much pork as possible for his or her own district. If all members of Congress spent all of their time getting pork and doing constituency service, then nothing that benefits the entire country would be accomplished.

Our legislative system also presents a principal-agent problem. The voters are the principals who elect members of Congress to be their agents and work on behalf of the people in the district. As we saw in Chapter 1, a principal-agent problem exists when principals cannot adequately observe the actions of agents. Voters evaluate members of Congress at election time and decide whether to keep them in office, yet voters may not have enough information to make intelligent voting decisions. And because voters cannot observe all that goes on in Congress, representatives may at times have incentives to act contrary to the interests of their districts—to vote against the wishes of a majority of their constituents, for instance. The principal-agent problem between voters and congressional representatives hinges on the degree to which voters can effectively monitor what happens in Congress.[23]

In Chapter 1, we discussed how various political institutions solve collective dilemmas. The way these institutions operate also has consequences. The details of the institutions determine who gets what in society and the quality of government policies. When Congress, for example, makes rules about who

pork barrel Government spending that benefits a narrow constituency in return for electoral support or some other kind of political support, including campaign donations.

---

[22] Morris Fiorina, *Congress: Keystone of the Washington Establishment*, 2nd ed. (New Haven, CT: Yale University Press, 1989).

[23] The principal-agent problem is also present in the relationship between congressional committees and other actors in the chambers. We will discuss these relationships later in the chapter.

can propose amendments to legislation and when they can propose them, those rules have implications for what legislation gets passed.

Three Models for Analyzing Congress

Although scholars generally agree that Congress faces collective dilemmas, that principal–agent problems exist in legislative politics, and that the internal institutional features of Congress help overcome these dilemmas, they come to different conclusions about which specific institutions are most important in Congress. They also disagree about the consequences of the institutions that make Congress operate. Various models of how congressional institutions work have been proposed. Here we consider three prominent models that help us gain a deeper understanding of the internal workings of Congress. All three models operate on the assumption that members of Congress want to be reelected, and for that reason want to be considered good representatives. Differences between the models have to do with how members go about improving their reputations.

distributional model
The view that the internal institutions of the congressional chambers are designed primarily to help members of Congress secure economic benefits for only their constituents, not the general public.

The Distributional Model. The **distributional model** of Congress focuses on the ways members of Congress help each other deliver specific benefits to specific groups of people.[24] Although valuable legislation that supports the general public is occasionally passed, congressional lawmakers devote much of their energy to securing programs that benefit their narrow constituencies and make sure that their own constituents do not face undue burdens in paying for government. Bills of broad national interest are frequently loaded with pork or with special provisions for relatively small groups of constituents, and members of Congress devote their time and their staffs' time to constituency service. This process, according to the model, is vital to understanding the workings of Congress.

logrolling An instance of two or more legislators agreeing to vote in favor of one another's proposed bills or amendments.

Why do members agree to each other's pork projects? The mechanism used to pass pork-barrel legislation is called **logrolling**. (The name comes from an era of timber cutting when men stood on logs floating in a river and helped each other roll their logs along the river toward the mill. It is an apt analogy for degislative voting behavior.) When members of Congress proposed to include billions of dollars in military construction to the spending bill, as discussed in the chapter opening, each member was asking fellow representatives to vote in favor of all the construction projects, even though only specific geographic areas benefited from them. The budget requests are made with the understanding that when a colleague's pet project is proposed, the other representatives will vote in its favor. It is a classic quid pro quo.

[24] Kenneth Shepsle and Barry Weingast, "The Institutional Foundations of Committee Power," *American Political Science Review* 81, no. 1 (1987): 85–104.

The Informational Model. The **informational model** of Congress proposes that members of Congress are mostly interested in gathering the best information possible to help them choose effective public policies that make voters happy and help incumbents win reelection.[25] According to this view, the institutions are designed to help Congress make more informed decisions. Given that it would be impossible for every member to become an expert on every issue, the only way Congress as a whole can make good public policy is to divide the tasks of determining which policies will work given the goals of the majority in Congress. Thus, when Congress is considering a bill to fund the Department of Defense, it must rely on members with some expertise in international aid and foreign affairs to play a large role in drafting the bill. Congressional leaders then can ensure that knowledgeable members on the appropriate committees review the bill.

This basic function of committees—to provide better knowledge—is the centerpiece of the informational model. Those who regard the informational model of Congress as the most convincing focus on how institutions, such as the CBO (discussed earlier), have grown within the chambers to help members navigate the complexities of modern policies. The expertise of staffers and research agencies helps make it possible for members to arrive at knowledgeable decisions.

> **informational model**
> The view that the internal institutions of the congressional chambers are designed to help Congress make more informed decisions.

The Partisan Model. The **partisan model** of Congress revolves around the significant role played by political parties, and especially party leaders, in the organization and work of the chambers. This model devotes attention to how intensely party leaders, especially in the House, try to control the agenda and enforce party discipline on key votes in Congress.[26] Advocates of the partisan model of Congress emphasize that party leaders stand at the center of congressional politics. In this view, the winners in the legislature are those currently represented by the majority party. Minority party members routinely lose in their efforts to pass legislation or gain pork for their district. Majority party leaders in Congress, when united as a group, rarely allow competing bills to reach the floor for a vote. Recall the role of the powerful Rules Committee as a strong tool that party leaders use in running the House. Moreover, research has shown that party leaders reward loyal party members by granting them their choice of committee assignments. They likewise punish those who have been disloyal by giving them undesirable committee assignments, thus using the committee assignment process as one tool to keep members in line. Leaders also devote considerable energy to crafting a theme for the upcom-

> **partisan model** The view that majority party leaders dominate the workings of Congress and ensure that most legislative benefits come to majority party members.

[25] Keith Krehbiel, *Information and Legislative Organization* (Ann Arbor: University of Michigan Press, 1992).

[26] Gary Cox and Mathew McCubbins, *Setting the Agenda: Responsible Party Government in the U.S. House of Representatives* (New York: Cambridge University Press, 2005).

ing election and assisting, both financially and administratively, loyal party members who are in danger of losing their seats.

The purpose of describing and comparing these three models is to give you some tools to evaluate Congress. No single model explains everything, but perhaps one or more of them captures the essence of how Congress works. These models are analytical tools that you can use to categorize information about Congress and try to fit that information into a coherent overall picture of the chambers. For our purposes, the models help you to understand the various moving parts of Congress in relation to each other—committees, party leaders, congressional elections, and voting on the floor of the chambers. Each model emphasizes different connections among these parts of Congress and ascribes different importance to each of them. For instance, consider the moment when a committee reports a bill to the floor in either the House or Senate. This process is where proponents of the informational model of Congress focus their attention. By sending a bill to the floor with a recommendation for passage, a committee is in effect saying, "We think this bill will make good law, and you should listen to us because we are specialists on the topic." If that is the main thing committees do—serve as filters to let good laws through and stop bad laws—then the informational model would seem to have considerable merit. In contrast, if the main thing committees do is take legislation and load it up with pork or with other kinds of special favors to specific constituents, then the distributional model seems more appropriate for describing Congress.

These three models are not entirely at odds with one another. They all make the case for the importance of congressional institutions in helping members to solve their collective dilemmas and accomplish their goals. Even the distributional model suggests that although members occasionally free ride off their colleagues, they also cooperate with each other to divide up the government largesse for their home constituents. Furthermore, your own analysis of Congress may combine aspects of more than one model. As an example, it is possible to propose a distributional-partisan model that emphasizes how majority party members secure pork for their own constituencies at the expense of the constituencies of minority party members.

Who Benefits from Congressional Institutions? The three models lead to different understandings of who benefits from congressional politics given the nature of the institutions. Under the distributional model, the winners are those people in geographic areas with effective representatives and senators who can bring specific benefits home to their districts or states. The losers are everyone else, and perhaps the taxpayers who foot the bill. This model makes sense to the degree that we see logrolling across groups of legislators on bills providing geographically specific benefits while less attention is paid to legislation with broad benefits across the entire country.

The informational model, in contrast, presumes that members structure lawmaking rules primarily to yield good information on the consequences of public policy, and they want to satisfy most voters. Some might consider the informational model a somewhat upbeat version of Congress, though such a conclusion depends on how other members use information from committees. If their fellow members learn from committees what will make effective public policy—meaning effective and helpful for a large proportion of people in the country—then the informational model presents Congress in a relatively positive light. If the information from committees is mostly used to improve the targeting of policies toward narrow interests, then this model is not much different from the distributive model—it differs only in the mechanisms used to serve narrow interests. For the distributional model, committee membership confers advantages by being present at the markup stage. For the informational model, all members in Congress benefit from other committees by learning how best to serve their specific constituencies.

The partisan model proposes an ideological, team-oriented approach to understanding Congress. Party members, when necessary, hold together to overcome their own collective dilemmas and then act in unison to enable Congress as a whole to get things done. The model is particularly apt if we emphasize the passage of the most bitterly contested bills, which pit the two parties against each other. In these cases, party leadership typically takes a firm, united position, demanding party discipline and staking the party's fortunes on the legislation's success. Winners under this model are the voters living in states and districts with representation by politicians from the majority party.

All three models assume that members of Congress are driven by their desire to win reelection, and their actions reflect that goal. Admittedly, these are simplistic versions of how Congress works. Those who subscribe to the partisan model do not believe that the distributional or informational models are irrelevant—that members of Congress are never motivated to understand or predict the consequences of proposed policies, or by the desire to bring pork to their districts. Likewise, the informational model does not suggest that political parties are irrelevant inside Congress. Rather, scholars who espouse these models claim that the assumptions and conclusions associated with them capture the essence of congressional politics better than other models. Strip away the details, and the favored model (one of the three) gets to the heart of the matter.

This discussion can have a historical angle. It may be that one model best describes Congress for a given era while another model is more apt for another era. Some scholars argue that the relevance of the partisan model has fluctuated, and that in our own era it matches the data best. Indeed, the partisan model recently has gained adherents among political scientists because of the partisan polarization that has occurred (see Figure 5.5; Chapter 12 covers this topic in more detail). Among members of Congress, since the 1980s Demo-

FIGURE 5.5

Party Polarization in Congress

Data for these charts and their basic design are from Voteview.com, maintained by Keith Poole at the University of Georgia. Shown are the mean values of DW-Nominate for each group in the Congress over time. DW-Nominate is a score given to each member of Congress based on roll-call voting and indicates underlying propensity to vote together (and often is interpreted to indicate ideology).

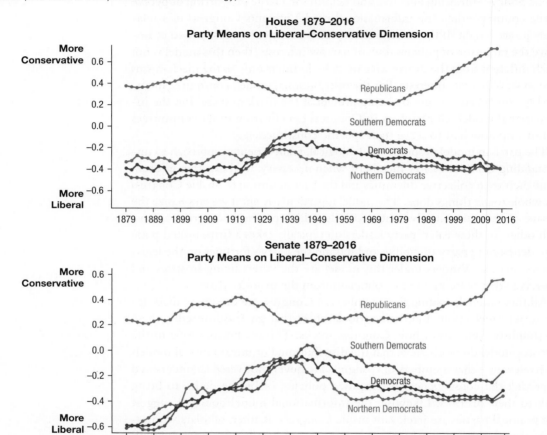

Source: Reprinted by permission of Jeffrey B. Lewis.

crats have become more uniformly liberal and Republicans have become more uniformly conservative. There are very few ideological moderates in either chamber, and this has meant less bipartisan cooperation on legislation, more floor and committee votes straight down party lines, and greater use of obstructive tactics by minority parties, especially in the Senate. Political scientists disagree on the causes and consequences of this polarization, but few of them dispute that it has occurred.

Let's now return to the puzzle at the beginning of this chapter: How does Congress overcome its collective dilemmas to work together? As we have seen, the answer is that members of Congress have together developed a set of internal institutions designed to overcome the body's collective dilemmas *and* enable members to sustain individual reputations that lead to reelection. Consider several specific institutional features. Having strong committees allows for party leaders to divide the legislative work. Then maintaining agenda control through the Rules Committee in the House and the office of the majority leader in the Senate helps coordinate and control floor action. These features help solve collective dilemmas. But having large numbers of staff also enables members of Congress to serve constituents directly and investigate opportunities to insert pork into bills. The institutionalization of staff working on committees and in members' offices sustains a system where high reelection rates are the norm.

Although scholars largely agree that the institutions of Congress enable it to accomplish as much as it does collectively—that is, the institutions allow the members to overcome their collective dilemmas as individually elected representatives and senators while continuing to get reelected—they disagree about the fundamental nature of those institutions, their operation, and their consequences. Hence the three different models of congressional institutions.

Final Thought: A Fourth Model? The three models described so far focus attention on the inner workings of Congress. There is a fourth, more directly critical view of Congress. These critics focus more attention on the process of election, particularly campaign finance, and less on the workings of internal congressional institutions. They charge that owing to the election process, the workings of Congress as a whole are geared toward maintaining a system of governmental benefits for those who are already privileged. They point to the basic fact that wealthy donors provide the vast majority of all the money contributed to congressional candidates. With little public funding for campaigns, American political parties and their candidates must curry the favor of and attract donations from wealthy voters to win elections.[27] A reasonable assumption is that these donors expect favorable legislation in return. Although research linking campaign contributions to legislative favors has largely been inconclusive, these critics argue that bias toward the wealthy is subtle and really comes in the form of agenda control. They typically conclude that policies intended to benefit the poor at the expense of the rich do not even make it onto the congressional agenda. The dominance of lobbying and campaign

---

[27] Kevin Phillips, *Arrogant Capital* (Boston: Little, Brown, 1994); Thomas Ferguson, *Golden Rule* (Chicago: University of Chicago Press, 1995).

contributions by wealthy corporations means that Congress stands at the center of a political system that maintains privilege for the wealthy in society.

In this chapter, we have analyzed the workings inside Congress, including three models proposed by political scientists, as well as the election process that shapes the nature of Congress as a representational institution. The ideas in this chapter—the three models and the criticisms of the election process just described—point to distinct consequences of congressional institutions and give different answers to the opening questions. Given the facts you have learned in this chapter, which ideas are most useful in answering the opening questions, describing Congress, and predicting how it will evolve in the future?

FURTHER READING

★ = Included in *Readings in American Politics*, 5th ed.

Cox, Gary, and Mathew McCubbins, *Legislative Leviathan* (New York: Cambridge University Press, 1992). An account of the House that strongly emphasizes how majority party leaders control committee assignments and other perks for their party members, and in this way influence the voting decisions of congressional representatives.

★ ———, *Setting the Agenda: Responsible Party Government in the U.S. House of Representatives* (New York: Cambridge University Press, 2005). An account that focuses attention on how leaders of the majority party in the House closely control the agenda and especially avoid having bills reach the floor that divide the majority party coalition.

Fenno, Richard, *Congressmen in Committees* (Boston: Little, Brown, 1973). A landmark study of how members of Congress use their prerogatives on committees to serve the specific needs of their constituents.

★ ———, *Home Style: House Members in Their Districts* (Boston: Little, Brown, 1978). A rich account of how members of Congress view their districts, and the kinds of representational styles they use to connect with constituents.

Grimmer, Justin, Sean Westwood, and Solomon Messing, *The Impression of Influence: Legislator Communication, Representation, and Democratic Accountability* (Princeton, NJ: Princeton University Press, 2015). In this extensive study, Grimmer, Westwood, and Messing analyze words in hundreds of thousands of press releases used by members of the House of Representatives to claim credit for national government spending in their electoral districts.

Krehbiel, Keith, *Information and Legislative Organization* (Ann Arbor, MI: University of Michigan Press, 1992). An account that focuses on how the majority must approve all decisions made by Congress, including the organization of the chambers—thus, the main purpose of any organizational feature of Congress is to enable the majority to make more informed decisions.

★ Mayhew, David R., *Congress: The Electoral Connection*, 2nd ed. (New Haven, CT: Yale University Press, 2004). A classic essay exploring the consequences of the basic assumption that members of Congress are primarily motivated by the desire to get reelected.

Swain, Carol, *Black Faces, Black Interests* (Cambridge, MA: Harvard University Press, 1993). A close exploration of the effects of redistricting efforts designed to increase representation of racial minorities; Swain argues that in some cases, the unintended consequences actually hurt the interests of minority constituents.

Swers, Michele, *The Difference Women Make* (Chicago: University of Chicago Press, 2002). Offers compelling evidence that women in Congress do vote differently than their male counterparts.

KEY TERMS

bicameral legislature (p. 150)

caucus (p. 173)

closed rule (p. 179)

cloture (p. 181)

conference committee (p. 171)

constituency service (p. 160)

delegates (p. 159)

distributional model (p. 190)

filibuster (p. 180)

gerrymandering (p. 156)

incumbency advantage (p. 161)

informational model (p. 191)

joint committee (p. 171)

logrolling (p. 190)

majority leader (p. 168)

markup (p. 178)

open rule (p. 179)

partisan model (p. 191)

party discipline (p. 168)

plurality rule (p. 152)

pocket veto (p. 185)

pork barrel (p. 189)

proportional representation (p. 152)

Reed's Rules (p. 168)

restricted (or modified) rule (p. 179)

single-member district (p. 152)

Speaker of the House (p. 168)

special (or select) committee (p. 171)

split referral (p. 178)

standing committee (p. 170)

trustees (p. 159)

unanimous consent agreement (p. 181)

whip (p. 168)

During his campaign, Donald Trump criticized President Obama's use of executive orders. As president, Trump used executive orders often on many controversial issues, including ones that put him at odds with Republicans in Congress.

6

The Presidency

 How and why has presidential power grown?

A major complaint by Republicans of Democratic president Barack Obama was that he overstepped his authority as president, especially in issuing executive actions and orders. Openly and without apology, Obama used the tool of executive action to enact policies that the Republican led Congress would not pass or even consider. In 2016, after Donald Trump won the election, it was the Democrats' turn to worry about executive authority.

Obama used executive actions many times during his two terms. He successfully ordered executive agencies to act on cyber security, student loans, minimum wage for federal contractors, and in support of behavioral science. One key example where he did not ultimately succeed occurred late in his second term when he unveiled a new plan for immigration enforcement known as the Immigration Accountability Executive Actions.[1] An aspect of this plan, called the Deferred Action for Parents of Americans and Lawful Permanent Residents (DAPA), granted "deferred action"—that is, temporary relief from deportation—to parents of children who are U.S. citizens or lawful permanent residents. Texas led a group of 26 states requesting a preliminary injunction to prevent the federal government from implementing it. The federal courts, including the Supreme Court, sided with the states, thus blocking the new policy.

Presidents can unilaterally use executive actions, including executive orders, to make policy, and such actions often hold up and survive attempts by Congress or the courts to stop them; most executive actions throughout history have withstood, or not even faced, challenges in the courts. When presidents do not like what Congress does or does not do, they simply change how the law is implemented without congressional approval.

[1] The White House, Office of the Press Secretary, "Fact Sheet: Immigration Accountability Executive Action," November 20, 2014, www.whitehouse.gov/the-press-office/2014/11/20/fact-sheet-immigration-accountability-executive-action (accessed 1/22/16).

OUTLINE

- Sources of Presidential Power

- Shaping the Modern Presidency

- Enhancing Presidential Power through Military and Economic Means

- Today's Powerful Presidency

- In Comparison: Executive Forms

- Checks on Presidential Power

What is to stop the president from doing this whenever Congress stymies what he or she wants? Legal challenges are one approach. Otherwise, Congress must pass a law to overturn an executive action. The president, however, can veto the law, requiring Congress to have the support of two-thirds of both chambers to overturn that veto. Another way, at least to the long-term effects of any executive action, is for new presidents entering the office to reverse the actions of previous presidents. Trump, after all, promised during his campaign to undo nearly all of Obama's executive actions soon after taking office.

In fact, Trump promised and tried to do many things upon taking office that he could likely do without congressional approval. He succeeded in renegotiating trade deals and arms agreements and imposing tariffs on China and Mexico. He used highly controversial executive orders on other immigration measures, including several overturned by courts. He failed to abolish the Affordable Care Act (ACA; also known as Obamacare) because Congress did not vote in support of his plan. Congress did not provide funding for a wall on the Mexican border. By and large, the things requiring congressional approval were the ones he was not able to accomplish, even though for two years his party had majorities in both chambers of Congress.

Congress, however, holds the purse strings of the government and needs to approve changes to policies such as the ACA, treaties like NAFTA, spending on infrastructure, and long-term foreign policies such as sustained military incursions against ISIS. Also, whether Trump's actions would survive legal challenges, should they arise, is hard to predict. What is clear though is that Trump will be as constrained as all previous presidents in enacting many of the policies he promised on the campaign trail.

While presidents can accomplish a lot on their own, the tools available to them do not give him or her complete authority to change how laws are executed; there are constraints on presidential action. With immigration and deportation, Obama was clearly trying to use his authority over executive agencies to bypass Congress, achieve his policy goals, and expand the power of the presidency. He was by no means the first president to try to do so, and many, including Obama, have succeeded in other areas. Obama, however, while running for president in 2008, criticized his predecessor's actions for overstepping the bounds of legitimate presidential authority, and promised to act differently, consult Congress, and stay well within the limits of the laws as written. Yet he maintained many of Bush's positions on presidential authority. Trump has acted as previous presidents have and has used presidential authority to bypass Congress when he can.

According to the Constitution, the presidency is at best equal in power to Congress, and evidence strongly suggests that the Founders generally wanted Congress to be the key decision-making branch. The Founders gave the presidency considerable powers, but they also intended for Congress and the courts to check those powers. Today, the American presidency is a far more powerful office than the Founders ever envisioned.

When do the other branches of government go along with strengthening the presidency as an institution? If the American people historically have been wary of centralized government power, why (and when) do they often support strong presidential powers?

Sources of Presidential Power

Presidential power derives from two main sources. First is the Constitution, which includes both enumerated (explicitly described) and implied powers. And second is the reputation built from a long history of being the one leader called upon and able to solve collective dilemmas among the states and across the various parts of the national government. Let's explore these sources.

Constitutional Bases of Presidential Power

The Constitutional Convention of 1787 featured intense debate over how to organize the executive branch. Delegates argued about whether a single person should serve as president or whether an advisory council would be more appropriate. They debated over how the executive was to be chosen—selected by Congress or elected by the people—and over the length of term of office.

Arguments in favor of having a single person as president—made during the Convention and afterward in the *Federalist Papers* by James Madison, Alexander Hamilton, and John Jay—were similar to those used to support a strong national government. Noting the problems that occurred under the Articles of Confederation, promoters of a strong presidency emphasized that states were not meeting their obligations to work toward the collective good of the Union, such as paying their debts from the Revolutionary War. What the country needed, they argued, was a strong executive who would respond decisively to crises, both domestic and foreign, and enforce the laws uniformly and fairly. Thus the most important aspect of the presidency—one person chosen to lead the executive branch—came about in response to the collective dilemmas that plagued the young United States. A single person given executive and police powers would be able to coerce conflicting groups to cooperate for the good of the whole country.[2]

Although they reached early agreement about having a single person serve as president, the Framers of the Constitution debated for another three months over the best method of selection and the length of presidential tenure. Ultimately, the constitutional delegates compromised on the following characteristics.

- *The presidency would not be too democratic.* The president would not be chosen through direct election by the people, in which each citizen has one vote. Rather, the president would be chosen for a four-year term by an appointed body known as the electoral college, which in principle represents the people. We say that the president is elected indirectly because there is a layer, the electoral college, between the voters and the choice

---

[2] See especially the *Federalist Papers*, Nos. 67–77, which focus on the presidency and the executive branch.

of president. The electoral college is formally a set of people chosen in their respective states to vote for the president, and the person winning a majority of electoral college votes becomes president. While it is not specified in the Constitution how electors are chosen by the state, in practice the states hold popular elections to choose a slate of electors pledged to support a particular presidential candidate. Thus, the Founders intended that the electoral college would be somewhat insulated from popular whim and choose a wise, discerning president regardless of who the people want. Usually today, except in rare circumstances (as in 2000 and 2016), the winner of the overall popular vote nationwide ends up being the winner of the electoral college vote.

- *The presidency would not be too beholden to the large states.* Recall from Chapter 2 that the Connecticut Compromise created a bicameral Congress, blending equal representation of all the states in the Senate with representation weighted by population in the House of Representatives. The compromise worked because it enabled the large states to predominate in the House and the small states to have at least equal power in the Senate. The results of the Connecticut Compromise are reflected in the electoral college as well. Representation in the college mirrors the voting weights given to the states in Congress. Each state has as many electoral votes to select the president as it has senators and representatives. Kansas, for example, currently has six electoral votes because it has four representatives in the House and two senators in the Senate. California has 55 electoral votes. Note how this system gives additional weight to larger states but reserves substantial voting power for smaller states, because every state is guaranteed at least three electoral votes. Even Wyoming has three electoral votes, which is substantially more voting weight in the electoral college than the state would have if the number of electoral votes were determined strictly by population size.

- *The presidency would be checked by the other branches.* The president would not be able to act alone. The president would need the approval of the House and Senate to raise money and declare war, and of the Senate to make appointments and treaties. Furthermore, the president could be impeached and recalled from office by Congress.

- *The presidency would check the other branches.* The Founders wanted the president to be involved in the affairs of the other branches of government. For instance, the office has important legislative powers. The president can force Congress to meet in formal session and can veto legislation (though Congress can override the veto by a vote of two-thirds of both chambers). The president is also authorized to appoint all federal judges and ambassadors (with Senate approval) and can issue pardons and reprieves for prisoners.

- *The presidency would play the primary role in the conduct of foreign policy and of the military.* The president would be authorized to make treaties with the "advice and consent" of the Senate (meaning that two-thirds of the senators approve), to receive ambassadors from other countries, and most important, to serve as commander in chief of the armed forces.

Despite the consensus on general characteristics of the presidency, the Constitution left many of the president's powers and responsibilities vague. The Founders envisioned a somewhat regal president, a man of unquestioned prestige who could rise above ordinary, day-to-day politics. George Washington, leader of the Continental army during the Revolution, set this tone immediately and was twice elected unanimously by the electoral college as the first president. Throughout his administration, from 1789 to 1797, Washington exercised his authority through subordinates, retained respect from people on all sides of the day's various debates, and excelled at ceremonial duties of the office. The Founders anticipated that the president would concentrate on foreign affairs and internal security, leaving most domestic policy matters to the Congress.

The Constitution lists two major roles for the president: executor (enforcer) of the laws, and commander in chief of the armed forces. It was not clear, even to the Founders, how the president would act in these roles. The Constitution says only that "the executive Power shall be vested in a President of the United States of America," that "he shall take Care that the Laws be faithfully executed," and that "the President shall be Commander in Chief of the Army and Navy of the United States, and of the Militia of the several States, when called into the actual Service of the United States." It says little about the specific powers the president can exercise, except for those of appointment, pardon, and treaty making.

This constitutional vagueness regarding presidential power—especially the "take Care" clause quoted earlier—has generally worked in the presidency's favor, providing openings for presidents to increase their powers and institutional capacities when they believed circumstances warranted such moves. As we have already seen in the opening story, presidents have taken advantage of this vagueness to assert their authority and at times act decisively without congressional approval.[3] Challenges to presidential power based on constitutional principles have often ended up in the courts. The Supreme Court has generally held that the scope of these powers depends on historical circumstances. The Court has stated that it prefers the president to act "concurrently" with the Congress, but that in some instances the president can act alone. This ambivalence can make Court rulings on presidential powers hard to predict.

---

[3] Stephen Skowronek, *The Politics Presidents Make* (Cambridge, MA: Belknap Press, 1997).

Know the FACTS — Constitutional Powers of the Presidency

ENUMERATED POWERS (EXPRESSED POWERS) Presidential powers explicitly stated in the Constitution

- **Power to execute the law:** The Constitution bestows on the president executive power and authority over government. (Article II, Section 1, and Article II, Section 3)

- **Power of military authority:** The Constitution defers authority over the nation's military to the president. (Article II, Section 2)

- **Power to pardon:** The Constitution gives the president power to pardon or grant reprieves. (Article II, Section 2)

- **Power of diplomacy:** The president is given considerable authority in dealing with the nation's foreign relations. The Constitution enables the president to meet with foreign ambassadors and to make treaties. (Article II, Section 3, and Article II, Section 2)

- **Power to veto legislation:** The Constitution gives the president some legislative authority through veto power. After Congress passes a bill, the president can veto it in an attempt to keep it from becoming law. However, Congress can overturn the veto when there is supermajority congressional support for the bill. (Article I, Section 7)

- **Power of appointment:** The president is given the power to nominate and appoint, with the Senate's advice and consent, various political officers, including members of the Supreme Court. (Article II, Section 2)

IMPLIED POWERS (INHERENT POWERS) Powers not explicitly stated in the Constitution, but rather inferred from it (These continue to be debated.)

- **Power to wage war:** The Constitution gives Congress the power to declare war. However, presidents have often engaged in military action without such congressional declaration. The president derives authority to take such unilateral military action and effectively "wage war" from the power implied by the title "Commander in Chief of the Army and Navy." Some argue that such action is an abuse of presidential power.

- **Power over domestic security:** Does the president have unilateral authority to dispatch federal troops to address domestic threats? Congress is given explicit constitutional authority to call forth the militia in response to insurrection and invasion. However, the president has called forth the National Guard in response to national emergencies such as Hurricane Katrina in 2005.

- **Power to issue executive agreements:** To avoid the need to obtain Senate approval for treaties, presidents have adopted the use of executive agreements. These agreements, though not addressed in the Constitution, have the effect of a treaty without requiring Senate approval.

- **Executive privilege:** Past presidents have maintained that, given the sensitive nature of information acquired by the executive, the office holds inherent privacy privileges. Presidents from George Washington to Barack Obama have evoked such executive privilege to keep documents and other information confidential despite congressional protests.

By and large, the Court has granted wider latitude to the president as military commander in chief than as executor of the laws. When President Truman issued an executive order seizing steel mills during the Korean War to prevent a general strike by steelworkers, his action was declared unconstitutional by the Supreme

Court on the grounds that he had overstepped his role as executor of the recently passed Taft-Hartley Act. The Court rejected the president's argument that he had acted as commander in chief to prevent disruption of the war effort. However, when Presidents Jimmy Carter and Ronald Reagan concluded an executive agreement with Iran concerning legal claims against the Iranian revolutionary government—a prerequisite for securing the release of American hostages in Tehran—the Court agreed that the president, as commander in chief, had such powers to resolve a foreign policy crisis.

Solving Collective Dilemmas and Principal-Agent Problems since the Founding

The Founders wanted a presidency that was relatively strong by the standards of the time, but the office has grown considerably stronger. The modern presidency emerged through a series of institutional changes that ratcheted presidential power higher in response to specific historical crises. Each crisis required cooperation and coordination among groups—states, members of Congress, bureaucracies, and members of political parties—that faced collective dilemmas. The president was and continues to be the primary solver of collective dilemmas not only in moments of deepest crisis but also in the achievement of political goals set by him and by his political allies.

Contrast the president with Congress. Because only one person occupies the presidency, the institution does not face the same kind of internal collective dilemmas as Congress. In Chapter 5, we discussed how Congress faces potentially severe collective dilemmas among its 535 members. We learned that Congress must sustain internal institutions that are designed to resolve these dilemmas.

The president encounters different kinds of problems because the executive branch is more hierarchical than the legislative branch.[4] As a single person overseeing a vast administration, the president faces more direct managerial challenges, including recurrent principal-agent problems. First, the president needs information from trusted agents. As the chief executive of the federal government, the president needs to make quick decisions on issues of foreign policy, national security, and the economy, and must have access to information from diverse, trusted sources. It is crucial that the president (the principal) has close advisers (agents) who are loyal and share the president's policy goals. To get useful information, presidents have surrounded themselves with a massive cadre of handpicked advisers working within the White House. We will discuss some of these White House staff members later in this chapter.

Second, the president (as principal) must try to coordinate the bureaucracy (as agents). There are natural coordination problems in the executive branch.

[4] For a comprehensive account of presidential authority, see Richard Neustadt, *Presidential Power and the Modern Presidents* (New York: Free Press, 1990).

To act effectively, the president must get the disparate parts of the executive branch to coordinate their decisions and actions by cultivating loyalty to certain policies among White House staff, among top executive-branch officials, and throughout the federal bureaucracy. Later in this chapter, we will discuss how the presidency over time has increasingly used the White House staff, and at times the vice president, to coordinate the federal bureaucracy.

Third, the president is needed to solve broad collective dilemmas, not just those occurring within his group of advisers. The creation—and evolution—of the presidency stemmed from the need to solve collective dilemmas among the states, within Congress, and among various groups within society. The justification among the Founders for having a single person as president was that it was an important component for developing a strong central government. Recall that they (the Federalists, at least) wanted a stronger central government to overcome collective dilemmas among the states. Over time, the president's ability to solve broad collective dilemmas has been an underlying cause of the growth in presidential power.

The solving of collective dilemmas and principal-agent problems occurred right away following the Founding. As the first president, Washington set a variety of important precedents. First, he instituted the cabinet system and met regularly with his closest advisers, some of whom were secretaries of such departments as Treasury and State. By creating the cabinet, Washington was attempting to coordinate the actions of the several executive departments. Second, he firmly maintained that the president had inherent powers that were implied, but not explicitly stated, in the Constitution. These inherent powers included the authorization to conduct a broad array of diplomatic relations with foreign countries, the negotiation of treaties before asking the Senate for approval, and the "federalization" of state militias to keep domestic peace. For example, Washington used state militias in 1794 to end the Whiskey Rebellion, a series of attacks by Pennsylvania farmers on officials charged with collecting federal excise taxes. True to the wishes of the Founders (and in contrast to the problems under the Articles of Confederation—see Chapter 2), Washington acted forcefully, coordinating the disparate state militias to quell internal unrest.

When George Washington was sworn in as president in 1789, most of the Founders wanted a stronger executive to help solve collective dilemmas. The Federalists believed that having a single president (rather than a multi-person executive council, for example) was important for a stronger central government.

Shaping the Modern Presidency

The American presidency as an institution has changed substantially over time because individual presidents responded to circumstances and built support for stronger institutional powers. The actions of several key presidents continued the trajectory Washington initiated, stretching and expanding the prerogatives of the office, making the presidency more partisan, more populist, and more powerful than the Founders intended.

Nineteenth-Century Changes

Three nineteenth-century presidents were especially influential in changing the institution. Andrew Jackson and Martin Van Buren made the presidency more populist and partisan than the Founders had intended; Abraham Lincoln then made the presidency more powerful, mostly through strong military action.

The President as the Voice of the People. Jackson served two terms as president, from 1829 to 1837, and profoundly changed the office. First, more than any previous president, he continually justified his actions as following the people's will. He considered himself the people's legitimate representative in opposition to the economically and politically well connected, and especially against Congress, which he berated as a bastion of special interests. Throughout his administration, he maintained that the presidency was equal to Congress and not subordinate to it. Jackson believed that only the president, as a single person representing the people, could overcome the delay and deadlock caused by disagreements among rival groups within Congress and among the states. In our contemporary terminology, he viewed himself as a solver of collective dilemmas.[5]

The Spoils System and Partisan Goals. Jackson also expanded and governed through use of the **spoils system**, which lasted in full until late in the nineteenth century and in some respects survives to this day. Under the spoils system, loyal partisans who support the president during campaigns for office gain government jobs after the elections. Jackson campaigned for the presidency by harshly criticizing the federal bureaucracy and promising to replace federal employees on a regular basis. The spoils system gave Jackson and subsequent nineteenth-century presidents many opportunities to fill government jobs with party supporters.

Van Buren, Jackson's second-term vice president, won the presidency in 1836 and used the spoils system to create mass parties. Following Jackson's

spoils system The practice of rewarding loyal partisans with government positions after they demonstrate their support during an election.

[5] For more on Jackson's populism, see Robert Remini, *The Life of Andrew Jackson* (New York: Harper and Row, 1998).

lead, presidential candidates like Van Buren offered federal jobs to supporters if elected. The spoils system helped presidents carry out their policies within the bureaucracy, but it also helped them solidify the loyalties of new voters toward the party in office. From this point forward, presidents routinely provided government jobs to people who supported them *and* their party.

Van Buren's genius was to exploit and build on the rapid expansion of voting rights that occurred in this era. Candidates for president, and the presidents themselves, needed to mobilize large numbers of voters to win mass elections and accomplish what they wanted to in office. Van Buren saw that the way to mobilize large numbers of voters was to link local, state, and national elections in a common partisan effort. State-level political parties would help themselves win state offices by helping the party's presidential candidate win the national office. Van Buren's goal was to mobilize a national organization in support of a single presidential candidate. It was to have a presence at all levels of government, and it would continue beyond the Van Buren presidency.

Voting in mass elections presents a collective action problem. Citizens always face the temptation to stay at home and avoid the costs of voting, such as the need in Van Buren's time to travel long distances to polling stations. It is tempting to free ride off the voting of fellow citizens. Parties and candidates must overcome these temptations and give citizens compelling reasons to act collectively by voting. In the 1830s and subsequently, they did so by organizing rousing parades, rallies, and pamphlets, by exaggerating the danger of voting for the opposing party, and by going door to door in their canvassing.

Furthermore, political parties in Van Buren's era had to convince state party leaders to support their presidential candidate because the state party leaders picked the delegates to the national convention. State party leaders across the country faced coordination problems in deciding which potential candidates to support. If they failed to agree on a candidate within their party, the opposition party would likely win. Thus, presidential candidates and their supporters needed to convince voters to turn out, and they also needed to coordinate their actions among state leaders.

Van Buren's efforts built a partisan presidency based on the mass support and mobilization of many new voters. Turnout for his election in 1836 was even higher than that of 1832, at the peak of Jackson's popularity. Van Buren approached the presidential contest as a partisan effort to gain mass support, and he succeeded in bringing many new participants into the political process.

The President as Military Leader. Lincoln's actions during the Civil War set key precedents for how executive power over the militia can solve the deepest of collective dilemmas. Lincoln faced the most serious crisis in American history when the southern states seceded from the Union in 1860–61 and declared themselves a separate country, the Confederate States of America. To defeat the southern rebels and reunite the country, he needed to invade the

South and protect the North. He was concerned not only about the Confederate army invading the North and capturing Washington, D.C., but also about southern infiltration and sabotage. He had to deal with northern states that were reluctant to send troops, money, and matériel for the war. There was strong resistance to the draft in the North, including violent draft riots. In other words, the northern states' leaders and populations faced deep collective action problems. They all wanted to defeat the South or end the war or both, yet it was costly to contribute to the effort and there were incentives to free ride.

Lincoln responded forcefully to overcome these problems. With the help of allies in Congress, he created what were at the time massive government bureaucracies to supply the army with troops, materials, food, and transportation and communication networks. When state governments in the North resisted his calls for more draftees to fight the war, he forced their hand by threatening arrests and armed intervention. And he went beyond the provisions of the Constitution in temporarily suspending the writ of habeas corpus, allowing federal troops and local officials to arrest people suspected of treason and hold them indefinitely without charge. In essence, he enforced the cooperation of people he needed to contribute to costly collective efforts.

Lincoln often faced a recalcitrant Congress, stubborn state leaders, and many critics within his own party and the army. He pushed on with the war effort, even when some of his own advisers urged him to settle with the South and end the conflict. Institutionally, he pushed the boundaries of presidential power during the Civil War by exploiting ambiguities in the Constitution (which we will discuss in the next section). He expanded the role of commander in chief far beyond what previous presidents had done, and he made policy decisions about the war within his administration and sometimes without full congressional approval.

Through Lincoln's efforts, and with the help of political allies who agreed with his political goals (though not necessarily with his institutional methods), the size of the national government and especially the powers of the president grew substantially during the Civil War era. In the years since Lincoln's presidency, Congress and the courts have given presidents more leeway to conduct foreign policy and make war than the Founders had likely intended. Although many of the bureaucracies Lincoln created to help prosecute the war were abolished after its conclusion, as we saw in Chapter 3, the size of the national government—in both spending and personnel—remained larger after the war than before it.

As this example shows, crises call for quick responses that often require coordination among, and even coercion of, diverse interests and political groups. After the crisis passes, there is often disagreement over whether to return to a weaker presidency or to maintain the new institutionalized powers of the executive office. Thus, we see a persistent dynamic in American political history: an emergency leads first to a stronger presidency and then to ongoing debates and political conflicts over continuing or rescinding presidential power. As illustrated by the cases of Lincoln in the Civil War and Obama with his many executive actions, the presidency has grown stronger largely due to individual presidents with enough political support from the other branches to solve collective dilemmas.

Through the Twentieth Century and into the Twenty-First

From Lincoln's actions during the Civil War, we have seen how presidents can increase their power in times of crisis. In the twentieth century, the presidency became powerful to a degree beyond the reckoning of the Founders and nineteenth-century Americans. In many ways, this development parallels the increasing power of the national government relative to the states, and especially the increasing power of the United States in world affairs. It was not inevitable, however, that the presidency would become as important as it has within the American political system.

Building on the Partisan Presidency. As a result of Jackson's and Van Buren's strategies in the nineteenth century, all successful presidential candidates since have had to gain leadership within one of the two major parties and help the party turn out the vote at the national, state, and local levels. As head of the party, the president is expected to solve collective dilemmas that arise from within the party.

The president today is the party leader in two arenas, elections and policy making.[6] Because the president is the public face of the party, his or her popularity shapes the party's fortunes in congressional and state elections. These election contests are deeply affected by people's attitudes toward the president. When the president is relatively popular, candidates for other offices running under the same party label typically benefit by "riding on the president's coattails." This means that candidates receive a boost in their own election fortunes simply by belonging to the same party as a popular president. On the flip side, members of the president's party can face difficulties when the president is relatively unpopular.

Some presidents have followed Van Buren's example and been important builders of political parties as organizations, helping candidates at all levels to mobilize voters, raise money, and create a more permanent party presence in the states and localities. Among recent presidents, Ronald Reagan was noteworthy for traveling around the country to help congressional and state candidates in their efforts to win elections. He spoke at numerous fund-raising events

---

[6] Sidney Milkis, *The President and the Parties* (New York: Oxford University Press, 1993); Scott James, *Presidents, Parties, and the State* (New York: Cambridge University Press, 2000).

for congressional candidates. Not all presidents relish this role, and some have been criticized for largely ignoring it. Richard Nixon was criticized by members of the Republican Party for not doing enough to help the party as a whole improve its capacity to win elections throughout the country. Barack Obama was criticized for not helping fellow Democrats enough in 2008 and 2012.

During presidential campaigns and in the several months after someone takes office in the White House, the president's initiatives shape the policy agenda not only of the party but also of the national government as a whole. Obama campaigned in 2012, as he had in 2008, on a platform of stimulating the economy and improving health care and education. His ideas dominated public debate after both elections

The president is a leader in both policy making and party politics. Donald Trump's White House Chief of Staff, John Kelly, was formerly the secretary of Homeland Security under Donald Trump.

and led to major shifts in government policy, including massive federal stimulus spending in 2009, an overhaul of health care in 2010, new immigration policies in 2013, and an education program that has affected every public school in the country. Obama's policy proposals and their aftermath will shape the Democratic Party's reputation for years. Donald Trump entered the office in 2017 with some policy goals that were consistent as well as at odds with fellow members of his party. He shared goals with his Republican colleagues in Congress to cut taxes and certain spending categories, especially domestic programs, and to reduce business regulations. But he departed from them in dramatically increasing the national debt and in adopting new restrictions on international trade.

The president relies on his own party members in Congress to support White House initiatives. Although they cannot expect unanimous support from all party members, presidents can count on much more support from members of their own party than from the opposition. Opposition-party members in Congress can be expected to oppose the president regularly, to criticize presidential policies and competence, and to try to thwart White House efforts.

Partly because presidents serve as leaders and standard-bearers for their political parties, they are deeply affected by the partisan makeup of Congress. Presidents can accomplish more of their goals when bargaining with the legislative branches if they have partisan allies at the table. Presidential success in bargaining depends substantially on whether the country has **divided** or **unified government**. The U.S. government is said to be divided when the presidency and at least one chamber of Congress are controlled by different political parties. Under divided government, presidents find it more difficult to get their

divided government A government whose president is from a different party than the majority in Congress.

unified government A government whose president is from the same party as the majority in Congress.

legislative priorities passed. We will consider this issue later in this chapter in our discussion of the president's veto power.

Developing the Populist Presidency. Although Jackson promoted the idea of the president as the voice of the people, most nineteenth-century presidents remained aloof, rarely making public appearances. It was considered undignified, for example, to campaign openly for reelection by giving speeches to the general public. Presidents seldom left Washington, D.C., even during campaign seasons.

In the twentieth century, the presidency became much more populist. Woodrow Wilson, who served two terms from 1913 to 1921, went beyond any previous president in his effort to reach the average man and woman "in the street." In part, this was because automobiles and improved roads gave him technological advantages over his predecessors. Moreover, Wilson's philosophy of democratic governance emphasized the value of direct contact between the president as leader and the people the president serves. He also gave many speeches in Washington trying to woo the press and interest groups in his favor over political opponents.

After Wilson, presidents increasingly reached out to the American people and sought their support as a way of increasing their own power. Presidents today use televised speeches and press conferences to communicate directly with citizens (Figure 6.1). Modern scholars call this **going public**. President Ronald Reagan, who was elected in 1980, raised this art to a new level. A former movie star, he had a warm smile and telegenic looks that endeared him to people and mobilized supporters. Reagan's ability to use his personal popularity to win over the general public, who would then pressure their members of Congress to follow his lead, is legendary. During one of his televised addresses to the country in 1981 about his proposed budget, which was stalled in Congress, he could not have been more explicit: "I urge you again to contact your senators and congressmen. Tell them of your support for this bipartisan proposal. Tell them you believe this is an unequaled opportunity to help return America to prosperity and make government again the servant of the people."[7] Reagan continually battered congressional opponents by encouraging constituents to inundate them with letters. Even after he had been in office for five years, one Democratic member of Congress admitted, "We're still a bit afraid of him."[8]

Besides talking to people directly, presidents—beginning with John F. Kennedy in the early 1960s—have increasingly conducted private polls to measure pub-

going public Action taken by a president to communicate directly with the people usually through a press conference, radio broadcast, or televised speech to influence public opinion and put pressure on Congress.

[7] Samuel Kernell, *Going Public: New Strategies of Presidential Leadership*, 3rd ed. (Washington, DC: CQ Press, 1997), p. 150. See also, Brandice Canes-Wrone and Kenneth Schotts, "Conditional Nature of Presidential Responsiveness to Public Opinion," *American Journal of Political Science* 48 (October 2004): 690–706.

[8] Kernell, *Going Public*, p. 140.

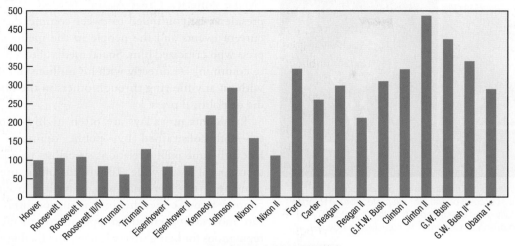

FIGURE 6.1

Presidential Public Activities in the United States (yearly average)*

Presidential Administration

* The yearly average number of public activities by presidents; includes major speeches, news conferences, minor speeches, and U.S. appearances, including those in Washington, D.C. Excludes specifically political activities.

** Through 2007 only. Data for Obama's first term are approximated from available data as of fall 2014. Data for Obama's second term are not available.

Source: Lyn Ragsdale, *Vital Statistics on the Presidency*, 3rd ed. (Washington, DC: CQ Press, 2009), p. 207.

lic opinion about their standing and their prospects for success with legislative initiatives. From new archival research, we now know that Kennedy conducted 15 private polls in less than three years in office, compared with Reagan's 204 in eight years.[9] Presidents use polls regularly to hone their communications with the general public and to gauge their popular approval. Bill Clinton reportedly favored pursuing policy goals that had the support of 60 percent of the public according to polls.

President Barack Obama, meanwhile, enthusiastically embraced social media to interact with the public and promote his legislative priorities. Obama communicated directly with nearly tens of millions of followers on Facebook and on Twitter. As part of his presidential campaign for reelection, his team developed its own social network, MyBarackObama.com. This strategy allowed the president direct contact with his supporters while also giving him access to information about his supporters to be used in the reelection campaign. No president used social media during a campaign as actively as Donald

[9] Lawrence R. Jacobs, "Communicating from the White House: Presidential Narrowcasting and the National Interest," in *The Executive Branch*, ed. Joel D. Aberbach and Mark A. Peterson (New York: Oxford University Press, 2005), pp. 174–218.

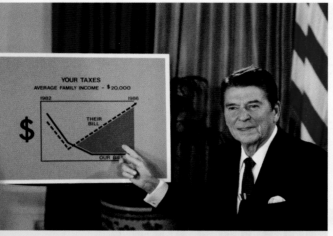

The president's connection to the people can be an important source of power. For example, Ronald Reagan successfully used direct appeals to the American people to pressure Congress to approve his policies.

Trump. He used his Twitter account to disparage opponents, tout his own ideas and accomplishments, and exhort his followers to join his movement to "Make America Great Again" (#MAGA). Even as president, he continued to tweet commentary about current events and the people in the media and the press who criticized him. Social media allowed Trump to communicate directly with his millions of followers without any filtering through others in the mass media or political press.

Presidents nowadays are often highly responsive to—and constrained by—public opinion.[10] They hire full-time public relations specialists to maximize their appeal nationwide. To win the office, presidents campaign in a personal way, traveling around the country to make speeches in as many localities as they can and crafting emotional appeals to enhance their reputations for being strong leaders and likable personalities. Once in office, they frequently leave Washington, D.C., to appear in person to announce new policy initiatives, pressure local members of Congress to vote their way, and raise money for congressional and presidential campaigns. They need to press the flesh constantly, be sure to give their speeches before the local television news deadlines, and present themselves in appealing settings such as school classrooms, factory floors, and fields of wheat and corn.

Enhancing Presidential Power through Military and Economic Means

Three presidents in the early twentieth century are noteworthy for changing the nature of presidential power: Theodore Roosevelt, Woodrow Wilson, and Franklin Delano Roosevelt. Republican Theodore Roosevelt served as president from 1901 to 1909. He created a personality cult around the office that had never before existed. An extraordinarily popular president, he was known as much for his larger-than-life personality as for his policies. "Teddy" Roosevelt projected an energetic, athletic, can-do spirit with the help of an increasingly aggressive press corps that covered his daily actions and utterances in detail. Like Andrew Jackson, he governed with the attitude that he alone represented the people.

[10] We will discuss the relationship between politicians and public opinion in Chapter 9.

Roosevelt made effective use of his "bully pulpit"—his privileged place as speaker on behalf of the American people—to pressure those who opposed his agenda. He was careful to cultivate the notion that the presidency was separate from Congress and that the president would not wait for Congress to act if he felt the action was in the people's best interest. Roosevelt demonstrated repeatedly that a president's personal charisma and popularity with the masses could be a powerful political tool. He had no qualms about stirring up popular support for his policies to pressure political opponents, even those within his Republican Party. The personality of the president, particularly his public approval and his performance in office, grew in importance following Roosevelt's tenure.

Like his successors, Roosevelt responded to collective dilemmas among various economic and political groups. The industrialization of the country had created an urban working class that was increasingly militant and demanded a share in the nation's wealth. It also gave rise to enormous industrial corporations (the "trusts") that Roosevelt considered dangerous to the country's economic and social well-being. Many people wanted to rein in these trusts, and a collective effort by various economic interests could have accomplished it. Such action, however, would have been costly because of the trusts' power and ability to punish opponents. Others wanted to counteract the increasing power of a small number of trade unions. Roosevelt responded to pressure from these constituencies by forming regulatory agencies and using litigation as a forceful tool.

For example, rather than wait for a foot-dragging Congress to legislate against the trusts—the huge monopoly corporations that he wanted to break up into smaller companies—Roosevelt decided to sue the trusts directly from the president's office. He initiated 44 lawsuits against companies in his first year in office, an unprecedented strong-arm tactic for any branch of the national government to undertake, let alone the presidency.

Institutionally, Roosevelt took major steps toward creating a national government bureaucracy to regulate the activities of American businesses. His executive branch increasingly regulated the railroads, oil companies, and some forestry industries. This policy expanded the role of the national government in the economy and gave the presidency a substantial boost in power. Although Teddy Roosevelt is credited with setting the regulatory wheels in motion, full-scale regulation of broad sectors of the economy did not come to fruition until after his cousin, Franklin Delano Roosevelt, became president in 1933.

We have already learned how Wilson advanced the populism of the office. In world affairs, Wilson changed the presidency in important ways during and after World War I. He sought to establish the American president as a major voice in international politics, on an equal footing with leaders of the great powers in Europe. He believed that one of his major roles following World War I was to help the European countries resolve their internal collective dilemmas.

Wilson emphasized an internationalist foreign policy and established regular contact with his counterparts abroad. His foreign policy had broad implications for the future of the presidency. Most presidents who followed Wilson, including those who served through the Cold War and into the 1990s, regarded maintaining the peace in Europe, Asia, and Latin America as a prime mission.

No president other than Washington has affected the nature of the office more than Franklin Delano Roosevelt (known as FDR, to distinguish him from Teddy). Starting in 1932, he won four elections—more than any president before or since—and served three full terms. (He died in 1945, about three months into his fourth term.) The two signature achievements of Roosevelt's presidency, the New Deal and the leadership of the Allies in World War II, led to massive increases in the size, reach, and importance of the national government.

After the Wall Street crash of 1929, the national government under President Herbert Hoover and the Republican Congress seemed unable or unwilling to respond effectively to the economic crisis. Political leaders and various economic interests disagreed over what the national government should do. The Democrats swept into power in the 1932 elections on a wave of optimism, but they too faced uncertainty and internal dissension. FDR devoted his efforts to solving collective dilemmas within his own party and across many diverse and competing interests. Within the first 100 days of taking office in 1933, he laid the groundwork for his New Deal, a set of policies intended to boost the American economy in the face of the Great Depression, to stabilize it once it was back on its feet, and to regulate further the activities of corporations. A by-product of the policies was to redistribute income in favor of retirees, widows, the disabled, and orphans.

The New Deal, discussed in detail in Chapters 3 and 15, was a major overhaul in how the national government operated within the American political system. It gave the executive branch greater authority than ever before. Under FDR, many new national bureaucracies were created to regulate the economy, with the result that the White House directed economic policies to an unprecedented degree. New Deal policies, including Social Security and unemployment insurance, increased both the taxes the national government collected from people and the benefits people received from the national government.

In the wake of FDR's New Deal, the political fate of all presidents—including reelection prospects, overall popularity, and ability to get legislation passed in Congress—has increasingly been tied to the state of the national economy. Because the presidency now wielded so much power, the American people could legitimately blame presidents when the economy was in trouble and reward them when times were good.

As during Lincoln's presidency, the Roosevelt administration's war effort also greatly expanded the size of the national government. The massive mo-

1787 The Constitution sets up a single executive elected by the electoral college and independent from the legislature.

1829–37 Andrew Jackson establishes the spoils system, rewarding individuals for their partisan loyalties and contributions.

1901–09 Congress empowers Theodore Roosevelt to set regulatory wheels in motion by establishing rules regulating railroads, oil companies, and some forestry industries.

1933–45 FDR, faced with economic turmoil during the Great Depression, makes sweeping regulatory reforms and expands the executive administration.

2001– George W. Bush and Barack Obama push the boundaries of authority over intelligence gathering and the detainment of prisoners while conducting the War on Terror.

1750　1800　1850　1900　1950　2000

1789–97 George Washington sets important precedents, including the establishment of a cabinet system.

1837–41 Martin Van Buren promises positions in federal office to his supporters and mobilizes voters through a national party that functioned at the national, state, and local levels.

1913–21 Woodrow Wilson campaigns directly to the people, marking the beginning of the populist presidency.

1981–89 Ronald Reagan takes the strategy of "going public" to the next level, using public pressure to get his policies passed.

bilization of more than 5 million U.S. soldiers and sailors during World War II (1941–45) necessitated a huge government bureaucracy to oversee their recruiting, training, supply, and transport. Unlike in the past, however, the military did not shrink after the war to a tiny peacetime force, but remained large and strong. FDR's successors, Presidents Harry S. Truman and Dwight D. Eisenhower, carried on many of his policies.

By the end of World War II, however, the country had largely abandoned its previous isolationist foreign policy and become deeply involved in international affairs on every continent. The national government spawned a huge military bureaucracy devoted to gathering intelligence, protecting Europe (and ultimately Korea) from communist aggression, and participating in new international organizations such as the United Nations (UN) and the North Atlantic Treaty Organization (NATO). The victory in World War II under FDR ushered in a new era of American leadership on the world stage, which in turn raised the American president to new heights of power and influence.

Growth of the federal government spilled over into the president's own office. FDR created a massive bureaucracy within the executive branch that was devoted to helping him make economic and foreign policy decisions in addition to implementing policies decided upon by the legislative branch. Figure 6.2 shows the current bureaucracy built around the office of the president. It is important to recognize that none of these bureaucratic institutions, other than the cabinet departments, existed before FDR took office.

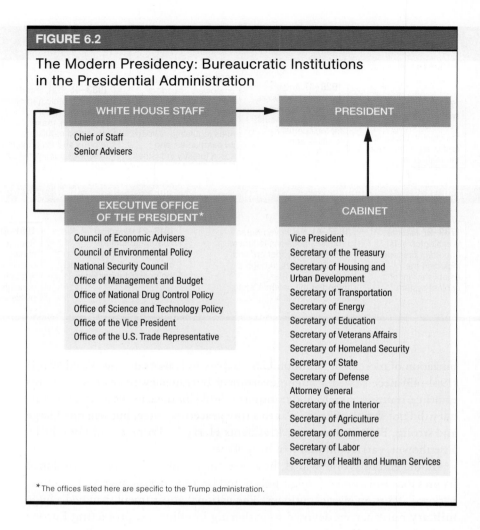

FIGURE 6.2

The Modern Presidency: Bureaucratic Institutions in the Presidential Administration

WHITE HOUSE STAFF

Chief of Staff
Senior Advisers

PRESIDENT

EXECUTIVE OFFICE OF THE PRESIDENT*

Council of Economic Advisers
Council of Environmental Policy
National Security Council
Office of Management and Budget
Office of National Drug Control Policy
Office of Science and Technology Policy
Office of the Vice President
Office of the U.S. Trade Representative

CABINET

Vice President
Secretary of the Treasury
Secretary of Housing and Urban Development
Secretary of Transportation
Secretary of Energy
Secretary of Education
Secretary of Veterans Affairs
Secretary of Homeland Security
Secretary of State
Secretary of Defense
Attorney General
Secretary of the Interior
Secretary of Agriculture
Secretary of Commerce
Secretary of Labor
Secretary of Health and Human Services

*The offices listed here are specific to the Trump administration.

Today's Powerful Presidency

The president has a variety of tools to wield authority, and many of these tools are oriented toward solving collective dilemmas and principal–agent problems. We can divide the tools into informal and formal (or enumerated) powers.

The president's position as head of a major political party and his ability to command public attention and communicate directly with citizens are key sources of presidential power. We call these *informal powers*, and they have grown over time with the actions of successive presidents. They enable the president to influence the actions of other branches of government, of state leaders, and of group leaders in society. When FDR needed the support of Democratic governors in the South for his New Deal policies, he leaned on them heavily, appealing to them as fellow Democrats and pointing out how popular some New Deal programs were among people in the South. He was actively trying to avoid having them defect from partisan cooperation on the New Deal. Barack Obama, like FDR and other presidents, used his informal powers to pressure Congress to adopt his policies. He too needed to overcome collective dilemmas, even among members of his own Democratic Party, to keep a coalition together. Obama achieved much of his early agenda, including a large stimulus spending plan, health care reform, and financial regulation reform, through a mixture of coaxing and public appeals to prod reluctant members of the House and Senate to vote in favor of his preferred bills.

A prominent theory of the presidency by Richard Neustadt proposes, in fact, that the president's informal powers of interpersonal persuasion are most important. Well beyond formal powers like the veto and appointment powers, the critical aspect of presidential leadership is the ability to persuade others that their interests lie in acting consistently with the president's goals. Presidents vary in their abilities to persuade, and thus in the effectiveness of their actions on policy. All presidents have similar formal powers that have changed only over long periods of time, but they differ in how well they wield their informal powers.[11]

In addition to the informal powers that Neustadt highlights, the president also exercises formal powers, sometimes called *enumerated powers*. These include powers specified by the Constitution and others that developed later and became codified into law through court rulings or statutes. Congress has delegated many powers to the executive branch, especially in the area of foreign policy, but also in domestic affairs. For example, early in the country's history the president's powers as commander in chief were expanded with congressional approval. On several occasions, most notably with the 1973 War Powers Act, Congress has tried to rein in the president's power to wage war, but these curbs have been largely ineffective. (See Chapter 17 for more on the War Powers Act.)

Furthermore, Congress and the courts have permitted the creation of **administrative law**, whereby Congress passes legislation to achieve broad policy goals, and the administrative agencies in the executive branch have the authority to fill in the legislative details. As we will see in Chapter 7, administrative decisions of the federal bureaucracies overseen by the president can have the force of law.

administrative law The body of law created by executive agencies with the purpose of refining general law passed in legislation.

Finally, in the early years of the Republic, Congress met for less than half the year. (Today Congress is in session almost continuously.) Many major decisions by early presidents, including Thomas Jefferson's Louisiana Purchase, which more than doubled the geographic size of the country, were made while

---

[11] Richard Neustadt, *Presidential Power and the Modern Presidents: The Politics of Leadership from Roosevelt to Reagan* (New York: The Free Press, 1990).

Congress was out of session. Because Congress was not always available to consult, presidents had more leeway to act. Over time, presidents seized these opportunities not only to make policy but also to increase the power of their office.

Let's now consider several of the president's formal powers in more detail. Some (the veto and the power to make appointments) are mentioned in the Constitution while others (executive orders and agreements, signing statements, and access to administrative resources) were asserted by presidents and later sanctioned by Congress and the courts.

The Veto

As we saw in Chapter 5, if Congress passes a bill, the president can either sign it into law or veto it. Congress can override a veto with a two-thirds vote in both chambers. If Congress overrides the president's veto, the bill becomes law without presidential signature. Presidents can also exercise a **pocket veto** by failing to sign legislation at the end of a congressional session. If Congress is not in session, then bills unsigned by the president 10 days after being passed by Congress are considered vetoed. Congress must pass the law again in the next session to keep the bill alive. In recent decades, the pocket veto has been rare because Congress has lately anticipated the president's possible action and scheduled legislative final votes to avoid the 10-day cutoff. This does not mean the pocket veto is now unimportant. Rather, the possibility of its usage shapes the nature of congressional action and spurs members to speed things along when the end of a session approaches.

The earliest presidents used the veto to nullify bills passed by Congress that they felt were unconstitutional. Andrew Jackson was the first president to justify the veto as a strategic tool to bring about policies more to his liking. He vetoed bills simply because he disagreed with them. In other words, Jackson considered the veto as a legislative procedure rather than merely a way to protect the Constitution. This rankled members of Congress at the time, but Jackson set a precedent that has been followed ever since.

Figure 6.3 shows how some presidents have regularly used the veto to bargain with Congress, while others have used it sparingly. What explains the differences? To answer this question, let's step back a bit and use the logic described earlier for the pocket veto. Contemporary scholars have studied how the mere *threat* of the veto can convince Congress to modify a piece of legislation. Thus presidents may not actually need to use the veto to achieve their goals. Presidents make so-called **veto threats** by publicly stating that if Congress passes a bill that the president dislikes, he or she will veto it. Scholars have shown that Congress tends to modify bills after presidents issue veto threats. This is a case of an institutional device, the veto, granting the president

pocket veto A veto that occurs automatically if a president does not sign a bill for 10 days after passage in Congress and Congress has adjourned during that 10-day period.

veto threat A public statement issued by the president declaring that if Congress passes a particular bill that he or she dislikes, it ultimately will be vetoed.

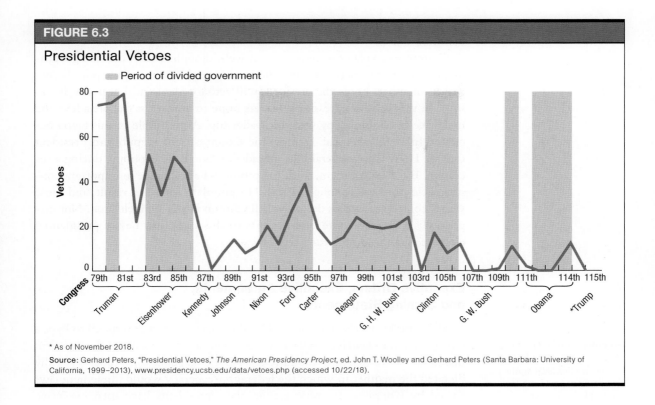

FIGURE 6.3

Presidential Vetoes

Period of divided government

*As of November 2018.

Source: Gerhard Peters, "Presidential Vetoes," *The American Presidency Project*, ed. John T. Woolley and Gerhard Peters (Santa Barbara: University of California, 1999–2013), www.presidency.ucsb.edu/data/vetoes.php (accessed 10/22/18).

considerable power over legislation; the president doesn't actually need to use it, but only to have it available for use if necessary. Thus, even though presidents seldom exercise the veto power, it is still considered an important tool.

Partisan control of Congress also helps explain differences in the use of the veto. In our discussion of divided government and unified government, we saw how partisan control of Congress can affect the success of the president's legislative initiatives. As we might expect, research has shown that presidents veto important legislation much more often under divided government than under unified government.[12]

Bargaining between the president and Congress becomes easier to manage when the president and Congress belong to the same party. The president can typically expect cooperation from members of his own party in Congress. Under unified government, Congress does not usually send the president a bill that is destined to be vetoed, because any differences between the two branches have already been smoothed over within the party. Under divided government, the two major parties spar more frequently over legislation, and

[12] Charles Cameron, *Veto Bargaining* (New York: Cambridge University Press, 2000).

the presidential veto or veto threat can be a powerful weapon in this partisan conflict.

Congress can play the veto game as well, though. Under divided government, Congress sometimes sends the president a bill that is quite popular but that its members know the president will veto for ideological or political reasons. In this way, congressional leaders hope to embarrass the president and make the public unhappy with his leadership. An example of this tactic occurred in 1992 when the Democratic Congress sent Republican President George H. W. Bush several bills intended to boost the economy during a recession. Bush vetoed them, fulfilling promises he had made to important constituencies in the Republican Party. His popularity fell as a result, and those vetoes contributed to his defeat by Bill Clinton in the 1992 election. Not surprisingly, Congress more often resorts to this tactic just before presidential elections than in other years.[13]

Executive Orders, Executive Agreements, and Signing Statements

executive order An official means by which the president can instruct federal agencies on how to execute the laws passed by Congress.

Modern presidents also have several legal maneuvers at their disposal to bypass Congress. An **executive order** is a regulation or a rule made by the president that has the force of law. In the early years of the Republic, such orders typically dictated the manner in which the federal bureaucracy would implement laws passed by Congress. In more recent years, presidents have used executive orders to make major policy changes and even exercise war powers. Examples include Harry S. Truman's order that desegregated the armed forces, Lyndon Johnson's order that the U.S. government adopt affirmative action, and Bill Clinton's order that led to the use of military force in Kosovo. (Technically, President Obama's action on immigration discussed in the opening story was not formally an executive order but simply a directive for an agency to follow and did not involve formal changes in any laws or regulations.)

All recent presidents have issued executive orders to avoid waiting for legislation that might not be forthcoming from a Congress controlled by the opposition party.[14] Sometimes resistance by members of the president's own party prompts the president to resort to an executive order. Truman desegregated the armed forces in 1948 after bills introduced in Congress to do the same were repeatedly stymied by southern Democrats. Another reason for the use of executive orders over the past century is that the United States has been engaged in many wars since the 1930s. Executive orders are issued frequently

[13] Tim Groseclose and Nolan McCarty, "The Politics of Blame: Bargaining before an Audience," *American Journal of Political Science* 45, no. 1 (2001): 100–119.

[14] William Howell, *Power without Persuasion* (Princeton, NJ: Princeton University Press, 2003).

during wartime because presidents do not feel they have the time to wait for congressional action.

The courts generally have upheld the right of presidents to issue executive orders, within limits. In two notable cases, however, federal judges have ruled that the president overstepped the bounds of executive authority and defied labor laws passed by Congress: Truman seized steel mills in 1952 to prevent a labor strike during the Korean War, and the court ruled that he was overstepping his role as commander in chief; and Clinton in 1996 ordered government agencies not to contract with organizations that had strikebreakers on their payrolls.

Congressional legislation can overturn an executive order, although such a law must generally survive a presidential veto. Thus, if a president is confident of having the support of at least one-third of the members of one chamber of Congress for a given action, an executive order is an effective way to make policy without requiring that a law be passed by Congress. George W. Bush made ample use of this maneuver, for example, when he limited funding for stem cell research through an executive order. Barack Obama used executive orders to reverse this and several other Bush policies (see the Interests, Institutions, and Outcomes box on page 226).

Presidents can also issue **executive agreements**, which are those made between the United States and foreign countries and that are concluded solely with presidential approval. Because such agreements are not treaties, they do not need Senate approval. As to how they are enforced and their legal status, there is not much difference between a treaty and an executive agreement, except that treaties are more prominent and are considered weightier and more enduring. Since the end of World War II, the United States has been party to more than 10,000 executive agreements involving trade, troop deployments in foreign countries, and cultural exchanges. The federal courts have repeatedly held that such agreements are constitutional.

Finally, presidents can issue **signing statements**. These are public declarations about how the president intends to interpret a law, and they can be controversial both legally and politically. Like their predecessors, George W. Bush and Barack Obama both used signing statements to communicate how laws should be interpreted by federal agencies and the courts. Most experts agree that such statements are within presidential prerogative. In his signing statements, President Bush also indicated which parts of laws he considered unconstitutional and would not enforce. Critics charged that this tactic gave him, in effect, a line-item veto, which is not allowed under current constitutional law. It is unclear whether the courts will allow this latter use of signing statements to continue, but President Bush often issued them in connection with foreign policy matters, where presidents historically have had great discretion. President Obama used signing statements mostly to clarify where he thought the

executive agreement An agreement between the United States and one or more foreign countries. Because it is not a formal treaty, it does not need Senate approval.

signing statement A public statement written by the president and attached to a particular bill to outline his or her interpretation of the legislation.

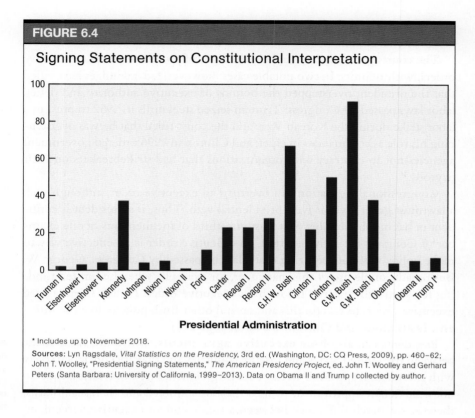

FIGURE 6.4

Signing Statements on Constitutional Interpretation

Presidential Administration

* Includes up to November 2018.

Sources: Lyn Ragsdale, *Vital Statistics on the Presidency*, 3rd ed. (Washington, DC: CQ Press, 2009), pp. 460–62; John T. Woolley, "Presidential Signing Statements," *The American Presidency Project*, ed. John T. Woolley and Gerhard Peters (Santa Barbara: University of California, 1999–2013). Data on Obama II and Trump I collected by author.

line was between executive authority and legislative authority. As Figure 6.4 shows, modern presidents have been increasingly likely to issue signing statements to address constitutional questions.

Appointments

The Constitution grants the president the power to make appointments to executive departments and other bureaus, and to the federal courts. Beginning with George Washington, presidents have shaped their governments by appointing people who agree with them on policy matters. With the growth of the federal government, this prerogative has become even more significant. Today, presidents make thousands of appointments to populate a much larger and more powerful national bureaucracy that affects the well-being of every community in the country

Historically, most presidential appointments that require the Senate's "advice and consent" have been routinely approved. High-profile positions, including cabinet secretaries and especially Supreme Court justices, can be controversial, and occasionally the Senate will reject a presidential appointment. But by and large, appointment of personnel at the top of the executive agencies and in the courts occurs as the president sees fit. Certain kinds of positions, especially ambassadorships to foreign countries, are often handed out as rewards to people who helped the president get elected. For example, President George W. Bush appointed David H. Wilkins, a major contributor to his 2004 campaign, as ambassador to Canada. Similarly, President Barack Obama appointed Dan Rooney, owner of the Pittsburgh Steelers football team and an early supporter of Obama's candidacy in Pennsylvania, to be ambassador to Ireland. Donald Trump focused his earliest appointments on those he considered were most loyal to him during the contentious 2016 campaign, such as Senators Jeff Sessions for Attorney General and Reince Priebus for chief of staff. He raised eyebrows when he appointed Steve Bannon, a fiery businessman linked to far-right media sites, to be his chief counselor. Bannon was controversial, but he had been loyal to Trump and it paid off. With exceptions, he mostly avoided the many Republicans who had been critical of him. These appointments followed a long, bipartisan tradition of handing out federal jobs to thank people and curry favor with donors and the party faithful. Although the spoils system is a shadow of what it was in the nineteenth century, vestiges of it survive in these presidential appointments.

In making most appointments, the president looks for candidates who not only have the necessary skills and prestige but also share his broader philosophical views. The president wants to use the appointments as ways to populate the leadership of the bureaucracy and the courts with people who think like the president does on overall policy and legal issues; this goes a long way toward solving a collective dilemma, effectively coordinating the executive and judicial branches on common political goals aligned with the president's goals. For instance, the first two Supreme Court justices that Obama appointed, Sonia Sotomayor in 2009 and Elena Kagan in 2010, were liberals who could be expected to support a range of legal interpretations sympathetic to Democrats and their policy agenda in such areas as abortion rights, gun control laws, and restrictions on campaign spending by corporations.

When appointing a federal judge, the president is choosing someone who may stay in that position for life. (Federal judges serve until they resign, die, or are removed from office as a result of an impeachment trial in Congress.) Thus, appointments to the judicial branch provide the president with an opportunity to leave a lasting legacy. In contrast, appointees who lead the bureaucracy and military usually serve much shorter terms. Not only are the heads of the federal bureaucracies typically replaced by new presidents when they come into office, but top officials routinely leave before serving an entire presidential term. Some appointees want to return to their previous careers; others are replaced because the president is displeased with their performance. For example, President Obama repeatedly replaced generals who were leading the war in Afghanistan.

The Collective Dilemma

The U.S. government provides substantial financing to social service agencies and organizations working in foreign countries, especially in poor, developing areas. One major controversy for decades has been whether government funding can go to organizations promoting family planning, including abortions. Since the 1980s, U.S. law has prohibited any federal money from going to pay for abortions, but it is a matter of interpretation whether that ban includes giving to organizations that support access to abortion services.

Interests

Opponents of abortion rights favor a strict enforcement of U.S. law, which means banning U.S. federal funds from going to any organization working overseas that promotes, in any overt way, abortion rights. Their support for banning government funds to these organizations is consistent with their support of other policies, such as banning government support to Planned Parenthood, a domestic organization that provides health care for women but also provides abortion services in certain locations.

Supporters of abortion rights find these kinds of bans counterproductive because it restricts funding to many organizations that provide health care to women and children overseas. And they make the same claims against threats to pull all funding from Planned Parenthood in the United States.

Institutions

One way that the rules on abortion funding, set by acts of Congress, can be altered is through the use of executive orders by the president. These orders have the force of law, and, historically, presidents have used them to direct the bureaucracy on how to implement the policy. More recently, however, presidents have issued orders that shift the direction of the policy.

Since the language of the rules about federal funding of abortions is ambiguous, it opens up the opportunities for presidents to shape the actual impact of the rules. For instance, the rules state that no funding can be used for abortions, but it says nothing about supporting organizations that sometimes provide abortion services or give advice about abortion.

Given these factors, executive orders are tools for presidents to avoid having to rely on congressional support. Also, executive orders are very difficult for Congress to overturn. Congress can reverse an executive order by passing a bill, but the president can veto that bill, which would then take two-thirds of both chambers of Congress to overturn.

Outcomes

The use of executive orders has caused abortion funding to come and go. Since President Ronald Reagan used an executive order in 1984 to establish what was called the Mexico City Policy—a policy banning U.S. Agency for International Development from allocating funds to organizations that advocate or perform abortions in foreign nations—the back and forth has coincided with the party of the president; Republican presidents have enforced it while Democratic presidents have not.

On January 22, 2001, just two days after he took office, President George W. Bush issued a memorandum restoring the Mexico City Policy, after President Clinton had revoked it. As a result, the United Nations Population Fund lost $34 million in U.S. aid.[a] On January 23, 2009, on his third day in office, President Barack Obama revoked Bush's policy, and in effect allowed the U.S. government to provide funds to family planning organizations overseas that include abortion services as part of their mission. The organizations that lost funding after Bush's executive order were once again eligible to receive them. Donald Trump reinstated the Mexico City Policy during his first week in office, and later expanded it to cover all global health organizations that receive aid from the United States.

Think About It

Will the Mexico City Policy and other similar rules continue to be repealed and reinstated every so often? What would have to happen to settle the policy one way or another? Should presidents have such powers through executive orders? What likely would have happened with this policy if Hillary Clinton had won the 2016 presidential election instead of Donald Trump?

a. Todd S. Purdum, "U.S. Blocks Money for Family Clinics Promoted by U.N.," *New York Times*, July 23, 2012.

During his campaign, Donald Trump said he would reverse many of President Obama's executive orders. Here, President Trump signs an executive order reinstating the Mexico City Policy.

Solving Collective Dilemmas with Administrative and Financial Resources

The power of the presidency has increased over time partly as a result of presidents reacting to crises, including wars, depressions, and civil unrest. One important way presidents respond to crises is to create new bureaucratic agencies designed to help them implement policy and make decisions. These agencies help coordinate government action across various parts of the government.

The growth of the federal bureaucracy has been particularly dramatic in recent years. When George Washington was president, his cabinet consisted of five people, and the national government's budget was a mere $4 million. (Even in the late eighteenth century, this was a small figure compared to the size of the American economy.) Today, Donald Trump presides over a vast federal bureaucracy with more than 2 million civilian employees and a budget of $4.4 trillion.

Because presidents have usually acted together with Congress in solving a crisis, the required congressional approval for these new agencies has sometimes been easy to obtain. For example, FDR established the Executive Office of the President (EOP) by executive order; Congress did not object and even approved money for the staff. A more recent example is George W. Bush's creation of the Department of Homeland Security, a cabinet department established in 2003 in response to the September 11 terrorist attacks and ongoing terrorist threats. A bill to create Homeland Security was first proposed publicly and then shepherded through Congress by Bush. As a result, existing agencies were reorganized and new resources were devoted to protecting the United States from attack and from natural disasters. President Obama created various new agencies to oversee implementation of his three main policy initiatives—reform of health care, financial regulation, and national education standards. For instance, he established the Consumer Financial Protection Agency inside the Federal Reserve Bank to implement aspects of the new financial regulations passed by Congress with his support. Although presidents often receive congressional approval, it is also true that the president's powers to issue orders in some areas can be controversial. Trump, for instance, eliminated or cut most funding for several of these agencies created by Obama.

Beyond the federal departments and agencies that execute national policies, such as Homeland Security, Defense, Treasury, Agriculture, and the Federal Reserve, presidents have their own staff and agencies to help them make decisions, manage information, and run the government. Presidents need a vast staff to solve collective dilemmas and principal-agent problems in the federal government. When different federal departments are at odds over national policy, who or what resolves the differences and forces them to coordinate? As an example, when the Department of the Treasury and the Federal Reserve Bank both have units to combat financial fraud within banks, how do they coordinate their actions, and also coordinate with the Department of Justice, to enforce the law effectively? President Obama had several economic advisers whose work included coordinating the actions of these three large federal bureaucracies on matters of financial fraud. The president also has advisers who do central clearance, which means that the White House monitors administrative proposals from federal departments to ensure that they comply with the president's policy goals. This is a form of solving principal–agent problems in which the president is principal and the bureaucracies are agents (see Chapter 7).

The president relies on staff to guide the bureaucracy and constantly seeks advice from them and other people. Three resources especially assist presidents in decision making and in solving collective dilemmas: the White House staff, the EOP, and the vice president.

White House Staff. The president relies mostly on White House staff to organize schedules and plot political, legislative, and international strategies. These advisers do not need Senate approval and serve at the pleasure of the president (the president can hire and fire them at will). They are the closest layer of government employees to the president. The White House chief of staff, for instance, controls access to the president and manages presidential duties. This person also is head of the EOP (discussed later). The national security adviser is in constant contact with the president to help manage foreign relations and the military aspects of the job. Recent presidents have also had political strategists, communications directors, spokespersons, and economic advisers (and their respective staffs) as part of the White House bureaucracy. Additionally, some members of the cabinet are part of the president's intimate circle of advisers. They are the front-line people for the president's desire to solve collective dilemmas and enable effective government action regarding his goals.

Trump's White House staff consisted of senior advisers and his chief of staff's office (see Figure 6.2). All told, Trump has around 500 people working for him as part of the White House staff. Besides security personnel, cooks, and personal assistants, most of them work for people who advise the president directly on policy matters.

Executive Office of the President. Formally, the White House staff is part of the EOP. We can think of it as the nerve center of the presidency, whereas the rest of the EOP provides expertise and continuity to the executive branch. The core parts of the EOP, such as the Office of Management and Budget (OMB) and the Office of the United States Trade Representative, stay in place from president to president. Because these offices were legislated into existence by Congress, the people appointed to head them require Senate approval. These are the exceptions, however. Much of the EOP is formed around the agenda of the current president, and the leaders of its various units serve at his pleasure. Obama, for instance, had an Office of Energy and Climate Change Policy, but his predecessor did not.

The EOP is a crucial intermediate layer between the president's core staff (in the White House) and the rest of the federal bureaucracy in the cabinet departments (discussed in detail in Chapter 7). Although all three layers report to the president, their independence from the president's political goals differs, becoming stronger as it moves from the White House staff to the EOP and then to the executive departments. The EOP carries out functions of both the White House staff and the executive departments. Like the White House staff, much of the EOP advises the president and helps with the president's policy agenda. But like the executive departments, the EOP also implements policy and supplies Congress with credible information.

A good example of this intermediate role is the OMB, which provides information about federal revenues and spending, as well as assists the entire national government with budget information.[15] The OMB is the primary source of information about the national government's finances. At the same time, it is a crucial source of advice for the president and helps craft the budget proposal sent to Congress every year. The head of the OMB works for the president and helps with the president's policy agenda. The OMB, by being part of the EOP, can be a source of reliable information and expertise for the entire government as well as an asset when the president plots and implements strategies for carrying out budget goals.

The Vice President. The vice presidency in the modern era is a major resource for the president. But the office hasn't always been this way—or, at least, it hasn't always been seen this way. The Constitution allows for the vice president to take office should the president die or be incapacitated. In the original document ratified in 1788, the vice president was the person who came in second place in the contest for the presidency. This structure presented problems because the president and vice president had just run against each other. For example, Thomas Jefferson became vice president when John Adams was elected president in 1796. Because they were bitter rivals, Jefferson could hardly be expected to help Adams with his policy programs. Nor would he have been likely to enact similar policies if he had been called upon as vice president to assume the powers of the presidency.

The Twelfth Amendment (1804) changed the procedure for choosing the vice president. Under the amendment, the vice president runs for election for that office concurrently with the president. In practice this means that, since the early nineteenth century, presidential and vice-presidential candidates have run together as a pair and been elected as a team. It was common in past eras for vice presidents to be chosen only to placate a disaffected wing of the presi-

---

[15] The Congressional Budget Office (CBO) is the legislative counterpart to the OMB, and it provides budget information. Often, the OMB and the CBO disagree about financial projections, but they both provide essentially the same data about past government spending.

The power of the vice president has grown over time, and recent vice presidents have been presidents' close advisers. Vice President Mike Pence has been an advocate for President Trump's policies on tax reform, health care, and immigration.

dent's party. According to the Twelfth Amendment, vice presidents must come from a different state than the president. It has made political sense for presidential candidates to choose vice-presidential running mates not only from different states but from different regions of the country in order to "balance" or broaden the appeal of the ticket.

Many vice presidents in the past had few qualifications for the office apart from their political appeal. In fact, over the years, the vice presidency has been the butt of jokes. One vice president even said the office wasn't worth a warm bucket of urine.[16] To comics and critics alike, vice presidents often seem to be idly waiting in the wings and acting as the president's lapdog. Dan Quayle, George H. W. Bush's vice president, was treated harshly by critics; comics and reporters skewered him for his tendency to misspeak and for his callow appearance. When Vice President Gerald Ford became president after Richard Nixon resigned, becoming the first nonelected president in American history, he was criticized for being unprepared for the office.[17]

---

[16] There are conflicting accounts as to whether John Garner told Lyndon Johnson that the vice presidency wasn't worth a bucket of "piss" or "spit." Most historians believe that he said "piss" and that the press made it more palatable by changing it to "spit."

[17] Nixon had appointed Ford as vice president after Spiro Agnew resigned.

However, contrary to the old jokes about the office, vice presidents today are powerful figures in the president's administration. Al Gore, Bill Clinton's vice president, was a key adviser throughout Clinton's two terms. Dick Cheney, the vice president for George W. Bush, played a particularly strong role, setting a new standard for being one of the president's closest advisers. Joe Biden, Obama's vice president, had a hand in changing the history of gay rights: his comment during a public interview supporting gay marriage forced Obama to take a position on the controversial issue during the heat of the 2012 presidential campaign. Shortly after Biden's interview, Obama expressed his support for gay marriage—a watershed moment for the gay rights movement.

In general, vice presidents today have four crucial roles. First, the vice president must be ready to take over the presidency should the president die or become incapacitated. Thus, he or she needs to be fully informed about all matters that the president deals with in case the vice president is called upon to assume control of the government. Second, the vice president is a key adviser to the president. Since the presidency of Harry S. Truman (1945–53), the vice president has sat on the National Security Council and has regularly counseled the president on foreign and domestic policy. Third, the vice president casts tie-breaking votes in the Senate, a power that has occasionally been historically important. For instance, Al Gore cast a tie-breaking vote in 1993 on a key budget bill.

Fourth, the vice president typically helps the president coordinate federal bureaucratic agencies to achieve presidential goals. Presidents entering office face a massive coordination problem in getting federal agencies focused on their policy agendas. Although vice presidents assume different specific responsibilities depending on who is president, they have in recent eras been active in promulgating the president's agenda and helping to solve coordination problems. Joe Biden helped Barack Obama considerably in foreign diplomacy. On the domestic side, Mike Pence assists Donald Trump in relations with Congress and the federal bureaucracy.

In Comparison: Executive Forms

The Founders chose the institutional form for the presidency, though it was not the only possible option. They had raised the possibility of a three-person executive, and some people advocated having a single person serve as president for life. Moreover, the nature of the American presidency, as it has evolved, reflects the particular historical trajectory since the Founding. Recall our discussion of path dependence in Chapter 1, the notion that past decisions about

Presidential democracies are rare, though they exist more frequently in Latin America. Here, then-candidate Donald Trump meets with former Mexican president Enrique Peña Nieto.

institutions leave legacies for the present that make it difficult to change direction. The American presidency has features distinctive from executives in other countries because of what the Founders decided and because of specific decisions by individual presidents as discussed throughout this chapter.

The Founders ultimately chose a system that stood in stark contrast to that of Britain, which had a king or queen who inherited the crown as well as a prime minister who was chosen by Parliament. The broad outlines of that system remain in place today in Great Britain, except that the contemporary monarch has no real political power. Great Britain remains a **parliamentary democracy**, which means that the legislature (in this case, the House of Commons) chooses the executive. As in much of Western Europe, as well as in Canada, Australia, Japan, and India, the prime minister and his or her government hold executive power by virtue of their leadership of the majority party in the national parliament. The most important decision the parliaments make in these countries is to elect the executive government. As discussed in Chapter 5, parliaments largely go along with the policies proposed by the executive once he or she is chosen.

Many other parliamentary democracies, like Italy and Israel, have presidents in addition to prime ministers. These presidencies are ceremonial posts held by appointees who wield little actual power. They are not the real

parliamentary democracy A form of democracy in which the executive is elected by the legislature and the government is responsible to the legislature.

executives of the government, although they are considered heads of state. Similarly, the British monarch is the (ceremonial) head of state, while the prime minister is head of government and de facto executive. When the president of the United States visits Britain, meetings about real foreign policy issues are held with the prime minister.

By contrast, the American president serves as *both* head of state and head of government. He or she is chosen by the electoral college, which in principle represents the people, and the president governs as the executive independently of Congress. Because the president's authority comes not from Congress but from the people, the United States is categorized as a **presidential system** of government with separation of powers.

France offers an example of a **mixed presidential system**, in which an elected president governs alongside a prime minister chosen by the National Assembly (the French parliament). By tradition, the French president is head of state and deals mostly with foreign affairs, while the French prime minister is head of government and deals mostly with domestic affairs.

Executive branch powers vary among presidential systems around the world. In Chile, for example, the president can legislate by decree on many important matters. This means that the Chilean president can make law independently of the legislature. If the legislature disapproves of a law, it must then vote to overturn the law, and it often takes more than a majority of legislators to revoke a presidential decree. Note how this practice is the opposite of that used in the United States, where the legislature makes laws and the president has the veto power.

Presidents in certain countries have sole power to propose legislation. In a common variation, presidents can exercise a partial veto, known as a **line-item veto**, to strike down specific parts of legislation passed by the legislature. This is a tremendous advantage for presidents because they do not have to accept a law in its entirety, but can choose the parts within the law they believe is acceptable and veto the other parts accordingly. An executive can virtually mold legislation to his or her liking. (The U.S. Congress approved the presidential line-item veto in 1996, when Bill Clinton was president, but the Supreme Court quickly ruled that it was unconstitutional.) In these countries, institutional rules concerning presidential powers of decree, of proposal, and of partial veto give the chief executive substantially more legislative powers than those granted to the American president.

Other nations' presidents have considerably *less* power than the American executive. In Poland and Portugal, for example, presidents have very limited veto powers and can apply them only to specific types of legislation. Some countries' legislatures have the power to dismiss executive cabinet members against the president's wishes. The French president—who, as mentioned earlier, governs in tandem with a prime minister—has only limited powers concerning domestic legislation.

presidential system A form of democracy in which the executive is elected independently and the government is not responsible to the legislature.

mixed presidential system A form of democracy in which the executive is elected independently and shares responsibility for the government with the legislature.

line-item veto A partial veto that allows the executive to strike specific passages from a given bill.

As we have seen in this chapter, executive orders offer a valuable tool for presidents to act unilaterally. When writing executive orders, presidents usually specify the agencies or departments that need to carry out the orders. This is called delegating statutory authority to an agency or department. An executive order about housing on military bases, for example, may specify that the Department of Defense, as opposed to the Department of Housing and Urban Development, carry out the order.

Political scientists have found that agencies and departments have political tendencies and ideological leanings. Some are liberal (e.g., the Environmental Protection Agency and the Department of Labor), moderate (e.g., the General Services Administration and the Department of Agriculture), or conservative (e.g., the Department of Defense and the Department of Commerce). Do these leanings influence which agencies presidents assign to enforce their executive orders? Does this vary by the president's party?

Political scientist Joshua Kennedy compiled executive-order data from 1989 to 2011 to try to answer these questions.[a] Note that 11 of the 24 agencies selected were considered conservative. Let's explore his data shown below.

Delegated Authority to Executive Bodies by Ideology across Presidents, 1989–2011

Number of Instances When the President Delegated to Each Category of Agency

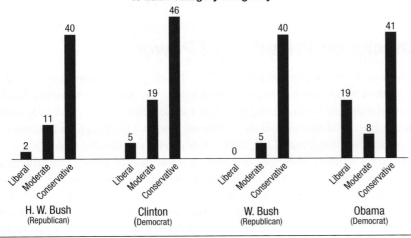

Think About It:

Why do you think that for each president the majority of delegations were to conservative agencies or departments? Based on these data, does political ideology have an effect on how presidents use executive orders? (*Hint:* Focus on liberal agency delegations.) Would you characterize this effect as strong or weak? Why?

a. Joshua B. Kennedy, "Who Do You Trust? Presidential Delegation in Executive Orders," *Research and Politics* 3, no. 1 (2016): 1–7. Replication data available at https://dataverse.harvard.edu (accessed 5/26/16).

Scholars of comparative government tend to believe that, on balance, American presidents—in comparison with their peers in other countries—have mid-level power relative to the legislature within their own political system.[18]

It is also interesting to compare the powers of the U.S. president to those of the American governors, who are the executives of the 50 state governments. Every state has a governor who is directly elected by voters rather than being chosen by the state legislature. Thus every state shares with the American national government a separation of powers system—though, unlike the national government, no state has the equivalent of an electoral college. Many formal powers of the governors are modeled after presidential powers, such as the power to veto legislation and the power of appointment. However, governors' powers vary from state to state. All but six governors have some form of line-item veto. More than half of the governors have sole power to propose state budgets. Governors without such powers are at a disadvantage compared with their counterparts. The governor of Vermont, for example, is considered institutionally weak in comparison with most of the others because the office does not have the line-item veto, and the legislature has full power to change the governor's proposed budget. When governors have these powers, they can gain an upper hand against the state legislature and direct their state's policies to a larger degree than governors without such powers.

Checks on Presidential Power

In light of the massive powers discussed in this chapter, it is sometimes said that the United States has an "imperial presidency," or "unitary presidency," indicating the degree to which the president can sometimes act unilaterally without congressional approval. Barack Obama, who had little support in Congress for most of his term, tested the limits of unilateral presidential action.

In some respects, these phrases make a good deal of sense. The American presidency revolves around an individual who holds vast powers to influence the course of the U.S. government. Moreover, given the dominant role that the United States plays in world affairs, the president's power *within* the American political system gives him enormous influence *outside* of the United States.

By certain criteria, the power of American presidents is unmatched. No executive anywhere in the world controls anything like the vast administrative and military machinery that the American president uses to influence domestic and world affairs. Since the early twentieth century, the American presidency has evolved into a vast bureaucracy that gives sitting presidents un-

---

[18] Mathew Shugart and John Carey, *Presidents and Assemblies: Constitutional Design and Electoral Dynamics* (Cambridge, UK: Cambridge University Press, 1992).

paralleled access to information, resources, and personnel. They are free to use these resources during times that they themselves define as crises. Although the American president does not have all of the constitutional powers within the political system that are granted to some other countries' chief executives, no reasonable comparison can be made to the sheer power of the American president to affect American and world politics.

The term *imperial* is misleading, however, if it is meant to imply that the president is detached from the American people and not subject to public pressure. That term, and *unilateral*, are also inappropriate if they are meant to imply that the president is unconstrained by the institutional design of the American government—namely, its separation of powers. Two simple but key factors prove these implications false. First, Congress can override presidential vetoes and withhold money for the president's policies. Second, as in any true democracy characterized by the rule of law, the president must obey the law and the Constitution.

Investigations and Impeachment

Courts have occasionally declared actions of the president unconstitutional. More important in recent times, Congress has shown the capacity and will to investigate the president's actions and even exercise its power of impeachment. It has become increasingly common for **special prosecutors** to investigate misdeeds among presidents and White House aides. These investigations— especially since the Nixon administration—have led to high-profile hearings, trials, and occasional prison sentences. They have also been a significant means for the two major political parties to attack each other and seek advantage in elections. The opposing party often tries to embarrass the president by exposing scandal, dishonesty, and betrayal in the administration.

special prosecutor Independent, private sector counsel hired by Congress to investigate government officials.

Reserved for the most serious offenses, **impeachment** is the process by which the House of Representatives formally charges a federal government official with, in the language of the Constitution, "Treason, Bribery, or other high Crimes and Misdemeanors." If a president is impeached by the House, the case then goes to the Senate, which votes on whether to recall the president from office. Although the impeachment procedure is rarely used, it represents a powerful check on the president's authority by the legislative branch.

impeachment Process by which the House of Representatives formally charges a federal government official with "Treason, Bribery, or other high Crimes and Misdemeanors."

No president has been forcibly recalled from office by a Senate vote, but three came close: Andrew Johnson (1868), Richard Nixon (1974), and Bill Clinton (1999). Johnson was impeached on a variety of charges, including conspiracy, but the Senate acquitted him by just one vote. Nixon was not formally impeached but resigned before the full House vote, which was certain to impeach him. Clinton was impeached by the House on two counts of perjury (lying under oath before a grand jury) about his affair with a White House staffer. He was acquitted by the Senate and served out his full term.

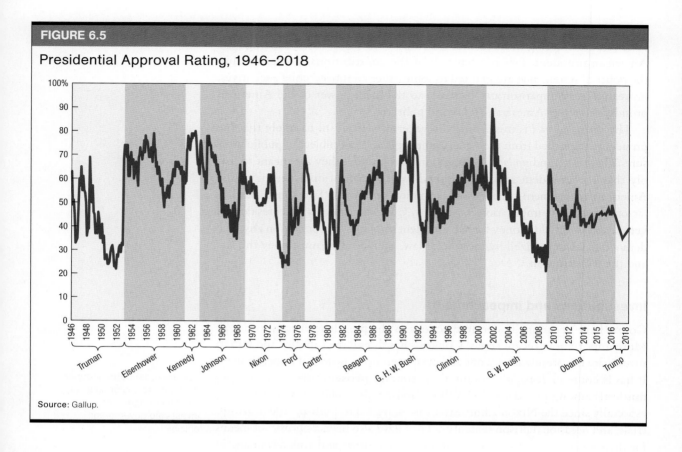

FIGURE 6.5

Presidential Approval Rating, 1946–2018

Source: Gallup.

It is interesting to place the Nixon and Clinton impeachment crises in the context of how public opinion and the modern political climate shaped decision making. Nixon's public approval ratings, as measured by opinion polls, had sunk to historic lows: only about one-quarter of those polled approved of his performance in office. His own Republican Party in Congress had made it clear that most would vote to recall him from office. Clinton's approval ratings, in contrast, remained at a high 60 percent throughout his ordeal (Figure 6.5). Not only did he carry on his normal duties as president, he steadfastly refused to respond directly to his Republican opponents about the charges against him. Most of his fellow Democrats in Congress supported him and voted against both impeachment in the House and removal from office in the Senate. Clinton reportedly said after surviving the vote in the Senate, "Thank God for public opinion."[19]

[19] Bob Woodward, *Shadow: Five Presidents and the Legacy of Watergate* (New York: Simon & Schuster, 1999), p. 513.

Electoral Pressures

Beyond the formal means of constraining the president—the veto override and other congressional checks, investigations, and impeachment—consider that the president needs to be elected and reelected by a people who are historically suspicious of centralized power, and presidential power in particular. The comparison between the Nixon and Clinton impeachment cases highlights the more general point that modern presidents carry out their duties under the watchful eyes of Congress and are highly responsive to shifting public opinion about their performance. Presidents, more than any other members of the U.S. government, are either encouraged or restrained by mass public opinion.[20] They are lightning rods for public anger, taking the blame when the economy turns bad or foreign policy initiatives do not work well. Yet they are heralded when they are seen to perform well, as illustrated by the initial popular support for George W. Bush's response to the September 11 attacks in 2001.

The American people seem to tolerate and even prefer a powerful and decisive president, as long as there are electoral and institutional checks on that power. In the terminology used by political scientists, the people (as principals) have an extremely powerful agent in the president, but one they ultimately want to be able to control at the ballot box.

The president as the elected representative of the entire country has a mandate different from any other, including that of Congress. Congress is composed of 535 people elected to represent specific subconstituencies, and these subconstituencies end up being quite different from one another. How Congress manages to make law given the different interests brought to its chambers by representatives and senators was the subject of Chapter 5. The president pursues policy goals and takes action on behalf of everyone, and this means ultimately that the president is the only person charged with being the agent of every single person regardless of where those people live in the country. It is difficult to nail down what this means in practice. As we will study in more detail in Chapter 13, whether elections end up choosing a president who represents the "average" person or voter, or who represents a specific partisan subset of the population, depends on how we think elections work. Prominent models of national elections—though not the only ones used by political scientists—depict the president as the winner of a contest for the allegiance of the average voter, where *average* is typically interpreted to mean "ideologically moderate." And if those models capture the essence of what actually happens, then the president does or should focus on pleasing the average, moderate person with policy actions; in theory, this person best represents what the

---

[20] Brandice Canes-Wrone, *Who Leads Whom? Presidents, Policy, and the Public* (Chicago: University of Chicago Press, 2006).

entire country deserves from government. As we'll see in Chapter 13, though, competing theories about elections propose different ideas about electoral pressures.

Institutionalizing Presidential Power to Solve Collective Dilemmas

 Let's now return to our puzzle from the beginning of this chapter. As we have seen, the power of the modern presidency is largely the result of presidents creating new institutions within the executive branch to solve collective dilemmas.

Presidents often expanded their authority in response to crises like the September 11 attacks or the recession of 2008–09 with the approval of Congress and the American people. Such crises demand collective action, yet it is difficult for rival political parties, competitors within the business community, and interest groups to coalesce behind a solution. At key moments in American history, the president's allies in Congress, the states, and society have demonstrated a belief that the presidency is the institution best equipped to solve collective dilemmas bedeviling a nation. Past presidents, like Obama, have relied on this belief to take unilateral actions in a range of policy areas, such as regulating immigration.

Even when the country is not in crisis, the power of the president to direct executive agencies in how to implement a law remains. Once the crisis is over, why has the power of the presidency not fallen back to its pre-crisis level? The answer has to do with the nature of the political institutions set up to assist presidents and maintain their power. By definition, institutions of government are designed to persist and address various political situations as they arise over time. Institutions are "sticky"; they do not come and go easily. Vestiges of institutions can remain in place long after the situation that compelled their creation has passed. As we will see in Chapter 7, many government institutions that persist—for instance, those created by presidents with the approval of Congress and public opinion—take the form of federal bureaucracies that the president can use to implement policy priorities.

FURTHER READING

★ = Included in *Readings in American Politics*, 5th ed.

Cameron, Charles, *Veto Bargaining* (New York: Cambridge University Press, 2000). A sophisticated look at presidents as legislators, and how they use the veto to influence legislation more to their liking than what Congress would do otherwise.

- ★ Canes-Wrone, Brandice, *Who Leads Whom? Presidents, Policy, and the Public* (Chicago: University of Chicago Press, 2006). A historical examination of twentieth-century presidents who sometimes followed public opinion and sometimes tried to lead public opinion.

  Druckman, James, and Lawrence Jacobs, *Who Governs?: Presidents, Public Opinion, and Manipulation* (Chicago: University of Chicago Press, 2015). Druckman and Jacobs analyze presidential archives to better understand how different presidents used public opinion information to craft their public statements and policy decisions.

- ★ Howell, William, *Power without Persuasion* (Princeton, NJ: Princeton University Press, 2003). A detailed look at the tools presidents use unilaterally to make policy, bypassing or forcing the hand of Congress.

  James, Scott, *Presidents, Parties, and the State* (New York: Cambridge University Press, 2000). A thoughtful history of how presidents have used the bureaucracy of the national government to serve the goals of their political parties.

  Kernell, Samuel, *Going Public: New Strategies of Presidential Leadership*, 4th ed. (Washington, DC: CQ Press, 2007). A book rich with data showing how presidents increasingly over the twentieth century spoke directly to the people to enhance their bargaining position with Congress.

  Madison, James, Alexander Hamilton, and John Jay. *Federalists Papers*, Nos. 67–77. Clear statements of support for a presidency checked by the other branches but also with enough autonomy to be decisive in times of crisis.

- ★ Neustadt, Richard, *Presidential Power and the Modern Presidents* (New York: Free Press, 1990). A classic explanation of how presidents wield power, arguing that executives are successful only to the degree that their personal charisma persuades people that helping the president achieve his or her goals is in their interests.

KEY TERMS

administrative law (p. 219)

divided government (p. 211)

executive agreement (p. 223)

executive order (p. 222)

going public (p. 212)

impeachment (p. 237)

line-item veto (p. 234)

mixed presidential system (p. 234)

parliamentary democracy (p. 233)

pocket veto (p. 220)

presidential system (p. 234)

signing statement (p. 223)

special prosecutor (p. 237)

spoils system (p. 207)

unified government (p. 211)

veto threat (p. 220)

The controversy around the Department of Health and Human Services's rule that would require health insurance pla[...] including those offered by Roman Catholic hospitals, universities, and charities—to offer free birth control to fe[...] employees illustrates the tensions bureaucrats face. While then secretary of HHS Kathleen Sebelius (left) had [...] appointed by President Obama, she said her department also had to be responsive to Congress and the public.

The Bureaucracy

Who controls the bureaucracy? And does it work?

During President Obama's first term in office, the U.S. Department of Health and Human Services (HHS) asked teams of prominent medical advisers to provide recommendations for improving women's health. The department then used these recommendations to create guidelines for all health care insurance plans adopted by employers. The HHS guidelines stated that all health care plans by employers should "cover women's preventive services such as well-woman visits, breastfeeding support, domestic violence screening, and contraception without charging a copayment, coinsurance, or a deductible."[1]

These regulatory guidelines met both praise—chiefly from those concerned with women's reproductive rights and preventative health care—and protest. One protesting voice came from the U.S. Conference of Catholic Bishops, who contended that the contraception mandate would force employers who oppose contraception on religious or moral grounds to "subsidize what they believe to be immoral."[2] Kathleen Sebelius, the secretary of HHS at the time, responded that the guidelines had "carved out" an exemption for religious organizations like churches that primarily employ people who subscribe to that faith. Yet for employers like Catholic hospitals and universities whose employees might be from any faith (including no religious faith), the guidelines eventually would need to be followed. Furthermore, there was no exemption for employers (nonreligious) who merely oppose contraception on moral grounds.

The exemptions did little to mollify the opposition. President Obama and Secretary Sebelius reconsidered the policy slightly and changed the regulations in 2012. The new regulations shifted the responsibility of providing free contraception from

[1] U.S. Department of Health and Human Services, "Affordable Care Act Ensures Women Receive Preventive Services at No Additional Cost," August 1, 2011, http://wayback.archive-it.org/3926/20140108162111/http://www.hhs.gov/news/press/2011pres/08/20110801b.html (accessed 5/11/16).

[2] Timothy Dolan, "HHS Contraception Mandate 'Un-American'," *USA Today*, January 25, 2012, http://usatoday30.usatoday.com/news/opinion/forum/story/2012-01-25/dolan-hhs-health-contraceptive-mandate/52788780/1 (accessed 4/20/16).

OUTLINE

- What Is the Federal Bureaucracy?

- Why Do We Need a Federal Bureaucracy?

- Principals and Agents in the Executive Bureaucracy

- How Has the Bureaucracy Changed?

- Shaping and Influencing the Bureaucracy

- In Comparison: Bureaucratic Traditions

- Two Views of Bureaucracy

the employer to the insurance companies. "Religious organizations won't have to pay for these services," the president said in describing the new HHS changes. "[A]nd no religious institution will have to provide these services directly,"[3] thus accommodating the concerns of religiously aligned hospitals, universities, and charities.

This shift in policy from HHS did not satisfy all opponents, but it did win over some Catholic women's groups, who split with the bishops and expressed satisfaction with the new regulations. Yet the way HHS handled the matter—first declaring a mandate for employers on providing contraception and then backtracking slightly to try to appease an important constituency—invited criticisms from members of Congress, both conservative Republicans and liberal Democrats. The HHS was caught between taking the recommendations of scientists and doctors from the medical community and responding to political pressures from important groups in society during a presidential election year. In subsequent years, the contraception mandate was still mired in legal challenges from religious organizations and employers who opposed contraception for moral reasons.

The HHS, as with all executive bureaucracies, is tasked with implementing legislation. But it can also establish the law, crafting new guidelines that impose certain standards and requirements on citizens to achieve policy goals. Thus bureaucrats sometimes are also policy makers, in that they refine and tailor vague legislation. However, bureaucrats are not elected, and it is not always clear to whom they answer, especially when Congress and the president are at odds. The House of Representatives, with a Republican majority at the time, had reasons to be strongly opposed to the contraception mandate; and indeed, the Republican leadership complained loudly. If executive branch bureaucrats have bosses both in Congress and the president, and those bosses disagree, how can they avoid defying their bosses?

[3] Barack Obama, White House address on the revision to the Department of Health and Human Services contraception mandate, "Video: President Obama on New Contraception Rules," Kaiser Health News, February 10, 2012, http://khn.org/news/president-obama-on-new-contraception-rules (accessed 4/20/16).

What Is the Federal Bureaucracy?

In Chapter 6 we focused on the president, who sits atop the executive branch and is chosen through the process of election. The president appoints a small portion of the people in the executive branch. Most people working in the executive branch, however, are not elected. They belong to the civil service and military bureaucracies and are not appointed by the president or any other elected official. Millions of people in these bureaucracies implement the policies decided upon by elected officials in Congress and the White House, and occasionally by judges. These are the people who, at the federal level, fight wars, protect borders, and regulate markets. They dispense Social Security payments, coin money and control the money supply, set interest rates for banks, and make loans to students, farmers, and small businesses. They finance science and applied research, operate national parks, investigate and prosecute federal criminal activity, and run prisons. At lower levels of government, in the states and localities, bureaucrats teach, enforce the law, clean streets, distribute driver's licenses, inspect restaurants, and distribute school lunches. Civilian and military bureaucrats have always been the workhorses of government.

In a democracy, a *bureaucrat* is anyone working for the government who is not elected or is not a judge in a court of law.[4] The **government bureaucracy** refers to the agencies and offices devoted to carrying out tasks for the government in a manner consistent with the law. Federal bureaucrats work in **government agencies**, which are the fundamental units of the national government that carry out duties prescribed by Congress or the president. Most bureaucrats in the national government work in the executive branch, although Congress and the courts also have their own small bureaucracies. All bureaucrats working for the government are agents in some way. Thus Congress and the president are the most important principals, and the bureaucrats are the agents.[5] As we will see, having two principals presents challenges for federal bureaucracies.

Agencies in the executive branch exist in one of three settings: within a department, as an independent agency, or as a government corporation. Some agencies are part of a **cabinet department**, such as the Department of Agriculture or the Department of Justice. Thus, the Food and Nutrition Service is an agency within the Department of Agriculture. Bureaucrats in the Food and Nutrition Service operate the Supplemental Nutrition Assistance Program

government bureaucracy Agencies and offices devoted to carrying out the tasks of government consistent with the law.

government agency An individual unit of the government responsible for carrying out the tasks delegated to it by Congress or the president in accordance with the law.

cabinet departments Departments within the executive branch that encompass many of the agencies that implement federal policy. Secretaries appointed by the president and confirmed by the Senate are given the responsibility of leading these departments and advising the president.

---

[4] For classic accounts of bureaucracy, see the following three texts: Max Weber, *From Max Weber: Essays in Sociology*, trans. H. H. Gerth and C. Wright Mills (London: Routledge & Kegan Paul, 1948); Woodrow Wilson, "The Study of Administration," *Political Science Quarterly* 2 (1887); and James Q. Wilson, *The Politics of Regulation* (New York: Basic Books, 1980).

[5] D. Roderick Kiewiet and Mathew McCubbins, *The Logic of Delegation* (Berkeley: University of California Press, 1991).

Three Types of Government Bureaucracy

Less
Independent

Cabinet Departments

The cabinet departments are government agencies that report directly to the president. The constitution establishes that the cabinet departments advise the president on subjects relating to the duties of their respective offices. The employment of cabinet officials as well as their job responsibilities rely heavily on the discretion of the president.

Examples:
Department of State, Department of the Treasury, Department of Defense, Department of Agriculture, Department of Justice, Department of the Interior

Independent Agencies

Independent agencies are established by congressional statutes to exist outside the cabinet departments. They are often headed by executive boards or commissions appointed by the president and confirmed by the Senate. The president's authority to remove board members or commissioners is generally subject to greater restriction than members of the cabinet. This restriction, among others, allows independent agencies more autonomy. Independent regulatory agencies have the most autonomy in this category as these are run by commissions or boards, and members can only be removed for cause.

Examples of independent agencies:
National Aeronautics and Space Administration, National Science Foundation, Environmental Protection Agency, National Archives, Central Intelligence Agency

Examples of independent regulatory agencies:
Federal Exchange Commission, Federal Trade Commission, Securities and Exchange Commission, Commodity Futures Trading Commission

Government Corporations

Federally owned corporations carry out businesslike tasks with the highest degree of agency independence. Generally, these corporations are motivated to generate revenue while achieving public service goals.

Examples:
U.S. Postal Service, Amtrak, Tennessee Valley Authority, Federal Deposit Insurance Corporation, Corporation for National and Community Service

More
Independent

(SNAP), which provides food for the poor and various school meals programs, among other things. The cabinet departments encompass hundreds of agencies. At the head of cabinet departments are secretaries appointed by the president, such as the secretary of agriculture and the attorney general (the "secretary" of justice). The heads of all the departments are part of the president's cabinet and can be close advisers to the president. (See the outline of cabinet departments in Chapter 6, Figure 6.2.)

Other agencies are considered to be independent, meaning they are not part of one of the cabinet departments. **Independent agencies** are granted more autonomy from the president and Congress than those within departments, and they are typically headed by boards or commissions appointed by the president and approved by the Senate. The Environmental Protection Agency (EPA) is an example of an independent agency. A subset of the independent agencies is made up of independent regulatory agencies, and these have the most autonomy among the independent agencies (see the Know the Facts box on page 246). An example of an independent regulatory agency is the Federal Communications Commission (FCC). All of these agencies usually regulate the conduct of business corporations in some way. The president and Congress are ultimately the principals over independent agencies, which are part of the executive branch. But because of how the laws setting up these agencies were written, the president has limited power to remove people who head these agencies.

independent agency An agency that exists outside the cabinet departments and is run with a larger degree of independence from presidential influence.

Government corporations are a third type of agency. They are given even more discretion than independent agencies and are charged by Congress with carrying out a task. Sometimes these tasks are regulatory, but often they are businesslike activities that the government wants done by a federal agency. Examples include the U.S. Postal Service and Amtrak, the passenger railway company. Although technically part of the government, these organizations conduct their affairs and run their businesses with relative independence. They may occasionally receive subsidies from the government, but the expectation is that they will generate enough revenue at least to break even. Their operations are heavily regulated in most cases. For example, the U.S. Postal Service could make more profits if it were allowed to abandon its least profitable rural routes. However, it is required to serve every address in the United States, and its rates are set by a government-appointed commission. Private companies by law are not allowed to compete with the Postal Service to deliver ordinary mail. In many aspects of its work, however, the service operates like a private company. Its overnight mail service faces competition from companies like UPS and FedEx, and it is allowed to charge market rates and compete against private companies for certain services. As with independent agencies, the president appoints the boards and commissions of the government corporations, and the appointments must be approved by the Senate.

government corporation A federally owned corporation that generates revenue by providing a public service, operating much like a private business and with a higher degree of autonomy than a cabinet department or an independent agency.

Why Do We Need a Federal Bureaucracy?

Bureaucracies are necessary because, while top government officials make broad policy decisions, someone or some set of people actually has to do the work of government. For instance, some bureaucratic agencies exist to redistribute resources. The Social Security Administration, an independent agency, is charged with using money collected through taxes to pay for retirement and disability benefits for millions of people.[6] It keeps records on everyone's payroll contributions and their age, and it sends people money according to formulas set by Congress.

It turns out that bureaucracies make policy decisions as well, as we will discuss shortly. In both implementing policies and in making certain decisions, bureaucracies are crucial parts of governments solving collective dilemmas.

Solvers of Collective Dilemmas

Recall from Chapter 1 that funding and creating public goods involve collective dilemmas. When it comes to public goods—benefits that anyone can enjoy, like national security or national parks—people are tempted to free ride and let others pay for or create them. Some public goods require coordinated action to produce. When government solves collective dilemmas, including those related to public goods, bureaucracies actually implement the solutions. Thus the main task of many bureaucratic agencies is implementing decisions (by Congress and the president) to create public goods. Consider the following examples of public goods and the government agencies or departments involved in providing them.

- *Scientific knowledge.* The National Aeronautics and Space Administration (NASA) is an independent agency that explores space to gather more knowledge of the physical world and the universe.

- *Security.* The Department of Defense prepares for and fights wars to keep the country and its interests abroad secure.

- *National parks.* The Department of the Interior manages parks to preserve natural resources and enable citizens to enjoy nature.

- *Public health.* The Centers for Disease Control and Prevention (part of the Department of Health and Human Services) conduct research to avoid epidemic outbreaks.

- *Funding for public goods.* The Internal Revenue Service is the part of the Treasury Department that collects taxes, a necessary task that makes possible everything the government does.

[6] See Martha Derthick, *Policymaking for Social Security* (Washington, DC: Brookings Institution, 1997), for a classic account.

Other bureaucratic agencies regulate private and commercial activities to make society function smoothly. They too are creating public goods, but to do so they typically solve coordination problems. The Federal Aviation Administration (part of the Department of Transportation), for example, hires air traffic controllers to manage the flow of airplanes into and out of airports. Without a public authority to help them coordinate, the airline companies, which compete against each other for business, for slots at airports, and for flying times, might bump into each other—both literally and figuratively—in their quest for profits. Air traffic controllers are government bureaucrats who solve coordination problems every day.

Coordination problems also need solving among the federal bureaucratic agencies. As chief executive of the national government, the president sets the direction for the executive branch and, in modern times, has a large White House bureaucracy to help make decisions.[7] Presidents and their staff must coordinate the actions of numerous agencies. At times, this work can be more than daunting. Take, for example, the government's response to a series of devastating storms hitting various parts of the country. In 2016, flooding, landslides, and mudslides in West Virginia and tornadoes in the Southeast led to massive destruction of property, natural habitats, and people's lives. Many national government agencies and tens of thousands

Scientific knowledge, including knowledge of the universe, is one public good that the government supplies through a bureaucratic agency, NASA. The information gathered through the Space Launch System and other NASA efforts benefits the country as a whole.

of national government employees became involved in responding to these emergencies. The White House relies to a large extent on the Federal Emergency Management Agency (FEMA) to organize the deployment of first responders, coordinate with state and local governments, and bring aid to thousands of people living in the affected areas. The White House also makes sure the EPA plays a role in sending scientists and inspectors to assess damage to coastlines and fragile ecosystems. Meanwhile, the U.S. Coast Guard responds to the dangers people face at sea during hurricanes. Without a major effort to coordinate their actions, these bureaucracies would have unclear lines of responsibility, duplicate efforts needlessly, and work at cross-purposes.

[7] Andrew Rudalevige, *Managing the President's Program* (Princeton, NJ: Princeton University Press, 2002); Joel Aberbach, "The U.S. Federal Executive in an Era of Change," *Governance* 16 (2003): 373–99; Terry Moe, "The Politicized Presidency," in *The New Direction in American Politics*, ed. John E. Chubb and Paul Peterson (Washington, DC: Brookings Institution, 1985), pp. 235–71.

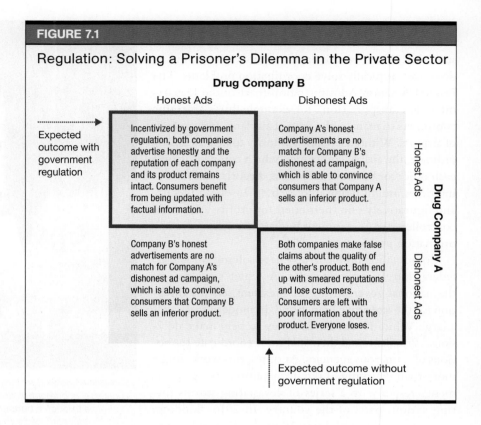

FIGURE 7.1

Regulation: Solving a Prisoner's Dilemma in the Private Sector

Drug Company B

	Honest Ads	Dishonest Ads
Honest Ads (Drug Company A)	Incentivized by government regulation, both companies advertise honestly and the reputation of each company and its product remains intact. Consumers benefit from being updated with factual information.	Company A's honest advertisements are no match for Company B's dishonest ad campaign, which is able to convince consumers that Company A sells an inferior product.
Dishonest Ads (Drug Company A)	Company B's honest advertisements are no match for Company A's dishonest ad campaign, which is able to convince consumers that Company B sells an inferior product.	Both companies make false claims about the quality of the other's product. Both end up with smeared reputations and lose customers. Consumers are left with poor information about the product. Everyone loses.

Expected outcome with government regulation →

Expected outcome without government regulation ↑

Sometimes regulatory agencies help solve prisoner's dilemmas.[8] This kind of collective dilemma is common among companies advertising against each other. Suppose two drug companies that make aspirin tablets compete intensely for customers. Because they make basically the same product, the companies must compete on the basis of price and product quality. It is always tempting for each company to exaggerate the claims of its product's superiority over the competition, or to claim that the other company's product is inferior or even dangerous. The Federal Trade Commission (FTC) is an independent regulatory agency charged with protecting consumers against unfair or deceptive practices, and this includes requiring that companies not lie in their advertising (Figure 7.1).

In policing the claims made by the two drug companies in their advertising, the FTC tries to move the companies away from the "defect-defect" equilibrium where they both lie to consumers. The FTC does this by suing (or threatening to sue) companies on behalf of the American people, claiming that the compa-

---

[8] For a general discussion of bureaucracy solving collective dilemmas, see Mathew McCubbins, Roger Noll, and Barry Weingast, "Structure and Process, Politics and Policy," *Virginia Law Review* 75 (1989): 431–82.

nies cannot back up the statements made in their advertisements. In the end, the two companies (not to mention consumers) are better off if they do not tear each other down with misinformation in advertising campaigns. Both companies can retain their reputation for safe products, and consumers can have confidence that they are not receiving false information. A regulatory agency is necessary to enforce and monitor this "cooperate-cooperate" outcome.

Principals and Agents in the Executive Bureaucracy

The Motivations of Bureaucrats

Contrary to their popular image of being boring and monotonous, bureaucracies in government can be scenes of considerable political conflict. First of all, bureaucrats, like others in government, have policy goals. And as employees, they generally want the same things other workers want from their jobs: clear instructions about what they are supposed to do, autonomy to carry out their tasks in the way they think best, and resources to accomplish their goals. Federal bureaucrats seldom get all three items on their wish list in the right proportions: *clarity in instructions* from Congress and the president, who often disagree and sometimes are from opposing parties; *autonomy* from too much intrusion by the people who pay their budgets and hire their bosses; and enough *resources* (money and staffing) allocated by people who find it easier to get reelected when they complain about spending within the bureaucracy.

But second, bureaucrats are not helpless; they can take actions to gain some autonomy and resources to do their jobs well. Political scientist Daniel Carpenter studied how upper-level civil servants in the early twentieth century cultivated allies across the national government, creating coalitions in favor of granting certain agencies more autonomy from political interference.[9] Until then, for example, the Department of Agriculture was dominated by political patronage appointments. Independent-minded bureaucrats like Seaman Knapp pushed for the department to make decisions based on the science of seeds, crops, and soils. In 1902–03, Knapp was instrumental in convincing members of both parties in Congress that the department deserved money and autonomy to help farmers increase their yields of crops and experiment with new techniques. Largely through the efforts of bureaucrats like Knapp, many parts of the Department of Agriculture gained stature as nonpartisan agencies that provided technical assistance to farmers regardless of their political affiliations,

---

[9] Daniel P. Carpenter, *The Forging of Bureaucratic Autonomy: Reputations, Networks, and Policy Innovation in Executive Agencies, 1862–1928* (Princeton, NJ: Princeton University Press, 2001).

and the department was able to expand with increased funding from Congress and new positions for scientists.

It is clear from Carpenter's research that bureaucrats can act like politicians—not in the sense of having to win elections, but in terms of building coalitions to bring about policy change. Bureaucrats, like all other citizens, have personal opinions and attitudes about policies and social goals. Sometimes they have to refrain from stating their political preferences in the workplace (and in some jobs, they cannot publicly advocate for or against certain controversial policies). Nevertheless, many bureaucrats can—and do—work harder at the tasks they believe they should be doing, and less hard at the tasks they believe they should *not* be doing.

Bureaucrats can also use their position to press for policy change that they see as desirable.[10] One advantage bureaucrats tend to have over members of Congress and the president is expert knowledge of a policy area and information about which policies work and do not work. They can use this information in their reports, in their publicity materials for the news media and for constituents, and in their communications with Congress. Furthermore, because bureaucrats are the government officials who are most directly in contact with the public, they can sometimes encourage people to communicate with Congress. Technically, members of the bureaucracy are not allowed to lobby members of Congress on behalf of their agencies, but they can, in a variety of ways, mobilize constituents to pressure Congress. The National Science Foundation (NSF), an independent agency constantly targeted for budget cuts, is masterful at letting university-based scientists and researchers know who in Congress is currently threatening the agency's independence or its budget (or both). The implication is clear: although the NSF cannot lobby, it can inform, and bureaucrats in the NSF hope that those they inform will act to pressure Congress.

Bureaucracy's Principal-Agent Problems

The principal-agent problem introduced in Chapter 1 sheds light on the politics of the bureaucracy. To reiterate briefly, principal-agent problems occur because principals cannot always observe what agents are doing. As a result, agents can shirk their duties and disobey their principals. Let's now consider one major factor that contributes to this problem in the context of the federal bureaucracy: the tendency of government agencies to "drift" from their defined missions.[11]

[10] Joel Aberbach, "The U.S. Federal Executive in an Era of Change," *Governance* 16 (2003): 373–99; Terry Moe, "The Politicized Presidency," in *The New Direction in American Politics*, ed. John E. Chubb and Paul Peterson (Washington, DC: Brookings Institution, 1985), pp. 235–71.

[11] William Niskanen, *Bureaucracy and Representative Government* (Chicago: Aldine, 1971); David Epstein and Sharyn O'Halloran, *Delegating Powers* (New York: Cambridge University Press, 1999).

We often think of elected officials—members of Congress and the president—as the principals, and the executive-branch bureaucrats as the agents. Problems arise when bureaucrats gradually change their behavior and stray from what the elected representatives want, working instead toward what the bureaucrats want. This phenomenon is sometimes referred to as **bureaucratic drift**, in that agents "drift" from the mandates given to them by principals.

Of course, there is another side to this story. A newly elected Congress or president may change policy preferences after an election and push the bureaucracy to alter its priorities. This situation, when the principals change but the agents stay the same, is known as **coalitional drift**. The agents are expected to adjust to the new political principals, but how quickly? And how completely? Note that coalitional drift could also be caused by cycling coalitions in Congress (recall cycling coalitions from Chapter 1). If new policies are repeatedly passed in Congress where the majority party loses its grip on the agenda and new coalitions regularly overturn previous legislation, the bureaucracy could have difficulty staying current with constant changes to the law. See Figure 7.2 for a comparison of bureaucratic and coalitional drift.

To illustrate how the principal-agent problem can apply to bureaucratic politics, let's consider a hypothetical example. Suppose Congress passes a law mandating that the EPA ensure factories do not dump mercury into rivers.

bureaucratic drift When government agencies depart from executing policy consistent with the ideological preferences of Congress or the president so as to execute policy consistent with their own ideological preferences.

coalitional drift When an ideological shift in elected branches creates disparity between the way an agency executes policy and the way new members of Congress or a new president believes the agency ought to execute policy.

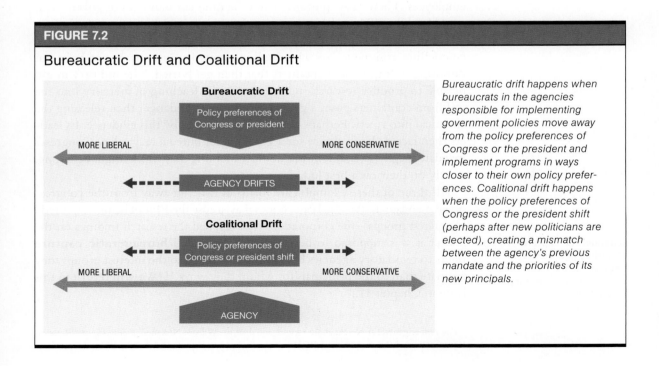

FIGURE 7.2

Bureaucratic Drift and Coalitional Drift

Bureaucratic Drift

Policy preferences of Congress or president

MORE LIBERAL   MORE CONSERVATIVE

AGENCY DRIFTS

Coalitional Drift

Policy preferences of Congress or president shift

MORE LIBERAL   MORE CONSERVATIVE

AGENCY

Bureaucratic drift happens when bureaucrats in the agencies responsible for implementing government policies move away from the policy preferences of Congress or the president and implement programs in ways closer to their own policy preferences. Coalitional drift happens when the policy preferences of Congress or the president shift (perhaps after new politicians are elected), creating a mismatch between the agency's previous mandate and the priorities of its new principals.

The EPA, as the agent, is supposed to do what Congress, as the principal, has asked it to do. Congress gives the EPA money to carry out these tasks. It instructs the EPA to notify companies of the rule changes, inspect factories regularly, monitor water quality in the rivers, and investigate possible illegal dumping of mercury.

The EPA could drift away from these duties for several reasons. First, the agency may be busy and its leaders may feel that they lack the resources to do all that Congress and the president ask. If they respond by making choices and prioritizing the agency's many tasks, they may delay implementation of the mercury regulation and focus on other tasks that they consider more urgent. Congress, however, may want immediate compliance with the mercury law and so view the agency as shirking its duty by delaying.

Second, the EPA has multiple principals who cannot always be satisfied simultaneously. This is a constant problem for executive-branch agencies. The EPA's leaders are appointed by the president but mandated to carry out laws passed by Congress (and usually signed by a president—one who may no longer be in office). If the mercury law was passed during a previous administration and the new president disagrees with it, the new president or the EPA leaders he or she appointed may instruct the EPA to drag its feet, go easy on offending companies, or simply ignore the law altogether. Although Congress typically sets out the details of the laws to be implemented and controls the budgets, the president nominates the leaders of the agencies and can fire top-level agency employees. These cross-pressures from the different branches of government could lead the EPA to drift away from its congressional mandate.

A third reason for drift could arise from corporations, which may provide compelling arguments for why dumping mercury in rivers is not as bad as disposing of it in waste containers that then get buried. The industry might be able to produce research indicating that the leaching of mercury into the soil from containers poses a greater environmental danger than releasing the chemical into rivers. Perhaps the EPA is convinced by this evidence. Its leaders then face a classic choice for a government bureaucracy: obey Congress's mandate strictly, even if it means doing something they think might be wrong, or rely on their own best judgment.

All three of these examples are forms of drifting away from the congressional mandate. In the third case, critics may accuse the EPA of being "captured" by interest groups—the corporations that supplied the research findings on the matter it was supposed to be regulating. So-called **bureaucratic capture** refers to regulatory agencies being more beholden to the interest groups they regulate than to the principals for whom they work.[12] (We will return to this issue in Chapter 11.)

bureaucratic capture When regulatory agencies are beholden to the organizations or interests they are supposed to regulate.

[12] For a more general argument about capture and drift, see William Niskanen, *Bureaucracy and Representative Government* (Chicago: Aldine, 1971).

A fourth, and more general, way for the EPA to shirk its duty as defined by Congress is to spend money it gets from Congress irresponsibly. In an ideal world, government bureaucracies would spend only as much as they need to accomplish their mandates and then return the rest to the public treasury. In doing so, the bureaucracies would be acting as responsible agents for the elected representatives. In the real world, many critics claim, government bureaucracies typically spend all of their money by the end of the fiscal year, regardless of whether the spending is efficient and rational. Then they complain to elected representatives that they do not have enough funding and ask for an increase for the following year. Elected officials cannot keep track of all the spending decisions of government bureaucracies to make sure they are always spending money responsibly.

Fifth, the EPA could simply be corrupt. Its personnel could take bribes from companies and allow illegal pollution of the rivers to go on. This kind of bureaucratic misconduct is rare, but hardly unheard of. In a major scandal exposed in 2015–16, dozens of U.S. Navy personnel were convicted of participating in a bribery and kickback scheme involving Leonard Glenn Francis, who had enormous contracts from the Department of Defense to maintain the Navy's ships throughout the Pacific region. Naval officers received money and gifts in exchange for classified information that helped Francis receive additional contracts and drive up costs, which increased his profits. The bribery scheme totaled at least $30 million.

You might ask, Why does Congress let agencies get away with such less than dutiful actions? The truth is that Congress passes so many rules and regulations that it cannot monitor everything that all the agencies do. To return to our hypothetical mercury regulation, Congress may not discover the EPA's shirking unless its members hear complaints about river pollution from environmental groups, or call on the agency to account for its implementation of the regulation. In fact, as we will see later in the section on congressional oversight, Congress has set up internal institutional rules precisely for the purpose of dealing with the fundamental principal-agent problem associated with bureaucratic agencies. Members of Congress want to be informed when agencies drift away and shirk the tasks assigned to them.[13]

The EPA example also shows how easily coalitional drift can occur in such situations. Consider a case involving the 2009 change in presidential administrations. Under George W. Bush, the EPA was given low priority for funding and other resources. When asked to regulate companies, the Bush White House pressured the EPA to be lenient and to give companies extra time to

[13] Kathleen Bawn, "Political Control versus Expertise: Congressional Choices about Administrative Procedures," *American Political Science Review* 89 (1995): 62–73; Mathew McCubbins, Roger Noll, and Barry Weingast, "Administrative Procedures as Instruments of Political Control," *Journal of Law, Economics, and Organization* 3 (1987): 243–77; David Epstein and Sharyn O'Halloran, *Delegating Powers* (New York: Cambridge University Press, 1999).

comply with regulations. Often, the EPA was instructed to put industry representatives on panels that made administrative laws on environmental issues. When Barack Obama took over as president, the EPA suddenly became a priority for the White House. The EPA was expected to be a more forceful advocate for communities and environmental groups against industry. The Obama White House undid many of the Bush policies concerning the EPA. In this instance, most employees of the EPA welcomed the change in administration because it seemed as though the Obama administration appreciated their main mission more than the Bush administration did. Nevertheless, the EPA employees had to adjust quickly to their new political principals, as they also did to the new Trump administration in 2017.

New presidential administrations sometimes seek to avoid the most jarring effects of coalitional drift, especially if the heads of agencies or departments are well liked by both political parties. It is not uncommon for new presidents, even those not from the party of their predecessor, to keep in place leaders in foreign policy and some key economic positions. Upon his election in 2009, Obama retained Bush's secretary of defense for a time and also nominated for a second term the chair of the Federal Reserve who had originally been appointed by Bush. Donald Trump, however, did not retain in his administration any of Obama's top bureaucrats or advisers.

Bureaucrats as Policy Makers

As mentioned, bureaucrats, like anyone else, have political goals and preferences, and moreover they are called upon to act as policy makers in certain ways. The shorthand version of policy making by the national government—Congress legislates and the president executes by relying on the executive-branch bureaucracy to enforce and implement the law—is overly simplistic. In reality, the executive branch conducts considerable lawmaking activity.

administrative law The body of law created by executive agencies with the purpose of refining general law passed in legislation.

rule making The process by which governmental agencies provide details on how laws passed by elected officials will be implemented.

We described **administrative law** in the previous chapter on the presidency. In fact, the vast majority of administrative law is made within the executive-branch bureaucracy, not within the White House. The making of administrative law is referred to as **rule making** by governmental agencies. Laws passed by Congress are often vague, requiring the government to establish a program or to regulate an aspect of commercial, private, or governmental behavior. If a law is vague, the bureaucracy must determine the specific details of the law as it is to be applied in practice.

Most of the rules and regulations for conducting commercial activities in the United States are actually drafted by administrative agencies doing rule making. Congress's immense workload makes it impossible for its members and their staff to write sufficiently detailed legislation. In addition, Congress does not have the technical or scientific expertise of the executive-branch agencies. Such expertise is necessary to write specific rules for, say, applying pesticides appropriately to avoid harming rare species, protecting workers in coal mines, or setting up the application process for students to request college loans. Interestingly, evidence shows that laws tend to be more vague under unified government than under divided government. This is probably because, under unified government, both branches are controlled by the same political party and Congress trusts the executive branch to implement the laws more faithfully than it would under divided government.[14]

The Administrative Procedures Act (APA) of 1946 established guidelines for agency rule making that are still followed. Specifically, the APA mandated, among other things, that agencies

- make records about all processes used to decide on regulations and rules fully transparent and accessible to the public;
- publish regulations in a timely manner and allow regulated persons time to comply;
- publish proposed regulations and allow public hearings before enforcement, during which the agency can make amendments in response to public comment;
- use trial-like procedures in many cases to adjudicate disputes, including protection for witnesses and defendants, and attorney-client privileges;
- report to Congress regularly on the effects of regulations.

Because of the APA guidelines, agencies first propose a new set of rules, then allow for citizens and interest groups to comment on the proposed rules, and then possibly amend the rules in response to comments. If public interest is high for a proposed rule, members of Congress usually weigh in and require hearings. As an example, the EPA and the U.S. Department of Transportation have proposed rules requiring that by 2025, all automobiles sold in the United States have a fuel efficiency of 54.5 miles per gallon. This set of rules was decided upon after long comments periods, during which the agencies and the department heard from hundreds of consumer groups, oil companies, auto companies, driver associations, and environmental groups, not to mention members of Congress. Note that the specific fuel standards were set by decisions of bureaucratic agencies and not legislation passed by Congress, and those fuel standard requirements for automobile companies have the force of law. The bureaucrats were given the mandate by previous laws to set standards to achieve goals set by Congress and the president—to reduce American dependence on fossil fuels, cut costs for consumers who drive automobiles, and improve the environment. It is a multistep process beginning with legislation that grants the bureaucrats the discretion to fill in the details with rule making later.

[14] John D. Huber and Charles R. Shipan, *Deliberate Discretion: The Institutional Foundations of Bureaucratic Autonomy* (New York: Cambridge University Press, 2002).

Besides rule making, bureaucrats act as policy makers in a more general, less formal way. Scholars sometimes refer to the people who most directly implement policies as "street-level" bureaucrats.[15] They staff the offices that interact with citizens and representatives from interest groups and companies; they conduct the inspections or experiments; they write the memos justifying decisions; and they organize small groups of bureaucrats to do the work of government. In each of these day-to-day actions, bureaucrats make important policy decisions. As an example, consider an inspector of meatpacking factories for the Department of Agriculture. He or she decides whether a slaughterhouse is clean enough for slaughtering cows and storing meat to satisfy federal regulations. Or consider a federal prosecutor deciding whether to charge someone with financial fraud. Is there enough evidence of fraud to proceed with charges? These are judgment calls made by individuals based on their knowledge of the laws and their observations. Through their everyday practices, they set standards and create routines of behavior by the government.

How Has the Bureaucracy Changed?

Now that we know what bureaucrats do and the challenges they face, let's examine how the bureaucracy has changed over time. These changes reveal that the challenges faced by bureaucrats have existed for centuries and that reforming the bureaucracy has long been a goal of politicians. Reforms are put forth as increasing efficiency and as being for the good of the American people, and often they are. But perhaps just as often, politicians want to reform the bureaucracy to achieve their own goals.

The Early Years

In the early years of the American republic, national government policies were administered by a few agencies led by groups of people appointed by the Continental Congress. As early as the 1780s, following the ideas of Alexander Hamilton and based on the British model of governmental administration, the government began to create "departments" headed by a single, appointed person called a secretary.

In 1789, there were three executive agencies—the State Department, the Treasury Department, and the War Department (later called Defense)—and the Office of the Attorney General (later a full-fledged department called Justice). The number of agencies and their scope grew slowly. Throughout the nineteenth century, the small size and focused work of the national agencies reflected

---

[15] Michael Lipsky, *Street-Level Bureaucracy* (New York: Russell Sage, 1980).

the limited scope of the national government. Most national bureaucrats in the nineteenth century were postal workers, soldiers, or customs officials. As the bureaucracy grew more quickly in the late nineteenth and early twentieth centuries, numerous reforms were proposed to make it more effective and efficient.

Growth in Size

In previous chapters, we studied the increasing nationalization of the American political system and the growing power of the presidency. Largely due to these trends, the bureaucracy has grown. By tracking the changes and large spikes in the size of the bureaucracy, it is possible to trace the major eras of reform, the wars, and the establishment of new programs (Figure 7.3).

The first major increase began in the late nineteenth century and continued through the Progressive Era in the early 1900s. The bureaucracy grew as the national government increasingly regulated the national economy and built a larger military. For regulation purposes, the government created a new type of bureaucracy: the independent agency (or commission). The first such agency, the Interstate Commerce Commission, was formed in 1887 to regulate railroads and later trucking and other surface carriers of goods and people. The Federal Trade Commission (1913) and the Federal Reserve Administration (1914) were created to regulate, respectively, financial transactions and the money supply for banks.

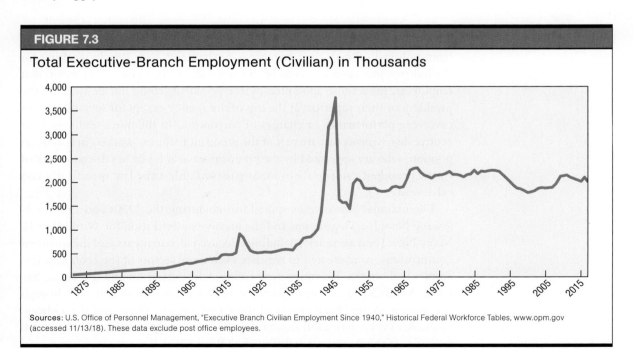

FIGURE 7.3

Total Executive-Branch Employment (Civilian) in Thousands

Sources: U.S. Office of Personnel Management, "Executive Branch Civilian Employment Since 1940," Historical Federal Workforce Tables, www.opm.gov (accessed 11/13/18). These data exclude post office employees.

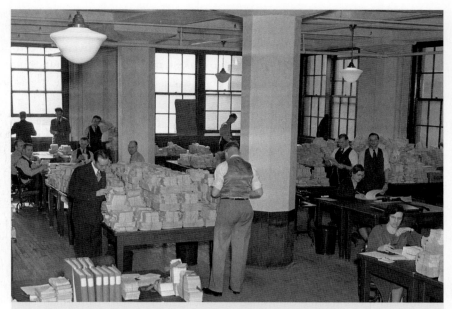

The New Deal programs of the 1930s vastly expanded the federal bureaucracy. One of the largest new programs administered by government agencies was the Social Security program. When the program went into effect in 1936, bureaucrats (like the workers in this Social Security office) had to set up and administer accounts for millions of Americans.

Independent agencies were ostensibly designed to have greater autonomy from political officials than executive departments had. People working for the independent agencies could be dismissed only "for cause." This means that employees, even those appointed by the president, could not be fired by the president or their superiors at the top of the agency except for specific reasons involving performance or charges of corruption. In the more traditional executive departments that are part of the president's cabinet, workers in leadership positions who are appointed by the president serve at his or her discretion—that is, the president can fire them for any reason unless the law specifically says otherwise.

The national bureaucracy spiked in size during the 1930s and 1940s, following New Deal legislation and the massive mobilization for World War II. Many New Deal agencies, including executive departments and independent commissions, were created to regulate even more sectors of the economy. Examples include the Transportation Safety Administration and the Social Security Administration. The Department of Defense was created in 1947 through the merger of the Departments of the Army and the Navy and the addition of the Air Force. Its establishment reflected the need to coordinate the global presence of the American military after World War II.

Another notable growth period of the civilian bureaucracy occurred in the 1960s and 1970s with Lyndon Johnson's Great Society programs and related new initiatives under Presidents Richard Nixon and Jimmy Carter. During that era, Congress passed laws creating agencies such as the Department of Housing and Urban Development, the EPA, and the Department of Education, which was spun off from the Department of Health, Education, and Welfare that had been created in 1953.

Since the 1960s the overall the size of the federal bureaucracy in terms of regular employees has plateaued, occasionally making small dips or increases. The minor growth in the civilian bureaucracy in the early 2000s resulted largely from the establishment of the new Department of Homeland Security (DHS). The department was created by splitting off some agencies from other parts of the executive-branch bureaucracy, bringing under its umbrella agencies that formerly stood alone and establishing new bureaucratic offices. The new Transportation Safety Administration is part of DHS, as is FEMA, once under the Department of Housing and Urban Development, which was a cabinet-level department before being absorbed into DHS.

Figure 7.3 reveals the link between major wars and the growth of the military bureaucracy. Large spikes occurred during the two world wars and the Korean, Vietnam, and two Iraq wars. During the Cold War (1946–90), the military stayed relatively large to manage American obligations around the world associated with the containment of communism. When the Cold War ended, the size of the military shrank briefly, only to grow again during the Gulf War (1991–92) and the war in Iraq that started in 2003.

The Spoils System

The nature of presidential appointments has also changed over time. Recall our discussion of Andrew Jackson's presidency in Chapter 6. Because Jackson believed that national bureaucrats should not hold government jobs for long periods, he used to great effect a rotation system that opened up positions for presidential appointments every four years or so. This timing conveniently aligned with presidential elections and, in effect, was a *patronage* or *spoils system*: to the victorious party (which won the presidency and did well in congressional elections) went the spoils (jobs). Thus in Jackson's era (1830s), the national bureaucracy was a favorite vehicle for elected presidents to reward their supporters with government jobs.[16]

This patronage-appointment system had a major impact on the federal bureaucracy, but its excesses soon became obvious as constant turnover and underqualified appointees interfered with effective implementation of

[16] Robert Remini, *The Life of Andrew Jackson* (New York: Harper and Row, 1998).

government policies. In the late nineteenth century, Congress passed laws establishing a professional civil service. However, vestiges of the spoils system still exist at the top of the bureaucracy. Presidents continue to fill several thousand leadership positions in the bureaucracy with men and women who either worked directly on or helped fund their campaigns, or who are known to be sympathetic to the president's ideological and political goals.

One problem with filling bureaucratic positions with political appointees is that campaign supporters and other ideological allies in those positions are not always knowledgeable or professionally trained to do their jobs. Presidents, for example, typically fill ambassador positions with people whose main qualification is that they helped him or her get elected. After his first election in 2008, President Obama appointed Matthew Barzun, an internet businessman, to be ambassador to Sweden after Barzun donated large sums of money to the Obama campaign. In 2012, Obama reappointed Barzun to the prestigious position of ambassador to the United Kingdom after he raised $2.3 million for Obama's reelection campaign. Nearly all presidents have made similarly embarrassing appointments, though in the heyday of the spoils system this kind of cronyism was more widespread and reached further down the bureaucratic ranks.

As the national government in the late nineteenth century increased its role in the economy and in building an infrastructure for commerce across regions, many government jobs required a measure of expertise. It became important, for example, for inspectors of meatpacking plants to know something about the science of pathogens and public health. In the 1880s, reformers known as *mugwumps* called for abolishing the spoils system and instituting a more merit-based bureaucracy. Mugwumps were mostly Republicans known for their willingness to support the Democrats when necessary to achieve reforms.[17] Reformers' appeals played well with segments of the population who were shut out from government jobs—pretty much anyone, that is, who was not active in the president's campaign or from a group considered crucial to the president's election efforts. Led by the mugwumps, reformers pressured the national government to take action in the 1880s to do away with the worst excesses of the spoils system. The core idea was to make the bureaucracy more professional and insulated from politicians who want to fill the jobs with their cronies.

Civil Service Reform

With the Pendleton Act of 1883, the national government began to institute a civil service system. The act made it illegal to require people to pay dues to political parties in order to get national government jobs, and it instituted

[17] *Mugwump* means "great man" in the Algonquin language. It eventually became a political slur, meaning someone who is indecisive or lacks ideological conviction.

layers of the national bureaucracy that are "protected," meaning they are not subject to political appointment and are classified or ranked by the skill and education levels required. Other countries, including Britain, France, and Germany, were instituting similar reforms at the same time.

All of these civil services are characterized by a system of evaluation and promotion from within the bureaucracies; tests and training take place to ensure that competent people fill the jobs. It is expected that employees in the bureaucracy can keep their job when a new president or new government is elected, but that the bureaucrats must work on behalf of whoever is in office. Salaries are allocated according to rank, and professional codes of conduct prohibit graft and political favoritism. Today, the vast majority of civilian bureaucrats in the U.S. government are civil servants—their jobs are protected from patronage and they cannot be fired by an incoming president for political reasons. Presidential appointees occupy only the top layers of a typical department.

Civil service reform sought to establish rational, routine procedures for conducting work, communicating among employees, hiring employees, setting salaries, and managing promotions and demotions (or layoffs). One goal was to minimize uncertainty in budgeting and to create a smoothly functioning bureaucracy in which people knew their jobs well and could coordinate their actions for the benefit of the organization. The increasingly technical nature of government work by the late nineteenth century provided further motivation to improve efficiency and performance within the government bureaucracy. Ideally, in jobs that required skill and specific knowledge, experienced bureaucrats who had learned how to do their jobs well would be able to retain those jobs and continue cultivating their expertise. Many people came to realize that it was wasteful for the government to remove a highly skilled worker, or someone who was successfully learning those skills, just to repay a political favor. The rapid turnover of qualified personnel in bureaucracies every time a new president took office represented a lost opportunity to build expertise in the bureaucracy.

Civil service reforms also served to break the grip that certain political party bosses had on specific segments of the national bureaucracy. It was well known in the nineteenth century that party bosses in New York had final say over who could fill the potentially lucrative national bureaucratic positions in the New York customhouses. These officials oversaw imports coming into the United States and collected customs and duties. Plum jobs in these houses afforded many opportunities to accept bribes from importers. The civil service reforms did not do away with all forms of bribery and patronage politics, but they did diminish their incidence and contributed to a much more professionalized, effective government bureaucracy, especially in those realms requiring expertise or some measure of political neutrality.

Beginning in the late 1890s, the Progressive Movement carried on this philosophy of scientific management as it applied to government bureaucracies. The Progressives, like their mugwump predecessors, believed fundamentally in the idea that government could and should be operated in an apolitical and nonpartisan manner based on scientific principles. In the first two decades of the twentieth century, especially with the elections of presidents Theodore Roosevelt and Woodrow Wilson, the national government continued shifting toward a civil service form of bureaucracy and setting up independent agencies. In fact, early in his career as a professor, Wilson had written famous works extolling the virtues of scientific management.

Modern Reforms of the Bureaucracy

Despite these reforms, and in part because the government bureaucracy at all levels grew throughout the twentieth century even with the implementation of the civil service model, the federal bureaucracy is widely seen today as bloated and inefficient. Many people complain that the bureaucracy grows but never shrinks (in fact, as noted later, its size has remained remarkably stable since the 1950s), and that large bureaucracies waste taxpayers' money and are inherently inefficient. It is often tempting for politicians running for office to tap into the public's wariness of large government agencies. The Republican Party has traditionally been the party of "small government," but throughout the twentieth century presidents of both major parties, as well as a number of third-party candidates, ran for office promising to clean up government "red tape" and provide the same or more government service for less tax money.

Ronald Reagan was openly hostile to government bureaucracy during his first campaign for president in 1980. He complained of runaway government budgets, bloated bureaucracy, regulations that hampered legitimate business activity, and corruption in the distribution of welfare benefits. He promised to reduce government regulation of businesses, cut taxes and government spending, and reorganize agencies to eliminate redundancy, waste, and fraud. Reagan's campaign struck a chord among people upset by media reports of $600 toilet seats purchased by the Department of Defense for government airplanes, or welfare cheats who drove fancy cars while taking advantage of generous government programs. Although some of these stories were exaggerated or untrue, many Americans agreed with Reagan that they paid too much in taxes for what they received in public goods and services.

As part of his effort to shrink the federal bureaucracy, Reagan was determined to weaken public employee unions. In 1981, he dramatically fired more than 11,000 federal air traffic controllers who had gone on strike over pay and working conditions. (National government employees were first

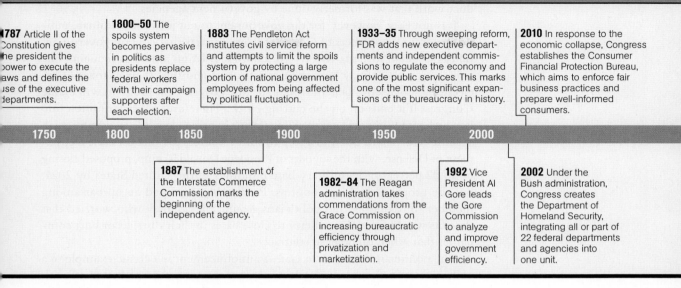

1787 Article II of the Constitution gives the president the power to execute the laws and defines the use of the executive departments.

1800–50 The spoils system becomes pervasive in politics as presidents replace federal workers with their campaign supporters after each election.

1883 The Pendleton Act institutes civil service reform and attempts to limit the spoils system by protecting a large portion of national government employees from being affected by political fluctuation.

1933–35 Through sweeping reform, FDR adds new executive departments and independent commissions to regulate the economy and provide public services. This marks one of the most significant expansions of the bureaucracy in history.

2010 In response to the economic collapse, Congress establishes the Consumer Financial Protection Bureau, which aims to enforce fair business practices and prepare well-informed consumers.

1750   1800   1850   1900   1950   2000

1887 The establishment of the Interstate Commerce Commission marks the beginning of the independent agency.

1982–84 The Reagan administration takes commendations from the Grace Commission on increasing bureaucratic efficiency through privatization and marketization.

1992 Vice President Al Gore leads the Gore Commission to analyze and improve government efficiency.

2002 Under the Bush administration, Congress creates the Department of Homeland Security, integrating all or part of 22 federal departments and agencies into one unit.

permitted to unionize in 1962—but unlike workers in the private sector, they were prohibited from striking.) In the wake of the strike, the Reagan administration decertified the controllers' union, fined senior union officials, and banned strikers from holding government jobs in the future.

In some cases, complaints about bureaucratic inefficiency and bungling are clearly justified. Individual government agencies often need reform, and the consolidation and coordination of the sprawling federal bureaucracy is an ongoing concern. For example, the September 11 terrorist attacks in 2001 highlighted the lack of communication among law enforcement and intelligence agencies spread across several departments, such as Defense, State, and Justice. Most analysts consider the collapse of financial markets in 2008–09 to have resulted in part because of failed coordination among, and weak enforcement of regulations by, agencies in various government departments.

Sometimes, members of Congress and the president move beyond campaign promises and actually work to reform the bureaucracy by improving laws and regulations or by cutting costs. Agencies are periodically consolidated and jobs eliminated. In fact, since the beginning of the twentieth century, there have been 11 major presidential commissions devoted to reforming the executive branch. These commissions made recommendations, many of them implemented by Congress and the president, to abolish certain agencies, consolidate others, and privatize much of the work of government.[18] Privatization means that the government contracts with private companies to conduct work that was formerly done by government agencies.

It is not easy, however, for the government to cut jobs and eliminate public programs.[19] Members of Congress from districts that contain government offices targeted for cuts will try to scuttle legislation aimed at reducing bureaucracy, since it may hurt their constituents and thus their chances of reelection. People who benefit from a specific government program will blame Congress if it ends up on the cutting block. Therefore, politicians often find it expedient to support bureaucratic reforms in principle while avoiding actual, specific reforms. In 2017, in a step to shift resources to other uses, the Department of Defense, with the support of President Donald Trump, proposed closing up to 22 percent of its military base buildings in the United States by 2021, but the proposal died in Congress. Predictably, it caused an uproar among members of Congress and politicians around the country who worried that the cuts would force the military to close bases in their districts or hurt companies that relied on defense contracts.

The politicians' reaction to Gates's announcement is a classic example of a collective action problem. Collectively, politicians would be better off with more efficient government, because they can all claim credit for making the government work better overall. But individually, politicians do not want the government to cut public jobs among their own constituents. So rather than cooperating, they "defect" and vote against reforms that might be unpopular with their constituents, even if the reforms would help the government and the country as a whole.

Nonetheless, many bureaucratic reforms have resulted in reducing the size of the bureaucracy, or slowing its growth. As Figure 7.3 shows, starting in the 1950s the overall size of the civilian bureaucracy leveled off at around 2 million workers. It has remained constant since then, even though the population it serves and the money the government spends have grown significantly.

How can the federal government spend so much more and serve so many more people with fewer workers in the bureaucracy? The gain in efficiency is partly due to technological advances. Computers, for example, have enabled fewer employees to do the work of collecting and distributing government benefits. Before the advent of computers, running the Social Security program entailed keeping paper records for each of the millions of employed,

[18] Paul Light, *The Tides of Reform* (New Haven, CT: Yale University Press, 1997). More recent data can be found in Daniel Carpenter, "The Evolution of National Bureaucracy in the United States," in *The Institutions of American Democracy: The Executive Branch*, ed. Joel Aberbach and Mark Peterson (New York: Oxford University Press, 2005), pp. 41–71.

[19] Hugh Heclo, *A Government of Strangers* (Washington, DC: Brookings Institution, 1977); Paul Light, *The Tides of Reform* (New Haven, CT: Yale University Press, 1997); Glenn Beamer, *Creative Politics* (Ann Arbor: University of Michigan Press, 1999).

retired, or disabled people in the United States. However, the reduced size of the bureaucracy is mostly the result of various programs of reform, especially since the 1980s, that limited the growth of the executive branch. These reform efforts have led to a decline in the number of employees and the elimination of many agencies. More than half (57 percent) of the federal agencies created between 1947 and 1998 have been abolished due to mergers of agencies, creation of new replacement agencies, or simply elimination altogether of the tasks.[20]

Privatization and Marketization

There has been a big push since the 1980s for the national government to privatize and marketize.[21] **Privatization** refers to having private sector companies or individuals implement government programs. **Marketization** refers to having government agencies adopt principles of private enterprise when making decisions and implementing policies.

Privatization takes numerous forms. One example is when the government hires a company or an organization on a **contract** basis to carry out a task, such as building roads, making military jets, or providing security in Iraq or Afghanistan for American diplomats and military leaders. Such contracts account for a significant portion of the federal government's budget—the 2016 figure was about $478 billion, or approximately 12.5 percent of the total budget—and have long been accepted practice.

Other types of privatization also account for a large proportion of government spending. The government can give **grants** to people and organizations to perform a task in the public interest, such as conducting research, experimenting with new policy initiatives, attending school, and making art. In 2016, government grants totaled roughly $600 billion. Sometimes, the government partners with private financial institutions to fund public projects. In recent years, this has included partnering with companies to build factories and housing that are jointly used by government agencies and by others. (An example is housing for military personnel and their families that is open to nonmilitary families as well.) The government can rely on volunteers and private donations to conduct work that is sanctioned by the government but directed by a private agency. For instance, the Red Cross is authorized by the government to provide relief to victims of disasters, but it is not formally a public entity. The government can also sell land and other assets to private companies or individuals, a form of privatization that increases government revenue.

privatization The contracting of private companies by the government to conduct work that was formerly done by government agencies.

marketization Government bureaucratic reform that emphasizes market-based principles of management that are common to the private sector.

government contract An agreement whereby the government hires a company or an organization to carry out certain tasks on its behalf.

government grant Money that the government provides to individuals or organizations to perform tasks in the public's interest.

[20] See Daniel P. Carpenter, "The Evolution of National Bureaucracy in the United States," in *The Executive Branch*, ed. Joel D. Aberbach and Mark Peterson (New York: Oxford University Press, 2005), pp. 52–53.

[21] Donald Kettl, *The Transformation of Governance* (Baltimore: Johns Hopkins Press, 2000).

In the Iraq and Afghanistan wars, the U.S. military hired private companies to do the work previously handled by government employees. For example, in Iraq, private contractors provided security services and even engaged in some combat operations, raising questions about accountability.

Since the 1980s, privatization reform has been a huge factor in reducing the growth of the government bureaucracy. Reagan appointed a prominent businessman, J. Peter Grace, to lead a commission devoted to reducing the size and cost of the executive branch. The Grace Commission (1982–84) made many recommendations for reform, focusing on the idea that the government should emulate the private sector more closely. This recommendation not only entailed privatizing many government tasks but also meant that government bureaucracies should adopt market-based principles of management widely used by private corporations (marketization).

One highly controversial example of marketization sometimes used at the state or local level is government-funded vouchers that parents can "spend" to send their children to private schools. The premise behind vouchers is that failing public schools will improve in order to compete for students and funding. Another example is the use of "pollution rights" that can be traded on the open market. Under these so-called cap-and-trade policies, companies (typically power plants) are allotted permits to pollute the environment with a certain quantity of emissions (up to a limit, or "cap"). They can buy other companies' emissions permits if they need to exceed the cap, or sell their own permits if they succeed in reducing emissions. In theory, the price of emissions permits should adjust so that supply meets demand, while the overall level of emissions (which is set by the government) gradually declines. Like school vouchers, pollution rights and emissions permits are controversial, but both the United States and the European Union have market-based emissions trading programs in place.

The Grace Commission's recommendations, and the underlying concepts of marketization and privatization, have influenced bureaucratic reform efforts by both Republican and Democratic administrations. Promoting privatization is a way for politicians to have their cake and eat it too. They can claim to keep the size of government in check while still maintaining the services that make constituents happy. Critics of privatization charge that private companies are more interested in profits than in the public good. Furthermore, private companies are much less accountable to elected officials than are government bureaucrats. During the Iraq War in the 2000s, for example, numerous private companies provided security for American government officials working in Iraq or actually carried out government-mandated rebuilding efforts in Iraq. There were instances of fraud and recurring complaints about a lack of oversight of these contractors. Without the direct control of the White House or a cabinet secretary, it can be difficult to monitor and coordinate these companies' actions.

Shaping and Influencing the Bureaucracy

We began this chapter by describing how the executive branch bureaucracy has two main principals, Congress and the president. Their direct influence over the bureaucracy occurs through the processes of appointments, budgeting, and oversight.

Appointments

Both the president and Congress (through the Senate) are involved in appointing the leadership of the bureaucracy; in general, the president proposes and the Senate approves. Although most of the people working in executive-branch agencies are civil service employees, the top positions are almost always filled by appointees. It is a matter of law which of these appointments must be approved by the Senate; generally, the higher up the positions are in a department or an agency, the more likely that the appointments must be approved by the Senate.

The appointment of cabinet secretaries, and perhaps of officials one or two layers further down in the hierarchy of an agency, can be politically controversial, especially under divided government. When the Senate was controlled by Democrats during President George W. Bush's tenure in office, the Senate stalled on many of Bush's appointment requests or turned them down.

A similar pattern occurred during the Clinton presidency when the Republicans controlled the Senate. Under President Obama, Republican senators, even when not in a majority, frequently filibustered to prevent selected appointments made by the president.

Moreover, after appointments are made, tension may arise between the professionals already working in the bureaucracy and the new political appointees.[22] Civil service workers are obligated to do what their superiors ask, regardless of whether they agree. Career bureaucrats in the EPA, who tend to have environmentalist backgrounds and sympathies, were known to resent top-level appointees of Presidents Reagan, George H. W. Bush, and George W. Bush. They viewed the political appointees as favoring business interests over environmental protection. Likewise, there is a long history of tension between professional military personnel in the Pentagon and their civilian bosses, the president and top-level presidential appointees.

Budgeting

Although the Senate's role in appointments is substantial, for Congress budgeting serves as its major control over the executive-branch bureaucracy. The president is involved as well in proposing an annual budget to Congress. Further, through the information provided by the Office of Management and Budget (OMB) and through the president's public statements, the president profoundly shapes the budgets of the various bureaucratic agencies. Nevertheless, Congress in the end controls the "purse strings" of government. The annual budgeting process includes deciding on specific budgets of all the executive-branch agencies.

There is an important distinction between Congress *authorizing* that something be done by the national government and Congress *appropriating* money to enable the national bureaucracy to implement the law. Even if something is authorized under law, until the money is appropriated by Congress to pay for it, the law will remain a dead letter. Thus Congress can pass a bill to authorize the building of a new type of aircraft carrier, but until a separate bill is passed that appropriates money for the new fleet of aircraft carriers, nothing can flow to the Department of Defense for that purpose. (Sometimes a single bill can both authorize and appropriate.)

Recall our earlier discussion about how bureaucracies are often accused of spending their full appropriations and then asking for increases the next year, regardless of whether it is the most efficient use of the government's resources. This approach to budgeting is actually acknowledged and indeed expected by elected representatives, who often lack the information they need to make

[22] Joel Aberbach, "The U.S. Federal Executive in an Era of Change," *Governance* 16 (2003): 373–99.

the most efficient spending decisions. In effect, as the principals (primarily Congress) asking the agents (bureaucracies) to spend money to solve problems, the principals cannot micromanage all the spending decisions involving many billions of dollars.

To deal with the difficulty of tracking the income and expenditures of government bureaucracies, elected officials have created a system of incremental budgeting. In this system, most government agencies in any given year can expect to receive approximately the same budget as the year before, with only a small, incremental increase. Thus, in the absence of a substantial change in the government's priorities, agency budgets tend to grow only modestly from year to year. Congress can eliminate any project simply by deleting the relevant line item in the agency's budget. Sometimes Congress may cut—or threaten to cut—an agency's entire budget. The national budget, however, provides departments and agencies with considerable discretion over their expenditures. This means that, short of a law requiring an agency to stop spending money on a particular action, the agency's leaders can often shift money from other parts of the agency to continue funding the project.

Oversight

Oversight refers to the monitoring of bureaucracies, and it is essentially how principals obtain information about the agents. Both Congress and the president oversee the workings of the bureaucracy, though Congress plays the more direct and public role through hearings and investigations. Even one executive-branch bureaucracy can oversee or investigate another. Sometimes the Justice Department investigates other agencies (or even its own subagencies or personnel) if criminal wrongdoing is alleged, and the General Accounting Office (GAO) oversees the accounting, human resources, and budgeting practices of most of the federal bureaucracies.

In delegating authority to the bureaucracy, lawmakers have set up institutional rules for how bureaucracies should conduct their rule making and adjudicating roles.[23] We have already discussed the APA (American Procedures Act) and the procedures it requires. Two other laws are also critical to bureaucratic oversight. The Freedom of Information Act, passed in 1966, requires that government agencies, upon request, disclose information (other than information vital to national security) on their activities if the information has not already been released through public reporting. The Sunshine Act, passed in 1976, requires that, with certain exceptions, all meetings of government agencies must be open to public observation.

---

[23] For a recent perspective on this topic, see Sean Gailmard and John W. Patty, *Learning while Governing: Information, Accountability, and Executive Branch Institutions* (Chicago: University of Chicago Press, 2013).

The Collective Dilemma

The U.S. Department of Defense (DoD) has a budget of approximately $500 billion, which is given to execute its missions to "provide the military forces necessary to deter war" and to "protect the security" of the country. A portion of its budget, however, has been spent on projects that seem, at best, tangential to military funding. For instance, its recent budgets allotted $20 million for alternative-energy research and $1 billion for health and disease research.[a] Previously, funds were allotted to study regional differences in Twitter slang, develop beef jerky, and operate a microbrewery.[b] Why do these kinds of projects find their way into the defense budget?

Interests

Expanding the DoD budget offers politicians from both parties an opportunity to advance their interests. For Democrats, it is an avenue through which federal funds can be secured for projects they support that are difficult to fund in other ways. The DoD budget appeals to Republicans because their party base stresses the importance of national security and the military[c]; thus, by supporting a large DoD budget, they appear to favor national-security interests. Further, opposing a strong DoD budget presents political risks for both parties. For instance, Allen West, a conservative political commentator, called previous defense secretary Chuck Hagel a "traitor" for proposing a DoD budget reduction,[d] which suggests that cutting the DoD budget can sometimes be viewed as a slight to the military and to patriotic Americans.

Institutions

Two features allow the DoD to fund a wide scope of projects. First is its bureaucratic autonomy. As with any large government bureaucracy, a principal-agent problem exists between the elected branches and the DoD. Congress and the president (the principals) have limited information regarding every facet of such an enormous department and budget; the DoD (the agent) has flexibility and discretion to set the boundaries on what it considers as part of its mission to defend the interests of the country. If the leaders want to spend some of the DoD's money on research, the DoD has enough autonomy to shift resources in that direction.

Second, the broad nature of the department's mission allows for a generous allocation from Congress. "Defense" can be broadly defined to include a number of items. For instance, some assert that poverty and terrorism are linked,[e] allowing one to argue, then, that human development—physical, intellectual, or economic—is within the purview of the DoD. It can be difficult to separate defense and nondefense related projects.

Finally, recall from Chapter 5 that individual members of Congress have incentives to secure "pork" into bills, bringing benefits to narrow constituencies through federal legislation. Larger pieces of legislation, like budgets and appropriations for the DoD, provide an opportunity to slip in tangential projects.

Outcomes

One obvious outcome is that the DoD enjoys a healthy budget. For the 2015 fiscal year, the DoD's budget exceeded the combined budgets of the next five largest departments: Departments of Transportation, Health and Human Services, Education, Veterans Affairs, and Housing and Urban Development.

Second, its sizeable budget enables the DoD to engage in projects that seem to overlap with the missions of other federal departments. As previously stated, the 2015 budget allotted $20 million to alternative-energy research,[f] even though there is a separate federal entity—the U.S. Department of Energy—that exists for energy-related initiatives.

Third, although it is common to hear statements about the need to cut the hefty DoD budget, doing so is politically contentious. In October 2015, President Obama issued his fifth veto halting the National Defense Authorization Act for 2016 from becoming law, in part, because he was displeased with the defense-spending levels.[g] On this veto, then speaker of the House John Boehner remarked, "By placing domestic politics ahead of our troops, President Obama has put America's national security at risk."[h] This kind of rhetoric is common when planning for DoD budgets, either cuts or expansions. The Trump administration, together with the Republican Congress during his first two years, increased the DoD budget by $82 billion by 2019, an increase of 18 percent from the 2017 defense budget.

Why does the DoD budget contain money for many projects, like alternative energy research, that are seemingly tangential to its mission?

Think About It

Is it likely that the DoD will continue to be able to fund governmental activities that are not strictly defense related? Why or why not? Should Congress rein in the department's budget? What are the downsides, if any, to having overlapping programs in different departments of the federal government?

a. Citizens Against Government Waste, 2015, "2015 Congressional Pig Book Summary," http://cagw.org/sites/default/files/pdf/Pig-Book-2015.pdf (accessed 10/1/15).

b. Tom A Coburn, "Department of Everything," Defense Technical Information Center, ADA570614, November 2012, www.dtic.mil/dtic/tr/fulltext/u2/a570614.pdf (accessed 9/24/15).

c. Pew Research Center, "Beyond Red vs. Blue: The Political Typology," June 26, 2014, www.people-press.org/files/2014/06/6-26-14-Political-Typology-release1.pdf (accessed 10/23/15).

d. Michael Ross, "Allen West Denounces Chuck Hagel as a 'Traitor' over Proposed Military Cuts," *Examiner*, February 26, 2014, www.examiner.com/article/allen-west-denounces-chuck-hagel-as-a-traitor-over-proposed-military-cuts (accessed 10/23/15).

e. See, for example, Joseph Kahn and Tim Weiner, "World Leaders Rethinking Strategy on Aid to Poor," *New York Times*, March 18, 2002, www.nytimes.com/2002/03/18/world/world-leaders-rethinking-strategy-on-aid-to-poor.html?pagewanted=all (accessed 11/20/15).

f. Citizens Against Government Waste, "2015 Congressional Pig Book Summary."

g. The White House, Office of the Press Secretary, "Remarks by the President at Veto Signing of National Defense Authorization Act," October 22, 2015, www.whitehouse.gov/the-press-office/2015/10/22/remarks-president-veto-signing-national-defense-authorization-act (accessed 11/20/15).

h. U.S. Speaker of the House, "Boehner: Defense Veto Must Not Stand," October 22, 2015, www.speaker.gov/press-release/boehner-defense-veto-must-not-stand (accessed 11/20/15).

fire-alarm oversight Congressional oversight that relies on interest groups and citizens to inform representatives of unwarranted action.

police-patrol oversight Congressional oversight that consists of actively monitoring agencies through routine inspection.

Scholars of bureaucracy have argued that the APA, the Freedom of Information Act, and the Sunshine Act constitute a system of congressional **fire-alarm oversight** of the bureaucracy. In other words, members of Congress hear from constituents when the bureaucracy does not do its job well or conform to congressional mandates. This contrasts with **police-patrol oversight**, in which members of Congress keep constant tabs on bureaucracies, routinely inspecting what they do. By mandating public comment periods before regulations are finally decided, and mandating public hearings in many cases, these laws allow aggrieved constituents to do the job of overseeing the bureaucracy and setting off alarms in Congress if bureaucrats drift too far from their principals' wishes.[24]

The Courts' Influence

Court decisions play a major role in shaping overall bureaucratic responsibilities and influencing their decisions. Lawsuits can lead to court interpretations of laws mandating that bureaucracies play a smaller or larger role in determining public policy. One key decision in 2007, for instance, substantially altered the prerogatives of the Environmental Protection Agency (EPA). During the George W. Bush administration in 2003, the EPA took the position that it did not have the authority to regulate pollutants for the purpose of controlling greenhouse gases and affecting climate change. A dozen states, including California, plus numerous cities sued, and in a 5–4 decision (labeled *Massachusetts v. EPA*), the Supreme Court sided with the states and local governments. The Court held that the Clean Air Act, originally passed in 1970 and amended since, required that the EPA regulate such pollutants.

An earlier Court decision set an important precedent for lawmaking in general. The 1984 Supreme Court decision in *Chevron v. the Natural Resources Defense Council* established a legal standard for upholding an agency's authority to write law in a specific area. If a person files a lawsuit challenging a bureaucratic agency's authority to write a rule following a congressional statute, the courts are first supposed to examine whether the congressional statute explicitly authorized the agency to write rules of implementation. If so, then the agency has considerable discretion. If, however, as is commonly the case, the legislation is not clear on this point, then the courts are to determine if the agency's interpretation of the statute is "reasonable" or "permissible." In the *Chevron* case, an environmental group had brought suit against the EPA in a lower federal court, arguing that the EPA's reinterpretation of part of the Clean Air Act of 1977 went beyond the agency's authority to interpret the

---

[24] Mathew D. McCubbins and Thomas Schwartz, "Congressional Oversight Overlooked: Police Patrols versus Fire Alarms," *American Journal of Political Science* 28 (1984): 165–79.

law. The lower court ruled against the EPA, and Chevron, as an affected party, appealed the decision to the Supreme Court. The Supreme Court sided with Chevron and ruled that the EPA had reasonably interpreted the Clean Air Act. Environmental groups liked neither the EPA's interpretation of the act nor the Court's decision, but the legal ruling set an important precedent about the authority of federal agencies.

Interest Groups

Although much interest group activity is focused on Congress, these groups lobby bureaucratic agencies as well. Groups try to influence those writing administrative laws and complain when their interests are threatened. Often, they enlist help from other parts of the government. Suppose a group of trucking companies is dismayed by the regulatory actions of the Department of Transportation. They may try to convince members of the specialized congressional transportation committees, who make most of the budgetary decisions affecting the department, that their complaints deserve attention. Another way to complain is to request a visit with someone in the White House; that person, assuming he or she agrees with the trucking companies, can pressure the Department of Transportation to alter its behavior. Or the trucking companies can take their grievances directly to the bureaucrats themselves and request hearings.

When scholars and other commentators speak of the "iron triangle," they are referring to the special relationships that develop among three types of actors: the interest groups representing the private sector that is being regulated by the government, the congressional committees and subcommittees that write laws regulating that sector, and the bureaucratic agency that implements the laws[25] (Figure 7.4). The concern is that these special relationships may lead to biased regulatory decisions. Specifically, the business interests being regulated by the government might have more "insider" status in the bureaucratic agency than the consumers whom the regulations are supposed to protect.

Iron triangles occur when a certain "coziness" develops among the three kinds of actors. People often switch jobs, moving from one corner of the triangle to another. It is common for someone who has worked in a government agency or as a staff member for a congressional committee to go to work as a lobbyist for a regulated business or industry. Lobbying organizations seek out such people because they know not only the laws and regulations but also the right people in the government to help advance their clients' interests. For instance, the lobbying firms representing defense contractors are filled with former members of the military and other government officials who have

---

[25] Hugh Heclo, *A Government of Strangers* (Washington, DC: Brookings Institution, 1977).

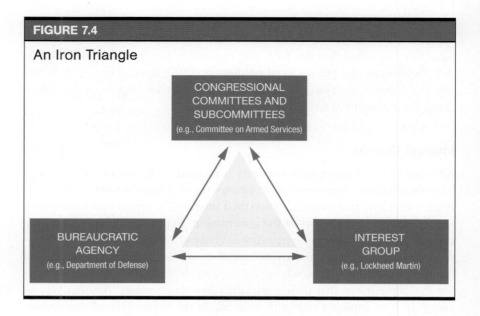

FIGURE 7.4

An Iron Triangle

CONGRESSIONAL COMMITTEES AND SUBCOMMITTEES
(e.g., Committee on Armed Services)

BUREAUCRATIC AGENCY
(e.g., Department of Defense)

INTEREST GROUP
(e.g., Lockheed Martin)

intimate knowledge of the process the Pentagon uses to award bids. Some observers believe that as consumer, environmental, and other public interest groups have gained power in the American political system since the 1970s, these classic triangular relationships have become less "ironclad," reducing the worst excesses of favoritism and "insiderism."

In Comparison: Bureaucratic Traditions

In all modern democracies, the bureaucracy is accountable to the elected branches of government, at least in principle. But the actual relationships between executive departments and parliaments, and the political power of the bureaucracy, vary across countries.

In parliamentary democracies, executive agencies are accountable only to the parliament, unlike in an American-style system of separation of powers where they have dual loyalties to the legislature and the president. In countries like Britain, when the government falls—that is, when the parliament votes to dismiss the current government—the ministers of all the executive departments are immediately fired and new people must be chosen by the parliament to replace them. In the American system, by contrast, if the majority party in Congress changes after a popular election but the president remains in office, the heads of the executive departments stay in place at the pleasure of the president.

Do Bureaucrats Behave Differently than Elected Officials?

Bureaucracy is supposed to be the apolitical arm of the federal government, tasked with carrying out the day-to-day operations that allow the government to function. Unlike the elected branches, bureaucrats' jobs do not depend on constituencies choosing whether or not to reelect them. Still, bureaucrats have political beliefs like everyone else, and they pay a lot of attention to politics and have opinions about the work they do. How do preferences and biases of bureaucrats manifest in their work? How does this differ from that of elected officials?

Let's start with elected officials. Political scientists Daniel Butler and David Broockman emailed state legislators a request for information on how to register to vote, using a name generally assumed to be white (Jake Mueller) and a name generally assumed to be black (DeShawn Jackson).[a] Figure A shows their findings for the entire sample of state legislators. The difference between the response rates is listed above the bar sets.

Now, let's compare with bureaucrats. Political scientists Katherine Einstein and David Glick studied racial biases of bureaucrats working in public housing.[b] They sent over 1,000 emails to public-housing authorities across the country, purporting to be a candidate for housing assistance. They experimented with supposedly white names (Emily Smith, Brett Smith), black names (Tyrone Johnson, Shanice Johnson), and Hispanic names (Santiago Martinez, Gabriela Martinez) to see if bureaucratic responsiveness differed by the name of the sender. Figure B plots the proportion of emails that received a response by the six names.

B. Proportion of Email Inquiries to Public-Housing Bureaucrats That Received a Response by Race/Ethnicity

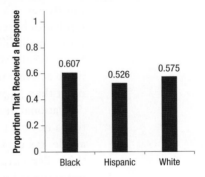

Source: Katherine Levine Einstein and David M. Glick, "Does Race Affect Access to Government Services? An Experiment Exploring Street-Level Bureaucrats and Access to Public Housing," *American Journal of Political Science* (forthcoming, 2016). Replication data available at https://dataverse.harvard.edu/dataset.xhtml?persistentId=doi:10.7910/DVN/1HOVTU (accessed 5/25/16).

Think About It

What does Figure A suggest about racial biases in response rates by the legislators? What does Figure B suggest about racial biases in response rates among bureaucrats? Do these two kinds of government officials react differently to requests from different racial groups? If so, why might that be?

A. Proportion of Email Inquiries to State Legislators that Received a Response, by Name of Sender

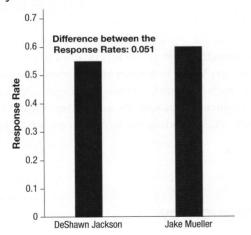

Source: Daniel M. Butler and David E. Broockman, "Do Politicians Racially Discriminate Against Constituents? A Field Experiment on State Legislators," *American Journal of Political Science* 55, no. 3 (2011): 463–77. Replication data available at http://isps.yale.edu/research/data#.V5dwergrl2w (accessed 7/26/16).

a. Daniel M. Butler and David E. Broockman, "Do Politicians Racially Discriminate Against Constituents? A Field Experiment on State Legislators," *American Journal of Political Science* 55, no. 3 (2011): 463–77.

b. Katherine Levine Einstein and David M. Glick, "Does Race Affect Access to Government Services? An Experiment Exploring Street-Level Bureaucrats and Access to Public Housing," *American Journal of Political Science* (forthcoming, 2016).

Japan, a parliamentary democracy, is well known for having a national bureaucracy that carries enormous influence at the national level. In particular, the Ministry of International Trade and Industry (MITI) controls so many aspects of economic regulation that at times in recent Japanese history it has exercised an effective veto over economic reforms of the government. Although in principle it is true that the MITI and other Japanese bureaucratic agencies serve under the government, the bureaucrats use their intimate knowledge of economic data and their connections to private industry to wield considerable power.

In many countries, bureaucratic institutions are the legacies of previous monarchical governments. France, for instance, has a long tradition of a strong centralized government since the 1500s and has always had a prestigious, well-educated bureaucracy that is widely seen as an elite segment of society. The United States has largely adopted the British civil service model, in which a modern, professional bureaucracy offers established career paths for people who mostly remain in nonelected government service. The French and Japanese models of bureaucracy have tended to lead to closer cooperation between the government and private sector corporations than that seen in the United States. Since World War II, the French and Japanese governments have been much more actively involved in investment decisions regarding industrial development than have governments in either the United States or Britain.

National bureaucracies in many developing countries are less well equipped to do government work than bureaucracies in the developed world. For example, tax compliance is much lower in parts of the developing world because the collection agencies (analogous to the U.S. Internal Revenue Service) are not equipped to gather all of the taxes that people are required to pay. Furthermore, bureaucratic agencies in much of the developing world are filled with patronage appointments. Similar to the earlier eras in the United States when the bureaucracy was filled by the spoils system, so it now goes in places like Nigeria, Bolivia, and the Philippines. When new governments come into power or new presidents are elected in such countries, wholesale changes often occur in the personnel of many government bureaucracies, and entire communities may feel a direct economic impact, depending on how their preferred party fared at the polls.

Two Views of Bureaucracy

Through legislative acts and court decisions, the American federal bureaucracy has been empowered in many instances to conduct work that touches on the three major realms of government activity. Agencies can write statutes or administrative law (legislate), hold hearings and decide cases (adjudicate as quasi-courts), and implement policies (as executive bodies). The last activity, implementation of policy, is the primary reason for the existence of the bureaucracy. Legislative and judicial powers have been specially delegated to bureaucracies by lawmakers on the grounds that the agencies have access to expertise that Congress and perhaps the courts do not have. Moreover, giving agencies rule making and adjudication powers relieves the burden on the other branches. Let the bureaucracies deal with the details, the thinking goes, while Congress, the president, and the federal courts deal with broad areas of policy.

Because they do the "grunt" work of government, bureaucrats at all levels often feel underappreciated. The words *bureaucrat* and *bureaucracy* can have negative connotations, especially in the United States, and especially in reference to government agencies. Many people have a view of bureaucrats as inefficient, impersonal, indifferent government workers who cannot be fired because of civil service laws, regardless of the service they provide to their fellow citizens. Government bureaucrats, especially those at higher levels in an agency, may also feel conflicted over certain responsibilities of their jobs. As the story of the HHS contraception mandate used at the beginning of this chapter highlights, there are two potentially competing visions of what public bureaucracies should do in a modern democracy. We will call them the "progressive" vision and the "democratic" vision.

The Progressive Vision of a Fair, Competent, and Impartial Bureaucracy

In the vision promoted by the mugwumps, and later during the Progressive Era in the early twentieth century, it was claimed that bureaucrats and government agencies should be fair, impartial, and competent. They should help resolve differences and even solve collective dilemmas among politicians and among groups in society in a reasonable and socially productive manner. A prosecutor, for example, should be able to investigate crimes without interference from politicians. A regulator of the oil companies should be free from political pressure by politicians from oil-rich states. The central bank president likewise should decide interest rates independent of any political pressure. Further down the ladder of the bureaucratic hierarchy, the person charged with checking your luggage at the airport should not care about your political party affiliation. It should not matter to the person inspecting industrial plants for pollution controls if the corporation's chief executive officer made campaign contributions to the president.

A bureaucracy independent of political meddling has advantages. By avoiding favoritism and bias, a specific agency can build a reputation across the political spectrum for expertise, integrity, and sound advice. Its staff can make decisions they feel are in the best interests of the country without regard to a particular party's political ideology. And the agency can be trusted to resolve collective dilemmas among social and political groups.

The Democratic Vision of a Bureaucracy Responsive to the Wishes of Politicians Elected by the People

This vision holds that because bureaucrats and government agencies are part of democratically elected governments, they should be responsive to what elected officials tell them to do. If the American people elect a new president from a party different from that of the previous president, they want the government to move in a different direction and the federal bureaucracy to follow suit. We need not return to the spoils system of the nineteenth century to have a bureaucracy responsive to election returns. It is enough to replace the top-level secretaries and have them give their subordinates directions on how to implement policy consistent with the president's wishes.

 Responsiveness may be desirable, but recall the problem of multiple principals that opened this chapter: What does responsiveness mean when principals are in conflict with each other, as was the secretary of HHS, Kathleen Sebeius, in the opening of this chapter? Like all employees of the bureaucracy, she worked for the president. However, Congress believes that people like Sebelius are tasked with carrying out laws that it wrote, amended, and passed. Because at times the executive-branch bureaucracy has two principals—the president and Congress—matters are considerably complicated for some employees of the U.S. government.

Sometimes political institutions have to change to allow bureaucrats to do their jobs better. During the Watergate scandal under President Richard Nixon in the early 1970s, a special prosecutor hired by Congress to investigate the White House was fired by the president because he did something the president did not like. This action, among others, eventually led to the president's resignation. For our purposes, the lesson is that certain situations reveal a flaw in institutional design. It became clear in the Watergate case that the president should not have the power to dismiss a federal prosecutor whom the president has appointed and who happens to be investigating the president's own actions. Four years after President Nixon resigned, a new law was passed that created the independent counsel's office. A special prosecutor in the independent counsel's office who is investigating high officials in the government could be dismissed only by the attorney general or a panel of three judges, not the president. This is a good example of a political institution being changed to fix a problem. In this instance, the institutional design of the bureaucracy, which can be depicted as a set of principal-agent relationships between the bureaucracy and the elected branches, was changed to eliminate a flaw. The statute expired in 1999, however, and the same functions are now performed by a special counsel office in the Department of Justice.

Nonetheless, the political conflicts within and between the executive and legislative branches continue to affect the bureaucracy. In 2016, Republicans in Congress were angry when the Justice Department decided not to bring charges against Hillary Clinton for allegedly sending and holding classified information on her personal email server during her tenure as Secretary of State. The Justice Department is required to conduct investigations and decide on criminal charges in a manner that is strictly politically neutral. Republicans accused the Justice Department, especially Attorney General Loretta Lynch, of declining to charge Clinton because she was the Democratic nominee for president. They felt that Lynch, appointed by Democratic president Obama, could not be politically neutral as required by law. The scandal led to a major showdown between the Democrats and Republicans in Congress and between the White House and Congress. The fundamental issue was whether the Justice Department had been appropriately independent from political pressures.

What is the right balance between the progressive and democratic visions of the bureaucracy? The answer boils down to a trade-off between loyalty and competence. In a democracy, bureaucrats should have a measure of loyalty to the goals of elected officials, and voters should be able to predict what the bureaucracy will do given the preferences of the people the voters elected. At the same time, bureaucrats should be competent, which sometimes means that they act in unexpected but valuable ways. After all, the bureaucrats are experts and often know how to respond to complex situations better than the elected officials.

Ideally, bureaucrats should try to achieve a balance by executing policies in a fair manner consistent with the law and responding to the goals of the elected officials who hire them.[26] However, at times it can seem impossible to do both well, and thus many bureaucrats work in a somewhat paradoxical way. How well they balance these sometimes competing pressures is critically important to the effective operation of the American political system. A key purpose of such institutions and procedures as the Administrative Procedures Act, the Freedom of Information Act, and the Sunshine Act has been to provide the right incentives so that bureaucrats can be effective while balancing these pressures. The government passed laws setting up institutional procedures to solve the difficult principal-agent problems inherent in the U.S. democratic political system.

---

[26] Discussion of the trade-off can be found in the following texts: Kathleen Bawn, "Political Control versus Expertise: Congressional Choices about Administrative Procedures," *American Political Science Review* 89 (1995): 62–73; Terry Moe, "Politics of Bureaucratic Structure," in *Can the Government Govern?* ed. John Chubb and Paul Peterson (Washington, DC: Brookings Institution, 1989), pp. 267–330; and David Epstein and Sharyn O'Halloran, *Delegating Powers* (New York: Cambridge University Press, 1999).

FURTHER READING

★ = Included in *Readings in American Politics*, 5th ed.

★ Carpenter, Daniel, *The Forging of Bureaucratic Autonomy* (Princeton, NJ: Princeton University Press, 2001). An in-depth historical account of secretaries at the top of the federal departments who pursued political clout during the Progressive Era so that they could be free from political meddling.

Epstein, David, and Sharyn O'Halloran, *Delegating Powers* (New York: Cambridge University Press, 1999). Highlights the trade-offs in designating institutions for preventing bureaucratic drift in democratic government.

Gailmard, Sean, and John W. Patty, *Learning While Governing: Expertise and Accountability in the Executive Branch* (Chicago: University of Chicago Press, 2013). An examination of how bureaucratic expertise develops on the job and the challenge of ensuring that bureaucrats remain loyal to the preferred policies of the president and Congress.

Gordon, Sanford C., "Politicizing Agency Spending Authority: Lessons from a Bush-Era Scandal," *American Political Science Review* 105, no. 4 (November 2011): 717–34. A case study from President George W. Bush's presidency that explores how an administration can apply electoral pressure to federal bureaucracies.

Heclo, Hugh, *A Government of Strangers* (Washington, DC: Brookings Institution, 1977). Describes the politics of bureaucratic agencies, paying special attention to iron triangle relationships among congressional subcommittees, bureaucratic agencies, and interest groups.

Huber, John, and Charles Shipan, *Deliberate Discretion* (New York: Cambridge University Press, 2002). A comparative study of different democratic systems and the degree to which legislatures seek to write laws constraining government bureaucracies.

Lipsky, Michael, *Street-Level Bureaucracy* (New York: Russell Sage, 1980). A detailed account of how the everyday actions of bureaucrats affect people's lives and set precedents for future government actions.

McCubbins, Mathew D., Roger Noll, and Barry Weingast, "Structure and Process, Politics and Policy," *Virginia Law Review* 75 (1989): 431–82. A classic article describing how codified administrative procedures solve principal-agent problems between Congress and bureaucracies.

★ McCubbins, Mathew D., and Thomas Schwartz, "Congressional Oversight Overlooked: Police Patrols versus Fire Alarms," *American Journal of Political Science* 28 (1984): 165–79. Describes the contrast between police-patrol and fire-alarm methods of monitoring bureaucratic agencies.

★ Moffitt, Susan, *Making Public Policy: Participatory Bureaucracy in American Democracy* (New York: Cambridge University Press, 2014). Moffitt argues that public committees and other elements of participatory bureaucracy not only allow bureaucratic leaders to *learn from* members of the public but also to *learn in* public.

Niskanen, William, *Bureaucracy and Representative Government* (Chicago: Aldine, 1971). A political economy of the inefficiencies inherent in government bureaucracy.

★ Wilson, James Q., *Bureaucracy: What Government Agencies Do and Why They Do It* (New York: Basic Books, 1989). A detailed examination of the goals of government bureaucracies and how those goals can be confusing given the different principals telling the agencies what to do.

————, *The Politics of Regulation* (New York: Basic Books, 1980). A classic account of the relationships between industries being regulated and the agencies designed to regulate them.

KEY TERMS

administrative law (p. 256)

bureaucratic capture (p. 254)

bureaucratic drift (p. 253)

cabinet departments (p. 245)

coalitional drift (p. 253)

fire-alarm oversight (p. 274)

government agency (p. 245)

government bureaucracy (p. 245)

government contract (p. 267)

government corporation (p. 247)

government grant (p. 267)

independent agency (p. 247)

marketization (p. 267)

police-patrol oversight (p. 274)

privatization (p. 267)

rule making (p. 256)

When it comes to highly controversial issues like same-sex marriage, Americans often look to the courts to be independent decision makers. But are the courts immune from politics?

8

The Judiciary

 Are the courts above politics?

A watershed moment in the gay rights movement was the Supreme Court decision, *Obergefell v. Hodges* (2015); a 5–4 decision that effectively legalized same-sex marriages everywhere in the United States. The case came to the highest court in the country after same-sex couples in Kentucky, Michigan, Ohio, and Tennessee sued their states, claiming that the states denied them the rights and liberties guaranteed by the Fourteenth Amendment. The couples filed with the Federal District Courts in their states and won, but in 2014, the Sixth Circuit Court of Appeals consolidated these cases and reversed their decision. In January 2015, the Supreme Court agreed to hear the group of cases together, and in its momentous decision, asserted that same-sex couples have the right to marry their partners and that all states must legally recognize same-sex marriages granted in other states.

In the opinion of the Court, Justice Kennedy argues that the Fourteenth Amendment—in particular, the due process clause—applies to same-sex marriage. As discussed in Chapter 4, the due process clause prohibits that "any State deprive any person of life, liberty, or property, without due process of law." Justice Kennedy states in his majority decision that these protected liberties include "certain personal choices central to individual dignity and autonomy, including intimate choices that define personal identity and beliefs." Invoking the texts from other cases, he affirms that "the Court has reiterated that the right to marry is fundamental under the Due Process Clause."[1]

According to Kennedy, four principles justify the Court's affirmation of same-sex marriage. The first is that marriage is a personal decision; innate to it is individual autonomy, and same-sex marriages are no exception. The second is that the "intimate association" that marriage affords to committed individuals is not exclusive to

[1] *Obergefell v. Hodges*, 576 U.S. ____ (2015).

OUTLINE

- Courts and Collective Dilemmas

- Constitutional Basis

- Establishing Judicial Power

- Organization of the American Judiciary

- Path of a Supreme Court Case

- In Comparison: The Judiciary

- How Political Are the Courts?

heterosexual partnerships. The third is that marriage engenders strong families. And the fourth is that marriage is central in maintaining social order.

Throughout his opinion, Justice Kennedy and his fellow justices in the majority wrestle with an underlying question that goes far beyond the issue of gay marriage: How does the Supreme Court interpret the Constitution and the Bill of Rights in light of changing attitudes? Kennedy writes, "The generations that wrote and ratified the Bill of Rights and the Fourteenth Amendment did not presume to know the extent of freedom in all of its dimensions, and so they entrusted to future generations a charter protecting the right of all persons to enjoy liberty as we learn its meaning." In writing this, he submits that enumerated liberties do not confine current understandings of what liberty entails or includes. He also suggests that the parameters of liberty cannot be removed from the context in which they are being discussed.

Critics of the decision charged the Supreme Court with a litany of offenses: re-defining marriage, bypassing the American public, and acting as an activist instead of legal arbitrator.[2] Some even questioned the legitimacy of the Supreme Court as an institution. In response to the *Obergefell v. Hodges* ruling, former Arkansas governor and Republican presidential hopeful Mike Huckabee said, "I will not acqui-esce to an imperial court any more than our Founders acquiesced to an imperial British monarch. We must resist and reject judicial tyranny, not retreat."[3] A former member of the George W. Bush administration claimed, "In one fell stroke, five Jus-tices short-circuited the democratic process."[4]

Justice Kennedy, foreseeing the criticism that the Supreme Court's decision cir-cumvented democratic processes and public will, addressed it in his opinion: "Of course, the Constitution contemplates that democracy is the appropriate process for change, so long as that process does not abridge fundamental rights."

The Supreme Court is the least democratic of the branches of the national gov-ernment: justices are appointed for life rather than being elected; and once ap-pointed, their decisions are not formally accountable to either the voters or the other branches of government. As the final arbiter on constitutional matters, the Court has an aura of independence; that is, of being "above" politics. Yet the story of the Court's decision in *Obergefell v. Hodges* highlights the fact that the Court is a major participant in American politics and policy making. And because its decisions have enormous political consequences, the executive and legislative branches try to in-fluence the Court, through criticism, appointments, and, in rare cases, even threats to change the way the Court acts. How has the Court maintained its aura of inde-pendence and its place as the respected arbiter of the Constitution despite these political pressures?

---

[2] Ryan T. Anderson, "Judicial Activism from the Court on Marriage: Here's How to Respond," *National Review*, June 26, 2015, www.nationalreview.com/article/420397/judicial-activism-court-marriage-heres-how-respond-ryan-t-anderson (accessed 1/4/16).

[3] Huckabee for President, "Huckabee Blasts SCOTUS," June 26, 2015, http://mikehuckabee.com/2015/6/huckabee -blasts-scotus-i-will-not-acquiesce-to-an-imperial-court-vows-to-resist-and-reject-judicial-tyranny (accessed 12/28/15).

[4] John Yoo, "The Court's Decisions Are Not Binding on the Executive and Congressional Branches," July 6, 2015, www.nationalreview.com/article/420810/judicial-supremacy-has-its-limits-john-yoo (accessed 12/28/15).

Courts and Collective Dilemmas

In any stable society, courts provide a means of settling disputes peacefully, enforcing contracts, interpreting the law, and holding persons accountable for their actions. As we discussed in Chapter 1, unfettered, ungoverned society is plagued by collective dilemmas. In an effectively governed society, courts are critical for solving certain kinds of collective dilemmas and allowing for productive interactions among people.

Prisoner's Dilemmas

Consider, for instance, the problem of enforcing contracts, which can be depicted as a prisoner's dilemma between any two or more people or groups in society. Suppose John agrees to sell his house to Julie for $200,000. They draw up a contract stating that Julie will pay John the money on July 1 and that John will vacate the house and Julie will have access to it on July 2. In the absence of a court of law, John might be tempted to "defect" from the agreement by taking Julie's money and then denying her access to the house. A court, however, enables Julie to sue John if he does not honor his obligations under the contract. If we depict the relationship between John and Julie as a type of prisoner's dilemma, then when courts enforce contracts, they are making sure the two sides cooperate even though they might be tempted to defect.

Coordination Problems

Courts also solve coordination problems. Judges interpret laws, including the Constitution, to give guidance to the rest of society, including other courts, police officers, prosecutors, and lawyers, on how law should be applied in real situations. The meaning of law emerges through court decisions. One Chief Justice of the Supreme Court, Charles Evans Hughes, said a long time ago, "The Constitution is what judges say it is."[5] As an example, does religious liberty enshrined in the Constitution include the right to sacrifice animals that in other circumstances are protected by laws against animal cruelty? The Supreme Court in 1993 interpreted this specific aspect of the First Amendment on religious liberty and said that under certain defined circumstances, animal sacrifices by religious groups should be permitted.[6]

Sometimes interpreting laws or constitutional provisions can be depicted as a coordination problem among different regulatory agencies and among groups

[5] Speech before the Chamber of Commerce, Elmira, New York (May 3, 1907); published in *Addresses and Papers of Charles Evans Hughes, Governor of New York, 1906–1908* (1908), p. 139.

[6] *Church of the Lukumi Babalu Aye, Inc. v. Hialeah*, 508 U.S. 520 (1993).

trying to comply with the law. Consider the McCain–Feingold campaign finance law that Congress passed in 2002, banning television advertisements for or against specific candidates or political parties by certain groups within 60 days of a general election. Broadly speaking, there were two different interpretations of the law. One side believed the law was narrowly tailored to ban only those advertisements by corporations and labor unions that mention a candidate or party and the election itself ("Vote for Troy Gamble on November 2"). The other believed the law was broadly intended to ban all advertisements that could hurt or hinder a candidate or party ("We urge you to support candidates

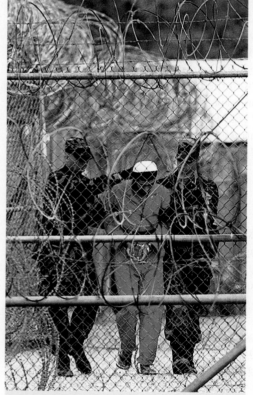

The independence of the judiciary from the other branches of government is especially important when government is a party to a case, as in the cases concerning the treatment of "enemy combatants" and American citizens charged with conspiring with the enemy. The independence of the judicial branch is established by the Constitution.

who are pro-labor"), even banning issue advertisements by corporations and labor unions within 60 days of the general election. After a series of lawsuits against the Federal Election Committee (FEC), the Supreme Court in *McConnell v. FEC* (2003) and *Citizens United v. FEC* (2010) sided with the first interpretation. In fact, the Court went even further, ruling that the broader interpretation, if enforced by the FEC, would violate the freedom of speech protected by the First Amendment. In *Citizens United*, the Court declared that those parts of the law that specifically banned advertisements sponsored by corporations and unions were unconstitutional.

The key insight here is that the courts coordinate people's interpretations of the law and the actions they take as a result.[7] If people are not coordinated on a common interpretation of the law, then the result is less effective enforcement: the law is applied differently in different parts of the country or by different government agencies. Everyone is better off with a common interpretation.

Independence and Legitimacy

For the rule of law to work for the benefit of society, people must have faith that the courts will be unbiased and rule fairly based on the law. Courts are central to modern societies because they play the role of impartial enforcers of contractual relationships among people, groups, and companies as well as between people and the government. It would not undermine the legitimacy of a legislature to craft a policy favoring one particular group simply because that group voted heavily for the majority party in the legislature. But it

[7] Keith Whittington, *Constitutional Interpretation* (Lawrence: University of Kansas Press, 1999).

would definitely be considered inappropriate for a court to decide in favor of one side or the other in a case because of that side's political support for particular judges. Economic historians claim that the establishment of courts with legitimacy in the eyes of society—that is, with a reputation for unbiased decision making—to settle disputes over contractual issues was essential to economic growth and the creation of capitalistic economies.[8]

In most modern democracies, the judiciary is independent of the elected branches and serves to check the authority of the government. By *independent*, it is meant that the courts are free to decide cases on their merits with limited or no pressure from the legislative or executive branches. As John Adams wrote in the Massachusetts Constitution (1780), which was a model for the U.S. Constitution, the democratic ideal was "a government of laws and not of men."

The importance of an independent judiciary is most evident when the government is a party in a court case. This is true in criminal trials—which always involve a government prosecutor who charges a person with a crime—or when people, organizations, businesses, and other levels of government sue or are sued by the national government. If the courts are truly independent, there should be no bias in the government's favor. That is the promise of an independent judiciary, yet it is violated routinely in many countries to the detriment of both democratic processes and the quality of life.

Constitutional Basis

Despite the central importance of courts in democratic societies, the U.S. Constitution says remarkably little about the role of the judicial branch. Article III states that judicial power shall be "vested" in the federal courts, which are headed by the Supreme Court. The Constitution lists the kinds of cases that fall under the jurisdiction of the national courts, including cases where one of the states is a party. The Constitution also requires that the courts be independent from the elected branches. Article III states that Supreme Court justices and lower-court judges are appointed and can hold their offices during good behavior—that is, for life if they are not impeached—and that their salaries cannot be reduced while they are in office. In other words, federal judges cannot be fired or have their pay cut just because Congress or the president becomes unhappy with a court's decisions.

At the same time, the Constitution binds the judicial branch to the other branches, consistent with the notion of checks and balances. Article II gives the president power to appoint Supreme Court judges and implies the same for the judges of any lesser courts established by Congress. The Senate is empowered to give "advice and consent" on such presidential appointments.

[8] We discuss the legitimacy of the courts in Chapter 4 as well.

The courts, as Congress likes to remind judges from time to time, rely on the legislative branch to fund the salaries of judges and prosecutors and maintain offices, courts, and jails.

Establishing Judicial Power

Regarding the judiciary's power to check the other branches, all the Constitution says is that the chief justice of the Supreme Court presides over impeachment trials in the Senate. The judiciary gained its most important powers over time as a result of court decisions that interpreted the Constitution and statutory laws. Foremost among those powers is *judicial review*, the power to determine if a law or an act of government conforms to the Constitution. A related power is enshrined in the concept of the *supremacy* of federal courts over state courts. Let's examine these powers in turn and then see how, beyond its powers to interpret the law, the Supreme Court acts as the court of last resort in settling disputes.

Judicial Review

Soon after the Founding, Congress passed the Judiciary Act of 1789, which laid the groundwork for the federal court system. It established circuit courts and other courts of appeal, and district courts throughout the states. One key aspect of the act was the provision enabling federal officials to apply to the Supreme Court for a writ of mandamus (a court order) if they believe they have been wronged. With a writ of mandamus, federal official A can ask the Court to order person B in the federal government or in a lower government to comply with the terms of official duties, for example, to appoint someone to a new position that the law requires. This provision of the act played a prominent role in establishing judicial review.

judicial review The authority of the judiciary to decide whether a law or any other government action is constitutional.

As we discussed in Chapter 2, the power of **judicial review** was first applied by the Supreme Court in the *Marbury v. Madison* decision in 1803.[9] The origins of this famous case go back to the bitter political battles waged during the administration of the second president, John Adams. Adams was a Federalist, as was his secretary of state, John Marshall. After Adams was defeated in his bid for reelection in 1800, but before his successor took office, he appointed Marshall chief justice of the Supreme Court. Marshall continued to serve in both capacities, only stepping down as secretary of state when Adams left office. Adams also decided to appoint 42 new justices of the peace for Washington, D.C., filling those positions with people sympathetic to the Federalist cause.

[9] For a classic account, see Alexander Bickel, *The Least Dangerous Branch* (Indianapolis: Bobbs-Merrill, 1962).

On March 3, 1801, the night before Adams turned the presidency over to Thomas Jefferson, the letters of commission granting the appointments for the justices of the peace were placed on a desk in the Department of State. They were supposed to be delivered to the appointees but were overlooked in the Federalists' haste to vacate the premises. Jefferson, the leader of the Democratic-Republicans, who had defeated Adams for the presidency in a bitter election, took office the next morning, March 4, and discovered the commissions on the desk. He decided not to deliver the letters, thus in his view voiding the appointments.

One of the Federalist appointees, William Marbury, brought suit against James Madison, Jefferson's secretary of state. Under the Judiciary Act, he asked the Supreme Court for a writ of mandamus to force Madison either to make the appointment or to compensate him for being wronged. The act, which gave the Court original jurisdiction in such cases, enjoyed broad support; but that support did not extend to the idea that the Supreme Court could override the states or was the final arbiter on legal matters. Marbury put the Court in a vulnerable position—if it was seen to overreach in deciding his case, it risked a backlash by the other branches of national government and by the states.

In historical terms, the Court's decision in *Marbury v. Madison* was extremely ambitious, but at the time it seemed somewhat convoluted. Chief Justice Marshall's majority opinion brimmed with irony and seeming contradiction. As a Federalist, Marshall blasted the Democratic-Republicans for violating the legal rights of the appointees, while simultaneously ruling that the Supreme Court did not have the authority to settle the matter. The Judiciary Act provision that the Supreme Court had original jurisdiction was invalid, Marshall reasoned, because the Constitution limited the Court to being an appellate court in such cases. Yet he also took the occasion to declare expansively that "it is emphatically the province and duty of the judicial department to say what the law is." In short, although Marshall and his fellow justices ruled that the Court was not empowered to adjudicate the controversy over the Adams appointments, it *was* empowered to declare laws passed by Congress and signed by the president unconstitutional. The decision narrowly diminished the Court's jurisdiction under the Judiciary Act, but it greatly enhanced the Court's powers to determine the constitutionality of all laws.

Although the idea of judicial review—especially the notion that the Supreme Court could declare acts of Congress unconstitutional—was highly controversial, it was hardly new. It had been mentioned in *Federalist 78* and was implicit in other writings of Alexander Hamilton and James Madison. Over the course of the nineteenth century, judicial review gradually became widely accepted as a legal concept. The Supreme Court's reasoning in the infamous *Dred Scott v. Sanford* (1857) decision, for example, relied directly on Marshall's logic in *Marbury v. Madison*. The Court declared that Scott, as a slave, was not entitled to the constitutional protections reserved for U.S. citizens. This decision depended on the assumption that the Supreme Court had the authority to invalidate the Missouri Compromise, a law passed by Congress in 1824. In ruling that the law was unconstitutional, the Court sealed Scott's legal fate and allowed him to be returned to Missouri as a slave.

The Court's use of judicial review fundamentally changed the nature of American government and federalism. Take, for instance, its revising of the interpretation of the commerce clause over time (see Chapter 2). The Court's revisions of the meaning of the commerce clause ultimately opened the door to expansive national power, but not without controversy and political wrangling. Through many decisions, the Court prevented the national government from regulating corporations until the late 1930s. In 1935, for instance, the Supreme Court began to strike down key parts of President Franklin Delano Roosevelt's New Deal programs as unconstitutional. In decision after decision, the Court ruled that legislative aspects of the New Deal overreached the constitutional powers of the national government to regulate commercial activity. According to the Court's interpretations of the commerce clause (Article I, Section 8) and the Fourteenth Amendment, the national government could regulate only some aspects of commerce between states, and commerce within states was mostly out of its reach.

The Court's decisions angered FDR, and he proposed the idea of expanding the size of the court to 15 justices, entailing his appointment of six new justices to reach that number. He wanted to try to change the Court's composition so that it would be more sympathetic to his policies.

The immediate political response to this court-packing plan, however, was decidedly negative. Even FDR's supporters in Congress felt that he had gone too far. The plan gathered little support in Congress and was not even approved by the Senate Judiciary Committee. Nevertheless, simply by proposing the plan, FDR seemingly had a major effect on the Court. Several months later, the same nine justices decided in favor of a minimum wage law in the state of Washington, reversing a previous ruling that had declared such laws unconstitutional. A key swing justice, Owen Roberts, changed his position on minimum wage laws generally and began to vote consistently with the liberals on regulatory questions. The Court, with what was now a 5–4 liberal majority, began to approve New Deal programs and eventually opened the way for Congress to

Despite their independence, as FDR's court-packing plan—and the response to that plan—indicated, the courts are still linked to the other branches of government and to the political goals of elected officials and other groups. In this cartoon, FDR and Congress are telling the judicial branch to "fall in" step with their goals.

regulate virtually any commercial activity in the country. Many people at the time considered Roberts's change of heart a response to FDR's intimidation of the Court. It was called "the switch in time that saved nine."

Why have the other branches of government accepted the Court's power of judicial review, even if reluctantly at times? This is an interesting question, one that we will try to answer toward the end of this chapter. Now let's consider another question concerning the power of the courts: How did the Supreme Court establish the supremacy of federal courts over state courts?

Supremacy of Federal Courts and Federal Law

Article VI of the Constitution says that all laws of the United States, and the Constitution itself, shall be "the supreme Law of the Land." After the Founding, however, it was not certain who would have the authority to interpret federal law and the Constitution. *Marbury v. Madison* presented the Marshall Court's view, generally supported by the Federalists, that the Supreme Court would interpret the Constitution as it applied to federal law and the actions of federal officials. But what about the Court's role in reviewing and potentially striking down state laws? Could state courts be the final arbiters about the degree to which state laws conformed to the federal Constitution? Through a set of key decisions after *Marbury*, the Court asserted strong powers of **federal court supremacy** over state law and state courts.

In *Fletcher v. Peck* (1810), the Court for the first time declared a state law unconstitutional. *Martin v. Hunter's Lessee* (1816) is particularly interesting for the language used by the Court when it established supremacy over state supreme courts. The Virginia supreme court had ruled that the Judiciary Act of 1789 was unconstitutional because it implied that the federal courts could overrule state courts. In the *Martin* decision, the U.S. Supreme Court viewed the potential problem of various state courts offering "jarring and discordant judgments" on the meaning of federal laws. The Court deemed it necessary for a single authority to review the laws so that interpretations would be harmonized. In other words, the Court recognized the dangers posed by coordination problems among different interpreters of law and declared the need for an authoritative court to coordinate on a single interpretation.

In two other famous cases, *McCulloch v. Maryland* (1819) and *Gibbons v. Ogden* (1824), the Marshall Court set precedents for defining the appropriate powers of Congress to regulate commerce, thus confirming the role of the federal courts in drawing the boundaries for relations between the states and the national government. *McCulloch v. Maryland* involved a state law that was intended to impede the operation of the Second Bank of the United States. The Court ruled that Congress, through the necessary and proper clause, has the authority to set commercial policies that do not violate the Constitution, even policies that might intrude on state sovereignty, so long as they serve a rational purpose.

federal court supremacy
The arrangement based on the supremacy clause in the Constitution that gives federal courts the authority to overturn state court decisions and to decide on the constitutionality of state laws and actions.

Federal courts even in our era are sometimes called upon to decide whether, in a given circumstance, it is appropriate to overturn state courts' decisions. Generally, federal courts would rather defer to the state courts if the matter is internal to the states and does not obviously violate national law. But assertions of supremacy occur and are noteworthy. In *American Tradition Partnership v. Bullock* (2012), the Supreme Court ruled that a Montana law banning corporate and union campaign contributions violated the interpretation of federal law given in *Citizens United v. FEC* (2010), discussed earlier. In doing so, the high court was reversing a decision of the Montana supreme court. It probably did not amuse the U.S. Supreme Court when the Montana court, in upholding the Montana law and before the case reached the national court, wrote that the logic of the *Citizens United* decision was "utter nonsense" and that the U.S. Supreme Court had a "crabbed view of corruption." When it invoked the supremacy clause and precedent, the higher court had the last word.

The Court of Last Resort

The Supreme Court's role as final arbiter of the laws, both state and federal, has put it at the center of numerous political controversies. The *Dred Scott* decision discussed earlier exacerbated regional tensions and contributed to the onset of the Civil War. In 1895, the Court ruled that a personal income tax passed into law by Congress was unconstitutional; that decision was eventually overridden by the Sixteenth Amendment to the Constitution in 1913.

Throughout the twentieth century, besides the interpretation of the commerce clause, the Court was embroiled in controversies over race and voting rights, segregation in schools, and the rights of criminal defendants. In recent years, the Court has decided on the constitutionality of abortion regulations, laws regulating homosexual conduct, campaign finance laws, affirmative action, antidiscrimination laws, and the rights of enemy combatants during wartime.

Beyond declaring specific laws unconstitutional, the Supreme Court has stepped in as the court of last resort to settle political disputes between the states and the national government, between different branches of government, and between major political parties or candidates. Few cases have been more controversial than the *Bush v. Gore* decision of 2000. That year's presidential election hinged on which candidate, Republican George W. Bush or Democrat Al Gore, had won more votes in Florida and would thus be awarded that state's electoral votes. The popular vote in Florida was almost evenly divided between the two candidates, and disputes arose in several counties over the validity of the ballots. The official count certified by Florida's attorney general came out in Bush's favor (by fewer than 1,000 votes), but the Democrats argued that many votes cast for Gore had not been counted accurately because of confusing ballots and voting machines in some counties. The Florida supreme court ordered a recount of

CONSTITUTIONAL POWER

Article III, Section 1

- Judicial power is vested in a Supreme Court as well as other inferior courts ordained and established by Congress.

- Judges of these courts will "hold their offices during good behavior." In other words, Supreme Court justices and other federal judges are appointed for as long as they are willing serve in good behavior.

Article III, Section 2

- This section defines what types of cases federal courts are allowed to hear. It outlines when the courts have original jurisdiction and when the courts have appellate jurisdiction.

JUDICIAL REVIEW

Marbury v. Madison (1803)
This case marked the first time that the Supreme Court struck down a federal law as unconstitutional, setting the precedent for judicial review.

Dred Scott v. Sanford (1857)
In deciding the case of Dred Scott, a slave who sued for his freedom, the Court ruled that Congress did not have constitutional authority to ban slavery in newly acquired territories (as Congress had attempted to do in the Missouri Compromise). This was the second time the Supreme Court struck down a federal law for violating the Constitution.

FEDERAL SUPREMACY

Fletcher v. Peck (1810)
The Supreme Court ruled that a Georgia state law violated the contract clause of the Constitution. This was the first time the Supreme Court ruled a state law unconstitutional.

McCulloch v. Maryland (1813)
The Supreme Court ruled that the Constitution allows Congress the authority to establish a bank in Maryland and protects the bank from being taxed by the state. The ruling not only strengthened the power of Congress and federal law under the Constitution, it also established the authority of federal courts to adjudicate disputes between state and federal governments.

Gibbons v. Ogden (1824)
The Court struck down a New York monopoly over steamboat ferry services and ruled that other steamboat ferry companies licensed by Congress could not be prevented from competing with companies licensed by New York. The congressional licenses were valid under the commerce clause of the Constitution. This is another prominent example of federal courts acting as the authoritative arbiter of disputes between state and federal governments.

ballots in certain counties. However, the Bush campaign appealed to the U.S. Supreme Court, which reversed the Florida court's ruling in a pair of decisions— by votes of 5–4 and 7–2—effectively awarding the presidency to Bush.

In deciding the key 5–4 decision, the more conservative members of the Supreme Court sided with Bush and the more liberal members with Gore. Many critics accused the Court of basing its decision more on politics than on legal reasoning. The majority opinion, written by Chief Justice William Rehnquist for the conservative bloc, stated that one main reason to overturn the

1789 Judiciary Act of 1789 establishes the federal judiciary system.

1810 For the first time, the Supreme Court overturns a state law for being unconstitutional in *Fletcher v. Peck*. A series of cases follow that establish the supremacy of federal law over state law.

1925 The Judiciary Act of 1925—also known as the Judge's Bill—gives the Supreme Court greater control over whom they choose to grant a writ of *certiorari* to.

2000 The opinions in *Bush v. Gore* reveal an ideologically rather than legally minded court.

1750   1800   1850   1900   1950   2000

1787 Article III of the Constitution vests judicial power in the Supreme Court and inferior courts set up by Congress. It defines the original and appellate jurisdiction of the courts and sets up life appointment and nondiminishing salaries for its judges.

1803 The *Marbury v. Madison* ruling sets precedent for judicial review, which allows the Supreme Court the power to decide on the constitutionality of a federal law or act of government.

1953–69 The Supreme Court under Chief Justice Earl Warren expands individual liberties, the scope of the First Amendment, and the right of individual expression, as well as the rights of the accused.

1986–2005 The Rehnquist Court is known for its emphasis on federalism, reducing the jurisdiction of the federal government and strengthening the rights of the states.

2005 The Roberts Court continues to limit the role of the commerce clause in permitting federal action over the states and strikes down regulatory laws on campaign finance, voting rights, and gay marriage.

Florida supreme court ruling was that the remedy it proposed, to recount the votes in only some but not all counties, violated equal protection of the laws.[10] Ironically, arguments based on equal protection of the laws, at least in voting rights cases, are typically made by more liberal groups in society. It has long been a liberal cause to ensure that the votes of all citizens are counted equally in elections. The liberal justices of the Court, in a heated dissent, argued that the majority's argument was flawed. They believed the case was about federalism and urged the Court to let Florida decide for itself how it ran its elections. Again, the irony was that arguments about federalism—states' rights to run their own affairs—are typically made by conservatives. Thus, for many the legal foundations of both the majority and dissenting opinions seemed to be simply partisan interest cloaked in convenient legal jargon. However, both sides in the case accepted the Court's decision, and Bush took office a few weeks later.

Bush v. Gore was an unusual case. But it highlights that, as the highest court in the federal judiciary, the Supreme Court is often asked to adjudicate disputes that other branches or levels of government do not have the legitimacy or the political will to resolve. Because it is the court of last resort in such cases, there can be no further legal appeals. People who are unsatisfied with a Court ruling, however, have several options to bring about future change. If it is a matter

---

[10] In fact, seven of the nine justices agreed that equal protection of voters had been violated by Florida's procedures, but two of the seven did not think it sufficiently serious to reverse the Florida court's ruling.

of interpretation of a statutory law, they can try to convince Congress to pass a different law. If it is a matter of constitutional interpretation, those who disagree with a ruling may have to wait for the composition of the Court to change as justices retire or die, and hope that the new justices will have a different point of view and be willing to overturn the precedent. Alternatively, opponents of a ruling can work to pass a constitutional amendment that overrides the Court's decision—something that is rarely achieved.

Organization of the American Judiciary

To understand how the courts carry out their roles in American society, we need to understand the basic characteristics of the American legal system, including the types of cases that come before the courts, standing and jurisdiction, the differences between federal and state courts, and common law and legal precedent.

Types of Cases

U.S. courts deal with two kinds of cases, criminal and civil. **Criminal cases** involve the government prosecuting a person for a crime against society. **Civil cases** involve one person suing another person for violating the civil code of conduct. It is important to note that under the law a *person* can be an individual, an organization, a business firm, or a government.

Both criminal and civil cases typically involve two parties: the plaintiff, who brings the charges, and the defendant, who is charged with violating the law. In a criminal case, the plaintiff is always the national or state government. The standard of proof in a criminal case at any level, except for military tribunals, is that a judge or jury must find a defendant innocent unless the evidence shows that she or he is guilty beyond a reasonable doubt. In a civil case, judges or juries merely decide which party's side is better supported by the evidence. In some situations in a civil case, courts use a standard of clear and convincing evidence to support one side over another.

criminal case A case in which the government prosecutes a person for a crime against society.

civil case A case in which at least one person sues another person for violating the civil code of conduct.

Standing and Class Actions

Standing refers to the official status of being a party to a case in court. Judges determine who has standing to sue or be sued. In lawsuits, huge groups can be granted standing in the same case, as when judges grant **class action** status to all individuals harmed by the actions of a corporation. Class action lawsuits arose from a section of the federal rules first promulgated in 1938. The intention was to streamline the hearing of cases in which multiple plaintiffs could press the same claim against a defendant. It is more efficient for multiple

standing The official status of a litigant who is entitled to have his or her case decided by the court.

class action A lawsuit in which the plaintiff or defendant is a collective group of individuals.

cases of harm to be dealt with in a single case. In some extreme situations, hundreds of thousands of people can be considered part of a class action lawsuit, as when all those taking a particular drug found to be harmful might be entitled to compensation from the drug manufacturing company.

Many class actions are initiated by an entrepreneurial lawyer or law firm that specializes in finding promising lawsuits to bring against corporations. These lawyers make their money by suing companies on behalf of groups of people who have allegedly been wronged. By granting class action status, a judge is declaring that these lawyers or law firms represent a class of people, even though those people may not be aware of the lawsuit or have never consented to it and might prefer different representation.

Note the potential collective action problem at the heart of class action lawsuits. The group of people who claim to have been harmed by a corporation or some other organization or government agency face a collective action problem. Who will bear the costs of hiring a lawyer to sue for damages on behalf of the larger group when there is no certainty of a favorable judgment and reward? Each person hopes someone else will take the time and pay the lawyer fees. The collective action problem is solved when the law firm agrees to organize the lawsuit for no fee in advance, providing that if the class action suit is successful, the law firm receives a portion of the financial damages awarded to the plaintiffs. The potential financial reward for the entrepreneurial law firm is enough incentive for it to solve the group's collective action problem.

Business organizations claim that too many class action lawsuits are frivolous and cost businesses huge amounts of money to defend against. In recent decades, some states have responded to business complaints by trying to restrict the ability of plaintiffs' lawyers to bring class action lawsuits without notifying or identifying each person in the class individually. Similar bills have been introduced in Congress as well. Critics of these moves by business organizations and state governments charge that such laws merely protect corporations and give them license to do harm.

Federal Courts

The U.S. Supreme Court is the only court specifically mentioned in the Constitution, although Congress was granted the power to establish lower federal courts. The Judiciary Act of 1789 did just that by creating district courts at the lowest level and circuit courts of appeal above them. Subsequent amendments to the act have expanded on that basic structure. Currently 94 federal district courts exist around the country, organized into 13 circuits that each host a court of appeal, meaning there are 13 circuit appeals courts. Appeals made following a district court verdict go to the circuit containing that district. Cases that reach the U.S. Supreme Court can originate in either state or federal courts. Either the Supreme Court or a federal circuit court of appeals can overrule findings of a state supreme court.

There are also two special courts with national jurisdiction. The U.S. Court of Federal Claims deals with most civil cases in which the national government is a party (usually the defendant). These cases are often disputes over business contracts between private firms and the government. The U.S. Court of International Trade deals with cases involving matters of trade and customs, often with foreign persons as a party.

State Courts and the Electoral Connection

Each state has its own hierarchy of courts, which includes a court of last resort (usually called the state supreme court) as the highest authority. At the bottom level are state trial courts, where 99 percent of all cases originate. State appellate courts stand between the trial courts and the state supreme court.

The most distinctive feature of state courts in the United States—which sets them apart from the federal courts and most courts around the world—is that a sizable proportion of their judges and prosecutors are elected by voters rather than appointed by elected officials. In 38 of the 50 states, at least some state judges are chosen by popular election; the remaining states appoint their judges (Figure 8.1 shows a map for state appeals courts). In many states, supreme court justices are elected. State prosecutors, especially district attorneys (the top prosecutors for particular regions in the state), are elected by voters in many states.

In some respects, the election of judges and prosecutors helps democratize the U.S. judicial system. Judges or prosecutors found to be corrupt or too far out of line with voters' preferences can be voted out of office. In general, voters appear to be satisfied with their state-level judges. Reelection for judges in many states is often routine unless a judge has been charged with corruption. Many judicial elections are uncontested, meaning that only the incumbent is on the ballot. District attorney jobs, however, are often hotly contested, and prosecutors get voted out of office more often than judges. In most states, judicial elections are nonpartisan, meaning that judges or prosecutors do not indicate on the ballot their political party affiliation.

However, this electoral connection has a more worrisome side as well. State-level judges and prosecutors must campaign for office, raise campaign funds, and woo interest groups and newspaper editorial boards for endorsements. In many judicial elections, candidates compete by bragging that they have put more people on death row than their opponents.[11] Although such campaigning gives voters some information about the judges' attitude toward the death penalty, it

[11] For a rigorous analysis of the role of elections on sentencing, see Gregory A. Huber and Sanford C. Gordon, "Accountability and Coercion: Is Justice Blind When It Runs for Office?" *American Journal of Political Science* 48 (2004): 247–63.

FIGURE 8.1

Judicial Selection for State Appellate Courts

Legend:
- Partisan election
- Nonpartisan election
- Legislative appointment
- Gubernatorial appointment
- Merit plan*

* Merit plans typically involve appointment by the governor from a list of candidates submitted by an independent or quasi-independent judiciary council or commission.

Source: Harold Stanley and Richard Niemi, *Vital Statistics on American Politics*, 2009–10 (Washington, DC: CQ Press, 2010), Table 7-1; "Judicial Selection in the States," Ballotpedia, ballotpedia.org/ (accessed 10/22/18).

also raises concerns about whether electoral pressures interfere with their incentives to act impartially. We may also ask whether voters have the information they need to make informed decisions about the performance of judges and prosecutors. Available evidence indicates that many voters ignore judicial elections on ballots more often than other races, and they often vote for the incumbent simply because they have heard his or her name.

Jurisdiction at the Federal and State Levels

As we saw earlier, federal law overrides state law, and the federal courts have jurisdiction to review both state law and legal findings in state courts (Figure 8.2). State courts deal with trials involving state law while federal courts deal with trials involving federal law. Nearly all felonies, such as murder, rape, robbery, burglary, and car theft, are prosecuted at the state level. In recent decades, however, Congress has legislated on some matters, such as drug offenses, that have traditionally been the province of the states. The federal courts, for example, have increasingly heard cases involving felonies related to drug offenses because the alleged crimes often involve criminal organizations that operate across several states. In addition, federal statutes usually provide more severe punishments for drug crimes than do state statutes, so state prosecutors often allow federal prosecutors to take over the cases.

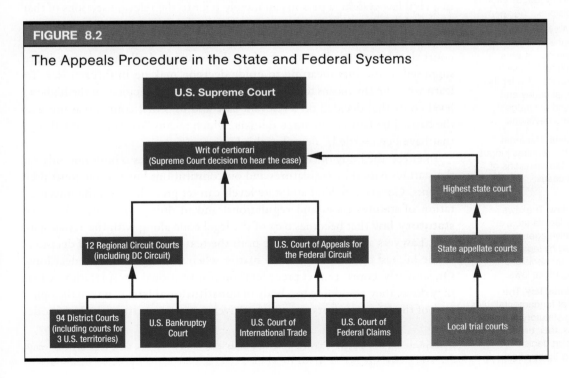

FIGURE 8.2

The Appeals Procedure in the State and Federal Systems

When courts have *original jurisdiction*, it means that cases start there. When courts have only *appellate jurisdiction*, it means that cases are brought there on appeal by either the plaintiff or the defendant after being decided in a lower-level court. No new evidence or witnesses are brought to an appellate (or appeals) court. The appeals court makes decisions based on the soundness of the procedures used to decide the case at the lower level. Some courts, like the U.S. Supreme Court and state supreme courts, have both original and appellate jurisdiction, depending on the nature of the case and the parties involved. In practice, however, federal and state supreme courts, which can rule on issues of fundamental federal or state constitutional law, almost always hear cases on appeal.

Common Law and Legal Precedent

The United States operates largely under a common law system, as opposed to the civil law system prevalent in Europe and other parts of the world. In a **common law** system, the judiciary at both the federal and state levels has the authority, when deciding cases, to declare how the law is to be interpreted. This contrasts with a **civil law** system, in which the law is described in a body of authoritative documents and judges apply the reasoning set forth in those documents to make decisions. Hence, to learn what the law means today in a civil law system, a person can merely refer to the relevant sections of that country's legal code.[12]

In a common law system, higher-level courts set legal precedents. When a court decides what a law means, then that court and all those below it are supposed to use that meaning to guide decision making in future cases. To learn what the law means today, a person refers to court decisions at the highest-level court that decided on a relevant case and uses that court's reasoning as the basis. The Latin term **stare decisis**, which means "to stand by the things that have been settled," describes this basic principle.

In effect, the body of laws governing the United States is built not only on the statutes passed by legislatures and on constitutions but also on court precedents. Courts at federal and state levels can set precedents on the interpretation of statutes (laws and regulations) and in doing so create a body of **statutory law** that becomes part of the legal code along with the actual statutes. Lawyers and judges then use both the text of the statutes and decisions of the highest court ruling on the matter when making their own decisions. Or, similarly, courts can set precedents on constitutional interpretation; when they do so, they are adding to a body of **constitutional law**, in which the opinions of the highest courts to rule on a given matter are part of the legal code.

common law A system of jurisprudence in which the judiciary has the authority to determine how the law is to be interpreted. Under this system, legal precedent established by judges informs future decisions.

civil law A system of jurisprudence in which authoritative documents determine how the law is to be interpreted. Under this system, legal codes and statutes (and not judges) inform future decisions.

stare decisis The legal principle that requires judges to respect the decisions of past court cases.

statutory law The laws passed by legislatures, or administrative agencies empowered by legislatures, and the court decisions interpreting those laws.

constitutional law The collection of fundamental rules for making statutory laws and regulations, their enforcement, and the court decisions interpreting those rules.

---

[12] Louisiana still uses aspects of civil law because of its legacy of French rule until the early eighteenth century.

In the somewhat rare cases when a legal precedent is overturned by the same level of court that set the original precedent, it is considered a serious decision by any court. Even the U.S. Supreme Court has reversed its own decisions. For example, the Constitution guarantees the right to counsel—that is, to have a lawyer represent you in court. In *Betts v. Brady* (1942), the Court ruled that states are not required to provide lawyers for defendants who are too poor to pay for legal services and that only the federal government is required to do so in cases at the federal level. Yet 20 years later, in *Gideon v. Wainwright* (1962), the Court ruled that the Constitution guarantees the right of counsel for defendants in felony cases at all levels of courts, including the state level. In another example, the Court's *Bowers v. Hardwick* (1986) ruling upheld a Georgia law banning sodomy; but in *Lawrence v. Texas* (2003), the Court struck down a Texas law banning sodomy between consenting adults of the same sex.

Although the *Gideon* and *Lawrence* decisions are noteworthy because they overturned precedents that were controversial and had garnered a lot of attention, they are often interpreted as examples of how the Court can be sensitive to the tides of public opinion. In both circumstances, the Court changed national legal standards following a period when gradual changes had been made in state laws around the country. For instance, in 1986, 25 states had laws against some form of sodomy; by 2003, only 13 states had such laws. There is little doubt that in the years between the *Bowers* and *Lawrence* rulings, American society became more tolerant of homosexuals and their private sexual conduct. Scholars of the Supreme Court disagree as to whether shifts in public opinion actually cause the Court to change direction. In this case, the evidence is compelling. Writing for the Court's majority in *Lawrence*, Justice Anthony Kennedy admitted that increasing tolerance toward homosexuals was a factor in his decision to vote to reverse *Bowers*. Changes of public opinion likely influenced the Court (and Kennedy, who wrote key opinions) when it made decisions in favor of gay marriage in 2013. We will have more to learn about the effects of public opinion later in this chapter.

Path of a Supreme Court Case

As we saw earlier, the Supreme Court is the court of last resort in the United States, deciding questions for which there are conflicting opinions among lower courts, or questions that cannot be resolved by the lower courts, the states, or other branches of government. The Court profoundly shapes the legal and political system of the United States, yet few Americans know much about how the justices reach their decisions. Let's take a look at this process, referring to the path of a typical Supreme Court case outlined in Figure 8.3.

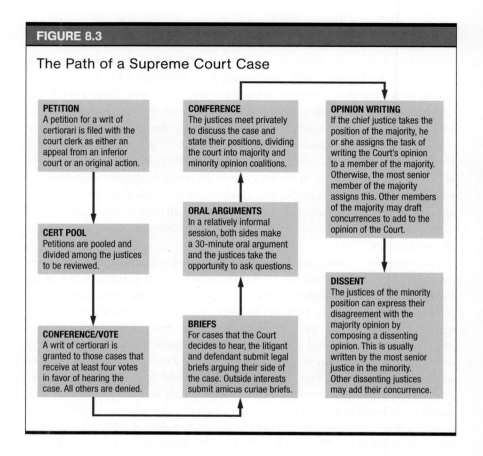

FIGURE 8.3

The Path of a Supreme Court Case

PETITION
A petition for a writ of certiorari is filed with the court clerk as either an appeal from an inferior court or an original action.

CERT POOL
Petitions are pooled and divided among the justices to be reviewed.

CONFERENCE/VOTE
A writ of certiorari is granted to those cases that receive at least four votes in favor of hearing the case. All others are denied.

CONFERENCE
The justices meet privately to discuss the case and state their positions, dividing the court into majority and minority opinion coalitions.

ORAL ARGUMENTS
In a relatively informal session, both sides make a 30-minute oral argument and the justices take the opportunity to ask questions.

BRIEFS
For cases that the Court decides to hear, the litigant and defendant submit legal briefs arguing their side of the case. Outside interests submit amicus curiae briefs.

OPINION WRITING
If the chief justice takes the position of the majority, he or she assigns the task of writing the Court's opinion to a member of the majority. Otherwise, the most senior member of the majority assigns this. Other members of the majority may draft concurrences to add to the opinion of the Court.

DISSENT
The justices of the minority position can express their disagreement with the majority opinion by composing a dissenting opinion. This is usually written by the most senior justice in the minority. Other dissenting justices may add their concurrence.

Choosing Cases

The Supreme Court hears cases for which it has jurisdiction, including cases involving federal law, cases between states, and cases that deal with a clear federal constitutional issue. (Note that this excludes the vast majority of court cases in the United States.) Since the early twentieth century (by act of Congress), the justices themselves have decided which cases they hear. Under the so-called rule of four, approval by four of the nine justices is required to grant a **writ of certiorari**, which means the Court will hear the case. (*Certiorari*, which means "to be informed of" in Latin, is the legal term for the Supreme Court's review of a lower court's decision.) Over the past few decades, the Court has typically accepted fewer than 80 cases per year out of the approximately 8,000 petitions it receives for a writ of certiorari.

The Supreme Court can decide not to hear a case because any decision would be considered **moot**, meaning that further legal proceedings would have no effect on at least one of the parties in the case. This can happen when a plain-

writ of certiorari An order by the Supreme Court directing an inferior court to deliver the records of a case to be reviewed, which effectively means the justices of the Court have decided to hear the case.

moot The status of a case in which further legal proceedings would have no impact on one or both parties.

tiff dies, or a new law passed by Congress changes the legal standards, or the matter in question is no longer relevant. A student suing over college admission standards, for example, may have been admitted in the meantime and thus the case can be declared moot. If a class action is involved, the Court may hear a case even when it is moot for the original plaintiff. In a lawsuit against tobacco manufacturers, for example, even if the original plaintiff has died and thus no longer represents the class of former smokers, the case may continue because of the many millions of former smokers who continue to have standing.

If the Supreme Court decides not to hear a case, the lower court's ruling automatically stands. This does not necessarily mean, however, that the Court upholds the lower court's reasoning or legal opinion. Rather, it could mean the Court does not want to deal with the constitutional questions raised by the case at that time.

Many cases the Court takes are those raising issues on which different federal courts or state supreme courts have made conflicting opinions. As an example, the Court agreed to take up the issue of the legal status of gay marriage in 2012 because courts around the country, both federal and state, were deciding on the legal merits in contradictory fashion. Its subsequent rulings in 2013 in favor of gay marriage were controversial within the Court (both major decisions were 5–4) and outside the Court. When courts below them conflict, the Supreme Court can in principle use the decisions of specific lower courts as cues about how to decide the case. For instance, conservative justices on the Supreme Court might pay more attention to the rulings of conservative-leaning circuit court opinions, and vice versa for liberal justices.

Legal Briefs

Once a case is granted a writ of certiorari, the two sides in the case submit written briefs (legal documents) arguing their positions. For appellate cases, the side challenging the lower court's ruling submits a brief first, and then the side urging the court to uphold the lower court's ruling responds.

Anyone who does not have a direct stake in the outcome of the particular case—including interest groups, government departments, members of Congress, and private citizens—can submit **amicus curiae** ("friend of the court") briefs. These are letters supporting one side or the other in the case. Some amicus briefs are requested by the Court. For instance, the justices might ask a historian or an economist to write a brief on an academic matter that would help them reach a decision.

amicus curiae Briefs (letters to the court) in which those who are not parties in a case provide their opinions on how the case should be decided.

In politically charged cases, it is common for many interest groups and private citizens to submit amicus briefs. In the famous *Brown v. Board of Education* (1954) decision that outlawed racial segregation in public education, according to later statements by several of the justices, amicus briefs documenting the harmful effects of segregation on African American children played a major role in the Court's decision.

Recent research into the effects of these legal briefs has shown that they can be influential in changing the minds of federal judges, especially when they are carefully written and come from organizations or law firms known to be knowledgeable about the specific topic. The research also shows that voluminous amicus briefs resulting from extensive mobilization by political groups have little effect on judges.[13]

Oral Arguments

After the written briefs are submitted, a clerk for the Supreme Court schedules a time for oral arguments. Each side has approximately half an hour to present its case, followed by questions from the justices. If the U.S. government is a party in the case, the solicitor general formally represents the government as its lawyer and will speak. Sometimes those submitting amicus curiae briefs are permitted to speak. These sessions are open to the public and are remarkably informal. Justices often interrupt to ask questions, make observations, or challenge attorneys' arguments. During these exchanges, justices may reveal how they are thinking on a case. During the 2012 oral arguments on the constitutionality of the individual health insurance mandate (requiring people to buy insurance under certain circumstances) in the Affordable Care Act, Justice Antonin Scalia inferred that the act was a power grab by the federal government, asking the solicitor general where the federal government would be limited if not with respect to mandating health insurance. Scalia questioned, "What is left? If the government can do this, what else can it not do?" Eventually, he suggested that if the government can make people buy health insurance, it would, by the same logic, be able to make people buy broccoli. In asking such questions, Scalia inferred that he thought the individual mandate was overstepping certain constitutional boundaries, indicating his position against the act.[14]

Although justices may reveal their predispositions during oral arguments, scholars have shown that what transpires during arguments can influence how a case is decided. Traces of the discussions between the advocates and the justices during oral arguments often emerge in the Court's majority opinions.[15] Evidence suggests that the Court is somewhat more likely to find for the side whose lawyer presents a higher-quality case during oral arguments.[16]

[13] Box-Steffensmeier, Janet, Dino Christenson, and Matthew Hitt, "Quality Over Quantity: Amici Influence and Judicial Decision Making," *American Political Science Review* 107 (August 2013): 446–60.

[14] Some justices rarely or never speak. Justice Clarence Thomas did not speak at all in oral arguments between 2006 and 2013.

[15] Timothy R. Johnson, *Oral Arguments and Decision Making on the U.S. Supreme Court* (Albany: State University of New York Press, 2004).

[16] Timothy R. Johnson, Paul J. Wahlbeck, and James F. Spriggs II, "The Influence of Oral Arguments on the U.S. Supreme Court," *American Political Science Review* 100, no. 1 (February 2006): 99–113.

David L. Franklin for state respondent
JANUS v. AFSCME, 2-26-18

During the oral argument phase of a Supreme Court case, some justices tend to ask many questions or address comments to the arguing attorneys while others, such as Justice Thomas, rarely speak. Here, attorney David Franklin speaks on behalf of the state respondents.

The Conference

After taking time—often many months—to consider the written and oral arguments, the justices meet in private conference to discuss the case and take a preliminary vote. Political scientists have outlined three principal models of judicial decision making. The **legal model** portrays Supreme Court decisions as determined by the facts of the case at hand in conjunction with the plain meaning of the relevant statutes and constitutional provisions, the intent of the framers of the Constitution, and legal precedent.[17] Most justices espouse this model publicly in explaining their decision-making process. Chief Justice John Roberts, for example, commented during his confirmation hearings in 2005 that a judge's job is like that of a baseball umpire who calls balls and strikes—that is, both of them are expected to decide neutrally based on how they see the facts.

Most political scientists, however, argue that justices are not simply neutral umpires, but political actors.[18] Supreme Court conferences often resemble

legal model A theoretical model where judicial decisions are primarily determined by the case, the plain meaning of the text from the Constitution and statutes, the intent of the framers, and/or legal precedent.

[17] See, for example, Ronald Dworkin, *Taking Rights Seriously* (Cambridge, MA: Harvard University Press, 1988).

[18] Howard Gillman, *The Constitution Besieged* (Durham, NC: Duke University Press, 1993); Larry Kramer, *The People Themselves* (New York: Oxford University Press, 2004).

"mini-legislatures," where justices bargain with each other over decisions, make strategic maneuvers to control the Court's agenda, and use complex processes of coalition building. According to the **attitudinal model** of judicial decision making, the individual justices' ideological biases and policy preferences shape how they interpret the facts of a given case and the decision they reach.[19]

This model is useful in grouping the justices into the ideological camps that tend to vote together. Figure 8.4 arrays the members of the Court in 2018 along an ideological spectrum. Justices Samuel Alito and Clarence Thomas anchor the conservative or right wing, while Sonia Sotomayor and Ruth Bader Ginsburg anchor the liberal or left wing. Anthony Kennedy, who retired in 2018 and was replaced by controversial justice Brett Kavanaugh, was considered a reliable swing vote.

Studies have shown a close correlation between the Court's voting patterns and the issues that divide the two major political parties. In abortion cases, for example, the conservative justices usually reflect the positions of the Republican Party, while the liberals reflect those of the Democratic Party. This is perhaps no surprise given that justices are appointed by presidents who are partisan politicians. The most conservative members of the Court were appointed by Ronald Reagan, George H. W. Bush, George W. Bush, and Donald Trump, the most recent Republican presidents. Most of the Court's liberal members were appointed by presidents Jimmy Carter, Bill Clinton, and Barack Obama, all Democratic presidents. But note that some justices appointed by Republican presidents ended up in the liberal wing of the Court, and some swing justices were appointed by Democrats. On closely argued cases, these swing justices play the decisive role in the final outcome.

For some political scientists, the explanation of justices' decisions as a reflection of their underlying political preferences is incomplete. Proponents of the **strategic (or rational choice) model** of judicial decision making emphasize the strategic nature of judicial behavior.[20] Justices, they argue, have personal policy goals that they wish to achieve. For a given justice to accomplish particular ends, he or she must consider the preferences and likely actions of fellow justices, but also the institutional context in which the Court operates. For example, under the rule of four—the requirement that at least four members of the Court must agree to hear a case—a justice who wishes a case to be considered needs the agreement of three fellow justices and therefore must tailor arguments to win over at least that many colleagues. The Court's place in the system of separation of powers also constrains its decision making; Congress, for example, can pass legislation that overrides a ruling of the

[19] Jeffrey A. Segal and Harold J. Spaeth, *The Supreme Court and the Attitudinal Model Revisited* (Cambridge, UK: Cambridge University Press, 2002).

[20] Lee Epstein and Jack Knight, *The Choices Justices Make* (Washington, DC: CQ Press, 1998); Forrest Maltzman, James Spriggs, and Paul Wahlbeck, *Crafting Law on the Supreme Court: The Collegial Game* (New York: Cambridge University Press, 2000).

Supreme Court. Justices keep Congress's potential legislative powers in mind as they write and decide on opinions. All of these constraints influence the way justices decide cases (Figure 8.5).

The dynamics of the strategic model can be seen in a recent landmark decision that affirmed the constitutionality of the Affordable Care Act, President Obama's signature health care law (sometimes called Obamacare). In the *National Federation of Independent Businesses v. Sebelius* (2012) decision, Chief Justice Roberts wrote the majority opinion supporting the law; in doing so, he made sure that the legal reasoning did not include an expansion of the commerce clause of the Constitution (recall the importance of the clause from Chapters 2 and 3). By most accounts, Roberts generally prefers that the Court limit the scope of the commerce clause through its decisions, including this one. But he also did not want the Court to overturn a major piece of social legislation that was passed by Congress and signed by the president. He thus chose to write the majority opinion in the case, so he could argue that the law could not be based on Congress's power to regulate commerce. Roberts was concerned, in this version of the story, that if someone else wrote the opinion or he joined the minority, another justice might convince a majority to sign on to an opinion leading to either one of two outcomes he did not want: to overturn the law based on the commerce clause or to expand the commerce clause to include regulating inactivity. Roberts pursued the best strategy he could by making sure he wrote the majority opinion.

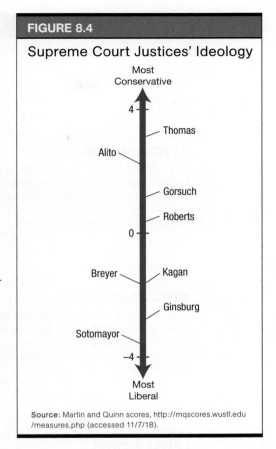

FIGURE 8.4

Supreme Court Justices' Ideology

Source: Martin and Quinn scores, http://mqscores.wustl.edu/measures.php (accessed 11/7/18).

Opinion Writing

During conference, one of the justices representing the majority is assigned to write the opinion justifying the ruling. As the preceding example illustrates, this choice can have significant consequences. If the chief justice is in the majority, he or she assigns a justice from the majority side to write the opinion. The chief justice can assign it to himself or herself, a key agenda-setting power. If the chief justice is not in the majority, then the senior justice on the majority side assigns the task to a justice representing the majority.

Any justice from the majority may also write a **concurring opinion** to explain why he or she is in the majority, but for different reasons than stated in the majority opinion. Likewise, any justice from the minority can write a **dissenting opinion** to give reasons for disagreeing with the majority. Concurrences

concurring opinion An opinion issued by a member of the majority of the Supreme Court that agrees with the decision of the majority but offers alternative legal reasoning.

dissenting opinion An opinion issued by a member of the Supreme Court in opposition to the majority, offering legal reasoning for the decision to oppose.

FIGURE 8.5

Judicial Decision Making

More
Autonomy

ATTITUDINAL MODEL

This model of judicial decision making posits that a judge's behavior can be predicted largely by his or her policy attitudes. It perceives judges of the court as motivated by policy goals and unconstrained by the law. Thus, they decide cases according to ideological preference rather than by the meaning or intention of legal texts or by precedent.

STRATEGIC MODEL

The strategic model acknowledges that judges seek to achieve policy goals. But it also acknowledges that they are subject to certain constraints in doing so. Since they cannot act simply according to preference, they must act strategically to achieve their goals given the constraints.

LEGAL MODEL

The legal model assumes that judges submit to the law when making decisions. If a judge has any personal preference for an outcome in a case, it is assumed that he or she leaves these preferences aside and defers to the facts of the case, the plain meaning of the Constitution or statute, the intention of its framers, or legal precedent when making his or her decision.

Less
Autonomy

and dissents often indicate how justices might try to craft a coalition in future cases on the same topic, or signal to Congress how it might write new legislation to overturn the Court's decision. In the early twentieth century, for example, Justice Oliver Wendell Holmes wrote several historic dissents that laid the groundwork for expanding freedom of speech in later Court majority decisions.

Even after the opinions are drafted, justices can change their minds before the Court's decision is announced. In one prominent example, certain justices (reportedly David Souter and Sandra Day O'Connor) belatedly convinced Anthony Kennedy to join them in upholding the logic of *Roe v. Wade*, the Court's landmark decision guaranteeing a woman's right to an abortion, in *Planned Parenthood v. Casey* (1992). Kennedy's shift gave those in favor of upholding abortion rights a majority in the case.

Once the justices have made their final decisions and written their opinions, the chief justice announces the case, and the author of the majority opinion reads it aloud in public session. Dissenting and concurring opinions may also be read aloud. Four-to-four decisions, which can happen if a justice is absent or recuses himself or herself because of conflict of interest, uphold the lower-court ruling. (In 2016, after the death of Antonin Scalia and the lack of action by the Senate on a new nominee, all cases involved at most eight justices, resulting in four-to-four decisions on several key cases.) The Court's opinions are then recorded in law indexes, and the majority opinion becomes the law of the land.

In Comparison: The Judiciary

We have already compared the American common law system (also used in Great Britain and most of its former colonies) with the civil law system in other countries. Now let's consider two other distinctive features of the American judiciary—the selection of judges and the concept of judicial review—from an international perspective.

Selecting Judges

The American courts, along with those in other countries in Europe, Japan, and Australia, are widely considered models of independence and professionalism. Compared with many other countries, especially in the developing world, there is less bribery and corruption in the ranks of courts in these democracies and less overt partisanship in judicial decision making. At the same time, there are differences even among advanced industrial democracies. The American judiciary is tied to the electoral process more closely than in other countries. Judges and prosecutors are either elected, as in some states, or appointed by elected officials.

In many other countries, special panels of fellow judges or lawyers—the equivalent of bar associations—appoint judges and prosecutors. This approach keeps politicians and voters out of the process of choosing judges. In France, judges are technically civil servants appointed by the president on the recommendation of a council of legal experts. A lawyer in France who wishes to become a judge must enter a special course of study at the National School for Magistrates. Similarly, lawyers in Germany who want to become judges must first gain experience as civil servants, working as prosecutors or in some other legal capacity within the government. Only then can they become eligible to be appointed as federal judges by either the upper or lower house of parliament.

From the outside, Great Britain's system looks similar to the American system in that the elected head of government, the prime minister, appoints judges. But in practice, the prime minister chooses from among candidates recommended by a nonpartisan commission in charge of judicial appointments. Most new democracies adopt a European-style judicial system based on the French, British, or German models, rather than an American-style model with elections and a highly politicized appointment process.[21]

Judicial Review

Compared with courts in some other countries, U.S. courts have relatively strong powers of judicial review. For example, in the British model, which is common around the world, judges do not have the power to review the constitutionality of acts of Parliament. British high courts can, however, review cases to clarify the meaning of laws passed by Parliament, and occasionally Parliament grants them authority to investigate alleged wrongdoing by members of the government. In both France and Germany, however, the high courts have powers of judicial review similar to that in the United States, and Germany's Constitutional Court is empowered much like the U.S. Supreme Court. In France, cases involving judicial review of government acts or laws arise from members of parliament petitioning the high court for an opinion on a pending piece of legislation, rather than from lower courts ruling on laws already passed.

In all countries of the European Union, the European Court of Justice is empowered to declare laws and actions of governments of the member states in violation of European law and European constitutional tradition. Thus the laws of each country, regardless of whether the countries have judicial review, are subject to judicial review with reference to European law. The United States does not formally recognize any international court as authorized to overrule the U.S. Supreme Court. However, as a party to various international treaties, the United States tends to abide by the rulings of several international courts. Under the North American Free Trade Agreement with Canada and Mexico, for example, international tribunals settle disputes among the three countries or among companies operating within them. When these tribunals make decisions, U.S. domestic courts are supposed to enforce them.

---

[21] For more on European legal traditions, see Alex Stone Sweet, *Governing with Judges* (New York: Oxford University Press, 2000).

The issue of whether the United States is required to abide by the rulings of international courts continues to be controversial, as illustrated by several recent cases involving potential litigation over the behavior of American soldiers during the Iraq War. Recent presidential administrations have firmly maintained that the United States can voluntarily comply with the rulings of international courts, but is not legally obligated to do so.

How Political Are the Courts?

American courts toe a difficult line in interpreting the law and maintaining their independence. If they stray too far from the path laid down by politics and public opinion, the courts can experience intense criticism and pressure to change or reverse course. They may lose legitimacy among some if they persistently make unpopular decisions. The courts grapple with problems balancing in three areas in particular: minority rights versus majority rule, judicial restraint versus judicial activism, and popular sovereignty versus the rule of law. In all three of these areas, federal courts are making decisions reacting to and also influencing the actions of Congress and the president, as well as the states.

Minority Rights versus Majority Rule

In some eras in American history, groups who felt excluded from the electoral process have used the courts as a means to change policy without having to rely on Congress and the president.[22] For instance, in the first half of the twentieth century, organizations focused on the rights of African Americans brought lawsuits in federal court to fight Jim Crow laws and violations of voting rights by the states. This strategy served two purposes. It was a way around having to win the support of the U.S. Senate, where civil rights laws had been blocked by southern senators for decades, and it enabled these organizations to avoid bringing the suits in biased state courts in the South. Through rulings like *Brown v. Board of Education*, the judiciary was extremely helpful to African Americans seeking to overturn discriminatory laws. That the courts gave such access to an oppressed minority is a credit to the federal judiciary of that era.

This example shows how an unelected branch of government can not only protect the rights and liberties of minorities from oppressive majorities but also define which rights and liberties need to be protected, the conditions under which they should be protected, and how to trade off rights and liberties against each other. Another set of unpopular minorities, criminal defendants, has an especially difficult time winning protection from legislatures and executives.

[22] Ronald Dworkin, *Taking Rights Seriously* (Cambridge, MA: Harvard University Press, 1978).

As a result, federal courts in the mid-twentieth century were instrumental in protecting the constitutional rights of defendants to a fair trial and to freedom from cruel and unusual punishment. In these cases, the courts acted to offset the tendencies of the other branches of government to be responsive to majorities who wanted to be harsh toward criminal defendants.

The courts have not consistently taken the lead in protecting minorities, of course. In fact, a substantial body of scholarship indicates that most changes in the direction of the Supreme Court have occurred *after* shifts in public opinion and majority sentiment. For example, the Court began to approve New Deal legislation only after it became popular and was supported by the other two branches of government. And the Court moved to protect the rights of African Americans *after* majority sentiment across the entire country turned against segregationist attitudes among southern whites.[23]

Some critics caution that groups in democracies who are simply disappointed because they lose in the legislative arena should not be encouraged to pursue their policy goals through the courts. In one example raised by the political scientist Robert Dahl, business groups in the late nineteenth and early twentieth centuries used the courts to keep anti–child labor regulations from becoming law, even though majorities in most states, as reflected in the overwhelming votes of state legislatures, wished to ban child labor. These critics argue that the courts should not be an alternative legislative system by which minorities, including privileged sectors of the business or investor communities, try to bypass the legitimate policy-making system.[24]

Analyzing Judicial Behavior

Judges, especially those in the federal circuit courts and in the state and national supreme courts, realize that their actions can have profound political consequences. Yet, in general, American judges do not consider themselves part of the ordinary political process. They often insist that they merely interpret the law and do not, or at least should not, make public policy. Judges likewise tend to be uncomfortable stepping into the electoral arena, as the Supreme Court was asked to do in *Bush v. Gore.*

Court observers, including political scientists, view judges as critical players in government, making highly political decisions. Observers often categorize judges according to their philosophical approaches to the law and to government in general.

---

[23] Gerald Rosenberg, *The Hollow Hope: Can Courts Bring about Social Change?* (Chicago: University of Chicago Press, 1991).

[24] Robert A. Dahl, "Decision-Making in a Democracy: The Supreme Court as a National Policy-Maker," *Journal of Public Law* 6 (1957): 279–95.

It is widely acknowledged that Supreme Court justices have political and judicial ideologies that shape their decisions. But there are constant debates about the consequences of specific Court members and the ideology of the Court. Political scientist Andrew Martin and law professor Kevin Quinn have tracked the opinions and decisions of specific justices over time, and given them ideological scores.

Figure A plots the ideological score of the median Supreme Court justice[a]—the person who falls between the four more liberal and four more conservative justices—calculated by Martin and Quinn. Negative numbers correspond to liberal justices and positive numbers correspond to conservative justices. The median justice represents the pivotal actor in decisions—that is, the justice whose vote is typically in the majority. Therefore, a higher ideological score for the median justice means that the court overall was more conservative; a lower ideological score for the median justice means that the court overall was more liberal. Figure B plots scores of recent justices.

Think About It

In looking at these figures, when was the most liberal Supreme Court? When was the most conservative Court? Who do you think has been the median justice on the Court recently? Which direction has the Court been trending? Which directions have the individual justices been trending? Do you think these trends will continue? Why or why not?

A. Ideological Score of Median Supreme Court Justices, 1937–2014

B. Ideological Scores of Recent Supreme Court Justices

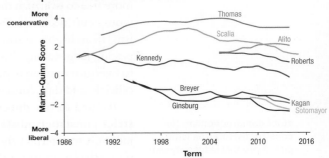

a. Andrew D. Martin and Kevin M. Quinn, "Dynamic Ideal Point Estimation via Markov Chain Monte Carlo for the U.S. Supreme Court, 1953–1999," *Political Analysis* 10, no. 2 (2002): 134–53. Data available at http://mqscores.berkeley.edu/measures.php (accessed 3/23/16).

Political Ideology. Like others in the national government, judges can be politically liberal or conservative. While judges may publicly deny it, evidence is substantial that political ideology influences judicial decisions. Federal judges appointed by Republicans systematically make different decisions than the federal judges appointed by Democrats.[25] In Chapter 9 and Chapters 15 and 16, we will learn more about the meanings of liberal and conservative in contemporary American politics. Briefly, liberals tend to support an active role of the government in the economy and less of a role of the government in enforcing traditional moral behavior, while conservatives prefer a smaller government role in the economy and use of government to uphold enforcement of traditional moral guidelines.

Role of Government. Also, judges differ on whether they tend to have expansive views of national governmental power or tend to decide to restrain the national government. Differences among judges along this dimension are less about classic liberal and conservative positions on public policy and more about the powers of the national government relative to state and local governments.

Restraint versus Activism. Finally, within the legal profession, a highly salient difference among judges is the degree to which judges defer to other branches and believe in a restrained role for the judicial branch, and a restrained role for judges at any given moment in time, versus more activist judges who feel more free to overturn the decisions of other branches of government and of previous court decisions. We can think about this as a dimension of judicial activism, from highly restrained on one end to highly activist on another. When placing judges along this dimension, political scientists look for judges' decisions to overturn or uphold (defer to) the decisions of legislatures and executive branch officials, and they consider the precedents set by previous court decisions.

Related to this dimension of difference, some judges refer to themselves as **strict constructionists (or constructivists)**, claiming that the proper role for judges is to interpret the law strictly in accordance with what the people who wrote the law meant at the time it was written. This includes both the Constitution itself and laws passed by Congress. Such judges claim that they exercise "judicial restraint" and do not enter into the policy-making process. Rather, they merely interpret what policy makers (or the Founders) wrote down. It is clear, however, from objective data that many federal judges claiming to be strict constructivists in recent years have shown considerable activism in overturning previous court precedents or overturning policies decided by other branches of government. This behavior can lead to confusion about the labels applied to judges, and it muddies the conclusions drawn about whether constructivists oppose judicial activism.

strict constructionism (or constructivism) The legal philosophy that judges should use the intentions of those writing the law or the Constitution as guides for how to interpret the law.

[25] A good place to start on demonstrating this can be found, using the Martin-Quinn scores, on http://mqscores.berkeley.edu.

The key distinction for constructivists is *where* they claim to look for guidance on decisions in controversial cases. Constructivists claim that they look to text for guidance on decisions. They, and their political supporters, criticize others and tag judges as "activist" when they go beyond the words of the law and consider how it should be interpreted and applied in light of historical changes. The implication often is that activist judges intrude in the process of policy making, which is properly the function of the legislative and executive branches. Judges have even been accused of inventing constitutional concepts to justify their rulings. Some judges are not ashamed of any of this, openly admitting to examining contemporary affairs and changing the meaning of a law because the times have changed; some even justify overturning precedents because of changing international legal norms.[26]

The judiciary may be the least politicized of the three branches of government, but it is still deeply political and its decisions are consequential for nearly all aspects of political life. Traditionally, the divide between strict constructionists and judicial activists mirrored political ideology—more liberal judges were comfortable making policy, while more conservative judges viewed such activity with discomfort and even disdain. Whether a judge is being activist or simply applying the language of the law is a judgment that in itself follows from the ideology of the person making the judgment. These ideological disputes are especially bitter in battles over abortion, the rights of criminal defendants, gun control, homosexual rights, affirmative action, and race.

Public Opinion, Congress, and the Federal Courts

Scholars over the last decade have also used new data to analyze the influences of public opinion and the elected branches (especially Congress) on federal court decision making. For a long time, scholars have posed a key question—Does the Supreme Court follow or lead public opinion?—and addressed it in several ways. First, some scholars focus especially on the role of Congress, which is typically highly responsive to public opinion, in taking actions to "curb" the Supreme Court when the court declares policies unconstitutional even when those policies tend to have broad public support. *Curbing* in this context means that Congress introduces bills or passes laws to reduce the budgets of courts or reorganize federal courts in some way, in response to unpopular Supreme Court decisions. Compelling evidence shows that the Supreme Court and other federal courts, when Congress curbs the courts, tend to reduce the frequency of decisions declaring acts of Congress unconstitutional in the years after the curbing takes place. In other words, the courts tend to avoid

[26] Justice Anthony Kennedy, in his majority opinions in *Lawrence v. Texas* (2003) and *United States v. Windsor* (2013), mentions prominently the idea that there was growing tolerance for homosexuals in the United States and in other countries and that this was a factor in his decision.

prolonged confrontation and defer to the legislative branch when Congress reacts negatively to the courts' decisions.[27]

Second, other scholars using historical data have linked negative public opinion to court decisions or to the court itself with more judicial deference to the other branches. There is disagreement about whether the primary element of public opinion that influences the courts is the public's attitude toward the Supreme Court as a whole or the public's attitude toward specific court decisions.[28] But political ideology clearly plays a role in public sentiment. When the Supreme Court makes a string of decisions in a liberal or conservative direction, ordinary citizens whose ideology opposes the Court's trend react negatively when asked about the Court's reputation. In turn, the Court in a perceptible way in historical data has usually shied away from additional unpopular decisions after negative public reaction to their actions.

In recent decades the Court has made decisions on highly controversial issues such as gun control, homosexual rights, abortion, health care policy, and freedom of speech. Some observers argue that the Court strongly influences public opinion. They point to the fact that the Court sometimes makes unpopular decisions that are then accepted by the public over time. The classic example is the set of school desegregation cases—starting with *Brown v. Board of Education* (1954)—that occurred during a major increase in toleration among whites for school desegregation. But how common is it for the Court's decisions to come before, rather than after or during, changes in public opinion?

The weight of evidence is that federal courts, including the Supreme Court, are sensitive to public opinion and to the prevailing sentiments of members of Congress. Moreover, this sensitivity means that the Court, on average, tends to follow public opinion rather than lead it. That is, although at times Court decisions have changed public attitudes on some topics, more often when the Court has to step into a politically charged issue, it seeks to defer to the political branches or makes decisions consistent with public opinion.[29] Most judges on the federal courts do not wish to be in the position of too often opposing the elected branches and consistently deciding against prevailing public opinion.

The Politics of Judicial Appointments

The most potent and long-lasting influence of the political branches on the federal courts is in the appointment of judges. In recent decades, presidential ap-

[27] Tom S. Clark, *The Limits of Judicial Independence* (New York: Cambridge University Press, 2011).

[28] Brandon L. Bartels and Christopher D. Johnston, "On the Ideological Foundations of Supreme Court Legitimacy in the American Public," *American Journal of Political Science* 57 (January 2013): 184–99. James Gibson and Michael Nelson, "Is the U.S. Supreme Court's Legitimacy Grounded in Performance Satisfaction and Ideology?" *American Journal of Political Science* 59 (January 2015): 162–74.

[29] Matthew Hall, "The Semiconstrained Court: Public Opinion, the Separation of Powers, and the U.S. Supreme Court's Fear of Nonimplementation," *American Journal of Political Science* 56 (April 2014): 352–66.

pointments to the federal judiciary have been politically contentious. The more openly ideological the judges, the more controversy they generate during Senate confirmation hearings and in the mass media. This is especially true of Supreme Court nominations, but confirmation rates for nominees to the lower federal courts have also fallen in recent years, as senators from the opposing party block nominations. Nominations to any federal court depend on whether there is unified or divided government.[30] The Republican-controlled Senate failed to approve many of Obama's judicial appointments to the federal court, including that of Supreme Court nominee Merrick Garland. Then, when Trump had a Republican Senate, he quickly filled the federal courts with numerous conservative judges, including two Supreme Court justices.

Some scholars claim that the judicial appointment process has always been highly political, for judges, the presidents who nominate them, and the senators who confirm or reject them are themselves political actors.[31] Others contend that the process has become intensely politicized only in recent years. They point to events such as the failed confirmation of Robert Bork to the Supreme Court in 1987, the stalling of Obama's judicial appointments, and the increasing emphasis placed on judicial nominations by interest groups as causing a breakdown in the norms of deference and restraint that previously governed the process.[32] Other scholars point to the existence of institutional hurdles such as the Senate's "blue slip" (enabling the senators from the state where a judgeship is located to veto a nomination), the majority party's control of the Senate Judiciary Committee, and the filibuster on the Senate floor. These procedural tools, when wielded in an environment marked by polarized parties that recognize the importance of judges in interpreting federal law, can cause the appointment process to grind to a halt.[33]

All federal judges can hold their office for as long as they are on good behavior (not impeached), which means that a given president's impact on the courts will last far beyond his or her term in office. In the New Deal era, both supporters and opponents of FDR's policies clearly recognized the political dimension of the Supreme Court and the long-range importance of judicial appointments. This remained the case when Barack Obama made his two successful appointments to the Supreme Court in his first term, and in his failure to sway the Senate to approve his appointment of Merrick Garland in his second term.

[30] Statistics from Sarah A. Binder and Forrest Maltzman, *Advice and Dissent: The Struggle to Shape the Federal Judiciary* (Washington, DC: Brookings Press, 2009).

[31] Lee Epstein and Jeffrey Segal, *Advice and Consent: The Politics of Judicial Appointments* (New York: Oxford University Press, 2005).

[32] See, for example, Wendy L. Martinek, Mark Kemper, and Steven R. Van Winkle, "To Advise and Consent: The Senate and Lower Federal Court Nominations," *Journal of Politics* 64, no. 2 (2002): 337–61; and Lauren Cohen Bell, *Warring Factions: Interest Groups, Money, and the New Politics of Senate Confirmation* (Columbus: Ohio State University Press, 2002).

[33] Binder and Maltzman, *Advice and Dissent*.

This discussion of appointments and of the role of the other branches, especially the president and Senate in the appointment process, brings us back to the questions posed at the beginning of this chapter. In principle, the Supreme Court should have the independence to make unbiased decisions based on its interpretation of the law. For it to do so, however, the president and Congress must refrain from pressuring the Court and need to respect its decisions even if they disagree with them. Though it is tempting to pressure the Court or threaten its independence in some way—such as when FDR threatened to pack the Court with additional justices judged friendly to his policies—by leaving the Court alone, the other branches receive the best long-term joint outcome. The situation thus represents a collective dilemma among people who might be tempted to interfere in the Court's business and pressure the Court beyond what is considered acceptable. If they interfere too much, it becomes a form of defection from a cooperative outcome. All are better off preserving the independence of the Court.

FDR's plan to change the composition of the Court during the New Deal Era was a defection in this interpretation. He saw the Court as an obstacle and was tempted, as players are in prisoner's dilemmas, to defect instead of cooperate, threatening to change the composition of the Court in an admittedly legal but politically unacceptable way. Many members of Congress, even from FDR's party, felt that he was violating long-standing norms and traditions that bound the legislative and executive branches to respect the Court's independence. Viewing this situation as a collective dilemma helps us to understand the anger of Congress and why people believed FDR was "defecting" from a cooperative outcome. As a blatant attempt to influence decisions of the Court, his plan offended their sense of how separation of powers ought to work. It would set a bad precedent by allowing the president to control the Court by "packing" it with judges favorable to his policies whenever he disagreed with Court decisions.

The reaction of New Deal supporters in Congress, especially the Senate, and among the general public is telling. A majority agreed with FDR's policy goals, and Congress might easily have approved his court-packing plan. Why, then, did they balk? More generally, why are the more political branches—Congress and president—reluctant to exert direct pressure on the Supreme Court, and why is the Court accorded such respect?

Opponents of same-sex marriage did not defect as FDR did, though they theoretically could have. The House of Representatives, which was controlled by Republicans, could have threatened to freeze judicial salaries or even instigate investigations into judicial conduct. But Republican Party leaders did not—and given the respect the Court enjoys, it clearly would have hurt the party's reputation for fair play. Republican leaders complained but begrudgingly went along with the decision and some vowed to try through elections and the legislative process to overturn the act itself.

Reactions to Kennedy's decision and to FDR's court-packing plan illustrate both the legitimacy of the Court in the eyes of the public and members of the

Judicial nominations, especially to the Supreme Court, are often controversial. Brett Kavanaugh, President Trump's nominee to replace Justice Anthony Kennedy, who announced his retirement in July 2018, faced a controversial confirmation process when he was accused of sexual assault, though he was ultimately confirmed by the Senate.

other branches and the difficulties courts face in acting independently. Although the courts are largely independent, they are simultaneously part of the national government under the system of separation of powers and intertwined with the other branches through checks and balances. This dichotomy—between the ideal of independent courts and the reality of their being tied up with the elected branches—provokes temptation among groups within government to interfere in the courts' business. Fortunately, the other branches of government rarely step over the line as FDR did. More often, the outcome is similar to what happened after *Obergefell*. Critics of the Court's decision raged, but they opted to try to influence the Court through well-accepted means: trying to capture the presidency and the Senate so that they could affect future appointments to the bench.

To what extent do the courts make decisions based on public or political pressure or judges' personal ideologies, instead of relying on the texts of laws, regulations, and the Constitution?[34] The answer depends on who sits on the

[34] For a discussion of these ideas set in historical perspective, see Bruce Ackerman, *We the People* (Cambridge, MA: Harvard University Press, 1991).

The Collective Dilemma

The Supreme Court is divided ideologically between conservative and liberal justices because the presidency has gone back and forth between Republicans and Democrats over the past three decades. Republican presidents appointed the conservative justices and Democratic presidents appointed the liberal ones. Many cases on the Supreme Court today, especially the politically sensitive ones, are decided 5–4 or 6–3 (or 4–4 when there is a vacancy), with the Court reflecting the partisanship of the appointing presidents.

Interests

When nominating a candidate to fill a vacancy on the Supreme Court, the president seeks a nominee who is first of all professionally competent. Given the nature of the job, professional competence means being well-versed and experienced in U.S. law. Also, since appointed justices help form the president's legacy beyond the term(s) of his or her office, it is important to the president that they generally share the same political and legal philosophies. But the president's interests are not the only ones that matter; his or her opposition in the Senate must also consider their own constituencies and reelection needs. Mounting a strong campaign against a nominee's judicial record or ideological orientation can be appealing to a senator's electoral base. Indiscriminate opposition to any nomination can appear petty or partisan to some in the Senate, but to others who oppose the president's agenda, it can appear to be standing on principle.

Institutions

The president must be strategic in his or her selection because of the fundamental institutional design of the confirmation process. The U.S. Constitution gives the president the power to nominate Supreme Court justices "by and with the advice and consent of the Senate,"[a] which means that the president's choice will prevail only upon the Senate's confirmation of the candidate.

A key institutional actor in the nomination process is the Senate Judiciary Committee, which holds confir-mation hearings for the president's nominee. These hearings are televised and receive a great deal of media attention. During the hearings, a nominee sits before the Judiciary Committee and is asked a number of questions about hot-button issues, such as abortion and the Second Amendment. Most commonly though, the questions pertain to civil rights, criminal justice, and the nominee's judicial philosophy.[b] After the hearings have concluded, the Senate votes on whether to confirm the nominee. Since the 1980s, the Senate confirmation votes have followed partisan lines.[c]

Outcomes

Because the selection of a new Supreme Court justice engages the executive and legislation branches, the process is highly political. In 2016, after the death of Justice Antonin Scalia, one of the conservative anchors on the Court, the Senate Majority Leader Mitch McConnell said in a speech, "The American people should have a voice in the selection of their next Supreme Court Justice. Therefore, this vacancy should not be filled until we have a new president."[d] Nevertheless, President Obama said he would nominate a candidate.[e] In an unprecedented move, the Senate Judiciary Committee unanimously recommended that there be no hearing no matter who Obama nominated.[f]

Obama briefly considered calling the Republicans' bluff by nominating Brian Sandoval, the Republican governor of Nevada.[g] But then he decided to nominate Merrick Garland, a widely respected, though generally liberal, federal judge. The Obama administration referred to Garland as a "consensus nominee" and cast him as a centrist. It was all for naught, however, as Senate leadership continued to take no action on the nomination.

The cases that reach the Supreme Court tend to deal with high-stakes political issues, so the Court nominations become greatly publicized forums for interest groups to press their views.[h] After Garland's nomination, conservative legal groups launched major social media and lobbying campaigns. Antiabortion groups attacked Garland for striking down regulations on partial-birth abortion in certain decisions. Anti–gun control groups claimed that with Garland as justice, Second Amendment rights (on gun ownership) will be "gutted."[i]

Garland's nomination sat for months and remained unresolved until after the presidential election. The Supreme Court thus had eight members instead of nine throughout 2016. Then, in 2017 and 2018, with control of both houses of Congress, the Republicans, led by President Donald Trump, placed two new, conservative Supreme Court justices, Neil Gorsuch and Brett Kavanaugh.

Think About It

What strategies should the president adopt to get the Supreme Court justices he or she wants? Did Obama make a mistake in nominating Garland? What kind of justice would the Senate have approved, if any?

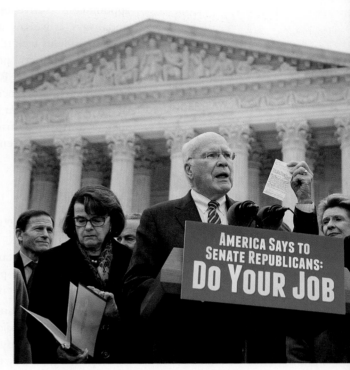

Republicans' refusal to consider President Obama's nominee incited harsh rebukes from Democrats like Senator Patrick Leahy (D-VT), a long-time member of the Senate Judiciary Committee.

a. U.S. Constitution, Art. II, § 2.

b. Lori A. Ringhand and Paul M. Collins Jr., "May It Please the Senate: An Empirical Analysis of the Senate Judiciary Committee Hearings of Supreme Court Nominees, 1939–2009," *American University Law Review* 60, no. 3 (2011): 589–640.

c. James B. Cottrill and Terri J. Peretti, "The Partisan Dynamics of Supreme Court Confirmation Voting," *Justice System Journal* 34, no. 1 (2013): 15–37.

d. Burgess Everett and Glenn Thrush, "McConnell Throws Down the Gauntlet: No Scalia Replacement under Obama," Politico, February 13, 2016, www .politico.com/story/2016/02/mitch-mcconnell-antonin-scalia-supreme-court -nomination-219248 (accessed 2/14/16).

e. The White House, Office of the Press Secretary, "Remarks by the President on the Passing of the U.S. Supreme Court Justice Antonin Scalia," February 13, 2016, www.whitehouse.gov/the-press-office/2016/02/13 /remarks-president-passing-us-supreme-court-justice-antonin-scalia (accessed 2/14/16).

f. U.S. Senate Committee on the Judiciary, Letter to Mitch McConnell, *New York Times*, February 23, 2016, www.nytimes.com/interactive/2016/02/23 /us/politics/document-Senate-SCOTUS-Letter.html (accessed 2/25/16).

g. Kevin Liptak, Manu Raju, and Tom LoBianco, "Obama Offers Supreme Court Hints; Top Democrat Suggests Republican Governor," CNN, February 24, 2016, www.cnn.com/2016/02/24/politics/obama-supreme -court-nominee (accessed 2/25/16).

h. Gregory A. Caldeira and John R. Wright, "Lobbying for Justice: Organized Interests, Supreme Court Nominations, and the United States Senate," *American Journal of Political Science* 42, no. 2 (1998): 499–523.

i. Judicial Crisis Network, "Judicial Crisis Network Launches Digital Ad Campaign Exposing Merrick Garland's Record as a Liberal," March 23, 2016, http://judicialnetwork.com/judicial-crisis-network-launches-digital-ad -campaign-exposing-merrick-garlands-record-as-a-liberal (accessed 3/29/16).

court and who appointed them, the partisan divides within and among the other branches of government, and on the specific policy issue involved in the court case. We are currently in an era where Republican presidents seek to appoint conservative justices to the Supreme Court who will generally (though not always, as we saw with Roberts) uphold conservative policies, and Democratic presidents seek to appoint liberal justices who will generally (but not always) uphold liberal policies. And in 2016, a sitting judge openly criticized Donald Trump, the Republican nominee for president. This was considered a breach of protocol. The Courts are respected and independent in terms of resisting pressure on specific cases, but at a time of deep partisan polarization such as ours, the nature of the judicial appointment process ensures that the courts will be firmly enmeshed in the divisive politics of society at large.

FURTHER READING

★ = Included in *Readings in American Politics*, 5th ed.

Ackerman, Bruce, *We the People* (Cambridge, MA: Harvard University Press, 1991). A detailed examination of how constitutional interpretation has gone through phases in American history in response to changes in historical circumstances.

Binder, Sarah A., and Forrest Maltzman, *Advice and Dissent: The Struggle to Shape the Federal Judiciary* (Washington, DC: Brookings Press, 2009). A study indicating the many constraints that elected officials face when they try to shape the judiciary through the appointment process.

Clark, Tom, *The Limits of Judicial Independence* (New York: Cambridge University Press, 2011). Analyzes in detail how Congress tries to constrain the federal courts and how the federal courts react to Congress.

Epstein, Lee, Andrew Martin, Kevin Quinn, and Jeffrey Segal, "Circuit Effects: How the Norm of Federal Judicial Experience Biases the Supreme Court," *University of Pennsylvania Law Review* 157, no. 3 (2009): 833–80. Many times, in cases that make their way to the Supreme Court via the circuit courts, justices are twice as likely to side with the position of the circuit court where they had previously worked than other justices.

Epstein, Lee, and Jeffrey Segal, *Advice and Consent: The Politics of Judicial Appointments* (New York: Oxford University Press, 2005). A systematic analysis of the relationship of the branches on judicial appointments, putting weight on political ideology as a motivation.

Johnson, Timothy, *Oral Arguments and Decision Making on the U.S. Supreme Court* (Albany: State University of New York Press, 2004). An innovative study of how oral arguments affect judicial decision making on the Supreme Court.

Kramer, Larry, *The People Themselves* (New York: Oxford University Press, 2004). A clear account of how courts respond to changes in public opinion and election results.

★ *Lawrence v. Texas* (2003). The ruling that overturned *Bowers v. Hardwick* (1986) and declared the sodomy law in Texas (and subsequently other states) unconstitutional.

★ *Marbury v. Madison* (1803). The ruling that established the Supreme Court's power of judicial review.

★ *National Federation of Independent Business v. Sebelius* (2012). The ruling that upheld major provisions of the Patient Protection and Affordable Care Act, including the individual mandate, but deemed its expansion of Medicaid unconstitutional.

★ Rosenberg, Gerald, *The Hollow Hope: Can Courts Bring about Social Change?* (Chicago: University of Chicago Press, 1991). A classic account questioning the notion that courts lead social change, arguing instead that courts have lagged behind the elected branches in responding to changing social conditions and enacting liberal policies.

Segal, Jeffrey A., and Harold J. Spaeth, *The Supreme Court and the Attitudinal Model Revisited* (Cambridge, UK: Cambridge University Press, 2002). A systematic analysis of decision making on the Supreme Court, treating the court like a mini-legislature where the justices act as though they "vote" on policies.

Whittington, Keith, *Constitutional Interpretation* (Lawrence: University of Kansas Press, 1999). A deep and convincing analysis of the changing interpretation of the Constitution throughout American history.

KEY TERMS

amicus curiae (p. 305)

attitudinal model (p. 308)

civil case (p. 297)

civil law (p. 302)

class action (p. 297)

common law (p. 302)

concurring opinion (p. 309)

constitutional law (p. 302)

criminal case (p. 297)

dissenting opinion (p. 309)

federal court supremacy (p. 293)

judicial review (p. 290)

legal model (p. 307)

moot (p. 304)

standing (p. 297)

stare decisis (p. 302)

statutory law (p. 302)

strategic (or rational choice) model (p. 308)

strict constructionism (or constructivism) (p. 316)

writ of certiorari (p. 304)

Many Americans have encouraged Congress to pass gun control legislations since the Sandy Hook shooting in 2012 and in the wake of more recent mass shootings. While Congressional Democrats have pushed in favor of restrictions, gun control laws have been unable to pass through a majority of Congress.

9

Public Opinion

 What is the link between public opinion and politicians' behavior?

I n December 2012, an armed man entered Sandy Hook Elementary School in Newtown, Connecticut, and killed 20 small children and 6 adults. This shocking event caused the issue of gun control to resurface as an agenda item in Congress. Six months after the shooting, the Senate took up a high-profile vote on gun control: the Public Safety and Second Amendment Rights Protection Act of 2013. This bill, which would have expanded background checks to include sales made at gun shows and on the Internet, failed to pass.

Polls conducted around this time conveyed overwhelming public support for stricter gun control measures. A poll by the *Washington Post* and ABC News found that 91 percent of Americans support a background check requirement for purchasing a gun.[1] A Gallup poll showed that 65 percent of Americans thought that the Senate should have passed this bill while only 29 percent did not.[2] In early May 2013, Pew Research Center asked a nationally representative sample of U.S. adults if they favored or opposed background checks for private sales and gun shows: 17 percent of the respondents opposed and 81 percent favored. Further, support and opposition were not clearly partisan: 83 percent of Democrats, 81 percent of Republicans, and 80 percent of independents supported the background check expansion.[3]

Gun violence, sometimes with heavy weapons wielded against strangers and large groups of people, continued throughout the decade, with scores killed in rampages in Orlando, Florida; San Bernardino, California; Las Vegas, Nevada; and Parkland, Florida. Public opinion continued to show support for background checks, but opposition to

[1] *Washington Post*, "March 2013 Post-ABC Poll," April 12, 2013, www.washingtonpost.com/page/2010-2019 /WashingtonPost/2013/03/12/National-Politics/Polling/question_10030.xml?tid=a_inl (accessed 1/31/16).

[2] Frank Newport, "Americans Wanted Gun Background Checks to Pass Senate," Gallup, April 29, 2013, www.gallup.com /poll/162083/americans-wanted-gun-background-checks-pass-senate.aspx (accessed 1/31/16).

[3] Pew Research Center, "Broad Support for Renewed Background Checks Bill, Skepticism about Its Chances," May 23, 2013, www.people-press.org/files/legacy-pdf/5-23-13%20Gun%20Policy%20Release.pdf (accessed 2/4/16).

OUTLINE

- Public Opinion in a Democratic System

- What Is Public Opinion?

- Measuring Public Opinion

- Where Do Political Attitudes Come From?

- Predispositions

- Opinions on Policies and Politicians

- Apathy and Lack of Knowledge

- In Comparison: Public Opinion

- Public Opinion and Policy Making

additional gun restrictions stayed steady and even rose according to some polls. Even legislation barring people on the no-fly list from owning guns in the United States because of suspicions of belonging to terrorist groups could not get through Congress. President Barack Obama grew increasingly frustrated and expressed his anger after the killings in several cities:

> We are the only country on Earth that sees mass violence erupt with this kind of frequency. It doesn't happen in other countries. It's not even close. And like I said, somehow, we become numb to it, and we start thinking that this is normal. And instead of thinking about how to solve the problem, this has become one of our most partisan, polarized debates.[4]

His fellow Democrats had often felt cross-pressured on gun control, with their constituents on both sides of the issue, some favoring stricter regulations and others adamantly opposed to any new restrictions. Yet in the mid-2010s, after the mass shootings, Democrats united and pushed hard for gun control legislation. House Democrats even conducted a sit-in on the House floor to pressure for a vote on one gun control bill. But Republicans, in majority control of the House and Senate, prevented any action.

Figure 9.1 shows evidence that, in fact, as seen in these data over many years, the public is split on gun control issues, with a slight majority favoring stricter laws. There was a spike in support for gun control in late 2012 after the Newtown killings, but combined support for keeping laws about the same or even less strict has been around 50 percent in recent years.

At times politicians seem quite concerned with following public opinion. Yet at other times they go against what a majority of people want, and in their statements try to sway the public. What is the link between public opinion and politicians' behavior and expressed views? Under what circumstances do politicians respond to the expressed opinions of the public? And when is the public influenced by elite rhetoric and decisions?

---

[4] Chris Tognotti, "The Most Jarring Quotes from Obama's Gun Control Speech Make Clear that Change Has to Come," *Bustle*, www.bustle.com/articles/133580-the-most-jarring-quotes-from-obamas-gun-control-speech-make-clear-that-change-has-to-come (accessed 9/15/16).

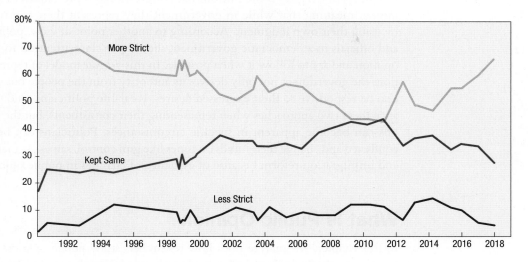

FIGURE 9.1

Public Attitudes on Gun Laws, 1990–2018

In general, do you feel that the laws covering the sale of firearms should be made more strict, less strict, or kept as they are now?

Source: Gallup, "Guns," www.gallup.com/poll/1645/guns.aspx (accessed 10/19/18).

Public Opinion in a Democratic System

In earlier chapters, we focused on the institutions of government, the rules and procedures that structure government action. We now switch to analyzing the external factors in society that both shape and are shaped by government action. This chapter is on the most general of these external factors, public opinion. As we saw with changing attitudes about same-sex marriage, public opinion is a crucial "input" in determining government action, but it is also affected by the actions of politicians and other leaders in society. The nature of public opinion, its nuances, how it is communicated, and how it changes over time have been the subject of intense study by social scientists. In later chapters, we will discuss specific means of transmitting public opinion and putting pressure on government, such as voting in elections and lobbying on behalf of various interest groups.

A core philosophical underpinning of the American political system—indeed, of any political system based on the concept of popular sovereignty—is that the government derives its authority from the people. In the modern era of scientifically valid surveys, summaries of public opinion serve almost as proxies for "the people." Policy makers and mass media communicators often use such measures of public opinion as indicators of what "the people" desire.

Politicians are sometimes criticized for being slaves to public opinion instead of leading based on their own opinions of what is the right thing to do. Recall from Chapter 5 the notion that congressional representatives can be *trustees*, meaning that while in government they represent their constituents by using their own judgment. According to another point of view, politicians and officials in a democratic government should pay close attention to public opinion and try to follow it when possible. In this *delegate* model of representation, the government not only derives its authority from the people but should also be responsive to their expressed desires. Real-life politicians tend to balance these two approaches when representing their constituents, but the trade-offs can become apparent in specific circumstances. Politicians can become conflicted and change their minds on issues like gun control, same-sex marriage, and immigration reform because of evidence of changes in public opinion.

What Is Public Opinion?

public opinion The collection of attitudes and preferences of the mass public.

In this chapter, we analyze both how researchers study public opinion (How are surveys conducted?) and what has been learned from that study (What does the public think about political issues and politicians?). Although researchers attempt to measure it by means of surveys and other methods, **public opinion** remains a fundamentally amorphous concept. It is typically defined as the collection of attitudes and preferences of the mass public.

We can further define an attitude in this context as coming in one of two forms. An opinion is an evaluation of a subject such as a politician or a policy. A predisposition is a deeper value or belief about politics that tends to be stable over time (such as an ideology or partisanship). Both opinions and predispositions fall under the broader concept of attitudes. Furthermore, preferences refer to how people rank outcomes or experiences. An example of a preference is "I prefer paying fewer taxes and therefore having fewer parks to paying more taxes and having more, high-quality parks." These various concepts are certainly related to one another, but noting their differences can help us understand how public opinion is formed and expressed, as we will learn shortly.

There has been a great deal of high-quality research on public opinion, and many polls about politics are conducted on a daily basis. Quantitative analyses of results from surveys and polls are the most common method of measuring and analyzing public opinion. As we will see, we tend to measure public opinion in terms of what opinion polls or surveys report in response to questions asked of random samples of people. Most of our attention will be on the use of surveys, though we summarize other methods later in this chapter.

The Challenge of Having Many Principals

The relationship between the public and the government can be viewed as a special kind of principal–agent problem. We might think of an elected politician as an agent with multiple principals. The president, for example, works for all the people. They "hire" the president through their ballots and can fire him or her at the next election. It is true that only approximately 65 million people may vote for the winning presidential candidate in a typical election (given recent turnout rates), but after taking office, the president represents more than 300 million principals. How does he or she know what these 300 million principals want? How does the president incorporate public opinion information into decision making? Members of Congress face a similar challenge: How can a senator from California, with close to 40 million principals, be a good agent? Can a representative in the House, typically having 650,000 constituents in his or her district, be responsive to all of them?

This challenge is all the more daunting because public opinion can be difficult to discern and follow with consistency. Consider a recent example using real public opinion data. The following two questions were asked of different national samples by different polling organizations between January 5 and 7 of 2016. Each question appears to measure public opinion about President Obama's executive actions on gun reform.

> *As you may know, this week (January 2016) Barack Obama announced several executive orders that change the nation's gun laws so that background checks are required for more gun purchases online and at gun shows, and which make it easier for the FBI (Federal Bureau of Investigation) to complete background checks efficiently. Overall, do you favor or oppose these changes?* (CNN/ORC International Poll)[5]

> Sixty-seven percent said they favor these changes, and 32 percent said they oppose them.

> *When it comes to gun control, should President Obama take action alone if Congress does not approve the initiatives he has proposed or should the government do only what the president and Congress agree on?* (Rasmussen Reports)[6]

> Thirty-four percent said Obama should act alone, and 58 percent said the government should implement what the president and Congress agree on.

Given these disparate survey results, how can we accurately gauge public attitudes on Obama's 2016 gun reforms? Is it reasonable to conclude that well over half of the country supports Obama's executive actions, or should we conclude that only 34 percent do? It is difficult to say. People's support for or

---

[5] Cable News Network, "CNN/ORC International Poll," January 5–6, 2016. ORC International [producer]. Cornell University, Ithaca, NY: Roper Center for Public Opinion Research, iPOLL [distributor], www.cnn.com/2016/01/07/politics/obama-guns-executive-action-poll-results (accessed 7/25/16).

[6] Rasmussen Reports, "Most Voters Oppose Obama Acting Alone on Gun Control," January 8, 2016, www.rasmussenreports.com/public_content/politics/current_events/gun_control/most_voters _oppose_obama_acting_alone_on_gun_control (accessed 5/18/16).

opposition to a policy often depends on how a question is posed. In this case, it matters that the second question highlights the unilateral nature of Obama's reforms. Among other aspects of survey design, question wording matters a lot in determining results. The two survey questions could be interpreted to indicate very different situations: response to the first question suggests that over half of the country supports Obama's executive actions while response to the second suggests that just over half opposes them. Such mixed signals make it hard for politicians to decipher public attitudes.

Moreover, the public can be fickle. Public opinion fluctuates even over relatively short periods. Consider the pattern of President Obama's and President Trump's approval ratings—the proportion of people who said they "approved" of the way they were running the country (Figure 9.2). Obama's ratings fluctuated throughout his presidency, often in response to events over which he had little control. Even if the public seems to approve of the job a politician is doing, or to support a particular policy, that approval can change relatively quickly.

Finally, many people are simply uninformed about government and politics, as we will discuss later in this chapter. For instance, pollsters in the 1960s discovered that a significant percentage of people gave what were essentially random answers to questions about their own preferences regarding public

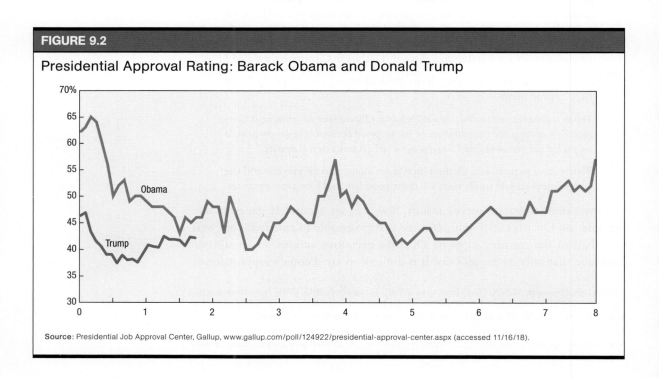

FIGURE 9.2

Presidential Approval Rating: Barack Obama and Donald Trump

Source: Presidential Job Approval Center, Gallup, www.gallup.com/poll/124922/presidential-approval-center.aspx (accessed 11/16/18).

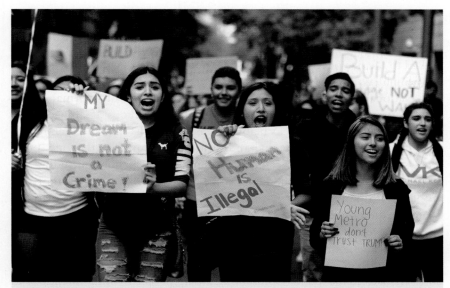

As agents (or representatives) of their constituents, policy makers find it difficult to follow the wishes of all their principals. For example, Americans were deeply split on immigration policy throughout the 2016 presidential campaign.

policies.[7] Contemporary surveys find low levels of factual knowledge among people about the basic workings of the government.

These challenges point to the complexity of public opinion. People are diverse in their opinions and attitudes (and political knowledge). When we summarize what millions of people think and then refer to a small set of numbers as reflecting public opinion, we can overlook the fundamental difficulties public officials have in responding to that opinion in a coherent way. Acknowledging these challenges may provide a clue as to why Congress has repeatedly failed to act on gun control. Perhaps they understand that public opinion on that issue was too complicated to be measured by a simple set of numbers derived from questions in several public opinion surveys.

Measuring Public Opinion

The study of public opinion is one of the most developed areas of research in the social sciences. Because of sophisticated methods of survey research and creative experimental techniques, we now know more than ever before about what people think and feel, as well as about the collective attitudes of the general public.

[7] Philip Converse, "The Nature of Belief Systems in Mass Publics," in *Ideology and Discontent*, ed. D. E. Apter (New York: Free Press, 1964), pp. 206–61.

Early Attempts at Measurement

Before the advent of scientific opinion polling, politicians and journalists looked to the size of crowds at rallies, the number of people buying and reading pamphlets, and the incidences of mob action as indicators of public opinion. National magazines regularly published the results of informal "straw polls." *Literary Digest*, for example, would mail out millions of sample ballots to its readers months or weeks before a presidential election and then record responses from those completed and returned. From 1920 through 1932, these straw polls predicted election results quite accurately, including the margins of victory. When the *Digest* failed to predict Franklin Delano Roosevelt's landslide victory over Alf Landon in 1936, however, these methods were called into question.

Straw polls, which were used as early as the nineteenth century, can get it right sometimes, but they are not scientifically valid in the sense that they are not consciously designed to represent the views of the electorate accurately. Since the late 1940s, public opinion, including people's voting intentions in upcoming elections, has routinely been measured through polling random samples of people and convincing them to respond to questionnaires. Polls in recent years have been remarkably accurate in predicting the election results in presidential races. Final poll results in the few days before the elections are

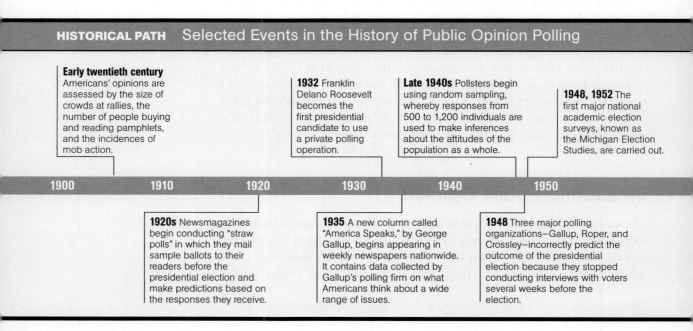

HISTORICAL PATH Selected Events in the History of Public Opinion Polling

Early twentieth century Americans' opinions are assessed by the size of crowds at rallies, the number of people buying and reading pamphlets, and the incidences of mob action.

1932 Franklin Delano Roosevelt becomes the first presidential candidate to use a private polling operation.

Late 1940s Pollsters begin using random sampling, whereby responses from 500 to 1,200 individuals are used to make inferences about the attitudes of the population as a whole.

1948, 1952 The first major national academic election surveys, known as the Michigan Election Studies, are carried out.

1900 1910 1920 1930 1940 1950

1920s Newsmagazines begin conducting "straw polls" in which they mail sample ballots to their readers before the presidential election and make predictions based on the responses they receive.

1935 A new column called "America Speaks," by George Gallup, begins appearing in weekly newspapers nationwide. It contains data collected by Gallup's polling firm on what Americans think about a wide range of issues.

1948 Three major polling organizations—Gallup, Roper, and Crossley—incorrectly predict the outcome of the presidential election because they stopped conducting interviews with voters several weeks before the election.

typically within one percentage point of the actual percentage of votes the winner and loser (or losers) receive on Election Day. Even among the widely criticized 2016 presidential election pollsters, many were within 1.5 percent of the popular vote.

Random Sampling

What accounts for the typical accuracy in predicting election results today? More generally, why can we have any confidence in results from surveys? National polls for the presidential election typically have between 500 and 1,200 respondents. This is an infinitesimal proportion of the voting population of approximately 130 million. It turns out that, with care, social scientists can get a fairly accurate picture of what an entire group will do by sampling a small fraction of randomly selected respondents from that group. The key lies in the tremendous value that comes from statistical analysis of random samples of data.

In the language of statistics, a **population** is the group you want to learn about. Suppose you want to know what proportion of the voters will choose the Democratic candidate for president. Your population is the set of voters in the presidential contest on Election Day. You are trying to predict in

population In statistical research, the entire group that you want to learn about, such as all adults living in the United States.

Mid-1960s As telephone ownership becomes near universal, an increasing number of surveys are conducted over the phone rather than face-to-face. Concerns about sufficiently sampling rural and low-income areas, and about the cost of long-distance calls, persist.

1980 Major polling organizations come under fire after the presidential election for substantially underestimating Ronald Reagan's margin of victory in their final polls before Election Day.

2000 The presidential campaign marks a new high point for the so-called daily tracking poll when each of three major polling firms conducts more than 35 such polls between Labor Day and Election Day.

2010s Increasing use of Internet polls, survey experiments, and brain imaging adds considerable sophistication to public opinion research.

1960   1970   1980   1990   2000   2010

1960 Polling during John F. Kennedy's campaign for president is conducted by Louis Harris, who introduces innovations such as state-level surveys and a focus on the "most important problem" facing the nation.

1977 All the television news networks and several major national newspapers have established consistent and frequent polling operations.

1990s Push polling—which involves wording questions in such a way as to elicit particular responses—becomes a widespread election tactic.

Mid-2000s An increasing proportion of polling is carried out over the Internet, but concerns about sample bias persist. Similarly, pollsters are concerned about the number of people, particularly young people, who own only cell phones.

sample In statistical research, a subset of the population chosen to provide information for research about the population.

random selection Choosing a sample such that each member of a population has an equal chance of being selected into the sample.

margin of error In statistical research, the range of outcomes we expect for a population, given the data revealed by a sample drawn from that population.

biased sample A sample that, because it does not accurately represent the overall population, is likely to lead to erroneous conclusions about the population.

advance the behavior of that population. A **sample** is a subset of the population chosen to provide information for analysis. A reputable pollster will choose a sample of people expected to vote in the election using methods of **random selection**, meaning that in principle each person in the population has an equal chance of being chosen to be part of the sample.

As the random sample gets larger, it increasingly approximates the entire population, but it does not need to be anywhere near the size of the true population for the sample data to offer a good approximation. In fact, if people are chosen randomly from the population and surveyed on their preference of presidential candidate, and if they answer the survey honestly and stick to their indicated choice when they actually vote, then a poll of approximately 1,200 respondents will predict the eventual popular vote winner in a typical presidential election nearly every time.

Well-done surveys that evaluate politicians, consumer products, and other matters of public opinion share similar features, such as selecting a truly random sample. If the sample is random and the responses are honest, then statistical summaries of the sample population will closely resemble characteristics of the entire population.

Information gleaned from samples is not perfectly accurate, of course. Pollsters refer to the **margin of error** as the range of outcomes in the population that we can expect to see given the data generated by the sample. As an example, in a typical presidential election poll surveying 1,200 voters, the margin of error is around 1.5 percent. This means that if a candidate, according to the sample of voters in a survey, will receive 47 percent of the vote on Election Day, we can confidently predict that the real election will lead to that candidate receiving between 45.5 and 48.5 percent of the vote (the range you get when you subtract 1.5 from 47 or add 1.5 to 47).

Possible Biases

Any attempt to measure public opinion will be inexact because measurements based on samples are unavoidably biased to a greater or lesser degree. In other words, they do not measure the truth about a population with 100 percent accuracy. Reputable researchers try to minimize bias, which is often unintentional and a natural outcome of the research process.

Biased Samples. A **biased sample** is one potential problem with polls. In sampling for any population you want to understand, the ideal is for each person in the population to have an equal chance of being selected to participate in the survey. This means not relying on biased sampling schemes where some kinds of people in the population are much more likely to respond to the survey than others. For example, if you wanted to understand the opinions of all college students, you would not simply go to the library on a Saturday evening to interview randomly selected students studying there. The library on Saturday evening draws a specific kind of student (more studious, less social?), and such a sample would be biased.

Unfortunately, many opinion polls reported in the media, and especially those used in marketing campaigns, rely on heavily biased sampling strategies. People should be suspicious of polls in which respondents are allowed to self-select by, for example, voluntarily responding to an email. Telephone surveys based on published phone directories are increasingly problematic due to the prevalence of people screening their calls or using cell phones rather than land lines. Before the 1970s, researchers encountered a different problem: a significant proportion of American households did not have phone service, either because it was too expensive or because the technology was not available in their area.

Response rates to phone surveys—the number of people who actually give interviews as compared to the number selected and solicited through a random process—have been declining for many years and now are below 30 percent. Low response rates can make it expensive to complete a survey because of the large number of people who need to be contacted to get a representative sample. Low response rates can also introduce substantial bias if those who respond to the survey are in some way different from those who do not respond. Consider a survey about transgender rights, for instance. If younger and older voters hold different opinions on the issue, the results may be biased because younger voters tend not to respond to surveys. Reputable survey companies work hard to minimize such bias. Phone surveys are still used for many purposes, but at some point response rates may become so low that other means will become the norm.

Internet polls are increasingly common. If they are not carefully designed, however, they can introduce even more serious biases than phone surveys. There is some evidence that improved methods of Internet surveys are providing opportunities to collect good samples. Companies like Qualtrics give thousands of people free Internet connections on the condition that they occasionally answer survey questions. Samples are often collected from the broad pool of people subscribing to the Qualtrics plan to mirror proportions in census categories. For instance, if we know from the census that approximately 13 percent of the U.S. population is African American, then companies like Qualtrics, knowing the demographics of its subscribers, can enlist 13 percent of any given national sample to be African American. Such techniques, including offering Internet access for free to people willing to answer surveys, can help to eliminate a built-in bias that arises because people with lower incomes are less likely to have Internet access that they pay for on a regular basis. As some research suggests, surveys that correct for this risk can provide samples that are as reliable as those produced by other, more traditional survey methods; but more research needs to be conducted on the differences among survey modes.[8]

Question Wording. The way questions are worded can introduce other kinds of biased responses in opinion polling. We have already seen how differences in wording affected the poll results about presidential action on gun control in 2016. Now consider these two differently worded questions about the death penalty:

> *Which punishment do you prefer for people convicted of murder; the death penalty or life in prison with no chance of parole?* (Quinnipiac University Polling Institute, 2015)[9]

> Forty-three percent said "death penalty," while 48 percent said "life in prison with no chance of parole."

> *Are you in favor of the death penalty for a person convicted of murder?* (Gallup, 2015)[10]

> Sixty-one percent said "yes."

There is no objective way to determine which preceding question is more "biased." But clearly if people wanted to demonstrate strong support for the death penalty, they would use the second question in their survey. In other words, survey information can be deliberately manipulated to yield results that are consistent with specific political goals. By wording a question in a particular way, interest group leaders can publicize results that are favorable to their policy interests. Even researchers who are trying to conduct an accurate, unbiased survey can inadvertently introduce bias depending on how they word their questions.

push polling Surveys or polls in which respondents are given information before answering an opinion question about a candidate, party, or political issue, where the information is given with the intention of influencing the opinion expressed.

The most egregious form of biased wording is **push polling**, which is not really polling at all, but rather a form of marketing and campaigning. In push polling, people are given information that reflects poorly or well on a particular candidate and then asked if they would vote for that candidate on the basis of that information. These survey "results" are highly misleading because they are based on responses influenced by selective information. During the 2000 Republican presidential primaries, for example, campaign consultants in favor of George W. Bush's election (possibly without the knowledge or involvement of his official campaign) conducted a poll in which potential primary voters were asked whether they would be likely to

---

[8] See, for example, Linchiat Chang and Jon A. Krosnick, "National Surveys via RDD Telephone Interviewing versus the Internet: Comparing Sample Representativeness and Response Quality," *Public Opinion Quarterly* 73, no. 4 (Winter 2009): 641–78.

[9] Quinnipiac University Polling Institute, May 19–26, 2015, Quinnipiac University Polling Institute [producer]. Storrs, CT: Roper Center for Public Opinion Research, iPOLL [distributor], www.qu.edu /images/polling/us/us06012015_Usknw84.pdf (accessed 7/25/16).

[10] Andrew Dugan, "Solid Majority Continue to Support Death Penalty," October 7–11, 2015, www .gallup.com/poll/186218/solid-majority-continue-support-death-penalty.aspx (accessed 12/3/15).

vote for or against John McCain after learning that his "campaign finance proposals would give labor unions and the media a bigger influence on the outcome of elections."[11] Clearly, the consultants' goal was not to find out how many people were going to vote for McCain, but to spread negative information about Bush's opponent while posing as pollsters, and eventually to publish poll results that showed McCain's drooping prospects. It is hard to know how widespread push polling is, but it definitely occurs and is troublesome for the polling industry because it heightens peoples' suspicions of pollsters.

Reputable, independent polling organizations, such as Gallup, Pew, and Roper, tend to use defensible methods and have long track records of relatively accurate polling results. By accurate, we mean that the results from polls show up consistently if the polling is repeated or changes in results can be explained. Academic polls such as the General Social Survey and the American National Election Survey are especially careful and have earned a reputation for providing high-quality data on public opinion about politics and public affairs.

Sometimes major gaffes happen, such as when pollsters badly overestimate or underestimate voter turnout in some populations. Preelection surveys can fail egregiously in predicting election outcomes, even when no obvious mistakes are made. The 2016 presidential election was incorrectly called by nearly all pollsters. All major polling companies predicted that Hillary Clinton would win, with popular vote margins of between 1 and 5 percent above Donald Trump. Clinton won the popular vote by about 2 percent but lost in the electoral college. The pollsters were wrong on the outcome but some were fairly close on the popular vote total (though all were wrong in the same direction). Another famous example occurred in 2015 in the United Kingdom national election. A majority of opinion surveys taken the week before the election showed a virtual tie in vote totals between the two major parties, Labour and Conservative. Some polls predicted a Labour win, and any major poll predicting a Conservative win indicated a very close election. The actual election in May of that year was considered a landslide by British standards: the Conservatives won by 6.5 percentage points and gained an outright majority of seats. In both cases, commentators and scholars tried to understand what went wrong, pointing to a possible late surge in the last few days by the winning sides and to the difficulties of surveying certain kinds of people. In the case of Michigan primary, younger people supported Sanders over Clinton and they are more difficult to track down by phone. For the United Kingdom, some observers believed that conservative-leaning voters do not answer their phones for pollsters as often as left-leaning voters.

---

[11] Matthew J. Streb and Susan H. Pinkus, "When Push Comes to Shove: Push Polling and the Manipulation of Public Opinion," in *Polls and Politics: The Dilemmas of Democracy*, ed. Michael A. Genovese and Matthew J. Streb (Albany: State University of New York Press, 2006), pp. 95–117.

To evaluate public opinion results reported in surveys, it is important to understand how surveys are conducted.

- Modern survey research usually relies on *samples from the overall population* of only 500 to 1,200 adults.

- *Numerous groups conduct political surveys*, including media outlets (such as television networks and newspapers), private polling firms, academic researchers, and interest groups. The Gallup Poll, for example, regularly publishes results on the president's approval rating.

- A political survey may ask questions about *policy attitudes* ("Do you support an expansion of offshore drilling?"), *evaluations of political figures* ("Do you approve of the job the president is doing?"), and *future political behavior* ("Which candidate do you intend to vote for in the November elections?").

- *A range of techniques may be used to obtain a sample* for a survey, from random-digit dialing (in which telephone numbers to call are generated at random) to self-selection on the part of the respondents. There is no consensus on the best way to select a sample, but it is clear that the results may be affected by the procedure used.

- *Survey questions may be developed in a number of ways*, including in a manner designed to elicit certain responses. In addition, questions about a given topic may be worded differently by different survey organizations.

- The *response rate*—the number of people from the selected sample who choose to cooperate with the survey—is also an important factor to consider when evaluating a survey. Although consensus exists on how to measure a survey's response rate, experts disagree on how much response rates affect the quality of results.

Alternative Methods to Surveys

It is worth noting that surveys are not the only methods for understanding public opinion. Although we cannot discuss all methods in detail, six deserve mention. First, researchers can conduct intensive interviews with people and analyze their answers to discover underlying predispositions and mental processes. Second, researchers can run focus groups, in which people gathered in a room discuss answers to questions posed by a moderator. This can help us learn how people express their views in groups, as opposed to in isolation with a survey interviewer or on a questionnaire. The third method offers similar advantages: listening to conversations among groups in everyday environments and discovering how people spontaneously express their political opinions during their ordinary routines. Fourth, researchers can run experiments to gain more knowledge of what affects the way people answer surveys or experience a particular emotion at one moment in time versus another, given a stimulus. Fifth, there has been increasing use of brain imaging (MRIs) to study mental processes as people hear or see political information. Sixth, researchers have examined the genetic makeup of people to learn if aspects of their political attitudes come from personality traits inherited from parents. Knowledge from all of these methods can complement the knowledge gained from surveys.

For these fifth and sixth sets of methods, brain imaging and genetic analysis, research has led to noteworthy findings that are spurring deeper study and analysis. Researchers are discovering, for instance, patterns linking specific genes to predispositions toward supporting liberal or conservative ideologies. Genetic attributes do not appear to determine political attitudes, but they do interact with and can be reinforced by social and environmental factors like family influences and traumatic events to tilt people in an ideological direction.[12]

Where Do Political Attitudes Come From?

Scholars of public opinion evaluate data of various kinds with the primary goals of describing people's attitudes and understanding what causes people to have certain attitudes. What are Americans' views toward government and politics? And where do these attitudes come from? In this section, we will summarize some of the fruits of this research, beginning with several fundamental factors that shape people's political attitudes: their backgrounds, underlying interests, group attachments, emotions, and the influence of political elites.

Socialization

Beyond the provocative idea that people might actually have genetically determined traits linked to their political attitudes (discussed earlier), research has shown that the information people are exposed to in their formative years—usually during the late teens or early twenties—matters tremendously in determining political attitudes, especially predispositions. Studies have found that parents play a primary role. Chances are high, for example, that if both parents are Democrats, their children will be Democrats as they reach adulthood—not because we can identify a "Democrat" gene, but because of the process of socialization. Likewise for Republicans, or for those who

---

[12] Peter K. Hatemi and Rose McDermott, "The Political Psychology of Biology, Genetics, and Behavior," *Political Psychology* 33, no. 3 (June 2012): 307–12; and Brad Verhulst, Peter K. Hatemi, and Lindon J. Eaves, "Disentangling the Importance of Psychological Predispositions and Social Constructions in the Organization of American Political Ideology," *Political Psychology* 33, no. 3 (June 2012): 375–93.

The Collective Dilemma

By the 1990s, the science of opinion surveys became good enough that most reputable survey companies were able to predict the winner of a presidential election in advance of the actual election itself. Unfortunately, producing quality survey data and forecasting election outcomes have become more difficult because potential respondents often do not answer their phones and may not even have ordinary phones. As a result, response rates to quality surveys have dropped. Furthermore, for the past three presidential elections, it has become more challenging to predict who will turn out in elections.

Interests

Subscribers to election polling information include candidates, campaign consultants, and journalists. Candidates and campaign consultants use this information to tailor the content of their campaigns and alter their election strategy. For journalists, polling figures are reportable news that indicates current political sentiment to viewers and readers.

Companies or organizations conducting opinion surveys want to earn money from clients and a reputation for providing accurate and valuable information. But targeted potential respondents of surveys and polls—generally, registered voters likely to vote—are reticent. Answering survey questions takes time and people, on average, prefer not to answer their phones and may not want to provide sensitive information (for example, their political preferences and the candidates they will vote for). The numerous media through which people can be reached—landlines, cell phones, emails, websites—mean that there are numerous occasions for people to feel burdened or bothered by requests for survey participation. It has become expensive to conduct high-quality polls.

Institutions

Many organizations and firms conduct polls. One of the most well-known names in the industry is Gallup, and up until the 2012 election, its predictions were considered a premier source of election forecasts. However, as of 2015, Gallup decided to no longer conduct election polling, aside from how Americans feel about candidates. Many attribute this decision to Gallup's poor predicting performance in the 2012 presidential election in which it incorrectly predicted that Mitt Romney would beat Barack Obama by one percentage point.

A new trend among institutions conducting surveys and election forecasting is the rise of meta-analysis. Meta-analysis forecasts election outcomes by using multiple survey results from a variety of sources. It differs from the work of individual firms like Gallup in that it analyzes the *aggregation* of polls. While the mathematical machinery is complex, the basic idea behind meta-analysis is simple. Consulting multiple results from different polls and combining them allows one to minimize a range of potential sources of bias. With meta-analysis, people can take into consideration not only poll results but also well-known patterns, such as voters' responses to new information about economic indicators or the tendency for voters in certain states to change their voting intentions in tandem. Moreover, people can use a given survey's degree of accuracy and make necessary statistical adjustments to correct for biases. Putting more weight on certain poll results and less weight on others, in effect, minimizes the opportunity for overall error.

Outcomes

The growing reliance on cell phones as people's primary phone is ushering changes in polling and surveying, forcing pollsters to question how to gauge people's attitudes in a changing technological environment. For example, Pew Research Center announced that 75 percent of phone interviews starting in 2016 will be through cell phones.[a]

Meta-Analysis: A Response to the Cell Phone Era

Other areas of change include the type of respondents being contacted and how these samples of respondents are gathered. In July 2014, on the heels of the midterm elections, the *New York Times* and CBS News announced they were collaborating with YouGov, a market-research firm, to change their methods for sampling that would depart from the traditional probability methods. The new method would include information from surveys that people opt into, that is, those who volunteer for polls. This announcement elicited strong reactions. Michael Link, president of the American Association for Public Opinion Research, called this "a black-eye" for the whole industry of public opinion,[b] while others lauded it as a practical choice in the face of changing technological realities.[c]

A well-known example of meta-analysis is the work of Nate Silver's FiveThirtyEight.com. In his analysis, Silver sometimes aggregates data from as many as 79 polls. Not all polls are treated equally in these models, and each source is assigned a weight. For instance, in one primary election that Silver analyzed, data from the pollster firm Public Policy Polling were given a weight of 1.62, while the data from Fox News were given 0.27. Silver's overall 2016 election strategy was to use two sets of formulas: polls-only and polls-plus forecasting. Polls-only forecasting uses polls from a particular state; polls-plus forecasting considers state and national polls in addition to endorsements received.

Meta-analysis is innovative in that it allows practitioners to identify shortcomings of sources of data and still use them by correcting for known biases. Still, meta-analysis does not evade the challenges of polling and surveying entirely, because it requires that data be collected. The key is that meta-analysis is an acknowledgement that no one polling source is accurate; all have errors, given the difficulties in reaching good samples. Thus, analyzing weighted averages of polling results leads to better overall results than relying on any one source. It is also less expensive for some to let others do the polling.

FiveThirtyEight and other poll aggregators fared poorly in the surprising 2016 election outcome. Since all the major polls were wrong in the same direction—

Statistician Nate Silver (center) and the staff at FiveThirty-Eight used meta-analysis techniques to forecast the outcomes of the 2016 presidential election. Poll aggregators, and pollsters in general, came under fire for their ultimately inaccurate predictions.

overestimating Clinton's final lead in the popular vote by 1 to 4 percent above the actual total in the election—these aggregators predicted a Clinton victory. Like the others, FiveThirtyEight's prediction was wrong, but it had 29 percent chance of Donald Trump winning the electoral college.

Think about It

What is the future for public opinion polling? Will researchers and survey companies be able to conduct surveys 20 years from now? How can we reach people to learn about their opinions and attitudes?

a. Kyley McGeeney, "Pew Research Center Will Call 75% Cellphones for Surveys in 2016," Pew Research Center, January 5, 2016, www.pewresearch.org/fact-tank/2016/01/05/pew-research-center-will-call-75-cellphones-for-surveys-in-2016 (accessed 2/3/16).

b. See, for example, Michael Link, "The Critical Role of Transparency & Standards in Today's World of Polling and Opinion Research," American Association for Public Opinion Research, August 1, 2014, www.aapor.org/AAPORKentico/AAPOR_Main/media/MainSiteFiles/Response-to-NYTimes_AAPOR-website-final_logo_01Aug14.pdf (accessed 9/24/15).

c. Andrew Gelman and David Rothschild, "Modern Polling Needs Innovation, Not Traditionalism," *Washington Post*, August 4, 2014, www.washingtonpost.com/blogs/monkey-cage/wp/2014/08/04/modern-polling-requires-both-sampling-and-adjustment (accessed 2/4/16).

One of the strongest influences on individuals' political views is their parents' political views. Most people—including former president George H. W. Bush and his sons, former president George W. Bush and former presidential candidate Jeb Bush—follow in their parents' footsteps when it comes to party identification.

describe themselves as liberals or conservatives. And we know from research that partisanship tends to persist over the course of a person's lifetime. Thus, the children of Democrats will typically grow up to be lifelong Democrats.[13] It is certainly the case that most people stay in place on both partisanship and ideology. (We will discuss partisanship and ideology in depth later in the chapter.)

The strong effect of parents' political views and the persistence of individuals' partisanship and ideology are the predominant patterns, but there are exceptions. Some people do change over time. Friends, coworkers, acquaintances, and others can influence a person's partisanship and ideology. When asked in surveys about with whom they discuss politics, people tend to identify one or two friends or coworkers who are particularly knowledgeable about politics. These knowledgeable people (often called "cue-givers," as we will see later) have been shown to influence the way their peers think about politics and their underlying attitudes toward public issues.[14]

There is evidence also that students who attend college at a liberal campus will tend to become more liberal during their college years, and vice versa for students who attend a conservative college.[15] Major world events such as wars, recessions, and social movements can change people's partisanship and ideology. So can personal events such as becoming a small business owner or a member of the military, which both tend to move people in a more conservative direction.[16] These are all factors in the process of socialization, in which the information and views that people are exposed to influence their attitudes and opinions.

Mass media can also be a source of individuals' attitudes. People tend to pay attention to media—newspapers, television stations, websites, blogs—that frame information in ways comfortable to them.[17] Thus Fox News, widely considered a conservative media outlet, attracts many more conservative viewers than liberal viewers. But it is not clear which way the relationship works.

[13] Richard G. Niemi and M. Kent Jennings, "Issues and Inheritance in the Formation of Party Identification," *American Journal of Political Science* 35, no. 4 (1991): 970–88.

[14] Robert Huckfeldt and John Sprague, *Citizens, Politics, and Social Communication: Information and Influence in an Election Campaign* (New York: Cambridge University Press, 1995).

[15] Theodore Newcomb et al., *Persistence and Change: Bennington College and Its Students after Twenty-Five Years* (New York: John Wiley & Sons, 1967).

[16] Richard G. Niemi and M. Kent Jennings, "Issues and Inheritance in the Formation of Party Identification."

[17] Norman H. Nie, Darwin W. Miller III, Saar Golde, Daniel M. Butler, and Kenneth Winneg, "The World Wide Web and the U.S. Political News Market," *American Journal of Political Science* 54, no. 2 (2010): 428–39.

Is Fox News causing people to be more conservative? Or are people who already hold conservative views choosing Fox News because they feel comfortable with the way it frames the news? The preponderance of evidence suggests that people tend to select media that they already agree with in general.

Interests and Rationality

One seemingly straightforward explanation for someone's expressed attitude in a survey or an interview is that it is "in his or her interest." This might be a way of saying that they have a preference for something, and that is that: "My preferences and attitudes follow from what my interests are." To what extent do self-interest and fixed preference determine political attitudes? Are people rational in making decisions based on their interests and preferences and the information that is available to them?

Material Interests. The notion of interest is hard to define precisely. It may seem easy to explain why poor people would prefer that the government increase spending on social welfare programs even if taxes need to be raised, and why the rich would prefer that the government cut taxes even at the cost of shrinking social welfare programs. Answers to many survey questions about economic and social issues depend on a person's income level. In surveys about health care reform in 2010, data showed that people in families with below-average incomes were significantly more likely to prefer mandatory, government-funded health insurance than were people in families with above-average incomes.[18] Public opinion data from surveys in all advanced industrial countries show that the higher the income or wealth of respondents, the more likely they are to say they prefer to cut taxes and reduce the size of government.

We might say that these preferences make sense because people prefer to be better off materially and thus prefer certain public policies that would accomplish this. In other words, they are protecting their interests and express their preferences accordingly. By similar reasoning, younger people tend to be more opposed to war than older people because younger people tend to do the fighting. Women prefer more public funding for child care than men do. Labor union members favor laws that make it easier for workers to unionize, while business owners do not. African Americans prefer tougher enforcement of racial discrimination laws.

If preferences and attitudes come purely from material interest, it almost inevitably follows that different groups of people will have conflicting preferences and attitudes. If you are taxed heavily to pay for a program that benefits

[18] Data analyzed from the Kaiser Family Foundation Tracking Poll (September 11–18, 2009), available from the Roper Center, http://webapps.ropercenter.uconn.edu (accessed 5/11/11).

others but not you, then you have an economic interest in changing either the program or the way it is funded.

Most public opinion researchers, however, broaden the definition of interests to acknowledge that many people have complicated policy preferences and attitudes that may conflict with their economic interests or their apparent self-interest. In other words, they might include nonmaterial benefits as part of their interests. This broader definition of interests might include altruism, among other things. The noted economist Albert Hirschman wrote that interests were "the totality of human aspiration, [but denoting] an element of reflection and calculation with respect to the manner in which these aspirations [are] to be pursued." Put another way, interests are what people prefer after careful consideration, not merely what they seek at the spur of the moment.[19]

Many researchers would go even further, for purposes of analysis, and argue that someone's interests are whatever he or she says they prefer in surveys or in other settings. Although the general patterns in survey data seem to indicate a relationship between material self-interest and opinions, there are many exceptions. Some rich people prefer even higher taxes than they currently pay, and some poor people prefer to reduce or even eliminate social welfare programs. Some African Americans and women wish to eliminate affirmative action programs, and some teachers prefer that less money be spent on public schools. Some might conclude that these people are stating policy opinions and preferences that run contrary to their interests. Others might argue that these respondents are not typical, but they are entitled to define and express their own interests.

Rationality. An idea related to interests is the assumption that people are rational. There is an ongoing debate in the social sciences about whether people's political behavior is fundamentally rational. Traditional models of political institutions often begin with the assumption that people are rational in the sense that they

- pay attention only to relevant information when making choices;
- make their decisions based on what is in their best interests;
- do not systematically make mistakes, but can correct past mistakes and improve decision making.

Researchers who use a "rational choice" framework to study public opinion and politics restrict their attention to interests and information. Given an individual's interests and given the information the individual has at his or her disposal, there is a rational choice to be made when faced with a decision. Deciding on the basis of **rationality** means making the best choice among available options given a person's interests and information.

rationality The habit of choosing the best choice among available options, given a person's interests and information.

[19] Albert Hirschman, *The Passions and the Interests* (Princeton, NJ: Princeton University Press, 1977), p. 32.

To test whether someone is being rational, we would need to have a complete understanding of their interests and all the information they have before them when making a decision. As a practical matter, since it is often difficult to define someone's interests, it generally makes sense for researchers to assume that people have a certain set of interests—that they prefer to make more money and work fewer hours, for example, or that members of Congress prefer to be reelected—and protect those interests by acting rationally. Given these assumptions, researchers can predict people's behavior.

However, there is considerable evidence that people violate the principle of rationality. As we will learn later, evidence from surveys shows that many people pay attention to irrelevant information when making their choice among options. Scholars disagree about how often and why people deviate from acting rationally, but much public opinion research is based on the assumption that people are not always rational in the way defined earlier.

Group Attachments

Researchers have discovered that many people express opinions and attitudes in surveys that are inconsistent with their own personal, material interests, but in accord with the collective interests of the groups with which they affiliate. Quite a few wealthy African Americans, for example, support more liberal social welfare policies than their wealthy white counterparts.[20]

In these cases, group interest, not mere self-interest, guides individuals' political attitudes and opinions. Often, group interests and self-interests are not in conflict, but when they are, surveys show that people tend to respond more in line with their group interests.

This finding can be explained in at least two ways. First, the public has a tendency to see the political world as made up of groups competing, forming coalitions, and winning or losing under each set of policies created by the government. That is, competition for resources at the political level tends to be among groups, not among individuals, and people orient themselves in the political world by connecting cognitively with groups.[21] Moreover, group leaders convince people, rightly or wrongly, that their individual interests are closely tied to group interests, and therefore it is usually best to support group goals. Second, group leaders' endorsements of particular policies (or stances against those policies) give shorthand cues to people to form opinions on topics they do not necessarily understand or pay much attention to. We examine the role of group endorsements as information cues in more detail later in this chapter.

[20] Michael Dawson, *Behind the Mule: Race and Class in African-American Politics* (Princeton, NJ: Princeton University Press, 1995).

[21] Donald Kinder and Cindy Kam, *Us Against Them: Ethnocentric Foundations of American Opinion* (Chicago: University of Chicago Press, 2010).

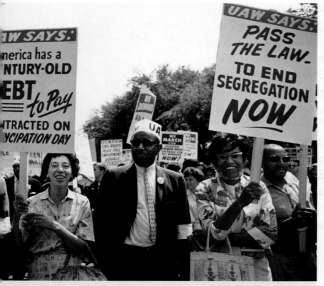

Were civil rights supporters motivated by self-interest and the desire for more opportunities as individuals? By group attachments? Or other factors? While researchers have identified numerous influences on individual opinions, it can be difficult to say which influences are decisive in a given instance.

Emotions

Political scientists and psychologists study in great detail how people make political decisions. In addition to the influences discussed earlier, researchers have discovered deeper mental processes that affect things like vote choices and survey responses. What causes some people to choose Republicans over Democrats? Why do some people vote while others do not? What causes some people to answer "very liberal" when asked about their political ideology?

There have been interesting research results, for instance, about the role of emotion (or "affect"). Some researchers who study political psychology have challenged the assumptions behind the concept of rationality. They have found that people do not always make political decisions based on objective consideration of the options and the information available. In particular, they emphasize that enthusiasm, fear, and other emotions can explain a great deal about attitudes and behavior that rationality cannot. The theory of affective intelligence, for instance, distinguishes between people's dispositions to act in normal situations and how those dispositions can be interrupted when emotion—such as the feeling of being threatened—comes into play.[22]

Researchers have also discovered patterns in how campaign advertisements trigger emotional responses and affect people's choices. Evidence shows, for instance, that positive advertisements laced with emotional images and music tend to make supporters and detractors more enthusiastic about their own positions. In other words, positive ads with emotional appeals polarize viewers. Negative ads have the opposite effect; their disturbing images and tense music tend to make people less certain of their convictions.[23] This area of research is ongoing, but the larger point is that, in addition to the other factors shaping political attitudes and decisions, emotion plays a role.

Influence of Elites

People's attitudes about politics can be affected by the way issues are presented to them by politicians, mass media personalities, pollsters, and interest

[22] George Marcus, Michael Mackuen, and W. Russell Neuman, *Affective Intelligence and Political Judgment* (Chicago: University of Chicago Press, 2000).

[23] Ted Brader, *Campaigning for Hearts and Minds: How Emotional Appeals in Political Ads Work* (Chicago: University of Chicago Press, 2006).

group leaders. Research into priming and framing is especially instructive. Let's first consider **priming**, which is the psychological process of shaping people's perceptions of a particular issue, figure, or policy. Suppose voters are being asked to decide whether to build a new county jail. Voters could be primed to think about this decision in a certain way based on how it is portrayed by those in government or in the media. Overt priming might take the form of negative coverage of the proposal to build the jail, influencing voters to view it negatively (and vice versa for positive coverage). More subtle priming might take the form of a photo of prisoners accompanying a news story about the proposal, cueing a negative connotation in voters' minds and thus *priming* them to consider the issue in a negative light. Conversely, a photo showing contented prison workers from another county might prime voters to consciously or subconsciously associate the building of the jail more positively.

priming The psychological process of shaping people's perceptions of a particular issue, figure, or policy.

Framing, meanwhile, has to do with establishing the context for an issue in such a way as to emphasize certain aspects over others. In our county jail example, the public could be cued by politicians, pundits, other public figures, and television ads to consider the proposal in terms of its effects on their taxes on the one hand, or as a way to increase the number of jobs available to potential guards, cooks, and social workers on the other. Which consideration ultimately dominates their thinking about the issue may shape their subsequent formation of an opinion on it.

framing Establishing the context for an issue in such a way as to emphasize certain aspects over others.

Priming and framing are related, and both can also play a role in measurements of public opinion. For example, in a survey, respondents could be primed to make a positive association with the jail proposal by framing the question in terms of the employment possibilities it offers rather than the higher taxes it threatens:

> To alleviate the county's unemployment problems, some have suggested trying to convince the state to build the new jail here. Do you support or oppose building a new jail in our county?

Framing can also affect how people assess various risks and rewards in politics and other arenas. In a famous survey experiment, the psychologists Daniel Kahneman and Amos Tversky asked a group of undergraduates the following questions, which were separated in the survey by filler questions:

> A: Would you accept a gamble that offers a 10% chance to win $95 and a 90% chance to lose $5?

> B: Would you pay $5 to participate in a lottery that offers a 10% chance to win $100 and a 90% chance to win nothing?

Objectively, these two questions describe the same options, but question A frames the $5 as a loss, while question B frames it as a cost incurred in playing a potentially lucrative lottery. In responding to the questions, more than half the subjects chose differently for the two questions, and among those, more than three-fourths answered no to A and yes to B. Kahneman and Tversky interpreted their results as highlighting two things: the key effect that framing choices has on influencing people's behavior, and the way in which people are biased against choices framed as losses rather than as potential gains.[24]

Whether framing matters, in surveys or in any setting where people are expressing opinions or acting on them, depends very much on the subject matter.[25] In the context of surveys, the more we know about the effects of framing, the more researchers can design surveys to avoid some biases in responses that hinder knowledge about what people really think and feel.

We can draw several larger lessons from our discussion of priming and framing. The first is the various biases that are introduced into polls by the possibilities of framing. It is important to be careful both in gathering data on public opinion and in interpreting it. For consumers of public opinion information, knowing the political interests of the people involved, especially those who are funding the research, is of key importance because, through manipulation of framing, researchers sometimes can get the results they want out of surveys.

Second, in the larger context beyond surveys, framing and attempted priming is done all the time by candidates, political parties, interest groups, advertisers, and public relations specialists. They seek to frame the controversy at hand in a manner favorable to them. Our earlier example of whether to build a new jail makes this point. On the issue of abortion rights, opponents frame it as an issue about the life of the fetus, hoping to tilt people's opinions one way, while supporters frame it as an issue about women's autonomy and life chances, hoping to tilt people's opinions the other way. These so-called wars of frames are intensely political and competitive with much at stake. Researchers have studied these situations in great detail; it is often difficult to predict in advance which framing will work for a given policy controversy.

Predispositions

Research on political attitudes shows that most Americans agree about certain topics. By and large, Americans appear to feel that their system of government is generally good, and they are comfortable with concepts like freedom of speech, religion, and the press. Because so few Americans depart from the norm when answering questions like these, polling firms seldom ask them anymore.

[24] Daniel Kahneman and Amos Tversky, *Choices, Values, and Frames* (New York: Russell Sage, 2000).

[25] See, for example, James N. Druckman, "Political Preference Formation: Competition, Deliberation, and the (Ir)relevance of Framing Effects," *American Political Science Review* 98, no. 4 (2004): 671–86.

What some scholars have called the American Creed is a set of widely shared values. According to some, this creed has been instrumental in allowing the United States to stay united and relatively free of group-on-group violence since the Civil War. There has not been much support for violent revolution in American society, even when it was quite popular in other countries in the early twentieth century. Nearly all people in the United States agree that on balance the political system works pretty well and is worth preserving. They especially believe in the First Amendment rights to freedom of expression and freedom of religion. These rights are ingrained in people at all levels of American society.

Of course, Americans differ in their opinions over what policies governments should adopt. In particular instances, even regarding First Amendment rights, there can be vigorous disagreement. In this section, we will discuss the other side of attitudes—predispositions. Ideology and partisanship are two fundamental predispositions that are usually long term and shape people's opinions toward specific politicians and government policies. By definition, ideology and partisanship divide people into different categories based on their overall perspectives on government and society.

Ideology

An **ideology** can be defined as a coherent, organized set of ideas founded on basic principles. Ideologies start with a core. When someone in the United States today professes to have a *conservative* ideology, for example, he or she is usually expressing a core preference for tradition—for preserving what currently works well or has worked well in the past. The value of tradition trumps the possibilities that might arise from changing to novel or untried policies. From that core, this individual might conclude that on specific public issues, it is best to let markets work unhindered by regulation and keep government small while allowing government to use the force of law to preserve moral standards in society. Note that conservatives can desire change, but usually they prefer to change back to a situation from a previous era.

Alternatively, when someone in the United States today professes to have a *liberal* ideology, he or she is usually expressing a fundamental optimism about change in a new direction and an enthusiasm for the possible benefits of redistribution of resources. From that core, this person might conclude that on specific public issues, government should be an active agent to improve society, especially economically, and that people should be free to experiment with lifestyles and private behavior without the government interfering in an attempt to protect traditional moral values.

Liberalism and conservatism anchor the predominant ideological differences that animate American politics. The political differences between liberals and conservatives in the modern United States are loosely related to concepts of

ideology A coherent, organized set of ideas and principles that functions as a core on which individuals draw when forming their attitudes about public affairs.

"left" and "right" that originated in prerevolutionary France. In the eighteenth century, members of the French Assembly who were more favorable to the king, the military, and the Church sat to the king's right, while the various representatives of the guilds and artisans, who tended to be critical of the king, sat to his left. The seating arrangements in the French Assembly continue along these lines today, but the meanings of left and right have evolved over time.

Since the mid-nineteenth century in Western political thought, the predominant set of political ideologies has ranged from communism on the far left (most closely identified with Marxism) to fascism on the far right. These extreme ideologies were discredited in the twentieth century by the actions of the fascist regimes in Germany and Italy, and of the communist regime in the Soviet Union. But communism as a state-sponsored ideology still persists in the world, most prominently in places like Cuba and North Korea.

As Figure 9.3 shows, ideological differences among the political parties in some other countries can be wider than in the United States. In Italy, for instance, some political parties in parliament and their supporters still espouse principles of communism. In Italy and Germany, something close to far-right fascism continues to have an appreciable following. In the United States, very few people—and none among serious candidates for national office—profess to support either communism or fascism. The most extreme politicians in the United States today who stand any chance of being elected to national office tend to be: On the left, democratic socialists like Bernie Sanders, a senator from Vermont who espouses a European-style social welfare system. He ran for president in 2016 as a Democrat but lost to Hillary Clinton for the party nomination. On the right, Ted Cruz, a determined archconservative who represents Texas in the Senate and supports policies such as abolishing the Internal Revenue Service and ending federal funding for education. He also ran for president in 2016 but lost in the Republican primaries to Donald Trump.

Although ideologies are abstract, they relate to opinions about concrete issues that confront the American government today. Survey research offers a way to conceptualize ideology in a systematic way and trace the connection between

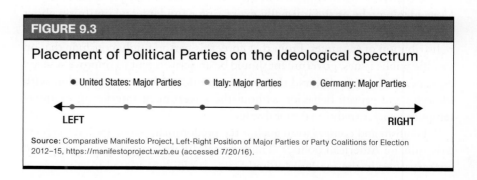

FIGURE 9.3

Placement of Political Parties on the Ideological Spectrum

● United States: Major Parties   ● Italy: Major Parties   ● Germany: Major Parties

LEFT   RIGHT

Source: Comparative Manifesto Project, Left-Right Position of Major Parties or Party Coalitions for Election 2012–15, https://manifestoproject.wzb.eu (accessed 7/20/16).

abstract principles and specific policy goals. Political scientist Philip Converse provided the concept of ideological "constraint," which means that preferences on one policy correlate with preferences on another policy issue.[26] People's opinion on the death penalty, for instance, might be constrained by their predisposition toward the rights of the accused or by their ideology.

Party Identification

Loyalty or psychological attachment to a political party is called **party identification (or partisanship)**. The following is one of the best-known questions in public opinion research because it has been asked regularly and tracked for many decades:

> Generally speaking, do you consider yourself a Democrat, a Republican, an independent, or what?

Public opinion researchers use the answer to this question to reveal the respondent's party identification. Figure 9.4 shows how responses to this question have changed since the 1950s. This figure does not tell us whether individuals are stable in their party identification, or whether they change much over time. Some people are changing, but how many? That number is difficult to pin down at any given time. Yet more in-depth analysis of party identification from survey research shows that individuals tend to be quite stable. Some do change over time, but most retain their party loyalties throughout adulthood.

Research in the 1950s at the University of Michigan showed that the best predictor of how someone would vote in a congressional or presidential election was their party identification, as given in an answer to the question earlier. It even trumped people's evaluation of a candidate's issue positions. The so-called Michigan model of voting, discussed in more detail in Chapter 13, posits that party identification is a psychological orientation to the political world that colors how people evaluate policies and candidates.[27]

Figure 9.4 shows that the percentage of survey respondents who identify with one or the other party has fluctuated over time. This change corresponds partially to the success or failures of presidents and to current events. Examine the trajectory in Figure 9.4. The proportion of Republicans relative to the proportion of Democrats drops after the Nixon Watergate scandals (mid-1970s) and during the second Iraq War (2006), but it rises during the Reagan administration (1980s) as Reagan succeeded in carrying out key parts of the Republican agenda.

party identification (or partisanship) Loyalty or psychological attachment to a political party.

[26] Converse, "The Nature of Belief Systems in Mass Publics."

[27] Angus Campbell, Philip Converse, Warren Miller, and Donald Stokes, *The American Voter* (New York: John Wiley & Sons, 1960).

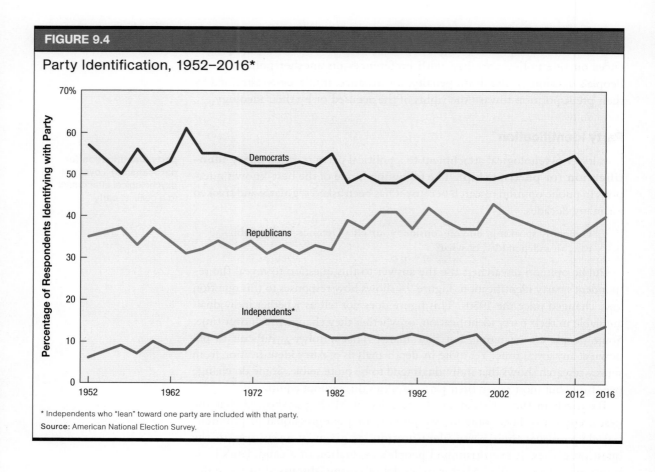

FIGURE 9.4

Party Identification, 1952–2016*

* Independents who "lean" toward one party are included with that party.

Source: American National Election Survey.

Other Predispositions

Besides ideology and partisanship, people's opinions are affected by deeply held predispositions. Research has shown, for instance, that some people have racist predispositions that are often not expressed openly (to pollsters, for example) but still affect opinions on policies and politicians and behaviors such as voting decisions.[28] More broadly, a person might have predispositions that stem from being a member of a particular ethnic or racial group. Many people's religious beliefs stay fixed over long periods, if not their lifetimes, and those beliefs shape opinions on issues—especially social issues having to do with marriage, reproduction, women's rights, gay rights, and the death penalty. As we discuss later, religion plays a distinctive role in American public opinion and political life compared to that of many other advanced industrial democracies.

[28] Kinder and Kam, *Us Against Them: Ethnocentric Foundations of American Opinion.*

Opinions on Policies and Politicians

When analyzing attitudes, in addition to predispositions such as ideology, religion, and party identification, we can also consider opinions toward current events and the policies of the government. These opinions are more amenable to change and may be shaped by a number of factors. The lack of durability of these opinions contrasts with the persistence of the predispositions discussed earlier.

Policy Opinions

Most people when asked will give an opinion about the latest major policy controversy rattling around Congress or in the White House. Their ideology and partisanship will shape those opinions and attitudes. For instance, if you are a lifelong Republican and the current Democratic president takes a firm position in favor of policy engagement with North Korea, partisanship may affect your opinion about the wisdom of this policy *just because the president, who is a Democrat, supports it* and you do not trust his or her judgment. In other words, our fundamental attitudes can, and often do, shape our more specific attitudes about policies and politicians.

Researchers and politicians are intensely interested in classifying people into categories or groups and using these classifications to examine differences and similarities in policy preferences. They do this in two general ways. The first is to examine the differences of opinions, attitudes, and behaviors between demographic groups. Are blacks, for example, more or less supportive of the death penalty than whites? Are women more likely than men to support the use of certain types of military action? Researchers start by segmenting people based on their relatively immutable or objective characteristics, and then compare their survey responses (see, for example, Tables 9.1 and 9.2).

TABLE 9.1

Differences in Attitudes between Racial Groups

"Do you favor or oppose the death penalty for murder?"

	Whites	African Americans
Favor (%)	57	29
Oppose (%)	35	63

Source: Baxter Oliphant, "Support for Death Penalty Lowest in More Than Four Decades," Pew Research Center, September 29, 2016, pewresearch.org (accessed 10/19/18).

TABLE 9.2

Differences in Attitudes between Genders

Support for using military force for specific types of military action.

	Men favor (%)	Women favor (%)
Naval forces	64	51
Increase troops	53	40
Sell or send arms	45	32
Air or missile strikes	64	52
Keep/maintain troops	52	40
War	48	39
Unspecified action type	54	44
Military action (general)	61	53
Presence of troops	52	45
Send troops	50	43
Provide advisers or training	48	41
Total	54	44

Source: These data are from Richard Eichenberg, "Gender Difference in American Public Opinion on the Use of Military Force, 1982–2013," *International Studies Quarterly* 60 (March 2016): 138–48. Eichenberg averaged results across nearly a thousand public opinion questions.

TABLE 9.3

Differences in Attitudes Leading to Differences in Behavior

"What if there was a measure on your local ballot to increase local parcel taxes to provide more funds for the local public schools? Would you vote yes or no?"

	Democrats	Republicans	Independents
Yes (%)	69	33	54
No (%)	29	65	43

Source: Public Policy Institute of California, 2013 Statewide Survey, www.ppic.org (accessed 5/22/13).

Another way is to classify people according to their opinions and attitudes (both fundamental and specific), and then examine the different behaviors of the various groups (Table 9.3). If people say they value environmental cleanup more than economic growth, for example, are they more willing to vote for tax increases to pay for the cleanup than the people who place a greater value on economic growth? Are liberals less willing to spend government money on crime control than conservatives?

Evaluations of Politicians and Government Institutions

Politicians and the people who work for them are often interested in learning how the public evaluates their performance. In the American political system, where reelection campaigns are constantly looming for members of Congress and first-term presidents, political leaders want to know if people are angry, frustrated, disappointed, or generally happy with how things are going. More specifically, they want to know how many people are evaluating them negatively and how many are satisfied enough to keep them in office.

One of the great predictors of how presidents will fare—in their reelection efforts, in their relationship with Congress, and in their efforts to convince citizens to support them in their policy goals—is the presidential approval rating. Here is the question Gallup asks a random sample of voting-age Americans at least once a month:

> Do you approve or disapprove of the job [X] is doing as president?

As we saw in Chapter 6, approval ratings shift, sometimes dramatically, during each president's term in office (Figure 6.5 tracks the approval ratings for American presidents from the 1950s to the present). Some scholars of voting behavior put great stock in predicting voting patterns by relying on people's evaluations of the performance of politicians, especially the president. As we will discuss in Chapter 13, voting behavior by people in elections can be partially predicted by learning how people evaluate an incumbent politician's past performance in office.

A related question, but one that earns less attention, asks about Congress:

> Do you approve or disapprove of the way Congress is handling its job? (CBS News, 2013)[29]

As we discussed in Chapter 5, people often give negative evaluations of Congress as a whole while giving a more positive evaluation of their individual representatives or senators. When the preceding question was asked in October 2013, only 9 percent of respondents said they approved of Congress's performance. However, when asked the following question, 46 percent said they approved:

> How about the representative in Congress from your district? Do you approve or disapprove of the way your representative is handling his or her job? (CBS News, 2013)

Most incumbents in the House are reelected easily, despite generally low evaluations of Congress as a whole, while senators face more competition

---

[29] CBS News Poll, October 2013, CBS News [producer]. Storrs, CT: Roper Center for Public Opinion Research, iPOLL [distributor], www.cbsnews.com/news/poll-post-shutdown-congress-disapproval-at -all-time-high/ (accessed 7/25/16).

but are usually reelected as well. Voters appear to separate their opinions about the entire legislative body from their evaluations of their own representatives.[30]

Apathy and Lack of Knowledge

In general, people readily give answers to survey questions, but can we trust their answers to reflect an informed opinion? What if people do not pay attention to politics and their answers simply follow from being polite to the interviewer? Research on the topic of political knowledge can lead to pessimistic conclusions.

We know from surveys, for example, that two-thirds of American adults cannot name the chief justice of the Supreme Court, and one-third cannot name the vice president. Even when shown a list of names, 40 percent of adults are unable to identify the Speaker of the House; more than one-fourth mention a branch other than the Supreme Court as having the final authority to declare laws unconstitutional; and nearly one-third are unable to name which political party controls the House of Representatives. Only a small percentage can name the leaders of Russia, Germany, China, Canada, Mexico, or France, and a vast majority cannot say with confidence whether Mexico holds elections for its president. (It does.)

The lack of knowledge revealed in these surveys is nothing new. Studies over the last 70 years have shown that a large percentage of Americans have little factual understanding of their government, the governments of other countries, and world affairs.[31] Research in the 1950s and early 1960s revealed not only factual ignorance but also a lack of basic understanding of the philosophical underpinnings of our government. These studies found that the majorities of those polled could not correctly indicate whether the Democratic or Republican Party was more conservative on economic issues. Many respondents could not even describe coherently what kinds of policies liberal or conservative politicians tend to pursue. As mentioned earlier, pollsters found that a significant percentage of people gave what were essentially random answers to questions about their own preferences on public policies.

If you happen to follow the news closely and are knowledgeable about politics, it is easy to be smug when you learn of such data. Yet the individual who does not follow the news closely and who would likely get many of the factual answers wrong in a political research poll could reason-

[30] John R. Hibbing and Elizabeth Theiss-Morse, *Congress as Public Enemy: Public Attitudes toward American Political Institutions* (New York: Cambridge University Press, 1995).

[31] Michael Delli Carpini and Scott Keeter, *What Americans Know about Politics and Why It Matters* (New Haven, CT: Yale University Press, 1997).

ably argue, "I am busy with other important things in my life. I know what I need to know to make good choices." Although some people may feel disappointed with their fellow citizens or even superior to them based on their lack of political awareness, others—including some public opinion researchers—contend that these citizens have enough knowledge to navigate their lives effectively, even if they cannot identify the current chief justice of the Supreme Court. Researchers are generally in agreement on the levels of ignorance about factual information, yet question whether such a prevalent lack of knowledge of public affairs is an important problem.

On the one hand, some analysts contend that we should be deeply worried that the American people may not be equipped intellectually to make good decisions in the voting booth and choose appropriately given their interests. Perhaps Americans are not up to the task of democracy, of guiding elected officials wisely through the ballot box, through their expressions of opinions in polls, and through lobbying efforts. The Founders expressed such concerns when they designed a set of governmental institutions that were originally quite removed from popular control. In the early years of the Republic, for example, the House of Representatives was the only element of the national government that was comprised of members directly elected by the people. Alexander Hamilton spoke for many political leaders of his generation when he reportedly referred to the people—those who would be the basis of popular sovereignty—as a "beast," a dangerous and unpredictable force that needed to be controlled rather than allowed to control leaders.

Who is this man? *In recent surveys, a majority of Americans are consistently unable to name John Roberts as the chief justice of the Supreme Court. Can citizens hold meaningful opinions about politics if they lack basic knowledge about government?*

Along the same lines, commentators in the early to mid-twentieth century worried that the populace's ignorance would make it easy for manipulative leaders to whip up support for oppressive policies, authoritarian leadership, and even fascism. They saw educating the public as necessary to preserve democracy. Some were deeply concerned that ignorance of public affairs—more pronounced among the uneducated, but also among the poor—only disadvantaged further those at the bottom rungs of society. Knowledge, it is said, is power, and in the American political system, knowledge means knowing when your interests are threatened and how to act to protect them.

A different perspective focuses less on what people do not know and more on whether they have the information they need to choose wisely. We might call this the need-to-know position. It is based on whether people can get the information they need to function properly in our society, and on how much information is widely available. Although many cannot name the chief justice or perhaps even their senator, maybe they can pick the correct party to vote for in the upcoming election, even if they cannot name the candidate. Since such decisions are often confined to a small number of options—should I vote for the Republican or the Democrat?—it might not be all that difficult for people to have just enough information to choose correctly, given their interests. There is also some evidence that people know more than has been concluded from analysis of surveys.[32]

It is puzzling that the level of public ignorance has remained roughly constant since quality surveys about politics began in earnest in the 1950s, while the education level of Americans has steadily increased over this same period. It is even more surprising given that consumption of media containing political news, especially television, has also increased during this period. Political news, while often crowded out by news of celebrities and sports, is widely available. Certainly it is not for lack of available information that people do not know much about politics.

Rational Ignorance?

One explanation for the low levels of knowledge among the general public focuses on a fundamental collective action problem. People can engage in what Anthony Downs called "rational ignorance" about politics by free riding off people who happen to like politics or need to know about politics for their jobs.[33]

To understand this concept, consider the following nonpolitical situation. You and seven of your friends are planning to take a flight to a warm destination over the holiday break. Only one of you needs to contact a travel agent and make the reservations for everyone in the group, and presumably that person will keep all the information about the travel arrangements. Your group faces a collective action problem. Who will take the time to book the reservations and keep all the materials and information together?

It turns out that one of your friends, Rita, volunteers and books everyone on the same flight, which leaves on a Friday. Rita informs you of the time of the flight, but you forget to write it down. Is this a big problem? Not really, as long as you can find out from Rita or the others in your party in enough time to make your flight. People ask you, "When is your flight Friday?" You reply, "I don't know. Rita knows. I'll check with her before Friday."

If you are confident that Rita is someone you trust to provide the correct information in time for you to catch your flight, you can free ride off her efforts. In fact, your ignorance about the time of the flight saves you the effort of tracking it until you actually need it.

[32] See, for example, Jeffery J. Mondak and Mary R. Anderson, "The Knowledge Gap: A Reexamination of Gender-Based Differences in Political Knowledge," *Journal of Politics* 66, no. 2 (2004): 492–512; and James L. Gibson and Gregory A. Caldeira, "Knowing the Supreme Court? A Reconsideration of Public Ignorance of the High Court," *Journal of Politics* 71, no. 2 (2009): 429–41.

[33] Anthony Downs, *An Economic Theory of Democracy* (New York: Harper & Row, 1957).

This way of thinking has led some researchers to a more benign conclusion about the levels of ignorance among the general public. As long as people can learn the necessary information to make wise choices from people they trust and who share their interests—called "cue-givers" because they give small, informative cues to people to help them make decisions—then general ignorance of politics is not a major problem. What matters is the quality of the specific knowledge people need to have and whether they can access that information in a timely manner.[34]

This view is contested by those who put more emphasis on the possibility that those people who know a lot about politics—the cue-givers—do not have the same interests as those who are less knowledgeable and receive the cues. Cue-givers typically include interest groups, politicians, media personalities, commentators, and even knowledgeable friends and relatives. Their cues, some argue, can manipulate situations and get people to make decisions that are not in their best interests.[35]

Apathy and Non-Attitudes

Some scholars are less concerned about the public's lack of knowledge than about its apathy. People simply may not care about politics, or they may display what scholars call **non-attitudes**. That is, people may answer survey questions about an issue even though they have never really thought about it. This could be the result of apathy or of a complete indifference to specific issues that might be of great import to others. We can think of a non-attitude as applying to an issue about which a person either has no opinion or does not let an opinion enter into his or her calculations about voting or taking some other political action. It is easy to imagine, for instance, that a typical college student has a non-attitude about policies having to do with specific tax formulas for retirement accounts. But this may not prevent the student from answering survey questions or voting in a referendum on the matter. It is highly likely that more college students have non-attitudes about this kind of policy issue than do people over the age of 65.

Some scholars have considered using the proportion of people who answer "don't know," "refuse to answer," or "no opinion" to a particular question as an indication of the size of the population with non-attitudes on a specific issue. For example, when asked about the nation's campaign finance laws—a policy issue that rarely bears directly on the quality of life of individual citizens—24 percent of respondents in a Gallup Poll reported having no

non-attitude A lack of opinion on an issue, or an opinion so weakly held that it does not enter into a person's calculations about voting or taking some other political action, even though the person may express an opinion to a pollster.

[34] See, for example, Benjamin Page and Robert Shapiro, *The Rational Public* (Chicago: University of Chicago Press, 1992).

[35] See, for example, Larry Bartels, "Uninformed Votes: Information Effects in Presidential Elections," *American Journal of Political Science* 40, no. 1 (1996): 194–230.

opinion.[36] The conclusion these scholars draw is that this issue is of little or no importance to a quarter of the American people.

However, researchers have learned to be careful about interpreting survey responses in this way. Evidence shows that the proportion of people who answer certain kinds of survey questions depends on the race, ethnicity, or sex of the interviewer. People may have strong opinions about some issues on the public agenda, and those opinions matter a lot in evaluating candidates and parties, but the survey respondents may not answer some questions because the issue is sensitive. For instance, people may not answer questions about policies regarding race or gender not because they have non-attitudes, but because of embarrassment or reticence. When samples of Americans were asked about government efforts to integrate schools racially through busing and redistricting, whites being interviewed by blacks are more likely to answer "don't know" than whites being interviewed by whites.[37] It is important, therefore, to be careful in interpreting nonresponses as non-attitudes. It depends on the topic being addressed.

Decisions over how to interpret the proportion of people giving specific answers are also related to question wording in surveys. Some survey questions do not even give the options "don't know" or "no answer," forcing people into options when they may not have much of an opinion at all. If a surveys asks, "Do you support or oppose policy X?" and no alternative is given for "don't know" or "no answer," perhaps a substantial portion of people giving the answers "support" or "oppose" do not really have an opinion and just give random answers. In survey design, most scholars believe that giving the full options including "don't know" and "no answer" is appropriate and provides more accurate estimates of populations' opinions on policies and politicians. It also allows for estimates of the proportion of the population with non-attitudes, and it even allows for research into whether people are embarrassed to give certain answers. Without those options, researchers lose information that can be gleaned from the survey data.

In Comparison: Public Opinion

To gain perspective on how Americans think about politics and their political system, we can examine the similarities and differences between the United States and other countries. We start with a puzzle. American society is in many respects more diverse than that of any other country. By just about any measure of diversity, the U.S. population is at or near the top of every inter-

[36] Gallup Poll, January 2008.

[37] Adam Berinsky, "The Two Faces of Public Opinion," *American Journal of Political Science* 43, no. 4 (1999): 1209–30.

national ranking. You might conclude that this diversity of wealth, ethnicity, and religion would be reflected in public opinion and that the population of the United States would hold highly diverse opinions about public policies and controversies, as well as a wide range of ideologies and perspectives.

To a degree, however, comparisons of surveys from around the world contradict this expectation. As we have already discussed, Americans as a group hold a near consensus of views about democracy and forms of government, though this is not always the case in other countries. We also learned earlier that Americans' ideologies, at least with regard to the candidates and policies they support, are not as widely spread on the spectrum from far left to far right as in other countries that have similar levels of economic development and democracy. So, in two important respects, Americans may have less diverse opinions about broad matters of politics than do residents of other countries.

This disparity could be explained by knowing that the United States was founded on basic principles that transcend ethnicity, religion, and class, whereas other countries were organized along ethnic or religious lines. The problem with this explanation is that even in countries like France that share with the United States basic principles of government, public opinion displays wider variation in key ideological dimensions.

The causes of the kind of consensus we observe in the United States relative to other countries is a matter of controversy in the political science literature. Some scholars find that the lack of diversity in some measures of public opinion in the United States stems from the rather bland political news coverage relative to that found in other countries.[38] Others believe there is plenty of diversity in public opinion in the United States, just not along the left–right continuum.[39] Still others think the lack of American support for socialist and far-left policies is the main difference between the United States and other countries.[40]

Recall our earlier discussion of redistributive policies and the relationship between social class and support for more active government policies for the poor. Such a relationship is even more pronounced in most other countries. Among the lower classes in Europe, and especially in the developing world, there is intense and consistent support for active government redistribution of income. In the United States, compared with nations with similar economic wealth in Europe, there is less support among the lower classes and more support among the upper classes for generous social welfare spending.

[38] For a summary of this argument, see Diana Mutz, *Impersonal Influence: How Perceptions of Mass Collectives Affect Political Attitudes* (New York: Cambridge University Press, 1998).

[39] See, for example, Robert Axelrod, "The Structure of Public Opinion on Policy Issues," *Public Opinion Quarterly* 31, no. 1 (1967): 51–60.

[40] Kay Lehman Schlozman and Sidney Verba, *Injury to Insult: Unemployment, Class, and Political Response* (Cambridge, MA: Harvard University Press, 1979).

In short, social class does not adequately explain support for leftist or rightist government policies.

Another point of comparison between the United States and other countries involves religion. In one important respect, the United States is markedly different from countries of similar wealth and economic development. Americans are decidedly more religious than Europeans, Canadians, Australians, and the developed countries of Asia (such as Japan). A vast majority of Americans (more than 85 percent) indicate in surveys that they believe in God, pray, and attend religious services often. In countries like Sweden, these numbers are much lower, well below 50 percent. The American pattern on religion surprises many scholars given that in most other societies, religious practice and belief have tended to decline as wealth has grown. In matters of religion, the United States more closely resembles the developing world than the industrialized nations.[41] And the religiosity of Americans appears to shape their opinions on issues such as whether public schools should allow prayer at official functions (most Americans say yes) and whether evolution should be taught in schools (a greater proportion of Americans say no, compared with publics in other countries). Certainly religious behavior correlates with political attitudes and voting behavior. Evidence is consistent that Americans who regularly attend religious services are on average more conservative politically than Americans who do not. This correlation shows up in Europe as well, but many more Americans attend religious services regularly compared with Europeans.

Public Opinion and Policy Making

 We have devoted attention to how the attitudes of individuals are measured. Some of our discussion has been about how those individual attitudes are combined into broader measures, such as presidential or congressional approval ratings, or the percentage of people who support or oppose specific policies. It is important to recognize the difference between analyzing individual opinions and aggregate (combined) opinions. The former analyzes how individuals learn about politics and form and express attitudes to each other, to pollsters, and to politicians, and how those attitudes affect decision making such as voting. The latter analyzes how large population-based shifts in opinion occur, whether those shifts move in response to events, and whether those shifts affect government decisions.

We end this chapter with a focus on large public opinion trends, and we can return to the question we posed at the beginning of the chapter: What is the

[41] World Values Survey, 2005–2008 wave.

Income, Policy Preferences, and Outcomes: Do the Rich Win?

Does wealth affect public opinion? Do the preferences of wealthier people influence policy stronger than those of other groups? Let's explore two data sets that try to answer these difficult questions.

First, consider Figure A, which separates attitudes toward Social Security spending by income group.[a]

groups support the bill in equal measure. If policy change only responds to affluent preferences, the green dots cluster above the line and the red dots below it—that is, bills that reflect preferences of affluent Americans pass, and bills that reflect preferences of median-income Americans do not.

A. Attitudes toward Federal Spending on Social Security by Income

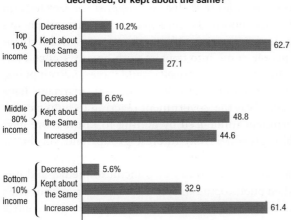

Should federal spending on Social Seurity be increased, decreased, or kept about the same?

Top 10% income
- Decreased: 10.2%
- Kept about the Same: 62.7
- Increased: 27.1

Middle 80% income
- Decreased: 6.6%
- Kept about the Same: 48.8
- Increased: 44.6

Bottom 10% income
- Decreased: 5.6%
- Kept about the Same: 32.9
- Increased: 61.4

B. Policy Support between Median-Income (x-axis) and Affluent Americans (y-axis)

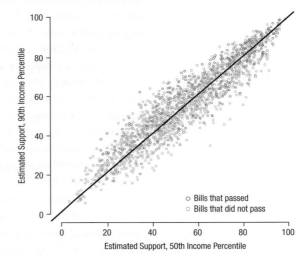

○ Bills that passed
○ Bills that did not pass

Estimated Support, 90th Income Percentile (y-axis)
Estimated Support, 50th Income Percentile (x-axis)

In addition to exploring whether or not wealthy people had different opinions on issues than lower-income people, researchers have also examined whether or not wealthy people's policy preferences were more likely to find support in Congress. One study by political scientists Branham, Soroka, and Wlezien used data on American policy preferences from 1981 to 2002 to create 1,779 "policy cases." They wanted to see whether a policy change for each policy case was implemented within four years of when the survey question was asked. Survey respondents were organized by income, and the researchers focused on two groups: the middle-income and the affluent Americans.[b]

Figure B shows Branham, Soroka, and Wlezien's data. The 45-degree line represents where both income

Think About It

After exploring the data in Figure A, what is the evidence that people of different income levels have different policy preferences? What do you think the chart would look like for defense spending instead of Social Security? Why? Based on Figure B, do policies more closely follow the preferences of the affluent or the middle-class Americans? Is there a difference? Why?

a. The American National Election Studies (ANES; www.electionstudies .org), The ANES 2012 Time Series Study [dataset]. Stanford University and the University of Michigan [producers].

b. J. Alexander Branham, Stuart N. Soroka, and Christopher Wlezien, "When Do the Rich Win?" *Political Science Quarterly* 132, no. 1 (Spring 2017): 43–62.

link between public opinion and politicians' behavior? Many citizens would hope, given the ideals of democracy at the heart of the American political system, that public opinion constrains the government, preventing it from enacting grossly unpopular policies on a regular basis. Politicians should *want* to please a majority of the public in order to win election and reelection, though they should not do so in ways that violate the fundamental rights of minorities.

Does Government Policy Follow Public Opinion or Vice Versa?

Public opinion is surely shaped by events, much as politicians' behavior is shaped by those same events. As an example, public support for more government surveillance of domestic groups increased substantially after the shooting of police officers in various cities in 2016, and support for stricter gun control rose after several mass shootings. Evidence shows that people are more likely to support same-sex marriage if they know gays and lesbians personally; thus, as more people come into contact with openly gay and lesbian people, public support for same-sex marriage should increase. Both public opinion and the government's actions regarding same-sex marriage have changed over the past decade. Was the government reacting to public opinion? Were people in government influenced by getting to know more gays and lesbians? Was it public pressure from interest groups and voters, or something else?

In many instances, politicians' reactions can be difficult to predict and understand. For politicians, when public opinion, events, and interests within one's own political party all point in the same direction—"support more gun control measures" or "support same-sex marriage"—they will likely move in that direction. For years, Democrats were not predictable on gun control because they were trying to be responsive to conflicting pressures from vocal supporters within their electoral coalition, their party, and the public. But as majorities among Democrats supported greater gun restrictions they became more predictable. Polls showing a new majority reinforced the views of key constituencies within their party to support more restrictions on gun ownership, but their efforts were thwarted by Republicans in Congress. Those Republicans, meanwhile, were following their own constituents' views on gun ownership.

The question posed at the opening of this chapter presumes that politicians can know with some degree of certainty what public opinion is on a given issue. But, as we have learned, public opinion data can either be unreliable or reflect a fickle public. As we have seen in exploring how surveys work, there can be biases (often unintentional) in representations of public opinion. It would be wrong to conclude that public opinion information from surveys and polls is always politically biased or useless. Despite the challenges of interpreting polls, enough good public opinion data evidently exists to motivate politicians to pay attention and even commission their own

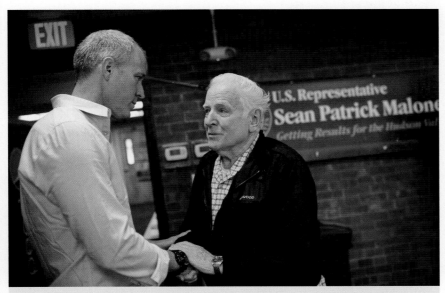

To what extent are governmental policies shaped by public opinion? Elected officials must always be mindful of how the policies they support will be perceived by constituents. However, they may focus on pleasing some constituents more than others. Here, Representative Sean Patrick Maloney (D-NY) meets with a senior citizen at a local town hall meeting.

private polls. But when information about public opinion sends conflicting signals, it grants leaders a certain freedom to make policy decisions based on other grounds. Although the principals (the public) can be difficult to read at times, the agents (people in government) are quite good at treading a middle ground between being responsive and being steadfast over spans of time.

One reason it is difficult to study the connection between public opinion and government action is that survey questions tend to ask about the broad direction of policy, rather than about specific, technical details that are the stuff of much of public policy making. If surveys reveal, for example, that a majority of people want more money to be spent on primary education, how should that money be spent? Should it be for new schools, more teachers, more rigorous curriculum development, or different programs?

Systematically measuring the actions of government poses another problem. If the government only slightly increases funding for primary school education to keep up with inflation, is that conforming to public opinion? Or is it actually just "standing pat" on policy when the public really seems to want a substantial increase? These kinds of measurement decisions for researchers who study public opinion and policy making are crucial to drawing conclusions that link public opinion to policy making.

Nevertheless, researchers have made some progress in measuring the extent to which government policy follows public opinion or leads it. In certain areas, government policy decidedly does not conform to majority opinion. Take the issue of prayer in public schools (see Chapter 4). The federal courts have interpreted the Constitution as forbidding formal prayers, and in some cases even silent prayers, in public schools. Yet public opinion data quite clearly shows that this policy contradicts majority views. When asked in surveys, between 55 and 75 percent of Americans (depending on question wording) support allowing prayer in public schools.

Yet this kind of issue is the exception that seems to prove the rule. On most politically debated policy issues, the government in fact does what the majority wants, at least according to systematic research on the subject. The political scientists Benjamin Page and Robert Shapiro studied public opinion data and policies across many issue areas and found that approximately two-thirds of the time the national government was responsive to public opinion.[42] When public opinion moved in one direction, government policy typically changed to accommodate that shift. Why the government responds to majority opinion on some issues and not on others remains a key question. This too is difficult to answer, but we will gain some insights in later chapters, especially Chapter 11, which focuses on interest groups.

In other research, scholars have studied broad patterns of opinion change that suggest the public has "moods" that make it more or less favorable to government activism in the economy. Scholars have been able to trace the relationship between these moods and actual government policies, and the results are striking. Through careful analysis, they have shown that government policy changes in a liberal or conservative direction on economic policy *after* a public opinion mood change in the same direction. This is further evidence of the overall responsiveness of the national government to public opinion.[43] Some scholars in the area refer to the public as a "sleeping giant" that can wake up at surprising moments and make politicians pay close attention to sharp changes in overall public mood.

As for whether the public is influenced by actions and statements of elites, there are compelling examples from numerous studies to indicate a responsive public. The public is not always movable (maybe even not often movable), but as research into priming and framing (discussed previously) shows, the potential is there. When people receive competing frames, however, and conflicting information or psychological cues, in general they retreat to their predispositions to guide them in what opinions to express and act on. As an example, if a staunchly conservative person hears information from credible

---

[42] Page and Shapiro, *The Rational Public*.

[43] James A. Stimson, Michael B. Mackuen, and Robert S. Erikson, "Dynamic Representation," *American Political Science Review* 89, no. 3 (1995): 545–65.

sources that raising taxes will lead to better schools in her area, she may be inclined to increase her support for higher local tax rates. But if she then hears information from competing credible sources that the money will be wasted on inefficient school bureaucracies, she will likely be inclined to follow her conservative predisposition and express opinions or vote against raising local taxes for schools. In a competition for people's allegiance involving different frames or competing information or cues, predispositions are hard to overcome. Liberals will not be able to sway this voter if conservatives get her ear as well.[44]

In sum, research shows that public opinion frequently, but not always, shapes government policy in the United States, and public opinion in turn has the potential to be shaped by elite rhetoric. To determine when and under what conditions this is true, we need to know more about the actual mechanisms that link public opinion to government policy and the actions of government and media elites. Public opinion is packaged and communicated to politicians by means that are not politically neutral. Interest groups, mass media, and partisan groups can shape the collection and communication of opinions in biased ways that have real consequences on how people in government perceive what the public wants. In later chapters, we will study these other mechanisms—elections, political parties, interest groups, and the mass media—in detail. These institutions provide focused, usable information for those who are most active in the political system as they attempt to respond to the people.

Furthermore, there is no *one* public opinion. Instead, there are multiple publics with different opinions, and politicians struggle all the time with how to be responsive to constituents who organize and present their opinions in packages. In other words, politicians, as the agents, want to make the principals happy, but understanding exactly which principals to focus on is a constant challenge.

To return to our opening story, Congressional actions on gun control should not be ascribed merely as a response to majority sentiment as expressed in public opinion surveys. Rather, the parties were reacting to the advice and political support they received from specific groups within their network of supporters and their own party leadership. Meanwhile, the initial answer to our question is that politicians' behavior does follow public opinion, but mostly in response to broad movements across many issues over relatively long spans of time, or sometimes in response to clear, reasonable, and measurably sharp movements within their bases of support. While Republicans in polls supported background checks after the Newtown killings, in later, more nuanced polls, Republicans questioned trusting the Obama administration to oversee such checks. The potential is there for public opinion to change with

---

[44] Druckman, "Political Preference Formation."

elite priming and framing, and with partisan cues. The mass public is constantly barraged by competing frames and new information and cues, but in general their predispositions (such as partisanship) hold their attitudes mostly in place.

A helpful way to conceptualize the role of public opinion within the American political system is to consider the attitudes of the public as forming a landscape upon which the main actors in the system operate. Features of the landscape make some tasks easier to accomplish and others more difficult. The landscape's basic contours are difficult if not impossible to change and shape. Some parts of the landscape are firm and immutable, while others are soft and can be changed with effort.

Some policies simply will not be possible for the government to pursue, because public opinion is constraining. If the government takes actions that are too much at odds with public opinion, it will ultimately fail unless public opinion changes to conform. The attempted prohibition of liquor production and transport in the early twentieth century offers an excellent example. Prohibition was a failure as a policy because enough people in the general public were adamantly opposed to it and were willing to break the laws associated with it. As a result, enforcement was impossible. The prohibition policy did not fit into the public opinion landscape.

FURTHER READING

★ = Included in *Readings in American Politics*, 5th ed.

★ Campbell, James, *Polarized: Making Sense of a Divided America* (Princeton, NJ: Princeton University Press, 2016). Campbell carefully shows that many more Americans today than in previous decades say they are ideologically either very liberal or very conservative. He argues that these measures from surveys reflect actual changes in American political attitudes with real consequences for politics.

Converse, Philip, "The Nature of Belief Systems in Mass Publics," in *Ideology and Discontent*, ed. D. E. Apter (New York: Free Press, 1964), pp. 206–61. A classic article with survey results indicating that many Americans have little knowledge or understanding of the political system and of electoral choices.

★ Cramer, Katherine, *The Politics of Resentment: Rural Consciousness in Wisconsin and the Rise of Scott Walker* (Chicago: University of Chicago Press, 2016). Drawing on fieldwork in rural Wisconsin, Cramer argues that the political attitudes of rural people, often simplified and sometimes ignored, deserve to be taken seriously. These people may be discounted, but when they find candidates that appeal to them, they make big waves that can roil national and state politics.

Kahneman, Daniel, and Amos Tversky, *Choices, Values, and Frames* (New York: Russell Sage, 2000). A deep analysis of how the framing of decisions affects people's choices.

★ Kinder, Donald, and Cindy Kam, *Us Against Them: Ethnocentric Foundations of American Opinion* (Chicago: University of Chicago Press, 2010). Many people conceive of the political world as comprising ethnic and racial groups that compete with one another, and their political attitudes are shaped by their degree of tolerance toward other groups.

★ Lupia, Arthur, and Mathew McCubbins, *The Democratic Dilemma: Can Citizens Learn What They Need to Know?* (New York: Cambridge University Press, 1998). This book counters the belief that Americans are ignorant about politics, arguing instead that Americans tend to get the information they need when they need it.

★ Zaller, John R., *The Nature and Origins of Mass Opinion* (New York: Cambridge University Press, 1992). A theory of how political attitudes are shaped by the combination of predispositions and new information, lending insight into who changes their attitudes and when.

KEY TERMS

biased sample (p. 336)

framing (p. 349)

ideology (p. 351)

margin of error (p. 336)

non-attitude (p. 361)

party identification (or partisanship) (p. 353)

population (p. 335)

priming (p. 349)

public opinion (p. 330)

push polling (p. 338)

random selection (p. 336)

rationality (p. 346)

sample (p. 336)

Voters wait in line in Maricopa County, Arizona, to cast their ballots in the 2016 Democratic and Republican primary elections. Long lines and other barriers to voting seemed to occur in areas with higher ethnic and racial minority populations.

10

Political Participation

 Why do groups with the greatest interest in changing the status quo have relatively low turnout rates?

On March 22, 2016, Arizona held its Democratic and Republican primaries for the presidential election; Hillary Clinton won the Democratic contest and Donald Trump won the Republican. In the months following, the Arizona primaries elicited heavy criticism, not because of who won but for how the elections were conducted. In the state's largest county, Maricopa, people had to wait for hours to cast their vote,[1] and many faced problems with registration because of mistakes by registrars. People who had been registered as Democrats were erroneously classified as independents. And since in Arizona independents cannot vote in primaries reserved for registered party members, these voters could not participate. While Maricopa County had at least 200 polling stations in 2012 primary elections, there were only 60 in 2016.

Voting rights activists claimed that areas with the longest lines were areas with the highest proportions of racial and ethnic minorities, and many called for Maricopa County recorder Helen Purcell to resign.[2] Meanwhile, the Justice Department requested data from election officials in Maricopa County to investigate what went wrong.[3] The Democratic National Committee initiated lawsuits against Arizona's Secretary of State and Maricopa officials,[4] and the campaigns of both Democratic contenders—Hillary Clinton and Bernie Sanders—agreed to join as plaintiffs.

[1] Ray Stern and Miriam Wasser, "Arizona Voters Brave Long Lines for Presidential Preference Election," *Phoenix New Times*, March 22, 2016, www.phoenixnewtimes.com/news/arizona-voters-brave-long-lines-for-presidential-preference -election-8159491 (accessed 3/30/16).

[2] Yvonne Wingett Sanchez and Caitlin McGlade, "Maricopa County Recorder Helen Purcell Takes Blame for Voter Lines, Says She Won't Resign," *Arizona Republic*, March 23, 2016, www.azcentral.com/story/news/politics/elections/2016/03 /23/maricopa-county-recorder-helen-purcell-admits-fault-long-primary-lines/82165730 (accessed 6/2/16).

[3] Chris Herren, Letter to Helen Purcell, U.S. Department of Justice, Civil Rights Division.

[4] Debbie Wasserman Schultz, "My Turn: Why Democrats Are Suing Arizona over Its Election," *Arizona Republic*, May 6, 2016, www.azcentral.com/story/opinion/op-ed/2016/05/06/arizona-primary-election-lawsuit-democrats/83854264 (accessed 5/31/16). Democratic National Committee, "DNC & DSCC File Joint Lawsuit with Arizona Voters, Arizona Democratic Party & Kirkpatrick for Senate," April 14, 2016, www.democrats.org/Post/dnc-dscc-file-joint-lawsuit-with -arizona-voters-arizona-democratic-party-ki (accessed 6/6/16).

OUTLINE

- Participation and Democratic Politics

- Collective Dilemmas in Participation

- Tallying the Costs and Benefits of Participating

- The Struggles for Voting Rights

- Patterns of Participation in the United States

- In Comparison: Political Participation

- The Crucial Role of Institutions and Mobilization

Was all this a result of poor planning on the part of the Maricopa County recorder? Or was it a calculated attempt to suppress voter turnout?

This story highlights several aspects of political participation. First, participating in politics requires time. For some Arizonians, voting took up to five hours. Second, turnout varies by socioeconomic status. Younger, poorer, and less educated Americans are less likely to vote than other groups. Thus, the voting trouble in Arizona may have disproportionately affected certain kinds of voters. Finally, election laws in the states and at the federal level matter for voter turnout. These laws put in place a set of institutions affecting who participates. For example, there have been recent changes in the enforcement of the Voting Rights Act, which was first approved in 1965 but amended many times and subject to occasional court reviews ever since. Following the Supreme Court's 2013 ruling in *Shelby County v. Holder* suspending a key element of the Act, states no longer need federal approval to alter election laws.[5] The 2016 election was the first in which the implications of the *Shelby County v. Holder* decision could be observed. Some critics of the decision claimed that voting restrictions in key states gave Donald Trump enough of an advantage to win and cost Hillary Clinton the election.

Which political institutions matter the most for turnout? Why are some groups affected more than others? How do the institutions at both the state and national levels change over time and shape political outcomes?

---

[5] *Shelby County v. Holder*, 570 U.S. ___ (2013).

Participation and Democratic Politics

In Chapter 9, we studied the attitudes and preferences of individuals toward government and politics. We now move to studying the participation of people trying to influence government. Our focus in this chapter is on general patterns of **political participation**, including the decision of whether to vote. We will study elections in more detail in Chapter 13.

As we have noted in previous chapters, democracy is based on the principle of **popular sovereignty**—the rule of the people. Citizens in a representative democracy rule by choosing their leaders through popular elections. The legitimacy of such governments depends on the participation of enough citizens at the polls. Voting in general elections serves as the central act of citizenship in modern democracies like the United States. When immigrants become U.S. citizens, the right to vote is heralded as a key element of their new status.

Political participation, however, is not just a matter of voting. It is also understood to include many other actions intended to influence the government, such as

- writing or contacting political representatives;
- attending rallies and protests;
- attending meetings of political organizations;
- writing to newspapers, magazines, or blogs about politics;
- wearing campaign buttons, posting political placards, or displaying political bumper stickers;
- giving money to campaigns and political organizations;
- talking to other people about politics.

The conventional forms of political participation listed here play important roles in determining the way democratic political systems function, because they communicate aspects of public opinion to the government or help people form their own opinions and hone their communication skills to pressure government. Most scholars of democratic politics believe that citizen participation is the lifeblood of a vibrant, democratic society. Diverse opinions are communicated through elections, peaceful mass action, deliberation in small or large groups, and direct contact with government representatives.

Some philosophers and political activists have expressed the view that participation makes individuals more public spirited and thus better citizens. The early democratic theorists Jean-Jacques Rousseau and John Stuart Mill believed that people who participate in politics, even if they are in the minority, more readily accept collective decisions. Moreover, those who participate have a heightened awareness of belonging to a community. Modern researchers have found evidence that people who participate in politics experience joy

political participation Activities citizens undertake to influence government behavior.

popular sovereignty The principle that the authority to make decisions on behalf of society belongs to the people.

in self-expression aimed at improving society. They learn about themselves and about government. They become more engaged with how government affects them and learn how to take advantage of what it has to offer. They acquire valuable skills in navigating government bureaucracy, pressing for change, and organizing others to do so. In short, they experience the full scope of citizenship, to the benefit of both themselves and society.[6]

To establish a successful participatory democracy, simply holding elections is not enough; people must be able to participate and organize freely, without fear. Governments in some countries vigorously repress dissent and citizens' participation, even though they may hold elections. In "democracies" like Iran, Pakistan, and Zimbabwe, citizens are typically intimidated by the government. Although they are allowed to vote, they are afraid to petition political leaders, organize political parties as rivals to the government, or openly express their frustration or anger with government. It is questionable whether such societies have a truly democratic political system. The popular legitimacy of any government depends on tolerance of dissent and criticism, and on freedom of the people to participate in choosing their leaders.

Conventional and Unconventional Participation

Throughout this chapter, we will focus on conventional (and what are generally considered legitimate) participatory acts during ordinary times. This does not include such acts of violence as rioting, vigilantism, terrorism, or insurgency. Although such actions can communicate opinions and preferences to the government and may be rationalized as necessary in extreme situations, they are not typically considered legitimate and do not ordinarily contribute to the functioning of a democratic system. Rather, they are unconventional and can generally be considered illegitimate because they detract from the functioning of a political system and a stable society. Examples would be the killing of doctors who provide abortions or the bombing of abortion clinics, actions that are widely condemned by antiabortion and pro-access to abortion groups alike.

Sit-ins and some kinds of strikes and protests are unconventional, but they represent a gray area between legitimate and illegitimate acts of civil disobedience. The nature of a political regime can lend an air of legitimacy to such acts, especially in retrospect. Consider the sometimes illegal protests of blacks in the South during the civil rights movement in the 1950s and 1960s, or the uprising of gays and lesbians against police raids of gay bars in the 1970s and 1980s. Today, these acts are widely judged to have been legitimate, given the oppression these groups were struggling to overcome. Determining what

[6] See, for example, Carole Pateman, *Participation and Democratic Theory* (New York: Cambridge University Press, 1970); and Robert Putnam, *Making Democracy Work* (Princeton, NJ: Princeton University Press, 1993).

constitutes a legitimate act of political participation can be controversial and often depends on context and timing. Long after the fact, for example, we can judge as legitimate the 1960 sit-ins by students at lunch counters in Greensboro, North Carolina, to protest "whites only" seating at restaurants and other Jim Crow barriers, even though those actions violated local laws, the rules of the local businesses, and local customs. We look back and judge these laws and rules of businesses to be unjust and immoral.

Clearly, the morality of existing laws and practices, and the legitimacy of such unconventional forms of political participation, ranging from one-day work stoppages that might be against the law to the nineteenth-century slave rebellions, are in the eye of the beholder. People who break local laws to block traffic (as environmentalists and antiwar protesters have done) or protest in front of abortion clinics believe they ought to be judged similarly as the sit-in leaders during the civil rights movement. Today, Americans venerate the revolutionaries who fought against the British in the American Revolution, but we note that they waged war against the established regime, and the British clearly believed the colonists' actions to be illegitimate. Regardless, our focus in this chapter is on conventional modes of participation that are generally considered legitimate in a functioning democracy.

Collective Dilemmas in Participation

Political participation presents a set of collective dilemmas. Voting, for example, is a collective action problem with incentives to free ride. Suppose an election for president is coming up. It is costly to vote (in terms of time and trouble), and your vote will almost never matter to the outcome. Therefore the best outcome, in strictly self-interested terms, is for a potential voter to let others vote and free ride off their efforts.

In what is sometimes called the **paradox of voting**, some scholars ask, "Why does anyone ever bother to vote in mass elections?"[7] On presidential Election Day, if you drive or take the bus, or walk anywhere that requires you to cross the street, the probability of a grave accident, though very small, is still much higher than the probability of swaying a national election with your single vote.

Recall that a presidential election consists of 51 separate elections (the 50 states plus Washington, D.C.). What does it mean to say that your vote could ultimately sway the national election? It means that in your state, the vote would have been a tie if you had not voted. That outcome is, of course, extremely unlikely. But compound that small likelihood by the chance that

paradox of voting The notion that people still vote even though the individual costs of voting likely outweigh the individual benefits.

---

[7] See, for example, Anthony Downs, *An Economic Theory of Democracy* (New York: Harper, 1957).

The Paradox of Voting

An individual's "utility" from voting in a general election can be understood as

$$p * B - C$$

p is the probability that an individual's act of voting will influence the outcome of the election.

B is an individual's share of the benefit derived from the election outcome occurring to his or her liking.

C is the costs of voting, including risks of harm, loss of wages, and time taken away from other activities.

Is the value of $p * B - C$ greater than or less than zero? If it is greater than zero, the individual will vote; if it is less than zero, the individual will not vote. The paradox is that, because *p* is typically so small, the costs (*C*) will almost always be larger than $p * B$, and the value will be less than zero—yet large numbers of people still vote.

Source: William Riker and Peter Ordeshook, "A Theory of the Calculus of Voting," *American Political Science Review* 62, no. 1 (1968): 25–42.

your state is the pivotal state in the national election, that by your one vote you swing the vote in your state, and that your state then swings the entire election. It is easy to see that the probability of such an outcome is very close to zero. The probability of your action being pivotal might be higher for local elections than for national elections, but it is still extremely small most of the time.

Given these odds, it may be reasonable to wonder why you should bother to vote when your vote will have a negligible effect on the outcome of the election. But if everyone thought that way no one would vote, and that would be bad for the country. Most people think it is good for a lot of people to vote because it shows their support for the democratic system. Nevertheless, individuals have an incentive to stay home and let others incur the costs.

The information in the Know the Facts box above makes this point more generally. In principle, this kind of calculation can apply to any act of political participation. The real monetary costs of donating to a political campaign, for example, or to an interest group, need to be weighed against other uses of that money. Why give to a political group if your donation will not make much of a difference? Why not let others do it? You could use your money for other things. Why write a letter to members of Congress to express your views on an issue that matters to you? Others will write such letters and yours probably won't matter much, unless you are a figure of importance like the president of a huge corporation, a celebrity, or a leader of a state or local government. If your letter will not matter much, why not spend your time in other ways?

For people who give money or spend time writing letters or attending rallies and protests, the cost of participation could potentially be much higher than that of voting. Why do people attend rallies and protests in authoritarian states, where police may be armed with batons, tear gas, or even live ammunition? The presence of one more or one less protestor is unlikely to affect the outcome. Yet people frequently risk their lives to participate in collective protests against government actions or regimes. In recent times in the United States, protests about race and the police have grown violent and some have died. When protestors have taken to the streets in Iran to rail against the governing regime, they have literally risked death. Many Syrians were killed by government-backed forces when their allegiance to the rebellion against the government became known. Syria's and Iran's governments have executed numerous people in recent years who have participated in or organized protest rallies or rallies in support of rebellion.

These examples focus our attention on the choices people make when faced with the collective action problem inherent in political participation. How large are the potential costs relative to the gain attained through an individual's participation?

Social scientists propose the collective action problem as a way to think about the act of voting and other forms of mass action, not as a suggestion that people ought to free ride. Most people who teach civics and who study political participation strongly encourage individuals to participate in the electoral process (and other conventional kinds of participation). They believe people should resist individual temptation and focus on the collective good engendered by widespread participation. And, of course, tens of millions of people in the United States, and hundreds of millions of people in other democracies around the world, participate in politics and overcome ordinary kinds of collective dilemmas such as those that occur in national elections.

Collective action problems are not the only kinds of dilemmas facing citizens when they consider political participation. They also face persistent coordination problems. Suppose you have decided to write a letter to members of Congress regarding an issue that you care strongly about. It would be most effective if others who share your goals sent letters saying similar things, or sent those letters to the same members of Congress on the same committees. Ideally, people who share views should coordinate their efforts and communicate a focused message. They should also target those communications to the members of Congress who are poised to do something about the issue in their favor. How do people who share the same political goals coordinate if they don't know each other or live in different parts of the country?

As we will see in Chapter 11, interest groups often solve coordination problems as a way to help mobilize people to participate in politics. To take a specific example, Planned Parenthood urged supporters in 2015 to "tell Congress that you stand with Planned Parenthood," providing a template letter for supporters to use. Their intention was to get their members to pressure their representatives in Congress. We see these kinds of communications—solutions to coordination problems, really—all the time in interest group flyers, newsletters, websites, and advertisements. Without this kind of coordination, like-minded people would be less effective in pressuring Congress because their messages would vary and would not target the same, pivotal legislators.

Analyzing participation through the lens of collective dilemmas focuses our attention on the costs and benefits of voting and of participation more generally. It also sheds light on the importance of mobilization, the active attempt by organizations and leaders to encourage people to participate. Mobilization can be seen as the effort both to reduce the costs of participating and to increase the perceived benefits. Let's analyze these costs and benefits in more detail, and discuss how mobilization might affect change.

Tallying the Costs and Benefits of Participating

People vote and participate in politics for many reasons, both individual and social. They feel a sense of duty. They are pressured to vote and participate by friends, family members, or coworkers. They do not want to be embarrassed to admit they did not vote. They want to indicate that they support their group. One way to explain why people vote and participate even when the possible costs appear likely to outweigh the benefits is that people do not always think strictly in terms of their own individual, instrumental benefits. Among the collective benefits of participation is the possibility that your action, in concert with the similar actions of others, could have an impact on government policies. If many members of a group vote and participate in disproportionately high numbers, this may sway government policies in that group's direction. In school board elections at the local level, for example, it is well known that teachers and school administrators turn out in high numbers relative to other groups in the community. Similarly, business owners and executives, highly paid professionals, scientists, community leaders, and other groups have good reason to feel that their participation in politics—especially in the forms of contacting elected officials, organizing campaign contributions, and writing blogs, op-eds, and letters to the editor—has a discernible impact on governmental decisions affecting their well-being.

These may all be valid benefits to consider, but the paradox presented in the Know the Facts box on page 378 exposes a central fact about the cost side of voting (and all forms of political participation): as the costs of participation rise, fewer people will participate because the costs will increasingly outweigh the likely benefits of a favorable outcome, as weighted by the probability that their actions will affect the outcome of the election or the outcome of any political process.

More important for our discussion, which focuses just on voting for the moment, the costs of voting do not have to be high to discourage some people from doing it, and institutional barriers can raise the costs to levels that inhibit voting by certain groups in society. Even minor personal and bureaucratic barriers can dampen participation, especially among those for whom the costs loom large in their lives and the benefits seem remote.

There are costs associated with voting. For example, Americans must register to vote in most elections.

Registering to Vote

U.S. citizens must register to vote, whereas most other nations permit their citizens to vote based simply on whether they are listed as residents and citizens of a town, city, or community. Under the requirements of **voter registration**, Americans who wish to vote must fill out forms and provide personal information to their state government. Citizens used to have to make a special trip to a local office to register. Nowadays, according to federal law, when you apply for a driver's license in your home state, you must be offered the chance to register to vote (called Motor Voter enacted in 1994). And some states now have same-day registration (SDR), which allows people to register at the polls immediately before voting.

The impacts of the Motor Voter law and SDR on voter registration and participation have been studied by political scientists, and their conclusions are mixed. Some scholars have provided evidence that Motor Voter registration has increased participation among those who voted only occasionally. However, the law appears to have done little to increase voting among those who never vote. In other words, even if people who habitually do not vote register when they get their driver's license, they still typically do not go to the polls on Election Day.[8] As for SDR, among states adopting this reform

voter registration A process by which citizens enroll with the government to gain permission to vote in an election.

[8] For a general discussion of how electoral reforms retain voters from election to election without expanding the population of those who participate, see Adam J. Berinsky, "The Perverse Consequences of Electoral Reform in the United States," *American Politics Research* 33, no. 4 (2005): 471–91.

(17 states and Washington, D.C., had done so as of fall 2018), voter turnout has been significantly higher than the average of the other states. But it is a matter of debate whether SDR caused this increase or whether the reform occurred in states with already high turnout rates.[9]

Gathering Information

political knowledge A general understanding of how the political system works, and who runs the government.

As we discussed in Chapter 9, the level of **political knowledge** varies widely within the population, and most people are not well informed. Some people like to follow politics, but most rely on friends or coworkers, or on simple "cues" from news stories or advertisements, to get the information they need to make political choices. Many people pay virtually no attention to politics.

People who habitually do not vote tend to pay little attention to politics. The same is true for people who almost never participate in any way in politics. This pattern raises some interesting questions. Is lack of information the cause or the effect of the failure to participate? Do people who find it too costly to become informed also find it too costly to vote? Do they simply believe that as uninformed people they should not vote? Or do people who do not vote tend to ignore politics because they know they will not participate in the process? These are difficult questions to answer with available data.

This much we do know: becoming informed about politics takes time and effort. Thus, the costs of becoming informed are higher for certain types of people than others. Wealthier and more-educated people know more about politics for a variety of reasons, including their schooling, jobs, and community organizations, and being routinely mobilized.[10] They also systematically follow political news in mass media more than other citizens. Alternatively, for the poor and less educated, becoming knowledgeable about politics often has to happen on their own, and they are not routinely mobilized. The individual costs for becoming informed on average are relatively higher, and they are exacerbated by the tendency of the less educated to choose entertainment over news in mass media. The discrepancies in the extent to which the wealthy and poor are mobilized perpetuate their different levels of participation. When people are mobilized to participate (to vote, attend meetings, and go to rallies) by organizations and personal contacts, they learn about politics, which further spurs them to continue participating in the future. So, if people consider being informed a prerequisite for participation, then the costs of gathering information will dampen participation among those who experience or perceive higher costs in becoming informed, specifically poorer and less-educated citizens.

[9] See www.projectvote.org/wp-content/uploads/2015/06/SameDayFactSheet-PV-Feb2015 (accessed 07/20/15).

[10] See, for example, W. Russell Neuman, *The Paradox of Mass Politics: Knowledge and Opinion in the American Electorate* (Cambridge, MA: Harvard University Press, 1986).

Voting

Casting a ballot is never completely without cost, but the burdens vary depending on the rules and procedures. In the United States, for instance, national Election Day always falls on a Tuesday in November. This day became traditional when the United States was an agrarian society because it was after the harvest season, was not on a Sunday (a holy day for the largely Christian country), and gave people relying on foot or horseback one full day after Sunday to travel to the polls. Voting at all levels and in other months (in primaries, for example) also tends to occur during the week and not on weekends, as in many other countries. For some people, missing work to vote is not a problem, but others might lose wages if they are paid hourly, or they might work in remote locations that make it difficult for them to get back to their polling place to vote.

States, moreover, can impose various rules at the polls that make it harder or easier to vote on Election Day. Some aspects of voting have become easier. We already discussed same-day registration (SDR). Casting absentee ballots has become widespread in recent elections as more people travel for work, and the military has pressed Congress to make it easier to allow troops overseas to vote. New voting machines, especially since the controversy surrounding the 2000 presidential election in Florida (see Chapter 8), have reportedly been easier to use than older machines.

Following the 2000 presidential election, Congress acted to help the states administer elections more effectively. The **Help America Vote Act of 2002** was intended to spur states to adopt electronic voting machines and to make it easier to vote in general. States could apply for federal funding to modernize much of their equipment at the polls, including purchasing or renting more accurate machines. This legislation has had at least one perverse effect. States have reduced the number of voting precincts by almost 40 percent because of the costs of updating voting equipment. Fewer precincts means fewer machines to buy and lower costs for the states, even with federal funding assistance. It also means that, as compared with the early 2000s, people now have fewer places to vote on Election Day, longer lines, and less convenient polling locations. In the 2016 national election, many voters, especially in large cities, complained about long voting lines.

Voting by mail is now permitted and even encouraged in a number of states, including Oregon, Washington, and Colorado. As with other reforms discussed earlier, the evidence on whether voting by mail leads to higher turnout is mixed. Early research suggested that voting by mail has increased turnout and encouraged people to become regular voters. It seemed that voting by mail lowered the costs of voting for enough people to make a difference. More recent research has questioned these findings and indicated that voting by mail has little to no effect on federal election turnout, but it can

Help America Vote Act of 2002 A federal law meant to reduce barriers to participation in elections.

vote by mail A program in many states that allows voters to mail in their ballots rather than appearing in person at a polling place.

Know the FACTS — Voting and Democracy

Democracy is based on the principle of popular sovereignty, meaning the people rule. In practice, the people generally do not make government decisions directly but instead elect leaders by voting in elections. Several factors may limit who participates through voting.

- **Formal barriers can limit voting.**
  - In most cases, an individual must be registered to vote.
  - For much of American history, women, nonwhites, and poor people without property were prevented from participating in elections.
  - Today, there are still some limits on who can vote. For example, many states bar convicted felons from voting. Americans under the age of 18 cannot vote.
  - Only citizens may vote, so immigrants who have not achieved citizen status cannot participate in elections.

- **There are costs associated with voting.**
  - Individuals may lack information about where and how to vote.
  - Individuals may lack information about which policies or candidates will best serve their interests.
  - Polls are typically open for only a few hours after regular work hours, which makes voting costly for those who cannot take time off to vote.

- **Electoral reforms and voter mobilization efforts are often aimed at removing barriers and minimizing the costs associated with voting.**
  - Civic organizations play a critical role in mobilizing citizens to participate in politics.
  - Older people are more likely to belong to these groups, and they participate in elections and politics at relatively high rates.
  - Young people are less likely to belong to a civic organization and are relatively less likely to vote or participate in politics.

boost participation in local elections that typically have low turnout.[11] Note that voting by mail can potentially increase turnout only among those who have already registered to vote; it can have no direct effect on people who have not registered, because ballots are mailed only to registered voters.[12]

The Help America Vote Act also permitted states to adopt antifraud measures that might not have been allowed under previous law. States increas-

---

[11] Kevin Arceneaux, Thad Kousser, and Megan Mullin, "Get Out the Vote-by-Mail? A Randomized Field Experiment Testing the Effect of Mobilization in Traditional and Vote-by-Mail Precincts," *Political Research Quarterly* 65 (2012): 882–94; and Thad Kousser and Megan Mullin, "Does Voting by Mail Increase Participation? Using Matching to Analyze a Natural Experiment," *Political Analysis* 15 (2007): 428–45.

[12] Adam J. Berinsky, Nancy Burns, and Michael W. Traugott, "Who Votes by Mail? A Dynamic Model of the Individual-Level Consequences of Voting-by-Mail Systems," *Public Opinion Quarterly* 65, no. 2 (2001): 178–97.

ingly require citizens to show proof of citizenship and identity in the form of a photo ID, passport, or birth certificate. The trend toward stronger anti-fraud measures tends to create an obstacle for those who do not drive or are elderly and may have difficulty finding their birth certificate. We discuss some of these measures again later.

Participation beyond Voting

The costs and benefits of participating in politics in other ways than voting vary from person to person and from one type of participation to another. Depending on a person's life circumstances, spending money or time tallies differently. People with plenty of money of course find it easier to donate money to political campaigns, organizations, and causes. So the difficulty of donating $100 to a candidate is lower for the rich than for the poor. As a percentage of income, spending that $100 is more "costly" for people the less money they have.

We discussed earlier in the context of political knowledge how costs and benefits fall differently on people. Similar patterns occur regarding time and skills. The following types of people, for instance, find it less difficult (and more beneficial) than the average person to contact elected officials directly through email, letters, personal visits, and petitions:

- Highly educated people
- People who write and fill out forms as a regular part of their job—that is, people in generally higher-paying jobs, as opposed to those who work mostly with their hands
- People who tend to join organizations or who are in leadership positions within organizations
- People who have experience communicating with public officials

On this last factor in particular (experience), note how the elderly might incur less "cost" in communicating with public officials compared with younger people simply because they have lived longer and have had more opportunities. Those who are more educated and wealthier may be more likely to attend the meetings of political organizations in part because they are more likely to make beneficial business contacts through such participatory actions. Who, for instance, would reap more benefits from regularly attending meetings of a local chapter of an environmental group—someone who owns her own business selling advertising for small businesses in the area, or someone who works in a factory piecing together components for television sets? The former will see political participation in such an organization not only as a good thing to do but also as a potential benefit for her business. She could get to know people who might become clients and buy her

The Collective Dilemma

Citizens in a democracy influence the government through political participation, especially by voting. However, some groups of citizens—for example, young adults, the poor, and racial and ethnic minorities—are less likely to vote than others, meaning that they have less of a say in government. Why do groups with the greatest interest in changing the status quo have relatively low turnout rates?

Interests

Different groups in society—categorized, for example, by age, economic status, immigration status, religion, and gender—can expect distinct benefits from the government. The poor and unemployed often rely on government assistance to support themselves. Students need loans to go to college. Religious people rely on tax exemptions to financially support their churches, synagogues, and mosques. Women, especially those raising children alone, rely on tax credits and exemptions for child care costs. And foreign-born citizens having difficulty finding jobs because of their accents and cultural ways need governmental assistance and publicly funded education.

Age is especially relevant when it comes to the likelihood of receiving government benefits. A typical 20-year-old in the United States might live for another 60 years or more and experience many years of potential benefits, while a typical 70-year-old might live for only another decade or so.

Different groups in society all rely on the government to some extent, and they each have a stake in making their collective voices heard in shaping government policy. But compared to other groups in society, the ones who need the government the most to live and even thrive are younger, poorer, and less stably employed or recent immigrants.

Institutions

As discussed toward the end of this chapter, mobilization of the poorer, younger, and minority voters is less successful and often less attempted by organizations than mobilization of the older, wealthier, and more stably employed. Certainly, the institutions that conduct mobilization drives find it more worthwhile to target groups that have stable incomes and residences (homeowners) and have experience with political participation, such as older people.

Of similar importance to these mobilization efforts by groups outside the government are laws and regulations governing voter registration and the act of voting. Take, for instance, the simple fact that a person must register to vote before casting a ballot. Combine that with rules regulating how long a person must live at a specific address before being able to register to vote in that locality's elections; some states have only a 10-day requirement while others have 30 days. For someone who moves often, these rules make it more costly in personal time to cast a ballot compared to someone who lived in the same location for a long time. People must register at each place they move, and young voting-age people undoubtedly move more often than older people; likewise, people with unstable jobs move more often, either because of eviction or in search of employment.

In addition to voter registration requirements, states have various rules for showing voter identification at polling stations, either for confirming a registration if the person has not voted in recent elections or for filling out forms to vote absentee or by mail. Each of these rules has an effect on the types of people who feel it is

Voter Turnout

worthwhile to take the time to register to vote. Scholars generally agree that these rules disproportionately burden people who are younger, poorer, less stably employed, recent citizen immigrants, and renters (compared to homeowners).

Outcomes

Voter turnout in the 2012 and 2016 elections dipped slightly from 2008. The high point in turnout in recent years came in 2008, especially among young people. In the 2008 presidential election, voter turnout among 18- to 24-year-olds reached its highest level since 1972. As shown in the figure on the right, 44 percent of eligible voters in this age group went to the polls, nearly 15 percentage points higher than in 2000. In a typical presidential election, 35 to 45 percent of all eligible voters in this age group vote, and evidence shows that only 43 percent voted in the 2016 election. These numbers stand in stark contrast to other age groups, especially the elderly. In 2016, evidence suggests that over 70 percent of those age 65 and older turned out to vote, roughly consistent with previous elections.

The patterns here need an explanation. Citizens in a democracy wield power through political participation, especially by voting—but some groups of citizens are less likely to vote than others. Besides age, we know that income, race and ethnicity, and education correlate with voter turnout. Wealthier and more educated people vote in higher proportions than poorer and less educated people. Northerners vote in higher proportions than southerners. Whites and African Americans vote in higher proportions than Latinos. And Jews vote in higher proportions than Catholics and Protestants. Many people who belong to groups that would seem to have the most to gain from changing the status quo—the poor, the young, racial and ethnic minorities, for

Voter Turnout by Age in Presidential Elections, 1972–2016

Source: U.S. Census Bureau, Voting and Registration, Historical Time Series Tables, Table A-9, www.census.gov (accessed 11/13/18).

instance—turn out to vote in lower numbers than other citizens.

Think About It

Demographic groups vary in terms of how they participate in politics. Why, generally, do the groups with the greatest interest in changing the status quo have lower turnout rates? What explains this disparity?

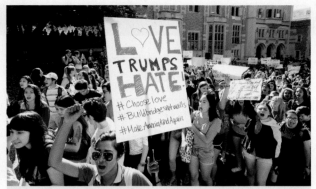
Political participation comes in many forms, including mass demonstrations and rallies.

advertising services. Small business owners, professionals, and entrepreneurs especially benefit from participating in local meetings because they can make personal contacts and market their services and products.

These examples help us to see how analyzing costs and benefits can help explain patterns in participation. We see a general pattern of costs and benefits falling favorably on those who are already advantaged in society. In other words, the individual costs are smaller and individual benefits potentially bigger for wealthier, more-educated people. Exceptions to the general pattern, however, can be seen in the acts of protesting or rallying. Largely because a major portion of protests and rallies in the United States are organized by labor unions in the form of strikes or walkouts, the costs of participating are somewhat equalized across different income groups in society. Labor unions substantially reduce the costs for unionized workers to learn about politics and to know how to participate to effect change. Working-class people, especially those in unionized jobs, have many opportunities to join in these kinds of collective efforts. Note, however, that these costs are not lowered for the poorest members of society—the unemployed and those in the lowest-wage, nonunionized jobs.

Social media and websites help people communicate easily about potential political action. Some people believe that the widespread availability of social media and handheld communication devices has lowered the costs of communicating so much that inequalities in participation might go away. Anyone can communicate rapidly with others and receive information about participation options. It no longer takes expensive organizations to mobilize people. The potential has been evident in the Syrian civil war,[13] for example. The availability of these means of communication allows organizers to communicate even though their governments might crack down on other forms of news dissemination. The Internet, they argue, has altered costs and benefits. This argument relies on the idea that the participation of people on the Internet and on phones is fundamentally different from, or has different effects than, more traditional, nonelectronic forms of participation.

Other arguments leading to the opposite conclusion fall along two lines. First, we know that social media is also available to the government and other

[13] Derek O'Callaghan, Nico Prucha, Derek Greene, Maura Conway, Joe Carthy, and Pádraig Cunningham, "Online Social Media in the Syria Conflict: Encompassing the Extremes and In-Betweens," arXiv (August 13, 2014): 1401.7535v3.

powerful institutions to monitor and possibly suppress dissent. We see in many countries, including Russia and China, the use of social media to harass people who dissent from government policy. Sometimes that harassment is government sponsored and sometimes not. Second, social media and the ability to express oneself easily through blogs and websites possibly has made people more passive and less willing to participate in actions in person.

A somewhat amusing term, "slacktivist," arose in the early 2000s to indicate someone who does not usually leave the home or apartment and whose political activism consists of posting politically charged items on social media platforms and hoping for the items to go viral. The term is meant to make fun, but note that throughout American history there is a proud tradition of writers, journalists, and activists using their written words to try to influence people. If anything is novel about this aspect of participation since the 1990s, it is simply the widespread availability of this option as a means of participating in politics. It is unclear whether fewer people participate *in person* in all aspects of politics post-1990s, in comparison to pre-1990s, due to existence of the Internet and social media.[14]

How people live, what kinds of jobs they have, and what resources they have affect whether they accept the costs of voting and other forms of participation as so minor that they participate anyway, or as so significant that they are discouraged from participating. But people who either are not allowed to participate or are discouraged from participating can overcome their collective dilemmas and push for change. Let's now consider struggles for equality of opportunity in political participation.

The Struggles for Voting Rights

Voting is the most fundamental participatory act in any democracy. The right to vote, also known as **the franchise (or suffrage)**, was denied to many types of people from the very beginning of the United States. Gradually, however, the country extended the franchise to the point where today virtually all American adults are eligible to vote.

the franchise (or suffrage)
The right to vote.

Restricting the Right to Vote

Democracies all over the world set boundaries on who can and cannot vote. Most advanced democracies allow citizens to vote by age 18 and have few

[14] Pippa Norris, "The Impact of the Internet on Political Activism: Evidence from Europe," *International Journal of Electronic Government Research* 1, no. 1 (2005): 19–39; W. Lance Bennett, Christian Breunig, and Terri Givens, "Communication and Political Mobilization: Digital Media and the Organization of Anti-Iraq War Demonstrations in the U.S.," *Political Communication* 25, no. 3 (2008): 269–89.

restrictions beyond that. In the American political system, the states formally control the franchise, but they must conform to federal law and the Constitution. States typically restrict voting to citizens who have resided in the state for a certain number of months—a common threshold is three months. States vary when it comes to extending voting rights to former prisoners with felony records and to those with mental illness. Voting restrictions based on mental capacities, criminal record, and residency have been deemed constitutional by courts, and the diversity of laws across states is widely acknowledged and accepted as complying with current constitutional law. Many laws affecting turnout were instituted during the Progressive Era in response to abuses by the political parties and candidate organizations that committed fraud or intimidated citizens. There is a long history of questionable election practices in the United States, especially in the nineteenth century.

Voting is subject to subtle restrictions that are considered questionable by the courts and affected groups. Certain laws and their implementation can indirectly disenfranchise specific population groups, or at least raise their costs of voting. Some restrictions are devised by local political parties, candidate organizations, or government officials with the obvious intent of limiting the franchise. Southern states in the twentieth century, for example, required that people registering to vote pay a poll tax or pass a literacy test. At the local level, these measures were implemented unevenly, and registrars required them more often of blacks than of whites. Even if they were implemented evenly, their effects fell disproportionately on blacks because of their poverty and lower educational status relative to whites in the South at the time.

Most of these kinds of restrictions were ultimately abolished by legislatures and the courts. The key legal change was the **Voting Rights Act of 1965**, which devised a wide-ranging set of federal protections of voting rights for minorities, especially in the South. Until 2013, due to their history of disenfranchising specific groups, parts of the South were designated as areas of special scrutiny by the U.S. Justice Department. The Justice Department was empowered to monitor and enforce equal voting rights for racial minorities in these areas. The Supreme Court in 2013 struck down continued application of the Voting Rights Act to these specific areas, but the Court invited Congress to use contemporary information to identify the targeted areas.

Some barriers are less obvious than poll taxes or literacy tests and may not be deliberate, yet they still result in unequal access to voting. In many states, for example, precincts in poorer neighborhoods have fewer voting machines and less up-to-date technologies for voting. This could be intentional, or it could be a result of more benign policy choices such as concluding that more and better voting technology is needed less in those neighborhoods where voter turnout tends to be lower. Whatever the motivation, the result is often that lines for voting are longer in poorer neighborhoods than in wealthier ones, and this may discourage some citizens from going to the polls.

Voting Rights Act of 1965
A federal law that made it a priority of the national government to enforce provisions of the Fourteenth and Fifteenth Amendments, leading to major improvements in voting rights for blacks, other minorities, and the poor.

In voting rights cases, the courts attempt to determine whether a given action by a local or state government should be struck down on constitutional grounds. If a state or local government designs and implements a system for voting that restricts the right to vote for minority groups that have been historically disenfranchised or underrepresented in government, then federal courts usually rule against the state or local government.

As we saw in Arizona in the opening story, in recent years, there has been intense controversy over the implementation of voter ID requirements at the polls. The laws, passed in some form by most states, require that voters present a government-issued photo identification to prove their identity and eligibility. The battles over these laws are occurring in state legislatures and state and federal courts, and they engender heated public debate. People disagree over whether this is a legitimate reform to combat voter fraud or an attempt to suppress turnout among population groups that are less likely to have ID or intimidated about showing ID. The federal courts have generally allowed the laws to exist at the state level, but permit the U.S. Justice Department to monitor how they are implemented.

Challenges to Reforms Intended to Increase Turnout

Some groups have been denied voting rights because others hold deep prejudices against them or find it politically advantageous to restrict the franchise. The Founders generally believed that only white male property owners, who (in their view) could be trusted to take the common good into account, should be eligible to vote. Racism and xenophobia led people to support restrictions on voting by blacks, Catholics, Mormons, Jews, and immigrants. Many people, including some women, argued that women should not be eligible to vote because they were inherently less intelligent than men. These prejudices have been, and continue to be, widespread in some parts of the world. They have often bolstered the case for restrictions on voting.

Overcoming such restrictions is complicated by the self-interest of incumbent politicians. Extending the franchise can be difficult because it typically requires the support of politicians who attained office when the restrictions were in place. When officials elected under one set of rules are asked to consider changing those rules to admit a new set of voters into the electoral process, they naturally tend to resist. The incumbent politician is likely to think, "Why rock the boat? Why not preserve the status quo? After all, the existing electorate elected me, so why should I take the risk and allow a new set of people to vote?"

When it comes to reforming voting rules, prejudices and self-interest often go hand in hand. For example, even after the Fifteenth Amendment stated in 1870 that voting rights could not be denied on the basis of race, white politicians in the South continued to resist removing the barriers that disenfranchised African Americans until the 1960s. Politicians elected in the South during this period used arguments about the inferiority of blacks as justification for withholding their voting rights. The politicians' self-interest in maintaining the status quo and their belief in racial inferiority caused them to restrict voting rights for blacks. Proponents of women's right to vote encountered similarly stiff resistance. They had to convince male lawmakers that it was right and just, as well as politically wise, to extend the franchise to women. It took more than seven decades for women to win the right to vote. The struggle began in earnest in the 1850s, when the argument for women's suffrage was linked to the abolition of slavery, and concluded with the passage of the Nineteenth Amendment in 1920.

Today it is common for the two major parties to disagree over proposed reforms that might affect the costs of voting. Republican candidates tend to attract voters on the higher end of the scale for income and wealth, while Democrats tend to attract voters at the lower end. Not surprisingly, Democrat-sponsored reforms aimed at making it easier to vote or to register to vote are frequently opposed by Republicans. Making it easier to register or to vote tends to boost turnout among those who are less inclined to turn out—that is, those lower down the income and wealth scale. This would likely increase support for Democrats, or so goes the thinking of many Republicans. Republicans often claim that making it too easy to vote invites fraud and have even proposed making it somewhat harder to vote, or at least harder to satisfy the requirements to be eligible to vote. Thus the conflict over voter ID laws continues. Not surprisingly, when introduced, these bills have typically been supported by Republicans and opposed by Democrats. Eric Holder, Obama's previous attorney general, compared such laws to the poll taxes of previous eras. The courts have generally upheld such laws, though some state supreme courts have recently overturned a few voter ID laws, and the Obama administration challenged laws in Texas, South Carolina, North Carolina, Ohio, and Wisconsin under the Voting Rights Act and the Fourteenth Amendment. Federal courts have issued conflicting opinions on specific instances, but as mentioned, states are permitted to have these laws if implemented in a way consistent with certain guidelines.

Removing Barriers to Voting

By the 1840s, nearly all the states had removed the requirement that only property owners could vote and had extended the franchise to all (white) free men. This was mostly because budding political parties—the Jacksonian Democrats and the Whigs—were in fierce competition and hungry to appeal to a new set of voters. Religious barriers took longer to dismantle. Even though Article VI of the U.S. Constitution states that "no religious Test shall ever be required as a Qualification to any Office or public Trust under the United States," Catholics were not allowed to vote or hold office in many states in the late eighteenth century, and Jews earned the right to vote in

Maryland only in 1828. Yet by the 1860s, the United States had the most expansive franchise in the world, meaning that larger percentages of the male population were allowed to vote than anywhere else.

After the Civil War, all African Americans were formally enfranchised by the Fifteenth Amendment (1870), which states: "The right of citizens of the United States to vote shall not be denied or abridged by the United States or by any State on account of race, color, or previous condition of servitude." Nevertheless, for more than 90 years many southern states continued to deny blacks their voting rights through intimidation and various legal and illegal barriers. In 1940, the state of Louisiana reported that 886 "colored" people had registered to vote, out of a population of 473,000 blacks in the state. Numbers in Mississippi, South Carolina, and Alabama were similar. Many whites were also effectively disenfranchised by some of these restrictions—voter turnout rates in the South were around 10 percent in some years—but blacks were denied more comprehensively based strictly on the color of their skin.[15]

Women were denied the right to vote in many states until the passage of the Nineteenth Amendment. From the mid-nineteenth century until the passage of the amendment in 1920, women's suffrage groups argued for this right.

Throughout the twentieth century, the franchise expanded through mass mobilization, court decisions, constitutional amendment, and the actions of the national government. As noted earlier, women were granted the right to vote in all federal and state elections upon passage of the Nineteenth Amendment (1920). The Voting Rights Act of 1965 made it a priority of the national government to enforce provisions of the Fourteenth and Fifteenth Amendments. Amendments to the act in 1970, 1975, and 1982 largely removed the barriers to voting that had disproportionately disenfranchised blacks in the South. While the Supreme Court in 2013 struck down specific parts of the Voting Rights Act, arguing that aspects of it were no longer relevant, in general, the Court's interpretations of the act and the Fourteenth Amendment (specifically the equal protection clause) have led to major improvements in voting rights for blacks, other minorities, and the poor. Today, voting rates among blacks across the country largely match those of other racial groups.

Group Struggles

Throughout American history, disenfranchised citizens have fought hard through the legal system, collective action, and political pressure on lawmakers to change the rules and allow new groups of people to vote. The legal

[15] V. O. Key, *Southern Politics in State and Nation* (New York: Knopf, 1949), p. 519.

foundation for opening the franchise could not have been established without group struggle. In the late 1960s, for example, college students in California launched a campaign called "Let Us Vote," or "LUV," to lower the minimum legal voting age from 21 to 18. The movement appealed to citizens of all ages and earned the support of such mainstream organizations as the League of Women Voters and the American Legion. Responding to public opinion and student pressure, Congress passed a law that mandated voting rights for 18- to 20-year-olds in all federal elections beginning in 1970. The Supreme Court, however, delivered a setback to this legislation, ruling that states had the right to set their own voting-age restrictions as long as they conformed to the Fourteenth Amendment, which mandated voting rights at age 21 for all elections, including state and local contests. This led to a bizarre situation in which some states were not coordinating effectively with the national government. Many young people on Election Day in 1970 had to be given separate ballots because they were permitted to vote only for the federal offices.

Congress quickly solved this coordination problem in March 1971 by passing a constitutional amendment that took just two months and seven days for 38 states to ratify (the shortest ratification time on record). The

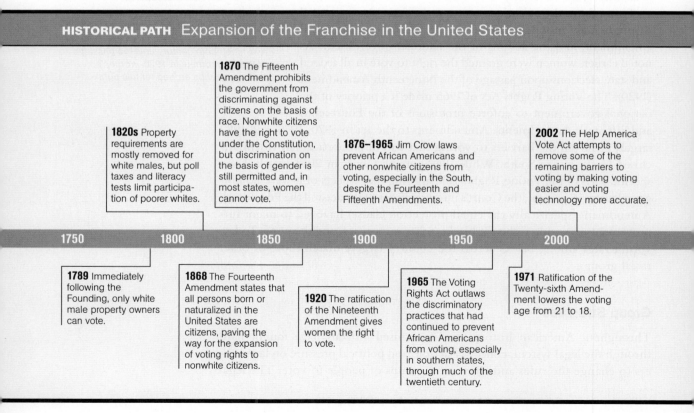

HISTORICAL PATH Expansion of the Franchise in the United States

1870 The Fifteenth Amendment prohibits the government from discriminating against citizens on the basis of race. Nonwhite citizens have the right to vote under the Constitution, but discrimination on the basis of gender is still permitted and, in most states, women cannot vote.

1820s Property requirements are mostly removed for white males, but poll taxes and literacy tests limit participation of poorer whites.

1876–1965 Jim Crow laws prevent African Americans and other nonwhite citizens from voting, especially in the South, despite the Fourteenth and Fifteenth Amendments.

2002 The Help America Vote Act attempts to remove some of the remaining barriers to voting by making voting easier and voting technology more accurate.

1750   1800   1850   1900   1950   2000

1789 Immediately following the Founding, only white male property owners can vote.

1868 The Fourteenth Amendment states that all persons born or naturalized in the United States are citizens, paving the way for the expansion of voting rights to nonwhite citizens.

1920 The ratification of the Nineteenth Amendment gives women the right to vote.

1965 The Voting Rights Act outlaws the discriminatory practices that had continued to prevent African Americans from voting, especially in southern states, through much of the twentieth century.

1971 Ratification of the Twenty-sixth Amendment lowers the voting age from 21 to 18.

Twenty-sixth Amendment mandated that people 18 years of age and older had the right to vote in federal, state, and local elections, thus coordinating voting ages among all the states and the federal government.

The students' activism paid dividends for future generations; they overcame their collective dilemmas to produce a public good (a protected right to vote for millions). Moreover, they acted at an opportune time. Politicians in both major parties realized that it looked good to be on record as supporting the lower voting age. They also calculated that giving 18- to 20-year-olds the right to vote would help them win future elections. It is important to note the two stages of participation at work here. People first had to participate in politics—mass action, protests, organizing, pressuring policy makers—to earn the second, more regular form of political participation: the opportunity to vote.

Patterns of Participation in the United States

Much like the study of public opinion, the study of political participation is quite advanced in the social sciences. Surveys reveal broad patterns of participation: what types of people tend to participate, how often they participate, and how participation compares over time and across countries. Much of this research focuses on voting habits, but we will also look at other forms of participation.

Trends in Voter Turnout

In the nineteenth century, American political parties and other organized movements expended massive efforts to turn out voters on Election Day. **Voter turnout**, as a percentage of those eligible to vote, reached a historic high at the end of the nineteenth century. Figure 10.1 shows a precipitous decline in participation levels in the early twentieth century, a pattern of ups and downs in the ensuing decades, and another steep drop in the 1960s and 1970s.[16]

voter turnout The proportion of potential voters who vote in a given election.

Part of the decline is attributable to the new groups that became eligible to vote but did not participate immediately in large numbers, causing the percentage of eligible voters who actually voted to drop even when more people were going to the polls. These newly enfranchised groups included women, immigrants who became citizens, southern blacks, and 18- to 20-year-olds. Between 1890 and 1920, some of the decline can be attributed to the increasingly effective denial of voting rights to African Americans in the South. In the latter half

[16] This discussion, including Figure 10.2, refers to the percentage of the voting-*eligible* population (VEP), counting only those citizens who are eligible to vote as the base. Slightly different percentages may be obtained if turnout is calculated as a percentage of the voting-*age* population (VAP), which counts all people of voting age as the base.

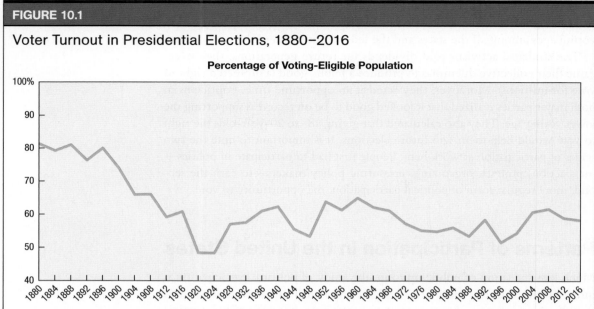

FIGURE 10.1

Voter Turnout in Presidential Elections, 1880–2016

Percentage of Voting-Eligible Population

Sources: For years before 1920, data are from Walter Dean Burnham, *Voting in American Elections* (Bethesda, MD: Academica Press, 2010). For years after 1920, data are from the United States Election Project, www.electproject.org/national-1789-present (accessed 11/15/16).

voter mobilization Efforts by organizations to facilitate or encourage voting.

of the twentieth century, the decline can also be linked to a falling off in **voter mobilization** efforts by political parties and other organizations.[17]

Recent years, however, have seen an overall rise and then decline in turnout in presidential elections. The major political parties have begun to conduct large-scale efforts, especially in key states like Ohio and Florida, to mobilize people who do not ordinarily vote. It is estimated that in Ohio, 600,000 more people voted in the 2004 presidential election than in 2000, thanks largely to the intense mobilization efforts of both parties (but primarily the Republicans). Moreover, there was an 11 percent increase between 2000 and 2004 in nationwide voter turnout in presidential elections, and another 2.5 percent increase between 2004 and 2008. There was a slight dip in national turnout in 2012 and another dip in 2016. Turnout in Ohio, meanwhile, was slightly lower in 2012 compared to 2008, but dropped substantially in 2016 (by 550,000 votes between 2012 and 2016).

Elections for the presidency and Congress have been extremely competitive since 2000. Margins of victory were small in the 2000 election in many races, which may help explain the upturn in voter participation in 2004. The 2016

[17] For one consideration of the participation of newly enfranchised groups, see J. Kevin Corder and Christina Wolbrecht, "Political Context and the Turnout of New Women Voters after Suffrage," *Journal of Politics* 68, no. 1 (2006): 34–49. For a treatment of the role of changing mobilization efforts, see Steven J. Rosenstone and John Mark Hansen, *Mobilization, Participation, and Democracy in America* (New York: Longman, 1993).

presidential election was extremely close nationally and state-level contests in key states were tight. Control of the Senate between the Republicans and Democrats hung in the balance for some time due to several states with very small margins between candidates.

Turnout for the 2016 presidential election was down, the likely reason being the unpopularity of both major candidates. However, research conducted on congressional elections shows that more competitive races tend to lead to increased turnout. If the races are expected to be close, then at least three related patterns emerge:

- Voters might believe their votes actually matter.

- Political organizations might expend greater effort to turn out voters because of heightened competition.

- The sense of drama causes the media to cover the race more closely, making it easier for people to get information and become excited about the race.

Two economists studying this phenomenon have analyzed data on different types of American elections and concluded that a 1 percent change in the predicted closeness of an election (toward a tied outcome) stimulated efforts by campaign organizations to mobilize more voters, leading to an average increase in turnout of 0.34 percent.[18]

The Demographics of Participation

In analyzing who participates and why, it is important to focus not only on the costs and benefits of participation generally but also on how different people respond to these costs and benefits. As noted earlier, the costs of political participation fall hardest on those who face other disadvantages in society, such as the poor, the unemployed, the least educated, and those whose English-language skills are weak. Wealthier, more-educated people tend to enjoy the lowest costs and the most benefits from participating.

Socioeconomic Status and Participation. Differences in the costs and benefits of voting go far back in American history. Consider this description of the act of voting just after the Founding in 1788:

> Voting . . . may require a lengthy ride from the farm to the county seat and back. Many . . . will be deprived of suffrage "by the necessity of traveling nearly fifty miles, passing over many mountains and cross many watercourses (frequently so high at the time of holding elections as to make it dangerous to pass the same)." Having reached the polling place, you may find it open or you may not: the length of the election (one to

---

[18] Ron Shachar and Barry Nalebuff, "Follow the Leader: Theory and Evidence on Political Participation," *American Economic Review* 89, no. 3 (1999): 525–47.

four days in Virginia) and the hours when the polls are open fluctuate according to the sheriff's humor and inclinations.[19]

Who would travel this far and be away from home for so long? Those who could afford to take time away from their work, those with healthy horses to transport them, or those with money to pay others to transport them. Among the landholding class eligible to vote, those near the top of the heap faced the fewest barriers. It is not so difficult to get to the polls today, but the costs of voting still fall differently across groups in the population.

socioeconomic status (SES) A measure of the way that individuals are regarded within a society by virtue of their wealth, income, education, and profession.

To help understand who is advantaged and disadvantaged in society, social scientists employ the concept of **socioeconomic status (SES)**—the relative degree of status persons enjoy in society by virtue of their wealth, income, education, and profession. The distribution of SES in the United States looks similar to that in other advanced industrial societies in Europe and Asia. Most people are middle class or below, and a smaller proportion earn high incomes and have advanced educational degrees. Studies dating back to the 1950s clearly show that the higher a person's SES, the more likely he or she is to be engaged in politics, to vote, and to join political organizations. In the language of social science, higher SES among people correlates positively with higher probabilities of voting and other kinds of political participation. This finding of class bias among those who turn out to vote, contact elected officials, donate money to campaigns and political parties, openly communicate their political views, and talk politics is robust and has changed little in the United States over the last 60 years.[20]

Studies of voting patterns in the United States have shown that educational status matters more than economic status in predicting voter turnout.[21] In other words, the key factor driving voter turnout is education; controlling for other factors such as wealth, income, race, region, and age, more-educated people turn out to vote more often than less-educated people.

Other Factors. Looking beyond SES and voting, we discover other factors that correlate with participation. Figure 10.2 shows patterns across different kinds of political participation (self-reported by survey respondents). We see, for example, that voting among Hispanics is lower than other racial or ethnic groups. This disparity is not surprising, given the language barriers that many immigrants in the Hispanic community face and their on average lower SES. The data on participation for African Americans is revealing, however. Studies have shown that African Americans tend to be mobilized quite effectively by

---

[19] Neil Spitzer, "The First Election," *The Atlantic* (November 1988): 18–19.

[20] See, for example, Sidney Verba and Norman H. Nie, *Participation in America* (New York: Harper & Row, 1972); or, more recently, Joe Soss and Lawrence R. Jacobs, "The Place of Inequality: Non-Participation in the American Polity," *Political Science Quarterly* 124, no. 1 (2009): 95–125.

[21] Raymond E. Wolfinger and Steven J. Rosenstone, *Who Votes?* (New Haven, CT: Yale University Press, 1980).

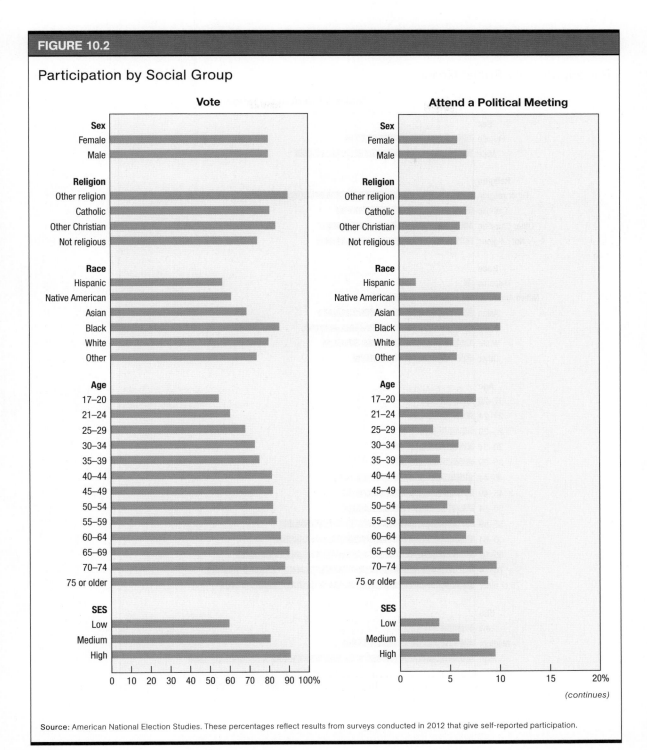

FIGURE 10.2

Participation by Social Group

Source: American National Election Studies. These percentages reflect results from surveys conducted in 2012 that give self-reported participation.

(continues)

FIGURE 10.2 (cont.)

Participation by Social Group

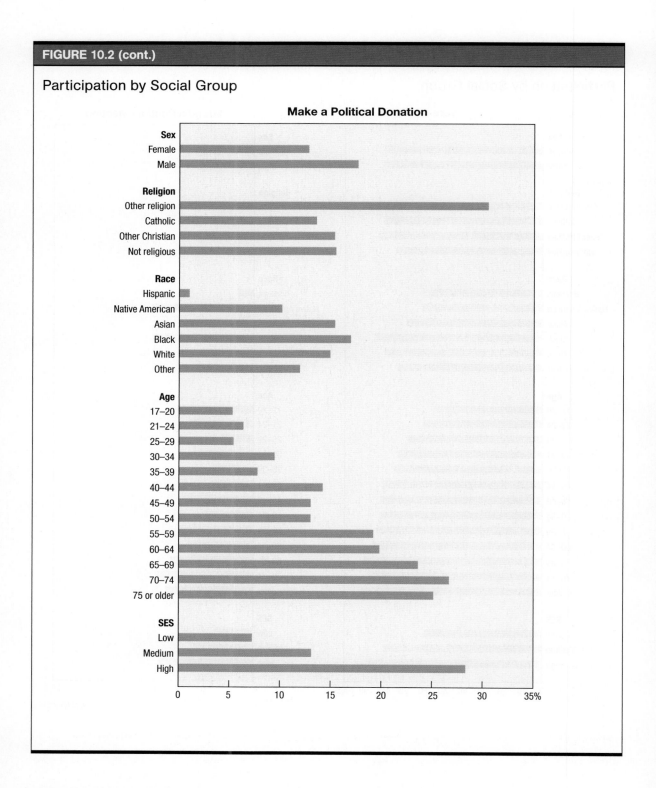

Make a Political Donation

civil rights organizations and churches, and thus, they actually have turned out in about the same as or even higher proportions than their white counterparts in recent national elections.

Lower voter turnout in southern states remains a persistent pattern (not shown). This is mostly due to the greater numbers of poor and rural residents in the region. Nationwide, participation outside the biggest cities continues to be higher among suburbanites than among rural citizens. Mainline Protestants and Jews (reflected in Other Christian and Other Religious categories) turn out in slightly higher numbers than Catholics, who turn out in higher numbers than evangelical Protestants (data not broken out). Evangelical Protestants are closing the gap, though, because of the intense mobilization of this group by the Republican Party in recent decades.

In the past, more men voted than women. In recent years, however, women have turned out in proportions roughly equivalent to those of men, if not higher in some elections, though any difference is very slight. The reasons for this change are unclear, but available evidence indicates that in some groups, especially among African Americans, women are mobilized effectively through church and other organizational affiliations.[22]

None of the differences across groups mentioned here compare to the differences between those whose education is above average and below average. If we control for education and, to some extent, wealth, then almost all of the other differences become insignificant. In other words, the different turnout rates between religious groups or regions to the country, for example, merely reflect differences across those groups in average levels of education and wealth.

The effect of SES on participation in activities other than voting is even clearer (Figure 10.3). Higher SES leads to substantially higher participation in such activities as donating money to campaigns and contacting public officials. More educated people join political organizations and attend meetings more often than those with less education. And people with higher SES participate in campaign activities more frequently than those with lower SES. As previously mentioned, the exception is that lower SES groups tend to protest and rally more often than those higher up on the SES scale.

In Comparison: Political Participation

In virtually every country where political participation has been surveyed and studied systematically, there is a correlation between status—measured by levels of education and income (or the equivalent of SES in other countries)—and rates of political participation. That is, the wealthier and

---

[22] Sidney Verba and Norman H. Nie, *Participation in America* (New York: Harper & Row, 1972); and Steven J. Rosenstone and John Mark Hansen, *Mobilization, Participation, and Democracy in America* (New York: Longman, 1993).

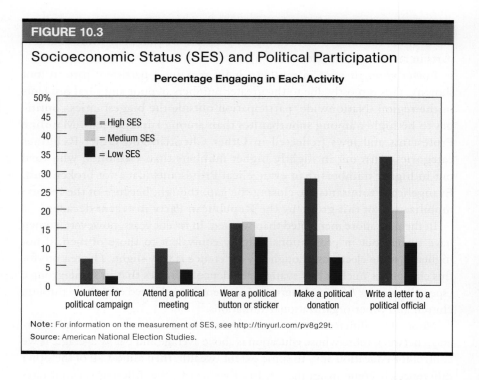

FIGURE 10.3

Socioeconomic Status (SES) and Political Participation

Percentage Engaging in Each Activity

Legend:
- = High SES
- = Medium SES
- = Low SES

Categories (x-axis): Volunteer for political campaign, Attend a political meeting, Wear a political button or sticker, Make a political donation, Write a letter to a political official

Note: For information on the measurement of SES, see http://tinyurl.com/pv8g29t.
Source: American National Election Studies.

more educated a person is, the more likely he or she will be to participate in politics, including voting, attending meetings, working on an electoral campaign, and directly contacting a public official. This pattern shows up repeatedly in data from democratic countries around the world. Some exceptions exist in India and parts of Latin America, where data show either no differences in turnout across SES groups, or slightly higher rates of voting participation among the rural poor than among wealthier people in the cities.

Yet there are differences in the overall levels of participation from country to country. We know from years of research that Americans consistently vote in smaller proportions than citizens in other countries. We also know that a higher proportion of Americans work in campaigns and belong to organizations than in other countries. How can we explain this seeming paradox? First let's consider voter participation. Figure 10.4 shows that Americans rank in the middle range in turnout rates compared with citizens of other countries. This may seem strange given that voting turnout correlates with wealth and education, and the United States is one of the wealthiest and best-educated countries in the world. Even more puzzling, education and wealth levels have been increasing in the United States faster than in other countries, yet participation rates here have fallen overall, despite recent increases.

There is more to this story, however. First, social scientists disagree about how to measure turnout, and there are disparities in how turnout is measured

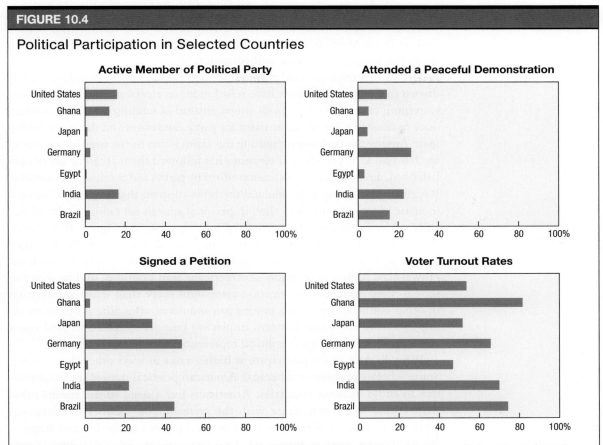

FIGURE 10.4

Political Participation in Selected Countries

Active Member of Political Party

United States
Ghana
Japan
Germany
Egypt
India
Brazil

0   20   40   60   80   100%

Attended a Peaceful Demonstration

United States
Ghana
Japan
Germany
Egypt
India
Brazil

0   20   40   60   80   100%

Signed a Petition

United States
Ghana
Japan
Germany
Egypt
India
Brazil

0   20   40   60   80   100%

Voter Turnout Rates

United States
Ghana
Japan
Germany
Egypt
India
Brazil

0   20   40   60   80   100%

Source: World Values Survey Wave 6 2010–2014, Official Aggregate v.20150418, World Values Survey Association, www.worldvaluessurvey.org. Aggregate File Producer: Asep/JDS, Madrid SPAIN (accessed 5/25/16). Data on turnout come from IDEA, www.idea.int/vt/ (accessed 5/25/16), except for the U.S. data, which come from the United States Election Project, www.electproject.org/home/voter-turnout/ (accessed 5/25/16). Turnout data shown are the most recently available from presidential elections under presidential systems and parliamentary elections under parliamentary systems. Voters are shown as a percentage of the voting-age population (VAP).

across countries. Most scholars who study turnout across countries believe that the typical way voting participation is measured in the United States understates real turnout, though controversy persists among scholars over which is indeed the best way to compare turnout across countries. The conclusion is that the gap between the United States and other countries is likely not as large as the most widely used measures indicate.

Second, even acknowledging the controversy that exists over measurement methods and accepting the commonly cited differences across countries, as it happens, voter turnout rates declined in all long-standing major democracies in the latter half of the twentieth century. Unfortunately, social scientists have no adequate explanation for this overall decline. Some claim that it is a result of the decline of labor unions around the world. Unions are a major source of voter mobilization among working-class voters; if they decline in numbers and importance, so does the mobilization of those who are below average in income and education.[23]

Others claim that political parties around the world have changed, as we will discuss in Chapter 12. Parties have relied more on electronic media, especially television, to communicate with voters, instead of sending campaign workers door to door to whip up enthusiasm for party candidates and the act of voting itself. Among the evidence supporting this claim is that the increase in turnout in the last two U.S. presidential elections has followed the increasing use of old-fashioned, direct-contact mobilization efforts by parties and political organizations. Recent studies using experimental methods confirm that in-person contacts increase voter turnout more than impersonal appeals on radio or television.

Now let's consider other kinds of participation. As Figure 10.4 shows, Americans belong to political parties and attend demonstrations less than people in some countries and much more than those in other countries. However, a higher proportion of Americans sign petitions, and in data not shown, they participate in election campaigns more than their counterparts in other countries by giving money to candidates, attending political meetings, wearing campaign buttons, displaying bumper stickers and yard signs, and writing letters to their political representatives.

Why do Americans participate at higher rates in ways other than voting? Some scholars propose that because American political parties are weak relative to those in other countries, Americans feel a need to use means other than voting to communicate with the government.[24] Other scholars emphasize the many different levels of electoral politics in the United States— school district, city, county, state, country—and the multiple times a year that Americans are confronted with candidates, elections, and campaigning. Americans in some states even elect county coroners and drain commissioners, something that is unheard of in other countries (see Chapter 13).

The ubiquity of elections in the United States might lead to voter fatigue. This, in turn, might explain the paradox mentioned earlier: even though Americans tend to turn out in relatively small numbers for national elections, they participate at relatively high levels in other activities that offer opportunities to work on behalf of friends, neighbors, or coworkers running for office.[25] Observers of American political life as early as Tocqueville (1830s) and

[23] Mark Gray and Miki Caul, "Declining Voter Turnout in Advanced Industrial Democracies, 1950 to 1997: The Effects of Declining Group Mobilization," *Comparative Political Studies* 33, no. 9 (2000): 1091–122.

[24] See, for example, Elisabeth S. Clemens, "Organizational Repertoires and Institutional Change: Women's Groups and the Transformation of American Politics, 1890–1920," *Civic Engagement in American Democracy*, ed. Theda Skocpol and Morris Fiorina (Washington, DC: Brookings Institution Press, 1999), pp. 81–110.

[25] See, for example, Richard W. Boyd, "The Effects of Primaries and Statewide Races on Voter Turnout," *Journal of Politics* 51, no. 3 (1989): 730–39.

DATA EXPLORATION Does the Cost of Voting Affect Turnout?

Voting is considered by many to be a duty of citizenship. It is reasonable to believe that minor inconveniences should not dissuade people from voting. Yet, it is also reasonable to expect that making voting inconvenient leads to lower voter turnout. Even dutiful citizens might be affected by the costs of voting. But how much does inconvenience matter in lowering turnout?

To answer this question, political scientists Henry Brady and John McNulty examined two elections in California, focusing on Los Angeles County turnout data.[a] California held a gubernatorial election in 2002, after which a recall election was held in 2003. (A recall election is when voters decide whether to fire the governor and hold a new election.) With the recall election, changes were made to the size of the voting precincts and the locations of the polls in Los Angeles. The situation offered a good opportunity for analyzing changing costs of voting.

The figure below shows Brady and McNulty's findings. It compares the change in voter turnout by change in distance to the polls from 2002 to 2003 for Los Angeles precincts. The dashed line indicates where there was no change in distance to the polls. In other words, points to the left of the line are where distance to the poll decreased in 2003, and points to the right of the line are where distance to the polls increased in 2003. Also, note that since the red line is below 0%, the overall turnout in 2003 was lower than in 2002.

Change in Voter Turnout by Change in Distance to Polling Location, 2002 to 2003

Think About It

After exploring these data, do you see evidence that change in the costs of voting affects voter turnout? If the distance to the polls increased by five miles instead of 1.1 (the maximum on this graph), how much lower would voter turnout have been in 2003?

a. Henry E. Brady and John E. McNulty, "Turning Out to Vote: The Costs of Finding and Getting to the Polling Place," *American Political Science Review* 105, no. 1 (2011): 115–34.

social capital The existence of organizations, clubs, and social venues that allow for citizens to interact together regularly to create bonds of social trust.

those in recent times (Robert Putnam in the 1990s) have noted how Americans have traditionally been "joiners" of organizations, creating a society with rich **social capital**. Few countries around the world have populations that belong to as many organizations and attend neighborhood meetings and churches as happens in the United States.[26]

The Crucial Role of Institutions and Mobilization

Comparing political participation across countries and over time helps us to understand the patterns and dynamics of the American political system. Based on such analysis, four patterns have been revealed:

- Wealthier and more highly educated people participate more in politics than others in the population. This is a widespread pattern in democracies around the world.

- Voter turnout—the percentage of those voting among those eligible to vote—declined overall in the United States from the late nineteenth century to 2000, but it has increased somewhat in recent presidential elections.

- Americans turn out to vote in lower percentages than people in most other democratic countries (even accounting for differences in measurement).

- Americans participate in campaigns and join organizations in higher percentages than people in most other democracies.

What explains these patterns? First, it is widely accepted that wealthier and more highly educated people face lower costs when voting and participating in politics in other ways. They find the bureaucracy of voting easier to navigate, including filling out forms, and salaried workers do not have to sacrifice wages when they leave their workplace to vote on a workday. People in this segment of society are generally more attuned to politics and current events than those making less money and with less education.

A second, related consideration is that organizations intent on mobilizing voters and participants in other kinds of activities find it easier to contact and convince people to participate if these people have above-average wealth and education. In other words, richer and better-educated people are generally more receptive to organizations' appeals to participate. It is more efficient—more successful mobilization of people at lower costs—to mobilize people higher up the status scale, which is why these types of people are mobilized more frequently.[27]

[26] Alexis de Tocqueville, *Democracy in America* (Chicago: University of Chicago Press, 2000); Robert Putnam, *Bowling Alone: The Collapse and Revival of American Community* (New York: Simon & Schuster, 2000).

[27] Steven J. Rosenstone and John Mark Hansen, *Mobilization, Participation, and Democracy in America* (New York: Longman, 1993).

Third, the kinds of organizations that specialize in mobilizing working-class and poorer people, such as unions and leftist, community-based organizations, have been declining in reach and importance in most developed democracies over the past 35 years.[28] Some argue that a consequence of this decline was a commensurate decline in participation in the United States and in other countries. The revival of such groups over the past decade—especially leftist organizations and church organizations devoted to mobilizing voting and campaign contributions—goes a long way toward explaining the upturn in voting rates.

Finally, not only was the decline of unions steeper in the United States than in other countries in the latter half of the twentieth century, but even going back 100 years, these kinds of American organizations have played a less powerful role in politics than their counterparts in other long-standing democracies.[29]

What about the high percentages of Americans belonging to organizations? Research shows that group members, especially those who attend meetings, are more likely to vote and participate in politics in other ways than those who do not belong to an organization.[30] Churches, for example, play a much greater role in educating people about politics and mobilizing them to participate in the United States compared with other democracies, and Americans tend to be more religious than citizens of other countries.

Participation in organizations is highly correlated with income, wealth, and education, and there has been a decline in organizational affiliation among Americans, along with a decline in voter participation. Church attendance is the exception. If Americans did not attend church in higher numbers than those in other countries, the data suggest that the differences in voter participation between the United States and other countries would be even greater.

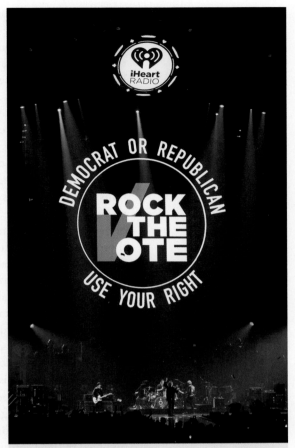

Concert tours are one way for organizations like Rock the Vote, a nonpartisan voter mobilization group, to connect and engage with young voters.

[28] See, for example, Michael Goldfield, *The Decline of Organized Labor in the United States* (Chicago: University of Chicago Press, 1987); and Benjamin Radcliff and Patricia Davis, "Labor Organization and Electoral Participation in Industrial Democracies," *American Journal of Political Science* 44 (2000): 132–41.

[29] Gary Marks, *Unions in Politics: Britain, Germany, and the United States in the Nineteenth and Early Twentieth Centuries* (Princeton, NJ: Princeton University Press, 1989).

[30] Sidney Verba, Kay Lehman Schlozman, and Henry E. Brady, *Voice and Equality: Civic Voluntarism in American Politics* (Cambridge, MA: Harvard University Press, 1995).

All this is to say that the patterns over time in political participation in the United States, and the differences between the United States and other countries, stem largely from differences in the nature of nongovernment institutions that mobilize people to participate in politics. Inequalities arise partly because poorer, less-educated people are less likely to participate in politics. But inequalities also stem from the different rates of mobilization by organizations such as political parties, interest groups, churches, and other associations. Moreover, these organizations continue to vary across countries in their commitments to mobilizing the working class and unemployed. As we have seen throughout this book, there are consequences when institutions constrain, encourage, and generally shape behavior within political systems. Most observers believe it matters a great deal that older, wealthier, more-educated people vote and participate in politics at much higher rates than others. It is hard to imagine that the government is not more responsive to those whose voices they hear and whose votes they seek than to those who fail to participate in the electoral process.

 To return to our puzzle at the beginning of this chapter concerning why the young, poor, and racial and ethnic minorities were most affected by Arizona' actions, we need to examine both the costs and the benefits of voting. On balance, young, poor, and racial and ethnic minorities are less likely to be mobilized by organizations and institutions. For one thing, these people are less likely to be employed. Employment not only connects people with others who share similar interests and discuss politics, it also directly connects government policies to financial well-being. Furthermore, these people are less likely to belong to associations that might mobilize them to vote and participate in politics.

Let's focus on age differences. As people age, they generally become more involved in their community, local schools, churches, and clubs, and in work-related organizations such as unions and trade associations. In contrast, the elderly not only have more time to gather information about politics but also generally have more money to devote to organizations, institutions, and politics. Perhaps most important, they are mobilized. They have the largest lobbying organization in the country, AARP (formerly the American Association of Retired People), along with many other similar organizations. The organizations and institutions that mobilize people to participate are more apt to target retired people who have the resources and time to help the organizations and institutions thrive.

Being mobilized reduces information costs because the mobilizing group is typically telling you how to vote or what to do in a participatory act ("Write to this senator on this Senate committee"). Being mobilized improves your knowledge of the benefits of your side winning the election while also increasing your own sense of efficacy and feelings of fulfilling your duty.[31] More important and

---

[31] Verba, Schlozman, and Brady, *Voice and Equality*; and Rosenstone and Hansen, *Mobilization, Participation, and Democracy in America*.

more generally, the costs of participation seem higher for the young, the poor, and the minorities than for other groups, and fewer organizations exist to lower those costs for them. In recent years, however, the increasing turnout among some of these groups seems to have encouraged organizations to make a greater effort to reach them, so perhaps the pattern will change.

FURTHER READING

★ = Included in *Readings in American Politics*, 5th ed.

Burns, Nancy, Kay Lehman Schlozman, and Sidney Verba, *The Private Roots of Public Action: Gender, Equality, and Political Participation* (Cambridge, MA: Harvard University Press, 2001). An extensive study of how women and men differ in their political participation.

Putnam, Robert, *Bowling Alone: The Collapse and Revival of American Community* (New York: Simon & Schuster, 2000). Shows extensive data indicating that American participation in voluntary organizations and in political participation more generally declined over the second half of the twentieth century. This had negative consequences for American civil life.

Rosenstone, Steven, and John Mark Hansen, *Mobilization, Participation, and Democracy in America* (New York: Longman, 1993). Presents convincing evidence that the decline in political participation in the second half of the twentieth century was because of declining mobilization by political organizations that in the past mobilized the poor and working class.

Verba, Sidney, Kay Lehman Schlozman, and Henry Brady, *Voice and Equality: Civic Voluntarism in American Politics* (Cambridge, MA: Harvard University Press, 1995). A complete analysis of who participates in American politics.

★ Wong, Janelle, S. Karthick Ramakrishnan, Taeku Lee, and Jane Junn, *Asian American Political Participation: Emerging Constituents and Their Political Identities* (New York: Russell Sage Foundation, 2011). An examination of Asian American political participation in the United States as captured in the 2008 National Asian American Survey.

KEY TERMS

the franchise (or suffrage) (p. 389)

Help America Vote Act of 2002 (p. 383)

paradox of voting (p. 377)

political knowledge (p. 382)

political participation (p. 375)

popular sovereignty (p. 375)

social capital (p. 406)

socioeconomic status (SES) (p. 398)

vote by mail (p. 383)

voter mobilization (p. 396)

voter registration (p. 381)

voter turnout (p. 395)

Voting Rights Act of 1965 (p. 390)

Here, Israeli Prime Minister Benjamin Netanyahu addresses the American Israel Public Affairs Committee (AIPAC) with a plea to block support of a nuclear arms treaty with Iran.

11

Interest Groups and Social Movements

 How can well-organized, narrow interests influence government in ways that go against the preferences of a majority of Americans?

I n July 2015, in Vienna, a number of the world's most powerful countries reached a consensus on the Joint Comprehensive Plan of Action (JCPOA), colloquially known as the Iran deal. This deal ended certain sanctions on Iran in exchange for limitations on Iran's enriched uranium and, above all, a commitment to nuclear nonproliferation.

American public opinion about the Iran deal was mixed. One survey found that 45 percent disapproved of the deal, over 30 percent approved, and almost 25 percent had no opinion.[1] An earlier piece of legislation, the Iran Nuclear Agreement Review Act of 2015, gave Congress the ability to review the deal and pass a resolution of approval or disapproval, or take no action.[2] Senate Republicans attempted to pass a resolution of disapproval but ultimately failed.

An ardent adversary of the Iran deal was a private interest group the American Israel Public Affairs Committee (AIPAC), which identifies itself as America's pro-Israel lobby. AIPAC was very active in its opposition and formed a special nonprofit organization just for this purpose called Citizens for a Nuclear Free Iran. It aired advertisements in California, Florida, Pennsylvania, and Texas where some Congressional members were undecided on how they would vote.[3] It is estimated that the organization spent between $20 and $30 million on these efforts.[4][5]

[1] Pew Research Center, "Support for Iran Nuclear Agreement Falls," September 8, 2015, www.people-press.org/files /2015/09/09-8-2015-Iran-release.pdf (accessed 1/15/16).

[2] U.S. Congress, *Iran Nuclear Agreement Review Act of 2015*, Pub. L. No. 114-17, 114th Congress, 1st Session.

[3] Catherine Ho, "Iran Deal Ads Running in at Least 23 States, Including Florida, Texas, California and Pennsylvania," August 20, 2015, www.washingtonpost.com/news/powerpost/wp/2015/08/20/iran-deal-ads-running-in-at-least-23 -states-including-florida-texas-california-and-pennsylvania (accessed 1/6/16).

[4] Jessica Schulberg, "AIPAC Throws in the Towel on the Iran Fight," *Huffington Post*, September 11, 2015, www.huffington post.com/entry/aipac-iran_us_55f33423e4b042295e3652c7 (accessed 1/19/16).

[5] M. J. Rosenberg, "AIPAC Spent Millions of Dollars to Defeat the Iran Deal. Instead, It May Have Destroyed Itself," *The Nation*, September 11, 2015, www.thenation.com/article/aipac-spent-millions-of-dollars-to-defeat-the-iran-deal-instead -it-may-have-destroyed-itself/ (accessed 1/6/16).

OUTLINE

- What Are Interest Groups, and What Do They Do?
- Collective Dilemmas and Interest Group Politics
- Determining Interest Group Influence
- Social Movements
- In Comparison: Group Politics
- Organized Forms of Public Pressure

AIPAC is widely recognized as one of the most powerful lobbying groups in Washington, D.C., with membership claims of more than 100,000 people.[6] (This figure is small compared to other well-known interest groups like the National Rifle Association [NRA], which claims to have a membership of 5 million people[7]; and the American Association of Retired Persons [AARP], which has almost 40 million members.[8]) It represents people and organizations that are pro-Israel, including many conservative Christians whose support for Israel follows for religious reasons.

AIPAC's main lobbying arm spends over $3 million annually,[9] a figure larger than that of the NRA.[10] Its influence is not only, or even primarily, financial; it relies heavily on mobilizing its members to pressure legislators through emails, phone calls, and letters.

For American politicians, being pro-Israel plays well. One expert on Washington politics says, "Today you cannot be successful in American politics and not be good on Israel. And AIPAC plays a key role in making that happen."[11] Some criticize AIPAC, alleging that it drives U.S. foreign policy where geopolitical strategy and shared cultural imperatives do not.[12] This assertion is very controversial, and AIPAC and other supporters of Israel claim that supporting Israel is in America's strategic interests. No one denies that AIPAC is a powerful voice in Washington, D.C., and often influences policy.

Still, AIPAC does not always succeed in securing its legislative goals—it lost on the Iran deal. Sometimes powerful interest groups win and sometimes they lose. AIPAC intensely lobbies members of Congress in person, and we see that direct, person-to-person lobbying is not always enough to convince members of Congress to support AIPAC's position. What conditions determine when powerful interest groups like AIPAC will be successful? What counts as success for an interest group? Why are some groups more successful at lobbying and influencing government than other groups?

[6] AIPAC, *The AIPAC Briefing Book: 2015 Edition*, 114th Congress, 1st Session, www.aipac.org/~/media/Publications/Policy%20and%20Politics/AIPAC%20Analyses/Issue%20Memos/2015/Briefing%20Book%202015%20final.pdf (accessed 1/6/16).

[7] Gregory Korte, "Post-Newton, NRA Membership Surges to 5 Million," *USA Today*, May 4, 2013, www.usatoday.com/story/news/politics/2013/05/04/nra-meeting-lapierre-membership/2135063 (accessed 1/15/16).

[8] Laura Johannes, "AARP Faces Competition from Conservative-Leaning Groups," *Wall Street Journal*, March 30, 2014, www.wsj.com/articles/SB10001424052702304704504579433343591891948 (accessed 1/14/16).

[9] U.S. Senate, The Lobbying Disclosure Act Database, http://soprweb.senate.gov (accessed 1/15/16).

[10] U.S. Senate, The Lobbying Disclosure Act Database.

[11] Aaron David Miller, *The Much Too Promised Land: America's Elusive Search for Arab-Israeli Peace* (New York: Bantam, 2008), p. 96.

[12] John J. Mearsheimer and Stephen M. Walt, "The Israel Lobby and U.S. Foreign Policy," *Middle East Policy* 13, no. 3 (2006): 29–87.

What Are Interest Groups, and What Do They Do?

This chapter focuses on *group politics*—the activities of interest groups and social movements. Unlike the relatively undifferentiated and unorganized general public that we considered in Chapter 9, these groupings of people are more organized in pressing their claims on the government. We start with analyzing interest groups. Social movements are discussed later in this chapter.

An **interest group** can be defined as any group other than a political party that is organized to influence the government. By implication, such groups are represented by formal organizations. Interest group politics occur primarily as interactions between organized groups (often represented by lobbyists working for those organizations) and people in government. It is important to note the distinction between interest groups and political parties. Parties, as we will learn in Chapter 12, are oriented toward gaining positions of power within the government. Interest groups, in contrast, do not seek positions in government, but rather try to influence those who are in government.

For many interest groups, seeking to influence the government is not their primary purpose, even though they engage in that activity. Labor unions, corporations, trade associations, nonprofit organizations, and foundations can all act as interest groups, even though their day-to-day work focuses on something else. The United Auto Workers is an interest group that tries to influence the government at times, but its main mission is to represent workers in their relations with their employers. Microsoft Corporation acts as an interest group, but it exists primarily to make and sell products and earn profits for its shareholders. Some interest groups do exist primarily to advocate policy goals to government officials—AIPAC is an example—but they are only a small portion of active interest groups.

Lobbying refers to attempts to influence public officials by speaking to them directly or by pressuring them through their constituents. Much lobbying in the United States is directed at Congress and the White House, or equivalently, at governors or state legislators within the states. In fact, the term *lobbying* originated from the notion that people trying to influence the legislative process speak to legislators outside of the chamber, in the lobby. As we will see, lobbying today involves much more than just talking to lawmakers in person. Also, groups lobbying the government can attempt to use the courts to promote their cause through lawsuits or court briefings. Likewise, lobbying can be directed at bureaucratic agencies, such as when a business trade group tries to influence the interpretation or setting of a rule or regulation by an executive branch agency when that rule would affect business firms.

Thousands of interest groups and lobbyists are active today in Washington, D.C., and many thousands more are found in state capitals. Interest

interest group Any group other than a political party that is organized to influence the government.

lobbying An attempt to influence public officials by speaking to them directly or by pressuring them through their constituents.

groups can either have their own staff lobbyists or hire lobbyists who work for professional lobbying firms, much like hiring a lawyer or an accountant. Thousands of groups have their headquarters in Washington, D.C., to be near government decision makers.

Most interest groups in the United States represent business corporations, business trade associations, and professional organizations. Large corporations such as Microsoft typically have their own lobbying units, but so do trade associations such as the American Petroleum Association, which represents numerous companies in the oil industry in pursuing their collective interests. Similarly, professional organizations such as the American Medical Association, representing medical doctors, can be quite powerful in lobbying on medical issues.

A smaller but still important portion of the interest group world is populated by labor unions and by what are called public interest groups. Public interest groups are defined as organizations that "seek a collective good, the achievement of which will not selectively or materially benefit the membership or activists of the organization."[13] The Child Welfare League of America, devoted to furthering the cause of foster children and other vulnerable children, is a classic example of a public interest group.

Figure 11.1 shows a distribution of spending on lobbying by interest group sector, according to published reports filed by lobbying firms and groups. Because more business groups are active than other kinds of groups, if we simply counted the number of groups we would get the impression that business interests are much more represented in the interest group community. Although this is undoubtedly true, determining the degree of imbalance between business interests and other types of interests or whether this imbalance gives businesses an unfair advantage in the policy-making process is not so easy. Many of the largest organizations are not business associations. For example, AARP (formerly the American Association of Retired Persons), which considers itself a public interest group in its lobbying role, has more than 37 million members. It is by far the largest voluntary interest group with dues-paying members in the country, dwarfing any specific business association. Likewise, the AFL-CIO claims to speak on behalf of all organized labor, and in some instances all workers, including nonunionized workers, not just its own members.

Nonetheless, by focusing on the money spent (Figure 11.1), we can see that a sizable majority of paid lobbyists and (in data not shown) the bulk of campaign contributions from interest groups are oriented toward the promotion of business interests. When those interests are united for or against a

[13] Jeffrey M. Berry, *Lobbying for the People: The Political Behavior of Public Interest Groups* (Princeton, NJ: Princeton University Press, 1977).

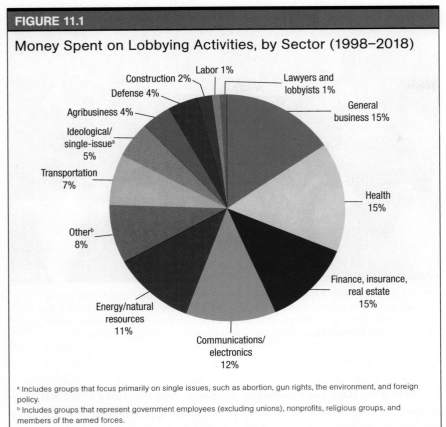

FIGURE 11.1

Money Spent on Lobbying Activities, by Sector (1998–2018)

- Labor 1%
- Construction 2%
- Defense 4%
- Agribusiness 4%
- Ideological/single-issue[a] 5%
- Transportation 7%
- Other[b] 8%
- Energy/natural resources 11%
- Communications/electronics 12%
- Finance, insurance, real estate 15%
- Health 15%
- General business 15%
- Lawyers and lobbyists 1%

[a] Includes groups that focus primarily on single issues, such as abortion, gun rights, the environment, and foreign policy.

[b] Includes groups that represent government employees (excluding unions), nonprofits, religious groups, and members of the armed forces.

Source: "Lobbying: Ranked Sectors," The Center for Responsive Politics, 2018, www.opensecrets.org (accessed 11/13/18). These data refer to spending on lobbying activities but do not include campaign contributions.

specific policy, it is hard for major political parties or Congress to ignore them. Such unity in the business community is extremely rare, however. Most of the time, industry lobbyists compete because various business interest groups find themselves on opposite sides of policy issues.

As an example, consider California, where the issue of beachfront development along the beautiful coastlines of the United States is particularly contentious. Luxury home and hotel builders, and the workers they employ, hire lobbyists who work to gain approval from local, state, and federal government agencies when those builders want to develop land along the Pacific coast and erect new homes and resorts. Susan McCabe, called one of the most influential lobbyists in California by the *Los Angeles Times*, is regularly hired by home-building companies to lobby the California Coastal

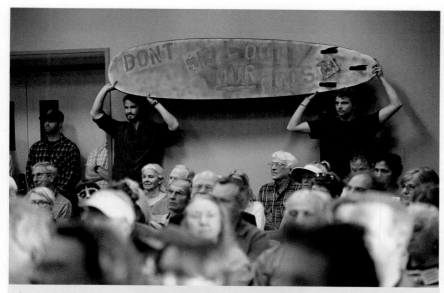

Construction projects along the California coast often prove controversial among residents, including surfers and existing businesses. Many developers who seek the California Coastal Commission's approval to build along the coast are represented by prominent lobbyist Susan McCabe, a former member of the Commission.

Commission, state environmental agencies, and the Environmental Protection Agency at the federal level, seeking approval for new building developments.[14]

Although opponents of these developments can be environmental organizations and sometimes government agencies, they also include other business interests. People and businesses with existing developments along the coast lobby against *new* developments because they do not want crowding and they want to enjoy the existing tranquility. Or, when McCabe lobbied on behalf of desalination companies in California (turning seawater into drinkable water for human consumption), she was opposed by existing utility companies and all the other companies that supply the existing water treatment plants from inland reservoirs of water.

As this example shows, there is typically no unified "business interest" with respect to a policy issue that is being debated and voted on at the local level or in Congress and discussed within presidential administrations. Instead, different industry groups usually compete for the attention of lawmakers.

[14] Kim Christensen, "The Most Influential Person on the Coastal Commission May Be This Lobbyist," *Los Angeles Times*, www.latimes.com/local/california/la-me-coastal-commission-lobbyist-20160424-story.html (accessed 6/1/16).

Inside and Outside Lobbying

Lobbying occurs at all levels of government. In fact, as the Susan McCabe example indicates, lobbying groups devote substantial resources to state-level efforts as well as to the federal level.[15] All lobbyists use a range of strategies and tools to influence policy makers. Some of these strategies involve direct contact with politicians, while others involve mobilizing constituents.

Interest group scholars refer to a "toolkit" that group leaders can draw from to influence policy makers. The kit includes two types of tools: inside and outside lobbying strategies. **Inside lobbying** refers to activities by lobbyists and interest group leaders who make direct contact with policy makers by speaking with them in person, testifying at committee hearings, or giving money to them at a fund-raiser. **Outside lobbying** refers to activities by group leaders to mobilize constituents and other people who are not part of the policy-making community to contact or pressure people inside the policy-making community. Examples of outside lobbying include organizing letter-writing or email campaigns for constituents to apply pressure on lawmakers, running advertisements on a policy issue, and leading protests or demonstrations.[16]

Both inside and outside lobbying are used in trying to influence Congress and the White House, and certainly groups often use inside lobbying in their interactions with bureaucratic agencies. As we learned in Chapter 7, these agencies have to pay attention to groups in society for multiple reasons. Groups unhappy with the decisions and actions of an agency can complain to Congress, and this can get agency leaders in hot water with the people who fund the agency. (Recall from Chapter 7 the fire-alarm model of monitoring the bureaucracy.) Alternatively, groups representing firms and organizations regulated by agencies can have productive and cooperative relationships with those agencies simply by staying in touch and keeping the lines of communication open with regulators, an important purpose of inside lobbying. Finally, groups often want to have their leaders and members comment on potential regulatory or rules changes proposed by agencies. As we know from Chapter 7, agencies are required to post potential rules and regulation changes and invite commentary from the public. Most such commentary occurring in hearings devoted to receiving this feedback comes from interest group leaders and spokespeople. Thus, participating in hearings at agencies is a major inside lobbying task of many interest groups.

When targeting bureaucratic agencies, outside lobbying is less effective and used less often by groups, because the leverage from outside lobbying comes from convincing elected officials that their constituents might care enough about the issue to alter their voting decisions in the next election. Bureaucrats

inside lobbying Activities by lobbyists and interest group leaders that involve direct contact with policy makers.

outside lobbying Activities by interest group leaders that seek to mobilize constituents and others outside the policy-making community to contact or pressure policy makers.

---

[15] Virginia Gray and David Lowery, *The Population Ecology of Interest Representation: Lobbying Communities in the American States* (Ann Arbor: University of Michigan Press, 1996).

[16] Ken Kollman, *Outside Lobbying* (Princeton, NJ: Princeton University Press, 1997).

Know the FACTS: Regulating Lobbyists

There are more than 12,000 active lobbyists in Washington, D.C., who seek to influence government on behalf of various interests. Thousands of lobbyists also are active at the state and local levels. The activities of these lobbyists are regulated under numerous laws and court decisions.

- The first federal law regulating lobbying activities was the Federal Regulation of Lobbying Act of 1946.

- Today, lobbyists' activities at the federal level are regulated under the Lobbying Disclosure Act of 1995 and the Honest Leadership and Open Government Act of 2007. For example, lobbyists must register with Congress and face restrictions related to lobbying former employers within the government. In addition, interest groups and lobbying firms that employ registered lobbyists must disclose the issues on which they lobby.

- Groups and individuals who lobby state and local governments are regulated by state and local laws.

- Participation by lobbyists and interest groups in the political process through campaign donations is also heavily regulated by the government. Interest group activity in campaigns for federal office is regulated through a combination of acts of Congress, such as the Federal Election Campaign Act of 1971 and the Bipartisan Campaign Reform Act of 2002, and decisions by the Supreme Court on the constitutionality of that legislation, such as *Buckley v. Valeo* (1976), *McConnell v. Federal Election Commission* (2003), and *Citizens United v. Federal Election Commission* (2010).

do not face reelection. Any outside lobbying directed at bureaucratic agencies would also usually have Congress or the White House as intended targets.

Another strategy that interest groups can use to influence policy does not fit easily into our typology of inside and outside lobbying: using the courts to promote an agenda. Interest groups use the courts in a number of ways to pursue their goals. They advocate for or against the confirmation of nominees for federal judgeships based on how they believe those nominees would rule on questions important to them.[17] They file amicus curiae, or "friend of the court," briefs in Supreme Court cases (see Chapter 8). These types of briefs allow individuals or organizations that are not party to a case, but who care about its outcome, to provide the Court with information that can aid its decision

---

[17] Lauren Cohen Bell, *Warring Factions: Interest Groups, Money, and the New Politics of Senate Confirmation* (Columbus: Ohio State University Press, 2002); and Nancy Scherer, Brandon L. Bartels, and Amy Steigerwalt, "Sounding the Fire Alarm: The Role of Interest Groups in the Lower Federal Court Confirmation Process," *Journal of Politics* 70 (2008): 1026–39.

making. Research suggests that these types of filings by interest groups do affect the Court's opinions[18]; in particular, evidence indicates that a litigant's status can be improved by the presence of an amicus brief filed by an interest group ally.[19] Interest groups may even go as far as filing their own lawsuits.[20] Scholars have found that this approach has been particularly popular with conservative groups and has been used less frequently on behalf of disadvantaged populations.[21]

Campaign Financing

One straightforward way of trying to influence a politician is to give money in support of his or her election or reelection. Under American law, and under the law of other democracies, outright bribery is illegal. Suppose a politician who receives a contribution from an interest group soon thereafter makes policy decisions unduly favorable to that group, and suppose someone (an accuser in court) can establish a direct cause-and-effect link between the contribution and the policy decisions. This is by definition a bribe.

Altogether, interest groups in the United States give billions of dollars a year to federal candidates, and they do not give that money for charitable reasons. They intend to spend their money in a way that will further the cause of their group interest.

In fund-raising situations, party leaders or candidates often come close to suggesting that large contributions to a campaign can result in favorable treatment by the government. "Please ask Panhandle Eastern Chairman Dennis Hendrix to donate $10,000 to join the Democratic Party's Business Council," read one internal memo to a National Democratic Party fund-raiser. "President Clinton . . . was instrumental in getting deep water drilling rights in the Gulf of Mexico through Congress."[22] The implication is clear: we, the Democrats, helped your company; now it's your turn to help us. (Republican politicians are no less averse to such quid pro quos, of course.) Scholars sometimes refer to this as the "holdup" potential by members of Congress, meaning that since they can influence the fortunes of any company or organization, they can virtually force an interest group to make campaign contributions, much as a robber can force a victim to hand over his or her money. Although such behavior may be unseemly at times, it is not illegal.

[18] Paul M. Collins Jr., *Friends of the Supreme Court: Interest Groups and Judicial Decision Making* (New York: Oxford University Press, 2008).

[19] Ryan C. Black and Christina L. Boyd, "U.S. Supreme Court Agenda Setting and the Role of Litigant Status," *Journal of Law, Economics, and Organization* (2010); first published online February 19, 2010.

[20] Frank R. Baumgartner and Beth L. Leech, *Basic Interests: The Importance of Groups in Politics and in Political Science* (Princeton, NJ: Princeton University Press, 1998), chap. 8.

[21] Karen O'Connor and Lee Epstein, "The Rise of Conservative Interest Group Litigation," *Journal of Politics* 45 (1983): 479–89; and Dara Z. Strolovitch, *Affirmative Advocacy: Race, Class, and Gender in Interest Group Politics* (Chicago: University of Chicago Press, 2007).

[22] Juliet Eilperin, "Old Memos Detail Link of Money to Influence," *Washington Post*, May 17, 2003.

The Collective Dilemma

Organizations and interest groups active in politics have to set priorities on how they raise and spend money, but the laws matter in shaping their choices. There are differences in how the law treats organizations and groups. Some face stringent rules, for example, about the information they are expected to disclose and the taxes they must pay; and some are tax exempt while others are not. What determines which groups enjoy lax disclosure rules and tax exemptions? What are the political implications of these benefits?

Interests

In the United States, religious organizations and those promoting the public good are often tax exempt. In general, organizations would prefer to have tax-exempt status because it allows them to keep the revenues to fund their activities and often allows special tax privileges to donors. For society, however, not all organizations can be tax exempt, and it is easy to see the underlying collective action problem: each group would like to be exempt, but if the federal government does not collect enough taxes to govern effectively, everyone suffers, including tax-exempt groups.

The Internal Revenue Service (IRS), tasked with collecting the taxes owed to the federal government from individuals and businesses, faces challenges when ruling on whether a particular group deserves tax exemption. It wants to be seen as fair and not unduly taxing a popular group that is seen as promoting the common good when enforcing the tax laws.

Institutions

The U.S. tax code and rulings by the IRS determine which types of groups are tax exempt and the conditions attached to these exemptions. Social welfare organizations are defined as "civic leagues or organizations not organized for profit but operated exclusively for the promotion of social welfare."[a] The IRS does not forbid these organizations from engaging in politics, but specifies that "political activities may not be the organization[s'] primary activities."[b] The question

then is: How much is "primary activity"? Is it less than 50 percent of an organization's work? Currently, there is no firm answer.

Further, the IRS holds different expectations for different kind of organizations. Take this important example: One kind of group—called 501(c)(4)s after the name of the tax code—gets special privileges but with reporting obligations, including notifying the IRS of disbursements, receipts, and gross income. But for the purposes of public disclosure, the IRS allows donor names to be redacted from publicly released forms, meaning that while these groups are required to report on spending and income, their donors can remain confidential.

Outcomes

Because there are different rules for organizations based on their purpose, it is common for groups to establish separate but related units to carry out different tasks. One example is Club for Growth, a conservative 501(c)(4). Its affiliates are Club for Growth Action, a $13 million expenditure-only committee, and Club for Growth PAC—both of which were actively engaged in the 2016 elections. Club for Growth refers to the other two as its "two political arms"[c] and information on all three groups are harbored on the same website. Legally, they are distinct entities; practically, they are coordinated by the same group of people.

There is concern that the rules enable political groups to take advantage of the tax and disclosure benefits by establishing themselves as social welfare organizations. For every political motivation, a vague and nonpolitical description can be written, which means that political groups can frame their mission to appear in line with the spirit of the 501(c)(4)s. In 2010, the IRS received 1,735 applications for 501(c)(4) status. In 2012, this number nearly doubled to 3,357 applications.[d]

Because 501(c)(4)s enjoy relatively lax disclosure rules, it is difficult to track just how much money is spent on political activities and who is doing the spending. Consider, for example, that 501(c)(4)s can contribute to super PACs. While super PACs must publicly disclose their donors, disclosing which 501(c)(4)s contributed relays very little information. By shrouding donors in anonymity, the rules for 501(c)(4) disclosure effectively obscure the money trail.

In 2013, a specific political controversy arose in the thicket of these complicated rules. The IRS began targeting 501(c)(4) applications of conservative-sounding groups—for example, ones containing "liberty," "patriot," or "Constitution"—applying extra scrutiny to see if they were truly in the spirit of the law about being social welfare groups. IRS officials stated that they had no prejudice in their approach and, instead, was seeking an effective way to sort the deluge of 501(c)(4) applications received. Republicans in Congress investigated the IRS and threatened litigation. The controversy eventually died down, but it changed the IRS's approach to regulating such groups.

The Obama administration came under fire when the IRS allegedly targeted conservative groups' tax-exempt status.

Think About It

Is there something intrinsically political about promoting social welfare? Do you feel it is important for organizations to disclose the names of their donors? Why or why not? How can the government effectively regulate these organizations and have a fair tax system?

a. U.S. Internal Revenue Service, "Types of Organizations Exempt under Section 501(c)(4)," January 22, 2016, www.irs.gov/charities-non-profits/other-non-profits/types-of-organizations-exempt-under-section-501-c-4 (accessed 6/29/16).

b. U.S. Internal Revenue Service, "Political Activity and Social Welfare," December 16, 2015, www.irs.gov/charities-non-profits/other-non-profits/political-activity-and-social-welfare (accessed 6/29/16).

c. Club for Growth, "About," www.clubforgrowth.org/about (accessed 7/5/16).

d. U.S. Treasury Inspector General for Tax Administration, "Inappropriate Criteria Were Used to Identify Tax-Exempt Applications for Review," Audit Report 2013-10-053, May 24, 2013, www.treasury.gov/tigta/auditreports/2013reports/201310053fr.html (accessed 7/7/16).

The American campaign finance system is unusual. In most industrialized democracies, the government distributes money to political parties to enable candidates to run for public office. In most developing countries that are democracies, money is funneled more or less secretly to candidates and political parties; the public knows little about where the money comes from and how much is raised. In the United States, by contrast, campaign money for candidates and parties mostly comes from wealthy individuals and interest groups. Since the 1970s, however, these contributions going directly to candidates have been heavily regulated, so we know a lot about where the money comes from and how much is given. As we will discuss in Chapter 13, contributions on behalf of candidates and certain issues are less regulated; thus, there remains much we do not know about a large portion of money coming from interest groups directed at politics when it is not given directly to candidates.

In private, Washington lobbyists often complain about having to attend so many fund-raisers. Many believe that their contributions will have little effect on an upcoming election or in changing policy. After all, if it takes hundreds of thousands, if not millions, of dollars to win a House or Senate seat, a lobbyist's $5,000 contribution will not make much difference.

Why, then, do lobbyists make any campaign contributions? This is not a straightforward question to answer, even if we approach it from the perspective of collective dilemmas. Consider, first, a collective action problem among interest group leaders and lobbyists who might in general be supportive of a particular candidate. Since any single lobbyist's contribution is small relative to the amount the candidate needs to campaign seriously for office, why don't lobbyists save their money and free ride off the efforts of others who are willing to contribute?

One answer is that campaign contributions, unlike many other types of collective action, *are* noticed by candidates, parties, and politicians. Candidates (and those who win and become public officials) pay attention to who gives and who does not. So it is not the case that a group's contribution will both be ineffective in determining the outcome and go unnoticed. On the contrary, as we noted in the previous section, the recipients often try to give the contributing group more access and perhaps more attention when considering policy decisions.

Two useful ways to understand campaign contributions are to consider these situations first as prisoner's dilemmas and second as opportunities to make investments. Let's start with considering prisoner's dilemma situations (Figure 11.2). Suppose there are two interest groups on opposite sides of an issue. If a member of Congress running for reelection receives money from only one group, then that member is more likely to invite that interest group in to talk about the issue, testify at hearings, and use that group's assistance in crafting legislation. But if both groups contribute, the member of Congress will gladly accept both contributions and be more evenhanded in the granting of access and in relying on both groups for advice. Thus, contribution-contribution is

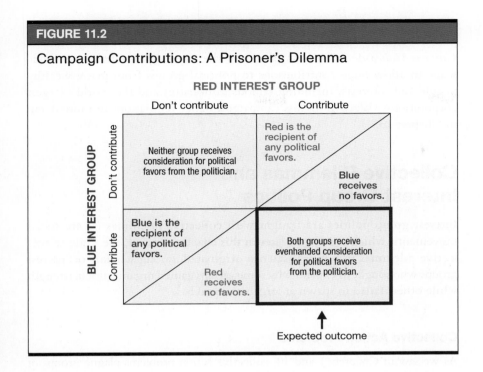

FIGURE 11.2

Campaign Contributions: A Prisoner's Dilemma

RED INTEREST GROUP

Don't contribute   Contribute

BLUE INTEREST GROUP

Don't contribute

Neither group receives consideration for political favors from the politician.

Red is the recipient of any political favors.

Blue receives no favors.

Contribute

Blue is the recipient of any political favors.

Red receives no favors.

Both groups receive evenhanded consideration for political favors from the politician.

Expected outcome

akin to a defect–defect outcome in a classic prisoner's dilemma situation. Each group is worse off if it doesn't contribute when the other group does.

If we consider contributions as investments, then an interest group is paying to support a politician who might win and also supports the group's goals. Especially important is investing in a politician early in his or her career because that investment may pay off for a long time if the politician makes a career out of being in government. As with any uncertain investment, there is risk of little or no return. Campaign contributions (as investments) may not pay off, where *paying off* means that the politician regularly grants the group's leaders access to discuss key issues or looks favorably on the group's proposals for changes in policy or for preventing changes in policy. Interest groups that can afford to give generously know the risks on return; and mindful that there is only the potential of reward, they invest in many different politicians, hoping that some portion will pay off, so to speak.

Finally, and relatedly, following the Supreme Court's decision in *Citizens United v. FEC* (2010), wealthy interest groups and wealthy people, including corporations, are permitted under the law to give unlimited contributions to groups that advocate on behalf of political ideas, ideologies, issues, and in support of candidates and parties. These relatively unregulated groups (often called super PACs) cannot give directly to candidates and parties, but they can advertise, mobilize, inform, and organize groups of citizens to promote political causes—that is, they can engage in forms of outside lobbying. The *Citizens United* decision has opened up the campaign contribution landscape to allow huge contributions to political groups from many wealthy people and interests, including famous billionaires and the world's largest corporations. (We will discuss campaign finance regulations in more detail in Chapter 13.)

Collective Dilemmas and Interest Group Politics

Interest group politics are fraught with collective dilemmas (as are social movements, which we discuss later in this chapter). In fact, the study of collective dilemmas in political science originated among scholars of interest groups who sought to explain why some groups gained organizational strength while others failed to spawn an organizational base.[23]

Collective Action Problems

As we saw in Chapters 1 and 10, collective action problems plague groups of people who share a common interest in trying to influence the government. To illustrate such problems and solutions, let's imagine you work in Greeneville, Tennessee, a town that depends on the zinc mining industry and on government contracts for zinc products. Greeneville is the home of Jarden Zinc Company, which manufactures products made from zinc for automobiles, coins, plumbing, and other products. Most of your friends and family are working in the zinc industry. Now suppose the government announces plans to stop using zinc for some of its products in the military. Suppose too that there is a bill pending in Congress to get rid of the penny coin, which includes zinc.

Leaders in Greeneville, and of Jarden Zinc, ask the citizens of the town to contribute to the common cause of preserving the economic health of the community. They form a group called Americans for Common Cents and try to enlist the support of people from the town and around the country to "save the penny" from elimination and showcase the value of zinc more generally. They ask for financial contributions from people like you to create an organization with headquarters in Washington, D.C.; to pay a lobbyist; and to run advertisements in specialized journals and magazines extolling the virtues of the penny and of zinc as the basis of industrial products.

Do you contribute financially to the cause? Do you agree to write to your member of Congress explaining how angry you are about the proposed bill, as

[23] Mancur Olson, *The Logic of Collective Action* (Cambridge, MA: Harvard University Press, 1971).

requested by the leaders of Americans for Common Cents? You see the common good it will do for your community if the group succeeds. Moreover, you personally will benefit if the group helps defeat the bill in Congress and convinces the government to continue using zinc in its military vehicles. But as one of the thousands of residents of Greeneville, your financial contribution will make little to no difference in the outcome. If the group succeeds in defeating the bill, but you do not contribute financially or give of your time, you will get the benefits from saving the government contracts for Jarden Zinc (and for your town) anyway. Why not free ride off the efforts of others?

This scenario is based on the true story of the Jarden Zinc Company, including its location in Tennessee, the 1989–90 bill to eliminate the penny (which was eventually defeated), and the name of the interest group formed and largely funded by Jarden.[24]

Overcoming Collective Action Problems

Groups facing common problems or seeking common goals constantly face collective action problems. The process of forming an interest group requires solving such problems and convincing people to contribute to a common cause despite the incentives to free ride. In this case, the residents of Greeneville shared an interest in protecting their jobs and local industry, but until they mobilized to form an organized group, that interest was merely **latent**. We say an interest is latent when the potential to form an active group and affect politics based on common interests exists, but that potential remains unrealized until the people take collective action.

Interest groups tend to be successful in organizing and in being active (as opposed to being latent) under two conditions.[25] First, groups are more likely to succeed in organizing on behalf of shared political interests if they exist primarily for reasons other than to influence politics. They may be corporations or business associations formed to share expertise among employees within an industry. They may also be labor unions formed to bargain collectively with companies on behalf of workers. The political activities conducted by such interest groups are **by-products** of organizing for other purposes. These groups were not formed by the voluntary contributions of members to further a political cause. Thus, they do not have to solve collective action problems in order to come together on behalf of shared political interests, because they are already organized for some other purpose.

The second condition related to success has to do with the problem of free riding: organizations that exist primarily for the purpose of political advocacy and that rely on the voluntary contributions of members are more likely to

latent interest A concern shared by a group of people on which they have not yet chosen to act collectively.

by-product A political activity conducted by groups whose principal organizational purpose is the pursuit of some nonpolitical goal.

[24] David Owen, "Penny Dreadful: They're Horrid and Useless. Why Do Pennies Persist?" *New Yorker* (March 31, 2008): 60.

[25] Olson, *The Logic of Collective Action.*

organize successfully if they have figured out a systematic method for overcoming people's incentives to free ride off others. Voluntary membership groups can overcome this kind of collective action problem through selective incentives, special donors, or entrepreneurs. Let's consider these strategies one at a time.

Recall that a public good is something that everyone can enjoy without necessarily having to pay for it, and for which one person's enjoyment of it does not inhibit the enjoyment of it by others (see Chapter 1). A **selective incentive**, in contrast, is a *private* good offered by group leadership to an individual on the condition that the individual contributes to group goals. This means an individual enjoys that good in such a way that others cannot enjoy it at the same time. For example, interest groups can offer benefits such as T-shirts, discounts on insurance, or journal subscriptions to entice potential members to participate in a collective effort. In other words, by creating selective incentives, groups offer private goods to get people to contribute toward the creation of a public good.

Selective incentives do not have to be material goods, such as financial discounts, vacation packages, or calendars. They can also be social goods, such as the private benefits you might get from attending meetings of the interest group. Perhaps you will make new friends at a meeting of an interest group on your campus, or you might make business contacts at a local meeting of an interest group.

Large or noticeable contributions from **special donors** can also make a difference in overcoming collective action problems. Groups can lean on potential participants who experience the lowest costs and/or derive the highest benefits from participation. In some instances, there are potential beneficiaries who might be willing to pay *all* the costs of the collective effort because the payoff is large enough for them. As an example, the executives of the Jarden Zinc Company might have been willing to pay the entire cost of lobbying Congress over the bill to eliminate the penny. The company's well-being depended on defeating the bill to such an extent that the temptation to free ride no longer existed. It made sense for the executives to contribute to the cause, both because they alone could fund the lobbying effort (they could afford it) and because their contribution made a huge difference in the success of the collective effort (they knew their money would matter).[26]

Groups may also rely on **entrepreneurs**, people who are so committed or so skilled in pursuit of a political goal that they do not need selective incentives. These political entrepreneurs are willing to join a common cause and take on the risks of failure and the high costs of starting something new. Because these people see the benefits as so compelling that just about any cost is worth paying, and they are skilled enough to seize the right opportunities when they arise, they are not (as) tempted to free ride. Although risk-taking political

selective incentive A benefit that a group can offer to potential members in exchange for participation as a way to encourage that involvement.

special donor A potential participant in a group for whom the cost of participating is very low and/or the benefits of participating are very high.

entrepreneur A leading group participant who is so committed to the group's goals and/or so skilled in the pursuit of those goals that he or she does not need selective incentives.

[26] Terry M. Moe, *The Organization of Interests: Incentives and the Internal Dynamics of Political Interest Groups* (Chicago: University of Chicago Press, 1980), esp. chap. 3; and Theda Skocpol, "Voice and Inequality: The Transformation of American Civic Democracy," *Perspectives on Politics* 2 (2004): 3–20.

entrepreneurs are rare, they have made a huge difference in the world. Martin Luther King Jr., who took enormous risks to create and sustain several organizations within the civil rights movement, is a canonical example of a political entrepreneur. He was likewise skilled at choosing protest strategies for maximum media impact. Ralph Nader, who started several consumer rights organizations in the 1960s, took fewer personal risks, but was skilled at publicity and pressuring the right corporations and policy makers at the right time.[27]

Coordination Problems

The collective action problem poses the main dilemma for latent groups with common interests in pressuring the government. However, groups also face coordination problems. Political action is most effective when groups can pressure the government in coordinated fashion, but different people or different groups might have different views of the best ways to coordinate.

Coordination means several things in interest group politics. First, it means finding a common message that can be delivered to government representatives from a variety of sources. Suppose two interest groups oppose a bill. One group says it opposes the bill because it is too expensive and prefers to support another, less costly bill. The other group says it opposes the bill not because of the price tag, but because it will spread those costs unequally across population groups. The people in government who hear these two different messages might become confused and ask, "Should we scrap the bill, or amend it? If the latter, how should it be changed?" Although the two groups agree on the ultimate policy goal, they advocate different strategies for amending the bill or introducing a new bill. It would be better for both groups, therefore, to coordinate on a common message to achieve their shared goal of killing the bill.

Second, coordination means organizing action to focus lobbying on the same key people in the government. If one group fighting a specific government regulation focuses its lobbying on the executive-branch agency in charge of interpreting and implementing the statutes while another focuses on the congressional committee charged with writing the statutes, the two groups might lack the coordination necessary to be effective. It would be better, therefore, for the groups to decide jointly on lobbying targets. Is the problem with the interpretation or implementation of the statute? (If so, then target the agency.) Is the problem with the statute itself? (If so, then target Congress.) Then the groups can join forces and apply pressure to the specific parts of the government that can further their cause.

[27] Jack L. Walker, *Mobilizing Interest Groups in America: Patrons, Professions, and Social Movements* (Ann Arbor: University of Michigan Press, 1991); and Kenneth T. Andrews et al., "Leadership, Membership, and Voice: Civic Associations That Work," *American Journal of Sociology* 115, no. 4 (2010): 1191–242.

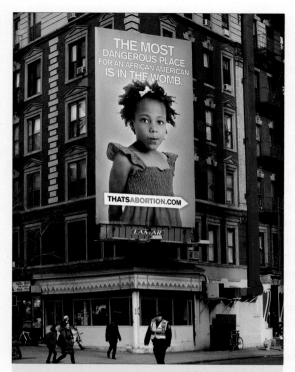

Groups on the same side of any given issue may have trouble coordinating on a strategy to influence policy makers. For example, when the antiabortion group Always Life put up billboards in African American communities highlighting the demographics of abortion, the strategy was controversial even among other antiabortion groups.

Third, coordination means organizing strategies to avoid overlapping too much or missing opportunities. For instance, two interest groups trying to influence Congress might divide tasks. One group might focus on lobbying members of Congress, meeting with them in Washington and providing written reports on the value of proposed legislation. The other group might devote more attention to rallying support for or opposition to a bill among the constituents of key legislators, using advertisements, email and web campaigns, and direct mail. Group leaders do well to coordinate their strategies with others.

Coordination problems are acute across interest groups. This is why organizations in Washington spend a lot of time working to form coalitions—groups of groups, if you will. Interest group leaders sometimes want to go it alone and lobby as they see fit, but often enough they join forces with other interest group leaders to create broader coalitions. This demonstrates to policy makers the breadth of concern across different kinds of groups representing different interests in society. Leaders of groups face recurrent coordination problems that need to be solved in order to make their activities effective.

Although these examples of collective dilemmas—both collective action problems and coordination problems—are drawn mostly from interest groups, the same logic applies to group politics in general. Leaders of social movements face the same types of dilemmas and need to find ways to solve them (as discussed later).

Determining Interest Group Influence

Washington, D.C., churns with group politics. While Congress is in session, thousands of lobbyists swarm the Capitol daily and make appointments to speak to executive-branch bureaucrats. They press their cases, provide information, and become friendly with politicians and their staff. They attend frequent fund-raisers, make donations to reelection campaigns, and in general show their support for politicians. The Mall, the large, grassy strip between the Capitol and the Lincoln Memorial, hosts protest groups on many weekends of the year. Demonstrators wave placards, march in unison, sing songs, and shout catchy slogans. Interest groups and the people mobilized by them create much of the buzz of Washington.

It is difficult to imagine that so much money and time would be invested in the formation of organized groups, and in lobbying activities and campaign contributions, if people did not think that lobbying mattered, or if people who contributed to causes or candidates did not believe that they would get a return on their investment. Do such groups really influence the decisions of policy makers? If so, which groups have influence over policy, and how much? These are difficult questions to answer, in part because it is hard to isolate the effects of lobbying from all the other influences on policy makers' decisions.

Consider, for example, the possible influences on a senator's decision to vote yes or no on a controversial bill. The senator could draw upon any of the following in making his or her decision: personal beliefs on the issue, constituents' opinions, pressure from party leaders, pressure from other senators, or lobbyists' activities. To claim that lobbying matters, we would need to identify specific situations in which the senator reversed his or her inclination to vote yes or no on the bill as a result of lobbying by interest groups. Unfortunately, in many instances we cannot know for sure that pressure from lobbyists was the deciding factor.

Because members of Congress are typically lobbied from various sides of an issue, a second, related problem arises. When the senator decides to vote one way or another, that action almost certainly will be consistent with the wishes of *some* lobbying group. The question is, How do we know the senator made that decision as a direct result of the lobbying group's actions?

Moreover, lobbyists tend to lobby legislators or agency bureaucrats who agree with them.[28] If an interest group wants a bill to pass, its lobbyists tend to focus on those legislators who are generally sympathetic to the group's goals. By making sure that it has the votes of these legislators, the group lays a solid foundation for its broader campaign. Given this tendency, it is hard to make the case that, absent the interest group's lobbying, the legislator would have chosen to do the opposite of what he or she actually did after being lobbied by the group.

It is likewise difficult to draw definitive conclusions about the impact of campaign contributions. Suppose you wanted to know whether a $5,000 contribution from an interest group influenced a candidate once he or she was in office. It is almost impossible to determine whether the contribution itself changed the actions of the member once in office, whether contributions from other groups mattered more or less than the $5,000 from this particular group, or whether the member of Congress would have acted this particular way regardless of the contribution. Scholars who have attempted to understand the

---

[28] Marie Hojnacki and David Kimball, "Organized Interests and the Decision of Whom to Lobby in Congress," *American Political Science Review* 92 (1998): 775–90.

relationship have generally found limited effects of campaign contributions on legislators' voting behavior.[29]

Despite the difficulties in linking groups' actions to legislative behavior, scholars have used creative research strategies to discern the effects of lobbying and of campaign finance. The political scientist Robert Dahl—in his book, *Who Governs?*—concluded that American government at its various levels was pluralist.[30] By this he meant that no one group dominated decision making; rather, within different policy areas certain groups were influential, but these groups did not all contain the same people. Dahl closely examined the decisions made by the city government of New Haven, Connecticut. He then connected those decisions to the various groups that were actively pressuring the mayor and city council. He found that each group sometimes was influential and sometimes not. His work refuted the widely held view that a small number of prominent people within towns and cities dominate the politics of those places. Dahl's study of New Haven was important because he appeared to capture how power was dispersed across groups in American politics, not only in New Haven but at all levels of government. It was also influential for its style of research: learning through interviews and observation what various groups want to achieve and then observing which groups win in any particular political conflict.

Building on Dahl's research, other pluralist scholars described American politics as an arena in which many groups were active, but none was dominant. Critics of the pluralist viewpoint, however, contended that Dahl and others missed the underlying bias in favor of the interests of the wealthy. As one scholar put it, "The flaw in the pluralist heaven is that the heavenly chorus sings with an upper-class accent."[31] Another set of scholars pointed out that Dahl and his fellow pluralists limited their studies to policy issues that were actually being proposed and debated. But what about those issues that never came up for consideration? Dahl's critics argue that dominant—that is, wealthy—interest groups keep controversial policies, particularly those that might redistribute wealth and income, off the legislative agenda.

The concept of pluralism is not as widely accepted among scholars of interest groups as it once was. Who has power in any given political situation has been difficult if not impossible to determine by rigorous scientific methods. Moreover, many scholars believe that power depends on institutional context—be it the U.S. House of Representatives, a city council, or an agency of the federal bureaucracy—and on the issue at stake. Scholars today

[29] Stephen G. Bronars and John R. Lott, "Do Campaign Donations Alter How a Politician Votes? Or, Do Donors Support Candidates Who Value the Same Things That They Do?" *Journal of Law and Economics* 40 (October 1997): 317–50; and Gregory Wawro, "A Panel Probit Analysis of Campaign Contributions and Roll-Call Votes," *American Journal of Political Science* 45, no. 3 (2001): 563–79.

[30] Robert Dahl, *Who Governs?* (New Haven, CT: Yale University Press, 1961).

[31] E. E. Schattschneider, *The Semisovereign People* (1960; repr., Hinsdale, IL: Dryden Press, 1975), pp. 34–35.

tend to focus on the potential influence of lobbying or campaign contributions in specific contexts, rather than making general claims about the power of one group in society over others across a wide range of issues.

Research in the past few decades has sharpened our knowledge of lobbying and the role of interest groups in campaign finance. We know, for instance, that interest groups are vital sources of information for policy makers as they try to predict the consequences of policy changes on industries, companies, communities, and groups in the population. Interest groups often act as proxy "staff" for a member of Congress. They can help write, amend, and lobby other members on behalf of a particular bill that the member wants passed. They can also help maneuver a bill through complex legislative processes. The groups and the member of Congress want the same thing, and the groups help the member achieve his or her goals. Of course, groups can give biased information, but policy makers repeatedly attest to the importance of dealing with lobbyists on a basis of mutual trust.[32] If a lobbyist misleads a policy maker even once, he or she loses credibility and jeopardizes future opportunities to enlist support.

To influence policy issues, people like Michael Correia (shown here), director of government relations for the National Cannabis Industry Association, regularly meet with legislators and their staff. The effects of direct lobbying on the outcome of legislation are unclear, though there is evidence that lobbyists can help legislators achieve policy goals by sharing information or helping to move a bill through the legislative process.

Research has also shown that when policy makers are subjected to "cross pressure" from various interest groups on opposite sides of an issue, those policy makers tend to decide consistently with public opinion in their district or with their political party leaders.[33]

Finally, there is some limited evidence that members of Congress tend to grant more direct access to two types of groups: ones that represent constituents, as opposed to ideological groups representing broad national goals[34]; and ones that contribute to their campaigns.[35] Similarly, White House officials tend to grant more direct access to groups that contribute to the president's

[32] Richard Hall and Alan Deardorff, "Lobbying as Legislative Subsidy," *American Political Science Review* 100 (2006): 69–84.

[33] John Kingdon, *Congressmen's Voting Decisions* (Ann Arbor: University of Michigan Press, 1989); and Gene M. Grossman and Elhanan Helpman, *Special Interest Politics* (Cambridge, MA: MIT Press, 2001).

[34] John R. Wright, "PAC Contributions, Lobbying, and Representation," *Journal of Politics* 51 (1989): 713–29; Michelle L. Chin, "Constituents versus Fat Cats: Testing Assumptions about Congressional Access Decisions," *American Politics Research* 33 (November 2005): 751–86; and Paul D. Jorgensen, "Campaigning on Fruit, Nuts, and Wine," *Political Research Quarterly* 63, no. 1 (2010): 16–22.

[35] John R. Wright, "Contributions, Lobbying, and Committee Voting in the U.S. House of Representatives," *American Political Science Review* 84, no. 2 (1990): 417–38; and Micky Tripathi, Stephen Ansolabehere, and James M. Snyder Jr., "Are PAC Contributions and Lobbying Linked? New Evidence from the 1995 Lobby Disclosure Act," *Business and Politics* 4, no. 2 (2002): 131–55.

campaign. In other words, if two groups seek a meeting with a policy maker and only one of them contributed money to that policy maker's campaign *and* represents constituents, that group is more likely to get the meeting.

Social Movements

Social movements are more difficult to define than interest groups, mostly because they lack clear boundaries. We can define a social movement as a loose coalition of groups and organizations with common goals that are oriented toward mass action and popular participation and share the intention of influencing the government. Interest groups can be part of a social movement, and new interest groups may be spawned by the activities of a broader social movement. But interest groups are formal organizations, while social movements are coalitions of many groups and individuals, some of them well organized and others less so.

Social movements are like the constellations of stars that make up a galaxy. Together, the clusters of various groups form a movement, but within the movement we can see all sorts of nuances and potential divisions. A major challenge for leaders of social movements is to coordinate the actions of disparate and sometimes competing organizations, all of which might agree on large philosophical goals and work toward common policy goals (Figure 11.3).

The quintessential example of a social movement is the civil rights movement, which began in the early 1950s and lasted as a major popular force until the late 1960s. The movement produced such monumental policy successes as the Civil Rights Act of 1964 and the Voting Rights Act of 1965, which shaped American politics and society as few other pieces of legislation have. Although the movement's most famous leader was Martin Luther King Jr., it was composed of many groups and encompassed many mass actions and leaders. Throughout the 1950s and 1960s, people and groups in the movement targeted racial segregation, unequal treatment of African Americans, and disparities in wealth and access to social advancement. Local leaders throughout the country (especially in the South) organized protests, sit-ins, boycotts, and educational forums to press the case that African Americans deserved the same rights to citizenship and the same privileges enjoyed by whites.

Heralded by some as a "new civil rights movement,"[36] Black Lives Matter is a recent example of a social movement. The Twitter hashtag #BlackLivesMatter was established in July 2013 after the acquittal of a Florida man, George Zimmerman, in the shooting death of teenager, Trayvon Martin.

[36] Elizabeth Day, "#BlackLivesMatter: The Birth of a New Civil Rights Movement," *Guardian*, July 19, 2015, www.theguardian.com/world/2015/jul/19/blacklivesmatter-birth-civil-rights-movement (accessed 6/3/16).

FIGURE 11.3

Social Movements and Interest Groups

Individuals share a common interest in an issue, such as civil rights.

INDIVIDUALS across the United States who were concerned about civil rights

They locate other individuals with similar interests and begin to organize into **groups**.

STUDENT GROUPS　　　**RELIGIOUS GROUPS**　　　**LIBERAL GROUPS**

These groups coordinate their actions to gain greater leverage for change and, in doing so, form a **movement**.

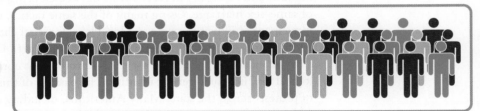

CIVIL RIGHTS MOVEMENT

Often, one or more **interest groups** related to the social movement become established as mainstream Washington organizations.

NAACP
National Association for the Advancement of Colored People

RAINBOW COALITION

MALDEF
Mexican-American Legal Defense and Education Fund

NOW
National Organization for Women

HUMAN RIGHTS CAMPAIGN

The movement gained national prominence in August 2014 after Michael Brown was shot and killed by a white police officer in Ferguson, Missouri.[37] Brown's death sparked massive protests in Ferguson. Black activists organized "freedom rides," busing people from cities across the country to Ferguson to join the protests. These protests continued for weeks after the shooting and were marked by tense exchanges with law enforcement. Then in 2015, the death of Freddie Gray in Baltimore sparked new protests, and the movement became even broader. The Black Lives Matter movement advocates for police reform to address the disproportionate killing of unarmed African Americans relative to the killing of unarmed white Americans by police. Sought-after reforms include better surveillance of police activity and the expedient punishment of offending police officers. The movement has a decentralized structure and a strong grassroots presence in the black community.[38]

Likewise, the transgender rights movement has classic elements of a social movement. It advocates for reform on a number of issues affecting transgender persons, including extending antidiscrimination policies to apply to them, making available affordable health care options for switching genders, promoting visibility of transgender persons, and highlighting the problem of violence against them. The movement follows on the heels of the movement for gay and lesbian rights, which for several decades has had success in changing laws and especially in recent years has helped bring about changes in favor of same-sex marriage. Using many of the same tactics, the transgender rights movement fought at the state and local level for legal changes. The movement became broader and more visible in 2016 when North Carolina implemented a law mandating that people use the bathroom that corresponds to their biological sex, not their gender identity. The passage of this law set off a number of protests across the state. Many Americans, including celebrities and leaders of large corporations, pledged to boycott North Carolina because of the law.

Prominent social movements such as the suffrage movement for women's right to vote, the civil rights movement, the consumer rights movement, and the Christian conservative movement have played major roles in American history. Movements come in different forms and have different modes of action. The civil rights movement had identifiable leaders and constituent organizations, was covered extensively by the mass media, used protest and nonviolent resistance as its main mode of operation, and—at least until the mid-1960s, a full 10 years after it began—had several clear policy goals that

[37] Deen Freelon, Charlton D. McIlwain, and Meredith D. Clark, "Beyond the Hashtags: #Ferguson, #Blacklivesmatter, and the Online Struggle for Offline Justice," Center for Media and Social Impact at American University, February 16, 2016, http://cmsimpact.org/wp-content/uploads/2016/03/beyond _the_hashtags_2016.pdf (accessed 6/3/16).

[38] Black Lives Matter, "11 Major Misconceptions about the Black Lives Matter Movement," http:// blacklivesmatter.com/11-major-misconceptions-about-the-black-lives-matter-movement (accessed 6/6/16).

drove members' participation, including the repeal of Jim Crow laws and full civil and political rights for African Americans.

The consumer rights movement also had several identifiable leaders, such as Ralph Nader, but it relied less on protest and disruption than on publications, demonstrations of product dangers for mass media consumption, and more traditional forms of lobbying. The Prohibition movement in the nineteenth and early twentieth centuries had a few identifiable leaders, such as Carrie Nation in the 1880s, but was oriented mostly toward convincing candidates for public office at all levels of government—from local city boards to Congress—to support a nationwide ban on the sale of alcoholic beverages. Again, some protests and social disruption by movement activists took place, but generally they worked through the electoral process and other accepted means to effect change.

Despite their diversity of form, social movements share certain features that set them apart from interest groups. One common feature is that social movements typically arise among groups of people who feel excluded, or have deliberately excluded themselves, from the mainstream political process. In fact, many scholars define a social movement as a form of resistance by disadvantaged segments of society.[39]

Just as protest is a staple of many, though not all, social movements, not all social movements are leftist in orientation—though most are. Recall from Chapter 9 that a leftist is someone who generally opposes inequalities of class, wealth, and status in society, and who advocates redistributing wealth to the poor and increasing the representation of the marginalized and disadvantaged. The leftist tendency of social movements occurs because groups that are part of social movements tend to use strategies and tactics outside the mainstream, since those who feel excluded from the centers of power regard those tools as the only ones available. In comparison with leftist groups, centrist or rightist organizations tend to have more support among those at the top of the social hierarchy and thus can work within the existing system of representation.

Exceptional rightist social movements—for example, Christian conservatives or Prohibitionists—arise and sustain themselves for the same reason as leftist groups. The Tea Party movement launched in 2009 helped coordinate the action of numerous local groups to pressure for policy changes, including balanced budgets, lower taxes, and traditional interpretations of the Bill of Rights. The movement devoted special attention to electoral politics—specifically, helping movement-backed candidates win Republican primaries and defeat Democratic candidates in elections. The Tea Party movement ultimately morphed into a faction within the Republican Party. By 2014, though it had elements remaining of a social movement—loosely organized

[39] This is sometimes referred to as a *political process approach* to social movements. See, for example, Doug McAdam, *Political Process and the Development of Black Insurgency, 1930–1970* (Chicago: University of Chicago Press, 1982); and Doug McAdam, Sidney Tarrow, and Charles Tilly, *Dynamics of Contention* (New York: Cambridge University Press, 2001).

1840–60s The women's suffrage movement begins.

1898–1914 Progressive movement

1920s–50s The labor movement emerges and grows in power.

1970s Rise of direct mail fund-raising gives conservative causes a new fund-raising advantage. Also, Christian evangelicals, known as the Christian Right, become active on the political and cultural right.

1850

1900

1950

1880s–1910s The Prohibition movement culminates with the ratification of the Eighteenth Amendment in 1918.

1955–70 The civil rights movement begins in the South and spreads nationwide.

1970s With the founding of Public Citizen by Ralph Nader in 1971, a "public interest" movement, focused on consumer and environmental protection, emerges.

groups around the country mobilized to achieve change and occasionally coordinating their actions—the strategic focus of its various groups became almost solely electoral victory in Republican primaries for its favored congressional candidates and pressure on existing members of Congress to stay firm on cutting the federal deficit and reducing the size of government.

The people behind the Christian conservative and Tea Party movements have felt excluded from decision making and often use protest to achieve their objectives. Protest from the right is commonly associated with the issues of abortion, health care reform, immigration, and government spending. Many Christian conservatives have also felt excluded by the mass media and some state-level political parties when it comes to decision making in local schools.

Two yardsticks are often used to measure the "success" of a social movement. First, a movement can succeed in mobilization by encouraging people to participate, by raising the profile of a cause, and by placing a specific set of policy changes on the agenda. Alternatively, a movement can succeed by changing government policy and achieving most of its desired reforms. The first kind of success does not automatically lead to the second kind. Not every social movement, even those that are large and mobilize many people, succeeds in achieving the goals of the groups under its umbrella. Nevertheless, social movements have profoundly shaped the political agenda and changed the nature of government and public policy. For example, in the absence of social movements that brought popular pressure to bear on the government, women would probably not have the right to vote, there would be few environmental laws, and labor unions would have a much more difficult time operating, if they were allowed to exist at all.

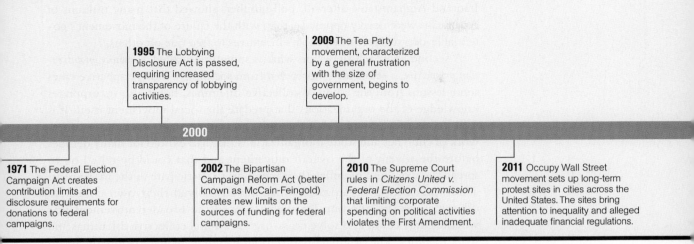

1995 The Lobbying Disclosure Act is passed, requiring increased transparency of lobbying activities.

2009 The Tea Party movement, characterized by a general frustration with the size of government, begins to develop.

2000

1971 The Federal Election Campaign Act creates contribution limits and disclosure requirements for donations to federal campaigns.

2002 The Bipartisan Campaign Reform Act (better known as McCain-Feingold) creates new limits on the sources of funding for federal campaigns.

2010 The Supreme Court rules in *Citizens United v. Federal Election Commission* that limiting corporate spending on political activities violates the First Amendment.

2011 Occupy Wall Street movement sets up long-term protest sites in cities across the United States. The sites bring attention to inequality and alleged inadequate financial regulations.

Deeper Analysis of Social Movements

Scholars ask some of the same questions about social movements that they ask about interest groups: Are social movements influential? If so, when and how? And why do some social movements get off the ground and take lasting shape while others do not?

We have defined a social movement as a loose coalition of groups and organizations with common goals, oriented toward mass action and popular participation. One question that continually intrigues scholars of mass behavior is, What explains why some social movements succeed in mobilizing people to participate while other movements fail? "Failed" social movements are usually hard to study because we do not hear about them, and they are not in our history books because they never got off the ground. In recent times, leaders of antiwar groups tried to mobilize a mass movement to oppose the wars in Iraq and Afghanistan, but by most measures they did not succeed. There were spotty protests, but little in the way of sustained, large-scale mass action against the wars.

Let's consider two approaches to the study of social movements that may help us understand why some succeed and some fail. In the first, we might focus attention on collective dilemmas—specifically, collective action problems. Explaining why some groups in society are able to organize for mass action and form successful social movements is analogous to explaining why some latent groups are able to overcome their collective action problems. Perhaps some groups are just lucky in having talented political entrepreneurs who are willing to pay the up-front costs of early organizing and then can use selective incentives to build the organizations. As for why the antiwar movement failed to gain traction, the explanation has less to do with people's opposition to the wars in Iraq and Afghanistan—after all, poll numbers showed that many millions of Americans were deeply opposed—than with the failure of the movement's potential leaders to overcome people's incentives to free ride off others.[40]

A second approach draws on what is sometimes called a *resource mobilization perspective*, a set of ideas borrowed from sociology. This perspective takes some lessons from the study of collective dilemmas, but it also incorporates knowledge of the organizations that predate the social movement itself. It is well known, for instance, that the civil rights movement was built on a network of churches and student organizations that had existed for many decades before the advent of the overall movement and that could be relied on to spread the word and mobilize their members to participate in the movement. These preexisting organizations had already solved their own collective dilemmas, so the question for the success of the broader movement was whether they could also solve cross-organizational collective dilemmas and work together. The original organizations had to be in place before the social movement could take shape. Thus, these organizations were the "resources" mobilized by movement leaders.[41]

From the resource mobilization perspective, social movements succeed or fail depending on the existence of established, organized groups that can be knit together to form a broader movement. For example, the failure of the antiwar movement is explained primarily by the weakness or nonexistence of peace-oriented organizations. Both of these approaches help us understand different aspects of social movements. The Tea Party movement, for instance, was sparked in January 2009 when the businessman and activist Karl Denniger used the Internet to urge readers to send tea bags to their congressional representatives to protest the government's bailout of large banks and auto companies. The symbolism of the tea bag was important. It referred to the Boston Tea Party of 1773, when colonists protested against onerous taxes imposed by the British Crown. Following Denniger's appeal, "tea parties" sprang up around the country.

Although the Black Lives Matter movement brought about the establishment of chapters across the country, it also depended on existing resources such as local civil rights organizations and churches. The movement relied

---

[40] See, for example, Dennis Chong, *Collective Action and the Civil Rights Movement* (Chicago: University of Chicago Press, 1991); and Marc Schneiberg, Marissa King, and Thomas Smith, "Social Movements and Organizational Form: Cooperative Alternatives to Corporations in the American Insurance, Dairy, and Grain Industries," *American Sociological Review* 73 (August 2008): 635–67.

[41] See, for example, John D. McCarthy and Mayer N. Zald, "Resource Mobilization and Social Movements: A Partial Theory," *American Journal of Sociology* 82 (1977): 1212–41; and D. Michael Lindsay, "Evangelicals in the Power Elite: Elite Cohesion Advancing a Movement," *American Sociological Review* 73, no. 1 (2008): 60–82.

on a number of organizations such as the Black Youth Project 100, the Dream Defenders, the Organization for Black Struggle, Hands Up United, and Millennial Activists United, among other local groups.[42] Preachers and members of predominantly black churches took part in the Ferguson demonstrations.[43] Elsewhere, churches remain a crucial part of the movement. The Concord Baptist Church of Christ in Brooklyn, for example, encouraged members to sign petitions and contact city officials in support of Black Lives Matter.[44]

The transgender rights movement, meanwhile, has relied in part on the existing infrastructure of the gay rights movement. Organizations such as the Human Rights Campaign, GLAAD, and the It Gets Better Project, which are seen mainly as gay rights organizations, are advocates in the transgender rights movement. The movement encompasses a number of trans-specific organizations like the National Center for Transgender Equality and the National LGBTQ Task Force. The movement includes a number of organizations that are not exclusively devoted to transgender rights, such as the American Civil Liberties Union (ACLU). The ACLU, which aims to fight civil rights violations across multiple social identities, filed a lawsuit against North Carolina for its 2016 bathroom bill that limits transgender people to the bathroom that corresponds to their biological sex. As one of the most visible organizations in American politics, the ACLU has become a key political voice for the transgender rights movement.

Building on the ideas of resource mobilization theories, Michael Heaney and Fabio Rojas argue that some social movements, when connected to a specific political party, can become what they call the "party in the street," helping and being helped by the national political party. The antiwar movement in the 2000s, for instance, was closely connected for a time to the Democratic Party as that party competed against President George W. Bush and the Republicans waging the wars in Afghanistan and Iraq. The antiwar movement helped the party mobilize activists and voters to elect candidates ostensibly opposed to those war efforts. One candidate the movement mobilized on behalf of was Barack Obama, who pledged as a presidential candidate to end those wars. Yet after Obama's election in 2008, he continued those wars for much of his first term (although he drew down the number of troops in both). Heaney and Rojas show data indicating how the antiwar movement, the Democratic Party in

[42] But one resource with which Black Lives Matter has an interesting and unclear relationship is the National Association for the Advancement of Colored People (NAACP), which has been the nation's leading voice on black rights. Some cite intergroup disillusionment over strategies and tactics, observing that the Black Lives Matter movement is forcing the NAACP to reclaim its relevance as a major actor in American politics. It remains to be seen how much of a "resource to be mobilized" the NAACP is to the Black Lives Matter movement.

[43] "11 Major Misconceptions about the Black Lives Matter Movement," http://blacklivesmatter.com /11-major-misconceptions-about-the-black-lives-matter-movement (accessed 6/6/16).

[44] Concord Baptist Church of Christ, "Black Lives Matter!" www.concordcares.org/social-justice--caring /black-lives-matter (accessed 6/9/16).

the street, died down after Obama's election and stayed limited in scope thereafter. The challenges, they argue, for social movements when they are tied to a specific party center on the difficulties of maintaining the energy of an opposition movement against the government when the party the movement is tied to becomes the incumbent party in government. Social movements can lose steam, as happened with the antiwar movement.[45]

These movements worked to establish local organizations ("resources") and then to solve broader collective action and coordination problems across those local groups. Their efforts at grassroots mobilization were mostly successful for a time. The transgender movement succeeded in changing public policy, though other political battles will loom for years ahead. It remains to be seen whether the Tea Party and Black Lives Matter—with broad, ongoing goals—will succeed in overcoming the underlying collective dilemmas facing them and have a lasting impact on American politics.

In Comparison: Group Politics

The American political system is widely considered to have more active and numerous interest groups than any other democratic country in the world. Scholars have explained this activity as a consequence of the many points of access in the U.S. national government. For instance, in the United States, if you want to change a particular regulatory rule that adversely affects your company, you can try to influence the bureaucrats in the regulatory agency to alter their interpretation and implementation of the rule. You can also try to influence the White House, and maybe even the president (if the company or industry is large and important enough and represents a huge constituency), to lean on the regulatory agency. Or you can try to influence the majority party leadership in Congress to make changing the rule a legislative priority. Another route is to try to influence the chairs or members of the relevant committees or subcommittees in Congress to attach an amendment to a future bill changing the rule. You may also try to take your case to court and influence the legal interpretation of the rule.

In other words, given the separation of powers in American government, you can seek access to all three branches of government, any one of which might be able to improve the lot of your company. In parliamentary democracies there are fewer points of access to influence the government. The governing cabinet tightly controls the flow of legislation in countries such as Britain, Germany, and Canada. Committees in these legislatures have little power. If you operate a company in Britain and you want to change a rule that affects your company, you have to make your case to a small number of people in the

---

[45] Michael Heaney and Fabio Rojas, *Party in the Street* (New York: Cambridge University Press, 2015).

What Does Lobbying Look Like Up Close?

Although lobbying is ubiquitous in American politics, it poses challenges for researchers who want to study the behavior because much of the work happens behind the scenes. The instances of lobbying that do make it into the public eye tend to be high profile and negative, offering a skewed or incomplete picture of what happens in Washington, D.C. The high-profile cases are also likely not representative of all, or even most, lobbying activities.

Five political scientists interviewed over 2,200 lobbyists to learn what issues were lobbied on for a typical day in Washington. The researchers asked the lobbyists to identify the most recent issues related to the federal government that they were actively lobbying on. Figure A reports 14 of the 98 causes that appeared in the sample and the percentage of lobbyists who identified each cause. For example, 3.4 percent of the lobbyists interviewed were working on the farm bill (the most frequent in the list of issues).

The researchers also constructed a measure—salience index—based on how much attention the cause received in the media and in Congress. They wanted to see if more important issues, as considered by the press and Congress, were the focus of the most lobbying efforts. So they calculated how many issues the lobbyists worked on were of high salience, low salience, and in-between (Figure B).

B. Number of Lobbyist Issues by Level of Salience

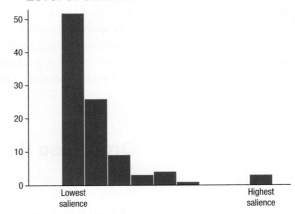

Source: Frank R. Baumgartner, Jeffrey M. Berry, Marie Hojnacki, David C. Kimball, and Beth L. Leech, *Lobbying and Policy Change* (Chicago: University of Chicago Press, 2009). Replication data available at http://www.unc.edu/~fbaum /books/lobby/documentation.html (accessed 7/8/16).

A. Percentage of Lobbyists Working on Select Causes

Cause	Percentage
Optometric funding	0.1
Public-safety officers	0.2
Clinical social workers	0.3
Credit-union membership	0.3
Cystic fibrosis research	0.3
Corporate average fuel economy	1.3
Low-power FM radio	1.3
Derivatives	1.3
Stock-option expensing	1.3
Math/science funding	2.2
Student visa/security	2.3
Medicare prescriptions	3.2
Managed-care reform	3.3
Farm bill	3.4

Source: Frank R. Baumgartner, Jeffrey M. Berry, Marie Hojnacki, David C. Kimball, and Beth L. Leech, *Lobbying and Policy Change* (Chicago: University of Chicago Press, 2009). Replication data available at www.unc.edu/~fbaum /books/lobby/documentation.html (accessed 7/8/16).

Think About It

Based on the data shown in Figure A, are most lobbyists focused on the same issues or is there a high level of diversity in lobbying activity? Based on the data shown in Figure B, were many of the issues salient and widely discussed in public? What do these data suggest about everyday lobbying in Washington?

cabinet, most likely the minister in charge of the bureaucratic ministry that directly regulates the industry or environment in which your business operates.

Furthermore, in many countries, laws severely restrict the kinds of lobbying that can occur. Many countries have what is called a corporatist style of interest representation. Under corporatism, the government grants recognition to a particular group to represent a set of people in society, and then the government grants access to that group alone. In Germany, for example, the government invites representatives from employer organizations and from labor unions to meet with government ministers to hash out legislation affecting workers. The government confers on specific interest groups the right to represent workers in society, and those interest groups are invited to such meetings.

This approach stands in contrast to American-style group politics, in which any group can form and press its cause on government officials. Under **pluralism**, as we saw earlier, groups compete with each other for influence, even within a particular policy realm and industry. There is no process that results in members of Congress granting access only to specific interest groups. In other words, the United States has a more laissez-faire system of interest representation.

pluralism A view of the American political system that emphasizes that a large number of diverse interest groups are involved in the political process, and that any given group may be influential on some occasions and not on others.

Organized Forms of Public Pressure

In Chapter 9, we explored how public opinion is studied and how it forms the basis of political competition. We compared public opinion to a landscape on which politics occurs. Public opinion sets the stage for what is possible in politics—for what kinds of constraints people in the government face when they try to make, implement, or interpret public policies.

How is public opinion actually communicated? We learned about polling as one method elected officials use to learn about public opinion. But it is more common for elected officials and upper-level bureaucrats in the government to hear from the representatives of groups in the population than from the people themselves.

If you ask a politician to specify how he or she learned about public opinion on a controversial policy issue, more often than not the politician will refer to interest group leaders who bring their concerns forward. "I heard from the local business community that this would be a bad bill for my state," is a typical response. Many different groups are trying to pressure the government, and the saying "The squeaky wheel gets the grease" is especially relevant to the American political system with its multiple levels and layers of authority. A group becomes "squeaky" when it acts collectively, hiring lobbyists or organizing protests or letter-writing campaigns, and puts pressure on government officials.

Interest groups and social movements can be thought of as organized clumps of public opinion. They help form the public opinion landscape. What politicians learn from interest groups is not always a fair rendering of public opinion. Often the opposite is true, in that the groups politicians hear from are those that have organized themselves most effectively to capture the attention of politicians. These interest groups, no matter how widespread, are not typically representative of the entire public. Thus, although interest groups seek to encapsulate public preferences in order to target government officials more effectively, their representations are hardly synonymous with public opinion. Many people in the population, including many directly affected by public policies in question, are not represented by any group active on a given issue. Interest groups and social movements represent the public in biased, unrepresentative ways, but in ways that are nevertheless important and deeply consequential.

Let's return to the example of AIPAC discussed at the beginning of this chapter. AIPAC members come from many different population groups in American society; a portion are Jewish but many are not. The group itself is very well organized. AIPAC, through its aim of holding politicians accountable and focusing intensely on politicians who waver on policies toward Israel, has gained a reputation for being able to influence election outcomes, even though its specific positions may not always be supported by either the general population or by the foreign policy establishment, including leaders in the State Department and the Department of Defense.

Groups like AIPAC and the NRA focus on grassroots organization that can mobilize voters based on their single issue (support for Israel for AIPAC and against gun control for the NRA). These groups convince their supporters to vote against politicians who waver or oppose their goals, and they raise and spend money to defeat these politicians *and* influence voters. Any group with that kind of organizational muscle and willingness to wade into the election process with gusto and mobilize voters and donors will be influential in American politics. Only a few groups wield such clout. AIPAC is successful because it repeatedly solves collective dilemmas among pro-Israel voters, targeting its efforts in a coordinated fashion and working to defeat its political foes in elections across the country. A well-organized and coordinated group of voters can achieve a reputation for voting as a bloc and swinging elections.

AIPAC and the NRA are unusual in that interest groups are rarely so successful at flexing their muscles so

Interest groups and social movements can be thought of as organized expressions of public opinion. As public opinion shifted more strongly in favor of civil rights in the 1950s and 1960s, the civil rights movement provided a dramatic expression of these preferences—and ultimately influenced public policy.

effectively during elections, mostly because it is hard to do and can be politically risky. If their targeted incumbents win they might then lose access in Washington. But when such groups display power and actually appear to swing elections, they can have enormous impact. One example from long ago is well known even today. In 1994, Speaker of the House Thomas Foley of Washington State lost his seat in Congress when he crossed the NRA on an assault weapons ban. These examples stick in the minds of politicians and become the stuff of lore in Washington, D.C. "Be careful of the interest groups you cross," politicians tell each other. "If the interest groups have enough clout with voters, they can cause you to lose your job."

Underlying whatever influence interest groups have over incumbents is the perception that they represent an important set of constituents whom incumbents want to keep happy. That constituency can represent a large number of voters or a significant bloc of campaign contributors. Either way, politicians pay attention to interest groups because they know that these groups can affect the outcome of an election.

It is important to keep this "ultimate weapon" in mind when assessing the impact of lobbying and campaign contributions, and social movement politics, on policy making by legislatures and executives. An interest group can try to work through the courts if the other branches are not receptive. But if there is no electoral connection whereby a politician sees the link between what a group wants him or her to do and what will happen in the next election, then the interest group will have little influence on legislatures and executives.

FURTHER READING

★ = Included in *Readings in American Politics*, 5th ed.

Ainsworth, Scott, *Analyzing Interest Groups: Group Influence on People and Policies* (New York: Norton, 2002). A comprehensive overview of theories of interest groups and lobbying.

Baumgartner, Frank R., and Beth L. Leech, *Basic Interests: The Importance of Groups in Politics and in Political Science* (Princeton, NJ: Princeton University Press, 1998). A broad overview of research findings on interest groups and campaign finance.

Dahl, Robert, *Who Governs?* (New Haven, CT: Yale University Press, 1961). A clear statement of pluralism, coming out of a study of political power in the city government of New Haven, Connecticut.

Gilens, Martin, *Affluence and Influence: Economic Inequality and Political Power in America* (Princeton, NJ: Princeton University Press, 2012). An analysis of political inequality and its impact on American democracy.

Goss, Kristin, *Disarmed: The Missing Movement for Gun Control in America* (Princeton, NJ: Princeton University Press, 2006). A detailed study comparing the success of pro- and anti-gun control organizations in mobilization and advocacy.

★ Kollman, Ken, *Outside Lobbying: Public Opinion and Interest Group Strategies* (Princeton, NJ: Princeton University Press, 1997). An analysis of interest group strategies with special focus on decisions to use grassroots mobilization as opposed to insider lobbying.

Moe, Terry M., *The Organization of Interests: Incentives and the Internal Dynamics of Interest Groups* (Chicago: University of Chicago Press, 1980). An analysis based on collective action; examines how interest group leaders persuade people to participate in group activities and lobbying.

★ Olson, Mancur, Jr., *The Logic of Collective Action: Public Goods and the Theory of Groups* (Cambridge, MA: Harvard University Press, 1971). A classic book describing the collective action problem and applying it to the study of political organizations.

Schattschneider, E. E., *The Semisovereign People* (1960; repr., Hinsdale, IL: Dryden Press, 1975). An account of popular mobilization that emphasizes the importance of who controls the participants in a political conflict; a critique of pluralism.

Strolovitch, Dara Z., *Affirmative Advocacy: Race, Class, and Gender in Interest Group Politics* (Chicago: University of Chicago Press, 2007). A creative study about organizations that advocate for the poor and marginalized, and about how well they represent the interests of the people they claim to represent.

KEY TERMS

by-product (p. 425)

entrepreneur (p. 426)

inside lobbying (p. 417)

interest group (p. 413)

latent interest (p. 425)

lobbying (p. 413)

outside lobbying (p. 417)

pluralism (p. 442)

selective incentive (p. 426)

social movement (p. 432)

special donor (p. 426)

12

Political Parties

Why are political parties and partisanship so widely criticized, but also so indispensable in a democratic system?

During the 2016 presidential campaign, Donald Trump railed against the Republican establishment and bragged that even though he was the Republican nominee he was running against ordinary politicians in Washington, D.C., including Republicans, and promised to upend politics in the capital. Hillary Clinton, meanwhile, repeatedly extolled the virtues of the Democratic party but promised to bring together members of both parties to solve the country's problems. She criticized the polarizing effects of partisan attacks in Congress.

Trump and Clinton are not alone. A favorite theme of recent candidates for president and Congress has been that they can rise above the bitter partisan atmosphere in Washington, D.C. The news media also play into concerns that party politics distracts government from important goals. Reporters and commentators often contend that the parties are merely interested in winning elections and not necessarily in doing what is good for the country. "Party Gridlock in Washington Feeds Fear of a Debt Crisis" and "Partisan Clashes Jeopardize Small Business, Energy Bills," declared two typical headlines.[1] Critics charge that leaders of the two major parties want to embarrass each other more than they want to work together to pass bipartisan legislation.

A large majority of Americans identify themselves in surveys as either Republicans or Democrats, but even among partisan loyalists, the two parties are usually seen as necessary evils. In fact, according to surveys, most Americans think that parties in general are bad for democratic politics—that they are corrupt, lead to gridlock in government, and make politicians inflexible in dealing with new problems as they arise. In recent surveys, about half of the respondents said they were angry at both parties, a much larger percentage than anger expressed at only one or neither party.[2]

[1] Jackie Calmes, *New York Times*, February 16, 2010; Naftali Bendavid and Stephen Power, *Wall Street Journal*, July 30, 2010.

[2] CNN/Opinion Research Corporation Poll, January 22–24, 2010.

OUTLINE

- What Are Parties?
- The History of the American Party System
- Why Two Parties?
- In Comparison: Parties
- Key Intermediate Institutions of Democracy

The tendency to deride political parties is not new. James Madison in *Federalist 10* describes the inevitability of factions (similar to what we know as political parties) competing for influence in a republic. He and the other Founders were motivated to design political institutions precisely to control and soften the negative effects of factional conflict. In one of his final public speeches as the country's first president, George Washington warned that parties were threatening the health of the young republic, and that if politicians continued to divide into parties they would damage the country's viability. In the late nineteenth and early twentieth centuries, election reforms were driven by a widespread perception that corruption in government was due largely to corruption among state and local party leaders. We continue to see this distrust today. When presidential candidates claim to be able to break through partisan conflict, they are tapping into a long-standing tradition of frustration with partisan rigidity in American history.

Most Americans seem to believe that partisan disagreement in Washington is bad for American democracy and that parties do more harm than good in the political system. Political scientists who study parties, however, usually make the opposite argument. They tend to agree with E. E. Schattschneider, who claims that "modern democracy is unthinkable save in terms of political parties."[3] Americans typically vote along partisan lines and, as we saw in Chapter 9, their attitudes toward policies and candidates are profoundly shaped by their partisanship. In fact, in the 2016 presidential election, partisanship (among all other variables typically studied) was the best predictor of someone voting for either Trump or Clinton. According to exit polls, Trump won the election with 90 percent of Republican voters supporting him, while 89 percent of Democratic voters supported Clinton. Meanwhile, politicians in Washington unite with fellow partisans to work toward common goals and thwart those of their opponents. Indeed, as we will learn in this chapter, parties solve a variety of collective dilemmas in the American political system, as well as in other systems, and grease the wheels of democracy. Why are parties and partisanship so widely criticized, yet so indispensable in a democratic system?

[3] E. E. Schattschneider, *Party Government* (New York: Farrar and Rinehart, 1942).

What Are Parties?

A **political party** can be defined as a group of candidates and elected officials organized under a common label for the purpose of attaining positions of public authority.[4] Parties are not formally part of the American government—the Constitution nowhere mentions them—yet they are key intermediate institutions in the American political system. They are intermediate in the sense that they mediate between the mass public and the government to help make democracy work.

Parties are ubiquitous in the national politics of representative democracies and, in the view of most scholars, essential to the functioning of elections and governing. Parties seem to "sprout and grow" under the right conditions, taking forms that are both influenced and shaped by that environment. In fact, data show that wherever mass elections are conducted freely and fairly, and wherever a legislature has meaningful policy power, political parties arise and play a central role. This is just as true in the newest democracies in the least developed parts of the world as it is in cities and most localities across the United States.[5]

The preceding definition seems simple enough, but it obscures a fundamental fact: parties are complex organizations, especially in the American political system. One reason many Americans view parties negatively is that they often do not understand what parties do. Parties organize politics in the American political system, but they are not singular, tightly unified organizations. Each of the major parties consists of multiple organizations that are linked by labels and by loose ideological affinity. These different organized elements of parties can work at cross-purposes with each other, even within a party. It can appear that parties create conflict—both across the two major parties but also within a given party—more often than they unify people around goals. As we have seen throughout this book, in Chapter 1 (Introduction) and Chapter 5 (Congress) for instance, examples of conflict *across* the two parties are front and center in American politics. But what can be confusing is conflict *within* a party. As an example, the Republican presidential campaign organization of Donald Trump in 2016 repeatedly clashed with specific Republican campaign organizations in Congress and with some state party organizations. The decentralized nature of how American parties are structured and organized makes it difficult to understand them and appreciate the purposes they serve in the political system.

political party A group of candidates and elected officials organized under a common label for the purpose of attaining positions of public authority.

---

[4] The party can include close supporters who work on behalf of candidates and public officials.

[5] Exceptions in American politics occur when states or localities mandate that elections be "nonpartisan," which means that candidates for office are not identified by party label on election ballots. In this case, laws inhibit some party functions. Many cities have formally nonpartisan elections for their city councils, and the Nebraska state legislature formally has nonpartisan elections at all levels, though it is important to note that within the legislature the members behave as though they belong to parties.

Scholars have sought to help people understand parties by dividing their functions and operations into three categories:

- *Parties in government.* Parties organize governmental action, especially in legislatures and parliaments. They influence how people in public office cooperate with one another to form teams and achieve policy goals.

- *Parties as organizations.* Parties organize efforts of candidates, politicians, and voters to win elections. They choose candidates to be on election ballots, help these candidates raise money, run campaigns, and turn out voters.

- *Parties in the electorate.* Parties orient voters' thinking by providing intellectual categories. Identifying with a party helps people link the party's values with their own beliefs and interests, engendering loyalty in the voting booth. Party labels also make it easier for citizens who share common beliefs and interests to coordinate their actions during elections, including voting and donating time and money, toward a unified goal.

These three functions reinforce each other. For example, the Democratic Party members in Congress and (when in power) in the presidency work together to enact (modern-day) liberal policies—robust government spending on infrastructure and redistribution, an internationalist U.S. foreign policy, and openness to new forms of social mores. This example illustrates the party in government.

Democratic members of Congress sit in those seats because Democratic Party organizations throughout the country appeal to people who want those things, and the party organizations try to get those people to donate to the party. The organizations distribute donated money among candidates, assist candidates in developing campaign advertisements touting liberal, progressive values, and help turn out left-leaning voters on election days. This is the party as organization, serving candidates and politicians in their desire to win and keep office.

The actions by Democrats in government also help increase the appeal of the party to voters who want liberal, progressive policies. These voters, in turn, develop loyalties to the Democratic Party. The party reputation among potential voters creates groups of loyal voters, and those groups of loyal voters make up the party in the electorate.

Success in one area contributes to success in the other two. Let's now discuss each of these functions in more detail, referring to Figure 12.1.

Parties in Government

In every mature democracy in the world, including the United States, national governments are run by political parties. That is, the leaders of the

Three Roles of Parties

Each part of a party affects the other parts. Parties operate in the electorate by shaping the way voters understand the political world. They are instruments of political identification, affiliation, and information for voters. Parties also are organizations by which candidates and interested citizens can aggregate to effect policy change. In this light, they serve as infrastructure for candidates to gather resources for elections. Parties organize government action in that collective decisions like passing legislation are made by coalitional work among like-minded lawmakers.

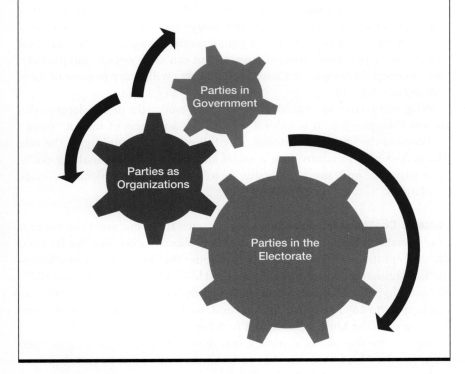

government are also leaders of their political parties, and they use the machinery of their parties to organize the activities of the government—to draft and pass legislation, to place top bureaucrats in the executive agencies, and to formulate broad policy goals.

Party leadership and governmental leadership are fused in most countries. In parliamentary democracies such as Britain, Germany, or Japan, the prime minister or other head of government is the leader of his or her party. If the party decides to change leaders, the prime minister steps down and gives way to the new party leader. Moreover, as we will discuss in more detail later, members of the parties in parliament almost always vote as blocs, with rare defections.

The role of parties in the U.S. government is more complicated due to the system of separation of powers. Generally, the president is considered the head of his or her party while the Speaker of the House and the Senate majority leader are among the top leaders in their parties. In light of the possibility of divided government—the situation in which one party controls the presidency while another controls at least one chamber of Congress—we cannot always say that one party or the other controls the national government. Only if one party controls the presidency, the House, and the Senate can we say that it controls the government. Moreover, party control of a chamber of Congress is by no means straightforward. Unlike legislators in many other countries, members of Congress do not always vote according to their party leaders' recommendations, and even presidents and Congress when controlled by the same party under unified government can clash openly and publicly. (We discussed these topics in Chapters 5 and 6 and will return to some of them later in this chapter.)

Why are parties so central to governing, especially in legislatures? To answer this question, it is helpful to consider a process of making policy decisions in the absence of parties. The following story highlights the role that parties play in controlling agendas and keeping policy-making coalitions together, and, more generally, in solving collective dilemmas inside legislatures.

Unstable Coalitions in Legislatures. In Chapter 1, we discussed the concept of an unstable coalition, which is one kind of collective dilemma. We revisited the concept in Chapter 5. Let's now reconsider the situation in a new hypothetical legislature, which we will call the House of Delegates (Figure 12.2). We use a hypothetical example to show that the insights gained from the example apply to any legislature in the world, to the U.S. Congress, to the state legislatures in the United States, and to other countries.

Suppose for the sake of argument that there are three roughly equal-sized groups in the House and that they each vote as blocs—that is, each legislator within a group votes as the leader of that group says to vote. One group represents students, another represents veterans, and another represents farmers. As expected, they legislate by majority rule, and here this means that any two of the groups joining together can pass a law. A bill can be proposed by any one leader of a group, and a vote is held—yea or nay—on the bill. Before voting on a bill, though, the leader of any other group can stand up and propose an amendment. Members can propose as many amendments as they wish. Each of the amendments must be approved or rejected before the final bill is voted on.

In our simple scenario, the members of the House are intent on passing legislation to benefit the people they represent. The ideal bill for, say, the students would tax farmers and veterans and give all the benefits to students. But such a bill would not be supported by the representatives of either the

FIGURE 12.2

Parties and Unstable Coalitions in Legislatures

Starting Coalition: Students introduce amendment that gives them 50% of all goods and 50% to the veterans.

Farmers introduce amendment that gives them 40% and increases veterans' share to 60% in order to gain their support.

The cycle of coalitions continues.

Coalition

Students **Veterans**

Coalition

Farmers **Veterans**

Coalition

Veterans **Farmers**

Students introduce amendment that gives them 50% and increases the farmers' 40% to 50%.

Veterans introduce amendment that gives them 50% and increases the farmers' share to 50%.

Coalition

Farmers **Students**

Coalition

Students **Farmers**

Farmers introduce amendment that gives them 40% and increases students' share to 60%.

Coalition

Students **Veterans**

Coalition

Veterans **Farmers**

Veterans introduce amendment that gives them 40% and increases the farmers' share to 60%.

Students introduce amendment that gives them 50% and increases veterans' share to 50%.

veterans or the farmers. The student group needs to propose legislation that at least one of the other two groups will support. So the student group proposes a bill to tax farmers and spread the benefits between students and veterans in a bid to get the support of the representatives of the veterans. In short, students and veterans get everything they want under this bill, and farmers get nothing but higher taxes.

Now let's say that the leader of the farmers' group proposes an amendment that effectively changes the entire bill. Under the amendment, veterans and farmers benefit from the public good and the taxes fall entirely on students. To win the support of the representatives of the veterans, the farmers' group offers slightly more of the public good to veterans than the previous students' bill was proposing. In short, veterans and farmers get everything they want, while students get nothing but higher taxes.

Before any of this can be voted on, however, the student group proposes an amendment to the farmers' amendment. As you might guess, the goal of the students is to entice the farmers to join with the students and to tax veterans. Then the representatives of the veterans respond by attaching an amendment to the students' amendment, this time proposing a coalition of veterans and farmers that entails students paying for the public good with taxes. In theory, this amendment process can go on forever. Note that eventually, the House will end up repeating the coalitions—sometimes students and farmers, sometimes students and veterans, and so on—as it repeats the process. The coalitions can "cycle" if no one controls the agenda.

In Chapter 1, we noted that putting institutions in place to assign agenda-setting control to specific members of a decision-making body can help prevent coalition cycles. In our simple example, policies and coalitions can cycle indefinitely and end up anywhere the process stops. Imagine how cycling could occur in a representative body as large as the U.S. House of Representatives, whose 435 members represent many more groups than students, veterans, and farmers! All it would take to upset any existing coalition in favor of a bill is for one person to propose an amendment.

Political parties are the key institutions that prevent coalition cycling in legislatures around the world. How do parties do this? Members who form parties essentially promise to support each other's bills most of the time and not to propose distracting or potentially divisive amendments. In our example, perhaps farmers and students create a durable coalition by promising to support each other's proposals most of the time, and not to propose something that will split their votes. In this way, parties create reputations for groups of politicians. Students and farmers could label their group something (the Liberal Party, for example) and try to convince voters that they are the reliable representatives for their districts. They signal to voters, "We will support each other in the legislature and thus pass helpful policies for you." The need for a positive reputation among voters gives them incentives to stay consistent in their support for certain kinds of policies and allied with others who tend to agree with them ideologically.

You might ask, why not form a universal party coalition with farmers, students, and veterans all together? Well, someone needs to pay for the benefits, and those who pay more than the others will need to be left out of the winning coalition and so will be unhappy and form the opposition. The view of those who are left out is that hopefully in the next round of elections, they can win enough seats to form a majority. The prospect of new elections avoids a situation where opposition parties believe they will be in opposition forever (and thus is the main difference between a one-party state and a true democracy).

The preceding scenario illustrates why parties are useful, and perhaps even necessary, in any legislative body. Although our example is greatly simplified, there is strong evidence that in the early sessions of Congress, just after the Founding, politicians formed parties in just this manner. At first there were many shifting coalitions, and members of Congress were unhappy with the uncertainty and the difficulty in getting things done. Then, as parties formed and Congress divided into stable coalitions under the party labels, Federalist and Republican—they did so to establish reputations to run for election against their opponents—Congress was able to pass key policies and avoid coalition cycles.[6] In the earliest Congress, the Federalists formed a majority and passed legislation whose costs were imposed primarily on the constituencies of the Republicans. Later, the Republicans won control of the Congress and turned the tables, passing the costs on to the constituencies of the Federalists.

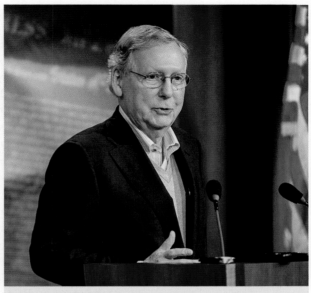

Party leaders in legislatures, like Senate Majority Leader Mitch McConnell, keep coalitions together by imposing discipline on their members. They may use pressure and enticements to ensure that their members vote in line with the party's overall goals.

The same function for parties holds true in modern times. We learned in Chapter 5 that parties are vital to the workings of Congress. Recall that the two major parties hold their own caucuses (meetings of all party members in Congress) and elect leaders, such as the speaker of the House (if the party holds the majority in that chamber) and the majority party leaders, whips, the committee and subcommittee chairs, and the leaders of the campaign committees. Of particular importance in the House is the Rules Committee (discussed in Chapter 5), which the majority party leadership uses to set the agenda for the entire chamber.

In the contemporary Congress, the Republicans have a challenging divide between mainstream Republicans, who tend to be strong on national defense and moderate to conservative on fiscal affairs, and Freedom Caucus (or Tea Party) Republicans, who favor much smaller government. Both factions within the Republicans tend to favor conservative policies on social issues. A major task of the leaders of the Republican Party is to hold their coalition together and avoid being divided by counterproposals from the Democrats. Similar problems arise for Democrats when they control either or both chambers of Congress. The moderate and more liberal wings of the Democrats, while united against the Republicans, usually struggle to find common ground on certain policy proposals. When the parties have such factional divides, the potential threat of "cycling" and unstable voting coalitions becomes more palpable, and

[6] John H. Aldrich, *Why Parties? A Second Look* (Chicago: University of Chicago Press, 2011).

the need within the party for strong agenda control of the legislative process becomes paramount.

Because political parties are present wherever there are free and fair elections and representative government, and because they largely succeed at controlling agendas, we rarely see the kinds of coalition cycles described earlier within legislative bodies. Parties actively seek to prevent their members from peeling away from coalitions by imposing as much discipline as possible, although, as we will discuss later, they do not always succeed. Besides agenda control, party leaders may apply pressure on reluctant members in the legislature or offer them enticements to vote for party-favored bills, such as pork-barrel projects for their districts (see Chapter 5) or funding for their reelection campaigns.[7]

Parties are also important for presidents and other executives (such as governors), especially in aligning their goals and actions with those of legislatures. President Obama, besides being identified and running for office as a Democrat, received assistance in enacting his policies from Democratic Party organizations both inside and outside Congress. He struggled and competed against the majority Republicans in the House of Representatives. Likewise, President Trump relied on Republicans in Congress and on Republican organizations around the country to help achieve his policy goals. He also faces opposition from Democrats in Congress, especially as the majority in the House.

Parties as Organizations

Outside of the government, the parties' activities mainly center on winning elections. Parties as organizations nominate candidates, help candidates get their messages out to potential voters and supporters, hire campaign workers, raise money, and turn out voters on election days. They do this at multiple levels. The national party organizations focus on presidential and congressional elections. State and local organizations focus on elections for state legislatures and governorships—and, to varying degrees across states, on helping to elect the presidential and congressional candidates in national elections.

Organizational Features. In general, American parties are quite loosely organized. They are not strongly hierarchical. The major American parties are large, sprawling, decentralized organizations, much like the government as a whole. In fact, the organizational chart of the Republican and Democratic parties reflects the structure of the federal system within which they operate (Figure 12.3).

[7] Gary Cox and Mathew McCubbins, *Legislative Leviathan: Party Government in the House*, 2nd ed. (New York: Cambridge University Press, 1993).

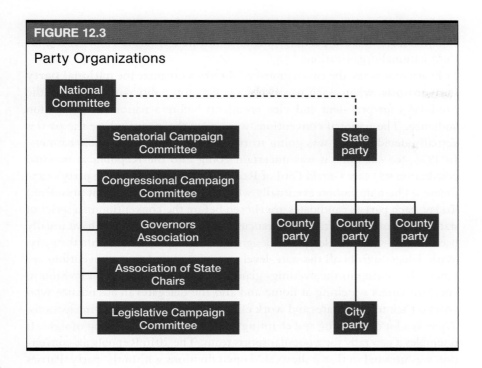

FIGURE 12.3

Party Organizations

In addition to the national party organizations, there are state-level party organizations, and within each state there are county-level and often city-level units. Local party offices help local candidates with fund-raising and public relations, answer questions from the press and from potential voters, and sometimes act as campaign offices for specific candidates. Candidates for federal office—either the presidency or Congress—also set up their own campaign organizations. So it is not unusual for a given city to have parallel offices supporting the same candidate—one for the candidate's campaign organization and one for the local party. The degree to which these offices coordinate with each other varies tremendously.

The Republican National Committee and the Democratic National Committee oversee the operation of their parties over the entire country. The two **national committees** plot their party's strategy, decide on rules for nominating elections and conventions, and try to coordinate candidates on common campaign themes. These committees are populated by politicians, activists, and major donors. The heads of the committees are often former politicians who have standing within the party and untarnished credentials as party loyalists and successful fund-raisers. They can be influential in reshaping the organization of the parties. In the 1980s, for instance, several leaders of the Republican National Committee pushed and prodded state and local party organizations to use direct mail fund-raising strategies to

national committee Officials who oversee the operation of their party nationwide.

increase revenues for election campaigns and voter-turnout drives. Similarly, today, leaders of both parties work to coordinate Internet fund-raising for their national organizations.

national party convention
The meeting where the party formally nominates its presidential candidate.

Every four years, the two national committees organize the **national party conventions**, where each party showcases its top politicians (including the candidates for president and vice president) before a nationwide television audience. The national conventions were once the events where the parties actually decided who was going to run for president under their banners. In 1976, for example, it was uncertain going into the Republican national convention whether Gerald Ford or Ronald Reagan would be the party's candidate. (The nomination eventually went to Ford, the incumbent president.) Today, each party's candidates are chosen before the convention in a series of state-level primary elections and caucuses. National conventions have usually become well-scripted celebrations designed to crown the victor within the party. With delegates from all the state-level parties in attendance, conventions are raucus, becoming in the evenings giant, noisy rallies shown on television to energize voters watching at home and also the delegates in attendance who will go back to their states and work on behalf of candidates to win elections. There is a lot of cheering and chanting, loud applause, and waving of signs. It resembles a pep rally for a popular sports team. The 2016 Republican convention was unusual in that it showcased open divisions within the party. Parties try to avoid exposing such divisions on television, but, because of Donald Trump's candidacy, the Republicans could not keep such divisions hidden.

In the daytime, attendees at the convention conduct the work of organizing the campaign efforts in committee meetings. Although the national committees set the rules for the national conventions (including who is invited), they have little operational control over lower-level party organizations. They occasionally use punishments or rewards in trying to compel lower-level units to comply with national standards or goals. When the national committee is displeased with a state or local organization, for example, it can refuse to seat the organization's delegation at the national convention. In the early 1960s, as the national Democratic Party became more liberal on racial issues, it closed the door to delegations from several southern states in which the local Democratic Party discriminated against black voters and candidates.

party professional A person who works directly for the party, is loyal to its goal of winning elections, and stays with it over long periods through multiple election cycles.

party amateur An issue activist who is mostly interested in specific policy areas and works for the party, or for specific politicians within the party, to advance these goals.

Political party organizations at any level—national, state, and local—consist of diverse people with various levels of commitment to the party. Political scientist James Q. Wilson draws a useful contrast between party professionals and party amateurs. **Party professionals** work directly for the party, are loyal to its goal of winning elections, and stay with it over long periods through multiple election cycles. **Party amateurs**, by contrast, are issue activists who are mostly interested in specific policy areas—such as environmentalism, pro-choice or pro-life abortion policies, gun control or gun rights, and health care reform—and work for the party, or for specific politicians within the party, to advance those goals. Amateurs have less direct loyalty to the party than professionals and are often paid by outside interest groups. Wilson's main point is that professionals make the parties run on a day-to-day basis, whereas amateurs push for change within parties when warranted, and sometimes even switch parties.[8]

Solving Collective Dilemmas among Candidates and Voters. Parties as organizations also solve two kinds of collective dilemmas: coordination problems among candidates and voters, and collective action problems among voters.

One of the major tasks political parties work on is coordinating candidates to run for office. Early in American history, party leaders chose candidates in meetings that were essentially private. These caucuses were often depicted as taking place in so-called **smoke-filled rooms**, where party leaders haggled and traded favors to get their chosen candidates on the ballots. Today, most state-level parties hold **primary elections** to choose candidates. As discussed in Chapters 5 and 13, primary elections occur months before Election Day and allow voters to select the candidates who will appear on the ballot under a given party label. In most states, voters can take part in only one of the two parties' primaries. Even when parties hold caucuses today, voters usually need to be registered party members to participate in the process of choosing party leaders. Thus, caucuses are no longer political horse-trading sessions so much as quasi-elections with a selective electorate.

By choosing only one candidate for each office to run under the party label, the party is, in effect, solving the coordination problem for its voters. Once again, let's consider a simplified example. Suppose three people want to win election to Congress from a given district; we'll call them Andy, Bob, and Carla. Andy and Bob are liberal and would like to be listed as Democrats on the ballot, while Carla is the lone conservative and would like to be listed as the Republican nominee. According to polls, 60 percent of the district's voters are liberals who generally vote Democratic and 40 percent are conservatives who generally vote Republican (Figure 12.4).

Early in the campaign, neither Andy nor Bob will step aside to let the other run as the sole liberal Democrat. If only one runs, he can virtually guarantee a victory over Carla, and the majority of liberals in the district will get their preferred ideology represented in Congress. If Andy and Bob both run, however, they may split the liberal vote and throw the election to Carla. The liberals in the district need to find a way to coordinate their efforts on a single candidate. If they fail to coordinate, they may lose the election even though a majority of voters in the district support their ideology. In this case, the local Democratic Party might, with the assistance of the state government,

smoke-filled room A situation in which party elites make important decisions away from the scrutiny or influence of party membership.

primary election An election held before Election Day to allow voters to select which candidates will appear on the ballot under a party label.

[8] James Q. Wilson, *Political Organizations* (Princeton, NJ: Princeton University Press, 1995).

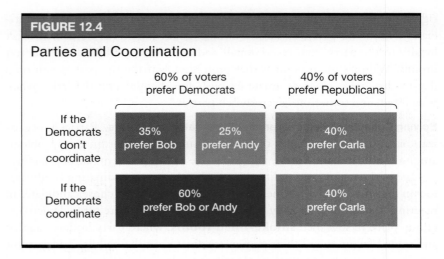

FIGURE 12.4

Parties and Coordination

	60% of voters prefer Democrats		40% of voters prefer Republicans
If the Democrats don't coordinate	35% prefer Bob	25% prefer Andy	40% prefer Carla
If the Democrats coordinate	60% prefer Bob or Andy		40% prefer Carla

hold a primary election or a caucus to determine which candidate should be listed on the ballot as the Democratic nominee.

There are two important caveats to the notion that parties solve these kinds of coordination problems. First, they need help from the laws regulating elections. The key to parties' ability to solve the coordination problem is that the election laws enforce the rule that the parties "own" their spots on the ballot. Thus, if Andy beats Bob in the party primary, then the Democrats mandate that Bob cannot run for election as a Democrat. The law enforces the rule that the parties control how many people can run under their labels. In principle, Bob could leave the party and run under another party label or as an independent, but unless he is extraordinarily popular, he will likely lose, given party loyalties in the electorate. It is rare in the United States for someone running for national or state office to lose a primary election and then quit the party to run under another party label.[9] In fact, some states have laws against so-called sore losers. These laws prohibit a candidate losing a state's primary election within a party from running in the general election, even for another party or as an independent.

Second, party organizations must do more than just solve coordination problems among candidates and voters; they must also solve such problems between voters, funders, and publicists. As we've seen, parties take strong action to set the agenda for voters, which essentially means choosing the set of candidates available on ballots. But beyond just the leaders of parties, other

[9] It can happen, of course. In 2006, Joe Lieberman, Democratic Senator from Connecticut, lost his party's primary during his bid for reelection. He ran in the general election as a third-party candidate against Republican and Democratic opponents and won.

elite actors—including the major funders, interest group leaders, and activists—play a predominant role in throwing their support behind a small number of viable candidates, signaling to primary voters and party leaders that these are the candidates on which to coordinate.[10]

Also, as we learned in Chapter 10, voters face a collective action problem in deciding whether to participate in elections. Because voting can be costly and elections almost never turn on a single vote, it may be rational for people to stay home, free ride, and let others vote. The problem for political parties is that they need "their" voters to turn out to defeat the other parties' candidates. The party that best solves the collective action problem among its loyal voters stands the best chance of winning the election. Thus, party organizations try to make it easier for voters to understand their options and get to the polls. They subsidize transportation to the polls, make phone calls to convince voters that their votes count, and highlight the benefits that the party's candidates will bring to the district (or the damage their opponents will do if they get elected).[11] Organizations advertise the parties' messages widely. They try to make voters see the high stakes involved in the election contests. Party organizations devote considerable efforts to convincing people to turn out to vote and not to free ride off others.

Parties in the Electorate

When scholars refer to parties in the electorate, they mean the large numbers of people with **party identification**, defined as attachment or loyalty to a political party. At any given moment, the political parties have a level of base support among the population—the proportion of people who consider themselves loyal to the party and nearly always vote for its candidates in elections. The Democratic Party, for example, has millions of people who consider themselves loyal Democrats, and that loyalty can be manifest in a variety of ways, from donating money to working for Democratic candidates, supporting the party itself, or simply voting consistently for Democrats. The same is true for the Republican Party.

In Chapter 9, we saw how party identification in the electorate as a whole fluctuates over time in response to world events and the actions of the government. The population samples used in Figure 9.4 are representative of millions of people. Switching our attention now to the individual voter, scholars conceive of party identification in various ways: as a psychological attachment, an informational shortcut, and a running tally of politicians' performance.

party identification Loyalty or psychological attachment to a political party.

---

[10] Marty Cohen, David Karol, Hans Noel, and John Zaller, *The Party Decides: Presidential Nominations Before and After Reform* (Chicago: University of Chicago Press, 2008).

[11] See the discussion of negative campaigning in Chapter 13.

Psychological Attachment. Many scholars think of party identification as a stable psychological attachment, the perceptual filter through which people learn about politics and evaluate government and politicians. As we learned in Chapter 9, this has been called the Michigan model, after a group of researchers at the University of Michigan in the 1950s and 1960s who promoted this view.[12] People have allegiances to particular parties, allegiances that color how they perceive the political world and how they make voting decisions. The key aspect of this approach is that party identification introduces a bias. When a Democrat learns of a policy action by President Barack Obama, he or she is more inclined than a Republican to trust the president and believe he is doing the right thing, even if the policy is moderately conservative. Although it is generally true that Democrats are more liberal and Republicans more conservative, party identification in this model is more than a proxy for ideology; it structures how individuals perceive the trustworthiness and incentives of people in government, and how they evaluate policies depending on who supports those policies. For Democrats, for example, Democratic politicians are "on their team," and thus Democrats trust that the Democratic politicians act more in their interest than Republicans do.

Informational Shortcut. A slightly different way to think about party identification is as an informational shortcut. As discussed in Chapter 9, many people do not pay much attention to politics. Even those who vote regularly often have difficulty grasping all of the information necessary to make good sense of the political system and how it operates. The American political system is complex; there are many different kinds of elections across all levels of government and numerous candidates and policies are at stake. Party identification in the electorate helps people make sense of this complexity. In recent decades, for example, Democratic candidates have generally supported abortion rights while Republican candidates have opposed them. People can reasonably categorize candidates and politicians simply on the basis of party labels. By making it easier to navigate the political world, such labels substantially reduce the costs of becoming informed.[13]

Running Tally. A third way to think about party identification in the electorate is as a "running tally" of the performance of party leaders. The thinking goes like this: I will be a Republican (or a Democrat) as long as the party leaders perform well and to my liking. If my party disappoints me repeatedly and I think the other party might offer better performance, I will switch my allegiance. In this respect, party identification is like loyalty to a brand or individual based on the consistent quality of their products. Just as with your

---

[12] Angus Campbell, Philip E. Converse, Warren E. Miller, and Donald E. Stokes, *The American Voter*, unabridged edition (Chicago: University of Chicago Press, 1980).

[13] Arthur Lupia and Mathew D. McCubbins, *The Democratic Dilemma: Can Citizens Learn What They Need to Know?* (New York: Cambridge University Press, 1998).

favorite video games, politicians with labels like Democrat or Republican have certain features that we rely on. We know, for instance, that our favorite video game franchise produces great new games in its series every so often, and so we continue to pay attention to what they produce and buy their new games. But if they make a string of changes, which we find detract from the quality of the game, the game platform might cease to be our favorite and we may choose not to buy new games in the series. A party label is not only an informational shortcut but also a marker of quality that has to be repeatedly earned by politicians.

Thinking of party labels as similar to brands helps explain why officials in the government have incentives to cooperate with one another. For instance, members of Congress from the same party tend to support each others' bills. Cooperation among politicians within the legislature makes it possible for voters to group them under labels such as Democrats (liberals) and Republicans (conservatives). By the same token, political parties seek to build brand loyalty and expand the number of people who support them. Thus Republicans and Democrats compete to improve their brand and so try to win people's loyalty and perhaps induce enduring party identification.

The two ways of considering party identification just described—as an informational shortcut and as a running tally (brand)—differ from the Michigan model in considering party identification less as a psychological bias than as a rational response to complex information or to the performance of people in government.[14] What is not in dispute among anyone who studies public opinion and voting behavior is that party identification is the best predictor of how people will vote in elections.[15] As we will discuss in Chapter 13, party identification within the electorate, in democracies across the world, is the most important factor in determining people's decisions at the polls. Even if a voter is a loyal Democrat who did not like the job that Barack Obama was doing, chances are quite strong that she voted for Hillary Clinton in 2016. Her party identification likely overrode her dissatisfaction with the president's performance.

Some scholars have tried to probe more deeply to understand how and why people develop party identification. Not surprisingly, if you are born into a household of loyal Republicans, you will tend to become a loyal Republican as you attain voting age and likely will retain your party loyalty for the rest of your life. That is the usual pattern, but the exceptions are noteworthy. Over the course of several elections, some people do switch their party identification. In the longer term, whole communities and regions commonly switch loyalties in response to changing circumstances. For example, African

[14] Morris Fiorina, "An Outline for a Model of Party Choice," *American Journal of Political Science* 21 (August 1977): 601–25.

[15] Larry M. Bartels, "Partisanship and Voting Behavior, 1952–1996," *American Journal of Political Science* 44 (January 2000): 35–50.

Americans largely switched from being loyal Republicans in the early twentieth century to being loyal Democrats by the mid-twentieth century. Conversely, white southerners became increasingly Republican between the 1960s and 1990s. Studies of new democracies have shown that for people voting in a country's first few elections, party identification appears to develop over multiple elections and not right away. The habit of voting for one party because the voter likes the ideology of its candidates tends to lead to lifelong partisan loyalty that often extends across generations as young people adopt the party identification of their parents.

The History of the American Party System

That parties sprout and grow as democratic processes unfold is illustrated by the early American experience. Also apparent throughout the history of American parties is the role that factional splits, and occasional third and minor parties, play in altering the popular coalitions that form around the two major parties.

The country's original two political parties, the Federalists and Republicans, developed in the 1790s, and many historians consider them the world's first two modern parties. Some earlier groups bore resemblance. In the 1600s and 1700s the British parliament had organized factions that were like parties, but they had no connection to popular elections. The American colonies had party-like organizations within their assemblies, and some of these party labels appeared on election ballots both before and after the Revolution. But such party-like groups were fundamentally different from political parties as we know them today. All modern parties combine the three functions described earlier: they organize government action, field slates of candidates to compete in mass elections, and appeal to voters based on labels. Such parties originated in the era immediately following ratification of the U.S. Constitution.

Political scientists divide the history of American political parties into six periods, or systems, that reflect the dynamics between the major parties.

The First Party System

Even though George Washington warned against the formation of parties, the Federalists and Republicans became locked in tight competition for control of Congress and the presidency in the second half of the 1790s. Both parties needed to mobilize voters throughout the country to win elections. Compared to contemporary parties, they operated on a small scale, even relative to the size of the country. As we learned in Chapters 2 and 10, few men were eligible to vote in the early years of the republic, and Congress was relatively small. Nevertheless, these two loosely organized parties resembled modern political parties in linking their partisan labels to policy programs and then asking voters to choose candidates on the basis of those labels. For instance, the Federalists favored a strong national government and leaned toward England, while the Republicans favored states' rights and leaned toward France. Scholars refer to the Federalist versus Republican era, roughly from 1796 to 1824, as the First Party System in the United States.

The Second Party System

By the 1820s, the Federalist Party had become defunct, having lost popular support because of its opposition to the War of 1812. During the "Era of Good Feelings" that followed, the Republicans faced little opposition. They were increasingly being called the Democratic-Republicans and eventually were known as the Democrats. The Second Party System began in 1832 with the rise of the Whig Party, which united remnants of the old Federalist Party with disenchanted Democratic-Republicans. The Democratic-Republicans split over presidential candidates in 1828 and 1832; those who followed the leadership of Andrew Jackson became the Democrats while most others became Whigs. The modern Democratic Party is the oldest active political party in the world, tracing its origins to the 1832 election (even though it emerged out of the older Republican Party).

This Second Party System of Whigs and Democrats lasted until 1860. The Whigs favored active commercial policies to assist manufacturers and business development in the West and Midwest while the Democrats opposed tariffs and supported states' rights on issues such as slavery. Most presidents in this era were Democrats, but the Whigs won a few presidential elections and controlled several sessions of Congress in the 1840s.

A major development in political parties occurred during the Second Party System. The Democrats, through state-level organizations and inspired by the candidacy of Andrew Jackson and later under the guidance of President Martin Van Buren, developed the capacity to mobilize tens of thousands of voters to win congressional seats and choose presidential electors. The parties became oriented toward solving collective dilemmas among voters and getting voters to the polls. This required tremendous organizing skills and the development of complex state-level party organizations. State party conventions not only served as forums to select candidates for election ballots but also became large, raucous affairs designed to stir up the party faithful and mobilize voters. The Democrats led the way in organizing, but the Whigs made similar gains. By the late 1840s, the Second Party System included two well-organized parties that were adept at turning out vast numbers of voters, or, as we would say today, "energizing their base." Many new voters entered the electoral process thanks to the mobilizing actions of these two parties. Patronage by presidents also helped in the process by giving citizens incentives to support one party or the other (see Chapters 6 and 7).

The Third Party System

The discord leading up to the Civil War on the issues of slavery and westward expansion split the two major parties and ultimately destroyed the Whigs as a party. Both Whigs and Democrats had anti- and proslavery factions, and the new Republicans—initially a third party challenging the Whigs and Democrats—emerged from the ashes of the Whig Party in the late 1850s as it split apart. The new Republicans' aim had been to unite antislavery voters from both parties with people who generally favored Whig economic policies, and indeed, most antislavery Democrats became Republicans. In a close race with multiple candidates, Abraham Lincoln won the presidency as a Republican in 1860.

Throughout the Civil War and well into the twentieth century, the Republican Party was identified as mostly northern and to some extent western, and it was in favor of national policies designed to help manufacturers and mining interests. The Democrats survived the Civil War intact. The South remained staunchly Democratic for another 110 years, largely because Republicans had been identified with the Union cause. The Democrats also began to prosper in the latter half of the nineteenth century in large northern cities. Among working-class and poor (mostly Catholic) immigrants, the Democrats were the partisan counterbalance to the mostly Protestant Republicans. What historians refer to as the Third Party System, which lasted from 1860 to 1896, was evenly balanced (after the Civil War) between

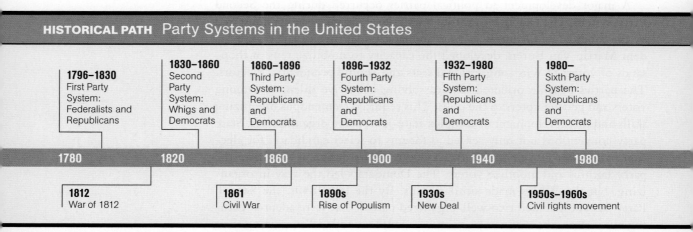

HISTORICAL PATH Party Systems in the United States

1796–1830 First Party System: Federalists and Republicans

1830–1860 Second Party System: Whigs and Democrats

1860–1896 Third Party System: Republicans and Democrats

1896–1932 Fourth Party System: Republicans and Democrats

1932–1980 Fifth Party System: Republicans and Democrats

1980– Sixth Party System: Republicans and Democrats

1780   1820   1860   1900   1940   1980

1812 War of 1812

1861 Civil War

1890s Rise of Populism

1930s New Deal

1950s–1960s Civil rights movement

Republicans and Democrats but had a strong sectional flavor. Republicans mostly dominated the Northeast and Midwest while Democrats were stronger in the South and in large cities. The two parties were more or less equally strong in the West.[16]

In this era, both parties, but especially the Democrats, developed a system of "machine politics" in northern cities such as Boston, New York, Baltimore, and Chicago. A **political machine** is a local organization with such broad control of the city or county government that it can reward whole neighborhoods, wards, and precincts with benefits such as jobs and government programs in return for supporting the party's candidates. Party machines relied on the use of patronage by local officials to win the loyalty of voters. In the late nineteenth century, political machines were often strong in cities that had large immigrant populations. They devoted considerable effort to obtain citizenship for immigrants so they could vote in elections and support the appropriate party's candidates. The incorporation of new immigrant voters into the electoral process fostered a strong connection between northern, urban Catholics and the Democratic Party.

political machine A local organization that controls the city or county government to such an extent that it can reward whole neighborhoods, wards, precincts, or other groups with benefits such as jobs and government programs in return for supporting the party's candidates.

The Fourth Party System

The election of 1896 was a watershed moment that ushered in the Fourth Party System. The election pitted William Jennings Bryan, nominated by both the Democrats and the Populists (a third party), against William McKinley, a pro-business Republican with ties to northern manufacturers and financiers who was intent on developing the West for the expansion of commerce. At stake in the election was the fate of a brand of government activism promoted by the Populists and some Democrats that would redistribute wealth and power from industrial titans to farmers and the poor. The Populist/Democratic coalition foundered on its own internal splits over racial issues (mostly between southern and northern wings of the Democrats) and over the specific policy proscriptions for redistribution. McKinley won the election by a decisive margin. There was continued sectionalism in this era as well—the South remained strongly Democratic, while the North and Midwest were strongly Republican.

Known mostly for Republican dominance of the national government for the next 34 years, the Fourth Party System saw the rise of the Progressives in 1912, the most potent third party in American history in terms of capturing votes in national elections. The Progressives were mostly former Republicans who mistrusted Democrats—and believed that machine-style politics was hopelessly corrupt—but were in favor of more government regulation than traditional Republicans.

[16] William E. Gienapp, *The Origins of the Republican Party, 1852–1856* (New York: Oxford University Press, 1994).

This image shows members of Tammany Hall, a powerful political machine in New York, helping to naturalize immigrants in exchange for votes for the Democratic Party in the 1856 election. As indicated by the man with a club in his hand, this process was not always an innocent one.

As a political party, the Progressives did not really become prominent until 1912, under the leadership of former President Theodore Roosevelt. But progressive ideals had been a focus of attention in American politics for more than a decade. For most of the nineteenth century, candidates were chosen either informally by local party leaders or by caucuses composed of party leaders and activists. During the first decade of the twentieth century, as part of progressive reforms to reduce corruption in politics, the parties began to use primary elections to choose candidates for the general election ballots. By 1920, most state parties had switched to using primaries for congressional candidates, and the trend in presidential elections during the early twentieth century was an increasing use of primaries. Although the Progressives succeeded in enacting many reforms, they did not last as a political party. Nevertheless, the Progressive reforms of electoral processes, including primaries, secret ballots, and anticorruption laws, eroded the strength of parties at the state and local levels, and strengthened the power of individual candidates vis-à-vis party organizations. Historians attribute a decline in voter turnout in the early twentieth century (see Chapter 10) to these Progressive reforms. Furthermore, the growing individualism of members of Congress in the twentieth century can be linked to the effects of these reforms (see Chapter 5).

The American Political Parties

- The United States has had two major parties throughout its history, though the identities of those two parties have changed. Currently, the Democratic and Republican parties dominate local, state, and national elections.

  - Other major parties have existed over the course of American history.

    - The Federalists, who were infuential in the decades following the Founding, were replaced by the Whigs, who were then replaced by the Republicans.

    - The Democratic Party emerged from the Democratic-Republicans, a party that first arose to compete with the Federalists early in American history.

- Third parties occasionally have influenced politics in the United States.

  - The Republicans began as a third party in the 1850s and replaced the Whigs by 1860 as the major party opposed to the Democrats. Thus, it is fair to say that the Republicans were the most successful third party in American history.

  - The Progressive Party, which emerged in the late nineteenth century, advocated for electoral reforms and for more government intervention in the economy. As with most third-party movements, elements of the Progressives' platform were incorporated into the major parties' platforms.

The American Party System

- Duverger's Law (named after the French political theorist Maurice Duverger) suggests that in a winner-take-all (plurality) electoral system like that of the United States, where the candidate with the most votes wins a single seat in an election, the number of parties competing to hold office will generally be two.

The Fifth Party System

The Fifth Party System, sometimes called the **New Deal Party System**, began in 1932 with the election of Democratic president Franklin Delano Roosevelt (FDR). It was solidified in 1936 with FDR's landslide reelection and the overwhelming victory of the Democrats in Congress. This system began to fray in the 1960s but lapsed more completely in the 1980s. FDR's New Deal coalition united several large voting blocs for the purpose of winning national elections:

New Deal Party System
A political alliance between southern Democrats, big-city Democrats, rural voters, and African Americans that endured for several decades after the election of Franklin Roosevelt in 1932.

- the southern wing of the Democratic Party
- big-city Democrats from the North and Midwest
- farmers who benefited from New Deal programs and policies
- increasing numbers of African Americans who favored the New Deal and began to see the Democrats as more supportive of their goals

The last two groups—farmers and African Americans—had favored Republicans before the 1930s, so FDR's success in earning many of their votes for Democrats was a major change. In fact, it ushered in nearly four decades of Democratic dominance of national government.

In the latter half of the twentieth century, as a result of the New Deal policies and the Fifth Party System, Democrats were clearly identified as the more liberal party. They emphasized active government intervention in the economy, civil rights for African Americans and other minorities, and openness to nontraditional social mores. Republicans were identified as the more conservative party, meaning that they preferred less government intervention in the economy, less government spending in general on domestic programs, and more traditional social values. In addition, during the Cold War, Republicans were seen by voters as the more anticommunist of the two parties, advocating an aggressive foreign policy against the Soviet Union.

The Democrats' New Deal coalition was the predominant partisan coalition in American politics in the mid-twentieth century. Between the 1960s and 1980s, however, largely because of the two parties' positions on civil rights, increasing numbers of southern whites switched their support to the Republicans, and by the mid-1990s the once "solidly Democratic" South had become solidly Republican. Meanwhile, Republicans improved their support among Catholics throughout the country. Many Catholics had left big cities to settle in the suburbs, and they supported Republicans because of their stand against abortion rights. The process of Republicans increasingly attracting white southerners and Catholics began under President Richard Nixon, who was first elected in 1968, and came to fruition in the 1980s, when Ronald Reagan won over many former Democrats and helped create the contemporary relationship between the parties. Completing a process begun in the 1930s, African Americans in all regions of the country overwhelmingly became Democrats by the 1960s because people saw that party as favoring strong government actions to address discrimination and supporting civil rights policies.

The Sixth Party System

Most scholars believe that we are now in the Sixth Party System (Table 12.1). It is characterized by many of the same policy positions the two parties took in the New Deal Era: Democrats generally favor more activist intervention

TABLE 12.1

The Sixth Party System

Democratic Votes Tend to Come from:	Republican Votes Tend to Come from:
Residents of the large cities of the East, Upper Midwest, and West Coast	White suburban residents
	White rural residents
African Americans	Whites in the South
Jews	Residents of the Mountain West and High Plains
Latinos	
Labor union members	Business owners and executives
Lower income earners	Wealthy retirees
Moderately paid professionals	Well-paid professionals
Gays and lesbians	Religiously observant Christians
Strong environmentalists	Conservatives
Liberals	

in the economy, and Republicans favor smaller government. Yet the breakdown of voters by region and locale (urban, suburban, and rural) has changed since the Fifth Party System. On average, suburban and rural voters are more Republican than big-city residents. Moreover, the South has switched sides, so to speak, from Democrat to Republican. It is important to emphasize, however, that this partisan imbalance springs from the overwhelmingly Republican leanings of white southerners; African Americans, Hispanics, Jews, and other groups in the South continue to favor Democrats.

A prominent feature of the Sixth Party System is that the national parties are stronger as organizations than they have ever been. Although they still cannot control lower-level parties to the degree that national parties can in other countries, they have more money and more influence than in any previous era. The strengthening of national party organizations was a key development of the 1980s. Until then, the Democratic and Republican parties functioned primarily as collections of state-level parties that met every four years to choose presidential candidates. Both national parties were relatively weak. They had small budgets, little power over state and local parties, and loose rules for how states chose delegates to the national conventions and candidates for national office.

By the 1980s, led by the Republicans, the two parties developed vast nationwide organizations to raise money for their candidates. The parties began to enforce national rules that reduced the autonomy of state-level parties. Whereas the state-level parties had been responsible for raising money and mobilizing voters for their own candidates and for presidential candidates, today's national organizations raise money and dispense it to congressional candidates throughout the country. They often set up their own organizations in the states to assist the party's presidential candidate. These national party organizations now work in parallel with state-level organizations.

As a result, the national parties' power today far exceeds the power they held in the nineteenth and early twentieth centuries. In the 2008 presidential primary season, for example, the national Democratic Party refused for a time to recognize delegates from Michigan and Florida because these states did not strictly follow national party guidelines for when they could hold their primary elections. It was not the first time something like this happened, but instances of the national party imposing its rules on state-level parties have become more frequent in recent decades.[17]

A continuing threat to the contemporary parties is the possibility of internal splits and even third and minor parties appealing to enough voters to thwart election victory. We have already discussed the role of the Tea Party in the Republican Party. Members of the Tea Party faction have remained mostly loyal to the Republicans in their general elections against Democrats, but in Congress and certainly during the party primaries to choose Republicans candidates, the presence of the Tea Party continues to challenge the Republican leadership as it tries to hold together a unified set of people and principles. Always looming is the possibility that some candidates will run as Tea Party candidates against Republicans and Democrats in races at the local, state, and federal levels; this idea fills Republican leaders with dread because support for the Tea Party would drain support mostly from Republicans. Meanwhile, Trump campaigned on policies directly opposed to Republican orthodoxy: against free trade and against international alliances and treaties like NATO and NAFTA. While he was able to attract new voters into the Republican column (some who previously voted Democratic) in 2016, the 2018 midterm election results showed that Republicans lost a consequential portion of those who had previously voted for Trump.

Though third parties have a very difficult time winning national or even statewide elections, they can influence election outcomes. Third-party candidate Ralph Nader ran for president in 2000 and 2004, and many believe he siphoned off just enough votes from the Democratic candidates to help Republican George W. Bush win both elections. In the 2016 election, Gary Johnson, the Libertarian candidate, got a consequential percentage of the vote (3.3%), likely from people turned off by both Clinton and Trump. And Bernie Sanders's long run against Hillary Clinton in the Democratic presidential primaries in 2016 exposed rifts within the party over how far left the party should go. Sanders put pressure on the national Democrats to adopt a more

[17] Aldrich, *Why Parties? A Second Look.*

left-oriented party platform than many in the party (including Clinton) would have adopted otherwise.

Since the 1990s, this Sixth Party System has also been characterized by more intensive ideological polarization between Democrats and Republicans than for most of the twentieth century. We discussed this topic and showed data about members of Congress in Chapter 5, and also discussed polarization in Chapter 9. At the level of elected officials, there are fewer moderates in either party in Congress as well as in state legislatures and governors' offices. Among the mass public, there is considerable evidence of more ideological uniformity among Republican and Democratic voters respectively, and hostility toward the opposite party (see Figure 12.5). That is, among ordinary citizens and elected leaders, compared with previous eras from which we have evidence in the twentieth century, conservatives cluster in the Republican Party and liberals cluster in the Democratic Party. Moreover, there are more extremely ideological people in each party with strongly held beliefs who are not counterbalanced by moderates willing to compromise with members of the other party.

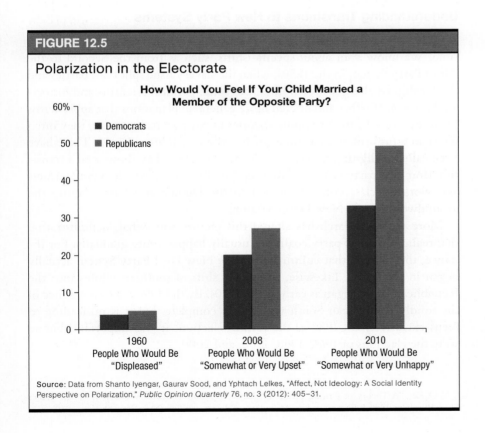

FIGURE 12.5

Polarization in the Electorate

How Would You Feel If Your Child Married a Member of the Opposite Party?

- ■ Democrats
- ■ Republicans

1960
People Who Would Be "Displeased"

2008
People Who Would Be "Somewhat or Very Upset"

2010
People Who Would Be "Somewhat or Very Unhappy"

Source: Data from Shanto Iyengar, Gaurav Sood, and Yphtach Lelkes, "Affect, Not Ideology: A Social Identity Perspective on Polarization," *Public Opinion Quarterly* 76, no. 3 (2012): 405–31.

This polarization has had profound implications for the two parties and for the political system, and provides a consistent theme in many of our chapters in this book. In the middle of the twentieth century, the major parties in Congress displayed ideological diversity and both parties contained liberals, moderates, and conservatives. Today there are no liberal Republicans or conservative Democrats, and few moderates of either party.

The parties are more unified within Congress, and they have been more effective there as agenda setters and disciplined voting blocs (Chapter 5). The party organizations push more consistent ideological messages on behalf of their candidates. Americans have less trust in the national government than before (Chapter 9); their attitudes toward elected officials are more negative, and they increasingly believe that politics in Washington signifies inaction, constant conflict, and ineffectiveness at solving the country's problems. Some political scientists point to the positive aspects of ideological polarization: today, ordinary people are less uncertain than those in the past concerning what the parties stand for ideologically. We return to this discussion about polarization at the end of this chapter.

Understanding Transitions to New Party Systems

Let's explore more systematically how party coalitions shift and change over time. We know a lot about specific shifts, such as from the Second to the Third Party System in the 1850s, when the slavery issue split both parties and they realigned along sectional lines. But some political scientists and historians have gone further and offered more general explanations that apply across historical periods. In developing theories of partisan realignment, they often focus on transformative elections, such as those of 1896 and 1932. These have been called realigning (or critical) elections because they showcased a transition from one party system to another.[18] In 1932, for example, many farmers and working-class voters switched to the Democratic Party, laying the groundwork for the New Deal coalition.

More recent research has altered this picture somewhat, demonstrating that realignments of party coalitions usually happen more gradually. For instance, the changes that culminated in the New Deal Party System actually began in the 1920s. Likewise, the steady shift of southern whites into the Republican Party began as early as the 1950s. By the 1990s, the emergence of the solidly Republican South was largely complete, but it is misleading to focus exclusively on 1980 as the critical election. It was important, but so were the elections of 1964, 1968, 1988, and 2000.

[18] V. O. Key, "A Theory of Critical Elections," *Journal of Politics* 17 (January 1955): 3–18; and Walter Dean Burnham, *Critical Elections and the Mainsprings of American Politics* (New York: Norton, 1970).

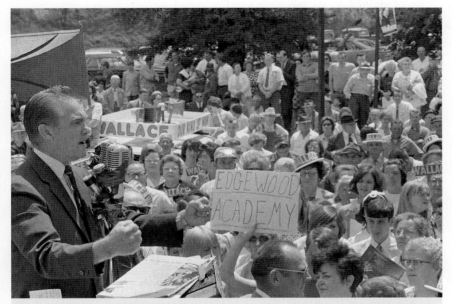

The American South experienced a strong party realignment. For the first half of the twentieth century, the South was solidly Democratic. Even segregationist candidates like George Wallace (pictured here campaigning for governor of Alabama) were Democrats. In light of the civil rights movement, this preference began to change; by the 1990s, the South was solidly Republican.

One group of scholars has proposed a theory of partisan coalition change that pays close attention to the role of activists within the parties in pushing for two kinds of alterations in party strategies. First, activists can convince political leaders within a party to exploit opportunities to win over voters from the other party. Second, activists can mobilize voters to switch party allegiance in line with the appeals of politicians.[19]

The abortion issue offers an excellent example. Many Democrats in the 1970s and early 1980s—especially Catholics, but also working-class evangelical Christians—became disenchanted with their party's position on abortion. The Democrats were pro-choice—that is, in favor of abortion rights and of upholding the *Roe v. Wade* Supreme Court decision. Antiabortion, or pro-life, activists convinced Republican leaders to back ardently antiabortion candidates within their party, such as Ronald Reagan, with the goal of winning over these Democrats. Meanwhile, these same Republican activists worked through church organizations and conservative political groups to convince voters that the Republican Party was more in tune with their values

[19] Norman Schofield and Gary Miller, "Elections and Activist Coalitions in the United States," *American Journal of Political Science* 51 (July 2007): 518–31.

than the Democratic Party. These activists worked at the elite and mass levels to gain many new voters for the Republicans. It can be said that pro-choice activists succeeded in doing the exact opposite for the Democrats—working at the elite and mass levels to convince pro-choice voters to become Democrats.

Abortion is only one of many major issues that have affected partisan coalitions. Race relations and civil rights, as discussed, realigned the parties toward the end of the twentieth century. In the late nineteenth century, the issue that divided the Democrats and strengthened the Republicans, leading to the Fourth Party System, was the controversy over the role of government in regulating the economy and redistributing wealth to poorer, more rural parts of the country. In the 1850s and 1860s, the issue of slavery altered the makeup of partisan coalitions.

We have told the history of American parties through the six party systems. By way of summary, let's now consider three long-term trends in the development of parties and the American party system:

- *Increasing democratization.* The parties became more oriented toward including all voters in their decision making over time, especially with the advent of primaries to choose candidates to run under the party labels. By the early twentieth century, the two major parties were mostly using primary elections instead of party caucuses (small meetings of party loyalists) to choose local candidates and candidates for Congress.

- *More centralized organizations.* The parties became more nationalized, as distinct from collections of local parties with little in common. Much of this change occurred in the last part of the twentieth century and paralleled the increasingly centralized nature of American federalism (see Chapter 3). These two trends are related, and there are strong reasons to believe that the centralization of the political system caused the nationalization of the political parties. This has especially been the case since the 1970s, when the major parties became adept at raising money for their congressional and presidential candidates.

- *The enduring two-party system.* There has been much turbulence and strife in American party history. Some parties failed to survive (the Whigs) and others rose (the modern Republicans); some parties were dominant for long periods, as the Republicans were between 1896 and 1932. But one thing has stayed constant: the number of serious competitors for control of Congress and of the presidency has always been limited to two.[20] Minor parties have played important roles at times and have even garnered a significant share of the vote in national elections. Nevertheless, the United States is undeniably the classic case of a two-party system.

[20] The one possible exception was in 1912, as we will see later.

Why Two Parties?

Ever since the First Party System pitted the Federalists against the old Republicans in the 1790s, the United States has generally been considered to have a two-party system. Although the names of the major parties have changed, at any given moment in history only two parties have stood a serious chance of capturing the presidency or Congress. Today, and historically since the early twentieth century, more than 95 percent of the votes cast in nearly all elections for national office are for Democrats or Republicans. The occasional exceptions when third parties do reasonably well in runs for president (1912, 1968, 1980, 1992, 2000), or when independents win statewide or congressional races, are newsworthy because they are unusual—and in the case of presidential third parties, consequential.

No one disputes that the United States has long had a two-party system. Yet throughout American history, minor parties have won a significant share of the popular vote in congressional and presidential elections. This was especially true during the political upheavals of the 1850s and 1890s, when such parties as the Greenbacks, the Union Party, the Populists, and the Progressives all won seats in Congress. Even in the twentieth century, the impact of third-party presidential candidates was significant at times. When Theodore Roosevelt ran as the Progressive candidate in 1912, he won more popular votes and considerably more electoral votes than the Republican incumbent, William Howard Taft, although he lost the election to Democrat Woodrow Wilson. In 1992, independent presidential candidate Ross Perot won 19 percent of the popular vote; in two states, he came in second to Democrat Bill Clinton and ahead of Republican George H. W. Bush (Maine and Utah, respectively).

Beginning in the 1920s, minor parties ceased to win many votes, at least in congressional races. But it is wrong to conclude from this fact that they have not been influential. It is common for minor parties to burst onto the scene, only to have their main issues taken up by the major parties. The income tax, for example, was first proposed by the Populist Party in the early 1890s, promoted by both the Democrats and Progressives, and eventually passed into law in the form of a constitutional amendment. Perot's third-party candidacy brought government deficits to the forefront of presidential politics in the early 1990s, but it was a Democratic president, Bill Clinton, who embraced the issue and balanced the federal budget.[21]

The two-party system is unusual outside the United States. Nearly every other country in the world that holds free and fair elections has more than two political parties that compete seriously for national office. It is true that in certain historical periods, two dominant parties in countries such as Great

---

[21] Note that the Tea Party movement was influential in the 2010–16 elections—not as a party, but as a movement within a party. This situation is akin to how the Progressives were a movement within the Republican Party in the early twentieth century. The Progressives only later became their own political party with a brief moment of influence on election outcomes.

Though third parties have a very difficult time winning national or even statewide elections, they can influence election outcomes. Third-party candidate Gary Johnson ran for president in 2016, and many believe he siphoned off just enough votes from Hillary Clinton to help Donald Trump win the election.

Britain, Uruguay, and Australia have competed for office with no serious opposition from smaller parties. But no other country has had as long a tradition of uninterrupted two-party dominance as the United States.[22] Scholars point to several possible explanations for this example of American exceptionalism, including the electoral system, the changing relationship between the national government and the states, and the actions of the major parties.

The Electoral System

It is well established that countries that hold elections for the national legislature on the basis of single-member districts and plurality voting have fewer political parties than countries that use proportional representation or have more than one representative per district. Put another way, one reason the United States has two major parties as opposed to three, four, or five is the use of single-member legis-

[22] Pradeep K. Chhibber and Ken Kollman, *The Formation of National Party Systems: Federalism and Party Competition in Canada, Great Britain, India, and the United States* (Princeton, NJ: Princeton University Press, 2004).

lative districts, in which only one candidate is elected to a given office and whoever gets the most votes wins. This regularity is sometimes referred to as **Duverger's Law**, after the political scientist Maurice Duverger, who wrote in 1954 that "the simple majority, single ballot system favors the two-party system."[23]

In an electoral system using plurality rule and single-member districts, any candidate who fails to win the most votes in a district receives no seat in the legislature or no position in the government. In other words, the losing candidate gets nothing in terms of representation, even though he or she may have received only slightly fewer votes than the winner of the election. This is sometimes referred to as the mechanical effect that contributes to Duverger's law.

On a psychological level, Duverger's Law predicts the response among voters to the "winner take all" effect of plurality elections in single-member districts. Suppose three people—Jack, Emilio, and Lisa—are running in a congressional district, and Jack is expected to get small numbers of votes relative to the other two candidates. Now consider all the voters who prefer Jack to the other two candidates; they might vote for Emilio or Lisa to make their votes matter in the election. If voters think their preferred candidate is unlikely to win, they are less likely to support that candidate, thus making the candidate even less likely to win. The candidate's chances of winning the election spiral downward because voters "drop off" in their support as they learn of others dropping off. As a result, only two major candidates are left to contest the election.

This is the heart of Duverger's argument: that voters do not like to waste their votes on candidates or parties that have little or no chance of winning an election, even if the voters prefer those candidates or parties to any other. When countries have proportional representation electoral systems, in contrast, voters can support a minor party and still receive representation. Under proportional representation, in principle, when a party receives 20 percent of the vote it receives 20 percent of the seats. It makes sense, then, that voters feel better about supporting minor parties in proportional representation systems than they do in plurality systems. They get representation despite supporting a party not at the top of the list of vote-getters. The tendency of voters to choose competitive candidates in a plurality system with single-member districts naturally leads to a two-party system, because parties that are expected to come in third (or further behind) in elections cannot convince voters to support them instead of one of the two front-runners.

National–State Political Relations

Some scholars point to the fact that most minor-party activity, especially in congressional elections, died out by the 1930s as evidence that the increasing

Duverger's Law A regularity that only two parties tend to compete for control of the government in countries that have single-member, plurality electoral systems.

[23] William Riker, "The Two Party System and Duverger's Law," *American Political Science Review* 76 (1982): 753–66; and Maurice Duverger, *Political Parties* (London: Methuen, 1954).

The Collective Dilemma

In 2015, the Republican National Committee (RNC) asked its candidates to sign a "loyalty pledge" affirming that, if the candidate fails to capture the party's presidential nomination, he or she will not run in the general election. Given that this pledge articulates the obvious—the winner moves on and those defeated do not—why was it necessary?

Interests

Each of the major parties, Democrats and Republicans alike, do not want one of their own to split off and run as a third-party candidate or an independent because doing so will likely siphon votes from that party's candidate. Yet, few losing candidates might be tempted to do just that. This is especially true for candidates who have an antiestablishment air about them; recent candidates about whom a third-party run was speculated include Ron Paul in 2012 and Donald Trump in 2016.

Institutions

Most states have some variation of what are called "sore-loser laws," which prohibit candidates from launching a bid in the general election after having already run in another party's primary. Only four states do not have sore-loser laws: Connecticut, Iowa, New York, and Vermont. And in almost every state with a sore-loser law, it does not apply to presidential elections.

Still, other challenges exist for the sore-loser presidential candidates; for example, to appear on the ballot, they must gather enough signatures by the specified dates of each state. Just like there is not one sore-loser law that every state follows, registration dates and rules vary across the country. Moreover, even within states, challenges exist. For instance, Vermont has a simultaneous-registration requirement, which means that major-party and independent candidates must file with the Vermont Secretary of State on the same day. So to keep open the possibility of a third-party or independent run, a candidate must have the foresight to cross-file (register with two parties at the same time).

Outcomes

Since sore-loser laws do not concern presidential candidates, it is possible for a candidate who ran in the Republican or Democratic primary to launch a third-party or independent run in the general presidential election. The Republican Party's 2015 loyalty pledge reflects this possibility and serves as a de facto sore-loser policy. All 17 GOP candidates eventually signed the pledge, although many were unsure if Donald Trump would sign it. Even after having signed the pledge, however, Trump publicly flirted with the idea of a third-party run in the general election.[a] Of course Trump's threat was not tested because he won the nomination and then the general election.

Because of the differences in states' sore-loser laws, the process may not be seamless. A recent example demonstrates this difficulty. In the Republican primary leading up to the 2012 presidential election, Gary Johnson registered to run in the Michigan's Republican primary but later submitted his withdrawal affidavit. But his submission was received three minutes past the withdraw deadline, which meant that technically he would appear on the primary ballot as a Republican contender. Michigan does not allow candidates to run on a party ticket in the general election if they ran

Sore-Loser Laws: Anti-Democratic, Smart Tactics, or Both?

in the primary of another party, so Johnson was ineligible to appear as the Libertarian party's candidate in the general election.

The most famous third-party candidates in recent U.S. presidential elections—Ross Perot in 1996, Ralph Nader in 2000, and Pat Buchanan in 2000—were not sore-loser candidates because they did not participate in a major party's primary the year they ran in the general election. They, too, likely siphoned votes away from major-party candidates and thus were termed "spoiler candidates," but they were technically not sore-loser candidates.

For some voters, sore-loser candidates mean making the choice between sincere and strategic voting. In sincere voting, a voter chooses the candidate closest to his or her ideal policies. Candidates' chances of winning are not incorporated into this voter's choice, so without a sore-loser law in place, the voter will have more options to vote sincerely. In strategic voting, a voter chooses the candidate—*among a number of viable candidates*—closest to his or her ideal policies. In other words, sincere voting asks voters to select the candidate whose preferences best mirror their own even though the candidate may or may not win; strategic voting asks voters to select the candidate whose preferences closely mirrors their own among several candidates who can actually win. Sore-loser laws use institutional means to eliminate minor-party candidates, thus eliminating the temptations for voters to vote sincerely. In effect, sore-loser laws force voters to have choices only among viable candidates.

Some are critical of sore-loser laws because they affect potential third-party or independent runners in congressional elections. They argue that these laws allow only the most ideological candidates to compete for the position[b] or that these laws circumvent democracy by not giving voters the full range of political choices.[c]

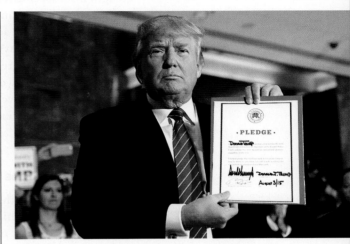

Before the 2016 nominating contests, presidential candidates were urged to sign a pledge to not run as an independent candidate were they to lose the nomination.

Think About It

Do sore-loser laws shortchange voters by limiting the number of general-election candidates as some critics charge? Or do these laws ensure that the most effective candidates run by filtering out those who could not win a major party's primary?

a. Eric Bradner, "Donald Trump Counters Condemnation with a Warning," CNN, December 9, 2015, www.cnn.com/2015/12/09/politics/donald-trump-republican-party-warning/index.html (accessed 1/19/16).

b. Barry C. Burden, Bradley Jones, and Michael S. Kang, "Sore Loser Laws and Congressional Polarization," *Legislative Studies Quarterly* 39, no. 3 (2014): 299–325.

c. Mickey Edwards, "Perverse Primaries," *New York Times*, January 23, 2014, www.nytimes.com/2014/01/24/opinion/perverse-primaries.html?_r=0 (accessed 1/18/16).

centralization of American politics at the national level has largely wiped out minor parties. In previous eras, they argue, minor parties tended to derive their strength from specific regions and states. But as power migrated from the states to the national government, voters and potential candidates saw the need to support strong parties across multiple regions, if not the whole country. The American two-party system—comprised of two dominant parties that compete to control Congress and the presidency—has always existed, but only since the 1930s have we had a deeper two-party system in which two major parties receive well over 90 percent of the national vote. This "deepening" of the two-party system, the argument goes, has been caused by political centralization.[24]

Major-Party Actions

A related argument is that the two major parties, in response to calls for cleaning up corruption within the parties during the Progressive Era, succeeded in passing state laws that made it difficult for minor parties to challenge them. Laws that require a high number of signatures on a petition, make it difficult for parties to get on general election ballots, or hinder minor parties in running their own primaries can solidify major-party dominance. Perhaps that is why minor parties competing for Congress and state offices "died out" starting in the 1910s, such that they were almost completely gone by the 1930s. This argument is appealing, but it has been challenged by scholars who point to the strength of several minor parties—the Progressives in 1912, the Socialists in the 1930s, and the Prohibitionists in the 1910s and 1920s—in many congressional races after restrictions on minor parties were common.

In Comparison: Parties

The durability of the American two-party system is unusual. Moreover, the makeup of the Democratic and Republican parties, and the way they operate, are unusual in comparison with parties in other countries.

Two Parties versus More Parties

Nearly every other democratic country in the world has more than two parties that compete seriously for seats in the national parliament and have a chance to participate in the government. Most advanced industrial de-

---

[24] Chhibber and Kollman, *The Formation of National Party Systems.*

mocracies have at least four major parties that win seats in the parliament. Furthermore, governments typically consist of multiple parties. That is, in most democracies, no one party controls a majority of seats in the parliament, and thus multiple parties join together to form a majority and elect the government.

There is great variation in party systems across the world. Germany has six parties that compete seriously for parliament and regularly win seats, while Italy has six parties that win seats in parliament, but more than 27 smaller parties that form coalitions with the six major parties. India has an unusually high number of parties in the national parliament (as many as 26 in recent years); this is largely because it has many state-level parties that send representatives to the national parliament. If the pattern in India were replicated in the United States, it would be as though many states had both national parties—the Democrats and Republicans—running candidates for office, but being challenged seriously by a state party with an entirely different label and pursuing state-specific interests. Imagine if Florida elected to Congress members of a party called the Florida First Party, and these members were not directly aligned with either major national party. This is what happens in India, and in a few other countries such as Brazil and Spain.

Party Discipline

Apart from the larger number of parties and the multiparty composition of governments, parties in other countries tend to be more ideologically cohesive, more centralized, and more disciplined than American parties. By discipline, we mean how often party members in the legislature vote together on bills. A party is said have strict **party discipline** if all its members routinely support its positions and vote accordingly. The degree of party discipline varies across countries. Once again, discipline—or the lack of discipline—is an unusual facet of the American political system in comparison with parties in other democracies.

party discipline The tendency for members of a legislative party to vote as a bloc.

It is relatively common in the United States for members of a given party in the House or Senate to be divided on a given bill, some voting yea and some voting nay. American politicians' party loyalty is often a matter of degree and depends on context.[25] American political parties are less disciplined in this sense than parties in most western European countries and in other advanced industrial democracies. In most other democracies, especially parliamentary democracies, it is rare for a member of parliament to vote against the wishes of his or her political party. In fact, some scholars have criticized

---

[25] Gary Cox and Mathew McCubbins, *Setting the Agenda: Responsible Party Government in the U.S. House of Representatives* (New York: Cambridge University Press, 2005).

American parties for being undisciplined and fostering an individualistic set of norms within Congress (see Chapter 5).

The difference in discipline between American parties and parties in other countries is directly related to the process by which candidates get on the ballots. In the United States, who appears on the ballot is determined either by many voters (in a primary election) or by many party members (in a party caucus). This means that if a member of Congress votes against his or her party leadership, it may not matter—in the sense that he or she cannot be left off the next election ballot—as long as voters or party members from the district or state choose that person to run again under the party label. The only people a member of Congress absolutely needs to please are his or her constituents.

To be sure, party leaders can make life uncomfortable for mavericks who vote against the party too often. Parties do this by, for example, funding an opponent in the primary or denying the member of Congress committee assignments that help him or her win reelection. But it is a matter of degree. In the American system, a politician who is popular with his or her constituents does not have to pay much attention to party leaders. This explains why American parties are not terribly disciplined in Congress, at least relative to parties in other countries. As we discussed in Chapter 5, unlike parliamentarians in other countries, members of Congress operate more as individual politicians with their own bases of popular support. That said, party discipline has been stricter in recent decades because of strong party leadership in Congress.

In contrast, in parliamentary democracies such as the United Kingdom, Canada, or Germany, the national party leaders determine who runs under the party label in various districts around the country. A member of parliament who votes against the party risks being dropped off the ballot under the party label. His or her political career depends directly on the good wishes of the top leaders of the party. This is because the parties are centralized, and they punish or reward their members depending on how often they vote with the rest of the party. In this rather simple way, parties in parliamentary democracies remain highly disciplined and vote as blocs.

confidence vote A vote held in a parliamentary system that, if it fails, brings on an election and possibly a new set of party leaders.

Parties in parliamentary systems are highly disciplined for another reason: if a majority party fails to support the government's position in a so-called **confidence vote**, as a result of which the government is forced to resign and call new elections, then members of parliament risk losing the party's endorsement in the next election. Parliamentarians from the majority are strongly motivated to support the government and so avoid the risk of new elections and the possibility of defeat.

Another way that American parties have differed from those in other countries, at least until recently, is in their increasing orientation toward high-profile, personalized campaigning by the parties' leaders. In any given national

Do the Rich (Candidates) Get Richer?
Fund-Raising and Political Parties

Parties serve multiple functions, but one of the most important is helping candidates raise funds to run for office. When multiple people run for the party nomination, parties use fund-raising to coordinate support around specific candidates and to signal to others which candidates the party leaders prefer. How successful are the major American parties in coordinating fund-raising efforts?

To answer this question, political scientist Hans Hassell took data from Senate primary contests (for both parties across all states) and calculated for each candidate the number of donors who contributed funds to both the candidate and the party's Senatorial Campaign Committee. The people who donate to the committees, which are dedicated to electing loyal party candidates to the Senate, can serve as a proxy for the party base. Thus, if many of the candidate's donors also donated to his or her Senatorial Campaign Committee, the candidate has received some degree of party support.

The left two bars in the figure below show the average amount of money raised by all Senate candidates, those who had 10 or fewer Senatorial Campaign Committee donors and those who had over 10 committee donors. The right two bars show the same data for campaigns where the candidates had the same level of political experience. Hassell provides a special focus on these races to see whether candidate quality was the main driver of fund-raising or if it was, in fact, the support of the party as represented by the Senatorial Campaign Committee donations.

Average Amount of Money Raised by Number of Party Donors

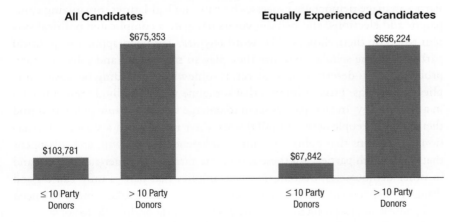

Source: Hans J. G. Hassell, "Party Control of Party Primaries: Party Influence in Nominations for the US Senate," *Journal of Politics* 78, no. 1 (2015). Replication data available at https://dataverse.harvard.edu/dataset.xhtml ?persistentId=doi:10.7910/DVN/EPEDIE.

Think About It

Why do you think donors pay attention to which candidates party insiders contribute to at an early stage? Based on this data, how big an effect does candidate quality have on fund-raising, as opposed to the early donations made by party insiders to one candidate over another?

election in the United States, the candidate for the presidency is the focus of attention and the most visible symbol of the party. He or she appears on television to represent the party's views and sets its priorities following the election. Parties in other democracies have traditionally been more team based. Candidates ran for election to the parliament under the party label and communicated with the public as a group on the basis of a party platform (a manifesto of policies the party will pursue once in office). The image of the party was what the party stood for collectively. This situation appears to be changing in many parts of the world. When commentators in other countries refer to the "Americanization" of national elections, they are referring in part to the increasing prominence of top party leaders as symbols of the parties—and they do not always mean it as a compliment.

Although there are differences across countries in how parties operate within parliaments and how they are organized, they all share certain common features: they solve collective dilemmas in government, in society at election time (as organizations), and among voters (within the electorate).

Key Intermediate Institutions of Democracy

Parties manage democratic processes by running legislatures, organizing campaigns and elections, and helping voters navigate a complicated political system to guide their choices. The word *ingenious* has been applied to political parties by some scholars because they play so many roles and solve so many problems. This description, however, is somewhat misleading because it implies two things. First, it implies that someone intentionally designed parties in a certain way. In fact, parties seem to emerge simply because politicians find them useful. People active in politics see their necessity in a variety of situations. It happens that politicians run as independents and win, and it happens that they switch parties, but these actions are rare in the American context and in other democracies. Second, *ingenious* implies that parties only cause good things to happen, and they always solve problems. Let's take a more balanced look, admitting to problems that parties either cause or do little to solve.

As we have said, political parties are "intermediate" institutions. That is, although they are not part of the formal institutions of government—to repeat, they are mentioned nowhere in the Constitution—they are key institutions that mediate between the public and the government to help make democracy work. Parties themselves operate within formal institutions, such as the legislature and system of elections, and serve to aggregate and represent broad interests in society.

To return to the question posed at the beginning of this chapter, we have learned why parties are useful, but why do some people react negatively to parties? Surely voters are uncomfortable with conflicts among politicians that seem to be based more on party labels than on policy positions. Parties can distort the truth to promote their candidates. They can intensify differences between people and make compromise difficult in policy making. They can highlight flaws in opponents and unifty their supports around feelings of resentment and fear. The two major political parties have, to some extent, caused and also benefited from the ideological polaralization of American politics. The heated 2016 presidential election not only added to party polarization, it was a reflection of it. Many Republicans and Democrats were deeply uncomfortable with their presidential candidates, and internal party divisions were on open display (especially on the Republican side). But in the end, as mentioned, party identification remained the best predictor of how people voted.

Even acknowledging the problems that parties can cause, and knowing how media portrayals of partisan bickering in Washington and in state capitals make people focus on these negative outcomes, we should not ignore the broader context—namely, the integral functions that parties perform in a democracy, indeed in any democracy in the world. They link voters to policy outcomes. Although voters often take their cues from journalists and commentators who complain about politicians being overly partisan, these same voters use party labels to make their decisions more manageable. A lot of information is contained in a single party label on a ballot. If all politicians were completely independent and no party labels were used, voters would be at a loss when trying to figure out who was responsible for what in the government.

Moreover, the conflict that takes place between the parties (and sometimes within the parties) has to be compared to other kinds of conflict that can happen, namely, violent conflict. Many political scientists believe that even though people get frustrated by partisan conflict—especially in our current, polarized era—we are better off with parties organizing their efforts to win elections and passing legislation against concerted opposition. Conflict is inevitable in any society. In democracies, parties channel that conflict into electoral and legislative divisions instead of violent opposition and separatism.

FURTHER READING

★ = Included in *Readings in American Politics*, 5th ed.

★ Aldrich, John H., *Why Parties? A Second Look* (Chicago: Chicago University Press, 2011). A direct and complete argument that political parties solve collective dilemmas in government and in society.

Bartels, Larry M., "Partisanship and Voting Behavior, 1952–1996," *American Journal of Political Science* 44 (January 2000): 35–50. Presents evidence from the 1990s that the Michigan model of voting held true in American elections.

Burnham, Walter Dean, *Critical Elections and the Mainsprings of American Politics* (New York: Norton, 1970). A readable account of transformative presidential elections (1800, 1828, 1860, 1896, 1932) shaping the party system.

★ Campbell, Angus, Philip E. Converse, Warren E. Miller, and Donald Stokes, *The American Voter*, unabridged edition (Chicago: University of Chicago Press, 1980). A classic book on voting behavior, influencing voting studies all over the world; presents the Michigan model of voting.

Chhibber, Pradeep K., and Ken Kollman, *The Formation of National Party Systems: Federalism and Party Competition in Canada, Great Britain, India, and the United States* (Princeton, NJ: Princeton University Press, 2004). Argues that the degree of political centralization explains why the United States has two parties, while other countries have more than two parties.

★ Cohen, Marty, David Karol, Hans Noel, and John Zaller, *The Party Decides: Presidential Nominations Before and After Reform* (Chicago: University of Chicago Press, 2008). An in-depth study of the presidential nomination process and the powerful way that parties wield influence.

Cox, Gary W., and Mathew D. McCubbins, *Legislative Leviathan: Party Government in the House*, 2nd ed. (New York: Cambridge University Press, 1993). A careful argument for parties organizing legislative action and serving the interests of party members.

Duverger, Maurice, *Political Parties* (London: Methuen, 1954). Discusses various facets of parties, especially their organization and the nature of party systems across countries.

Schattschneider, E. E., *Party Government* (New York: Farrar and Rinehart, 1942). A classic argument in favor of the responsible party model of democratic government.

Schofield, Norman, and Gary Miller, "Elections and Activist Coalitions in the United States," *American Journal of Political Science* 51 (July 2007): 518–31. Ties the behavior of party activists to the shifting policy positions of the Democrats and Republicans.

Sundquist, James L., *Dynamics of the Party System: Alignment and Realignment of Political Parties in the United States* (Washington, DC: Brookings Institution, 1983). An insightful study of shifting party coalitions in American history.

KEY TERMS

confidence vote (p. 484)

Duverger's Law (p. 479)

national committee (p. 457)

national party convention (p. 458)

New Deal Party System (p. 469)

party amateur (p. 458)

party discipline (p. 483)

party identification (p. 461)

party professional (p. 458)

political machine (p. 467)

political party (p. 449)

primary election (p. 459)

smoke-filled room (p. 459)

Hillary Clinton and Donald Trump, shown here at the second of three presidential debates during the 2016 presidential campaign, spent over $1 billion on advertising, travel, and extensive campaign organizations. But did all this campaigning

13

Elections and Campaigns

 Do campaigns matter in national elections, and if so, how?

In 2016, Hillary Clinton and Donald Trump mounted massive fund-raising appeals to win the presidency. Together, their campaigns collected $1.3 billion in contributions from thousands of individuals and groups. The money was used for large-scale campaign organizations, for travel and staff salaries, and especially for advertising to promote their candidacies. Moreover, groups outside the candidates' campaign organizations spent an estimated $6 billion to try to convince voters to support one or the other of the candidates.

Presidential campaigns have been called the grand feasts of American democracy. They rouse millions of people to participate in the political process. In the months and weeks preceding elections, potential voters are bombarded with messages, either from the candidates themselves or from people commenting on the election. Ideally, if not always in practice, presidential campaigns constitute ongoing conversations in which the candidates and the American people deliberate over challenging issues about governance and the country's priorities.

Yet, the election campaign was especially nasty and personal. Each presidential candidate tried to define the other as unfit for office. Clinton's campaign tagged Trump as being racist, unpredictable, and out of touch with ordinary Americans. Clinton charged that Trump's business experience was mostly in sham enterprises and that he inherited his money and did not earn it, while she had a steady hand in government. She stressed that her many years of experience as secretary of state, U.S. senator, and first lady gave her the kind of knowledge necessary to lead the government in these complex times. Furthermore, she emphasized key themes of her Democratic Party: the need for infrastructure and educational spending and to examine international trade agreements carefully to make sure they did not harm job prospects for Americans. Trump focused on how many people were "forgotten" under the Democratic presidency of Barack Obama, even though the economy was growing according to data. He tried to turn his business experience to his advantage,

491

OUTLINE

- What Do Elections Accomplish?
- American Electoral Institutions
- American Electoral Campaigns
- In Comparison: Elections
- Is There a Need for Reform?

claiming he knew how to create jobs. He also complained about trade agreements, going even further than Clinton in arguing that the United States was continually cheated by foreign countries in many international treaties and agreements. Above all, Trump attacked Clinton as "crooked" and corrupt, saying repeatedly that she "should be in jail." His theme was "Make America Great Again," implying that the United States had gone off course and that Washington insiders like Clinton were the main problem. Both candidates traveled the country, campaigning right up to the morning of Election Day.

Do campaigns matter for the outcome of national elections? Did they matter in 2018, when the Democrats took back control of the House and Republicans retained control of the Senate? These questions may seem strange, given the resources devoted to campaigns and the attention they garner. Consider, however, that the two major-party presidential candidates are usually household names by the time they campaign in the general election. The typical voter tends to know the candidates' positions on the issues of most importance to the voter. Unlike in most presidential primary elections, where the candidates are all from the same party, in general elections, party identification matters a great deal in determining how individuals vote (see Chapters 9 and 12). Evidence shows that in national elections for the presidency and Congress, as many as 85 percent of voters have made up their mind well before Election Day. Moreover, according to researchers who study public opinion trends and campaign rhetoric, few voters are swayed by campaigns in the general election at the presidential level. There is no guarantee that the money candidates spend campaigning will translate into votes—the presidential candidate who spent more money in 2016, Hillary Clinton, lost the election. The state of the economy and people's attitudes toward the incumbent administration are much more important than campaign messages. Finally, most states are sewn up by one candidate by early fall, leaving only a few states up for grabs. Why, then, do candidates and parties raise and spend billions of dollars in national campaigns? Why do they continue to seek national media attention up to the day of the election? If campaigns do in fact sway enough undecided voters to influence the outcome of elections, how does this happen?

What Do Elections Accomplish?

Popular elections are the means by which "government by the people" becomes reality. According to the ideals of democracy, the people should have the final say over who governs them, and this is accomplished through voting in elections. In this chapter, we will analyze the conduct and consequences of American electoral institutions and electoral campaigns. We bring together many of the concepts and topics we have already studied in previous chapters, such as political parties, public opinion, interest groups, and participation. This chapter serves partially as the culmination of earlier topics of study, though it offers new concepts and ways to understand elections and campaigns at a deeper level.

Let's first consider the fundamental purposes of elections. If elections are central to democracy, what do they accomplish? Put another way, what consequences should we expect from our elections? Wise, efficient government decisions? Government that is responsive to public opinion? Scholars have different views about the role of elections in the American-style two-party system, and in democracy in general. We will focus on using a principal-agent framework to gain a deeper understanding of elections. Voters (as principals) choose representatives and leaders (as agents) to work on their behalf.

Determining Policy Direction and Ideology

An intuitive and common understanding is that through mass elections, people choose representatives to carry out specific policies—in other words, elections communicate policy intent and steer the directions of government ideologically. Representatives in government can move the country in a liberal direction or a conservative direction, or pursue more moderate policies, depending on the voters' wishes.

By way of illustration, we will consider two approaches to American national elections that link election outcomes and the ideological direction of government. These two approaches focus on the competition between the two national parties for control of the presidency and Congress.

One approach examines the pressures of the two parties to converge on moderate positions. This approach is an extension of a famous argument from theoretical economics called the **median voter theorem**. The theorem holds that if voters are arrayed along a line according to their ideology, and none of the voters controls the agenda, the voter at the exact midpoint of that line will get exactly the policies he or she favors. The median voter's most preferred ideology will prevail. The logic is that any majority coalition of voters supporting a proposal would have to include the median voter, who can "hold out" until exactly what he or she wants is proposed. This approach assumes

median voter theorem A mathematical result showing that the voter with the ideological preference in the middle of the ranking of voters must be satisfied and approve of a majority-rule winning outcome.

that politics can be depicted as a competition along a single-dimension line and that no voters abstain.[1]

A corollary to the median voter theorem holds that if two candidates are competing for votes and can shift their ideological positions to attract new voters, their only equilibrium position is that held by the median voter. This means that if either candidate campaigns based on a position that is not the position of the median voter, then he or she has an incentive to shift toward the median voter and do better in the election. So, using this way of thinking, we can predict that candidates in two-party elections will converge on the median voter (again, assuming that no one abstains). And moreover, the median voter is the one principal that the winning candidate (as the agent carrying out policy once in office) has to please.

If all these assumptions hold, we can expect the two candidates to end up being moderate and trying to win over moderate voters, instead of taking ideologically extreme positions. In two-candidate elections, if everyone votes, the voters at the extremes have no choice but to vote for the candidate who is closer to them; hence, a candidate can feel comfortable moving as close to the other candidate as possible without crossing over to his or her ideological side. The other candidate is in the same situation. The two parties are locked in competition to attract a majority of voters. To win, they need to convince the most persuadable voters, the middle-of-the-roaders who may be open to voting for either party depending on how much they like a certain candidate. Thus, the candidates converge on the median voter because to move anywhere else along the line would spell certain defeat.

There is undoubted validity to this line of thinking. In comparison with political parties in other advanced industrial democracies, especially in Europe, the two major American parties are moderate, as we learned in Chapters 9 and 12. There is evidence that presidential candidates seek their nominations by appealing to the party base in primary elections and then moderate their rhetoric to win over the moderate voters in the general election. Consider this all-too-common scenario: In the primary elections, candidates need to appeal to the median voter *in their parties* to win the nomination; if they win the nomination, they must then appeal to the median voter *in the electorate as a whole*. This means that candidates tend to be more extreme ideologically in primary elections and then moderate their stands during general elections. By the end of the campaign, the candidates will not be very far apart on policy issues; they will both moderate their positions to try to attract independent voters because they know they have their partisans locked up. Following this argument, the policies that gain prominence will not be all that different no matter which party controls the presi-

---

[1] Duncan Black, "On the Rationale of Group Decision-Making," *Journal of Political Economy* 56 (1948): 133–46; Anthony Downs, *An Economic Theory of Democracy* (New York: Harper, 1957).

In primary elections, candidates from the same party compete with one another. Here, 2016 candidates for the Republican nomination for president square off in a televised debate before the Florida primary.

dency and Congress.[2] Consider that during the 2016 presidential election campaign season, by one interpretation Donald Trump had to diverge toward extreme Republican primary voters to win the Republican nomination, but then during the general election—facing the Democrats Hillary Clinton and Tim Kaine—Trump and his running mate Mike Pence faced pressures to appear more moderate and soften their previously strong conservative positions on issues like immigration, law enforcement, and international alliances.

An alternative approach focuses on pressures for candidates or parties to diverge toward the ideological extremes in order to win elections. Candidates and parties need the support of intense partisans, generous donors with strong policy views, and people on the more extreme ends of the ideological spectrum who might not participate if the parties become too moderate. Parties, this line of thinking emphasizes, will respond to their core supporters and will seek to deliver policies favoring distinct industry and population groups (see Figure 13.1). Proponents of this way of thinking about elections note that the two parties often advocate contrasting positions on major policy questions. In the 2016 campaign, for example, Clinton and Trump took opposing positions on the Obama health care reforms that had passed in 2010 (Trump promised to repeal the plan if elected, but he failed), on the desirable size of government, and on weighing women's right to abortion

[2] For a classic account of this process, see Benjamin I. Page, *Choices and Echoes in Presidential Elections* (Chicago: University of Chicago Press, 1978).

FIGURE 13.1

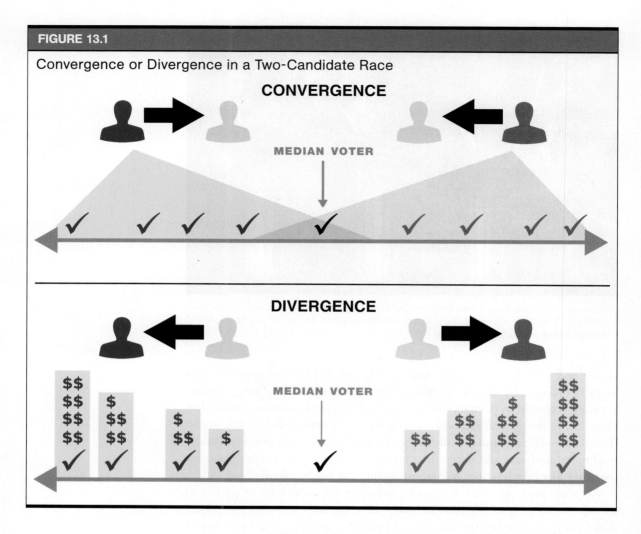

Convergence or Divergence in a Two-Candidate Race

CONVERGENCE

MEDIAN VOTER

DIVERGENCE

MEDIAN VOTER

against the possibility of government regulation of abortion. Determining what policies will be pursued after an election depends on which party gets elected; Democrats will adopt different kinds of policies than Republicans.[3]

Which approach to elections and ideological outcomes makes more sense? The different approaches are intended to provide insight into election processes, not to predict outcomes for a specific election. But the reasonable answer to the question is that each approach makes sense in specific contexts. Where candidates end up ideologically in American elections depends largely on how voters at the ideological extremes behave, and on which issues are important to voters and are being considered. If voters at the extremes abstain when candidates get

[3] J. M. Snyder, "Safe Seats, Marginal Seats, and Party Platforms: The Logic of Platform Differentiation," *Economics & Politics* 6, no. 3 (1994): 201–13.

too far from them ideologically, or voters at the extremes are the ones donating money and expecting policies in return for campaign contributions, then the theory that candidates will diverge toward the extremes will prevail. If voters at the extremes vote anyway and are resigned to candidates appealing to moderate voters, and if campaign contributions come from voters across the ideological spectrum, then perhaps the theory that candidates will converge toward the center (that is, the median voter) makes more sense.

Choosing Competent, Non-Corrupt Leaders

Some people argue that elections are not effective at steering government in particular ideological directions because ordinary voters do not understand enough about government, and circumstances change so much that elected leaders cannot keep their promises to voters once in office. An alternative argument is that elections are not about guiding the direction of policy, but rather that they are primarily about preventing corruption or promoting competence in government, or both. That is, because politicians generally want to win election (and reelection) and stay in office, they have incentives to behave in a manner that pleases constituents. Incompetence and corruption surely are present in politics, but if the electoral institutions are operating properly, most dishonest or incompetent politicians should be weeded out by losing elections.

If promoting competence in government and reducing corruption are the main purposes of democratic elections, then we have two additional ways to consider how elections work. Elections can be a good means for selecting the right types of people to be in office (selection), or they can be a good means for giving incentives to people in office to work hard or be honest (accountability). Let's consider these possible functions of elections using the principal-agent framework that we introduced in Chapter 1 and discussed in detail in Chapter 7.

The selection effect assumes that the goal of elections is to choose good leaders. If we consider voters to be the set of principals who hire an agent to represent them, then as we learned, the agent is an elected official—a member of Congress, a governor, or the president. Recall that the principal-agent "problem" is that agents do not always act the way principals want them to behave. Usually, this is because they do not have exactly the same preferences. The politician may not pay attention to issues that the voters care about, may not want to work as hard as the principals expect, or may want to get rich rather than pass good public policy.

The key is the information about candidates that is revealed *before* the election. When campaigns are truly informative for voters about candidates' strengths and weaknesses, and the parties end up nominating strong candidates, then elections enable the voters (as principals) to choose good government officials (as agents). Voters can make good choices, and the electoral system works. We would say that elections select good politicians and do not select bad ones. Politicians come in different types—some are corrupt or incompetent, for example, and some are neither. The selection effect assumes elections are screening devices to filter out the wrong types of politicians.[4]

The accountability effect assumes that the main function of elections is to give leaders the right incentives. In this view, the reason to have regular elections is to ensure that badly behaving or incompetent government officials are thrown out of office—that is, they are defeated in their bids for reelection. The prospect of losing the next election focuses elected officials on staying honest and working hard to represent voters well. Elections hold politicians accountable once they are in office. The selection effect has to do with what happens before and during the election—choosing good government officials on the basis of the information voters have *before* they vote. The accountability effect, by contrast, focuses on what happens *after* the election—encouraging government officials to avoid the temptation to be lazy or corrupt, and helping voters be aware of how incumbents have been behaving.[5]

What is at stake in depicting elections as mechanisms of either selection or accountability? They offer insight into the kinds of reforms that might be called for when elections do not work well. If elections too frequently lead to the choosing of corrupt politicians—politicians who were corrupt even before the election—we might question the parties' nominating procedures and ask why voters did not have enough information to avoid electing these characters. It could be that the election system is not doing a good job of selecting the right types of politicians. In contrast, politicians may tend to become corrupt once they are in office and then secure reelection time and again because of built-in biases in the system. In that case, we would say that the election system does not do a good job of holding politicians accountable. Is the problem the lack of information during campaigns or the lack of information about what government officials do once in office? Neither way of conceptualizing elections is always valid, and you do not need to choose either the selection approach or the accountability approach as accurate or inaccurate.

It is worth making some intriguing connections from the overall discussion here of the purposes of elections (see Figure 13.2). We have discussed four approaches overall, two having to do with whether election processes and outcomes guide the government ideologically and two having to do with whether elections hinder corruption and promote competence. Note that if

[4] James Fearon, "Electoral Accountability and the Control of Politicians: Selecting Good Types versus Sanctioning Poor Performance," in *Democracy, Accountability, and Representation*, ed. Adam Przeworski, Susan C. Stokes, and Bernard Manin (New York: Cambridge University Press, 1999), pp. 55–97.

[5] Morris P. Fiorina, *Retrospective Voting in American National Elections* (New Haven, CT: Yale University Press, 1981).

FIGURE 13.2

What Do Elections Accomplish?

Convergence
The two candidates appeal to moderate voters.

Divergence
The two candidates appeal to more extreme voters.

Elections

Determine policy direction

Give incentives to politicians to avoid corruption

Selection effect
Avoiding the election of incompetent or corrupt politicians in the first place

Accountability effect
Avoiding reelecting incumbent politicians who are incompetent or corrupt

in two-candidate elections the candidates converge on a common ideological position for the reasons discussed earlier, then competence or corruption may be the only feature that distinguishes one from the other. Put simply, if both candidates end up advocating similar issue and ideological positions, then voters have only competence or other nonissue characteristics to use in judging the candidates.

Furthermore, if we focus on how the candidates are pressured to diverge ideologically by activists and donors, then consider the following. Suppose that changing circumstances—recessions, wars, terrorist threats—move the median voter right or left, depending on the specific election year. If the two major parties are divergent from each other (both not moderate), then in any given election year, one or the other party will be close to the median voter (but not both parties), and thus the winning party represents quite well the average preference of the electorate in that specific moment in history. In other words, divergence of the parties could link government policies to the median voter because the median voter moves ideologically toward one or the other party given historical events. This is yet another way to think about voters and parties: the parties stay relatively fixed (and separated ideologically) while the voters move in ideological space over time.

American Electoral Institutions

Elections can lead to desirable goals only if the rules for the conduct of elections are generally fair and work reasonably well in practice. These rules constitute some of a country's most important political institutions, and they give advantages to some people while disadvantaging others. This does not mean the institutions are necessarily unfair (though they can be at times), but rather that, like all political institutions, their particular features have consequences for who gets what in society, consequences that are not always well understood even by those participating in the electoral processes.

Electoral rules account for the following:

- *How votes are counted and seats are allocated in legislatures.* In the United States, most elections for government office are conducted under plurality rules, which means the person with the most votes wins. There are no runoff elections; and there are single-member districts, meaning that for a given office, only one person is elected from the district.

- *How executives are chosen.* State governors are typically chosen according to plurality rules in statewide elections. The U.S. president is chosen by the electoral college. Electoral college members are elected by plurality rules in most states. This means that the presidential candidate with the most votes in the statewide election wins all the electoral college votes from that state. The candidate with the majority vote of the electoral college then wins the presidency.

- *Whether, when, and how direct democracy is practiced.* Some elections held in the United States at the state or local level do not elect representatives or executives to office, but rather allow citizens to vote directly on policy issues. Such elections are of two types: referendums and initiatives.

- *How eligible electorates are determined.* The states are charged with maintaining voter registration rolls. Certain federal laws control who is eligible to vote and who must be permitted easy access to voting, but the states still have some leeway to set rules for eligibility. (See Chapter 10 for more discussion of voter eligibility and turnout.)

Voting in elections is a hallmark of American democracy, but the institutions of American elections have evolved over time. For example, in the nineteenth century, before the introduction of the "Australian ballot," votes were not private and political parties often printed their own ballots.

These institutional details have important implications for politics and policy. For instance, in some states former felons cannot vote, although in other states they can. It has been shown that countries (like the United States) with single-member districts tend to have fewer political parties than other countries, and that the presence of fewer parties tends to lead to more pro-business economic policies compared with countries that have more political parties.[6] These are just a few examples of how the nature of the electoral institutions shapes the outcomes that citizens experience in the American political system.

Let's now take a closer look at three aspects of American elections: the role of state-level election laws, plurality rules, and election ballots.

State-Level Election Laws

In the United States, as mandated by the Constitution, elections are regulated and operated at the state level. This is true even for elections to national office. In presidential elections, for instance, the Constitution specifies how the electoral college works, how many votes each state has in the college, and what occurs if no candidate receives a majority of the votes (Figure 13.3). The Constitution does not, however, indicate how states should choose their electors for the college. That they are chosen by plurality vote within the states has become customary over time.[7]

By the same token, nothing in the Constitution mandates how states should elect members to the House of Representatives; it says only that they are to be chosen "by the people of the several states." Nevertheless, the Constitution does grant Congress broad powers to regulate state-level elections for national office. Article I, Section 4, states: "The Times, Places and Manner of holding Elections for Senators and Representatives, shall be prescribed in each State by the Legislature thereof; but the Congress may at any time by Law make or alter such Regulations."

The states control how electoral districts are drawn for Congress and for state legislatures. Depending on who draws the district boundaries, this system can greatly benefit one or the other political party. We have already discussed in Chapter 5 how gerrymandering works and how, to correct for discrimination against disadvantaged minorities, national courts have regulated some aspects of how states draw district boundaries. Seats in Congress are reapportioned every 10 years following the national census, and district boundaries for state legislatures and for Congress are often redrawn afterward. Because state governments control the process of drawing district boundaries, the political party in control of a state's government in the few years after a census has the power to draw districts to its advantage. The states also regulate voter registration,

---

[6] Torsten Persson, Gerard Roland, and Guido Tabellini, "Electoral Rules and Government Spending in Parliamentary Democracies," *Quarterly Journal of Political Science* 2 (2007): 1121–61.

[7] States can alter the methods of choosing electors; in Maine and Nebraska, for instance, electors are chosen in districts, so it is possible that Maine and Nebraska's electoral college votes can be split across multiple candidates (which occurred in Maine in 2016). But this is not the typical practice among the states.

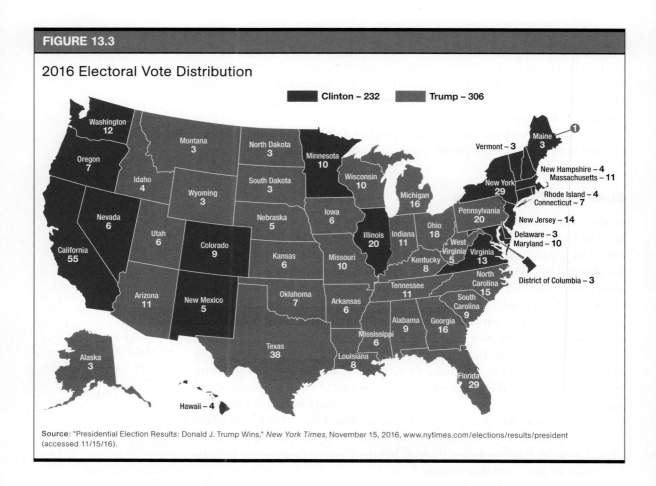

FIGURE 13.3

2016 Electoral Vote Distribution

Clinton – 232   Trump – 306

Washington 12 · Montana 3 · North Dakota 3 · Minnesota 10 · Vermont – 3 · Maine 3 · ① · Oregon 7 · Idaho 4 · Wyoming 3 · South Dakota 3 · Wisconsin 10 · Michigan 16 · New Hampshire – 4 · Massachusetts – 11 · New York 29 · Rhode Island – 4 · Connecticut – 7 · Nevada 6 · Utah 6 · Nebraska 5 · Iowa 6 · Ohio 18 · Pennsylvania 20 · New Jersey – 14 · California 55 · Colorado 9 · Kansas 6 · Missouri 10 · Illinois 20 · Indiana 11 · West Virginia 5 · Kentucky 8 · Virginia 13 · Delaware – 3 · Maryland – 10 · North Carolina 15 · District of Columbia – 3 · Arizona 11 · New Mexico 5 · Oklahoma 7 · Arkansas 6 · Tennessee 11 · South Carolina 9 · Alabama 9 · Georgia 16 · Mississippi 6 · Texas 38 · Louisiana 8 · Florida 29 · Alaska 3 · Hawaii – 4

Source: "Presidential Election Results: Donald J. Trump Wins," *New York Times*, November 15, 2016, www.nytimes.com/elections/results/president (accessed 11/15/16).

ballot counting, staffing of polling places, and—to varying degrees—campaign finance for state office and the operation of primary and general elections.

Beginning in the late nineteenth century, the national government started to mandate certain features of state elections. By the 1960s, the federal government was closely monitoring the effects of state electoral institutions on participation and representation of certain groups, especially African Americans. As a result of congressional statutes, electoral rules have become highly uniform across the 50 states. Congress passed a series of laws requiring the states to hold elections for national office on specific dates, to use single-member districts, and, in recent decades, to manage voter registration in certain ways (for example, the Motor Voter Bill, discussed in Chapter 10). Furthermore, national laws and Supreme Court interpretations of the Constitution have compelled states to change electoral procedures because those procedures resulted in systematic discrimination against certain population groups, or violated either the principle of one person, one vote, or the First

Votes and Seats

- Nearly all winners of American elections for legislatures and governors are determined in single-member districts and are elected directly by plurality rule with no runoffs.

- The president and the vice president are elected indirectly by an electoral college. Each state is allocated a number of electors equal to the total number of its members in the House and Senate. Each elector is given one vote for the president and one vote for the vice president, and the candidates with an absolute majority of the electoral votes in their respective contests win the presidency and vice presidency. (The Twelfth Amendment outlines the procedure invoked when no candidate wins a majority of electoral votes.)

- Currently, all states choose their electors by a popular vote.

How Districts Are Drawn

- States divide their seats for the House of Representatives into geographic regions called districts. Each district must be of roughly equal population size. However, where the district boundaries are drawn is left primarily to the discretion of state governments.

- Members of the legislature can use the power to redraw district boundaries in a way that advantages them or their party in future elections. When states draw strangely shaped districts to give a political advantage to one group, it is called gerrymandering.

How Candidates Are Chosen

- Parties do not want more than one of their members running for a given office at once. Parties hold internal elections to determine their candidates. The elections vary in form.

- **Primaries** are mass public elections that take place through the ballot process before an election for public office.

- Primaries can either be **open** or **closed**. If only party members are allowed to vote in their party's primary, then the primary election is considered closed. If any registered voters can choose to vote in a party's primary, regardless of membership, then the primary election is considered open.

- **Caucuses** are formal gatherings of party members who convene to elect their party's candidate for office. Rather than through a public ballot, voting takes place in a private venue (or multiple private venues) where members are asked to vote for the candidate they want to run under the party label.

Amendment protections of freedom of speech and association. As we saw in Chapters 4 and 10, much of the federal oversight of state elections resulted from discrimination against African Americans, often in the South.

Nevertheless, the states continue to have wide latitude in running elections. Through the Help America Vote Act of 2002, for example, they can receive money from the national government to improve technology for voting and counting ballots. States that apply for federal funding choose which voting machines to use, how many polling stations to set up, and how to monitor them. In recent years, states set new regulations for voting, some struck down by federal courts and some allowed. Virginia, for example, in one simple rule change by the order of their Democratic governor, allowed hundreds of thousands of former felons to vote. Republican lawmakers in Virginia sued, and the state courts said the governor could not restore voting rights all at once, so he restored thousands of voting rights to former felons one at a time. In sum, the details of elections are mostly decided on and entirely implemented by the states, though with federal judicial oversight.

Plurality Rule

plurality rule A method for determining an election's winner in which the candidate who receives the most votes wins.

single-member district An electoral district in which a single person is elected to a given office.

Most American elections for national office are conducted according to **plurality rule** in **single-member districts**. Typically, each electoral race is for a single office from a district or state. The person who receives the most votes wins the election, and there is no runoff to obtain a majority. If more than two candidates run for the office, it is not uncommon for the winner to receive less than 50 percent of the vote.

We have already discussed how elections using single-member districts shape the incentives of members of Congress (Chapter 5) and tend to lead to the two-party system (Chapter 12). Under plurality rule and especially single-member districts, members of Congress work hard to develop reputations for individual competence and willingness to fight for the interests of their single district or state. Moreover, plurality rule combined with single-member districts tends to drive out minor parties because those parties cannot win any representation in Congress unless they win the most votes in district elections.[8] In proportional representation systems with multi-seat districts, by contrast, small parties can gain seats with small proportions of the vote.

Increasingly, however, states, especially in the South and West, are moving toward a runoff system: the candidates who finish in first and second place but do not receive a majority of votes must face a runoff election to determine the winner. The number of states using this system especially for state and local offices has grown, but it is still small relative to the number using plurality rules. In the 2016 federal elections, 12 states used some form of these runoff rules for state-level or congressional seats.

In Georgia, for example, a victorious Senate candidate has to receive at least 50 percent of the vote. If no candidate receives 50 percent, a runoff election must be held between the top two vote-getters. Louisiana, California, and Washington State hold an unusual kind of election for national, state, and local offices: Candidates from all parties, including multiple candidates from the same party, run together in one primary election. If any candidate receives more than 50 percent of the vote, he or she wins the office. If no one receives more than 50 percent of the vote, there is a runoff between the top two vote-getters, regardless of their party affiliation. So two people from the same party could conceivably face each other in the general election, which is what happened in the 2018 California race for the Senate when two Democrats squared off in the final round.

[8] Maurice Duverger, *Political Parties* (New York: John Wiley & Sons, 1963); Gary Cox, *Making Votes Count* (Cambridge, UK: Cambridge University Press, 1997).

Election Ballots

Political parties played a major role in organizing events on Election Day until the end of the nineteenth century. Not surprisingly, elections were frequently marred by corruption and bias, as each party tried to skew the results in its favor. For instance, party leaders often handed out distinctively colored party ballots (or had them printed in newspapers) for voters to take into the voting booth. Alternatively, people were simply asked at the voting booth to state their voting intentions orally. Either way, it was difficult in many cases to know if people were being coerced into voting for a particular party. Moreover, because voters' choices were not private, party officials could reward their own voters with bribes or punish voters for the other parties.

As a result of reforms passed during the Progressive Era (in the late nineteenth and early twentieth centuries), state governments stepped in to regulate elections and loosen the grip of the two major parties on the vote-counting process and the allocation of government positions. Supporters of the progressive reforms were primarily motivated by a philosophical preference for transparency in government and fairness in electoral systems, but many progressives also wanted to end the domination of the Republicans and Democrats and open the way for minor parties like the Progressive Party.

One key reform was the introduction of the **Australian ballot**, so named because it was first widely used in that country. The Australian ballot, in contrast to a party ballot, is printed by the state government and contains the names of all the candidates or parties participating in the election. Because all ballots look the same, and because voters mark their ballots in the privacy of a voting booth, no one else can know how they voted. This reform greatly reduced the incidence of fraudulent elections. It also enabled voters to "split" their ballots by voting for candidates from different parties instead of having to choose a single party's slate of candidates for all offices. The Australian ballot is now widely used around the world.

Australian ballot A type of ballot that lists all candidates running for each office and allows voters to cast their votes secretly and for specific individual candidates.

Direct Democracy

Voters who participate in referendums and initiatives are exercising a form of direct democracy that was once common—in ancient Greece, for example—but is relatively rare in the modern world. The initiative and referendum were among the major institutions championed by progressive reformers in the early twentieth century as a way of making the political process more transparent and responsive to the popular will.

Referendums enable voters to accept or reject legislative acts—either laws or constitutional amendments—that have been passed by the state legislature. The legislature controls the agenda in this institutional setup, in the sense that voters react to what has been proposed rather than proposing

referendum An election in which citizens vote directly on whether to overturn a bill or a constitutional amendment that has been passed by the legislature.

legislation themselves. In some states, referendums are held in response to petitions signed by voters who are reacting to what the legislature has done; in other states, the legislature sets the process in motion by, for example, passing a bill that includes a provision mandating a popular referendum on whether it should ultimately become law. **Initiatives** enable voters to decide on questions proposed by a group of citizens. A petition containing a certain number of signatures is required to get a question on the ballot (the number varies from state to state). Through the initiative process, citizens can place items on the agenda with or without the support of the government in power. State commissions uphold requirements and standards for ballot initiatives, such as ensuring that the question on the ballot is clear and not self-contradictory.

The 50 American states differ on what kinds of direct democracy they allow. Some states hold only referendums, some hold only initiatives, some allow for both, and some do not permit either. The national government does not hold referendums or initiatives.

Direct democracy is controversial. In some quarters, these elections, especially initiatives, are seen to be dominated by special interest groups that pay companies to gather signatures supporting a ballot initiative. Initiatives are often originated by organizations such as environmental or gun control groups or groups seeking to change a state's constitution regarding such matters as abortion rights or same-sex marriage. Some referendums or initiatives attract a great

initiative An election held to vote directly on a ballot question that was proposed by a group of individuals.

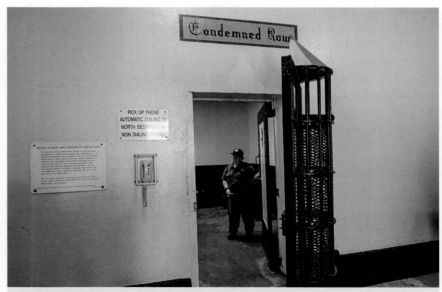

States employ varying methods of direct democracy, including referendums and initiatives. In 2016, the California electorate weighed in on whether to keep or repeal the death penalty. Proposition 62, an initiative put on the ballot that would have repealed the death penalty if passed, was rejected by 54 percent of voters.

deal of media attention and cause voters to turn out in high numbers to vote on that one issue. There have been numerous state referendums and initiatives on such controversial issues as medical and recreational marijuana, gay marriage, affirmative action, and immigration reform. But many pertain to low-profile issues that few voters care about, or that are arcane or technical. In 2018, voters in California rejected an obscure initiative to regulate the profits of dialysis clinics. Not surprisingly, there was not much media coverage on this initiative (or the initiatives on marijuana in other states) relative to the congressional election, though politicians and state-level bureaucrats in state capitals cared a great deal.

Some researchers believe that fears of special-interest dominance in direct democracy are largely unfounded. They point to the following common pattern as an example: An initiative is proposed that sounds reasonable, and opinion polls show that voters favor it. Interest groups on both sides of the issue air television advertisements, which give citizens the opportunity to learn about both sides of the argument and make decisions that are on average consistent with their economic interests. Many initiatives fail because the more citizens learn about the consequences of passage, the more skeptical they become. In other words, most voters, using the cues from advertisements on ballot issues, tend to "get it right" in the voting booth. Instead of being persuaded to vote one way or another against their own interests, they learn a good deal from the campaigning on the issue.[9]

American Electoral Campaigns

When voters are choosing representatives or executives in elections, candidates for those positions work hard to win. Winning office through election in the American political system is usually an arduous process involving numerous steps. Candidates must obtain a position on the ballot, raise money, decide on a strategy for appealing to voters, get their message out to voters, and let the voters decide. In this section, we take a closer look at each of these steps.

Getting on the Ballot

For elections to accomplish something meaningful, voters must have meaningful options on the ballots. How do states determine which choices—both for political parties and individual candidates—to present to voters?

In a typical presidential election, numerous political parties other than the Democrats and Republicans are listed on the ballot. (This is also true in elections

---

[9] Elisabeth Gerber, Arthur Lupia, Mathew McCubbins, and Roderick Kiewiet, *Stealing the Initiative* (New York: Prentice Hall, 2000); Arthur Lupia and Mathew D. McCubbins, *The Democratic Dilemma: Can Citizens Learn What They Need to Know?* (New York: Cambridge University Press, 1998).

for Congress or state-level offices.) In 2016, for instance, it was common to see candidates representing the Greens, the Libertarians, or the Independent Party. The names of the parties on the ballot vary from state to state, but the Democratic and Republican parties always appear.

States have generally made it difficult for independent candidates (those who are not affiliated with an organized party) to obtain positions on the general election ballot. Both new parties and independent candidates must satisfy one of two general conditions. Either they need to have secured a certain percentage of the vote (between 5 and 15 percent) in the previous election for the same office, or they need to submit a petition requesting a space on the ballot signed by a certain number of registered voters. The required number of signatures varies across the states; naturally, the larger it is, the more onerous and expensive is the process of getting on the ballot.

As we discussed in Chapter 12, a key task of political parties is to choose candidates to run under party labels on election ballots. When several people want to run for the same office under the same party label, the party must have some means of choosing among them. Otherwise, the votes of party supporters would be divided among candidates in the general election, which would reduce the party's chances of winning. By choosing who runs under their label in the general election, parties are essentially performing a key act of agenda control in the American political system. They are determining the slate of candidates that voters can choose among on the general election ballot. Sometimes the parties choose their candidates through meetings (called caucuses, as discussed in Chapter 12) that are open only to formal party members. But more often, parties choose their candidates through primaries.

Recall that primary elections are used in most states to choose candidates for Congress, for state and local offices, and for delegates to the national political conventions that nominate presidential candidates. A primary is a form of mass election, and the ballot process is generally open to the public. (In a few states, candidates are selected by party caucuses composed of party members.) Some states hold **open primaries** in which any registered voter can vote, while others hold **closed primaries** in which only those voters registered with a specific political party can vote. By tradition, most states use plurality rules, and the candidate receiving the most votes wins.

There are other differences between primary elections and general elections. In primaries, at least two serious candidates within the same party often compete. Primaries also generate lower voter turnout than general elections. Research has shown that the average voter in a primary election tends to be more committed to the party cause, more ideologically motivated and extreme, and more affluent and educated than the average voter in a general election,[10]

open primary A primary election in which any registered voter can vote, regardless of party affiliation.

closed primary A primary election in which only voters registered with the party can vote.

[10] See, for example, Barbara Norrander, "Ideological Representativeness of Presidential Primary Voters," *American Journal of Political Science* 33, no. 3 (1989): 570–87.

though more recent work suggests that this trend may be changing.[11] Primary elections thus tend to be battles among candidates who claim to be the most authentically committed to the party's goals, but who also must appear to have a good chance of winning the general election against the opposition party's candidate. At this stage in the electoral process, candidates tend to describe themselves less in terms of moderation than in terms of devotion to policy goals that energize activists and garner votes in the primary election.

The nomination of presidential candidates is a long process, beginning in earnest the year before the election. Many candidates may compete to become the party's nominee, and in its early stages the competition can seem like a free-for-all. In 2016, sixteen candidates entered the race for the Republican presidential nomination. Candidates run in state-level contests, either primary elections or in party caucuses, to earn seats at the national party convention for "their" delegates. The delegates formally select the party's nominee at the convention, but the primary and caucus outcomes before the convention make the outcome of the convention a foregone conclusion.

Candidates "test the waters," usually in the Iowa caucuses and the New Hampshire primary, two of the earliest contests. During this preliminary phase of the election, the presidential candidates focus on appealing to core party constituencies and often end up criticizing members of their own party. The state contests proceed at a rapid pace. On several key dates, multiple contests are held that often tip the balance toward one of the party's candidates. While Iowa and New Hampshire are important, they are not determinative. Among a crowded field of 16 candidates with his party, Ted Cruz won Iowa in the 2016 Republican nomination process but ended up losing the nomination. After a lengthy battle throughout the winter, including winning New Hampshire, Donald Trump surged ahead of his remaining rivals in late April 2016 with big wins in five states in one day. The wins that day essentially locked up the Republican nomination.

Over time, the presidential nomination process has vacillated between granting power to voters and ensuring that key party officeholders have a strong voice in the nomination. In the nineteenth century, nominations often resulted from bargaining among state party chairs and congressional leaders in back rooms at the national conventions; power was clearly in the hands of party leaders. During the twentieth century, the states steadily moved toward adopting primaries and letting the voters choose candidates. This trend culminated in the 1970s when a number of victorious "dark horse" candidates took party leaders by surprise. In 1972, for example, George McGovern won the Democratic nomination, but lost badly in the general election to Richard Nixon.

The parties reacted by changing the rules in the 1980s and 1990s to offset the power of voters in the primaries. The goal was to give party leaders, who

[11] See, for example, Alan Abramowitz, "Don't Blame Primary Voters for Polarization," *The Forum* 5, no. 4 (2008).

presumably have a better understanding of candidates' "electability" than rank-and-file voters, a larger say in the nomination process. As a result, the modern system of nominating presidential candidates is once again tilted in favor of party power brokers. The Democrats grant heavily weighted votes to so-called PLEO (party leaders and elected officials) delegates to the national convention. The Republicans award states bonus delegates in proportion to how well they delivered Republican votes in previous national elections. Hence, these bonus delegates represent the strongest Republican states with visible, relatively loyal Republican Party leaders. During and after the 2016 election, there were many calls for reforms in both parties in the processes for choosing delegates and running primaries within the states. Especially on the Republican side—with Trump winning the nomination even as he savagely criticized party insiders and other Republican candidates and Republican members of Congress—party leaders sought ways to unify the party earlier in the primary process. Trump was seen as a critic of his own party who won the nomination in unorthodox fashion, including adopting many policy positions at odds with the preferences of the traditional party base. Moreover, his statements during the campaign season, especially during the primaries, seen as derogatory to Latinos, immigrants, racial minorities, and women were considered counterproductive to Republican efforts over the past decade to improve its standing among minority and female voters.

Raising Campaign Money

It costs a lot of money to run a campaign and win office at the national level in the United States. Candidates in Senate races typically raise and spend millions of dollars. House races involve somewhat lower expenditures (the average in the 2016 election cycle was $393,000 for major-party House candidates). Presidential campaigns are vastly more expensive. All told, major-party candidates in the 2016 presidential election, including campaigns for primaries and the general election, raised nearly $1.3 billion.

Election campaigns for Congress and the presidency are largely funded by private contributions. Only presidential candidates are eligible to receive public funding, though the major-party candidates tend not to take the public funds (discussed later). Federal candidates use the money they raise to hire campaign staff, rent offices and equipment, travel, run advertisements, and make and distribute lawn signs, bumper stickers, and T-shirts. Most campaign contributions come from wealthy individuals, interest groups, or groups of wealthy individuals who have a large stake in policies adopted by the national government. Candidates and parties raise money through fund-raising events, direct mail solicitations, and—increasingly—Internet and email appeals.

Private campaign financing flows through various organizational channels. Individuals can donate directly to a candidate or party. **Political action com-**

political action committee (PAC) A type of organization regulated by the Federal Election Commission that raises money from donors to support the election campaigns of federal political candidates.

mittees (PACs) are organizations that raise money for candidates or parties. They can be set up by the employees of a company, members of a union, or any other set of people with common interests. An interest group will often form a PAC (a side organization) with the express purpose of enabling its members to contribute to candidates or parties because the interest group itself is not permitted to give directly. Not surprisingly, the groups that give the most money to candidates in federal elections are those with a huge financial stake in the policy decisions made in Washington, D.C. (Table 13.1).

TABLE 13.1

Top Hard-Money Contributors to Federal Candidates in the 2016 Election Cycle

	Total Expenditures	Percentage to Democrats	Percentage to Republicans
Comcast	$11,489,697	74	27
AT&T	$11,408,788	33	67
Commonwealth of Pennsylvania	$10,217,932	100	0
Jobs Ohio	$10,001,000	0	100
Blue Cross/Blue Shield	$8,814,264	56	44
City of Philadelphia, PA	$8,680,464	100	0
International Brotherhood of Electrical Workers	$6,672,376	98	1
Microsoft	$6,530,890	51	49
Alphabet Inc.	$6,441,120	69	31
Honeywell International	$6,077,593	35	65
National Association of Realtors	$5,742,917	41	59
Renaissance Technologies	$5,165,846	56	44
Lockheed Martin	$4,836,270	40	60
Bank of America	$4,795,839	48	52
National Beer Wholesalers Association	$4,631,488	43	57
Goldman Sachs	$4,461,605	36	64
Philadelphia Convention & Visitors Bureau	$4,448,499	100	0
Koch Industries	$4,182,574	1	99
Deloitte	$4,160,508	40	60
Exelon Corp.	$4,107,852	73	27

Source: The Center for Responsive Politics, "Top Organization Contributors: Hard Money," www.opensecrets.org (accessed 11/13/16).

Campaign Contribution Limits (2017–18)

Donors	Recipients			
	Candidate Committee	PAC[1]	State, District, and Local Party Committee	National Party Committee
Individual	$2,700* per election	$5,000 per year	$10,000 per year combined limit	$33,900* per year
State, District, and Local Party Committee	$5,000 per election combined limit	$5,000 per year combined limit	Unlimited transfers to other party committees	
National Party Committee	$5,000 per election	$5,000 per year	Unlimited transfers to other party committees	
PAC, Multicandidate[2]	$5,000 per election	$5,000 per year	$5,000 per year combined limit	$15,000 per year
PAC, Not Multicandidate	$2,700* per election	$5,000 per year	$10,000 per year combined limit	$33,900* per year

* These limits are increased for inflation in odd-numbered years.
[1] A contribution earmarked for a candidate through a political committee counts against the original contributor's limit for that candidate. In certain circumstances, the contribution also may count against the contributor's limit to the PAC.
[2] A multicandidate committee is a political committee with more than 50 contributors that has been registered for at least six months and, with the exception of state party committees, has made contributions to five or more candidates for federal office.
Source: Federal Election Commission, "Contribution Limits for 2017–18," www.fec.gov (accessed 10/19/18).

Federal Election Commission (FEC) The federal agency that regulates campaign donations to and spending by candidates for Congress and the presidency.

Since 1974, all such private donations have been regulated by the **Federal Election Commission (FEC)** through a series of laws passed in response to the Watergate scandal. In the first of a series of rulings, the Supreme Court in *Buckley v. Valeo* (1976) established the important precedent that expenditures on behalf of candidates but independent of them could not be regulated because they qualify as political speech protected by the First Amendment. The Court did, however, allow the FEC to limit and regulate campaign contributions made directly to candidates and parties. (The Know the Facts box above summarizes the regulations as of 2018.) Some regulations limit the amount an individual or organization can give to a political campaign; others prohibit certain kinds of organizations, such as corporations and unions, from contributing directly to candidates or parties.

When the major Supreme Court decision *Citizens United v. FEC* (2010) was announced, striking down many regulations limiting contributions of corporations and unions, the lid was off for campaign contributions. As a result of the ruling, spending "on behalf of" candidates or parties—that is, spending not directly given to candidates or parties or coordinated with them—has no limit even for corporations and unions. Thus, spending by independent groups, especially in television advertising, increased dramatically, to an estimated $1.4 billion for the 2016 federal elections ($1.1 billion in the 2018 midterm elections). This does not count dollars spent on state and local campaigns by independent groups.

Individual donations toward candidates and parties are still regulated, but donors can get around many of these legal restrictions by setting up PACs or acting as "bundlers" to provide more money to their favored candidate or party. Less formal than PACs, bundlers coordinate the donations of many individuals and channel them to specific candidates. Through fund-raisers, bundlers combine these individual donations—which are limited by law to $2,700 per candidate—into one lump sum, often tens of thousands of dollars. Jeffrey Katzenberg, chief executive officer of DreamWorks Animation, raised millions of dollars as a bundler in the 2016 election for Hillary Clinton's presidential campaign. And so-called **super PACs** are those created to spend money independent of the candidates or parties. Following the various court rulings and the resulting hands-off approach of the FEC, there is no limit to how much individuals, corporations, unions, and organizations can donate to and spend through a given super PAC. Ordinary PACs are regulated by the FEC and generally give directly to candidates and parties, while super PACs are subject to very light regulation and spend on behalf of candidates or parties, or in favor of one side on an issue or in favor of an ideological approach.

In the parlance of campaign finance, donations by individuals or PACs to parties or candidates are considered **hard money**, as distinct from **soft money**, which is not given directly to a candidate or party (see Table 13.1 for a list of top hard-money contributors in 2016). Soft money is spent on advertising, voter mobilization drives, or other efforts to promote the candidacy of specific people or parties. Much soft money is associated with organizations called **527s** (after the section of the tax code that applies to them) and super PACs, which advocate publicly in favor of a candidate or a position on a ballot initiative. Some of these nonparty organizations have created television ads that are more notable than what the candidates or parties themselves create.

In the 2016 election cycle, for example, outside groups spent more than $1 billion dollars to support or criticize federal candidates. Outside groups in the 2016 presidential election ran advertisements claiming that Hillary Clinton was lying about her private email server while working as secretary of state; others claimed Donald Trump was a misogynist and a racist, and was responsible for running casino companies into the ground on purpose to receive tax breaks. Many of these commercials were criticized for being misleading, but they were more memorable (and arguably more effective) than other commercials coming from the specific campaign organizations or parties. A recent innovation in political finances comes from the invention of political entities classified as "social welfare" nonprofit groups under the tax code as opposed to 527 groups, which have electoral aims as their primary purpose. By law, these groups are not required to reveal their donors. Their

super PACs A type of organization regulated by the Federal Election Commission that can spend unlimited sums of money to advocate for the election or for the defeat of a candidate but is prohibited from contributing funds directly to federal campaigns and parties.

hard money Campaign funds that are given directly to candidates or parties to support a particular candidate and thus are subject to FEC regulations.

soft money Campaign funds that are given to parties or other organizations to support voter mobilization or voter education activities and thus typically not subject to FEC regulations.

527s Organizations that are independent of any party or candidate and thus not regulated by the Federal Election Commission; they do not advocate publicly for or against specific candidates, parties, or policies.

activities, however, have called into question their proper classification (as either political or social welfare) and, earlier in the decade, the IRS began to closely scrutinize groups like Crossroads GPS, a conservative social welfare nonprofit group headed by former George W. Bush advisers that spent millions advocating against Democrats.

A few states, including Maine, Vermont, Connecticut, and Arizona, have public funding of election campaigns. Candidates who qualify are given money by their state governments to run their campaigns. Public funding for presidential elections is provided by a special program instituted in the 1970s. The amount of money available is determined by the number of people who check off a special box on their income tax returns indicating that they want to allocate a certain amount (currently $3) of their taxes to the presidential candidates. Under this system, candidates who win a certain proportion of the votes during the primaries can tap into the national treasury to pay for their campaigns. In addition, the major-party candidates who end up winning their parties' nominations automatically qualify for a large amount of public funding to run their summer and fall campaigns.

If a state-level candidate accepts public money from his or her state, or if a presidential candidate accepts money from the national government, the candidate must abide by spending limits. Neither Hillary Clinton nor Donald Trump accepted public money, and therefore they could spend as much as they wanted. John McCain, likely the last major candidate to do so under the existing system, accepted public money in the 2008 presidential campaign and was able to spend $83 million on the general election. In 2008 Barack Obama chose to forgo public money from the U.S. Treasury. This decision gave him a huge financial advantage in the general election, as he was able to spend nearly three times more than McCain. Presidential candidates from major parties have since then decided that it gave them more freedom and resources to avoid taking public funds.

Citizens United v. FEC (2010) has clearly changed the campaign finance landscape. In striking down existing FEC restrictions on corporate and union spending on campaigns, the Court ruled that corporations and unions were "persons" deserving equality under the law and should not be prohibited from exercising their right of free speech in election campaigns, including the right to advertise on behalf of a candidate or party. Some have concluded that the *Citizens United* decision will give a huge advantage in the political system to wealthy corporations and wealthy people. All told, about $7 billion was spent on federal election campaigns in 2016—a record amount by far, even factoring in inflation—and much of that money was given by rich people and rich organizations (though to both major parties). Approximately $5.2 billion was spent on the 2018 federal elections. Yet how much it has or will bias election outcomes systematically has yet to be determined and will be difficult to determine with confidence. Until several campaign cycles have occurred, we will not be able to evaluate the implications of this important ruling by the Court. It is worth noting that many thought the ruling would favor the Republicans, but at least for the presidential elections in 2012 and 2016, pro-Democratic and pro-Republican groups spent approximately the same amount. In 2016, the Democrats spent more on the presidential race, but for all other federal elections combined, spending by the parties, candidates, and outside groups was roughly equal between the two parties and their supporters.

Campaign Rhetoric and Prisoner's Dilemmas

With money available for campaigning, candidates need to get out their message and motivate their supporters to turn out on Election Day. Candidates have to be strategic in their campaign messages, to consider carefully what the other candidates are communicating, and to react quickly at times. They typically use a mixture of messages in their campaigns. For example, they can

- promote their own qualities and positions on issues (what we might call positive campaigning);
- criticize their opponents for their character and/or their stands on issues (negative campaigning);
- criticize politicians and government in general and claim to be reformers.

Generally, once in the electoral arena, candidates for the major parties consider winning as the ultimate goal. If they believe that negative campaigning will improve their chances of winning, more often than not they will do it. When pressed, many candidates after the election say that they regret having to "go negative." All things being equal, they seem to want to run positive campaigns. However, most candidates would prefer to win by running a negative campaign than to lose by running a positive campaign.

Campaigns between two candidates are like prisoner's dilemmas. In Chapter 1, we discussed the example of two candidates facing off in an election and having to decide whether to spend money and time on campaigning. If neither campaigned, the outcome might turn out the same as if they had. But if one campaigns and the other does not, then the campaigning candidate will surely win. One possible reason researchers do not detect many effects of campaigns on election outcomes is that we so rarely observe the situation where only one candidate campaigns. Instead, we observe both candidates campaigning and the outcome being virtually the same as if neither had campaigned. In this situation, the two campaigns "cancel each other out."[12]

---

[12] John Sides and Lynn Vavreck, *The Gamble: Choice and Chance in the 2012 Election* (Princeton, NJ: Princeton University Press, 2013).

The Collective Dilemma

During presidential elections, the Iowa caucus and New Hampshire primaries are mainstays of the process. Considering the relatively small size of these states, why do these contests garner so much attention? And what determines timing of these events in other states?

Interests

States want to hold their caucuses or primary elections early in presidential election years because going early brings widespread attention to their state. Media travel to these states and report exit-poll numbers, and results make national headlines. Local economies also benefit because the increased activity translates into business for shops and restaurants where candidates host local events.[a]

Party leadership, meanwhile, is interested in organizing and maintaining control of which states hold their events on which days. Not only do the results of these caucuses and primaries matter but so does the timing; what happens at each state's events contributes to the party's image.

Likewise, candidates care about which states hold their caucuses or primaries first. If an early state happens to be populated by the demographic group to which a candidate mainly appeals, this bodes well for the candidate's chance of winning that primary or caucus.

Institutions

In some cases, state law mandates early events. The first-slot caucus is codified into Iowa law:

> Delegates to county conventions of political parties and party committee members shall be elected at precinct caucuses held not later than the fourth Monday in February of each even-numbered year. The date shall be at least eight days earlier than the scheduled date for any meeting, caucus, or primary which constitutes the first determining stage of the presidential nominating process in any other state, territory, or any other group which has the authority to select delegates in the presidential nomination.[b]

Similarly, New Hampshire law specifies that the primary "shall be held on the second Tuesday in March or on a date selected by the secretary of state which is 7 days or more immediately preceding the date on which any other state shall hold a similar election."[c] These laws establish that Iowa holds the first political event that contributes to parties' presidential nominations and that New Hampshire holds the first primary election. Political scientist Elaine C. Kamarck describes these as "automatic triggers,"[d] meaning that when another state moves its event to a time before Iowa or New Hampshire, these two states automatically move theirs even earlier, maintaining their positions as first caucus and primary.

The two national party organizations influence caucus or primary dates in states and they can punish states that try to contravene the rules. It is not illegal for states to try to move their primaries or caucuses up, but the parties can threaten to reduce the number of convention delegates from the state or even strip a state of convention delegates altogether. The dates of primaries and causes do move around, but the party organizations constrain the movements.

Outcomes

The Iowa caucus and New Hampshire primary each enjoy their own special day, unlike many states that share dates with other states. "Super Tuesday," for instance, happens in February or March, and as many as 24 states hold their nominating events, none of which can receive the kind of attention as Iowa and New Hampshire. Two scholars described the New Hampshire primary this way: "Every four years during the primary election season, the ninth-smallest state in the union captures the attention of the national press and television to a degree unmatched in vast more populous locales."[e]

More broadly, the sequenced nature of political events like caucuses and primaries means that in most presidential election years the results of later states matter less than results of earlier ones. Yet, winning Iowa does not guarantee the party nomination, although "increased media attention associated with their Iowa performance propelled their candidacies into New Hampshire, and in some cases beyond." This is because a win in the earliest races signals "how voters perceive the viability and electability of candidates."[f]

There have been debates about the future influence of the early events. Often, there are rumblings that the status quo will change. In 2016, Chairman of the Republican Party Reince Priebus remarked, "I don't think there should ever be any sacred cows as to the primary process or the order."[g] Some are critical of the early-state events because neither Iowa nor New Hampshire is representative of the country's population, and the timing affords an arbitrary sample of citizens an undue influence.[h]

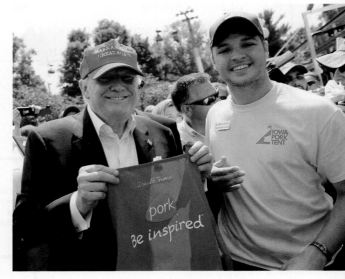

Candidates spend a good deal of time campaigning in Iowa and New Hampshire in the months leading up to the primaries and caucuses because they know that winning these early contests may bode well for victories in other states. The Iowa State Fair is a popular campaign stop for candidates hoping to win their party's presidential nomination.

Think About It

Is it unfair for Iowa and New Hampshire to enjoy the early slots at every presidential election? If so, what would "fair" timing look like? What kinds of states should hold elections early in the process?

a. Brianne Pfannenstiel, "How Are Candidates Spending Ahead of the Caucuses?" *Des Moines Register*, December 10, 2015, www.desmoines register.com/story/news/elections/presidential/caucus/2015/12/05/caucus-spending-iowa-rarely-large-times-odd/76379652/ (accessed 1/08/16).

b. Iowa Code §43.4.

c. New Hampshire Code §653:9.

d. Elaine C. Kamarck, *Primary Politics: How Presidential Candidates Have Shaped the Modern Nominating System* (Washington, DC: Brookings Institution Press, 2009), p. 71.

e. Gary R. Orren and Nelson W. Polsby, "New Hampshire: Springboard of Nomination Politics," in *Media and Momentum*, ed. Gary R. Orren and Nelson W. Polsby (Chatham, NJ: Chatham House Publishers, 1987), p. 1.

f. David P. Redlawsk, Caroline J. Tolbert, and Todd Donovan, *Why Iowa? How Caucuses and Sequential Elections Improve the Presidential Nominating Process* (University of Chicago Press, 2011), p. 159.

g. Tim Alberta, "RNC Chair: Iowa and New Hampshire Aren't 'Sacred Cows' After 2016," *National Review*, September 29, 2015, www.nationaljournal.com /s/73980/rnc-chair-iowa-new-hampshire-arent-sacred-cows-after-2016 (accessed 1/7/16).

h. See Elaine C. Kamarck, *Primary Politics*, pp. 51–80.

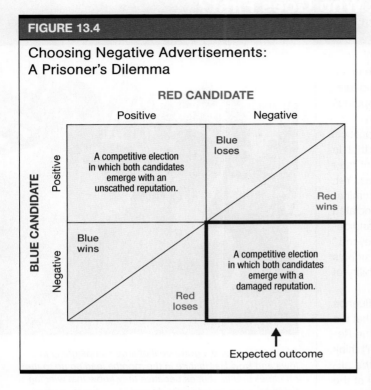

FIGURE 13.4

Choosing Negative Advertisements: A Prisoner's Dilemma

RED CANDIDATE

Positive / Negative

BLUE CANDIDATE — Positive / Negative

A competitive election in which both candidates emerge with an unscathed reputation.

Blue loses

Red wins

Blue wins

A competitive election in which both candidates emerge with a damaged reputation.

Red loses

Expected outcome

Now consider a related situation, this time involving two candidates who are deciding whether to campaign positively or negatively. Suppose, for the sake of argument, that both candidates believe that negative campaigning works better than positive campaigning in persuading voters, but also that negative campaigning harms the overall electoral process.

In Figure 13.4, each of the two candidates has to choose between positive and negative campaigning. All things being equal, both candidates would prefer to campaign positively. Voters would like that too—it would keep the debate surrounding the election enlightened and civil. However, it is all too tempting to campaign negatively. If only one candidate goes negative, he or she wins handily. If they both go negative, the election results (in terms of vote percentages and who wins) are pretty much what they would have been if both stayed positive, but the tone of the election becomes degrading and turns off many voters (and pundits in the media). The equilibrium outcome is negative campaigning by both because they are locked in a situation comparable to the prisoner's dilemma. The temptation to go negative is too great because of the potential payoff.

As in all our prisoner's dilemma depictions, Figure 13.4 leaves out complicating factors. Suppose, for instance, that one of the candidates in the preceding story uses more effective negative campaigning and so the two campaigns do not cancel each other out but instead give one candidate an advantage that would not have occurred without the campaigning. Our depiction here leaves out that factor in order to keep matters simple and to focus on explaining this puzzle: Why would candidates simultaneously campaign negatively and complain about having to do it?

Campaigning with Modern Technologies

A vast majority of elections in the United States, particularly for state and local offices, are conducted on a small scale—handshakes at fairs, door-to-door leaflet drops, and yard signs and bumper stickers. In nearly all federal elections and statewide elections, by contrast, candidates rely considerably on electronic media to communicate with voters. These means of electronic communication have profoundly shaped the way campaigns for public office are conducted. (We will discuss the topic of journalism and the general mass media in more detail in Chapter 14.)

We can think of electronic or mass media campaign messages as being relayed to voters in one of two ways: directly, in the form of advertising and speeches; or indirectly, through coverage by journalists, pundits, or bloggers. The former is considered "paid" media, the latter "free" media. Obviously, candidates appreciate free media that portrays them in a positive light. The problem is that they cannot control what others say about them. With paid media, candidates can at least control the messages they are sending to voters.

Before the age of electronic media—that is, before the advent of the telegraph in the mid-nineteenth century—presidential candidates could travel to different places and say different things to different groups of people. A candidate could promise one group of voters a vigorous stand against competition from imported goods, then travel down the road and promise another group of voters a set of policies designed to encourage foreign trade. Since neither group knew what the other had been told, it was unlikely that they would hold the candidate's words against him. Speeches in public squares and essays published in local party newspapers were the primary means of communicating with voters in this era.

Contrast this decentralized mode of campaigning with the situation today, when electronic media transmits a candidate's words around the world in a matter of seconds. This phenomenon began with the telegraph and was extended with the advent of radio, television, the Internet, and now text messaging and social media. Words spoken by or written about politicians can reach all kinds of voters virtually instantaneously. Consequently, candidates are obliged to send out consistent messages, avoid contradictory rhetoric or promises to different groups of voters, and be mindful of the diverse groups that will end up hearing, seeing, or reading a given speech.

This simple observation—that electronic communication has forced candidates to be more careful in what they say—illustrates a broader point: specific kinds of electronic media have changed the nature of campaigns and elections in many fundamental ways. For example, the rapidity with which messages or images can be transmitted has forced candidates to tighten control over the campaign promises they make to voters. It has imposed a certain kind of discipline on candidates and their supporters—a need to stay focused on common themes and messages, and to control the content of all communications.

The advent of television was perhaps the most important turning point in election campaigns. Television offers a highly intimate and immediate method of communication. Beginning in the 1950s and especially the 1960s, when most American families owned televisions, politicians not only had to be eloquent, they also had to look good on the television screen. They needed to

1860s Former slaves granted suffrage formally through constitutional amendment

1880s–1890s Adoption of the Australian ballot, moving election administration from the political parties to state governments

1913 The direct election of senators is mandated by constitutional amendment.

1920 Women's suffrage is granted by constitutional amendment.

1970s The beginning of federal regulation of campaign finance for federal offices; the Federal Election Commission is established.

1993 The Motor Voter Act is intended to make it easier for people to register to vote.

2002 The Help America Vote Act is intended to improve access to polls and voting technology, and the McCain-Feingold Act is intended to improve regulation of campaign finance for federal offices.

1820	1860	1900	1940	1980

1820–1850 Expansion of male franchise beyond white propertied males

1880s–1960s Jim Crow laws and other discriminatory laws greatly limit actual voting rights of African Americans.

1962–1963 The Supreme Court mandates that all electoral constituencies for legislatures (except for U.S. Senate seats) must be of equal population size within states.

1965 The Voting Rights Act makes the federal government the main enforcer of voting rights and promoted suffrage of minorities, especially African Americans.

2010 The Supreme Court greatly restricts federal government from regulating campaign finance due to First Amendment concerns.

communicate in a way that conveyed the force of facial image, voice, and gesture to appeal simultaneously to vast numbers and different kinds of voters. In short, television caused politicians to become mass-marketed products with a consistent brand image across all parts of the country.

Political debates began to be televised in the 1960s. The first televised presidential debates, between Richard Nixon and John F. Kennedy in 1960, were noteworthy for the respective powers of television (visual) and radio (audio). According to polls conducted afterward, more voters watching the debates on television thought Kennedy performed better than Nixon, while more voters listening on the radio thought Nixon performed better than Kennedy. Kennedy, as the more telegenic candidate, represented the wave of the future. Ever since then, presidential candidates have had to "win" on television. In the 2016 campaign, both major party candidates were well known to nearly everyone going in. Donald Trump was a celebrity from reality TV and a major businessman in New York, while Hillary Clinton was a former secretary of state, U.S. senator, and first lady. Neither needed to be introduced to the public, yet their performances in debates were hugely important. In the primary elections, Trump gained advantage over his rivals by belittling them and boasting about his business success during numerous de-

Today, candidates take advantage of social media to reach new voters and mobilize supporters. Donald Trump's active and prolific use of Twitter was one of his key campaign strategies. He frequently engaged with media outlets, other politicians, and his over 13 million followers throughout his campaign. His victory message on election night is shown above.

bates, sometimes with eight candidates on stage. Clinton struggled sometimes in debates with her rival Bernie Sanders during the primary election debates, but she performed better in the general election debates against Donald Trump, and was widely seen to have made him seem inexperienced and easily ruffled. Telegenic candidates can overcome a lack of experience in the national government or national exposure through powerful performances in this hugely popular format.

Television is also the preferred medium for the short, 15- or 30-second advertisements that are the staple of modern campaigning. Increasingly, television ads are migrating to the Internet through forums like YouTube. These ads range from attacks on opponents to feel-good messages with pleasant images and upbeat music. The creators of these ads use subtle devices to evoke certain emotions or responses from viewers, in much the same way that television commercials deliberately manipulate our feelings about certain products or services. It has been demonstrated, for example, that when viewers are shown images of racial minorities in campaign advertisements, they tend to use more racist reasoning in making political choices, such as voting or expressing support for certain policies. These same viewers indicate that they are not conscious of the effects of the advertisements on their choices. In other words, much like in product advertising in the business world, political advertising provokes subconscious feelings that affect choices and attitudes.[13]

Beyond the use of television, candidates and parties are increasingly deploying social networking feeds and cell phones to raise money, communicate their positions on issues to voters and journalists, and mobilize voters. In 2016, both the Trump and Clinton campaigns used social media and email to connect with potential supporters. The two candidates set up sophisticated websites; promoted themselves on Twitter, YouTube, and Facebook; and stayed in touch with supporters by means of cell phones and text messaging. Trump used his Twitter account relentlessly, and kept the Clinton campaign guessing about his strategies with provocative tweets. Such creative use of social media allowed the Trump campaign to interact with supporters, as well as to reach and mobilize his audience that normally fails to turn out in large numbers at the polls.

Voter Decision Making

We began this chapter by asking whether campaigns matter for the outcome of presidential elections. Let's now rephrase the question and ask whether they matter for the outcome of *any* election. We have already noted that many people vote based on their partisanship and are not persuaded by campaigns. Furthermore, many make up their minds early on or live in states where the election results are foregone conclusions.

Of course, campaigns are not just about persuading people to vote for one candidate or another. They are also about exciting people, mobilizing them to go to the polls, and convincing them to vote for one particular party. In a larger sense, campaigns are part of the process of defining the problems and issues that voters want the government to address.

In some instances, elections come down to a very small number of voters who are genuinely undecided. Swaying a comparative handful of voters in key states could make the difference between winning and losing an election. This happened in the 2000 presidential contest when George W. Bush narrowly won Florida's popular vote by only a few hundred votes (and thus its all-important votes in the electoral college), and again in 2008 when Al Franken won a Senate seat in Minnesota by a paper-thin margin of 312 votes (out of roughly 3 million votes cast). The 2016 presidential election was quite close. The final popular vote difference was over 2.5 million, or about 2 percent. More importantly, key swing states like Michigan, Pennsylvania, and Wisconsin were decided by small margins. This explains why late in the fall of an election year, candidates tend to focus their attention on the few

[13] Nicholas Valentino, Vincent Hutchings, and Ismail White, "Cues that Matter: How Political Ads Prime Racial Attitudes during Campaigns," *American Political Science Review* 96, no. 1 (2002): 75–90.

geographical areas where undecided voters live. Presidential candidates continue to advertise nationally to make sure voters stay engaged, even in states where they seem to have a secure lead, but they spend most of their time visiting and giving speeches in the so-called swing states.

In earlier chapters on public opinion (Chapter 9) and political parties (Chapter 12), we discussed how different groups in the population develop loyalties toward one party or the other. Party identification, we learned, is the best predictor of how most people will vote on Election Day. Other factors matter as well, however, such as evaluations of the incumbents, candidates' positions on issues, and news about corruption and scandal. Voters have been shown to depart often enough from their partisan leanings that the outcome of elections cannot be predicted simply by counting the number of Democrats and Republicans in a given state or congressional district. People might lean toward one party, but in a given election they may vote for the other party's candidate based on his or her trustworthiness or competence. Moreover, we must not forget that many voters are truly independent and show no consistent preference for one party over another. By one estimate, independent voters comprise roughly 12 percent of the electorate nationwide.

To explain why individuals vote in a certain way, political scientists have developed theories of voter decision making. The following are the five most prominent models of voting that appear in the social science literature.

The Partisan Model. This model, also known as the Michigan model, was developed by researchers at the University of Michigan in the 1950s and culminated in publication of the classic book *The American Voter*. The model emphasizes that party identification is a deep psychological attachment to a particular party, and that a voter's partisanship shapes his or her perceptions of facts and issues. For example, Democrats and Republicans will observe certain economic data—say, a troublesome rise in inflation—and assign blame differently to politicians. Democrats are inclined to blame Republicans for causing the inflation, while Republicans are inclined to blame Democrats. The point is that people filter information through their partisanship and come to biased conclusions.[14]

The Retrospective Voting Model. This model emphasizes the many ways in which voters rely on politicians' past performance to make judgments about their competence in office. If the economy is doing poorly, then voters of either party are inclined to blame the incumbent president, or the incumbent president's party, for the problems, and be less inclined to support that party

[14] Angus Campbell, Philip E. Converse, Warren E. Miller, and Donald Stokes, *The American Voter* (New York: John Wiley & Sons, 1960).

in the next election. Voters look to the past to predict how politicians will fare in the future. The model's logic is rooted in the competence and skill of politicians rather than party identification as a psychological category leading to biased assessments.[15]

The Valence Model. This model is similar to the retrospective voting model in that it focuses on the competence and skills of candidates. Valence, however, refers to characteristics of candidates or parties that nearly all voters wish for in leaders, such as strength of character, honesty, or charisma. Voters ascribe reputations to specific candidates or parties for having certain of these characteristics. If a candidate or party has a valence advantage over the other(s), it means that this draws voters from across the ideological spectrum to the advantaged candidate or party. While the retrospective voting model focuses on previous performance by an incumbent party, the valence model focuses on reputations of candidates or parties that do not necessarily follow from past outcomes. Many of the valence characteristics will come from voters observing candidates on television or other forms of electronic communication during campaigns.[16]

The Spatial Model. This model considers issues or ideology to be the most important factors in influencing a person's vote. It is called spatial because researchers depict voters and politicians as existing in a common space of competition. It is assumed that people vote for the candidate or party closest to them in ideological space. As we discussed in the section on elections as a determinant of policy and ideology direction, competition for office among politicians can be depicted as a movement along an imaginary ideological line in an effort to win over voters. In this model, the key to understanding voting is the assumption that voters know which competitor is closest to them on the line and vote accordingly. In other words, they weigh the candidates' issue positions or ideologies heavily in deciding how to vote.[17]

The Directional Model. This model also focuses on issues and ideology, but it offers a different interpretation of voting decisions than the spatial model. Voters are interested in knowing in which direction the various parties will shift policy. Voters to the left of the current policy want a party that will be dedicated to moving the policy to the left, while voters to the right of the current policy want a party that will move the policy to the right. The key is not how far away a party or candidate is in a policy space in comparison to the voter's preferred positions (as in the spatial model), but rather how intensely a party pursues these policies. Thus, leftist voters want candidates or

[15] Fiorina, *Retrospective Voting in American National Elections.*

[16] Harold D. Clarke, David Sanders, Marianne C. Stewart, and Paul F. Whiteley, *Political Choice in Britain* (New York: Oxford University Press, 2004).

[17] Anthony Downs, *An Economic Theory of Democracy* (New York: Harper, 1957).

parties to prioritize leftist policies, and vice versa for rightist voters. In spatial terms, leftist voters want parties that are far to the left.[18]

Although political scientists might hold that one or another of these theories is best at explaining voting decisions, it is possible to compromise among several of them. Evidence remains strong, for example, that party identification is the best predictor of voting, but many scholars have argued that party identification *summarizes* or encompasses these other concepts. That is, voters develop loyalties to parties because those parties appeal to them on the issues, or have in their fold competent incumbent government officials.

Recent research has provided further insight into the conditions under which campaigns can matter in influencing voters. Some scholars have suggested that the presence of a field operation in an area can yield modest effects on a candidate's vote share,[19] while other research has found that both door-to-door canvassing and commercial phone-bank calls can have strong effects on voting choices.[20] In addition, a recent study of presidential campaign advertising suggests that ads can persuade enough voters to swing some elections, even if they do not increase the overall turnout.[21]

In Comparison: Elections

As we have seen in this and previous chapters, American elections have certain well-known features: two-party dominance; candidate-centered elections; freewheeling, open-ended campaigning; fund-raising from private sources; and multiple elections for offices at all levels of government. These features are not found everywhere. Through knowledge of other countries, we can become informed about the consequences of the specific aspects of American institutions, and about what changes might be possible to the American system.

Different Formal Electoral Institutions

The range of electoral rules across countries is too vast to detail here, but we can offer several generalizations. First, several major countries hold single-

[18] George Rabinowitz and Stuart Elaine Macdonald, "A Directional Theory of Issue Voting," *American Political Science Review* 83 (1989): 93–121.

[19] Seth E. Masket, "Did Obama's Ground Game Matter? The Influence of Local Field Offices during the 2008 Presidential Election," *Public Opinion Quarterly* 73, no. 5 (2009): 1023–39.

[20] Kevin Arceneaux, "I'm Asking for Your Support: The Effects of Personally Delivered Campaign Messages on Voting Decisions and Opinion Formation," *Quarterly Journal of Political Science* 2, no. 1 (2007): 43–65.

[21] Gregory A. Huber and Kevin Arceneaux, "Identifying the Persuasive Effects of Presidential Advertising," *American Journal of Political Science* 51, no. 4 (2007): 957–77.

member plurality elections for the national parliament: the United States, Great Britain, India, and Canada are four examples. This type of electoral system is unusual, however, and is mostly restricted to Britain and its former colonies. Second, it is common for countries to have some form of proportional representation in which the proportion of seats a party holds in parliament is related to the proportion of votes it receives in elections. Third, many countries have complicated voting systems whereby voters can vote for multiple candidates or parties or can specify a second-favorite choice so that their votes can be transferred to more competitive parties. Fourth, electoral systems around the world tend to encourage the establishment of multiple political parties and to lead to governments in which multiple parties are knit together to form a majority in the parliament. The United States and a few other countries, such as Britain and Canada, are unusual in having single-party majorities controlling the national parliament most of the time.

Party-Centered, Ideological Elections

We discussed in Chapter 12 that national elections in other countries are usually tied more directly to parties and their platforms than to individual politicians. This kind of party-centered election is common in long-standing industrial democracies in Europe, as well as in Australia, Canada, and Japan. In parliamentary contests in the Netherlands, Israel, Italy, or Sweden, voters hardly know the names of the candidates; rather, their vote is based on their favored party. Moreover, voting in other countries tends to involve making selections for a party overall (like voting straight tickets in the United States), while U.S. voters typically choose individual candidates in dozens of elections for various offices. Voters in Oregon, for example, often have more than 100 choices to make on Election Day.

Party-centered campaigning in other countries is more prevalent than in the United States, in part because these nations have more competing parties. We described earlier how in the United States, candidates of the two major parties have incentives to move to the middle to appeal to moderate voters, taking it for granted that voters who hold more extreme beliefs will vote for them anyway. When there are many parties competing, each party attempts to win as many voters as it can in a relatively narrow range of the ideological space. Party ideology rarely moves much compared to the ideologies of U.S. presidential candidates, which tend to shift toward the moderate center of their party's ideological spectrum. By not shifting positions, the parties in other countries emphasize their ideological credentials.

Campaign advertising can be considered a prisoner's dilemma. Two competing candidates each have an incentive to use negative advertisements even though both would be better off if neither used them.

Two political scientists, Zachary Auter and Jeffery Fine, categorized the nature of Facebook posts by 78 Senate candidates during their campaigns. Auter and Fine defined negative posts as ones that attacked the opponent's character or competency for the job or highlighted the opponent's stance on an unpopular policy.

Figure A shows the average number of weekly negative Facebook posts by the competitiveness of the race. Figure B shows the relationship between the number of negative Facebook posts and the timing, as the election nears for underdogs and front-runners; moving from left to right means we are getting closer to the election.

A. Average Number of Weekly Negative Facebook Posts by Senate-Race Competitiveness, 2010

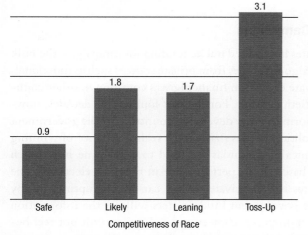

B. Number of Weekly Negative Facebook Posts during Each Week of "Safe" Senate Races, 2010

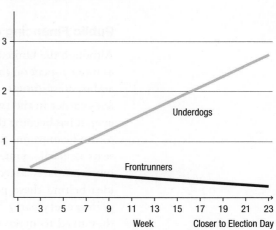

Source: Zachary J. Auter and Jeffrey A. Fine, "Negative Campaigning in the Social Media Age: Attack Advertising on Facebook," *Political Behavior* (2016): 1–22. Replication data available at https://dataverse.harvard.edu/dataset.xhtml?persistentId=doi:10.7910/DVN/TGKZ2T (accessed 6/15/16).

Think About It

When and under what circumstances do you see the most negative advertisements among Senate candidates? Which kinds of candidates make the most use of negative advertisements? What does this tell you about how candidates view the impact of negative campaigning?

Limited Campaigning

In many other countries, campaigning for national elections is heavily regulated by the government. For instance, it is common to limit the campaign period to several months before the election. Advertising on television, posting signs, and holding campaign rallies are prohibited before and after the campaign period. Many countries do not allow campaign commercials in the few days before an election. All of this might seem appealing to Americans, who experience nearly two years of campaigning for the presidential elections. In South Korea and a few other countries, candidates cannot attack each other verbally. This restriction is interpreted and enforced quite strictly. In political debates, South Korean candidates must stick to descriptions of their policy programs, and they are not permitted to question the character or judgment of the opposition candidates. Such regulations on campaigning are unheard of in the American system, where the legal system places tremendous value on the freedom of political speech.

Public Financing of Campaigns

Although the United States has limited public funding for campaigns, the bulk of money spent on campaigning comes from private sources such as individuals and interest groups. Private campaign financing was common in other countries earlier in the twentieth century. For the past four or five decades, however, it has become the norm in other developed countries for the government to fund campaigns for political parties that stand a realistic chance of winning seats in parliament. Typically, formulas are used to determine how much money a party receives based on its performance in previous elections. The idea behind these policies is that private money can be corrupting. So, by giving every party some government funds, voters will get the information they need to make the appropriate choices and politicians will not feel beholden to special interests that donated to their campaign. There is no consensus among scholars, and no definitive evidence, that public financing changes the nature of campaigns and candidates.

In sum, from a comparative international perspective, American elections and campaigns are unusual. Other countries have different features, often stemming from changes to their election rules in the twentieth century designed to achieve specific purposes. Are there aspects of American elections and campaigns that could be improved? Put another way, what, if anything, can we learn from other countries?

Is There a Need for Reform?

We began this chapter with a question: Do campaigns matter? There are two ways of approaching an answer. First, we can summarize research on how individual voters react to campaign messages. We have learned that campaigns probably do not matter for most voters, but for the small number who might switch from one party to another, they can be decisive. In two-party elections, under the ideas that follow from the median voter theorem discussed earlier in the chapter, the parties can be similar in their ideologies. Furthermore, it might be the perceptions among voters about competence or corruption that distinguish the parties or candidates. Thus, if we accept the convergence theory and the selection effect, elections can hinge on that small number of voters who listen to campaign messages about the individual characteristics of the candidates. So, yes, campaigns can change some voters' minds, though that number is relatively small.

Second, we can think about campaigns in terms of their overall effects on election outcomes, and also on candidates' motivations for campaigning in particular ways. A prisoner's dilemma framework is useful here. If only one of the two major-party candidates conducted a vigorous campaign, then campaigning would likely matter. But since ordinarily both major-party candidates campaign with intensity, the two campaigns may cancel each other out, and it can seem as though campaigning does not matter much. In fact, campaigning matters for each candidate in canceling out the effects of the campaigning of the other. If, however, campaigns reveal information about candidates that tilt voters toward one candidate or the other, then campaigns do not cancel each other out but can shift the outcome. The 2016 election campaign for president had many twists and turns, with new revelations about both major candidates upending the polls and shifting momentum. The outcome, a Trump victory, was a surprise to nearly everyone, and it is hard to argue that events that occurred during the campaign did not matter, as surely they did. But that is not the same as knowing the measurable effects that the campaign strategies of each candidate had on the eventual outcome.

Now consider a different question: Do the specific electoral institutions in the United States matter? The institutions we have studied throughout this book address a range of collective dilemmas relating to how political parties are organized and mobilize voters; how interest groups and PACs endorse and fund candidates; how mass media outlets inform voters; how primary elections or party caucuses lead to voter and candidate coordination; and how state-level regulations, intraparty organizations, and campaign finance affect elections.

Some of these institutions or institutional features are more successful than others. The American political parties do quite well in coordinating voters and candidates and in mobilizing fund-raisers. They perhaps do less well in mobilizing voters, but maybe well enough, given the limited number they expect to support them in elections. It is safe to say that the institutions of American electoral democracy do not do terribly well in preventing campaigns in which the two major-party candidates hurl personal and often untrue or misleading accusations at each other. During the 2016 election, the presidential candidates accused their opponents of lying, corruption, and even criminality. There were many instances in 2016 of name-calling and personal attacks, often based on flimsy or false information.

Beyond considering what discourse is appropriate in election campaigns, we need to ask a more general question: Do American elections work as they should? Do they choose capable, responsive leaders? What reforms, if any, are called for?

Before we start to answer these questions, let's step back for perspective. We need to acknowledge the way constitutional law set boundaries on reforms. Contemporary electoral campaigns, and the institutions and decision making that shape them, have been profoundly affected by Supreme Court interpretations of the First Amendment over the past half century. In general, the Supreme Court in its decisions beginning in the 1970s and through *Citizens United* (2010) has sided strongly with the view that political speech, including spending money to broadcast that speech, deserves the utmost protection from government regulation. Repeatedly, federal courts have struck down efforts to regulate either the funding of campaigns or when or where people or organizations can say whatever they want about candidates.

The following electoral reforms have been proposed in recent decades. Although all have been adopted in other countries, there is little or no chance that any of them will soon be adopted in the United States, given the current political climate. The reforms are listed in order from the least likely to the most possible.

- Limit campaign rhetoric to positive messages. This change would certainly be found to violate the First Amendment protection of political speech.

- Move toward proportional representation and away from plurality voting. This would require changes in state laws.

- Abolish the electoral college in favor of a pure popular voting system for president. This would require a constitutional amendment because the Constitution specifies that the president is to be chosen by the electoral college.

- Limit the amount of time for campaigning by prohibiting campaign advertisements and public messages before a certain date before the election. This would possibly be found unconstitutional under the First Amendment's protection of political speech, but it could conceivably be achieved by congressional statute.

- Fund all campaigns for federal and state office with public money provided by the government. This could be mandated by congressional statute.

- Make it easier for third and minor parties to get on election ballots. This would require changes in state laws.

- Adopt further limits on the amount of money candidates or parties, and other people, can raise and spend in or on behalf of campaigns. This would require new congressional statutes and state laws, and a different constitutional interpretation by the Supreme Court of whether corporations and unions are persons under the law and thus deserve protection of freedom of speech under the First Amendment.

- Adopt regulations promoting more transparency and public information about who gives money to candidates and parties, and how that money is spent. This would require new congressional statutes.

Would any of these reforms improve elections in the United States? If so, what would the consequences be?

FURTHER READING

★ = Included in *Readings in American Politics*, 5th ed.

★ Achen, Christopher, and Larry Bartels, *Democracy for Realists: Why Elections Do Not Produce Responsive Government* (Princeton, NJ: Princeton University Press, 2016). Achen and Bartels take a pessimistic view of whether voters understand enough to choose their leaders wisely in a democracy and challenge us to confront the reality that elections often do not work to produce effective, responsive government.

Brader, Ted, *Campaigning for Hearts and Minds* (Chicago: University of Chicago Press, 2006). A detailed study of the role of emotion in determining how voters respond to campaign advertisements.

★ Campbell, Angus, Philip E. Converse, Warren E. Miller, and Donald Stokes, *The American Voter* (New York: John Wiley & Sons, 1960). A classic book on voting behavior, influencing voting studies all over the world; presents the Michigan model of voting.

★ *Citizens United v. Federal Election Commission* (2010). The ruling that declared that corporations and unions share similar First Amendment rights as individuals, including the right to advertise on behalf of a candidate or party during election campaigns.

Cox, Gary, *Making Votes Count* (Cambridge, UK: Cambridge University Press, 1997). A detailed study of how electoral systems affect the number of parties and candidates in elections around the world.

Downs, Anthony, *An Economic Theory of Democracy* (New York: Harper, 1957). Gives a rational choice account of democracy with a special focus on electoral processes.

Duverger, Maurice, *Political Parties* (New York: John Wiley & Sons, 1963). A classic book on various facets of parties, especially their organization and the nature of party systems across countries.

Fiorina, Morris P., *Retrospective Voting in American National Elections* (New Haven, CT: Yale University Press, 1981). A study of voting behavior, arguing that many voters choose candidates based on past performance of incumbents.

★ Fox, Richard, and Jennifer Lawless, "Gendered Perspectives and Political Candidacies: A Central Barrier to Women's Equality in Electoral Politics," *American Journal of Political Science* 55 (2011): 59–73.

Gerber, Elisabeth, Arthur Lupia, Mathew McCubbins, and Roderick Kiewiet, *Stealing the Initiative* (New York: Prentice Hall, 2000). Shows in detail the process that occurs when referendums and initiatives are proposed to great fanfare and then lose at the polls.

Huber, Gregory A., and Kevin Arceneaux, "Identifying the Persuasive Effects of Presidential Advertising," *American Journal of Political Science* 51, no. 4 (October 2007): 957–77. A careful analysis of which voters are swayed by campaign advertisements.

Magleby, David, *The Change Election: Money, Mobilization, and Persuasion in the 2008 Federal Elections* (Philadelphia: Temple University Press, 2010). Explains well the innovations in campaign strategy employed across a number of federal elections in 2008.

Page, Benjamin I., *Choices and Echoes in Presidential Elections* (Chicago: University of Chicago Press, 1978). An account of how presidential candidates become more moderate over time to try to win general elections.

Rabinowitz, George, and Stuart Elaine Macdonald, "A Directional Theory of Issue Voting," *American Political Science Review* 83 (1989): 93–121. The original article espousing the directional model of voting, where candidates seek to appeal to ideological voters.

Sides, John, and Lynn Vavreck, *The Gamble: Choice and Chance in the 2012 Presidential Election* (Princeton, NJ: Princeton University Press, 2012). The issues, events, and campaign strategies in the 2012 presidential election.

Sulkin, Tracy, *The Legislative Legacy of Congressional Campaigns* (New York: Cambridge University Press, 2011). Examines how reliable congressional members have been in fulfilling campaign promises, finding that congressional promises are good indicators of what policies an elected official will pursue.

Valentino, Nicholas, Vincent Hutchings, and Ismail White, "Cues that Matter: How Political Ads Prime Racial Attitudes during Campaigns," *American Political Science Review* 96, no. 1 (2002): 75–90. Experiments show that voters unconsciously respond to racial appeals in campaign advertisements and sometimes change their voting behavior.

KEY TERMS

527s (p. 513)

Australian ballot (p. 505)

closed primary (p. 508)

Federal Election Commission (FEC) (p. 512)

hard money (p. 513)

initiative (p. 506)

median voter theorem (p. 493)

open primary (p. 508)

plurality rule (p. 504)

political action committee (PAC) (p. 510)

referendum (p. 505)

single-member district (p. 504)

soft money (p. 513)

super PACs (p. 513)

Since leaking classified information from the National Security Agency in 2013, Edward Snowden has been a fixture of press coverage on mass surveillance, national security, and information privacy, although not all media outlets have covered his revelations and their consequences in the same way. Here, Snowden speaks virtually with Jane Mayer of *The New Yorker* in 2014.

14

Mass Media and the Press

Is media bias a problem in American politics?

T he *Guardian* and the *Washington Post* published articles in 2013 alleging that the National Security Agency (NSA) had been conducting extensive surveillance of U.S. citizens. The NSA required cell phone carriers to provide the agency with the phone records of millions of Americans, "indiscriminately and in bulk."[1] Through a program called PRISM, the agency also required access to the data of Internet firms like Google.[2]

The publications revealed their source: Edward Snowden, a 29-year-old NSA contractor,[3] whose work as an analyst gave him access to the inner workings of the surveillance. Snowden found the surveillance unethical and undemocratic, and he exposed the program out of his own sense of duty.[4] Snowden's conduct exposed him to the risk of being charged with treason, and he fled the United States, eventually finding asylum in Russia.

The Snowden leaks were one of the largest news stories for several years. The story amplified the national debate on the trade-offs between civil liberties and security (see Chapter 4), but it also raised questions about the role and potential bias of the media in national and international politics. People get most of their information about government and politicians from mass media companies, but are

[1] Glenn Greenwald, "NSA Collecting Phone Records of Millions of Verizon Customers Daily," *Guardian*, June 6, 2013, www.theguardian.com/world/2013/jun/06/nsa-phone-records-verizon-court-order (accessed 10/1/15).

[2] Barton Gellman and Laura Poitras, "U.S., British Intelligence Mining Data from Nine U.S. Internet Companies in Broad Secret Program," *Washington Post*, June 7, 2013, www.washingtonpost.com/investigations/us-intelligence-mining-data -from-nine-us-internet-companies-in-broad-secret-program/2013/06/06/3a0c0da8-cebf-11e2-8845-d970ccb04497 _story.html (accessed 10/1/15).

[3] Barton Gellman, Aaron Blake, and Greg Miller, "Edward Snowden Comes Forward as Source of NSA Leaks," *Washington Post*, June 9, 2013, www.washingtonpost.com/politics/intelligence-leaders-push-back-on-leakers-media /2013/06/09/fff80160-d122-11e2-a73e-826d299ff459_story.html (accessed 10/1/15).

[4] Laura Poitras and Glenn Greenwald, "NSA Whistleblower Edward Snowden: 'I Don't Want to Live in a Society That Does These Sort of Things'—Video," *Guardian*, June 9, 2013, www.theguardian.com/world/video/2013/jun/09/nsa -whistleblower-edward-snowden-interview-video (accessed 10/1/15).

OUTLINE

- Mass Media and the Press in a Democracy

- Trends in Media and the Press

- Mass Media Companies and the Profit Motive

- Government Regulation

- In Comparison: Mass Media

- Are the American Press and Mass Media Biased?

- Media Effects

- The Media as Principals and Agents

those companies presenting information accurately and fairly? People sympathetic to Snowden found the news coverage heavily biased against him, while people angry at Snowden found the news coverage too sympathetic to him.

More generally, politicians and commentators in the United States often complain about partisan or ideological media bias. Conservatives claim that the political news reporting has a liberal bias, and liberals claim that large media corporations report news in a manner favorable to big business. A major complaint of the Donald Trump presidential campaign was that the press was biased against him and the kinds of people he claimed to represent. Who is right amid such counterclaims?

Critics charge that American press content has, at times, a "patriotic bias." Reporters have made stylistic choices like using *we* or wearing the American flag in times of war or national crisis.[5] These choices are subtle but may have implications for how American audiences receive the news.

Scholars of political news and media analyzed in detail the press coverage of the Snowden leaks. The *Columbia Journalism Review*, for example, found that in four leading U.S. newspapers—the *New York Times*, *USA Today*, *Los Angeles Times*, and *Washington Post*—terms like *security* and *terrorism* were more likely to be used than were words like *privacy* and *civil liberties* in stories about Snowden.[6]

The coverage surrounding Edward Snowden's revelation suggests that media bias may not always, or primarily, be about partisanship or ideology. Media companies and reporters face different kinds of pressures to cover the news in particular ways for American audiences, sometimes even directly from the government.

What are the pressures that media producers face in reporting political content? What explains the consistent complaints over ideological bias when, as evidenced by coverage of the Snowden leaks, other biases might be present?

[5] April Eisman, "The Media of Manipulation: Patriotism and Propaganda—Mainstream News in the United States in the Weeks Following September 11," *Critical Quarterly* 45 (2003): 55–72; Jim Rutenberg and Bill Carter, "Draping Newscasts with the Flag," *New York Times*, September 20, 2001, www.nytimes.com/2001/09/20/business/a-nation-challenged-the-media-draping-newscasts-with-the-flag.html (accessed 10/14/15).

[6] Albert Wong and Valerie Belair-Gagnon, "On the NSA, the Media May Tilt Right," *Columbia Journalism Review*, October 23, 2013, www.cjr.org/the_kicker/news_media_pro_surveillance_bi.php (accessed 10/1/15).

Mass Media and the Press in a Democracy

The term *media* can be confusing. **Media**, strictly defined, refers to the methods or technologies people use for communication, such as phones, radio, newspapers, television, or the Internet. The term *media*, as used colloquially in American politics, is really a reference to the **press**: the people and organizations that provide content—news and commentary—that is disseminated across media.[7] When people say, "The media" is reporting on something, they are referring to the press. For clarity in this discussion, we will refer to the media as the means of communication, and the press as the people and organizations whose purpose is primarily to provide content. This chapter focuses mostly on the role of the press in using mass media to disseminate political news. But since media is a *means* to communicate, note that the press is not the only provider of content. Government and ordinary citizens use media to communicate about politics too.

The media as the means of communication is vitally important to understand as a component of American politics. For instance, when we refer to *private media* (like phones or private email), we know that these means enable people to communicate information with an understanding that it will not necessarily be shared with others. Information disseminated by **mass media**, in contrast, is intended to be publicly available, or at least targeted at large numbers of people.

Early in American history, political information was commonly transmitted by means of letters sent on foot or on horseback across large distances. As media technologies changed, they transformed the nature of politics. For example, the rise of cheap daily newspapers in the late nineteenth century brought readable political information to millions of people quickly for the first time. The increasing prominence of television, starting in the 1950s, dramatically affected the way candidates and political parties campaigned for public office. And the Internet, which became widely used in the late 1990s, created new possibilities for organizing mass action and raising money for campaigns and political causes.

Although people receive the bulk of their political news and commentary through mass media, they can learn about politics and public affairs through private media as well. The difference between private and mass media can be subtle, and the lines blurred. Certain contemporary technologies are used for both. Corresponding privately through email, the Internet, or Twitter is different from sending out massive numbers of emails, tweets, or Facebook notices. Blogs may or may not be read by a broad audience, but they are public in the sense that they are typically available to anyone who wants to find

media The methods or technologies people use for communication, such as phones, radio, newspapers, television, and the Internet.

press The people and organizations that provide content about public affairs—news and commentary—that is disseminated across media.

mass media Media that is intended to be publicly available, or at least targeted at large numbers of people.

---

[7] The press is distinct from paid consultants, who are hired to provide content that is intended to be used by those with political interests.

them. Blogs, mass emails, and tweets would usually be considered mass media, while directed email and Facebook notices would usually be considered private. Another example of private media is someone who posts information about an upcoming political event on a personal site on Facebook, but allows only friends access to that site.[8]

Regardless of the specific media used, a free press is vital to modern democracy. The word *free* means that news, information, and commentary can be gathered and disseminated without being subject to government controls. If the government can censor the press or control content, it may be able to maintain its authority without being checked by an informed people. Citizens are directly involved in choosing government leaders in a democracy, and they need information to choose and evaluate their leaders. Effective rule by the people requires a free press leading to an informed citizenry. Let's now explore in more detail what a free press through mass media can do.

Providing Essential Information

At a minimum, mass media ought to do two things in a democracy. First, it should enable politicians to communicate with the people. The mass media can be a means for candidates and parties to make their case for why they should be in government, while giving citizens the information they need to evaluate their options on Election Day. Second, the mass media, usually through the press, should provide information to citizens about their communities, their country, and the wider world so they can form reasonable policy opinions and preferences. How do you find out about what your state government is doing, or about a new war brewing in the Middle East? Through mass media. Even if you learn about political news from friends, they have usually been made aware of the story by the press through mass media.

These two basic functions—providing information about potential leaders and about events in the world—are considered necessary in a democracy. This is why freedom of the press is guaranteed in the First Amendment (and in similar clauses in other democratic countries' constitutions).

Evaluating and Interpreting

The press does more than passively report events and the actions of governments and people. It also actively monitors and investigates the government and interprets developments in government and society.

In serving as a "watchdog," operating independently of opposing political parties, the press can monitor and evaluate government officials and expose

---

[8] In our era, private media exchanges can fall into the wrong hands and be made public as content for mass media. Politicians and those in government need to be aware of this possibility.

wrongdoing or incompetence. In 1972 and 1973, Bob Woodward and Carl Bernstein of the *Washington Post* pursued evidence linking associates of President Richard Nixon to a break-in at the Watergate Hotel and other illegal activity—an investigation that ultimately led to Nixon's resignation. In 2012, when a U.S. ambassador was killed in Benghazi, Libya, reporters from CNN uncovered discrepancies between the statements of government officials and what actually happened. The incident and allegedly misleading statements by State Department officials were major points of contention between congressional Republicans and the Obama administration during Obama's second term, and with Hillary Clinton during her campaign for president. An independent government report, it turns out, confirmed CNN's information and corrected the State Department's official stance.[9]

The press through mass media also helps people interpret information. If the only information you received about your local government's budget was a set of numbers with no context and no interpretation, the numbers would not be very useful. Mass media can help you learn, for example, why this year's budget is larger than last year's. Media stories may help you plan your household finances by indicating the likelihood that your taxes will go up this year based on the local government's budget. The press can also provide a more pointed interpretation by, say, observing that "the city government's budget is full of giveaways to friends of the mayor," which might make you decide to vote against the mayor in the next election.[10]

Helping Solve Collective Dilemmas

As we know, people face various kinds of collective dilemmas in politics. Access to reliable information from mass media plays a major role in solving these dilemmas.

Even if people are willing to participate in political action, they may not know enough about the urgency of a situation, what their fellow citizens are doing, or the trustworthiness and competence of people in government. This kind of information is nearly always conveyed to citizens through the mass media. For individuals contemplating strategies for political behavior (Which candidate should I vote for? Should I attend a certain rally?), it is especially

---

[9] Investigative Reporters and Editors, Inc., "2012 IRE Award Winners," www.ire.org/awards/ire-awards /winners/2012-ire-award-winners (accessed 7/31/13).

[10] In a related vein, the press can help people orient their own opinions and values to the values of the community. Political theorist Harold Lasswell called this the media's socialization function. People, especially if they are young or new to a community, can use mass media to become more familiar with and accustomed to the culture in a society. See Harold Lasswell, "The Structure and Function of Communication in Society," in *The Process and Effects of Mass Communication*, ed. Wilbur Schramm and Donald F. Roberts (Urbana: University of Illinois Press, 1971), pp. 84–99.

The Collective Dilemma

During campaigns, candidates make claims about their own or their opponents' records. In 2016, Donald Trump said that Hillary Clinton pledged "totally open borders" with Mexico.[a] Hillary Clinton, meanwhile, said that Trump "praised the Chinese government for massacring protesters in Tiananmen Square [in 1989]."[b] Are these statements accurate? How do we know? Are there institutions in place to check the facts?

Interests

Candidates want to win, and in the heat of competition they will say what is necessary to boost their chances. Most voters, meanwhile, want candidates to be truthful, or at least not be outright liars. And members of the media have several interests that can be in tension. First, they want to maximize the number of viewers (or readers) for their news programs and thus want to report compelling claims made by politicians. Second, they want to demonstrate concern for truth to their audience and thus want to offer factual corrections. Third, some media personalities hold ideological positions and thus publicize their opposition to specific candidates, becoming persistent critics of one side or the other in election campaigns.

Institutions

There is a proliferation of "fact checking" in contemporary political news outlets, whereby fact checkers affirm or deny the validity of statements made by candidates. Most news shows, newspapers, and websites have devoted space to separating defensible statements from bogus claims. PolitiFact, for instance, is a project of the *Tampa Bay Times* that won the Pulitzer Prize for National Reporting for its coverage and fact checking during the 2008 presidential election; and FactCheck.org is a nonpartisan, nonprofit "consumer advocate" for voters, sponsored by the Annenberg Public Policy Center of the University of Pennsylvania. The 2016 presidential campaign, seen by many as the most negative and personal in recent U.S. history, created a situation where fact-checking websites and organizations went into overdrive.

Outcomes

If it emerges as a trusted source, a fact-checking project may not only help voters make informed decisions but it may also give candidates incentives to minimize false claims and misleading exaggerations. The experience of the 2016 campaign, however, belied the assumption that the scrutiny of fact checkers among political media may compel candidates to be more truthful.

By one reckoning, Donald Trump promulgated approximately 250 distinct statements that were untruthful during his campaign.[c] For example, he said to Clinton during a debate, "Just like when you ran the State Department, $6 billion was missing. How do you miss $6 billion? You ran the State Department, $6 billion was either stolen—they don't know. It's gone, $6 billion."[d] This claim was debunked as completely false by numerous sources. Hillary Clinton's distinct, questionable claims were much less numerous, but she did repeat several highly misleading statements, such as that Trump wanted to adopt pro-Kremlin (Russian) policies in office, and that he

Verifying Political Statements

wanted to ban all Muslims from entering the United States.

The increasing presence of fact checking among political media programs reflects a desire for more objective coverage among an important set of media consumers and voters. Considering the current climate of hyper-partisan political news, there is a (perhaps growing) niche for outlets catering to voters who want more objectivity.

Of course, fact checkers themselves may not necessarily maintain that objectivity. They too can cater to biases and, as a result, their findings may amplify ideologically charged coverage. A fact checker could, for instance, neglect to reveal one candidate's misstatements while exposing only those of the other candidate.

The 2016 presidential election campaign occurred *after* the proliferation of many fact-checking organizations and websites, and given the voluminous number of lies told during the campaign, it perhaps can be argued that they have done little to improve the truthfulness of campaign statements. Instead, fact checking perhaps hardens opposition to either side of an election campaign, thus becoming yet another means of polarizing the mass public and politicians. In the end, it is clear that the 2016 presidential candidates were not much influenced by fact-checking organizations.

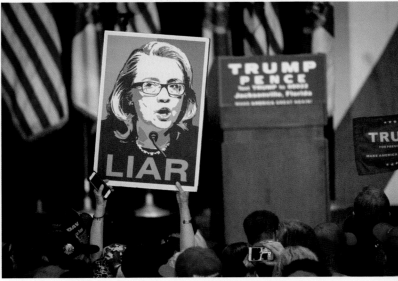

More and more political fact-checking organizations have emerged. Did they influence the tone or content of the 2016 presidential campaign?

Think About It

Will vigilance by some media companies against false statements improve the tenor of campaigns and make them more informative? Are fact checkers subject to (or contributors to) the same biases found in other media outlets?

a. www.youtube.com/watch?v=3hheSZg72Qc&feature=youtu.be&t=57m16s (accessed 11/22/16).

b. www.youtube.com/watch?v=3QhnlnNrP6s&feature=youtu.be&t=21m7s (accessed 11/22/16).

c. www.politico.com/magazine/story/2016/10/one-month-253-trump-untruths-214369 (accessed 11/22/16).

d. Transcript of the third and final presidential debate between Hillary Clinton and Donald Trump, www.washingtonpost.com/news/the-fix/wp/2016/10/19/the-final-trump-clinton-debate-transcript-annotated (accessed 11/22/16) useful to rely on information about politics and public affairs that others receive as well.

The press can help citizens prioritize the various problems that need to be solved. In recent years, press coverage of potential flu epidemics has spurred tens of millions of Americans to get flu shots, and it also has led to pressure on the government to ensure that sufficient vaccine supplies are available even if private companies cannot provide enough. The local and national press can convey the urgency of the situation ("This year's flu strain is potentially deadly") and provide information about which public officials you and other interested citizens can contact to give your opinions on the need for vaccine supplies.

The press can also coordinate the actions of citizens who want to influence politics but do not know how. Modern forms of media, both broadcast (radio and television) and the Internet, give ordinary people the means to work together for political action. If you are worried about the quality of the schools in your town, for example, you and others who share your concerns will be much less effective in pressuring the local government if you fail to coordinate your efforts and inadvertently split into different groups that meet in more than one location. Better to join forces in common meetings, decide on a common message, and present a united front to the local school board or the local or state government.

Of course, in providing information that might lead to effective collective action, the press can exaggerate and mislead, as we will discuss later. The more trustworthy the media source, the more helpful the information will be in solving a collective dilemma.

Trends in Media and the Press

Media technologies in the United States have evolved over time, and this process has had implications for politics. In the nineteenth century, handwritten letters gave way to typed and printed handbills, newsletters, newspapers, and magazines. Later, radio and television became the primary sources of information, and now we have the Internet. Any technological means of communicating political news and commentary can be more or less objective. Historically, technological changes in media have gone hand in hand with changes in the professional norms of the press, especially in news reporting. In brief, we can divide the history of American political mass media into three eras:

- The country began with a highly partisan press that communicated through print media.

- The trend toward more objective reporting by the press coincided with the appearance of large-scale, mass-appeal media outlets based on electronic technologies (such as newspaper wire service reports, radio, and television) in the twentieth century.

- Today we live in an era when many kinds of media coexist: professionalized, intentionally objective news reporting, mostly promulgated through corporate television, Internet, and hard-copy outlets, exists alongside plenty of ideologically charged, partisan news and commentary distributed through a variety of electronic sources, including cable television and the Internet.

The Eighteenth and Nineteenth Centuries

Americans in the late eighteenth and early nineteenth centuries received much of their political news by word of mouth, or by attending local meetings and rallies. Mass media primarily took the form of an unapologetically partisan press operating through print outlets, such as newspapers and party pamphlets. Many party-sponsored newspapers or pamphlets slanted political coverage to be as critical as possible of the other parties and candidates and as laudatory as possible of the sponsoring party. There was no expectation of objectivity in the press.

Commercial newspapers became increasingly popular during the nineteenth century. To sell as many copies as possible, stories were written to appeal to consumers of various political persuasions. At the same time, the telegraph, which became widely used in the 1840s, made it possible for news to travel over long distances almost instantaneously. The people who produced the news in printed form responded by focusing on straightforward facts about events across the country that local reporters could shape to their own purposes. The founding of the Associated Press in 1848 heralded a new era of centralized gathering and dissemination of relatively unbiased news. This is not to say that partisan bias disappeared entirely, however. Most towns still had competing newspapers that openly supported one political party or another.

By the late nineteenth century, the costs of printing, and of sharing information via telegraph or telephone, had become low enough that newspapers like the *New York Sun* could be sold for a penny—a fraction of the price papers had charged a few years earlier. The era of truly mass media had begun. The "penny press" specialized in reporting bizarre occurrences, society gossip, and sensational news. In a famous example, William Randolph Hearst's *New York Journal* criticized Spain for sinking the U.S. battleship *Maine* in 1898, despite a lack of conclusive evidence. Most historians today consider the explosion in Havana harbor an accident. Nevertheless, the newspaper's tendentious coverage was instrumental in stirring up public opinion in favor of starting the Spanish-American War later that year.

Alongside the sensational press, there arose in the late nineteenth century a new breed of professional journalists working for prestigious, nonpartisan newspapers like the *New York Times* and the *Chicago Daily News*. New codes of journalistic conduct emphasized objective reporting. Professional journalism societies and schools sprang up throughout the country, and journalists increasingly resisted pressure from media owners and editors to publish news with an obvious partisan or ideological slant. By the mid-twentieth century, openly biased reporting was frowned upon at magazines like *Time* and *Newsweek*, and at newspapers like the *New York Times*, *Los Angeles Times*, and *The Christian Science Monitor*.

Network Television Comes to Predominate

Beginning in the 1920s, radio became an important medium for disseminating political news. Some large stations broadcast objective news reporting and commentary, much like the big-city newspapers mentioned earlier. Other stations, many of which had smaller audiences, provided content geared toward specific population groups. The different parts of the radio spectrum, and the relatively low cost of radio transmission, encouraged such specialized programming.

After television sets became common in American homes in the 1950s, television quickly replaced newspapers and radio as the main source of political news for most Americans. Because the cost of producing programs for television was considerably higher than for radio, a few large media companies came to dominate television news. By 1960, more than 80 percent of American households owned a television that received the nightly news broadcasts aired by the three major national networks: CBS, ABC, and NBC. The number of competitors was limited both by technology and by government regulation of the television industry; as a result, the content of network news programs was generally politically moderate, neither strongly conservative nor strongly liberal. At the very least, network news programs generally presented two sides of a controversial issue corresponding to the mainstream ideological positions of the two major political parties. These same limitations encouraged large numbers of

In the late nineteenth century, the "penny press" frequently published sensational, highly biased stories. The New York Journal's misleading coverage of the sinking of a U.S. battleship notoriously whipped up support for the Spanish-American War in 1898.

citizens who were only slightly interested in politics, but who enjoyed watching network television, to become better informed about public affairs.

The norm of unbiased news coverage—meaning nonpartisan and reasonably objective in reporting the facts—was well established in television news by the 1960s. In the latter third of the twentieth century, the three national networks covered the news in a manner that attracted huge nightly audiences. They presented war footage, political news, personal interest stories, and health information. They also covered the news in a relatively unbiased way—at least, the reports were ostensibly nonpartisan in tone. Government regulation contributed to this state of affairs, a topic discussed in more detail later.

Thus, through big-city newspapers, radio, and the national television networks, national political news in the late twentieth century typically was presented in a manner meant to appeal to people from either party—liberals and conservatives alike—and avoid offending large groups of citizens. There were important exceptions to this model, however. In several large cities, thriving black newspapers competed with the mainstream media for business among African Americans. The *Chicago Defender* and the *New York Amsterdam News* provided alternative points of view on politics, entertainment, and sports. Black radio and (after the advent of cable) television stations similarly targeted the African American community. Other minority groups, especially those with large numbers who spoke a language other than English at home, developed their own media outlets.

Rise of New Media

The contemporary era can be said to have begun with the rapid rise of cable television in the 1980s. Suddenly, dozens and then hundreds of television stations were competing with the three major networks. As a result, programmers were free to appeal to specific groups of people with particular tastes—and, in the realm of news and commentary, particular political attitudes.

Equally important, people with only a slight interest in politics were no longer exposed to political news just because they felt like watching network television. The proliferation of cable stations meant that viewers could opt for biased news, or for entertainment of an entirely different sort—a cooking show, for instance. As we will discuss later, cable television led to the development of "soft news" programs, or "infotainment."

The expansion of the Internet in the 1990s magnified this trend by enabling media companies and individuals supplying political news and commentary to target ever-smaller slivers of demographic groups. The Internet has altered the mass media landscape in two significant ways. First, there are now few limits on reaching specific segments of the population instantaneously through websites, email, cell phones, and social networking groups. So it is easier than ever to tailor narrow messages to specific people. Second, the

1784 *The Pennsylvania Packet* is the first daily newspaper in the United States.

Mid-nineteenth century The telegraph allows newspapers across the country access to a common set of facts about an event. Newspapers begin to appeal to broader audiences in search of higher profits.

1898 The *New York Journal's* sensationalist reporting of the explosion of the *U.S.S. Maine* helps shift American public opinion in favor of the Spanish-American War.

Early twentieth century Commercially licensed radio broadcasting provides Americans with a new way to consume news.

Late twentieth century Cable news channels and the Internet give Americans the opportunity to access news information on demand while also allowing them to select news with a point of view.

2012 One-third of Americans report going online and using the Internet as their primary source for political news.

1750   1800   1850   1900   1950   2000

Late eighteenth to early nineteenth century The media landscape is dominated by press outlets that publish explicitly partisan content.

1848 The *Associated Press* is founded in New York.

Late nineteenth century Technological advances, including the telephone and improved printing presses, drive down the costs of transmitting information and publishing newspapers.

1920 Pittsburgh radio station KDKA broadcasts the results of the 1920 presidential election for four hours on the night of Election Day.

Mid-twentieth century By 1960, more than 80 percent of American households own television sets. Television has replaced radio and print media as the main source of political news for most Americans.

1980 CNN is founded as the first 24-hour news channel in the United States.

2008 Forty-four percent of Americans report going online for political news—nearly 11 times the number who did in 1996.

costs of sending out information to large numbers of people have dropped, and virtually no marginal costs are incurred in reaching more people directly after the content is produced and disseminated. Each additional email, tweet, or Facebook contact costs nothing to post beyond the time it takes to find the address and add it to a contact list.

The Internet now plays an enormous role in the conduct of elections and in political fund-raising. People can get up-to-date information on politics instantaneously through news websites and sites sponsored by interest groups, parties, and private individuals. As more and more information about politics flows through the Internet, television has had to play catch-up and repeat what has already been reported on websites. Television programs, newspapers, and magazines typically have their own websites that continuously update information and post news instantaneously. These websites are now vital means of marketing and staying in contact with readers and viewers. And naturally, candidates post their policy stances and their answers to critics on their web pages and Twitter accounts. Barack Obama made history in 2008 by raising hundreds of millions of dollars from Internet appeals, and nearly all candidates today follow his lead. Donald Trump personally wrote hundreds of tweets throughout his presidential campaign. All serious presidential candidates in 2016, of course, from the Republican and Democratic primaries through the general election, used websites and Twitter feeds to raise money, post information about their policy positions, answer questions, and coordinate supporters.

The Internet has dramatically altered how the press is organized and how media companies operate. Scores of major newspapers around the United States either have gone out of business or have severely limited their print versions because more and more people are getting their news from the Internet instead of buying print newspapers. Print magazines struggle to survive as businesses. No longer is it necessary for journalists to join a large news organization to write and spread their content. Blogging has become a standard form of professional journalism, allowing individuals to set up their own websites and seek dedicated audiences.

At the same time, there has been somewhat of a return to an era of available partisan sources of the news.

With the rise of new media and mobile technology, political news is accessible nearly all the time. In addition, more and more politicians are using text messaging and social media to connect with supporters, and campaigns have developed mobile applications to allow volunteers to make phone calls and share campaign messages easily.

This is not because traditional newspapers and magazines have become more politically biased. Rather, it is due to the rise of certain heavily subscribed news outlets, most of which are on the Internet or cable television, that offer openly biased, partisan news and opinion programming. We will have more to say about this trend later in this chapter.

Researchers continue to study how "new media" have transformed the spread of political news. There is little question that the Internet, increasingly accessed through cell phones, has become a central outlet for news. The proportion of Americans using the Internet is fast approaching 90 percent, and most of those not using the Internet are elderly. Increasing numbers of people use their cell phones to keep up with political news. Television remains a popular source of political information, but phones and Internet connections of various kinds are becoming the common means for people, especially younger people, to follow politics. Social media sites like Facebook regularly communicate vast amounts of political information among groups of friends and acquaintances, and from celebrities and political leaders to mass publics.[11]

Generational differences appear to carry over to new forms of civic engagement unique to the Internet. In areas where the Internet simply provides a new way to carry out long-established political activity, such as making a donation or contacting an elected official, both old and young citizens use it at similar rates. But in instances where the Internet allows for a new kind of activity—social networking and blogging, for example—young people use it

---

[11] Pew Research Center, "15% of Americans Don't Use the Internet. Who Are They?" www.pewresearch.org/fact-tank/2015/07/28/15-of-americans-dont-use-the-internet-who-are-they/ (accessed 7/25/16).

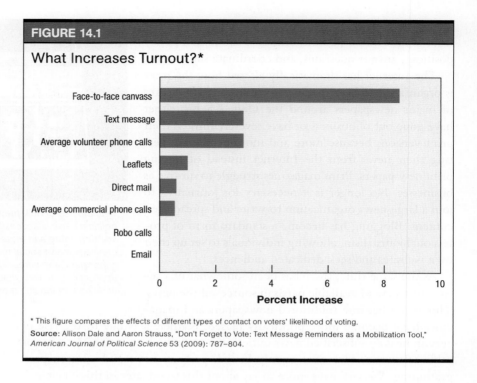

FIGURE 14.1

What Increases Turnout?*

Face-to-face canvass
Text message
Average volunteer phone calls
Leaflets
Direct mail
Average commercial phone calls
Robo calls
Email

0 2 4 6 8 10

Percent Increase

* This figure compares the effects of different types of contact on voters' likelihood of voting.

Source: Allison Dale and Aaron Strauss, "Don't Forget to Vote: Text Message Reminders as a Mobilization Tool," *American Journal of Political Science* 53 (2009): 787–804.

much more than their elders.[12] As Figure 14.1 shows, some forms of new media can be effective in encouraging people to vote.

As was the case with the rise of cable television, the greater volume of accessible information does not mean that people are learning more about politics. Whereas network television, when it dominated political news, tended to expose all sorts of people to daily political happenings, viewers now have a wider range of entertainment options with which political news must compete. Recent surveys suggest that people interested in politics are learning more about it than ever before, but that people with other primary interests know less about politics than in the past.[13] These interests and knowledge levels correlate with people's education and economic status. As discussed in Chapter 10, the more education and income people have, the more likely they are to seek out political news and entertainment that includes political commentary; in contrast, the less education and income people have, the less likely they are to seek out political news and instead watch and listen to en-

[12] For more on the role of the Internet in politics, see the Pew Internet and American Life Project, "The Internet and Civic Engagement," www.pewinternet.org/2009/09/01/the-internet-and-civic-engagement -2/; and "The Internet's Role in Campaign 2008," www.people-press.org/2008/01/11/internets-broader -role-in-campaign-2008 (accessed 9/1/16).

[13] Markus Prior, *Post-Broadcast Democracy: How Media Choice Increases Inequality in Political Involvement and Polarizes Elections* (New York: Cambridge University Press, 2007).

tertainment that has little political content. Research also suggests that people who get their political news mostly from cable television and the Internet receive different information than those who get their political news mostly from network television. As an example, network news overwhelmingly focuses on the president and the White House while cable news covers a broader range of governmental institutions and Washington agenda setters.[14]

Mass Media Companies and the Profit Motive

The United States, despite the availability of much free content on the Internet, still has a vibrant private media industry. Some media companies that provide political content are struggling to make money through the Internet, but the industry as a whole is thriving in the sense that competing publications, networks, and mass media companies continue to provide content through multiple channels. Most people get their political news and commentary from private media businesses, as opposed to public media companies that are common in other countries. And while there is a huge number of private sources of political news as opposed to public (that is, government owned) media companies, and each source that survives finds its audience (whether large or small), the overwhelming size of web and television audiences for news programming produced by a few corporate conglomerates dwarfs the audience sizes for all the other sources combined. Political news produced by, for example, the News Corporation (which owns Fox News and the *Wall Street Journal*), The Disney Company (which owns ABC), The New York Times Company, The Washington Post Company, Gannett, CBS, and General Electric (which owns NBC) collectively reaches, through multiple media platforms, vastly more people with their political programming than all other sources put together.

There is a publicly owned side of media in the United States as well. The U.S. government supports public television and radio enterprises through the Corporation for Public Broadcasting, which receives funding from both public and private sources. Although the government funds these public enterprises, and at times, politicians pressure public broadcasters, in practice there are few restrictions on the content they provide. In addition, most cities and towns have community-based "public access" television and radio stations that document the affairs of local governments and offer citizens the chance to present their views.

[14] Matthew Baum and Sam Kernell, "Has Cable Ended the Golden Age of Presidential Television?" *American Political Science Review* 93 (March 1999): 99–114.

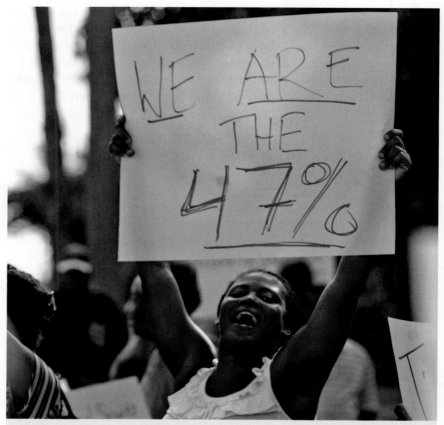

Because they seek to hold an audience's interest, the news media tend to focus on stories that involve controversy, conflict, and scandal. In 2012, the press devoted considerable attention to controversial private remarks made by Mitt Romney that 47 percent of Americans are dependent on government and would automatically vote for Obama.

The vast majority of journalists who cover American politics are either employed by private, for-profit companies or work for these same companies as independent freelancers. The underlying profit motive means that these outlets are compelled to present the news in ways that sell newspapers and magazines, get people to watch or listen to a particular news program, or attract people to a particular website. When people joke that "if it bleeds, it leads," they are referring to the tendency of local news programs to put lurid, graphic news—typically violent crime stories—up front to grab and hold viewers' attention. In similar fashion, newspaper headlines and magazine covers often highlight conflict, controversy, and scandal. News stories need a narrative hook, a way to capture an audience that is willing to pay. This makes it worthwhile for journalists to cover stories that are of interest to large numbers of people, preferably those targeted by advertisers—that is, people with money to spend on certain consumer products. The local government's budgeting process that affects people's taxes and education goals may be quite important, but it is not likely to push sports, crime, or scandal off the front page, or bump the top story from the local television newscast.

The drive for profits also determines how media companies allocate resources. These resources can be personnel (journalists and editors), space in publications or time in newscasts, or money spent on travel. Few American newspapers or news websites devote nearly as many resources to international news coverage or national political news as they do to sports, fashion, food, or celebrity gossip. Most often, the news that gets covered is a function of what will sell rather than what is most critical to a reader's well-being. Consumers of news might well know that the local government's budget process is important, but they might reason, "I don't need to know much about it, and I find it boring to read about."

Journalists often draw a distinction between news and entertainment, but the line is clearly blurred in practice. It is entertaining to read news about celebrities, but it may not be the kind of news that will improve our decisions as citizens. In contrast, it may be entertaining or depressing, depending on one's point of view, to read about scandals involving politicians, but this kind of news may actually help us make better choices in elections.

Infotainment has become an increasingly important way for Americans to get their political news and commentary. Infotainment refers to mass media programming that is intended primarily to entertain, but also provides political news. Shows like *60 Minutes* and *Dateline* mix in political news with news about celebrities and health. Quite a few young people today receive the bulk of their political news from comedy shows or web content such as *Last Week Tonight with John Oliver, The Daily Show with Trevor Noah,* or *The Onion,* in which entertainers and writers comment on the current news in a way that is both funny and informative. The two shows spoof the press and news, but also provide content in the process. Audiences for some of these shows are relatively large and, importantly for advertisers, include disproportionately high numbers from groups such as 20- to 35-year-olds who are hard to reach with more straightforward news programming.[15]

infotainment Mass media programming that is intended primarily to entertain but also provides political news.

Government Regulation

Because of the First Amendment and the tradition of a free press, governments at various levels in the United States are severely restricted from interfering

---

[15] Matthew Baum, "Sex, Lies, and War: How Soft News Brings Foreign Policy to the Inattentive Public," *American Political Science Review* 96 (2002): 91–109.

Government Regulation of Mass Media

- Until 1987, the *Fairness Doctrine*, which stated that holders of broadcast licenses were required to present information on important issues in a way that was honest, equitable, and balanced, was enforced by the Federal Communications Commission (FCC) and influenced American media coverage. The Fairness Doctrine is now defunct.

- Another important provision still somewhat enforced by the FCC is the *Equal Time Rule*, which requires broadcasters to give equal time to competing candidates for political office. For example, if a television station gives one candidate a free minute of airtime, then the station must make the same free airtime available to his or her opponent(s).

- In the broadcasting realm, most current government regulation falls under the purview of the *Telecommunications Act of 1996*, which sought to remove regulatory entry barriers for new firms in the media marketplace.

- A key legal doctrine involves *prior restraint*, which refers to the ability of governmental actors to prevent media outlets from publishing particular material because the government believes that information will jeopardize public safety and/or national security. Federal courts in the United States have ruled that prior restraint may be exercised only in extraordinary circumstances.

with the content and dissemination of political information. But this does not mean that government actions do not matter. Government regulation has had an impact on what political information people receive and how it is conveyed by the press. Such regulation of the press and mass media in the United States has focused almost entirely on television and radio broadcasters, as opposed to print media. Newspapers and magazines have been largely protected from government regulation because of First Amendment guarantees. The situation is different for broadcast media because, under U.S. law and the laws of most other countries, the airwaves for television or radio are public property. The rationale for making companies pay for airwave space is that, since the airwaves are publicly owned, the government has the right to sell off and regulate their use. Also, in the absence of government regulation, private companies might trample on each other's airwave space. This is a classic coordination problem. Radio and television stations are all better off with a means of dividing up the airwaves and permitting every station to be heard without interference from other broadcasts. Government regulation is seen as necessary to enforce coordinated use of the airways.

Since the early twentieth century, the federal government has sold to media companies rights of access to specific portions of the airwaves, in return for which the companies have agreed to codes of conduct. For many decades, these codes stipulated that the airwaves be used to promote the common good and provide information useful to all citizens. In practice, this meant that radio and television stations were required to produce news programming and make some time slots available to nonprofit organizations or local governments. In addition, the Federal Communication Commission's Fairness Doctrine, which stood in place until 1987, required that television and radio stations present at least two sides of every controversial public issue. By the same token, if one candidate for office was interviewed on a news program, the other viable candidates for that same office had to be invited for an interview as well.

As a result of trends toward deregulation in business law—and consensus among politicians from both major political parties that the Fairness Doctrine was unworkable, unwise, or both—the federal government has largely ceased regulating content of mass media. The Fairness Doctrine was abandoned after having been left mostly unenforced by the Reagan administration in the 1980s.[16] "Public interest" broadcasting requirements began to be interpreted very broadly. Today there are few restrictions on content for mass media in the United States. Many scholars argue that the rise of cable television and the Internet—media that do not face the same public domain issues as traditional broadcasting—made those restrictions irrelevant anyway.[17]

Likewise, government regulations regarding media ownership, which were on the books and enforced for many years, have largely been abandoned. Strict rules against ownership of multiple broadcast companies by a single group or individual, for example, arose from attempts to avoid concentrating control over the flow of information to the public in a few hands. The rules loosely applied to print media as well. Since the 1980s, however, these regulations have fallen out of favor, and many have been repealed.

As a result, concentrated ownership of major media outlets has become the norm. Large media conglomerates now own newspapers, radio stations, television stations, and cable television stations across multiple states and within the same urban areas. By the 1990s, it had become common for the same company to own the one or two dominant local newspapers in the same town, eliminating any sense of competition between them. Today, many cities have either one or no daily newspaper. Even if one survives, it is likely to be owned by the same company that owns one of the main television stations in town.

The consequences of concentrated media ownership on public discourse and political knowledge are unclear. Some scholars argue that with less competition within local areas, the quality of political information has declined.[18]

[16] See the discussion in Chapter 7 about Reagan's broad attack on the federal bureaucracy in the 1980s, including his complaints about government regulation.

[17] See, for example, Brian Lehrer, "A Million Little Murrows: New Media and New Politics," *Media Law and Policy Review* 17 (September 2008): 1–18.

[18] See, for example, Peter Clarke and Eric Fredin, "Newspapers, Television, and Political Reasoning," *Public Opinion Quarterly* 42, no. 2 (1978): 143–60; and Martin Gilens and Craig Hertzman, "Corporate Ownership and News Bias: Newspaper Coverage of the 1996 Telecommunications Act," *Journal of Politics* 62 (2000): 369–86.

Evidence of such an effect is hard to come by, however, in part because of the survival of some small-scale media. Certainly, in smaller cities and towns there is little competition among private companies providing local political news. But on the national level, the mass media landscape contains numerous relatively small companies around the country that find their own niche consumer bases, mostly around certain issues people care about. More importantly, national political news and news in large cities is dominated by programming produced by about five or six enormous conglomerates that compete among themselves for huge audience shares. Thus, some argue, competition exists across media companies of various sizes, and, it may be argued, competition at any level causes media companies to provide quality programming. We return to this discussion about the effects of media concentration shortly.

In Comparison: Mass Media

Journalists and media companies in other parts of the world often envy the freedom of their American counterparts to publish what they want. In countries like Iran or China, the government owns nearly all the mass media and closely controls access and content. Even in countries that are considered partial democracies, journalists are arrested and jailed for writing or broadcasting information that offends the government.

In many countries, the media and press are more heavily regulated than in the United States. When news outlets in Iran were prevented by the government from covering protests in Tehran in 2010, people used cell phones to send images and information outside the country.

Differences across democracies in the conduct of the press and in mass media mostly stem from how media companies are owned and regulated. In the United States, a multitude of private media companies, sometimes regulated but not controlled by the government, compete with each other for consumers of news and entertainment. The sheer number and the overwhelming presence of private media companies are unusual features of the American political system.

In many other democracies, public media companies are at the center of political news gathering. Many people might think that such publicly owned companies would be beholden to the government and rarely criticize its leaders, but this is not the case, particularly in long-standing democracies. The British Broadcasting Corporation (BBC), for example, has earned a reputation as an aggressive news gatherer. In general, the BBC has complete freedom to cover and comment on the news as it wishes. It is seen as acting independently of the government and more than willing to criticize. A similar claim can be made for the public media companies in Canada, France, Australia, and other countries.

In a few countries, private ownership is concentrated in the hands of a small number of individuals, a situation that would probably not be permitted under American antitrust laws. Such concentration can be problematic, especially when the individuals are members of the government. In Italy in the early twenty-first century, for example, Prime Minister Silvio Berlusconi owned four of the five major television companies. Again, the consequences of concentrated media ownership are unclear. Critics are quick to show evidence that the media in countries like Italy offers either bland or biased news coverage, but scholarly research has not established this definitively across various countries or over time.[19]

Many countries have government-enforced restrictions on political content in the media that would not be allowed in the United States because of the First Amendment. Thus, as discussed in Chapter 13, political campaigning—when and where it takes place, and what is said—is heavily regulated in most other democracies. Even political advertisements need to be approved by government regulators in other countries—something unheard of in the United States.[20]

Ironically, in the realm of private media, the United States has been somewhat more open to government regulation and monitoring of individuals

[19] See, for example, Kees Brants, "Who's Afraid of Infotainment?" *European Journal of Communication* 13, no. 3 (1998): 315–35.

[20] U.S. television and radio stations have been permitted to refuse to broadcast offensive images or words, even when coming from a political candidate, but this practice has been challenged and sometimes the courts have sided with the candidates. One candidate in 1992 wanted to show bloody fetuses in a campaign ad to highlight his opponent's pro-choice stance. A federal appeals court in *Becker v. FCC* ruled that broadcasters had to allow the ads. See Carol Lomicky and Charles Salestrom, "Anti-Abortion Advertising and Access to the Airwaves: A Public Interest Doctrine Dilemma," *Journal of Broadcasting & Electronic Media* 42, no. 4 (1998): 491–506.

and to corporate monitoring than other countries, especially in comparison with Europe. First, the U.S. government and military branches have aggressively prosecuted individuals accused of leaking classified military and diplomatic information to the entire world community through the Web (through sites such as WikiLeaks). Second, the United States has led the way in allowing government agencies to monitor the emails, tweets, cell phone calls and texts, and blogs of people suspected of crimes, especially of abetting terrorism. Third, the U.S. government has been reluctant to pass additional regulations prohibiting companies like Google, Facebook, and Microsoft from collecting personal information on software users so that those companies can market products and advertise more efficiently through their own software portals. On the one hand, this last example is unusual in that, contrary to the norm, the U.S. privacy protections for individuals are less strict than Europe's protections. On the other hand, it is consistent with a broader difference between the United States and Europe: in Europe, there is more widespread acceptance of corporate regulations.

Are the American Press and Mass Media Biased?

We now return to the subject of our opening story—media bias—in light of our discussion of the history of the press and media. With this context in mind, we can consider the nature of media bias and findings from systematic research.

Discerning Bias

Scholars of media and politics agree that media bias is difficult to discern, let alone define consistently. We might say for our purposes that bias is the notion that someone is being subjective in a way that serves his or her political interest. If a conservative journalist writes a blog that consistently criticizes liberal politicians and praises conservatives, we can confidently say that he or she has an ideological bias. Likewise, if a liberal journalist selectively chooses to report only facts that make liberals look good and conservatives look bad, this reflects a bias. Or, if a news outlet owned by a large corporation always reports in a manner that reflects well on that corporation and avoids reporting negative factual information that is actually in the public's interest to know, then we would say this news outlet is biased.

Bias is not inherently bad. Many publications are widely considered to have an ideological bias and openly admit to it. *National Review* is a conservative magazine, the *Nation* a leftist magazine. The *Rachel Maddow Show* reflects a liberal point of view, *Tucker Carlson Tonight* a conservative one. Fox News is conservative and pro-Republican, and it has an enormous following in relative terms, while MSNBC has been quite liberal and pro-Democratic in recent years, but with much less market share than Fox News. CNN was long considered to be more balanced and ideologically neutral, but critics contend that it has recently become more liberal. Many people would argue that, as in a judicial setting where both sides have an opportunity to make their best case, an adversarial system in the press is the best means of uncovering information relevant to the political process. Certainly ideological bias, especially one that is known and acknowledged, is less troublesome than bias by a news outlet against reporting important negative news about its parent corporation.

In fact, most major national news producers, such as the *New York Times* or the *Wall Street Journal*, take pains to avoid the appearance of bias. Even the "liberal" *Times*, which generally supports Democratic candidates over Republicans on its editorial page, would deny having a partisan bent toward the Democrats. The *Times* prides itself on presenting differing points of view in its news stories and routinely publishes unedited comments from a "public editor" charged with investigating bias in the paper's reporting. At the same time, its editorials and other opinion columns clearly lean to the left. The line between news reporting and opinion writing can be blurry at times, but people in the news business, especially at prestigious newspapers and national television networks, try hard to maintain it.

Even when reporters try to avoid bias, they cannot escape making choices about content that are shaped by their own values and experiences. Consider the reporting of facts. What information should be reported when a given event occurs? In theory, any statement, even a purely factual one, is biased because the reporter chooses to report some facts instead of others. Suppose a television reporter noted that "Twelve American soldiers were killed in Iraq yesterday." This sentence, if true, would be considered unbiased by most observers. But suppose that 100 ISIS fighters were killed as well. Someone might say that the news report focused on the American deaths and thus distorted what happened. Now suppose someone stated on television, "Twelve soldiers of the American occupying army were killed by noble ISIS fighters yesterday." Quite biased, you might say. But what about not covering the story at all? Is that biased? Or what if the reporter said, "Twelve American soldiers were killed in Iraq yesterday, the largest one-day toll in months." Is that biased? It may be biased because highlighting a one-day surge in deaths may lead people to believe the American military engagement is going badly.

Journalism has professional norms of conduct that require disclosure and honesty to a degree rare in other professions. Journalists known for unbiased reporting are praised and rewarded by their peers. Prominent television journalists in recent years have been fired after others discovered that they had made campaign contributions to candidates. The point is that they had violated both a norm in the profession and a corporate policy about the "appropriate," unbiased behavior of journalists who cover politics. Nevertheless, it is hard to refute a charge of bias if someone wants to make one. Such judgments are themselves subjective and depend on individual point of view.

Ideological versus Other Kinds of Bias

We can divide types of bias along several lines. Let's first contrast ideological bias from other kinds. Allegations of media bias by both liberals and conservatives are common in the United States. Both sides have some reason to be concerned. Surveys reveal the press to be, on the whole, more liberal than conservative,[21] suggesting that, consciously or not, individual journalists' decisions about which stories to cover and how to cover them might take on a liberal flavor (Figure 14.2). Yet publishers and owners of media organizations are businesspeople, typically a conservative constituency, and conceivably they exert a subtle influence on how editors, anchors, and reporters convey the news.

Note that the liberal–conservative dimension is not the only area in which the media can potentially exhibit bias. Various scholars have argued, for instance, that the media is biased in favor of capitalism, nationalism, and minimal government. Another vein of research finds that the local media's emphasis on crime has led to an unfavorable, distorted picture of minorities.[22] These quandaries over what is biased and what is not are no easier to sort out than the liberal–conservative divide. When Donald Trump and his supporters complained about the press, their complaints were of bias against him and also against his brand of anti–free trade, more isolationist foreign policy. They complained that the press failed to cover the misdeeds of their Democratic opponents.

In fact, most scholars of the mass media would focus less on ideological bias of the sort that divides Republicans from Democrats, and the typical Fox News watcher from the typical reader of the *New York Times*. This kind of ideological difference gets attention in political circles because politicians can gain some traction among constituents by complaining about news coverage and media bias, but its impact in reality is much less notable. Instead, scholars tend to focus attention on the pressures of private companies to gain more market share and expand their audiences. This biases coverage toward what is sensational and attention-grabbing, and in turn gives incentives for politicians and other government officials to shape their information in certain ways to grab the attention of news reporters hungry for news that sells.

[21] David Domke, Mark D. Watts, Dhavan V. Shah, and David P. Fan, "The Politics of Conservative Elites and the 'Liberal Media' Argument," *Journal of Communication* 49, no. 4 (1999); David Niven, *Tilt: The Search for Media Bias* (Westport, CT: Praeger, 2002).

[22] R. M. Entman and A. Rojecki, *The Black Image in the White Mind: Media and Race in America* (University of Chicago Press, 2000).

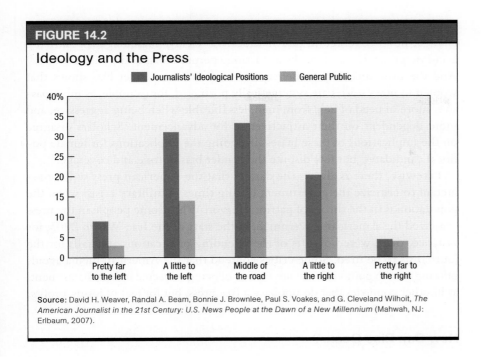

FIGURE 14.2

Ideology and the Press

■ Journalists' Ideological Positions   ■ General Public

	Pretty far to the left	A little to the left	Middle of the road	A little to the right	Pretty far to the right

Source: David H. Weaver, Randal A. Beam, Bonnie J. Brownlee, Paul S. Voakes, and G. Cleveland Wilhoit, *The American Journalist in the 21st Century: U.S. News People at the Dawn of a New Millennium* (Mahwah, NJ: Erlbaum, 2007).

Finally, some critics of American media believe that bias among the press is quite subtle. As we have learned, in terms of content and media ownership, mass media in the United States is less regulated than in other countries. There are thousands of mass media outlets peddling political news, but a few huge companies dominate the market. Ironically, given the plethora of private media in the United States, many observers believe that Americans actually receive less diversity of viewpoints *on selected topics* than people in other countries. For example, most media companies that create and disseminate political news derive the bulk of their profits from advertising. Private media companies might shy away from criticizing the actions of corporations for fear of offending advertisers or potential consumers.[23]

Moreover, there is evidence of bias with racial and gender implications. A study of local news coverage in Los Angeles sought to demonstrate the accuracy of portrayals of different racial groups in the categories of crime victims, perpetrators, and police officers. The study shows that whites in Los Angeles local news in the 2000s were disproportionately shown as victims and police officers in crime stories, while Latinos especially were disproportionately underrepresented in studies of victims and police officers. African Americans

[23] See, for example, James T. Hamilton, *All the News That's Fit to See: How the Market Transforms Information into News* (Princeton, NJ: Princeton University Press, 2004), especially chap. 3.

were generally portrayed in accurate proportions, but this has been a recent change; news coverage in past decades was clearly biased against showing accurate proportions of blacks as victims, perpetrators, and police officers.[24] And the overwhelming evidence from research on gender bias shows that women in news stories are systematically portrayed, for example, as more passive, more in need of help from men, less likeable when being aggressive, and more dependent on their attractiveness for advancement. Scholars disagree on the implications of these biases, including the implications for female political candidates, but few dispute the gender bias in tone and coverage.[25]

Likewise, there is always the danger that the American press will be reluctant to criticize the government during times of military crisis, when the population is in the throes of patriotic fervor. When some people in the press criticized the American government at the start of the Iraq War in 2003, for instance, there were boycotts of the offending publications and calls for the journalists to be fired. Some critics contend that the American media avoids offering certain points of view not for fear of being subjected to legal harassment, as in other countries that do not have a free press, but for fear of losing profits.

How Can Bias Occur?

Scholars have another way of dividing media bias; they specify three categories for how it occurs: gatekeeping bias, coverage bias, and statement bias. **Gatekeeping bias** is the tendency to avoid reporting stories of a particular nature. In the absence of gatekeeping bias, media organizations can still exhibit **coverage bias**, whereby certain kinds or aspects of stories receive less attention in column space or airtime. Finally, the media can exhibit **statement bias**, the interjection of opinions into the coverage of an issue.[26]

This classification is far from perfect. To measure gatekeeping bias, for instance, researchers need to know how many stories *might* have been reported, which is inevitably a matter of opinion. To measure coverage bias, they need to decide whether certain aspects of a given story require more attention because of their novelty or complexity. Still, where researchers have undertaken to sort out these issues, a fairly positive picture emerges. Across dozens of studies, newspapers and magazines exhibited no consistent bias in one direction or another. Television networks exhibited slight liberal coverage and statement biases, but on balance it seems that, according to researchers, both liberals and

gatekeeping bias The tendency for the media, or a specific media outlet, not to report stories of a particular nature.

coverage bias The tendency for the media, or a specific media outlet, to give less attention in terms of column space or airtime to certain kinds of stories or aspects of stories.

statement bias The tendency for the media, or a specific media outlet, to interject opinions into the coverage of an issue.

[24] Travis L. Dixon, "Good Guys Are Still Always in White? Positive Change and Continued Misrepresentation of Race and Crime on Local Television News," *Communications Research*, April 2, 2015, 1–18.

[25] See, for example, J. S. Aubrey, "The Role of the Media in Body Image Concerns among Women: A Meta-Analysis of Experimental and Correlational Studies," *Psychological Bulletin* 134, no. 3 (2006): 460–76.

[26] On this type of bias in presidential election coverage, see Dave D'Alessio and Mike Allen, "Media Bias in Presidential Elections: A Meta-Analysis," *Journal of Communication* 50, no. 4 (2000): 133–56.

conservatives have ample opportunity to be heard.[27] Voices on one side or the other may be louder and drown out the opposition at times, but the available studies do not add up to a conclusion that one side consistently overwhelms the other in politics.

Media Effects

So far in this chapter, we have focused on the evolution of mass media content, media companies, and government regulation of media. That is, we have studied the *supply* side of media. What about the *demand* side? What is the nature of media consumption? How has consumption of media content changed over time, and what does that mean for politics?

There has been much research on the effects of media on individuals and public opinion. For example, researchers have conducted careful experimental studies of people's responses to campaign advertising. Others have analyzed what people know about politics and how that relates to their choice of media sources. Some of the findings from this research have already been summarized in Chapters 9 and 13.

For our purposes, we can divide questions about media effects into two types: those that ask what media people use and why, and those that ask how specific kinds of media content affect people's attitudes, opinion, and actions. The former type of question examines the decisions people make to read newspapers, watch television, or browse the Internet for information about politics, as well as which newspapers, television programs, or websites they select. The latter type examines the consequences of those decisions on how people think and reason.

Who Chooses Which Media Content and Why?

Researchers have explored three different hypotheses about why people choose specific media outlets. The *partisan hypothesis* says that people choose media programming on the basis of its partisan or ideological slant. Although this seems plausible on the surface—after all, Fox News clearly attracts more conservative and more Republican viewers (in fact, many more viewers, period) than does MSNBC—studies provide little support for this hypothesis. Participants in experiments typically appear to choose media content for other reasons.[28]

The *agenda hypothesis* asserts that people choose media programming on the basis of personal interest in the issues and policy areas the outlet tends to

[27] D'Alessio and Allen, "Media Bias in Presidential Elections."

[28] See, for example, Shanto Iyengar, Kyu S. Hahn, Jon A. Krosnick, and John Walker, "Selective Exposure to Campaign Communication: The Role of Anticipated Agreement and Issue Public Membership," *Journal of Politics* 70 (2008): 186–200.

Do people choose to watch the Rachel Maddow Show *because they want political information with a liberal slant? Do they choose* Tucker Carlson Tonight *for a conservative slant? Research shows that factors other than partisanship or ideology may be more important.*

emphasize. A news outlet that devotes considerable attention to health care stories, for example, will attract viewers or readers who are especially interested in such stories (such as the elderly). The same appears to be true of such issues as foreign policy, environmentalism, hunting, sports, or local business reports. Experimental and survey evidence strongly supports this agenda hypothesis.[29]

The *engagement hypothesis* contends that some people are generally interested in politics while others are not. Nearly everyone (or at least some members of each household) is interested in some combination of weather, movies, sports, scandal, and celebrity gossip, but consuming in-depth political news and commentary is almost like a hobby for "political nerds." To show which media outlets people gravitate toward, we can simply find out how interested people are in politics in general and then anticipate that they will access those outlets that offer the corresponding amount of political coverage, from very little (for those uninterested in politics) to very much (for those highly interested in politics).[30]

This last hypothesis turns out to be largely confirmed, and the consequences are important for political equality. Consider the well-known pattern discussed in Chapters 9 and 10: Interest in politics is highly correlated

[29] See, for example, Doris Graber, *Processing the News: How People Tame the Information Tide* (New York: Longman, 1984).

[30] Markus Prior, *Post-Broadcast Democracy: How Media Choice Increases Inequality in Political Involvement and Polarizes Elections* (New York: Cambridge University Press, 2007).

with higher levels of education and income. And as a result, because interest in politics leads to people seeking out information about politics, political knowledge is significantly higher among those who are more educated and wealthier. Evidence from surveys and experiments overwhelmingly supports these patterns. Exceptions can occur during heated presidential campaigns or times of economic or foreign policy crisis, when people from all income, wealth, and education groups seek out more political news and commentary.[31]

It is hard to square the minimal evidence for the first hypothesis with the incontrovertible fact that conservatives tend to watch conservative shows on channels like Fox News more than liberals while liberals prefer to watch liberal shows on such channels as MSNBC or read the *New York Times*. Perhaps different ideological groups pay more attention to different issues, and the various media outlets take advantage of these different focuses. Thus, perhaps Fox News covers wasteful government spending and budget deficits more than MSNBC because Fox viewers, being more conservative, focus their attention on issues related to taxation and spending. This explanation could make sense of the agenda hypothesis and the different viewer bases of various cable channels.

What Is the Effect of Specific Media Content?

In recent decades, researchers have conducted many experiments and surveys to try to understand what difference specific content makes in individual decision making.

Some scholars have studied whether media content is both informative and persuasive. If media stories are informative, then people learn new facts about the world that they did not know before watching or reading them. Not surprisingly, evidence suggests that people learn most of what they know about current events from the media, as opposed to from direct observation or from neighbors or coworkers.[32] Evidence for the educational value of media overall is more mixed than some people might imagine, however. Many studies have shown that people who are generally uninformed about politics retain very little factual information even a short time after observing media content; the information does not stick for long among vast portions of the general public.[33]

---

[31] On the relationship between education, income, and political knowledge, see Michael X. Delli Carpini and Scott Keeter, *What Americans Know about Politics and Why It Matters* (New Haven, CT: Yale University Press, 1996). On media usage being stratified by income and education, see H. Brandon Haller and Helmut Norpoth, "Reality Bites: News Exposure and Economic Opinion," *Public Opinion Quarterly* 61, no. 4 (1997): 555–75. On media consumption during times of crisis, see Scott L. Althaus, "American News Consumption during Times of National Crisis," *PS: Political Science & Politics* 35, no. 3 (2002): 517–52.

[32] Shanto Iyengar and Donald R. Kinder, *News That Matters* (University of Chicago Press, 1987).

[33] See, for example, W. Russell Neuman, "Patterns of Recall among Television News Viewers," *Public Opinion Quarterly* 40, no. 1 (1976): 115–23.

Some researchers think this finding slights people's ability to learn about politics. They may not remember rote facts, but this does not mean that media content did not help them form considered opinions. Think about a movie you saw five years ago. Although you may have forgotten many details of the characters and plot, you probably still remember whether you liked or disliked it. There is evidence that much political information works this way: people discard the details once they have used them to update their *feelings* toward a person or party.[34]

As for persuasion, research has shown that single news stories are rarely enough to make people change their minds about whom to vote for or how to evaluate candidates or government officials. But repeated exposure to negative information about a candidate reduces enthusiasm for voting for that candidate. In other words, mass media content can persuade people to be more or less supportive of something, but usually this occurs only through repetition.[35] But as with other findings, some groups of people are more easily persuaded than others. Interestingly, both the people who are least informed and the people who are the most informed about politics tend to be difficult to persuade. The former (least informed) are difficult to persuade with information from media because they are less engaged and pay less attention. The latter (most informed) are difficult to persuade with information from media because their advanced levels of knowledge mean that additional information is only a small part of all the considerations they use to make decisions. It is the group in the middle—the moderately informed, who occasionally pay attention to politics and know some but not a great deal about politics—that is most amenable to being persuaded by new information provided in news programming via mass media.

Agenda setting by the mass media has also been a focus of research. People place increased importance on certain social problems and government agenda items based on media coverage. As one scholar observed, "The media may not be successful much of the time in telling people what to think, but [it] is stunningly successful in telling its readers what to think *about*."[36] This is especially true when people are incessantly exposed to a variety of media sources that agree on the need to tackle a given problem. For example, surveys show that most people believe that violent crime is a growing problem, even though the incidence of such crime has actually fallen in the country as a whole.

[34] Milton Lodge, Kathleen McGraw, and Patrick Stroh, "An Impression-Driven Model of Candidate Evaluation," *American Political Science Review* 83, no. 2 (1989): 399–419; Milton Lodge, Marco Steenbergen, and Shawn Brau, "The Responsive Voter: Campaign Information and the Dynamics of Candidate Evaluation," *American Political Science Review* 89, no. 2 (1995): 309–26.

[35] Benjamin I. Page and Robert Y. Shapiro, *The Rational Public: Fifty Years of Trends in Americans' Policy Preferences* (University of Chicago Press, 1992).

[36] Bernard C. Cohen, *The Press and Foreign Policy* (Princeton University Press, 1963), p. 13; emphasis in original.

Do Fact-Checking Organizations Change Candidate Behavior?

Organizations like FactCheck.org and PolitiFact, and media outlets like Politico, the *Washington Post*, and the *New York Times*, conduct fact-checking on the statements of candidates. Does the threat of being fact-checked deter politicians from making untrue statements?

Two political scientists ran an experiment on real politicians to answer this question. Brendan Nyhan and Jason Reifler sampled 1,169 state legislators in nine states and randomly assigned them to three groups. In the treatment group, legislators were sent letters about the reputation costs of having false claims refuted by fact-checkers; these letters also reminded them that a PolitiFact affiliate exists in their state. In the placebo group, legislators were sent a letter to notify them about a study on accuracy in politicians' statements, but the letter made no reference to fact-checking.[a] And in the control group, no letters were sent to the legislators. After the letters were sent (or not sent in the case of the control group), Nyhan and Reifler then examined whether the politicians' statements were criticized for being untrue by fact-checking media organizations during the campaign period. Here's what they found:

Legislator's Probability of Receiving Accuracy Criticism

Source: Brendan Nyhan and Jason Reifler, "The Effect of Fact-Checking on Elites: A Field Experiment on U.S. State Legislators." *American Journal of Political Science* 59, no. 3 (2015): 628–40. Replication data available at https://dataverse.harvard.edu/dataset.xhtml?persistentId=doi:10.7910/DVN/26867 (accessed 5/27/16).

Think About It

What can we conclude from this graph about politicians being reminded of fact-checking media organizations? What seemed to matter more, the reminders of the presence of fact-checking organizations, or the notification that a study was being conducted on accuracy in politicians' statements?

a. The purpose of the placebo group was to account for the tendency to behave differently because they are being observed.

Why this disconnect between facts and perceptions? Scholars point to data showing the increased coverage of violent crime in the mass media over the 1990s and 2000s, which clearly influenced people en masse to prioritize crime fighting on the government's agenda.[37]

Priming and framing research offers telling insights into media impact (see Chapter 9). *Priming* is the psychological process of shaping people's perceptions of a particular issue, figure, or policy. Research shows that mass media reports have a direct bearing on whether people focus on personal character, appearance, performance, competence, or other attributes when evaluating political candidates. The more media content highlights an individual politician's philandering, for instance, the more likely people are to view that politician negatively despite other qualities that might recommend him or her. Moreover, people will be more likely to judge *all* politicians by that criterion.[38]

In much the same way, media reports can influence the weight people attach to certain aspects of a complicated problem or policy issue. The actions by those giving the information, such as reporters and media personalities, is known as *framing*. Research shows that the effects of framing can be very large in shaping people's attitudes. These effects can be attenuated, and in some rare instances eliminated altogether, when people are exposed to multiple media sources that display different ideological or partisan biases.[39] (See Chapter 9 for more discussion of framing.)

What media content people use and how it influences their political behavior is one of the more exciting areas of research in the social sciences. Scholars of media effects generally agree that mass media profoundly affects public opinion, at least at the level of framing specific issues in certain ways and shaping attitudes toward certain politicians; they study the details of how, when, and to whom such effects occur. New survey and experimental techniques have given us deeper insight into the causes and consequences of individuals' access to different kinds of political news and commentary.

Politicians and the Government as Sources

An inescapable fact for the press and media companies in the American political system is that a large amount of political information of use to reporters comes straight from politicians and the government. The relationships between

[37] Maxwell E. McCombs, *Setting the Agenda: The Mass Media and Public Opinion* (Malden, MA: Blackwell Publishing, 2004), chap. 2.

[38] See, for example, James N. Druckman, "Priming the Vote: Campaign Effects in a U.S. Senate Election," *Political Psychology* 25, no. 4 (2004): 577–94; and Nicholas A. Valentino, "Crime News and the Priming of Racial Attitudes during Evaluations of the President," *Public Opinion Quarterly* 63, no. 3 (1999): 293–320.

[39] James N. Druckman, "Political Preference Formation: Competition, Deliberation, and the (Ir)relevance of Framing Effects," *American Political Science Review* 98, no. 4 (2004): 671–86.

politicians and the press can be, at times, cooperative or adversarial, but there is no denying that they need each other. Politicians need the press, and successful politicians use the press and various forms of media to their advantage. They cultivate relationships with trusted reporters, giving them access when they travel and hold meetings, granting them one-on-one interviews, and sometimes hiring them away from media companies as spokespeople. Meanwhile, successful political reporters have to walk a fine line. They cannot alienate politicians and members of the government too much, lest the politicians stop talking and giving access. Yet the reporters cannot appear too biased toward or cozy with politicians, lest their potential audiences or critics accuse them of pandering with no independence. Nevertheless, reporters need information and sources for stories, and they do not want to be shut off.

Donald Trump during his 2016 presidential campaign actually banned certain reporters and media companies from attending his semiprivate media sessions. These reporters, he claimed, were unfair in their coverage of him. This is unusual behavior by an American politician. Politicians do not usually need to ban specific reporters from press events. They just need, subtly, to reward the friendlier (but still respected) reporters with more access, and journalists get the message.

While politicians need the press and vice versa, politicians can avoid the filtering that takes place through the press and write directly on Twitter, Facebook, or their own blogs and websites. Today's major candidates commonly use social media to communicate directly to supporters and potential donors.

The Media as Principals and Agents

We began this chapter by posing questions about bias in mass media content and later analyzed the concept of bias in some detail. Some scholars of media politics concede that many Americans are often getting news with a strong partisan bias but question whether this is a problem.[40] Consumers may choose sources that reinforce their own biases. But to call people biased simply means that they have a specific point of view that is shaped by their preferences for political outcomes. Evidence shows that partisan-biased television shows get people engaged in politics and may in fact mobilize them to participate more.[41] As long as people have access to multiple news sources with different biases, then a partisan press may produce a more engaged and active

[40] Shanto Iyengar and Jennifer A. McGrady, *Media Politics: A Citizen's Guide* (New York: Norton, 2006).
[41] See, for example, Stefano DellaVigna and Ethan Kaplan, "The Fox News Effect: Media Bias and Voting," *Quarterly Journal of Economics* 122, no. 3 (2007): 1187–234.

citizenry.[42] It may also be that other kinds of bias, besides the ideological kind, are more consequential.

Let's return to the "why" of our opening puzzle: What explains the nature of American coverage of Edward Snowden and the larger issues his behavior invoked? What motives drive media companies and reporters? The major answer from our analysis in this chapter is that today companies find it both possible and profitable to tailor their content for specific audiences. But part of the answer also lies in the fact that people appear to find it interesting or useful to read, watch, or listen to political content created by those who share their own political attitudes. In this case, concerns about national security were likely more salient to consumers of American mainstream media than were concerns about government surveillance.

As consumers of political news and commentary, it behooves us to pay close attention to the media sources we use, and especially to their motivations. Reporters have incentives to get an interesting story and are usually in a hurry to get it. They interview and gather information from a variety of sources—the more convenient, the better. As discussed, much of their information comes from people in the government, who generally seek to avoid negative coverage. Reporters also get information from candidates and parties challenging incumbents, who naturally want to make the incumbent party and the government look bad. Finally, reporters get information from interest group leaders, who also have incentives to influence how the news is framed for public consumption.

To communicate their content to mass audiences, reporters rely on mass media companies, which have their own complicated set of incentives. In understanding the roles these companies play, it helps to draw on insights from the principal–agent problem we discussed in previous chapters (see especially Chapters 1 and 7). American mass media companies, both public and private, play multiple roles and affect the political system in multiple guises. At times, they act as principals; at other times, as agents.

The Press and Mass Media as Principals

Mass media companies *control the means of communication* between people, and between institutions and people. They own the television and radio stations, operate the cables and cable boxes that deliver television programs, license portions of the public airwaves and satellite frequencies, create the technology and towers for cell phone transmissions, and own the billboards and periodicals bearing political advertisements. Mass media companies and their personnel also *produce programming content about politics*, including news programs,

[42] How informed that citizenry becomes because of the press is a different matter, as addressed in Chapter 9 and earlier in this chapter.

opinion and talk shows, written stories and editorials, blogs, and candidate debates. In other words, media companies make products that are disseminated through the forms of transmission mentioned earlier. In this capacity, media companies can act as principals when their own employees produce commentary, news, and forums for debate and discussion.

Like other interest groups, mass media companies try to influence the government to protect and advance their interests by lobbying, making political donations, and appealing to the public. In this respect, they are similar to auto or oil companies, or any other businesses. But unlike any other type of interest group, media companies can use their capacities as owners of means of communication and producers of content to bolster their political influence.

Despite the strong tradition in the journalistic profession of separating business decisions from editorial decisions, there is little question that some media owners use their companies to promote certain lines of argument in politics. For example, Rupert Murdoch, the owner of many newspapers (including the *Wall Street Journal*) and other mass media outlets (including Fox News) in the United States, England, and Australia, is known to be politically conservative and to push his publications to favor conservative points of view. He openly supports Republican candidates in elections and donates to the Republican Party.

The Press and Mass Media as Agents

The government, interest groups, political parties, and candidates all communicate to the mass public through radio, television, the Internet, cell phones, and public billboards and notices. The public communicates with political elites using some of the same means. In other words, media companies allow for communication in several directions. We can say that, in this guise, media companies are the agents, hired by principals (candidates, for example) to carry their messages or to bring them messages.

If mass media producers are merely agents of other principals—such as political parties, candidates, or the government—then the question of bias is really about who gets access to the most effective means of mass communication. We know partisan elites are biased; we expect them to be. In the same way, media producers can shape the news in biased ways by deciding which voices are heard.

In sum, media companies act both as principals *and* as agents, and it is hard to fault them for doing what we, as consumers, encourage them to do when we select content that agrees with our own attitudes. But when critics of the media allege media bias, are they referring mostly to the selective access they give politicians and other political organizations that actually supply the content? Or are they referring to the media companies themselves, producing their own content through their paid journalists and commentators? If the former, then perhaps a return to something like the Fairness Doctrine would improve public discourse. If the latter, new regulations would almost certainly run afoul of interpretations of the First Amendment protections of the press and recent Supreme Court rulings, making it difficult to impose any changes in news content.

FURTHER READING

★ = Included in *Readings in American Politics*, 5th ed.

★ Baum, Matthew, *Soft News Goes to War* (Princeton, NJ: Princeton University Press, 2003). A detailed study of how people learn about international news from soft news, which is media programming that is intended to entertain but contains political information.

Delli Carpini, Michael X., and Scott Keeter, *What Americans Know about Politics and Why It Matters* (New Haven, CT: Yale University Press, 1996). Indicates the deep inequalities in political knowledge, and how this inequality tilts government programs toward the more knowledgeable.

Druckman, James, "Political Preference Formation: Competition, Deliberation, and the (Ir)relevance of Framing Effects," *American Political Science Review* 98 (2004): 671–86. Presents experimental evidence demonstrating that framing effects on people's political attitudes depend on whether they receive one-sided frames or counteracting frames.

Entman, R. M., and A. Rojecki, *The Black Image in the White Mind: Media and Race in America* (Chicago: University of Chicago Press, 2000). Discusses evidence that media coverage of crime and government social welfare programs reinforces racism among certain segments of society.

Hamilton, James T., *All the News That's Fit to Sell: How the Market Transforms Information into News* (Princeton, NJ: Princeton University Press, 2004). Probes deeply into the incentives of media companies and the press to report political facts.

Iyengar, Shanto, and Donald R. Kinder, *News That Matters* (Chicago: University of Chicago Press, 1987). Describes how the reporting of political information shapes perceptions of social groups, reinforces stereotypes, and shapes political choices.

Iyengar, Shanto, and Jennifer A. McGrady, *Media Politics: A Citizen's Guide*, 2nd ed. (New York: Norton, 2011). A comprehensive resource for the current state of knowledge on media and politics.

Ladd, Jonathan M., *Why Americans Hate the Media and How It Matters* (Princeton, NJ: Princeton University Press, 2012). An argument contending that increased competition within the media and political parties has amplified citizens' distrust of the mainstream media.

Lodge, Milton, Marco Steenbergen, and Shawn Brau, "The Responsive Voter: Campaign Information and the Dynamics of Candidate Evaluation," *American Political Science Review* 89, no. 2 (1995): 309–26. Presents evidence that people retain very little information about candidates from campaign advertising.

Niven, David, *Tilt? The Search for Media Bias* (Westport, CT: Praeger, 2002). Data showing that reporters tend to be slightly more liberal than the general population, and that editors and owners of media companies are slightly more conservative than the general population.

Prior, Markus, *Post-Broadcast Democracy: How Media Choice Increases Inequality in Political Involvement and Polarizes Elections* (New York: Cambridge University Press, 2007). An argument that usage of new media has improved political knowledge among those voters already informed and has reduced political knowledge among those less informed.

Valentino, Nicholas A., "Crime News and the Priming of Racial Attitudes during Evaluations of the President," *Public Opinion Quarterly* 63, no. 3 (Fall 1999): 293–320. Argues that people unconsciously absorb racial cues in news coverage, and these cues shape people's evaluations of politicians.

KEY TERMS

coverage bias (p. 560)

gatekeeping bias (p. 560)

infotainment (p. 551)

mass media (p. 537)

media (p. 537)

press (p. 537)

statement bias (p. 560)

Governments use an array of tools and approaches to achieve economic goals. Some politicians, like President Obama, have advocated raising the federal minimum wage as a way to help combat income inequality.

15

Economic Policy

 What can governments do about the economy? Why do they sometimes favor one approach over another?

T he American economy showed signs of growth in the mid-2010s, but that growth was too slow for many people, and evidence accumulated that much of the benefits occurred among the top income earners. Wages for many people in the lower ranges of the income distribution were not increasing. Working class and poor people felt that their financial situations were not getting any better; this was especially true for young people. Across the country people continued to feel strapped by stagnant income growth and steadily rising costs for education, energy, housing, and basic services. Congressional candidates from both major parties in 2018, despite data showing a growing economy, devoted much of their time in speeches focusing on how the economic conditions of Americans were precarious, and the benefits of growth grossly uneven.

In fact, data show that inequality among Americans is at levels not seen since the late nineteenth and early twentieth centuries. Measures often compare the incomes and wealth of the top 10 percent compared with the bottom 50 percent. Best-selling books by economists in 2015 and 2016 called for dramatic policy changes to tax the rich and shift resources to improve the circumstances of those at the bottom of the income scale.[1] That both major party presidential candidates put inequality at the top of their agendas in 2016 highlights how economic inequality has become a major topic of public discussion and political competition in recent years among many different groups in the population, including conservative Republicans. Complaints about the economy were widespread in 2016, especially among voters for Donald Trump.

We discussed economic issues and ongoing budget crises in Chapter 1. Now we will probe more deeply into the government's actions and the underlying politics of economic policy making. The government's response to economic troubles in

[1] Thomas Piketty, *Capital in the 21st Century* (Cambridge, MA: Harvard University Press, 2014); Joseph Stiglitz, *The Price of Inequality* (New York: W. W. Norton & Company, 2013).

OUTLINE

- Government and the Economy: Ideas and Historical Trends

- Benefits and Costs

- Purposes of Economic Policies

- Types of Policies

- In Comparison: Economic Policy

- The Politics of Economic Policy Making

the early 2010s was to spend over a trillion dollars in "stimulus" money for programs intended to create jobs and get money circulating again. The stimulus plan focused on funding for education, research, transportation, and so-called knowledge industries, with special emphasis on potential technological breakthroughs in key areas such as solar energy, electric cars, and biomedical products. At the same time, the government bailed out banks and auto companies to keep the largest (by number of employees) afloat until the economy improved. In terms of keeping the companies going and allowing them to become profitable again, the strategy largely worked, with the survival of General Motors and Bank of America as two examples. During the recession, and then when the economy recovered with slow growth through 2018, the government kept interest rates extremely low and worked to keep inflation low.

It is not difficult to understand why the government generally emphasizes improving the economy, especially during downturns. The state of the economy directly affects people's jobs, income, and wealth. A poor economy leads to unhappy voters who want to vote incumbent politicians out of office. But the specific form of government responses throughout the recession and at times of growth requires explanation. Why does the government pay attention to specific industries, like banking, housing, automobiles, energy, defense, and high technology? Why, in times of recession, does the government sometimes believe that spending government money to stimulate the economy would work? Why are low interest rates and low inflation seen as means of continued economic growth?

Governments have an array of tools and approaches they can use to influence the economy. During economic downturns or periods of slow growth, they can try to boost specific sectors of the economy or influence the money supply. They can cut taxes, spend money on new government projects, or increase entitlements. During periods of high inflation, they can also influence the money supply and the supply of key products in the economy such as oil or food.

Why do they sometimes favor one approach over another? And why does the government intervene in some areas of the economy but not in others? To answer these questions, we need to learn about economic policies and how politics affects economic policy making.

Government and the Economy: Ideas and Historical Trends

In every modern democratic country, including the United States, government intervention in the economy is pervasive and enormously consequential. Among the world's advanced industrial democracies, the total amount of taxpayers' money that governments spend is between one-third (in the United States) and two-thirds (in Sweden, for example) of the entire national economy. To put it another way, on average 50 cents of every dollar of wealth created in industrial democracies is spent by governments. Especially during times of recession or slow growth, most people expect their government to take significant action to improve economic conditions. However, the U.S. government has not always been deeply involved in the economic markets. Around the time the country was founded, British philosopher Adam Smith published his famous book *The Wealth of Nations*, in which he argued in favor of **laissez-faire** capitalism: the idea that if left alone from government interference, economic markets will efficiently create greater wealth for the society as a whole. Many of the Founders would have been well aware of Smith's ideas after the publication of his book, and the virtues of capitalism were mostly taken for granted in the early years of the Republic. Let's look closer at this and other economic philosophies and then turn to the changing nature of economic policy in American history.

laissez-faire An economic philosophy advocating that the government take a noninterventionist approach to the economy, leaving market forces alone to determine the economic behavior of people and business firms.

Prominent Economic Philosophies

Promoters of capitalism favor widespread private ownership of **capital** and generally leaving the government out of decisions over what goods are produced and consumed by people. *Capital* refers to goods, both public and private, used to produce other goods that we consume directly, such as food, clean air, roads, clothing, medicines, toys, books, and automobiles. Land, factories (and the machinery within them), mines, construction equipment, office furniture, computers—all these can be considered capital. In nineteenth-century terminology, capital is sometimes referred to as the *means of production*. These means can be owned either privately or collectively by all the people in a community. In the modern world, collective ownership of capital means that it is owned and operated by the government.

capital Goods used to create other goods in an economy.

The free market, according to a capitalistic view, should be allowed to operate with little or no government interference. Economists consider a market *free* when people, not governments, decide what and how much to trade, buy, produce, and consume, and what prices are charged for those goods.

Challenges to Smith's ideas of capitalism came from German economic philosopher Karl Marx, who in the mid-nineteenth century advocated socialism as a means of creating a more just society. The philosophy of Marxism seeks collective ownership of capital. In its purest form, Marxism (or communism) promotes the abolition of private ownership of property in favor of state ownership of all "means of production."[2] In theory, Marxism places control of capital directly in the hands of the people. What this means in reality is greater emphasis on centralized planning in determining how much of specific goods to produce and how much people will pay for them.[3]

Marxism espouses virtually complete government control over the economy, while pure laissez-faire capitalism was an ideal target for those opposed to government intervention. Given changes in American society by the late nineteenth century, it became all but inevitable that government would intervene more directly in the economy and move away from laissez-faire. Industrialization in Europe and North America in the nineteenth century saw the rise of massive corporations and unfettered capitalism, along with widespread exploitation of workers and damaging effects on the environment and consumers. Large trusts (or monopolistic corporations) were able to dominate a particular market, drive out competitive companies, and raise prices and exploit workers. For example, Standard Oil in the 1890s and first few years of the twentieth century came to dominate the markets for crude oil and in the process to wield unparalleled influence over the entire American economy. The political reaction to these effects was increased popular pressure on governments, including the U.S. national government, to regulate these firms and markets. The Progressive movement, for instance (discussed in Chapters 3, 6, and 12, especially), was partially motivated by a sense that the trusts needed to be broken up and that the government needed to set up regulatory agencies to balance against the power of large corporations.

The appeal of socialism became more acute among Americans by the early twentieth century, but neither major political party truly espoused moving the American economy toward European-style socialism. By the late 1920s, a somewhat hybrid economic philosophy became popular and influenced policy makers. Called Keynesianism after its main proponent, British economist John Maynard Keynes, it proposes that government spending be used to regulate the ups and downs of economic cycles that lead to fluctuations in unemployment. In particular, Keynesianism promotes active government intervention, mostly spending on new government programs, during economic downturns. The government should feel free to borrow money to permit this spending, or to raise taxes on the wealthy. The idea is to create government jobs even if their purpose isn't completely necessary, thus giving people money that they will spend on goods produced by private companies, leading those

---

[2] Karl Marx, *Capital: A Critique of Political Economy* (1867–94; repr., New York: Penguin Classics, 1993).

[3] See Joseph Schumpeter, *Capitalism, Socialism, and Democracy*, 3rd ed. (New York: Harper Perennial, 1962).

private companies to hire workers to make those goods. So-called Keynesian (that is, government) spending during economic recessions or depressions would stimulate the economy to spur growth. Once the economy was growing again, government spending could (and perhaps should) tail off toward normal levels, and perhaps borrowing also would decrease and even government debts would be paid off.

Toward the late twentieth century, counterreaction to Keynesianism came in several forms. Some economists promoted monetarism, a philosophy that says the key to prosperity is maintaining a supply of money in the society that matches the productive capacity of the society. In practical terms, this means keeping inflation low and regulating the amount of money in the society closely. It is always tempting for governments to print more money to pay off their debts or to inflate the currency to allow debt holders in society to pay off their fixed debts more easily. Monetarists decry this temptation and urge governments to be disciplined about their money supply.

Another alternative to Keynesianism is supply-side economics. Keynesianism relies on spurring growth through putting more money into people's pockets so that they spend more as consumers. This is called demand-side stimulation. In contrast, supply-side economists believe that it is better to keep taxes low and avoid excessive government borrowing. Low taxes are especially important to wealthier segments of society, because then people who own capital will have more money to invest in new business ventures and to expand existing businesses. Growth happens, in this view, when the "supply" side of the economy—meaning companies and people that own capital leading to final products—have money to use to expand that capital.

Related to both of these is the so-called Austrian school, identified closely with the ideas of Ludvig von Mises and Friedrich Hayek. A set of theorists and philosophers trained in Vienna have influenced (mostly conservative) economists with an emphasis on individual and corporate autonomy from government interference, a rejection of collectivist (that is, socialist) solutions to economic problems, and a heavy emphasis on the ethical value of human freedom. The Austrian school's philosophy is often set as the main alternative to both modern forms of socialist and Keynesian philosophies of economic governance.

These various economic philosophies map onto our notions of left and right, liberal and conservative. In modern political parlance, the terms *left* and *right*, *liberal* and *conservative* are often used to characterize people as favoring more or less redistribution of wealth. In fact, we can think of the major economic philosophies as arrayed along an ideological spectrum.

At the far right is pure laissez-faire capitalism, which is predicated on private ownership of nearly all forms of capital except for a few items the government must own, like military capital and police stations.[4] In a traditional

---

[4] See Milton Friedman, *Capitalism and Freedom* (1962; repr., University of Chicago Press, 2002).

capitalist society, and in societies governed by believers in monetarism and supply-side economics, the government would avoid large-scale redistribution. Thus, today an economic conservative is someone who believes that the free market should determine who gets what in society and therefore opposes redistributive policies.

Meanwhile, at the other end of the spectrum are leftists or liberals who prefer more government redistribution from the wealthy to the poor, accomplished through tax or spending policies. Most do not advocate anything as extreme as pure Marxism, though, which has largely been discredited. This is partly because nearly all avowedly Marxist countries have set up nondemocratic governments that own a large portion of business activity and suppress challenges by opposition parties and other groups. It is also because many economists and policy makers believe that too much centralized planning for the economy has historically led to bad outcomes. Milder forms of socialism, however—often described as democratic socialism—promote active government redistribution through generous welfare programs (see Chapter 16).

In contemporary American politics, to be called a "socialist" is usually derogatory (though not for everyone) and describes someone far to the left and out of touch with the views of most Americans. Bernie Sanders, for instance, ran for the Democratic presidential nomination in 2016 openly claiming to be a democratic socialist. He lost the nomination to Hillary Clinton, though he successfully pressured the Democrats to adopt more leftist economic policies in its platform during the presidential campaign. In Europe, however, a socialist tends to mean a leftist who is more moderate (centrist) than a Marxist or communist. Keynesians can be considered somewhat between left and right, and the philosophy's location on this ideological dimension depends on the nature of the government programs pursued through spending.

To summarize, for the past four decades on the conservative side of American politics, a basket of ideas are associated with the Republican Party in general: supply-side, pro-capitalism, Austrian economics, and monetarism. On the more liberal side of American politics, Keynesian, pro-regulatory, and pro-redistribution (some say democratic socialist) policies are associated with the Democratic Party.

We now turn to the development of American economic policy. The government's role in the economy evolved in response to specific historical events and forces, including the promulgation of these economic philosophies.

Economic Policy in the Early United States

From the Founding to the late nineteenth century, the government's role in the economy was modest. Government budgets at the national and state levels were small relative to the size of the economy. Mostly the government

In the nineteenth century, government involvement in the economy was focused largely on transportation and communication infrastructure, such as canals, railroads, and telegraph and telephone networks. The Erie Canal (completed in 1824) connected the Great Lakes to waterways leading to the Atlantic coast, making it possible to ship goods to and from the interior states by boat.

built transportation and communication infrastructure—canals, roads, railroads, harbors, telegraph and telephone networks—and periodically altered tariff rates to help American companies and farmers. Sometimes the government raised tariffs to protect domestic companies from foreign competition, and sometimes the government lowered tariffs to help American companies buy cheaper raw materials from overseas and sell their products to foreigners. Public money was raised through tariffs and customs duties on imports.

Although the individual states played a smaller role in economic policy making than they do today, they were more directly involved in economic policy making than the national government. The states had the authority to license and tax businesses, and to regulate how products and money flowed within state boundaries. Partly because federal courts interpreted the Constitution to prohibit much national government regulation of economic activity (see Chapters 3 and 8), and partly because it was not widely seen as the prerogative of the national government, economic policy making was highly decentralized and inconsistent across regions. Different states had different rules governing how businesses could compete and how they treated their workers. For the most part, the doctrine of laissez-faire capitalism reigned in the North with little state intervention except to protect companies in their quests for profits and growth.[5] A different system prevailed in the South, where the predominantly agricultural economy was based on slave labor until the 1860s.[6] Even after the abolition of slavery, a quasi-feudal economy persisted for decades in the South. Former slaves were tied to the land and more or less forced to continue working for a specific landowner (often their former master).

Policy areas that were required by the Constitution to be managed at the national level, such as customs duties and tariffs on imports, were highly contentious and led to some of the deepest political splits of the nineteenth century. As a trade policy issue, "the tariff" polarized economic interests on both sides of the partisan divide. High tariffs benefit local industries that sell mostly to domestic consumers while low tariffs benefit exporting industries. Thus, when the presidency and Congress were controlled by parties that drew significant support from exporting states—namely, the Democratic-Republicans and then the Democratic Party—tariffs tended to go down. Conversely, when importing, manufacturing states got the upper hand in the national government—that is, when Whigs and Republicans were in power—tariffs tended to go up. Many electoral battles at the state and national levels were won depending on the state of the economy and the numbers favoring higher or lower tariffs.

A Growing Role for Government

As discussed in Chapter 3 and in this chapter, the national government became more enmeshed in economic regulation starting in the late nineteenth century, especially with regard to railroads, telephones, mining, and forestry. During the Progressive Era, the government began to regulate food and drugs, protected the rights of workers (especially child laborers), and permanently instituted a national banking system with the Federal Reserve Bank at its center. Finally, the national government gained the power to levy income taxes on corporations and individuals, enabling it to tap into huge sources of funding for its programs. In the 1890s, the Supreme Court had ruled that an income tax violated the Constitutional mandate that no "direct, Tax shall be laid" unless it be in proportion to the population of the state as determined by the census.[7] This decision eventually led to the passage of the Sixteenth Amendment in 1913, allowing the federal government to raise revenue through an income tax. Income taxes had become the chief source of government revenue by the time the United States entered World War I in 1917.

---

[5] Robert L. Heilbroner and Aaron Singer, *The Economic Transformation of America: 1600 to the Present*, 4th ed. (Fort Worth, TX: Harcourt Brace, 1999).

[6] Ira Berlin, *Many Thousands Gone: The First Two Centuries of Slavery in North America* (Boston: Belknap Press, 2000).

[7] See *Pollock v. Farmers' Loan and Trust Company*, 158 U.S. 601 (1895).

Not until the 1930s, however, was the national government expected to be the key driver of economic growth throughout the entire country. During the New Deal (see Chapters 3, 5, and 6), the national government stepped up its regulation to encompass a wide spectrum of industries, including the regulation of labor relations. And Keynesian ideas were widespread among government economists at that time; they justified the spending policies of the federal government in response to the Great Depression as adopting Keynesianism. Starting in the 1940s, the national government protected workers when they tried to form labor unions. (Because some state governments were more cooperative than others, these protections varied across industries and regions.) By the 1950s, one-third of American wage laborers were unionized.

The Social Security program, enacted in 1935, directly tied the economic well-being of all retirees and disabled people to that of the national government. Moreover, the government developed new programs to promote small-business development, education, research, and massive infrastructure projects. Every president since Franklin Delano Roosevelt has devoted enormous attention and resources to managing the economy.

In the mid-twentieth century, the government's growing involvement in the economy was reflected in the massive amount of public money spent on military equipment and personnel and on scientific research in space programs, medicine, and the basic material sciences. Such government spending touched every corner of the country, and the economies of many communities and regions came to depend on it to greater or lesser degrees. For example, the spectacular growth of Los Angeles after World War II was largely the result of government spending on aerospace technology, which fueled job creation in industries in southern California.

Throughout the twentieth century, state and local governments also became increasingly involved in the economy, especially in promoting industrial zones to attract businesses and in providing basic poverty relief. In short, government at all levels took a more active role in managing and promoting economic growth.

One exception to this trend is that in the area of protective tariffs and restrictions on trade with foreign countries, the government has become not more but less active. By the second half of the twentieth century, tariffs ceased being a highly contentious domestic issue and instead became more of a foreign policy tool. The past several decades have seen a worldwide movement to reduce trade barriers and promote the free exchange of goods, services, and money across international borders. The United States has played a central role in promoting this trend and is the major player in organizations such as the World Trade Organization (WTO), which monitors and regulates compliance with trade treaties. The United States has also promoted the reduction of barriers to foreign investment and the worldwide

1913 Establishment of the Federal Reserve Bank

1929 Great Stock Market Crash and the beginning of the Great Depression

1950–60s Major expansion of government funding for defense and technological research

1980s Cuts in programs reduce the welfare state; income tax rates are lowered.

1990s Vigorous economic growth and increasing economic inequality

2000s Recession and then growth with tax cuts for upper-income families

1900	1920	1940	1960	1980	2000

1913 Establishment of the Federal Income Tax

1932–38 The New Deal created a massive regulatory system and the Social Security program.

1960s Great Society programs increased fiscal transfers to states and set up Medicare and Medicaid.

1970s Oil crisis led to periods of high inflation and low growth.

2008 Large global recession led by collapse of U.S. housing market

2010 Government stalemates on economic policies, continuing increases in inequality

distribution of products (especially cultural and intellectual ones) with as much copyright protection as is possible given other countries' policies and legal capacities.

The growth of government taxing and spending has slowed in recent decades relative to the size of the economy, but it is still much larger than earlier generations of Americans ever imagined. We live in a time when our prosperity, for better or worse, is intimately tied to the specific economic policies of all levels of government, but especially the national government.

Nevertheless, political battles continue over the overall growth of the government's role in the economy, whether the government should cut back, whether taxes should be cut, whether more government investment is necessary, and whether the wealthy should pay more taxes than they currently do. Generally, Republicans today tend to adopt supply-side economics as their guiding philosophy while Democrats tend to favor a more robust Keynesianism that tolerates a larger role for government. Both parties in the United States are still coming to terms with political forces shaped by increased inequality in the American population. The 2016 presidential campaign altered the overall connection between Republicans and pro-capitalism somewhat. Republican presidential nominee Donald Trump espoused policies that can only be considered anticapitalist, such as trade protection and limiting labor mobility.

As president, Trump pursued some policies that followed through on those campaign promises, especially on trade and limiting immigration. Deficits and debt increased substantially in his first two years. But he also worked with Republicans in Congress to pass a large tax cut, and he supported deregulation of many industries.

Benefits and Costs

To better understand economic policies, a few basic concepts from economics are helpful. Economics concerns how benefits (often called goods) and costs are distributed in a society. Things or experiences that we want more of are called benefits. They are generally desired by people, and the more the better. Costs are things or experiences that we want less of. Spending your own money is by definition a cost, but so are things like polluted air, noisy neighbors, and bad experiences such as disease or violent conflict. People obviously seek to minimize costs, but many costs are unavoidable, as in the old adage about the two universal experiences in life: death and taxes.

Recall our discussion from Chapter 1 in which we distinguished between private goods and public goods. **Private goods** are those things that, when we consume or use them, cannot be consumed or used by anyone else. A meal we enjoy is a private good, as is our own automobile or pajamas. The government can provide private goods, such as a paycheck from working at a government job or a publicly funded health checkup. **Public goods** are those benefits that we can consume or enjoy without keeping others from consuming or enjoying them too. Pure public goods are described as *nonrival* (if one person is enjoying them, it does not preclude someone else from enjoying them) and *nonexcludable* (people cannot be kept from enjoying them if they want to).

private good A product or benefit provided such that its enjoyment can be limited to specific people, and one individual's consumption of it precludes others from consuming it.

public good A benefit provided to a group of people such that each member can enjoy it without necessarily having to pay for it, and one person's enjoyment of it does not inhibit others from enjoying the benefit.

Types of Public Goods

There are few pure public goods. Clean air is one; national security (that is, safety from foreign invasion or terrorism) is another. Other things we call public goods share certain aspects of private goods. A public beach that everyone can enjoy is a special kind of public good, which economists call a **common good**. A common good is one that is subject to crowding, so that although no one can be kept from enjoying it (it is nonexcludable), enjoyment by too many people cuts into enjoyment by others (it is rival). Another kind of benefit is a **club good**, which is excludable but nonrival, such as satellite television. You have to pay for it (and thus can be excluded if you don't pay for it), but once you pay, your enjoyment does not diminish the enjoyment of anyone else who has also paid for it (Table 15.1).

common good A variant of a public good; a benefit provided to a group of people such that each member can enjoy it without necessarily having to pay for it, but one individual's consumption of it limits or precludes others from consuming it.

club good A variant of a public good; a product or benefit provided such that its enjoyment is exclusively for those who paid for it, but one person's enjoyment of it does not inhibit others from enjoying the benefit.

Although economists distinguish pure public goods from common and club goods, in discussing economic policy we will refer to all three kinds as public goods. Most benefits involving the government are characterized by a blend of excludability and rivalry. A city's football stadium can be considered a club good that you and many others can enjoy while attending a game, but it has a limited number of seats, and each seat is a private good. The Internet is mostly a public good, but when too many people from your neighborhood try to download movies at the same time and the Internet is slow, then, because of

TABLE 15.1

Four Kinds of Goods

	Nonexcludable *No one can be excluded from enjoying it.*	**Excludable** *Some people, such as those who don't pay, can be excluded from enjoying it.*
Nonrival *One person's enjoyment of the good doesn't prevent others from enjoying it.*	**Public good** (example: clean air)	**Club good** (example: satellite television)
Rival *One person's enjoyment of the good limits or precludes enjoyment by others.*	**Common good** (example: a public beach)	**Private good** (example: shoes)

crowding, each measure of used capacity becomes a private good for local Internet surfers.

The distinction between private goods and public goods is fundamental to understanding modern economics and economic policy. As we have seen in earlier chapters (especially Chapter 1), producing public goods requires some kind of institutional or collective solution. The creation of public goods often presents a collective action problem because some people are tempted to free ride. Whenever possible, people will avoid paying the costs of producing pure public goods and common goods, because they can enjoy them regardless of whether they paid for them. If we were not required to pay taxes, how many of us would voluntarily pay our fair share of the cost of the aircraft carriers that the U.S. government operates as part of its national security strategy? Closer to home, how many would voluntarily pay for the upkeep of our local parks? Some of us might, but others would let their neighbors pay while continuing to picnic and play games in the park.

Without the involvement of governments, it is doubtful that many public goods, such as parks, schools, or roads, would be built and operated. But in taxing people to pay for such public goods, governments take money out of the economy that would otherwise be spent to produce and buy private goods. People need both public and private goods to lead satisfactory, happy lives, but what is the proper mixture? This question is at the heart of economic policy making. It is easy to see the difficulties governments face in deciding how much to spend on public goods; people disagree vigorously over which public goods are worth having and how much to pay for them. Later we will discuss economic philosophies that place different priorities on government spending and involvement in the economy.

Externalities

Both the benefits people enjoy and the costs people pay can have spillover effects, sometimes called **externalities**. Of most concern are costly externalities, which occur when production or consumption of a public or private good imposes costs not only on the people producing or consuming the good but on others as well. A classic example is automobile pollution. When we drive a car (a private good), we pollute the air that is breathed in by others. Our benefit—driving the car—causes someone else to experience a cost—polluted air to breathe. Another example is noise pollution. When you and your friends enjoy loud music at a party late at night, your neighbors also experience that noise and may not appreciate it. Your enjoyment of a benefit—music played loudly—spills over to affect others who consider it a cost at 2:00 A.M. In such situations, the enjoyment of certain goods gives rise to costly externalities.

Externalities can occur in the production of goods as well. Factories regularly release pollution into the air, water, or ground in the process of making their goods. These pollutants are costly externalities for others. Say a factory in Ohio pollutes the air and water that flow into Kentucky and Indiana. Not only is the factory creating costly externalities, but the state government of Ohio, if it does not regulate its factories well enough, is allowing those externalities to affect the residents of other states.

As we will see in the next section, a large portion of all government regulation of business is intended to manage bad externalities. For example, when a concrete company releases pollutants into a river, it affects another company downstream that runs a fish farm and sells fish for people to eat. The concrete company upstream imposes costly externalities on the fish company, which earns lower profits, and on the consumers who might ingest the pollutants through eating the fish. The government can pass laws and enforce strict regulations governing which pollutants and what quantities are permitted to be released by companies upstream. When people encourage the government to regulate business more tightly, they usually have a sense that too many costly externalities are caused by private businesses unconcerned about the effects of those externalities on others.

externalities Effects on people, good or bad, arising from the economic behavior of others. Also known as *spillover effects*.

Purposes of Economic Policies

Economic policies can serve five broad purposes: distributing benefits, redistributing benefits, stabilizing the economy, regulating commerce, and promoting economic growth. These purposes frequently overlap and occasionally conflict.

Distributing Benefits

Many policies provide public goods or even private benefits to wide swaths of the population, paid for by taxes that are in turn charged to wide swaths of the population. Because benefits and costs are widely distributed, these policies are known as **distributive policies**. For example, the benefits of basic defense spending to protect the United States are widely enjoyed by all people within its borders, and defense policies are not primarily intended to transfer benefits from one population group to another. Likewise, federal highway programs provide government money and administration to build and repair highways in every state. The resulting highway system is one of the most extensive in the world, linking regions of the United States economically so that trucks can deliver products, buses can transport people, and tourists can drive anywhere in the country efficiently and safely.

distributive policy A government policy intended to provide benefits to large portions of the population.

Redistributing Benefits

Some policies impose costs on one group—typically in the form of taxes—while the benefits mostly accrue to another group in the population. These are known as **redistributive policies**. Thus, Medicaid programs that provide health care to poor people are paid for by taxes that fall mostly on people who do not receive Medicaid. Many similar social welfare programs are redistributive, in the sense that most of the costs fall on people who do not benefit from them directly.

redistributive policy A government benefit provided to some people that is paid for by another group of people.

These differ in intention from distributive policies because redistributive policies impose costs on one set of people while the direct benefits flow to another. With distributive policies, the intention is for costs to be shared by many people and the benefits shared by many of the same people paying the costs. National parks and clean water supplies are provided thanks to distributive policies, while school breakfast and lunch programs for poor children are provided thanks to redistributive policies.

Redistributive policies are the most controversial of government policies in that they generally pit one group in society against another. Wealthy people may not like to be taxed at high rates to pay for schools in poorer areas, when the people living in those poor areas pay little or no taxes. It may rankle people to pay for health care, education, or jobs programs from which they will never benefit directly.

Many economic policies have both distributive and redistributive elements. If public goods or benefits are enjoyed widely, they are distributive, but if the benefits and costs of policies are enjoyed unequally across the population, then they are redistributive. It is easy to see that this can be a matter of degree. When the government backs student loans, it benefits many people and probably benefits society as a whole in making college widely accessible. But people without college-age children pay more for this program than they receive. Thus, it is partly a redistribution from the people who pay taxes but do not need college loans to those who have children and need such loans.

In fact, because redistribution is generally controversial, those in favor of certain policies tend to frame them as a distribution of benefits rather than as redistribution. Consider the Social Security program: people who currently work are taxed at a flat-rate percentage of their income, and those funds are paid out to retirees, their widows or widowers, and the disabled (see Chapter 16). In other words, money is redistributed directly from those who are working to those who are not working, and from the younger to the older. But this is not the way the Social Security program is generally understood. Most people consider Social Security to be a form of insurance that they will benefit from if they live long enough. Workers pay into the program now and receive the benefits when they retire. This is more or less true as long as the program continues. So most people see the distributive aspect of Social Security, in which the costs are dispersed broadly to all workers. The degree to which Social Security is redistributive or distributive is thus a matter of perception, and such perceptions matter politically. The politics of Social Security depends on the degree to which people come to believe that they will receive benefits later in life that roughly correspond to the financial sacrifices they made earlier in life when they paid Social Security taxes.

Stabilizing the Economy

Some policies are intended to steer economies within relatively narrow ranges of growth and decline, keeping economic downturns mild. It makes sense to try to avoid severe downturns. When the economy contracts too intensely, it can throw many people out of work suddenly and lead to a cascade of business closures. When people are out of work, they cannot afford to buy goods that companies make, and thus many companies do not sell enough to keep their employees, leading to more layoffs and less spending on other goods, and so on.

Why societies should avoid sharp upturns in economic growth is a more difficult question. The answer is that if the economy grows too fast, it can lead to debilitating inflation. **Inflation** occurs when the supply of money in the economy grows faster than the supply of goods and services produced and consumed, causing prices to rise and eroding the value of savings. For consumers, inflation leads to the purchasing value of a unit of currency, such as the dollar, declining to the extent that goods and services cost more of the currency. Mild inflation is generally considered acceptable and natural in an economy. But rampant inflation reduces the value of everyone's wealth too quickly and makes it difficult for people to buy goods unless their incomes increase at least as fast as the inflation rate. When inflation spirals out of control, people may lose confidence in the currency and hoard goods for fear of further inflation.

inflation When the purchasing value of a unit of currency, such as the dollar, declines so that goods and services cost more of the currency.

FIGURE 15.1

U.S. Inflation Rates, 1914–2018

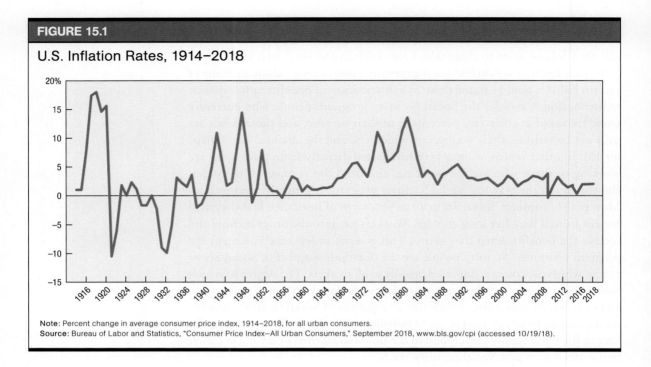

Note: Percent change in average consumer price index, 1914–2018, for all urban consumers.
Source: Bureau of Labor and Statistics, "Consumer Price Index–All Urban Consumers," September 2018, www.bls.gov/cpi (accessed 10/19/18).

Historically, periods of very high inflation have led to social unrest, both in the United States and in other countries (Figure 15.1).

A major goal of governments today is to keep economies growing steadily, with relatively low inflation, and when downturns come, to keep them mild. Stable periods with manageable growth are generally desirable. Most economists think it is impossible to avoid "business cycles," in which periods of growth alternate with periods of contraction. But the intensity of these swings matters a great deal. Mild contractions of the economy can be managed and people can often recover, but extreme swings can be devastating. Consider the difference between companies having to lay off workers temporarily during a downturn but rehiring them when the economy improves (common during mild downturns), and companies going bankrupt and having everyone who works there lose their jobs permanently. The latter is more common during severe recessions or depressions. When recessions or depressions are deep and sustained, many companies fail and never recover, and people can be out of work for a long time or lose their savings and assets permanently.

Societies can become unstable when they have continuous cycles of deep recessions or depressions followed by periods of rapid economic growth. In fact, one of the great success stories of modern social science has been the use

FIGURE 15.2

U.S. GDP: Annual Change*

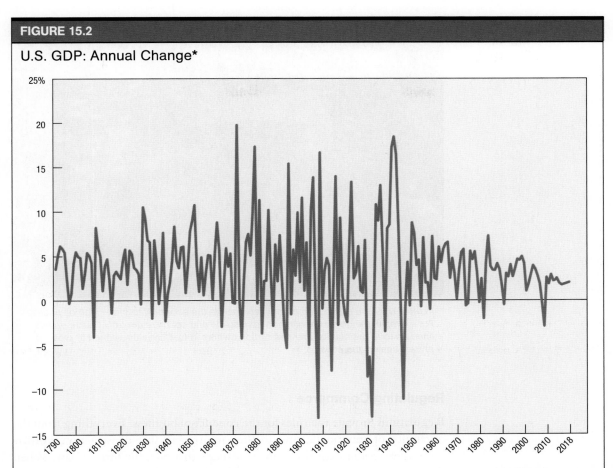

* GDP, or gross domestic product, is the value of all goods and services produced within a country's borders. The annual change in GDP, measured here as the percentage of increase or decrease each year relative to the preceding year, offers a way to compare changes in the strength of the economy over time. Data for 2016 are through the third quarter.

Source: Richard Sutch, "National Income and Product," in *Historical Statistics of the United States, Earliest Times to the Present: Millennial Edition,* edited by Susan B. Carter, Scott Sigmund Gartner, Michael R. Haines, Alan L. Olmstead, Richard Sutch, and Gavin Wright (New York: Cambridge University Press, 2006); U.S. Department of Commerce, Bureau of Economic Analysis, www.bea.gov/national/index.htm (accessed 10/19/18).

of economic theory to guide policy makers in "smoothing" out the business cycle. Since the 1930s, economic swings in advanced industrial democracies have been less dramatic than before. As Figure 15.2 shows, dramatic economic shifts in the 1870s, 1890s, and 1930s were all much more severe than anything we have seen since. The exception is the deep downturn in 1945, but that was a temporary result of the end of World War II. Later in this chapter, we will discuss various policy tools that are used to stabilize the economy.

In the 1970s, the U.S. government intervened in the economy to offset high oil prices. For example, the government rationed gasoline and set price controls. These drivers lined up to fill their tanks after gas station owners in California threatened to close in protest against the policies.

Regulating Commerce

Regulations provide the rules for the conduct of business. Everything from the durability of automobile tires to the requirement that construction workers wear safety helmets results from regulations that take the form of law. When the national government requires that businesses selling food or pharmaceuticals follow strict guidelines for the safety or health information provided on product labels, the benefits to society are obvious. For example, people with peanut allergies need to know if a candy bar contains peanuts, so that information must be listed on the label. Just as these regulations can be critically important to individuals' well-being, so are many business regulations vital to modern economies and to public safety. Regulations in general are intended to protect consumers, workers, businesses, and investors. Of course, it may be debatable whether specific regulations are necessary, achieve their desired goals, or cause more harm than good in some circumstances. When business leaders believe they are overregulated and do not have enough freedom to develop new products or find less expensive ways to produce goods, it can have a negative impact on the economy and end up hurting workers and investors.

Compared to programs like Social Security, Medicare, or national defense, regulations are inexpensive for the government to create and enforce. The costs of complying with regulations are typically borne by private businesses.

The government pays for hiring bureaucrats and lawyers to regulate businesses, and for operating the offices, vehicles, and machinery necessary for their work. But regulatory policies do not involve paying out billions of dollars to recipients, as with Social Security, or designing and building extremely expensive aircraft carriers or jets. This is not to say that regulations do not have enormous economic consequences (they do), only that they are not expensive for the government to administer compared to other kinds of policies.

A useful example to consider is the role of environmental policies. Some environmental policies regulate business and personal conduct to prevent degradation of the environment, including investigating and enforcing violations of environmental laws by any person or organization. Other policies clean up past pollution. There are government programs to support research into better techniques for environmental protection, and others to manage natural areas so they are not overused or exploited to the detriment of the public good.

Environmental laws and regulations spring from different motivations. Some people support them because they are good for humans, while others support them out of concern for the natural environment (including non-human animals) and a desire to protect that environment from humans.

Environmental problems and the regulations designed to alleviate them do not affect all people equally. Often dangerous environmental areas are clustered near poorer communities, leading to degraded resources and public health. Such was the case in Flint, Michigan, where many residents live near or below the poverty line, after state and local officials failed to adequately respond to complaints of lead-contaminated tap water from residents for several months. Here, Flint resident, Jessica Owens, shows Sen. Gary Peters (D-MI) a bottle of contaminated water after a federal hearing on the Flint water crisis.

Using our knowledge of collective dilemmas, we can see that environmental laws can be necessary for various reasons. Without environmental laws, many people (including those who lead large businesses) will act in their own self-interest; they will overuse natural resources and abuse the environment, believing either that their actions will make little difference in the broad scheme of things, or that the abuses are necessary to produce goods at a lower expense. But the result of many such individual and business actions will be a degraded environment and depleted resources. This poses a collective action problem for people who wish to enjoy the goods provided by nature and also wish to have access to inexpensive products: without an enforcer of rules about access to those goods, individuals and companies will eventually degrade the environment to the point where everyone loses.

Another aspect of environmental laws deserves mention. Environmental problems do not hurt people equally. Some suffer more than others from dirty air and water, giant and dangerous trash heaps, and radiation fallout from nuclear accidents. Historically, governments have concentrated pollution and trash dumps in geographic areas near where poor people live. Hence, poor people, and especially poor minorities, have been underserved by environmental laws. This problem has received more attention in recent decades; clean-up efforts in large cities have specifically targeted "brownfield" sites, which tend to be distant from commercial centers and affluent residential neighborhoods. Environmental cleanup and prevention policies inevitably help some areas and industries more than others, and in this way these policies have a redistributive aspect. Political fights over priorities are as common in environmental policy as in any other area.

Many environmental problems cross state boundaries and require the Environmental Protection Agency (EPA) to step in. Each state has its own version of the EPA, and there can be close cooperation across the states and between the states and the national government. Quite often the EPA supervises or overrules the workings of state-level agencies because federal environmental laws are typically stricter than state laws. A few states, however, have stricter environmental laws in some areas than the national government. California, for instance, has had stricter regulations on permissible auto emissions. Interestingly, studies have shown that when states adopt stronger laws on the environment, the national government tends to end up adopting the stricter standards.[8]

Promoting Economic Growth

Some policies are intended to develop a country's or region's infrastructure, to support research and education, or to encourage new investment in busi-

---

[8] Johannes Urpelainen, "Explaining the Schwarzenegger Phenomenon: Local Frontrunners in Climate Policy," *Global Environmental Politics* 9, no. 3 (2009): 82–105.

nesses. They promote economic growth by making it more attractive for businesses to set up new headquarters, plants, and stores, and by improving the skills and knowledge of employees and consumers. One example is when a local government sets up new industrial parks or enterprise zones, paying the initial costs and developing the land and perhaps offering companies tax breaks to locate offices there. At the national level, the government offers tax breaks for companies to experiment with new sources of energy, on the principle that global business opportunities are available to American companies with innovative energy technologies.

As the example in energy indicates, promotion policies can take forms similar to stabilization policies. Governments can spend money on new programs that will have multiplier effects in the private sector. Funding for health care research can improve health and also lead to new discoveries that can be sold all over the world. New medicines and medical devices are often discovered in research programs funded by the government. Newly discovered medical technology can then be manufactured and distributed by private companies. The difference is that promotion policies are more directly oriented toward promoting growth, whereas stabilization policies are oriented toward preventing instability, which can include promoting growth but also slowing down the economy. Although the end results may be similar, the overall goals are somewhat different.

State governments and leaders of larger cities specialize in promotional policies that are intended to attract companies to set up shop within their borders. State and city leaders compete for business investment by offering companies tax breaks and generous public goods for their employees.

Types of Policies

How do governments achieve these five purposes? We can divide the tools available to government into three categories: monetary policies, fiscal policies, and trade policies.

Monetary Policies

Monetary policies involve the supply of money in the economy. In relation to the broad purposes discussed earlier, monetary policy is mostly intended to stabilize the economy, though it can also have a strong side effect in promoting growth. We divide our discussion of monetary policy into three areas: controlling inflation, the role of interest rates, and regulating banks.

monetary policy Government management of the supply of money in the economy, which affects prices, interest rates, and the availability of loans.

Controlling Inflation. The money supply relates directly to inflation. Inflation can occur for several reasons; let's consider two of them. First, the government can simply print too much money, causing inflation. The supply of money is regulated in part through the determination of how much currency to coin and print. The Department of the Treasury is in charge of making such decisions. Second, economic growth can happen rapidly, leading to low unemployment because businesses need employees to expand in response to growing demand. When unemployment is very low, wages become higher because businesses have to offer more wages to attract and keep employees. When wages rise, prices increase for consumer goods because they cost more to make. And when prices rise higher than wages (even slightly), it leads to inflation. Thus, economic growth can sometimes, if not matched with appropriate monetary policies, lead to inflation.

Though there are exceptions, most governments prefer that the real rate of inflation be close to, but not quite at, zero percent. And they try to control inflation through the rate at which they print money, through the regulation of banks (discussed later), and in influencing the markets for government bonds. During periods of sustainable growth, inflation tends to fluctuate between 2 and 4 percent. Yet, the opposite of inflation is bad too. This is called **deflation**, when people and companies cannot borrow or earn enough money to make economic transactions that match the level of productivity. When deflation becomes a concern, governments can pump more money into the economy.

deflation When the purchasing value of a unit of currency, such as the dollar, increases so that goods and services cost less of the currency.

Interest Rates. When the economy is not growing fast enough or is not growing at all—or perhaps is even contracting, as occurred in the late 2000s—governments can lower interest rates to make it easier for businesses and consumers to borrow money for investments and purchases. When businesses and consumers borrow money, they hire people and buy products, which spurs business growth and total economic growth. Depending on circumstances, governments can also raise interest rates. Governments do not want interest rates to fall so low that they deter investors from buying government bonds, the chief method for governments to borrow money. In sum, under various circumstances—high inflation, slow growth, or both—governments can manipulate interest rates, mostly by changing the rates they charge banks to borrow money from the Federal Reserve, to try to stabilize the economy.

Regulating Banks through the Federal Reserve. Banking regulations are vitally important to the supply of money in the economy. By and large, banks are regulated at the national level through the **Federal Reserve System**. In previous eras, independent state-level banks provided almost all banking services for the country. Now nearly all banks, even those that are state chartered, are part of a national system run by the **Federal Reserve Board** (known as the Fed).

Federal Reserve System
Network of U.S. government banks that loan money to and regulate the commercial behavior of private banks.

Federal Reserve Board
Board of directors, consisting of seven members appointed by the president, in charge of policies for the Federal Reserve System.

The modern Federal Reserve was set up in 1913 to create a common national system of banking. Any bank doing business in multiple states must join. Smaller local banks are not required to take part, but most of these also join the system. In return for complying with national regulations, banks get access to loans from the central bank (in other words, the 12 Federal Reserve

Banks scattered around the country serve as banks to other banks), a check-clearing system that provides insurance against widespread fraud, and access to currency to make payouts. Consumers who deposit money in banks belonging to the Federal Reserve System have their savings and checking accounts insured against bank failures up to $250,000.

The Fed also regulates banks and any businesses that loan money. These regulations are used by the Fed to try to stabilize or stimulate the economy. As an example, the Fed requires that banks have enough money on hand to pay out to depositors (although the definition of "enough" can change). These reserve requirements are important in regulating the money supply. By requiring banks to keep more money in their vaults, the Fed can effectively pull money out of the economy (thus slowing down inflation). Conversely, by loosening reserve requirements, the Fed can pump more money into the economy, which usually leads to lower interest rates and easier access to loans.

The Federal Reserve Board is in charge of the 12 regional Federal Reserve Banks. Each of the seven board members is appointed by the president and confirmed by the Senate for a 14-year term. The chair of the Fed is appointed from among those members and leads for a four-year term, which

---

Know the FACTS The Federal Reserve

- The Federal Reserve sets monetary policy in the United States. The Federal Reserve has several tools at its disposal to manipulate the money supply. The supply of money in the economy determines the rate of inflation. When there is relatively more money, inflation increases; and when there is relatively less money, inflation decreases.
  - The Federal Reserve may change the *discount rate*, the rate at which commercial banks borrow money from the Federal Reserve.
  - The Federal Reserve may change the *reserve requirement*, which is the minimum amount of money a commercial bank must have on hand to meet depositors' demands.
  - By buying and selling treasury bonds through *open-market operations*, the Federal Reserve may influence the supply of money in the economy.

- The Federal Reserve System consists of 12 Federal Reserve banks that are headquartered in business centers around the United States.

- The Federal Reserve is governed by the Federal Reserve Board, which consists of the 12 governors of each of the Federal Reserve banks and the chairman of the Federal Reserve Board. This board, which is appointed by the president, is responsible for making decisions about the discount rate, reserve requirement, and open-market operations carried out by the Federal Reserve System.

can be renewed. The chair of the Federal Reserve is one of the most important economic figures in the world. He or she leads the board that determines the interest rates banks charge, loan requirements, reserve requirements, and more generally the supply of money in the American economy, which is the largest and most influential in the world.

By virtue of being the "bank to the banks" and having most of the banks in the country under its regulatory umbrella, the Fed has enormous influence on all aspects of finance. With that influence comes responsibility and, inevitably, criticism. By law, the Fed is supposed to be independent of political pressure, meaning that its decisions do not need to be approved by the president or Congress. The members of the boards of the various Fed banks, and the members of the Fed Board, cannot be fired during their terms for policy decisions they make, and they are not partisan politicians. They are instructed to make decisions in the interest of ensuring a stable economy.

Yet, the Fed is not completely insulated from politics. After all, politicians determine who runs this "independent" banking system, and naturally the White House chooses people who share the president's overall economic philosophy. Moreover, Congress exercises formal oversight over the Fed's operations. Fed members are respected economists who may lean one way or the other politically but are usually considered moderate. Significantly, a Fed chair appointed by a president of one political party is often reappointed by a president of the other party. Democrat Bill Clinton stuck with Alan Greenspan even though Greenspan was originally appointed by Republican Ronald Reagan and served under two Republican presidents. Reagan himself reappointed Paul Volcker, the chair he inherited from his Democratic predecessor, Jimmy Carter. And Ben Bernanke was first appointed by George W. Bush in 2006 and then reappointed by Barack Obama.

The Fed can generate controversy, especially when the economy is not doing well. It was heavily criticized in the 2010s, for instance, for having inadequate regulations in place for home mortgage loans. Many observers believe that, in the years leading up to 2008, the Fed's policies encouraged speculation and irresponsible lending, leading to the collapse in home prices and, ultimately, to the financial crisis that erupted in 2008. At various moments in recent history, members of Congress have called for abolishing the Fed or for making its decisions subject to congressional approval. Criticisms of the Fed have come from elements of both the Republican and Democratic parties. Some

When the U.S. housing market imploded in 2008, leading to rampant foreclosures, many people were critical of the Fed's lack of regulation of banks' mortgage lending policies, which critics blamed for the crisis. Some politicians have even called for abolishment of the Fed itself or making its decision subject to congressional approval.

Republicans, including Donald Trump, have argued that the government's intrusion into the economy, led mostly by the Fed, has been a drag on the entrepreneurial spirit of Americans and thus has slowed economic growth. Some Democrats have argued that the Fed too often sides with the financial industry and fights inflation too hard at the expense of encouraging Keynesian-style fiscal stimulus (see next section).

Board members and economists might agree with certain criticisms of specific decisions by the Fed, but they will usually counter that the Fed is necessary and needs to be independent from the more politicized institutions of government in order to make responsible monetary policies.

Fiscal Policies

Fiscal policies have to do with taxing and spending by governments. Let's take these policies in turn.

fiscal policy Taxing and spending decisions by governments.

Taxation. Tax policies can accomplish three tasks. First, they raise money for the government. Second, they can redistribute wealth, because money that is raised from taxes on one group can be spent on another group. Third, they can encourage or discourage certain behaviors.

A classic example that illustrates all three tasks is the levying of heavy taxes on the sale of cigarettes by state and federal governments. This revenue makes it unnecessary for governments to raise an equal amount from other kinds of taxes (task number 1 earlier); much of the money raised goes to health care or education for everyone, thus shifting resources from smokers to the entire population (task number 2); and the main reason taxes on the sale of cigarettes are much higher than ordinary sales taxes is to discourage people from smoking (task number 3).

Modern democratic governments raise money through several types of taxes.

- *Income and payroll taxes.* Governments can tax a percentage of income earned. This can be either a flat percentage (say, 4 percent of a person's income) or a percentage that increases as a person's income increases (say, 4 percent on the first $15,000 earned, and 6 percent on earnings above $15,000). At the national level, income tax rates (in 2018) vary from 10 to 37 percent, depending on income level. Since the 1910s, income and payroll taxes have been the largest source of tax revenue for the national government.

- *Sales taxes.* Governments can levy a tax on consumer purchases. This is a common method for raising money among the states, cities, and counties in the United States. The rates vary from one locality to another. Say you buy a piece of clothing in Michigan and the price tag says it costs $100. The cashier rings up that amount plus $6 in tax. In New Jersey, the sales

The Collective Dilemma

The Federal Reserve System in the United States (the Fed) is the "bank to the banks." It is a public institution that helps private banks operate smoothly. These central banks, however, can be run in different ways with different priorities, and their actions and independence can become controversial.

Interests

Everyone benefits when the economy is growing or downturns are mild and short. Yet, different groups in a society have different financial and economic priorities. People in debt but with steady jobs can manage moderate inflation levels better than people to whom those debts are owed and those on fixed incomes, such as retired people. More highly skilled people are less affected by increasing unemployment than people with basic skills. And people who own businesses are more sensitive to higher interest rates on loans. Meanwhile, elected officials know that, to a great extent, their reelection hinges on the overall health of the economy.

Fed officials for their part value their independence from the elected branches of government and the banks they regulate. The economists in the Fed want to be free from political and public pressures and to rely solely on objective economic information to craft policies. In general, governors and officials at the Fed want stability in the economy, and do not want inflation, unemployment, interest rates, and government revenues to be extremely high or low.

Institutions

Legislation establishing the Fed states that the bank's purpose is to secure "maximum employment and stable prices."[a] To do this, economists argue, it must be independent from political pressures and partisan interests, because politicians are often interested in short-term fixes that might have negative long-term consequences. The Fed is independent in that Congress does not appropriate its funds; instead, it is funded primarily by the interest it accumulates on U.S. government securities. The leadership structure of the Fed also gives it independence. The Board of Governors is comprised of seven individuals, each with a 14-year term. The president appoints a governor, who must then be confirmed by the Senate. The governors' terms are staggered; that is, the terms do not have a uniform expiration date. This staggering avoids the situation where one president could appoint all seven governors at once. Importantly, since governors are not elected officials, they do not have incentives to cater to short-term populist political sentiment.

Despite its independence, the Fed is held accountable. It makes many of its operations public by reporting its monetary policy plans biannually and undergoing an annual audit by an independent auditor. The Fed's existence and mission result from congressional statute, so Congress does have the ability to alter its role and scope. The Fed is aware that some members of Congress and a portion of the public are critical of it and so devotes resources to public relations, and its governors often speak in public to justify its actions.

Outcomes

The reputation of the Fed is generally positive, largely because it is considered independent of partisan pressures. It also has a reputation for running the economy in a relatively moderate fashion, and evidence is strong that its actions have limited the depth of economic downturns since the 1930s. Moreover, all over the world, investors and governments look to the Fed as a source of stability and guidance on monetary policy.

In recent years, however, the Fed has come under intense scrutiny, with some critics calling for it to become less independent. The argument is that the Fed is too concerned with stability and not enough on overall economic growth or on producing jobs. Thus, the Fed is influenced by politics, especially by the fact that the president appoints and the Senate approves the nominees to the various Fed boards. When the president and the Senate are at odds over economic policy making, the makeup of the Fed boards can be severely affected; when both major political parties fail to agree on acceptable candidates to fill positions, important slots are left vacant for an extended period of time. In fact, in the last few years of President Obama's second term, Senate Republican committee chairs held up Obama's appointments to the Fed. Continuing the politicization of the Fed, Donald Trump stridently criticized the Fed during his presidential campaign, especially Janet Yellen, chair of the Fed under the Obama administration. Trump's presidency saw even more political attacks on the Fed, further threatening its independence.

Though the Fed is largely insulated from partisan pressures, it is accountable to Congress. As seen above, Fed Chairman Janet Yellen often reports to Congress on the Fed's actions and priorities.

a. U.S. Federal Reserve, "About the Fed," May 23, 2013, www.federalreserve.gov/faqs/about-the-fed.htm (accessed 9/9/16).

Think About It

Critics of the Federal Reserve believe that it has skewed priorities toward slow economic growth and that it is too powerful for being an unelected, independent body. Are these criticisms valid? How would the Fed's actions change if its Board of Governors were elected?

tax rate is slightly higher, and you would pay $7 in tax on a similar $100 purchase. Revenues from sales taxes go to the state or local government, depending on where you buy the item. The United States has no national sales tax.[9]

- *Property taxes.* Governments can tax land, automobiles, or other property on the basis of its fair market value. This is the most common way for state and local governments in the United States to pay for schools and other local public goods.

- *Customs duties and tariffs.* These taxes are a percentage of the value of imported goods. Duties and tariffs were by far the largest source of revenue for the American national government throughout the nineteenth century and until the 1910s. This method of taxation is also an important tool that governments use to protect domestic industries from foreign competition. Many industry lobbyists have worked hard to preserve the market share of domestic companies by encouraging Congress to raise tariffs on the goods of foreign competitors. But, as discussed earlier in this chapter, restrictions on imports (including taxing them with tariffs or duties) have been quite low for many decades relative to previous eras.

- *Inheritance taxes.* Governments can tax money or property on a percentage basis when it is passed on from someone who has died to his or her heirs. Thus, in the United States in 2018, if a deceased person had an estate worth $11.2 million or more to pass on to his or her heirs, the federal and/or state government will take a certain percentage of it in inheritance taxes (also known as estate or "death" taxes).

Taxation is a deeply political issue. Taxes fall differently on various groups in the population, and those groups regularly pressure the government to shift the tax burden away from them onto others, or to reduce taxes overall. Tax policies are said to be **progressive** if the tax burden falls more heavily on higher-income and wealthier people and more lightly on the poor, relative to their income levels. They are said to be **regressive** if the burden falls more heavily on those lower down on the income scale. In contemporary societies, poor people on average nearly always pay less in total taxes (in dollar amounts) than wealthy people do on average; the difference between progressive and regressive taxes has to do with the proportion of income that goes toward taxes. Tax policies are more progressive to the degree that poorer people pay a lower share of their income on taxes compared to wealthier people, and they are more regressive to the degree that poorer people pay a higher share of their income on taxes compared to wealthier people.

progressive tax A tax that places a greater financial burden on the wealthy than on the poor and the middle class.

regressive tax A tax that places a greater financial burden on the poor and the middle class than on the wealthy.

[9] In Europe, a related tax—known as a value-added tax (VAT)—is applied to any increase in value when a product is sold or resold, including wholesale and retail sales.

The progressivity of income taxes can vary dramatically. Figure 15.3 shows the highest income tax rates across selected countries. Inheritance taxes are generally progressive because only wealthy people tend to have much to pass on to heirs.

The progressivity of tax policies is a matter of degree. In general, income taxes tend to be progressive, and sales taxes tend to be regressive. Everyone in a state pays the same sales tax rate; thus, people with lower incomes spend a greater proportion of their money on sales tax than wealthier people.

Spending. Spending by the government can promote any of the five purposes discussed earlier in this chapter. It is easy to see that it costs money to achieve the first two purposes, *distributing* and *redistributing benefits*. The government employees who operate our various public goods—park rangers, military and law enforcement officers, airline security personnel—need to be paid. Social Security benefits are basically financial transfers from government to individuals. Spending can

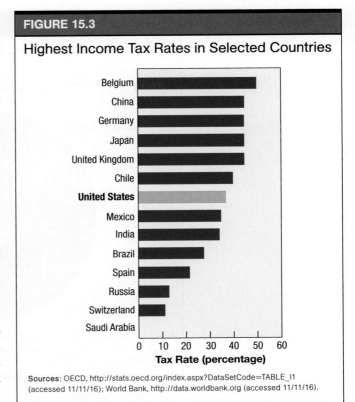

FIGURE 15.3

Highest Income Tax Rates in Selected Countries

Sources: OECD, http://stats.oecd.org/index.aspx?DataSetCode=TABLE_I1 (accessed 11/11/16); World Bank, http://data.worldbank.org (accessed 11/11/16).

also be used to *stabilize* the economy. For example, Obama's 2008 stimulus plan was an attempt to spend government money to lift the economy out of a recession. *Regulating* business costs money, mainly to pay employees and operate regulatory offices. Finally, governments at all levels invest in grants, low-interest loans, and planning commissions; the purpose of these expenditures is to *promote* certain kinds of industries and thus economic growth.

It is often said that spending reflects priorities. A glance at the U.S. government budget would suggest that its priorities are to have a strong military, to provide for the elderly and the poor, and to be able to borrow money because taxes are not high enough to cover all spending. Figure 15.4 shows the various budget categories and the levels of spending in a typical budgetary year. Some of the largest items are national defense, Social Security, Medicare and Medicaid (programs that provide subsidized health care for the elderly and poor), and interest on borrowed money. Programs like Social Security and Medicare are hugely expensive, but attempts to scale them back invariably meet with vigorous and widespread public disapproval. These popular programs are highly valued not only by the elderly who benefit immediately, but by younger people who expect the programs to be in place when they retire.

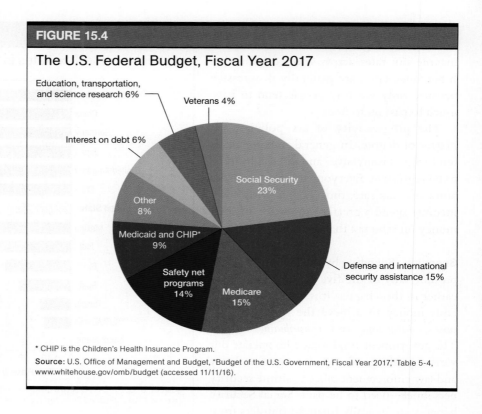

FIGURE 15.4

The U.S. Federal Budget, Fiscal Year 2017

Education, transportation, and science research 6%

Veterans 4%

Interest on debt 6%

Social Security 23%

Other 8%

Medicaid and CHIP* 9%

Defense and international security assistance 15%

Safety net programs 14%

Medicare 15%

* CHIP is the Children's Health Insurance Program.

Source: U.S. Office of Management and Budget, "Budget of the U.S. Government, Fiscal Year 2017," Table 5-4, www.whitehouse.gov/omb/budget (accessed 11/11/16).

Since the early 2000s, the national government has spent much more than it takes in from taxes and other forms of direct income (such as payments on debt and fees). To make up the difference, the government borrows from people, banks, and other institutions and governments by selling government bonds. (A *bond* is like a loan in which the purchaser provides the government with funds to finance current expenditures at a fixed rate of interest.) Interest payments on government bonds account for a substantial portion of the annual budget, nearly 9 percent in 2019. The difference between government revenue and expenditure in a given year is called the **national deficit**; since 2002, the annual deficit has been quite large, even relative to the size of the economy (Figure 15.5). The total cumulative debt owed by the government is called the **national debt**. It too is quite large and has fluctuated (Figure 15.6).

Although budgets often do reflect priorities, it is also true that some vitally important government functions are relatively inexpensive in the context of the entire budget. We have already noted how little it costs to regulate certain industries, and how significant the resulting benefits for society can

national deficit The difference in a given year between what the government raises in taxes and fees and what the government spends.

national debt The total amount owed to those who have loaned money to the government.

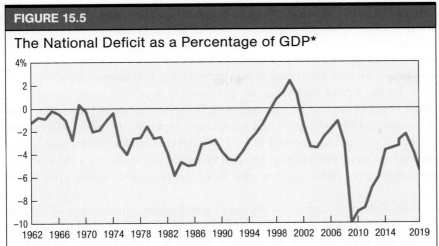

FIGURE 15.5

The National Deficit as a Percentage of GDP*

* The total government deficit, including Social Security and the U.S. Postal Service, as a percentage of GDP. Positive numbers indicate a surplus, and negative numbers indicate a deficit.

Source: U.S. Office of Management and Budget, "Budget of the U.S. Government, Fiscal Year 2016," Table 5-1, www.whitehouse.gov/omb/budget (accessed 11/11/16).

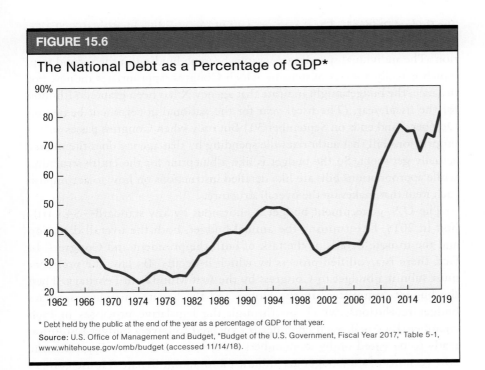

FIGURE 15.6

The National Debt as a Percentage of GDP*

* Debt held by the public at the end of the year as a percentage of GDP for that year.

Source: U.S. Office of Management and Budget, "Budget of the U.S. Government, Fiscal Year 2017," Table 5-1, www.whitehouse.gov/omb/budget (accessed 11/14/18).

be. It would be misleading to suggest, on the basis of the U.S. government budget, that national defense has a much higher priority than a functioning judicial system. Both are central to modern government, but national defense happens to cost a lot more.

There is an important connection between tax policies and spending policies. To the extent that taxes are progressive, nearly all government programs, even those that benefit everyone, have redistributive properties. This is because people who pay the lowest taxes, typically the poor, still receive the benefits of public goods. Even tax policies that are less progressive spread the costs of government programs and thereby make them more distributive, or perhaps even redistribute wealth from the poor and middle class to the rich.

Redistribution can occur through tax policies, spending policies, or both. When President Reagan took office in 1981, he accomplished two things that made the U.S. government budget less redistributive: he lowered the top income tax rate on rich people, and at the same time cut government programs for poor people. Reagan defended these actions by saying that money needed to be put into the hands of people who would invest in new businesses; furthermore, he claimed that certain government programs for the poor were inefficient and counterproductive. (We will discuss the politics of welfare policies in Chapter 16.)

The Budget Process. There are two steps to any spending by the national government. Congress first sets forth the overall budget in the form of a resolution. The individual spending decisions become binding in the second step, which is really a series of steps by which Congress appropriates money. For instance, the budget might indicate that agency X has been granted $1 billion for the fiscal year. (The fiscal year for the national government begins on October 1 and ends on September 30.) But only when Congress passes an appropriations bill that authorizes the spending by that agency does the money actually get spent. So the budget is like a blueprint for the entire structure, while appropriations bills are like detailed instructions on how to accomplish each item that makes up the overall structure.

The U.S. government budget is enormous by any standard—$4.1 trillion in 2018. Determining the annual budget, both the overall direction and the minute details, is the task of both the president and Congress. In fact, there is a codified process by which it occurs. By law, the president must submit a budget to Congress by the first Monday in February. Then the budget committees in the House and the Senate introduce separate budget resolutions, which go through the legislative processes in each chamber. By April, each chamber is expected to have a budget resolution ready to be voted on by its members on the chamber floor. Typically, the two versions of the budget are submitted to a joint Senate–House conference committee, which reconciles any differences between them. The final version of the budget, identical across both chambers, is then passed by both houses.[10]

The federal budget is not a law in the ordinary sense, however; in fact, it does not need to be signed by the president. Rather, it is a resolution, which is binding on Congress when it makes appropriations decisions. It is these congressional appropriations bills that become the law of the land.

Nevertheless, few legislative items attract as much attention as the budget. Leaders of the various federal agencies seek increases for special initiatives and fight to avoid cuts when the economy is in trouble. But programs that consistently enjoy strong support from specific constituencies—agricultural subsidies, for instance—tend to be funded either at the same level, or with slight increases to offset inflation, year after year. When the president proposes large increases or cuts in any given item, it is big news in Washington, as might be expected. But the president's budget proposal is only the starting point. It is Congress that takes out the scalpel and makes surgical changes, after listening carefully to interest groups and constituents. With some well-known exceptions, the final budget usually reflects congressional priorities more than the president's. The president can be virtually helpless in the face of united congressional opposition to major budget cuts, particularly when they involve pork-barrel projects (see Chapter 5). Or, alternatively, the president can face opposition to his favored programs by a Congress committed to budget cuts. The intense budget battles in the 2010s pitted a solid Republican majority in the House devoted to cutting the budget substantially and preserving tax cuts against the White House desperately trying to save certain domestic programs (as discussed in Chapter 1). Donald Trump shifted budget priorities and succeeded in lowering taxes and cutting programs he did not like.

Trade Policies

As mentioned previously regarding "the tariff," trade policies have long been contentious in American politics. In fact, trade policies are typically contentious in most countries. Trade policies involve tariff rates (taxes on imports) on specific products, numerical limits on imports of certain kinds, subsidies for domestic companies to compete with foreign competitors, and agreements between countries to promote trade or to restrict trade. The last topic, international agreements on trade, is discussed in Chapter 17.

Governments can promote trade by lowering tariffs and having little or no limits on imports, or they can restrict trade by raising tariffs or numerical goals for imports. When governments subsidize their own companies to

[10] See Chapter 2 in Walter Oleszek, *Congressional Procedures and the Policy Process*, 8th ed. (Washington, DC: CQ Press, 2010).

compensate them for perceived unfair competition from foreign companies, this can be seen as a trade restriction; it may not level the playing field but tips the balance in favor of domestic producers. Typically, governments of foreign countries retaliate against trade restrictions of their exports to the United States by raising their own trade barriers regarding American exports to their domestic markets.

Recall our discussion of the Founding in Chapter 2. One motivation for crafting and ratifying the Constitution was that the states competed against one another for trade with foreign countries. By lowering tariffs relative to the tariffs other states charged, a state could get an advantage and attract more foreign trade. Thus, the Founders decided that trade policies would be set at the national level; the Constitution mandated that the states could not set their own tariffs and limit trade between states or develop any formal trade policies on their own. Absent such an arrangement by the Constitution, if states set their own trade policies, they would all face a collective action problem, among other collective dilemmas. Better to have one common policy to solve the dilemmas.

Tariffs and other trade restrictions generally raise the prices of goods for consumers because they limit competition. That is, companies that face limited competition can raise their prices and still have consumers buy their goods, for lack of an alternative source. Sometimes tariffs and other trade restrictions are seen as necessary if foreign countries or foreign companies use unfair trading practices. But most often tariffs are used to curry favor with a particular constituency and are considered by economists to be bad public policy (at least bad for consumers and bad for economic efficiency).

The Constitution solved the dilemma among the states on trade policies, but collective dilemmas persisted and continue to persist mostly across industries and regions of the country. If Congress passes a tariff to protect steel manufacturers against foreign competition, this creates higher prices for industries that rely on steel for their products, and those prices get passed on to consumers in the form of higher prices. For example, automakers would then have to charge more for their cars because steel was more expensive than it would be if foreign competitors were allowed to compete to sell their steel to automakers. Similarly, the American automakers at one time lobbied and successfully convinced Congress to pass limits on the number of foreign automobiles that could be sold in the United States. This was a boon to American automakers, but most economists considered it bad for U.S. consumers. Each industry prefers to have its products protected against foreign competition, but everyone is better off with freer trade—low or no tariffs and no limits on imports—because then prices are set according to the free market, meaning that they come from supply and demand unfettered by political manipulation through trade policies.

Trade has been a contentious issue since America's founding. There has long been a tension between free-trade policies that promote growth and worries about externalities like unfair labor practices, loss of American jobs, and environmental damage.

An alternative view holds that foreign competition hurts American workers, because many foreign countries do not require their companies to have appropriate safety standards for their workers, or health standards for products, or other kinds of regulations that cause American companies to pay more costs to manufacture their products. There are many complaints by American interest groups that foreign governments subsidize their companies, giving them an unfair advantage. Companies given subsidies can charge lower prices and still stay in business. Perhaps, then, American companies go out of business because foreign competitors can undercut them on price. Thus, some unions and some companies pressure the government for trade restrictions against certain countries and companies, targeting the ones that perhaps can offer cheaper products to American consumers but violate principles of "fair trade."

It can be difficult to parse the validity of claims that interest groups make in favor of trade restrictions: Do they have legitimate concerns about the fairness of foreign competitors' trading practices, or are they simply trying to protect their own companies so they can charge higher prices? In each case, which view is correct is a political question whose solution is in the eye of the beholder. The most important fact about the politics of trade in the

American political system (that is, economic policy) as opposed to between countries (foreign policy) is that although most economists and observers agree with the principle that overall consumers and societies would be better off with free and fair trade, there are nonetheless strong incentives to argue for trade protection in response to unfair practices by the other side in foreign countries. Many industrial interest groups, both labor and business, lobby intensely to seek trade protection, and the U.S. government often listens—as do the governments in other countries—to its own interest groups.

In Comparison: Economic Policy

Like much of the rest of the industrialized democratic world, the United States has an economic system that is primarily capitalist but allows extensive government intervention in the economy. Some people refer to this system as *liberal capitalism*. Quite a few countries (such as Sweden or Denmark) lean more toward socialism than the United States, but only a handful (such as Cuba or North Korea) are fully Marxist in the sense that the government owns the vast majority of capital and sets prices for private goods. Even China, which still calls itself a communist country, has paradoxically adopted capitalist economic policies.

It was once fashionable to consider the United States exceptional in its economic policies and to distinguish it in this respect from other advanced industrial democracies. Since World War II, the U.S. government has indeed spent less money than the typical western European country on social welfare policies, nationalized health care, and public education, both on a per capita basis and as a percentage of **gross domestic product** (the total amount of goods and services produced in a year, usually abbreviated as GDP). But if we broaden our comparison to include democracies in Asia and Latin America, and base it on spending at all levels of government, then the United States does not seem so exceptional (Figure 15.7).

A more nuanced picture of how the economic policies of the United States compare to those of other countries emerges when other criteria are considered.

gross domestic product (GDP) The value of all the goods and services produced by an economy within its borders.

- As the most powerful country in the world in international affairs, especially military affairs, the United States spends far more on defense than any other country. In fact, the United States spends more on its military than the next 10 countries combined (see Chapter 17).
- In terms of the proportion of GDP that flows through government coffers in taxes, spending, and borrowing, the United States ranks near the middle

of all democracies. If we limit our comparison to advanced industrialized democracies, however, it ranks near the bottom, and its highest marginal tax rate is at the lower end of the spectrum (see Figure 15.3).

- Subnational (state and local) governments account for approximately 40 percent of all government spending in the United States. This is a much higher proportion than in most other advanced industrialized democracies, even federations such as Germany and Switzerland, which have relatively weak national governments. (Canada, however, resembles the United States in this regard.)

- The United States is considered to have one of the most reliable and stable currencies in the world. The U.S. dollar is widely used in developing countries as the currency of choice among the people, and many countries peg their currency's exchange rate to the dollar rather than other currencies. They have confidence in the dollar because the United States has never defaulted on its bonds or experienced a serious threat to its constitutional system since the mid-nineteenth century. Moreover, it has one of the most independent central banks in the world, offering assurance to investors that the government will not inflate the dollar for short-term political gain (see our discussion of inflation earlier).

- Compared to many other industrial democracies, the United States is more committed to free-trade policies and has more bilateral trade agreements with countries all over the world. As a result, the imports and exports that flow across American borders are largely unimpeded by high customs duties and tariffs.

- The debt the U.S. national government owes to borrowers is moderate in comparison with other countries. The U.S. debt (including government owned) is just over 100 percent of GDP. This amount is less than in some countries—such as Italy, where government debt is 132 percent of GDP— but higher than in more fiscally responsible countries like Australia, where it is 40 percent.

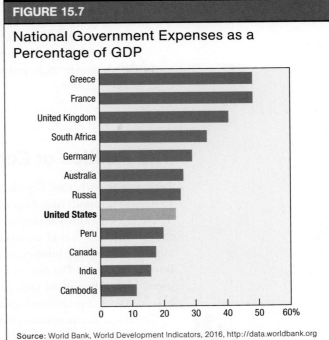

FIGURE 15.7

National Government Expenses as a Percentage of GDP

Source: World Bank, World Development Indicators, 2016, http://data.worldbank.org (accessed 11/11/16).

- The United States remains somewhat exceptional by virtue of the free-wheeling lobbying environment that exists in Washington, D.C., and in many state capitals (see Chapter 11). In many other countries, economic pressure groups operate less openly, and they focus less on specific legislative committees and more on governing parties than in the United States.

The Politics of Economic Policy Making

Let's now use what we have learned about economic policies and philosophies to deepen our understanding of economic policy making in the United States. There is a consensus among mainstream politicians in both major parties that the government should try to keep the economy within certain bounds, maintaining stability for business investment while preventing people from falling into dire poverty. No one in either party wants less growth, high unemployment, high inflation, or high government deficits, but they disagree on how to balance these concerns and relieve economic goals.

To return to our opening story, it was not inevitable that inequality that has been increasing since the 1970s would become a major political issue for presidential candidates in 2016. But economic issues are usually front and center in American political campaigns. As social scientists and politicians know, voters as a group weigh economic outcomes more heavily than any other factor when evaluating the performance of incumbent politicians. This is especially true when the economy is in recession or only weakly growing, but it is even true during times of growth. Many Americans for various reasons felt economically insecure even in 2018 during times of rapid growth.

Given the role of governments in economies around the world, in times of economic problems people expect the government to take action to improve matters. Financial traders, consumers, and private companies all have collective dilemmas that prevent them from working together to solve large-scale economic problems. Some economists, especially those advising Democrats, believe that a hands-off approach by the government is generally not feasible, while others, especially those advising Republicans, believe that a hands-off approach is precisely what is needed. In times of growth, when the topic of debate has been focused on inequality, the two parties disagree on whether the ways to improve the conditions of the poor and working class people include government investment in the economy or getting the government out of the economy and letting private business do the main work.

Between 2008 and 2011, the American government took actions that marked the largest government interventions to financial markets in world history. Yet they were not as massive or dramatic as they might appear. By

DATA EXPLORATION Income Inequality and Politics

Many people are concerned with growing economic inequality and its effect on politics and public policy in the United States. Scholars have focused on the wealthiest families and individuals, and many argue that their political influence has increased dramatically compared to other Americans. Is this true? If so, what are the consequences for American politics and policy?

Figure A shows income inequality over time. We see that the average income of the top 1 percent of Americans has grown much faster than the average income of the remaining 99 percent since the 1970s. The ratio of the average incomes of these two groups is similar now to what it was in the 1920s. Today, American families in the top 0.01 percent of income are especially wealthy, with annual incomes of $30 million or more. The share of the top 0.01 percent of income has grown somewhat in the past few decades, but the share of campaign contributions from that group has grown much more. As you can see in Figure B, the proportion of campaign contributions coming from the wealthiest 0.01 percent of Americans has increased rapidly, especially since 2000.

A. Income Inequality

Note: Shown is the ratio of the average income of the top 1 percent of income-earning families to the average income of the remaining 99 percent of income-earning families (includes capital gains).

Source: Emmanuel Saez and Thomas Piketty, "Table A4: Top Fractiles Income Levels (Excluding Capital Gains) in the United States (Adjusted for Price Inflation)," in *Income Inequality in the United States, June 2015,* http://eml.berkeley.edu/~saez/ (accessed 1/22/16).

B. Wealthiest Americans' Share of Campaign Contributions and Income

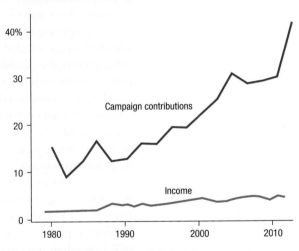

Source: Adam Bonica, Nolan McCarty, Keith T. Poole, and Howard Rosenthal, "Why Hasn't Democracy Slowed Rising Inequality?" *Journal of Economic Perspectives 27,* no. 3 (2013): 103–24.

Think About It

People across the ideological spectrum find the rising inequality in both incomes and in campaign giving worrisome. What consequences should we expect, knowing that the wealthiest 0.01 percent give 40 percent of all campaign contributions in the United States? Can a case be made that these two increasing trends reinforce each other—that is, each causes the other to increase? If so, why?

most measures, those interventions increased government involvement in the economy by no more than a few percentage points of GDP. Even with the major spending packages passed, the United States continued to lag far behind many other industrialized democracies in the size of government spending relative to the overall economy. Thereafter, the government retrenched somewhat and cut some spending, mostly because of intense pressure by House Republicans. The president and Congress together form fiscal policy, and cuts in spending in the 2010s resulted from intensive bargaining between the branches. Again, the overall role of the government in the economy was not changing all that much even with the budget cuts.

It would be simplistic to associate the U.S. government's current level of intervention in the economy with a leftist ideology or Democratic partisanship coming out of the Obama administration. The stimulus policies by Obama were initiated before he took office, at the tail end of Republican George W. Bush's administration. Bush, by reputation an economic conservative and averse to government intrusion on private markets, oversaw a massive government investment in bank stocks and huge infusions of government loans to keep banks afloat. That a Republican president would instigate these policies shows how serious people of all political stripes saw the crisis, and how the American people expected the government to steer the economy regardless of which party controlled the White House or Congress. Donald Trump, likewise, promised to bolster infrastructure spending but was unable to pass such policies even with a Republican majority in both houses of Congress.

Although some kind of government intervention is inevitable, especially during troubled economic times, the specific policies that governments pursue are harder to predict. Certain policies may be forced on politicians by necessity, but it is the configuration of American governmental institutions that determines *which* policies are chosen and to whom the benefits flow. These are not merely technical bureaucratic but deeply political decisions that spread costs and benefits differently across population groups. The partisan devils are in the economic details—which industries will suffer lost profits when regulations change, which government agencies and their clienteles will lose when government budgets are cut, and which interest groups will benefit from new programs.

The economic policies the government chooses are not always the ones that make the most sense from a purely economic standpoint. Some policies reflect the strong influence that certain economic interests and their lobbyists have over aspects of the budget or the regulatory regime. Sugar farmers, for instance, receive generous subsidies from the government and benefit from high tariffs on foreign imports. There is no way to explain this redistributive policy in terms of public goods. Sugar prices would almost certainly be lower for everyone if these subsidies and tariffs did not exist. Yet many farmers in politically sensitive states, such as Florida and Georgia, would lose part of their livelihoods if the policy were reversed. Politicians in Washington are keen to make their constituents happy, especially if they can protect jobs at the same time. Consumers of sugar, including companies that use sugar in their products, could learn a lesson from sugar farmers when it comes to applying political pressure on their members of Congress.

Industries are prepared to lobby whichever party is in power. Consider what happened when a few years ago the government discussed insuring deposits made into money market mutual funds in the same way it insures standard bank savings accounts. Realizing that this would give people incentives to move their money from bank accounts into investment accounts, the banking industry mobilized quickly, arguing that the policy would defeat the government's purpose of stabilizing the banks so they could lend more money to businesses. As a result, the government backed off the proposal.

Any president's economic policies reflect the political coalition that was put together to win votes for the winner nationwide in the previous election. Financial sectors that stand to benefit from government intervention have enough sway within the two party coalitions to pressure the national government to adopt certain kinds of policies. Many jobs in key industries reside in key "battleground" states in national elections.[11] It is not hard to see that a lot of what government does has redistributive consequences, and that political calculations strongly influence which way the resources flow.

As discussed in Chapter 1, conservative Republicans, including President Trump, continue to take stands against government spending, but Democrats continue to hold firm on certain fiscal priorities. Partisan and ideological conflict over the size of the government and the nature of the government's economic policies will continue to define the main fault lines in Washington.

FURTHER READING

★ = Included in *Readings in American Politics*, 5th ed.

Banerjee, Abhijit, and Esther Duflo, *Poor Economics: A Radical Rethinking of the Way to Fight Global Poverty* (New York: PublicAffairs, 2011). Two established economists analyze numerous studies indicating what makes anti-poverty programs work or fail.

Friedman, Milton, *Capitalism and Freedom* (1962; repr., Chicago: University of Chicago Press, 2002). A classic argument in favor of laissez-faire capitalism and monetarism (small government with careful control of the money supply).

[11] For an insightful and entertaining analysis of the winners and losers from the 2008 financial crisis, see Michael Lewis, *The Big Short: Inside the Doomsday Machine* (New York: W. W. Norton & Company, 2010).

Hibbs, Douglas, *The American Political Economy* (Cambridge, MA: Harvard University Press, 1987). A clear and thorough description of the link between partisan politics and economic policy making.

Keynes, John Maynard, *The General Theory of Employment, Interest, and Money*, 1935. A classic argument in favor of government intervention to keep unemployment levels low.

Lewis, Michael, *Boomerang: Travels in the New Third World* (New York: W. W. Norton, 2011). An engaging account of the global financial crisis.

Marx, Karl, *Capital: A Critique of Political Economy* (1867; repr., New York: Penguin Classics, 1993). A full explication of the Marxist doctrine.

Scheve, Kenneth, and David Stasavage, *The Submerged State: How Invisible Government Policies Undermine American Democracy* (Princeton, NJ: Princeton University Press, 2016). Scheve and Stasavage argue that taxes on the rich have tended to go up when many people feel that the government has been unequal in the treatment of different classes, favoring the rich over the poor.

Schumpeter, Joseph, *Capitalism, Socialism, and Democracy*, 3rd ed. (New York: Harper Perennial, 1962). A creative work of political economy, laying the foundation for future scholars and linking election outcomes to economic policy making.

KEY TERMS

capital (p. 575)

club good (p. 583)

common good (p. 583)

deflation (p. 594)

distributive policy (p. 586)

externalities (p. 585)

Federal Reserve Board (p. 594)

Federal Reserve System (p. 594)

fiscal policy (p. 597)

gross domestic product (GDP)
(p. 608)

inflation (p. 587)

laissez-faire (p. 575)

monetary policy (p. 593)

national debt (p. 602)

national deficit (p. 602)

private good (p. 583)

progressive tax (p. 600)

public good (p. 583)

redistributive policy (p. 586)

regressive tax (p. 600)

Abortion and federal funding for Planned Parenthood have proven to be some of the most divisive issues facing Americans today, with very vocal pro-life and pro-choice advocates on either side of the debate. This conflict has manifested itself in Congress in recent years, as several bills have been proposed—but none passed—to keep Planned Parenthood from receiving federal funds.

16

Social Policy

 Why are social policies so controversial?

T he U.S. House of Representatives in 2015 passed a bill called the Defund Planned Parenthood Act. The bill would have banned the nationwide organization Planned Parenthood, one of the largest providers of women's health care, from receiving federal funds for one year if the organization continued to offer abortion services. Later that year, the Senate passed the Restoring Americans' Healthcare Freedom Reconciliation Act, which essentially incorporated elements of the House bill and would have kept Planned Parenthood from receiving federal funds. The catalyst for this legislation was an undercover video released by an anti-abortion group that allegedly showed Planned Parenthood staff offering to sell aborted fetal tissue.

The video footage and the subsequent defunding attempts received substantial media attention. During the 2016 election campaigns, candidates from both parties for president and Congress weighed in, with Republicans typically voicing support for defunding Planned Parenthood and Democrats typically opposing defunding efforts. For its part, Planned Parenthood and its supporters claimed that the video footage was doctored.[1] They also stressed the wide range of women's health issues covered by Planned Parenthood and that federal funding accounts for one-third of its budget. The cuts would, therefore, damage women's health. Advocates for Planned Parenthood took to social media, using the hashtag #StandwithPP and "pinking out" profile pictures on Facebook to affirm support.

This was not the first time attempts were made to defund Planned Parenthood. A similar battle over funding occurred five years earlier when other compromising videos were released by antiabortion groups. Planned Parenthood receives about $450 million from the U.S. budget, a tiny fraction (0.0001%) of the over $4 trillion

[1] Planned Parenthood, "Statement from Eric Ferrero, Vice President of Communications, Planned Parenthood Federation of America," July 14, 2015, www.plannedparenthood.org/about-us/newsroom/press-releases/statement-from-planned -parenthood-on-new-undercover-video (accessed 1/4/16).

OUTLINE

- What Are Social Policies?

- Historical Perspective

- Major Areas of Social Policy

- Political Ideologies and Social Policies

- In Comparison: Social Policy

- Interest Groups, Parties, and Social Policy Making

- Explaining Political Outcomes

budget total. Thus, the issues at stake fundamentally are not about money but ideology. Defunding Planned Parenthood is emblematic of larger concerns: how to prioritize social issues, how to address them once prioritized, and how to fit them into larger values of society.

Yet, like with almost all social policies, money is not absent from the controversy. In the heat of the Planned Parenthood defunding dispute, Republican presidential candidate Jeb Bush said, "I'm not sure we need half a billion dollars for women's health issues, . . . [but] if you took, dollar for dollar, there are many extraordinary fine organizations, community health organizations, that exist, federally sponsored organizations, to provide quality care for women on a variety of health issues."[2] He was criticized for implying that women's health is something that does not merit half a billion dollars. Although Bush later said he misspoke,[3] his initial remarks reflect the fact that addressing social issues costs money.

Abortion politics is always controversial, but the situation was also about government-provided health care. For many decades, and especially since the Affordable Care Act (also known as Obamacare) was passed in 2010, the role of government in health care provision has been at the forefront of political battles in Washington. In fact, the role of government in many areas of everyday life—housing, safety, education, poverty relief—has been contentious for over a hundred years. What is it about social policies that leads to divisive and prolonged political battles?

[2] Michael Barbaro, "Jeb Bush Causes a Stir on Women's Health Issues," *New York Times*, August 4, 2015, www.nytimes.com/politics/first-draft/2015/08/04/jeb-bush-suggests-womens-health-issues-are-overfunded/ (accessed 1/6/16).

[3] Jeb 2016, Inc., "Jeb Bush Statement on Federal Funding for Planned Parenthood," August 4, 2015, https://jeb2016.com/statement-federal-funding-planned-parenthood/?lang=en (accessed 1/6/16).

What Are Social Policies?

In Chapter 15, we learned about the role of the government in guiding the economy to stabilize prices and interest rates, and to ensure a steady supply of jobs, goods, and currency. We also learned about taxing and spending by governments. We now analyze social policies, which account for some of the largest spending items in budgets at every level in the United States. **Social policies** can be defined as government actions to provide a basic income level for certain categories of people, and to ensure that people are safe, educated, fed, housed, and healthy. These policies are intended to bring about an orderly, just society, where "order" and "justice" are more broadly conceived than simple economic efficiency and smooth commercial transactions. In other words, these policies are not explicitly justified by their implications for the economy.[4]

Recall that pure public goods can be enjoyed by people regardless of whether they pay for the goods. From one perspective, many social policies can be considered public goods, such as the existence of public schools, police forces for crime prevention, social insurance, and health care clinics. These policies provide private benefits to individuals—an education or a doctor's visit, for instance—but they also are good for society as a whole. Living in a society with educated, safe, and healthy people who are reasonably taken care of benefits everyone, even if any given set of people did not contribute much to paying for these goods. Social policies can provide public goods to the extent that everyone benefits from having them in place if they need them, even if the *direct* benefits are not targeted at everyone.

There are important economic aspects to social policies. These policies often provide direct services to people who are especially vulnerable to the vagaries of the free-market economy. Not everyone in the United States has access to jobs or enough money to clothe, feed, house, and educate themselves. Many social policies, such as Social Security for the aged, government-funded housing and health care, and basic income insurance for the poor, are designed to mitigate the sometimes harsh effects of capitalism.

In Chapter 15, we learned that redistributive policies—those that provide one group of people with benefits that are paid for by another group—are generally among the most controversial. The people who pay for redistributive policies that provide goods for others often do not favor these kinds of policies. (Whether the existence of redistributive policies can be considered a public good is itself a matter of ideological dispute, as we will discuss later

social policy Government actions intended to provide a basic level of assistance with income, safety, education, housing, and health care for certain categories of people at risk.

---

[4] The terminology here can be confusing given what is often referred to as "social issues" in contemporary political discourse in the mass media and in electoral campaigns. Sometimes, people refer to social issues when speaking or writing about "culture war" controversies over reproductive rights, gun control, religious freedom, and cultural matters like gay and transgender rights. Those issues, and others like them, are treated in depth in Chapter 4 on civil rights and liberties.

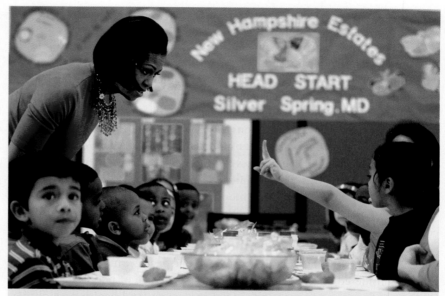

Many social policies—such as the Head Start program that provides education, health, and nutrition services to children from low-income families—are based on the belief that it benefits the country as a whole when people are healthy, educated, and safe. Here, former First Lady Michelle Obama visits students in a Head Start program in Maryland.

in this chapter.) Social policies typically blend distributive (benefiting nearly everyone) and redistributive (benefiting specific groups) characteristics. Education programs, for instance, are intended to help all children; it benefits society as a whole to have all children educated, so in this respect the policy is distributive. But the federal government, through certain educational programs like Head Start and free school lunch programs, focuses on low-income children who are especially at risk academically. Thus, education policy is also redistributive and has aspects not only of private goods but also of private goods targeted at the poor.

Similarly, health care policies that manage flu epidemics, such as through vaccines or public education campaigns about infection, are primarily distributive in the sense that nearly everyone benefits. However, programs specifically designed to go into poor sections of inner cities and give free flu vaccines are redistributive because specific urban dwellers reap most of the benefits while all taxpayers bear the costs.

Redistribution is the primary function of some social policies. The **Temporary Assistance for Needy Families (TANF)** program, for example, provides federally funded cash assistance to families below a certain income level who reside in "suitable homes." This is the type of purely redistributive benefit that people sometimes refer to as "welfare," and as we would expect, the program is controversial. Determining the budget for antipoverty pro-

Temporary Assistance for Needy Families (TANF) A federal government program that provides temporary income assistance to the poor.

grams like TANF and implementing those programs in each state are some of the most controversial and divisively partisan of all government actions at any level in the United States. We will take up the debate over redistributive policies later in this chapter.

Historical Perspective

Before the twentieth century, the few social policies that existed were enacted almost entirely at the state and local levels. The national government in the nineteenth century played virtually no role in poverty relief, education, and crime prevention, areas that states had been involved in from the Founding.

Social Policies at the State and Local Levels

By modern standards, state and local programs in the nineteenth century were small and sporadic. Many states had limited programs for poverty relief, including government support for almshouses, food distribution centers, and pensions for mothers and veterans. These state- and city-level policies were often implemented in close cooperation with private charitable organizations.

In two social policy areas, education and crime prevention, states have always been and continue to be primarily responsible for financing and implementing programs. States have been heavily involved in public education since it was first promoted as a public good by people like Horace Mann, a member of Congress from Massachusetts and an influential proponent of education reform in the early nineteenth century. By the 1850s, many states mandated that local communities provide compulsory education for all children up to a certain age. States did not themselves have much financial or bureaucratic capacity to assist local communities, but they did enforce laws requiring the establishment of schools, and there were credible state-level education standards for literacy, mathematics, writing, and learning of classic works of literature.

Responsibility for public safety (as distinct from national defense) has always been shared by the states and localities; this includes the training, staffing, and oversight of police forces. More generally, maintaining the peace—which includes general crime control, prosecutions, the housing of prisoners, and surveillance of criminal organizations—has been the province of the states for much of American history.

As we learned in Chapter 4, the states have protected citizens from each other and from governments with varying degrees of effectiveness. The protection or violation of civil rights and liberties is related to the nature of state social policies. During the nineteenth century, governments permitted laws

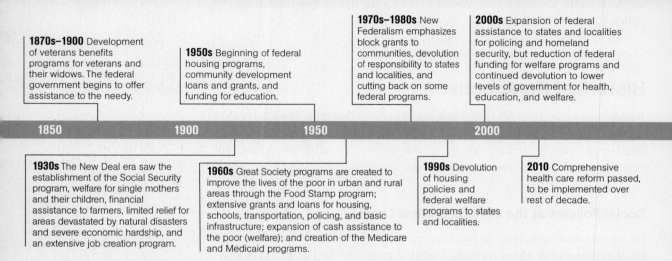

1870s–1900 Development of veterans benefits programs for veterans and their widows. The federal government begins to offer assistance to the needy.

1950s Beginning of federal housing programs, community development loans and grants, and funding for education.

1970s–1980s New Federalism emphasizes block grants to communities, devolution of responsibility to states and localities, and cutting back on some federal programs.

2000s Expansion of federal assistance to states and localities for policing and homeland security, but reduction of federal funding for welfare programs and continued devolution to lower levels of government for health, education, and welfare.

1850   1900   1950   2000

1930s The New Deal era saw the establishment of the Social Security program, welfare for single mothers and their children, financial assistance to farmers, limited relief for areas devastated by natural disasters and severe economic hardship, and an extensive job creation program.

1960s Great Society programs are created to improve the lives of the poor in urban and rural areas through the Food Stamp program; extensive grants and loans for housing, schools, transportation, policing, and basic infrastructure; expansion of cash assistance to the poor (welfare); and creation of the Medicare and Medicaid programs.

1990s Devolution of housing policies and federal welfare programs to states and localities.

2010 Comprehensive health care reform passed, to be implemented over rest of decade.

and practices that today seem archaic and cruel. Although this has much to do with our changing concepts of civil rights and liberties, it also reflects the ways in which states used social policies to create an orderly society. Southern states allowed whites to enslave blacks until the 1860s and afforded slaves no benefits from social policies. Catholics, atheists, and Jews could not teach in public schools in some states for many decades. There were no provisions for divorce in many states, and women could be jailed for cheating on their husbands while men were free to have dalliances. The police forces in many states routinely mistreated immigrants, blacks, Chinese, and accused criminals. States were often directly involved in pervasive violations of rights and liberties, including inequalities in the implementation of social policies. Many of these practices continued into the twentieth century. Until the 1960s, southern states continued to enforce state laws treating blacks differently from whites in the legal, educational, and political systems. In some states, homosexual sodomy was a crime until 2003, when the Supreme Court ruled such bans unconstitutional.[5]

Partly because of changes in federal law and oversight of state actions related to the Fifth and Fourteenth Amendments, and partly because of changes

[5] See *Lawrence v. Texas*, 539 U.S. 558 (2003).

in the mores of modern societies generally, states today protect the constitutional rights of citizens better—and provide social policy benefits more equitably across population groups—than in the past. Yet state laws still vary with regard to what is considered illegal and what is worthy of attention by state and county prosecutors. Definitions of murder, manslaughter, rape, robbery, and burglary can vary slightly, but more dramatic differences exist across states in liquor and drug laws, privacy protections, the death penalty, body cameras on police, marriage laws, and general behavioral proscriptions. In some places, spitting on the sidewalk is a crime; in others, it is illegal to wear pants too low down on the buttocks. As these examples illustrate, the states are their own realms when it comes to day-to-day keeping of an orderly society. States have authority over many areas of social policy, and they differ in their approaches to such highly contested issues as the legality of medical marijuana, the use of bathrooms by transgender persons, or the death penalty. These issues not only involve civil rights and liberties but also relate to state-level social policies having to do with medical care, sex/gender relations, and criminal justice.

In the nineteenth century, the national government was less involved in addressing social problems than it is today. For example, aid to the needy was often provided by churches or other private groups. In this image, bread is distributed to poor children by the Ladies Mission in New York City, 1871.

The Growing Role of the National Government

The national government did play a small role in the nineteenth century in certain key areas of social policy, such as higher education. The states have generally run their own state-level universities and colleges. But beginning in the nineteenth century, the national government granted states federally owned land for the purpose of setting up colleges and research stations to develop new agricultural and mining techniques. These "land grant" universities were instrumental in giving the United States the most extensive system of higher education in the world. Although the national government's role was mostly passive in the beginning (it merely granted federal land to the states), by the 1880s the states could receive financial support from the national government for agricultural research. Some of today's largest and most prestigious universities and colleges were established as land-grant institutions, including Massachusetts Institute of Technology (MIT), Cornell, Michigan State University, the Ohio State University, the University of Hawaii, the University of Illinois at Urbana–Champaign, and Kansas State University.

Poverty relief is another area in which the national government's involvement in the nineteenth century was selective and incremental. Some historians date the beginning of the national government's involvement in poverty policy that affected people directly (as opposed to working through the states) to the provision of veterans' benefits following the Civil War. These included benefits to the widows and children of fallen soldiers. The national government gradually took on this role, relieving the states of this responsibility.[6]

In the early twentieth century, the U.S. government, like the governments of many European countries, responded to strong labor movements and developed general policies that provided a social safety net for people who were out of work, disabled, aged, or sick. The national government's role in social policy grew dramatically in the 1930s, and again in the 1960s. The New Deal programs that solidified a large national presence in social policy were part of a trend across North America and Europe to develop what has been called a **welfare state**.[7] Until the 1930s, educating children, helping the poor and aged, protecting the environment, and preventing crime were not part of what most people expected the national government to do. If these activities were properly the concerns of government at all (and many did not believe that they were), they fell within the purview of states and localities. The Great Society, begun under the presidential administration of Lyndon Johnson (1963–69), had as its main goal the elimination of poverty, and it entailed scores of new federal programs in cooperation with states and cities seeking to improve the lives of rural and urban poor people. Its lasting policy legacies include the Medicare program and huge expansions in the Social Security program.

As we know from previous chapters, by the latter half of the twentieth century social programs, especially insurance programs for the aged, accounted for huge portions of the national budget. A major dynamic in the nationalization of the American political system, discussed in detail in Chapter 3, was the creation and implementation of national social programs. Figure 16.1 shows federal and state governments' increased spending on social insurance and health care since the 1930s. In all major areas of social policy (which we examine in the next sections), the national government set up new agencies or cabinet-level departments, spent billions of dollars, and imposed an enormous volume of new regulations on state and local governments. Today, the national government is the major provider of social insurance, health care, and civil rights protection. The states still play a role in these policy areas, but mostly at the direction of, or with funding from, the national government.

welfare state The programs of the government devoted to social policies.

---

[6] Theda Skocpol, *Protecting Soldiers and Mothers: The Political Origins of Social Policy in the United States* (Cambridge, MA: Belknap Press, 1995).

[7] In most other countries, the term *welfare state* does not have the negative connotation that *welfare* tends to have in American political discourse. It refers to the commitments by governments to provide basic social security, poverty relief, and unemployment insurance. It may also include guarantees of food, health care, and housing.

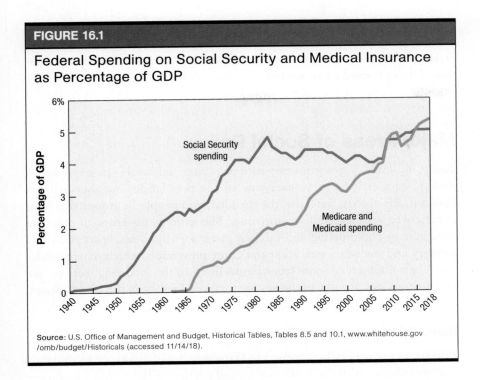

FIGURE 16.1

Federal Spending on Social Security and Medical Insurance as Percentage of GDP

Source: U.S. Office of Management and Budget, Historical Tables, Tables 8.5 and 10.1, www.whitehouse.gov /omb/budget/Historicals (accessed 11/14/18).

Furthermore, the national government plays a larger role than ever before in what the states do to keep the order. It closely monitors how states protect civil rights and liberties, for example, and is deeply involved in policies to fight terrorism and organized crime.

The national government's role in social policies has not increased consistently. Figure 16.1 shows growth in dollars, but as a percentage of GDP (value of all the goods and services produced by an economy within its borders), growth in spending on social programs slowed after the early 1980s. This slowdown was a result of a backlash against generous social policies, although the total amount of spending continued to increase modestly. Ronald Reagan, first as a presidential candidate and then as president, focused public attention on waste and abuse in social programs and highlighted their expense. He pushed budget cuts through Congress that decimated some programs, especially in housing and urban development, and reduced spending in many other programs.[8] There has been renewed pressure to cut back on social

[8] Paul Pierson, *Dismantling the Welfare State? Reagan, Thatcher, and the Politics of Retrenchment* (New York: Cambridge University Press, 1994).

programs since the Republican surge in the 2010 elections for Congress.[9] Recent federal budgets, as a result of a Republican-controlled House and Senate and the Republican-controlled White House, generally reflect a continued drive toward more austerity.

Major Areas of Social Policy

Today, all levels of government—national, state, and local—are expected to provide certain benefits to everyone in the population, but especially to children, the elderly, veterans, the disabled, and people in groups that have experienced widespread discrimination. The national government plays the main role in coordinating and funding many social policies, apart from elementary and secondary education and crime prevention, which remain under state control subject to some federal guidelines. In the following sections, we take a closer look at some of the key areas of social policy in the United States.

Basic Provisions for the Poor

Americans are generally surprised to learn that direct assistance to the poor (not including health care) takes up a small portion of the national budget—never more than 3 percent historically. In the United States, we usually refer to such assistance as welfare. Some would argue that health care should be included in measures of spending to combat poverty. Including Medicaid (government-funded health insurance for the poor), the portion of the budget allocated to poverty relief has remained at approximately 10 percent in recent decades.

means-tested program A government policy that applies to people based on whether they qualify according to a quantitative measure, such as income level.

Supplemental Nutritional Assistance Program (SNAP) A federal government program that provides electronic debit cards for poor people to buy food (formerly known as the Food Stamp program).

Medicaid and other poverty relief programs are means tested. A **means-tested program** has an income threshold for eligibility—that is, people qualify for benefits only if they earn less than a certain amount. Besides Medicaid, the key national-level poverty programs are the Temporary Assistance for Needy Families (TANF), the Earned Income Tax Credit (EITC), and the **Supplemental Nutritional Assistance Program (SNAP)**.

Federal welfare began in earnest during the New Deal era and involved cash payments to families living below the poverty line as defined by the federal government. Starting in 1997, as part of an overhaul of welfare, the federal government made TANF cash assistance "temporary" in the sense that cash payments are made for a limited time—typically five years maximum, but states can alter that length in some circumstances. After that time, needy families must find other means of support. TANF works as block grants given to the states.

[9] Lori Montgomery, "Republicans Map Out Their Agenda of Less," *Washington Post*, November 6, 2010.

States have discretion within limits on how the funds can be spent to alleviate poverty and promote the welfare of children. States are supposed to spend the funds on families with children or on programs to reduce nonmarital childbearing and promote two-parent families.

Under the EITC, individuals or couples (with children living at home) who earn less than a certain amount of income receive tax credits toward their tax bill. This program greatly reduces the tax burden on low-income families; some pay no income taxes at all. The amount of the tax credit depends on formulas that take into account the number of children in the household and the family's income level. The EITC program costs the U.S. Treasury approximately $70 billion a year and is one of the most important national antipoverty policies in the United States. Several states have their own versions of the EITC as well.

SNAP is administered by the U.S. Department of Agriculture. It provides electronic debit cards that people living near or below the poverty line can use in grocery stores and food banks to buy basic food items. (Before 2008, recipients used paper stamps—thus the original name of the program, food stamps.) Various forms of food stamps began circulating in the 1930s, but the program did not become nationwide until the early 1960s. In recent years, restrictions have been placed on the kinds of foods the poor can buy through the program, with an emphasis on healthier foods.

The origins and recent politics of the SNAP program are an interesting example of how political coalitions involving diverse groups can lead to major policy changes. Advocates for the poor and for children teamed up with advocates for farming interests in the early 1960s to create a program that would enable food producers to sell more of their products and feed the neediest people in the country. Government directly subsidizes the poor in their attempts to eat nutritious food and indirectly subsidizes the food industry by enabling people to buy more products. In effect, the program raises income for farmers and other food producers by increasing demand for agricultural products. The association between poverty relief through SNAP and agricultural subsidies has frayed in recent years. In the 2010s, the federal government cut the budget for SNAP while maintaining robust agricultural subsidies. For instance, a major agricultural bill passed in 2014 cut $8 billion from SNAP per year but at the same time reorganized and increased agricultural subsidies to the total amount of $1 trillion over four years.

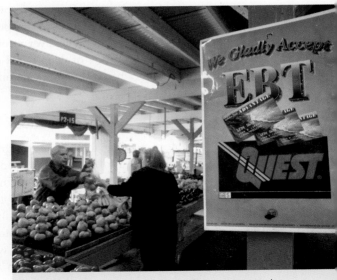

SNAP, formerly known as the Food Stamp program, is one way the federal government provides help for low-income Americans. Recipients can use their SNAP EBT card to purchase food, using up to a certain dollar value every month.

Despite the relatively small percentage of the federal budget devoted to poverty relief, few government programs have been as controversial as those involving direct assistance for the poor. The controversy stems, first, from basic differences in political ideologies. Recall our discussion in Chapter 15 of how ideologies affect attitudes toward redistributive policies. Supporters of generous welfare programs mostly justify the policies out of a basic moral conviction that society should help those in need. Others feel strongly that government intervention to redistribute goods leads to economic inefficiencies and is ultimately ineffective. They contend that overly generous programs cause people to lose their incentives to work and encourage them to become dependent on the government. Some people distinguish between "deserving" and "undeserving" poor, but there is no consensus about what these terms mean. Is someone who suffers from an alcohol addiction deserving of aid? Or what about a mother who cannot work because she has to stay home to care for her children?

A second source of controversy about poverty relief has to do with the correlation between race and poverty levels. In the United States, debates over the wisdom, ethics, or practicality of direct assistance to the poor have often taken on racial overtones. Research indicates that many whites view antipoverty programs negatively because they perceive them as disproportionately benefiting members of racial minorities, who are on average poorer than white Americans.[10] Several studies have shown that when people learn that most recipients of government aid are in fact white, a substantial portion of whites think more positively of these programs. Such attitudes muddy the waters whenever reforms of poverty programs are proposed. The historical legacy of deep racial divisions and resentment has complicated and exacerbated the political conflict that surrounds the issue of "welfare."

Social Insurance

Social insurance programs are intended to provide benefits to people based on a formula determined mostly from the contributions they made previously. These benefits are financed through money accumulated in "trust funds," which are created by law to be separate from general government cash holdings and revenues.

Social Security A federal government program that provides basic income assistance to retired elderly people and the disabled.

The largest and most politically secure of all social policies is the **Social Security** program, which provides cash income to all elderly and retired people over a certain age (usually 67, although the limit varies), as well as to many disabled people. The program was created in the 1930s to help alleviate the crushing poverty of those who were disabled or too old to work and

[10] Martin Gilens, *Why Americans Hate Welfare: Race, Media, and the Politics of Antipoverty Policy* (Chicago: University of Chicago Press, 1999).

did not have younger family members to support them. In the United States, as in all advanced industrial democracies, social security programs for the elderly are popular and relatively generous. They have formed the basis of the modern welfare state since the early twentieth century.

Levels of benefits from Social Security in the United States are partly determined by how much income an individual's family earned before retiring. Social Security benefits are funded by a payroll tax paid by both workers and employers. These payroll taxes are paid as a flat percentage of a person's income regardless of income level, and they are paid half by the employee and half by the employer. Income someone earns above a certain amount ($128,400 in 2018) is not subject to Social Security payroll tax. The program, however, is not means tested, and all elderly people receive a certain minimum benefit regardless of their work history. Put another way, Social Security is universal in the sense that everyone over a certain age is eligible for benefits. The program currently accounts for 24 percent of the national budget, which translates into $1.05 trillion in the 2019 budget.[11]

Social Security has been called the "third rail" of American politics because it is dangerous to touch (as is the case with electrified third rails on some railroads). Politicians who try to reform the Social Security system—by making it more equitable, taxing benefits, or reducing payments to certain beneficiaries— can put their careers at risk. Largely because Social Security is universal, and the benefits are understood to have been earned through payroll taxes throughout a person's employment lifetime, the program enjoys widespread support that cuts across party and generational lines. Not only the elderly (who, as we saw in Chapter 10, vote in very high numbers) but also young people support Social Security because it provides income for their parents and grandparents, and it will also provide income for them in the future.

Recently, many Americans have worried that the Social Security program is headed toward insolvency and will no longer exist when today's young people grow old. According to recent estimates by the Social Security Administration, the program under existing levels of taxes and payments will have trust funds that remain solvent until 2033, after which it may be unable to pay out the promised benefits. This position is controversial; scholars have questioned the methods used by the government to arrive at the year 2033, claiming that the fund will run out well before that.[12] Regardless of who ends up being right about the health of the fund, given the popularity of the program, adjustments likely will be made to ensure its survival—for example, by having working people pay more in taxes to support the system.

[11] U.S. Office of Management and Budget, "Budget of the U.S. Government, Fiscal Year 2017," www .whitehouse.gov/omb/budget (accessed 11/15/16).

[12] Konstantin Kashin, Gary King, and Samir Soneji, "Explaining Systematic Bias and Nontransparency in U.S. Social Security Administration Forecasts," *Political Analysis* 3, no. 23 (2015): 336–62.

Another key form of social insurance involves payments to people who are unemployed. These unemployment insurance programs are jointly funded and regulated by the states and the national government. They are paid for by contributions made by employers as a percentage of each employee's wages up to a set level. The federal government, for instance, in 2019 collects 6 percent of the first $7,000 in every employee's wages from employers and devotes that to the trust fund used for unemployment benefits. States also collect some funds from employers in addition to the federal program. Benefits given to individuals when they become unemployed through no fault of their own are the combined amounts from federal and state. These unemployment cash benefits are given only for a set period, and they are not intended to replace wages at their former levels but rather to provide subsistence for living. Recipients must be actively looking for work to qualify.

Education

Most primary and secondary education in the United States is funded and implemented at the state and local levels. In most other countries, national governments play a much larger role in education policy. This is one area in which American-style decentralized federalism is alive and well.[13]

American local school districts hold elections for their school boards or councils, which make policy decisions for the schools. States typically mandate curricular standards, numbers of school days and hours of instruction, and teacher certification. The national government historically has not interfered much with local control of education. As a result, there is tremendous variation across school districts, and across states, in how well public schools are funded and how successful they are at educating children. Education is one of the major areas of inequality in American society. Some wealthy school districts spend three or four times as much as poorer districts do in educating each child.

There have been some national-level regulations and programs in recent decades. The U.S. Department of Education was detached from the former Department of Health, Education and Welfare (established in 1953) and made a separate cabinet-level department in 1980. It has numerous programs in the areas of teacher training, grants to states and schools for curricular initiatives, and assistance in infrastructure improvements. The department has taken the lead on a variety of literacy and school lunch programs (in collaboration with the Department of Agriculture), many of which provide the states with funding to target poor children and children of immigrants.

In 2001, Congress passed the controversial No Child Left Behind Act, which mandated that states grade public schools on the basis of student achieve-

[13] Jennifer L. Hochschild and Nathan Scovronick, *The American Dream and the Public Schools* (New York: Oxford University Press, 2004).

ment and allocate funds accordingly. In extreme cases, schools can be closed for failing to improve student achievement. The national-level policies that followed passage of the act were contentious among educators and the general public, and by 2015, all national-level aspects of the program were eliminated by various legislative actions.[14] States are now free to enact elements of the policies.

Partly as a replacement to the defunct No Child Left Behind, groups of state governors and state educational officials have promoted Common Core standards, suggestions for all states to adopt as part of their educational curriculum. The Common Core provides guidelines for learning goals in English language arts and mathematics for K-12 students. The impetus behind the Common Core has also been divisive and has sparked controversy, especially within the Republican Party.

The controversy over the Common Core raises difficult questions about federalism, indicating that the states themselves face some of the same federalism issues as the federal government. Which level of government should decide school curriculums? Some conservatives have promoted the Common Core heavily because the standards arose from outside the government among educational professionals while others have claimed that they are "federal" wolves in sheep's clothing—another attempt by national level groups (in this case, organizations of educators) to impose uniform standards on the states and on local school districts. In truth, the Common Core is simply a set of suggestions, not mandates, by the federal government. The controversies end up being played out at the state level in discussions over whether states should adopt them or not and impose them on local school districts.

Some national policy programs have been those providing student loans and grants for college and graduate school. The government for a long time guaranteed loans that banks and other lending institutions made to college students, but in 2010 the federal government took over the lending task and now makes the loans to students through the Federal Direct Student Loan Program. In addition, students from relatively low income families can earn Pell Grants and Supplemental Education Opportunity Grants (up to $10,095 in total across both grant programs in 2019). These loans and grants have the effect of redistributing wealth to students and their families from other taxpayers, who foot the bill for the grants and for the loans when students default.[15]

Health Care

The national government became directly involved in health care provision during the Progressive Era in the early twentieth century, when it began to

[14] Bill Swindell, "States Eager to Retake Lead in School Policy," *Congressional Quarterly* (February 28, 2005): 492–93.

[15] See also the discussion of school voucher programs in Chapter 7.

protect consumers from badly produced or bogus products that could harm health. In that era, the Department of Agriculture began to inspect and grade meat products, and the Food and Drug Administration (FDA) started to license drugs and evaluate the safety of cosmetics. In the 1940s and 1950s, national programs were instrumental in building hospitals in all parts of the country, especially in rural areas.

But it was not until the 1960s that health care became a major priority as reflected in the federal budget. Two areas stand out: research and health insurance. The national government, in establishing the National Institutes of Health (NIH), became the major funder of medical research, a priority that continues to this day. In 2019, the NIH budget for research grants was approximately $38.3 billion. This compares to the $7.47 billion that the government allocated to the National Science Foundation to fund all of its basic science programs combined.

Medicare A federal government program that provides basic health care insurance to the elderly.

Medicaid A government program, cofunded by the federal government and state governments, that provides basic health insurance to the poor.

Medicare and **Medicaid**, two large, complex programs that are formally part of Social Security legislation, were begun in 1965 following acrimonious debate in Congress that reflected conflicts among the various interest groups concerned with health care. These same fundamental conflicts persist today. Doctors, nurses, and other providers; hospitals; insurance companies; pharmaceutical companies; and advocates for consumers of health care all have competing interests to advocate and protect. As a result, they often differ over the appropriate role of government and the right way to spend money on health care.

Together, Medicare and Medicaid take up a huge portion of the national budget. Medicare provides guaranteed health insurance for all Americans over the age of 65; in 2018, its total costs were $583 billion, approximately 14 percent of the federal budget. Medicaid, as discussed previously, is a means-tested program of health insurance for all Americans below a certain income level, with special assistance for children of poor families. Responsibility for Medicaid is shared by the states and the national government. States vary in the generosity of their Medicaid coverage, but the national government mandates minimum levels of coverage. The program's total costs by the national government and the states in 2017 were estimated to be $577 billion (the federal government paid $355 billion of that total).

Under both Medicare and Medicaid, the government reimburses health care providers for specific services to the elderly, children, and the poor. Furthermore, portions of both programs are operated in close cooperation with private insurance companies. For instance, the elderly can buy supplemental Medicare insurance that is a mixture of public and private insurance regulated by the government.

People across the political spectrum in the United States believe that the health care system in the United States is in trouble. There are two main problems: overall costs are rising much faster than the rate of inflation every year, and health care is poorly apportioned—those who need health care most often do not get quality care. A long-running problem has been the relatively large percentage of Americans without health insurance. When uninsured, people get their health care, if at all, from a variety of sources; but the treatment they receive is relatively expensive, inefficiently administered, and of lower quality than that received by people with insurance. The Affordable Care Act (ACA) targeted this problem specifically, and by 2018 had already reduced the number of uninsured by around 20 million. It was projected to reduce the number of people without health insurance from 45 million in 2012 to less than 18 million by 2023.[16] The Trump administration chipped away at aspects of the ACA, but it was still in place in 2019.

The cost of health care makes up a huge proportion of the U.S. economy—by some measures, 16 percent of GDP, which is higher than in most other countries. Experts disagree about the reasons for the high cost of health care in the United States. One basic issue for reformers is how the United States can rein in its health care costs without sacrificing the quality of care (and in certain areas, improving care). This may sound like a technical question for experts and number crunchers, but answers quickly revert to positions that reflect political ideologies, as we will discuss in more detail later in this chapter.

Two factors are important to note at this point. First, it is typical for western European countries, and for many other countries around the world, to have universal health care coverage provided by the government. Second, the national government in the United States, in conjunction with the states, is in fact the largest provider of health insurance in the country due to the size and reach of the Medicare program. That said, in comparison with other advanced industrial democracies, the American medical system is much more privatized. The government does not mandate the prices of procedures, the salaries of medical professionals, or the kinds of procedures that people can have.

Although the government does not *mandate* prices, the national government does affect how health care is provided in many ways; and under the ACA, those effects became more profound. As an example, the government reimburses doctors and hospitals at a fixed rate for procedures or medicines given to people on Medicare (that is, the elderly). That reimbursement rate is important in determining, indirectly, how much doctors and hospitals charge for those procedures, and the prices that pharmaceutical companies charge for medicines, for people who are not on Medicare. These prices largely determine the costs of health care all over the country, even in transactions involving people enrolled in private insurance.

---

[16] Congressional Budget Office, http://cbo.gov/publication/43900 (accessed 8/5/13).

The Collective Dilemma

There are deep, persistent inequalities in the quality of America's schools. What causes this inequality?

Interests

Society benefits when children receive quality education. Employers want an educated workforce to have well-trained and knowledgeable employees. Educated citizens make better choices in civic and private life. Yet, while there is broad consensus that quality education is important, interests diverge when it comes to allocating resources and deciding how to achieve the best schools. Parents, in particular, are most concerned with education of their *own* children. Those with high relative income and wealth can pay more in local taxes to bolster the quality of local schools, but they may not want to pay even higher taxes to support schools in less affluent neighboring communities. Those with low relative income and wealth cannot afford to live in communities with top quality schools and want funding from elsewhere—the state or the federal government—to equalize the quality of schools across districts. Teachers, meanwhile, want robust salaries and benefits. If they currently have high relative salaries, they do not want to see those salaries and benefits reduced to pay for equality across all districts. If they have lower than average salaries, they want the government to make pay more equitable across districts. Moreover, people without children and people who send their children to private schools generally want low local taxes and less spending on public education.

Institutions

In the United States, tradition and legal standing of local control of schools has a major impact on the inequality in education. Section 9527 of the Elementary and Secondary Education Act of 1965 codifies this tradition, prohibiting the Department of Education from endorsing or sanctioning a curriculum to be implemented in schools. It also forbids any claim requiring

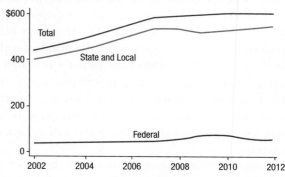

Revenues for Public Elementary and Secondary Schools, 2002–12 (in billions)

Source: National Center for Education Statistics, *Digest of Education Statistics 2015*, Table 235.10, http://nces.ed.gov/programs/digest/d15/tables/dt15_235.10.asp (accessed 6/20/16).

states to submit their curricula for federal approval.[a] This tradition of local control is manifest most clearly in the general opposition to centralized control. For example, in the Republican presidential primaries in 2016, several candidates, including at one point Donald Trump, pledged to abolish the U.S. Department of Education.[b] This antipathy toward federal control of education is reflected in spending. As the figure above shows, federal funds account for a small portion of public elementary and secondary schools.

Indeed, local governments play a major role in public education in the United States. Communities elect their own school boards and local property taxes typically pay for the schools, including administrative and teacher salaries, building maintenance, and supplies. Not surprisingly, wealthier areas can generate more property tax revenue to fund their schools, which places residents in these areas at an advantage.

Inequality in Public Education: Roots and Reforms

Outcomes

Differences in spending per pupil has been thought to be a key measure of disparities in education. Consider the table on the right, which contains data on spending per pupil in three Ohio school districts. In Parma, Ohio spent $7,858 per pupil on classroom instruction ($10,709 per pupil in total spending); and in Beachwood, a nearby district, $11,026 per pupil on classroom instruction ($16,809 per pupil in total spending). These two cities, both suburbs of Cleveland, are only about 15 miles apart, but there are significant differences in spending per pupil as well as in achievement indicators, with Beachwood outperforming Parma.[c] Equal spending, however, may not be sufficient or even an effective way to reduce educational inequalities; Avon Local also outperformed Parma on achievement indicators despite spending less per pupil than Parma. These data on spending per pupil reflects a larger truth: educational success and inequality across schools are multifaceted, and while school resources play a role in shaping education inequality, it is difficult to know how resources should be allocated to achieve the best outcome.

Given the localized nature of education in the United States, it is difficult for federal programs to fix inequalities. Consider, for instance, Race to the Top, one of Obama's education policies, which provided grants to states willing to adopt certain standards; adoption of these standards were voluntary. Although the federal government was able to give states incentives to comply with its standards in the form of grant money, it was not able to force the states to adopt them. The federal government's limited role in education allows state and local governments to have their say; state courts and state education boards have wide authority to rule and govern on education matters.[d]

Finally, educational reforms at federal, state, and local levels end up being politically contentious. Consider the controversy over the Common Core Standards, state-authored education policies designed to coordinate curricula across the country. These standards

Spending per Pupil in Three Suburban Cleveland School Districts in 2015–16

School District	Spending per Pupil on Classroom Instruction	Total Spending per Pupil
Beachwood	$11,026	$16,809
Parma	$7,858	$10,709
Avon Local	$5,639	$7,909

Source: Ohio Department of Education, Interactive Local Report Card Home, http://reportcard.education.ohio.gov (accessed 9/26/16).

were bitterly contested partly because they were seen as federal interference in local control of education. The initiative had to affirm that "[t]he federal government played no role in the development of the Common Core. State adoption of the standards is in no way mandatory."[e] The fact that the initiative must explicitly distance itself from the federal government to earn legitimacy is evidence of the general hostility and suspicion among many people in the United States of the federal government's role in education. Those proposing federal policies to improve education and equalize spending have to confront these political realities.

Think About It

What are politically feasible solutions to the problems of vast inequalities in the quality of education in the United States? Is there any role for the federal government, or is this solely a state and local matter?

a. Elementary and Secondary Education Act of 1965, § 9527.

b. Ted Cruz made such a pledge in the 2016 presidential primary, as did Michele Bachman and Rick Perry in 2012.

c. Ohio Department of Education, Interactive Local Report Card Home, http://reportcard.education.ohio.gov (accessed 9/26/16).

d. David A. Gamson, Kathryn A. McDermott, and Douglas S. Reed, "The Elementary and Secondary Education Act at Fifty: Aspirations, Effects, and Limitations," *Russell Sage Foundation Journal of the Social Sciences* 1, no. 3 (2015): 1–29.

e. Common Core State Standards Initiative, "Myths vs. Facts," www.corestandards.org/about-the-standards/myths-vs-facts (accessed 9/26/16).

Housing

Both state and national housing policies have made the United States a country of widespread home ownership. Approximately two-thirds of American families own their own homes. In a typical European country such as Germany, by contrast, the rate of home ownership is around 52 percent. By far the most important policies in encouraging home ownership have been the generous subsidies that the national government provides to people who take out mortgages (loans) to buy homes. Since the 1930s, the national government has subsidized and guaranteed mortgage loans, as well as offering tax deductions for the interest paid on those loans. These are significant taxpayer-funded subsidies to homeowners. Most economists understand them as a major redistribution of income from the average taxpayer to people who take out the largest home mortgages. Although these policies are typically justified as promoting a noble social goal, they mostly benefit those at the upper end of the income scale.

Since 2008, the government's role in the mortgage industry has undergone an overhaul. The crisis in the industry in 2008–09 was widely understood to have precipitated a major economic recession. Many economists argue that the crisis was caused by weak financial regulations on the part of the national government. Mortgage companies granted too many loans to people who were not capable of paying them back if the value of their property declined. At the same time, financial companies traded instruments that included large numbers of mortgage-backed securities (notes promising repayment of loans). The value of these instruments peaked in 2007 and then fell rapidly in 2008 as investors lost faith in the value of real estate.

Following the 2008–09 crisis, attempts have been made to improve national government regulations of the mortgage industry and of financial companies trading in mortgage-backed securities. The national government has tightened loan requirements and changed the incentives for investors to speculate on real estate.[17] These reforms are ongoing.

Despite the national government's role in encouraging home ownership, many poor Americans continue to live in substandard housing. National government involvement in housing for the poor began in 1937 with several New Deal programs. Most of these involved the building of rental units for low-income families by the newly established Federal Housing Administration (FHA). The FHA ran into many difficulties, including recalcitrant local zoning boards, real estate interests, and a variety of local laws that promoted racial segregation and effectively corralled the poor into ghettos. The agency itself reflected the racial divisions in the country. For instance, from the 1930s through the 1950s, official FHA policy was to avoid mixing blacks and whites in public housing because of the social problems it caused.[18] After the Civil Rights Act of 1964, which banned racial discrimination in housing, the national government became an enforcer of rules protecting the rights of minorities to rent or own where they wished, including in public housing projects.

[17] Helene Cooper, "Obama Signs Overhaul of Financial System," *New York Times*, July 21, 2010, www .nytimes.com (accessed 2/25/11).

[18] James O. Midgley and Michelle M. Livermore, eds., *The Handbook of Social Policy* (New York: Sage Publications, 2009), p. 406.

Recently, public housing priorities have changed. Government funds are no longer going to large high-rise housing complexes, but to smaller low-rise public housing like this development in San Francisco, California, and to rent subsidies for poor people.

Legislation enacted in 1949 pledged the government to provide a "decent home and suitable living environment for every American family." For the next several decades, the national government devoted substantial resources, through state grants and direct federal programs, to build housing for the poor. The Department of Housing and Urban Development (HUD), which subsumed the FHA, became a cabinet-level department in 1965. HUD programs for razing substandard housing and building new housing for the poor were among the centerpieces of the Great Society initiatives by the federal government in the 1960s (see Chapter 3). But local standards and constraints often clustered HUD housing units into urban ghettos, and many of these public housing projects became dilapidated and crime ridden.

Since the mid-1970s, the emphasis of federal housing programs has been on subsidizing rents for the poor (through the so-called Section 8 program begun in 1974) and on assisting localities in building housing for a mixture of income groups. There are regulations today, for example, that require new urban development schemes intended to attract wealthy people also to include new housing for the poor. The goal is to promote mixed neighborhoods, keeping the poor from becoming isolated in run-down sections of urban areas.

In recent decades, overall government funding for housing for the poor has declined relative to other priorities. Backlash against welfare in the 1980s, discussed earlier, hit HUD particularly hard as the successive Republican administrations of Ronald Reagan and George H. W. Bush emphasized private solutions to housing problems. Even the Democratic Clinton administration did not restore previous levels of funding for housing. In a sign of the times, by the 1990s some of the most notoriously run-down federal housing projects, such as Cabrini-Green in Chicago, were being torn down to make way for luxury housing developments. Housing advocates have complained for the last few decades of inadequate funding for HUD, and of inadequate commitment in general by the national government to improving housing for the poor.

Another category of Americans in need is the homeless—people who neither own a home nor have any permanent dwelling. Some are temporarily homeless and looking for jobs, but others are chronically homeless, including many veterans with injuries, addicts, and mentally ill people. The national government has at various times encouraged the states to assist the homeless directly by providing shelters and food banks, remedial job training programs, and drug and alcohol rehabilitation centers. But little money has come from Washington for such programs. Thus, resources devoted to aid for the homeless vary greatly and depend almost entirely on the priorities of the local governments when allocating spending from their own city and county budgets.

Crime Prevention

States and localities operate most of the governmental machinery for controlling domestic crime. The vast majority of police and court personnel, judges, and prosecutors are city, county, or state employees.

The national government steps into domestic crime control when criminals break federal laws concerning bank robbery, tax evasion, misdeeds in financial markets, drug trafficking, support for terrorism, and criminal organizations and activities that routinely cross state boundaries. For example, investigating Mafia and Mafia-like organizations since the 1920s has been mostly a national government responsibility.

The national government first became involved in this area when the Interstate Commerce Act of 1887 authorized the Justice Department to prosecute interstate crime. The investigative agencies of the department at first dealt with companies violating federal regulations, especially antifraud statutes. Later, they became involved in investigating and prosecuting prostitution rings, bank robbers who crossed state lines, liquor production and sales during Prohibition (1919–33), and organized crime more generally. The Justice Department's main investigative arm was named the Federal Bureau of Investigation (FBI) in 1935, and it has been the key crime-control force within the national government ever since.

State and local crime control is in some areas shaped and coordinated by actions of the national government. The Justice Department, for instance, was a major promoter of the concept of "community policing," an approach to crime control that places police in neighborhoods and among people while walking or driving their beats. The department awarded grants to states to teach local police forces how to shift their focus toward community policing. Some studies have indicated that this kind of proactive, high-visibility policing—as opposed to traditional methods of crime control, in which police show up only after crimes have been committed—helps to reduce fear of crime and even reduces certain kinds of crime, especially property crimes such as robbery and burglary.

Since 2003, the national government has subsidized local crime control largely through the Department of Homeland Security, the agency in charge of fighting terrorism activity on American soil. States and localities can obtain grants for equipment, vehicles, weapons, and even additional personnel to try to prevent terrorist violence and other kinds of disruptions. These efforts by Homeland Security and by the states have expanded in recent years to include fighting illegal immigration. Some tension has developed between state and national agencies on issues surrounding illegal immigration. Notably, Arizona passed an aggressive state law targeting illegal immigrants, parts of which the Supreme Court declared to be unconstitutional and parts of which it upheld. State leaders, however, insist that it is meant to reinforce federal immigration law.[19]

Crime rates fluctuate over time. A spike in murders and gun violence, including mass killings by lone gunmen, occurred in 2015–16, driven by a variety of factors including gang warfare in major cities and a heroin addiction epidemic. The last major spike before that in violent crime occurred in the 1980s and early 1990s, when the crack cocaine epidemic and resulting gang wars led to a dramatic rise in murders in urban areas and thefts by addicts. Since the mid-1990s, violent crime rates have fallen overall. (This is true even despite the 2015–16 spike in gun deaths, which has been an increase from historic lows.) Yet public opinion surveys indicate that fear of crime has increased. The reason for this paradox remains something of a mystery. According to one theory, local television stations increasingly highlight sensational crime stories in an effort to appeal to the shrinking audience for television news. People believe the crime problem is worse than it is because of what they are exposed to in the media.[20]

For our purposes, it is important to note that fear of crime drives public support for certain crime prevention policies, especially harsh sentencing of convicted criminals. Beginning in the early 1990s, the states built many new prisons. Largely as a result of policies against illegal drug trafficking, which have led to a large number of arrests and convictions, the prison population has increased by almost 1 million over the past two decades. Today, the United

[19] See Randal Archibold, "Arizona Enacts Stringent Law on Immigration," *New York Times*, April 23, 2010, www.nytimes.com (accessed 2/25/11).

[20] This effect has been demonstrated in several studies on the effects of the media on public opinion. See, for example, Lutz Erbring, Edie N. Goldenberg, and Arthur H. Miller, "Front-Page News and Real-World Cues: A New Look at Agenda-Setting by the Media," *American Journal of Political Science* 24, no. 1 (1980): 16–49. For another good example of a study on media effects on perceptions of crime rates, see Shanto Iyengar, Mark D. Peters, and Donald R. Kinder, "Experimental Demonstrations of the 'Not-So-Minimal' Consequences of Television News Programs," *American Political Science Review* 76 (December 1982): 848–58.

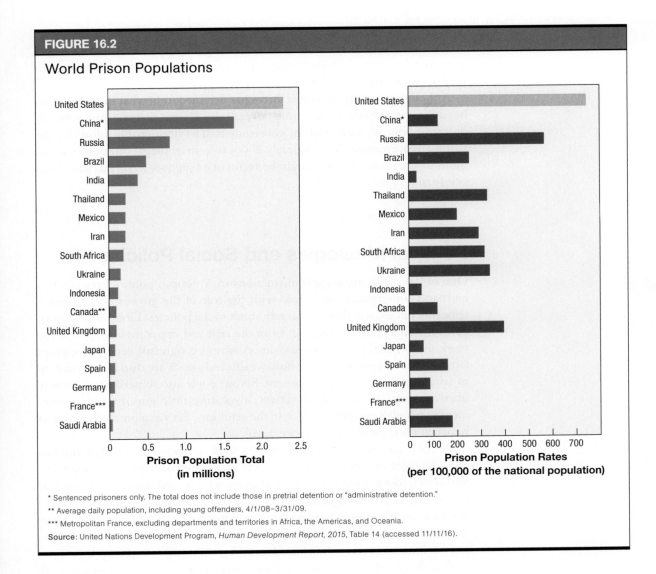

FIGURE 16.2

World Prison Populations

Prison Population Total (in millions) — bar chart showing countries from top to bottom: United States, China*, Russia, Brazil, India, Thailand, Mexico, Iran, South Africa, Ukraine, Indonesia, Canada**, United Kingdom, Japan, Spain, Germany, France***, Saudi Arabia. X-axis: 0, 0.5, 1.0, 1.5, 2.0, 2.5

Prison Population Rates (per 100,000 of the national population) — bar chart with same countries. X-axis: 0, 100, 200, 300, 400, 500, 600, 700

* Sentenced prisoners only. The total does not include those in pretrial detention or "administrative detention."

** Average daily population, including young offenders, 4/1/08–3/31/09.

*** Metropolitan France, excluding departments and territories in Africa, the Americas, and Oceania.

Source: United Nations Development Program, *Human Development Report, 2015*, Table 14 (accessed 11/11/16).

States has one of the highest incarceration rates in the world. A higher percentage of Americans are in prison—2.2 million, or about 0.8 percent of the population—than in any other country for which reliable statistics are available. The next highest is Russia, which has 0.62 percent of its population behind bars (Figure 16.2). The large American prison population strains resources, and in May 2011 the U.S. Supreme Court found California's prison system to be overcrowded to the point of violating the constitutional protections against cruel and unusual punishment.

By 2014, the large incarceration rate had become a major political issue, especially with regard to race and ethnicity. The high incarceration rates among

African Americans and Latinos led to reforms and calls for reexamination of long prison sentences for relatively minor drug offenses. States by 2015 began to release prisoners held for minor drug crimes, and some states continue to reform sentencing procedures.

Although spending on police forces has declined somewhat in recent years because of state budget constraints, overall the United States spends robustly on crime control at all levels of government. The high profile efforts by the national government since the early 2000s to restrict illegal immigration and monitor organizations that might be terrorist or support terrorism have been prioritized in national budgets.

Political Ideologies and Social Policies

One of the major ideological distinctions in American politics between liberals and conservatives has to do with the role of the government in redistributing goods, and thus it is largely about social policies. Liberals (or leftists) generally support redistribution from the rich and upper middle class to the working class and poor, whereas conservatives (or rightists) generally support letting free markets determine how wealth and goods are distributed, instead of assigning that task to government. Some people also subscribe to a form of libertarianism, an ideological variant advocating little government involvement in people's everyday lives or in the economy. Let's explore the differences between these ideologies in more detail.

Political theorists have long posited a trade-off between equality and liberty: the more liberty there is in a society for people to change jobs, open new businesses, move around in search of more wealth, and use their property as they see fit, the more economic inequalities will arise. Those with more talent and luck, and the ability to work hard, will gain more wealth over time, given the freedom to seek it. Moreover, their gain often affects other people. When one business succeeds, others may fail, and people may lose their jobs.

Proponents of redistributive policies argue that the government can curb such inequalities by redistributing wealth, restricting people's ability to earn a lot of money at the expense of others, or assisting the poor in gaining access to paths to wealth (which can mean less access by the nonpoor). Critics of such policies contend that government efforts to address inequality necessarily inhibit liberty. By heavily taxing the wealthy to provide goods for the poor, for example, the government may not only reduce the incentives of the wealthy to work hard and look for new opportunities for economic growth but also inhibit their freedom to do what they want with their money (Figure 16.3).

In fact, all governments redistribute resources to some extent. There is no way to avoid redistribution completely if the government is to provide a mini-

FIGURE 16.3

The Trade-Off between Liberty and Equality

Active government
intervention to tax wealth and redistribute to the poor—reduces inequality, but people are less free to do what they want with their money and may have fewer incentives to work hard.

Complete freedom
for individuals to acquire resources and spend money as they wish with low taxes—leads to inequalities.

MORE EQUALITY   MORE FREEDOM

mal level of public services and public goods. Even providing national defense, education, roadways, and waterways is redistributive to a certain extent. This is because not everyone pays equally for the production of those goods, and some people—those who get the government contracts to build the public goods, for instance—benefit more than others. Of course, virtually all governments pursue policies that are intentionally redistributive, such as health care clinics for the poor, literacy programs for children at risk, and affirmative action programs. As we will see, countries vary tremendously in how actively governments have redistributed benefits and costs, wealth, or opportunities for wealth.

We noted in Chapter 4 that the United States is widely considered to be among the freest countries in the world in terms of civil rights and liberties. This is also true in the realm of economic and social policies. The United States is renowned for championing, and even concretely assisting, entrepreneurship—enabling new businesses to start and helping people with potentially lucrative ideas gain access to business loans. Compared to other countries, fewer regulations stand in the way of starting a new business in the United States (though it varies across states). In countries like Italy or France, by contrast, entrepreneurs and new business owners must obtain many permits and approvals, and the costs of hiring new workers and complying with government regulations are generally much higher than in the United States.

In short, Americans enjoy considerable liberty in the realm of economics, but the United States also has a relatively high level of economic inequality. Perhaps that is the trade-off Americans have made, or at least the trade-off the government has made for them. The extent to which any specific trade-off enjoys broad public support is difficult to determine. Opinion polls show consistent majority support for receiving generous—and even increasing—Social Security benefits, health care insurance (even if government provides it), and generous benefits like student loans and school lunch programs. But if asked about paying taxes to fund these things, supporting more welfare (using specifically that word), or creating a more equal society through government programs, public support drops below a majority.

People who pressure the government to redistribute wealth to the poor through social policies tend to believe that inequality is a problem. What kind of problem? Some consider inequality a moral problem. In their eyes, it is intrinsically wrong and urgently needs to be set right. Others believe that inequality is a practical problem. They claim that it leads to undesirable consequences for society as a whole, over and above the neediness of individuals. For instance, too much inequality might lead to social unrest and even revolution.

Others argue that posing the problem as a trade-off between liberty and equality is misleading. In fact, they say, true liberty comes only when people have enough material resources to enjoy life. So inequality actually provides more liberty to those at the upper end of the income and wealth scale, but much less liberty to the poor. Alternatively, equality offers more liberty to the poor than they currently enjoy. The poor cannot exercise their liberty because they are poor, even if they live in a society that supposedly is quite free. People who hold these views would be called liberals in American politics (that is, they are on the left-hand side of the ideological spectrum), or social democrats in Europe. They might be called socialists if they thought that government ownership of major industries was the solution to inequality.

On the other side of the ideological spectrum, some conservatives (or rightists) believe the government should stay out of the business of redistributing wealth. Some conservatives would argue that inequality is natural, unavoidable, and even just. Goods should flow to those who have more talent or commitment, or who work hard. Many libertarians and conservatives argue that government redistribution is counterproductive because it saps people's will to work hard and earn a living. Moreover, it leads to inefficiencies in society because goods and costs are not distributed according to free markets. In a variant of this view, some conservatives say it is immoral for the government to take money from some and give it to others.

People who call themselves libertarians—a category that includes some conservatives—can be motivated by both practical and ethical concerns. The more practical libertarians (and many conservatives) argue that government redistribution does not ultimately work or costs a lot more than the benefits it yields for society. The more ethics-based libertarians argue that government redistribution is unjust in that it takes property away from someone who has earned it.

To the extent that libertarians focus on economic matters, they generally agree with the policy goals of those we would call conservatives in today's terms. However, other strains of libertarianism focus more narrowly on people's private lives. People who embrace both forms of libertarianism are difficult to fit into today's major political parties (and a contemporary Ameri-

TABLE 16.1

Modern American Ideologies

		Economic Behavior	
		Government stays out	Government regulates/redistributes
Social Behavior	Government stays out	**Libertarian**	**Liberal**
	Government regulates	**Conservative**	(Statism)*

* Statism is much less prominent as an ideology, but it is one way to describe a belief in government regulation of the economy and people's everyday lives.

can left/right or liberal/conservative spectrum) because they believe that government should stay out of people's lives as much as possible in all realms. Thus, if we are referring to personal, noneconomic conduct—private behavior such as sexual relations or drug use—then libertarians might agree more with liberals than with conservatives (Table 16.1).

Many modern American conservatives agree that government can make people more equal in material terms. But in doing so the government may need to curb the liberty that many people enjoy, at least in the economic realm, and conservatives generally believe that this is wrong, counterproductive, or both. Notably, many conservatives believe that, rather than direct welfare programs that deliver benefits to the poor, it is better to have more indirect programs that give tax credits and other kinds of financial incentives to people and organizations. We discuss these indirect forms of poor relief shortly.

The differences between liberal and conservative ideologies raise fundamental questions about human nature and about politics and government. If indeed there is a trade-off between liberty and equality, then no "solution" to the problem of inequality will please everyone. We cannot all be free to do what we want and also be equal in wealth and status. All we can do is try to insist that our government enact and implement public policies that place us, metaphorically speaking, where a majority of Americans want to be on the trade-off line, as shown in Figure 16.3.

In Comparison: Social Policy

The United States is widely reputed to have less generous social policies (or, to put it another way, a small welfare state), at least in comparison with western European countries, Australia, and Canada. This reputation is accurate if we focus on unemployment and health insurance, cash assistance for the poor, and other policies that protect the jobs of the lower and working classes. To the puzzlement of some, the United States, as the world's largest economy with many of the world's richest people, has a larger proportion of poor people than other advanced industrial societies. Indeed, by the most commonly used measures of inequality, the United States is a highly unequal society (Figure 16.4). Moreover, poverty in the United States has lethal consequences. For example, the rate of infant mortality—the proportion of babies who die before their first birthday—is relatively high, especially among poor and immigrant families who cannot afford or do not have access to quality prenatal care.

Furthermore, inequality in the United States has been increasing since the 1970s, and all signs indicate that it will continue to increase given broad trends in the economy. Scholars disagree over the root causes of the trend toward more inequality; some are focusing on the basic economic forces and technological changes occurring worldwide. After all, inequality has been increasing in nearly every developed country in the world, and in many underdeveloped countries as well. The argument is that technological changes push in two directions: reducing the need for highly paid working-class employees through automation, and enabling the wealthy to shift their money around the world to reap better investment gains and avoid taxes.

An alternative argument is that inequality has increased because governments, including those at all levels in the United States, have reduced their commitments to provide for the poor and unemployed. For a variety of reasons discussed in Chapter 15 (such as the decline in the appeal of socialism worldwide), nearly all countries have embraced more market capitalism as ways to grow their economies, although the costs fall on the poor and the opportunities come to the wealthy. Few disagree that even though many countries have reduced commitments to the poor, the United States still remains low in its direct governmental commitments to poverty relief relative to most other wealthy countries.

However, such comparisons are not as straightforward as they seem, especially if we broaden the basis of comparison and examine what these measures actually indicate. It is largely true that direct social policies are not as targeted toward the poor as is the case in many other countries. But many American social policies are carried out in two related ways that are in fact indirect. The first is through tax credits. Programs like the Earned Income Tax Credit (discussed earlier) are in fact indirect forms of poverty relief. Other tax credits give companies and individuals breaks in their taxes if they contribute to nonprofit organizations dedicated to serving the poor. The second way is through efforts conducted by private organizations and corporations, where the allocation of

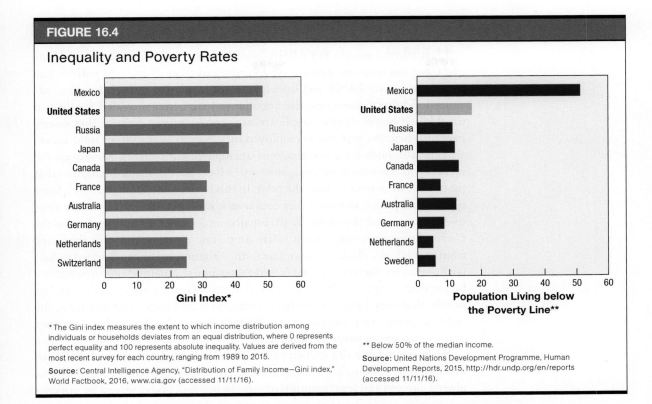

FIGURE 16.4

Inequality and Poverty Rates

Gini Index*

Mexico
United States
Russia
Japan
Canada
France
Australia
Germany
Netherlands
Switzerland

0 10 20 30 40 50 60

Population Living below the Poverty Line**

Mexico
United States
Russia
Japan
Canada
France
Australia
Germany
Netherlands
Sweden

0 10 20 30 40 50 60

* The Gini index measures the extent to which income distribution among individuals or households deviates from an equal distribution, where 0 represents perfect equality and 100 represents absolute inequality. Values are derived from the most recent survey for each country, ranging from 1989 to 2015.
Source: Central Intelligence Agency, "Distribution of Family Income—Gini index," World Factbook, 2016, www.cia.gov (accessed 11/11/16).

** Below 50% of the median income.
Source: United Nations Development Programme, Human Development Reports, 2015, http://hdr.undp.org/en/reports (accessed 11/11/16).

resources is determined partly by financial incentives provided by government policy and partly by private bureaucracies. We can say that there is an American-style welfare state, one implemented by employers and private charities and sometimes by local governments, that is subsidized heavily by the national and state governments. We can think of this as a form of privatized bureaucracy that is publicly subsidized.

This privatized bureaucracy makes decisions that have deep consequences. One of these is that many middle- and upper-middle-class people benefit from an indirect version of the American welfare state, and the poor do not receive as much as they might if the orientation were more redistributive. But the poor do receive considerable benefits, and many lower- and working-class people in the United States receive excellent health care, education and worker training benefits, and food assistance, largely through their employers.

Nevertheless, certain particularly vulnerable groups are undeniably underserved by the American welfare state: the unemployed, those with mental illnesses that push them out of the workforce though they are not sick enough to be in homes for the mentally ill, and undocumented immigrants or immigrants without work visas who cannot receive benefits through employers.

Unemployed people can receive benefits from the government for a limited time, but they are then cut off according to recently enacted policies (see the discussion of TANF and unemployment insurance earlier). In other advanced industrial countries, the unemployed are better provided for than in the United States. Some people (mostly conservatives) believe that overly generous benefits give the unemployed little reason to search for jobs. Liberals generally push for more generous unemployment benefits. Moreover, the mentally ill rely mostly on the generosity of local governments or charities that receive tax incentives to assist the poor. In this respect, the United States is fairly typical, except that in some other countries it is more usual for families to routinely take care of the mentally ill. Finally, undocumented immigrants in the United States must rely almost solely on private charities and cash they earn from menial jobs. This too is similar to the situation in other advanced industrial countries. In fact, in the United States undocumented immigrants fare better than in many other countries. It is not that they are treated well, but simply that they have certain legal protections and rights (for example, the right to elementary education for their children) that few other countries grant to people in these circumstances.

So in comparing the redistributive social policies in the United States to those in other countries, we can mark three major differences. First, unemployed citizens and legal immigrants are, in general, better served by government assistance in other countries of comparable wealth than they are in the United States. Second, other countries' governments tend to be more generous in providing health care and housing to the poor. Third, a great deal of the overall commitment in American society to aid the poor comes in indirect forms or through private organizations.

A final difference between the United States and other countries deserves mention, and we will discuss it in more depth in the next chapter. The United States spends more on defense and national security than all the other major countries of the world combined. And many other countries have their own national security linked to American military commitments. Thus, some would argue, these other countries to which the United States is compared on social policies can afford to be more generous with their welfare states because they do not have to spend on defense due to American protection. This is a controversial argument, and a counterargument made is that American military spending is a choice and not a necessity (at least at its current high levels); these robust defense budgets enjoy healthy support from the public, partly because such expenditures represent in themselves a form of government economic support for specific communities and sectors of the population. Regardless of whether the U.S. government has a meaningful option to reduce its defense budgets substantially, there is no denying the stark trade-off

Social scientists refer to *deservingness* as a factor in people's attitudes about how much the government should provide for citizens and who is entitled to these provisions. Deservingness, researchers say, is a mental shortcut we use to form an opinion on who deserves what when limited information is available.[a] Deservingness has been shown to be strongly related to whether people believe the situation—sickness or unemployment, for instance—was randomly determined or caused by one's own actions that could have been avoided. It has been shown that people feel that those in situations perceived to have come through randomness rather than their own doing deserve more government support.

Two social scientists conducted research to see how deservingness shapes attitudes about unemployment and sickness.[b] Based on answers to survey questions, they created a specific measure on the degree to which unemployed people are viewed as victims of random events the same as those who are sick. Data were collected from representative samples of adults in Denmark, the United States, and Japan, and the figure below shows some of their results. The *y*-axis displays the average values for their measure, where higher values indicate that respondents viewed the subject as a victim of uncontrollable events—and thus high on deservingness.

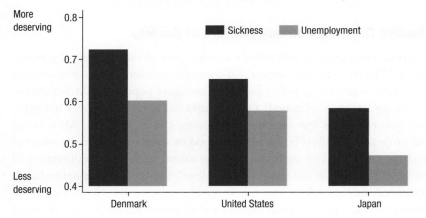

Deservingness: Comparing Sickness and Unemployment in Denmark, the United States, and Japan

Source: Carsten Jensen and Michael Bang Petersen, "The Deservingness Heuristic and the Politics of Health Care," *American Journal of Political Science*, early view (2016). Replication data are available at https://dataverse.harvard.edu /dataset.xhtml?persistentId=doi:10 .7910/DVN/TIXGF8 (accessed 6/8/16).

Think About It

How do Americans compare to people in Denmark and Japan on their attitudes about deservingness for the unemployed and the sick? What might explain the differences across countries? What might explain the differences in attitudes about unemployment and sickness? Which country do you think has the highest level of social services for people who are sick and unemployed? Which do you think has the lowest?

a. Michael Bang Petersen, Rune Slothuus, Rune Stubager, and Lise Togeby, "Deservingness versus Values in Public Opinion on Welfare: The Automaticity of the Deservingness Heuristic," *European Journal of Political Research* 50, no. 1 (2010): 24–52.

b. Carsten Jensen and Michael Bang Petersen, "The Deservingness Heuristic and the Politics of Health Care," *American Journal of Political Science*, early view (2016).

between each government dollar going toward defense or toward traditional social policies such as those described in this chapter.

Some scholars attribute the distinctiveness of American social policies in part to long-standing historical antecedents. They note that the United States had a weaker labor movement than European countries, and as a result the "leftist" American party (the Democrats) never fully embraced European-style democratic socialism. Other scholars argue that the disparities have more to do with Americans' deep-seated suspicion of government and centralized power, a suspicion that goes all the way back to the Founding.

Interest Groups, Parties, and Social Policy Making

Let's now look into some explanations for the current state of social welfare policies in the United States and return to our opening puzzle. In doing so, we will refer to collective dilemmas and also return to the trade-off between liberty and equality. We'll start with collective dilemmas and link them to interest group conflict over social policies.

Collective Dilemmas among Sectors of Society

Social policies in general will remain a major part of the budgets of governments at all levels, yet controversies will continue over how they are structured and targeted. Some social policy programs are quite popular and in little danger of being seriously trimmed. Even in tight budgetary times, for instance, Social Security faces few challenges of being cut or reduced. Most other social programs see their budgets threatened or reforms potentially enacted that change formulas or methods of governance. Education programs will never be cut to zero at the state and local level, but they can be centralized, reorganized, or cut back.

Nevertheless, a fundamental aspect to the interest group politics of social policies centers at least as much on who will pay for the programs and which programs deserve scrutiny or more bolstering. In other words, how much will the various sectors in society bear in their taxes to pay for social programs, and who will benefit from social programs? It is straightforward to see that with redistributive questions like these, many individuals in society would prefer to have access to generous social programs and be able to avoid paying taxes for those programs. But individuals cannot avoid paying taxes they are legally required to pay without risk of arrest or fines; they can, however, join with others to try to change tax policies or reduce the costs of programs that do not benefit them.

When interest groups organize to represent sectors of society, they often lobby and pressure to minimize the costs borne by their own sectors and argue against programs that their members do not benefit from. This presents, of course, classic collective action problems, both within groups and across groups. Within a group, each member prefers that others in the group bear the costs of organizing to lobby for lower taxes on its group overall. As we know from Chapter 10, smaller groups and wealthy groups have an easier time overcoming their collective action problems. But more importantly for this chapter, each sector of society wishes to avoid taxes and have other sectors pay most of the costs of social policies (and other policies as well). And naturally, the wealthier segments of society need social policies less than poorer segments, and they pressure the government to keep taxes that are progressive (like income taxes and capital gains taxes) low.

Alternatively, as we learned in Chapter 10, poorer segments of society have difficulty organizing effectively to lobby the government, and they also have to argue in ways that cut against the grain of American political culture. When they can organize, or have their interests represented by public interest groups or unions, they often have to make the case in favor of generous social programs that require other segments of society—the wealthy and middle class—to pay for them. The poor simply do not have the income and wealth to tax at the appropriate levels to pay for many social programs. Thus, the poor have to rely on the willingness of other segments of society to pay much of the costs. In terms of political rhetoric, the wealthy can argue against taxes (always a popular argument) while those representing the poor have to argue in favor of government programs that redistribute (often unpopular in the United States).

The Major Parties and Social Policies

Some people highlight the important distinction between equality of opportunity and equality of result. Both Democrats and Republicans today are generally comfortable with the notion that the government should be in the business of assuring equality of *opportunity*. There is agreement across the political spectrum on the importance of providing basic elementary education and health services—emergency care and prenatal care, for example—for everyone, regardless of wealth or status. The role of government in redistribution is huge, and some of these policies are in little danger of being repealed. Most Republicans acknowledge the popularity of certain programs, such as Social Security and Medicare, and know that they should not try to change them. Likewise, most Democrats have moderate tendencies and are not proposing much in the way of expensive redistributive programs to relieve poverty.[21]

---

[21] Margaret Weir, ed., *The Social Divide: Political Parties and the Future of Activist Government* (Washington, DC: Brookings Institution Press, 1998).

Where the parties differ most clearly is in their attitude toward equality of *result*. Democrats in general want the government to work more actively to assure equal results. Whether this is possible, let alone desirable, is a matter of spirited debate. Some conservatives argue that any government programs intended to bring about equal results are destined to fail for the simple reason that people are not equally endowed to take advantage of those benefits or to sustain the lifestyles required to make them permanent.

Most major social policies that have been added to the government's agenda since the 1930s have occurred when liberals, and specifically Democrats, have gotten the upper hand in Congress and in the national government more generally. There are a few exceptions. President Nixon, who was a Republican, significantly increased payments for Social Security and even proposed several antipoverty programs that were quite bold. George W. Bush pushed through the No Child Left Behind Act and was instrumental in placing many new health care clinics in poor areas. He also dramatically increased medical benefits to the elderly through generous prescription drug entitlements. Donald Trump, during his presidential campaign in 2016, advocated new trade policies to protect low-wage workers from layoffs and also suggested that all Americans should be provided with basic health care for free. But in general, conservatives have tended to cut back or eliminate specific social policies. Leaders in both parties have worked to amend social policies, usually through tightening standards, working to make them run more efficiently, or decentralizing them to give more control to the states.

Thus, social policies are contested by partisan groups that disagree deeply and fundamentally over the appropriate trade-off between equality and liberty. If we had to pinpoint the one major difference between Democrats and Republicans that has been constant since the 1930s, it would be over the degree to which the government should try to assure equality of economic results through social policies.

Explaining Political Outcomes

To return to our opening story, health care is one of the most complex of all policy areas. The debates and conflicts over government support for health care and for organizations like Planned Parenthood will undoubtedly continue for many years. The ideologies we have discussed translate into the different prescriptions concerning health care.

Liberals (or leftists), mostly Democrats, tend to support not only abortion rights but also universal health care provided by doctors, hospitals, nurses, and other health professionals funded by the government. They believe that health care can be more equitably provided by government than by the pure

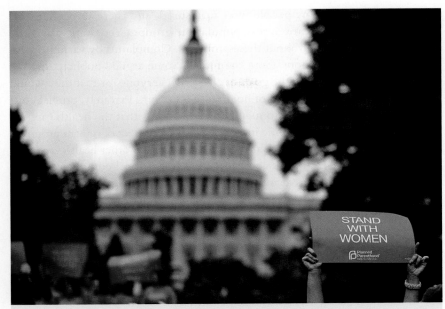

In July 2013, when members of Congress considered introducing a bill that would ban abortions after 20 weeks, supporters of Planned Parenthood gathered on Capitol Hill in protest. Will conflict over abortion policy continue under President Trump, with Republicans in control of both houses of Congress?

free market. Conservatives (or rightists), mostly Republicans, tend to oppose abortion, but they also support a free-market system of medical care provided by doctors and hospitals that charge for their services according to the law of supply and demand. Many people have health insurance of some kind, which means that health providers are funded directly by insurance companies that charge premiums to people. Rightists are typically comfortable with this arrangement as long as the insurance companies are themselves private companies that compete for customers in a free market. In other words, the government should not be the sole insurer—as would be the case in universal health care provision—or even the largest and most important insurer.

It would be easy to dismiss either of these ideological preferences as simplistic or dogmatic. But for the most part, the people who hold them genuinely want all Americans to be healthy and to have access to quality health care. Their differences stem from disagreements over means, priorities, and the cherished ideals of democracy—liberty and equality. To understand why certain social policies actually get passed and implemented, we need to pay attention to who is represented, who pays for what, and who benefits.

In the debate leading to the health care reform bill that Congress passed in 2010, everyone agreed that there were deep problems in health care: costs were too high, too many people were uninsured, and there were shameful inequalities in health care across population groups. Yet there was little agreement on what to do about these problems. Complaints by various interests focused on expectations about the future. Some argued publicly that the reforms would not achieve the goals of covering everyone, or that they would inflate health care costs instead of holding them down. Privately, crucial constituency groups complained to members of Congress that the health care reforms threatened their economic interests. For every aspect of reform proposed and amended, some large group in society—doctors and other health care professionals, hospitals, insurance companies, pharmaceutical companies, health equipment companies, government, and finally health care consumers—did not like it. The health care debate was a classic situation in which many powerful groups were unhappy with the status quo, but many were even unhappier with specific proposals for reform. That health care reform passed in some form is a testament to the shared sense among many that the health care system was broken. The final bill establishing Obamacare was a compromise that left few people fully satisfied. And price increases for insurance under the ACA prompted many to turn away from the policy.

Considering the politics surrounding health care reform and many other social policies, any student of policy making would be forced to conclude that the poorest and most vulnerable members of society are less well represented, in either party, than the rest of the people. Whatever one's views on abortion, it is well known that Planned Parenthood provides extensive health care to poor women. Furthermore, the Affordable Care Act of 2010 was designed to lead to health insurance for nearly everyone. But pervasive inequalities in the provision of care will likely persist—the very poorest will get the bare minimum—and the ACA is now at risk of elimination. Given what we know about the structure of American government—how Congress and the president in particular respond to the voices of constituents—and about the low participation rates of the poor in elections, it is not easy to see how enough political pressure will come about to cause more generous social policies for the poor in the near future.

FURTHER READING

★ = Included in *Readings in American Politics*, 5th ed.

★ Bartels, Larry, *Unequal Democracy: The Political Economy of the New Gilded Age* (Princeton, NJ: Princeton University Press, 2008). Explores the ways in which the policies of the national government, and the economic philosophies of the two major parties and their voters, have significantly affected income inequality in the United States.

Baumgartner, Frank R., and Bryan D. Jones, *Agendas and Instability in American Politics*, 2nd ed. (Chicago: University of Chicago Press, 2009). An examination of why certain social problems arise on the national government's agenda and how they are transformed by the pressure from interest groups.

Fine, Doug, *Too High to Fail* (New York: Gotham Books, 2012). An argument, both economic and moral in aim, for the federal legalization of marijuana.

Gilens, Martin, *Why Americans Hate Welfare: Race, Media, and the Politics of Antipoverty Policy* (Chicago: University of Chicago Press, 1999). Presents compelling evidence that people's attitudes toward welfare are deeply affected by their racial attitudes.

Hacker, Jacob, and Paul Pierson, *Winner-Take-All Politics* (New York: Simon & Schuster, 2010). The political challenges of mobilizing for government-led redistribution, viewed from a liberal perspective.

Hochschild, Jennifer, and Nathan Scovronick, *The American Dream and the Public Schools* (New York: Oxford University Press, 2003). Examines inequality in the American educational system and various reform efforts.

MacDonald, Heather, *The Burden of Bad Ideas* (Chicago: Ivan Dee, 2000). A discussion of social policies that created more problems than they solved, from a conservative perspective.

Pierson, Paul, *Dismantling the Welfare State? Reagan, Thatcher, and the Politics of Retrenchment* (New York: Cambridge University Press, 1994). Examines the policies in the 1980s in the United States and Britain that reduced the size of the welfare state.

Skocpol, Theda, *Protecting Soldiers and Mothers: The Political Origins of Social Policy in the United States* (Cambridge, MA: Belknap Press of Harvard University Press, 1995). A comprehensive history of early welfare spending, indicating that pensions for veterans and widows of soldiers were the first federal cash transfers to individuals.

KEY TERMS

means-tested program (p. 626)

Medicaid (p. 632)

Medicare (p. 632)

social policy (p. 619)

Social Security (p. 628)

Supplemental Nutritional Assistance Program (SNAP) (p. 626)

Temporary Assistance for Needy Families (TANF) (p. 620)

welfare state (p. 624)

Many critical players and agencies are involved in formulating the U.S. policy against ISIL. Targeted air strikes of ISIL strongholds in Syria have been led by the Department of Defense, with the support of the White House and Congress.

17

Foreign Policy

 What tools does the United States have to craft foreign policy? When and why does it use them?

T he United States faces numerous foreign policy challenges, and President Donald Trump and Congress rely on a vast array of departments, agencies, committees, and advisers working in specific areas to make policy decisions. Challenges include threats of terrorism, wars in parts of the world such as the Middle East that affect American interests, recalcitrant countries such as North Korea and Iran that pose threats to American allies and regional stability, and difficult but important trading partners such as China that need constant diplomatic attention. For each challenging policy domain—security, trade, diplomacy, and international regulation—specialized parts of the government are handling some aspect.

Take, for example, the situation involving the Islamic State of Iraq and the Levant (ISIL, often referred to as ISIS). The influence of the group and its use of wanton violence has stirred international concern and united many countries, including Russia and the United States, in an effort to fight the group. From the perspective of the U.S. government, ISIL is a threat both to the stability of the Middle East and the safety of U.S. citizens. ISIL-inspired terrorist attacks in North America and Europe roiled both continents throughout 2015 and 2016.

Responses by the U.S. government to ISIL have been complex and multifaceted, and the White House and Congress have sought cooperation both outside and inside the government. Outside the government, mostly through the diplomatic activities of the president and the former secretary of state John Kerry, American politicians sought the cooperation of governments around the world in containing and eliminating the threat of ISIL.[1] Inside the government, the White House and Congress sought to enlist and coordinate the support of various agencies and departments. The U.S. conducted targeted air strikes in Syria and Iraq in a mission called Operation

[1] The White House, Office of the Press Secretary, "Fact Sheet: The 2015 G-20 Summit in Antalya, Turkey," November 16, 2015, www.whitehouse.gov/the-press-office/2015/11/16/fact-sheet-2015-g-20-summit-antalya-turkey (accessed 2/3/16).

OUTLINE

- Collective Dilemmas and Foreign Policy

- Theories and Strategies of Foreign Policy

- Historical Perspective

- Tools of Foreign Policy

- Making Foreign Policy

- Foreign Policy Doctrines

- Domestic and International Constraints on Foreign Policy

Inherent Resolve, which is managed by the Department of Defense. Meanwhile, ISIL terrorists are recruited and dispersed throughout the world, requiring the U.S. government, mostly through the FBI and Homeland Security, to monitor ISIL-recruited Americans from going overseas to participate in terror.[2] The Department of the Treasury also identified and imposed sanctions on ISIL affiliates in order to weaken ISIL's finances.[3]

The media does not always acknowledge the many tools and aspects of American foreign policy, preferring instead to focus on dramatic events like wars, terrorist attacks, and diplomatic tensions. Well known are the Central Intelligence Agency (CIA), the Defense Department handling war policy, the State Department spearheading diplomatic efforts, congressional committees devoted to setting spending priorities on foreign policy and defense, and the various White House groups like the National Security Council plotting grand strategy with the president. Less well known are the parts of the Departments of the Treasury, Agriculture, Commerce, Justice, Health and Human Service, and Transportation that handle numerous foreign policy issues, interacting with their counterparts in foreign countries and setting policies affecting foreign entities.

The dispersion of foreign policy expertise and authority across parts of the government, exemplified in the U.S. response to ISIL, raises several questions. Given these different parts of the government and the variety of tools available in foreign policy, how do government leaders in Congress and the presidency craft coherent policies? What doctrines have guided American foreign policy, and have principles been applied consistently and effectively? What explains the differences in actions taken against various threats? Have President Trump's policies differed from those of previous presidents?

[2] Homeland Security Advisory Council, "Foreign Fighter Task Force: Interim Report, Spring 2015," U.S. Department of Homeland Security, Spring 2015, www.dhs.gov/sites/default/files/publications/DHS-HSAC-Foreign-Fighter-Task-Force-Interim-Report-May-2015.pdf (accessed 1/28/16).

[3] David S. Cohen, "Combating the Islamic State of Iraq and the Levant's Access to Financing," U.S. Department of the Treasury, September 10, 2014, www.treasury.gov/connect/blog/Pages/Combating-ISIL-.aspx (accessed 2/3/16).

Collective Dilemmas and Foreign Policy

We learned in earlier chapters about the political pressures that various groups put on Congress and the president; these pressures help shape government policies, which in turn affect the lives of all Americans. We have focused mostly on domestic political pressures and domestic policies. However, many political events that determine government policy and affect the lives of Americans happen outside the borders of the United States.

Foreign policy, which can be defined as government actions affecting the country's relationships with other countries and regions, differs from economic policy and social policy in certain fundamental respects. The focus of policy is in protecting Americans at home as well as American interests abroad. The United States is militarily the most powerful country, and its interests, both economic and military, extend to every region in the world. The U.S. government cannot ignore the actions and preferences of foreign governments, nor can it ignore what happens in locations outside of its borders. Foreign governments and organizations may be suspicious of American motives or hostile to American interests. American foreign policy is shaped by the actions of other countries and of entities (like terrorist groups) that reside abroad, and the details for foreign policies are determined at least as much by events occurring outside of U.S. borders as they are by domestic political pressures.

foreign policy Government actions affecting a country's relationships with other countries and regions.

We have also learned throughout this book that political institutions and policy decisions are often responses to collective dilemmas. Both domestic and international collective dilemmas matter in making foreign policy. Let's consider the impact of collective dilemmas among three kinds of actors—the American states, members of Congress, and the countries of the world—on foreign policy.

Domestic Dilemmas

As we saw in Chapter 2, the Framers of the Constitution were concerned that if each state engaged in its own foreign policy, the states would compete with each other instead of cooperating on outcomes beneficial to all. This concern was one of the reasons that the Framers wanted a stronger central government than the one that was in place under the Articles of Confederation; it also explains why they made foreign policy the exclusive province of the national government. The states, subject to federal guidelines, can have their own social policies and their own taxing and spending policies. But to avoid the consequences of uncoordinated or competitive foreign policy among the states, they are forbidden under the Constitution to engage in foreign policy. In this way, the Constitution solved a collective dilemma among the states when it came to foreign policy.

The Navy Seals' assault on Osama Bin Laden's home (leading to his killing) in 2011 is a prime example of how a president can take swift action in foreign affairs.

Another way that collective dilemmas matter in foreign policy making is related to the roles of the president and Congress in making foreign policy; over time, the president has become predominant in this area. The shift toward a greater role for the president in foreign policy follows from the differences between the two branches of government. Most members of Congress recognize that in times of international crises and wars, it is important to have a single leader making quick decisions and devising strategy in foreign policy. Legislatures require time for bargaining to solve collective dilemmas among their members. In the U.S. Congress, it can take weeks or months to enact a law that establishes a given policy. Thus, legislatures are not the best units of government to respond quickly and decisively to the actions of foreign governments. The Constitution granted certain foreign policy powers to the president, but these powers also grew over time as the American people looked to the president rather than to Congress to take the lead in most areas of foreign policy. In other words, recognition of the collective dilemmas inherent within Congress channeled power to the presidency in matters of foreign policy.

These two aspects of foreign policy making have to do with collective dilemmas *within* the United States—between the states and within Congress. The need to solve these internal collective dilemmas has shaped the American institutions of government that are involved in making foreign policy. To understand contemporary American foreign policy more deeply, however, we must learn about what happens *outside* the United States, especially the underlying collective dilemmas among countries.

International Dilemmas

In Chapter 1, we discussed the need for a sovereign authority to enforce rules to protect people from violence and oppression. We learned about the theories of Thomas Hobbes, who argued that in an anarchic world without a sovereign authority, life would be "nasty, brutish, and short" because of fear, hatred, and repeated vengeance. Without a higher authority, people or groups are like the players in a prisoner's dilemma, who will defect on each other (in other words, be unable to reach a cooperative outcome that makes both of them better off). The prisoner's dilemma is a two-player situation, but the same logic applies to larger numbers of actors in a social system.

The international system is inherently anarchic. Each country claims sovereign authority over its own territory, but there is no sovereign authority over the entire world. Thus, when countries interact, they have no one to help them solve the dilemma in a way that benefits all. There is no one authority, such as a higher-level government, to prevent countries from attacking or stealing from one another in the pursuit of their respective interests.

The lack of a sovereign in the international system makes the relative stability of the global order somewhat puzzling.[4] If Hobbes was right about behavior and social systems in the absence of a sovereign (and many political scientists agree with him in principle), then why do countries frequently cooperate instead of "defect" on each other (that is, in the international context, attack or steal from each other) all the time? The facts would seem to contradict Hobbes: there is no sovereign, yet there is a degree of order and certainly not constant widespread warfare. The answer to this question is debated among scholars and politicians, and it bears directly on the principles that guide American foreign policy.

Thomas Hobbes's Leviathan (1651) argued that in the absence of a sovereign government, anarchy would reign. There is no sovereign authority over the international system—only individual sovereign countries—and yet the constant chaos and fighting Hobbes predicted does not occur. Why?

Theories and Strategies of Foreign Policy

Theories of foreign policy and international politics serve two purposes. The first is to help social scientists and analysts better understand the international system. The second is to guide decision making by foreign policy professionals and leaders of countries. These purposes are related; after all, decision makers also want to better understand the international system and often rely on the writings and advice of social scientists. The following approaches to foreign policy can be seen as serving both purposes to varying degrees, sometimes intended mostly as frameworks for understanding and sometimes intended as the means for guiding actual foreign policy decisions. We begin with realism and idealism, two classic approaches.

[4] See, for example, Robert Axelrod and Robert Keohane, "Achieving Cooperation under Anarchy," *World Politics* 38, no. 1 (1985): 226–54.

Realism

Realism assumes that countries typically seek to increase their own power relative to that of other countries. Power—primarily military, but also economic—rules the international system. Because that system has no sovereign authority, realists believe that it could possibly become "nasty" and "brutish" in Hobbesian terms. Nonetheless, countries are constrained in their pursuit of self-interest by the possibility that other states will act against them. They will not attack or harm another country if they expect a harsh reprisal. Moreover, they may cooperate with other countries as a way to counteract a threat from a more powerful country. Thus, according to realists, what holds order in place and allows for cooperation is fear of military reaction by more powerful states. Realists believe that the United States should maintain a robust military and may need to back up its threats with force.[5]

Idealism

In contrast to realism, **idealism** (sometimes called liberalism or neoliberalism) assumes that countries most often have common interests and can work together to avoid war through robust international organizations and even international governments. Unlike realists, idealists place their faith in international institutions such as the United Nations (UN) to police the behavior of individual countries. Idealists do not consider the quest for national power to be the key motivation in international affairs. Furthermore, idealists believe that the United States can best influence the behavior of other countries not through military force, but through example, and through diplomatically pressuring countries to adopt democratic principles and improve their human rights records.[6]

Internationalism versus Isolationism

Most foreign policy makers, whether realists or idealists, agree that the United States should remain actively engaged in the international community. By *engaged*, they mean being **internationalist**, or actively involved in the affairs of other countries and in maintaining world order. As we will learn shortly, the United States has throughout its history, especially since the early twentieth century, become the most active country in the world in participating in international organizations, affecting the politics and conflicts within and

[5] Realism has often been associated with the foreign policy of the Richard Nixon administration (1969–74) due to the influence of Henry Kissinger, a notable realist scholar and diplomat who served as Nixon's national security adviser and secretary of state.

[6] Idealism has often been associated with the administrations of Woodrow Wilson (1913–21), Jimmy Carter (1977–81), and Barack Obama (2009–17).

across other countries, and paying for the military and diplomatic collective efforts on a global scale.

But some Americans are **isolationists**, who propose that it is in the best interests of the United States to stay out of the affairs of other countries, and more generally to remain disengaged from international organizations and conflicts. Although this view is not widely held by policy makers in the United States today, in the past many Americans argued that meddling in international conflicts (such as World Wars I and II) was damaging to the country's welfare and interests. Isolationism has been on the rise in recent years in American political discourse and is popular among certain segments of society. Donald Trump ran for president with a strongly isolationist theme that the United States was paying far too much for its alliances and foreign policy entanglements. As president he has repeatedly advocated that the United States should substantially pull back from commitments overseas, including key alliances like those with Europe and in East Asia.

isolationism An approach to foreign policy that advocates for a country to stay out of international affairs.

One underlying assumption of isolationism is that if countries focused more fully on their own affairs, the world would be a more peaceful place. Hence, the best contribution the United States can make to international stability is to deal with its own domestic problems. For advocates like President Trump, another assumption is that the United States would be better off if it paid less money for internationalist foreign policies, and that alone is sufficient justification for isolationism.

Disagreements about whether isolationism or internationalism is best for the United States have continued throughout American history (as we discuss again later). Most often, isolationism has emerged from specific domestic constituencies that for various reasons opposed American participation in foreign wars, in trade agreements, or in costly alliances.

Unilateralism versus Multilateralism

Among foreign policy specialists and certain domestic constituencies, there are splits between those advocating a more unilateral approach to foreign policy and those advocating a more multilateral approach. The former approach refers to the United States making its own decisions on foreign policy and acting on those decisions despite the wishes and pledged support of the leaders of other countries. **Unilateralism** springs largely from a realist point of view— that the United States needs to pursue its own interests regardless of the interests of other countries—and, in current times, from recognition that as the most powerful country in the world, the United States *can* successfully carry out many of its foreign policy goals without the approval or concrete support of other countries. Thus, when the United States decided to invade Iraq in 2003, it did so without the cooperation or approval of the other major world powers, including its own allies in Western Europe.

unilateralism An approach to foreign policy that is informed primarily by a nation's own interests and means, relying little on the approval or support of other nations.

multilateralism An approach to foreign policy that considers and depends on the perspectives and resources of multiple nations.

Multilateralism, in contrast, tends to come from an idealist perspective. Seeking the cooperation and coalitional support of other countries in foreign policy actions benefits the United States. It is not good, in this view, for the United States to be alone in foreign policy ventures, especially in military ventures. Long-run stability for the United States relies on the goodwill of allies, and that goodwill is gained over time with careful alliance building before taking bold action. For example, when the United States intervened militarily in Libya in 2011 and in Syria in the years following, it did so as part of a large international coalition following a United Nations resolution supported by some of the countries of the Arab League and nearly all countries in the North Atlantic Treaty Organization (NATO). Multilateralism also includes having the United States participate willingly in international organizations and forums, a topic we take up later in this chapter.

The Democratic Peace as a Motivation

Starting with nineteenth-century philosopher Immanuel Kant, observers noted that no major wars had occurred between two democratic countries.[7] Democracies have fought in wars, of course, but always against nondemocratic countries, or so the argument goes. Scholars disagree over how to define democracy, and some question the claim that democracies have "never" fought each other. But the evidence supporting the **democratic peace** is compelling.

democratic peace The observation that historically it has been extremely rare for democracies to fight wars against other democracies.

Why do democracies tend not to fight each other? Realists and idealists would have different explanations for the pattern. Some argue that authoritarian regimes, in line with realist thinking, often seek to enhance their relative power on the world stage by initiating wars. Democracies, by contrast, have more complicated national interests, as defined by the populations that elect their governments. Hence, they tend to pursue goals that can be achieved by peaceful means, such as gaining more wealth, so that more people within society will benefit. Both realists and idealists can agree that if more countries in a given region become democratic, they will be more constrained by their own populations and less prone to resort to irrational aggression in comparison with authoritarian countries. But a realist maintains that power is the currency of international politics and that all countries, regardless of regime type, seek more power. Thus, democracies would seek additional power in other ways besides war. An idealist, on the other hand, claims that power is just one motivation for democracies to avoid war; but perhaps an additional motivation is that their populations seek things other than power, such as wealth and overall better living standards.

[7] See Immanuel Kant, "To Perpetual Peace: A Philosophical Sketch," in *Perpetual Peace and Other Essays on Politics, History, and Morals*, ed. Ted Humphrey (1795; repr. Indianapolis: Hackett, 1983).

Contemporary Political Science Approaches

Today political scientists tend to approach the study of international relations and foreign policy from one of two perspectives, both of them leading to more nuanced understandings of the international system than previous theories based on realism and isolationism. Some depict relations between countries to be constant **bargaining** over the desired goods at stake in the international system—land, wealth, autonomy, influence, raw materials, and prestige. In bargaining relationships, the two or more actors involved have some common and opposing interests, but most importantly, they are trying to divide something they both want. For instance, two countries both want peace (the common interest) but also both want the same piece of land. The key to foreign policy from an individual country's perspective is to bargain effectively, first to be sure to achieve the common goals with other countries, but second to get as much as possible out of the bargain in their country's favor. Political scientists using a bargaining perspective will examine the multiple tools available to countries—diplomacy, threats, sanctions, warfare, alliance building, trade (all discussed later)—as they seek peaceful bargaining outcomes that advantage them. In studies of bargaining between countries, scholars focus on the various moves and countermoves that nearly always remain peaceful but not quite fully cooperative. Countries generally do not want war or violence, but they threaten war and occasionally end up using warfare and violence as part of an overall bargaining strategy. Peaceful bargaining can break down due to miscalculations and intransigence, and war can result.

Alternatively, some political scientists pay close attention to domestic pressures and factors as the keys to understanding foreign policy. This approach is not necessarily at odds with a bargaining approach, and the two approaches can be combined. Among the domestic factors that are often seen to matter are the basic political institutions, such as whether the country is a democracy or some kind of autocracy, or whether as a democracy it is a presidential system as opposed to a parliamentary system; public opinion that is strongly in favor or opposed to going to war (especially in democracies); powerful interest groups that pressure the government on specific elements of foreign policy; and the economic health of the country. (We address some of these later in this chapter.) Political scientists analyze which of these domestic factors correlate with which foreign policy behavior. One correlation we have already discussed—the presumed democratic peace. In

bargaining Actors (e.g., countries) advance their own interests while working toward a specific common objective with other actors (e.g., other countries).

German Chancellor Angela Merkel (right) and French President Emmanuel Macron (left) at a European Union summit. Though democratic countries disagree—often bitterly—about foreign and economic policy, they usually end up working together when faced with international crises. Moreover, many have observed that democratic nations tend not to go to war against each other.

other research, political scientists have found a relationship between public opinion, as expressed through polls, and escalation or demobilization of war efforts.[8]

Historical Perspective

A historical perspective on American foreign policy indicates that many of these approaches have been influential within the national government. The United States came into existence as a small country that feared being bullied by the major European powers of the day—Great Britain, France, and Spain. For years after winning its independence, the new country remained vulnerable to attack. One key motivation for writing and ratifying the Constitution in the late 1780s was the need for a stronger national government that could maintain a powerful military to protect American interests. Security concerns continued to motivate American foreign policy after the Founding, but although Alexander Hamilton and the Federalists pushed for deep economic engagement with other countries to build up the American economy, Thomas Jefferson and the Democratic-Republicans generally took a more isolationist position.

The United States enjoyed several unusual advantages that limited its vulnerability: an ocean that buffered it from the European powers; a vast, relatively undeveloped wilderness to the west (especially after the Louisiana Purchase in 1803); and, after California became a state in 1850, another ocean guarding its western border. As a result, unlike many countries, the United States has never had to worry about being "squeezed" from different sides by allied opponents invading by land. Indeed, since the early nineteenth century no country has seriously threatened to invade and occupy the United States. This fact has enabled isolationism to take hold among politicians at various points in American history, especially during World War I and just before World War II, but also today.

Relative safety from invasion does not, however, mean that the United States is invulnerable. The Pearl Harbor attack by Japan in 1941 and the 2001 terrorist attacks in New York and Washington, D.C., occurred in American territory. Moreover, the United States has interests all over the world that are exposed to attack and need to be protected. In recent years it has had ambassadors killed (for example, in Libya in 2012) and military bases attacked (in Afghanistan repeatedly in 2015–17). Thus, despite the low threat of foreign invasion and the strain of isolationism, the United States has been deeply

---

[8] John Mueller, *War, Presidents, and Public Opinion* (New York: John Wiley & Sons, 1973).

involved in international affairs and military conflict throughout its history because of its international ambitions and reach.

In the nineteenth century, most such conflicts occurred on the American continent: the United States fought Great Britain in the War of 1812, Mexico in the 1840s, and various Native American tribes throughout the century. A brief war with Spain beginning in 1898 resulted in the United States becoming a colonial power, foreshadowing several American military interventions in Latin America in the early twentieth century. But it was U.S. involvement in the two world wars, in 1917–18 and 1941–45, that put foreign policy at or near the top of the government's agenda. These two global conflicts made the United States the major political, economic, and military force in Asia and Europe, as well as in its own hemisphere.

In both wars, U.S. military intervention was decisive in ending German aggression. After World War II, American military bases dotted Europe, and millions of American soldiers were stationed there. The United States played the leading role in maintaining the peace, supporting the democratic regimes of Western Europe (both economically and militarily), and securing their borders against perceived threats of Soviet aggression during the Cold War. After the defeat of Japan in 1945, American forces occupied that country and projected American power throughout Asia and the Pacific. The American guarantee of Japanese nonaggression set the stage for the economic and political rise of other Asian countries, such as China, South Korea, Singapore, Indonesia, and Taiwan. Even in the twenty-first century, the United States is seen as a vital guarantor of political and military stability in both Europe and Asia.

The top priority for American foreign policy and the U.S. military is no longer to protect the country from invasions by foreign countries. Rather, it is to (1) safeguard and advance American interests overseas; (2) maintain international stability; and (3) protect American interests and Americans from terrorist attacks. Realists and idealists in various presidential administrations and in Congress have pulled foreign policy in different directions. Realists have been more prone to pursue military action, and when they get the upper hand politically, it has often led to war. Since World War II, the United States has engaged in major wars and minor military actions on four continents besides North America (Figure 17.1). In each case, U.S. troops fought to secure what were seen at the time as key national interests. Between 1948 and 1990, these conflicts centered on the Cold War rivalry with the Soviet Union. Since the collapse of the Soviet Union in 1991, the United States has been involved in numerous conflicts to settle regional wars or to protect American interests in the Middle East and other regions.

Of course, military action is not the only way the United States engages in international conflict and cooperation. Idealists emphasize trade and diplomacy as instruments of foreign policy. As a trading nation, the United

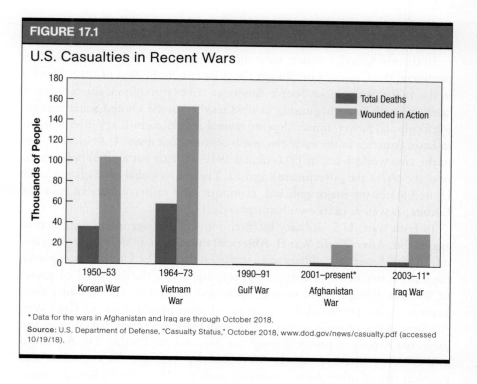

FIGURE 17.1

U.S. Casualties in Recent Wars

Legend:
- Total Deaths
- Wounded in Action

Y-axis: Thousands of People (0 to 180)

X-axis categories:
- 1950–53 Korean War
- 1964–73 Vietnam War
- 1990–91 Gulf War
- 2001–present* Afghanistan War
- 2003–11* Iraq War

* Data for the wars in Afghanistan and Iraq are through October 2018.

Source: U.S. Department of Defense, "Casualty Status," October 2018, www.dod.gov/news/casualty.pdf (accessed 10/19/18).

States has always been deeply involved in the global flow of goods. Since the mid-twentieth century, it has played a central role, if not the preeminent role, in the World Trade Organization (WTO), the UN, and numerous other international organizations. The United States has worked to resolve intractable conflicts in Sudan, Israel and Palestine, and Northern Ireland. It has distributed humanitarian, political, and military aid to countries worldwide. We will discuss these aspects of foreign policy in more detail later in this chapter.

Although isolationism has been a recurring theme of U.S. foreign policy, it has never been a consistent stance. The isolationism of the early twentieth century, for example, pertained mainly to conflicts among the Great (European) Powers. In matters having to do with Asia and Latin America, the United States has been interventionist and even militarily aggressive since the nineteenth century. Under the so-called **Monroe Doctrine**, enunciated in 1823 by President James Monroe, the United States claimed the entire Western Hemisphere as its exclusive sphere of influence. A large portion of the southwestern United States, including Texas and much of California, was captured from Mexico by aggressive American militaries during the Mexican-American War (1846–48). The United States also intervened in limited but important ways in

Monroe Doctrine Enunciated in 1823 by President James Monroe, the notion that the United States could claim the entire Western Hemisphere as its exclusive sphere of influence.

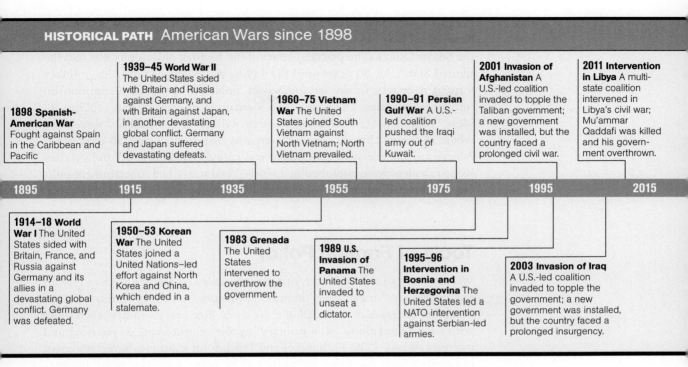

1898 Spanish-American War Fought against Spain in the Caribbean and Pacific

1939–45 World War II The United States sided with Britain and Russia against Germany, and with Britain against Japan, in another devastating global conflict. Germany and Japan suffered devastating defeats.

1960–75 Vietnam War The United States joined South Vietnam against North Vietnam; North Vietnam prevailed.

1990–91 Persian Gulf War A U.S.-led coalition pushed the Iraqi army out of Kuwait.

2001 Invasion of Afghanistan A U.S.-led coalition invaded to topple the Taliban government; a new government was installed, but the country faced a prolonged civil war.

2011 Intervention in Libya A multi-state coalition intervened in Libya's civil war; Mu'ammar Qaddafi was killed and his government overthrown.

1895   1915   1935   1955   1975   1995   2015

1914–18 World War I The United States sided with Britain, France, and Russia against Germany and its allies in a devastating global conflict. Germany was defeated.

1950–53 Korean War The United States joined a United Nations–led effort against North Korea and China, which ended in a stalemate.

1983 Grenada The United States intervened to overthrow the government.

1989 U.S. Invasion of Panama The United States invaded to unseat a dictator.

1995–96 Intervention in Bosnia and Herzegovina The United States led a NATO intervention against Serbian-led armies.

2003 Invasion of Iraq A U.S.-led coalition invaded to topple the government; a new government was installed, but the country faced a prolonged insurgency.

China, Russia, and many Central American countries in the nineteenth and early twentieth centuries.

As these examples show, internationalism (as opposed to isolationism) has long been at the core of U.S. foreign policy, though that has changed somewhat under President Trump. Even as a young and relatively weak nation, the United States became enmeshed in the affairs of other countries and the conflicts of other regions. It first aspired to become a great power around the turn of the twentieth century, in the aftermath of the Spanish-American War. With the decline of Britain as the world's predominant power and the defeat of Germany in two world wars, the United States in the 1940s emerged alongside the Soviet Union as a full-fledged superpower. Since the dissolution of the Soviet Union in 1991, the United States has stood alone, with far more military capability than any other country and economic, military, and diplomatic involvement in every region of the world. Only China, growing as an economic and military power, will rival the United States any time soon. Conflicts within the U.S. government over foreign policy typically hinge on how to maintain the country's superpower status and advance its interests by using this massive power responsibly.

There is an interesting parallel between the ideas animating American foreign policy during the Cold War and the ideas alive today. George Kennan became a dominant thinker in U.S. foreign policy circles after World War II. Kennan in 1947–48 advocated foreign policies to contain the ambitions of the Soviet Union. The practical effect of the Kennan philosophy was that the United States, for 50 years until the 1990s, was willing to use U.S. military force if necessary to thwart any Soviet ambitions to advance communism into more countries. The Korean and Vietnam Wars were legacies of Kennan's ideas. Today, the United States is often willing to use military force anywhere to thwart threats, especially terrorist threats, to American interests or Americans themselves. This stance was called "containment" policy after Kennan's ideas were published in 1946–47, and today U.S. containment policies are directed not at the Soviets, but at international terrorist organizations.

Tools of Foreign Policy

We now turn to the tools that, in principle, every country can use in foreign policy. We say "in principle" because in practice, not every country has the capability or freedom to use all of these tools. Not every country, even those with large populations, has a military capable of protecting its territory and interests abroad. (The Philippines and Poland, for example, have very small militaries.) Such countries are protected by other countries or by international entities like the Association of Southeast Asian Nations (ASEAN) or the North Atlantic Treaty Organization (NATO). The United States, however, has unparalleled capability to use all of these tools thanks to its status as the world's largest economy and sole superpower.

Basic Tools

We start with the basic tools of foreign policy that are in constant use in international politics: bilateral diplomacy, intelligence gathering, multilateral diplomacy and participation in international organizations, trading relationships, and foreign aid.

diplomacy Peaceful negotiations and interactions among countries.

Bilateral Diplomacy. Diplomacy refers to peaceful negotiations and interactions among countries in which information is exchanged, differences are discussed and possibly resolved, and occasionally decisions are made to cooperate. Bilateral diplomacy occurs between two countries at a time. At the top of the American diplomatic hierarchy is the president, who engages with other heads of state or government on the broadest level. Directly below the president is the secretary of state, the nation's chief diplomat, who is usually chosen because he or she is respected around the world. The president can appoint special envoys with responsibility for particular trouble spots—for instance, former senator George Mitchell was sent by President Obama to help with peace talks in Northern Ireland, Sudan, and the Middle East. Deputy secretaries of state also carry out high-level talks with top government officials in other countries. The U.S. trade representative, another presidential appointee, leads bilateral and multilateral trade negotiations and is granted considerable discretion to make trade deals. In addition, there are hundreds of ambassadors—either political appointees or career diplomats—who head U.S. embassies around the world.

Formal interactions with other countries can take the form of bilateral negotiations between high-level elected and appointed political officials. On a day-to-day basis, however, lower-level professional diplomats conduct most such intergovernmental business. As the first line of diplomacy, ambassadors and embassy staffs handle routine communications with the leaders of other countries. The same function is performed by the representatives of foreign governments, whose embassies are located in Washington, D.C.

The United States maintains diplomatic relations with nearly every country in the world. For countries with which it has no formal diplomatic relations, such as North Korea, the American government communicates through various informal channels, such as an American "interest section" housed in the embassy of a third country.

Intelligence Gathering. A major part of modern foreign policy is intelligence gathering, a mission carried out by various agencies spread across the Departments of State, Defense, and Homeland Security, among others (see the Know the Facts box on page 672). Unlike the depictions in popular spy movies, the bulk of intelligence work involves mundane tasks such as reviewing government reports, reading newspapers, and talking to knowledgeable people about what other governments are doing.[9] Most intelligence gathering is overt, meaning that the materials are not classified and the work is done openly. But some intelligence work, the most sensitive and dangerous kind, is covert and involves conducting secret surveillance and interrogations and writing classified reports. The Central Intelligence Agency (CIA) has the primary responsibility for gathering covert intelligence.[10] Nearly every day, the president receives a secret intelligence briefing that summarizes key findings from the previous 24 hours, collected from across the many intelligence units in the government.

Multilateral Diplomacy. Diplomacy can also be multilateral—that is, it can involve more than two countries at a time. Most often, multilateral diplomacy occurs within forums sponsored by international organizations, and the meetings are well publicized and widely covered by the media.

[9] See Richard Betts, "Analysis, War, and Decision: Why Intelligence Failures Are Inevitable," *World Politics* 31, no. 1 (1978): 61–89.
[10] See Robert M. Gates, "The CIA and Foreign Policy," *Foreign Affairs* (Winter 1987/88): 215.

Know the FACTS — Agencies and Departments Involved in Gathering Intelligence

Office of the Director of National Intelligence–adviser to the president and coordinator of intelligence agencies throughout the federal government

Central Intelligence Agency (CIA)

Department of Defense
- Defense Intelligence Agency (DIA)
- National Security Agency (NSA)
- National Geospatial-Intelligence Agency (NGA)
- National Reconnaissance Office (NRO)
- Air Force Intelligence, Surveillance and Reconnaissance Agency (AFISR or AIA)
- Army Intelligence and Security Command (INSCOM)
- Marine Corps Intelligence Activity (MCIA)
- Office of Naval Intelligence (ONI)

Department of State
- Bureau of Intelligence and Research (INR)

Department of Justice
- Federal Bureau of Investigation (FBI), Directorate of Intelligence
- Drug Enforcement Administration (DEA), Office of National Security Intelligence

Department of Energy
- Office of Intelligence and Counterintelligence (OICI)

Department of Homeland Security
- Coast Guard Intelligence (CGI)
- Office of Intelligence and Analysis (I&A)

Department of the Treasury
- Office of Terrorism and Financial Intelligence (TFI)

Source: Eric Rosenbach and Aki J. Peritz, *Confrontation or Collaboration? Congress and the Intelligence Community*, a publication of The Intelligence and Policy Project of Harvard Kennedy School's Belfer Center for Science and International Affairs, 2009, http://belfercenter.ksg.harvard.edu (accessed 2/28/11).

Organizations such as the UN, WTO, World Bank, International Telecommunications Union, and Arab League are increasingly important players in world politics. But they have distinctive features from those of the other players (usually countries) in international affairs. International organizations are formed through treaties and agreements among nation-state governments. Many of them are granted powers to pass regulations and international laws, and to enforce those laws through lawsuits and court-like proceedings. Yet these organizations have no real sovereign authority; they depend instead on their members to use their own militaries or police forces to enforce international law.

Note that enforcement of rules passed by international organizations involves collective action problems among countries. Which countries will put in the resources, or the military might, to enforce international rules? Most of the time, solving such collective action problems is not a big issue, because countries help enforce the rules on a voluntary or nearly voluntary basis. The United States, as perhaps the key country in many international organizations (it typically contributes the most money, personnel, and equipment), has been central to putting the rules into effect. It has led many important UN missions during conflicts in places like Korea and the Middle East. It has been the most important voice in the World Bank and International Monetary Fund, as well as a leader within the WTO, for most of its history.

Nevertheless, the United States has complicated relationships with organizations like the UN. Some presidential administrations are more comfortable than others with participating in and leading international organizations, depending on whether idealists or realists have the upper hand. In general, recent Democratic presidents (Bill Clinton and Barack Obama) have regarded American involvement in international organizations positively, whereas recent Republican presidents (especially George W. Bush, but also Ronald Reagan and Donald Trump) have been more wary and have actively undercut the work of some of these organizations. The Republican argument, which has resonated among many voters, has been that these international organizations encroach on the sovereign authority of the United States, or that the United States pays much more than its fair share. Donald Trump's criticisms of NATO and the UN included accusations that other countries were free riding off the United States. In saying this, he was trying to motivate voters to support his policies of either renegotiating the international agreements underlying these alliances and organizations or withdrawing from them altogether.

Trading Relationships. Trade policy has long been among the most political and delicate of any policy that the national government undertakes. In global terms, trade can take on the character of multiple prisoner's dilemmas between countries. We discuss this aspect of trade in Chapter 15 as well. Every country individually would be better off if its domestic industries were protected from competition from foreign companies, provided those same domestic industries could have access to another country's markets. "Defecting" occurs when one country closes its markets but benefits from the open markets of another country. Because every country is tempted to close its own markets to foreign competition, it is widely recognized that it is best for all concerned to have trade agreements and an international body to enforce them.[11] The WTO plays this role to some extent. It can levy fines on countries that close their markets or permit trade sanctions by other countries in retaliation, but in the face of a world power's intransigence, the WTO is largely helpless.

Trade policy is important for three reasons. First, it is vital to maintaining good relations with other countries. Trading relationships that are healthy—meaning that goods and money flow relatively freely across national boundaries—tend to tie the fates of countries together and discourage them from going to war. War becomes costlier as trade increases because countries have a lot to lose economically from breaking off trade relations. Second, trade is vital to economic growth in other countries. To the extent that the United States benefits from increasing wealth in other countries—which leads to political stability and also to those countries buying more American-made goods and allowing American investment—trade helps make the world more peaceful and prosperous. Third, and of most importance domestically, free trade benefits U.S. companies on the whole and increases the wealth of Americans. From a foreign policy professional's perspective, a strong American economy yields many benefits: more money for military spending, more attention paid by the president to diplomacy and foreign policy in general (because less attention is paid to economic crises), and a happier Congress that is willing to spend on foreign aid, new embassies, and other things that help smooth relations with other countries.

Insofar as trade policy is a domestic matter, it may not seem to bear much discussion in a chapter on foreign policy. Yet perhaps the key fact about trade policy is that domestic economic interests put enormous pressure on Congress and the president to adopt policies favorable to their interests. Furthermore, politicians, including both Donald Trump and Hillary Clinton in the 2016 presidential campaign, regularly complain about the costs of existing trade agreements on certain vulnerable sectors among American workers. Foreign competition can put American companies out of business and workers out of jobs. Complaints about free trade resonate among workers either laid off or fired from companies that lose out to foreign competitors.

Pursuing policies opposed to free trade, or policies to try to renegotiate existing trade agreements, can be motivated in several ways. First, it can be a form of economic isolationism; the U.S. economy does not need to trade

[11] See Thomas Oatley, *International Political Economy: Interests and Institutions in the Global Economy* (New York: Pearson/Longman, 2004), pp. 42–51.

much with other countries in order to thrive. Most economists reject this argument, and instead claim that trade overall helps the U.S. economy and creates more jobs than are lost by foreign competition. Yet the argument has favor among many people in the United States, both Democrats and Republicans. (It especially resonated in 2016 among supporters of Donald Trump on the Republican side and Bernie Sanders during his bid for the Democratic presidential nomination.) Second, existing trade agreements are in fact flawed and need renegotiation. Third, free trade in general is acceptable, but specific industries need protection from foreign competition because of the special needs of the industry or the vulnerability of the workers. An example in the United States is the steel industry that receives ongoing trade protection because of (alleged) evidence that some countries regularly dump their excess steel on American markets at very low prices.

In regard to focused domestic political pressure, exporting companies and industries, and their workers, want policies that maintain open foreign markets.[12] Importing companies and industries want low tariffs and customs fees on products that they sell or need for assembling their own products. And domestic companies endangered by foreign competitors want high tariffs or product quotas (limits on imports of foreign goods) from foreign countries so that they can sell more easily to American consumers.[13]

In the end, the national government has to walk a fine line to satisfy all these goals—keeping domestic industries satisfied, maintaining good relationships with foreign countries, and participating in good faith in international organizations devoted to free trade and promoting the common good. Thus, trade policy is one of the most complicated of all policy areas, foreign or domestic.

Foreign Aid. The United States dispenses billions of dollars in aid to foreign countries every year.[14] Although several countries devote a higher percentage of their gross domestic product (GDP) to foreign aid than the United States does, only the European Union comes close to the total amount that the United States doles out. Most Americans, when asked in polls, rank foreign aid low in priority among all the items in the government budget. Some argue that such spending takes funds away from important domestic programs,[15] even though foreign aid accounts for less than 1 percent of the federal budget.

[12] Michael Gilligan, *Empowering Exporters* (Ann Arbor: University of Michigan Press, 1997).

[13] See, in particular, Ronald Rogowksi, "Political Cleavages and Changing Exposure to Trade," *American Political Science Review* 81, no. 4 (1987): 1121–37; and E. E. Schattschneider, *Politics, Pressures, and the Tariff* (New York: Prentice-Hall, 1935).

[14] For the politics of foreign aid, see Bruce Bueno de Mesquita and Alastair Smith, "A Political Economy of Aid," *International Organization* 63, no. 2 (2009): 309–10.

[15] For more on U.S. public opinion and the distribution of foreign aid, see Helen Milner and Dustin Tingley, "The Political Economy of U.S. Foreign Aid: American Legislators and the Domestic Politics of Aid," *Economics and Politics* 22, no. 2 (2010): 200–232.

American aid has various goals. By far, the largest amount of money is for military aid to Israel and Egypt (Figure 17.2). This aid began in the 1940s and escalated dramatically in the early 1970s as tensions and war in the Middle East threatened the stability of the region and world oil prices. Giving aid to both Israel and Egypt was intended to sustain the balance of power in the Middle East. The United States signed an historic agreement in 2016 with Israel to provide that country with $38 billion in aid over ten years. Today, substantial American aid also flows to Jordan and Pakistan to help those countries against aggressive neighboring countries and to fight extremist groups endangering the international economy.

Smaller amounts of aid are earmarked for humanitarian assistance and the promotion of democracy; for example, the United States gives money to Uganda to help run peaceful elections. In Nigeria, Kenya, and Haiti, U.S. aid promotes citizens groups and provides medical supplies and food for the poor. The United States has given money for disaster relief to countries such as Indone-

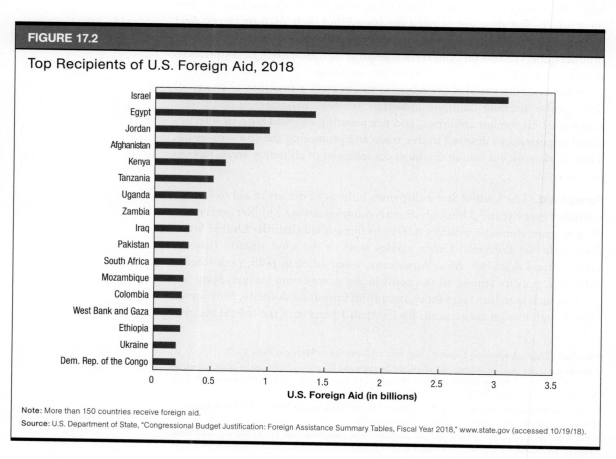

FIGURE 17.2

Top Recipients of U.S. Foreign Aid, 2018

Note: More than 150 countries receive foreign aid.

Source: U.S. Department of State, "Congressional Budget Justification: Foreign Assistance Summary Tables, Fiscal Year 2018," www.state.gov (accessed 10/19/18).

sia (after the 2005 tsunami), Pakistan (after the earthquakes of 2008 and 2010), and Japan (after the earthquake of 2011). Humanitarian aid may spring from motives that are genuinely humanitarian and not directly linked to the national interests or the global economic stability. Military aid, however, is clearly intended to advance American national interests as defined by Congress and the president. Similarly, aid to promote democracy abroad can be seen as having foreign policy implications.

Domestic politics plays a role in this area of foreign policy as well. Some American aid to other countries has had strings attached that reflect politicians' domestic agendas. As an example, for most of the 2000s, under an executive order issued by President Bush, no U.S. money was to be spent on organizations that promoted abortions, in keeping with the views of many Republican voters who oppose abortion. (President Obama rescinded this policy; see Chapter 6.) In the early years of the Trump administration, the government pulled back on foreign aid commitments to help other countries cope with the effects of climate change. This position reflects the skepticism among some Republicans about the seriousness of climate change, and the skepticism among other Republicans that government action would do much to reverse climate change in any event.

Crisis Tools

So far, we have discussed foreign policy tools that are ongoing and relatively routine. When crises develop between the United States and other countries, or among countries other than the United States where potential military conflict threatens American interests, two major alternatives to diplomacy are available: economic pressure and military action. In both cases, the intention is to influence the behavior of other countries, usually in response to circumstances deemed threatening to American interests, but sometimes in response to how governments are treating their own people.

Economic Pressure. Economic pressure represents an intermediate level of action between diplomacy and military engagement.[16] Such pressure usually takes the form of sanctions—for example, freezing the bank accounts and assets of a particular country in banks outside of its borders, forbidding the country's leaders or citizens to travel to certain countries, or imposing trade restrictions between the country and much of the rest of the world.[17] In extreme cases, the United States or other countries can enforce a blockade to

---

[16] See David A. Baldwin, *Economic Statecraft* (Princeton, NJ: Princeton University Press, 1985).

[17] See Daniel Drezner, *The Sanctions Paradox: Economic Statecraft and International Relations* (New York: Cambridge University Press, 1999); and Gary Clyde Hufbauer, Jeffrey Schott, Kimberly Ann Elliott, and Barbara Oegg, *Economic Sanctions Reconsidered*, 3rd ed. (Washington, DC: Institute for International Economics, 2007).

prevent goods from moving into or out of the country, but this usually falls into the category of military action. In sum, the United States and its allies can try to impose various degrees of economic isolation on a country as punishment for not abiding by the wishes of the United States or the international community.

In recent years, the United States and other countries have imposed various economic sanctions on North Korea and Iran as a result of a widespread belief that they were preparing to develop nuclear weapons in defiance of international treaties. In the 1980s, South Africa came under intense economic pressure from other countries as part of a campaign to abolish apartheid—a system that denied blacks fundamental rights of citizenship. Sudan, Zimbabwe, Syria, Burma, Libya, and Egypt have recently experienced international economic pressure because their governments have taken actions that were seen to violate norms of human rights. In 2016, many of the onerous sanctions were lifted for Iran after an agreement was reached between Iran and the major world powers that Iran would halt its nuclear program in exchange for releasing financial resources that had been held up in the West since the 1970s and 1980s.

Enforcing international economic pressure involves another collective action problem among countries. Any individual country would benefit by trading with a rogue country or welcoming the rogue country's money for investment, especially if all the other countries were shunning the rogue country. Thus, there are strong temptations to free ride off the sanctions of other countries and reap the rewards of being the only country (or one of the few countries) with economic ties to the rogue country.

The United States is often the instigator of economic sanctions and uses its immense influence to pressure other countries to enforce them. Thus, various American laws impose economic penalties on countries that violate sanctions against Iran, North Korea, and other rogue countries. These actions by the American government should be seen as attempts to enforce a collective action against targeted countries, such as Iran, and thus prevent defection not directly by Iran, but by other countries tempted to engage with Iran. Note that other countries may not see violating the sanctions as wrong or as "defecting" from a collective agreement. After all, economic sanctions are blunt and hurt people across the targeted society, including many innocent people who are the intended (long-term) beneficiaries of the sanctions.

Military Action. Economic sanctions are an example of the use of **soft power** in foreign policy.[18] **Military action**, defined as the organized use of deadly force by a government, is the opposite of soft power. It is the last resort in foreign policy and naturally carries enormous costs and risks. The wars in Iraq and Afghanistan resulted in the injury or death of thousands of American

soft power The use of nonmilitary pressure such as economic sanctions, diplomatic isolation, or public shaming against another country.

military action The organized use of deadly force by a government.

[18] Joseph Nye, "Soft Power and American Foreign Policy," *Political Science Quarterly* 119, no. 2 (2004): 255–70.

soldiers, not to mention the huge military and civilian casualties suffered by Iraqis, Afghanis, and citizens of other countries. By 2019, the two wars combined had cost U.S. taxpayers over $4 trillion (including payments on debt to pay for them), an enormous sum that is more than the entire annual GDP of Germany, the world's fourth-largest economy. Military action carries other costs as well; the invasion of Iraq by American-led coalition forces in 2003 led to serious ruptures in diplomatic relations with governments in Europe and parts of the Middle East.

Huge financial costs are incurred not only in waging wars but also in preparing for them. The United States has by far the most powerful standing military in the world. It spends more than 40 percent of the world's total on military technology, weapons, personnel, and facilities. Its military has a global reach with military bases on five continents; more than 300,000 American servicemen and women (out of more than a million active military personnel) are stationed in countries other than the United States and its territories (Figures 17.3 and 17.4).

As a tool of foreign policy, military action can serve various goals, including the acquisition of territory. In the last 100 years, however, U.S. military actions have been intended to protect American interests overseas (Gulf War); to defeat global forces of fascism or communism (World War II, Korea,

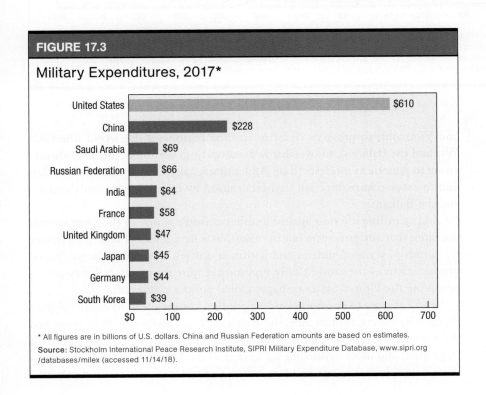

FIGURE 17.3

Military Expenditures, 2017*

Country	Expenditure
United States	$610
China	$228
Saudi Arabia	$69
Russian Federation	$66
India	$64
France	$58
United Kingdom	$47
Japan	$45
Germany	$44
South Korea	$39

* All figures are in billions of U.S. dollars. China and Russian Federation amounts are based on estimates.

Source: Stockholm International Peace Research Institute, SIPRI Military Expenditure Database, www.sipri.org /databases/milex (accessed 11/14/18).

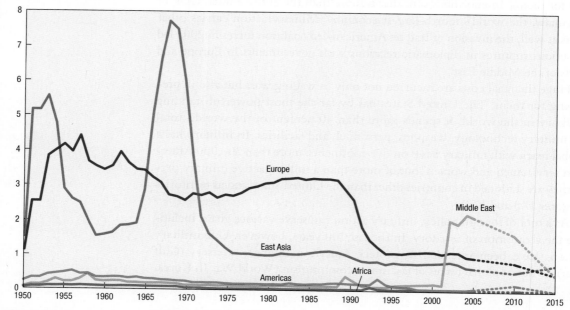

FIGURE 17.4

U.S. Troops Deployed Overseas, 1950–2015 (in hundreds of thousands)

Europe

Middle East

East Asia

Africa

Americas

Note: Data are unavailable for 2006–11 and 2013–14.

Source: Calculations by Tim Kane, Ph.D., The Heritage Foundation, based on annual records from the Department of Defense, 2007; "U.S. Military Deployments Overseas Mapped: How Have They Changed under Obama?" *The Guardian*, October 23, 2012, www.theguardian.com/news/datablog/interactive/2012/oct/23/us-military-deployments-overseas (accessed 8/15/13). 2015 data from the Department fo Defense Manpower Data Center (accessed 11/11/16).

and Vietnam); to preserve order in specific regions of the world (the Gulf War and the Balkans); to overthrow dictators or governments deemed threatening to American interests (Iraq, Afghanistan, Libya, Panama, and Grenada); and to resolve humanitarian disasters caused by bad governments (Somalia and the Balkans).

Taking military action against another country is one of the most serious decisions that any government can make. Wars have a way of reshaping power relationships across countries and within countries. Given the United States' unique status as the world's only superpower, just about any military action involving the United States reshapes global politics profoundly.

Severe threats to the homeland by another country lead to relatively predictable decisions; for instance, the attack on Pearl Harbor in 1941 prompted the United States to declare war on Japan the next day. Much more difficult to predict, and more agonizing for leaders in the U.S. government, are decisions over whether to use military action to protect people in foreign countries. The United States in 1994 declined, for a variety of logistical and political reasons, to intervene militarily in Rwanda to try to stop the genocide that killed hundreds of thousands of people. President Bill Clinton, both in office and since leaving office, has indicated his regret at not using American military force in that situation. His decision illustrates a difficult political reality: as valuable as it is to save lives, there is sometimes no obvious way to articulate what is at stake for American national interests in such humanitarian disasters.

Furthermore, it is important to recognize that in recent decades most American military action has been undertaken in coalition with other countries. This includes not only the wars in Iraq and Afghanistan, and the bombing action in Libya, but also the Korean War (1950–53), the Gulf War (1991), the military action in the Balkans (1997–98), the enforcement of the no-fly zones in Libya and Syria (2011–14), and drone attacks on ISIL and other groups (2012–18). Thus, the lead-up to military action often involves intensive diplomacy to convince potential allies to join American forces in combat. One of the major contemporary challenges for the United States is that it is engaged in a low-level military conflict with loosely organized, decentralized terrorist groups like Al Qaeda.

The United States routinely uses two other kinds of military actions, though the second might not qualify as strictly "military." First, the United States uses bombardments by unmanned aircraft (drones) to cross into the airspace of a foreign country and kill leaders and operatives of these "non-state" actors. (*Non-state* meaning that they are not acting in the interests of any given country, but rather in pursuit of extremist religious or ideological goals.) This military conflict with non-state actors represents a novel, but global, effort requiring different strategic thinking. Second, the United States engages in cyber warfare, which entails electronically invading computer networks in foreign countries, especially in the military and intelligence units in foreign countries, to disrupt hostile behavior. The United States has been the subject of cyber attacks (from North Korea, China, and Russia, for instance) and has worked with other countries like Israel to attack Iran and other Middle East countries.

Our theories of international relations are not yet equipped to fully understand this new kind of conflict. Drone strikes represent a method of warfare that can kill people without much risk to a group's own soldiers, so the typical constraints (for example, fear of casualties in that group) do not apply. Similarly, cyber warfare has few limits on applications and the potential for attacks on the infrastructure of entire countries, including electricity, water and sewage stations, and dams. In both cases, troubling ethical issues are raised; but the United States and other countries, including its adversaries (North Korea) and competitors (China and Russia), continue the technological advancement and usage of these military actions.

Making Foreign Policy

Who and what determines which tools of foreign policy are used, and how they are used? Let's divide our discussion of making foreign policy into three categories: the role of elected leaders—the president and Congress—in setting direction; the role of the bureaucracies that implement foreign policy; and the domestic political pressures that influence all levels of the national government that decide and implement foreign policy.

Elected Leaders

The president is indisputably predominant in the setting of foreign policy. Under the Constitution, he or she is head of state and commander in chief.[19] This makes the president both the nation's lead diplomat (above the secretary of state) and lead military decision maker. As head of state, the president is charged with representing the United States abroad in meetings such as those of the G8 or G20, which involve the heads of government or state of the 8 or 20 largest economies in the world. As commander in chief, the president is head of the armed forces and has final responsibility for the use of military force. Although the president delegates the tactical and many of the strategic decisions about the conduct of war, he or she has final responsibility for major strategic decisions. In addition, recall from Chapter 6 that the president has political authority that is not stated in the Constitution. As the leader of his or her party, for instance, the president sets the agenda for legislation regarding foreign policy and for communicating foreign policy goals to the people. In all of these roles, the president has dozens of advisers within the White House who liaise with various agencies and help make weighty decisions.

Congress, of course, also plays a major role in foreign policy. Although Congress can seem to be a distant second behind the president in this area,[20] it comes to the fore at key moments. Under the Constitution, for instance, Congress has to declare war or authorize the president to use military force. Formally, Congress has declared war only five times, but it has been directly involved in all other decisions to use military force. At times presidents have not sought prior congressional approval for relatively small military actions, but such instances were rare and justified by the need for speed and secrecy. The **War Powers Act** of 1973 requires the president to notify Congress and

War Powers Act Legislation passed in 1973 requiring that the president notify Congress and seek its approval within 48 hours after ordering military action.

[19] See Louis Henkin, "Foreign Affairs and the Constitution," *Foreign Affairs* (Winter 1987/88): 284.

[20] For more on the view of Congress as subservient to the president in foreign policy, see Stephen R. Weissman, *A Culture of Deference: Congress's Failure of Leadership in Foreign Policy* (New York: Basic Books, 1995). For more on the view that Congress can check the power of the president, see Stephen Krasner, *Defending the National Interest: Raw Materials Investments and U.S. Foreign Policy* (Princeton, NJ: Princeton University Press, 1978). Also see William G. Howell and Jon C. Pevehouse, "Presidents, Congress, and the Use of Force," *International Organization* 59 (Winter 2005): 209–32.

seek its approval within 48 hours of ordering military action, and presidents have complied with this aspect of the act. Thus the president can, under certain circumstances, gain congressional authorization after the fact. For example, President Reagan first decided to invade Grenada, then notified Congress afterward and obtained the necessary approval under the War Powers Act. Similarly, President Obama joined in the multinational force in Libya in 2011 before seeking any approval from Congress, a move that angered congressional leaders from both political parties.

Congress approves budgets for defense and for all the other aspects of foreign policy, such as diplomatic missions, foreign aid, and intelligence. In this way, Congress can, in principle, cut off funds for any presidential action it disagrees with. However, this course of action can be politically difficult, especially if voters interpret cutting off funding as increasing the risks to soldiers and to American interests. Furthermore, congressional approval is required for presidential appointments to key foreign policy posts, including those of secretaries of state and defense, ambassador to the UN, director of the CIA, and some cabinet-level advisers to the president.

The Constitution stipulates that the Senate must approve all treaties between the United States and foreign countries. The two-thirds voting requirement in the Senate ensures that such intergovernmental treaties are rare. (Recall from Chapter 6 how presidents in recent decades have used executive agreements more often than treaties because of the difficulty of obtaining Senate approval.) Finally, Congress has general oversight of the federal bureaucracy. It exercises influence over foreign policy in conducting investigations and overseeing the work of the foreign policy bureaucracies and of other executive branch actors (including the president and vice president) to monitor compliance with the law.

Although the states are forbidden under the Constitution to engage in foreign policy, state governments do become involved in matters overseas. In particular, nearly all the states actively seek to attract foreign investment. Governors often visit with or host foreign leaders to market the virtues of investing in businesses in their states.

Bureaucracies

Many crucial foreign policy decisions are made within the bureaucratic agencies of the national government.[21] The high degree of bureaucratic expertise required to conduct certain aspects of foreign policy, especially military affairs and diplomacy, means that executive departments are granted more discretion in foreign policy than in some other areas. In this respect, foreign policy

---

[21] See Graham Allison, "Conceptual Models and the Cuban Missile Crisis," *American Political Science Review* 63, no. 3 (1969): 689–718.

is more like economic policy than social policy. Of particular note are the departments of Defense and State. These two bureaucracies are at the center of the permanent staff within the government devoted to foreign policy. The Department of Defense prepares and operates the military while the State Department has charge of diplomatic efforts.

The Department of Defense is by far the largest and most expensive of all the executive-branch departments. Besides deciding on and implementing war strategy, it staffs and equips the armed forces. Through the department, the government relies on private companies to build, deliver, maintain, and repair military hardware—weapons, vehicles, aircraft, ships, special uniforms, and communications equipment. The department also oversees military bases within the United States and around the world.

In principle, decisions concerning weapons, military bases, and the number of military personnel needed at any given time are made for reasons having to do with broad foreign policy goals set by the president and Congress. In practice, however, Defense Department bureaucrats make a multitude of decisions affecting the particular character of the American military that never reach the level of congressional or presidential decision making. When Congress does get involved (see the following), issues of national interest can get pushed aside in favor of domestic political considerations.

The State Department is also highly professionalized, with a corps of diplomats known for their specialized expertise. The department has the primary responsibility for staffing diplomatic missions abroad and carrying out the wishes of the president in diplomacy. The president, secretary of state, and various deputy secretaries of state are all deemed "political" (that is, noncareer) diplomats. Below them are the professional civil servants who run American embassies and are part of the civil service. In each embassy, for instance, an ambassador appointed by the president, sometimes assisted by a deputy ambassador, sets the overall tone, but civil servants hired and trained by the Department of State mostly handle day-to-day relations with other countries. In Washington, D.C., large teams of professionals with expertise on specific countries advise the president and the various embassy employees. They maintain contacts with foreign countries, monitor other governments on a regular basis, and help the political diplomats prepare for negotiations and make decisions.

Recall what we learned in Chapter 7 about bureaucratic politics. Bureaucracies have their own

Former secretary of state John Kerry (right), pictured here with Libyan Prime Minister Ali Zeidan, was the United States' chief diplomat from 2013 to 2017. Several federal departments have a role in foreign policy. The State Department leads the way in diplomatic affairs, and the Department of Defense heads up the U.S. military.

Many actors and interests contribute to American foreign policy. The president's lead role in military and diplomatic affairs is unmistakable. The president sets foreign policy tenor and appoints leaders of key entities such as the Department of Defense and the Department of State.

How is the influence of other actors and interests compared with that of the president in the eyes of the general public? The figure below shows data from the 2014 Survey of American Public Opinion and U.S. Foreign Policy, produced by the Chicago Council on Global Affairs.[a] A sample of Americans were asked to gauge the foreign policy influence of each of the nine groups or actors plotted on the *x*-axis on a scale from 0 to 10. Not surprisingly, the president ranked first among the actors, earning an average score of 7.5.

American Perceptions of Foreign Policy Influence

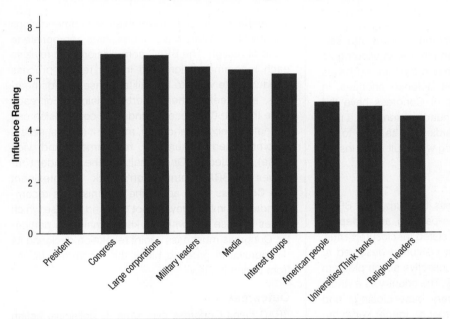

Think About It

Besides the president, what other actors or interests are most and least influential according to the public? Does the public perception fit with what you have learned about foreign policy's key players and influences in this chapter? Why do you think public perception diverges from the reality of foreign policy making?

a. Survey of American Public Opinion and U.S. Foreign Policy, 2014. Produced by the Chicago Council on Global Affairs, ICPSR36216-v1. Distributed by Ann Arbor, MI: Inter-university Consortium for Political and Social Research, 2015-08-06. http://doi.org/10.3886/ICPSR36216.v1 (accessed 6/17/16).

The Collective Dilemma

The United States' proposed budget for the 2016 fiscal year included a new round of Base Realignment and Closures (BRAC) with the goal of making the Department of Defense (DoD) more efficient. This kind of proposal from the executive branch is not uncommon. However, BRAC commissions have been assembled only five times since 1988, the most recent in 2005. Why are they commonly proposed, and what prevents them from coming to fruition? Further, when they are successfully gathered, what determines which bases are to close or to shrink in size?

Interests

BRAC commissions are commonly called into service because the DoD has an interest in allotting its resources efficiently, which may mean closing bases that no longer serve national-defense priorities. In contrast, individual members of Congress have the incentive to support the continued existence of a military base in their district, regardless of its utility to the military, because a base closing will result in job losses in the district.

Institutions

Established in 1988 by Congress, the purpose of BRAC is to provide "an objective, non-partisan, and independent review" of military bases slated for closure.[a] Thus, we can think of BRAC as an institution designed to overcome the congressional collective action problem innate to military base closings. The country as a whole stands to benefit from military base closings and restructuring. Closing bases that no longer serve the defense priorities (for example, training soldiers to fight in warmer climates as opposed to cold ones) means that funds can be spent on other bases. This, in turn, enhances the military's ability to use funds efficiently and defend the country.

In order for a BRAC commission to assemble, Congress must appropriate funds for it. Once funds are appropriated, a BRAC commission works in the following manner. The DoD assembles recommendations about which military bases it considers appropriate to close or realign. The BRAC commission then reviews each recommendation, and in this review process conducts site visits to the military bases, holds hearings, and seeks other experts' opinions. For each base that the DoD recommends, the commission can accept the recommendation, modify it (that is, slate a recommended closure for realignment and vice versa), or reject it. Once finalized, the president receives the BRAC commission's work. The president and Congress must adopt the commission's recommendations in full; they cannot pick and choose which bases to close and which to keep running. In particular, Congress must pass a joint resolution declaring its disapproval in order to block the recommendations from becoming law.

Outcomes

BRAC helps Congress overcome its collective action problem by giving the task of choosing closures to an independent board that is not beholden to a specific constituency. However, Congress is able to forbid funds from being used for BRAC by inserting language into the National Defense Authorization Act. For example, the budget for the 2015 fiscal year called for two rounds of BRAC, one for 2015 and the other for 2017; the budget for the 2017 fiscal year called for BRAC in

2018, as did the budget for the 2018 fiscal year. But the 2015 National Defense Authorization Act contained language explicitly prohibiting BRAC: "Nothing in this Act shall be construed to authorize an additional Base Realignment and Closure (BRAC) round."[b] Thus, we commonly observe a tension between government branches, with the executive pushing for BRAC and the legislative denying the funds for it.

It is expected that members of Congress will publicly oppose proposed rounds of BRAC and will fight for their district's base if a BRAC round threatens it. Members make strong public statements against BRAC rounds and sometimes offer amendments to prohibit them. In February 2012, 42 members of Congress signed and published a letter to President Obama in bipartisan opposition to the proposed rounds of BRAC.

One obvious outcome from BRAC is that military bases close because of this institution. In 2005, the commission approved 21 of the 33 recommended major bases for closure, changed seven of the 33 to realignments, and rejected the remaining five. This fact is central to the tension between the executive that calls for BRAC rounds and the legislature that, on average, opposes them. In the 2005 letter to President Bush, the commission articulated the reality of this: "We recognize that our final recommendations will have profound effects on many communities and the people who bring them to life."[c]

a. U.S. Defense Base Closure and Realignment Commission, www.brac.gov (accessed 10/4/15).

b. National Defense Authorization Act for Fiscal Year 2015, §2711.

c. Defense Base Closure and Realignment Commission, Letter to the President, September 8, 2005, www.brac.gov/docs/final/Volume1BRACReport .pdf (accessed 10/4/15).

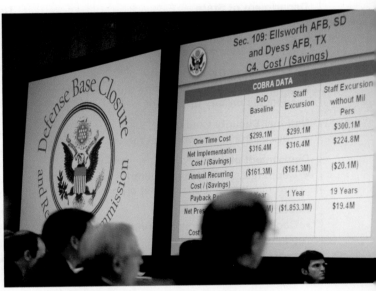

The independent BRAC commission, shown here considering Air Force bases in South Dakota and Texas, helps make military base closings easier by insulating politicians representing affected districts from decision making.

Think About It

Is the back and forth between the executive and legislative branches evidence that BRAC is insufficient to overcome the collective action problem of military base closings? Or does the Congress serve as a necessary check by representing certain constituencies who would be disproportionately harmed by military base closings?

interests, which may or may not be consistent with what political leaders see as the national interests. Moreover, overlapping responsibilities exist among many departments and agencies involved in foreign affairs. The Commerce Department, for instance, is mostly in charge of promoting economic growth, which can include promoting American companies overseas. But there is also the U.S. trade representative, a cabinet-level presidential adviser whose office is responsible for promoting American interests in international forums. The tasks carried out by these two bureaucratic units—one a department, the other a White House agency—often overlap, and although they can coordinate their efforts, they can also interfere with each other's work.

When the lines of responsibility among various agencies get blurred, it can affect foreign policy both directly and indirectly. For example, both the Defense and State departments have intelligence units that gather covert and publicly available information about foreign countries. Then there is the CIA, an independent executive-branch agency that conducts most of the covert intelligence gathering. Long-standing rivalries between the intelligence units in Defense and State, and between them and the CIA, have led to inefficiencies and occasionally to errors that have had serious consequences.

These rivalries between departments and agencies can matter a great deal.[22] To some degree, how intelligence is gathered and disseminated to the president and Congress depends on whether it originated with the Pentagon, the CIA, or the State Department. Leaders receive information from and have decisions framed for them by these bureaucracies. Defense Department intelligence is generally seen as tending to suggest military solutions to problems, while State Department intelligence is more cautious about recommending military action. And the president relies on his own National Security Council for advice largely *because* of the known and acknowledged differences and rivalries between Defense and State.

Domestic Political Pressures

The president and Congress respond to domestic constituencies when crafting and implementing foreign policy.[23] Public opinion on major questions of war and peace, as expressed in polling numbers and election results, fundamentally shapes the decisions of elected officials, especially the president.

On specific matters, presidents, bureaucrats, and members of Congress are lobbied by interest groups and corporations. In this respect, foreign policy closely resembles other areas of policy, except that the White House is more often the target of lobbying. Examples of foreign policy lobbyists include companies and allied interests seeking lucrative military contracts; ethnic and religious groups who want the government to support particular countries or groups in diplomatic, trade, and military matters; and ideological interest groups promoting non-nuclear policies, free trade, humanitarian aid, or other policies.

The bureaucracies, especially the Department of Defense, feel popular pressure mostly through the requests by members of Congress for special consideration for their states or districts. Decisions about spending on weapons and military bases can be highly politicized. Interest groups linked to weapons companies and labor unions exert enormous pressure on Congress to choose their specific model of military hardware. For example, after vigorous debate in Washington, the State Department approved the sale of new F-16 fighter jets to Pakistan. The sale, which enjoyed support from both congressional Republicans and Democrats after robust lobbying, equips a country that has a troubled diplomatic and military alliance with the United States with additional advanced machinery. The sale might, some reasoned, reward

---

[22] See Theodore Sorensen, "The President and the Secretary of State," *Foreign Affairs* (Winter 1987/88): 231.

[23] For a recent treatment of the influence of domestic political pressure on foreign policy, see Helen Milner and Dustin Tingley, "Who Supports Global Economic Engagement? The Sources of Preferences in American Foreign Economic Policy," *International Organization* 65, no. 1 (2011): 37–68.

an ally that has wavered on fighting U.S. enemies like the Taliban and has a poor human rights record.

The location of military bases is especially contentious. Within the United States, political interests fight among themselves to secure bases. When budget cutters in Congress move to close military bases in a state, members of Congress (especially senators) from that state can be counted on to complain vociferously about the potential loss of jobs and revenue for that area of the country. Overseas, the hosting of an American military base can be an equally politically charged issue. Countries such as Turkey and South Korea have sizable constituencies that pressure their governments to oppose allowing U.S. military bases on their territory.

Washington insiders and scholars disagree about whether pressure from domestic constituencies distorts American foreign policy in ways that are harmful to the national interest. Why did the United States side with Israel in the 1967 and 1973 Arab–Israeli wars? Was it because of pressure from pro-Israeli lobbyists among American citizens?[24] Or was it because of the value the U.S. government saw in having a stable democracy in the oil-rich Middle East? Why did the United States not punish Ireland following World War II, when it was widely recognized that Ireland had been sympathetic to Nazi Germany (mostly because of Germany's war with Britain, Ireland's colonizer and perceived oppressor)? Was it because of the many Irish Americans who would have reacted negatively to any punitive actions? Or did the United States act as it did to avoid recriminations and give Europe a fresh start toward peace? Does the growing political clout of Mexican Americans affect the foreign policy of the United States toward Mexico, over and above the general U.S. interest in maintaining good relations with its southern neighbor?

There is little question that leaders in the national government have domestic political considerations in mind when they make foreign policy. The question is, which domestic interests matter for which foreign policies? Do specific ethnic groups have more voice in determining the foreign policy toward their ancestral countries than the broader population? Although such claims have been made repeatedly, they are hard to substantiate. The rationale for foreign policy decision making is often opaque, in part because every decision arises from a unique set of circumstances that makes it almost impossible to compare one decision directly with another. In sum, scholars have a difficult time gauging the proper weight to attach to domestic political pressures and international political considerations in explaining foreign policy decisions.

---

[24] See John Mearsheimer and Stephen Walt, *The Israel Lobby and U.S. Foreign Policy* (New York: Farrar, Straus, and Giroux, 2007).

Foreign Policy Doctrines

American foreign policy sometimes swings with the professed doctrines of presidents. Doctrines are meant to reflect national interests, at least as those interests are understood by the people who promote them. And they also follow from some of the theories discussed previously.

Policy makers within both the Bush and Obama administrations, for instance, justified the wars in the 2000s in Iraq and Afghanistan along both realist and idealistic lines. The **Bush Doctrine**, articulated by President George W. Bush, was a complicated blend of realism and idealism. It was developed mostly by foreign policy makers steeped in the realist tradition. The realists within the Bush administration who favored invading Iraq argued that foreign countries, when faced with the choice between cooperating and not cooperating with the United States, respond only to force or the threat of force. Yet other elements of the Bush Doctrine were consistent with an idealist approach. The emphasis on regime change—the use of outside intervention to transform countries like Iraq into stable, peaceful democracies—as a foreign policy objective grows out of the idealist tradition.

Then advisers in the Obama administration saw promoting democracy in the Middle East as the best way to promote peace in that region.[25] In many ways, Obama's foreign policy was not all that different from his predecessors. He pulled troops out of Afghanistan and Iraq but arguably a Republican president would have done likewise. He attacked terrorist leaders using drones, and clearly used covert and overt operations to disrupt the activities of groups in many foreign countries. President Donald Trump pulled back from some international commitments, but he especially criticized allies for not paying enough into alliances like NATO. He was also unilaterally more aggressive against certain foreign enemies, like Iran.

Other doctrines or predictions based on notions such as the democratic peace have been identified with earlier presidential administrations. For example, the Reagan Doctrine toward the end of the Cold War opposed the global influence of the Soviet Union; hence the United States fought proxy battles against the Soviet Union in places like El Salvador and Nicaragua. The Carter Doctrine emphasized rewarding countries with good human rights records. Doctrines sometimes come and go as new presidents enter and leave office. They are useful in spelling out the country's priorities and communicating American intentions and justifications to the world.

Doctrines guide decision making overall, but they do not always determine behavior in specific instances. Although the Bush Doctrine seemed to

Bush Doctrine An approach to American foreign policy developed during the George W. Bush administration that advocates preventing terrorism through active intervention in foreign countries, including pressuring or even invading foreign countries and using military force against terrorists where they live and train; the doctrine also advocates maintaining a stronger military than any other country.

---

[25] See James Lee Ray, *Democracy and International Conflict: An Evaluation of the Democratic Peace Proposition* (Columbia: University of South Carolina Press, 1995); and Bruce Russett and John Oneal, *Triangulating Peace: Democracy, Interdependence, and International Organizations* (New York: Norton, 2001).

guide decision making from 2003 (when the United States invaded Iraq and toppled its government) until 2008 (when Bush left office), it did not lead the Bush administration to invade Pakistan, Iran, or Syria, even though those countries satisfied as many of the criteria for invasion under the doctrine as did Iraq.

In another area of foreign policy, the United States places many restrictions on trade and other exchanges with countries like Cuba or Syria because of their human rights records, but does not do the same with China, even though China arguably has a poor record as well. The United States generally encourages democracy in other countries, devoting resources to programs that promote democratic institutions such as political parties, parliaments, and independent judicial systems. Yet when election outcomes are not to the liking of the United States, it has sometimes intervened and played a role, either openly or covertly, in ousting regimes and preventing election winners from remaining in office.

The bottom line is that American foreign policy is seldom as consistent as the doctrines behind it. Foreign policy decisions are constrained by practical considerations, such as the availability of economic and material resources. Moreover, foreign policies are subject to the vagaries of coalition politics, both domestic and international. Presidents listen to various advisers who may give different rationales for taking or not taking a specific action. They pay close attention to international coalitions that the United States needs to maintain in order to accomplish its foreign policy goals. Often, American foreign policy seems to work at cross-purposes with itself. For example, the U.S. invasion of Iraq in 2003 damaged our relations with France and Germany, whose cooperation the United States needed to impose effective sanctions on Iran.

Domestic and International Constraints on Foreign Policy

The United States is not alone in making decisions that are occasionally at odds with its professed doctrines and that seem inconsistent across situations. The tension between principle and practice will always be present in foreign policy. Advocates for various policy decisions can hold elected officials accountable for either violating some well understood principle or making practical mistakes in the world of international affairs. President Carter was criticized for taking an overly principled approach to other countries' progress toward democracy and improved human rights, while at the same time being criticized on practical grounds for not being clever enough in balancing authoritarian regimes against each other in some regions to achieve peace.

The range of action available to the president and Congress in setting foreign policy is more limited than in domestic policy. It is rare for a newly elected president or majority party in Congress to dramatically change the course of American foreign policy. The United States is part of an international political system with persistent problems that do not lend themselves to quick solutions. Foreign policy presents few opportunities for a president to make sweeping new initiatives in his first 100 days in office, as Franklin D. Roosevelt did with the first stages of the New Deal, and Donald Trump tried to do with immigration policies. Other countries' leaders do not bend easily to American wishes, nor do they always respond well to abrupt changes in American foreign policy. Furthermore, the U.S. government's foreign policy bureaucracies have their own system of decision making that even presidents find hard to change.

An announced shift in foreign policy took place when George W. Bush entered office in 2001. He pledged to get the United States out of the business of "nation building"—meaning that it would not interfere in other countries' affairs as much as previous administrations had done—and pull back U.S. involvement in international organizations. In the wake of the terrorist attacks in New York and Washington, D.C., however, the Bush administration quickly discovered that these new policies were difficult to sustain. In the aftermath of the invasions of Afghanistan and Iraq, U.S. leaders believed they had to engage in nation building, and the United States needed other countries' support to conduct both wars.

Domestic interests can have a strong impact on U.S. foreign policy. Here, Vice President Mike Pence speaks to the American Israel Public Affairs Committee (AIPAC), a powerful pro-Israel lobbying group.

Domestic politics also looms large in foreign policy making. Presidents and especially members of Congress feel tremendous pressure from specific ethnic or cultural constituent groups over foreign policy matters. In recent years, Armenian Americans have pressured Congress and presidents to side with them against Turkey in declaring that the 1918 massacres of Armenians in parts of the Ottoman Empire constituted genocide. African Americans lobbied for the United States to support the antiapartheid movement in South Africa in the 1980s and early 1990s. Many Jewish groups regularly pressure the government to favor Israel in its policies.[26] Likewise, Greek Americans lobby for closer alliance with Greece.

To return to our opening story and the questions asked, we can start with doctrines. Doctrines loosely guide but do not determine policy choices. Obama

[26] See, again, Mearsheimer and Walt, *The Israel Lobby and U.S. Foreign Policy*.

as a presidential candidate criticized the Bush administration's conduct of foreign policy, and Donald Trump promised he would change the country's foreign policy direction once in office. Obama, however, largely maintained his predecessor's policies. Even today, it is hard to define a distinctive "Obama Doctrine." He departed only marginally from Bush's foreign policy without making a major change, with one notable exception. He has shown more reluctance to attack other countries, like Iran or Syria, even though they present threats similar to those perceived from Iraq and Afghanistan among policy makers in the early 2000s. This is not to say that Obama shied away from military force. He used aerial bombing in Libya, Iraq, and Syria.

History shows that the relative continuity between presidential administrations is the norm rather than the exception. Foreign policy is less subject to changes in party or administration than economic and social policies, partly because the U.S. government has less freedom of action in foreign affairs than many people suppose, and partly because foreign policy making is guided more by specific circumstances than by overarching doctrines or ideologies. Perhaps a Republican presidential administration would have been militarily more aggressive toward Syria than the Obama administration, but more likely the policy decisions toward Syria would have been similar under either party controlling the White House. As far as what determines American foreign policy choices, abstract doctrine is usually not as influential as the tools available to the government and the specific circumstances that shape government officials' assessments of whether those tools will be successful in achieving key goals. The Trump administration, in its first two years, was more isolationist in tone and substance than recent past administrations, but Trump was also thwarted in some of his foreign policy goals (such as pulling out of South Korea and cutting foreign aid substantially) by a stubborn Congress and foreign policy bureaucracy.

FURTHER READING

★ = Included in *Readings in American Politics*, 5th ed.

Allison, Graham, "Conceptual Models and the Cuban Missile Crisis," *American Political Science Review* 63, no. 3 (1969): 689–718. A classic article describing different models of foreign policy decision making.

Mead, Walter Russell, *Special Providence* (New York: Knopf, 2001). Examines four different strands of American foreign policy throughout history.

Mearsheimer, John, and Stephen Walt, *The Israel Lobby and U.S. Foreign Policy* (New York: Farrar, Straus, and Giroux, 2007). A controversial book claiming that pro-Israeli lobbyists in the United States distort American foreign policy priorities.

Nye, Joseph, "Soft Power and American Foreign Policy," *Political Science Quarterly*, 119, no. 2 (Summer 2004). An article laying out the case for using soft power instead of hard (military) power to advance American interests.

Page, Benjamin, and Marshall Bouton, *The Foreign Policy Disconnect* (Chicago: University of Chicago Press, 2006). Presents evidence showing that the U.S. government conducts foreign policy against the wishes of the majority of the public.

Power, Samantha, *A Problem from Hell: America and the Age of Genocide* (New York: HarperPerennial, 2003). A strong critique of the United States' failure to stop genocide throughout the twentieth century, arguing that leaders claimed an inability to intervene while the reality was a lack of political will.

Russett, Bruce, and John Oneal, *Triangulating Peace: Democracy, Interdependence, and International Organizations* (New York: Norton, 2001). A thorough examination of the democratic peace hypothesis.

Yoo, John, *The Powers of War and Peace: The Constitution and Foreign Affairs after 9/11* (Chicago: University of Chicago Press, 2005). A controversial argument for the constitutional legitimacy of expanded presidential power in foreign and military policy.

KEY TERMS

bargaining (p. 665)

Bush Doctrine (p. 691)

democratic peace (p. 664)

diplomacy (p. 670)

foreign policy (p. 659)

idealism (p. 662)

internationalism (p. 662)

isolationism (p. 663)

military action (p. 678)

Monroe Doctrine (p. 668)

multilateralism (p. 664)

realism (p. 662)

soft power (p. 678)

unilateralism (p. 663)

War Powers Act (p. 682)

APPENDIX

The Declaration of Independence

In Congress, July 4, 1776

The unanimous Declaration of the thirteen united States of America,

When in the Course of human events, it becomes necessary for one people to dissolve the political bands which have connected them with another, and to assume among the powers of the earth, the separate and equal station to which the Laws of Nature and of Nature's God entitle them, a decent respect to the opinions of mankind requires that they should declare the causes which impel them to the separation.

We hold these truths to be self-evident, that all men are created equal, that they are endowed by their Creator with certain unalienable Rights, that among these are Life, Liberty and the pursuit of Happiness.—That to secure these rights, Governments are instituted among Men, deriving their just powers from the consent of the governed.—That whenever any Form of Government becomes destructive of these ends, it is the Right of the People to alter or to abolish it, and to institute new Government, laying its foundation on such principles and organizing its powers in such form, as to them shall seem most likely to effect their Safety and Happiness. Prudence, indeed, will dictate that Governments long established should not be changed for light and transient causes; and accordingly all experience hath shewn, that mankind are more disposed to suffer, while evils are sufferable, than to right themselves by abolishing the forms to which they are accustomed. But when a long train of abuses and usurpations, pursuing invariably the same Object evinces a design to reduce them under absolute Despotism, it is their right, it is their duty, to throw off such Government, and to provide new Guards for their future security.—Such has been the patient sufferance of these Colonies; and such is now the necessity which constrains them to alter their former Systems of Government. The history of the present King of Great Britain is a history of repeated injuries and usurpations, all having in direct object the establishment of an absolute Tyranny over these States. To prove this, let Facts be submitted to a candid world.

He has refused his Assent to Laws, the most wholesome and necessary for the public good.

He has forbidden his Governors to pass Laws of immediate and pressing importance, unless suspended in their operation till his Assent should be obtained; and when so suspended, he has utterly neglected to attend to them.

He has refused to pass other Laws for the accommodation of large districts of people, unless those people would relinquish the right of Representation in the Legislature, a right inestimable to them and formidable to tyrants only.

He has called together legislative bodies at places unusual, uncomfortable, and distant from the depository of their public Records, for the sole purpose of fatiguing them into compliance with his measures.

He has dissolved Representative Houses repeatedly, for opposing with manly firmness his invasions on the rights of the people.

He has refused for a long time, after such dissolutions, to cause others to be elected; whereby the Legislative powers, incapable of Annihilation, have returned to the People at large for their exercise; the State remaining in the mean time exposed to all the dangers of invasion from without, and convulsions within.

He has endeavoured to prevent the population of these States; for that purpose obstructing the Laws for Naturalization of Foreigners; refusing to pass others to encourage their migrations hither, and raising the conditions of new Appropriations of Lands.

He has obstructed the Administration of Justice, by refusing his Assent to Laws for establishing Judiciary powers.

He has made Judges dependent on his Will alone, for the tenure of their offices, and the amount and payment of their salaries.

He has erected a multitude of New Offices, and sent hither swarms of Officers to harrass our people, and eat out their substance.

He has kept among us, in times of peace, Standing Armies without the Consent of our legislatures.

He has affected to render the Military independent of and superior to the Civil power.

He has combined with others to subject us to a jurisdiction foreign to our constitution, and unacknowledged by our laws; giving his Assent to their Acts of pretended Legislation:

For Quartering large bodies of armed troops among us:

For protecting them, by a mock Trial, from punishment for any Murders which they should commit on the Inhabitants of these States:

For cutting off our Trade with all parts of the world:

For imposing Taxes on us without our Consent:

For depriving us in many cases, of the benefits of Trial by Jury:

For transporting us beyond Seas to be tried for pretended offences:

For abolishing the free System of English Laws in a neighboring Province, establishing therein an Arbitrary government, and enlarging its Boundaries so as to render it at once an example and fit instrument for introducing the same absolute rule into these Colonies:

For taking away our Charters, abolishing our most valuable Laws, and altering fundamentally the Forms of our Governments:

For suspending our own Legislatures, and declaring themselves invested with power to legislate for us in all cases whatsoever.

He has abdicated Government here, by declaring us out of his Protection and waging War against us.

He has plundered our seas, ravaged our Coasts, burnt our towns, and destroyed the lives of our people.

He is at this time transporting large Armies of foreign Mercenaries to compleat the works of death, desolation and tyranny, already begun with circumstances of Cruelty & perfidy scarcely paralleled in the most barbarous ages, and totally unworthy the Head of a civilized nation.

He has constrained our fellow Citizens taken Captive on the high Seas to bear Arms against their Country, to become the executioners of their friends and Brethren, or to fall themselves by their Hands.

He has excited domestic insurrections amongst us, and has endeavoured to bring on the inhabitants of our frontiers, the merciless Indian Savages, whose known rule of warfare, is an undistinguished destruction of all ages, sexes and conditions.

In every stage of these Oppressions We have Petitioned for Redress in the most humble terms: Our repeated Petitions have been answered only by repeated injury. A Prince whose character is thus marked by every act which may define a Tyrant, is unfit to be the ruler of a free people.

Nor have We been wanting in attentions to our Brittish brethren. We have warned them from time to time of attempts by their legislature to extend an unwarrantable jurisdiction over us. We have reminded them of the circumstances of our emigration and settlement here. We have appealed to their native justice and magnanimity, and we have conjured them by the ties of our common kindred to disavow these usurpations, which, would inevitably interrupt our connections and correspondence. They too have been deaf to the voice of justice and of consanguinity. We must, therefore, acquiesce in the necessity, which denounces our Separation, and hold them, as we hold the rest of mankind, Enemies in War, in Peace Friends.

We, Therefore, the Representatives of the United States of America, in General Congress, Assembled, appealing to the Supreme Judge of the world for the rectitude of our intentions, do, in the Name, and by Authority of the good People of these Colonies, solemnly publish and declare, That these United Colonies are, and of Right ought to be Free and Independent States; that they are Absolved from all Allegiance to the British Crown, and that all political connection between them and the State of Great Britain, is and ought to be totally dissolved; and that as Free and Independent States, they have full Power to levy War, conclude Peace, contract Alliances, establish Commerce, and to do all other Acts and Things which Independent States may of right do. And for the support of this Declaration, with a firm reliance on the protection of divine Providence, we mutually pledge to each other our Lives, our Fortunes and our sacred Honor.

The foregoing Declaration was, by order of Congress, engrossed, and signed by the following members:

John Hancock

NEW HAMPSHIRE
Josiah Bartlett
William Whipple
Matthew Thornton

MASSACHUSETTS BAY
Samuel Adams
John Adams
Robert Treat Paine
Elbridge Gerry

RHODE ISLAND
Stephen Hopkins
William Ellery

CONNECTICUT
Roger Sherman
Samuel Huntington
William Williams
Oliver Wolcott

NEW YORK
William Floyd
Philip Livingston
Francis Lewis
Lewis Morris

NEW JERSEY
Richard Stockton
John Witherspoon
Francis Hopkinson
John Hart
Abraham Clark

PENNSYLVANIA
Robert Morris
Benjamin Rush
Benjamin Franklin
John Morton
George Clymer
James Smith
George Taylor
James Wilson
George Ross

DELAWARE
Caesar Rodney
George Read
Thomas M'Kean

MARYLAND
Samuel Chase
William Paca
Thomas Stone
Charles Carroll, of Carrollton

VIRGINIA
George Wythe
Richard Henry Lee
Thomas Jefferson
Benjamin Harrison
Thomas Nelson, Jr.
Francis Lightfoot Lee
Carter Braxton

NORTH CAROLINA
William Hooper
Joseph Hewes
John Penn

SOUTH CAROLINA

Edward Rutledge
Thomas Heyward, Jr.
Thomas Lynch, Jr.
Arthur Middleton

GEORGIA

Button Gwinnett
Lyman Hall
George Walton

Resolved, That copies of the Declaration be sent to the several assemblies, conventions, and committees, or councils of safety, and to the several commanding officers of the continental troops; that it be proclaimed in each of the United States, at the head of the army.

The Articles of Confederation

Agreed to by Congress November 15, 1777; ratified and in force March 1, 1781

To all whom these Presents shall come, we the undersigned Delegates of the States affixed to our Names, send greeting. Whereas the Delegates of the United States of America, in Congress assembled, did, on the fifteenth day of November, in the Year of Our Lord One thousand Seven Hundred and Seventy seven, and in the Second Year of the Independence of America, agree to certain articles of Confederation and perpetual Union between the States of Newhampshire, Massachusetts-bay, Rhodeisland and Providence Plantations, Connecticut, New-York, New-Jersey, Pennsylvania, Delaware, Maryland, Virginia, North-Carolina, South-Carolina and Georgia in the words following, viz. "Articles of Confederation and perpetual Union between the states of Newhampshire, Massachusettsbay, Rhodeisland and Providence Plantations, Connecticut, New-York, New-Jersey, Pennsylvania, Delaware, Maryland, Virginia, North-Carolina, South-Carolina and Georgia.

Art. I. The Stile of this confederacy shall be "The United States of America."

Art. II. Each state retains its sovereignty, freedom and independence, and every Power, Jurisdiction and right, which is not by this confederation expressly delegated to the United States, in Congress assembled.

Art. III. The said states hereby severally enter into a firm league of friendship with each other, for their common defence, the security of their Liberties, and their mutual and general welfare, binding themselves to assist each other, against all force offered to, or attacks made upon them, or any of them, on account of religion, sovereignty, trade, or any other pretence whatever.

Art. IV. The better to secure and perpetuate mutual friendship and intercourse among the people of the different states in this union, the free inhabitants of each of these states, paupers, vagabonds and fugitives from Justice excepted, shall be entitled to all privileges and immunities of free citizens in the several states; and the people of each state shall have free ingress and regress to and from any other state, and shall enjoy therein all the privileges of trade and commerce, subject to the same duties, impositions and restrictions as the inhabitants thereof respectively, provided that such restriction shall not extend so far as to prevent the removal of property imported into any state, to any other state, of which the Owner is an inhabitant; provided also that no imposition, duties or restriction shall be laid by any state, on the property of the united states, or either of them.

If any Person guilty of, or charged with treason, felony, or other high misdemeanor in any state, shall flee from Justice, and be found in any of the united states, he shall, upon demand of the Governor or executive power, of the state from which he fled, be delivered up and removed to the state having jurisdiction of his offence.

Full faith and credit shall be given in each of these states to the records, acts and judicial proceedings of the courts and magistrates of every other state.

Art. V. For the more convenient management of the general interests of the united states, delegates shall be annually appointed in such manner as the legislature of each state shall direct, to meet in Congress on the first Monday in November, in every year, with a power reserved to each state, to recall its delegates, or any of them, at any time within the year, and to send others in their stead, for the remainder of the Year.

No state shall be represented in Congress by less than two, nor by more than seven Members; and no person shall be capable of being a delegate for more than three years in any term of six years; nor shall any person, being a delegate, be capable of holding any office under the united states, for which he, or another for his benefit receives any salary, fees or emolument of any kind.

Each state shall maintain its own delegates in a meeting of the states, and while they act as members of the committee of the states.

In determining questions in the united states, in Congress assembled, each state shall have one vote.

Freedom of speech and debate in Congress shall not be impeached or questioned in any Court, or place out of Congress, and the members of congress shall be protected in their persons from arrests and imprisonments, during the time of their going to and from, and attendance on congress, except for treason, felony, or breach of the peace.

Art. VI. No state without the Consent of the united states in congress assembled, shall send any embassy to, or receive any embassy from, or enter into any conference, agreement, or alliance or treaty with any King, prince or state; nor shall any person holding any office or profit or trust under the united states, or any of them, accept of any present, emolument, office or title of any kind whatever from any king, prince or foreign state; nor shall the united states in congress assembled, or any of them, grant any title of nobility.

No two or more states shall enter into any treaty, confederation or alliance whatever between them, without the consent of the united states in congress assembled, specifying accurately the purposes for which the same is to be entered into, and how long it shall continue.

No state shall lay any imposts or duties, which may interfere with any stipulations in treaties, entered into by the united states in congress assembled, with any king, prince or state, in pursuance of any treaties already proposed by congress, to the courts of France and Spain.

No vessels of war shall be kept up in time of peace by any state, except such number only, as shall be deemed necessary by the united states in congress assembled, for the defence of such state, or its trade; nor shall any body of forces be kept up by any state, in time of peace, except such number only, as in the judgment of the united states, in congress assembled, shall be deemed requisite to garrison the forts necessary for the defence of such state; but every state shall always keep up a well regulated and disciplined militia, sufficiently armed and accoutred, and shall provide and constantly have ready for use, in public stores, a due number of field pieces and tents, and a proper quantity of arms, ammunition and camp equipage.

No state shall engage in any war without the consent of the united states in congress assembled, unless such state be actually invaded by enemies, or shall have received certain advice of a resolution being formed by some nation of Indians to invade such state, and the danger is so imminent as not to admit of a delay, till the united states in congress asssembled can be consulted; nor shall any state grant commissions to any ships or vessels of war, nor letters of marque or reprisal, except it be after a declaration of war by the united states in congress assembled, and then only against the kingdom or state and the subjects thereof, against which war has been so declared, and under such regulations as shall be established by the united states in congress assembled, unless such state be infested by pirates; in which case vessels of war may be fitted out for that occasion, and kept so long as the danger shall continue, or until the united states in congress assembled shall determine otherwise.

Art. VII. When land-forces are raised by any state for the common defence, all officers of or under the rank of colonel, shall be appointed by the legislature of each state respectively, by whom such forces shall be raised, or in such manner as such state shall direct, and all vacancies shall be filled up by the state which first made the appointment.

Art. VIII. All charges of war, and all other expences that shall be incurred for the common defence or general welfare, and allowed by the united states in congress assembled, shall be defrayed out of a common treasury, which shall be supplied by the several states in proportion to the value of all land within each state, granted to or surveyed for any Person, as such land and the buildings and improvements thereon shall be estimated according to such mode as the united states in congress assembled, shall from time to time direct and appoint.

The taxes for paying that proportion shall be laid and levied by the authority and direction of the legislatures of the several states within the time agreed upon by the united states in congress assembled.

Art. IX. The united states in congress assembled, shall have the sole and exclusive right and power of determining on peace and war, except in the cases mentioned in the sixth article—of sending and receiving ambassadors—entering into treaties and alliances, provided that no treaty of commerce shall be made whereby the legislative power of the respective states shall be restrained from imposing such imposts and duties on foreigners, as their own people are subjected to, or from prohibiting the exportation of any species of goods or commodities -whatsoever—of establishing rules for deciding in all cases, what captures on land or water shall be legal, and in what manner prizes taken by land or naval forces in the service of the united states shall be divided or appropriated—of granting letters of marque and reprisal in times of peace—appointing courts for the trial of piracies and felonies committed on the high seas and establishing courts for receiving and determining finally appeals in all cases of captures, provided that no member of congress shall be appointed a judge of any of the said courts.

The united states in congress assembled shall also be the last resort on appeal in all disputes and differences now subsisting or that hereafter may arise between two or more states concerning boundary, jurisdiction or any other cause whatever; which authority shall always be exercised in the manner following. Whenever the legislative or executive authority or lawful agent of any state in controversy with another shall present a petition to congress stating the matter in question and praying for a hearing, notice thereof shall be given by order of congress to the legislative or executive authority of the other state in controversy, and a day assigned for the appearance of the parties by their lawful agents, who shall then be directed to appoint by joint consent, commissioners or judges to constitute a court for hearing and determining the matter in question: but if they cannot agree, congress shall name three persons out of each of the united states, and from the list of such persons each party shall alternately strike out one, the petitioners beginning, until the number shall be reduced to thirteen; and from that number not less than seven, nor more than nine names as congress shall direct, shall in the presence of congress be drawn out by lot, and the persons whose names shall be so drawn or any five of them, shall be commissioners or judges, to hear and finally determine the controversy, so always as a major part of the judges who shall hear the cause shall agree in the determination: and if either party shall neglect to attend at the day appointed, without shewing reasons, which congress shall judge sufficient, or being present shall refuse to strike, the congress shall proceed to nominate three persons out of each state, and the secretary of congress shall strike in behalf of such party absent or refusing; and the judgment and sentence of the court to be appointed, in the manner before prescribed, shall be final and conclusive; and if any of the parties shall refuse to submit to the authority of such court, or to appear to defend their claim or cause, the court shall nevertheless proceed to pronounce sentence, or judgment, which shall in like manner be final and decisive, the judgment or sentence and other proceedings being in either case transmitted to congress, and lodged among the acts of congress for the security of the parties concerned: provided that every commissioner, before he sits in judgment, shall take an oath to be administered by one of the judges of the supreme or superior court of the state, where the cause shall be tried, "well and truly to hear and determine the matter in question, according to the best of his judgment, without favour, affection or hope of reward:" provided also, that no state shall be deprived of territory for the benefit of the united states.

All controversies concerning the private right of soil claimed under different grants of two or more states, whose -jurisdictions as they may respect such lands, and the states which passed such grants are adjusted, the said grants or either of them being at the same time claimed to have originated antecedent to such settlement of jurisdiction, shall on the petition of either party to the congress of the united states, be finally determined as near as may be in the same manner as is before prescribed for deciding disputes respecting territorial jurisdiction between different states.

The united states in congress assembled shall also have the sole and exclusive right and power of regulating the alloy and value of coin struck by their own authority, or by that of the respective states—fixing the standard of weights and measures throughout the united states—regulating the trade and managing all affairs with the Indians, not members of any of the states, provided that the legislative right of any state within its own limits be not infringed or violated—establishing and regulating post-offices from one state to another, throughout all the united states, and exacting such postage on the papers passing thro' the same as may be requisite to defray the expences of the said office—appointing all officers of the land forces, in the service of the united states, excepting regimental officers—appointing all the officers of the naval forces, and commissioning all officers whatever in the service of the united states—making rules for the government and regulation of the said land and naval forces, and directing their operations.

The united states in congress assembled shall have authority to appoint a committee, to sit in the recess of congress, to be denominated "A Committee of the States," and to consist of one delegate from each state; and to appoint such other committees and civil officers as may be necessary for managing the general affairs of the united states under their direction—to appoint one of their number to preside, provided that no person be allowed to serve in the office of president more than one year in any term of three years; to ascertain the necessary sums of Money to be raised for the service of the united states, and to appropriate and apply the same for defraying the public expenses—to borrow money, or emit bills on the credit of the united states, transmitting every half year to the respective states an account of the sums of money so borrowed or emitted,—to build and equip a navy—to agree upon the number of land forces, and to make requisitions from each state for its quota, in proportion to the number of white inhabitants in such state; which requisition shall be binding, and thereupon the legislature of each state shall appoint the regimental officers, raise the men and cloath, arm and equip them in a soldier like manner, at the expense of the united states; and the officers and men so cloathed, armed and equipped shall march to the place appointed, and within the time agreed on by the united states in congress assembled: But if the united states in congress assembled shall, on consideration of circumstances judge proper that any state should not raise men, or should raise a smaller number than its quota, and that any other state should raise a greater number of men than the quota thereof, such extra number shall be raised, officered, cloathed, armed and equipped in the same manner as the quota of such state, unless the legislature of such state shall judge that such extra number cannot be safely spared out of the same, in which case they shall raise officer, cloath, arm and equip as many of such extra number as they judge can be safely spared. And the officers and men so cloathed, armed and equipped, shall march to the place appointed, and within the time agreed on by the united states in congress assembled.

The united states in congress assembled shall never engage in a war, nor grant letters of marque and reprisal in time of peace, nor enter into any treaties or alliances, nor coin money, nor regulate the value thereof, nor ascertain the sums and expenses necessary for the defence and welfare of the united states, or any of them, nor emit bills, nor borrow money on the credit of the united states, nor appropriate money, nor agree upon the number of vessels of war, to be built or purchased, or the number of land or sea forces to be raised, nor appoint a commander in chief of the army or navy, unless nine states assent to the same: nor shall a question on any other point, except for adjourning from day to day be determined, unless by the votes of a majority of the united states in congress assembled.

The congress of the united states shall have power to adjourn to any time within the year, and to any place within the united states, so that no period of adjournment be for a longer duration than the space of six Months, and shall publish the Journal of their proceedings monthly, except such parts thereof relating to treaties, alliances or military operations, as in their judgment require secrecy; and the yeas and nays of the delegates of each state on any question shall be entered on the Journal, when it is desired by any delegate; and the delegates of a state, or any of them, at his or their request shall be furnished with a transcript of the said Journal, except such parts as are above excepted, to lay before the legislatures of the several states.

Art. X. The committee of the states, or any nine of them, shall be authorised to execute, in the recess of congress, such of the powers of congress as the united states in congress assembled, by the consent of nine states, shall from time to time think expedient to vest them with; provided that no power be delegated to the said committee, for the exercise of which, by the articles of confederation, the voice of nine states in the congress of the united states assembled is requisite.

Art. XI. Canada acceding to this confederation, and joining in the measures of the united states, shall be admitted into, and entitled to all the advantages of this union: but no other colony shall be admitted into the same, unless such admission be agreed to by nine states.

Art. XII. All bills of credit emitted, monies borrowed and debts contracted by, or under the authority of congress, before the assembling of the united states, in pursuance of the present confederation, shall be deemed and considered as a charge against the united states, for payment and satisfaction whereof the said united states and the public faith are hereby solemnly pledged.

Art. XIII. Every state shall abide by the determinations of the united states in congress assembled, on all questions which by this confederation are submitted to them. And the Articles of this confederation shall be inviolably observed by every state, and the union shall be perpetual; nor shall any alteration at any time hereafter be made in any of them; unless such alteration be agreed to in a congress of the united states, and be afterwards confirmed by the legislatures of every state.

And Whereas it hath pleased the Great Governor of the World to incline the hearts of the legislatures we respectively represent in congress, to approve of, and to authorize us to ratify the said articles of confederation and perpetual union. Know Ye that we the undersigned delegates, by virtue of the power and authority to us given for that purpose, do by these presents, in the name and in behalf of our respective constituents, fully and entirely ratify and confirm each and every of the said articles of confederation and perpetual union, and all and singular the matters and things therein contained: And we do further solemnly plight and engage the faith of our respective constituents, that they shall abide by the determinations of the united states in congress assembled, on all questions, which by the said confederation are submitted to them. And that the articles thereof shall be inviolably observed by the states we respectively represent, and that the union shall be perpetual. In Witness whereof we have hereunto set our hands in Congress. Done at Philadelphia in the state of Pennsylvania the ninth day of July, in the Year of our Lord one Thousand seven Hundred and Seventy-eight, and in the third year of the independence of America.

The Constitution of the United States of America

PREAMBLE

We the People of the United States, in Order to form a more perfect Union, establish Justice, insure domestic Tranquility, provide for the common defence, promote the general Welfare, and secure the Blessings of Liberty to ourselves and our Posterity, do ordain and establish this Constitution for the United States of America.

Article I

SECTION 1

[LEGISLATIVE POWERS]

All legislative Powers herein granted shall be vested in a Congress of the United States, which shall consist of a Senate and House of Representatives.

SECTION 2

[HOUSE OF REPRESENTATIVES, HOW CONSTITUTED, POWER OF IMPEACHMENT]

The House of Representatives shall be composed of Members chosen every second Year by the People of the several States, and the Electors in each State shall have the Qualifications requisite for Electors of the most numerous Branch of the State Legislature.

No Person shall be a Representative who shall not have attained to the Age of twenty five Years, and been seven Years a Citizen of the United States, and who shall not, when elected, be an Inhabitant of that State in which he shall be chosen.

Representatives and *direct Taxes*[1] shall be apportioned among the several States which may be included within this Union, according to their respective Numbers, *which shall be determined by adding to the whole Number of free Persons, including those bound to Service for a Term of Years, and excluding Indians not taxed, three fifths of all other Persons.*[2] The actual Enumeration shall be made within three Years after the first Meeting of the Congress of the United States, and within every subsequent Term of ten Years, in such Manner as they shall by Law direct. The Number of Representatives shall not exceed one for every thirty Thousand, but each State shall have at Least one Representative; *and until such enumeration shall be made, the State of New Hampshire shall be entitled to chuse three, Massachusetts eight, Rhode-Island and Providence Plantations one, Connecticut five, New-York six, New Jersey four,*

[1] Modified by Sixteenth Amendment.

[2] Modified by Fourteenth Amendment.

Pennsylvania eight, Delaware one, Maryland six, Virginia ten, North Carolina five, South Carolina five, and Georgia three.[3]

When vacancies happen in the Representation from any State, the Executive Authority thereof shall issue Writs of Election to fill such Vacancies.

The House of Representatives shall chuse their Speaker and other Officers; and shall have the sole Power of Impeachment.

SECTION 3

[THE SENATE, HOW CONSTITUTED, IMPEACHMENT TRIALS]

The Senate of the United States shall be composed of two Senators from each State, *chosen by the Legislature thereof*[4] for six Years; and each Senator shall have one Vote.

Immediately after they shall be assembled in Consequence of the first Election, they shall be divided as equally as may be into three Classes. The Seats of the Senators of the first Class shall be vacated at the Expiration of the second Year, of the second Class at the Expiration of the fourth Year, and of the third Class at the Expiration of the sixth Year, so that one third may be chosen every second Year; *and if Vacancies happen by Resignation, or otherwise, during the Recess of the Legislature of any State, the Executive thereof may make temporary Appointments until the next Meeting of the Legislature, which shall then fill such Vacancies.*[5]

No Person shall be a Senator who shall not have attained to the Age of thirty Years, and been nine Years a Citizen of the United States, and who shall not, when elected, be an Inhabitant of that State for which he shall be chosen.

The Vice President of the United States shall be President of the Senate, but shall have no Vote, unless they be equally divided.

The Senate shall chuse their other Officers, and also a President pro tempore, in the Absence of the Vice President, or when he shall exercise the Office of President of the United States.

The Senate shall have the sole Power to try all Impeachments. When sitting for that Purpose, they shall be on Oath or Affirmation. When the President of the United States is tried, the Chief Justice shall preside: And no Person shall be convicted without the Concurrence of two thirds of the Members present.

Judgment in Cases of Impeachment shall not extend further than to removal from Office, and disqualification to hold and enjoy any Office of honor, Trust or Profit under the United States: but the Party convicted shall nevertheless be liable and subject to Indictment, Trial, Judgment and Punishment, according to Law.

---

[3] Temporary provision.

[4] Modified by Seventeenth Amendment.

[5] Modified by Seventeenth Amendment.

SECTION 4

[ELECTION OF SENATORS AND REPRESENTATIVES]

The Times, Places and Manner of holding Elections for Senators and Representatives, shall be prescribed in each State by the Legislature thereof; but the Congress may at any time by Law make or alter such Regulations, except as to the Places of chusing Senators.

The Congress shall assemble at least once in every Year, and such Meeting shall be on the first Monday in December, unless they shall by Law appoint a different Day.[6]

SECTION 5

[QUORUM, JOURNALS MEETINGS, ADJOURNMENTS]

Each House shall be the Judge of the Elections, Returns and Qualifications of its own Members, and a Majority of each shall constitute a Quorum to do Business; but a smaller Number may adjourn from day to day, and may be authorized to compel the Attendance of absent Members, in such Manner, and under such Penalties as each House may provide.

Each House may determine the Rules of its Proceedings, punish its Members for disorderly Behaviour, and, with the Concurrence of two thirds, expel a Member.

Each House shall keep a Journal of its Proceedings, and from time to time publish the same, excepting such Parts as may in their Judgment require Secrecy; and the Yeas and Nays of the Members of either House on any questions shall, at the Desire of one fifth of those Present, be entered on the Journal.

Neither House, during the Session of Congress, shall, without the Consent of the other, adjourn for more than three days, nor to any other Place than that in which the two Houses shall be sitting.

SECTION 6

[COMPENSATION, PRIVILEGES, DISABILITIES]

The Senators and Representatives shall receive a Compensation for their Services, to be ascertained by Law, and paid out of the Treasury of the United States. They shall in all Cases, except Treason, Felony and Breach of the Peace, be privileged from Arrest during their Attendance at the Session of their respective Houses, and in going to and returning from the same; and for any Speech or Debate in either House, they shall not be questioned in any other Place.

No Senator or Representative shall, during the Time for which he was elected, be appointed to any civil Office under the Authority of the United States, which shall have been created, or the Emoluments whereof shall have been encreased during such time; and no Person holding any Office under the United States, shall be a Member of either House during his Continuance in Office.

---

[6] Modified by Twentieth Amendment.

SECTION 7

[PROCEDURE IN PASSING BILLS AND RESOLUTIONS]

All Bills for raising Revenue shall originate in the House of Representatives; but the Senate may propose or concur with Amendments as on other Bills.

Every Bill which shall have passed the House of Representatives and the Senate, shall, before it become a Law, be presented to the President of the United States: If he approve he shall sign it, but if not he shall return it, with his Objections to that House in which it shall have originated, who shall enter the Objections at large on their Journal, and proceed to reconsider it. If after such Reconsideration two thirds of that House shall agree to pass the Bill, it shall be sent, together with the Objections, to the other House, by which it shall likewise be reconsidered, and if approved by two thirds of that House, it shall become a Law. But in all such Cases the Votes of both Houses shall be determined by yeas and Nays, and the Names of the Persons voting for and against the Bill shall be entered on the Journal of each House respectively. If any Bill shall not be returned by the President within ten Days (Sundays excepted) after it shall have been presented to him, the Same shall be a Law, in like Manner as if he had signed it, unless the Congress by their Adjournment prevent its Return, in which Case it shall not be a Law.

Every Order, Resolution, or Vote to which the Concurrence of the Senate and House of Representatives may be necessary (except on a question of Adjournment) shall be presented to the President of the United States; and before the Same shall take Effect, shall be approved by him, or being disapproved by him, shall be repassed by two thirds of the Senate and House of Representatives, according to the Rules and Limitations prescribed in the Case of a Bill.

SECTION 8

[POWERS OF CONGRESS]

The Congress shall have Power

To lay and collect Taxes, Duties, Imposts and Excises, to pay the Debts and provide for the common Defence and general Welfare of the United States; but all Duties, Imposts and Excises shall be uniform throughout the United States;

To borrow Money on the credit of the United States;

To regulate Commerce with foreign Nations, and among the several States, and with the Indian Tribes;

To establish an uniform Rule of Naturalization, and uniform Laws on the subject of Bankruptcies throughout the United States;

To coin Money, regulate the Value thereof, and of foreign Coin, and fix the Standard of Weights and Measures;

To provide for the Punishment of counterfeiting the Securities and current Coin of the United States;

To establish Post Offices and post Roads;

To promote the Progress of Science and useful Arts, by securing for limited Times to Authors and Inventors the exclusive Right to their respective Writings and Discoveries;

To constitute Tribunals inferior to the supreme Court;

To define and punish Piracies and Felonies committed on the high Seas, and Offences against the Law of Nations;

To declare War, grant Letters of Marque and Reprisal, and make Rules concerning Captures on Land and Water;

To raise and support Armies, but no Appropriation of Money to that Use shall be for a longer Term than two Years;

To provide and maintain a Navy;

To make Rules for the Government and Regulation of the land and naval Forces;

To provide for calling forth the Militia to execute the Laws of the Union, suppress Insurrections and repel Invasions;

To provide for organizing, arming, and disciplining, the Militia, and for governing such Part of them as may be employed in the Service of the United States, reserving to the States respectively, the Appointment of the Officers, and the Authority of training the Militia according to the discipline prescribed by Congress;

To exercise exclusive Legislation in all Cases whatsoever, over such District (not exceeding ten Miles square) as may, by Cession of particular States, and the Acceptance of Congress, become the Seat of the Government of the United States, and to exercise like Authority over all Places purchased by the Consent of the Legislature of the State in which the Same shall be, for the Erection of Forts, Magazines, Arsenals, dock-Yards, and other needful Buildings;—And

To make all Laws which shall be necessary and proper for carrying into Execution the foregoing Powers, and all other Powers vested by this Constitution in the Government of the United States, or in any Department or Officer thereof.

SECTION 9

[SOME RESTRICTIONS ON FEDERAL POWER]

The Migration or Importation of such Persons as any of the States now existing shall think proper to admit, shall not be prohibited by the Congress prior to the Year one thousand eight hundred and eight, but a Tax or duty may be imposed on such Importation, not exceeding ten dollars for each Person.[7]

The Privilege of the Writ of Habeas Corpus shall not be suspended, unless when in Cases of Rebellion or Invasion the public Safety may require it.

No Bill of Attainder or ex post facto Law shall be passed.

No Capitation, or other direct, Tax shall be laid, unless in Proportion to the Census or Enumeration herein before directed to be taken.[8]

[7] Temporary provision.

[8] Modified by Sixteenth Amendment.

No Tax or Duty shall be laid on Articles exported from any State.

No Preference shall be given by any Regulation of Commerce or Revenue to the Ports of one State over those of another; nor shall Vessels bound to, or from, one State, be obliged to enter, clear, or pay Duties in another.

No Money shall be drawn from the Treasury, but in Consequence of Appropriations made by Law; and a regular Statement and Account of the Receipts and Expenditures of all public Money shall be published from time to time.

No Title of Nobility shall be granted by the United States: And no Person holding any Office of Profit or Trust under them, shall, without the Consent of the Congress, accept of any present, Emolument, Office, or Title, of any kind whatever, from any King, Prince, or foreign State.

SECTION 10

[RESTRICTIONS UPON POWERS OF STATES]
No State shall enter into any Treaty, Alliance, or Confederation; grant Letters of Marque and Reprisal; coin Money; emit Bills of Credit; make any Thing but gold and silver Coin a Tender in Payment of Debts; pass any Bill of Attainder, ex post facto Law, or Law impairing the Obligation of Contracts, or grant any Title of Nobility.

No State shall, without the Consent of the Congress, lay any Imposts or Duties on Imports or Exports, except what may be absolutely necessary for executing its inspection Laws: and the net Produce of all Duties and Imposts, laid by any State on Imports or Exports, shall be for the Use of the Treasury of the United States; and all such Laws shall be subject to the Revision and Control of the Congress.

No State shall, without the Consent of Congress, lay any Duty of Tonnage, keep Troops, or Ships of War in time of Peace, enter into any Agreement or Compact with another State, or with a foreign Power, or engage in War, unless actually invaded, or in such imminent Danger as will not admit of delay.

Article II

SECTION 1

[EXECUTIVE POWER, ELECTION, QUALIFICATIONS OF THE PRESIDENT]
The executive Power shall be vested in a President of the United States of America. *He shall hold his Office during the Term of four Years, and, together with the Vice President, chosen for the same Term, be elected, as follows*[9]

Each State shall appoint, in such Manner as the Legislature thereof may direct, a Number of Electors, equal to the whole Number of Senators and

---

[9] Number of terms limited to two by Twenty-second Amendment.

Representatives to which the State may be entitled in the Congress: but no Senator or Representative, or Person holding an Office of Trust or Profit under the United States, shall be appointed an Elector.

The electors shall meet in their respective States, and vote by ballot for two Persons, of whom one at least shall not be an Inhabitant of the same State with themselves. And they shall make a List of all the Persons voted for, and of the Number of Votes for each; which List they shall sign and certify, and transmit sealed to the Seat of the Government of the United States, directed to the President of the Senate. The President of the Senate shall, in the Presence of the Senate and House of Representatives, open all the Certificates, and the Votes shall then be counted. The Person having the greatest Number of Votes shall be the President, if such Number be a Majority of the whole Number of Electors appointed; and if there be more than one who have such Majority, and have an equal Number of Votes, then the House of Representatives shall immediately chuse by Ballot one of them for President; and if no Person have a Majority, then from the five highest on the List the said House shall in like Manner chuse the President. But in chusing the President, the Votes shall be taken by States, the Representation from each State having one Vote; A quorum for this Purpose shall consist of a Member or Members from two thirds of the States, and a Majority of all the States shall be necessary to a Choice. In every Case, after the Choice of the President, the person having the greatest Number of Votes of the Electors shall be the Vice President. But if there should remain two or more who have equal Votes, the Senate shall chuse from them by Ballot the Vice President.[10]

The Congress may determine the Time of chusing the Electors, and the Day on which they shall give their Votes; which Day shall be the same throughout the United States.

No Person except a natural born Citizen, or a Citizen of the United States, at the time of the Adoption of this Constitution, shall be eligible to the Office of President; neither shall any Person be eligible to that Office who shall not have attained to the Age of thirty five Years, and been fourteen Years a Resident within the United States.

In Case of the Removal of the President from Office, or his Death, Resignation, or Inability to discharge the Powers and Duties of the said Office, the Same shall devolve on the Vice President, and the Congress may by Law provide for the Case of Removal, Death, Resignation or Inability, both of the President and Vice President, declaring what Officer shall then act as President, and such Officer shall act accordingly, until the Disability be removed, or a President shall be elected.

The President shall, at stated Times, receive for his Services, a Compensation, which shall neither be increased nor diminished during the Period for which he shall have been elected, and he shall not receive within that Period any other Emolument from the United States, or any of them.

---

[10] Modified by Twelfth and Twentieth Amendment.

Before he enter on the Execution of his Office, he shall take the following Oath or Affirmation:—"I do solemnly swear (or affirm) that I will faithfully execute the Office of President of the United States, and will to the best of my Ability, preserve, protect and defend the Constitution of the United States."

SECTION 2

[POWERS OF THE PRESIDENT]

The President shall be Commander in Chief of the Army and Navy of the United States, and of the Militia of the several States, when called into the actual Service of the United States; he may require the Opinion, in writing, of the principal Officer in each of the executive Departments, upon any Subject relating to the Duties of their respective Offices, and he shall have Power to grant Reprieves and Pardons for Offences against the United States, except in Cases of Impeachment.

He shall have Power, by and with the Advice and Consent of the Senate, to make Treaties, provided two thirds of the Senators present concur; and he shall nominate, and by and with the Advice and Consent of the Senate, shall appoint Ambassadors, other public Ministers and Consuls, Judges of the supreme Court, and all other Officers of the United States, whose Appointments are not herein otherwise provided for, and which shall be established by Law: but the Congress may by Law vest the Appointment of such inferior Officers, as they think proper, in the President alone, in the Courts of Law, or in the Heads of Departments.

The President shall have Power to fill up all Vacancies that may happen during the Recess of the Senate, by granting Commissions which shall expire at the End of their next Session.

SECTION 3

[POWERS AND DUTIES OF THE PRESIDENT]

He shall from time to time give to the Congress Information of the State of the Union, and recommend to their Consideration such Measures as he shall judge necessary and expedient; he may, on extraordinary Occasions, convene both Houses, or either of them, and in Case of Disagreement between them, with Respect to the Time of Adjournment, he may adjourn them to such Time as he shall think proper; he shall receive Ambassadors and other public Ministers; he shall take Care that the Laws be faithfully executed, and shall Commission all the Officers of the United States.

SECTION 4

[IMPEACHMENT]

The President, Vice President and all civil Officers of the United States, shall be removed from Office on Impeachment for, and Conviction of, Treason, Bribery, or other high Crimes and Misdemeanors.

Article III

SECTION 1

[JUDICIAL POWER, TENURE OF OFFICE]

The judicial Power of the United States, shall be vested in one supreme Court, and in such inferior Courts as the Congress may from time to time ordain and establish. The Judges, both of the supreme and inferior Courts, shall hold their Offices during good Behaviour, and shall, at stated Times, receive for their Services, a Compensation, which shall not be diminished during their Continuance in Office.

SECTION 2

[JURISDICTION]

The judicial Power shall extend to all Cases, in Law and Equity, arising under this Constitution, the Laws of the United States, and Treaties made, or which shall be made, under their Authority;—to all Cases affecting Ambassadors, other public Ministers and Consuls;—to all Cases of admiralty and maritime Jurisdiction;—to Controversies to which the United States shall be a Party;—to Controversies between two or more States;—*between a State and Citizens of another State;*—between Citizens of different States,—between Citizens of the same State claiming Lands under Grants of different States, *and between a State,* or the Citizens thereof, *and foreign States, Citizens or Subjects.*[11]

In all Cases affecting Ambassadors, other public Ministers and Consuls, and those in which a State shall be Party, the supreme Court shall have original Jurisdiction. In all the other Cases before mentioned, the supreme Court shall have appellate Jurisdiction, both as to Law and Fact, with such Exceptions, and under such Regulations as the Congress shall make.

The Trial of all Crimes, except in Cases of Impeachment, shall be by Jury; and such Trial shall be held in the State where the said Crimes shall have been committed; but when not committed within any State, the Trial shall be at such Place or Places as the Congress may by Law have directed.

SECTION 3

[TREASON, PROOF, AND PUNISHMENT]

Treason against the United States, shall consist only in levying War against them, or in adhering to their Enemies, giving them Aid and Comfort. No Person shall be convicted of Treason unless on the Testimony of two Witnesses to the same overt Act, or on Confession in open Court.

The Congress shall have Power to declare the Punishment of Treason, but no Attainder of Treason shall work Corruption of Blood, or Forfeiture except during the Life of the Person attainted.

---

[11] Modified by Eleventh Amendment.

Article IV

SECTION 1

[FAITH AND CREDIT AMONG STATES]

Full Faith and Credit shall be given in each State to the public Acts, Records, and judicial Proceedings of every other State. And the Congress may by general Laws prescribe the Manner in which such Acts, Records and Proceedings shall be proved, and the Effect thereof.

SECTION 2

[PRIVILEGES AND IMMUNITIES, FUGITIVES]

The Citizens of each State shall be entitled to all Privileges and Immunities of Citizens in the several States.

A Person charged in any State with Treason, Felony or other Crime, who shall flee from Justice, and be found in another State, shall on Demand of the executive Authority of the State from which he fled, be delivered up, to be removed to the State having Jurisdiction of the Crime.

No person held to Service or Labour in one State, under the Laws thereof, escaping into another, shall, in Consequence of any Law or Regulation therein, be discharged from such Service or Labour, but shall be delivered up on Claim of the Party to whom such Service or Labour may be due.[12]

SECTION 3

[ADMISSION OF NEW STATES]

New States may be admitted by the Congress into this Union; but no new State shall be formed or erected within the Jurisdiction of any other State; nor any State be formed by the Junction of two or more States, or Parts of States, without the Consent of the Legislatures of the States concerned as well as of the Congress.

The Congress shall have Power to dispose of and make all needful Rules and Regulations respecting the Territory or other Property belonging to the United States; and nothing in this Constitution shall be so construed as to Prejudice any Claims of the United States, or of any particular State.

SECTION 4

[GUARANTEE OF REPUBLICAN GOVERNMENT]

The United States shall guarantee to every State in this Union a Republican Form of Government, and shall protect each of them against Invasion; and on Application of the Legislature, or of the Executive (when the Legislature cannot be convened), against domestic Violence.

---

[12] Repealed by the Thirteenth Amendment.

Article V

[AMENDMENT OF THE CONSTITUTION]

The Congress, whenever two thirds of both Houses shall deem it necessary, shall propose Amendments to this Constitution, or, on the Application of the Legislatures of two thirds of the several States, shall call a Convention for proposing Amendments, which, in either Case, shall be valid to all Intents and Purposes, as Part of this Constitution, when ratified by the Legislatures of three fourths of the several States, or by Conventions in three fourths thereof, as the one or the other Mode of Ratification may be proposed by the Congress; *Provided that no Amendment which may be made prior to the Year One thousand eight hundred and eight shall in any Manner affect the first and fourth Clauses in the Ninth Section of the first Article;*[13] and that no State, without its Consent, shall be deprived of its equal Suffrage in the Senate.

Article VI

[DEBTS, SUPREMACY, OATH]

All Debts contracted and Engagements entered into, before the Adoption of this Constitution, shall be as valid against the United States under this Constitution, as under the Confederation.

This Constitution, and the Laws of the United States which shall be made in Pursuance thereof; and all Treaties made, or which shall be made, under the Authority of the United States, shall be the supreme Law of the Land; and the Judges in every State shall be bound thereby, any Thing in the Constitution or Laws of any State to the Contrary notwithstanding.

The Senators and Representatives before mentioned, and the Members of the several State Legislatures, and all executive and judicial Officers, both of the United States and of the several States, shall be bound by Oath or Affirmation, to support this Constitution; but no religious Test shall be required as a Qualification to any Office or public Trust under the United States.

Article VII

[RATIFICATION AND ESTABLISHMENT]

The Ratification of the Conventions of nine States, shall be sufficient for the Establishment of this Constitution between the States so ratifying the Same.[14]

---

[13] Temporary provision.

[14] The Constitution was submitted on September 17, 1787, by the Constitutional Convention, was ratified by the conventions of several states at various dates up to May 29, 1790, and became effective on March 4, 1789.

Done in Convention by the Unanimous Consent of the States present the Seventeenth Day of September in the Year of our Lord one thousand seven hundred and Eighty seven and of the Independence of the United States of America the Twelfth. *In Witness* whereof We have hereunto subscribed our Names,

G:⁰ *WASHINGTON*—
Presidt. and deputy from Virginia

NEW HAMPSHIRE
John Langdon
Nicholas Gilman

MASSACHUSETTS
Nathaniel Gorham
Rufus King

CONNECTICUT
Wm. Saml. Johnson
Roger Sherman

NEW YORK
Alexander Hamilton

NEW JERSEY
Wil: Livingston
David Brearley
Wm. Paterson
Jona: Dayton

PENNSYLVANIA
B Franklin
Thomas Mifflin
Robt. Morris
Geo. Clymer
Thos. FitzSimons
Jared Ingersoll
James Wilson
Gouv Morris

DELAWARE
Geo: Read
Gunning Bedford jun
John Dickinson
Richard Bassett
Jaco: Broom

MARYLAND
James McHenry
Dan of St Thos. Jenifer
Danl. Carroll

VIRGINIA
John Blair—
James Madison Jr.

NORTH CAROLINA
Wm. Blount
Richd. Dobbs Spaight
Hu Williamson

SOUTH CAROLINA
J. Rutledge
Charles Cotesworth Pinckney
Charles Pinckney
Pierce Butler

GEORGIA
William Few
Abr Baldwin

Amendments to the Constitution

Proposed by Congress and Ratified by the Legislatures of the Several States, Pursuant to Article V of the Original Constitution.

Amendments I–X, known as the Bill of Rights, were proposed by Congress on September 25, 1789, and ratified on December 15, 1791.

Amendment I

[FREEDOM OF RELIGION, OF SPEECH, AND OF THE PRESS]
Congress shall make no law respecting an establishment of religion, or prohibiting the free exercise thereof; or abridging the freedom of speech, or of the press; or the right of the people peaceably to assemble, and to petition the Government for a redress of grievances.

Amendment II

[RIGHT TO KEEP AND BEAR ARMS]
A well regulated Militia, being necessary to the security of a free State, the right of the people to keep and bear Arms, shall not be infringed.

Amendment III

[QUARTERING OF SOLDIERS]
No Soldier shall, in time of peace be quartered in any house, without the consent of the Owner, nor in time of war, but in a manner to be prescribed by law.

Amendment IV

[SECURITY FROM UNWARRANTABLE SEARCH AND SEIZURE]
The right of the people to be secure in their persons, houses, papers, and effects, against unreasonable searches and seizures, shall not be violated, and no Warrants shall issue, but upon probable cause, supported by Oath or affirmation, and particularly describing the place to be searched, and the persons or things to be seized.

Amendment V

[RIGHTS OF ACCUSED PERSONS IN CRIMINAL PROCEEDINGS]
No person shall be held to answer for a capital, or otherwise infamous crime, unless on a presentment or indictment of a Grand Jury, except in cases arising

in the land or naval forces, or in the Militia, when in actual service in time of War or in public danger; nor shall any person be subject for the same offence to be twice put in jeopardy of life or limb; nor shall be compelled in any criminal case to be a witness against himself, nor be deprived of life, liberty, or property, without due process of law; nor shall private property be taken for public use, without just compensation.

Amendment VI

[RIGHT TO SPEEDY TRIAL, WITNESSES, ETC.]
In all criminal prosecutions, the accused shall enjoy the right to a speedy and public trial, by an impartial jury of the State and district wherein the crime shall have been committed, which district shall have been previously ascertained by law, and to be informed of the nature and cause of the accusation; to be confronted with the witnesses against him; to have compulsory process for obtaining witnesses in his favor, and to have the -Assistance of Counsel for his defence.

Amendment VII

[TRIAL BY JURY IN CIVIL CASES]
In suits at common law, where the value in controversy shall exceed twenty dollars, the right of trial by jury shall be preserved, and no fact tried by a jury, shall be otherwise reexamined in any Court of the United States, than according to the rules of the common law.

Amendment VIII

[BAILS, FINES, PUNISHMENTS]
Excessive bail shall not be required, nor excessive fines imposed, nor cruel and unusual punishments inflicted.

Amendment IX

[RESERVATION OF RIGHTS OF PEOPLE]
The enumeration in the Constitution, of certain rights, shall not be construed to deny or disparage others retained by the people.

Amendment X

[POWERS RESERVED TO STATES OR PEOPLE]
The powers not delegated to the United States by the Constitution, nor prohibited by it to the States, are reserved to the States respectively, or to the people.

Amendment XI

[Proposed by Congress on March 4, 1794; declared ratified on January 8, 1798.]

[RESTRICTION OF JUDICIAL POWER]

The Judicial power of the United States shall not be construed to extend to any suit in law or equity, commenced or prosecuted against one of the United States by Citizens of another State, or by Citizens or Subjects of any Foreign State.

Amendment XII

[Proposed by Congress on December 9, 1803; declared ratified on September 25, 1804.]

[ELECTION OF PRESIDENT AND VICE PRESIDENT]

The Electors shall meet in their respective states and vote by ballot for President and Vice-President, one of whom, at least, shall not be an inhabitant of the same state with themselves; they shall name in their ballots the person voted for as President, and in distinct ballots the person voted for as Vice-President, and they shall make distinct lists of all persons voted for as President, and of all persons voted for as Vice-President, and of the number of votes for each, which lists they shall sign and certify, and transmit sealed to the seat of the government of the United States, directed to the President of the Senate;—the President of the Senate shall, in presence of the Senate and House of Representatives, open all the certificates and the votes shall then be counted;—The person having the greatest number of votes for President, shall be the President, if such number be a majority of the whole number of Electors appointed; and if no person have such majority, then from the persons having the highest numbers not exceeding three on the list of those voted for as President, the House of Representatives shall choose immediately, by ballot, the President. But in choosing the President, the votes shall be taken by states, the representation from each state having one vote; a quorum for this purpose shall consist of a member or members from two-thirds of the states, and a majority of all the states shall be necessary to a choice. And if the House of Representatives shall not choose a President whenever the right of choice shall devolve upon them, before the fourth day of March next following, then the Vice-President shall act as President, as in the case of the death or other constitutional disability of the President.—The person having the greatest number of votes as Vice-President, shall be the Vice-President, if such number be a majority of the whole number of Electors appointed, and if no person have a majority, then from the two highest numbers on the list, the Senate shall choose the Vice-President; a quorum for the purpose shall consist of two-thirds of the whole number of Senators, and a majority of the whole number shall be necessary to a choice. But no person constitutionally ineligible to the office of President shall be eligible to that of Vice-President of the United States.

Amendment XIII

[Proposed by Congress on January 31, 1865; declared ratified on December 18, 1865.]

SECTION 1

[ABOLITION OF SLAVERY]

Neither slavery nor involuntary servitude, except as a punishment for crime whereof the party shall have been duly convicted, shall exist within the United States, or any place subject to their jurisdiction.

SECTION 2

[POWER TO ENFORCE THIS ARTICLE]

Congress shall have power to enforce this article by appropriate legislation.

Amendment XIV

[Proposed by Congress on June 13, 1866; declared ratified on July 28, 1868.]

SECTION 1

[CITIZENSHIP RIGHTS NOT TO BE ABRIDGED BY STATES]

All persons born or naturalized in the United States, and subject to the jurisdiction thereof, are citizens of the United States and of the State wherein they reside. No State shall make or enforce any law which shall abridge the privileges or immunities of citizens of the United States; nor shall any State deprive any person of life, liberty, or property, without due process of law; nor deny to any person within its jurisdiction the equal protection of the laws.

SECTION 2

[APPORTIONMENT OF REPRESENTATIVES IN CONGRESS]

Representatives shall be apportioned among the several States according to their respective numbers, counting the whole number of persons in each State, excluding Indians not taxed. But when the right to vote at any election for the choice of electors for President and Vice-President of the United States, Representatives in Congress, the Executive and Judicial officers of a State, or the members of the Legislature thereof, is denied to any of the male inhabitants of such State, being twenty-one years of age, and citizens of the United States, or in any way abridged, except for participation in rebellion, or other crime, the basis of representation therein shall be reduced in the proportion which the number of such male citizens shall bear to the whole number of male citizens twenty-one years of age in such State.

SECTION 3

[PERSONS DISQUALIFIED FROM HOLDING OFFICE]

No person shall be a Senator or Representative in Congress, or elector of President and Vice-President, or hold any office, civil or military, under the

United States, or under any State, who, having previously taken an oath, as a member of Congress, or as an officer of the United States, or as a member of any State legislature, or as an executive or judicial officer of any State, to support the Constitution of the United States, shall have engaged in insurrection or rebellion against the same, or given aid or comfort to the enemies thereof. But Congress may by a vote of two-thirds of each House, remove such disability.

SECTION 4

[WHAT PUBLIC DEBTS ARE VALID]
The validity of the public debt of the United States, authorized by law, including debts incurred for payment of pensions and bounties for services in suppressing insurrection or rebellion, shall not be questioned. But neither the United States nor any State shall assume or pay any debt or obligation incurred in aid of insurrection or rebellion against the United States, or any claim for the loss or emancipation of any slave; but all such debts, obligations and claims shall be held illegal and void.

SECTION 5

[POWER TO ENFORCE THIS ARTICLE]
The Congress shall have power to enforce, by appropriate legislation, the provisions of this article.

Amendment XV

[Proposed by Congress on February 26, 1869; declared ratified on March 30, 1870.]

SECTION 1

[NEGRO SUFFRAGE]
The right of citizens of the United States to vote shall not be denied or abridged by the United States or by any State on account of race, color, or previous condition of servitude.

SECTION 2

[POWER TO ENFORCE THIS ARTICLE]
The Congress shall have power to enforce this article by appropriate legislation.

Amendment XVI

[Proposed by Congress on July 2, 1909; declared ratified on February 25, 1913.]

[AUTHORIZING INCOME TAXES]
The Congress shall have power to lay and collect taxes on incomes, from whatever source derived, without apportionment among the several States, and without regard to any census or enumeration.

Amendment XVII

[Proposed by Congress on May 13, 1912; declared ratified on May 31, 1913.]

[POPULAR ELECTION OF SENATORS]

The Senate of the United States shall be composed of two Senators from each State, elected by the people thereof, for six years; and each Senator shall have one vote. The electors in each State shall have the qualifications requisite for electors of the most numerous branch of the State legislatures.

When vacancies happen in the representation of any State in the Senate, the executive authority of such State shall –issue writs of election to fill such vacancies: Provided, That the legislature of any State may empower the executive thereof to make temporary appointments until the people fill the vacancies by election as the legislature may direct.

This amendment shall not be so construed as to affect the election or term of any Senator chosen before it becomes valid as part of the Constitution.

Amendment XVIII

[Proposed by Congress December 18, 1917; declared ratified on January 29, 1919.]

SECTION 1

[NATIONAL LIQUOR PROHIBITION]

After one year from the ratification of this article the manufacture, sale, or transportation of intoxicating liquors within, the importation thereof into, or the exportation thereof from the United States and all territory subject to the jurisdiction thereof for beverage purposes is hereby prohibited.

SECTION 2

[POWER TO ENFORCE THIS ARTICLE]

The Congress and the several States shall have concurrent power to enforce this article by appropriate legislation.

SECTION 3

[RATIFICATION WITHIN SEVEN YEARS]

This article shall be inoperative unless it shall have been ratified as an amendment to the Constitution by the legislatures of the several States, as provided in the Constitution, within seven years from the date of the submission hereof to the States by the Congress.[1]

---

[1] Repealed by the Twenty-first Amendment.

Amendment XIX

[Proposed by Congress on June 4, 1919; declared ratified on August 26, 1920.]

[WOMAN SUFFRAGE]

The right of citizens of the United States to vote shall not be denied or abridged by the United States or by any State on account of sex.

Congress shall have power to enforce this article by appropriate legislation.

Amendment XX

[Proposed by Congress on March 2, 1932; declared ratified on February 6, 1933.]

SECTION 1

[TERMS OF OFFICE]

The terms of the President and Vice President shall end at noon on the 20th day of January, and the terms of Senators and Representatives at noon on the 3rd day of January, of the years in which such terms would have ended if this article had not been ratified; and the terms of their successors shall then begin.

SECTION 2

[TIME OF CONVENING CONGRESS]

The Congress shall assemble at least once in every year, and such meeting shall begin at noon on the 3d day of January, unless they shall by law appoint a different day.

SECTION 3

[DEATH OF PRESIDENT-ELECT]

If, at the time fixed for the beginning of the term of the President, the President elect shall have died, the Vice President elect shall become President. If a President shall not have been chosen before the time fixed for the beginning of his term, or if the President elect shall have failed to qualify, then the Vice President elect shall act as President until a President shall have qualified; and the Congress may by law provide for the case wherein neither a President elect nor a Vice President elect shall have qualified, declaring who shall then act as President, or the manner in which one who is to act shall be selected, and such person shall act accordingly until a President or Vice President shall have qualified.

SECTION 4

[ELECTION OF THE PRESIDENT]

The Congress may by law provide for the case of the death of any of the persons from whom the House of Representatives may choose a President whenever the right of choice shall have devolved upon them, and for the case of the death of any of the persons from whom the Senate may choose a Vice President whenever the right of choice shall have devolved upon them.

SECTION 5

[AMENDMENT TAKES EFFECT]

Sections 1 and 2 shall take effect on the 15th day of October following the ratification of this article.

SECTION 6

[RATIFICATION WITHIN SEVEN YEARS]

This article shall be inoperative unless it shall have been ratified as an amendment to the Constitution by the legislatures of three-fourths of the several States within seven years from the date of its submission.

Amendment XXI

[Proposed by Congress on February 20, 1933; declared ratified on December 5, 1933.]

SECTION 1

[NATIONAL LIQUOR PROHIBITION REPEALED]

The eighteenth article of amendment to the Constitution of the United States is hereby repealed.

SECTION 2

[TRANSPORTATION OF LIQUOR INTO "DRY" STATES]

The transportation or importation into any State, Territory, or Possession of the United States for delivery or use therein of intoxicating liquors, in violation of the laws thereof, is hereby prohibited.

SECTION 3

[RATIFICATION WITHIN SEVEN YEARS]

This article shall be inoperative unless it shall have been ratified as an amendment to the Constitution by conventions in the several States, as provided in the Constitution, within seven years from the date of the submission hereof to the States by the Congress.

Amendment XXII

[Proposed by Congress on March 21, 1947; declared ratified on February 27, 1951.]

SECTION 1

[TENURE OF PRESIDENT LIMITED]

No person shall be elected to the office of President more than twice, and no person who has held the office of President or acted as President, for more than two years of a term to which some other person was elected President shall be elected to the office of the President more than once. But this Article shall not apply to any person holding the office of President when this Article was proposed by the Congress, and shall not prevent any person who may be holding the office of President, or acting as President, during the term within which this Article becomes operative from holding the office of President or acting as President during the remainder of such term.

SECTION 2

[RATIFICATION WITHIN SEVEN YEARS]
This article shall be inoperative unless it shall have been ratified as an amendment to the Constitution by the legislatures of three-fourths of the several States within seven years from the date of its submission to the States by the Congress.

Amendment XXIII

[Proposed by Congress on June 16, 1960; declared ratified on March 29, 1961.]

SECTION 1

[ELECTORAL COLLEGE VOTES FOR THE DISTRICT OF COLUMBIA]
The District constituting the seat of Government of the United States shall appoint in such manner as the Congress may direct:

A number of electors of President and Vice President equal to the whole number of Senators and Representatives in Congress to which the District would be entitled if it were a State, but in no event more than the least populous State; they shall be in addition to those appointed by the States, but they shall be considered, for the purposes of the election of President and Vice President, to be electors appointed by a State; and they shall meet in the District and perform such duties as provided by the twelfth article of amendment.

SECTION 2

[POWER TO ENFORCE THIS ARTICLE]
The Congress shall have power to enforce this article by appropriate legislation.

Amendment XXIV

[Proposed by Congress on August 27, 1962; declared ratified on January 23, 1964.]

SECTION 1

[ANTI-POLL TAX]
The right of citizens of the United States to vote in any primary or other election for President or Vice President, for electors for President or Vice President, or for Senator or Representative of Congress, shall not be denied or abridged by the United States or any State by reason of failure to pay any poll tax or other tax.

SECTION 2

[POWER TO ENFORCE THIS ARTICLE]
The Congress shall have power to enforce this article by appropriate legislation.

Amendment XXV

[Proposed by Congress on July 6, 1965; declared ratified on February 10, 1967.]

SECTION 1

[VICE PRESIDENT TO BECOME PRESIDENT]
In case of the removal of the President from office or his death or resignation, the Vice President shall become President.

SECTION 2

[CHOICE OF A NEW VICE PRESIDENT]
Whenever there is a vacancy in the office of the Vice President, the President shall nominate a Vice President who shall take the office upon confirmation by a majority vote of both houses of Congress.

SECTION 3

[PRESIDENT MAY DECLARE OWN DISABILITY]
Whenever the President transmits to the President pro tempore of the Senate and the Speaker of the House of Representatives his written declaration that he is unable to discharge the powers and duties of his office, and until he transmits to them a written declaration to the contrary, such powers and duties shall be discharged by the Vice President as Acting President.

SECTION 4

[ALTERNATE PROCEDURES TO DECLARE AND TO END PRESIDENTIAL DISABILITY]
Whenever the Vice President and a majority of either the principal officers of the executive departments, or of such other body as Congress may by law provide, transmit to the President pro tempore of the Senate and the Speaker of the House of Representatives their written declaration that the President is unable to discharge the powers and duties of his office, the Vice President shall immediately assume the powers and duties of the office as Acting President.

Thereafter, when the President transmits to the President pro tempore of the Senate and the Speaker of the House of Representatives his written declaration that no inability exists, he shall resume the powers and duties of his office unless the Vice President and a majority of either the principal officers of the executive department, or of such other body as Congress may by law provide, transmit within four days to the President pro tempore of the Senate and the Speaker of the House of Representatives their written declaration that the President is unable to discharge the powers and duties of his office. Thereupon Congress shall decide the issue, assembling within forty eight hours for that purpose if not in session. If the Congress, within twenty one days after receipt of the latter written declaration, or, if Congress is not in session, within twenty one days after Congress is required to assemble, determines by two-thirds vote of both Houses that the President is unable to discharge the powers and duties of his office, the Vice President shall continue to discharge the same as Acting President; otherwise, the President shall resume the powers and duties of his office.

Amendment XXVI

[Proposed by Congress on March 23, 1971; declared ratified on July 1, 1971.]

SECTION 1

[EIGHTEEN-YEAR-OLD VOTE]
The right of citizens of the United States, who are eighteen years of age or older, to vote shall not be denied or abridged by the United States or by any State on account of age.

SECTION 2

[POWER TO ENFORCE THIS ARTICLE]
The Congress shall have power to enforce this article by appropriate legislation.

Amendment XXVII

[Proposed by Congress on September 25, 1789; declared ratified on May 8, 1992.]

[CONGRESS CANNOT RAISE ITS OWN PAY]
No law varying the compensation for the services of the Senators and Representatives, shall take effect, until an election of representatives shall have intervened.

The Federalist Papers

No. 10: Madison

Among the numerous advantages promised by a well constructed Union, none deserves to be more accurately developed than its tendency to break and control the violence of faction. The friend of popular governments never finds himself so much alarmed for their character and fate, as when he contemplates their propensity to this dangerous vice. He will not fail therefore to set a due value on any plan which, without violating the principles to which he is attached, provides a proper cure for it. The instability, injustice, and confusion introduced into the public councils have, in truth, been the mortal diseases under which popular governments have everywhere perished, as they continue to be the favorite and fruitful topics from which the adversaries to liberty derive their most specious declamations. The valuable improvements made by the American constitutions on the popular models, both ancient and modern, cannot certainly be too much admired; but it would be an unwarrantable partiality to contend that they have as effectually obviated the danger on this side, as was wished and expected. Complaints are everywhere heard from our most considerate and virtuous citizens, equally the friends of public and private faith and of public and personal liberty, that our governments are too unstable, that the public good is disregarded in the conflicts of rival parties, and that measures are too often decided, not according to the rules of justice and the rights of the minor party, but by the superior force of an interested and overbearing majority. However anxiously we may wish that these complaints had no foundation, the evidence of known facts will not permit us to deny that they are in some degree true. It will be found, indeed, on a candid review of our situation, that some of the distresses under which we labor have been erroneously charged on the operation of our governments; but it will be found, at the same time, that other causes will not alone account for many of our heaviest misfortunes; and, particularly, for that prevailing and increasing distrust of public engagements and alarm for private rights which are echoed from one end of the continent to the other. These must be chiefly, if not wholly, effects of the unsteadiness and injustice with which a factious spirit has tainted our public administration.

By a faction I understand a number of citizens, whether amounting to a majority or minority of the whole, who are united and actuated by some common impulse of passion, or of interest, adverse to the rights of other citizens, or to the permanent and aggregate interests of the community.

There are two methods of curing the mischiefs of faction: the one, by removing its causes; the other, by controlling its effects.

There are again two methods of removing the causes of faction: the one, by destroying the liberty which is essential to its existence; the other, by giving to every citizen the same opinions, the same passions, and the same interests.

It could never be more truly said than of the first remedy, that it is worse than the disease. Liberty is to faction what air is to fire, an aliment without which it instantly expires. But it could not be a less folly to abolish liberty, which is essential to political life, because it nourishes faction, than it would be to wish the annihilation of air, which is essential to animal life, because it imparts to fire its destructive agency.

The second expedient is as impracticable, as the first would be unwise. As long as the reason of man continues fallible, and he is at liberty to exercise it, different opinions will be formed. As long as the connection subsists between his reason and his self-love, his opinions and his passions will have a reciprocal influence on each other; and the former will be objects to which the latter will attach themselves. The diversity in the faculties of men, from which the rights of property originate, is not less an insuperable obstacle to a uniformity of interests. The protection of these faculties is the first object of Government. From the protection of different and unequal faculties of acquiring property, the possession of different degrees and kinds of property immediately results; and from the influence of these on the sentiments and views of the respective proprietors, ensues a division of the society into different interests and parties.

The latent causes of faction are thus sown in the nature of man; and we see them everywhere brought into different degrees of activity, according to the different circumstances of civil society. A zeal for different opinions concerning religion, concerning Government, and many other points, as well of speculation as of practice; an attachment to different leaders ambitiously contending for pre-eminence and power; or to persons of other descriptions whose fortunes have been interesting to the human passions, have in turn divided mankind into parties, inflamed them with mutual animosity, and rendered them much more disposed to vex and oppress each other, than to co-operate for their common good. So strong is this propensity of mankind to fall into mutual animosities, that where no substantial occasion presents itself, the most frivolous and fanciful distinctions have been sufficient to kindle their unfriendly passions, and excite their most violent conflicts. But the most common and durable source of factions has been the various and unequal distribution of property. Those who hold and those who are without property have ever formed distinct interests in society. Those who are creditors, and those who are debtors, fall under a like discrimination. A landed interest, a manufacturing interest, a mercantile interest, a moneyed interest, with many lesser interests, grow up of necessity in civilized nations, and divide them into different classes, actuated by different sentiments and views. The regulation of these various and interfering interests forms the principal task of modern Legislation, and involves the spirit of party and faction in the necessary and ordinary operations of Government.

No man is allowed to be judge in his own cause, because his interest would certainly bias his judgment and, not improbably, corrupt his integrity. With equal, nay with greater reason, a body of men are unfit to be both judges and parties at the same time; yet what are many of the most important acts of legislation but so many judicial determinations, not indeed concerning the rights of single persons, but concerning the rights of large bodies of citizens; and what are the different classes of legislators but advocates and parties to the causes which they determine? Is a law proposed concerning private debts? It is a question to which the creditors are parties on one side and the debtors on the other. Justice ought to hold the balance between them. Yet the parties are, and must be, themselves the judges; and the most numerous party, or in other words, the most powerful faction must be expected to prevail. Shall domestic manufacturers be encouraged, and in what degree, by restrictions on foreign manufacturers? are questions which would be differently decided by the landed and the manufacturing classes, and probably by neither with a sole regard to justice and the public good. The apportionment of taxes on the various descriptions of property is an act which seems to require the most exact impartiality; yet there is, perhaps, no legislative act in which greater opportunity and temptation are given to a predominant party to trample on the rules of justice. Every shilling with which they overburden the inferior number is a shilling saved to their own pockets.

It is in vain to say that enlightened statesmen will be able to adjust these clashing interests and render them all subservient to the public good. Enlightened statesmen will not always be at the helm. Nor, in many cases, can such an adjustment be made at all without taking into view indirect and remote considerations, which will rarely prevail over the immediate interest which one party may find in disregarding the rights of another or the good of the whole.

The inference to which we are brought is that the *causes* of faction cannot be removed and that relief is only to be sought in the means of controlling its *effects*.

If a faction consists of less than a majority, relief is supplied by the republican principle, which enables the majority to defeat its sinister views by regular vote. It may clog the administration, it may convulse the society; but it will be unable to execute and mask its violence under the forms of the Constitution. When a majority is included in a faction, the form of popular government, on the other hand, enables it to sacrifice to its ruling passion or interest both the public good and the rights of other citizens. To secure the public good and private rights against the danger of such a faction, and at the same time to preserve the spirit and the form of popular government, is then the great object to which our enquiries are directed. Let me add that it is the great desideratum by which alone this form of government can be rescued from the opprobrium under which it has so long labored and be recommended to the esteem and adoption of mankind.

By what means is this object attainable? Evidently by one of two only. Either the existence of the same passion or interest in a majority at the same time must be prevented, or the majority, having such co-existent passion or interest, must be rendered, by their number and local situation, unable to concert and carry into effect schemes of oppression. If the impulse and the opportunity be suffered to coincide, we well know that neither moral nor religious motives can be relied on as an adequate control. They are not found to be such on the injustice and violence of individuals, and lose their efficacy in proportion to the number combined together, that is, in proportion as their efficacy becomes needful.

From this view of the subject it may be concluded that a pure Democracy, by which I mean a Society consisting of a small number of citizens, who assemble and administer the Government in person, can admit of no cure for the mischiefs of faction. A common passion or interest will, in almost every case, be felt by a majority of the whole; a communication and concert results from the form of Government itself; and there is nothing to check the inducements to sacrifice the weaker party or an obnoxious individual. Hence it is that such Democracies have ever been spectacles of turbulence and contention; have ever been found incompatible with personal security or the rights of property; and have in general been as short in their lives as they have been violent in their deaths. Theoretic politicians, who have patronized this species of Government, have erroneously supposed that by reducing mankind to a perfect equality in their political rights, they would at the same time be perfectly equalized and assimilated in their possessions, their opinions, and their passions.

A Republic, by which I mean a Government in which the scheme of representation takes place, opens a different prospect and promises the cure for which we are seeking. Let us examine the points in which it varies from pure Democracy, and we shall comprehend both the nature of the cure and the efficacy which it must derive from the Union.

The two great points of difference between a Democracy and a Republic are: first, the delegation of the Government, in the latter, to a small number of citizens elected by the rest; secondly, the greater number of citizens and greater sphere of country over which the latter may be extended.

The effect of the first difference is, on the one hand, to refine and enlarge the public views by passing them through the medium of a chosen body of citizens, whose wisdom may best discern the true interest of their country and whose patriotism and love of justice will be least likely to sacrifice it to temporary or partial considerations. Under such a regulation it may well happen that the public voice, pronounced by the representatives of the people, will be more consonant to the public good than if pronounced by the people themselves, convened for the purpose. On the other hand, the effect may be inverted. Men of factious tempers, of local prejudices, or of sinister designs, may, by intrigue, by corruption, or by other means, first obtain the suffrages, and then betray the interests of the people. The question resulting is, whether small or extensive Republics are most favorable to the election of proper guardians of the public weal; and it is clearly decided in favor of the latter by two obvious considerations.

In the first place it is to be remarked that however small the Republic may be, the Representatives must be raised to a certain number in order to guard against the cabals of a few; and that however large it may be they must be limited to a certain number in order to guard against the confusion of a multitude. Hence, the number of Representatives in the two cases not being in proportion to that of the Constituents, and being proportionally greatest in the small Republic, it follows that if the proportion of fit characters be not less in the large than in the small Republic, the former will present a greater option, and consequently a greater probability of a fit choice.

In the next place, as each Representative will be chosen by a greater number of citizens in the large than in the small Republic, it will be more difficult for unworthy candidates to practise with success the vicious arts by which elections are too often carried; and the suffrages of the people being more free, will be more likely to centre on men who possess the most attractive merit and the most diffusive and established characters.

It must be confessed that in this, as in most other cases, there is a mean, on both sides of which inconveniencies will be found to lie. By enlarging too much the number of electors, you render the representative too little acquainted with all their local circumstances and lesser interests; as by reducing it too much, you render him unduly attached to these, and too little fit to comprehend and pursue great and national objects. The Federal Constitution forms a happy combination in this respect; the great and aggregate interests being referred to the national, the local and particular to the State legislatures.

The other point of difference is the greater number of citizens and extent of territory which may be brought within the compass of Republican than of Democratic Government; and it is this circumstance principally which renders factious combinations less to be dreaded in the former than in the latter. The smaller the society, the fewer probably will be the distinct parties and interests composing it; the fewer the distinct parties and interests, the more frequently will a majority be found of the same party; and the smaller the number of individuals composing a majority, and the smaller the compass within which they are placed, the more easily will they concert and execute their plans of oppression. Extend the sphere and you take in a greater variety of parties and interests; you make it less probable that a majority of the whole will have a common motive to invade the rights of other citizens; or if such a common motive exists, it will be more difficult for all who feel it to discover their own strength and to act in unison with each other. Besides other impediments, it may be remarked, that where there is a consciousness of unjust or dishonorable purposes, communication is always checked by distrust in proportion to the number whose concurrence is necessary.

Hence, it clearly appears that the same advantage which a Republic has over a Democracy in controlling the effects of faction is enjoyed by a large over a small republic—is enjoyed by the Union over the States composing it. Does this advantage consist in the substitution of representatives whose enlightened views and virtuous sentiments render them superior to local prejudices and to schemes of injustice? It will not be denied that the representation of the Union will be most likely to possess these requisite endowments. Does it consist in the greater security afforded by a greater variety of parties, against the event of any one party being able to outnumber and oppress the rest? In an equal degree does the increased variety of parties comprised within the Union increase this security? Does it, in fine, consist in the greater obstacles opposed to the concert and accomplishment of the secret wishes of an unjust and interested majority? Here again the extent of the Union gives it the most palpable advantage.

The influence of factious leaders may kindle a flame within their particular States but will be unable to spread a general conflagration through the other States: a religious sect may degenerate into a political faction in a part of the Confederacy; but the variety of sects dispersed over the entire face of it must secure the national Councils against any danger from that source: a rage for paper money, for an abolition of debts, for an equal division of property, or for any other improper or wicked project, will be less apt to pervade the whole body of the Union than a particular member of it; in the same proportion as such a malady is more likely to taint a particular county or district than an entire State.

In the extent and proper structure of the Union, therefore, we behold a republican remedy for the diseases most incident to Republican Government. And according to the degree of pleasure and pride we feel in being republicans ought to be our zeal in cherishing the spirit and supporting the character of federalist.

PUBLIUS

No. 51: Madison

To what expedient, then, shall we finally resort, for maintaining in practice the necessary partition of power among the several departments as laid down in the constitution? The only answer that can be given is that as all these exterior provisions are found to be inadequate the defect must be supplied, by so contriving the interior structure of the government as that its several constituent parts may, by their mutual relations, be the means of keeping each other in their proper places. Without presuming to undertake a full development of this important idea I will hazard a few general observations which may perhaps place it in a clearer light, and enable us to form a more correct judgment of the principles and structure of the government planned by the convention.

In order to lay a due foundation for that separate and distinct exercise of the different powers of government, which to a certain extent is admitted on all hands to be essential to the preservation of liberty, it is evident that each department should have a will of its own; and consequently should be so constituted that the members of each should have as little agency as possible in the appointment of the members of the others. Were this principle rigorously adhered to, it would require that all the appointments for the supreme executive, legislative, and judiciary magistracies should be drawn from the same fountain of authority, the people, through channels having no communication whatever with one another. Perhaps such a plan of constructing the several departments would be less difficult in practice than it may in contemplation appear. Some difficulties, however, and some additional expense would attend the execution of it. Some deviations, therefore, from the principle must be admitted. In the constitution of the judiciary department in particular, it might be inexpedient to insist rigorously on the principle: first, because peculiar qualifications being essential in the members, the primary consideration ought to be to select that mode of choice which best secures these qualifications; second, because the permanent tenure by which the appointments are held in that department must soon destroy all sense of dependence on the authority conferring them.

It is equally evident that the members of each department should be as little dependent as possible on those of the others for the emoluments annexed to their offices. Were the executive magistrate, or the judges, not independent of the legislature in this particular, their independence in every other would be merely nominal.

But the great security against a gradual concentration of the several powers in the same department consists in giving to those who administer each department the necessary constitutional means and personal motives to resist encroachments of the others. The provision for defence must in this, as in all other cases, be made commensurate to the danger of attack. Ambition must be made to counteract ambition. The interest of the man must be connected with the constitutional rights of the place. It may be a reflection on human nature that such devices should be necessary to control the abuses of government. But what is government itself but the greatest of all reflections on human nature? If men were angels, no government would be necessary. If angels were to govern men, neither external nor internal controls on government would be necessary. In framing a government which is to be administered by men over men, the great difficulty lies in this: You must first enable the government to control the governed; and in the next place oblige it to control itself. A dependence on the people is, no doubt, the primary control on the government; but experience has taught mankind the necessity of auxiliary precautions.

This policy of supplying, by opposite and rival interests, the defect of better motives, might be traced through the whole system of human affairs, private as well as public. We see it particularly displayed in all the subordinate distributions of power, where the constant aim is to divide and arrange the several offices in such a manner as that each may be a check on the other; that the private interest of every individual may be a sentinel over the public rights. These inventions of prudence cannot be less requisite in the distribution of the supreme powers of the State.

But it is not possible to give to each department an equal power of self-defense. In republican government, the legislative authority necessarily predominates. The remedy for this inconveniency is to divide the legislature into different branches; and to render them, by different modes of election and different principles of action, as little connected with each other as the nature of their common functions and their common dependence on the society will admit. It may even be necessary to guard against dangerous encroachments by still further precautions. As the weight of the legislative authority requires that it should be thus divided, the weakness of the executive may require, on the other hand, that it should be fortified. An absolute negative on the legislature appears, at first view, to be the natural defense with which the executive magistrate should be armed. But perhaps it would be neither altogether safe nor alone sufficient. On ordinary occasions it might not be exerted with the requisite firmness, and on extraordinary occasions it might be perfidiously abused. May not this defect of an absolute negative be supplied by some qualified connection between this weaker branch of the stronger department, by which the latter may be led to support the constitutional rights of the former, without being too much detached from the rights of its own department?

If the principles on which these observations are founded be just, as I persuade myself they are, and they be applied as a criterion to the several State constitutions, and to the federal Constitution, it will be found that if the latter does not perfectly correspond with them, the former are infinitely less able to bear such a test.

There are, moreover, two considerations particularly applicable to the federal system of America, which place that system in a very interesting point of view.

First. In a single republic, all the power surrendered by the people is submitted to the administration of a single government; and usurpations are guarded against by a division of the government into distinct and separate departments. In the compound republic of America, the power surrendered by the people is first divided between two distinct governments, and then the portion allotted to each subdivided among distinct and separate departments. Hence a double security arises to the rights of the people. The different governments will control each other, at the same time that each will be controlled by itself.

Second. It is of great importance in a republic not only to guard the society against the oppression of its rulers, but to guard one part of the society against the injustice of the other part. Different interests necessarily exist in different classes of citizens. If a majority be united by a common interest, the rights of the minority will be insecure. There are but two methods of providing against this evil: The one by creating a will in the community independent of the majority—that is, of the society itself; the other, by comprehending in the society so many separate descriptions of citizens as will render an unjust combination of a majority of the whole very improbable, if not impracticable. The first method prevails in all governments possessing an hereditary or self-appointed authority. This, at best, is but a precarious security; because a power independent of the society may as well espouse the unjust views of the major as the rightful interests of the minor party, and may possibly be turned against both parties. The second method will be exemplified in the federal republic of the United States. Whilst all authority in it will be derived from and dependent on the society, the society itself will be broken into so many parts, interests and classes of citizens, that the rights of individuals, or of the minority, will be in little danger from interested combinations of the majority. In a free government the security for civil rights must be the same as that for religious rights. It consists in the one case in the multiplicity of interests, and in the other in the multiplicity of sects. The degree of security in both cases will depend on the number of interests and sects; and this may be presumed to depend on the extent of country and number of people comprehended under the same government. This view of the subject must particularly recommend a proper federal system to all the sincere and considerate friends of republican government: Since it shows that in exact proportion as the territory of the Union may be formed into more circumscribed Confederacies, or States, oppressive combinations of a majority will be facilitated; the best security, under the republican form, for the rights of every class of citizens, will be diminished; and consequently the stability and independence of some member of the government, the only other security, must be proportionally increased. Justice is the end of government. It is the end of civil society. It ever has been and ever will be pursued until it be obtained, or until liberty be lost in the pursuit. In a society under the forms of which the stronger faction can readily unite and oppress the weaker, anarchy may as truly be said to reign as in a state of nature, where the weaker individual is not secured against the violence of the stronger: And as, in the latter state, even the stronger individuals are prompted, by the uncertainty of their condition, to submit to a government which may protect the weak as well as themselves: So, in the former state, will the more powerful factions or parties be gradually induced, by a like motive, to wish for a government which will protect all parties, the weaker as well as the more powerful. It can be little doubted that if the State of Rhode Island was separated from the Confederacy and left to itself, the insecurity of rights under the popular form of government within such narrow limits would be displayed by such reiterated oppressions of factious majorities that some power altogether independent of the people would soon be called for by the voice of the very factions whose misrule had proved the necessity of it. In the extended republic of the United States, and among the great variety of interests, parties, and sects which it embraces, a coalition of a majority of the whole society could seldom take place on any other principles than those of justice and the general good; and there being thus less danger to a minor from the will of the major party, there must be less pretext, also, to provide for the security of the former, by introducing into the government a will not dependent on the latter, or, in other words, a will independent of the society itself. It is no less certain than it is important, notwithstanding the contrary opinions which have been entertained, that the larger the society, provided it lie within a practicable sphere, the more duly capable it will be of self-government. And happily for the *republican cause*, practicable sphere may be carried to a very great extent by a judicious modification and mixture of the *federal principle*.

PUBLIUS

GLOSSARY

527s Organizations that are independent of any party or candidate and thus not regulated by the Federal Election Commission; they do not advocate publicly for or against specific candidates, parties, or policies.

administrative law The body of law created by executive agencies with the purpose of refining general law passed in legislation.

affirmative action Efforts to redress previous discrimination against women and minorities through active measures to promote their employment and educational opportunities.

agenda setter An authority that controls what options are decided on by a group.

amicus curiae Briefs (letters to the court) in which those who are not parties in a case provide their opinions on how the case should be decided.

Antifederalists Those who opposed adopting the Constitution as written because they feared that it created an overly strong national government.

Articles of Confederation The constitution drafted by the Second Continental Congress in 1777 and ratified by the states in 1781. It set up a weak central government consisting of a congress with limited legislative power and virtually no authority over the execution of its laws.

attitudinal model A theoretical model where judicial decisions are primarily determined by the policy goals and ideological agendas of judges.

Australian ballot A type of ballot that lists all candidates running for each office and allows voters to cast their votes secretly and for specific individual candidates.

authoritarianism A political system in which there is no expectation that the government represents the people, and the institutions of government do not give the people a direct voice in who will lead.

ballot initiative An election in which citizens vote directly on a proposition raised by a group of fellow citizens.

bargaining Actors (e.g., countries) advance their own interests while working toward a specific common objective with other actors (e.g., other countries).

biased sample A sample that, because it does not accurately represent the overall population, is likely to lead to erroneous conclusions about the population.

bicameral legislature A legislature consisting of two chambers or houses.

Bill of Rights The first 10 amendments to the Constitution, which enumerate a set of liberties not to be violated by the government and a set of rights to be protected by the government.

block grants Sums of money transferred to lower-level governments such that, as long as the general purpose of the grant is met, the lower-level governments are allowed considerable freedom in deciding how the money is spent.

bureaucracy An agency or office devoted to carrying out tasks for the government in a manner consistent with the law.

bureaucrat Any government employee who is not part of the ruling powers.

bureaucratic capture When regulatory agencies are beholden to the organizations or interests they are supposed to regulate.

bureaucratic drift When government agencies depart from executing policy consistent with the ideological preferences of Congress or the president so as to execute policy consistent with their own ideological preferences.

Bush Doctrine An approach to American foreign policy developed during the George W. Bush administration that advocates preventing terrorism through active intervention in foreign countries, including pressuring or even invading foreign countries and using military force against terrorists where they live and train; the doctrine also advocates maintaining a stronger military than any other country.

by-product A political activity conducted by groups whose principal organizational purpose is the pursuit of some non-political goal.

cabinet departments Departments within the executive branch that encompass many of the agencies that implement federal policy. Secretaries appointed by the president and confirmed by the Senate are given the responsibility of leading these departments and advising the president.

capital Goods used to create other goods in an economy.

categorical grants Grants that narrowly define how the funds are to be spent. These grants normally come with conditions that need to be satisfied in order for the money to be used.

caucus In a legislature, a group of legislators that unites to promote an agenda not pursued within the parties or the legislative committees.

checks and balances An arrangement in which no one branch of government can conduct its core business without the approval, tacit or expressed, of the other branches.

civil case A case in which at least one person sues another person for violating the civil code of conduct.

civil law A system of jurisprudence in which authoritative documents determine how the law is to be interpreted. Under this system, legal codes and statutes (and not judges) inform future decisions.

civil liberties Freedoms protected from interference by the government, such as freedom of speech, the right to bear arms, and freedom of religion.

civil rights Rights that (1) enable individuals to engage in activities central to citizenship or legal immigrant status, such as voting or petitioning the government; (2) ensure all individuals receive due process and equal treatment under the law; or (3) guarantee freedom from discriminatory actions by others that seek to deny an individual's full status as an equal member of society.

civil rights movement A social movement of the 1950s and 1960s focused primarily on the situation of African Americans, but also promoting the goals that all people be treated as equals under the law and that discrimination based on race, religion, ethnicity, gender, and place of origin be eliminated.

class action A lawsuit in which the plaintiff or defendant is a collective group of individuals.

closed primary A primary election in which only voters registered with the party can vote.

closed rule A provision that allows no amendments to be proposed once a bill comes to the chamber floor.

cloture A rule that limits the debate on a bill to a specific number of hours. Senate rules require 60 senators to support such a motion to end the debate (including filibusters) and proceed to a vote.

club good A variant of a public good; a product or benefit provided such that its enjoyment is exclusively for those who paid for it, but one person's enjoyment of it does not inhibit others from enjoying the benefit.

coalitional drift When an ideological shift in elected branches creates disparity between the way an agency executes policy and the way new members of Congress or a new president believes the agency ought to execute policy.

collective action problem A situation in which people would be better off if they all cooperated; however, any individual has an incentive not to cooperate as long as others are cooperating.

collective dilemma A situation in which there is conflict between group goals and individual goals or self-interest.

commerce clause An enumerated power listed in Article I, Section 8, of the Constitution that grants Congress the power to "regulate Commerce with foreign Nations, and among the several States, and with the Indian Tribes."

common good A variant of a public good; a benefit provided to a group of people such that each member can enjoy it without necessarily having to pay for it, but one individual's consumption of it limits or precludes others from consuming it.

common law A system of jurisprudence in which the judiciary has the authority to determine how the law is to be interpreted. Under this system, legal precedent established by judges informs future decisions.

concurring opinion An opinion issued by a member of the majority of the Supreme Court that agrees with the decision of the majority but offers alternative legal reasoning.

confederation A political system with multiple levels of government in which lower-level governments retain full sovereignty and cannot be compelled by the national government to act.

conference committee A meeting of legislators from the House and Senate to reconcile two bills passed on the same topic.

confidence vote A vote held in a parliamentary system that, if it fails, brings on an election and possibly a new set of party leaders.

Connecticut Compromise An agreement reached at the Constitutional Convention to establish a bicameral legislature with an upper house (the Senate) composed of equal representation from each state and a lower house (the House of Representatives) composed of representation from each state in proportion to its population.

constituency service A legislator directly helping a constituent in dealing with government bureaucracy.

constitutional law The collection of fundamental rules for making statutory laws and regulations, their enforcement, and the court decisions interpreting those rules.

cooperative federalism A political system in which both levels of government—national and state—are active in nearly all areas of policy and share sovereign authority.

coordination problem A situation in which two or more people are all better off if they coordinate on a common course of action, but there is more than one possible course of action to take.

coverage bias The tendency for the media, or a specific media outlet, to give less attention in terms of column space or airtime to certain kinds of stories or aspects of stories.

criminal case A case in which the government prosecutes a person for a crime against society.

deflation When the purchasing value of a unit of currency, such as the dollar, increases so that goods and services cost less of the currency.

delegates Representatives who listen carefully to what their constituents want and make decisions based on feedback from constituents.

democracy Rule by the people; in practice today, this means popular election of the government and basic protections of civil rights and liberties.

democratic peace The observation that historically it has been extremely rare for democracies to fight wars against other democracies.

dictatorship An authoritarian political system in which sovereign power is vested in one individual.

diplomacy Peaceful negotiations and interactions among countries.

dissenting opinion An opinion issued by a member of the Supreme Court in opposition to the majority, offering legal reasoning for the decision to oppose.

distributional model The view that the internal institutions of the congressional chambers are designed primarily to help members of Congress secure economic benefits for only their constituents, not the general public.

distributive policy A government policy intended to provide benefits to large portions of the population.

divided government A government whose president is from a different party than the majority in Congress.

dual federalism A political system in which each level of government—national and state—is sovereign in its own sphere of policy authority.

due process The right to legal protections against arbitrary deprivation of life, liberty, or property.

Duverger's Law A regularity that only two parties tend to compete for control of the government in countries that have single-member, plurality electoral systems.

elastic clause (necessary and proper clause) The provision in Article I, Section 8, of the Constitution stating that Congress can make whatever laws are "necessary and proper" to provide the means to carry out its enumerated powers.

electoral college The electors appointed by each state to vote for the president.

entrepreneur A leading group participant who is so committed to the group's goals and/or so skilled in the pursuit of those goals that he or she does not need selective incentives.

equal protection The principle that laws passed and enforced by the states must apply fairly to all individuals.

executive agreement An agreement between the United States and one or more foreign countries. Because it is not a formal treaty, it does not need Senate approval.

executive order An official means by which the president can instruct federal agencies on how to execute the laws passed by Congress.

expressed powers (enumerated powers) Those powers specifically described in the Constitution.

externalities Effects on people, good or bad, arising from the economic behavior of others. Also known as *spillover effects*.

federal court supremacy The arrangement based on the supremacy clause in the Constitution that gives federal courts the authority to overturn state court decisions and to decide on the constitutionality of state laws and actions.

Federal Election Commission (FEC) The federal agency that regulates campaign donations to and spending by candidates for Congress and the presidency.

Federal Reserve Board Board of directors, consisting of seven members appointed by the president, in charge of policies for the Federal Reserve System.

Federal Reserve System Network of U.S. government banks that loan money to and regulate the commercial behavior of private banks.

federal system A political system with multiple levels of government in which each level has independent authority over some important policy areas.

federalism A political system with multiple levels of government in which each level has independent authority over some important policy areas.

Federalists Those who favored adopting the Constitution as written because they believed that a strong national government was needed to solve the collective dilemmas facing the states.

filibuster Instances in which senators, once recognized to speak on the floor, talk for an extended period ("hold the floor") in an attempt to block the rest of the Senate from voting on a bill.

fire-alarm oversight Congressional oversight that relies on interest groups and citizens to inform representatives of unwarranted action.

fiscal policy Taxing and spending decisions by governments.

foreign policy Government actions affecting a country's relationships with other countries and regions.

framing Establishing the context for an issue in such a way as to emphasize certain aspects over others.

the franchise (or suffrage) The right to vote.

free riding Benefiting from a public good while avoiding the costs of contributing to it.

gatekeeping bias The tendency for the media, or a specific media outlet, not to report stories of a particular nature.

gerrymandering Drawing strangely shaped district boundaries to gain political advantage.

going public Action taken by a president to communicate directly with the people usually through a press conference, radio broadcast, or televised speech to influence public opinion and put pressure on Congress.

government agency An individual unit of the government responsible for carrying out the tasks delegated to it by Congress or the president in accordance with the law.

government bureaucracy Agencies and offices devoted to carrying out the tasks of government consistent with the law.

government contract An agreement whereby the government hires a company or an organization to carry out certain tasks on its behalf.

government corporation A federally owned corporation that generates revenue by providing a public service, operating much like a private business and with a higher degree of autonomy than a cabinet department or an independent agency.

government grant Money that the government provides to individuals or organizations to perform tasks in the public's interest.

grants-in-aid Money that is distributed to lower-level governments with the purpose of funding special projects.

gross domestic product (GDP) The value of all the goods and services produced by an economy within its borders.

hard money Campaign funds that are given directly to candidates or parties to support a particular candidate and thus are subject to FEC regulations.

Help America Vote Act of 2002 A federal law meant to reduce barriers to participation in elections.

home rule The constitutional or legal authority held by local governments that allows them to govern themselves with little or no interference from the state.

idealism A philosophy about international politics based on the assumption that countries have common interests and can work effectively together, often through international organizations. Also known as *liberalism*.

ideology A coherent, organized set of ideas and principles that functions as a core on which individuals draw when forming their attitudes about public affairs.

impeachment Process by which the House of Representatives formally charges a federal government official with "Treason, Bribery, or other high Crimes and Misdemeanors."

incorporation The process by which rights and liberties established by the Bill of Rights are applied to state and local governments through the Fourteenth Amendment.

incumbency advantage The advantage current officeholders have in an election, in particular as it relates to the high rates at which congressional legislators win reelection.

independent agency An agency that exists outside the cabinet departments and is run with a larger degree of independence from presidential influence.

inflation When the purchasing value of a unit of currency, such as the dollar, declines so that goods and services cost more of the currency.

informational model The view that the internal institutions of the congressional chambers are designed to help Congress make more informed decisions.

infotainment Mass media programming that is intended primarily to entertain but also provides political news.

initiative An election held to vote directly on a ballot question that was proposed by a group of individuals.

inside lobbying Activities by lobbyists and interest group leaders that involve direct contact with policy makers.

institutions Rules or sets of rules or practices that determine how people make collective decisions.

interest group Any group other than a political party that is organized to influence the government.

intergovernmentalism A system in which multiple levels of government are active in a given policy area.

intermediate scrutiny An intermediate standard used by the Supreme Court to determine whether a law is compatible with the Constitution. A law subject to this standard is considered constitutional if it advances "an important government objective" and is "substantially related" to the objective.

internationalism An approach to foreign policy that advocates for a country to engage actively with other countries and to become involved in international organizations.

isolationism An approach to foreign policy that advocates for a country to stay out of international affairs.

Jim Crow laws Laws passed after the Civil War to establish a system of segregation of public facilities and private establishments that made African Americans second-class citizens.

joint committee A committee made up of members of both the House and Senate.

judicial review The authority of the judiciary to decide whether a law or any other government action is constitutional.

laissez-faire An economic philosophy advocating that the government take a noninterventionist approach to the economy, leaving market forces alone to determine the economic behavior of people and business firms.

latent interest A concern shared by a group of people on which they have not yet chosen to act collectively.

legal model A theoretical model where judicial decisions are primarily determined by the case, the plain meaning of the text from the Constitution and statutes, the intent of the framers, and/or legal precedent.

line-item veto A partial veto that allows the executive to strike specific passages from a given bill.

lobbying An attempt to influence public officials by speaking to them directly or by pressuring them through their constituents.

logrolling An instance of two or more legislators agreeing to vote in favor of one another's proposed bills or amendments.

majority leader The head of the party holding a majority of seats and, in the Senate, the leader of the Senate. In the House, the majority leader is second to the Speaker of the House.

margin of error In statistical research, the range of outcomes we expect for a population, given the data revealed by a sample drawn from that population.

marketization Government bureaucratic reform that emphasizes market-based principles of management that are common to the private sector.

markup A committee or subcommittee process where committee members edit and amend bills.

mass media Media that is intended to be publicly available, or at least targeted at large numbers of people.

means-tested program A government policy that applies to people based on whether they qualify according to a quantitative measure, such as income level.

median voter theorem A mathematical result showing that the voter with the ideological preference in the middle of the ranking of voters must be satisfied and approve of a majority-rule winning outcome.

media The methods or technologies people use for communication, such as phones, radio, newspapers, television, and the Internet.

Medicaid A government program, cofunded by the federal government and state governments, that provides basic health insurance to the poor.

Medicare A federal government program that provides basic health care insurance to the elderly.

military action The organized use of deadly force by a government.

minimum winning coalition The smallest-sized coalition necessary to achieve a goal.

mixed presidential system A form of democracy in which the executive is elected independently and shares responsibility for the government with the legislature.

monarchy A political system in which a ruler (usually a king or queen) is chosen by virtue of being the heir of the previous ruler.

monetary policy Government management of the supply of money in the economy, which affects prices, interest rates, and the availability of loans.

Monroe Doctrine Enunciated in 1823 by President James Monroe, the notion that the United States could claim the entire Western Hemisphere as its exclusive sphere of influence.

moot The status of a case in which further legal proceedings would have no impact on one or both parties.

multilateralism An approach to foreign policy that considers and depends on the perspectives and resources of multiple nations.

national committee Officials who oversee the operation of their party nationwide.

national debt The total amount owed to those who have loaned money to the government.

national deficit The difference in a given year between what the government raises in taxes and fees and what the government spends.

national party convention The meeting where the party formally nominates its presidential candidate.

New Deal Party System A political alliance between southern Democrats, big-city Democrats, rural voters, and African Americans that endured for several decades after the election of Franklin Roosevelt in 1932.

New Jersey Plan A plan proposed at the Constitutional Convention by William Paterson of New Jersey to amend, rather than replace, the standing Articles of Confederation. The plan called for a unicameral legislature with equal representation among the states, along with a plural (multi-person) executive appointed by the legislature.

non-attitude A lack of opinion on an issue, or an opinion so weakly held that it does not enter into a person's calculations about voting or taking some other political action, even though the person may express an opinion to a pollster.

oligarchy A political system in which power resides in a small segment of society.

one-party state A political system in which one party controls the government and actively seeks to prevent other parties from contesting for power.

open primary A primary election in which any registered voter can vote, regardless of party affiliation.

open rule A provision that allows any amendment to be proposed once a bill comes to the chamber floor.

outside lobbying Activities by interest group leaders that seek to mobilize constituents and others outside the policy-making community to contact or pressure policy makers.

paradox of voting The notion that people still vote even though the individual costs of voting likely outweigh the individual benefits.

parliamentary democracy A form of democracy in which the executive is elected by the legislature and the government is responsible to the legislature.

partisan model The view that majority party leaders dominate the workings of Congress and ensure that most legislative benefits come to majority party members.

party amateur An issue activist who is mostly interested in specific policy areas and works for the party, or for specific politicians within the party, to advance these goals.

party discipline Pressure on party members to vote on bills that have the support of the party leadership. Also, the tendency for members of a legislative party to vote as a bloc.

party identification (or partisanship) Loyalty or psychological attachment to a political party.

party professional A person who works directly for the party, is loyal to its goal of winning elections, and stays with it over long periods through multiple election cycles.

path dependence The notion that earlier events or decisions deeply affect current and future policy decisions or outcomes.

pluralism A view of the American political system that emphasizes that a large number of diverse interest groups are involved in the political process, and that any given group may be influential on some occasions and not on others.

plurality rule A method for determining an election's winner in which the candidate who receives the most votes wins.

pocket veto A veto that occurs automatically if a president does not sign a bill for 10 days after passage in Congress and Congress has adjourned during that 10-day period.

police-patrol oversight Congressional oversight that consists of actively monitoring agencies through routine inspection.

political action committee (PAC) A type of organization regulated by the Federal Election Commission that raises money from donors to support the election campaigns of federal political candidates.

political knowledge A general understanding of how the political system works, and who runs the government.

political machine A local organization that controls the city or county government to such an extent that it can reward whole neighborhoods, wards, precincts, or other groups with benefits such as jobs and government programs in return for supporting the party's candidates.

political participation Activities citizens undertake to influence government behavior.

political party A group of candidates and elected officials organized under a common label for the purpose of attaining positions of public authority.

political system The way a society organizes and manages its politics across various levels of public authority.

politics The process of making collective decisions, usually by governments, to allocate public resources and create and enforce rules for the operation of society.

popular sovereignty The principle that the authority to make decisions on behalf of society belongs to the people.

population In statistical research, the entire group that you want to learn about, such as all adults living in the United States.

pork barrel Government spending that benefits a narrow constituency in return for electoral support or some other kind of political support, including campaign donations.

preferences The outcomes or experiences people want or believe they need.

presidential system A form of democracy in which the executive is elected independently and the government is not responsible to the legislature.

press The people and organizations that provide content about public affairs—news and commentary—that is disseminated across media.

primary election An election held before Election Day to allow voters to select which candidates will appear on the ballot under a party label.

priming The psychological process of shaping people's perceptions of a particular issue, figure, or policy.

principal–agent problem (delegation problem) An instance in which one actor (a principal) contracts another actor (an agent) to act on the principal's behalf; but the actors may not share the same preferences, and the principal lacks the means to observe all of the agent's behavior.

prisoner's dilemma An interaction between two strategic actors in which neither actor has an incentive to cooperate even though each of them would be better off if they both cooperated.

private good A product or benefit provided such that its enjoyment can be limited to specific people, and one individual's consumption of it precludes others from consuming it.

privatization The contracting of private companies by the government to conduct work that was formerly done by government agencies.

progressive tax A tax that places a greater financial burden on the wealthy than on the poor and the middle class.

proportional representation A method for allocating seats in a legislature in which the number of seats a party receives in a district or nationwide is proportional to the votes it receives in the elections.

public good A benefit provided to a group of people such that each member can enjoy it without necessarily having to pay for it, and one person's enjoyment of it does not inhibit others from enjoying the benefit.

public opinion The collection of attitudes and preferences of the mass public.

public policies Programs and decisions by the government that are enforced by the rule of law.

push polling Surveys or polls in which respondents are given information before answering an opinion question about a candidate, party, or political issue, where the information is given with the intention of influencing the opinion expressed.

random selection Choosing a sample such that each member of a population has an equal chance of being selected into the sample.

rational basis test The lowest-level standard used by the Supreme Court to determine whether a law is compatible with the Constitution. A law subject to this standard is assumed to be constitutional as long as its goals are clearly linked to its means.

rationality The habit of choosing the best choice among available options, given a person's interests and information.

realism A philosophy about international politics based on the assumption that countries primarily seek to increase their own power relative to other countries.

recall election An election during the term of an elected government official in which citizens vote directly on whether to remove the individual from office.

redistributive policy A government benefit provided to some people that is paid for by another group of people.

Reed's Rules Procedural guidelines used by the majority party leadership for determining who sits on which committees, how the order of business should be decided, and how the majority party should limit the powers of the minority party.

referendum An election in which citizens vote directly on whether to overturn a bill or a constitutional amendment that has been passed by the legislature.

regressive tax A tax that places a greater financial burden on the poor and the middle class than on the wealthy.

republic A political system in which public officials are chosen to represent the people in an assembly that makes important policy decisions.

reserved powers Those powers not granted to the national government by the Constitution, and therefore reserved to the states.

restricted (or modified) rule A provision that allows only certain kinds of amendments to be proposed once a bill comes to the chamber floor, typically only amendments that pertain to the original purpose of the bill.

revenue sharing A principle whereby the national government and the lower-level governments cooperate in funding a project.

rule making The process by which governmental agencies provide details on how laws passed by elected officials will be implemented.

rule of law A system in which all people in a society, including governing officials, are subject to legal codes that are applied without bias by independent courts.

sample In statistical research, a subset of the population chosen to provide information for research about the population.

selective incentive A benefit that a group can offer to potential members in exchange for participation as a way to encourage that involvement.

separation of powers An arrangement in which specific governmental powers are divided among distinct branches of government; typically, this means having an executive who is chosen independently of the legislature, and thus executive power and legislative power are separated.

signing statement A public statement written by the president and attached to a particular bill to outline his or her interpretation of the legislation.

single-member district An electoral district in which a single person is elected to a given office.

smoke-filled room A situation in which party elites make important decisions away from the scrutiny or influence of party membership.

social capital The existence of organizations, clubs, and social venues that allow for citizens to interact together regularly to create bonds of social trust.

social movement A loose coalition of groups and organizations with common goals that are oriented toward using mass action to influence the government.

social policy Government actions intended to provide a basic level of assistance with income, safety, education, housing, and health care for certain categories of people at risk.

Social Security A federal government program that provides basic income assistance to retired elderly people and the disabled.

socioeconomic status (SES) A measure of the way that individuals are regarded within a society by virtue of their wealth, income, education, and profession.

soft money Campaign funds that are given to parties or other organizations to support voter mobilization or voter education activities and thus typically not subject to FEC regulations.

soft power The use of nonmilitary pressure such as economic sanctions, diplomatic isolation, or public shaming against another country.

Speaker of the House The constitutionally designated leader of the House of Representatives. In the modern House, he or she is always the leader of the majority party.

special (or select) committee A committee appointed to consider a special issue or serve a special function that disbands once it has completed its duties.

special donor A potential participant in a group for whom the cost of participating is very low and/or the benefits of participating are very high.

special prosecutor Independent, private sector counsel hired by Congress to investigate government officials.

split referral A rule (in place since 1975) that permits the Speaker to split a bill into sections and give sections to specific committees.

spoils system The practice of rewarding loyal partisans with government positions after they demonstrate their support during an election.

standing The official status of a litigant who is entitled to have his or her case decided by the court.

standing committee A group of legislators given permanent jurisdiction over a particular issue area or type of policy.

stare decisis The legal principle that requires judges to respect the decisions of past court cases.

statement bias The tendency for the media, or a specific media outlet, to interject opinions into the coverage of an issue.

statutory law The laws passed by legislatures, or administrative agencies empowered by legislatures, and the court decisions interpreting those laws.

strategic (or rational choice) model A theoretical model where judicial decisions are primarily determined by the policy goals of judges and the various constraints that stand in the way of achieving those goals.

strict constructionism (or constructivism) The legal philosophy that judges should use the intentions of those writing the law or the Constitution as guides for how to interpret the law.

strict scrutiny The highest-level standard used by the Supreme Court to determine whether a law is compatible with the Constitution. A law subject to this standard is considered unconstitutional unless it advances a "compelling state interest" and represents the least intrusive means.

super PACs A type of organization regulated by the Federal Election Commission that can spend unlimited sums of money to advocate for the election or for the defeat of a candidate but is prohibited from contributing funds directly to federal campaigns and parties.

Supplemental Nutritional Assistance Program (SNAP) A federal government program that provides electronic debit cards for poor people to buy food (formerly known as the Food Stamp program).

supremacy clause The section of Article VI of the Constitution stating that the Constitution and the subsequent laws of the United States are to be the "supreme law of the land," meaning that they supersede any state and local laws.

Temporary Assistance for Needy Families (TANF) A federal government program that provides temporary income assistance to the poor.

transaction costs The challenges people face when they try to exchange information or use other means to cooperate with each other.

trustees Representatives who make decisions using their own judgments about what is best for their constituents.

unanimous consent agreement Rules under which the Senate debates, offers amendments, and votes on a given bill. All members of the chamber must agree to them, so any senator can object and halt progress on a bill.

unified government A government whose president is from the same party as the majority in Congress.

unilateralism An approach to foreign policy that is informed primarily by a nation's own interests and means, relying little on the approval or support of other nations.

unitary system A political system in which the national government holds ultimate authority over all areas of policy and over the actions of subunit governments.

unstable coalition An instance in which three or more people must make a collective choice from a set of alternatives, but any voting coalition in favor of an alternative can be divided by consideration of another alternative.

veto threat A public statement issued by the president declaring that if Congress passes a particular bill that he or she dislikes, it ultimately will be vetoed.

Virginia Plan A plan proposed at the Constitutional Convention by Edmund Randolph of Virginia outlining a stronger national government with an independent executive and a bicameral legislature whose membership in both houses would be apportioned according to state population.

vote by mail A program in many states that allows voters to mail in their ballots rather than appearing in person at a polling place.

voter mobilization Efforts by organizations to facilitate or encourage voting.

voter registration A process by which citizens enroll with the government to gain permission to vote in an election.

voter turnout The proportion of potential voters who vote in a given election.

Voting Rights Act of 1965 A federal law that made it a priority of the national government to enforce provisions of the Fourteenth and Fifteenth Amendments, leading to major improvements in voting rights for blacks, other minorities, and the poor.

War Powers Act Legislation passed in 1973 requiring that the president notify Congress and seek its approval within 48 hours after ordering military action.

welfare state The programs of the government devoted to social policies.

whip A member of the House or Senate who is elected by his or her party to help party leaders coordinate party members' actions, including enforcing party discipline.

writ of certiorari An order by the Supreme Court directing an inferior court to deliver the records of a case to be reviewed, which effectively means the justices of the Court have decided to hear the case.

CREDITS

FIGURES

Figure 2.4 (p. 67): José Antonio Cheibub, Zachary Elkins and Tom Ginsburg, "Beyond Presidentialism and Parliamentarism," *British Journal of Political Science*, Vol. 44, No. 3, pp. 515–544, © Cambridge University Press 2013, reproduced with permission; **Figure 5.5 (p. 194):** From Voteview.com. Reprinted by permission of Jeffrey B. Lewis; **Figure B in Chapter 9 Data Exploration box (p. 365):** "Figure 1: Policy Support for People with High and Middle Incomes, 1,779 Issues," J. Alexander Branham, Stuart N. Soroka, and Christopher Wlezein, "When Do the Rich Win?" *Political Science Quarterly* 132, no. 1 (Spring 2017): 43–62. Reprinted with permission.

PHOTOS

Chapter 1: p. 2: Spencer Platt/Getty Images; p. 5: Bill Pugliano/Stringer/Getty Images; p. 8 (left): Getty Images/Tetra Images RF; (right): AP Photo/J. Scott Applewhite; p. 13: Scott Olson/Staff/Getty Images. **Chapter 2:** p. 32: Granger, NYC/The Granger Collection; p. 36: Granger, NYC/The Granger Collection; p. 37: Granger, NYC/The Granger Collection; p. 48: Granger, NYC/The Granger Collection; p. 59: AP Photo; p. 63: AP Photo/John Locher; p. 66: Chuck Nacke/Alamy. **Chapter 3:** p. 70: Erich Schlegel/Getty Images; p. 81: CSU Archives/Everett Collection; p. 83: Granger, NYC/The Granger Collection; p. 95: AP Photo; p. 102: REUTERS/Anthony Bolante/Newscom. **Chapter 4:** p. 106: Bill O'Leary/The Washington Post/Getty Images; p. 115: Pornchai Kittiwongsakul/AFP/Getty Images; p. 116: Tami Chappell/Reuters; p. 123: AP Photo/Charles Gorry; p. 125: AP Photo; p. 135: vm/Getty Images; p. 137: Astrid Riecken For the Washington Post via Getty Images. **Chapter 5:** p. 146: Tom Williams/Contributor/Getty Images; p. 153: Whitney Curtis/Getty Images; p. 170: Susan Walsh/AP Photo; p. 173: Bloomberg/Contributor/Getty Images; p. 175: Mark Wilson/Staff/Getty Images; p. 183: UPI/Newscom. **Chapter 6:** p. 198: Chip Somodevilla/Getty Images; p. 206: Granger, NYC/The Granger Collection; p. 211: Chip Somodevilla/Staff/Getty Images; p. 214: David Hume Kennerly/Getty Images; p. 227: Bloomberg/Contributor/Getty; p. 231: BRENDAN SMIALOWSKI/AFP/Getty Images; p. 233: Daniel Cardenas/Anadolu Agency/Getty Images. **Chapter 7:** p. 242: Stephen Crowley/The New York Times/Redux; p. 249: NASA; p. 260: AP Photo/Henry Griffin; p. 268: AP Photo/Gervasio Sanchez; p. 273: Ethan Miller/Staff/Getty Images. **Chapter 8:** p. 284: Fredric J. Brown/Staff/Getty Images; p. 288: Chris Hondros/Getty Images; p. 292: Granger, NYC/The Granger Collection; p. 307: Art Lien; p. 321: Chip Somodevilla/Staff/Getty Images; p. 323: Jim Watson/Stringer/Getty Images. **Chapter 9:** p. 326: Chip Somodevilla/Getty Images; p. 333: Alex Milan Tracy/Sipa USA/Newscom; p. 343: Andrew Toth/Stringer/Getty Images; p. 344: Newport News Daily Press/Contributor/Getty Images; p. 348: Steve Schapiro/Corbis via Getty Images; p. 359: Larry Downing-Pool/Getty Images; p. 367: Tom Williams/CQ Roll Call/Getty Images. **Chapter 10:** p. 372: AP Photo/Matt York, File; p. 381: Joe Raedle/Getty Images; p. 388: FREDERIC J. BROWN/AFP/Getty Images; p. 393: Chusseau-Flaviens/George Eastman House/Getty Images; p. 407: Ethan Miller/WireImage/Getty Images. **Chapter 11:** p. 410: Nicholas Kamm/AFP/Getty Images; p. 416: Al Seib. Copyright © 2016. Los Angeles Times. Reprinted with permission; p. 421: Tom Williams/CQ Roll Call/Getty Images; p. 428: Mario Tama/Getty Images; p. 431: The Washington Post/Contributor/Getty Images; p. 443: Flip Schulke/Corbis/Corbis via Getty Images. **Chapter 12:** p. 446: Joe Raedle/Getty Images; p. 455: Zach Gibson/Stringer/Getty Images; p. 468: Everett Collection/Agefotostock; p. 475: AP Photo; p. 478: Helen H. Richardson/The Denver Post via Getty Images; p. 481: Spencer Platt/Staff/Getty Images. **Chapter 13:** p. 490: Paul J. Richards/AFP/Getty Images; p. 495: Carolyn Cole/Contributor/Getty Images; p. 500: Granger, NYC/The Granger Collection; p. 506: David Paul Morris/Bloomberg via Getty Images; p. 517: Win McNamee/Getty Images; p. 521: Amer Ghazzal/Alamy Stock Photo. **Chapter 14:** p. 534: Bryan Bedder/Stringer/Getty Images; p. 541: Jabin Botsford/The Washington Post via Getty Images;

p. 544: Granger, NYC/The Granger Collection; p. 547: Clynt Garnham Technology/Alamy Stock Photo; p. 550: Patrick Farrell/MCT/Newscom; p. 554: Reuters via Your View; p. 562 (left): Virginia Sherwood/NBC/NBCU Photo Bank via Getty Images; (right): AP Photo/Richard Drew. **Chapter 15:** p. 572: Jewel Samad/AFP/Getty Images; p. 579: Granger, NYC/The Granger Collection; p. 590: Getty Images; p. 591: Mark Wilson/Getty Images; p. 596: David Zalubowski/AP; p. 599: Alex Wong/Getty Images; p. 606: Bloomberg/Contributor/Getty Images. **Chapter 16:** p. 616: Olivier Douliery/Getty Images; p. 620: Alex Wong/Getty Images; p. 623: Granger, NYC/The Granger Collection; p. 627: AP Photo/Rich Pedroncelli; p. 638: Kim Steele/Alamy Stock Photo; p. 653: Mark Wilson/Getty Images. **Chapter 17:** p. 656: Gokhan Sahin/Getty Images; p. 660: Ramin Talaie/Contributor/Getty Images; p. 661: Design Pics/Contributor/Getty; p. 665: Thierry Monasse/Contributor/Getty Images; p. 684: AP Photo; p. 687: Mark Wilson/Getty Images; p. 693: Chip Somodevilla/Staff/Getty.

INDEX

[Note: Page numbers in *italics* refer to tables, figures, and photos.]

527s, 513

AARP (American Association of Retired Persons), 414
Abbott, Greg, 71
abortion rights
    conservatives and, 653
    executive orders and, 226–27
    in government response to discrimination, 132–36
    liberals and, 652–53
    political parties and, 133, 475–76
    politics and, 132–36
    unconventional political participation and, 377
ACA (Affordable Care Act), 200, 306, 309, 618, 633, 654
accountability effect, 498
Adams, John, 39, 113, 230, 289, 290–91
Adams, Samuel, 38
administrative law, 219, 256
Administrative Procedures Act (APA), 257
affirmative action, 131–32
Affordable Care Act (ACA), 200, 306, 309, 618, 633, 654
Afghanistan
    government contracts, 267
    military action in, 678–79, 681
    military base attacks, 666
    nation building in, 693
African Americans
    affirmative action and, 131–32
    civil rights and liberties and, 117–18
    civil rights movement, 122–24
    congressional districts and, 156
    discrimination against, 88, 126–27
    Fifth Amendment and, 393

group attachments, 347
incarceration rates, 641–42
lobbying for support of antiapartheid movement, 693
mass media bias and, 559–60
political participation, 398–401
political parties, 463–64, 470
school integration, 313
slavery and, 118–19
agenda hypothesis, 561–62
agenda setting, 20–21, 564–66
agents. *See* principal-agent problems
Agriculture, Department of
    education programs and, 630
    functions of, 636
    meat product inspection/grading, 632
    in state coordination, 103
    stature of, 251
AIPAC (American Israel Public Affairs Committee), 411–12, 443
Alien and Sedition Acts (1798), 113, 114, 118, 121
Alito, Samuel, 308
Al Qaeda, 681
ambassadors, 666
amendments
    killer, 21
    methods of, 51–52
    proposal of, 52
    See also specific amendments
American Civil Liberties Union (ACLU), 439
American Creed, 351
American embassies, 684
American Israel Public Affairs Committee (AIPAC), 411–12, 443
Americanization of elections, 486
Americans with Disabilities Act (ADA), 134

American Tradition Partnership v. Bullock (2012), 294
The American Voter, 523
amicus curiae, 305
Amtrak, 247
Antifederalists
    defined, 52
    Federalists versus, 52–54
    national government power and, 79
antiwar movement, 437, 439
APA (American Procedures Act), 271–74, 281
apathy, 361–62
appeals procedure, 298–99, *301*
appellate jurisdiction, 302
appointments
    congressional, 269
    government bureaucracy, 269–70
    judicial, 318–24
    patronage system, 261–62
    presidential, 224–25, 269–70
    Supreme Court justices, 286, 308
Appropriations Committee (House of Representatives), 170
approval ratings, presidential, 238
Aquinas, Saint Thomas, 143
Arab-Israeli wars, 690
Argentina, 188
Articles of Confederation
    agreement to, 34
    Congress established by, 41
    currency under, 36, *36*
    defined, 40
    national government and states relationship, 36
    overview of, 40–41
    Shays's Rebellion and, 33
    timeline, 54
Association of Southeast Asian Nations (ASEAN), 670
attitudinal model, 307–8, *310*

Australia
 mass media in, 555
 as parliamentary democracy, 233
 party-centered elections, 526
 public opinion in, 364
 social policies, 645
 two-party system, 478
Australian ballot, 505
Austrian school, 577
Auter, Zachary, 527
authoritarianism, 26, 35

Baker v. Carr (1962), 91, 155, 188
Balkans, military action in, 681
ballot initiatives, 91
ballots
 access, 484
 Australian, 505
 getting on, 507–10
 overview of, 505
bank regulation, 594–97
Bannon, Steve, 225
bargaining, 665
Barron v. Baltimore, 126
Barzun, Matthew, 262
Base Realignment and Closures
 (BRAC), 686–87
BBC (British Broadcasting
 Corporation), 555
Beard, Charles, 68
Belgium, 99
Benghazi, Libya, 539
Berlin, Isaiah, 143
Berlusconi, Silvio, 555
Bernanke, Ben, 596
Bernstein, Carl, 539
Betts v. Brady (1942), 303
biased samples, 336–38
biases
 coverage, 560
 discerning, 556–58
 gatekeeping, 560
 how they occur, 560–61
 ideological, 558–60
 of mass media, 556–61
 of press, 556–61
 in public opinion measurement,
  336–39
 question wording, 338–39
 reinforcement of, 567
 sample, 336–38
 statement, 560
 types of, 560–61
bicameral legislature, 47, 150
Biden, Joe, 232, *693*
bilateral diplomacy, 670–71

Bill of Rights
 civil liberties and, 62–63
 consequences of, 67–68
 decentralization of power and, *80*
 defined, 40, 54, 111
 egregious violations of, 121
 Fourteenth Amendment and, 126–28
 governmental power limits, 55–56
 historical path, 127
 major provisions of, *112*
 overview of, 54–56
 ratification of, 54
 rights and liberties in, 111
 See also specific amendments
bills
 committee action, 178
 conference committees, 184–85
 congressional committees and,
  170–73
 floor action, 184
 killer amendments, 21
 in lawmaking process, *177*
 logrolling, 190
 moving to floor, 178–80
 pork-barrel, 189
 presidential signature, 185
 proposals for, 176
 referrals for, 176–78
 roll-call voting, 184
 scheduled for markup, 178
 Senate distinctiveness, 180–81
 split referral, 178
 veto power of presidency, 185
 volume of proposed, 176
bills of attainder, 149
Bipartisan Campaign Reform Act
 (2002), 418
Black Lives Matter, 13, *13*, 432–34,
 438–39, 440
block grants, 86
"blue slip," 319
Bolivia, 278
Bollinger cases (2003), 132
bonds, 602
Bork, Robert, 319
Boston Tea Party, 37
Bowers v. Hardwick (1986), 303
BRAC (Base Realignment and
 Closures), 686–87
Brady, Henry, 405
Brandeis, Louis, 103
Brazil, 57, 139, 188, *403*
British Broadcasting Corporation
 (BBC), 555
British House of Commons, 154
Broockman, David, 277

Brown v. Board of Education (1954), 131,
 305–6, 313, 318
Bryan, William Jennings, 467
Buckley v. Valeo (1976), 418, 512
budgetary crises, 30
budget process
 authorization versus appropriation,
  270
 collective dilemma, 272–73
 discretion in, 271
 in fiscal policies, 604–5
 government bureaucracy and,
  270–71
 as source of conflict, 3
 tax policy and, 4
 See also federal budget
"bully pulpit," 215
bureaucracies. *See* government
 bureaucracy
bureaucratic budget battles, 272–73
bureaucratic capture, 254
bureaucratic drift, 253
bureaucratic misconduct, 255
bureaucrats
 autonomy and, 251
 clarity of instructions and, 251
 defined, 22, 245
 elected official behavior versus, 277
 "grunt" work of, 279
 lobbying and, 252
 motivations of, 251–52
 negative connotation of, 279
 policy change and, 252
 as policy makers, 256–58
 resources and, 251
 rulemaking, 256–57
 "street-level," 258
Burma, 678
Bush, George H. W.
 on housing problems, 638
 political influences, *344*
 Supreme Court appointments, 308
 vice president, 231
Bush, George W.
 2000 election, 294–95, 338, 522
 appointments, 225, 269
 approval ratings, 239
 Bush v. Gore (2000), 294–97
 Department of Homeland Security
  creation, 228
 economic stimulus policies, 85
 EPA and, 274
 executive orders, 223
 Fed chair, 596
 foreign policy, 693
 international organizations and, 673

political influences, *344*
signing statements, 223
Supreme Court appointments, 308
third-party candidate and, 472
vetoes, 222
vice president, 232
Bush, Jeb, *344*
Bush Doctrine, 691
Bush v. Gore (2000), 294–97, 314
Butler, Daniel, 277
by-products, 425

cabinet department
defined, 245
examples of, 245, 246
See also specific departments
campaign financing
American system as unusual, 422
contribution impact, 429–30
contribution limits, 512
contribution pay off, 423
Federal Election Commission and
(FEC) and, 512
finance laws, 163
hard money, 513
income inequality and, 611
interest groups and, 419–24
political action committees (PACs),
510–11
prisoner's dilemma and, 422–23
public, 514, 528
soft money, 513
super PACs, 421, 423–24, 513
campaigns and campaigning
accountability effect, 498
advertising, 513, 518, 523, 527
candidates strengths and weaknesses
and, 497–98
collective dilemmas, 516–17
elections, 516–17
emotions and, 348
fact-checking, 540–41
finance laws, 195–96
getting on the ballot, 507–10
incumbency advantage, 161–63
limited, 528
with modern technologies, 518–22
negative, 518
in other countries, 482–86, 525–28
political debates, 520–21
prisoner's dilemma, 515–18
raising campaign money, 510–15
reform, 529–31
rhetoric, 515–18
selection effect, 498
voter decision making, 522–25

Canada
ballot access in, 484
civil rights and liberties in, 138–39
decentralization of power and, 98
electoral institutions in, 526
federation formation, 98–99
group politics in, 440
legal traditions in, 139
mass media in, 555
national government, 609
North American Free Trade
Agreement (NAFTA) and, 312
as parliamentary democracy, 233
party-centered elections in, 526
public opinion in, 364
social policies in, 645
candidates
collective dilemmas among, 459–61
electability, 510
"going negative," 527
presidential, nomination process, 509
strengths and weaknesses of, 497–98
"testing the waters," 509
See also campaigns and campaigning
capital, 575
capitalism, 575, 577–78, 608, 646
Carpenter, Daniel, 251–52
Carter, Jimmy
Fed chair and, 596
on foreign policy, 692
Iran agreement and, 205
Supreme Court appointments, 308
categorical grants, 86
caucuses, 173, *175*, 503, 516–17
CBO (Congressional Budget Office),
175, 191
CBS network, 544, 549
Centers for Disease Control and
Prevention, 248
Central Intelligence Agency (CIA),
658, 671, 688
centralization of power, *75*, *80*
checks and balances
defined, 49
presidential power, 49–50, *50*,
236–40
Cheney, Dick, 232
*Chevron v. the Natural Resources Defense
Council*, 274
Chicago Daily News, 544
Child Welfare League of America, 414
Chile, 234
China
cyber attacks from, 681
foreign policy and, 657
government institutions in, 26

human rights record, 692
mass media in, 554
military expenditures, 679
as military rival, 669
rise of, 667
U.S. intervention in, 669
Chong, Dennis, 16
Christian conservative movement,
435–36
The Christian Science Monitor, 544
CIA (Central Intelligence Agency),
658, 671, 688
Citizens United v. FEC (2010), 288,
294, 418, 423–24, 512, 514
city governments, 93–96
civil cases, 297
civil law, 302
civil liberties
around the world, 138–40
Bill of Rights on, 62–63, 111
defined, 27, 109
of the disabled, 134–35
ethnicity and, 119–20
evolution of legal doctrine and, 128
failures in, 120–22
firearms, 107–8
Fourteenth Amendment and,
126–28
Fourth Amendment and Bill of
Rights and, 126–28
government responses to
discrimination, 128–38
government trade-offs, 131
incorporation of, 127–28
laws concerning, 112
national security and, 141
origins of, 110–13
race and, 117–19
reasons for protecting, 142–44
social policies and, 622
special role of courts in, 113–17
technology and social norms and,
114, *115*
See also democracy
civil rights
around the world, 138–40
Bill of Rights on, 111
defined, 109
ethnicity and, 119–20
evolution of legal doctrine and,
128
failures in, 120–22
Fourteenth Amendment and,
126–28
Fourth Amendment and Bill of
Rights and, 126–28

civil rights (*continued*)
  government responses to
    discrimination, 128–38
  government trade-offs, 131
  incorporation of, 127–28
  laws concerning, 112
  origins of, 110–13
  popular demands for more, 122–25
  race and, 117–19
  reasons for protecting, 142–44
  special role of courts in, 113–17
  technology and social norms and,
    114, *115*
  See also social movements
Civil Rights Act (1964), 128, 172, 432
civil rights leaders, 123, 124
civil rights movement
  defined, 122
  overview of, 122–24
  role in American history, 434
civil service reforms, 262–64
Civil War, 73–74, 208–10, 466
class actions, 297–98
Clay, Henry, 184
Clean Air Act (1977), 274–75
cleavages, Constitutional Convention,
  44, *45*
Clinton, Bill
  1992 election, 222
  appointments, 270
  approval ratings, 238
  balancing of federal budget, 477
  executive orders, 222–23
  Fed chair, 596
  impeachment, 237–38
  international organizations and, 673
  public policy support, 212
  on Rwanda decision, 681
  Supreme Court appointments, 308
Clinton, Hillary
  2016 election, 374, *490*, 491–92, 495
  advertisements against, 513
  Bernie Sanders and, 472–73, 578
  Democratic Party and, 447
  electoral college and, 8
  in helping fellow Democrats, 211
  personal email server, 281
  political debates, 520–21
  polling predictions and, 339
  public money and, 514
  questionable claims, 540
  on trade policies, 674
closed primaries, 503, 508
closed rule, 179
cloture, 181
club good, 583

CNN, 539, 546, 557
coalitional drift, 253
coalition raiding, 20
coalitions, 428
Cold War, 261, 667, 669, 691
Cole Memorandum II (2013), 95
collective action problems
  class actions and, 298
  coordination problems comparison,
    18–19
  defined, 12, 20
  examples, 29
  interest groups and, 420, 422
  overview of, 12–13
  in political participation, 378–79
  political parties and, 459–61
  prisoner's dilemma and, 14, *15*
  social movements and, 437–38
  voters, 461
collective dilemmas
  bureaucratic budget battles, 272–73
  campaigns and campaigning, 516–17
  collective action problems, 12–13,
    18–19, 20
  Congress, 165–66, 188–96
  congressional elections, 152
  coordination problems, 16, 18–19, 20
  courts, 287–89
  defined, 10, 20
  Democratic sit-in, 182
  federal and state conflicts over
    marijuana, 94–95
  federalism as response to, 75–76
  Federal Reserve, 598–99
  foreign policy, 659–61, 686–87
  government bureaucracy and,
    248–51
  inequality in public education,
    634–35
  institutions and, 23–24
  interest groups and, 424–28
  judicial confirmations, 322–23
  mass media and, 539–42
  meta-analysis, 342–43
  military base closings, 686–87
  need for government and, 9–11
  political participation, 377–80
  political parties, 459–61
  presidency and, 205–6
  prisoner's dilemma situations,
    13–16, 20
  religion and, 58
  rights of the disabled, 134–35
  social movements and, 437–38
  social policies, 634–35
  sore-loser laws, 480–81

tax-exempt status, 420–21
trade policies, 606
types of, 12–21
unstable coalitions, 19–21, 165–66
voting, 386–87
colonial charters, 40
commerce, regulation of, 590–92
Commerce, Science, and
  Transportation Committee
  (Senate), 170
commerce clause
  decentralization of power and,
    79, *80*
  defined, 61, 79
  revision of interpretation of, 292
committees
  action in lawmaking process, 178
  basic function of, 191
  conference, 171, 184–85
  consequences of system, 172–73
  joint, 171
  membership, 172
  national (political party), 457–58
  special (select), 171
  standing, 170–71
committees, congressional
  examples of, *174*
  overview of, 170
  role of, *173*
  types of, 170–71
Common Core, 631
common good, 583
common law, 302
community policing, 639–40
competition, fostering, 101–2
concurring opinion, 309–11
Confederate States of America, 73
confederation
  defined, 73
  European Union (EU) as, 74–75
  federation and, 73–76
conference committees, 171, 184–85
conferences, Supreme Court, 307–9
confidence vote, 484
Congress, U.S.
  administrative law, 219
  analysis models, 190–95
  authorization versus appropriation,
    270
  Base Realignment and Closures
    (BRAC) and, 686–87
  as bicameral, 47, 150
  bill proposal statistics, 167
  bureaucracies and, 23
  campaign finance and, 195–96
  caucuses, 173, *175*

checks and balances, 49–50, *50*
codes of behavior, 167
collective dilemmas, 165–66, 182–83, 188–96
commerce clause, 61, 79, *80*
committees, 170–73
comparison of legislative institutions, 186–88
competing visions of representation, 159
congressional elections, 151–65
congressional staff, 173–75
constituencies, 239
constituency service, 160–61
Constitution and, 149–51
demographics of, 164–65
distributional model of, 190, 192
elastic clause, *50*, 79
energy expenditure, 148
established by Articles of Confederation, 41
first meeting of, 166
foreign policy and, 659, 683
on gun control, 333
historical path timeline, 169
ideological moderates and, 194–95
as increasingly institutionalized, 166–67
individualism in, 152–59
informational model of, 191, 193
internal institutions of, 165–75
internal makeup of, 173
lawmaking function, 150–51
lawmaking process, 176
lobbying and, 151, 195–96, 417, 428–29, 440
major developments in, *169*
McCarthy era, 114–15
meetings with constituents, *153*
oversight, 271–74
partisan control of, 221
partisan model of, 191–92, 193
party discipline in, 168
party leaders, 168–69, *170*
party polarization in, *194*
presidential power and, 151
presidential veto and, 151
principal-agent problems, 21–24, 189
public opinion and, 317
relative powers, 57–61
research services, 175
in school system operation, 77–78
seat reapportionment, 501
separation of powers and, 185–86
in session, 219–20

Supreme Court and, 308–9
as trustees, 330
unstable coalitions, 165–66
vetoes and, 220–22
women in, 163–65, *164*
See also House of Representatives; Senate, U.S.
Congressional Black Caucus, 163, 173
Congressional Budget Office (CBO), 175, 191
congressional districts
drawing boundaries, 154–58
gerrymandering and, 156
partisan redistricting, *155*
single-member, 152–53
Supreme Court and, 155, 156–57
congressional elections
as candidate-centered, 158
collective dilemmas, 152
drawing district boundaries, 154–58
financing of, 158
general, 154
incumbency advantage, 161–63
minority representation, 163–65
other electoral factors, 158–59
overview of, 151–52
plurality rule, 152–53
primary elections, 153–54, 160
representing districts or states, 159–65
single-member districts, 152–53
Congressional Hispanic Caucus, *175*
congressional staff, 173–75
Connecticut Compromise, *43*, 44, 47, 202
conservatives
on abortion rights, 653
economic policy, 577
equality in material terms and, 645
on health care, 653
ideology, 351–52
public opinion and, 369
redistributive policies and, 644
constituency service, 160–61
Constitution, U.S.
agreement and signing of, 46
amendments, 51–52
background, 36–46
bicameral legislature, 47
checks and balances, 49–50
colonial and state constitutions and, 40
comparison with national constitutions, 56–57
on conduct of foreign affairs and defense, 61

Congress and, 149–51
consequences of, 63–68
criticism of, 68
evolution of, 57–63
federalism and, 50–51
foreign policy and, 659
independent judiciary, 48–49
institutional features of, 46–52
institutions specified by, 9, 24
length of, 57
in military decision making, 60
overview of, 33
president as executive, 47
presidential power and, 201–5
presidential debate, 52–56
ratification of, 46, 54, 666
relative powers of branches of government, 57–61
religion in politics and, 59
reputation, 66–67
separation of powers, 49
signing of, *48*
skeleton analogy, 35
on tariffs, 606
text of, 46
unicameral, 33
Virginia Plan and, 42, *43*
Constitutional Convention (1787)
cleavages, 44, *45*
compromises, 44–46
Connecticut Compromise, *43*, 44
constitutional debates, 41–43
executive branch and, 47
Founders' task at, 34
on institutional design, 24
on institutions of government, 34
overview, 36–37
slavery compromise, 45–46
slavery outlaw proposals, 118
timeline, 54
constitutional debates, 41–43
constitutional evolution, 57–63
constitutional law, 302
constitutions
accomplishments of, 35
colonial, 40
longer, costs and benefits of, 65, 66
national, 56–57
state, 40, 65
constructivists, 316–17
Consumer Financial Protection Agency, 228
consumer rights movement, 434
Continental Congress, 37–38, 41
Controlled Substance Act (1970), 96
Converse, Philip, 353

"cooperate-cooperate" outcome, 251
cooperative federalism, 77
coordination problems
    collective action problems
        comparison, 18–19
    concept in context, *17*
    courts and, 287–88
    defined, 16, 20
    government bureaucracy, 249
    interest groups and, 380
    overview of, 16–18
    political participation, 379–80
    political parties and, 18, 460
    prisoner's dilemma and, 17
    See also collective dilemmas
corporate style of interest
        representation, 442
Correia, Michael, *431*
council-managers, 93
courts
    civil rights and liberties and, 113–17
    collective dilemmas, 287–89
    constitutional basis, 289–90
    Constitution and, 78–81
    coordination problems, 287–88
    federal, 290, 293–94, 298–99
    in government bureaucracy, 274–75
    independence and legitimacy, 288–89
    interest groups and, 418–19
    jurisdiction of, 301–3
    lobbying and, 413
    politics and, 313–24
    prisoner's dilemmas, 287
    state, 290, 299–301
    See also judicial branch; Supreme
        Court, U.S.
coverage bias, 560
crime prevention, 621–22, 638–42
crime rates, 640
criminal cases, 297
crisis tools, 677–81
Cruz, Ted, 352
Cuba, 608, 692
cue-givers, 361
currency, 36, 609
customs duties, 600
cyber warfare, 681

Dahl, Robert, 314, 430
Davids, Sharice, 153
Davis, Kim, 138
Deal, Nathan, 71
debt, national, 602, *603*, 609
decentralization of power, 79, *80*
Declaration of Independence, 39–40,
    54, 110–11

"defect-defect" equilibrium, 250
Defense, Department of
    budgets, 272–73
    creation of, 260
    domestic pressures, 689–90
    foreign policy and, 683, 684
    functions of, 688
    intelligence, 689
    military base closings, 266
    as original executive agency, 258
    overview of, 684
    as solvers of collective dilemmas, 248
    Syrian airstrikes led by, *656*
Defense of Marriage Act (DOMA), 137
Deferred Action for Parents of
        Americans and Lawful
        Permanent Residents (DAPA),
        199
deficit, national, 602, *603*
deflation, 594
Defund Planned Parenthood Act
        (2015), 617–18
delegated authority, 235
delegate model of representation, 330
delegates, 508–10, 516
delegation problems. *See* principal-
        agent problems
demand-side stimulation, 577
democracy
    bureaucracies in, 22
    defined, 26
    direct, 505–7
    elections and, 493
    emerging, 64–66
    institutional features of, 26–28, *28*
    mass media and press in, 537–42
    practice determination, 500
    public opinion and, 329–30
    voting and, 384
    war and, 664
    See also parliamentary democracies
Democratic National Committee, 457
Democratic Party
    on abortion rights, 133
    antiwar movement and, 439
    brand, 463
    coalitions, 455–56
    in Congress, 4, 450
    emergence of, 469
    equality of opportunity, 651
    equality of result, 652
    on government spending, 4
    minority representation, 163–64
    New Deal coalition, 470
    performance in congressional
        elections, *187*

presidential candidates, 510
    sit-in for gun control, 182–83
    social policies and, 652
    voter attraction, 392
    on voting rights, 373–74
    See also political parties
democratic peace, 664
demographics, of political participation,
    397–401
Denmark, 139, 608
Denniger, Karl, 438
depressions, 588
deservingness, 649
dictatorships, 26, 35
dilemmas. *See* collective dilemmas
Dillon's Rule, 96
diplomacy
    bilateral, 670–71
    multilateral, 671–73
    as presidential power, 204
    vice presidents in, 232
diplomatic relations, 671
direct democracy
    as controversial, 506–7
    defined, 505
    initiatives, 506
    referendums, 505–6
    special-interest dominance and,
        507
    See also elections
direct elections, 62
directional model, 524–25
disabilities, people with, 135–36
discrimination
    government responses to,
        128–38
    Supreme Court on, 129
    See also specific types of discrimination
The Disney Company, 549
dissenting opinion, 309–11
distributional model, 190, 192
distributive policies, 586, 601
diversity, preservation of, 100–101
divided government, 211–12, 221
doctrines, foreign policy, 691–92,
    693–94
DOD. *See* Defense, Department of
Donnelly, Joe, 160
Downs, Anthony, 360
Dred Scott v. Sanford (1857), 117–18, 291,
    294, 295
drift, 253–54
dual federalism, 76–77
due process, 126
Duverger, Maurice, 469
Duverger's Law, 469, 478–79

Earned Income Tax Credit (EITC),
   626, 646
economic growth, 592–93
economic philosophies, 575–78
economic policy
   benefits and costs, 583–85
   call for changes, 573
   collective dilemmas, 598–99
   distributing benefits, 586
   in early United States, 578–80
   externalities, 585
   fiscal policies, 597–605
   growing role in government,
      580–82
   historical path timeline, 582
   monetary policies, 593–97
   politics of policy making, 610–13
   presidency and, 613
   prominent philosophies, 575–78
   promoting economic growth with,
      592–93
   purposes of, 585–93
   redistributing benefits, 586–87
   in regulating commerce, 590–92
   stabilization of economy with,
      587–89
   stimulus plans, 574, 612
   types of, 593–608
economic pressure, 677–78
economic stimulus policies, 85
Education, Department of, 261, 630,
   634, 636
education policy
   inequality and, 634–35
   No Child Left Behind Act, 630–31
   reforms, 634–35
   state enactment of, 631
Egypt, 403, 678
Eighth Amendment, 62, 112, 130
Einstein, Albert, 121
Eisenhower, Dwight D., 81
EITC (Earned Income Tax Credit),
   626, 646
elastic clause (necessary and proper
   clause), 47, 79, 80
elections
   accomplishments of, 493–99
   accountability effect and, 498
   Americanization of, 486
   arguments, 497
   campaigns and campaigning, 516–17
   comparing with other countries,
      525–28
   competent, non-corrupt leaders and,
      497–99
   congressional, 151–65

democracy and, 493
direct, 62
direct democracy, 505–7
election ballots, 505
electoral campaigns, 507–25
electoral institutions, 500–507
electoral rules, 500
historical path timeline, 520
ideology and, 493–97
incumbent administration and, 492
as institutional check on power, 100
Internet role in, 546
party-centered, ideological, 526
plurality rule, 504
policy direction determination,
   493–97
presidential, 239–40, 377, 396–97
primary, 153–54, 160, 459, 495,
   503, 508, 516–17
recall, 91
selection effect and, 498
state courts and, 299–301
state-level laws, 501–4
two-candidate, 494, 496, 515–18
ubiquity of, 404
voter decision making, 522–25
voter turnout and, 396–97
electoral college
   2016 vote distribution, 8, 339, 502
   Constitution and, 501
   defined, 47
   functioning of, 503
   plurality rules and, 500
electoral institutions
   candidate selection, 503
   comparing with other countries,
      525–26
   direct democracy, 505–7
   drawing of districts, 503
   election ballots, 505
   electoral rules, 500
   overview of, 500–501
   plurality rule, 504
   state-level election laws, 501–4
   votes and seats, 503
electoral reforms, 529–31
electoral system, 478–79
electorate
   eligibility determination, 500
   polarization in, 473–74
   political parties in, 450, 461–64
electronic media. See mass media
elites, influence of, 348–50
El Salvador, 691
emotions, public attitudes and, 348
Energy, Department of, 688

engagement hypothesis, 562
Engel v. Vitale, 117
entrepreneurs, 426–27
enumerated powers (expressed powers),
   47, 204, 219
environmental policies, 591–92
Environmental Protection Agency (EPA)
   Clean Air Act (1977) and, 274
   creation of, 261
   as independent agency, 247
   principal-agent problems and,
      254–56
   role of, 249
   rulemaking, 257
   state boundaries and, 592
   in state coordination, 103
equality
   liberty trade-off, 644
   of opportunity, 651
   of result, 652
equal protection, 126
Equal Rights Amendment (1972), 125
Equal Time Rule, 552
Estelle v. Gamble (1976), 130
ethnic discrimination, 119–20
Europe
   civil rights and liberties in, 138–40
   party-centered elections, 526
   political parties in, 494
   public opinion in, 363–64
   social policies, 645
   See also specific European countries
European Court of Justice, 312
European Union (EU)
   as confederation, 74–75
   federations and, 98
   foreign aid, 675
   judicial system, 312
Evers, Medgar, 124
evolution, constitutional, 57–63
executive actions, 199–200
executive agencies, 258, 276
executive agreements, 222–23
executive branch
   administrative law, 219
   civil rights and liberties and, 113–14
   Constitutional Convention and, 47
   decision coordination, 206
   employment, 259
   institutional feature of Constitution,
      47
   New Jersey Plan on, 42, 43
   oversight, 271–74
   separation of powers, 49
   Virginia Plan on, 42, 43
   See also presidency

Executive Office of the President
(EOP), 228, 229–30
executive orders, 222–23, 226–27, 235
expressed powers (enumerated powers),
47, *204*, 219
externalities, 585

fact-checking, 540–41, 565
Fairness Doctrine, 552, 553
fascism, 352
FBI (Federal Bureau of Investigation),
121, 639
FCC (Federal Communications
Commission), 247, 552, 553
FDA (Food and Drug Administration),
632
FEC (Federal Election Commission
and), 512
Federal Aviation Administration, 249
federal budget, *602*, 604–5
federal bureaucracy. *See* government
bureaucracy
Federal Bureau of Investigation (FBI),
121, 639
Federal Communications Commission
(FCC), 247, 552, 553
federal courts
appeals procedure, *301*
circuit appeals, 298
jurisdiction of, 301–3
overview of, 298–99
public opinion and, 318
special, 299
supremacy of, 290, 293–94
See also judicial branch
Federal Election Campaign Act (1971),
418
Federal Election Commission (FEC),
288, 512
Federal Emergency Management
Agency (FEMA), 249
federal financing, 85–88
Federal Housing Administration
(FHA), 637–38
federalism
American, 76–78, 97–104
avoiding tyranny, 99–100
"back and forth" swings, 77
comparison of, 97–99
cooperative, 77
courts and Constitution, 78–81
defined, 73
as difficult but important balance,
104
dual, 76–77
evaluation of, 99–104

federal financing, 85–88
federation and confederation,
73–76, *75*
fostering competition, 101–2
on immigration policy, 71–72
institutional feature of Constitution,
50–51
jurisdiction and, 81
legalized marijuana and, 94–95
local governments and, 92–97
in national coordination, 76
negative consequences of, 103–4
negative externalities, 101
preserving diversity, 100–101
promoting unity and
experimentation, 102–3
questions, resolution of, 72
race and, 88–90
as response to collective dilemmas,
75–76
with separation of powers, 53–54
state governments and, 90–92
stronger national government and,
82–85
Federalist Papers
on avoiding tyranny, 99–100
on constitutional authority, 149
defined, 53
on federalism advantage, 90
Marbury v. Madison (1803), 291–92
overview of, 53–54
on presidency, 201
Federalists
Antifederalists versus, 52–54
defined, 44, 52, 469
passing of legislation, 455
on strength of national government,
63–64
Federal Reserve Administration, 259
Federal Reserve Banks, 228–29,
594–95
Federal Reserve Board (Fed)
2008 housing market and, *596*
chair of, 596
collective dilemma, 598–99
composition of, 595
controversy, 596–97
defined, 594
functions of, 594–95
independence and accountability at,
598–99
politics and, 596
Federal Reserve System, 594, 595
federal system, 7–8
Federal Trade Commission (FTC),
250, 259

FHA (Federal Housing
Administration), 637–38
Fifteenth Amendment, 111
Fifth Amendment, *112*, 126, 137, 393,
622
Fifth Party System, 469–70
filibusters, 180–81
Finance Committee (Senate), 171
Fine, Jeffery, 527
fire-alarm oversight, 274, 417
firearms, possession of, 107–8
First Amendment, *112*, *116*, 117, 138,
551–52
First Party System, 464–65
fiscal policies
budget process, 604–5
defined, 597
spending, 601–4
taxation, 597–601
See also economic policy
Fisher cases (2013 and 2016), 132
527s, 513
Fletcher v. Peck (1810), 293, 295
floor action, 184
floor debates, 184
Foley, Thomas, 444
Food and Drug Administration (FDA),
632
Food Stamp program, 626–27
Ford, Gerald, 231, 458
foreign aid
amount of, 675
domestic politics and, 677
goals of, 676
recipients of, *676*
foreign competition, 607
foreign policy
ambassadors and, 666
American perceptions of influence,
685
bargaining and, 665
bilateral diplomacy, 670–71
bureaucracies and, 683–89
collective dilemmas, 659–61,
686–87
conflicts in government over, 669
contemporary political science
approaches, 665–66
crisis tools, 677–81
decisions, 692
defined, 659
democratic peace and, 664
doctrines, 691–92
domestic dilemmas, 659–60
domestic pressures and, 665, 689–90
economic pressure, 677–78

elected leaders and, 682–83
foreign aid, 675–77
historical perspective, 666–70
humanitarian, 676–77
idealism, 662
intelligence gathering, 671, 672
international dilemmas, 660–61
internationalism, 662–63, 669
ISIL example, *656*, 657–58
isolationism, 663, 668
making, 682–90
military action, 678–81
military base closings, 686–87
multilateral diplomacy, 671–73
multilateralism, 664
presidency and, 693
presidential power and, 203, 209
realism, 662
soft power, 678
theories and strategies of, 661–66
tools of, 670–81
top priority for, 667
trade policies, 605–8
trading relationships, 673–75
unilateralism, 663
Foreign Relations Committee (Senate), 170
Fourteenth Amendment
    Bill of Rights and, 111, 126–28
    civil rights and liberties and, 126–28, 285
    enforcing, 88
    equal protection clause, 393
    federalism and, 112
    same-sex marriages and, 137, 285
    slavery and, 111
    social policies and, 622
Fourth Amendment, *112*
Fourth Party System, 467–68
Fox News, 344–45
framing, 349–50, 566
France
    civil rights and liberties in, 138–40
    ideology, 352
    judge selection, 311–12
    judicial review, 312
    legislative institutions in, 186–88
    mass media in, 555
    mixed presidential system, 234
    national bureaucracy, 278
    new business regulations in, 643
    religion in politics and, 58–59
    religious freedom in, 140
the franchise, 389
Francis, Leonard Glenn, 255
Franklin, David L., *307*

Freedom of Information Act (1966), 271, 274, 281
freedom of speech, 115–16
free riding, 12, 76
free speech, 142
fund-raising
    contribution limits, 512
    Federal Election Commission and (FEC) and, 512
    hard money, 513
    political action committees (PACs), 510–11
    political parties and, 485
    soft money, 513
    super PACs, 421, 423–24, 513
    top contributors, 2016 election cycle, *511*
    See also campaign financing

Gannett Company, Inc., 549
Garland, Merrick, 319, 322–23
gatekeeping bias, 560
Gates, Robert, 266
gay, lesbian, and transgender rights, 125, 136–38
GDP (gross domestic product), *589*, *603*, 608, *609*
gender, differences in attitudes between, *356*
gender discrimination, 124–25
general elections, 154
General Electric, 549
Germany
    ballot access in, 484
    civil rights and liberties in, 138–40
    fascism, 352
    group politics in, 440, 442
    home ownership rate, 636
    judge selection, 312
    judicial review, 312
    national government, 609
    party leaders, 451
    political participation in, *403*
Gerry, Elbridge, 156
gerrymandering, 156, 187
Ghana, *403*
Gibbons v. Ogden (1824), 79, *80*, 293–94, 295
Gideon v. Wainwright (1962), 303
Ginsburg, Ruth Bader, 308
going public, 212
Gore, Al, 294–97
Gorsuch, Neil, 323
government
    analyzing, 29–30
    divided, 211–12, 221

economic goal of, 588
in external authority role, 16
national, strength of, *55*
"natural law" independent from, 110
need for, 9–11
political parties in, 450–56
role in economies, 610–12
role of, judge ideology and, 314, 316
size debates, 11
strong, liberty versus, 41–42
unified, 211, 221
unitary system, *75*, 98
government, U.S.
    authority from the people, 329–30
    branches of, 6–7
    control, 98
    in domestic crime control, 639
    early economic policy role, 580–82
    economy and, 575–82
    federal grant money allocation, 89
    Great Society Era, 83
    growing role in social policies, 623–26
    health care and, 633
    historical path timeline, 54, 84
    media and press regulation, 551–54
    as media content source, 566–67
    New Deal Era, 82–83
    Progressive Era, 82
    public relationship with, 331
    recent trends, 84–85
    redistribution of goods, 636
    relative powers, 57–61
    responses to discrimination, 128–38
    responsibilities of, 77
    rise of power, *84*
    spending, 601–4
    states' rights versus, 61–62
government agencies
    consolidation of, 265
    defined, 245
    lobbying and, 417–18
    rulemaking, 256
government bureaucracy
    appointments, 269–70
    budgeting, 270–71
    changes in, 258–69
    civil service reform, 262–64
    comparison of traditions, 276–78
    Congress and, 23
    coordination problems, 249
    courts' influence, 274–75
    defined, 22, 243
    Democratic vision of, 280–81

government bureaucracy (*continued*)
early years of, 258–59
foreign policy and, 683–89
growth in size, 259–61
historical path timeline, 265
inefficiency, 265
interest groups, 275–76
modern reforms of, 264–67
need for, 248–51
negative connotation of, 279
oversight, 271–74
overview of, 245–47
principal-agent problems, 252–56
privatization and marketization, 267–69
Progressive vision of, 279–80
role in redistribution, 651
shaping and influencing, 269
as solvers of collective dilemmas, 248–51
spoils system, 207, 261–62
types of, *246*
views of, 278–81
of voting, 406
White House, 229, 249
government contracts, 267
government corporations, 246, 247
government grants, 267
Grace, J. Peter, 268
Grace Commission (1982–1984), 268–69
grants-in-aid, 86
Great Britain. *See* United Kingdom
Great Depression, 216
Great Society Era
housing programs, 638
overview of, 83–84
programs, 261
social policies and, 624
Greenback Party, 477
Greenspan, Alan, 596
Griswold v. Connecticut, 63, 113
gross domestic product (GDP), *589*, *603*, 608, *609*
group attachments, 347
group politics. *See* interest groups; social movements
group struggles, voting rights and, 393–95
Gulf War, 681
gun control
Congress failure to act on, 333
gun violence and, 327–28
public attitudes on, 328, *329*
public policy and, 366, 369
sit-in for, 182–83

Haiti, 676
Hamilton, Alexander
Federalist Papers, 53, 149, 201
on foreign policy, 666
on governmental administration, 258
on judicial review, 291
on legislative branch, 149
people as a "beast," 359
on presidency, 201
Hancock, John, 38
hard money, 513
Hayek, Friedrich, 577
Head Start program, *619*
Health and Human Services (HHS), Department of, 243–44, 636
health care
comparing with other countries, 648
conservatives and, 653
cost of, 633
liberals and, 652–53
national government and, 633
in Progressive Era, 631–32
reform, 653–54
Heaney, Michael, 439
Heller, Dick, 107–8
Help America Vote Act (2002), 383, 384–85
Henry, Patrick, 42
Hispanic Americans
incarceration rates, 641–42
political clout of, 690
political participation, 398
historical path timelines
American wars, 669
Congress, U.S., 169
economic policy, 582
elections, 520
founding, 54
government, U.S., 54, 84
government bureaucracy, 265
judicial branch, 296
mass media, 546
political parties, 466
public opinion polling, 334–35
social movements, 435–36
social policies, 622
voting rights, 394
Hobbes, Thomas, 10–11, 660–61
Holder, Eric, 392
Holmes, Oliver Wendell, 310–11
Homeland Security, Department of
creation of, 228, 261
function of, 640

state budget money, 85
in state coordination, 103
home rule, 96
Honest Leadership and Open Government Act (2007), 418
Hoover, Herbert, 216
House of Representatives
bicameralism and, 150
committees, 170–72
direct elections, 62
impeachment and, 237
majority leader, 168
overview of, 150
party leaders, 168–69
peak and cap of membership, 166
presidential power and, 202
Reed's Rules, 168
Rules Committee, 171–72, 179–80, 191, 195, 455
Speaker of the House, *8*, 168, 176, 452
whip, 168
See also Congress, U.S.; legislative branch
Housing and Urban Development, Department of, 261, 636, 637–38
housing programs, 636–39
Hughes, Charles Evans, 287
humanitarian aid, 676–77
Hussein, Saddam, 60

idealism, 662, 667
ideological moderates, 194–95
ideology
bias, 558–60
conservative, 351–52
defined, 351
liberal, 351–52
median voter theorem, 493–94
modern American ideologies, *645*
predispositions and, 351–53
press and, *559*
social policies and, 642–45
two-candidate elections, 499
voters and, 496–97
immigration policies
amnesty, 160
Donald Trump and, 693
federalism and, 71–72
illegal immigrants, 160
special districts and, 97
treatment of immigrants, 119–20, 127
impeachment, 237–38
income and payroll taxes, 597
income inequality, 611

income tax rates, by country, *601*
incorporation, 127–28
incumbency advantage, 161–63
independent agencies, 246, 247
independent judiciary, 48–49
India
    civil rights and liberties in, 139
    electoral institutions, 526
    executive form, 233
    legal traditions in, 139
    political participation in, *403*
    voter turnout in, 402
inequality
    income, campaign financing and, 611
    increase of, 646
    poverty rates and, *647*
    in public education, 634–35
inflation
    controlling, 593–94
    defined, 587
    rates, *588*
influence
    of courts, 274–75
    of elites, 348–50
    interest groups, 428–32
    Supreme Court decisions, *81*
informal powers, 218
informal shortcut, 462
informational model, 191, 193
infotainment, 551
inheritance taxes, 600
initiatives, 506
inside lobbying, 417–19
institutions
    collective dilemmas and, 23–24
    comparison of, 25–28, *28*
    defined, 6
    designing, 23–25
    electoral, 500–507, 525–26
    as empowered (obligated), 128
    evaluations of, 357–58
    examples of, 7, *8*, 9
    informal, 7
    legislative, comparison of, 186–88
    mobilization and, 406–9
    overview of, 6–9
    political outcomes and, 8
    in political system, 7–8
    principal-agent problems, 23–24
    as restrained, 128
    state government, 91
    as "sticky," 240
intelligence gathering, 671, 672
interest groups
    bureaucratic agencies and, 417–18
    campaign financing, 419–24, 431

collective action problems, 424–27
collective dilemmas and, 424–28
comparing with other countries,
    440–42, 608–10
coordination problems, 380, 427–28
courts and, 418–19
"cross pressure," 431
as cue-givers, 361
defined, 413
economic policy and, 612–13
entrepreneurs and, 426–27
examples of, 413
government bureaucracy and,
    275–76
influence on decisions, 428–32
iron triangle and, 275–76
latent interest, 425
lobbying by, 275, 413–19
organized forms of public pressure,
    442–44
overview of, 413–16
pluralism and, 430
by-products, 425
public opinion and, 442–43
selective incentive, 426
social movements and, *433*
social policies and, 650–51
special donors and, 426
"toolkit," 417
trade policies and, 607–8
by type, *415*
White House and, 431–32, 440
interest rates, 594
intergovernmental failure, 104
intergovernmentalism, 77
Interior, Department of, 248
intermediate scrutiny, 130
Internal Revenue Service (IRS), 248
international conflicts, 667–68
internationalism, 662–63, 669
Internet
    Barack Obama appeals, 546
    press and, 547
    as public good, 583
    rise of new media, 545–46
    role in elections, 546
Interstate Commerce Act (1887), 639
Interstate Commerce Commission,
    77, 258
Iran
    constitution, 56–57
    economic sanctions on, 678
    executions in, 379
    mass media in, 554
    power in, 57
    protests in, 379

Iraq
    airstrikes in, 657–58
    government contracts and, 267
    military action in, 678–79, 681
    nation building in, 693
    U.S. invasion of, 663, 692
Iraq War, 313
iron triangle, 275–76
IRS (Internal Revenue Service), 248
ISIL, *656*, 657–58
isolationism, 663, 668
Israel
    Arab-Israeli wars, 690
    constitutional structure, 56
    executive form, 233–34
    party-centered elections, 526
Italy
    executive form, 233–34
    fascism, 352
    mass media in, 555
    new business regulations, 643
    party-centered elections, 526

Jackson, Andrew, 207–8, 220, 465
Japan
    centralization of political control, 98
    civil rights and liberties in, 140
    national bureaucracy, 278
    as parliamentary democracy, 233
    party-centered elections, 526
    party leadership and government
        leadership, 451
    Pearl Harbor attack, 666
    political participation in, *403*
    public opinion in, 364
    sovereign authority of government,
        98
Jay, John, 53, 149, 201
Jefferson, Thomas, 39, 219, 666
Jim Crow laws
    defined, 119
    lawsuits against, 313
    repeal and social movements, 434–35
    states' rights and, 88–90
Johnson, Andrew, 237
Johnson, Gary, *478*
Johnson, Lyndon B., 83, 129, 144, 222,
    261, 624
joint committees, 171
Joint Comprehensive Plan of Action
    (JCPOA), 411
Joint Select Committee on Deficit
    Reduction, 171
Jordan, 26
judicial appointments, 318–24
judicial behavior, 314–16

judicial branch
  case types, 297
  checks and balances, 49–50
  civil rights and liberties and, 113–17
  collective dilemmas, 287–89,
    322–23
  common law and legal precedent,
    302–3
  comparison of systems, 311–13
  constitutional basis, 289–90
  court of last resort, 294–97
  development timeline, 296
  federal courts, 290, 293–94, 298–99
  historical path timeline, 296
  independence, 288–89
  institutional feature of Constitution,
    48–49
  judge selection, 311–12
  judicial confirmations, 322–23
  judicial review, 290–93, 312–13
  jurisdiction, 301–3
  in lawmaking process, 185
  minority rights versus majority rule,
    313–14
  organization of, 297–303
  politics and, 313–24
  power, establishing, 290–97
  relative powers, 57–61
  role of, 289
  separation of powers, 49
  standing and class actions, 297–98
  state courts, 290, 299
  See also Supreme Court, U.S.
judicial decision making, 307–9, *310*
judicial power
  court of last resort, 294–97
  establishment of, 290–97
  federal court supremacy, 293–94
  judicial review, 290–93, 312–13
  overview of, 290
  sources of power, 295
judicial review, 290–93, 312–13
Judiciary Act (1789), 290, 293, 298
Judiciary Committee (Senate), 319, 322
Justice Department
  on community policing, 639–40
  criminal investigations, 281
  FBI as investigative arm, 639
  foreign policy and, 688
  Pentagon Papers and, 121
  in voting rights enforcement, 390

Kagan, Elena, 225
Kahneman, Daniel, 349–50
Kaine, Tim, 495
Kamarck, Elaine C., 516

Kaptur, Marcy, 161
Katrina response, 103–4
Kavanaugh, Brett, 308, *321*, 323
Kelly, John, *211*
Kennan, George, 669–70
Kennedy, Anthony, 285–86, 303,
  308, 311
Kennedy, John F., 16, 83, 128, 212–13,
  214, 520
Kenya, 676
Kerry, John, 657, *684*
Keynesianism, 576–77, 581
killer amendments, 21
Kim Jong-un, 26
King, Martin Luther Jr., 121, 123, 129,
  427, 432
Kirk, Mark, *321*
Knapp, Seaman, 251
knowledge
  lack of, 358–62
  political, 382
  as power, 359
  scientific, 248
Korean War, 670, 681
Korematsu v. United States, 120
Kucinich, Dennis, 161
Ku Klux Klan, 139

Labor, Department of, 636
laissez-faire capitalism, 575, 577–78
Landon, Alf, 334
Lasswell, Harold, 5
latent interest, 425
lawmaking process
  committee action, 178
  committee system, 172–73
  conference committees, 184–85
  Democratic sit-in and, 182
  floor action, 184
  illustrated, *177*
  moving bills to floor, 178–80
  overview of, 176
  presidential signature, 185
  proposals, 176
  referrals, 176–78
  Senate distinctiveness, 180–81
  separation of powers and, 185–86
  split referrals, 178
  volume of proposed bills, 176
  See also Congress, U.S.
Lawrence v. Texas (2003), 303
legal briefs, 305–6
legal model, 307, *310*
legislative branch
  administrative law, 219
  as bicameral, 47, 150

checks and balances, 49–50
civil rights and liberties and, 113–14
in foreign policy, 659
institution comparison, 186–88
lobbying, 151, 195–96
New Jersey Plan on, 42, *43*
oversight, 271–74
separation of powers, 49
unstable coalitions in, 452–56
Virginia Plan on, 42, *43*
See also Congress, U.S.
"Let Us Vote" ("LUV"), 394
Leviathan (Hobbes), *661*
liberal capitalism, 608
liberals
  on abortion rights, 652
  economic policy, 577
  on health care–3, 652–53
  ideology, 351–52
  public opinion and, 369
  redistributive policies and, 644
libertarians, 644–45
liberty and equality trade-off, *643*, 644
Libya, 678, 681
Lincoln, Abraham
  Civil War actions, 208–10
  succession and, 74
  Third Party System, 466
line-item veto, 234
lobbying
  bureaucrats and, 252
  campaign financing and, 419–24,
    431
  Congress and, 428–29, 440
  coordination problems, 427–28
  courts and, 413
  economic policy and, 613
  government agencies and, 417–18
  influence on decisions, 428–29
  inside, 417–19
  by interest groups, 275, 413–19
  legislative branch and, 151, 195–96
  money spent on, 414, *415*
  outside, 417–19
  regulating, 418
  statistics, 441
Lobbying Disclosure Act (1995), 418
local governments
  cross-state, 93
  home rule, 96
  responsibilities of, 77
  revenue and expenditures, *92*
  special districts, 96–97
  types of, 93
Locke, John, 39, 40
logrolling, 190

Los Angeles Times, 536, 544
Loving v. Virginia (1967), 286
Lugar, Richard, 160
Lynch, Loretta, 281

Macron, Emmanuel, *665*
Madison, James, 41, 53, 149, 201, 291, 448
majority leader, 168, 176, 452
majority whip, 168
Maloney, Sean Patrick, *367*
Mann, Horace, 621
Marbury, William, 291
Marbury v. Madison (1803), 290–92, 295
margin of error, 336
marketization, 267–69
markup, 178
Marshall, John, 126, 290–91
Martin, Andrew, 315
Marx, Karl, 575–76
Marxism, 352, 576, 578
Massachusetts Constitution (1780), 289
Massachusetts v. EPA, 274
mass media
    agenda setting by, 564–66
    biases, 556–61
    campaigning with, 519–22
    centralized ownership
        consequences, 553–54
    comparing with other countries,
        554–56
    content selection, 561–63
    control the means of
        communication, 568
    coverage of Edward Snowden story,
        535–36
    defined, 537
    in a democracy, 537–42
    eighteenth and nineteenth centuries,
        543–44
    evaluating and interpreting
        information, 538–39
    fact-checking, 540–41, 565
    framing, 566
    government regulation of, 551–54
    historical path timeline, 546
    infotainment, 551
    Internet and, 547
    media effects, 561–67
    persuasion, 564
    political attitudes and, 344–45
    priming, 566
    as principals and agents, 567–70
    profit motive, 549–51
    programming content about
        politics, 568–69
    providing essential information, 538

public interest broadcasting
        requirements, 553
    reporter incentives, 568
    rise of new media, 545–49
    in solving collective dilemmas,
        539–42
    television, 544–45
    trends in, 542–49
    verifying political statements, 540–41
material interests, public attitudes and,
        345–46
McCabe, Susan, 415–16
McCain, John, 339, 514
McCain-Feingold campaign finance
        law, 288
McCarthy, Joseph, 114
McCarthy, Kevin, *153*, *170*
McConnell, Mitch, 322, *455*
McConnell v. FEC (2003), 288, 418
McCulloch v. Maryland (1819), 79, *80*,
        293–94, 295
McDonald v. Chicago, 108
McGovern, George, 509
McKinley, William, 467
McNulty, John, 405
means-tested programs, 626
measuring public opinion
    alternative methods to surveys,
        340–41
    brain imaging, 341
    early attempts at, 334–35
    experiments, 341
    focus groups, 340
    framing and, 349–50
    genetic makeup, 341
    historical path timeline, 334–35
    intensive interviews, 340
    Internet polls, 337–38
    listening to conversations, 340–41
    meta-analysis, 342–43
    overview of, 333–34
    phone surveys, 337
    possible biases, 336–39
    priming and, 349–50
    push polling and, 338–39
    random sampling, 335–36
    surveys, 340
media, 537. *See also* mass media
media content
    about politics, 568–69
    agenda hypothesis, 561–62
    effect of, 563–66
    engagement hypothesis, 562
    partisan hypothesis, 561
    politicians and government as
        sources, 566–67

selection of, 561–63
    See also mass media
median voter theorem, 493–94
Medicaid
    defined, 632
    as means-tested program, 626
    in national budget, 632
Medicare
    cut-backs, 29
    defined, 632
    federal spending on, *625*
    in national budget, 632
Merkel, Angela, *665*
meta-analysis, 342–43
Mexican-American War (1846–48),
        668
Mexico
    foreign policy towards, 690
    North American Free Trade
        Agreement (NAFTA), 312
Michigan model, 353, 523
military action
    Congress and, 60
    costs of, 678–79
    cyber warfare, 681
    defined, 678
    drone strikes, 681
    in foreign policy, 678–81
    historical path timeline, 669
    in international conflict, 667
    military expenditures and, *679*
    no-fly zone, 681
    realists and, 662
    seriousness of, 680
    types of, 681
    U.S. casualties, *668*
    uses of, 679–80
    U.S. troops deployed overseas, *680*
military base closings, 686–87
military base locations, 690
military contracts, 689
Mill, John Stuart, 143, 375
minimum wage, 76
minimum winning coalition, 19
minority leader, 169
minority representation, 163–65
minority rights versus majority rule,
        313–14
minority whip, 169
von Mises, Ludvig, 577
Mitchell, George, 670–71
mixed presidential system, 234
monarchies, 26
monetary policies
    bank regulation, 594–97
    controlling inflation, 593–94

monetary policies (*continued*)
  defined, 593
  Federal Reserve and, 594–97,
    598–99
  interest rates, 594
  See also economic policy
Monroe, James, 668
Monroe Doctrine, 668
Montesquieu, 40
moot, 304
mortgage industry, 637
Motor Voter, 381, 502
Mourdock, Richard, 160
mugwumps, 262
multilateral diplomacy, 671–73
multilateralism, 664
Murdoch, Rupert, 569
Murphy, Chris, 180

Nader, Ralph, 427, 435, 472
Nation, Carrie, 435
National Aeronautics and Space
    Administration (NASA), 25,
    248, *249*
national bureaucracies, 276–78. *See also*
    government bureaucracy
national committees, 457–58
national debt, 602, *603*, 609
national deficit, 602, 603
*National Federation of Independent
    Businesses v. Sebelius* (2012),
    84, 309
National Institutes of Health (NIH),
    632
national parks, 248
national party conventions, 458
National Review, 556
National Rifle Association (NRA),
    443–44
National Science Foundation (NSF), 252
National Security Agency (NSA), *534*,
    535
National Security Council, 232, 658,
    688
national–state political relations,
    479–82
Nation magazine, 556
Native American rights, 125
NATO (North Atlantic Treaty
    Organization), 217, 664, 670
"natural law," 110
Nazis, 139
NBC network, 544, 549
necessary and proper clause (elastic
    clause), 47, 79, *80*
need-to-know position, 359

negative externalities, 101
Netanyahu, Benjamin, *410*
Netherlands, 526
Neustadt, Richard, 219
New Deal Era
  courts and, 292
  economic policy, 581
  government bureaucracy, 260
  judicial appointments, 320
  overview of, 82–83
  policies, 216
  political parties, 469–70
  Supreme Court and, 319–20
New Deal Party System, 469–70, 474
New Jersey Plan, 42, *43*
News Corporation, 549
Newsweek magazine, 544
New York Journal, 543, *544*
New York Times, 536, 544, 557, 558, 563
The New York Times Company, 549
New Zealand, 56
Nicaragua, 691
Nieto, Enrique Peña, *233*
Nigeria, 278, 676
Nineteenth Amendment, 62, 111, 393
Ninth Amendment, *112*
Nixon, Richard M.
  1972 election, 509
  impeachment and, 237–38
  political debates, 520
  resignation of, 231
  social policy and, 83
  Watergate scandal, 280, 539
No Child Left Behind Act, 78, 630–31,
    652
"no fly, no buy," 182
non-attitudes, 361–62
North American Free Trade Agreement
    (NAFTA), 312
North Atlantic Treaty Organization
    (NATO), 217, 664, 670
North Korea
  constitution, 56
  cyber attacks from, 681
  as dictatorship, 26, 56
  diplomatic relations and, 671
  economic sanctions on, 678
  as Marxist, 608
Norway, 139
NRA (National Rifle Association),
    443–44
NSF (National Science Foundation), 252

Obama, Barack
  2016 election and, 491
  antiwar movement and, 439–40

appointments, 225, 270
approval ratings, 332
Benghazi story and, 539
campaigning, 211
DAPA and, 199
democracy in Middle East and, 691
Democratic Party and, 211
economic stimulus policies, 85
EPA as priority, 256
executive actions, 199
executive orders, 222–23
federal bureaucracy, 228
on financial fraud, 229
foreign policy, 693–94
on gun control, 328, 331–32
health care law, 309
HHS and, 243–44
informal powers, 219
international organizations and, 673
Internet appeals, 546
on minimum wage, *572*
new agencies, 228
on same-sex marriages, 137
signing statements, 223–24
social media and, 213
stimulus policies, 160, 612
Supreme Court appointments, 308,
    319
Supreme Court decisions and,
    84–85
Syrian refugee crisis response and,
    72
unilateral presidential action, 236,
    240
vice president, 232
war powers, 60
White House staff, 229–30
Obergefell v. Hodges (2015), 137,
    285, 286
O'Connor, Sandra Day, 311
Office of Management and Budget
    (OMB), 175, 229–30, 270
Office of the Trade Representative,
    688
oligarchies, 26
one-party states, 26
open primaries, 503, 508
open rule, 179
Operation Inherent Resolve, 657–58
opinions, 330
opinion writing, 309–11
oral arguments, 306, *307*
organizations
  centralized, 476
  political parties as, 450, 456–61
original jurisdiction, 302

outside lobbying, 417–19
oversight, 271–74

PACs (political action committees),
510–11
Pakistan, 376
paradox of voting, 377, 378
parliamentary democracies
ballot access in, 484
confidence vote, 484
defined, 233
examples of, 233–34
executive agencies and, 276
national bureaucracy and, 276–78
party leaders, 451
political parties in, 484
presidential systems and, 233–34
See also democracy
parliamentary systems, 67
partisan hypothesis, 561
partisan model, 191–92, 193
partisanship. See party identification
party discipline, 168, 483–86
"Party Gridlock," 447
party identification
cooperation and, 463
defined, 353, 461
development of, 463–64
graph, 354
informational shortcut, 462
political parties and, 447
psychological attachment, 462
public opinion and, 353
running tally, 462–63
party professionals, 458
path dependence, 25
patronage system. See spoils system
Pearl Harbor attack, 666, 680
Pelosi, Nancy, 8, 182
Pence, Mike, 71, 231, 495, 693
Pendleton Act (1883), 262
Pentagon, 270, 276
Pentagon Papers, 121
Perot, Ross, 477
Peters, Gary, 591
Peterson, Paul, 102
Philippines, 278, 670
Planned Parenthood, 380, 616, 617–18,
654
Planned Parenthood v. Casey (1992),
311
pluralism, 430, 442
plurality rule, 152–53, 504
pocket veto, 185, 220
Poland, 234, 670
police-patrol oversight, 274

policy making
"cross pressure," 431
economic, 610–13
public opinion and, 364–70
political action committees (PACs),
510–11
political attitudes
"cue-givers," 344
from emotions, 348
framing and, 349–50
by gender, 356
from group attachments, 347
from influences of elites, 348–50
from interests and rationality,
345–47
leading to differences in behavior,
356
mass media and, 344–45
priming and, 349–50
by racial groups, 355
from socialization, 341–45
See also public opinion
political debates, 520–21
political ideology, judges, 315
political knowledge, 382
political machine, 467
political outcomes, 652–54
political participation
actions of, 375
barriers to, 372, 373–74
beneficiaries of, 385–88
beyond voting, 385–89
collective action problems, 378–79
collective dilemmas, 377–80
comparing with other countries,
401–6
contacting of officials and, 385
conventional and unconventional,
376–77
coordination problems, 379–80
costs and benefits of, 380–89
defined, 375
democratic politics and, 375–77
demographics of, 397–401
institutions and mobilization and,
406–9
patterns of, 395–401
political knowledge and, 382
in selected countries, 403
by social group, 399–400
socioeconomic status (SES) and,
397–401, 402
voter mobilization and, 384, 386
voter registration and, 381–82
voting and, 385–89
voting rights and, 386–87, 389–95

political parties
2016 election, 487
ballot access, 484
coalitions and, 452–56
collective action problems, 459–61
collective dilemmas, 459–61
comparing with other countries,
482–86
coordination problems, 18, 460
defined, 449
democratization, increasing, 476
deriding, 447–48
Duverger's Law, 478–79
electoral system, 478–79
in electorate, 450, 461–64
Fifth Party System, 469–70
First Party System, 464–65
Fourth Party System, 467–68
fund-raising and, 486
in government, 450–56
historical path timeline, 466
history of, 464–76
on ideological spectrum, 352
importance of, 456
as ingenious, 486
as intermediate institutions, 486–87
major-party actions, 482
membership control, 456
national committees, 457–58
national party conventions, 458
national politics, 449
national-state political relations,
479–82
organizational features, 456–59
as organizations, 450, 456–61
overview of, 449–50
party amateurs, 458–59
party discipline, 168, 483–86
"Party Gridlock," 447
party identification and, 447,
461–64
party leaders, 451–52
party professionals, 458
problems caused by, 487
roles of, 451
Second Party System, 465–66
separation of powers and, 452
Sixth Party System, 470–74
socialization and affiliation, 341–44
social movements and, 439–40
social policies and, 651–52
Third Party System, 466–67
transitions to new party systems,
474–76
trends in, 476
two-party system, 476–82

political parties (*continued*)
    unstable coalitions in legislatures
        and, 452–56
    voter attraction, 392
    See also Democratic Party;
        Republican Party
political rights, 28
political science, 29–30
political systems
    American, origins of, 36–46
    comparison of, 25–28
    defined, 5
    institutions in, 7–8
politicians
    evaluations of, 357–58
    as media content source, 566–67
    public opinion on, 330, 355–58
politics
    abortion rights and, 132–36
    analyzing, 29–30
    courts and, 313–24
    defined, 5
    in distribution of benefits and
        costs, 6
    of economic policy making, 610–13
    of executive orders, 235
    income inequality and, 611
    institutions, 6–9
    of judicial appointments, 318–24
    political parties in, 449
    principal-agent problem in, 21–22
    prisoner's dilemma in, 14–16
    religion in, 58–59
    strategies of judicial confirmations
        and, 322–23
    of trade, 607–8
    understanding, 5–9
    unstable coalitions in, 21
pollution rights, 268–69
populations, 335
Populist Party, 477
pork-barrel bills, 189
Portugal, 57, 234
poverty
    basic provisions, 626–28
    inequality and, *647*
    lethal consequences of, 646
    redistribution programs and, 651
    relief, 646–47, 651
    unemployment and, 647–48
Powell, Adam Clayton, 16
prayer in public schools, 117, 367
predispositions
    defined, 330
    ethnic and racial group, 354
    ideology and, 351–53

overview of, 350–51
party identification, 353–54
racist, 354
religion and, 354
preferences, 5–6
presidency
    administrative and financial
        resources, 228–32
    appointments, 224–25
    approval ratings and, *238*
    Base Realignment and Closures
        (BRAC) and, 686
    bureaucratic institutions and, *218*
    characteristics of, 201–3
    checks and balances, 49–50, 236–40
    collective dilemmas and, 205–6,
        226–32
    comparison of executive forms,
        232–36
    constitutional powers of, 201–5
    crises and, 209–10
    economic policy and, 613
    electoral pressures, 239–40
    enhancing presidential power,
        214–18
    enumerated powers, *204*, 219
    executive agreements, 223
    executive orders, 222–23, 226–27
    foreign policy and, 203, 209, 659,
        693
    implied powers of, *204*
    informal powers, 218
    institutional feature of Constitution,
        47
    institutionalizing power of, 240
    interest groups and, 431–32, 440
    investigations and impeachment,
        237–38
    in lawmaking process, 185, 186
    lobbying and, 417
    modern, shaping of, 207–14
    nineteenth-century changes, 207–10
    oversight, 271–74
    partisan, building on, 211–12
    populist, developing, 212–14
    power of, 200
    president as military leader, 208–10
    presidential signature, 185
    principal-agent problems and,
        205–6
    public activities, *213*
    public opinion and, 214
    relative powers, 57–61
    roles, 203
    signing statements, 223–24
    sources of power, 200

    today's powerful, 218–32
    veto power of, 151, 185, 220–22
    War Powers Act (1973) and, 683
    White House staff, 229
    See also executive branch; *specific*
        presidents
presidential systems
    defined, 234
    mixed, 234
    in parliamentary democracies,
        233–34
    parliamentary systems versus, *67*
press
    as agents, 569–70
    biases, 556–61
    defined, 537
    in a democracy, 537–42
    eighteenth and nineteenth centuries,
        543–44
    evaluating and interpreting
        information, 536–37
    freedom of, 551–52
    government regulation of, 551–54
    ideology and, *559*
    Internet and, 547
    as principals, 568–69
    profit motive, 549–51
    in solving collective dilemmas,
        539–42
    trends in, 542–49
    See also mass media
Priebus, Reince, 225
primary elections
    2016 election cycle, *495*
    closed, 503, 508
    collective dilemma, 516–17
    defined, 503
    general elections versus, 508–9
    open, 503, 508
    overview of, 153–54
    state-level parties, 459
    voters, 160
priming, 349–50, 566
principal-agent problems
    in Congress, 23, 189
    defined, 21
    Environmental Protection Agency
        (EPA), 254–56
    government bureaucracy, 252–56
    institutions and, 23–24
    mass media, 567–70
    overview of, 21
    in politics and government, 22–23
    presidency and, 205–6
    public opinion, 331–33
    See also collective dilemmas

prisoner's dilemma
    in American politics, 14–16
    campaign financing and, 422–23
    campaigns and campaigning and,
        515–18
    collective action problem and, 14, *15*
    concept in context, *15*
    coordination problem and, 17
    courts and, 287
    defined, 14, 20
    negative advertisements, 518
    overview of, 13–16
    regulatory agencies and, 250
    See also collective dilemmas
prison populations, by country, *641*
private goods, 12, 583, 584
private media, 537
private polls, 212–13
privatization, 267–69
Progressive Era
    on break-up of trusts, 576
    government bureaucracy and,
        279–80
    government regulation in, 580
    health care provision, 631–32
    overview of, 82
    scientific management, 264
Progressive Party, 467–68, 469, 477
progressive tax policies, 600, 601
Prohibition movement, 435
property taxes, 600
proportional representation, 152–53
proposals, bill, 176
protests, 376, 379, 435
psychological attachment, 462
public campaign financing, 528
public goods
    club good, 583
    common good, 583
    defined, 12, 583
    examples of, 248
    funding for, 248
    government agencies/departments
        that supply, 248
    as nonexcludable, 583
    as nonrival, 583
    redistribution of, 636
    types of, 583–84
public health, 248
public opinion
    alternative methods to surveys,
        340–41
    apathy and lack of knowledge and,
        358–62
    biases, 336–39
    classification by, 355–56

communication of, 369
comparison of other countries,
    362–64
complexity of, 333
Congress and, 317
defined, 330
in democratic system, 329
diversity in, 363
early attempts at measurement,
    334–35
events in history of polling, 334–35
federal courts and, 318
fluctuation of, 332
foreign policy and, 685
government authority and, 329–30
on gun control, 328, *329*
interest groups and, 442–43
measuring, 333–41
policy making and, 364–70
on politicians, 330, 355–58
polls, 330, 334–35
predispositions, 330, 350–54
presidents and, 214
principal-agent problem, 331–33
private goods comparison, 584
public policy and, 355–58, 366–70
random sampling, 335–36
religion and, 354
role of, 370
social movements and, 442–43
Social Security program, 643
sources of political attitudes, 341–50
study of, 329, 330
Supreme Court and, 303, 314, 317–18
surveys, 340
wealth and, 365
public policies
    defined, 24
    public opinion and, 355–58, 366–70
    standing pat on, 367
public pressure, organized forms of,
    442–44
public safety, 621–22
push polling, 338–39
Putnam, Robert, 406

Qaddafi, Mu'ammar, 60
Quayle, Dan, 231
question wording, 338–39
Quinn, Kevin, 315

race discrimination
    affirmative action and, 131–32
    civil rights and liberties and, 117–19
    federalism and, 88–90
    gerrymandering, 156–57

housing and, 637
predisposition, 354
school integration and, 81
voting rights and, 391
Rachel Maddow Show, 556–57, *562*
racial groups
    differences in attitudes towards, *355*
    predisposition and, 354
random sampling, 335–36
random selection, 336
rational basis test, 130
rational ignorance, 360–61
rationality, 346–47
Reagan, Ronald
    1976 party nomination, 458
    on abortion rights, 475
    on drinking-age standard, 86
    in election campaigning, 210–11
    Fed chair, 596
    going public, 212, *214*
    government bureaucracy and, 264
    Grenada invasion, 683
    on housing problems, 638
    international organizations and, 673
    Iran agreement, 205
    Supreme Court appointments, 308
Reagan Doctrine, 691
realism, 662, 667
recall elections, 91
recessions, 588
Red Cross, 267
redistributive policies, 586–87, 601,
    620, 642–44
Reed, Thomas, 168
Reed's Rules, 168
referendums, 91, 505–6
referrals for bills, 176–78
Refugee Act of 1980, 71
Regents of the University of California v.
    Bakke (1978), 132
regressive tax policies, 600
regulations
    bank, 594–97
    business, 601
    commerce, 590–92
    environmental, 591–92
regulatory agencies, 250–51
Rehnquist, William, 295
relative powers, 57–61
religion
    collective dilemmas and, 58
    expression of, 58–59
    freedom of, 138–40
    in politics, 58–59
    public opinion and, 354, 364
    voting right barriers and, 392

religious freedom, *116*
Republican National Committee, 457–58, 480
Republican Party
   on abortion rights, 133
   brand, 463
   coalitions, 455
   divide, 455
   economic philosophies, 578
   emergence of, 469
   equality of opportunity, 651
   on government spending, 4
   on gun control, 369–70
   loyalty pledge, 480
   national conventions, 458
   presidential candidates, 510
   in Sixth Party System, 471–72
   small government and, 264
   social policies and, 652
   Tea Party movement and, 435–36, 440, 472
   voter attraction, 392
   See also political parties
republican system, 64
republics, 26
research services, congressional, 175
reserved powers, 51
resource mobilization perspective, 438–40
Restoring Americans' Healthcare Freedom Reconciliation Act, 617
restraint versus activism, judges, 316–17
restricted (or modified) rule, 179
retrospective voting model, 523–24
revenue sharing, 86
Revolutionary War, 37–39, 40, 54, 201
rights of the disabled. *See specific rights*
Roberts, John, 307, 309, 324, *359*
Roberts, Owen, 292
Roe v. Wade (1973), 132–36, 311, 475
Rojas, Fabio, 439
Romney, Mitt, 342
Roosevelt, Franklin Delano
   1936 election, 334
   court-packing plan, 292, 320–21
   enhancing presidential power, 216–17
   informal powers, 218–19
   judicial appointments, 320
   New Deal Party System, 469–70
   New Deal programs, 82–83, 292, 693
   war effort, 216–17
Roosevelt, Theodore, 82, 214–15, 264
Rosen, Jacky, *63*
Rousseau, Jean-Jacques, 375

rulemaking, 256, 257
rule of law, 35, 41, 66
Rules Committee (House of Representatives), 171–72, 179–80, 191, 195, 455
running tally, 462–63
Russia
   centralization of power and, 99
   cyber attacks from, 681
   inequality and poverty rates, *647*
   prison population in, 641
   U.S. intervention, 669
Rwanda, 681
Ryan, Paul, 182

sales taxes, 597–600
same-day registration (SDR), 381–82, 383
same-sex marriages
   civil rights and liberties and, 137–38
   legalization of, 285–86
   public opinion and, 320
   Supreme Court on, 138, 285–86, 305
samples, 336
Sanders, Bernie, 352, 472, 578, 675
Sandoval, Brian, 322
Sandy Hook shooting, *326*, 327
Saudi Arabia, 26
Scalia, Antonin, 108, 306, 311, 322
Schattschneider, E. E., 448
school integration, 81
school system operation, 77–78
Science Committee (House of Representatives), 170
scientific knowledge, 248
Scott, Rick, 72
Sebelius, Kathleen, 243, 280
Second Amendment, *112*, 126
Secondary Education Act (1965), 634
Second Party System, 465–66
security, 248
selection effect, 498
selective incentive, 426
Senate, U.S.
   "advice and consent," 289
   appointments, 269
   approval of treaties, 683
   bicameralism and, 150
   "blue slip," 319
   committees, 170–72
   direct elections, 62
   filibusters, 180–81
   institutional design of, 24, 25
   in judicial appointments, 320
   killer amendments, 21
   majority leader, 168, 176, 452

moving bills to floor, 180–81
   overview of, 150
   party leaders, 168–69
   presidential power and, 202
   unanimous consent agreements, 181
   See also Congress, U.S.; legislative branch
Senatorial Campaign Committee, 485
separation of powers
   checks and balances and, 49
   defined, 49
   federalism with, 53–54
   judicial branch, 309
   in lawmaking process, 185–86
   New Jersey Plan and, 42
   origins of, 40
   political parties and, 452
SES (socioeconomic status), 397–98
Sessions, Jeff, 225
Seventeenth Amendment, 47, *63*, 152
Seventh Amendment, *112*
sexuality rights, 136–38
Shays, Daniel, 33
Shays's Rebellion, *32*, 33, 64
Shelby County v. Holder (2013), 157, 374
Shelling, Thomas, 10
signing statements, 223–24
single-member districts, 152–53, 504
sit-in for gun control, 182–83
sit-ins, 376
Sixth Amendment, *112*, 580
Sixth Party System
   defined, 470–71
   national party organization strength, 471
   polarization and, 473–74
   vote sources, *471*
"slacktivist," 389
Slaughter-House Cases, 126
slavery
   African Americans and, 118–19
   compromise on, 45–46
   constitutional debates over, 42–43
   Constitution sanctioning of, 68
   economic policy and, 580
   legacy as systemic failure, 119
Smith, Adam, 575
Smith, Howard, 172
smoke-filled rooms, 459
SNAP (Supplemental Nutrition Assistance Program), 245, 626–27
Snowden, Edward, *534*, 535–36, 568
social capital, 406
social insurance programs, 628–30
socialism, 576, 578

socialization, 341–45
social media
    2016 campaign, 522
    candidate use of, *521*
    in harassment, 389
    Obama and, 213
    political participation and, 388
    Trump and, 213–14
social movements
    analysis of, 437–40
    civil rights, 122–24
    collective action problems, 437–38
    collective dilemmas, 437–38
    comparing with other countries,
       440–42
    defined, 432
    examples of, 432–36
    exclusion and, 435
    "failed," 437
    historical path timeline, 435–36
    interest groups and, *433*
    leftist, 435
    means-tested programs, 626
    modes of action, 434
    nuances and political divisions, 432
    political parties and, 439–40
    public opinion and, 442–43
    resource mobilization perspective,
       438–40
    rightist, 435–36
    right to vote, 125
    sexuality rights, 136–38
    success measurement, 436, 437–40
    women's rights, 125
social policies
    basic provisions for the poor,
       626–28
    collective dilemmas, 634–35
    comparing with other countries,
       645–50
    crime prevention, 621–22, 639–42
    defined, 619
    Democratic Party and, 652
    distributive and redistributive
       characteristics, 620
    economic aspects of, 620
    education, 630–31
    growing role of national
       government, 623–26
    health care, 631–33
    historical path timeline, 622
    historical perspective, 621–26
    housing, 636–39
    interest groups and, 650–51
    major areas of, 626–42
    overview of, 619–21

political ideologies and, 642–45
political parties and, 651–52
pressure to cut back, 625–26
reasons for passage and
    implementation, 653
redistribution function, 620–21
social insurance programs, 628–30
social policy making, 650–52
at state and local levels, 621–23
See also health care
Social Security Administration, 248,
    260, 636
Social Security program
    challenges to, 650
    defined, 628
    effects of, 216
    establishment of, 581
    federal spending on, *625*
    insolvency, 629
    levels of benefits, 629
    politics of, 587
    public opinion, 643
    as redistributing benefit, 587
    running of, 266–67
    as "third rail," 629
social services, deservingness, 649
socioeconomic status (SES), 397–401,
    402
soft money, 513
soft power, 678
sore-loser laws, 480–81
Sotomayor, Sonia, 225
South Africa, 678, 693
South Korea, 528
sovereignty, 104
Soviet Union
    Cold War, 261, 667, 691
    collapse of, 99, 667
Spanish-American War, 669
spatial model, 524
Speaker of the House, *8*, 168, 176, 452
special (select) committees, 171
special districts, 96–97
special donors, 426
special prosecutors, 237
spending policies
    defined, 601
    national debt and, 602, *603*
    national deficit and, 602, *603*
    purposes of, 601
    redistribution and, 604
    tax policies and, 604
    See also fiscal policies
spillover effects, 585
split referrals, 178
spoils system, 207, 261–62

standing, 297
standing committees, 170–71
stare decisis, 302
state autonomy, 84–85
state budgets, 85
state courts
    appeals procedure, *301*
    electoral connection, 299–301
    federal court supremacy over, 290
    hierarchy, 299
    judicial selection for, *300*
    jurisdiction of, 301–3
    overview of, 299–301
    See also courts; federal courts
State Department
    domestic pressures, 689
    foreign policy and, 684
    functions of, 688
    military action and, 689
    overview of, 684
state governments
    constitutions (1776–1780), 40
    constitutions, length of, 65
    early economic policy, 579–80
    electoral politics, 91
    electoral rules, 500
    executive selection, 500
    federal financing and, 85–88
    federalism and, 90–92
    institutions of, 91
    legalized marijuana and, 94–95
    national authority over, 50–51
    power of, 92
    reserved powers, 51
    responsibilities of, 77
    revenue and expenditures, *92*
    revenues from intergovernmental
       federal transfers, *87*
    voter registration roles, 500
state-level election laws, 501–4
statement bias, 560
State of Iraq and the Levant (ISIL), *656*,
    657–58
states' rights
    Jim Crow laws and, 88–90
    national power versus, 61–62
statutory law, 302
stimulus policies, 574, 612
strategic (rational choice) model, 308–9,
    310
straw polls, 334
"street-level" bureaucrats, 258
strict constructionism (constructivism),
    316–17
strict scrutiny, 129–31
strikes, 376

Sudan, 678
suffrage, 389
Sunshine Act (1976), 271, 274, 281
super PACs, 421, 423–24, 513
Supplemental Nutrition Assistance
    Program (SNAP), 245, 626–27
supply-side Keynesianism, 577
supremacy clause, 51, 78, *80*
Supreme Court, U.S.
    on abortion rights, 132–36
    on Affordable Care Act, 309
    case selection, 304–5
    on centralization of power, 79, *80*
    changing attitudes and, 286
    checks and balances, 49–50
    commerce clause and, 61–62,
        79–80
    conferences, 307–9
    Congress and, 308–9
    on congressional districts, 155
    constitutional basis, 289–90
    coordination problems and, 287–88
    as court of last resort, 294–97
    on discrimination, 129
    on EPA, 274
    on federal powers, 92
    First Amendment interpretations,
        530
    on freedom of speech, 115–16
    "friend of the court" briefs, 418
    on gerrymandering, 156–57
    on homosexual sodomy, 622
    on immigration policies, 120
    influence of decisions, *81*
    institutional feature of Constitution,
        48–49, 57
    intermediate scrutiny, 130
    judicial confirmations, 322–23
    judicial decision making, 307–9, *310*
    judicial review, 290–93
    jurisdiction, 302
    justice appointments, 286, 308
    justice ideology, 308, 315
    legal briefs and, 305–6
    on national government
        encroachment, 100
    New Deal Era and, 319–20
    on one person, one vote, 188
    opinion writing, 309–11
    oral arguments and, 306, *308*
    path of a case, 303–11
    on possession of firearms, 107–8
    on presidential power, 203
    Progressive Era and, 82
    public opinion and, 303, 314,
        317–18

rational basis test, 130
    on reserved powers, 51
    on rights and liberties, 62–63, 114,
        115–17
    on same-sex marriages, 138, 285–86
    on state autonomy, 84–85
    strict scrutiny, 129–31
    trade-offs in rulings, 142
    on voting rights, 390
    See also judicial branch
surveys
    design, 362
    public opinion, 340, 367
    question formation, 332
    response interpretation, 362
Sweden
    party-centered elections, 526
    socialism and, 608
Switzerland
    as decentralized country, 98, 99
    direct democracy and, 26
    national government, 609
Syria
    airstrikes in, 657–58
    economic pressure on, 678
    executions in, 379
    no-fly zone, 681
    policy doctrine towards, 694
    trade restrictions, 692
Syrian refugee crisis, 71–72

Taft, Howard, 477
Taft-Hartley Act, 205
"take care" clause, 203
Tammany Hall, *468*
Taney, Roger, 117
TANF (Temporary Assistance for
    Needy Families), 620–21, 626,
    648
tariffs, 580, 581, 600
tax policies
    accomplishments of, 597
    budgets and, 4
    overview of, 597
    progressive, 600, 601
    redistribution and, 604
    regressive, 600
    spending policies and, 604
    tax-exempt status, 420–21
    tax types and, 597–600
    See also fiscal policies
Tea Party movement, 85, 435–36, 438,
    440, 472
technology
    campaigning with, 518–22
    civil liberties and, 114, *115*

television
    campaigns and, 519–20
    predominance of, 544–45
Temporary Assistance for Needy
    Families (TANF), 620–21, 626,
    648
Tenth Amendment, 51, 79, 80, *112*
Third Amendment, *112*
third parties, 472
Third Party System, 466–67
Thirteenth Amendment, 111
Thomas, Clarence, 308
Thurmond, Strom, 180
Tiebout, Charles, 101–2
Time magazine, 544
trade policies
    collective dilemmas, 606
    defined, 605
    foreign competition and, 607
    foreign policy and, 673–75
    free and fair trade, 608, 674–75
    importance of, 674
    interest groups and, 607–8
    restrictions, 606, 607
    tariffs, 605–6
transaction costs. *See* collective
    dilemmas
transfers, 86
transgender rights movement, 434, 439
Transportation, Department of, 103,
    249, 257
Transportation Safety Administration,
    260, 261
Treasury, Department of
    controlling inflation, 593–94
    financial fraud and, 228–29
    foreign policy and, 688
    Internal Revenue Service (IRS),
        248
    as original executive agency, 258
Truman, Harry S., 222–23, 232
Trump, Donald
    2016 election, 374, *490*, 491–92,
        495, 567
    advertisements against, 513
    appointments, 225
    approval ratings, 332
    budget priorities and taxes and, 605
    economic policies as candidate, 582
    on education, 634
    electoral college and, 8
    on Federal Reserve, 597
    on foreign policy, 694
    on immigration policies, 693
    on infrastructure spending, 612
    isolationist campaign theme, 663

NATO criticisms, 673
political debates, 520–21
promise of change, 3
promises on taking office, 200
public money and, 514
Republican Party and, 447, 449, 472, 510
republican primary, 352
social media use, 213–14
on trade policies, 652, 674
"unified" government, 4
untruthful statements, 540
white house staff, 229
trustees, 159
Tucker Carlson Tonight, 557, *562*
Tversky, Amos, 349–50
Twelfth Amendment, 230–31
Twenty-fourth Amendment, 111
Twenty-sixth Amendment, 111
Twitter, 546
two-candidate elections, 495, *496*, 515–18
two-party system
deepening of, 482
Duverger's Law and, 478–79
major-party actions and, 482
more parties versus, 482–83
national-state political relations and, 479–82
reasons for, 477–82
United States as, 476, 477
See also political parties

UN (United Nations), 217, 662, 673
unanimous consent agreements, 181
unconventional political participation, 376–77
unemployment insurance, 216, 630
unicameral, 33
unified government, 211, 221
unilateralism, 237, 663
Union Party, 477
unitary system, *75*, 98
United Kingdom
ballot access in, 484
civil service model, 278
constitutional structure, 56
electoral institutions, 526
group politics in, 440
judge selection in, 312
judicial review in, 312
as parliamentary democracy, 233
party leaders, 451
polling in, 339
two-party system, 477–78
War of 1812, 667

United Nations (UN), 217, 662, 673
United States v. Jones (2012), 114
United States v. Lopez (1995), *80*, 84
United States v. Texas, 84–85
unity, promoting, 103
unstable coalitions
Congress, 165–66
defined, 20
overview of, 19–21
in politics, 21
stabilization of, 20
Uruguay, 478
USA PATRIOT Act, 121
USA Today, 536
U.S. Court of Federal Claims, 299
U.S. Court of International Trade, 299
U.S. Internal Revenue Service, 278
U.S. Postal Service, 247

valence model, 524
Van Buren, Martin, 207–8, 465
Velázquez, Nydia, *175*
Veterans' Affairs, Department of, 636
Veterans Affairs Committees (House and Senate), 175
vetoes
Congress and, 151, 220–22
line-item, 234
pocket, 185, 220
by president, *221*
veto threats, 220–21
vice presidency, 230–32
Vietnam War, 670
Virginia Declaration of Rights (1776), 40, 111
Virginia Plan, 42, *43*
Volcker, Paul, 596
voter mobilization
defined, 396
efforts, 384, 386
role of institutions and, 406–9
voter registration, 381–82, 500
voters
collective action problem, 461
collective dilemmas among candidates and, 459–61
decision making, 522–25
ideology and, 496–97
participation and, 385–89
voter turnout
2016 election, 397
challenges to reforms for, 391–92
close races and, 397
collective dilemma, 387
cost of voting and, 405
defined, 395

methods to increase, *548*
in presidential elections, *396*
removing barriers to, 392–93
in southern states, 401
trends in, 395–97
voter ID laws and, 391
voting
bureaucracy of, 406
collective dilemma, 386–87
cost and benefits of, 383, 405
democracy and, 384
directional model, 524–25
as duty of citizenship, 405
as the franchise, 389
by mail, 383
Michigan model of, 353, 523
paradox of, 377, 378
political knowledge and, 382
retrospective model, 523–24
spatial model, 524
valence model, 524
See also political participation
voting rights
barriers, 390–91
barriers, removing, 392–93
enforcement of, 390
expansion of, 111
expansion timeline, 394
Fifteenth Amendment and, 111
Fifth Amendment and, 393
group struggles, 393–95
group struggles and, 393–95
ID requirements and, 391
Nineteenth Amendment and, 62, 111, 393
poll taxes and, 390
race discrimination and, 391
restricting, 389–91
Twenty-fourth Amendment and, 111
Twenty-sixth Amendment and, 111
women and, 62, 434
Voting Rights Act (1965), 90, 157–58, 163, 374, 390, 393, 432
vouchers, 268

Wallace, George, *475*
Wall Street Journal, 557, 569
War Department, 258
war powers, 57, 60
War Powers Act (1973), 682–83
Washington, George, 54, 60, 206, 228
Washington Post, 535–36
The Washington Post Company, 549
Watergate scandal, 280, 539
Water Resources Reform and Development Act of 2014, 88

Ways and Means Committee (House of Representatives), 166, 170
wealth
    campaign contributions and, 611
    ideologies and, 642
    public opinion and, 365
The Wealth of Nations (Smith), 575
welfare state, 624, 647
Wesberry v. Sanders (1964), 91, 155, 188

Whig Party, 144, 465, 466
whip, 168–69
Whiskey Rebellion, 60, 206
White House. *See* presidency
Wilson, James Q., 458
Wilson, Woodrow, 212, 215–16, 264, 477
women
    abortion rights, 132–36
    in Congress, 163–65, *164*

voting rights, 125
Woodward, Bob, 539
World Trade Organization (WTO), 581–82, 668, 673, 674
writ of certiorari, 304

Yellen, Janet, 599

Zeidan, Ali, *684*
Zimbabwe, 376, 678